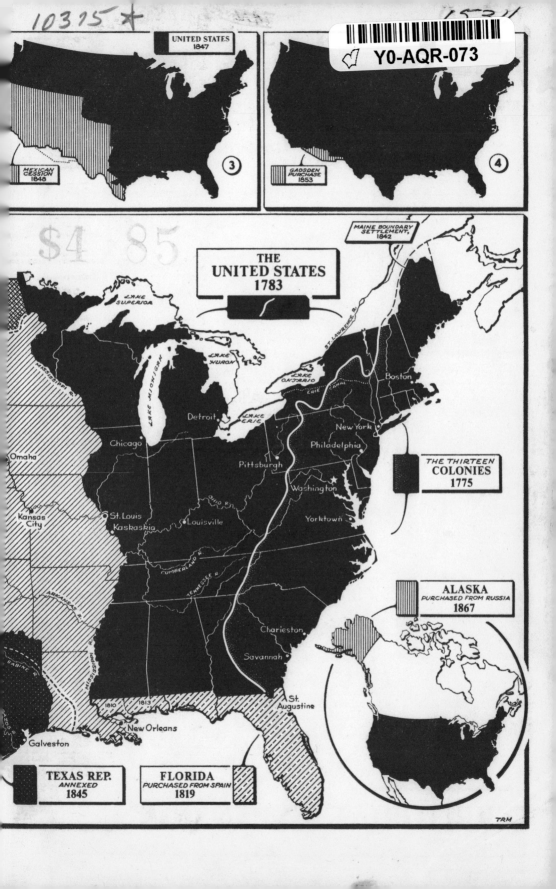

UNITED STATES
1847

MEXICAN CESSION
1848

③

GADSDEN PURCHASE
1853

④

MAINE BOUNDARY SETTLEMENT, 1842

THE
UNITED STATES
1783

THE THIRTEEN
COLONIES
1775

ALASKA
PURCHASED FROM RUSSIA
1867

TEXAS REP.
ANNEXED
1845

FLORIDA
PURCHASED FROM SPAIN
1819

LAKE SUPERIOR

LAKE MICHIGAN

LAKE HURON

LAKE ONTARIO

LAKE ERIE

ERIE CANAL

ST. LAWRENCE R.

Boston

Detroit

New York

Chicago

Philadelphia

Pittsburgh

Washington

Yorktown

Omaha

St. Louis
Kaskaskia

Louisville

OHIO R.

Kansas City

CUMBERLAND R.

TENNESSEE R.

Charleston

Savannah

MISSISSIPPI R.

ARKANSAS R.

SABINE R.

BRAZOS R.

1810   1813

New Orleans

Galveston

St. Augustine

TRM

THE

United States

O F

America

*

A HISTORY

HENRY BAMFORD PARKES

NEW YORK UNIVERSITY

THE

United States

OF

America

*

A HISTORY

SECOND EDITION, REVISED

ALFRED A. KNOPF: NEW YORK

1960

L. C. Catalog card number: 59–6118

© *Alfred A. Knopf, Inc., 1959*

THIS IS A BORZOI BOOK,
PUBLISHED BY ALFRED A. KNOPF, INC.

Published 1953. Reprinted seven times

Second Edition, Revised, 1959

Reprinted 1960

Preface

Eᴀʀʟʏ in the seventeenth century a few small groups of pioneers
sought new homes on the Atlantic coastline of North America. This
was the beginning of an astonishingly rapid process of expansion, which in
less than three and a half centuries, has brought nearly 40 million immigrants across the ocean, carried all the institutions of civilization 3,500
miles across the continent to the Pacific, and made the United States
incomparably the richest and most powerful nation in the world. In contrast with the Europeans and Asiatics, and even with their neighbors in
Mexico and the southern continent, the Americans are still a relatively
young people. Their rise to world leadership is one of the most important
events in the recent history of the human race.

The special qualities that differentiate the society of the United States
from that of older nations stem from two primary factors. First, the
United States was settled by men and women who came from other parts
of the world and belonged to many different ethnic and cultural groups.
Although some of them were transported to America by force, the majority came of their own volition in the hope of finding security against
persecution and wider opportunities for economic and social advancement
and self-expression. This meant that the Americans from the beginning
were an active and enterprising people, who had confidence in their own
powers, who believed in resisting oppression rather than submitting to it,
and who were not disposed to accept unnecessary limitations upon their
freedom. In the course of time they evolved a system of government that

protected the rights of individuals more fully and effectively than any other in the world. Faith in free institutions became the main formative principle of the new American nationality. Unlike the European peoples, the Americans were unified not by any community of ancestry and tradition but by common ideals and hopes for the future.

The second major factor in the evolution of American society has been the abundance of fertile land and natural resources. The pioneers who explored and colonized North America found millions of square miles of virgin forest, rich soils suitable for almost all forms of agriculture, broad rivers providing communication with the heart of the continent, vast grassy plains, and almost every mineral known to man. There was no easy way to develop these resources; but opportunities unique in human history awaited men and women who had the necessary courage and initiative, and above all, the capacity for hard work. The natural wealth of the continent strengthened the optimistic and individualistic spirit of the American people, promoted social and political equality, and enabled them to achieve both the highest general standard of living ever known and the material power needed for world leadership.

Since the changing attitudes and preoccupations of the present cause us to look at the past from new perspectives, history has to be constantly rewritten. Most historical scholars of earlier generations were concerned with government and interpreted the growth of different nations mainly in terms of political development. Historians of today study the evolution of society as a whole instead of concentrating on its political institutions. This more comprehensive scope is especially appropriate in writing about the people of the United States, since they have been engaged in creating not only a new kind of government but a new way of life.

Throughout the nineteenth century it was possible to describe the growth of the United States with relatively little reference to events in other parts of the world. Once the American people had won their independence from European control, their development for several generations was determined chiefly by internal factors. In the shrinking world of the twentieth century, however, the United States could no longer separate herself from other countries; she could achieve security only by assuming international responsibilities. Looking back on American history from this modern perspective we can see that, in actuality, the United States was never so isolated as was formerly supposed and that in spite of her political independence and the special qualities and values of her society, she was always deeply affected by economic and cultural trends in the other nations of the Western world.

In describing the growth of the United States from the first small settlements of the seventeenth century to the world power of the twentieth, this book presents the essential facts of her political history, but it also discusses economic and social development, the movement of beliefs and ideas, and the expression of the American spirit in literature and the arts. Regarding the Atlantic Ocean as a means of communication rather than a barrier, this book emphasizes the constant interaction between the United States and Europe and the common cultural heritage of all the Western peoples.

On the whole, the building of civilization in the United States can justly be regarded as a remarkable demonstration of human energy, intelligence, and idealism. American society has had its failures and short-comings, which we should not attempt to condone or conceal. But in confronting the heavy responsibilities of today, the American people can legitimately find guidance, inspiration, and encouragement by studying the record of their past.

Preface to the Second Edition

NEARLY six years have elapsed since this book was first published, but so far no change of perspective seems to be called for. Internally, the United States has continued, on the whole, to move forward towards a fuller realization of her national ideals of freedom and democracy. Externally, she has maintained her associations with the like-minded nations of western Europe and the Western Hemisphere, and still faces the respon-sibilities of international leadership and the problems of working out a new kind of world order appropriate to the atomic age. A new administra-tion in Washington has brought some changes of method but no funda-mental change of objectives. Possibly its most significant achievement has been to demonstrate that the political conflicts among the American people are relatively superficial and that they are substantially united in support of policies of progressive reform at home and international coop-eration abroad.

For this edition I have included a section covering the first five and a half years of the Eisenhower administration, and have also added some new material to the last chapter. Several books written since 1952 have added appreciably to our knowledge of the American past, and in the earlier chapters I have made some revisions in order to incorporate new facts or interpretations. I have also revised some of the chapter bibliog-raphies, and have corrected any erroneous or misleading statements that have been called to my attention. Several new maps and map captions have been added. I should like to thank all those persons—teachers, students, and general readers—who have written to me to point out misstatements, inform me of new materials, and agree or disagree with my opinions. Such communications from an author's unseen audience are always a welcome indication that his book is being read with interest and attention.

H.B.P.

CONTENTS

I.   THE EXPANSION OF EUROPE   *3*
     1. *The European Background*   *3*
     2. *The Development of England*   *10*
     3. *The Opening of the New World*   *13*

II.   THE FOUNDING OF THE COLONIES   *20*
     1. *The Beginnings of Colonization*   *21*
     2. *The Chesapeake Colonies*   *28*
     3. *The New England Colonies*   *33*
     4. *The Later Colonies*   *42*

III.   THE LATER COLONIAL PERIOD   *48*
     1. *The Expansion of the Colonies*   *48*
     2. *The British Imperial System*   *53*
     3. *Internal Conflicts*   *58*
     4. *The Conflict with France*   *68*

IV.   THE AMERICAN ENLIGHTENMENT   *75*
     1. *The Meaning of the Enlightenment*   *76*
     2. *The Diffusion of Culture*   *79*
     3. *The Development of Religion*   *80*
     4. *Social Theory*   *83*
     5. *Science and Philosophy*   *85*
     6. *Literature and the Arts*   *87*

V.   THE REVOLUTION   *93*
     1. *The Causes of the Revolution*   *93*
     2. *The Course of the Controversy*   *95*
     3. *The Outbreak of the War*   *101*
     4. *The War of Independence*   *105*

VI.   THE CONFEDERATION AND THE CONSTITUTION   *116*
     1. *The Conflict of Ideals*   *117*
     2. *Reforms of the Revolutionary Period*   *120*
     3. *The Confederation Period*   *122*
     4. *The Movement for a New Government*   *126*

5. *The Making of the Constitution*   128
6. *Ratification*   134

VII.   FEDERALISTS AND REPUBLICANS   137
1. *The New Nation*   138
2. *Washington's Administration*   139
3. *Washington's Foreign Policy*   146
4. *The Adams Administration*   149
5. *Jefferson's First Administration*   153

VIII.   EMERGENT NATIONALISM   160
1. *Neutral Rights*   160
2. *The War of 1812*   163
3. *Foreign Policy of Monroe and Adams*   168
4. *Nationalism and Sectionalism*   174

IX.   THE SETTLEMENT OF THE MISSISSIPPI VALLEY   181
1. *The Westward Movement*   182
2. *Kentucky and Tennessee*   183
3. *The Role of the Federal Government*   185
4. *The Old Northwest*   189
5. *The Old Southwest*   195
6. *Results of the Westward Movement*   200

X.   THE OLD SOUTH   203
1. *The Rise of King Cotton*   203
2. *The Revival of Slavery*   206
3. *Southern Economic Problems*   209
4. *Southern Society*   211
5. *Southern Political Interests*   216

XI.   THE INDUSTRIAL REVOLUTION   219
1. *The Revolution in Transportation*   220
2. *The Revolution in Manufacturing*   223
3. *The Growth of the Laboring Class*   228
4. *Foreign Trade and Shipping*   231

XII.   THE JACKSONIAN PERIOD   235
1. *New Political Forces*   235
2. *The Rise of Jacksonian Democracy*   239
3. *Jackson's Two Administrations*   243
4. *Van Buren, Harrison and Tyler*   250

XIII.   THE GROWTH OF SOCIAL IDEALISM   254
        1. *Social Trends*   254
        2. *Religion*   257
        3. *Movements for Reform*   264
        4. *Education and Science*   269

XIV.   AMERICAN ROMANTICISM   274
        1. *Factors in Literary Development*   274
        2. *Early New York Writers*   277
        3. *The Flowering of New England*   281
        4. *Writers of the Southern and Middle States*   286
        5. *The Other Arts*   291

XV.   THE CONQUEST OF THE WEST   298
        1. *Early Activities in the Far West*   298
        2. *The Texas Question*   304
        3. *The Transcontinental Migration*   307
        4. *Expansionism in American Politics*   311
        5. *The War with Mexico*   315

XVI.   THE SECTIONAL CONFLICT   321
        1. *Causes of the Conflict*   321
        2. *The Compromise of 1850*   326
        3. *The Rise of the Middle West*   332
        4. *The Conflict Revived*   337
        5. *The Buchanan Administration*   343

XVII.   THE CIVIL WAR   349
        1. *Secession and War*   349
        2. *Behind the Lines*   356
        3. *From Bull Run to Gettysburg*   360
        4. *Diplomacy of the War*   366
        5. *From Gettysburg to Appomattox*   368
        6. *The War and the Northern Economy*   371

XVIII. THE POSTWAR SOUTH   375
        1. *After Appomattox*   376
        2. *Johnson and the Radicals*   378
        3. *Radical Reconstruction*   383
        4. *Economic Trends*   387
        5. *The Populist Movement*   390

XIX.   THE GROWTH OF INDUSTRY   395
        1. *Factors in Industrial Growth*   396

2. The Expansion of the Railroads   *401*

3. Industrial and Financial Development   *406*

4. Problems of Labor   *414*

XX.   THE END OF THE FRONTIER   *422*

1. The Completion of Western Settlement   *422*

2. The Farmer in Industrial Society   *431*

3. The Closing of the Frontier   *440*

XXI.   FROM GRANT TO MCKINLEY   *443*

1. The Political System   *444*

2. Presidential Parade   *448*

3. The Revolt of the Farmers   *457*

XXII.   SOCIAL CHANGES IN THE INDUSTRIAL ERA   *464*

1. The Growth of Cities   *465*

2. Immigration   *468*

3. Religious Organizations   *472*

4. Education and Science   *476*

5. The Press   *481*

XXIII.   NEW WAYS OF THINKING   *484*

1. The Reign of Orthodoxy   *484*

2. The Impact of Darwinism   *486*

3. New Ways in Sociology and Economics   *490*

4. New Ways in Philosophy   *495*

5. New Ways in History   *500*

XXIV.   REALISM IN THE ARTS   *503*

1. Literature after the Civil War   *503*

2. Two Masters   *506*

3. The Movement Towards Realism   *508*

4. Painting, Architecture, and Music   *512*

XXV.   THE UNITED STATES BECOMES A WORLD POWER   *518*

1. The New Power Politics   *519*

2. Overseas Expansion   *521*

3. The Open Door in China   *527*

4. Caribbean and Mexican Policy   *529*

5. Relations with Japan   *537*

start 3rd term

XXVI.   THE PROGRESSIVE PERIOD   *543*

1. *The Progressive Spirit*   *543*
2. *Progressivism in Municipal and State Politics*   *547*
3. *The Roosevelt Administration*   *551*
4. *The Taft Administration*   *555*
5. *The Wilson Administration*   *560*

XXVII.   THE FIRST WORLD WAR   *565*

1. *The Road to Belligerency*   *565*
2. *The United States at War*   *574*
3. *The Treaty and the League*   *580*

XXVIII.   POSTWAR POLITICS   *588*

1. *From Harding to Hoover*   *589*
2. *Legislation*   *593*
3. *Problems of Individual Liberty*   *597*
4. *Foreign Policy*   *600*

XXIX.   PROSPERITY AND DEPRESSION   *610*

1. *Economic Advances*   *611*
2. *Weaknesses in the Economic System*   *614*
3. *The Depression*   *621*

XXX.   THE NEW DEAL   *628*

1. *The Hoover Administration*   *628*
2. *Roosevelt and His New Deal*   *630*
3. *New Deal Legislation*   *635*
4. *Foreign Policy During the New Deal Period*   *645*

XXXI.   THE SECOND WORLD WAR   *648*

1. *The End of Neutrality*   *649*
2. *The United States at War*   *656*
3. *Planning a New World Order*   *669*

XXXII.   SINCE THE WAR   *675*

1. *Domestic Affairs*   *675*
2. *Two Worlds*   *681*
3. *The Eisenhower Administration*   *693*

XXXIII.   THE ARTS IN A BUSINESS CIVILIZATION   *704*

1. *Literary Trends*   *705*

Mid Term

2. Criticism   706
3. The Novel   709
4. Poetry   713
5. The Theater   715
6. Painting and Sculpture   716
7. Architecture   719
8. Music   720

XXXIV.   Society at Midcentury   724
1. The Churches   725
2. Education   727
3. Problems of Equality   729
4. Changing Morals   734
5. Threats to Individual Independence   737
6. The Advance of the Sciences   741
7. Conclusion   744

Appendix I.   The Declaration of Independence   745

Appendix II.   The Constitution of the United States of
                 America   748

                 Tables   763

                 Bibliography   779

                 Index   *follows page* 783

ILLUSTRATIONS

FACING PAGE

New Amsterdam about 1650 (*Museum of the City of New York*)   *82*

Westover (*Museum of Modern Art, New York*)   *83*

Rotunda of the University of Virginia (*Brown Brothers*)   *83*

Mrs. Sylvanus Bourne, by JOHN SINGLETON COPLEY (*Metropolitan Museum of Art, New York*)   *98*

The Peale Family, by CHARLES WILLSON PEALE (*New-York Historical Society*)   *98*

George Washington, by CHARLES WILLSON PEALE (*Pennsylvania Academy of the Fine Arts, Philadelphia*)   *99*

Thomas Jefferson, by REMBRANDT PEALE (*New-York Historical Society*)   *99*

Tontine Coffee House, by FRANCIS GUY (*New-York Historical Society*)   *242*

Engagement of the *United States* and the *Macedonian*, by THOMAS BIRCH (*New-York Historical Society*)   *243*

Fulton's *Clermont* (*Stokes Collection, New York Public Library*)   *243*

Verdict of the People, by GEORGE CALEB BINGHAM (*Boatmen's National Bank of St. Louis*)   *258*

A Camp Meeting (*New-York Historical Society*)   *259*

A Lyceum Lecture (*Museum of the City of New York*)   *259*

A Mountain Man (*New-York Historical Society*)   *338*

Fur Traders Descending the Missouri, by GEORGE CALEB BINGHAM (*Metropolitan Museum of Art, New York*)   *338*

Caravan en Route, by ALFRED JACOB MILLER (*Walters Art Gallery, Baltimore*)   *339*

xv

President Lincoln on the Battlefield of Antietam (*Brown Brothers*)   *354*

Robert E. Lee (*Bettmann Archive*)   *355*

Ulysses S. Grant (*Brown Brothers*)   *355*

Plains Indians Hunting Buffaloes, by KARL BODMER (*New York
    Public Library*)   *426*

Across the Continent (*New York Historical Society*)   *427*

Wholesale (*Culver Service*)   *458*

A Painful Position for Nurse McKinley (*Bettmann Archive*)   *458*

The World's Constable (*Culver Service*)   *459*

Walt Whitman, by THOMAS EAKINS (*Pennsylvania Academy of the
    Fine Arts, Philadelphia*)   *562*

The Gulf Stream, by WINSLOW HOMER (*Metropolitan Museum of Art,
    New York*)   *562*

Agricultural Hall, Columbian Exposition, Chicago, 1893 (*Bett-
    mann Archive*)   *563*

Robie House, by FRANK LLOYD WRIGHT (*Museum of Modern Art,
    New York*)   *563*

Woodrow Wilson (*Brown Brothers*)   *578*

Franklin D. Roosevelt (*Brown Brothers*)   *578*

Brooklyn Bridge, New York City (*Brown Brothers*)   *579*

Hoover Dam, Nevada (*Brown Brothers*)   *579*

MAPS

BY THEODORE R. MILLER

	Territorial Expansion	front end papers
1.	Physical Contour Map of the United States	xxi
2.	The New World Before 1600	19
3.	Colonial Settlement, 1607–1760	47
4.	The Struggle for America	71
5.	The War of Independence in the North	107
6.	The War of Independence in the South	157
7.	Routes to the West, 1760–1840	191
8.	New States, 1789–1850	199
9.	Trans-Mississippi Routes to the West	297
10.	The Mexican War	317
	Mexico City Campaign (inset)	
11.	Slave and Free Territories, 1850–54	331
12.	Railroads in Operation, 1850, and Railroad Construction, 1850–60	334
13.	Railroads in Operation, 1870, and Railroad Construction, 1870–90	335
14.	The Civil War	363
15.	Agricultural Regions of the United States	433
16.	The Growth of Farm Tenancy	439
17.	The Caribbean since 1895	531
18.	American and Japanese Expansion in the Pacific	539
19.	America's Expanding Population	587

20.   *American Productive Capacity, 1920*   *608–9*

21.   *Western Fronts, 1942–45*   *663*

22.   *Pacific Theater, 1941–45*   *667*

23.   *The World after World War II*   *686–7*

24.   *Continental United States in the Mid-twentieth Century*   *723*

      Admission of States   *rear end papers*

TABLES

I.	Admission of States to the Union	763
II.	United States Population, 1790–1950	764
III.	Presidents of the United States	770
IV.	Chief Justices of the Supreme Court	771
V.	Presidential Elections, 1789–1956	772
VI.	Public Elementary and Secondary Schools—Summary, 1870–1947	776
VII.	American Recipients of the Nobel Prize	777

1. *Physical Contour Map of the United States*

THE DEVELOPMENT OF THE UNITED STATES WAS PROFOUNDLY INFLUENCED BY THE physiographic features of the North American continent. Since most Americans came originally from Europe, the movement of expansion was, in most instances, from East to West. As they worked their way across the continent, the pioneers passed through a series of different regions, running parallel to each other from North to South, each of which presented individual problems.

The Atlantic Coastal Plain was the first area to be occupied. Because it had plenty of timber, abundant rainfall, and a number of navigable rivers, this was settled relatively easily. But throughout the colonial period, expansion westward was blocked by the Appalachian Mountains and by the fact that the French, who had settled around the Great Lakes and at the mouth of the Mississippi, were trying to control the whole of the trans-Appalachian country.

During the half-century following the Revolution pioneers were moving into the Gulf Coastal Plain, where the hot and humid climate was suitable for cotton growing, and into the Central Lowlands. The physiographic features of the Central Lowlands were not essentially different from those of the Atlantic Coastal Plain, and the small homestead remained the chief unit of settlement. For a long time economic progress was impeded by transportation problems, which were not finally solved until the building of railroads began in the 1840's and 1850's.

In the next two main regions, the Great Plains and the Rocky Mountains, timber was scarce and rainfall averaged less than twenty inches a year. This meant that the agricultural methods applied in the East, whether on the plantation or on the homestead, were no longer practicable. In preference to settling in this arid country pioneers of the 1840's and 1850's moved across to the Pacific coast in caravans of covered wagons. The need for quicker transcontinental communication was met after the Civil War by the railroads.

During the 1870's the cattle kingdom, originating in Texas close to the Rio Grande, spread northward through the High Plains. At the same time agricultural settlement in this region was made possible by new techniques of irrigation and dry farming, and by the invention of barbed wire, which took the place of timber for fencing. The Rocky Mountain region was settled largely by miners, many of whom moved eastward from California; but the whole of the arid Western half of the United States still remains much more thinly populated than the East.

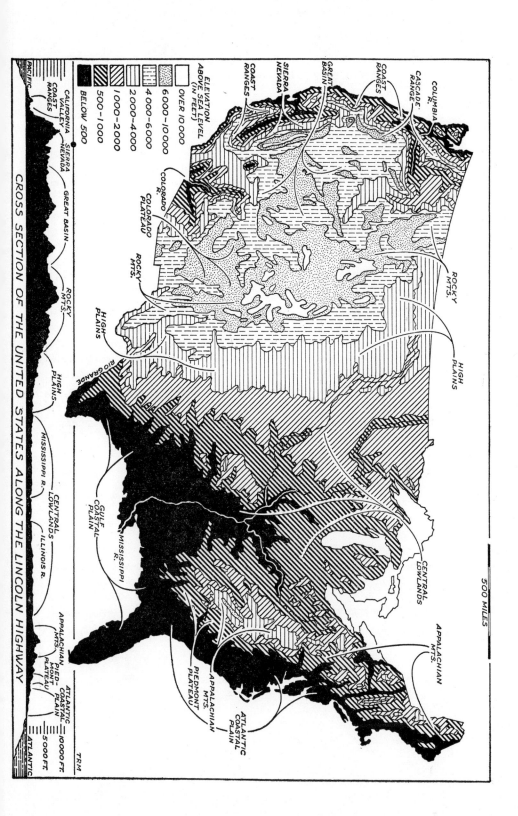

CROSS SECTION OF THE UNITED STATES ALONG THE LINCOLN HIGHWAY

ELEVATION
ABOVE SEA LEVEL
(IN FEET)

OVER 10,000
6,000–10,000
4,000–6,000
2,000–4,000
1,000–2,000
500–1,000
BELOW 500

500 MILES

PACIFIC

COAST
RANGES

CALIFORNIA
VALLEY

SIERRA
NEVADA

GREAT BASIN

ROCKY
MTS.

HIGH
PLAINS

MISSISSIPPI R.

CENTRAL
LOWLANDS

ILLINOIS R.

APPALACHIAN
MTS.

PIED-
MONT
PLATEAU

ATLANTIC
COASTAL
PLAIN

ATLANTIC

10,000 FT.

5000 FT.

TRM

COAST
RANGES

SIERRA
NEVADA

GREAT
BASIN

COAST
RANGES

CASCADE
RANGE

COLUMBIA R.

COLORADO R.

COLORADO
PLATEAU

ROCKY
MTS.

HIGH
PLAINS

RIO GRANDE

GULF
COASTAL
PLAIN

MISSISSIPPI
R.

CENTRAL
LOWLANDS

ROCKY
MTS.

HIGH
PLAINS

CENTRAL
LOWLANDS

APPALACHIAN
MTS.

APPALACHIAN
MTS.

PIEDMONT
PLATEAU

ATLANTIC
COASTAL
PLAIN

THE

United States

OF

America

*

A HISTORY

I

The Expansion of Europe

1. THE EUROPEAN BACKGROUND

2. THE DEVELOPMENT OF ENGLAND

3. THE OPENING OF THE NEW WORLD

IN ORDER to understand the development of the United States, it is necessary to know something about the European countries from which her people originally came. The Americans derived their basic ideals and institutions from the European background, although these were considerably modified during the experience of building a new society in the New World. Throughout her history, in fact, the United States has remained an integral part of the Western, or Atlantic, civilization that originated in Europe, growing during the past three hundred years from a handful of colonies on the periphery of the Western world into its strongest power and the principal guardian of its cultural heritage.

1. THE EUROPEAN BACKGROUND

WESTERN civilization began to expand from Europe to other parts of the world in the fifteenth and sixteenth centuries. This period was marked by far-reaching changes in the whole economic, political, and cultural fabric of European society. The feudal institutions established during the early

SELECTED BIBLIOGRAPHY: E. P. Cheyney, *European Background of American History, 1300–1600* (1904), and the early chapters in C. P. Nettels, *The Roots of American Civilization* (1938), are good general surveys of the reasons for European expansion. J. H. Randall, Jr., *The Making of the Modern Mind* (revised edition, 1940), is a useful survey of European intellectual history. The best short account of English history is J. A. Williamson, *The Evolution of England* (1931). Spanish exploration and the building of the Spanish Empire in North America are described in J. B. Brebner, *The Explorers of North America* (1933), F. A. Kirkpatrick, *The Spanish Conquistadores* (1934), and H. I. Priestley, *The Coming of the White Man* (1930). The standard work on the Spanish colonial system is C. H. Haring, *The Spanish Empire in America* (1947).

Middle Ages were disintegrating under the impact of commercial growth and the rise of the bourgeois, or middle, class, while the peoples along the Atlantic seaboard were organized into unified national states governed by strong monarchies. Meanwhile, the otherworldly emphasis of medieval thought was giving place to the optimistic humanism of the Renaissance, and in the sixteenth century the authority of the Catholic Church was challenged by the Protestant Reformation. All of these movements stimulated a spirit of individual independence and made men more mobile, more adventurous, and more confident of their own powers. All of them contributed to the expansion of European civilization to the Western Hemisphere.

The Growth of Trade.   When the civilization of Europe first began to take shape after the chaos and barbarism of the Dark Ages, most of the population lived as peasants in isolated village communities, society was dominated by the unruly feudal aristocracy, and there was little trade or manufacturing. In a few areas, however, especially in Italy, there were cities inhabited by traders and craftsmen; and as conditions became more stable, this bourgeois class slowly expanded and became richer and more influential. Especially important, both in promoting economic progress and, in the long run, in leading to the expansion of European civilization to other parts of the world, was the development of trade with the richer and more advanced civilizations of the Orient.

This was initially due mainly to the crusades, a series of military expeditions for the purpose of conquering the Holy Land from the Mohammedans. The first crusade, launched in 1096, set up the Christian kingdom of Jerusalem and was followed by commercial contacts with Asia. Europeans bought various manufactured articles and, more especially, pepper and other spices which would relieve the monotony of a medieval diet. Many of these commodities originated as far to the east as India, China, and Indonesia, and were transported by land routes across Asia to the Mediterranean seaports. There they were bought by merchants from Venice and other Italian cities and were then distributed throughout Europe. As early as the thirteenth century a few European merchants, such as the Venetian Marco Polo, actually visited China and brought back fascinating stories of its luxury and sophistication. Favored by geography, the Italians were able to dominate the Mediterranean trade and collect heavy middlemen's profits; and by the fourteenth and fifteenth centuries northern Italy was far ahead of the rest of Europe in wealth and culture.

Meanwhile, cities were developing and a wealthy bourgeois class was rising to prominence in countries along the Atlantic seaboard. The accumulation of fluid capital in these countries made it possible to finance trading expeditions to distant lands in the hope of profits; and in the fifteenth and sixteenth centuries their merchants began to invest money in searching for direct sea routes to the spices and other riches of the Orient.

This was the principal motive for the voyages of discovery that resulted in the colonization of America. The voyages were facilitated by certain technical advances. During the later Middle Ages navigation became easier as a result of several new inventions, especially that of the compass, while the introduction of gunpowder gave Europeans a decisive military advantage over other peoples they encountered.

The Decline of Feudalism. Another important factor in promoting the expansion of Europe was a change in the system of land-holding. The feudalism of the early Middle Ages had been a static form of social and economic organization in which the peasants were attached to the soil and had no freedom of movement, the functions of each individual were fixed by heredity, and there was little incentive for economic progress. The lands belonging to each village community were held and cultivated in common; part of them were set aside as the demesne of the lord, and the peasants were obligated to spend several days a week in working for him. During the later Middle Ages this system began to be transformed by the increased use of money, a change which occurred especially rapidly in England. Instead of continuing to exact labor from the peasants in accordance with traditional practice, many lords found it more convenient to ask for cash payments. This process of "commuting" the customary services into money changed the feudal relationship of lord and serf into one of landlord and tenant. It was usually advantageous to both parties, since the lord could now hire wage laborers to work on his demesne, while the peasant was no longer bound to the soil and acquired more personal freedom. At the same time the community lands were often broken up into separate farm properties belonging to individual families.

The effect of these economic changes was to give men more independence and mobility. In place of peasants attached to the soil, there were now growing numbers of free farmers and wage laborers who could, if they chose, seek better conditions by moving to new countries. Thus, while the growth of trade and the merchant class led to the discovery of America, it was the disintegration of feudalism that enabled America to be colonized. And since the upper class, while surrendering its feudal rights, retained ownership of a large part of the land, along with extensive social and political privileges, men born into the poorer classes had strong inducements for seeking broader opportunities in a new world. Down to the nineteenth century, in fact, the European structure of class privilege derived from the feudal background was a main cause for the migration of European peasants and workers to America. Thus feudalism had a vast indirect influence on American development, even though it was one European institution that was never transplanted into the soil of the United States.

The Rise of National States. While economic developments made Europe ripe for expansion, it was the political situation that made expan-

sion actually possible. Men could not have explored and conquered the
New World if they had not been backed by the power and resources of
strong national governments.

In the early Middle Ages Europeans had regarded themselves primarily as members of the Christian community and had not developed
much sense of national differences. And while each country had its king,
he had rarely been able to enforce his authority over the feudal lords. In
several western countries, however, especially in Spain, France and England, there was a steady trend towards national unification under the rule
of strong kings. This growth of royal power was supported by the bourgeoisie, who wanted a form of government capable of enforcing law and
order and protecting trade and recognized that this could be achieved
only through extending the authority of the Crown. By the end of the
fifteenth century, in fact, the kings of Spain and France had become
virtually absolute rulers, claiming that they were responsible to God
alone and could not be called to account by their subjects. Germany and
Italy, on the other hand, did not develop effective central governments
until the nineteenth century, and hence did not acquire American colonies.

The rise of national states was not wholly beneficial, since it weakened the traditional belief in the unity of European civilization. People
began to think of themselves primarily as Spaniards, Frenchmen, and
Englishmen, and to give their main loyalty to their own government, no
longer recognizing the claims of any broader ideal. This resulted in a series
of conflicts between different nations which have continued into the
twentieth century. But there can be no doubt that, by contrast with the
anarchy of feudalism, the national state marked a step forward towards
more orderly and efficient government.

In addition to enforcing order, the royal governments supervised economic development in a most elaborate fashion. The notion that economic
matters should be left to the free play of supply and demand had been
wholly alien to medieval ways of thinking, and it had always been assumed that the authorities should control prices and wages and protect
the general welfare. Each of the new royal governments now assumed
these regulatory functions and also sought to increase the wealth and
power of its own nation at the expense of her foreign competitors. It was
for this reason that they assisted the merchants in searching for new trade
routes.

This attitude of economic nationalism developed into the "mercantilist" economic policies that were adopted by all the leading European
states through the sixteenth, seventeenth, and eighteenth centuries. According to mercantilist thinking, the nation should aim at economic independence, seeking to produce all necessities within her own territories;
she should try to accumulate gold and silver by selling to competing nations more than she bought from them; and she should lay special empha-

sis on the production of any goods needed for war purposes. Mercantilist economic policy was a most important factor in the colonization of America. Colonies were regarded as valuable because they could supply necessary raw materials not produced at home. After the discovery of the New World each of the new national states set out to acquire American colonies and monopolize their trade, and the consequent imperialistic rivalries led to a series of general wars.

Cultural Changes. These economic and political developments were accompanied by changes in men's intellectual attitudes and beliefs. The exploration of the New World was due not only to economic pressures and political ambitions but also to the growth of a new spirit of optimism, adventurousness, and self-confidence.

During the early Middle Ages all intellectual and aesthetic activities had been dominated by religious belief, and the world had been regarded in gloomy terms. On account of human sinfulness, this life was not capable of much improvement and was primarily a mere preparation for the life to come; the highest form of earthly existence was that of the monk who renounced all worldly desires in order to devote himself to the worship of God. Medieval ways of thinking, moreover, were unscientific, since nature was viewed teleologically; in other words, each natural object was defined in terms of the end or purpose for which God had made it.

In spite of the otherworldly emphasis of medieval thought, however, its permanent contribution to the heritage of Western civilization should not be overlooked. The great Scholastic philosophers of the Middle Ages, fusing the Jewish, Greek, and Roman elements in the European tradition, interpreted the universe as the creation of a rational Being who governed by law rather than by arbitrary fiat. Human societies, they believed, should conform to this divine law, which was also a law of nature and of reason; and it should be binding upon kings as well as upon their subjects. Most medieval thinkers regarded monarchy and class privilege as in accord with divine law; but in spite of their conservative inclinations they believed that power should always be limited. This doctrine of a fundamental law of God, nature, and reason has continued, in different forms, to be one of the main principles of Western civilization down to the present day. The American belief in the supremacy of law, derived immediately from the English political tradition, comes more remotely from the thought of the Middle Ages and of the ancient world.

As wealth and orderly government increased, the pessimism of medieval thinking gave place to a new emphasis on the potentialities of life in this world, the result being the many-sided cultural movement known as the Renaissance. Originating in the rich cities of northern Italy, where it led to a great artistic efflorescence, the Renaissance spread to other parts of Europe in the late fifteenth and sixteenth centuries. Its leading figures manifested an exuberant delight in intellectual and aesthetic exploration, and thought less of the salvation of their souls in an after life and more of the earthly immortality to be derived from fame and worldly achievement.

One of the main elements in the Renaissance was a revival of the literature and learning of ancient Greece and Rome. "Humanist" scholars turned back to the classics in order to escape from the otherworldliness of medieval thinking and recapture more optimistic views of human life. This led to a reform of education which had lasting effects. Idealizing the gentleman rather than the ascetic, the Humanists believed that education should promote a well-rounded development of all sides of human nature and that this could best be accomplished through the study of the classics. Whereas in Italy the Renaissance led to much outright paganism, in England and other northern countries its chief manifestation was a Christian Humanism which placed the classics almost on a level with the Bible and regarded the rational appreciation and improvement of life in this world as consistent with devout religious belief.

The chief figures of the Renaissance were the great artists and writers of Italy, Spain, France, and Elizabethan England. But the explorers of the New World manifested a similar confidence in man's capacities and in the limitless possibilities of the material world. The culture of the early American colonies, moreover, was a product of the Renaissance. Their first schools and colleges were imbued with the spirit of Christian Humanism.

Although the Renaissance was not primarily a scientific movement, it led indirectly to a new approach to the natural sciences. Before the end of the sixteenth century a few men were beginning to suggest that, by abandoning the teleological emphasis of medieval thought and studying the causes of natural phenomena, it might be possible to increase human power immeasurably. Interpreting the concept of natural law in a new way, they were beginning to see the material world as a complex of forces operating by immutable chains of cause and effect and to realize that exact measurement was the key to its interpretation. But the sciences were not placed on firm foundations until the seventeenth century.

Religious Changes.   Even more important than the Renaissance in shaping the view of life of the early American colonists was the Protestant Reformation. The Catholic Church had retained its authority down to the end of the Middle Ages, although it was admittedly corrupt and in need of reform, while its claims to universality conflicted with the growing spirit of nationalism. Early in the sixteenth century the Reformation was precipitated by the German theologian Martin Luther, and within a few years most of the countries of northern Europe repudiated the supremacy of the Pope and set up their own Protestant churches. The Catholic Church then rallied her forces, purified abuses through the Catholic Reformation, and endeavored to win back her lost provinces. For more than a hundred years much of Europe was involved in intermittent religious wars. When the spirit of religious fanaticism finally grew less intense in the middle of the seventeenth century, the Catholic Church retained the allegiance of southern Europe and also of two northern peoples, the Poles and the Irish, while Great Britain, Holland, Scandinavia, and northern Germany remained Protestant.

To a considerable extent the Reformation was a political and economic movement, supported by men who wished to strengthen national independence and to strip the Church of much of her wealth. But it also introduced new conceptions of religious belief and experience and of church organization. Luther and other early Protestant theologians did not share the optimism of the Renaissance, and emphasized human sinfulness in the most uncompromising terms; but by insisting that man could be redeemed only if he felt a sincere faith in Jesus Christ, and that he could not earn salvation simply by obeying the rules prescribed by the Church, they made religion more individualistic.

After Luther the most influential Protestant leader was the Frenchman Jean Calvin, who published the first edition of his *Institutes of the Christian Religion* in 1534 and subsequently became the dominating figure in the city-state of Geneva, Switzerland. Calvin's view of the world was extremely gloomy. Denying free will and declaring that all men were "predestined" either for Heaven or for Hell, he regarded redeeming faith as the free gift of God to those whom he had "elected" for salvation. Yet in spite of its severity, the Calvinist creed had a strong appeal to the middle classes; and when its adherents experienced what they believed to be redeeming faith and felt assured of their own election, they displayed an extraordinary moral energy and crusading fervor. The ethical doctrines of Calvinism condemned worldly pleasures and amusements, inculcated industry and thrift, and promoted a kind of asceticism of daily life, as contrasted with the medieval asceticism of the monastery. God, it was declared, required man to work conscientiously at the business or profession to which he had been "called." And whereas most other forms of Protestantism put the Church under the control of the secular authorities, Calvinism declared that kings and magistrates should be guided by the will of God as interpreted by the Church and that the Church consisted of the whole community of the elect, devout laymen sharing with the clergy in its government. Thus, while Calvinist ethics tended to sanctify the activities of the businessman, Calvinist views of church government had revolutionary implications. Calvinism spread to middle-class groups in France, England, Scotland, Holland, and southwestern Germany, and led everywhere to rebellions against kings who refused to do the will of God as interpreted by the Calvinist churches.

In spite of the pessimism and moral severity of Calvinism, it made a great contribution to the progress of Western civilization. By teaching thrift and hard work, it stimulated economic growth. By encouraging revolution against impious rulers, it led indirectly to more democratic forms of government. And by requiring the individual to live strictly, constantly examining his conscience and regulating his behavior by the will of God, it promoted higher standards of personal integrity. The strict Calvinist was not very tolerant or warmhearted; but he was a man of strong character and a useful citizen.

Both Lutheranism and Calvinism, like Catholicism, believed that what they regarded as religious truth should be enforced by the secular authorities. But some other Protestant groups declared that religion consisted essentially of a mystical communion between God and the individual, and went on to argue that no elaborate church organization was required, that the state should not interfere with religious beliefs, and that force and compulsion in any form were inherently evil. Some of them, such as the Anabaptists, repudiated all secular authority and looked forward to the rapid approach of the Kingdom of God on earth. These mystical sects spread especially among peasants, craftsmen, and other humble people in western Germany and the Netherlands. Persecuted by the authorities and generally regarded as crazy and subversive, they foreshadowed the liberalism and humanitarianism of the future.

All these varieties of religious belief were brought across to America. The settlement of the American colonies was, in fact, greatly stimulated by religious dissensions. While the expansion of the Spanish and French colonies was hastened by the militant faith of the Catholic Reformation, represented by the friars who traveled through the forests and across the mountains to convert the Indians, some of the English colonies were settled by minority Protestant groups who wished to worship God in their own way. While New England was founded as a model Calvinist community, Pennsylvania became a place of refuge for the mystical sects, both English and German. The institutions of all the early colonies, moreover, whatever form of religion they professed, were products of a society which had a vital belief in an after life and regarded the propagation of true beliefs as man's most important duty.

2. THE DEVELOPMENT OF ENGLAND

OF THE various European nations which contributed to the settlement of America, England has, of course, a special importance for the history of the United States. The political and social development of England differed in significant ways from that of the continental countries; her government was less authoritarian, and class distinctions were less rigid. American traditions of freedom and equality grew from English seeds.

Political Institutions.   At the end of the Middle Ages, England, like Spain and France, achieved unity under a strong monarchy. The rulers of the Tudor dynasty, the greatest of whom were Henry VIII (1509–47) and Elizabeth I (1558–1603), enforced order, promoted commerce, and made themselves the focuses of national loyalty. But the English monarchy, unlike that of continental countries, never became absolute. In England alone the medieval belief in the supremacy of law had become effectively embodied in political institutions. A bicameral Parliament, with a House of Lords composed of members of the aristocracy and a House of Commons made up of elected representatives of the bourgeoisie and the country gentry, had become a regular part of the government, and the principle had been established that the king could not make new laws or impose new taxes without its consent. The English common law, moreover, gave more protection to individuals than did the legal system of any continental country. Although the English were in no sense a democratic people, they prided themselves on being a free people and on the security given to private citizens through trial by jury and the independence of the judiciary. Ever since King John had been compelled to sign the Magna Carta in 1215, the tradition had been maintained that citizens had certain legal rights which the Crown could not violate.

In spite of the extensive powers of the Tudor monarchs, they governed with the aid and approval of Parliament; and although they dealt sternly with powerful offenders, they usually respected the rights of plain citizens. They were, in fact, wholly dependent upon popular support. The Crown had no large bureaucracy or standing army, and was constantly short of money even for the ordinary expenses of government. One of the most important features of the Tudor system was that most of the work of administration, especially in local government, was entrusted not to salaried royal officials but to private citizens who were not paid for their services. In every English county the local gentry, serving as justices of the peace, administered justice and enforced the decisions of Crown and Parliament. Ordinary citizens sat on juries, and were called for service in the militia during insurrections or times of national danger. Thus government in England was not an alien power represented by a separate bureaucratic and military class but was broadly based on popular approval and participation.

The men who settled the early American colonies brought with them all these English traditions—limitation of executive power, a bicameral legislature, trial by jury, protection of individual rights by the common law, reliance on the militia rather than on a standing army for defense and on justices of the peace rather than on salaried officials for local administration. The American system of government was built on these English foundations.

Economic Development.   Economic conditions in sixteenth-century England were peculiarly favorable to overseas expansion. Feudalism had disappeared more rapidly and completely than on the continent, and the peasants had been transformed into free yeoman farmers, tenants, or wage laborers. Although a small upper class owned much of the land, there was no sharp distinction between the nobility and the rich bourgeoisie; city merchants and lawyers sometimes bought land and acquired titles, and many noblemen were interested in commercial profits and became partners with merchants in new economic enterprises. English society, in fact, had become predominantly business-minded. The later Tudor period was one of rapid economic progress; foreign trade and domestic industries, especially the cloth industry, were expanding, and capital was being accumulated. Especially important was the formation of joint-stock commercial companies for trade with distant countries. These were chartered by the Crown and usually received monopolistic privileges. By organizing a company, merchants and noblemen were able to pool their capital resources for new and ambitious commercial enterprises.

While rich men accumulated profits, however, many of the poorer classes were in acute distress. The growth of the woolen industry made sheep-herding an especially profitable activity, and many large landowners began to use their estates for sheep instead of for agriculture. For the same reason they appropriated and enclosed some of the common lands formerly available for the use of the small farmers. Since sheep-herding required relatively little labor, the result of these economic changes was widespread rural poverty and unemployment. Rural England appeared to be overcrowded, and its surplus population began to flow into the cities to seek jobs in industry.

Thus, by the end of the sixteenth century, England was ready to take advantage of the opening of the New World. On the one hand, rich men had capital to invest, and had discovered how to finance large-scale enterprises by means of joint-stock companies. On the other hand, there was a relatively large body of laborers and small farmers who had the requisite mobility and strong inducements for emigration.

The Growth of Puritanism.   One other feature of English development was of special importance in stimulating migration to America. This was the growth of religious conflicts. The Church of England, or Anglican Church, set up by the Tudors during the Reformation, was controlled by the Crown and the bishops, permitted considerable divergences of belief, and made little attempt to enforce a strict morality. But during the reign of Elizabeth I, Calvinist doctrines won steadily increasing support, especially among the middle classes and the rural gentry. The English Calvinists, who became known as Puritans, remained within the Church of England but wished to make drastic changes in its organization and principles. The Church, they declared, should be controlled by the ministers and devout laymen instead of by the Crown, and the whole community should be compelled to accept the theology of Calvinism and its strict ethical code. Both the revolutionary program of church government put forward by the Puritans and their theological and moral intolerance made conflict with the monarchy inevitable, although the issues did not become sharply defined until after the death of Elizabeth.

In 1603 the crown passed to the Scottish Stuart dynasty, thereby bringing about a union of the crowns of England and Scotland (although the two countries continued to have separate governments until 1707).

The early Stuart kings, James I and Charles I, strongly opposed the Puritans and tried to prevent them from propagating their beliefs. They also antagonized many Englishmen who cared more about liberty than about religion by disregarding the rights of Parliament, interfering with the law courts, and claiming absolute powers. Charles I's policies led finally to the Civil War, which broke out in 1642. Meanwhile, many Englishmen, especially among the Puritans, had strong religious and political motives for moving to America.

The main religious conflict was between the supporters of the established Anglican Church and the Puritans, neither of whom believed in religious freedom. But meanwhile a few obscure groups, some of them influenced by the German Anabaptists, began to separate completely from the established Church and to form their own religious congregations. One of these groups has a special place in American history since it was responsible for the voyage of the *Mayflower*. Another early seventeenth-century separatist group, who rejected the traditional belief in infant baptism, became the founders of the Baptist Church. In the 1640's the Society of Friends, better known as the Quakers, was founded under the leadership of George Fox. These new organizations, with their emphasis on freedom of opinion, won support at first only among humble farmers and craftsmen and were regarded by both Anglicans and Puritans as dangerously subversive; yet in the retrospect of history it can be seen that they pointed the way to the liberalism of the future.

A new kind of society was, in fact, taking shape in the England of the Tudors and early Stuarts—a society in which government would be responsible to the will of the people, opinions would be free and uncontrolled, and the individual's place in society would depend on his abilities rather than on hereditary class and rank. It was a long time before this new society was fully achieved. Most Englishmen of the early seventeenth century still thought largely in medieval terms, accepting hereditary class distinctions and religious intolerance as in accord with the will of God. But the concepts of a free society were already germinating in English soil. Wherever Englishmen settled in other parts of the world, they carried with them the seeds of liberty.

3. THE OPENING OF THE NEW WORLD

The Role of Portugal.   The little country of Portugal, fronting the Atlantic and remote from the wars in which most other European peoples were involved, took the lead in the voyages of exploration. Early in the fifteenth century Portuguese sea captains began to sail down the African coast, hoping to open up new trade routes to the East, discover new countries, and spread the knowledge of Christianity. The early expeditions were organized by a Portuguese prince, Henry the Navigator, who founded a school for geographical and nautical studies at Sagres in southern Portugal about the year 1420. At the time of his death in 1460 Portuguese ships had not yet crossed the equator, but other men continued his efforts. In 1488 Bartholomeu Dias reached the Cape of Good Hope at the southern end of Africa, and in 1498 Vasco da Gama made the first voyage round Africa to India. The cargo of spices which he brought back with him was sold at a profit of 6,000 per cent, thus showing the enormous value of a direct sea route to Asiatic markets. For nearly a century thereafter Portugal dominated the trade with the Orient and acquired a number of possessions in the East Indies, though she lacked the population and resources to retain her leadership after other European nations had begun to challenge it.

The Discovery of America.   The first Europeans to reach America had been Norse seamen from Iceland and Greenland about the year 1000; but their discoveries had never become known in the rest of Europe and had been forgotten even by the Norwegians. By the fifteenth century, however, a number of people in Europe were considering the possibility of reaching Asia by sailing westwards. Geographers believed that the world was round and generally underestimated its size, and there were legends of islands out in the Atlantic which might serve as calling points in a voyage to the Orient. Both Portuguese and English seamen, in fact, sailed considerable distances into the Atlantic but became disheartened by the unending expanse of water and turned back. What was needed was somebody bold enough to put the theories of the geographers to a conclusive test. Columbus had the necessary skill in seamanship; but he earned his place in history primarily by his self-confidence and courage.

Born in Genoa, Italy, Columbus worked for a number of years as a seaman and cartographer in the employment of the Portuguese. In 1484 he asked the Portuguese government to give him financial backing in a westward voyage. His petition rejected, he turned next to Spain, which had not hitherto shown much interest in maritime expansion; and after seven years of frustration at the Spanish court he finally captured the interest of Queen Isabella and obtained a grant from the royal treasury. He set sail from Palos in southern Spain with three small ships on August 3, 1492. On October 12, thirty-three days after leaving the Canary Islands, the expedition touched land in the West Indies.

Columbus believed that he was close to the mainland of Asia and never realized that he had discovered a whole new hemisphere. In three later voyages he explored a large part of the Caribbean, but failed to find the route through to China for which he was looking. Not until 1522, when the survivors of the Magellan expedition reached Spain after the first voyage round the world, did it become known how vast an ocean lay between America and the Orient. But Spanish colonists occupied the larger West Indian islands and established plantations for growing sugar and other tropical crops. The Indians of the islands, a primitive and unwarlike people, were reduced to servitude; and when they began to die off, Negro slaves were imported from Africa to take their places. Spain claimed exclusive rights over most of the New World by virtue of a grant from the Pope. By the papal line of demarcation of 1493, modified a year later by the Treaty of Tordesillas, the non-European world was divided between Spain and Portugal. While most of America was granted to Spain, the eastern part of Brazil fell on the Portuguese side of the line.

The Spanish Empire on the Mainland.   For a generation after the first voyage of Columbus, Spain derived little profit from his discoveries; and by contrast with the achievement of Vasco da Gama, they seemed relatively disappointing. But in the year 1519 Hernán Cortés, leading an expedition from Cuba, landed on the mainland of Mexico, made his way into the mountains of the interior, and discovered the rich and powerful empire of the Aztecs. This part of the New World had been a center of advanced Indian cultures for thousands of years. The Spaniards could scarcely believe their eyes when they first saw the Aztec city of Tenochtitlán, with its handsome buildings, stores of gold and silver, and sophisticated way of life. Aided by Indian tribes who hated the Aztecs, they won control of southern Mexico within the next three years, and its silver mines soon became a source of immense profits for Spain.

After the discovery of Tenochtitlán the Spaniards believed that the possibilities of America were limitless, and during the next three quarters of a century, searching for new Indian civilizations and for marvels like El Dorado, the country of the Amazons, and the Fountain of Perpetual Youth, they explored and conquered an area larger than the whole of Europe. From their base in southern Mexico they steadily expanded northwards, reaching the borders of New Mexico and California before the end of the century, while in 1565 they took possession of Florida, where they founded St. Augustine, the first white settlement in any part of the United States. Exploring expeditions led by Hernando de Soto and Francisco Vásquez Coronado had already ranged over large areas of the Mississippi Valley and the Great Plains, and Spanish ships had sailed up both the Atlantic and the Pacific seacoast almost into Canadian waters. In South America, Francisco Pizarro, setting out from Panama in 1531, conquered the empire of the Incas in Peru, which was even richer in gold and silver than that of the Aztecs, while other leaders carried Spanish dominion into the mountains of what is now Colombia and Venezuela, made their way down the Pacific coast into the rich valley of central Chile, and founded cities on the Río de la Plata in the plains of Argentina. By the end of the century Spain was the owner of an empire stretching from the Rio Grande and the Gulf of California down to Buenos Aires and Santiago, nearly six thousand miles from north to south. This was as much as she could effectively hold, though she continued to claim the whole of the Western Hemisphere except Brazil. After 1600 there was little further expansion, and the Spaniards settled down to develop and enjoy the riches of their empire.

The most important factor in the development of Spanish America was the presence of large Indian populations, accustomed to agriculture, who could be compelled to labor for their white conquerors. Most of the Spanish colonists who settled in the New World became wealthy land-owners or mine-owners, supported by Indian dependents. Thus society remained divided by sharp distinctions of class and race. The Spanish Crown, moreover, imposed an absolutist form of government, and all authority was concentrated in the king and the officials he dispatched to the colonies. For these reasons the development of Spanish America was very different from that of the English colonies which became the United States; the Spanish colonial system prohibited the growth of any spirit of equality or democracy. Yet Spain did much to promote civilization throughout her empire. Spanish officials and clergy encouraged arts and sciences, founded schools and universities, built cathedrals that were architectural masterpieces, converted the Indians to Christianity, taught them new handicrafts and agricultural techniques, and made sincere, though often unsuccessful, efforts to protect them from excessive exploitation by the Spanish colonists.

Thus changes in the economic and political structure of European society had stimulated some of its peoples to explore and conquer new countries, while its cultural development had given it a dynamic power with which no other existing society could compete. Western civilization was launched on a process of expansion which eventually brought almost all non-European peoples within its scope and made it virtually world-wide.

2. The New World Before 1600

EUROPE IS THE SMALLEST OF THE FIVE CONTINENTS AND INCLUDES ONLY A TINY fraction of the total land area of the globe. Nevertheless the civilization that developed in western Europe acquired a dynamic and expansionist quality that eventually made it almost world-wide. Down to the end of the Middle Ages the chief centers of economic and cultural advance were along the shores of the Mediterranean, and the main trade routes were those connecting Italy with the East. After the voyages of discovery supremacy shifted to the peoples fronting the Atlantic, especially to those of Spain, France, and England, each of whom acquired colonial possessions many times larger than their homelands.

Located at the southwestern extremity of Europe, Portugal and Spain were well situated to assume priority in the discoveries. Portugal's main ambition was to find a sea route to India around Africa, and this was accomplished by Vasco da Gama in 1498. She also acquired the right to settle Brazil, which fell east of the demarcation line established between Portugal and Spain by the Treaty of Tordesillas of 1494. The Brazilian coast was first explored by Cabral in 1500. Probably this expedition was planned by the Portuguese government, although it was formerly believed that Cabral had been blown off his course while sailing down Africa and had thus discovered Brazil by accident. The first colonies were established in Brazil in the 1530's.

After the voyage of Columbus, Spain claimed the whole of the New World except Brazil, and before 1600, had explored and colonized a large part of it. By that time she controlled most of the area now divided among the different Spanish-speaking republics, with the exception of southern Chile and Argentina, which were held by unconquered Indian tribes until the late nineteenth century. The two main centers of Spanish power were Mexico (then known as New Spain) and Peru, each of which contained rich gold and silver mines and advanced Indian civilizations. Thus European civilization has a much longer history in Hispanic America than in the United States. A map of the New World in 1600 shows that the Spanish and Portuguese empires covered wide areas, although the regions north of Florida still had no white inhabitants.

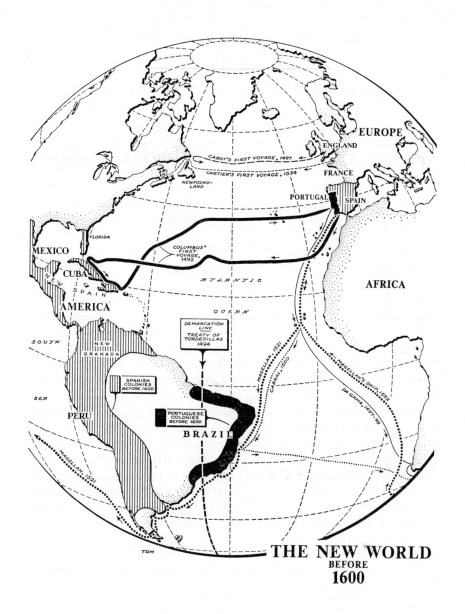

CABOT'S FIRST VOYAGE, 1497

CARTIER'S FIRST VOYAGE, 1534

NEWFOUND-
LAND

EUROPE

ENGLAND

FRANCE

PORTUGAL SPAIN

MEXICO

FLORIDA

CUBA

NEW SPAIN

COLUMBUS'
FIRST
VOYAGE,
1492

ATLANTIC

AFRICA

AMERICA

OCEAN

SOUTH

NEW
GRANADA

DEMARCATION
LINE
TREATY OF
TORDESILLAS
1494

SPANISH
COLONIES
BEFORE 1600

MAGELLAN 1521

CABRAL 1500

MAGELLAN'S SHIP 1522

DA GAMA, 1497-'98

SEA

PORTUGUESE
COLONIES
BEFORE 1600

PERU

BRAZIL

MAGELLAN 1521

TRM

THE NEW WORLD
BEFORE
1600

II

The Founding of the Colonies

1. THE BEGINNINGS OF COLONIZATION

2. THE CHESAPEAKE COLONIES

3. THE NEW ENGLAND COLONIES

4. THE LATER COLONIES

For more than a hundred years after the voyage of Columbus, the Spaniards were the only people who founded permanent colonies in North America. Other European nations, especially the English and French, were by no means willing to allow Spain a monopoly of all the wealth of the New World; but for a long time the other nations devoted their main efforts not to the planting of colonies but to piracy at Spanish expense and to the search for a sea route to the Orient around North America. The main reason was that the Spaniards had already occupied the most attractive parts of the New World. In the northern areas that the Spaniards had left unsettled there were no advanced Indian communities to be conquered and exploited, and no gold or silver mines which would provide immediate profits, so that colonies could not become paying

SELECTED BIBLIOGRAPHY: The best one-volume survey of colonial history is C. P. Nettels, *The Roots of American Civilization* (1938). The most authoritative longer study is C. M. Andrews, *The Colonial Period in American History* (4 vols., 1934–37). H. L. Osgood, *The American Colonies in the Seventeenth Century* (3 vols., 1904–07) is still useful. Two volumes in *A History of American Life* cover the early colonial period: H. I. Priestley, *The Coming of the White Man* (1929); and T. J. Wertenbaker, *The First Americans, 1607–1690* (1927). Under the general title *The Founding of American Civilization*, T. J. Wertenbaker has written *The Middle Colonies* (1938), *The Old South* (1942), and *The Puritan Oligarchy* (1947), which stress cultural as well as political development. The best study of the founding of the Southern colonies is W. F. Craven, *The Southern Colonies in the Seventeenth Century, 1607–1689* (1949). The most convenient history of early New England, J. T. Adams, *The Founding of New England* (1921), is unsympathetic to the Puritans. The balance can be redressed by reading it in conjunction with S. E. Morison's charming *Builders of the Bay Colony* (1930). The most useful survey of Puritanism is the introduction of P. G. E. Miller and T. H. Johnson (eds.), *The Puritans* (1938).

propositions quickly. But after several unsuccessful attempts, the English and French founded lasting colonies on the North American mainland early in the seventeenth century, while smaller enterprises were launched by the Dutch and Swedes.

1. THE BEGINNINGS OF COLONIZATION

Problems of Colonization.   That part of North America that faces Europe consists chiefly of a coastal plain, most of which was originally thickly forested. To the west the land rises slowly as far as the Appalachian ranges, which stretch from the St. Lawrence almost to the Gulf of Mexico. For a long time these mountains blocked any advance from the coastal regions into the Mississippi Valley. Along much of the coastline the soil is not very fertile, although it becomes richer inland, particularly in the valleys east of the main Appalachian ranges.

For several reasons it was not very easy to establish colonies in this region. Although the climate was generally similar to that of western Europe, the winters in the north were longer and more severe, while the south suffered from much hotter and more humid summers. A number of the areas first settled proved to be unhealthful, containing disease germs to which Europeans had not acquired immunity. The thick forests, moreover, impeded overland communication, so that early colonization was limited to the coastal areas and to sites on rivers and inlets of the sea which provided easier communication by water. Thus the French settled on the St. Lawrence, the Dutch on the Hudson, the Swedes on the Delaware, and the English on the rivers emptying into Chesapeake Bay. Early exploration and expansion westwards moved mostly along the different river systems.

The main obstacles to colonization, however, were economic. Colonies, like other economic enterprises, required considerable investments of capital and could not flourish unless they quickly produced profits. It was therefore necessary to find products for which there was a demand in Europe. But what Europe chiefly needed was commodities, such as sugar and spices, which could be produced only in a tropical climate. For this reason the development of trade with the East Indies and the settlement of the West Indies proved for a long time to be more attractive to European investors than the colonization of North America.

In the beginning, the greatest source of wealth in North America was the fur trade. The whole continent was rich in furry animals, particularly beavers, and there was a steady market for their skins throughout Europe. But an exploitative occupation like fur-trapping did not make a good foundation for permanent prosperity. Fur-traders would open up a new country, but would move elsewhere as soon as the supply of wild animals began to diminish. There were similar objections to lumbering, which also attracted some European capital. No colony could have a healthy development until profitable forms of agriculture or industry were established, but this was a slow process.

The Organization of Colonies.   England and France both laid claims to considerable areas of North America; and the legal theory on which colonization proceeded was that all land in these areas was initially the property of the Crown. Grants of North American land were made by the Crown either to commercial companies or to individual proprietors, who might then transfer it to settlers. Legal titles could not be obtained in any other way. In practice, however, this legal theory was frequently difficult to enforce. Once colonists had established themselves in America, they were likely to move out into unoccupied territory and take possession of attractive land without any regard for titles of ownership. A man who had discovered a section of fertile ground and had cleared it by his own labor was inclined to feel that it was now his own property, and that the government could not afterwards dispossess him or compel him to pay rent for it. The conflict between the squatter and the man who claimed land by legal title was to be an important factor in American development for two and a half centuries.

When a group of men received a charter to establish a colony, they did not merely acquire ownership of the land; they also received the power to govern it. Thus political authority over the colony belonged to the men who invested money to establish it, and most of them usually remained in Europe. These men would then appoint a governor and other officials to exercise authority in America. In the French and Dutch colonies this despotic system of government was accepted by the colonists without serious protests. In all the English colonies, on the other hand, it soon proved to be unworkable. By the seventeenth century English people were accustomed to certain guarantees of liberty and were not willing to forfeit them on moving to America. They insisted that they should continue to enjoy the protection of the common law, and that executive power should be limited by an elected legislature. The organizers of the English colonies quickly realized that they could not attract settlers unless they gave them the political and legal rights enjoyed by English people at home.

Since the Dutch and Swedes lacked the population and resources for large-scale expansion and Spain already had as large an empire as she could control, England and France became the major claimants for domination of what is now the United States, and the issue between them, often leading to violent conflict, was for a long time in doubt. By establishing themselves on the St. Lawrence, which enabled them to by-pass the Appalachian barrier and enjoy easy access by way of the Great Lakes into the heart of the continent, the French acquired a great strategic advantage. English settlers did not begin to cross the mountains until the middle of the eighteenth century, long after the French had taken possession of the Mississippi Valley. Yet in the end it was the English who became predominant. The main reason for this was that, from the beginning of the period of colonial expansion, English people migrated to America in much larger numbers than the French. Most Frenchmen were peasants who preferred to stay on their own land. In England, on the other hand, economic changes had created a large dispossessed class lacking adequate means of support. England, unlike France, appeared to be overcrowded.

The Indians. Before proceeding to the details of colonization, a few words should be given to the original settlers of North America. In the sixteenth century the region which is now the United States probably had less than 1,000,000 Indian inhabitants, divided into a number of different tribes with distinct languages and cultural characteristics. By contrast with Indian peoples like the Mayas and Aztecs of Mexico and the Incas of Peru, who had created high civilizations, all of the North American Indians had remained on a more primitive level of development. The tribes scattered through the eastern forest zone lived partly by the cultivation of corn and partly by hunting. Most of them were relatively peaceful, though a few, like the Iroquois in what is now upstate New York, became highly militant. Their political organization was simple and fairly democratic. The chieftain of an Indian tribe had limited powers, and important decisions were made by the tribal council. Fields and hunting-grounds were held by the tribe in common and were not divided into private properties. Agriculture was often left mainly to the women, while the men concentrated on hunting and fighting.

Colonists from Europe learned much from the Indians. They learned, for example, how to grow corn and a number of other vegetables, and how to use many plants with medicinal or narcotic properties, particularly tobacco. Early colonial organizers usually hoped to establish good relations with the Indians and aspired to convert them to Christianity. But it proved to be impossible for the two races to live peacefully side by side. As the white men cut down the forests and expanded the land under cultivation, they diminished the grounds over which the Indians could hunt. Constant misunderstandings were caused, moreover, by the fact that the Indians had no conception of private property in land; Indian chieftains would agree that white settlers could make use of part of their tribes' hunting grounds, and would then discover that the whites were clearing the land, fencing it in, and treating it as their private property. White settlers interested primarily in the fur trade or in hunting could usually establish friendly relations with the Indians, but wherever the whites developed agriculture, conflicts developed quickly.

Almost from the beginning, therefore, there was fighting between the two races. The whites soon found that the Indians could be remarkably cruel to their enemies and began to retaliate in the same manner. Governments, both during the colonial period and afterwards, often tried to protect the Indians from unfair treatment; but the average colonist, living in fear of being killed and scalped, usually came quickly to the conclusion that the only good Indian was a dead Indian. For nearly three hundred years the record of white-Indian relations in the United States was a tragic story of misunderstandings, broken agreements, treacheries, and massacres. Eventually the white peoples took possession of almost the whole country, and the surviving Indians, reduced to one-fifth of their original number as a result not only of warfare but also of the liquor and diseases brought by the white men, were herded on to reservations.

Early English Activities.   The English made their first attempt to explore America almost as soon as they heard the news of Columbus's discovery. In 1497 and 1498 John Cabot, a Venetian seaman employed by King Henry VII, made two voyages to Newfoundland and parts of the mainland. This gave the English Crown a claim to sovereignty over much of North America, but Cabot's expeditions were not followed up by any efforts at colonization. During the next eighty years fishermen from the English West Country regularly took their tiny vessels across the North Atlantic to the banks of Newfoundland to fish for cod, but the English government was preoccupied, first with wars on the European continent and afterwards with the Reformation and the ensuing religious conflicts.

By the 1570's, under the rule of Elizabeth, the country had achieved more stability, and commerce and industry were increasing rapidly. A number of prominent individuals, partly at the royal court and partly among the London merchants, then began to advocate a policy of imperial expansion. Initially, their main hope was to find a northwest passage which would lead to the spices of the Orient. In 1576 Martin Frobisher explored the coast of Labrador, and during the next half-century he was followed by John Davis, Henry Hudson, William Baffin, and others. Most of the desolate bays and islands to the north of Canada gradually acquired English names, and the English developed an interest in the region which led to the establishment of fur-trading stations on Hudson Bay in the year 1670. Otherwise the search for a passage had no tangible results. Meanwhile, other Englishmen organized piratical expeditions to attack Spanish ships and to raid settlements in the Caribbean and on the mainland of South America. This was justified largely on religious grounds and had a strong appeal to the more militantly Protestant elements among the English people.

Although piracy promised much more dazzling rewards than colonization, it could not be regarded as a satisfactory basis for lasting national greatness. Far-sighted Englishmen realized that only permanent colonies would establish English power in the New World. Colonization was advocated by influential men at the royal court, while arguments for it were put in writing and presented to the general public by two men, an uncle and a nephew, both called Richard Hakluyt. The younger and better-known of the Hakluyts, a clergyman and university scholar, published his great collection of *Principal Navigations, Voyages, Traffiques, and Discoveries of the English Nation* in order to stimulate popular interest in empire-building.

Colonies in America might serve as bases for the search for a northwest passage and for further attacks on Spain; but, as the Hakluyts pointed out, they would also serve more constructive purposes. The enclosures and other economic changes had created a large dispossessed and unemployed class, who had become a serious social problem. Such persons could find a new livelihood in America. Colonies might produce various commodities (such as sugar, wine, olive oil, silk, and vegetable dyes) which the English were in the habit of buying from Spain and other southern countries; and in the course of time they would provide a market for the rapidly growing English industries, particularly the cloth industry. Thus a colonial empire would make England economically independent of foreign countries, and therefore richer and more secure. These arguments for colonization, first stated by the Hakluyts, were to remain the main principles of British colonial policy for the next two hundred years.

Queen Elizabeth, although sympathetic, was not willing to invest any royal money in colonizing projects, which had therefore to be financed from the resources of private citizens. The first attempt to found an English colony was made by Sir Humphrey Gilbert, who acquired a charter from the Crown empowering him to take possession of any unoccupied land in America. Gilbert led a preparatory expedition across to Newfoundland in 1583, but on the return voyage his ship sank with all on board. His rights then passed to his half-brother Sir Walter Raleigh. Statesman, general, admiral, poet, historian, patron of literature and science, and royal favorite, Raleigh was the most versatile and variously gifted Englishman of his time. As a result of royal generosity he was a very wealthy man, and he was willing to invest much of his fortune in colonial enterprises.

In 1584 Raleigh dispatched an exploring expedition, which chose the country south of the Chesapeake as the best location and named it Virginia in honor of Elizabeth, who liked to be known as the "Virgin Queen." The following year he sent a party of colonists who settled on Roanoke Island, in what is now North Carolina, but returned home after a discouraging winter. This party included the artist John White, who brought back paintings which became the conventional portrayals of the North American Indian for centuries to come. A new group of colonists, including women and children as well as men, was sent to Roanoke Island in 1587. As a result of war with Spain, no further expedition was dispatched until 1591, and by that time the original colonists had totally disappeared.

What happened to this unfortunate party is a mystery that has never been solved. After these discouraging experiences Raleigh abandoned the whole project.

The French in Canada.   Expeditions sent out by the French government began to explore the North American coastline in the 1520's. In 1535 Jacques Cartier sailed up the St. Lawrence and picked Quebec as the best site for a colony; and in 1541 he returned with the intention of founding a permanent settlement. But after two winters of starvation his party abandoned the project. For the remainder of the century France was preoccupied with religious civil wars, although French pirates continued to attack Spanish ships in the Caribbean, and French fishermen made regular visits to the St. Lawrence.

In the final years of the sixteenth century, with the re-establishment of peace under the rule of Henry IV, the French again became interested in Canada. Apart from the continued hope of a northwest passage, the main economic inducement was the fur trade, which was to become the most important Canadian activity for the next two hundred years. Financed by French merchants, a series of exploring expeditions were led by Samuel de Champlain, one of the ablest and most attractive figures in early American history. Champlain founded permanent colonies at Port Royal in Acadia (the modern Nova Scotia) in 1605 and at Quebec in 1608. These colonies continued to be owned and governed by a series of commercial companies until 1663, when they passed under the direct rule of the Crown.

From Quebec, French explorers quickly found their way up the St. Lawrence into the country north and south of the Great Lakes. Although Champlain made the serious mistake of antagonizing the Iroquois, the most formidable Indian warriors in the entire region, the French were able to form friendly relationships with most of the other Indian tribes. Fur-traders, known as *voyageurs* and *coureurs de bois*, were soon ranging over immense areas of North America, buying furs from the Indians, adopting much of the Indian way of life, and begetting half-breed children. But the fur trade was not the only dynamic force in French Canada; equally important was the missionary zeal engendered by the Catholic Reformation. A number of highly educated members of the Jesuit and other religious orders resolved to devote their lives to the conversion of the Indians, and some of them traveled through the forests and across the lakes almost as widely as the fur-traders, preaching to Indian tribes, enduring almost unbelievable hardships, and not infrequently ending their lives in martyrdom.

In spite of this rapid extension of French influence, the colony itself had a very slow growth. As late as 1663 its total population numbered only about 2,500, almost all of whom were fur-traders, clerics, and officials. They were not yet self-supporting and still imported food from France. When the royal government assumed control, it set to work to build up the colony, giving subsidies and generous land grants to immigrants, encouraging agricultural and industrial development, and sending out shiploads of unmarried girls from whom settlers could choose wives. By the end of the century the population had risen to about 7,000. A feudal form of land tenure was established; the land was divided into large estates known as *seigneuries*, the holders of which had extensive powers over the peasant farmers (*habitants*) who cultivated the land. The social organization of the colony was thus modeled on that of France. Government belonged exclusively to the royal officials, and the whole life of the colony was supervised by the Catholic Church. The moral standards of French Canada (exclusive of the fur-traders, whose manner of living evoked vigorous clerical disapproval) were almost as strict as those of Puritan New England; there was little of the traditional Gallic *joie de vivre* in this offshoot of French civilization.

New Netherland and New Sweden. The Dutch had developed into a great maritime nation during their struggle for independence from Spain, and in the early seventeenth century their ships were going to almost all parts of the known world. Their main colonial activities were in the East Indies, where they ousted the Portuguese and built up the rich empire which they continued to hold until the twentieth century. They became interested in America chiefly through attacks on Spanish commerce in the West Indies.

In 1609 the English navigator Henry Hudson, who had been hired by Dutch merchants to search for a passage to the Orient, sailed a long way up the river which bears his name before abandoning the hope of finding a route to China. Hudson reported that the region was rich in furs, and in 1624 the Dutch West India Company sent across a party of colonists. New Amsterdam, at the southern end of Manhattan Island, became the capital of the colony (which was named New Netherland), while settlements were also made on the site of Albany and on the Delaware and Connecticut Rivers.

The Dutch gradually spread over parts of Long Island, New Jersey, and the Hudson Valley, but New Netherland never became really prosperous. All authority was vested in the governor, the colonists having no political rights; and none of the governors appointed by the West India Company displayed much ability or integrity. The colony was primarily a fur-trading station, and few inducements were offered to settlers interested in farming. In 1629 the Company adopted a policy of offering large estates to individuals who would bring across tenant farmers; these big landowners were to be known as patroons, and could collect rents and exercise essentially feudal powers over their tenants. Only one person, however, Kiliaen Van Rensselaer, succeeded in establishing a patroonship. The progress of the colony was further checked by Indian wars; the Dutch established friendly relations with the Iroquois, and thereby became involved in conflicts with Indian tribes hostile to the Iroquois. As late as 1667 the total white population of New Netherland was only about 8,000, and a large number of these were not of Dutch origin. It was said that no fewer than eighteen languages were being spoken around New Amsterdam. Thus Manhattan Island had already acquired that cosmopolitan flavor which it has retained through its later history.

Sweden made her one attempt at American colonization in 1638, when a settlement was made on the Delaware River, on the present site of Wilmington, the primary objective being the fur trade. The total population of the colony eventually reached about 400. The Dutch regarded this as an infringement upon their territorial rights, and in 1655 a Dutch fleet seized the colony and added it to New Netherland. These Swedish settlers, however, made one interesting contribution to American development: they brought with them the practice of building cabins out of logs instead of hewn boards. Since log cabins gave better protection against the weather, they were afterwards adopted by pioneers in other colonies.

2. THE CHESAPEAKE COLONIES

Foundation of Virginia.   The early years of the seventeenth century were a period of large-scale English emigration. This was due not only to the scarcity of land in England and the prevalence of unemployment but also to widespread discontent with the political and religious policies of the Stuart kings. By 1642, when the movement was ended by the outbreak of the Civil War, about 65,000 English people had come to different parts of America. Nearly half of them settled on the mainland, while the remainder went to the West Indies.

The advance guard of the migration consisted of a party of 104 persons, who reached Virginia in the year 1607 and founded a settlement which they called Jamestown. Raleigh's project had now been taken over by a commercial company, which had received a charter from King James I in the previous year. The stockholders included both merchants and noblemen, but the leading spirit was Sir Thomas Smith, the greatest English businessman of his time. Large profits were confidently expected from Virginia, chiefly from the growing of various crops suitable for a warm climate. Most of the colonists were shipped across at the expense of the company, and were to work as servants under the direction of company officials.

This first English colony was by no means an immediate success. On the contrary, its early history was chiefly a dreary record of famine, disease, and death. Few of the early colonists had either the skill or the moral stamina needed for survival in the wilderness; and since they were merely employees of the company, they lacked any sufficient incentive for hard work. Moreover, the site which they had chosen was unhealthful, and the Indians in the neighborhood quickly became hostile. Two-thirds

of the first party died within a few months, and the death rate among the
later arrivals was almost equally high. For a variety of reasons none of the
crops envisaged by the organizers of the colony proved to be successful,
and almost no profits were earned. Within a few years, in fact, most of the
London merchants lost faith in the possibilities of Virginia and turned to
the development of Bermuda and the West Indies.

The colony was kept in existence only through stern government by
a series of company officials. Twice a day the colonists were summoned
by the beat of a drum to march out into the fields, and twice a day they
were marched back to Jamestown to eat and pray. Eventually a basis for
prosperity was discovered in the growing of tobacco. First introduced
into England in the 1560's, tobacco-smoking was now becoming fashionable,[1] and the fortunes of Virginia soon came to depend upon it. One of
the Virginia colonists, John Rolfe (who is also famous because he married
the Indian princess Pocahontas), began experimenting with tobacco in
1613, and after a few years a method of curing it was developed which
made it palatable to English smokers. In 1618 the colony exported 50,000
pounds. Nine years later this had increased to 500,000.

By this time the Virginia Company had come under new management. About the year 1618 a group headed by Sir Edwin Sandys ousted
Smith from leadership and embarked on a new and ambitious program for
building up the colony. In order to encourage immigrants of a better
type, two changes of great importance were planned. Colonists were to
be given land of their own and were to have a voice in the government.
Every person already in the colony was to receive one hundred acres, and
in the future every person who emigrated at his own expense would receive fifty acres (known as a "head-right") for himself and an additional
fifty acres for every servant he brought over. Servants shipped across at
Company expense would receive land when their period of service ended,
but would pay quitrents for it.[2] The government of the colony was lib-
eralized by the establishment of a representative assembly. The Virginia
House of Burgesses, the first legislative body anywhere in the New
World, held its first meeting on July 30, 1619.

The Sandys group sent across colonists in large numbers—nearly
5,000 (most of them servants) before 1623—and also spent a good deal of
money in the hope of creating a more diversified economy and ending the
dependence upon tobacco. But these plans met with little support in the
colony. The colonists could not easily feed and house the new arrivals,
and, having found a dependable cash crop, were unwilling to resume ex-

---

[1] In spite of the disapproval of King James I, who wrote a pamphlet describing it as
"a custome lothsome to the eye, hatefull to the Nose, harmefull to the braine, dangerous to
the lungs, and in the blacke stinking fume thereof, neerest resembling the horrible Stigian
smoke of the pit that is bottomeless."

[2] Quitrents were a relic of feudal land laws. They differed from ordinary rents in that
the individuals paying them were "quit" of all other obligations, and were therefore regarded
in other respects as owners, not as tenants. When Virginia became a royal colony, the quitrents were paid to the government and hence became a kind of land tax.

perimentation. In 1622, moreover, 350 people were killed, and every settlement outside Jamestown was destroyed, in an Indian war. Meanwhile, Sandy's opponents in the Virginia Company were complaining of extravagance and mismanagement. In 1624 the King intervened by revoking the charter and placing the colony directly under royal rule. Since the new government did not interfere with the land grants or the House of Burgesses, the Virginians appear to have been pleased by the change. Thenceforth, until the Revolution, Virginia had a royal governor, usually an English nobleman. The Anglican Church had already been established, and taxes were imposed for the support of its clergy.

During the eighteen years of its existence the Company had invested in Virginia about 100,000 pounds (an immense sum in those days) and earned virtually no profits. It had sent to the colony about 7,000 persons, of whom only 1,200 were still alive. Virginia, however, was now securely established and able to continue growing without further financial aid from London. By 1640 its population had increased to about 8,000, and by 1700 to 72,000.

Foundation of Maryland.   The early history of Jamestown was a useful example of how not to start a colony, and later organizers were able to profit by its experience. It was apparent that settlers of a good type could be attracted only by giving them their own land and a share in the government. These lessons were applied in the second of the Southern colonies, Maryland. This was founded, not by a commercial company, but by an individual proprietor. In 1632 Cecilius Calvert, the second Lord Baltimore, received from King Charles I title to land north of Virginia, along with the right to govern it and other privileges of a feudal character. A convert to Roman Catholicism, Baltimore intended that his colony should become a refuge for English Catholics. But, since few of his coreligionists were willing to emigrate, he recognized that Protestants also must be welcomed and a policy of religious toleration adopted. Actually, from the beginning Maryland contained a majority of Protestants. In order to safeguard the Catholic minority, Baltimore saw to it that toleration was formally established by law in 1649.

The first group of colonists arrived early in 1634. They received land (although Baltimore charged quitrents higher than those collected in Virginia), and in the following year a legislative assembly held its first meeting. Concentrating on tobacco production, the colony soon began to prosper, and there was no "starving time." By 1689 population had increased to about 25,000.

The political history of Maryland was somewhat stormy, chiefly because of resentment against the powers exercised by Baltimore and his heirs. The proprietors continued to collect quitrents and to entrust most of the official positions in the colony to their relatives. Trouble was also caused by the immigration of a number of Puritans who regarded all Catholics as anti-Christian and disapproved of religious toleration. There were several popular revolts against the proprietary government. In 1691 Maryland came under the direct rule of the Crown, after which the Anglican Church was officially established. But in 1715 the current Lord Baltimore regained his hereditary feudal rights, which continued until the Revolution.

Economic and Social Development.   A significant feature of the subsequent development of Virginia and Maryland was that they remained almost wholly rural. The growing of tobacco continued to be the basic occupation; the tobacco was shipped to England, and manufactured goods were imported in return. Most of the early settlements were along the banks of navigable rivers, so that it was possible for ships to go directly to the plantations instead of loading at a central seaport. There were no large towns, and almost no manufacturing. Most inhabitants of the region lived by the land; and although they raised food for themselves and occasionally engaged in fur-trading, they were mainly dependent upon their one cash crop. Producers of raw materials have almost always been at a disadvantage in dealing with traders (a fact abundantly illustrated throughout history, from Biblical and Greek times to the present), and these tobacco-growers were no exception. As prices fell because of increasing production, the growers began to fall into debt to London business houses.

For two or three generations Virginia and Maryland continued to consist mainly of small farms, worked partly by their owners and partly by white servants. Servants were brought from Great Britain by shipowners who paid the costs of transportation and then sold them (usually at a considerable profit) to colonial employers. According to the terms of the contract (known as an indenture) a servant was normally obliged to work for at least four years after reaching America and was then set free with a gift of tools, clothing, and a year's supply of grain. Throughout the seventeenth century most of the immigrants who arrived in Virginia and Maryland were servants. Exploitation and ill treatment, both on shipboard and in the colonies, were frequent; but this was the one way by which vigorous young Englishmen without resources could get to the New World. Many former indentured servants eventually rose to prosperity and even to high political and social positions. In 1663, for example, it was noted that, of the thirty members of the Virginia House of Burgesses, thirteen had formerly been servants.

Unfortunately, tobacco-growers wanted a more permanent labor force and began to find it in Negro slavery. The first cargo of Negroes reached Virginia from Africa in 1619, but by 1650 there were only 200 in the colony. Nor was there at first any provision for slavery in the laws of the colony; legally, the slave had the same status as the servant, although in practice a definite racial line seems to have been drawn from the beginning. By 1680, however, Virginia had 3,000 Negroes, and in the early years of the eighteenth century the Negro almost completely re-

placed the white servant. With scarcely any thought for future consequences, English slave-traders and American planters were led by economic interest to fasten upon American society an institution which was
to cause irreparable harm for many generations to come.

Meanwhile, a plantation-owning aristocracy was slowly emerging.
The cultivation of tobacco quickly diminished the fertility of the soil; and
this, along with falling prices, made it difficult for the small farmer to
maintain himself and led to a concentration of landownership. This occurred especially in Virginia; in Maryland the policies of the proprietors
made it more difficult for colonists to acquire large estates. By the end of
the seventeenth century there were planters in the tidewater region of
Virginia who counted their acres in thousands instead of hundreds, and
who were building large homes modeled after those of the English gentry,
buying libraries, and cultivating the amenities of civilization. A few of
these men had come to America with money and social prestige; a larger
number rose to prosperity by their own industry and shrewdness. Southerners of a later generation liked to believe that their ancestors had sprung
from the English aristocracy and, unlike the New Englanders, had been
"cavaliers" (i.e., upper-class supporters of the monarchy in the English
Civil War); but this social myth does not have much factual support.
Most of the early Virginians, like most of the early settlers in all the other
colonies, were originally farmers, craftsmen, or laborers.

In accordance with the English feudal tradition, it was generally assumed in Virginia and Maryland that wealthy landowners were entitled
to exercise leadership and become a ruling class. The most important unit
of local government was the county; and, as in Tudor and Stuart England,
the most prominent citizens of each county served as justices, with broad
administrative and judicial powers. Counties were subdivided into
parishes, each of which was governed by a vestry chosen from the chief
local planters. These same individuals were usually elected to the colonial
legislatures (voting for which was restricted by property qualifications).
Controlling the government, the members of this ruling class were able
to acquire additional economic privileges: in particular, they could often
become owners of large stretches of unsettled land on easy terms or as
payment for political services.

Probably the average small farmer accepted upper-class rule as being
in accord with the laws of God and nature; but when his own rights were
not protected, he could become indignant. There was an explosion in
Virginia in 1676, caused mainly by the failure of the dominant group to
give protection against the Indians to outlying settlements. Indignation
was directed especially against the royal Governor, William Berkeley;
but Berkeley was closely associated with the rich families of the colony,
who, because of their fur-trading interests, wanted to keep the Indians
friendly. Nathaniel Bacon, a young man from an aristocratic English
family, who had come to Virginia only two years earlier, assumed the role

of a radical leader, collected a volunteer army to fight the Indians, and subsequently led his men to Jamestown and seized control of the government. But when he died of a fever, his followers lost all sense of discipline, and Berkeley was easily able to regain control. Thirty-seven of the rebels were then hanged, and the old system was re-established. Though often interpreted as a protest against British rule, in actuality Bacon's rebellion was primarily an outbreak of class conflict between different groups of Virginians.

3. THE NEW ENGLAND COLONIES

The Plymouth Pilgrims.   While the Virginia Company was struggling to build a colony on the Chesapeake, several groups of merchants and noblemen were forming projects for colonies in New England and sending out expeditions to explore the coastline. But the region could not produce any crops for which there was a market in Europe, and its economic possibilities seemed to be limited to fish and furs, neither of which could support a large population. By 1625 there were several small fishing settlements, with a total population of about fifty. Any large migration to New England would have to be motivated by other than purely economic considerations.

The first people to demonstrate that it was possible to make a living in New England by agriculture were the *Mayflower* Pilgrims. The nucleus of the *Mayflower* party consisted of some members of a separatist congregation which had been established at Leyden in Holland in 1608 by religious refugees from England. About the year 1618 thirty-five of these people, finding it difficult to make a living in a foreign country, decided to go to Virginia. Returning to England, they obtained money by becoming partners with some London merchants in an unincorporated joint-stock company, joined forces with a number of other emigrants, chartered the *Mayflower*, and set sail in the late summer of 1620. The original passenger list numbered one hundred, and two more were born during the voyage. But the *Mayflower* was blown off its course, and just as winter was setting in, it reached land, not in Virginia, but on the desolate shores of Cape Cod. Since they were in a country where there was no legal authority, and since it was essential to maintain discipline, the leaders of the party drew up an agreement by which they formed a "civil body politic" and accepted the principle of majority rule. This was the famous *Mayflower* Compact. They then chose Plymouth as the site of their colony.

Nearly half of the party died during the first winter; and except on special occasions (like the first Thanksgiving Day in the autumn of 1621), it was several years before anybody at Plymouth had a satisfying meal. The supplies which they had brought from England were altogether inadequate; and, being city people, they lacked skill in farming, hunting, and fishing. Fortunately, the Indians in the neighborhood were friendly and showed them how to grow corn; otherwise they would probably have died of starvation. But unlike some other groups of early colonists, they did not suffer from any failure of discipline or morale. The Leyden group, especially William Bradford, who served as governor after 1621, provided excellent leadership and imbued the whole colony with their own sense of religious dedication. A few other parties arrived, and by 1630 Plymouth had a population of about 300 and was no longer in any danger of famine. They were able to free themselves from their financial obligations to the London merchants, canceling the major part and paying off the remainder through fur-trading. Land was distributed freely in small lots; and as the colony expanded, a system of representative government was evolved.

The voyage of the *Mayflower* has acquired a special place in the imagination of modern Americans, partly because it was the independent enterprise of a group of very humble people, unsupported by any powerful commercial company or aristocratic proprietor, and partly because of the courage and idealism with which the Pilgrims faced the privations of the early years. But Plymouth was always a small and unimportant colony, and in its own time it attracted little attention.

Foundation of Massachusetts.   The much more important colony of Massachusetts Bay was founded not by separatists but by Puritans— in other words, by people who, instead of seceding from the established Church of England, wished to remain within it and reorganize it in accordance with their ideals. In the 1620's and 1630's, however, it seemed unlikely that the Puritans would ever achieve power in England. On the contrary, the Stuart monarchy was making it difficult for them to propagate their opinions; Puritan ministers could no longer preach freely, and Puritan gentlemen had little opportunity to participate in government. A group of Puritan ministers, merchants, and country gentlemen then decided to establish a colony where they could put their beliefs into practice and exercise their talents for preaching and political leadership. Their leader was John Winthrop, a well-to-do landowner and a man of high moral character, capacity for statesmanship, and (in spite of his strict beliefs) unusual humanity and generosity. A land grant was obtained in 1628, and in the following year the Massachusetts Bay Company was formed, with a royal charter. How this group of the King's political enemies was able to get a charter has remained a mystery.

The founders of the colony issued a good deal of promotional literature, depicting New England as a kind of paradise in which it would be easy for everybody to live in comfort, stressing the fact that land would be given free, but not mentioning the long winters or the stony soil. It was made plain, however, that nobody would be welcome who would not accept the beliefs and moral discipline of Puritanism. Probably most of the people who came to New England had economic motives for leaving home, but chose New England rather than Virginia or the West Indies for religious reasons. Most of the early settlers were middle-class farmers or craftsmen, and brought wives and children with them. Relatively few of them were servants.

The advance guard of the Puritan migration, led by John Endicott, made a settlement at Salem in 1628. Two years later came a fleet of eighteen ships, carrying some 900 passengers, among them Winthrop and other organizers of the colony. Boston was chosen as the site of the main settlement. Immigrants continued to arrive until 1640, to a total of perhaps 18,000 or 20,000. The customary hardships had to be endured during the early winters; food was scarce, and the death rate was high. But within a few years the colonists were growing enough corn and catching enough fish to support themselves, and could claim that their standards of living were higher than they had been at home.

Massachusetts was unique among the major colonies in that its leading organizers came to the colony themselves and brought their charter with them. Stockholders of the Massachusetts Bay Company who wished to remain at home sold out their rights to those who wished to go to America. This meant that legal ownership and control of the colony were transferred from London to Boston, so that for a long time Massachusetts was almost completely independent of English authority. Although the colony had been organized in the form of a commercial enterprise, its promoters were interested not in profits but in putting their ideals into practice. They had no intention, however, of establishing a democratic government; Winthrop and his associates had organized and financed the migration in the expectation of keeping control in their own hands. They spoke of religious freedom, but they very definitely meant freedom only for themselves, not for non-Puritans.

Almost from the beginning, however, the rank and file of the colonists began to complain of authoritarian government, and through a series of concessions the charter of the Massachusetts Bay Company gradually evolved into the constitution of the colony. According to the charter, all power belonged to the stockholders, or "freemen," who were authorized to elect a governor and a board of "assistants." In 1630 a number of the settlers were made freemen, but were given only the right to fill vacancies among the assistants. Four years later the freemen insisted on seeing the charter (which Winthrop had hitherto managed to keep hidden) and discovered that they were entitled to make the laws of the colony. This led to the establishment of the General Court, in which the assistants met with deputies elected by the freemen (this was divided into two houses in 1644). Henceforth the governor and other officials were elected annually. But the Puritan character of the colony was ensured by the device of restricting political rights to church members. Church membership was a privilege open only to persons of good character and sound doctrine, as certified by the ministers. Under this system about one-fifth of the adult male population of Massachusetts seems to have acquired the franchise.

Other New England Colonies.   Several other parts of New England were colonized during the period of the great migration. In 1636 the Reverend Thomas Hooker, who had originally settled near Boston but had developed some minor economic and religious disagreements with the Massachusetts authorities, led a party across land to the Connecticut River and founded the town of Hartford. A few years later this Connecticut colony absorbed a small settlement which had been made by Puritans from England at Saybrook. In 1639 another group, headed by the Reverend John Davenport, founded the colony of New Haven. While the institutions of Connecticut and New Haven were similar to those of Massachusetts, the former was slightly more liberal and the latter somewhat more authoritarian. They were combined into a single colony in 1662.

Rhode Island was settled in the 1630's by several persons who, with their followers, were expelled from Massachusetts for stirring up religious dissensions. The most interesting of them were Anne Hutchinson and Roger Williams. Mrs. Hutchinson was a baffling character who has been variously appraised as a religious mystic, a pioneer of women's rights, and a neurotic troublemaker. After settling in Boston with her husband (a mild man who followed her leadership) she began to arouse conflict by declaring that almost all the Massachusetts clergy had never genuinely experienced divine grace and were therefore leading their congregations to Hell. The theological questions involved baffled most people then and have done so since (even Winthrop confessed that he did not understand them); but obviously the clergy could not tolerate this challenge to their authority. When Mrs. Hutchinson claimed that she knew the will of God through personal revelation, they accused her of antinomianism (i.e., of declaring that individuals in a state of grace could ignore moral laws) and had her banished from the colony.

About Roger Williams, on the other hand, there are today no differences of opinion. Courageous, warm-hearted, intellectually gifted, and often indiscreetly outspoken, he was undoubtedly one of the most interesting and attractive figures in early American history. He came to Massachusetts as a Puritan minister; but he had a restless and inquiring mind, and soon reached the embarrassing conclusion that neither the Puritans nor any other religious group really had any certain knowledge of the will of God. Since the truth was not yet known but was still in process of being discovered, there should be complete intellectual and religious freedom. He also began to ask inconvenient questions—for example, about the right of the Puritans to settle on land belonging to the Indians. Since Williams was incapable of keeping his mouth shut, it is not surprising that the authorities (although personally fond of him) finally ordered him to leave.

Under Williams's leadership the different groups who had settled in Rhode Island came together and set up a united government on democratic principles. A charter was obtained from the English Parliament in 1644. Church and state were separated and religious freedom guaranteed. Many of the early settlers were Baptists, but the colony became a refuge for eccentrics of all kinds, and was regarded with profound disapproval by its more respectable neighbors. Williams defended his views in *The Bloudy Tenent of Persecution for Cause of Conscience*, in which he argued that any group of people could come together and form a church, which should have the same status as any other private corporation. When the Boston minister John Cotton wrote a pamphlet denouncing this subversive doctrine, Williams replied with *The Bloudy Tenent Yet More Bloody from Mr. Cotton's Attempts to Wash It White in the Blood of the Lamb*. Regarded by his contemporaries as a dangerous radical, he ranks today as the first great exponent of the American tradition of intellectual freedom.

Several Englishmen had claims to northern New England by virtue of royal land grants, and a few settlements were made along the coast by non-Puritans from England. In the 1640's, during the English Civil War, however, the Massachusetts government assumed control over the whole region, and Massachusetts colonists began to move into it. Later in the century the English claimants initiated a series of lawsuits, as a result of which New Hampshire was declared independent and given a royal government in 1679. Maine, on the other hand, remained a part of Massachusetts until 1820.

Through the later seventeenth century the New England settlements were slowly spreading through eastern Massachusetts, along the Maine coast, up the valley of the Connecticut, and along Long Island Sound. By 1689 the population had reached about 80,000. This process caused two wars with the Indian tribes in the region, the Pequot War of 1637 and a war in 1675 with a chieftain known as King Philip. On each occasion the death rate among the colonists was high, and they retaliated by massacring their Indian opponents with very little compunction. The expansion of New England also caused hostility with the Dutch in New Netherland and led to conflicts on the northern frontier with French missionaries and fur-traders from Canada. In 1643 the need for defense caused the four leading colonies (Rhode Island being excluded for religious reasons) to come together in the New England Confederation, which lasted until 1684.

Economic Development. The New England colonies were decidedly different from those on the Chesapeake not only in their animating ideals but also in their methods of settlement and expansion. Although the organizers of the Puritan migration believed that political responsibility should belong only to a small ruling group, they established economic institutions which promoted an attitude of equality. Thus New England became more democratic than the South. It was also less individualistic, retaining much of that collectivist spirit which had been characteristic of the medieval village community.

Land was granted by the colonial governments not to separate individuals but to towns. A group of people would obtain permission to establish a new town, and, having acquired land, would divide part of it into separate farms and keep the remainder for collective use or for distribution later when the population increased. Each member of the group became a freeholder and had no rent obligations. Local government and control of the common lands were initially vested in the town meeting, in which all freeholders had voting rights. This system was not wholly equalitarian, since persons of greater wealth and social prestige received larger farms; but there were no sharp class distinctions. And since all the houses in the town were usually built around a central plot of common land, instead of being scattered over the countryside, all the inhabitants were definitely members of a single community and had to conform to accepted mores and beliefs.

Thus, except on the seacoast, early New England became a country of small farmers, who carried on a diversified agriculture primarily for their own subsistence. There were no basic cash crops, no big estates, and no large servant class. Although the church members constituted an elite group in that they alone could be enfranchised, this political right did not carry economic privileges with it. And a foundation for democracy was established in the land system and the town meeting.

Meanwhile, the more ambitious and enterprising of the New Englanders turned towards the sea. Fishing, carried on at the banks of Newfoundland by fleets of ships from the Massachusetts coastal towns, became so important to the prosperity of the colony that the codfish was placed on its official coat of arms. Shipbuilding began as early as 1631, when craftsmen built a thirty-ton vessel for Governor Winthrop. Before long Massachusetts was constructing ships not only for its own merchants but for sale abroad. Boston quickly developed commercial interests with other parts of the world, particularly with the Caribbean. Exporting fish, timber, and foodstuffs to the West Indies, Boston shipowners also acquired a considerable carrying trade. By the later decades of the seventeenth century a number of merchants had acquired considerable fortunes.

Since New England produced little which could be sold in Europe, its capacity to buy manufactured goods was limited. This stimulated the growth of local industries. Most farm families produced at home almost everything they needed, thus becoming independent of the market except for a few raw materials and an occasional luxury; the farmer built his own house and constructed his own tools and furniture, and his wife made the clothing and preserved food for the winter. But there were a number of professional craftsmen, some of them migratory and others established in the larger towns, who engaged in such occupations as weaving, carpentry, shoemaking, hatmaking, and the manufacture of silverware and pottery. As in medieval England, the prosperous craftsmen gave employment to apprentices and wage earners, but their employees normally expected to become independent after they had acquired enough experience.

Religious Institutions. In the seventeenth century everybody except a few eccentrics still assumed that social order was impossible without an established religion and that regular church attendance and adherence to the accepted rules of morality must be enforced by law. These beliefs were put into effect in early Virginia no less than in early New England. In Virginia, however, the official religion never had much vitality. The clergy were always too few to provide adequate services, and were frequently men of low moral and intellectual caliber. And although the early laws of the colony had a strongly puritanical flavor, they were difficult to enforce in territory where the population was so scattered.

Early New England, on the other hand, was permeated with the beliefs and moral discipline of Puritanism. Calvinism in its various forms has, in fact, been one of the most potent influences in the shaping of American civilization in general. This was partly because New England has exercised a deep cultural and economic influence on other sections of the country, and partly because Calvinist beliefs were brought to the Middle and Southern colonies by later immigrant groups during the eighteenth century.

Throughout Massachusetts and Connecticut every town was required to establish a church, pay the salary of a minister, and build a meetinghouse. The system of church government was, in theory, Congregationalist. The English Puritans had split into two main groups: the more authoritarian Presbyterians, who believed that all churches should be controlled by a central synod; and the more democratic Congregationalists, who declared that each congregation should be self-governing. The founders of New England had belonged before the migration to the second of these groups. In practice, however, their adherence to Congregationalist principles proved to be decidedly limited. No new churches could be set up without the consent of the government; meetings of ministers were held periodically to formulate principles of theology and ethics; and individual ministers and congregations were not permitted to deviate from accepted standards of orthodoxy. Thus a rigid uniformity was maintained everywhere except in Rhode Island (the original differences between the Puritans and the separatists at Plymouth soon became unimportant).

In view of the influence of the ministers, early New England has often been described as a theocracy. This influence was exercised not only through their control of the qualifications for church membership, and hence for the franchise, but also more directly in giving advice to secular officials. The leading ministers of the first generation (John Cotton in Massachusetts, Thomas Hooker in Connecticut, and John Davenport in New Haven) were regularly consulted by the governors of the respective colonies. In the second generation Cotton's position of leadership was inherited by Increase Mather. And since the Puritan ministers were convinced that they knew the will of God, they did not permit any advocacy of what they regarded as false doctrine. Four persons were put to death in Boston in the years 1659–61 for preaching Quakerism, and Baptist preachers were whipped and expelled from Massachusetts.[3]

Puritan Beliefs.   The beliefs of the New Englanders were not wholly identical with those originally stated by Calvin. Calvinist doctrine had been modified by a number of French and English theologians, and there was now less emphasis on man's inability to save himself and on the more emotional and mystical elements in religious experience. New England thinking was dominated by the notion of a "covenant" (or contract). God had promised that those persons who obeyed his will would receive guidance and protection in this world and salvation in the hereafter. Religion thus meant primarily a sober decision to trust in God and conform to his moral laws. The tendency to think in terms of a contract also influenced New England conceptions of social organization. When men and women came together to form a new colony or a new town or congregation, they were making a covenant with each other, and the relationship between government and people was formulated in the same manner. This type of thinking was destined to have a great influence on American political theory.

The New England ethos, however, was still Calvinist. By nature, it was believed, man was wholly sinful and could achieve good only by severe and unremitting discipline. Hard work was a religious duty; and profanation of the sabbath day, blasphemy, fornication, drunkenness, playing of games of chance, and participation in theatrical performances were penal offenses. These rules were enforced throughout New England, in most areas until after the Revolution. As in Virginia, the punishment of offenders was entrusted to prominent citizens serving as justices in the county courts. This legal code was accepted by the mass of the people with remarkably few complaints, and serious violations were extremely rare.

One should not exaggerate the severity of life in early New England. The morality of the original Puritans was in some respects milder than

[3] Another, though less valid, proof of Puritan intolerance was provided by the witchcraft persecutions. Between 1647 and 1662 fourteen persons were hanged (not burnt) for witchcraft in Massachusetts and Connecticut. Later in the century the fear of witchcraft was revived by writings on the subject by Increase Mather and his son Cotton. In 1691 and 1692 there was an outbreak of panic in the neighborhood of Salem, Massachusetts, during which twenty persons were hanged. In fairness to the Puritans, it should be remembered that belief in witchcraft was still almost universal, even among scientists; that many thousands of persons were put to death for it in seventeenth-century Europe; that Cotton Mather wanted accused persons to be fairly tried, and did not approve of the proceedings at Salem; and that nearly everybody involved, among both the clergy and the laity, recognized afterwards that serious injustice had been done. Many people in rural New England continued to believe in witchcraft until the nineteenth century, but after 1692 nobody was hanged for it.

that of their modern successors. While they disapproved of getting drunk, they enjoyed good liquor; and while they believed that persons guilty of extramarital sexual relations should be punished, they discussed sexual problems with a quite remarkable frankness. Dancing and some other forms of recreation were permitted, although any unrestrained gaiety was frowned upon. But perhaps the most significant aspect of the Puritan view of life was not its code of behavior, which was by no means narrowly ascetic, but its emphasis on constant self-examination and self-discipline. Since man by nature was wholly sinful, he must never allow himself to be spontaneous; and since God alone was worthy of love, he must not feel too much affection for another human being. Puritan beliefs thus had the effect of inhibiting natural emotions. This process began in early childhood, since even small children would be damned if they died in a state of sin.

One of the more attractive aspects of Puritanism was its encouragement of education. Since God's will was recorded in the Bible, everybody must be taught to read it, while scholars were needed in order to expound its deeper meanings. Every town was legally required to maintain a school; and although the law was not fully enforced, most New Englanders learned to read and write. Harvard College, intended primarily to provide the churches with ministers who knew theology and the classical languages, was founded as early as 1636. No less than 130 college graduates came to New England during the great migration; and the tradition of scholarship which they established was maintained by later generations. The first printing press was set up in Boston in 1639, and the output of printed matter was voluminous. Most of these products of the New England mind were sermons and theological treatises, but leading clergymen like Increase Mather and his son Cotton were also interested in science and history, although their main motive was always to discover the workings of the divine will. Some New Englanders, laymen as well as ministers, read widely and displayed some of the tolerant humanist spirit of the English Renaissance; and a number of them like to compose verses.

Probably the most enduring manifestations of Puritanism were in the economic sphere. By teaching hard work and thrift, it promoted qualities which made for economic success. This did not mean that businessmen could make profits by fraudulent or unjust methods. In accordance with medieval traditions, both the ministers and the magistrates in early New England condemned monopolistic price-fixing and other forms of extortion. But Puritanism declared that the man who devoted himself wholeheartedly to his business or profession was doing the will of God, and that in most instances material success was a sign of divine favor. This attitude contributed to the rapid growth of wealth and prosperity in colonial New England. At a later date it was a potent force in shaping the ethos of American society in general.

4. THE LATER COLONIES

The Carolinas.   The outbreak of the English Civil War in 1642 put a stop to emigration, and for a few years the colonies were left wholly to their own resources and became self-governing in all but name. The Civil War ended in the defeat of King Charles I (who was beheaded in 1649), after which power was assumed by the Parliamentary army, composed largely of left-wing Puritans. Its leader, Oliver Cromwell, served as Lord Protector from 1653 to 1658. Cromwell required the colonies to give formal acknowledgment to his government, but did not otherwise interfere with them. After his death, a more moderate group took control and restored the monarchy, though with guarantees that the king would henceforth govern with the cooperation of Parliament. In 1660 the son of Charles I was installed as Charles II. The Restoration was followed by a resumption of colonial expansion, new land grants being made by the King to a number of wealthy promoters.

The first of these grants covered a vast stretch of land south of Virginia. This was given in 1663 to a group of eight proprietors, most of whom held high offices in the English government, and was named Carolina. The Carolina proprietors regarded their colony primarily as a real-estate venture; they proposed to let colonists assume most of the risks and expenses of colonization and then collect quitrents from them. They adopted a land policy modeled on that of Virginia, every settler being promised so many acres for himself and so many extra for each servant or slave he imported. Land grants varied according to the wealth and importance of the individual, and ambitious plans were drafted for the creation of a ruling class of big landowners. It was necessary, however, to attract more humble settlers, and the proprietors promised a legislature and religious freedom (although the Anglican Church was to be supported by the government).

The first settlement was made in the southern part of the colony in 1670. After some years of hardship and much experimentation, the colonists turned to rice as a staple cash crop suitable to the soil and climate. For about a century this remained the basis of the economy of South Carolina, although there was also a good deal of fur-trading with the Indians, chiefly in deer skins. The methods of rice cultivation led quickly to the growth of large plantations and the employment of slave labor. By 1700 the area had a population of 5,000, of whom no less than half were Negro slaves. Almost from the beginning, therefore, South Carolina society acquired an aristocratic flavor, and the institution of Negro slavery became more deeply rooted than in Virginia. Another distinctive feature of South Carolina was the development of Charleston into an urban center where the planters built themselves houses and enjoyed an active social life. The heirs of the original proprietors sold their rights in 1719, and South Carolina then became a royal colony.

The northern part of Carolina, cut off from the Atlantic by a line of islands and sand banks, had a very different development. It was settled largely by people who wanted to be left alone; these included a number of small farmers who drifted down from Virginia in order to escape debts and taxes, and groups of Quakers seeking freedom from persecution. The Carolina proprietors set up a government in this area, but exaction of quitrents was almost impossible. North Carolina remained primarily a country of small farmers with few plantations and few slaves. At the time of the Revolution it ranked fourth among the colonies in population, but was one of the most backward in economic and cultural development. It became a royal colony in 1728.

New York. Shortly after the Carolina grant the whole middle region between Connecticut and Maryland was assigned to the King's brother, the Duke of York. All this area was claimed by the Dutch; but commercial rivalries brought about war between England and Holland, and in 1664 an English fleet forced the surrender of New Netherland, the Dutch government being too weak and too unpopular to attempt any real resistance. Selling the southern part of his territory, the Duke retained ownership of the northern part and renamed it New York.

The new government of New York proved at first to be as authoritarian as that of the Dutch. The Dutch policy of encouraging the growth of big estates continued; and a few favored families—De Lanceys, Livingstones, Morrises, Schuylers, and others—acquired ownership of enormous stretches of land in the Hudson Valley. Most of their land remained uncultivated; but they collected rents from enough tenant farmers to enable them to live in an aristocratic style. The Duke's officials worked in close cooperation with the landowners and with the fur-traders of Albany and the merchants of New York City, and these groups were permitted to exploit the small farmers and the urban craftsmen. Protests about taxation without representation, chiefly from New Englanders who had settled in Long Island, brought about the meeting of the first legislature in 1683, but no further meetings were permitted until the 1690's, by which time the colony had come under royal government.[4] As a result of these political and social conditions, New York attracted relatively few immigrants. Parts of the colony, as also of New Jersey, continued to be Dutch-speaking until the nineteenth century.

The Quaker Colonies. In 1664 the New Jersey region was sold by the Duke to two English noblemen, both of whom subsequently transferred their rights to groups of Quakers. The region already contained a few Dutch and Swedes. Subsequent immigrants included a number of old-fashioned Puritans from New Haven who regarded the Connecticut government as too liberal. The Quaker proprietors established legislatures; but opposition to quitrent collections and trade conflicts with New York caused frequent disturbances, and in 1702 they agreed that a single

[4] See page 55.

royal government should be established over both sections of the colony.

Meanwhile, a much more ambitious Quaker enterprise was taking shape farther south. When first preached in England by George Fox during the period of the Civil War, Quakerism (like similar movements in Germany a century earlier) had appealed only to the poorer classes; but its tolerant, optimistic, and humanitarian doctrines were now winning converts among rich merchants and even among members of the ruling class. Among these latter was William Penn, the son of an admiral closely associated with the Duke of York. In 1681 Penn acquired ownership of the territory which he christened Pennsylvania. By an additional grant a year later he also became the proprietor of Delaware, which was given a separate government in 1703.

The foundation of Pennsylvania was a bold experiment in social idealism. More fully than any of the other colonies, it represented the liberalism of the future rather than the authoritarianism of the medieval background. In drafting the institutions of his colony, Penn explicitly affirmed his faith in man's natural goodness and in complete religious freedom, and welcomed settlers of all races and all creeds in the confidence that they could learn to live together in cooperation and equality. The system of government was not fully democratic, since voting was restricted by property qualifications, and considerable power was retained by the proprietor; but the first code of laws was more humane than any other in existence. Penn also recognized the rights of the Indians, buying land from them instead of appropriating it, and scrupulously adhering to treaty agreements. Philadelphia, laid out by Penn himself in 1682, with straight streets and plenty of open space around each house, was the first American town that was planned instead of being allowed to grow at random.

Pennsylvania had a remarkably rapid growth. A colonist who wanted more than fifty acres was required to pay for it, and quitrents were collected; but land could be obtained more cheaply than in other colonies. A number of the early settlers were Quakers; but as early as 1683 a group of German Mennonites arrived, and these proved to be the advance guard of a large migration of non-English colonists seeking freedom from persecution. Philadelphia became a seaport and trading center, while the fertile back country was settled by small farmers. Quaker idealism was manifested in the rapid development of educational and scientific activities and institutions. Within two generations from its foundation Philadelphia had become the chief cultural center in the colonies.

Like a good many aristocratic idealists, Penn was apt to show a lack of practical common sense. His later life was unhappy. By 1689 he had spent 30,000 pounds on his colony, and a few years later he was heavily in debt and even spent some time in a debtors' prison in London. The agents whom he appointed to govern his colonies were not wisely chosen, and he became involved in a number of conflicts with the Pennsylvania and Delaware legislatures. After his death his rights passed to his sons, who did not share his idealism. Conflicts between the colonists and the proprietors over quitrents and other matters continued until the Revolution.

Thus before the end of the seventeenth century the English had established firm footholds on the American continent, and had planted a line of settlements along a thousand miles of the Atlantic seaboard from Maine to South Carolina. By 1689 the total population amounted to about 220,000. The colonists, moreover, had set up political institutions which were eventually to evolve into the American system of government, while significant differences had already appeared between the Northern and the Southern colonies. These seventeenth-century beginnings already foreshadowed much of the later history of the United States.

3. Colonial Settlement, 1607–1760

THE FIRST SETTLEMENTS IN NORTH AMERICA WERE MADE ALONG THE EASTERN SEA coast and up navigable rivers. It should be remembered that it was much easier to travel and transport goods by water than by land, since no hard-surfaced roads were built until the end of the eighteenth century. The black area indicates approximately the regions occupied during the first half-century of colonization. In Virginia and Maryland settlements were made along the shores of Chesapeake Bay and up a number of river estuaries. In New England towns were planted along the coastline and up the Connecticut River, while pioneers from Connecticut moved across to the eastern end of Long Island. The Dutch established themselves at the mouth of the Hudson River, at Albany, and on the Delaware, and the Swedes founded a colony on Delaware Bay.

By 1700 the settled area had become considerably larger but was still close to the sea. Much of New Jersey and eastern Pennsylvania had been occupied. South Carolina had been colonized around Charleston, and small farmers from Virginia had moved down into North Carolina.

During the next sixty years, as a result of the high birth rate and the heavy German and Scotch-Irish immigration, the settled area more than doubled. Almost all of southern New England was occupied, and a number of farmers from Massachusetts and Connecticut moved into southern New Hampshire and Vermont. In New York settlers pushed up the Mohawk River. Pennsylvania and Virginia expanded westward almost as far as the Appalachian Mountains, and settlements were made, chiefly by the Scotch-Irish, in the Great Valley lying between the Blue Ridge and the main Appalachian ranges.

Except in the South, most of the good land east of the mountains was occupied before 1760; what remained consisted mostly of hill country or pine barrens unsuitable for agriculture. Thus pressure developed, especially in Virginia, for western expansion. This was an important influence in both the struggle with France and the Revolution.

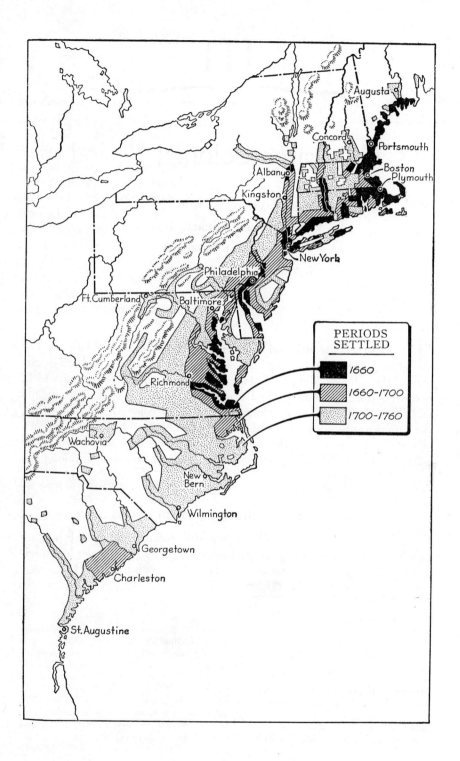

PERIODS
SETTLED

1660

1660-1700

1700-1760

Augusta

Concord

Portsmouth

Albany

Boston
Plymouth

Kingston

New York

Philadelphia

Ft. Cumberland

Baltimore

Richmond

Wachovia

New
Bern

Wilmington

Georgetown

Charleston

St. Augustine

III

The Later Colonial Period

1. THE EXPANSION OF THE COLONIES

2. THE BRITISH IMPERIAL SYSTEM

3. INTERNAL CONFLICTS

4. THE CONFLICT WITH FRANCE

THE late seventeenth and early eighteenth centuries were a period of steady growth in the population, economic resources, and self-assurance of the colonies. Meanwhile, two main lines of conflict appeared, which, in conjunction, led finally to the Revolution. While successive governments in London built up a more elaborate system of colonial administration, the Americans began to demand broader powers of control over their own affairs. At the same time the dominance of upper-class groups within the colonies was challenged by an emerging spirit of democracy among the mass of the people.

1. THE EXPANSION OF THE COLONIES

Population Growth.   Throughout the colonial period the population increased at a more rapid rate than during any later epoch of American history, reaching a total of more than 1,500,000 by 1763. Until near

---

SELECTED BIBLIOGRAPHY: In addition to the works by C. P. Nettels and C. M. Andrews cited on page 20, the student may consult H. L. Osgood, *The American Colonies in the Eighteenth Century* (4 vols., 1924–27), and L. H. Gipson's massive *The British Empire before the American Revolution* (1936–   ), of which nine volumes have been completed so far. J. T. Adams, *Provincial Society* (1927), is the appropriate volume in *A History of American Life.* The most useful study of British administration is L. W. Labaree, *Royal Government in America* (1930). Immigration is discussed in the early chapters of M. L. Hansen, *The Atlantic Migration, 1607–1860* (1940). Economic development is described in the early chapters of E. C. Kirkland, *History of American Economic Life* (revised edition, 1951), and H. U. Faulkner, *American Economic History* (revised edition, 1949), and interpreted in L. M. Hacker, *The Triumph of American Capitalism* (1940).

the end of the seventeenth century most of the colonists still lived close to the sea, and the interior was settled only along such navigable rivers as the Connecticut, Hudson, Delaware, Potomac, and James. Much of the back country remained thickly forested and unexplored, and only a few fur-traders from Virginia crossed the Appalachian ranges. By 1763, on the other hand, except at the northern and southern extremities of the colonies, the settled area had been extended westwards as far as the mountain barrier, and most of the fertile land between the ocean and the Appalachians had been transformed from forest into farms and plantations. Forward-looking traders and investors were already making plans for the settlement of the rich plains and river valleys beyond the mountains.

This growth of population was due not only to immigration but also to the remarkably high birth rate. In a country where land was abundant and labor was scarce, there were strong economic inducements for raising large families. A farmer could put his sons and daughters to work while they were still children, and could be confident that there would be new land available for them when they reached the age of independence. Most colonial families had a child every two years, and in many this process continued over a period of twenty or thirty years. A man frequently married two or three times in the course of his life, and raised a family with each successive wife. As in all countries, before the development of modern medicine, the infantile death rate was high, and probably more than a quarter of the children never reached maturity. But enough survived to bring about a doubling of the population every twenty-five or thirty years.

Meanwhile, men and women continued to cross the Atlantic in search of economic opportunities and freedom from persecution. Many of them came not from England but from other parts of the British Isles or from the European continent. Emigration from England never wholly ceased; but with the growth of English industry and other changes, the country no longer seemed overcrowded. In the eighteenth century the government took steps to prevent the emigration of skilled craftsmen and other desirable citizens. But some English people still wanted to leave home, and others were transported to America against their will; many persons convicted of minor crimes were shipped to the Southern colonies by the government and sold as indentured servants.

Foundation of Georgia. One new English colony was founded during this period. In 1732 the territory south of the Carolinas was granted to a group of proprietors and given the name of Georgia. The British government was interested in preventing the region from coming under Spanish or French control, but the main interest of the proprietors was philanthropic. Their leader, General James Oglethorpe, envisaged the colony as a refuge for persons liable to imprisonment for debt and for other deserving but unfortunate characters. By the terms of their grant, the proprietors, known as trustees, could not make profits from the colony, and their expenses were met partly by annual subsidies from the government and partly by private contributions.

In the autumn of 1732 Oglethorpe conducted the first party of colonists across the Atlantic and laid out the town of Savannah. But the colony grew slowly, and relatively few of the early settlers were actually debtors or in need of philanthropic assistance. According to Oglethorpe's plans, Georgia was to become a community of small farmers, for which reason large land grants and the importation of Negro slaves were forbidden. These and other paternalistic regulations (such as the prohibition of rum) soon provoked complaints. In soil and climate, eastern Georgia was similar to South Carolina, and was more suited to rice plantations than to small farming. During the 1740's the original plans were gradually abandoned, and large plantations and Negro slavery were permitted. Finally, in 1751, Georgia became a royal colony with a governor and an elected legislature.

The French.   Of the non-English immigrant groups, the first were the French. In 1685 King Louis XIV revoked the Edict of Nantes, which had given toleration to the French Protestants (known as Huguenots), and reverted to the old policy of religious persecution. In spite of the prohibition of emigration, many of the Huguenots eventually succeeded in escaping to other countries, and a few of them came to America, particularly to Boston, Charleston, and New York. The Huguenots in France had been primarily a middle-class group of merchants and craftsmen, and like all Calvinists they were hard-working, sober, and conscientious. In America, Huguenot families like the Faneuils of Massachusetts, the Bayards of New York, and the Laurenses and Manigaults of South Carolina soon rose to affluence. Their economic and religious background was similar to that of the English Puritans, and they quickly became assimilated instead of remaining a separate ethnic group.

The Germans.   A much more numerous body of immigrants came from southwestern Germany, especially from the area known as the Palatinate, and from Switzerland. In both Germany and Switzerland the mass of the people were exploited by landowning aristocracies whose privileges had originated in medieval times. Parts of Germany, moreover, were several times ravaged and laid waste in wars provoked by the ambitions of Louis XIV of France. These economic motives for leaving the mother countries were reinforced by religious troubles. Some of the peasants were Lutherans or Calvinists, while others belonged to the mystical sects—Mennonites, Dunkers, Amish, and others—which had originated during the Reformation. At the beginning of the eighteenth century these were being persecuted by Roman Catholic rulers. As the news of the freedom and opportunities available in the New World spread through the Rhineland, there began a migration which after about 1710 assumed mass proportions.

Many of the Germans could reach America only as indentured servants. The whole migration was, in fact, stimulated by shipowners who made a business of selling servants in the colonies and employed agents to tour the Rhineland and make extravagant promises to prospective emigrants. The emigrants were conducted to Rotterdam and packed into ships for transportation across the Atlantic. During a voyage which sometimes lasted for several months, at least a third of them often died from malnutrition, scurvy, or some infectious disease, while the remainder, after being put ashore in the colonies, were auctioned off to employers. Yet, despite the horrors of this traffic in human beings, those who were hardy enough to survive could in the end look forward to being free and owning their own land.

Some German and Swiss groups went to North Carolina, Georgia, and upstate New York, but the migration soon concentrated on Pennsylvania, which offered religious freedom, a liberal land policy, and plenty of employment opportunities. Much of the country immediately west of Philadelphia, along the Susquehanna and Schuylkill Rivers, became almost wholly German.

The Germans had learned from their religious beliefs, both Lutheran and mystical, to take little part in political activities, and many of them remained completely unassimilated. They continued to speak their own language, maintain their own religious institutions, and preserve their old-fashioned and sometimes eccentric customs. Many of their descendants (misleadingly known as the Pennsylvania Dutch) have continued to live in the same fashion down to the twentieth century. But they were excellent farmers, much more careful and efficient than the English, and some of them were highly skilled craftsmen. German and Swiss mechanics made Lancaster into one of the most important manufacturing centers in the colonies. Two of their products were destined to figure prominently in the history of American western expansion. They were probably the best gunsmiths in the world, and their rifles (often known later as Kentucky rifles) became the favorite weapons of the frontiersmen. And they manufactured the Conestoga wagons which carried pioneer families into the West and eventually across the continent to the Pacific.

The Scotch-Irish. Comparable in importance to the migration from Germany was that of the Scotch-Irish from northern Ireland. Early in the seventeenth century, after a series of rebellions by the Catholic Irish against English rule, much of the land in the northern province of Ulster had been confiscated by the government and assigned to Protestant settlers from Scotland. These people were Calvinists, with a Presbyterian form of church organization, and they quickly made Ulster into a thriving center of agriculture and industry. Then, at the end of the century, their prosperity was abruptly destroyed by English laws, passed for the protection of English farmers and manufacturers, which deprived them of their export markets. Since many of them were tenants of English landlords, who evicted them when they could not pay their rents, they were faced with total ruin. The first group of Scotch-Irish emigrants left Belfast for America in 1714, and during the next half-century tens of thousands of others followed their example. Mingled with the Scotch-Irish came an indeterminate number of the Catholic Irish; but since they were not permitted to maintain their own religion in most parts of the colonies, they soon lost their identity and did not constitute a distinct group.

The Scotch-Irish came to all the colonies from New Hampshire down to Georgia, but like the Germans they soon found Pennsylvania the most attractive. A considerable part of central Pennsylvania, west of the German country, became filled with Scotch-Irish farmers. They organized Presbyterian churches and generally followed the guidance of their ministers rather than of any secular officials. They were a vigorous, combative, and ambitious people, and unlike the Germans they took a most active part in political conflicts. Few of them were ever willing to acquire legal titles to their land by buying it or paying quitrents for it; God, they declared, had provided the land for the use of his disciples, not to provide profits for English proprietors.

From Pennsylvania, Scotch-Irish families soon began to move southwards into the Shenandoah Valley of western Virginia and thence into the Carolinas. This stream of migration created in the back country of the South a small-farmer society very different from that of the plantation regions along the seacoast. By the period of the Revolution almost the whole of the southern frontier line had been occupied by the Scotch-Irish, and they afterwards played a most prominent role in the history of western expansion.

Thus the people of the colonies, in addition to being English, Dutch, and Swedish, were also French, German, Swiss, Scotch, and Irish. Nor were these the only European ethnic stocks to be represented. Groups of Sephardic Jews settled in Rhode Island, New York, and South Carolina; and there were scattered immigrants from Italy and several other countries. Long before the Revolution the process of intermingling and intermarriage had begun. The French writer Crèvecœur, who spent fifteen years in the colonies, commented on "that strange mixture of blood, which you will find in no other country." "Here," he declared, "individuals of all nations are melted into a new race of man. . . . I could point out to you a family whose grandfather was an Englishman, whose wife was Dutch, whose son married a French wife, and whose present four sons have now four wives of different nations." In 1776 Tom Paine could truthfully declare that all Europe, and not England alone, was the real "parent country" of America.

Negro Slaves.   Much the largest of the eighteenth-century additions to the population remains to be mentioned. In 1700 the total number of slaves in the colonies was about 20,000. During the next three-quarters of a century shipowners in Great Britain and New England made a regular business of buying slaves from Negro chieftains along the coast of West Africa and transporting them to the West Indies and the Southern colonies. Through much of the eighteenth century importations to the mainland averaged 3,500 a year, and by 1763 the total Negro population of the thirteen colonies was probably close to 400,000. There were 150,000 Negroes in Virginia and 70,000 in South Carolina.

Slavery existed in all the colonies, but north of Maryland and Delaware it was not an integral part of the economy; Negroes were employed chiefly as household servants for wealthy families, and never became numerous. In the plantation regions along the southern seacoast, on the other hand, they soon outnumbered the whites. Elaborate legal codes were drafted in order to keep them in subjection, with severe penalties for any insubordination. There were a number of small-scale rebellions or attempts at rebellion, and the participants were hanged or, in a few instances, burned alive.

Before the Revolution a few persons, chiefly among the Quakers of Pennsylvania, were beginning to declare that slavery was an evil which ought to be abolished. But most white Americans had come to regard the Negro races as inferior and drew a rigid color line, according to which anybody with any Negro ancestry was classified as wholly Negro. By colonial laws children of a white father and a slave mother inherited the status of the mother. This attitude of race discrimination proved to be an insuperable obstacle to any peaceful abolition of slavery in those areas where there was a large Negro population. Even those Southerners who disapproved of slavery in principle did not believe that the two races could live together as equals; emancipation, they declared, must be accompanied by a removal of the Negro population back to Africa or to some other part of America. Such a proposal was, of course, not a practical possibility.

2. THE BRITISH IMPERIAL SYSTEM

Origins of the Navigation Code. In accordance with the prevalent mercantilist theory, all British governments assumed that colonies should be kept in subordination to the mother country and that their main function was to be a source of necessary raw materials. These should be shipped to England, and English manufactured goods bought in return, thus making the Empire, as far as possible, a self-sufficient economic unit, independent of her foreign rivals. This policy was enforced by means of the Acts of Trade and Navigation. From the beginning the control of economic development caused some resentment in the colonies, though it was not until the 1770's that the divergence of interests became so serious as to precipitate open conflict.

The first step towards the regulation of colonial trade was taken soon after the foundation of Virginia. During the 1620's it was ordered that Virginia tobacco should be exported only to England and that it must be carried in English ships. These rules fell into abeyance after the outbreak of the Civil War, during which much of the trade of the Chesapeake colonies was taken over by the Dutch. In 1650 the government of the Commonwealth adopted a Navigation Act prohibiting foreign vessels from trading with the English colonies, but Cromwell made no serious effort to enforce it. After the restoration of the monarchy, this legislation was considerably strengthened. In 1660 a new Navigation Act declared that all colonial trade had to be carried in either English or colonial ships, and that certain "enumerated" commodities produced on the mainland and in the West Indian colonies, including tobacco and sugar, could be exported only to England. In 1663 Parliament added a Staple Act, according to which the colonies could not buy goods directly from any European country except England, with the exception of certain articles imported from southern Europe, such as Madeira wine.

Thus the original navigation code included three main items: the colonies must do all their trading in British ships; they must do most of their buying from the mother country; and they must do most of their selling to the mother country. The most obvious result was to enable English merchants to profit through control of colonial trade. The colonies, however, were permitted to trade freely with each other and (with some restrictions) with such non-European areas as the West Indies.

The navigation code was enforced, on the whole, in the Chesapeake colonies, but was persistently violated in New England. Prior to 1660 the New England colonies had acquired the habit of doing as they pleased, and they showed no willingness to surrender their liberties after that date. Boston merchants, for example, regularly disobeyed the Navigation Act by shipping enumerated articles, such as Virginia tobacco and West Indian sugar, to continental Europe. Royal officials made a long series of attempts to enforce obedience in this and other matters. Finally, in 1684, the charter of Massachusetts was declared to be forfeited, and the colony was placed under a royal governor. Two years later all the New England colonies were combined into a single Dominion of New England, to which New York and New Jersey were added later, and Sir Edmund Andros was appointed governor with autocratic powers. Andros never enforced his authority over Connecticut and Rhode Island, but in Massachusetts he levied taxes without the consent of any representative body, questioned the validity of all land titles, exacted quitrents, and offended the Puritan ministers by introducing Anglican church services, theatrical performances, and other abominations.

The Revolution of 1688.   The Andros regime was brought to an end as a result of political changes in England. The restoration of the monarchy in 1660 had not stabilized the relations between King and Parliament; both Charles II and his brother James II, the former Duke of York, who succeeded Charles in 1685, had worked to increase royal power, and James II had also aroused opposition by supporting Roman

Catholicism. Finally, by a bloodless revolution in 1688, James was expelled from the throne, which then passed to his Dutch nephew, William of Orange, who became King William III. The main result of the revolution was to establish Parliamentary supremacy; although it was several generations before the methods of parliamentary government were fully worked out, England henceforth was ruled by the party that won a majority in the House of Commons, and the monarchy gradually faded into a mere symbol of national unity.[1] The accession of William III was followed by the enactment of a Bill of Rights summarizing all the liberties that Englishmen had gained during their long political evolution, and by a Toleration Act giving religious freedom to all Protestants.

The news of the revolution reached Boston in 1689, and was immediately followed by a popular rising which overthrew the Andros regime and re-established the old Puritan regime. Increase Mather, the leading figure in the theocracy, then traveled to London to negotiate with the new English government for a restoration of the charter. But Massachusetts was not permitted to regain such complete autonomy as in the past. By a new charter, issued in 1691, the colony was to have a royal governor, the right of voting was to be based on property and no longer on church membership, and freedom of worship was to be given to all Protestant churches. Plymouth was permanently united with Massachusetts, but Connecticut and Rhode Island were allowed to keep their original charters.

The Revolution also had repercussions in New York, where popular indignation had been growing against the royal officials and the wealthy merchants and landowners who cooperated with them. In 1689 a rising of urban craftsmen and shopkeepers, assisted by small farmers, overthrew King James's officials and set up a more democratic regime headed by a German merchant, Jacob Leisler. But when a new governor arrived from England in 1691, he quickly formed an alliance with the local aristocrats. Leisler was executed on a charge of treason; and although a legislature henceforth met regularly and made a few reforms, New York continued to be controlled and mostly owned by a few wealthy families.

The Expansion of the Navigation Code. The revolution of 1688 was of small importance in the history of the colonies except for the changes brought about in New England. Although the English people had taken a decisive step forward in their progress towards political liberty, English colonial policy remained essentially unchanged. Commercial and financial interests dominated the English government even more fully than in the past, and its attitude continued to be strictly mercantilist. The system of trade regulation was therefore maintained and extended, and new machinery was set up to enforce obedience.

In 1696 supervision of colonial economic development was entrusted

---

[1] Two political parties had taken shape during the reign of Charles II. The Tories had supported the King, while the Whigs wished to limit his power.

to a group of officials known as the Board of Trade and Plantations, which assumed very broad powers over American affairs, while a supplementary Navigation Act provided for stricter enforcement of the regulations. In the following year it was ordered that special admiralty courts, controlled by the British government and not allowing trial by jury, should deal with merchants accused of illegal trade. The list of enumerated articles which could be shipped only to England was steadily extended, and eventually included all important colonial exports except fish, grain, and rum. The development of colonial industry was checked by the Woolen Act of 1699, which forbade the colonies to export woolen goods. A law of 1732 extended the same prohibition to the products of colonial hatmakers, and a law of 1750 rigorously restricted the right of the colonies to manufacture iron goods.

Of all the British acts of trade, however, the most unpalatable was the Molasses Act of 1733, which was designed to end the trade between the colonies and the French and Spanish West Indies. Prohibitive duties were to be paid on all sugar, molasses, and spirits imported from foreign plantations, the purpose being to compel colonial merchants to buy solely from the British islands. Since the French and Spanish trade was extremely profitable, especially to the New Englanders, effective enforcement would have meant serious losses. But like some other items in the navigation code, the Molasses Act was persistently and successfully violated.

As a result of the navigation laws the colonies received less for some of their exports and paid more for some of their imports than they might have done if they had been permitted to trade freely. The laws were drafted and administered in England, and the interests of the mother country took precedence over those of the colonies. Although, prior to 1764, England did not attempt to collect revenue from the colonies through taxation, her indirect profits through control of colonial trade were considerable. But the system was by no means wholly one-sided, and the colonies received a number of benefits from it. Their shipping was encouraged equally with that of the mother country, and they had a protected market for their products. Englishmen, for example, were not allowed to grow tobacco at home, and were discouraged by heavy duties from buying it from foreign producers. Duties on foreign commodities imported into the colonies by way of England were often refunded, so that the colonists could obtain them more cheaply, and bounties were paid to colonial producers of goods needed for naval construction.

Defenders of the navigation code argued that the colonies had been built up by English capital, much of which had never brought in any direct profits, and that they were under the protection of British armed forces, to which they were not required to contribute. It should be remembered, moreover, that the mercantilist economic theory was at that time accepted almost universally, and that the English colonies were subject to much less stringent regulation than the Spanish and the French. Down to the Revolution there was much grumbling in the colonies against the details of the navigation code, and much violation of laws, such as the Molasses Act, which seemed especially oppressive; but there was little disposition to criticize the system in principle or as a whole.

The Political Evolution of the Colonies. While the economic development of the colonies was subject to this elaborate regulation, in political matters they became largely self-governing, not because the English authorities approved of colonial autonomy but rather because they were unable to prevent it.

Every colony had its legislature, which was generally bicameral in accordance with the British model. The lower house, usually known as the assembly, was elected by qualified voters, whose number was everywhere restricted by property qualifications, while the upper house of councilors or assistants consisted of prominent citizens nominated by the governor. Connecticut and Rhode Island elected their own governors, as provided by their original charters, but in all the other colonies the governor was nominated from England, either by the Crown or by proprietors. Maryland, Pennsylvania, and Delaware were, however, the only colonies that retained proprietary rule down to 1776. The English Parliament assumed the powers of a supreme legislature for the Empire and could legislate directly for the colonies, while colonial legislation might be vetoed by the English Privy Council, usually on the advice of the Board of Trade.

The main trend in the political evolution of the colonies through the early eighteenth century was a gradual shift in power from the governors and councilors to the elected assemblies. The colonies were generally inclined to regard the governors with suspicion as representatives of an alien authority; and in many instances this attitude had much justification. While some of the governors were men of ability and integrity, a large number were minor politicians, owing their appointments solely to influence, who frequently antagonized the Americans by their arrogance and sometimes by corruption. Following precedents set by the English House of Commons in its struggle with the Stuart kings, the assemblies quickly realized the importance of control of the purse; they claimed that they had the exclusive right to vote taxes and appropriate money, including money for the governor's salary, and insisted that all money grants had to be renewed annually. Royal and proprietary governors fought a long series of battles over this issue; but since they were financially dependent upon legislative grants and could use as weapons only the negative powers of proroguing the assemblies or vetoing their bills, they were generally defeated. Having established control of the purse, the assemblies then began to claim a share in the formulation of policy on numerous other questions.

Although the growth of the power of the assemblies was of great importance in the evolution of American political institutions, it should be remembered that these bodies were by no means democratic. The power lost by the royal governors was assumed not by the mass of the people but by the wealthier classes in the different colonies. Meanwhile, these upper classes were themselves being challenged by the spokesmen of the craftsmen and the farmers, so that political conflicts in eighteenth-century America often became three-cornered, the struggle for colonial rights against British interference running parallel with a more fundamental internal struggle between different groups of Americans.

3. INTERNAL CONFLICTS

Democratic Tendencies.   As the people of the colonies became more numerous and more prosperous, they began to acquire a new outlook. Belief in the need for hereditary class distinctions and for authoritarian government became weaker, and men began to acquire a faith in the capacity of the average man and in his right to freedom and economic opportunity. This growth of democratic sentiments was strongest in the newly settled regions of the back country. Along the eastern seaboard, on the other hand, traditional European attitudes were more deeply rooted, and wealthy families continued to defend aristocratic principles. The resultant conflict between the new spirit of democracy and the traditional belief in aristocracy was one of the main factors in American political development both before and after the Revolution.

Perhaps the most striking feature of the new American society was the lack of extreme economic inequalities. In a country where land was cheap and abundant nearly every white person could become independent, and no large class of dependent laborers could develop. Some families were relatively rich and others poor; but the difference between them was smaller than in Europe, and the vast majority of the white population occupied a middle position, being neither exploiters of other men's labor nor themselves the victims of exploitation. In America, said Benjamin Franklin, there were "few people so miserable as the poor of Europe," and "very few that in Europe would be called rich. . . . It is rather a general happy mediocrity that prevails."

This "general happy mediocrity" was exemplified among the craftsmen who composed the bulk of the urban population in the New England and Middle colonies. But it was most evident in the rural back country, which was inhabited mostly by small farmers everywhere from New Hampshire down to Georgia. Many of those attitudes which we think of as distinctively American first originated in the colonial farmer's way of life.

The Farm Population.   This life was by no means easy; it was filled with unremitting toil throughout the year. But the rewards were often substantial. In most regions a farmer could acquire as much land as he and his family could cultivate, and—barring some natural catastrophe—he could raise food in a variety and an abundance which had been unknown among his European ancestors. Nor was rural life devoid of gaiety, even among the stern New England Puritans and the Scotch-Irish Presbyterians. There were periodic religious or family festivals, when the supply of rum or whisky was unlimited and men and women entertained themselves with the traditional dances and folk songs that had been handed down from medieval or Tudor times.

A number of the colonial farmers incurred debts which they were never able to pay off. But if they could avoid debts, they could expect to enjoy economic independence to an extent almost unknown in the modern world. Producing almost all the necessities of life for themselves, they needed to sell only a small surplus in order to pay their taxes or quitrents and to buy gunpowder, salt, metal, and a few luxuries such as tea or coffee. So long as they could meet these small obligations, they had remarkably little cause for anxiety.

This independence did not mean isolation. Except in parts of the South, men lived close to their neighbors, and cooperation and generous hospitality became customary. Families regularly assisted each other in the performance of such tasks as the raising of the framework of a new house or barn, which required collective effort. Local government and defense were largely joint responsibilities, instead of being left to some separate group of officials. Every citizen had certain duties, such as service in the militia and on juries, and in each community the more prominent and respected individuals acted as justices of the county court, officers of the militia, and representatives to the colonial legislature. In addition to the legal machinery of self-government, rural communities often had their own extralegal methods of maintaining order. Criminals and troublemakers might be beaten, stripped naked, ridden on rails, tarred and feathered, or driven out of town. Under such conditions there was no obvious need for elaborate political institutions or for salaried officeholders. Organized government could do little for the citizens of a rural community which they could not do more cheaply and effectively for themselves. Rural Americans were likely to feel that the best government was one which left individuals free to manage their own affairs and interfered with them as little as possible.

The American Spirit. The "general happy mediocrity" of rural society did not mean any complete equality. There were always some individuals, shrewder and more ambitious than their neighbors, who were rising to wealth and prominence; they might become country merchants as well as farmers, engage in trade with the Indians or in land speculation, and assume political leadership. At the other extreme, there were many people who were content to scrape a meager living from small forest clearings to which they never acquired legal titles, or who preferred to move out beyond the frontier line into unsettled country where they could live like the Indians and be free from the discipline of civilized white society. Similarly, among the urban craftsmen a few enterprising persons rose above the general level and became employers of labor on a considerable scale, while some others remained wage earners all their lives. But what was important was that the status of each individual depended largely upon his own efforts and abilities, not merely upon his ancestry. Unlike Europe, with its more rigid class lines, colonial America had great social mobility.

Franklin summarized this tendency of American life when he warned any European "who has no other quality to recommend him but his birth" to stay at home. "In Europe it has indeed its value; but it is a commodity that cannot be carried to a worse market than that of America, where people do not inquire concerning a stranger: *What is he?* but: *What can he do?* If he has any useful art, he is welcome; and if he exercises it, and behaves well, he will be respected by all who know him; but a mere man of quality, who on that account wants to live upon the public, by some office or salary, will be despised and disregarded. The husbandman is in honor there, and even the mechanic, because their employments are useful."

The men and women who grew up in America came to believe that courage, industry, and perseverance would usually ensure success, and that, if an individual remained poor, it was usually because of his own weaknesses. Men were admired if they showed enterprise and ambition, instead of accepting their hereditary status in the social order as their European ancestors did. America became a country where the son, instead of merely succeeding to his father's position, was expected to surpass him.

According to Crèvecœur, it was the growth of this sense of limitless opportunity that transformed the European immigrant into an American.

An European, when he first arrives, seems limited in his intentions, as well as in his views; but he very suddenly alters his scale. . . . He no sooner breathes our air than he forms new schemes, and embarks in designs he never would have thought of in his own country. . . . He begins to feel the effects of a sort of resurrection; hitherto he had not lived, but simply vegetated; he now feels himself a man, because he is treated as such. . . . Judge what an alteration there must arise in the mind and thoughts of this man; he begins to forget his former servitude and dependence, his heart involuntarily swells and glows; this first swell inspires him with those new thoughts which constitute an American. . . . The American is a new man, who acts upon new principles; he must therefore entertain new ideas, and form new opinions. From involuntary idleness, servile dependency, penury, and useless labor, he has passed to toils of a very different nature, rewarded by ample subsistence.

Thus, throughout the colonial period, Americans were learning from their daily experience that the average citizen was entitled to opportunities for self-expression and advancement; that he could, on the whole, be trusted with freedom and the power to regulate his own affairs; and that he need not be controlled by a ruling class or an authoritarian government. In the course of time this attitude gradually crystallized into a system of political doctrines which became the main formative principles of the new American nation.

Sectional and Class Conflicts. This growth of democratic attitudes, however, was a slow process, and for a long time it was held in check by the representatives of upper-class rule. Most of the colonies had been founded by men who believed that only "gentlemen" were qualified for political leadership, and had at first been governed by men who had belonged to the upper classes in England. These original ruling groups had afterwards been enlarged by families who had acquired wealth and privilege after the migration. In the eighteenth century aristocratic principles were represented by the merchants of New England and Pennsylvania, the merchants and landowners of New York, and the planters of the South. Largely controlling the different colonial governments, these wealthy families had a tendency to copy the beliefs and way of life of the English gentry.

Conflict between aristocratic and democratic tendencies had already shown itself in the seventeenth century in Bacon's Rebellion in Virginia and in the Leisler episode in New York. During the eighteenth century there were similar controversies in most of the colonies, although none of them reached the point of violence until the Revolutionary period. These controversies revolved around four main issues: political rights, the ownership of land, the currency, and religion.

Political Rights. In all the colonies the right to vote was restricted by property qualifications which excluded many of the farmers and craftsmen. Perhaps even more important was the unequal distribution of seats in the legislature. Everywhere the seaboard regions had many more representatives in proportion to population than did the back country. The political predominance of the seaboard was further increased by the location of the capitals, all of which were on the coast or close to it. At a time when there was no means of rapid communication, this was much more important than it would be today.

In general, questions of political rights seem to have been of more interest to the craftsmen than to the farmers. By the middle of the eighteenth century craftsmen in urban centers like Boston, New York, and Philadelphia were taking an active part in politics and beginning to assert themselves as a distinct group with interests of their own.

Ownership of Land. A question of more widespread concern was that of ownership of unsettled lands. The farmer was likely to believe that settlers should have free access to western land, and that the land should

belong to those who put their labor into it. By occupying a section of
forest, clearing the trees, building a house, and growing crops, he felt,
the individual settler established a property right which ought to take
precedence over any title of ownership acquired by merely legal processes.
This point of view was directly contrary to that of the wealthy men who
engaged in land speculation. Just as in the seventeenth century English
noblemen had acquired American land from the Crown, so in the eighteenth century merchants and planters obtained western land titles from
the colonial governments. This resulted in frequent conflicts with the
settlers from whom they tried to collect rents.

This was largely a question of divergent economic interests, but involved in it were far-reaching issues of public policy. Was it better for the
future of the country that squatters should be allowed to move into new
country and take possession of it as they pleased? Or should the process
of expansion be controlled by business groups who would invest capital
in the development of the land, provide for orderly settlement, make
agreements with the Indian tribes, and then earn profits through sales
or rents?

Almost every prominent individual in eighteenth-century America
became interested in western land, either individually or as a stockholder
in a company, and the pervasive importance of the question can scarcely
be over-estimated. The conflict between different groups of speculators
for the control of the West, and the more fundamental conflict between
the speculator and the settler, were factors in almost every political controversy throughout the century.

The Currency.   In some of the colonies there was a similar conflict
of interests in the currency question. Since the colonies had no gold or
silver mines, and since they generally bought from abroad more than they
sold, there was always a serious scarcity of hard money, especially among
the farm population. This meant that substitutes had to be adopted. A
good deal of business was done by barter. In Virginia, for example, hogs-
heads of tobacco were regularly used as money, while in the back country
of Pennsylvania debts could be paid with whisky. The chief substitute,
however, was some form of paper money. Beginning with Massachusetts
in 1690, a number of the colonial governments paid their debts by issuing
promissory notes in anticipation of tax collections. These were known as
"bills of credit" and circulated freely.

Closely connected with the problem of the currency was that of
agricultural credit. Farmers often needed to borrow money, and could
apply only to individual storekeepers or merchants, who charged high
interest rates. There were no commercial banks in America until after the
Revolution. Debt was a more serious matter then than it is today because
persons unable to meet their obligations might go to jail as well as lose
their farms. In order both to increase the supply of money and to relieve
the distress of the farmers, several colonial legislatures established what

were known as "land banks." These institutions issued notes, backed not by gold or silver but by land, with which loans could be made to farmers.

The need for some form of paper money was initially recognized by merchants as well as by farmers, and in some of the colonies, such as Pennsylvania, bills of credit circulated smoothly and evoked no serious controversy. In Massachusetts and Rhode Island, on the other hand, they were issued in such quantities as to cause a serious degree of inflation. This worked to the benefit of debtors and the detriment of creditors, and aroused acute sectional and class conflicts. Eventually the British government, anxious to maintain a stable currency in order to protect the interests of merchants exporting goods to the colonies, intervened to prevent any further inflation.

The Great Awakening. The conflict between upper-class and democratic attitudes also spread to religion. The Congregationalist churches in Massachusetts and Connecticut, and the Anglican Church in parts of New York and in the South, were tax-supported institutions, and their clergy were often closely allied with the mercantile and planting interests. In the 1730's and 1740's the colonies were swept by a series of religious revivals known as the "Great Awakening." Precipitated by a number of different evangelists, the most prominent of whom was a visitor from England, George Whitefield, the revivals began in New England, New Jersey, and Pennsylvania at about the same time, and spread afterwards to the South. They affected chiefly the urban craftsmen and the back-country farmers, not the wealthier classes, and led to the growth of more democratic forms of religion and to demands for the separation of church and state.

The theology of the revivalists was old-fashioned Calvinism, with an emphasis on the emotional and mystical aspects of religious experience. Man, they declared, could not obtain salvation unless he was converted, and conversion was essentially an emotional convulsion, not merely a sober decision to obey God's moral law. Preachers soon discovered that the most effective way to bring about conversions was to create a state of mass hysteria by emphasizing the terrors of Hell. Entire congregations would start screaming and falling in convulsive fits, and would finally achieve a conviction of divine grace. Persons converted in this manner felt that they had direct contact with the divine spirit and were therefore more enlightened than those upper-class and better-educated groups, both lay and clerical, who had never passed through this kind of experience. They began to join new religious organizations in which control belonged to the entire body of members, not to the ministers alone, and to refuse payment of taxes to the established churches. In New England the Congregationalist churches were split into "new light" (revivalist) and "old light" groups, while many people seceded altogether from the established order and either became Baptists or formed new "separatist" congregations of their own. In the Middle colonies the Presbyterian

Church was similarly split, while in the South many of the small farmers joined either the Presbyterian or the Baptist Church and became vigorous opponents of the privileged position of the Anglicans.

New England.   Few non-English immigrants came to New England in the eighteenth century, so that this remained, both racially and religiously, the most homogeneous section of the colonies. It was the scene, nevertheless, of sharp internal conflicts.

The clergy had now lost most of their political influence, and the dominant class were the merchants of the seaboard towns, whose wealth was derived mainly from the West India trade. New England ships carried timber and foodstuffs to sugar planters in the Islands, and came back loaded with silver dollars and with molasses, most of which was distilled into rum. Even more profitable was the triangular trade by which rum was shipped to West Africa, and slaves then transported across the middle passage to the West Indies. In this way, a number of mercantile families acquired large fortunes, part of which they spent in building large houses and maintaining an aristocratic style of living, while part was spent for investment at home.

Although there were some profitable industrial enterprises in colonial New England, such as shipbuilding and the mining and manufacturing of iron, the chief investment opportunities were in real estate. As the settled area of New England expanded, landownership became less democratic. Instead of giving land to townships for distribution among individual settlers, as the practice had been in the seventeenth century, the legislatures began to sell it to wealthy men interested in speculation. Thus seaboard merchants became owners of new township lands in western Massachusetts and northern Connecticut, and farmers who wished to settle there were required to pay rents. Conflicts were also caused by the apportionment of the common lands in the older towns; these were generally claimed by the descendants of the original proprietors, newcomers being excluded from any share in the distribution.

By the 1730's a number of the back-country farmers were in economic difficulties and were falling into debt to the merchants. This caused them to support land-bank projects and to demand an increase in the quantity of money in circulation, although the colonial paper currencies were already seriously depreciated. In Rhode Island inflation went on until the British government put a stop to it in 1751. In Massachusetts debtor-class leaders won control of the popular branch of the legislature in 1740 and set up a land bank; after a bitter controversy, almost resulting in civil war, the British authorities intervened on the side of the creditor interests, and the land bank was ended by order of Parliament in 1741. In 1751 the New England colonies were forbidden to issue any further legal tender bills, and in 1764 this prohibition was extended to all colonies.

Meanwhile, the upper classes were also becoming alarmed by the spread of religious revivalism. In 1735 Jonathan Edwards, minister of the church at Northampton, had brought about a revival in the Connecticut Valley, chiefly by horrifyingly vivid descriptions of hell-fire; and in the autumn of 1740 George Whitefield preached in every part of New England and precipitated a general excitement. Thousands of people underwent the experience of conversion, after which many of them broke away from the established Congregationalist churches, declaring that salaried and college-educated clergymen were unnecessary and that once any individual had received divine grace, he could know the will of God by direct revelation. Both in Massachusetts and Connecticut the authorities regarded such tendencies as a threat to social order. The new "separatist" and Baptist congregations were denied legal status, and persons who refused to pay taxes for the support of the regular clergy were subjected to the penalties of the law. During the 1740's and 1750's there was religious persecution, especially in Connecticut.

The most conspicuous result of these internal tensions was the stimulation of migration. During the middle decades of the eighteenth century, thousands of farmers from southern New England moved northwards in search of vacant land and the right to worship God as they pleased. They began to fill up the back country of New Hampshire and the area now known as Vermont (which then belonged to New Hampshire, although part of it was also claimed by New York), defying the authority of the New Hampshire legislature and the property rights of land speculators. Thus, at the outset of the Revolutionary period, conflicts were developing in northern New England.

The leadership of the mercantile class was also challenged from another direction. Boston, which by the middle of the century had a population of nearly 20,000, was much the largest town in New England; yet, like the small rural townships, it was still governed by its town meeting. Attended chiefly by the craftsmen and other middle-class citizens, the Boston town meeting became a vehicle for the expression of popular opposition to the policies of the colonial government. This democratic gathering provided opportunities for political leaders of a new kind—men who did not belong to the charmed circle of the mercantile families and who were skilled in the use of oratory and the arts of political management. By the end of the 1750's the town meeting was largely controlled by a group of such men, who were known as the Caucus club. The principal organizer of this political machine, Samuel Adams, devoted his life almost exclusively to agitation, first against the ruling families of Massachusetts and afterwards against British control.

The Middle Colonies. In the Middle colonies farmers and craftsmen had even more cause for discontent but fewer opportunities for expressing it. This was particularly true in New York, where the franchise was narrowly restricted and aristocratic institutions were well established. By the middle of the century a large part of the land in the colony was owned by only thirty families, three of which had more than 1,000,000 acres each. These families, along with their allies among the merchants of Manhattan Island, controlled the government and competed with each other for offices and economic privileges. Resentment against upper-class rule was spreading both among the craftsmen and small tradesmen of New York City (which by 1774 had a population of nearly 30,000) and among the tenant farmers in the Hudson Valley; but until the outbreak of the Revolution it remained largely inarticulate.

New Jersey was in a state of turmoil through the middle decades of the century as a result of conflict about rents and land titles between the farm population and the heirs of the original proprietors. During the same period Pennsylvania was disturbed by a three-cornered conflict among the Penn family, the Quaker merchants, and the back-country farmers. Merchants and farmers were agreed in opposing the proprietary government and its attempts to collect quitrents, but were bitterly opposed to each other on all other issues.

Philadelphia, which contained close to 40,000 inhabitants at the outset of the Revolution, had become the largest city in the colonies; but unlike Boston it had no town meeting and was governed by a small closed corporation, the majority of its citizens being disfranchised. It had grown rapidly, chiefly because it was surrounded by the richest farming country in America; its merchants exported grain and other foodstuffs to Europe and the West Indies. This part of the colonies was also a center of manufacturing, largely as a result of the skill of German craftsmen; a few establishments, like the Stiegel glass plant at Mannheim, which employed 120 workers, and some of the iron foundries, were large-scale enterprises.

Enriched by these activities, the first families of Philadelphia and its environs became even more conservative and more class-conscious than their counterparts in Boston and New York. They controlled the legislature and were accused by the farmers, particularly the Scotch-Irish, of making the back country pay an unfairly large share of taxes and of failing to provide for its defense against Indian raids. Both these accusations were true, although, in reply to the second of them, the merchants correctly pointed out that they, as Quakers, had conscientious objections to warfare, and that the Scotch-Irish themselves provoked the Indians by encroaching on their lands.

The South.   South of the line drawn by two surveyors, Mason and Dixon, in 1767, a society was developing which became steadily more divergent from that of the Northern and Middle colonies. This was only partially true in the border area of Maryland, because Baltimore was the commercial rival of Philadelphia and was also a center of manufacturing. But from Virginia southwards there were few merchants and little industry, and the dominant class were the slave-owning planters.

Eighteenth-century Virginia was divided into three sections: the seaboard region known as the Tidewater; the region stretching inland as far as the Blue Ridge, which was known as the Piedmont; and the Shenandoah Valley. Most of the Tidewater was now owned by plantation aristocrats who lived with a graciousness and an easygoing generosity unparalleled elsewhere in the English colonies. Economically, however, their position was far from being secure. Tobacco cultivation had a tendency to exhaust the soil, and much of the Tidewater land was rapidly losing its fertility. British trade regulations kept the planter families dependent upon mercantile firms in London, and most of them were now heavily in debt. These debts were handed down from generation to generation.

As agriculture in the Tidewater became less profitable, the more enterprising planters began to move inland into the Piedmont. Some of them, like George Washington, abandoned tobacco cultivation altogether and began to grow wheat. But, as elsewhere, the easiest and most obvious source of wealth was not agriculture but land speculation, and a number of the planters acquired ownership of territories in the western part of the colony. And, as elsewhere, this caused conflicts between the upper class and the small farmers.

In addition to the question of landownership, the farmers of the Piedmont and the Shenandoah Valley were aggrieved by their inadequate representation in the House of Burgesses, by the unfair incidence of taxation, and by the collection of taxes for the support of the Anglican clergy. Shortly before the outbreak of the Revolution their discontent was beginning to find political expression. A back-country lawyer with remarkable powers of oratory, Patrick Henry, became their spokesman in the House of Burgesses and in the law courts, while they also won support from some of the younger and more liberal-minded planters, such as Richard Henry Lee and Thomas Jefferson.

In the Carolinas the division between the seaboard and the back country was even sharper. South Carolina was dominated by rice-planters and fur-traders. In North Carolina, where a large majority of the population were small farmers, the government had come under the control of a small group of tobacco-planters, merchants, land speculators, and officials. As the back country filled up, largely with Scotch-Irish and German immigrants, conflicts developed over rents, taxes, protection against Indian raids, and other questions.

Early in the eighteenth century South Carolina was disturbed by a long controversy about inflation, ending in a victory for the creditor party in 1731. In North Carolina the grievances of the back-country farmers became so acute that they finally resorted to violence. In the 1760's, oppressed by rent collections, unfair taxes, and legal fees, these farmers formed an association, known as the Regulators, which used force to intimidate tax-collectors, judges, and other officials. In 1771, after some years of virtual civil war, the Regulators were crushed in the battle of Alamance by an army recruited in the seaboard regions and commanded by the royal Governor.

4. THE CONFLICT WITH FRANCE

THESE internal tensions could be reduced in the end only through the opening of new territories for settlement, and the migration of discontented groups across the Appalachian barrier. But this did not become possible until after the claims of the French to the Mississippi Valley had been disposed of.

European Claims to the West.   The St. Lawrence provided easy access to the western country, and as early as the middle of the seventeenth century French explorers, fur-traders, and missionaries were opening up trails south of the Great Lakes into what is now the Middle West. In 1673 Marquette and Joliet reached the Mississippi River from Lake Michigan and paddled down it as far as Arkansas; and in 1682 La Salle, greatest of the French explorers, made a complete crossing from Canada to the Gulf of Mexico and proclaimed French sovereignty over Louisiana. A few years later he led a party of colonists from France to take possession of the country, but this attempt ended in disaster and in his own death at the hands of his followers. In 1697, however, Iberville successfully planted a French colony on the Gulf, and in 1718 the city of New Orleans was founded. Although the French were primarily interested in the fur trade, the colonists around New Orleans established plantations for various tropical foodstuffs, and imported Negro slaves. The city soon acquired a cosmopolitan flavor, and its relaxing climate and mixed population led to the growth of a sophisticated and easygoing way of life, very different from the severity of life in French Canada.

The French hoped to retain control of the whole western country and to prevent the British from crossing the Appalachians. They built forts at various points between Canada and Louisiana, and established settlements of fur-traders and farmers at Kaskaskia and other places in the valley. The number of French colonists was always small, but (with the notable exception of the Iroquois in western New York) most of the Indian tribes became dependent upon them, selling them furs in exchange for firearms, liquor, and other luxuries. By the middle of the eighteenth century French influence was established over an immense area, extending westwards as far as Saskatchewan and the Dakotas.

Meanwhile, two other European powers were interested in parts of what is now the United States. Spain had held Florida since the sixteenth century, and the Spanish officials competed with the Carolina fur-traders for control of the Indians in the back country of Georgia. Farther to the west, Spaniards from Mexico took possession of New Mexico during the seventeenth century, and early in the eighteenth a Spanish colony was planted on the coast of Texas. Spanish missionaries and traders were active in the whole southwestern country, and in the year 1776 a party of colonists founded the city of San Francisco. This movement was undertaken to forestall the Russians, who had been advancing eastwards across

Asia for generations and were now threatening to enter America from Siberia. In 1741 a Russian expedition had crossed the Bering Strait into Alaska—possibly the first group to do so for twenty thousand years— and in the late eighteenth century Russian merchants were developing commercial relations with Indian tribes in the Oregon country.

The Cycle of Wars. Population statistics made it inevitable that, sooner or later, most of the western country should become English-speaking. The French were outnumbered in North America by at least twenty to one. Yet nearly a century of warfare elapsed before they lost control of the Mississippi Valley. While this conflict was of primary importance in the development of the American colonies, it was only one aspect of a world-wide struggle for supremacy. Under Louis XIV (1643–1715) France had become the dominant power on the European continent, and the ambitions of the French monarchy provoked a series of wars with France's European neighbors. At the same time the French were competing with the British for possession not only of the North American fur trade but also of the sugar plantations of the Caribbean and the rich and varied markets of India. Between 1689 and 1763 these dynastic and mercantile rivalries resulted in four world wars, each of which was fought partly in Europe and partly on the seas and in the colonies. The final victory of the British was probably due mainly to the fact that they could concentrate most of their energies on maritime and colonial warfare; the French, on the other hand, were fighting for supremacy on the European continent as well as in India and America.

The struggle for North America was conducted partly by the British government and partly by the thirteen colonies. But for a number of reasons the efforts of the colonies were not very effective. Their governments found it difficult to raise enough money to finance ambitious military operations, and they had no professional armies. All able-bodied citizens belonged to the militia and were liable to be called for service when necessary; but militia regiments were deficient in training and discipline, and rarely gave a good account of themselves when opposed by regulars. Although they were often good marksmen, they could not be relied upon to obey orders and were likely to succumb to panic during a battle.

Another handicap was the lack of any central coordinating authority. Some of the colonies contributed more than their share to the common cause—notably Massachusetts, which was concerned with the fisheries off the Canadian coast and the security of the northern frontier, and South Carolina, because of her interest in the southern fur trade. But there was little cooperation from regions which felt more secure. Some other colonies, moreover, especially Virginia and Pennsylvania, became involved in competition with each other for control of western territories. Their boundary lines had never been definitively drawn, and Virginia, on the basis of early charters, laid claim to the whole of the Ohio Valley.

4. The Struggle for America

THE CONFLICT BETWEEN BRITAIN AND FRANCE WAS OF VAST IMPORTANCE FOR THE future history of the United States, since the main question at issue in North America was whether the British colonies would be able to expand westward across the Appalachians or whether the Western country would be settled by the French. The map indicates approximately the areas under British, French, and Spanish control in 1754 at the beginning of the final phase of the conflict.

With colonies in Canada along the St. Lawrence River and at New Orleans near the mouth of the Mississippi, the French hoped to maintain control of the whole Mississippi Valley and keep the British east of the Appalachians. Their missionaries and fur-traders established friendly relations with Indian tribes over a vast area in the heart of the continent, and made settlements at various points south of the Great Lakes and on the Mississippi. In 1749 the French began to move into the Ohio Valley, and in 1754 they built Fort Duquesne where Pittsburgh now stands. This put them directly athwart the westward expansion of Virginia and Pennsylvania and meant that the plans of speculative land companies in the British colonies could not be fulfilled. It was therefore in this region that the war started, when on July 3, 1754, George Washington, in command of a force of Virginia militiamen, fought a skirmish with the French at Great Meadows close to Fort Duquesne.

In the South Spain held Florida, and the boundary line between Florida and the British colony of Georgia was unsettled. Fur-traders from South Carolina competed with the Spaniards for influence over the Indian tribes in the Georgia back country. During earlier periods there had been conflicts between France and Spain, and the Spaniards had regarded the French position at New Orleans as a threat to their control of Texas and Florida. But in the eighteenth century Spain and France were usually allied with each other against the British.

The British won the war in the end by assaulting the main French strongholds in Canada. After losing Quebec in 1759 and Montreal in 1760, the French could not longer hope to hold any part of the Western country. By the Treaty of Paris of 1763 everything east of the Mississippi became British, and the French possessions west of the Mississippi were transferred to Spain.

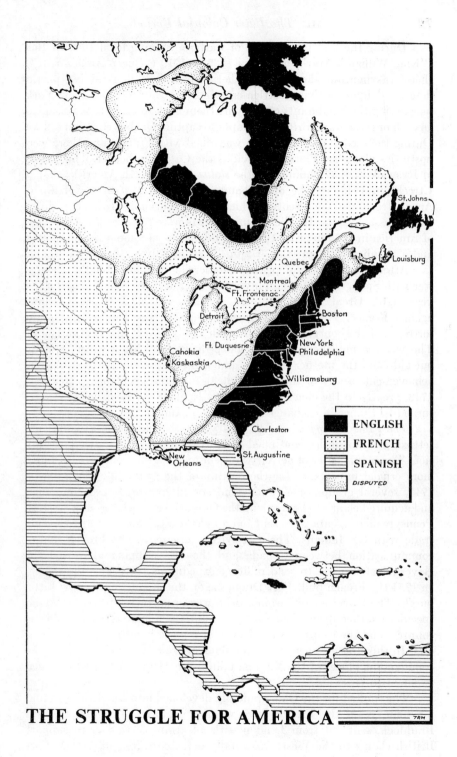

St.Johns

Louisburg

Quebec

Montreal
Ft.Frontenac

Detroit

Boston

Ft. Duquesne
Cahokia
Kaskaskia

New York
Philadelphia

Williamsburg

Charleston

New
Orleans

St.Augustine

	ENGLISH
	FRENCH
	SPANISH
	DISPUTED

THE STRUGGLE FOR AMERICA

TRM

During the first two periods of warfare, running from 1689 to 1697 ("King William's War") and from 1702 to 1713 ("Queen Anne's War"), there was fighting along the northern frontier. Indian raiding parties descended upon outlying settlements in New England and New York, massacring the inhabitants or carrying them back to Canada as prisoners. In each of these wars, British attempts to capture Quebec ended in failure. During the second of them Spain was allied with France, and there were hostilities along the Florida as well as the Canadian border. The Treaty of Ryswick in 1697 maintained the *status quo* in North America; that of Utrecht in 1713, on the other hand, established British ownership of Acadia (renamed Nova Scotia), which had been occupied by an expedition from Massachusetts. Its French inhabitants were removed to other parts of America in 1755 in order that they might not become fifth columnists, and a number of them (the "Cajuns") eventually settled in Louisiana.

After a generation of peace, commercial conflicts brought about a war with Spain in 1739, again involving the Southern colonies, and a few years later Great Britain entered another general European conflict against France. The principal American episode was the capture of the fortress of Louisbourg, which the French had built on Cape Breton Island. This was accomplished by a militia expedition from Massachusetts, without aid from the mother country, and was perhaps the greatest colonial achievement in any of the wars. But at the subsequent peace treaty in 1748, greatly to the chagrin of the New Englanders, Louisbourg was returned to France in exchange for Madras in India.

The Final Struggle.   The treaty left the fundamental issues unsettled, and hostilities continued in North America with little interruption. The main center of activity now shifted to a different area, of much more crucial importance for the destiny of the continent. Beginning in 1747, several groups of Virginia land speculators organized companies and acquired claims to lands along the Ohio River, in what is now western Pennsylvania; agents were sent out to explore the country and develop trade with the Indians. These activities threatened the French line of communication between Canada and the Mississippi, and caused the Governor of Canada to send military expeditions to occupy the region. In 1754 the French built Fort Duquesne on the site of what is now Pittsburgh. The Governor of Virginia, who was in partnership with the land speculators, then dispatched a body of militiamen in an effort to hold the country, and the result was a skirmish at a place known as Great Meadows. In this first engagement in the final struggle for North America the commanding officer of the Virginia militia was George Washington, then twenty-two years old.

The conflict for the Ohio gradually developed into a general war, and for some years the French were winning victories. In 1755, General Braddock, sent out from London with an army of regulars to support British claims to the West, was totally defeated a few miles from Fort

Duquesne; and expeditions against French outposts in northern and western New York could make little headway. These events enabled the French to strengthen their influence over most of the Indian tribes, and opened the frontiers of all the Northern and Middle colonies to raids and massacres. Through 1756 and 1757 the French held the initiative; an army from Canada under General Montcalm, coming by way of Lake Champlain, advanced to within sixty miles of Albany; and both New England and New York were threatened with invasion. Meanwhile, the British government, hoping that the colonies could be induced to co-ordinate their efforts, had sponsored a congress at Albany in 1754; but only seven of the legislatures sent delegates, and although the congress approved a plan for a federal union, drafted by Benjamin Franklin, the colonies were not willing to surrender their powers to any central authority.

War was officially declared and spread to Europe in 1756, Great Britain and Prussia being combined against France and Austria, afterwards joined by Spain. In the following year a new and inspiring leader assumed direction of British war activities. This was William Pitt the elder, subsequently known as the Earl of Chatham. Giving help to Prussia in order to keep France busy in Europe, establishing British naval control of the Atlantic, and sending new armies under young and vigorous officers to America, Pitt quickly reversed the course of events and provided the British with decisive victories.

In 1758 a British expedition recaptured Louisbourg, while combined British and American forces took Fort Duquesne. This was followed by a three-pronged invasion of Canada by way of the St. Lawrence, Lake Champlain, and Lake Ontario. In 1759 the St. Lawrence expedition, commanded by General Wolfe, captured Quebec (both Wolfe and the French commander, Montcalm, being killed in the decisive engagement); and in 1760 the surrender of Montreal to General Amherst put an end to all French resistance. Many of the western Indians were still sympathetic to the French; but in 1763 a widespread Indian rising, under a chieftain called Pontiac, was suppressed by British troops. Meanwhile, Great Britain had also expelled the French from India and won victories in the Caribbean.

The Peace of Paris was signed in 1763, its most important provision being the extinction of French sovereignty on the mainland of North America. Canada and the western country as far as the Mississippi became British. Spain ceded Florida to Great Britain and received Louisiana from France in compensation. Thus North America was now divided between Great Britain and Spain, the Mississippi River becoming the boundary line.

The expulsion of France from North America led directly to the Revolution, partly because the British government, having a much larger American empire under its control, began to reorganize its system of administration in ways that conflicted with colonial liberties, and partly because the Americans no longer felt dependent upon British military assistance and were therefore more inclined to demand autonomy. For a full understanding of the Revolution, however, we must consider not only the political and economic interests of the colonies but also their intellectual and cultural development.

IV

The American Enlightenment

1. THE MEANING OF THE ENLIGHTENMENT

2. THE DIFFUSION OF CULTURE

3. THE DEVELOPMENT OF RELIGION

4. SOCIAL THEORY

5. SCIENCE AND PHILOSOPHY

6. LITERATURE AND THE ARTS

THE early eighteenth century was a period not only of material growth but also of considerable intellectual and aesthetic achievement. But in order to understand this development, we must first form some conception of what was happening in Europe. Culturally, as well as politically, the colonies were largely dependent upon the mother country; they read English books and were influenced by new European trends of thought. In the American environment some European ideas were more influential than others, and some of them were reformulated and modified by American thinkers, so that in the course of time Americans began to exert a reciprocal influence upon Europe. But throughout the colonial period the cultural center of gravity of Western civilization was on the European side of the Atlantic.

SELECTED BIBLIOGRAPHY: Max Savelle, *Seeds of Liberty: The Genesis of the American Mind* (1948), is a comprehensive study of thought and culture before the Revolution. V. L. Parrington, *Main Currents in American Thought*, Vol. 1 (1927), deals with colonial literature mainly in terms of its intellectual content, while Merle Curti, *The Growth of American Thought* (revised edition, 1951), is the best general survey of intellectual history. The standard history of literature is R. E. Spiller and others (eds.), *Literary History of the United States* (1948). For colonial philosophy, see the early chapters of H. W. Schneider, *A History of American Philosophy* (1946); for economic theory, Joseph Dorfman, *The Economic Mind in American Civilization*, Vol. 1 (1946); for art and architecture, the early chapters of O. W. Larkin, *Art and Life in America* (1949), which can be supplemented with J. T. Flexner, *America's Old Masters* (1939), and H. S. Morrison, *Early American Architecture* (1952). The best biography of the leading figure in the American Enlightenment is Carl Van Doren, *Benjamin Franklin* (1938).

1. THE MEANING OF THE ENLIGHTENMENT

THE eighteenth century was the age of the Enlightenment. This word refers to the growth of certain new intellectual attitudes closely associated with the progress of the natural sciences. Having abandoned the teleological emphasis of medieval thought and discovered the value of exact observation and experiment, a series of investigators had devoted themselves to explaining natural phenomena in terms of invariable sequences of cause and effect. Their efforts culminated in the great work of Sir Isaac Newton, whose *Principia Mathematica* was published in 1687. Newton portrayed the universe as a kind of vast mechanism in which all the movements of matter were in accord with a few simple natural laws and could be expressed by means of mathematical formulas. This vision of an orderly and intelligible cosmos dominated the mind of western Europe throughout the eighteenth century.

The faith of the scientists in natural law was derived from the Christian tradition; like the medieval Scholastics, they believed that the world was the creation of a divine mind. But the new concepts seemed incompatible with the notion that God continued to intervene in worldly affairs after he had set the cosmic machine in motion. Eighteenth-century thinkers were frequently deists: they believed in the existence of God but not in any religion (such as Christianity) which inculcated faith in miracles or revelation. And while most deists accepted the doctrine of personal immortality, they were concerned primarily with the improvement of this life rather than with salvation in the hereafter. A new and optimistic faith in the progress of the race began to take the place of other-worldly religion in giving meaning to human life.

The Growth of Liberalism.   In the Newtonian universe the stars and planets moved independently, yet harmony was maintained by the workings of natural law. The thinkers of the Enlightenment hoped that, in a similar way, freedom and order could be reconciled in human society if the appropriate natural laws were discovered and obeyed. The most influential exponent of this view was John Locke, the English Whig philosopher, who wrote his two *Treatises on Civil Government* primarily in order to justify the Revolution of 1688. According to Locke, men were endowed with certain natural rights, of which the most fundamental were those to life, liberty, and property. They had agreed with each other to establish governments in order that these rights might be protected, from which it followed that any government which violated the rights of citizens should be changed or overthrown. Government was therefore based on a "social contract"; it was not, as more conservative theorists affirmed, the divinely created expression of the organic unity of society. In Locke's theory the individual was prior to the state, and not vice versa.

This individualistic approach implied that each person should be free to do as he pleased as long as he respected the rights of others. Traditional Christianity, declaring that man had an innate bias towards evil, had insisted that he needed authoritative guidance and discipline. But Locke interpreted human nature in more optimistic terms. In his philosophical writings he argued that the mind at birth was like a blank sheet of paper and was therefore not already tainted with original sin. The character of each individual was due wholly to post-natal experience, so that a good environment would make good human beings. Many eighteenth-century thinkers went further and argued that man had an innate moral sense which, if not perverted by bad institutions, would make him naturally virtuous.

Similar conceptions were applied to economics. Writers began to argue that individuals should be allowed free play for the exercise of enterprise and initiative, instead of being controlled by mercantilist governments. A group of French economists who called themselves Physiocrats were the first to present a systematic criticism of the traditional belief in economic regulation and to preach the new doctrine of *laissez faire*. They also argued that land was the only source of wealth and that nations could become truly prosperous only by the encouragement of agriculture.

The most influential advocate of *laissez faire* was the Scotsman Adam Smith, who published his *Wealth of Nations* in 1776. Smith declared that if each individual were left free to pursue his own self-interest, the processes of competition would promote the general welfare; the "invisible hand" of God had established a harmony between the interests of each and those of all. Smith insisted that economic injustice and exploitation were due to governmental interference with the workings of economic law; in a regime of free competition, he believed, profits and wages would always tend to equalize. Writing before the Industrial Revolution had made large-scale enterprise necessary, Smith saw no need for corporations, and favored an economic system in which production and trade could be carried on by a multitude of independent small owners.

Thus the thinkers of the Enlightenment, like those of the Middle Ages, believed that human welfare could be promoted by following the laws of God, nature, and reason. But whereas medieval philosophy had interpreted these laws so as to justify established institutions, the Enlightenment stimulated political and social change. Since men were naturally inclined toward good, an ideal society, it was believed, could be created by allowing them to pursue happiness as they pleased. Authoritarian institutions were contrary to natural law. Such doctrines were preached by a great number of writers, particularly by the French *philosophes*, of whom Voltaire was the most prominent. Their criticisms of traditional forms of government prepared the way for the French Revolution and the liberal movements of the nineteenth century.

Much of the literature and art of the eighteenth century was in accord with this intellectual atmosphere. Aesthetically, it was a period of classicism. Just as the philosophers believed that men could be happy by following a few simple laws of nature, so critics identified beauty with adherence to certain rules of good taste which were supposed to be universal and innate. This emphasis on a code of rules inhibited poetic spontaneity; but prose-writers cultivated an admirable elegance and clarity of style. And the cultivation of formal harmony had highly satisfying results in music (as in the work of Bach and Mozart) and in architecture.

The Enlightenment in America.   The Enlightenment had a deep and lasting influence on American ideals and institutions. The main reason for this was that colonial society, with its growing emphasis on individual freedom and equality, and its spirit of optimism and enterprise, was already developing in the same direction. European thinkers like Voltaire were, in fact, inclined to idealize America as a country where men could live freely, naturally, and virtuously. And the Americans welcomed the doctrines of man's natural goodness and the progress and perfectibility of the human race because they seemed to give intellectual justification to the attitudes which they had already acquired in settling the New World.

This harmony between American life and eighteenth-century thought was well exemplified in the career of Benjamin Franklin. For Franklin was both the representative figure of colonial civilization and a very typical product of the Enlightenment. Born in Boston in 1706, he found its Puritan atmosphere somewhat oppressive, and moved to Philadelphia at the age of seventeen. By occupation he was a printer, and after he had become rich and famous, he never forgot that he had begun life as a craftsman working with his hands. By 1730 he had become owner of his own business, and proprietor and editor of a newspaper; and after his skillful journalism had made him a well-known figure, he engaged in an extraordinary variety of other activities. He was continuously engaged in Pennsylvania politics; he wrote voluminously about politics, economics, and innumerable other subjects; he became famous in Europe as a result of his scientific researches into the nature of electricity; he helped to found several institutions of learning and civic improvement; he was in charge for several years of the colonial post office; he accumulated a considerable fortune through investment in various enterprises; and he invented (among other things) the lightning rod, the Franklin stove, a new musical instrument, and bifocal glasses.

In all his activities Franklin displayed a confidence in human reason and in the infinite possibilities of human progress that was typical of the Enlightenment. Personally, he was always good-humored, tolerant, sagacious, witty, and remarkably free from any kind of internal conflict. He was typical of the Enlightenment also in his deficiencies: his optimism was sometimes a little shallow; his trust in the reasonableness of human nature was a little cold-blooded; and he had little sympathy for the poetic and mystical side of human life.

2. THE DIFFUSION OF CULTURE

THROUGHOUT the colonial period the American mind was primarily concerned with activities that seemed to have immediate practical value. There was widespread interest in religious and political theory (both of which were regarded as necessary for successful action), in applied science, and in such useful arts as architecture. But as long as people were engaged mainly in the task of settling a new continent, little energy could be spared for abstract philosophical speculation, pure science, or the more imaginative forms of literature and art. Nor was there any way by which creative writers and artists could have acquired economic support. There were no well-established aristocratic groups interested in giving patronage, no ecclesiastical or academic foundations with money to spend on such purposes, and no large popular market.

But although colonial America did not produce any creations of the first rank, it was culturally more democratic than Europe. Literacy was more widely diffused, and intellectual leaders maintained a more vital interest in the needs and sentiments of the mass of the people. Many individuals, moreover, developed a quite extraordinary versatility. While they did not equal the greater Europeans in any one line of endeavor, they had broader interests and a more many-sided humanity.

Education. Although education did not become universal until the twentieth century, there was already a growing conviction of its importance, for both religious and practical reasons. In New England each town was required to establish a school, although the rule was not always obeyed. In the other colonies there were a number of free schools, mostly maintained by religious groups, and some academies for paying pupils. Wealthy parents, particularly in the South, usually employed private tutors, and often sent their sons to English schools and colleges to complete their educations.

Higher learning was represented in the seventeenth century by Harvard (founded in 1636) and William and Mary (founded in 1693). By the end of the century the Harvard faculty was developing rationalistic tendencies, so in 1702 a group of conservative Puritans established Yale, hoping that it would remain a stronghold of orthodoxy. Between 1740 and 1770 no less than six new colleges were founded: Pennsylvania, Princeton, Columbia, Brown, Rutgers, and Dartmouth (some of them originally under different names). All of them except Pennsylvania were originally affiliated with different religious denominations. The classics and theology continued to be the chief subjects of study, but college curricula were steadily broadened by the addition of courses in different sciences and other modern branches of learning.

Books and Newspapers.　　The first printing press was set up at Cambridge, Massachusetts, in 1639. There were presses at Philadelphia and New York before the end of the century, and in eleven of the colonies before 1765. The output of the colonial presses was quite large, especially in Massachusetts, but consisted mostly of sermons and political pamphlets. More important in the diffusion of culture was the importation of books from England. Most significant English books, both in imaginative literature and in science and philosophy, eventually reached the colonies, although there was sometimes a time lag of twenty years or more. A few Americans gathered large private libraries: early in the eighteenth century Cotton Mather in Boston and William Byrd in Virginia each owned more than 4,000 volumes. Some of the college libraries were well stocked, and by the middle of the eighteenth century there were circulating libraries in a number of towns.

The first successful newspaper was the Boston *News Letter*, founded in 1704. By 1765 there were twenty-five newspapers, each of them appearing once a week, in eleven different colonies. Initially, almost all of their material was reprinted from English sources, but there was a steady increase in the coverage of American news and the space given to American contributors. As a result of the Zenger case in New York in 1733, in which a jury decided (contrary to British legal practice) that criticisms of public officials were not libelous if they could be shown to be true, the American press acquired considerable freedom.

The first attempt to produce a literary magazine was made in 1741, but the most ambitious and mature colonial periodical was the *American Magazine* of 1757–58, edited by William Smith, provost of the College of Philadelphia (afterwards the University of Pennsylvania). On a more popular level, the various almanacs had a wide circulation and provided the reading public with vast quantities of useful information and moral advice. The best-known was *Poor Richard's Almanac*, edited by Benjamin Franklin.

3. THE DEVELOPMENT OF RELIGION

IN QUANTITY, although not perhaps in quality, writings about religion continued to outweigh those on all other subjects. This was partly because of the general belief in the paramount importance of religion, and partly because the clergy were the only large professional class with lesiure for literary composition.

The Growth of Rationalism.　　As the ideas of the Enlightenment spread to the colonies, there was a considerable growth of religious skepticism among the wealthier and more sophisticated groups. A large number of the leading figures of the Revolutionary period were inclined towards deism. Although they discussed their beliefs in private, they did not, in general, care to arouse popular opposition by any public avowal.

The first open criticism of Christianity was *Reason the Only Oracle of Man*, written by the Vermont Revolutionary leader Ethan Allen and published in 1784.

More widely influential were certain clergymen who began to introduce liberal and rationalistic attitudes into theology itself. This occurred particularly in eastern Massachusetts. The first definite departure from Puritan orthodoxy (as represented by such clergymen as Increase and Cotton Mather) was the foundation of the more liberal Brattle Street Church in 1699 by a group of Boston merchants. By the middle of the eighteenth century a number of the clergy around Boston had abandoned the Calvinist doctrine of predestination and were affirming that salvation depended on man's free choice—a belief known as Arminianism. They interpreted religion as primarily an ethical code designed to promote human happiness, and declared that this was the best of all possible worlds and that God wished all men to be saved. The most influential of these theological optimists were Charles Chauncy (whose *Benevolence of the Deity* was written about 1750, although not published until 1784) and Jonathan Mayhew. This trend eventually developed into Unitarianism, although there was no open profession of such an attitude until after the Revolution.

In New York and in the South the more educated classes were mostly Episcopalian. This form of religion was generally so tepid that it scarcely conflicted with the growth of rationalism. It was beginning to acquire a new vitality, however, as a result of the adherence of several former New England ministers who had repudiated Calvinism. The most influential of them was Samuel Johnson, who left the Congregational Church in 1722 and subsequently became the first president of King's College (afterwards Columbia) in New York.

The Quakerism of the Philadelphia area was already characterized by an optimism, simplicity, and emphasis on practical benevolence that could easily be harmonized with the Enlightenment. To a lesser extent this was also true of some of the German mystical sects in eastern Pennsylvania. One of the best expressions of both Quakerism and eighteenth-century humanitarianism was the *Journal* of the New Jersey tailor John Woolman, who was led by his belief in the inner light to become an active opponent of slavery and other social and economic injustices.

New Trends in Calvinism.   Meanwhile, the majority of the population throughout New England and the back country of Pennsylvania and the South continued to accept some form of Calvinism. Calvinist beliefs, with a more emotional and democratic emphasis than in the past, were revitalized by the Great Awakening. The hysteria of the Awakening and its insistence on the sinfulness of human nature horrified the exponents of rationalistic religion. For this reason the movement was vigorously denounced by Chauncy and Mayhew, as well as by upper-class conservatives who were afraid of anarchy. Yet its effects were liberal in many ways. Regarding religious conversion as a private transaction between God and the individual, the revivalist preachers weakened traditional forms of authority and stimulated demands for religious freedom and political and social democracy.

The greatest figure associated with the Awakening was Jonathan Edwards. Although Edwards spent his life defending Calvinism, he was also deeply influenced by the Enlightenment. Educated at Yale, he spent twenty-one years as minister at Northampton, Massachusetts; in 1750 a dispute with his congregation brought about his dismissal, and he then became a missionary to the Indians at Stockbridge and (for a short period) President of Princeton. In his private life he was always cheerful, patient, hard-working, wholly devoted to his wife and children, and not unduly severe. The main purpose of his voluminous writings was to reinterpret Calvinist doctrine in order to confute the optimism of the Boston Arminians, while at the same time avoiding the anarchical disorderliness of some of the New Light groups. But he had also studied the works of Newton, Locke, and other forerunners of the Enlightenment, and his theology differed more than he realized from that of the original Puritans.

Edwards was the most profound thinker produced by colonial America, and his *Freedom of the Will* (in which he argued that since the will was always determined by the strongest motive, freedom of choice was a meaningless conception) was a masterpiece of logical virtuosity. More widely influential was his *Treatise Concerning Religious Affections*, in which he insisted that religion was essentially an emotional experience, not a matter for sober and rational decision. God communicated the knowledge of his beauty to those whom he had elected for salvation, and they were then irresistibly drawn to love and obey him. Goodness meant a complete surrender to the will of God. In other writings Edwards portrayed the natural universe and the course of human history as expressions of God's attributes, insisting that the world and man himself were deeply tainted with evil but that ugliness and sin were necessary in order that God's beauty and justice might be made manifest.

In attempting to explain and justify the entire cosmos in terms comprehensible to the human mind (instead of assuming, as the original Calvinists did, that God's purposes were mysterious), Edwards showed himself to be a product of the Enlightenment. And in defining religious belief as due to "a spiritual and divine light immediately imparted to the soul," he contributed to the growth of liberal individualism. The mystical meditations on the beauty of God and God's universe that fill his writings have an extraordinary charm and intensity of feeling. And although his portrayal of God as deliberately condemning a majority of his creatures to eternal torment in Hell in order to manifest his own righteousness is a horrifying conception, his view of life seems today more realistic than that of his opponents. We may be repelled by Edwards's explanation of suffer-

NIEUW AMSTERDAM ofte NUE NIEUW IORX ofT TEYLANT MAN

NEW AMSTERDAM ABOUT 1650

Early colonists built in styles to which they had been accustomed in Europe. This painting,
by an unknown Dutch artist, shows New Amsterdam similar to a city in Holland.

WESTOVER

A great plantation mansion in Virginia, built in 1730 in colonial Georgian style.

ROTUNDA OF THE UNIVERSITY OF VIRGINIA

Designed by Jefferson and built in the 1820's in the Greek Revival style, which was popular in the early nineteenth century.

ing and evil, but unlike the Boston Arminians he did not try to evade the
tragic element in human experience.

Edwards's theological writings had little influence in his lifetime. He
left, however, a small group of devoted disciples, the most important of
whom were Joseph Bellamy and Samuel Hopkins. These men continued
the task of reinterpreting and rationalizing Calvinism, and Edwards's
"new divinity" gradually permeated the Congregationalist and—to a
lesser extent—the Presbyterian Church. By the end of the eighteenth
century almost all the New England clergy (except in the Boston area)
and a number in the Middle states were preaching Edwardean doctrines.
Their efforts resulted in a new series of religious revivals, running from the
1790's down to the Civil War, which greatly strengthened the influence of
the Protestant churches and had important effects on American social and
political development.[1] Edwards is thus a significant figure not only because of the intrinsic interest of his writings but also because of his place
in American cultural history.

4. SOCIAL THEORY

THE output of books and pamphlets on political and economic questions
was second only to that of sermons and theological treatises. Dealing
generally with specific controversies, most of it had little permanent
value. But it was important in so far as it helped to shape the American
mind and prepare the way for the Revolution.

The Doctrine of Natural Rights.   A few persons, most of them government officials or Episcopalian clergymen, maintained that the people
owed an unlimited obedience to constituted authority, as represented by
the British Crown; government was created by God, and its jurisdiction
was prior to the rights of individuals. But this Tory, or conservative,
theory of politics, still widely prevalent in Europe, never appealed to
many Americans, either before the Revolution or afterwards. Most
Americans always preferred to believe that individuals had certain in-
alienable rights and that government was a man-made institution designed to promote individual welfare. Derived originally from the liberal
tendencies in the English tradition, and also from the Puritan theory of a
covenant, this attitude was repeatedly reinforced during the process of
colonization. In episodes like the signing of the *Mayflower* Compact and
the settling of frontier areas, Americans could see for themselves how men
agreed to set up governments for the sake of their own protection.

It is not surprising, therefore, that the political theory of John Locke
was quickly accepted in the colonies. One of its first and most forceful
exponents was John Wise, minister of the Congregationalist Church at
Ipswich, Massachusetts, who restated it early in the eighteenth century

[1] See pages 257-9.

in two books written in opposition to a proposal of the Mathers for setting up a more authoritarian system of church government. Another vigorous liberal spokesman was Jonathan Mayhew, of Boston, who in 1750 preached a famous sermon declaring rebellion against an unjust government to be not only a right but a duty.

Before the Revolution, in fact, American political thinking on all levels, from the most popular to the most intellectual, was permeated with the doctrine of natural rights. It was generally believed that these rights were incorporated into the British constitution and guaranteed to the Americans by their colonial charters, and that the powers of the British government were limited by fundamental law. In this respect American political theory deviated in a very significant fashion from that of the English, who believed that there were no limits whatever to the authority of Parliament. This divergence became apparent during the Revolution.

Although almost all Americans believed in the theory of rights, there was much room for argument about its application. Consistently interpreted, the theory seemed to imply not only that the people should control their government but also that all men were entitled to take part in politics. Nevertheless, both Locke himself and his eighteenth-century disciples were inclined to argue that rights were more secure under a government controlled by the wealthy classes than under a system of outright majority rule. Only substantial property-owners, it was felt, had enough of a stake in the community and could be trusted to display enough wisdom and self-restraint. Except in the writings of Roger Williams (who had little influence outside Rhode Island) and John Wise, there was little open advocacy of democratic theory in colonial America, in spite of the strong forces making for democracy in practice.

Economic Attitudes.   In their economic thinking the Americans were slowly abandoning the medieval doctrine of social regulation of business activity, and were coming to believe instead that each person should be free to do as he pleased with his property. In the early colonial period medieval attitudes were still prevalent. New England ministers, for example, declared that governments should fix prices and wages and punish businessmen who sought profits by unjust methods. In the eighteenth century this kind of regulation was by no means wholly abandoned; but the general climate of economic opinion was changing. There was more emphasis on government aid for business enterprise and less on regulation to protect the general welfare.

Trade regulation by the British government was accepted in principle by most Americans until the Revolution, though criticized in detail. A few writers, however, boldly advocated complete commercial freedom. The most notable of these was Franklin, who had reached this conclusion by 1751. Some of Franklin's essays were probably the ablest and most original contributions to economic theory made during the colonial period.

He was a vigorous participant in the paper-money controversy, arguing that economic progress would be impeded unless money was sufficiently plentiful, and opposing the doctrine that gold and silver were the only safe circulating media. He also acquired from the French Physiocrats the notion that land was the only source of wealth and that farmers were therefore the only people who were genuinely productive, merchants being essentially parasitical. Such a theory had a wide appeal in America because it served to justify the rural population in its opposition to the moneyed interests, both British and native.

5. SCIENCE AND PHILOSOPHY

THE history of science in America began with the first settlements. In the earliest colonies there were individuals who studied the natural phenomena of the New World in a scientific spirit and reported their findings to English savants. During the seventeenth century, however, little or no original work was done in America, and scientific investigations were curiously mingled with superstitions and magical conceptions surviving from earlier periods.

The Natural Sciences. The ablest scientist of the first generation was John Winthrop, Jr., Governor of Connecticut, who was probably the first American member of the British Royal Society. Later in the seventeenth century Puritan ministers like the Mathers made scientific observations and kept abreast of English developments in astronomy and physics. But although they showed no reluctance to accept the latest hypotheses, their main purpose was to study the workings of divine providence. While adopting the scientific explanations of comets and earthquakes, for example, they continued to insist that these things were at the same time warnings to sinners and were always followed by catastrophes. They also kept records of occasions when God had intervened directly in earthly affairs in order to protect the righteous and to punish sinners. God, they believed, used natural law for moral purposes.

In the eighteenth century interest in science increased, and a more genuinely scientific spirit was displayed. Beginning with Harvard in 1728, universities began to establish professorships in different branches of natural science, and learned societies were founded. In 1744 Franklin started the organization that eventually developed into the American Philosophical Society. Philadelphia became the leading scientific center, partly because of its tolerant atmosphere and partly because of Franklin's leadership, with Boston and Cambridge a close second. The plantation society of the South remained closer perhaps to the Renaissance than to the Enlightenment, continuing to emphasize the study of the classics and the humanistic ideal of the gentleman, and making relatively few contributions to science.

The leading colonial scientist was John Winthrop IV, Hollis Professor at Harvard, who did original work in astronomy and seismology. Another important astronomer was the self-taught David Rittenhouse, who became a professor at the College of Philadelphia. In New York, many new observations and hypotheses, including a bold attempt to improve upon the Newtonian theory, were made by the versatile Cadwallader Colden, a physician who was also a mathematician, physicist, botanist, anthropologist, philosopher, and Lieutenant-Governor of the colony. In contributions to knowledge, however, none of these men were equal to Benjamin Franklin, whose researches into the nature of electricity, presented in a paper written in 1751, had a great effect upon both theoretical development and practical application.

The development of physics had a significant incidental effect in weakening the more superstitious forms of religious belief. Franklin's lightning rod, for example, was important not only in protecting buildings from destruction; it ended the fear of lightning as an instrument of divine anger. The spread of rationalistic attitudes can conveniently be measured by means of two earthquakes in eastern Massachusetts. An earthquake in 1728 caused most of the population to fly to the churches and engage frantically in prayer, and was followed by a large number of conversions. In 1755, on the other hand, a more severe earthquake resulted in no increase in church membership, Professor Winthrop's scientific explanation of it being generally accepted.

Another branch of science to which Americans made important contributions was botany. The Quaker John Bartram of Pennsylvania made a vast collection of American plants; his work was continued by his son, William Bartram, whose *Travels* (appearing in 1791) were widely read. Another colonial botanist was Dr. Alexander Garden of Charleston, after whom the gardenia was named. There were also some badly needed attempts to apply science to the improvement of agriculture, most notably by James Logan in Pennsylvania and Jared Eliot in Connecticut.

Medicine.   Meanwhile, medicine was making progress, although it was still impeded by the lack of any valid theory regarding the cause of infection. Most doctors still relied mainly upon bleeding and purging and upon dosing their patients with fantastic medicines, the more repellent the better, and probably did more harm than good. But there were a number of American physicians, like William Douglass in Boston and John Morgan in Philadelphia, who made careful observations of different diseases in a scientific spirit.

The first American hospital was built in Philadelphia in 1752, and the first medical schools were founded in Philadelphia in 1765 and in New York in 1767. The training of students, however, was impeded by a strong popular prejudice against autopsies. Probably the greatest medical advance was the introduction of inoculation against smallpox. This occurred first in Boston in 1721. Oddly enough, its most prominent supporter was the chief spokesman of orthodox religion, Cotton Mather, for which reason it was vehemently opposed as unscientific by William Douglass and other exponents of the scientific attitude.

Philosophy. Most American thinkers were more interested in the practical applications of new ideas than in their theoretical elaboration. Apart from the work of Edwards and his disciples, there was little American philosophy. Some individuals, however, were concerned with the controversy between materialism and idealism, which was perhaps the main metaphysical problem of this period in Europe. Ever since the seventeenth-century French thinker Descartes had made a sharp separation between mind and matter, philosophers had been trying to bridge the gap between them, arguing either that the mind was wholly material or that matter was a mental illusion. In America, Cadwallader Colden presented a somewhat materialistic interpretation of human nature, while Samuel Johnson, of King's College, wrote in defense of idealism.

In 1768, John Witherspoon, an immigrant from Scotland, became President of Princeton and introduced what was known as the Scottish or common-sense school of philosophy. This school held that mind and matter both existed independently of each other, and that the beliefs of the plain citizen, including particularly his religious beliefs, were philosophically valid. Brushing aside abstruse metaphysical problems and subtleties, this common-sense approach was welcomed by American students, and continued to be the dominant trend in American academic philosophy for about a hundred years.

6. LITERATURE AND THE ARTS

Imaginative Literature. In imaginative literature the record of colonial America was almost wholly blank. There was a considerable market for English novels, but Americans were too concerned with more necessary occupations to produce any fiction of their own. The first American novel (William Hill Brown's *Power of Sympathy*) was not published until 1789. Vast quantities of verse were written, but very little of it had any literary value. Two New Englanders, Anne Bradstreet in the first half of the seventeenth century, and the Reverend Edward Taylor in the second half, wrote religious poetry in the Elizabethan manner with a real poetic intensity, but neither of them was born in America. In the 1750's a group of young men around William Smith, of the College of Philadelphia, began to show an enthusiasm for poetry, but were unable to break through the strait jacket of classicist formalism. Perhaps the first genuine American poet was Philip Freneau, who began writing while a student at Princeton early in the 1770's.

In spite of religious hostility, a considerable interest in the theater developed. Early in the eighteenth century English professional companies began to tour the Middle and Southern colonies, performing the plays of Shakspere and those of contemporary English dramatists. The first play by an American author was Thomas Godfrey's *Prince of Parthia*, produced in 1767. But the American drama did not achieve serious literary status until the twentieth century.

   History and Autobiography.   Many colonial Americans, nevertheless, wrote extensively, although their purpose was to present information or to inculcate beliefs rather than to appeal to the imagination. The period of the early colonization produced a number of narratives describing the experiences of the early settlers and conveying their wonder at the phenomena of the New World. The style often had both the exuberance and the long-winded complexity that characterized Elizabethan prose. Outstanding works were William Bradford's *History of Plymouth Plantation* and the *Journal* of John Winthrop.

   Later writers continued to be concerned with the history of the colonies. Cotton Mather celebrated the virtues and achievements of the Puritans in his long *Magnalia Christi Americana*. Many New Englanders kept diaries in order to record their spiritual experiences and the workings of divine providence, among them being Cotton Mather and his contemporary, Judge Samuel Sewall. The eighteenth century saw a number of histories in which some attempt was made at scientific objectivity; there were works on Massachusetts by Thomas Prince and Governor Thomas Hutchinson, on New York by William Smith, on the Iroquois Indians by Cadwallader Colden, on Pennsylvania by Richard Jackson, and on Virginia by Robert Beverley and William Stith. William Douglass produced a history and description of all the thirteen colonies, in which he gave vigorous expression to his deistical antipathy to religion. Less serious, but more entertaining and more skillfully written, were the descriptive and autobiographical writings of the rich Virginia planter William Byrd.

   In the eighteenth century, for the first time, English prose style achieved clarity and simplicity as well as force and elegance; and American writers began to imitate the latest English models, particularly the essays of Addison, with admirable results. The general level of American political writing during the Revolutionary period was extremely high. At the same time the American language was beginning to deviate in certain ways from standard English and to acquire a more exuberant and picturesque vocabulary. New words (from Indian, Dutch, German, French, and provincial English sources) and new constructions were becoming current, and English purists were already complaining of Americanisms. The best qualities of eighteenth-century American writing— its clarity and its colloquial vigor—were well represented in the essays, proverbs, and miscellaneous writings of Benjamin Franklin and in his classic *Autobiography*.

   Visual Arts.   In general, colonial Americans had little interest in artistic activities that did not serve some useful purpose. But while this attitude ruled out certain forms of artistic creativity, it also had positive advantages. It encouraged honest craftsmanship and tended to eliminate meretricious ornamentation and display. The best colonial art displayed technical skill, strength and simplicity of design, and natural good taste.

Not only the social conditions under which Americans lived but their religious beliefs were responsible for the American attitude towards art. In earlier societies the primary function of art had been to assist in religious worship: architecture, painting, sculpture, music, and some forms of literature had been used to promote reverence and to provide human beings with sensuous representations of supernatural powers. Most forms of Protestantism, however, insisted that this was unnecessary: the soul could communicate with God directly, and sensuous intermediaries were positively harmful. The Puritans regarded religious pictures and statues as idolatrous and preferred to worship in plain meeting-houses, in which they sang the psalms without instrumental accompaniment. The higher forms of art thus lost what had formerly been their main social justification. The Puritans were not hostile to the fine arts; but having divorced them from religion, they considered them only agreeable recreations. On the other hand, the seriousness and the honesty of the Puritan mind contributed largely to the high quality of the useful arts in America.

Painting. The main function of the colonial painter was to make portraits of prominent citizens, and his customers expected the portraits to be as accurate as possible. There was no market for landscapes or for more imaginative pictures.

A number of portraits have survived from seventeenth-century New England and New York, none of which display much technical skill or aesthetic sensitivity. Most of them were the work of "limners" whose main occupation was the painting of signs to hang outside shops or taverns. Somewhat greater competence was shown by a few New Yorkers of Dutch origin, who had been influenced by the artistic tradition of Holland.

In the early eighteenth century, English portrait painters began to discover that there was a market for their services in the colonies; and while they generally displayed a tendency to sentimentalize and prettify their sitters, they also introduced a knowledge of professional techniques into America. John Smibert settled in New England in 1729, and his portraits of Boston merchants and clergymen served as models for native craftsmen. Some of his disciples were able to combine his technical accomplishment with an uncompromising realism and a respect for individuality that were products of their American background.

Among a number of New England painters, two did work of outstanding value: Robert Feke of Newport, who was active during the 1730's and 1740's; and John Singleton Copley. Copley painted his first picture in 1753, when he was fifteen, and he was busy for the next twenty years portraying Boston merchants and their families. In 1774 he left for England in search of wider opportunities. He won fame and money in

London, but the quality of his work deteriorated; he is remembered today for the strength and honesty of his early portraits.

Outside New England, Philadelphia was the only area where native work was encouraged. The first talented figure in this region was Benjamin West. But West went to Europe in 1760, and, like Copley later, gained material success while losing his artistic integrity. In the opinion of modern critics the best of the Philadelphia artists was Charles Willson Peale, who was active through the Revolutionary period and is chiefly remembered for his portraits of George Washington. Peale's work combined a realism like that of the New Englanders with a warmth and gaiety which may have been derived from his Maryland upbringing.

Architecture.   Colonial architecture had a similar development. During the seventeenth century most buildings were small, crudely constructed, and lacking in decoration. The initial tendency of each group of settlers was to reproduce the kind of architecture they had been accustomed to at home, although with much less elaboration. Thus early Boston recalled Elizabethan England, early New York looked like a city in Holland, and sections of Pennsylvania resembled the Rhineland. The first houses often had features which had been appropriate to life in a crowded medieval city but were no longer functional in America.

Colonial carpenters gradually learned to adapt their techniques to the new environment, and American dwelling houses, while remaining simple, began to acquire more pleasing lines and proportions. Eventually the growth of wealth made more ambitious projects possible. In the eighteenth century Southern planters and Northern merchants were able to spend money on palatial private houses, and there was a demand for more elaborate churches and government buildings. People turned for guidance to books of architectural designs which had been published in England. These designs were copied, with modifications, by American builders (there were no professional architects in the colonies).

The result of this fusion of English forms with American craftsmanship was the colonial Georgian style, which prevailed, with some regional variations, throughout the thirteen colonies. The great age of colonial building was from about 1740 until the Revolution. Georgian was a development of the Renaissance style which had been introduced into England in the seventeenth century by Inigo Jones and Sir Christopher Wren. This style made a sharp break with the medieval Gothic tradition, emphasizing horizontal rather than vertical lines (although many churches still had towers and spires); buildings were generally rectangular, had little detailed ornamentation, and were designed with formal regularity and symmetry. Colonial Georgian is best exemplified in the red brick houses built by rich Virginia planters, in government buildings like Independence Hall in Philadelphia and the Governor's Palace at Williamsburg, and in the white wooden churches erected throughout southern New England. Simple, harmonious, and dignified, such buildings reflected the good taste and the optimistic self-assurance of the eighteenth-century mind. It would be easy to argue that later American architects have never surpassed these achievements of the colonial craftsmen.

On a smaller scale, similar qualities were displayed in the construction of furniture and utensils. Copying and modifying the work of Englishmen like Chippendale and Sheraton, carpenters in Pennsylvania and New England made superbly designed chairs and cabinets. German artisans produced decorated pottery and glassware. In Boston, silversmiths like Jeremiah Dummer and the famous Paul Revere excelled in the making of tankards and other household articles. There was also a flourishing market for carvers in stone, metal, and wood, who could decorate fireplaces, tombstones, weather vanes, and the prows of merchant ships.

Music.   In music the record was much less impressive. Colonial Americans liked to sing, and many of them learned to play an instrument; but there was virtually no original work.

The early settlers brought English folk songs and dances, and these continued to provide popular entertainment in all parts of the colonies, including Puritan New England. The favorite instruments were fiddles and fifes. American dancing seems to have become more boisterous than that of England, while American singers were more inclined towards a melancholy tone. But throughout the colonial period there was no addition to the repertory. The first American folk song, *Springfield Mountain*, was certainly not earlier than the Revolution, and may belong to the early nineteenth century.

Another form of popular music, the singing of hymns, did not begin until the eighteenth century. New Light groups after the Great Awakening liked to express their religious fervor by singing hymns composed by Englishmen like Isaac Watts and Charles Wesley; and some of them, particularly among the Baptist congregations along the frontier, gradually evolved compositions of their own. In the nineteenth century these spread to the slave population in the South and resulted in the Negro spiritual. Meanwhile, the more orthodox New England congregations gradually became willing to accept instrumental music and hymns in the church service. During the later years of the eighteenth century William Billings of Boston composed about three hundred hymn tunes and did much to improve the standards of congregational singing.

Music of a higher quality won appreciative audiences among the upper classes, especially in South Carolina (the Cecilia Society was founded in 1762 in Charleston) and other Southern colonies. Concerts and performances of ballad operas were frequent and well attended. But much the finest colonial music came from the Pennsylvania Germans, particularly from the Moravians who settled at Bethlehem (bringing with them Bach's works) and from the Dunker community at Ephrata.

The first native composer was the Philadelphian Francis Hopkinson, one of Provost William Smith's young men, who in 1759 wrote music for the song *My Days Have Been So Wondrous Free*, and afterwards composed an opera. With typical eighteenth-century versatility, Hopkinson also wrote poems, painted pictures, served in the Continental Congress, designed the American flag, and eventually became a judge. But no American composer of serious music achieved high rank until the twentieth century.

V

The Revolution

1. THE CAUSES OF THE REVOLUTION

2. THE COURSE OF THE CONTROVERSY

3. THE OUTBREAK OF THE WAR

4. THE WAR OF INDEPENDENCE

T HE American Revolution was brought about by the development of
new attitudes in the colonies and in Great Britain. On one side the
Americans were becoming increasingly unwilling to accept a subordinate
position within the British Empire. On the other side British governments,
after 1763, adopted new policies designed to control the colonies more
stringently than before. The result was a conflict which in the end could
be settled only by force.

1. THE CAUSES OF THE REVOLUTION

American Attitudes. The remarkable material and cultural progress of the colonies during the middle decades of the eighteenth century
was accompanied by the growth of a new kind of self-assurance. Surveying
their past achievements and future prospects, many Americans felt that

SELECTED BIBLIOGRAPHY. The most recent general history of the Revolution is
the two-volume work of J. C. Miller, *Origins of the American Revolution* (1943) and *The
Triumph of Freedom, 1775–1783* (1948). An older general history is C. H. Van Tyne, *The
Causes of the War of Independence* (1922) and *The War of Independence* (1929). Among the
numerous works dealing with the controversies leading to the Revolution, two are especially important: C. W. Alvord, *The Mississippi Valley in British Politics* (2 vols., 1917),
and A. M. Schlesinger, *The Colonial Merchants and the American Revolution, 1763–1776*
(1917). C. L. Becker, *The Declaration of Independence* (1922), is a classic. Internal development during the period of the Revolution is discussed in J. F. Jameson, *The American Revolution Considered as a Social Movement* (1926), and in E. B. Greene, *The Revolutionary
Generation, 1763–1790* (1943), "A History of American Life," Vol. IV. The best full-length
biography of Washington is the seven-volume work of D. S. Freeman (1948–57), and perhaps
the most useful of the numerous shorter biographies is by N. W. Stephenson and W. H.
Dunn (1940).

they were fully capable of controlling their own destiny and that they were developing a way of life of their own which made them more than merely transplanted Europeans. This new spirit was very evident in the newspapers and other political writings of the 1740's and 1750's.

This attitude was not at first accompanied by any desire to repudiate the British political connection or the British heritage. For reasons of both sentiment and material interest almost all Americans wished to remain within the British Empire. But some of them were beginning to feel that they were entitled to full self-government and to equality with the people of Britain, and that the affairs of the Empire should no longer be administered so exclusively for British advantage. Forward-looking men like Franklin dreamed of a perpetual partnership of the English-speaking peoples in which leadership might eventually pass to the western side of the Atlantic.

Certain kinds of people, particularly those who were more enterprising and ambitious, were especially affected by this new spirit. The more vigorous of the Southern planters, for example, were eager to escape from their burden of debt to British merchants, and hopeful of finding new opportunities in the settlement of the rich lands across the Appalachians. The more energetic Northern merchants felt that their expanding business activities were restricted by the British system of trade regulation and the British limitations on colonial manufacturing. Conflict on these issues had been prevented before the 1760's only because many of the trade laws were inadequately enforced and the merchants were able to violate them with impunity.

Meanwhile, many of the urban mechanics and some of the farmers were demanding wider economic opportunities and more political rights. They wished to end the special privileges of the colonial ruling classes and bring about more political and economic democracy. They found, however, that these ruling classes were supported by the British officials in America and the British Parliament in London, so that the struggle for colonial democracy had also to become a struggle for colonial self-government.

These were the groups who took the lead after 1763 in asserting American rights and finally in establishing independence. The American Revolution was therefore a complex struggle with two objectives: it was partly a revolt of planters and merchants against the restrictions imposed upon American economic growth by British mercantilism, and partly a revolt of farmers and mechanics against aristocratic privilege. To a considerable extent, of course, these two movements pointed in different directions, and throughout the Revolutionary period there were conflicts between upper-class and democratic elements within the colonies.

By no means all the people of the colonies shared these sentiments. Probably a majority of the farmers took no interest in politics. Among the richer classes there were many who were content with things as they were and were more afraid of democracy in America than of British control. When war came, a large part of the American people remained apathetic, and many others actively supported the British government. The American Revolution was the work of a minority of the total population; but this minority included the men of superior ability, courage, liberality, and dynamic enthusiasm.

The British Attitude. While this new spirit was developing in America, the British still adhered to the prevalent mercantilist theory, according to which colonies existed primarily for the benefit of the home country and must therefore be kept in subordination. Nor did they recognize any limitations whatever upon the power of Parliament. They did not share the American belief that Parliament's authority was restricted by some kind of fundamental law. Upon these basic principles there was no difference of opinion among British political leaders. But whereas some of them (such as <u>Edmund Burke</u> and the <u>Earl of Chatham</u>) felt that it would be unwise to make any change in the relationship as it had existed before 1763, others believed that the colonies ought to be more strictly supervised.

As a result of the war with France, Great Britain now had a much larger American empire to govern; she also had a heavy war debt. It therefore seemed desirable to many British officials to reorganize imperial administration and to require the colonies to pay part of the cost of imperial defense. And since experience during the war had shown that the colonies were very reluctant to cooperate with each other for mutual protection, and to pay any additional taxes, it seemed necessary for the British government to resort to compulsion. Meanwhile, it was notorious that the trade regulations were habitually violated, and British merchants were complaining of colonial competition and of colonial trading with the enemy during the war. This situation called for action to prevent smuggling.

From their own point of view British governments after 1763 were not acting illegally, nor were they trying to reduce the Americans to slavery. But they were seeking to hold the colonies in their traditional position of subordination just at the time when the most vigorous elements in the colonial population were beginning to feel themselves entitled to equality.

2. THE COURSE OF THE CONTROVERSY

British Politics. In view of the fundamental differences between the British and American conceptions of the nature of the Empire and the powers of Parliament, it seems unlikely that conflict could have been avoided permanently. The lack of statesmanship in London during the 1760's and 1770's was, however, an important contributory factor in precipitating the Revolution.

For a long time prior to 1760 Great Britain had been governed by cabinets representing the majority party in the House of Commons rather than by the king. But the year 1760 marked the accession of King George III, a young man who was by no means willing to remain a mere figurehead. He had few of the qualities needed for governing an empire, but he was pertinacious and hard-working; and the unusual virtue of his private life made him popular with the middle classes. He set out to win control over Parliament by undermining the dominant Whig Party and by building up a body of personal adherents. The first decade of his reign was a period of political instability; largely as a result of the King's intrigues there were frequent changes of government, and nobody stayed in power long enough to work out and administer an effective colonial policy. By 1770 George had succeeded in his objective, and for the next twelve years he was the effective head of the British government; the Prime Minister, Lord North, usually followed his advice, while "the King's friends" controlled the House of Commons. Liberal Englishmen have always blamed George III for the American Revolution. This is not wholly fair, however, since the King was not responsible for the initial attempts to tax the Americans, and the fundamental issues at stake went deeper than any question of personality.

New Colonial Policies.   The first move towards tighter British control of the colonies was made before the end of the war with France. Since many colonial merchants habitually evaded the regulations which prohibited trading with the enemy, customs officials were given "writs of assistance," or general search warrants, empowering them to search ships and warehouses for smuggled goods. This aroused vigorous opposition, especially in Boston, where the lawyer James Otis defended the merchants with great force and eloquence. According to Otis, the writs of assistance violated the fundamental rights of British citizens and were therefore illegal. This argument reflected the American conviction that the powers of the British government were limited by fundamental law.

At the end of the war the most immediate problem confronting the British authorities was a decision about the disposition of the trans-Appalachian territories from which the French had now been expelled. On the one hand, the land was claimed by several of the colonies, particularly by Virginia; and a number of colonial land companies, some of which were in conflict with each other, were hoping to secure titles to parts of it and organize settlements. On the other hand, British fur-trading companies, which were planning to take the place of the French at Montreal, wanted agricultural settlers excluded and the territories reserved for their own activities. Meanwhile, there were a number of Indian tribes in the region, some of which had recently participated in the Pontiac rising and needed careful handling. Reconciliation of these conflicting interests was obviously a complicated problem, so in 1763 the British government issued a proclamation prohibiting any settlement beyond the

Appalachian watershed. This was intended merely as a temporary measure while British officials studied the question and worked out a program of expansion.

During the next few years British officials made progress in negotiating treaties with Indian tribes under which lands were to be opened for white settlement, and in 1768 the proclamation line was moved farther to the west. Meanwhile, the agents of colonial land speculators hopefully continued to lobby in London for validation of their titles. But the British government was slow to reach any decision on these questions, partly because of the influence of the fur-traders and of groups at home who argued that colonial western expansion was contrary to British economic and political interests. The delay exasperated influential groups in the colonies, especially in Virginia, and made them feel that the whole western question should be left to the Americans to handle by themselves instead of being controlled by British officials. Their resentment became more acute in 1774 when the Quebec Act declared all the lands north of the Ohio to be part of the province of Quebec, and thus wiped out the claims to the region of several of the colonies. By this time a number of frontiersmen, not waiting for legal titles, had already crossed the mountains and made settlements in the Ohio Valley and the Kentucky-Tennessee region.

The British government of 1763 also decided to maintain an army of 10,000 troops in North America, in order to guard against possible Indian raids and French attempts at reconquest. These were to be posted mainly in Canada, Nova Scotia, and New York. And since (in the British view) they were needed for the defense of the colonies, this led to the momentous decision that the colonies should be required to pay part of the cost. The prime minister responsible was George Grenville, an honest, hard-working, but unimaginative official who had no understanding of the kind of people he was dealing with.

The Grenville Measures.   One of the acts of trade which American merchants most consistently violated was the Molasses Act of 1733. According to this act a duty of sixpence a gallon was to be paid on molasses bought from the French and Spanish West Indies, the purpose being to compel American merchants to buy solely from the British planters. Since the French and Spanish trade was extremely profitable, effective enforcement would mean serious losses to the merchants. Grenville, however, decided that this might be a source of revenue. In 1764 he put through Parliament the Sugar Act, which reduced the duty on foreign molasses from sixpence to threepence but set up machinery by which the duty could actually be collected. Duties were also imposed on some other colonial imports. This was followed in 1765 by the Stamp Act, which declared that stamp duties were to be paid on newspapers and legal and commercial documents. Grenville calculated that these measures would bring in about one-third of the cost of the army stationed in America. Although some indirect taxes had been a part of the system of trade regulation, this was the first time that any British government had laid a direct tax on the colonies.

When the news of the Stamp Act reached the colonies, the indignation seems to have been nearly unanimous. The Americans did not regard a British garrison as either necessary or desirable. Suffering from a chronic shortage of currency and from a post-war economic depression, they felt that the act would drain the colonies of money and make their debts to British merchants even more intolerable. And they had learned from the long experience of colonial legislatures in dealing with royal governors the importance of retaining the power of the purse. Taxation without representation, they believed, was tyranny. While they accepted trade regulation by the British Parliament as legitimate (although often unjust in detail), they insisted that Parliament's imposition of direct taxes was contrary to fundamental law and natural right.

What was surprising to almost everybody was the violence of the opposition. It took the form not only of resolutions by colonial assemblies (beginning with the Virginia House of Burgesses, which was carried away by the eloquence of Patrick Henry), and of a collective protest drafted by a congress of delegates from nine colonies, which met at New York in October 1765, but also of riotous popular demonstrations. Groups, composed mainly of urban mechanics, made life miserable for the agents who had undertaken to sell the stamps, and for customs collectors and British officials generally. In Boston the house of Thomas Hutchinson, a leader of the Massachusetts upper class and Chief Justice of the colony, was partially destroyed by a mob. These popular demonstrations were as alarming to some of the colonial conservatives as to the British government. Calling themselves Sons of Liberty, and led by men like Sam Adams in Boston, Isaac Sears and John Lamb in New York, Charles Thomson in Philadelphia, Samuel Chase in Baltimore, and Christopher Gadsden in Charleston, insurgent farmers and mechanics were to play a prominent role during the events of the next ten years.

The most effective weapon used against the Stamp Act, however, was a general agreement to stop importing British goods. British merchants suffered heavy losses and urged the government to give way. By this time Grenville had been succeeded as prime minister by the Marquis of Rockingham. In March 1766 the Rockingham government repealed the Stamp Act, lowered the molasses duty to one penny (to be paid on all molasses, British as well as foreign), and passed a Declaratory Act affirming the principle of Parliamentary supremacy over the colonies. Delighted with their victory, the Americans enthusiastically asserted their loyalty to the mother country and paid no attention to the Declaratory Act.

The Townshend Duties.   At this point wise British leadership might have capitalized on this sense of gratitude. Unfortunately, Rockingham was quickly replaced by the Earl of Chatham, who fell ill and was unable to keep control over his cabinet. The minister in charge of

MRS. SYLVANUS BOURNE,
by JOHN SINGLETON COPLEY
(1738–1815)

    The vigor and honesty with which Copley conveyed the personalities of his sitters made him the greatest of the colonial portrait painters.

THE PEALE FAMILY, *by* CHARLES WILLSON PEALE (1741–1827)

    Peale was inferior to Copley in craftsmanship, but his work had more warmth and gaiety.

GEORGE WASHINGTON, by CHARLES WILLSON PEALE (1741–1827)
Painted in 1787. Peale's portraits of Washington are less idealized than the better-known paintings of the Father of our Country by Gilbert Stuart.

THOMAS JEFFERSON, by REMBRANDT PEALE (1778–1860)
Painted in 1805 by a son of Charles Willson Peale. The mature Jefferson, about the time of his second inauguration.

finances was the ambitious and unstable Charles Townshend. Parliament reduced taxes in England, so Townshend, with a deficit to make up, turned to the colonies. In 1767 a number of new duties were imposed on colonial imports, and new administrative machinery was set up to make sure that they would be paid. Townshend explained that, in refraining from direct taxation and levying only import duties, he was complying with the viewpoint of the colonists. Townshend was also responsible for the suspension of the legislature of New York because it had refused to provide supplies for the troops stationed in the colony.

The Townshend duties remained in force for three years. The most effective statement of the American case during this period was the series of *Letters from a Farmer*, written by a conservative Pennsylvania lawyer, John Dickinson. Dickinson still accepted the right of Parliament to regulate trade, but denied that it could levy taxes, direct or indirect. New agreements were made to refrain from importing British goods, and in a number of seaports, merchants engaged in illegal trade were protected from customs officials by the Sons of Liberty. Such incidents were especially frequent in Boston, where the richest of the smuggling merchants, John Hancock, was closely associated with the popular organization directed by Sam Adams.

In 1768 two regiments of British regulars were stationed in Boston to prevent smuggling. The Sons of Liberty did everything possible to arouse popular hostility to these unwanted guests, and finally, on March 5, 1770, some of the soldiers, goaded beyond endurance by snowballs and stones thrown by a crowd of jeering men and boys, used their guns. In this so-called Boston Massacre four or five persons were killed. In retrospect, what seems most remarkable about this episode is the moderation displayed by both sides after the event. The Governor withdrew the troops from the city; the soldiers responsible were put on trial; they were tried fairly, and all were acquitted except two, who received mild penalties for manslaughter.

Meanwhile, the British government had again decided to give way. Lord North was now prime minister, and on the day the Boston Massacre occurred he recommended the repeal of the Townshend duties. One small duty on tea, however, was retained in order to assert the principle of Parliamentary authority. Many of the Americans refused to pay the duty, drinking only tea smuggled in from Holland. But the non-importation agreements were abandoned, and a large number of merchants, alarmed by the growth of the Sons of Liberty, tried to prevent any further agitation.

The Final Crisis. It was obvious, however, to such popular leaders as Sam Adams that none of the basic issues had been settled. These leaders used this period of calm to prepare for the next crisis. Adams was a master of the arts of propaganda, and in speeches at the Boston town meeting and in numerous newspaper articles he continued to accuse the

British government and its Massachusetts representatives (especially Hutchinson, who was now Governor of the colony) of all kinds of wicked designs against American liberties. In 1772 Adams and his associates set up throughout Massachusetts a network of "committees of correspondence," composed of men who would carry on agitation and, if necessary, organize resistance. This idea was imitated by Henry and Jefferson in Virginia and by similar leaders in other colonies, so that a real intercolonial political organization began to take shape.

The British government made its next and most crucial mistake in 1773. The East India Company was in financial trouble, and its stockholders, who included some very influential men, demanded assistance. Since the Company had a large supply of surplus tea on its hands, Lord North decided that it should be allowed to ship and sell it directly to agents in the colonies, paying the small American duty but not the larger duty previously collected at British ports. Thus the Americans would get their tea at much lower prices and would, it was hoped, drink the Company out of its difficulties. What made the plan unacceptable to the Americans was that the East India Company would acquire a virtual monopoly of the colonial tea market; neither the smuggling nor the law-abiding merchants would be able to sell their tea cheaply enough to compete with it. The result was that many of the merchants again joined forces with the Sons of Liberty. The plan, moreover, was generally interpreted in the colonies as an attempt to bribe them into accepting the principle of Parliamentary taxation.

The first shipments of tea arrived in the autumn, and everywhere the popular organizations prevented any duty from being paid. In some places the ships' captains agreed to return to England without unloading, but in others there was violence. In Boston, Governor Hutchinson insisted that the tea should be landed, whereupon a group of men, following orders from Adams and his associates, disguised themselves as Indians, boarded the ships, and threw the tea into the harbor. This destruction of property met with vigorous criticism from other colonies, but when news of the British reply arrived, it became obvious to all liberty-loving Americans that they must stand together.

The King and Lord North felt that this challenge to their authority must be met with a strong hand. Early in 1774 a series of four "coercive acts" were passed. The most important of these "intolerable" acts closed the port of Boston to commerce until the tea was paid for, and made various changes in the Massachusetts political and legal system so as to increase the authority of the royal governor. Four regiments of troops were sent to Boston, and the British General Gage replaced Hutchinson as Governor. About the same time Parliament also passed the Quebec Act, which alarmed the Americans not only because it annulled the colonial claims to the lands north of the Ohio, but also because it provided for an autocratic regime in Canada and gave a privileged position to the Catholic

Church in the province. In actuality both these provisions were in accord with the wishes of the French-Canadian population, but colonial propagandists seized upon them as proofs that Lord North proposed to abolish all colonial liberties and to promote Catholicism. Thus the Quebec Act seemed to the Americans to be quite as "intolerable" as the Coercive Acts.

The Coercive Acts made it quite plain that, in the opinion of the British government, the Americans had no political or legal rights that were not subject to revocation at the pleasure of the British Parliament. The basic issue of the whole controversy thus became so clear that nobody could fail to see it. The Virginia House of Burgesses passed a resolution calling for a congress, and the committees of correspondence industriously circulated it throughout the colonies. Delegates were chosen from every colony except Georgia—in some cases by the legislatures, in others by self-appointed committees or by mass meetings. Numbering fifty-six in all, the delegates assembled at Philadelphia on September 5, 1774.

3. THE OUTBREAK OF THE WAR

The First Continental Congress.   The members of the Continental Congress found themselves divided into two groups. On one side were the radicals who felt that the time had come for resistance by force. The most prominent of these were the Massachusetts delegates, especially Sam Adams and his young cousin John Adams, and the Virginia delegates Patrick Henry and Richard Henry Lee. Most of the radicals had previously been spokesmen of popular opposition to upper-class rule in the colonies. On the other side were moderates, such as John Dickinson of Pennsylvania, who were still hoping for some kind of compromise settlement. Most of the moderate party were wealthy men who had supported the conservative viewpoint in colonial politics. The radicals had a small majority, but they had to proceed cautiously in order to preserve unity.

The radicals won an initial victory when the Congress accepted the Suffolk Resolves, which had been passed by a convention in Suffolk County (the county in which the town of Boston was located). The Resolves declared that America should refuse to obey the Coercive Acts. This appeared to be an endorsement of armed resistance, and was so interpreted by the Massachusetts delegation; but most members of the Congress were not yet willing to recognize that war was inevitable. Instead, they hoped that a commercial boycott would again induce the British government to give way. It was agreed that Americans should stop all trading with Great Britain, and that committees of "safety and inspection" should be elected in every town and county with authority to see that this decision was obeyed and prevent merchants from violating it. This agreement was known as the Continental Association. The Congress also drafted a Declaration of Rights and Grievances and—in order to please the moderates—sent a petition to the King. In these documents the right of Parliament to regulate trade was still accepted. A compromise proposal put forward by the moderates was defeated by only one vote. This was Joseph Galloway's Plan of Union, according to which a continental government would be set up consisting of a grand council representing the colonial legislatures and a president-general appointed by the Crown. Authority over the colonies was to be shared between the council and Parliament.

By this time, however, clear-sighted Americans were reaching the conclusion that the real issue was not whether there should be limits to Parliamentary authority over the colonies but whether Parliament should have any authority at all. Perhaps the Americans should be associated with the home country solely through a common allegiance to the Crown. This theory (according to which the colonies were entitled to full rights of self-government in the same manner as the British dominions of the twentieth century) had already been suggested by Benjamin Franklin. The early history of the colonies seemed to give it some legal validity, for initially they had received their charters not from Parliament but from the Crown, and Parliament had assumed legislative power over them only at a later date. In 1774 and 1775 this conception of the status of the colonies was put forward in pamphlets written independently of each other by three of the ablest young men in America: James Wilson of Pennsylvania, Thomas Jefferson of Virginia, and John Adams of Massachusetts. In the final stages of the controversy it was adopted by the Continental Congress.

There was, of course, not the slightest possibility that either King George or any other person of influence in Great Britain would accept this novel view. Even those leaders who (like Burke and Chatham) felt that the British government was to blame for provoking the colonies, still believed in Parliamentary supremacy. Nor was the King willing to give way. He declared that the time for compromises was past and that the colonies must "either submit or triumph." Early in 1775 Lord North proposed that, if any colony would itself contribute money for imperial defense (the amount to be fixed by the British government), then it would be exempt from Parliamentary taxation. Obviously this proposal did not represent any real concession.

Lexington and Concord.   The Massachusetts delegates came home from the Philadelphia congress assured that they would have the support of the other colonies in opposing the Coercive Acts. While General Gage and his army occupied Boston, the lower house of the Massachusetts legislature reorganized itself as a provincial congress and appointed a committee of safety, headed by John Hancock, to assume executive power and make plans for resistance. Through the winter Gage had control only over the town of Boston, while elsewhere the militia of the colony prepared for war and gathered supplies of guns and ammunition. Armed conflict was plainly imminent.

It began in the early morning of April 19, 1775. Gage sent out a body of troops from Boston to destroy an ammunition dump at Concord and, if possible, to arrest Hancock and Sam Adams. Two of the Boston Sons of Liberty, Will Dawes and Paul Revere, had ridden out during the night to give warning; and when the British reached Lexington they found a company of militia waiting for them. Here (in the words of Emerson) was "fired the shot heard round the world." The British succeeded in reaching Concord and destroying the ammunition, but on the march back to Boston they were attacked by American marksmen from behind walls and houses and suffered more than 200 casualties. After these events some 20,000 men from all the New England colonies gathered at Cambridge, and the British found themselves besieged in Boston.

The Second Continental Congress. In May another Continental Congress assembled at Philadelphia. It was a more radical body than its predecessor, and included some distinguished newcomers, notably Benjamin Franklin, who had spent most of the previous eighteen years as agent for the Pennsylvania legislature in London, and Thomas Jefferson. With little opposition the Congress voted to give full support to Massachusetts and to assume the direction of the war and the responsibilities of a central government. The New England militia were to become the nucleus of a continental army. On June 15, at the suggestion of John Adams, George Washington was appointed commander-in-chief.

Even at this stage very few Americans were openly in favor of independence, but with the outbreak of war all British authority in the colonies rapidly disappeared in fact, if not yet in theory. The royal governors were ejected, the legislative assemblies of the different colonies assumed the powers of provincial congresses, and committees of safety were appointed to carry on executive functions. Orders issued by these authorities were enforced by the local town and county committees which had been set up by the First Continental Congress. Thus a new and essentially revolutionary government came into existence throughout the thirteen colonies.

Meanwhile, the British government ended the hesitation of the moderates by declaring the colonies in a state of rebellion and (at the end of 1775) by interdicting all trade between the colonies and the mother country. John Adams declared that this "throws thirteen colonies out of the royal protection, and makes us independent in spite of supplications and entreaties."

Patriots and Loyalists. Now that the shooting had started, every individual of any prominence was confronted with the necessity of choosing sides and declaring himself either an American patriot or a loyalist. There were many for whom this choice was not easy. In general, the most militant support for the American cause came from the democratic organizations among the Northern farmers and craftsmen, and from Northern merchants and Southern planters who resented the restrictions of British mercantilism. But many upper-class citizens in the North preferred the rule of King George to that of the revolutionary committees; and many prosperous farmers, especially in the Middle colonies, saw no reason for repudiating British authority. In the South, on the other hand, the fact that the planters were mostly patriots caused a number of the back-country farmers, especially among the Regulators of North Carolina, to become loyalist. Thus the Americans were by no means divided along class lines, although on the whole the patriots tended to be more democratic and the loyalists more aristocratic.

Nobody knows what proportion of the population were inclined towards loyalism, but it may have been as much as one-third. Seventy or eighty thousand persons were so strongly loyalist that they went into exile after the war, going mostly to Canada. Yet nowhere in the colonies were they ever strong enough to retain control without the aid of British troops. This was largely because, unlike the patriots, the majority of the loyalists lacked vigor and enterprise and were inclined to remain passive.

Most of the loyalists, especially in the Middle colonies, were not molested. But at the outbreak of the war the revolutionary committees took action against the more outspoken leaders, sometimes putting them in prison or organizing mob action to intimidate them. At a later date, when some of them were suspected of giving information to the British generals and many were serving in the British army, state legislatures adopted severely repressive legislation, depriving them of political rights and confiscating their property. This was ruthless procedure, but it appeared to the patriots to be necessary. And although militant loyalists were made to suffer acutely for being on the wrong side, they were treated more mildly than similar groups in other revolutions. In the American Revolution (unlike the French and Russian Revolutions) there was no reign of terror. Very few loyalists were executed, and none without real justification.

Independence. As the war continued and the attitude of the British authorities made it more obvious that no concessions could be expected, the idea of complete independence began to win more support. This was hastened by the publication, in January 1776, of the pamphlet *Common Sense*, written by the English immigrant Tom Paine. *Common Sense* lived up to its title. Paine abandoned the legalistic arguments the Americans had relied on before this, and stated their case in terms of the liberal idealism of the Enlightenment. In clear and vigorous language he insisted that the colonies could govern themselves better than the British could do it for them, and that they had a magnificent opportunity to create a new society, free from the tyranny and exploitation of the European background. The pamphlet was sold in hundreds of thousands and must have been read by almost every literate patriot.

At late as the autumn of 1775 the legislatures of five colonies went on record against independence; and the groups who controlled the Middle colonies continued to oppose it almost to the end. But in May 1776 the Continental Congress advised the colonies formally to establish independent governments; and in June it began discussion of a motion for independence presented by Richard Henry Lee of Virginia. One of the strongest arguments for such a step was that it would make it easier for the Americans to secure help from France. A committee headed by Thomas Jefferson was appointed to draft a formal declaration. Lee's motion was carried on July 2, with the support of every colony except New York, and on July 4 the Congress adopted the Declaration.

Jefferson's task had been to give expression to the political sentiments generally held by his fellow-Americans. In simple and dignified terms the Declaration summarized the political philosophy characteristic of the Enlightenment: the belief that all men were endowed by God with inalienable rights, that governments were instituted in order to protect these rights, and that men could alter or abolish any government which became destructive of them. The Americans had derived this theory mainly from John Locke, but Jefferson made one interesting change in Locke's list of natural rights. Making no mention of the right of property, he spoke instead of "the pursuit of happiness," thereby justifying the Revolution in more liberal and more comprehensive terms. Another significant feature of the Declaration was that, in listing the specific grievances of the colonies, Jefferson referred only to King George, not to Parliament. This was because the Continental Congress had now adopted the theory that Parliament had never had any legitimate authority over the colonies, their only legal tie with Great Britain being their allegiance to the Crown.

Thus the United States began its career as an independent nation with a ringing affirmation of faith in human rights. All men, according to the Declaration, were "created equal," and all governments derived "their just powers from the consent of the governed." The traditional beliefs in hereditary inequalities and in authoritarian government were repudiated. The subsequent history not only of the United States but of the whole human race has consisted largely of an unending struggle to transform the ideals stated in the Declaration into effective realities.

4. THE WAR OF INDEPENDENCE

THE War of Independence dragged on through seven dreary years chiefly because until 1781 neither side was able to accumulate enough military strength to win a decisive victory. The British won most of the battles but were never able to hold more than a small area of the United

5. The War of Independence in the North

DURING MOST OF THE WAR OF INDEPENDENCE, THE BRITISH RETAINED THE initiative. Their most important advantage was control of the sea, which enabled them to land or withdraw troops wherever they pleased along the Atlantic coastline. Their forces, moreover, were better trained and equipped than those of the Americans, and often more numerous. But although they won most of the battles, they were never able to destroy Washington's army or maintain control over any large segment of American territory.

During the first phase of the war, Massachusetts was the main scene of action. When fighting started in the spring of 1775, the only large British army in the colonies was stationed in Boston. The city had little strategic value; nor could the British hope for much support elsewhere in New England. Besieged by Washington's forces, the British army was evacuated by sea to Nova Scotia in March, 1776.

During the second phase of the war, operations took place mainly in the Middle States. The British concentrated their efforts on this section partly because of its strategic and economic importance and partly because it had a considerable Tory population. By controlling the Hudson Valley and establishing communications with Canada, they hoped to isolate New England from the South. In 1776 General Howe, returning by sea from Nova Scotia, captured New York City and drove the American army southwards across New Jersey. At the end of the year, the Americans successfully struck back at British detachments at Trenton and Princeton and were able to establish winter quarters at Morristown. In 1777 Howe's objective was Philadelphia, and rather than fighting his way across New Jersey, he went around by sea to the head of Chesapeake Bay. Defeating the Americans at Brandywine and Germantown, the British took possession of the city while the Americans settled at Valley Forge. Meanwhile, General Burgoyne, marching down from Canada into the Hudson Valley, was defeated and compelled to surrender at Saratoga, the British forces left in New York being too weak to give him effective assistance. Howe's decision to take the bulk of his army to Philadelphia instead of waiting to cooperate with Burgoyne was one of the major British mistakes of the war. It was formerly—and incorrectly —supposed that the British War Office had failed to keep him informed of Burgoyne's plans.

In 1778, with the entry of France into the war, Britain had to reduce her operations in America. Clinton, replacing Howe, evacuated Philadelphia and moved back to New York, repelling an American attack at Monmouth. Henceforth, there was relatively little fighting in the North. The British sent out raiding parties and hoped to wear down the American will to resist. The American forces, posted at various points in the Hudson Valley and New Jersey, with headquarters at White Plains, were too weak to take the offensive, but were always able to keep open communications between New England and the South.

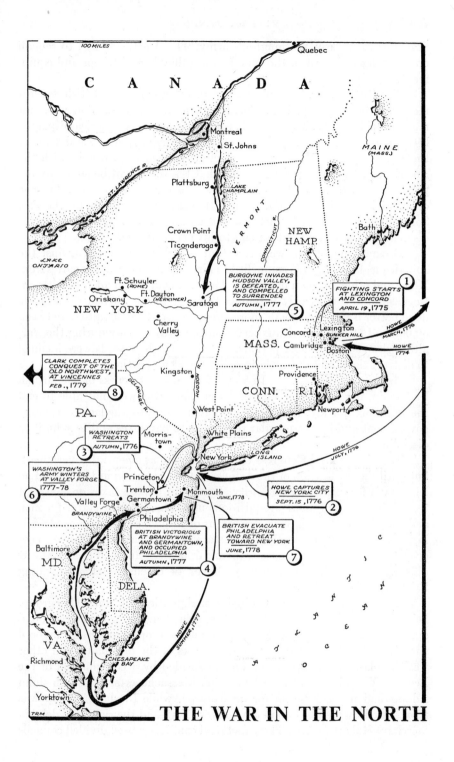

100 MILES

Quebec

C A N A D A

MAINE
(MASS.)

Montreal
St. Johns

ST. LAWRENCE R.

Plattsburg
LAKE
CHAMPLAIN

VERMONT

CONNECTICUT R.

NEW
HAMP.

Bath

Crown Point
Ticonderoga

LAKE
ONTARIO

Ft. Schuyler
(ROME)
Ft. Dayton
(HERKIMER)
Oriskany
NEW YORK
Saratoga

**BURGOYNE INVADES
HUDSON VALLEY,
IS DEFEATED,
AND COMPELLED
TO SURRENDER**
AUTUMN, 1777
⑤

**FIGHTING STARTS
AT LEXINGTON
AND CONCORD**
APRIL 19, 1775
①

Cherry
Valley

Concord
Lexington
BUNKER HILL
MASS. Cambridge
Boston

HOWE
MARCH, 1776

HOWE
1774

**CLARK COMPLETES
CONQUEST OF THE
OLD NORTHWEST,
AT VINCENNES**
FEB., 1779
⑧

Kingston

HUDSON R.

DELAWARE R.

Providence

CONN.
R.I.

PA.

West Point

Newport

**WASHINGTON
RETREATS**
AUTUMN, 1776
③

Morris-
town

White Plains

LONG
ISLAND

HOWE
JULY, 1776

New York

**WASHINGTON'S
ARMY WINTERS
AT VALLEY FORGE**
1777-78
⑥

Princeton
Trenton
Germantown

Monmouth
JUNE, 1778

**HOWE CAPTURES
NEW YORK CITY**
SEPT. 15, 1776
②

Valley Forge

BRANDYWINE

Philadelphia

**BRITISH VICTORIOUS
AT BRANDYWINE
AND GERMANTOWN,
AND OCCUPIED
PHILADELPHIA**
AUTUMN, 1777
④

**BRITISH EVACUATE
PHILADELPHIA
AND RETREAT
TOWARD NEW YORK**
JUNE, 1778
⑦

Baltimore

MD.

DELA.

VA.

HOWE
SUMMER, 1777

Richmond

CHESAPEAKE
BAY

Yorktown

TRM

THE WAR IN THE NORTH

States or to destroy Washington's army. The Americans had to remain on the defensive most of the time because they lacked troops and equipment.

The British Side.   The conduct of the war by the British government was not very efficient. The King's ministers in London were not men of much ability. The generals who commanded in America displayed little energy and were too fond of comfort to move quickly, and some of them (like General Howe) were reluctant to deal too severely with the Americans because they were hoping that the war might be ended by negotiation. Although most Englishmen supported the traditional doctrine of colonial subordination, there was little popular enthusiasm for the war. Some English liberals, in fact, wanted an American victory in order to discredit the King and put an end to his personal rule.

Because the British were reluctant to enlist for service against the Americans, the King was compelled to hire nearly 30,000 mercenaries from Hesse and other German provinces. These, of course, fought with little enthusiasm and could easily be induced to desert. The British would have done better if they had made more effective use of the loyalists. Between 30,000 and 50,000 Americans served in the British army during the war, although mostly for short periods. But the British generals were inclined to distrust them and did little to enlist their cooperation.

American Problems.   In view of the ineffectiveness of the British leadership, it seems surprising that the Americans were not able to end the war more quickly. But they were handicapped by the lack of a strong government and by the popular reluctance to pay taxes and to submit to discipline.

The Continental Congress tried to function as a central government, but until the ratification of the Articles of Confederation in 1781 it had no legal basis for exercising authority. Unable to impose taxes or conscript troops, it could only make requisitions upon the different states for men and supplies, without having any means of enforcing its decisions. And as in the French and Indian Wars, the state governments often failed to cooperate; all of them had acute economic difficulties and had to struggle at different times with their own problems of defense against invading British troops.

Congress was also impeded by internal political divisions. One group, being inclined to regard the Revolution as a struggle for democracy, disapproved in principle of strong government; an opposing group favored effective central government in the interests of the merchants and other wealthy classes. The former group was headed by a combination of the Lees of Virginia and the Adamses of Massachusetts (although John Adams had no enthusiasm for democracy), while the latter group was represented by men like John Jay of New York and the rich Philadelphia merchant Robert Morris. These factional conflicts caused divided councils about the conduct of the war and about the choice of generals and diplomats.

Lack of money was the most serious problem of the Congress. Because there was little gold or silver in America, it was necessary to resort to the printing press, and this quickly led to uncontrolled inflation. Close to $250,000,000 of Continental paper money was issued by 1780, while more than $200,000,000 was issued by the state governments. The paper money rapidly depreciated in value, so that by 1781 a Continental dollar was worth one cent in silver. In the end the paper money disappeared from circulation, and most of it was not redeemed. The Congress also financed the war through some internal borrowing, by running up debts, by making direct requisitions upon the states for money and supplies, and through loans from France, Spain, and Holland.

Lack of money made it difficult for the Americans to raise and maintain an army of any size. Soldiers were paid only in depreciated paper money; after 1780, in fact, many of them were not paid at all. Even more discouraging was the lack of supplies. Thanks to French aid, the army usually had enough guns and ammunition, but it was almost always short of food and clothing. There were periods when the men lived for days without meat and could survive at all only by raiding neighboring farms. Many of them never received uniforms, and wore their own clothes until they were torn to rags. Soldiers sometimes had to sleep on frozen ground without blankets and make long marches without boots. Parts of the army were sometimes unable to take the field because of considerations of decency: the men did not even have enough clothing to cover themselves with. These hardships were not due to any lack of food or clothing in America; the British army was always well fed. But the British paid in hard cash for what they needed, while the Americans could offer only depreciated paper.

Under such circumstances few men could be induced to enlist for any long period in the Continental Army, or to refrain from deserting at the end of a summer. Each state was supposed to provide its quota of enlistments, but in spite of bounties, promises of free land, and other inducements, the quotas were rarely filled. Washington's army was always small and sometimes in danger of complete extinction. More than 200,000 men saw service at one time or another; yet Washington rarely had more than 16,000 under his command at the same time, and during a difficult winter the number sometimes dropped to less than 3,000. There were times when there may have been about as many Americans serving in the British army as in the American. During periods of warfare the army could be supplemented by the militia; but although these men sometimes fought well in defense of their own home territories, they could not be relied upon for a long campaign. Meanwhile, the British armies in America usually totaled 30,000 or more.

On the whole, it must be said that there was a deplorable lack of public spirit during the War of Independence. In spite of the inflation, most of the civilian population continued to live comfortably, and a number of people made fortunes. Merchants found it very profitable to send out privateers to raid British commerce, and some of them had no scruples about charging excessive prices for supplies sold to the government. Many government contracts were tainted with graft and peculation. The later war years were, in fact, a period of business expansion and widespread prosperity in areas where there were no military campaigns. Almost the only people who did not have enough to eat were the small group of men who continued to fight for the independence of the United States.

The Military Leaders. Washington's most essential service was to keep an army of some kind in existence. He had been appointed general largely because he was a Virginian; since the war had begun in Massachusetts, it had seemed advisable to nominate somebody who would ensure Southern support. The choice proved to be extremely fortunate. Although Washington generally showed good judgment, he was not a military genius, and he might have been more successful in preventing desertions if he had been less insistent on imposing strict discipline and maintaining distinctions of rank between officers and men. But his forceful personality inspired confidence and obedience, and he possessed to a superlative degree the essential moral qualities of honesty, courage, and determination. Of equal importance for the future was his complete devotion to republican principles of government; there was no danger that he would ever become a military dictator.

Writers have so often depicted Washington as a man of superhuman perfection that it has become difficult to see him as he really was. Generally shy and reserved, somewhat mistrustful of his own ability, inclined to be pessimistic, and occasionally resentful and suspicious of criticism, he had strong emotions which found an outlet in a few personal friendships and, on certain memorable occasions, in violent explosions of anger. He enjoyed hunting, dancing with pretty women, and—above all—managing his Virginia plantation, developing improved methods of scientific farming, and acquiring more land. Although he was by no means lacking in ambition, the happiest days of his life were those he spent at Mount Vernon.

There were few other Americans who had ever commanded troops, so the Congress initially gave high positions to two men who had held commissions in the British army and now professed to believe in the American cause: Charles Lee and Horatio Gates. Both of these men proved to be incompetent, and Lee was suspected, rightly or wrongly, of treason. Eventually Washington found a number of able subordinates among men without previous military experience, particularly the Rhode Island Quaker Nathanael Greene; but this process took time. Unlike the professional soldiers against whom they were fighting, the Americans, both officers and men, had to learn warfare as they went along. Yet in the end the best of the American generals proved to be more resourceful and imaginative than the British.

Aid from France. The final American victory, however, would have been impossible without French assistance. The French government was eager to avenge the defeat it had suffered in 1763. Also, many of the French middle class were sympathetic to the ideals expressed in the Declaration of Independence. Both these sentiments were ably cultivated by Benjamin Franklin, who was sent to France in 1776 and rapidly made himself one of the best-known and most popular figures in the country.

Almost from the beginning of the war the French secretly supplied the Americans with war materials, while a number of volunteers (such as Lafayette) served in the American army, as did also some from Prussia, Poland, and other countries. In 1778 France became an open belligerent, dividing the energies of the British, challenging their control of the sea, and giving direct aid to Washington, particularly in the final Yorktown campaign. Spain also entered the war in 1779, and Holland in 1780. Thus in the final stages of the struggle the British had to fight at Gibraltar and in the West Indies as well as in North America.

The First Two Years. When Washington assumed command of the army in Massachusetts, at the end of June 1775, the battle of Bunker Hill had already been fought. In this engagement the Americans had been driven from positions which they had occupied in Charlestown, overlooking Boston Harbor. But although the British had gained their objective, they had suffered extremely heavy losses. Possibly because of this experience, General Howe (who replaced General Gage as British commander) remained on the defensive in Boston for the remainder of the year. Washington spent this period in a heartbreaking struggle to organize the men under his command into something resembling an army, and was soon making the most pessimistic complaints about the dishonesty of contractors and speculators and the general lack of cooperation and public spirit.

Meanwhile, an expedition against Quebec was defeated and driven back, in spite of brilliant leadership by Benedict Arnold. Contrary to American hopes, the French Canadians showed no interest in rebelling against British rule. Nor did the Americans receive any support from other British colonies, such as Nova Scotia and Bermuda, both of which had been similarly subjected to Parliamentary taxation.

By March 1776, Washington was ready to take the offensive. Threatened with bombardment, General Howe decided to evacuate Boston, and the British army was transported to Nova Scotia. It was accompanied by about 1,000 loyalists, many of whom were from wealthy and distinguished New England families.

For the next few years the main center of the war was New York.

The British decided to make it their headquarters partly because of its excellent harbor and partly in the hope of separating New England from the rest of the country. Its population, moreover, included a large number of loyalists. General Howe, with an army of 30,000 and a large fleet, arrived in New York Harbor from Nova Scotia in June 1776. Anticipating his arrival, Washington had hurried down from Boston and posted his troops partly in Manhattan and partly across the East River in Brooklyn.

During the next few months the British won a series of victories. Howe defeated the forces in Brooklyn, occupied Manhattan, drove the Americans across the Hudson, and through the autumn was pursuing them southwards across New Jersey. Washington's army began to disintegrate, and a number of the New Jersey patriots, convinced that the war was lost, hastened to swear allegiance to the King. Then, at the end of the year, after the British had gone into winter quarters, Washington suddenly turned the tables by attacking and defeating detachments at Trenton and Princeton. This daring and brilliant operation re-established American morale.

In 1777 Howe decided to take Philadelphia; and since he chose to go by sea, the operation took him most of the summer. Landing his forces at the head of Chesapeake Bay, he defeated Washington at Brandywine and again at Germantown. He and his army then settled down to enjoy the pleasures of Philadelphia society, while the Americans camped a few miles away at Valley Forge. Meanwhile, another British army, under General Burgoyne, had been ordered to march down from Canada and establish control of the Hudson Valley. Burgoyne, who liked to enjoy all the comforts of London, was encumbered with a heavy baggage train, and the Americans had time to assemble a large militia army from New York and New England. In October 1777, after suffering several defeats, Burgoyne was compelled to surrender at Saratoga. Horatio Gates was the official American commanding officer, but this major American victory was due largely to the leadership of Benedict Arnold.

The End of the War.   Saratoga convinced the French that the American cause was worth supporting and brought them openly into the war. This compelled the British to reduce their operations in North America, and in 1778 Sir Henry Clinton, who replaced Howe, was ordered to evacuate Philadelphia and concentrate on holding New York. As the British retreated across New Jersey, Washington met them at Monmouth, but failed to win a victory, apparently because Charles Lee disobeyed orders to attack.

For the remainder of the war the British in New York remained largely inactive, although they occasionally sent out raiding parties to lay waste sections of the country. And for the next three years Washington, who established headquarters at White Plains, was too busy with the unending task of keeping his men fed and clothed, and preventing them from deserting, to be able to undertake major offensive operations. This was perhaps the gloomiest period of the war for the Americans. Few people retained much enthusiasm for the cause, and some of the troops, contrasting their half-starved condition with the comforts enjoyed by the civilian population, actually mutinied. It was in 1780 that Benedict Arnold, heavily in debt as a result of luxurious living, and resentful because his services had not been more fully rewarded, sold himself to the British.

The only important operation of this period was undertaken under the direction not of Washington and the Continental Congress but of the government of Virginia. British officers and fur-traders in the West had encouraged the Indians to enter the war. Frontier communities had been exposed to Indian attacks, and some of them had been massacred. In 1778 a frontier leader, George Rogers Clark, was commissioned by Virginia to lead an expedition against the British in the Illinois country. After covering immense distances with extreme rapidity and enduring extraordinary hardships, Clark and his men captured the three posts held by British troops in Illinois. Fighting continued in the West until the end of the war; the British held Detroit and six other places close to Canada, and made some gains. But most of the western country remained under American control.

The final campaigns took place in the South. In the spring of 1780 a British army captured Charleston, and under the leadership of General Cornwallis began to move northwards in the hope of conquering each state in turn. In August, Cornwallis completely defeated Gates at the battle of Camden, in North Carolina. But the British were not numerous enough to hold any large area; and although they were supported by loyalist elements among the back-country farmers, they could not put an end to patriot resistance. For the next two years there was a ferocious civil war in the Carolinas; both loyalists and patriots formed guerrilla bands which plundered and killed each other with little compunction. In South Carolina the patriots gradually gained the upper hand under such chieftains as Marion, Sumter, and Pickens. In North Carolina patriot frontiersmen, having decisively defeated a loyalist army at King's Mountain in October 1780, kept control of the western part of the state.

Meanwhile, Nathanael Greene, ablest of the American generals, assumed command in the South; and although Cornwallis defeated him in the battle of Guilford Court House in March 1781, the British suffered such heavy losses that they had to abandon all hope of holding the Carolinas. Eventually Cornwallis decided to push on into Virginia, where he established himself with about 7,000 men on the seacoast at Yorktown.

This led to the final and decisive episode of the war. French troops had landed in New England, and they now made plans with Washington for a joint attack on Cornwallis. Several previous attempts at Franco-American cooperation had turned out unfortunately, but this time everything went smoothly. A French fleet drove away British ships attempting to relieve Cornwallis and blockaded Yorktown by sea, while American and French troops came down by land, skillfully outwitting Clinton in New York. On October 19, 1781, Cornwallis, surrounded and heavily out-numbered, was compelled to surrender. Although British troops continued to hold New York, Charleston, and Savannah, there was little further fighting.

The Peace Treaty.   Yorktown was a small-scale engagement, even by eighteenth-century standards; but it was large enough to convince the British that it was futile to continue the struggle. Widespread popular discontent brought about the resignation of Lord North, and King George lost his control over the House of Commons. The new British prime minister, Lord Rockingham, began peace negotiations. The British were holding their own in the West Indies and other parts of the world, but they were now willing to concede American independence. Continuance of the war might lead to the loss of India and other colonies to the French. British merchants, moreover, had been suffering heavy losses from commerce raiding by American privateers (which numbered about 2,000) and by the small but active Continental Navy.

Franklin, John Adams, and John Jay represented the United States at the peace negotiations, which took place in Paris. According to the terms of the French alliance and the instructions of Congress, they were required to make no agreement without the consent of France. But Jay and Adams (with good reason) distrusted the French government, suspecting that it was opposed to American expansion into the Mississippi Valley, so they insisted on negotiating a separate treaty without consulting their allies. The British, fearing a permanent Franco-American alliance, were eager to encourage dissensions between their opponents and were therefore disposed to be generous.

A preliminary treaty was signed in November 1782. Considering the military situation, the terms were remarkably favorable to the Americans. Great Britain not only conceded American independence but also surrendered her claims to the whole of the western country south of the Great Lakes. The Mississippi River was therefore to be the western boundary of the United States. At the insistence of John Adams, American citizens were allowed to retain their fishing rights off Newfoundland and in the Gulf of the St. Lawrence. There were only two things which caused trouble: the British insistence that debts owing to British merchants should be paid and that the loyalists should regain their property. Since these matters were within the jurisdiction of the different states, not of the Congress, the American delegates could not undertake binding commitments. It was agreed in the peace treaty that creditors should not be prevented from collecting their debts, and that the Congress should recommend to the state governments the restoration of loyalist property; but the state governments paid little attention to either of these clauses.

In the end the debts owed to British merchants were paid by the Federal government, a final settlement being made in 1802; and the British government had to take care of the loyalists.

A general peace treaty was signed in the following year. In the agreements between the European powers the only clause of interest to the Americans was the restoration of Florida to Spain.

Thus the Americans had established their right to control their own destiny, and a new nation, based on new principles, had come of age. It now remained to be seen whether the manifold problems of political unification, economic growth, and western expansion, which British governments before the Revolution had failed to handle satisfactorily, would be successfully solved by the Americans themselves. The destructive phase of the Revolution had ended; its more important constructive phase had scarcely begun.

VI

The Confederation and the Constitution

1. THE CONFLICT OF IDEALS

2. REFORMS OF THE REVOLUTIONARY PERIOD

3. THE CONFEDERATION PERIOD

4. THE MOVEMENT FOR A NEW GOVERNMENT

5. THE MAKING OF THE CONSTITUTION

6. RATIFICATION

DURING the Revolutionary period it did not seem likely that the Americans would succeed in creating a stable central authority to replace that of the British Crown, and there were many gloomy predictions that the new nation would dissolve into anarchy. Yet within a few years of the winning of independence it created a government which combined freedom with order, and local self-government with national unity,

SELECTED BIBLIOGRAPHY: The leading authority on the Confederation period is Merrill Jensen, who has written *The Articles of Confederation* (1940) and *The New Nation* (1950). Internal changes during the Revolutionary period are described in the works by J. F. Jameson and E. B. Greene cited on page 93 and in Allan Nevins, *The American States During and After the Revolution* (1924). The proceedings of the Philadelphia Convention are described in Carl Van Doren, *The Great Rehearsal* (1948), and analyzed in C. A. Beard, *An Economic Interpretation of the Constitution of the United States* (1913), an epoch-making work, though its thesis is somewhat over-stated, and in R. L. Schuyler, *The Constitution of the United States: An Historical Survey of Its Formation* (1923). Irving Brant, *James Madison* (5 vols., 1941–1956) is an outstanding biography. *The Federalist*, by James Madison, Alexander Hamilton, and John Jay, has been often reprinted and has been regarded as a classic ever since it was written; it should be read by all students of the Constitution, but with a realization that it was written primarily as propaganda. In order to find out why and how the Constitution was made and ratified, one should read the fascinating *Records of the Federal Convention*, edited by Max Farrand (4 vols., 1911–37), and J. Elliot (ed.), *The Debates of the Several State Conventions on the Adoption of the Federal Constitution* (5 vols., 1836–45).

thereby demonstrating to the rest of the world the effectiveness of republican institutions. This achievement was the more remarkable in view of the deep politico-economic conflicts among the American people.

1. THE CONFLICT OF IDEALS

The central factor in the internal political development of the United States during the Revolutionary period, and for a long time afterwards, was the interplay between two opposing movements. These may be roughly (although not quite accurately) described as democratic and aristocratic, radical and conservative, or agrarian and mercantile.

The Democratic Tendency.   The democratic movement was represented in the early stages of the Revolution by Sam Adams, Patrick Henry, and other leaders of the Sons of Liberty. After the adoption of the Constitution its greatest champion was Thomas Jefferson, while in the 1820's democratic tendencies found expression in the party headed by Andrew Jackson. These men believed that government should be controlled by the mass of the people, that its powers should be strictly limited, and that economic policy should aim at protecting the interests of the average citizen rather than those of the wealthy class. While their ideals can be regarded as, in large measure, a product of the American environment, in which the abundance of land and economic opportunities had promoted democratic attitudes, they were also an expression of the Enlightenment. Such leaders as Jefferson, like the philosophers of eighteenth-century Europe, believed that men were naturally good and could be trusted with freedom, and that if they repudiated the traditions of the past and relied on the powers of human reason, they could create a new and better society.

In analyzing the doctrines of these democratic spokesmen, it is important to remember that their ideal citizen was the small, independent property-owner, especially the farmer. Men like Jefferson regarded economic independence as a prerequisite for political freedom, and were doubtful if political rights could safely be entrusted to propertyless wage-earners, who, they felt, would be controlled either by their employers or by demagogues. They wanted the United States to remain a country in which everybody owned property or could easily acquire it, and believed that if a large urban proletariat developed, liberty would probably be destroyed. Thus their faith in democracy had significant limitations. In this respect there is a fundamental difference between the liberalism of the eighteenth century and that of the twentieth.

The Aristocratic Tendency.   The aristocratic movement was supported during the Revolutionary period by a number of merchants and landowners; after the adoption of the Constitution its outstanding spokesman was Alexander Hamilton. Hamilton and his associates argued that the mass of the people were too ignorant and lacking in self-discipline to be entrusted with political power, and that outright majority rule would lead to the robbery of the rich by the poor, and to the destruction of individual rights and of all civilized standards of behavior. Society, they declared, should be governed by an elite group composed of "the gentlemen of principle and property" or of "the wise, the rich, and the well-born." They favored strong government, controlled by an upper class, which would give adequate protection to the privileges and property of the rich. Skeptical of the optimistic doctrines of the Enlightenment, they wished the United States to retain some of the traditional institutions of Europe and to be guided by European experience.

Economic Conflicts.   Perhaps the most essential difference between these two groups was in economic policy. Both groups believed in the protection of private property; but while one of them wished property to be widely distributed, the other favored a concentration of wealth in the hands of an upper class.

Democratic leaders supported legislation that would bring about the division of big estates; they wished the western lands to be accessible to settlers; they were inclined to support monetary and financial policies that would make it easier for debtors to meet their obligations; and they were opposed to the granting of special privileges to merchants and financiers. In general, the kind of private property which they wished to protect was that of the farmer who owned and cultivated a piece of land. While some of them favored direct government aid for farmers and debtors, others (including Jefferson) were sympathetic to the new *laissez-faire* doctrine, arguing that government intervention in economic matters usually had the effect of enriching some favored group at the expense of the mass of the people.

Their opponents, on the other hand, advocated various forms of assistance to the moneyed class. Government, they believed, should protect the property rights of businessmen, in particular by enforcing the obligations of commercial contracts; it should adopt a financial policy beneficial to creditors, and should support the claims of speculators in western lands; and it should give merchants and financiers positive aid and encouragement in new commercial and industrial enterprises. Instead of adopting a strict *laissez-faire* attitude, they argued that government should promote business expansion by means of navigation laws, protective tariffs, subsidies, grants of monopoly rights, and other measures.

Political Conflicts.   This conflict about economic questions was accompanied by equally wide differences of attitude towards government. In general, the democratic group regarded all government with suspicion, as a necessary evil at best, in the belief that it was always likely to be controlled by some privileged class. They wanted the functions of the government to be strictly limited by law, in order to prevent it from becoming oppressive. And they were particularly suspicious of any tendency towards the centralization of power. Government, they argued, should be local as far as possible, in order that the people might more easily keep control over it. They could see little need for any remote central authority in the United States, and wished to preserve the powers of the separate states.

For the same reason most supporters of upper-class rule, especially among the Northern merchants, wanted state powers to be limited and a strong national government created. During the 1780's they came to believe that a central government was less likely to be dominated by agrarian and debtor groups and would be more responsive to upper-class interests. And only a strong central authority, they felt, could give adequate protection to commercial and industrial enterprises. Navigation laws for the protection of American shipping, protective tariffs, and the maintenance of a sound currency should not be left to the thirteen different states, all of which were likely to pursue different policies.

Thus in the eighteenth century it was, on the whole, the wealthy business groups who favored a strong national government and argued that it should guide and direct economic development, while it was the more democratic elements who wanted the government's powers to be strictly limited and who were more sympathetic to the doctrine of *laissez faire*. In the twentieth century, of course, these attitudes have been reversed. A movement like the New Deal can be considered Jeffersonian in so far as it endeavored to limit the powers of the wealthy class and promote the welfare of the mass of the people; yet the New Dealers advocated an increase in Federal power and criticized *laissez faire*, while their business opponents talked in Jeffersonian terms about the dangers of strong government. This change was due mainly to the transformation of American society by industrialism and the consequent growth of a new kind of liberalism, based not on the small independent property-owner but on the wage-earner. It is misleading to apply the statements of eighteenth-century statesmen to modern problems without making allowances for this change of attitudes.

Each of these movements made an essential contribution to the development of the United States, and it is important that due credit should be given to both sides. It was the democratic Jeffersonian movement that chiefly shaped the distinctive ideals of the American people, but it was the opposite movement that gave them an effective central government and brought about the growth of national wealth and power. Jeffersonianism kept American society fluid, free from rigid class barriers and privileges; but it was the policies of men like Hamilton that made possible the accumulation of capital and its investment in productive enterprise. Without the Jeffersonian faith in human freedom and equality American civilization might have had little spiritual meaning or vitality; but without the Hamiltonian emphasis on efficient organization and business expansion the United States would not have become a world power or achieved its high standard of living.

2. REFORMS OF THE REVOLUTIONARY PERIOD

Political Changes.   In the early years of the War of Independence democratic tendencies were gaining ground. Many of the men who assumed leadership in the provincial congresses and local committees were spokesmen of popular rights, while in some of the states the aristocratic elements were weakened by the fact that many of their members were either loyalist or decidedly lukewarm towards independence. At the outset of the war, in fact, there was in some areas a period of what seemed to conservatives to be outright mob rule. Law courts ceased to function, debts could no longer be collected, and radical committeemen maintained order by dictatorial methods. A number of leading loyalists, most of them wealthy men, were tarred and feathered, ridden on rails, or arbitrarily put in prison. But these highhanded procedures antagonized many people, and there was a marked reaction to more conservative leadership during the later war years.

The permanent effect of the Revolution on American internal development was to bring about a considerable advance towards democracy, although this went much further in some states than in others. But the tradition of aristocratic rule was by no means brought to an end. Many of the men who had taken the lead in the movement for independence belonged to the upper class, especially in the South, and they successfully resisted pressure for drastic reforms. Moreover, the whole political scene was still in a state of flux; clear-cut parties with definite programs had not yet emerged, and few individual leaders were guided by any clearly formulated body of principles.

All the states except Connecticut and Rhode Island had formerly had royal or proprietary governors, and therefore had to revise their consitutions. In most instances, this was done by the provincial congresses. Massachusetts, however, adopted a method that has since been generally accepted; the drafting of a new constitution by an especially elected convention, followed by ratification by a popular vote.

Democratic leaders generally wished to extend the franchise to all property-owners, give adequate representation to the western areas, provide for annual elections, entrust power mainly to the legislature rather than the executive, and impose limitations upon government authority through a bill of rights. These ideas were most fully realized in the new Pennsylvania constitution of 1776. Other states which made similar changes included New Hampshire, Delaware, North Carolina, and Georgia. Elsewhere, especially in Massachusetts, New York, Virginia, and South Carolina, the upper classes retained much of their authority, and reforms were mild. The franchise was more restricted, and the seaboard regions retained more than their fair share of seats in the legislatures.

Perhaps more significant than these legal reforms was the election of men of relatively humble origins to high office. Political leadership was no longer a monopoly of the upper class. This occurred even in states which remained relatively conservative. The first elected governors of Virginia and New York were Patrick Henry and George Clinton, each of whom was a back-country lawyer without hereditary advantages. Another interesting change, indicative of a shift of power from the seaboard to the back country, was the movement inland during the 1780's and 1790's of a number of the state capitals.

Changes in Landownership.   The Revolution brought some changes in the ownership of property. In particular, a number of large estates that had belonged to loyalist families were confiscated. But since most of them were bought by speculators, this did little to bring about a more democratic system of land distribution.

Of greater significance were reforms in the inheritance laws. The feudal principles of entail and primogeniture had formerly been established in New York and in the South. Entail meant that the owner of an estate could not sell or give away any part of it, while primogeniture meant that on his death it was inherited, without division, by his eldest son. During the Revolutionary period most states abolished entail and provided that when a landowner died intestate, his estate should be divided among all his sons. These changes tended to prevent any landowning aristocracy from becoming permanently established in the United States.

Separation of Church and State.   The Revolution stimulated the movement for complete religious freedom, and led to the separation of church and state everywhere except in New England. The Episcopalian Church had formerly been a tax-supported institution in parts of New York and in all the states from Maryland southwards. Its connections with the British government and the loyalist sympathies of most of its clergy weakened its position, and the movement to deprive it of its privileges was completely successful. The most eloquent statement of the ideal of religious and intellectual freedom was the Virginia Statute of Religious Liberty, written by Jefferson in 1779, although not passed by the legislature until 1786.

In Congregationalist New England, on the other hand, the established church had more popular support, and very few of its clergy were loyalist. Taxes for the maintenance of the church were therefore retained, although individuals belonging to other religious organizations were permitted to earmark their contributions for their own ministers. Church and state were not completely separated until 1817 in New Hampshire, 1818 in Connecticut, and 1833 in Massachusetts.

Slavery.   The liberal idealism of the Revolutionary period found expression also in a widespread movement for the abolition of slavery. In the North, where slaves were few in number and of little economic importance, one state after another provided for either immediate or gradual emancipation. In Massachusetts, for example, all slaves were declared

free as a result of a judicial decision in 1781. New Jersey, the last Northern
state to act, provided for gradual emancipation by a law passed in 1804.

In the South the problem was much more complex, and liberal
leaders like Jefferson recognized that there was no possibility of immediate
abolition. But in the tobacco colonies there were no longer strong economic inducements for slavery, and very few people defended the system
in principle. Although action against slavery itself was postponed until
some later period, all states except South Carolina and Georgia passed
laws prohibiting the importation of new slaves from abroad.

3. THE CONFEDERATION PERIOD

The Articles of Confederation.   The first central government in the
United States was established by the Articles of Confederation. These
were drafted mainly by John Dickinson; and after being severely amended
in order to strengthen the powers of the states, were accepted by the
Continental Congress in 1777. In their final form the Articles reflected the
popular distrust of centralized authority. The Confederation was to control foreign policy, defense, and some other things; but it was not allowed
to exercise two of the essential attributes of sovereignty: the power to
tax and the power to regulate trade. Its revenues were to be derived from
requisitions on the different states. No provision was made for separate
executive and judicial branches of government, all the authority of the
Confederation being vested in a Congress. In this body each of the thirteen
states had one vote, and at least nine votes were required for important
decisions. The Articles could not be amended without the consent of all
thirteen. The Confederation was thus not much more than a mere league,
and power remained, on the whole, with the states.

Ratification was delayed until 1781, as a result of a controversy
which had important implications. Virginia and some other states continued to claim western lands. A group of land speculators from Pennsylvania and other Middle states argued that these claims should be
annulled and the western lands made the common property of the Confederation, and Maryland insisted that this should be a condition of
ratification. Virginia eventually gave way in part, and all the lands north
of the Ohio River were turned over to the Confederation, with the understanding that they should eventually be organized into new states instead
of being controlled by any of the existing thirteen. This region north of
the Ohio and east of the Mississippi became known as the Northwest
Territory. It was primarily the self-interest of the Middle-state speculators that was responsible for the decision; but its beneficial effects were
incalculable. It meant that the manifold dangers of state imperialism had
been averted.

Economic Progress.   The Confederation lasted from 1781 until
1789. Historians have frequently depicted this as an unhappy period of

economic depression, internal conflict, and lack of constructive leadership. Yet in actuality much was accomplished. The gloomy portrayals of this period have been derived mainly from the propaganda of the group working for a stronger central government; this has been accepted by many writers quite uncritically. Unquestionably there was need for a more effective union, without which certain important problems had to remain unsolved. But in many ways the Confederation period was one of rapid progress.

The transition to peace inevitably caused economic dislocations. As soon as the war ended, there was a heavy importation of goods from Great Britain, and the country was drained of specie in order to pay for them. Lack of money then put a stop to this process, and 1784 and 1785 were years of general depression. But there was a quick recovery, as enterprising merchants began to discover new markets. Americans were soon taking advantage of their new freedom from the restrictions of British mercantilism. Many foreign countries opened their ports to American traders with few limitations, while at the same time Americans were allowed to trade with Great Britain on the same terms as during the colonial period. The only important impediment was that American ships were no longer admitted to the British West Indies; this was a serious matter to the New England and Middle-state shipowners, but in practice the rule was partly evaded by smuggling. Before the end of the decade foreign trade was booming, and sailings from every important American seaport were considerably larger than they had been during the colonial period. Merchants, moreover, had opened up a new trade route which was to bring in big profits during the next half-century. In 1784 the *Empress of China*, sailing from New York with a cargo of ginseng, made the first passage across the Pacific to China and the East Indies.

The benefits of independence were similarly manifested in internal development. There was a rapid growth of manufacturing, and a widespread interest in its encouragement. Several states adopted tariffs against foreign goods, while admitting goods freely from other parts of the United States (the notion that there were serious barriers to interstate commerce under the Confederation is a myth). A number of companies were chartered for building roads and bridges; and commercial banks, the first in America, were founded in Philadelphia, New York, and Boston.

Western Expansion. Meanwhile, as soon as the war ended, there began a large-scale movement of settlers out into the West, some of them traveling across Pennsylvania to the Ohio River, while others crossed from Virginia into Tennessee by way of the Cumberland Gap. The migration was well under way before the Congress formulated a policy about the settlement of the West. While it had been agreed that the West should eventually be organized into new states, it remained to be decided on what terms public land should be distributed. Involved in this question was the perennial conflict of interest between the settler and the speculator.

In 1784 Congress adopted an ordinance, drafted by Jefferson, according to which settlers in the Northwest Territory were to have full self-government immediately, and the Territory was eventually to be divided into ten or more states. In accordance with his democratic convictions Jefferson believed that land should be free. Congress, however, decided otherwise, partly through the influence of speculators, and partly because of its need for money, and the result was the Land Ordinance of 1785, which provided for the sale of public land. After being surveyed, the Territory was to be divided into townships, each containing thirty-six square miles. Four square-mile sections in each township were to be reserved for the United States government, and one was to be used for the support of a school. The remaining thirty-one were to be sold at auction. The price was to be not less than a dollar an acre, and nobody could buy less than one section. Such an arrangement meant, in practice, that most of the land would go to speculators, because the average settler would not wish to buy a whole square mile of land.

After the adoption of the Land Ordinance, Congress arranged for the surveying of the Territory, and also sent out troops to burn the cabins of the squatters who had already settled there. But surveying was necessarily a slow process, and meanwhile the speculators were impatient and the Confederation needed money. In 1787 Congress, in response to skillful lobbying, agreed to an immediate sale of about 1,500,000 acres of unsurveyed land to an influential group of New England merchants, ministers, and ex-officers who had organized the Ohio Company; the price worked out at less than nine cents an acre. Similar grants were made to two other large concerns, the Scioto Company, of New York, and a New Jersey group headed by John Cleves Symmes, though both of them failed in the end to fulfill the terms of their contracts.

This made it necessary to provide immediately for some kind of government. By the Northwest Ordinance of 1787 (which replaced Jefferson's more liberal Ordinance of 1784) the Territory was initially to have a governor and judges appointed by Congress. When it had 5,000 adult male inhabitants, it would elect a territorial legislature with limited powers. Eventually the Territory was to be divided into not less than three nor more than five states, which were to be admitted into the Union on a basis of complete equality with the existing states. A population of 60,000 was to be the qualification for statehood. The Ordinance also included a statement about the encouragement of public education, and—a provision of great importance—it prohibited slavery throughout the Territory.

These two ordinances were the most notable accomplishments of the Confederation. And in spite of the preference given to speculators over the actual settlers, they were, on the whole, products of enlightened statesmanship. They meant that the American government had adopted a new kind of colonial policy. A colony was to be an extension of the nation and was eventually to be admitted to full equality; it was not, as with the

European empires, to be held in a position of permanent inferiority and kept subject to permanent exploitation. This policy made it possible for the United States to expand across the continent during future generations with remarkably little friction.

Projects for New States. Meanwhile, settlers in certain other territories, not controlled by the Confederation, were already claiming rights of self-government. These movements cannot be regarded as pure manifestations of the democratic spirit, since they were largely instigated by speculators whose primary interest was to secure validation for claims to land.

The people of Vermont, led by Ethan Allen and his brother (who wanted legal title to about 300,000 acres of central Vermont), had already assumed the rights of statehood and drafted a constitution in 1777. Since New York was unwilling to give up its claims to part of the Vermont land, the new state was not recognized and admitted to the Union until 1791. Prior to that date Vermont was virtually an independent republic, and its leaders even conducted secret negotiations with the British in their efforts to secure support for their interests.

Under the Confederation there were similar movements in the Kentucky-Tennessee country south of the Ohio River. This had not been included in the territory ceded to the Confederation, and belonged partly to Virginia and partly to North Carolina. But the governments of these states were unable to maintain any effective control over the remote Western regions, and in practice the settlers were left to their own resources, both for the maintenance of law and order and for protection against Indians. Under the Confederation there were short-lived attempts to organize separate state governments in both Kentucky and Tennessee; but the land speculators who assumed leadership played a double game, and eventually found it expedient to re-establish the jurisdiction of Virginia and North Carolina.

Diplomatic Problems. One other Western problem was the threat of encroachment by European imperialisms. Great Britain held Canada, and Spain held Florida and Louisiana, and both powers were hostile to American western expansion.

The British ministers responsible for ending the war left office in 1783, and their successors, feeling that the treaty had been unnecessarily generous, refused to evacuate the posts held by British troops at Detroit and other points south of the Great Lakes.. They claimed that the Americans had not fulfilled their engagements with respect to the loyalists and the debts; but this was a mere pretext. By maintaining their relations with the Indians, the British hoped to keep indirect control over a good deal of the Northwest Territory, with its valuable fur trade.

Meanwhile, Spanish officials at New Orleans were similarly building up influence with the Indians in what was legally United States territory and—an even more serious matter—refused to allow the Western settlers to ship goods down the Mississippi. The right to free trade on the Mississippi was vitally important to the economic development of the West, because transportation of heavy goods across the Appalachians was too expensive to be practicable.

The government of the Confederation was not strong enough to win the respect of the European powers. Moreover, the New Yorker John Jay, who was in charge of foreign affairs after 1785, was unsympathetic to Western interests. Many of the seaboard conservatives disliked western expansion, partly in the belief that it would add to the strength of the democratic movement, and partly because they wished to maintain land values and keep a supply of labor in the East. In 1786 Jay negotiated a treaty with the Spanish minister Gardoqui in which he accepted the closing of the Mississippi in return for concessions to American merchants trading with Spain. This provoked an explosion of indignation throughout the South and West, and the treaty was never submitted to Congress. Westerners began to talk of seceding from the Confederation and either driving the Spaniards out of New Orleans or coming to terms with them independently. Some of them entered into secret negotiations with Spanish officials and even spoke of joining the Spanish Empire. Obviously, what was needed was a central government responsive to all national interests and capable of protecting them.

4. THE MOVEMENT FOR A NEW GOVERNMENT

The Federalists.   Throughout the Confederation period a relatively small but influential group of men were working for an effective federal government. Support for this movement came primarily from merchants and large landowners, while it was opposed by political leaders who claimed to represent the farmers (such as Patrick Henry and Richard Henry Lee of Virginia, and Governor Clinton of New York). The active leadership was supplied mainly by young men who had not been prominent in the controversies preceding the Revolution and who, growing to maturity during the disillusioning years of the war, felt that what the country needed now was more unity and discipline rather than more liberty. Among them were James Madison of Virginia and Alexander Hamilton of New York.

The Federalist group hoped at first to make the Articles of Confederation the basis of a real union. In 1781 they were strong enough to oust the Lee-Adams party from control of Congress and appoint conservative leaders with broad powers to control different branches of the administration. In particular, Robert Morris, the wealthiest merchant of the time (and incidentally a war profiteer), became Superintendent of Finance. Morris brought a much-needed business skill and efficiency to the operations of his department. But attempts to amend the Articles in order to give the Confederation the right to levy import duties were defeated; all thirteen states had to approve amendments, and there was always at least one state voting in the negative. After the peace treaty, moreover, the need for strong government was less apparent, and the Federalist group lost control of Congress within two or three years. After further failures to secure for the Confederation the power to impose taxes and regulate trade, they began to favor the creation of a wholly new government.

Stronger government was needed for a number of purposes: for example, to protect commerce, shipping, and manufacturing; to prevent interstate conflicts; and to provide for national defense, especially in the West. But the two issues that excited most concern were the public debt and the currency.

Problems of Finance. During the war the Confederation had accumulated a considerable debt, partly foreign and partly internal, and the soldiers of the Continental Army had not received their full pay. When the war ended, some members of the Federalist group urged the soldiers to refuse to be demobilized until they had been paid, hoping to use their grievances as a lever for bringing about a stronger government. But Washington refused to support any proposal involving disobedience to legal authority, and in a meeting at the army headquarters at Newburgh in 1783, he persuaded the soldiers to return peacefully to their homes. The soldiers received certificates stating that the government owed them money, and the army was disbanded. Many of these certificates were subsequently bought up by speculators at heavy discounts.

Unable to levy taxes, the Confederation could not pay its debts, and was partially in default even on interest payments, although a good deal of necessary work was done by its officials in examining claims and settling accounts. The public creditors, eager for a government capable of meeting its obligations, composed a pressure group that could be relied upon to support the Federalist program.

More disturbing to propertied men was the perennial problem of the currency. By the end of the war, the Continental paper, now virtually worthless, ceased to circulate, and gold and silver became again the main media of exchange. As in the colonial period, the consequent scarcity of both money and credit caused severe hardships to the farmers, especially during the depression years of 1784 and 1785. Seven of the states therefore made new issues of paper money, part of which was loaned to farmers who could offer land as security. Three of these states adopted adequate safeguards against inflation, but in the others, especially in Rhode Island, the value of the paper depreciated, and creditors who were required to accept it in payment of debts complained that they were being cheated. Some states, moreover, passed "stay" laws suspending the foreclosure of mortgages for unpaid debts. Such legislation was alarming to creditors, who felt that all property rights and contractual obligations were becoming insecure.

In Massachusetts the government was controlled by mercantile interests and no relief was given to debtors. The state began to pay off its debt, much of which was held by wealthy speculators, and a large share of the consequent burden of taxation was shifted to the farmers. Taxes had to be paid in specie, and often amounted to no less than one-third of the farmer's total income. A number of farmers lost their land through foreclosures, and others went to jail on account of unpaid debts. In 1786 farmers in the Connecticut Valley, feeling that the situation had become unbearable, began to use force to prevent the law courts from hearing debt cases; and in the autumn, after the government took action to protect the courts, the farmers resorted to open rebellion under the somewhat unwilling leadership of an ex-officer of the Continental Army, Daniel Shays. The movement was quickly crushed by the state militia; and after order had been re-established and a new and more liberal legislature had been elected, the rebels were pardoned, and some concessions were made to debtors. But Shays's Rebellion had an influence far in excess of its real importance. The threat of civil war caused general alarm throughout the country and made it possible for the Federalist group to win wide support in their campaign for a stronger government, not only among the wealthy class but among the mass of the people.

In September 1786, a convention, attended by delegates from five states, met at Annapolis to consider problems of interstate commerce. The convention decided that such questions could not be effectively dealt with unless the Articles of Confederation were revised, and adopted a recommendation, proposed by Alexander Hamilton, that a convention of all the states should be held for this purpose. The Congress of the Confederation accepted the proposal and made the necessary arrangements.

5. THE MAKING OF THE CONSTITUTION

Purposes of the Federal Convention.   The convention met at Philadelphia, the first session taking place on May 25, 1787. At different periods it was attended by a total of fifty-five delegates from twelve of the states (all except Rhode Island), most of whom belonged to the wealthier and more conservative classes. Radical leaders either had failed to be elected or (like Patrick Henry) had refused to participate. Jefferson was out of the country, as minister to France. Among more conservative statesmen the only outstanding figures who were absent were John Adams, who was envoy to Great Britain, and John Jay, who was still Secretary of Foreign Affairs. The convention consisted preponderantly of practical men, experienced in the management of business or of public affairs, who were concerned not with enunciating noble sentiments but with drafting a concrete and workable plan of action. Many of them were relatively young men, the average age being forty-two. Washington was elected presiding officer. Madison, who had a vast fund of historical knowledge about the theory and practice of different governments, was the most active and useful member.

Most of the delegates were in substantial agreement as to what they hoped to accomplish. In the first place, they wanted to create a central government strong enough to maintain order, pay its debts, promote economic development, and protect American interests abroad. At the same time they recognized that if they ignored the popular sentiment in favor of states' rights, their proposals would have little chance of acceptance. Hamilton argued that effective government was impossible unless state sovereignty was wholly abolished, but the rest of the convention felt that this attitude was much too extreme. What was necessary was to devise a federal system in which sovereignty would be divided between the nation and the states. This was a delicate operation, and the examples from similar experiments in past history showed chiefly what things should be avoided. A successful federal system would be an almost unique achievement.

In the second place, the convention wished to limit outright majority rule, in the belief that it would endanger property rights and destroy wise and enlightened leadership. A number of the members expressed a distrust of democracy. Since the convention met behind closed doors and none of its proceedings were made public, it was possible for them to speak frankly. They believed (in the words of Edmund Randolph of Virginia) that "the evils under which the United States labored" were due to "the turbulence and follies of democracy," and that "some check therefore was to be sought for against this tendency of our government." Their primary motive, according to Madison, was "the necessity of providing more effectively for the security of private rights and the steady dispensation of justice. Interferences with these were evils which had, more perhaps than anything else, produced this convention." And by private rights they meant especially rights of property. Madison declared that one of their aims should be "to protect the minority of the opulent against the majority."

These statements should not be misinterpreted. The members of the convention wished only to limit majority rule, not to destroy it. And their fear of "the turbulence and follies of democracy" did not mean that they would have preferred any authoritarian form of government. On the contrary, authoritarianism was precisely what they were trying to avoid; one of their main objectives was to protect the rights of individuals and of minorities, both "the minority of the opulent" and also other minorities. The theory on which the Constitution was based was explained most clearly by Madison, both in speeches to the convention and in his contributions to *The Federalist.* Regarding most political conflicts as having an economic basis, Madison argued that society always became divided into different economic groups: rich and poor; debtors and creditors; landowners, merchants, and manufacturers; and so on. One of the purposes of a good constitution was to prevent any one of these groups from acquiring exclusive control of the government and then oppressing the others. The rights of all could be protected only by a balancing of different interests. In particular, property and numbers should be balanced against each other, in such a way as to prevent both the exploitation of the poor by the rich and the robbery of the rich by the poor. Madison suggested that such a balance of interests could be achieved more easily in a federal union than in the states, since it would include a greater variety of different sectional groups.

This emphasis on balance was characteristic of much eighteenth-century thinking. It had been derived largely from Sir Isaac Newton, according to whom God maintained the harmony of the universe by balancing different physical forces against each other. The makers of the American Constitution thought in Newtonian terms. They believed that the statesman, like God, should create a balance of forces. It followed from this belief that the statesman should be above parties and should not himself be identified with any particular group. The constitution-makers recognized that "factions" were inevitable, but felt that they were dangerous and should not be allowed to control the government. A political leader, they believed, should be the representative of the whole community, not merely of a particular sectional or class interest.

The members of the convention were also in agreement about the framework of the new government. They believed that government was divided into three parts, a legislative branch, an executive branch, and a judicial branch, and that these parts ought to be, as far as possible, independent of each other. The most influential exponent of this theory of "separation of powers" was the French writer Montesquieu, who believed (incorrectly) that it was exemplified in the British government. But the Americans had already become accustomed to such a separation during the colonial period. The independence of the judiciary is, of course, one of the fundamental features of a free government; under a dictatorship the law courts are controlled by the executive. But a separation between the legislature and the executive is not essential, as has been shown by the success of parliamentary government in Great Britain and other European countries. In 1787, however, the virtues of the British system were not yet apparent. Experience under the Confederation, moreover, had shown the need of a strong and separate executive.

Conflicting Viewpoints.   The most difficult of the problems confronting the convention was the decision regarding representation in the legislature: should it be based wholly on population, as was desired by the large states, or should each state have equal power, as the small states insisted? Delegates from the small states felt that if population alone were taken into consideration, they would be consistently outvoted and discriminated against by the large states. They appear to have been thinking largely of the ubiquitous question of western land claims. Since one of them made the revolutionary suggestion that all existing boundaries be wiped out and the country redivided into thirteen regions of mathematically equal size, they do not seem to have been motivated by states' rights sentiment.

The convention began by considering a draft of a constitution, presented by the Virginia delegation, in which voting was to be based on population. Alternative proposals, representing the small states' point of view, were then put forward by the New Jersey delegation. Discussion of the issue continued through most of June and July; hot weather caused hot tempers, which led to widespread pessimism, and the deadlock seemed to be unbreakable. Eventually, however, both sides accepted a compromise sponsored by Connecticut. It was agreed that the legislature should have two houses, and that seats in the House of Representatives should be allotted on a basis of population, while in the Senate each state should be equal. This compromise was regarded, on the whole, as more of a victory for the small states.

There were also some conflicts between Northern and Southern states. The North was interested in the protection of American shipping, while the South, living almost exclusively by agriculture, disliked anything that might interfere with the export of its products to Europe. A compromise was agreed upon by which (for the benefit of the North) the Federal government might make navigation laws, while (to reassure the South) export taxes were prohibited and the importation of slaves into the country might not be prohibited for at least twenty years. Another question was whether, in determining the number of Congressmen the Southern states were entitled to, the slaves should be included as part of their population. It was agreed that three-fifths of the slaves should be so counted.

These were the only major conflicts, although there were many differences of opinion about details. The convention finished its work on September 17. Nobody regarded the proposed Constitution with complete approval, but thirty-nine of the delegates agreed to sign it and give it their support. Three had more serious objections, and the remaining thirteen had already dropped out of the convention. It was decided that ratification should be by conventions especially elected in the several states (this seemed more likely to produce a favorable result than submission either to the state legislatures or to direct popular vote), and that approval by nine states should be considered sufficient. This was, of course, contrary to the Articles of Confederation, but, in view of the attitude of Rhode Island, to abide by the rule of unanimity meant almost certain defeat.

The Framework of the Constitution. The most distinctive feature of the Federal Constitution was the division of authority between the Union and the states. Within its own sphere of action the Federal government was to exercise full rights of sovereignty. It was to have direct coercive power over individuals; Federal laws and treaties were to be binding upon state officials and law courts; and the state militia could be called upon by the Federal government to enforce Federal authority. The Union was thus much more than a mere league of states. If any state disobeyed Federal laws, its officials could be held personally responsible. The constitution-makers clearly recognized that the Union would not be effective if it did not have direct authority over individuals (a truth which has been repeatedly illustrated in the history of leagues and federations, including the League of Nations and the United Nations). But the Federal government was to have jurisdiction only within clearly prescribed limits. A number of the rights of sovereignty remained with the states.

Like the Confederation, the Federal government was to control foreign policy and national defense. It also acquired a number of new powers, the most important of which were those of taxation (limited by the rule that direct taxes must be apportioned among the states in proportion to population) and regulation of foreign and interstate commerce. And it was authorized to make any laws necessary for carrying its powers into execution, a clause which gave the Constitution enough elasticity to meet the needs of later generations.

The state governments were forbidden to do a number of things which might interfere with Federal authority or threaten national unity. They were also deprived of any power to coin money or issue paper money and were prohibited from passing any "law impairing the obligations of contracts." These clauses reflected that desire to protect property rights which had been largely responsible for the meeting of the convention. The statement about contracts, particularly after Chief Justice Marshall in the Dartmouth College case of 1819 interpreted it to cover the charters of corporations, became one of the most important items in the whole Constitution.

The convention discussed the possibility of limiting majority rule by giving direct representation to wealth: for example, by laying down high property qualifications for election to the Senate. In the end they relied mainly on a system of indirect elections. In Madison's words, they adopted "a policy of refining the popular appointments by successive filtrations." The House of Representatives, chosen directly by the people for two-year terms, would be the democratic part of the government. Voting qualifications were to be determined by the states. The Senate, on the other hand, would be more independent of popular pressure, partly because its members would be chosen by the state legislatures, not by popular vote, and partly because the Senators were to have six-year terms.

The President was even further removed from the people. He was to be chosen by an electoral college; and since it was expected that each state would put forward a candidate of its own, a somewhat complicated method of election was devised. Each member of the college was to vote for two candidates, at least one of whom was to come from another state. If no candidate received a majority of the votes, the House of Representatives, voting by states, was to make the final choice. The candidate with the second-highest vote would become Vice-President. Initially (although this was not stated in the Constitution) the members of the electoral college were chosen by the state legislatures. It was, of course, assumed that they would genuinely use their own judgment in deciding who was best qualified for the presidency. The four-year presidential term, with no bar to re-election, was a compromise between those who wanted a single term and those who favored election for life.

Thus new laws would normally have to be approved by three different authorities, two of which were not directly chosen by the electorate. In this way the will of the people, while ultimately supreme, would be checked, delayed, and (as Madison said) "refined."

The Constitution was perhaps most open to criticism in so far as it was based on the theory of the separation of powers between legislature and executive. This separation was, of course, not complete. The President had a limited veto on legislation; and the Senate had to give its consent to executive appointments and to treaties. Congress, moreover, could put pressure on the executive through its control of revenue. But no method was provided for settling disputes between the two branches of the government. There could be no immediate appeal to the people, since elections could be held only at two- and four-year intervals. Nor could the President be removed from office unless he were impeached for "treason, bribery, or other high crimes and misdemeanors" (this was a relic of English Parliamentary procedure under the Stuart kings). Conflicts between President and Congress, making it impossible for either to carry through any consistent and effective program, have proved, in practice, to be the greatest weakness of the American form of government.

Several features of the Constitution did not work out according to plan. In particular, the electoral college quickly became a mere mechanism for registering the decisions of the electorate. Contrary to both the wishes and the expectations of the constitution-makers, politicians became divided into national parties, and state divisions lost much of their importance. As early as 1796 the members of the college were pledged to vote for their party candidates and ceased to exercise any independent judgment. This made necessary the Twelfth Amendment, adopted in 1804, by which they balloted separately for President and Vice-President.

Another deviation from the original intention occurred in the control of foreign policy. According to the Constitution the President was to make treaties "by and with the advice and consent of the Senate." The Senate, in other words, was to act as a council of state cooperating with the executive in the conduct of diplomacy. But when Washington became President, he found it impossible to get effective cooperation from the Senate. The making of treaties became at once a purely executive function, although they still had to be submitted afterwards to the Senate for ratification. The requirement of a two-thirds majority was a relic of the Jay-Gardoqui negotiations; the South wanted to be sure that no treaty could be made without its consent.

In general, however, the members of the convention were remarkably successful in framing a constitution that would stand the test of time. This was largely because they restricted themselves, on the whole, to essentials, and allowed plenty of leeway for change and development.

6. RATIFICATION

Federalists and Antifederalists.   In the campaign for ratification the defenders of the Constitution could count on the approval of most of the wealthier class. They also won considerable support among two groups who were normally on the more democratic side: the urban craftsmen, who wanted a government capable of protecting American industry; and the settlers in the West, for whom national defense was a vital concern. Opposition came mostly from the farmers and their political spokesmen, and from state officials who were reluctant to surrender any of their powers to a new federal authority. To a considerable extent the contest was between the back country (exclusive of the more westerly sections) and the seaboard.

The opponents of the Constitution—men like Patrick Henry, Richard Henry Lee, and George Mason of Virginia, and George Clinton of New York—insisted that the country was sufficiently prosperous and orderly under the existing system. They suggested that the new government had been planned by a small group of ambitious men who wanted to exploit the mass of the people, and that it would quickly result in the establishment of an oppressive aristocracy or a dictatorship. They also complained of the absence of a bill of rights guaranteeing popular liberties. Other arguments were based more directly on economic interest. According to Madison, the two clauses which excited the most antagonism were the one making treaties binding on the states and the one prohibiting any impairment of contracts. The former meant that, in accordance with the peace treaty of 1782, debts due to British merchants would have to be paid, while the latter meant that no relief could be given to debtors by state legislatures.

It is quite possible that a majority of the population were initially opposed to ratification. The Federalists, however, could more easily mobilize their supporters, who were strongest along the seaboard, while their opponents were scattered through the back country. The leading Federalist spokesmen, moreover, were superior in political skill and in the clarity and reasonableness of their arguments. Particularly notable, as an exposition of the Constitution and as a permanent contribution to political theory, was the series of papers known as *The Federalist*, written for a New York newspaper by Madison, Hamilton, and Jay. In several states the conventions seemed likely at first to vote against ratification but were won over by the effective speeches and political management of the Federalists in the course of the sessions. In the end the Federalists succeeded in winning a favorable vote in every one of the state conventions.

Delaware was the first state to ratify, in December 1787. By July 1788, Pennsylvania, New Jersey, Georgia, Connecticut, Massachusetts, Maryland, South Carolina, New Hampshire, Virginia, and New York had followed in that order, making a total of eleven. In several conventions the vote was close: it was 187 to 168 in Massachusetts, 89 to 79 in Virginia, and 30 to 27 in New York. The two remaining states, North Carolina and Rhode Island, accepted the Constitution only because it was now certain to go into effect anyway.

The Bill of Rights. Five of the states ratified with the understanding that the Constitution should be amended by the addition of a bill of rights —a stipulation which some of the Federalists accepted. Ten amendments were therefore added in 1791. This Bill of Rights was based on a theory representing the point of view of the more democratic groups—a theory which had been explained very clearly in the debates of the ratifying conventions. Believing in the doctrine of a social contract, these groups insisted that sovereignty belonged only to the people and could not be alienated, and that government could exercise only those powers that the people delegated to it. There was always the danger that government would become too oppressive, and it was therefore necessary to prescribe very clearly what it could and could not do.

The Bill of Rights was based on English and American experience in dealing with oppressive governments during several centuries. The most important of its articles were the First, which prohibited Congress from abridging freedom of religion, speech, and press, and the rights of assembly and petition; the Fifth, which declared (among other things) that no person could be "deprived of life, liberty, or property without due process of law"; and the Sixth and Seventh, which guaranteed trial by jury. These were regarded as popular rights necessary for the protection of the people against corrupt or tyrannical officials. The authors of the Bill of Rights were not thinking of civil liberty in its more modern meaning, as a safeguard for individuals or minorities holding unpopular opinions. They were concerned with the protection of the majority from a minority invested with political power. These forms of freedom were considered primarily as means toward maintaining popular control of government. It did not occur to anybody in the eighteenth century that freedom of speech and press might be claimed by groups wishing to destroy rather than to defend majority rule.

The Success of the Constitution. After the Constitution had been ratified and the new government set up, the Antifederalists ceased to oppose it. This was largely due to the confidence inspired by Washington as the first President, to the competence of his administration, and to the fortunate fact that he took office at a time of rising prosperity. But it was also a proof of the political maturity of the Americans. They recognized that once a definitive decision had been reached by legal methods, it was incumbent upon all groups to accept it without further argument. The success of the Constitution should, in fact, be attributed to the character of the American people quite as much as to its intrinsic merits. As has been shown in the history of many other countries, the most perfect frame of government will fail if it is not in accord with the habits of the citizens.

Through a long period of past history, first in medieval, Tudor, and Stuart England, and afterwards in the colonies, the Americans had acquired the habits needed for successful self-government. They had become accustomed to settling disputes as far as possible by free discussion followed by balloting, not by violence; to conceding to their opponents the same rights they claimed for themselves; and to respect for the law. Eighteenth-century Americans, like all men everywhere, were largely motivated by self-interest. Their political spokesmen recognized this fact quite frankly, without hypocrisy. But they also accepted the interests of the community as paramount; with few exceptions, they did not seek personal aggrandizement to a point that would endanger national welfare and stability. They knew that, in the last resort, the success of a free government depends upon the wisdom and the self-restraint of each individual citizen.

VII

Federalists and Republicans

1. THE NEW NATION

2. WASHINGTON'S ADMINISTRATION

3. WASHINGTON'S FOREIGN POLICY

4. THE ADAMS ADMINISTRATION

5. JEFFERSON'S FIRST ADMINISTRATION

IN VIEW of the character and traditions of the American people, the success of the Constitution seems, in retrospect, easy to understand. But in 1789 it looked like a very hazardous experiment. In almost all other countries monarchy was still regarded as the normal and only effective form of government. Throughout previous history republics had usually shown a lack of concerted energy and an inability to maintain the unity that is essential to peace and progress; and the republican form of government had rarely proved successful in any area larger than a city state. How then could a republican government hope to keep control over a country so vast and so undeveloped as the United States? The early years of the Constitution were of crucial importance in demonstrating that free institutions were not incompatible with the maintenance of national solidarity or with vigorous and efficient administration.

SELECTED BIBLIOGRAPHY: C. G. Bowers, *Jefferson and Hamilton* (1925), is a lively account of political history from 1789 to 1801, but is strongly biased in favor of Jefferson. The same author's *Jefferson in Power* (1936) continues the story down to 1809. The most useful biography of Hamilton is by Nathan Schachner (1946). The standard work on Jefferson is Dumas Malone, *Jefferson and His Times* (1948–), of which two volumes have appeared so far. A. Koch and W. Peden (eds.), *The Life and Selected Writings of Thomas Jefferson* (1944), is a useful anthology. Henry Adams, *A History of the United States of America During the Administrations of Thomas Jefferson and James Madison*, first published between 1889 and 1891, is a classic, and the first volume contains an outstanding portrayal of American society in 1800. L. D. White's two books, *The Federalists* (1948) and *The Republicans* (1951), deal with the important and often-neglected subject of administrative methods. For foreign affairs, there are two excellent one-volume surveys: T. A. Bailey, *Diplomatic History of the American People* (revised edition, 1955), and S. F. Bemis, *Diplomatic History of the United States* (revised edition, 1955).

1. THE NEW NATION

BEFORE turning to the organization of the new government, let us look briefly at this new member of the concert of nations. Its area at the time of the adoption of the Constitution was about 800,000 square miles, less than half of which had so far been organized into states. According to the first census, taken in 1790, the population was less than 4,000,000, among whom nearly 800,000 were Negroes. Close to 2,000,000 lived in the New England and Middle Atlantic states, and 1,850,000 in the South, while scarcely 100,000 persons had settled in the Western territories. In all sections the vast majority were still rural and agricultural. Only 5 per cent of the total population lived in urban areas, and only six towns in the whole country had more than 8,000 inhabitants, these being (in order of size) Philadelphia, New York, Boston, Charleston, Baltimore, and Salem.

Effective central government was likely to be difficult in a country where a relatively small population was scattered over a wide area, particularly in view of the difficulties of communication and transportation. There were no hard-surfaced roads; all roads were merely dirt tracks, likely to be impossible for wheeled traffic in rainy or snowy weather. Before 1800 more or less regular stagecoach services were in operation between cities as far apart as Boston and Baltimore, but coaches frequently took as many days as the hours needed by a modern railroad. Travelers generally went by horseback, while heavy goods could be transported only by water along the seacoast or up navigable rivers. It took no less than twenty-nine days for news of the completion of the Constitution to be carried from Philadelphia to Charleston. The discomforts of travel were greatly increased by the lack of good hotel accommodations. Inns were generally filthy; food was poor; and several people often had to sleep not only in the same room but even in the same bed. Under such conditions few people visited far from their homes; and the average American, having no personal acquaintance with other parts of the country, was likely to think in local rather than national terms.

Economic methods and ways of living were, by twentieth-century standards, equally primitive. Most of the burdensome tasks had not yet been eased by the advance of science and technology. Life for the mass of the people was somewhat less arduous than in Europe, chiefly because of the abundance and fertility of the land; the average American farmer had more to eat, and labored less incessantly, than the European peasant. But he still relied on the same implements that his ancestors had used for thousands of years, and enjoyed none of those mechanical contrivances that his modern descendants have learned to take for granted. His diet consisted mainly of corn and salt pork, with vegetables only in the appropriate season; and he usually grew up, raised children, and died without benefit of professional medical attention.

In the towns life was somewhat more luxurious, at least for the wealthy class. Yet if any modern American were transported back to the Philadelphia or New York of 1789, he would be horrified by the manifold discomforts. Scarcely any organization had yet been set up to deal with the problems of urban life. There were no sewers, and garbage was thrown into the streets to be eaten by wandering herds of pigs. Housewives in need of water had to go to the nearest pump, which might be several blocks away. Fires, which were frequent, were dealt with by volunteer fire brigades; and although a watchman was employed to patrol the un-lighted streets at night, there was no regular police force. Having no sound ideas about sources of infection, the people in eighteenth-century cities suffered from frequent outbreaks of smallpox, cholera, yellow fever, and other diseases. Philadelphia, in 1793, for example, was attacked by a yellow-fever epidemic which killed a tenth of its inhabitants. During the 1780's and 1790's a number of cities were incorporated by state legis-latures, thereby acquiring power to elect their own officials and exercise other rights of self-government. But urban population increased too fast for civic organization to keep abreast of it.

The eighteenth-century American differed from his modern successor not only in his lack of scientific and technological knowledge but also in his social attitudes. His mind had not yet been permeated by the new revolutionary doctrine of the rights of man. The concept of democracy was new and untried, and for many people obviously dangerous. Class lines were sharply drawn and were emphasized by wide differences of clothing, manners, and ways of living. Wealthy merchants and planters still took it for granted that they had the right to rule, and their claims to leadership were accepted by many of the poorer classes. The general tone of eighteenth-century life, moreover, would appear somewhat brutal by modern standards. People took physical suffering for granted, and society recognized little responsibility for alleviating it. For example, criminals were still flogged or executed in public. Dueling was still an ac-cepted method for settling quarrels among the upper classes in New York and the South, while among the lower classes, especially on the frontier, there was much rough-and-tumble fighting of an extremely savage kind.

During the past century and a half Western civilization in the United States and elsewhere has been transformed by the combined impact of the Industrial Revolution, the growth of democracy, and the spread of humanitarian ideas. These have brought about more fundamental changes in ways of living than any previous development in human his-tory since the discovery of agriculture. But these forces could become fully effective only as a result of the establishment of political institutions under which order and security were combined with individual liberty.

2. WASHINGTON'S ADMINISTRATION

Launching the New Government. The Federal government went into operation in the spring of 1789, New York City being the first capital.

Washington had, of course, been the unanimous choice of the electoral college for the presidency, while John Adams of Massachusetts became the first Vice-President. Convinced that his abilities would not be equal to the task ahead of him, and declaring that he felt like a criminal going to his execution, Washington left Mount Vernon to assume his new duties with the greatest reluctance. In his inaugural address he gave expression in memorable words to the immense importance of the responsibility entrusted to him, declaring that "the preservation of the sacred fire of liberty and the destiny of the republican model of government are justly considered, perhaps, as *deeply*, as *finally* staked on the experiment entrusted to the hands of American people."

The first few months were necessarily devoted to the enormous task of getting the new government organized. Congress, under the leadership of Madison, quickly voted tariff duties which provided enough revenue for immediate expenses. Meanwhile, Washington himself had to create an administration and select all its officials before any important measures could be executed. Himself an excellent administrator, he insisted on equally high standards among his subordinates, and made every effort to give appointments only to men of ability, good reputation, and complete integrity. In eighteenth-century Europe honesty among public officials was a somewhat rare phenomenon, and the standard set by the new American government was undoubtedly far higher than that of any other country in the world except Prussia. Probably it was higher under Washington than it has ever been since. The only criticism that may be made of Washington's methods is that he appointed only men who had supported the Constitution. But in view of the bitter controversy over this document and the precarious margin of its adoption, such a policy seemed necessary for the success of the new government, even if it meant that the Federal bureaucracy represented only one side of public opinion.

The two chief positions in the administration, those of Secretary of State and Secretary of the Treasury, were given to Thomas Jefferson and Alexander Hamilton. The first Cabinet also included General Henry Knox of Massachusetts as Secretary of War and Edmund Randolph of Virginia as Attorney General. A Cabinet had not been prescribed by the Constitution; but Washington always preferred to seek advice before making any decision, and from the beginning the Cabinet became part of the machinery of government.

The Constitution had also left vague the organization of the judiciary; but the gap was filled by the enactment in 1789 of a Judiciary Act, which declared that the Supreme Court was to have six members and also set up thirteen district and three circuit courts. John Jay of New York was Washington's choice for Chief Justice. The Judiciary Act made it plain that Federal judges were to interpret the Constitution as the supreme law, and as early as 1791 and 1792 circuit courts exercised this function by invalidating state laws and also an act of the Federal Congress.[1] Thus the doctrine of judicial review, which had already been stated by Hamilton in one of the *Federalist* papers, quickly became a part of the Federal system of government, although its importance was not recognized until it was asserted by the Supreme Court in the case of Marbury v. Madison in 1803.

Alexander Hamilton. The main task confronting the new government was to work out a program for dealing with financial and economic problems. This was the responsibility of Alexander Hamilton, whose recommendations were generally accepted by Washington and who quickly became a dominating figure in the administration. In lucidity of mind and administrative ability no American statesman has surpassed him. On the other hand, he thought in traditional European terms, and was totally lacking in sympathy with the emergent spirit of democracy that distinguished American society.

Born in the West Indies in 1757, Hamilton had come to New York while still a boy to seek his fortune; and after serving through most of the War of Independence as an officer on Washington's staff, he had married into the wealthy, landowning Schuyler family and become a lawyer in New York City. Believing that the mass of mankind were incapable of governing themselves, and despising democratic idealists as doctrinaire and impractical, he felt that law, order, good government, and individual liberties could be preserved only through the rule of an aristocracy. The main purpose of his financial policies was, therefore, to establish an alliance between the Federal government and the wealthy class. Hamilton was arrogant and ambitious, but there is no reason to doubt the sincerity of his beliefs, which he expressed with a frankness that was often indiscreet. He was a man of great personal charm and superlative courage, and his financial integrity, though sometimes challenged, appears to have been complete.

Public Credit. Hamilton's financial program was embodied in a series of reports submitted to Congress during 1790 and 1791. In the first of them, the Report on Public Credit, he recommended that the debt inherited from the Confederation (totaling about $50,000,000) should be funded at its face value and that the Federal government should also assume the debts of the states (which amounted to an additional $20,-000,000). The Treasury, he believed, could raise enough money by taxation to make regular interest payments and eventually to pay off the principal. Such a policy would strengthen the Federal government by winning the support of all public creditors, while at the same time it would provide the moneyed classes with capital for new business enterprises.

The main objection to this plan was that much of the public debt was now held by a relatively small number of speculators, who had bought

---

[1] In the first Hayburn case, in 1792, a circuit court refused to execute an act of Congress requiring the courts to pass on pension claims, on the ground that such a duty was beyond the scope of the judiciary.

up at heavy discounts many of the certificates held by veterans. Men who had acquired certificates for as little as 20 per cent of their face value would now receive 100 per cent in return, the community as a whole being taxed to pay them. For Hamilton, however, this was a positive advantage: money spread through the nation would be spent on consumption, but money accumulated in the hands of a small class would be available for investment.

Congress voted by a substantial majority to fund the debt of the Confederation, the passage of the measure being considerably eased by the fact that nearly half the members of the House of Representatives were themselves holders of certificates. But the proposal to assume the state debts aroused more antagonism, chiefly because the debts of the Northern states were much larger than those of the South. It was therefore opposed by Southern Congressmen, who were beginning to feel that Hamilton's program was designed mainly for the benefit of Northern business groups. Hamilton, however, arranged a bargain through Jefferson, who had not yet made up his mind about the policies of his colleague. Congress was also debating the location of the new Federal capital provided for by the Constitution. Jefferson persuaded some of the Virginia Congressmen not to vote against the assumption plan, while in return Hamilton, through his influence with the Pennsylvania Congressmen, arranged that the Federal capital should be built on the Potomac rather than farther north. The government moved to Philadelphia in 1790 and to the new city of Washington in 1800.

The Excise.   In a report on taxation, Hamilton recommended that, in addition to the tariff, the government should raise money through an excise duty on whisky, not only for financial reasons but also to strengthen Federal power through the back country. In general, Hamilton regarded taxes as positively beneficial, since they would compel people to engage in productive enterprise and make it impossible for them to live merely by subsistence farming. The duty was voted by Congress, and caused trouble in western Pennsylvania. In 1794 attempts to collect the duty led to open defiance of Federal authority, chiefly among the Scotch-Irish, wherupon Hamilton persuaded Washington to call out the militia of four states to enforce obedience. This demonstration of Federal authority speedily put an end to this so-called "Whisky Rebellion" and showed that the new government was capable of enforcing obedience to its decisions.

The Bank.   In another report Hamilton recommended the establishment of a bank. Like the rest of his program, the proposal was based largely on British experience. The projected Bank of the United States, like the Bank of England, was to assist the government by holding its funds, and, when necessary, by making loans. By issuing notes that would circulate as money, the bank would help to maintain an adequate and stable currency; and by extending credit to businessmen engaging in new enterprises, it would promote economic expansion. One-fifth of the capital was to be contributed by the government, and four-fifths by private investors, so that ownership and control of the bank would be predominantly in private hands.

In order to understand Hamilton's arguments for the bank, it should be realized that the Treasury proposed to restrict its issue of money to the coinage of gold and silver, and not to print any paper money. According to orthodox economic doctrine, precious metal was the only reliable form of currency, though it could be supplemented by bank notes as long as these could always be redeemed for gold or silver and were issued in strictly limited quantities. During the eighteenth century the American people had had unhappy experiences with paper money not backed by gold or silver, and it was assumed that, as a result of lack of public confidence, such money could never serve as a reliable medium of exchange. Thus the amount of money in circulation must always be limited by the amount of precious metal available. Later generations, through the nineteenth and twentieth centuries, were to see prolonged and bitter controversies between supporters of a currency based on precious metal and groups who wished the government to increase the amount of money in circulation by issuing notes not redeemable in gold or silver.

Hamilton's bank plan was opposed by Jefferson, who by this time had developed a number of objections to the whole Hamiltonian program. Jefferson felt that the bank would give excessive power over the national economy, and too many opportunities for making large profits, to a small group of private investors. But he chose to oppose the bank on the ground that the chartering of it was not explicitly authorized by the Constitution. To Jefferson's argument that the functions of the Federal government should be limited by a "strict construction" of the words of the Constitution, Hamilton replied by developing a theory of "implied powers." Washington supported Hamilton, and in 1791 the bank was established by Congress with a charter to run for twenty years.

Aid for Manufacturing. In his final report Hamilton recommended Federal aid to manufacturing. Criticizing the *laissez-faire* doctrine of Adam Smith, he argued that infant industries in a young country needed protection, and that the United States ought to aim at greater economic independence of Europe. He suggested a higher protective tariff, direct subsidies, and various other measures. This report, however, had little immediate effect. The two economic groups with the greatest influence in Congress were the Northern merchants (who had secured a Navigation Act for the protection of American shipping in 1789) and the Southern planters; and neither was interested in proposals which would tend to reduce foreign trade. The manufacturing interest did not become strong enough to obtain much government protection until after the War of 1812.

Formation of Political Parties. In spite of the general belief that political parties necessarily led to corruption and to government in the interests of a dominant faction rather than of the community as a whole, the divergent ideals and economic interests among the American people quickly caused them to become divided into two opposing groups. Hamilton's financial program served as a catalyst. Its supporters, being largely the same men who had campaigned for the ratification of the Constitution, continued to call themselves Federalists, while their opponents assumed the name of Republicans.[2]

Hamilton's political theories, and the policies that implemented them, appealed to those who believed in government by "the wise, the rich, and the wellborn," and who felt that democracy meant mob rule and anarchy. His policies benefited merchants, financiers, and manufacturers rather than planters and farmers, and were thus more advantageous to the North than to the more exclusively agricultural South. The Federalist Party therefore represented aristocracy as opposed to democracy, and business as opposed to agriculture; and while it had some support from wealthy men in the South, it was predominantly a Northern party. The backbone of the organization consisted of the Northern merchants, especially in New England.

The opposition to Hamilton began among the Southern planters. Madison, who had originally been the spokesman for the administration in the House of Representatives, had turned against Hamilton in 1790 during the debate on the public-credit proposals. Although he had been a leading Federalist during the making of the Constitution, Madison was quite consistent in his views; he believed in a balance between opposing interests, whereas Hamilton's program appeared to mean an exclusive domination by the moneyed interest. During the controversy about the bank, Madison was joined by Jefferson; and the two men then set out to find allies. They could already count on the support of most of the South, and in the North there were a number of influential men who had either political or personal reasons for disliking Hamilton. In particular, there was George Clinton, who was still (in spite of his opposition to the Constitution) Governor of New York; while in New York City there was a rising young lawyer named Aaron Burr, who was soon to develop some useful connections with a democratic political club known as the Tammany Society. An alliance between the Virginians and the New Yorkers thus became the nucleus of the new Republican Party. Jefferson and Madison also won support from democratic elements in New England (including the elderly Sam Adams and his followers) and in Pennsylvania (which supplied Albert Gallatin, a young immigrant from Switzerland who became the party expert on finance).

The new party was far from being an embodiment of pure idealism.

[2] This original Republican Party corresponds to the present Democratic Party, the name being changed during the Jacksonian period. The modern Republican Party was founded in 1854.

It included a fair proportion of ambitious office-hunters who were interested in patronage rather than in principles. Aaron Burr, for example (despite an ancestry heavily studded with Puritan ministers and college presidents), was an unscrupulous adventurer, endowed with great personal charm but with no morals whatever. For such leaders as Jefferson and Madison, however, the purpose of Republicanism was to maintain the ideals of the American Revolution: the ideals of popular government, the rights of man, and protection for the interests of the mass of the people rather than of a privileged upper class. Jefferson believed that Hamilton was secretly seeking to destroy republican government in the United States and set up a monarchy on the European style, and that his doctrine of "implied powers" would undermine those limitations of Federal authority upon which popular liberty depended. For this reason the Republicans (at any rate as long as their opponents controlled the Federal government) continued to preach "strict construction," declaring that Federal power must be limited in accordance with the words of the Constitution, and that the rights of the states must be scrupulously defended.

In actuality, of course, Hamilton had no such sinister intention. Although he frankly avowed his admiration for the British form of government, he was loyal to the Constitution as he understood it. But whereas for Jefferson the key word was always "liberty," Hamilton thought mainly of discipline. Unable to believe that any educated man could sincerely believe in rule by the people, he described Jefferson as a "contemptible hypocrite," and was convinced that his impractical doctrines would lead to general anarchy, followed probably by the dictatorship of some power-hungry demagogue or military chieftain.

The two party organizations began to take shape in 1791. Members of Congress and of the state legislatures affiliated themselves with one party or the other, and organized "caucuses" to decide on party policies and to choose candidates for forthcoming elections. Each party established its own newspapers (the editor of the principal Republican paper being the poet Philip Freneau), which engaged in the unrestrained vituperation that has always characterized American political journalism. Thus the American people became divided into two groups, each regarding the other with intense suspicion. While wealthy mercantile families in cities like Philadelphia and New York refused to have any relations with men suspected of being "democrats" (a word whose connotations were similar to those of "radical" today) and accused them of plotting to subvert all law and order and bring about anarchy, Republican craftsmen and farmers were convinced that American liberties were endangered by a monarchist conspiracy.

Washington, although generally sympathetic with the Federalists, did not believe that the government should be exclusively controlled by either party, and therefore kept both Hamilton and Jefferson in the

Cabinet. In 1792 he reluctantly agreed to accept a second term at the request of both men, neither of whom felt that the government could stand the strain of a disputed election for the presidency.

At the end of 1793 Jefferson, finding himself consistently outvoted at Cabinet meetings, finally induced Washington to allow him to resign. He was replaced by another Virginia Republican, Edmund Randolph. But Randolph was quickly ousted by the Federalists by means of charges (since proved false) of corrupt connections with the French minister, and his successor was an extreme Federalist from Massachusetts, Timothy Pickering. Thus the attempt to maintain a bipartisan Cabinet was finally abandoned, and the administration became exclusively Hamiltonian.

3. WASHINGTON'S FOREIGN POLICY

The French Revolution.   Throughout Washington's administration, and for a long time afterwards, the dominating factor in Western civilization was the French Revolution, which began in the spring of 1789. In the long run this cataclysmic event led to the overthrow of absolute monarchy and the spread of liberal institutions throughout western Europe, but its immediate results were much less desirable. After a three-year period of relatively moderate reforms, power was assumed in 1792 by a group of radical Jacobins, who professed to believe in the democratic doctrines of Jean-Jacques Rousseau. They crushed opposition groups in a ruthless reign of terror, became involved in a conflict with Great Britain and most of continental Europe, and proclaimed their intention of abolishing monarchy and spreading the ideals of the Revolution throughout the world. This was followed by twenty-three years of almost incessant war, in the course of which the Jacobin program of liberating the people of other countries gradually degenerated into French imperialism, while the Jacobins themselves gave place in 1795 to the more moderate but very corrupt government of the Directory and in 1799 to the personal rule of the most successful of the French generals, Napoleon Bonaparte. Peace was not finally re-established until Napoleon's defeat at Waterloo in 1815.

Americans of all classes were deeply interested in the progress of the Revolution, and after the rise of the Jacobins, there were sharp divergencies of opinion. While many of the Republicans continued to regard the French as engaged in a struggle for the rights of man, the Federalists were horrified by the Jacobin reign of terror and alarmed by the Jacobin program of world-wide revolution, and they interpreted events in France as a corroboration of all their fears of democracy and of the doctrinaire rationalism of the Enlightenment. Thus the Revolution did much to sharpen party differences in the United States.

Meanwhile, the long European war meant both problems and opportunities for American diplomacy. Both the British and the French showed little respect for the rights of neutrals and interfered with American trade. On the other hand, their preoccupation with the struggle in Europe meant that they could no longer pay much attention to the affairs of the Western Hemisphere. By refusing to become involved with either side, the United States was able to strengthen her position on the North American mainland.

Washington's Neutrality Policy. Washington closely supervised the foreign policy of his administration, displaying an invaluable realism and coolness of judgment. One of his primary concerns was to make it plain that the United States was a genuinely independent country, concerned with the defense of her own interests, and no longer the subsidiary of any European power. This lesson, he felt, must be learned by the Americans themselves, some of whom still had a colonial psychology and kept a traditional attachment to Great Britain, while others were too passionately concerned with the conflict of ideologies in Europe. As he declared in his Farewell Address, "Nothing is more essential than that permanent, inveterate antipathies against particular nations and passionate attachments for others should be excluded; and that in place of them just and amicable feelings towards all should be cultivated." While Washington was not opposed to war and to temporary alliances with other countries when American interests were at stake, he believed that the United States needed a long period of peace in order to build up her strength, even if this meant some temporary surrender of American rights. He therefore resisted both Federalist pressure for involvement on the side of Britain and Republican pressure for aid to France.

When the war started, the French apparently assumed that the treaty of alliance of 1778 was still in force; while they did not expect the United States to become a belligerent, they were hoping for sympathy and economic assistance. The first diplomatic representative of the French Republic, Edmond Charles Genêt, tried to use American ports as bases for French privateers, enlisted American citizens for a projected invasion of the Spanish colonies, and meddled in American internal politics on the side of the Republicans. But in April 1793 Washington issued a proclamation affirming American neutrality; and when Genêt continued his activities, Washington asked for his recall. Fearful of being guillotined if he returned to France, Genêt remained in the United States as a private citizen, marrying a daughter of Governor Clinton and settling down as a farmer in the Hudson Valley.

Controversies with Britain. The next threat to American neutrality came from the British navy, which established a blockade of France and the French colonies, including those in the West Indies. The British began to seize American ships carrying goods that belonged to French citizens or bringing to French ports articles declared to be contraband.

American protests that "free ships make free goods" and that only goods destined for the use of armed forces could fairly be considered contraband were disregarded.

An even more flagrant violation of neutral rights was the British practice of impressment. The British government insisted that any of its subjects found among the crews of neutral ships might be impressed for service in the British navy, and regarded anybody of British birth as still a British subject, refusing to recognize any right to change citizenship by naturalization. British naval officers in need of men therefore began to stop American ships and search them for British subjects, and in a number of instances they proceeded to impress men of bona fide American birth.

In addition to the blockade and impressment, other American grievances were the continued British occupation of posts south of the Great Lakes and the British assistance given to Indian tribes in the Northwest Territory. In 1791 Indians equipped with British weapons had defeated Arthur St. Clair, Governor of the Territory, in a battle in what is now western Ohio.

By the spring of 1794 the two countries were dangerously close to war. Washington, however, was determined to try to negotiate a settlement, and was supported by the Federalists, who were motivated not only by their fear of revolutionary France but also by economic considerations. The New England merchants carried on valuable trade with Great Britain, and much of it was financed by British bankers. In spite of British confiscations, they were making big profits as a result of the war, and much preferred taking their chances with the British navy to having any breach of commercial relations. Washington therefore dispatched Chief Justice John Jay as envoy extraordinary to Great Britain. Jay's task was rendered easier by events in the Northwest Territory. In the summer of 1794 General Anthony Wayne defeated the Indians in the battle of Fallen Timbers—an event which ended British hopes of keeping control of the Territory.

Jay's Treaty, signed in November 1794 and ratified the following year, was a diplomatic defeat for the United States. This was not wholly Jay's fault, since Hamilton threw away his one trump card by assuring the British minister in Philadelphia that under no circumstances would the United States join forces with Britain's opponents. The British did agree to evacuate the Northwest Territory. On the other hand, Jay accepted the British position on neutral rights of trade and failed to secure any substantial commercial concessions. In the United States the treaty was vehemently denounced by the Republicans as a surrender to Britain. Washington, however, decided that it was preferable to war, and at his recommendation the Senate ratified it. Most historians have felt that this was a wise decision.

Pinckney's Treaty. This diplomatic failure in London was followed by a success at Madrid. Since the beginning of his administration Washington had been attempting to secure the opening of the Mississippi to American trade. In 1795 Spain became an ally of France, and her government, anticipating war with Great Britain, resolved to establish friendly relations with the United States. The American minister, Thomas Pinckney, was able to negotiate a treaty by which Americans could have unlimited use of the Mississippi and could deposit at New Orleans, duty-free, goods intended for export. Spain also promised to restrain the Indian tribes on the American frontier, and agreed to a boundary settlement in accordance with American claims.

Thus, before the end of Washington's administration, much had been done to establish American security in the West. In the long run, control of the Northwest Territory and free navigation of the Mississippi were much more vital to American development than neutral rights of trade.

Washington's Retirement. Worn out by the duties of an office which he had never wished to occupy, Washington insisted on retiring at the end of his second term in 1797. He died two years later. On leaving public life, he summarized his political beliefs in a Farewell Address. Like most presidential state papers, this was a cooperative product (both Madison and Hamilton helped to write it), but the ideas were Washington's. The most famous passage in the address dealt with foreign policy. "Europe," he declared, "has a set of primary interests, which to us have none, or a very remote relation . . . 'Tis our true policy to steer clear of permanent alliances with any portion of the foreign world. . . . We may safely trust to temporary alliances for extraordinary emergencies." In expressing these sentiments Washington was thinking primarily of the dangerous partisanships excited among the American people by the French Revolution. He believed that the best interests of the United States would be served, as long as she remained a relatively weak country, by remaining aloof from European entanglements. His doctrine of isolation was intended as a temporary expedient, not as a permanent policy for the guidance of future generations after the United States had become one of the world's great powers.

4. THE ADAMS ADMINISTRATION

The Election of 1796. With the country divided into militant factions, the presidency now became a party question. The Federalists decided to vote for John Adams, who was not closely identified with the party but was likely to be a much more popular candidate than Hamilton, while the Republicans supported Jefferson. Sixteen state legislatures took part in the choice of the electoral college, Vermont, Kentucky, and Tennessee having now been added to the original thirteen. The result was a narrow victory for Adams, the vote in the electoral college being 71 to 68.

Founder of a family which was to play a distinguished part in American life for a century and a half, Adams was an able lawyer, an accomplished student of political theory, belligerently outspoken, and incorruptibly honest. Although he had first entered politics as the protégé of his cousin Sam, he had no faith in the wisdom of the majority; on the other hand (unlike the more extreme Federalists), he was not tempted to identify wisdom with riches and aristocratic lineage. Like many of the constitution-makers, he believed that liberty could be preserved only by balancing wealth against numbers.

Unfortunately for his success as President, Adams often showed poor judgment in practical questions. His first mistake was to retain Washington's Cabinet, the members of which continued to look to Hamilton for leadership. Hamilton himself, unable to support his family on his salary, had returned to his law practice in January of 1795. But even out of office he still directed the policy of Federalist legislators and administrators. Until 1799, when Adams finally asserted his control, it was mainly Hamilton who shaped the program of the administration.

Controversies with France.   The next two years were occupied mainly with foreign affairs. Washington's restraining hand having been removed, the Federalists now moved towards war with France, and the French government seemed willing to meet them halfway. The French were indignant with the United States for accepting the British blockade policies in Jay's Treaty, and regarded America as virtually an ally of Britain. French privateers therefore began to attack American merchant ships, and had seized more than three hundred of them by the summer of 1797. When Adams dispatched a mission of three men (John Marshall, C. C. Pinckney, Elbridge Gerry) to negotiate with the French government, they were unable to see any high officials but were visited instead by three anonymous Frenchmen (always referred to in official documents as Messrs. X, Y, and Z), who explained that a bribe for the French foreign minister and a loan for the French government were prerequisites for negotiation, and hinted that if the Federalists did not comply with French wishes, they might be overthrown by a revolution in the United States. The American envoys refused to do business on these terms; and when, in the spring of 1798, their report of the X.Y.Z. affair was made public, there was a burst of popular indignation. "Millions for defense, but not one cent for tribute" became the slogan of the moment.

War indeed appeared imminent. The Federalists seemed to want it for political reasons, as a means of checking the growth of Republicanism, and also because they were genuinely alarmed by the French program of world-wide revolution. In anticipation of hostilities, the navy was enlarged and merchant ships were armed; and for a year there was actually an undeclared naval war in the West Indies, in which eighty-four French ships, most of them privateers, were captured by the Americans. War with

France would mean war also with her ally Spain, and the Federalists made ambitious plans for an attack on Spain's American colonies. Hamilton was scheduled to take command of the American army in the field, and he began to dream of winning a military glory that would make him indisputably the leading figure in the country.

The Alien and Sedition Acts. Meanwhile, measures were taken to suppress what the Federalists regarded as revolutionary propaganda and to deal with the French agents who were allegedly undermining American institutions. In 1798 Congress passed the Alien and Sedition Acts. The Alien Act empowered the President to expel foreigners by executive decree, although Adams, who disapproved of such legislation, never made use of this power. The Sedition Act was more important. Intended in part to provide machinery for dealing with revolutionary conspiracies, it also prescribed penalties for anybody who spoke or wrote against President or Congress with the intention of bringing them "into contempt or disrepute"—a phrase vague enough to make it a threat to anyone engaging in public criticism of the administration.

This act was clearly a violation of the first article of the Bill of Rights. It was, moreover, enforced with excessive severity by the judges, most of whom were strong Federalists. Twenty-four Republican newspaper editors, along with many other individuals, were arrested under the Sedition Act, and ten of them were fined or imprisoned. Obviously, the Republican leaders had to find some way of reasserting their constitutional liberties; and since nothing could be expected from the Federalist Supreme Court, they turned instead to the state legislatures. The legislatures of Virginia and Kentucky denounced the Alien and Sedition Acts in two sets of resolutions, written, respectively, by Madison and by Jefferson. According to the argument of the Kentucky Resolutions, when the Federal government transgressed the powers delegated to it by the Constitution, it was the duty of the states to unite in declaring such Federal acts void and demanding their repeal. No other state responded to this suggestion, however; and Jefferson and Madison (unlike later exponents of the states' rights theory, such as John C. Calhoun) did not believe that the states could nullify Federal legislation unless all of them took action together.

Peace with France. Fortunately for American liberties, the expected war with France never materialized. The Federalists had expected that the French would begin it. But early in 1799 the French government indicated that it was willing to negotiate a settlement, and that if a new American mission were sent to Paris, there would be no repetition of the X.Y.Z. affair. Greatly to the disgust of the Federalists in Congress and in his Cabinet, John Adams insisted that this offer should be accepted. For the first time, he now asserted his control of his own administration, dismissing Secretary of State Pickering when he refused to agree to this change in policy. Adams recognized that in making peace with France he was playing into the hands of the Republicans, who had insisted all along that war was unnecessary, and was thereby jeopardizing his own chances of re-election; but he refused to be deflected by personal or party interest from doing what he regarded as his duty.

When the new American envoys reached Paris, they found Napoleon in power, and were unable to do much more than sign an agreement stating that the two countries were at peace with each other. But by this time any popular desire for war in the United States had completely evaporated.

The Election of 1800.   The Federalist caucus reluctantly agreed to support Adams for re-election in 1800, although Hamilton hoped that if they won a majority in the electoral college, they might contrive to give the presidency to the man who was nominally their vice-presidential candidate, C. C. Pinckney. The Republicans nominated Jefferson and Aaron Burr. The election provoked bitter class feelings, and some of the New England Federalists, still suffering from their alarm about the French Revolution, accused Jefferson of being in league with the Jacobins. An American dictatorship, a reign of terror, and the abolition of religion and of marriage were declared to be probable consequences of a Republican victory. But such attempts to stir up panic had little effect. The Federalists had lost too much of their popular support as a result of their war program and their attack on civil liberties. The Republicans won control of most of the Middle and Southern states, with a majority in the electoral college of 73 to 65.

As a result of a legal complication, Jefferson was not immediately declared the next president. According to the Constitution, each member of the electoral college voted for two candidates, and each of the Republicans (with an unprecedented display of party regularity) voted for both Jefferson and Burr, thereby causing a tie. This meant that the final choice had to be made by the House of Representatives, which was about equally divided between the two parties. The Federalist Congressmen decided to vote for Burr, who seemed willing to betray his own party and come to terms with them. Thirty-five ballots were taken, without a majority for either candidate. Eventually the deadlock was broken by the intervention of Hamilton, who recognized the dangers of this cynical attempt to frustrate the intention of the electorate. At his behest enough of the Federalists cast blank ballots to give a majority to Jefferson. In 1804 the Twelfth Amendment made any repetition of such a situation impossible. Henceforth the electoral college balloted separately for president and vice-president.

Although the Federalists had to surrender their control of the executive and legislative branches of the government, they set out before leaving office to entrench themselves in the judiciary. John Adams was still President until midnight on March 3, 1801; and during the last days of his administration he was able to appoint many new Federal judges. By the Judiciary Act of 1801, passed by the lame-duck Congress, the number of district and circuit judges was considerably enlarged. All of these so-called "midnight appointments" went to determined Federalists.

Adams was able also to appoint a new Chief Justice of the Supreme Court, and the nomination went to John Marshall, a Virginia Federalist who had succeeded Pickering as Secretary of State. This was possibly the most important action taken by Adams during his presidency. In the long run, the decisions handed down by Marshall and other Federalist judges probably had more influence on American development than the policies pursued by Jefferson. Under Marshall's leadership the courts interpreted the Constitution in such a way as to extend Federal powers and limit those of the states. They also gave maximum protection to the property rights of the business classes. The Federalist Party never won another national election, but through its control of the judiciary it had a continuing effect on American institutions.

5. JEFFERSON'S FIRST ADMINISTRATION

Thomas Jefferson.   Jefferson owes his special place in history primarily to the fact that, with the possible exception of Lincoln, he could express ideas more pointedly and unforgettably than any other American statesman; and some of his phrases are inseparably associated with the democratic faith. Throughout his long career he continued to assert that all men, not merely a privileged few, were endowed with rights, and that the protection of these rights was the primary purpose of government and social organization. Animated by the optimism of the Enlightenment, he insisted that men were naturally good and inclined to follow the guidance of reason, although he also believed that they might be corrupted by bad institutions. He shared, however, some of the limitations of his time and background. A product of the agrarian society of Virginia, he idealized agriculture as the only way of life that prompted moral and political virtue. Big cities, he believed, made men corrupt; neither the urban business class nor the urban proletariat could be trusted to defend free institutions. This meant that Americans would keep their liberties only as long as they continued to be mainly farmers and there was enough territory to prevent overcrowding of the land. "When we get piled upon one another in large cities, as in Europe," Jefferson declared, "we shall become corrupt as in Europe, and go to eating one another as they do there."

Jefferson was typical of the Enlightenment not only in his view of life but also in the extraordinary breadth of his interests. The most variously gifted of American presidents, he was equally at home in the arts and in science. He wrote an essay on English poetry, collected pictures, had a passion for music, and was the finest architect of his time. Interested in everything that promised to improve human life, he was a philosopher, a naturalist, and a scientific agriculturalist. He invented an improved kind of plow and experimented with plants of all sorts, and being as gadget-minded as Franklin, he filled his home at Monticello with novel labor-saving devices. In his old age he founded the University of Virginia, personally designing the buildings, selecting the faculty, and planning the curriculum.

He was more effective, however, as a thinker than as a man of action. Too thin-skinned to enjoy a fight, he often preferred to evade or compromise an issue rather than meet it directly. His policies as President, therefore, turned out to be much milder than his statements had led people to expect. He sincerely believed, moreover, that the best government was that which governed least, and that this applied particularly to the Federal government. So, although he claimed that the election of 1800 was the equivalent of a revolution, he contented himself with reversing some of the Federalist policies and made few positive innovations. In this policy of moderation he was supported by his two chief advisers, Madison as Secretary of State and Gallatin as Secretary of the Treasury. Some of the more extreme Southern Republicans, on the other hand, soon began to complain that he was little better than a Federalist.

Domestic Affairs.   Having won control of both houses of Congress, the Republicans abolished the whisky excise and allowed the Alien and Sedition Acts to expire, while Gallatin severely cut government expenditures, especially on the army and navy, and planned to pay off the debt as rapidly as possible. Presented with a bureaucracy composed wholly of Federalists, Jefferson dismissed some in order to make room for Republicans, and retained others, thereby offending extremists in both parties. This middle-of-the-road program made such a startling contrast to the extravagant predictions of national ruin which had been made by the Federalist leaders during the campaign that many of their followers began to reconsider their party allegiance. This tendency was encouraged by Jefferson, who regarded the Republicans as the true representatives of the American people and the average Federalist voter as a well-meaning citizen led astray by monarchist conspirators.

The only domestic issue that led to serious conflict was the power of the judiciary. The bench was manned almost wholly by Federalists, who had shown a marked partisanship in enforcing the Sedition Act. The Republicans regarded their conduct as an abuse of judicial power and were further alarmed when, in the case of Marbury v. Madison in 1803, Chief Justice Marshall made a forceful assertion of the right of the Supreme Court to invalidate acts of Congress.

Marbury was one of the men appointed to the bench during the last days of the Adams administration, but he never received his commission, which was withheld by Secretary of State Madison. Marbury thereupon appealed to the courts for a writ of mandamus which would compel Madison to deliver the commission, and in accordance with a section of the Judiciary Act of 1789, he brought his case directly to the Supreme Court. The decision of the Court, written by Chief Justice Marshall, was a masterpiece of both legal reasoning and political dexterity. The gist of it was that the Court had no constitutional authority to issue writs of mandamus and hence that the section of the Judiciary Act in question was invalid. By refusing to order Madison to deliver the commission, Marshall avoided a direct conflict with the administration. At the same time, by asserting the power of the Court to review legislative acts, he made it plain that there were limits to the power of the Republican majority in Congress.

The Republicans decided finally to proceed against the judiciary by the method of impeachment. In 1804 a district judge who had clearly become insane was successfully impeached; and proceedings were then started against Justice Chase of the Supreme Court. But although Chase had certainly shown political bias, for example by denouncing the Republicans while addressing juries, it could not be proved that he had committed any crime or misdemeanor. The prosecution, moreover, was mishandled by John Randolph of Roanoke, the brilliant but very erratic Virginia planter who led the Republicans in the House of Representatives. Chase was therefore acquitted.

After this failure Jefferson could hope only for a gradual transformation of the judiciary through the appointment of Republicans. Unfortunately, many of the Federalist judges proved to be very long-lived (notably Marshall himself, who served as Chief Justice until 1835). Thus few judgeships opened up for Republican appointments. Moreover, such Republican judges as were appointed did not always remain loyal to their party principles after being exposed to Marshall's influence. Thus, for decades of Republican rule, the judiciary continued to interpret the Constitution according to Federalist principles. Yet Jefferson's attack on the Court did accomplish one important objective—judges henceforth were more careful to show a proper impartiality and to refrain from direct participation in political conflicts.

The Louisiana Purchase. The most important achievement of Jefferson's administration was in diplomacy. In 1800, by the Treaty of San Ildefonso, Louisiana was transferred from Spain to France. The treaty was kept secret, Spanish officials continuing to govern the territory, but news of it soon leaked out. In 1802, moreover, the right of deposit at New Orleans, which the United States had obtained from Spain in 1795, was suspended. This presented the United States with an alarming prospect: France, unlike Spain, was a vigorous and expansionist power, and if she proposed to use control of the mouth of the Mississippi to block the development of the American West, the United States must inevitably be drawn into European conflicts. "The day that France takes possession of New Orleans," declared Jefferson (in spite of his previous sympathy for the

6. The War of Independence in the South

DURING THE THIRD AND FINAL PHASE OF THE WAR, THE SOUTH WAS THE MAIN scene of activity. Much of the fighting was a guerrilla struggle between small bodies of patriots and Tories. As in the earlier phases, sea power was a decisive factor.

The British captured Savannah and restored royal government in Georgia in 1778. Early in 1780 a British army, despatched by sea from New York, landed in South Carolina, captured Charleston, and won control of most of the state, receiving considerable assistance from local Tories. The British commander, Lord Cornwallis, then planned to march northwards, conquering each state in turn.

In August, 1780, General Gates, sent by Congress to assume command in the South, was decisively defeated at Camden. Cornwallis then advanced into North Carolina, but was compelled to retreat when a force of Tories, moving parallel to the main British army but farther to the west, was completely destroyed by patriot militiamen at King's Mountain. Early in 1781 Cornwallis received fresh troops and resumed his advance, while another British force led by Benedict Arnold was shipped from New York to raid Virginia. Nathanael Greene, replacing Gates as American commander, planned to harass Cornwallis's flanks and communication. After Daniel Morgan had cut to pieces a British detachment at Cowpens, Cornwallis, pursuing Morgan, came up with Greene's main army at Guilford Court House. The British were victorious, but suffered such heavy losses that Cornwallis decided to retire to the seacoast at Wilmington to recuperate. Greene then moved into South Carolina, which was held by Tories and small British garrisons. During the summer of 1781, after bitter fighting, the patriots regained control of all the Carolinas and Georgia except the seaport towns. The British defeated Greene in battles at Hobkirk Hill and Eutaw Springs, but were unable to hold their own against the guerrilla tactics of the Americans.

Meanwhile Cornwallis, abandoning the lower South, advanced into Virginia, where he joined Arnold's forces and established a base at Yorktown at the mouth of the York River. At this juncture the arrival of a French fleet under Admiral De Grasse deprived the British, for a brief but decisive period, of their control of the sea. After considering an attack on Clinton in New York, the American and French leaders decided to concentrate on Yorktown. On September 5, De Grasse defeated the British Admiral Graves in the Battle of the Capes of Chesapeake and blockaded Yorktown by sea, thus making it impossible for Cornwallis's army to be evacuated. A large American and French army, much of it transported partly by sea, was ready for action by September 28. Successful siege operations brought about Cornwallis's surrender on October 19.

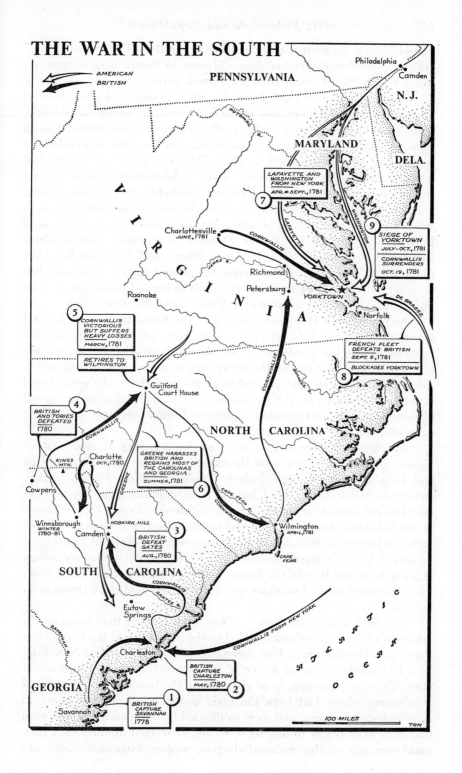

THE WAR IN THE SOUTH

AMERICAN
BRITISH

PENNSYLVANIA

Philadelphia
Camden

N.J.

MARYLAND

DELA.

VIRGINIA

⑦ LAFAYETTE AND
WASHINGTON
FROM NEW YORK
APR. & SEPT., 1781

⑨ SIEGE OF
YORKTOWN
JULY–OCT., 1781

CORNWALLIS
SURRENDERS
OCT. 19, 1781

Charlottesville
JUNE, 1781

CORNWALLIS

LAFAYETTE

Richmond

Petersburg

YORKTOWN

DE GRASSE

Roanoke

Norfolk

⑤ CORNWALLIS
VICTORIOUS
BUT SUFFERS
HEAVY LOSSES
MARCH, 1781

RETIRES TO
WILMINGTON

FRENCH FLEET
DEFEATS BRITISH
SEPT. 5, 1781

BLOCKADES YORKTOWN

⑧

Guilford
Court House

CORNWALLIS

ROANOKE R.

④ BRITISH
AND TORIES
DEFEATED
1780

CORNWALLIS

NORTH   CAROLINA

KINGS
MTN.

Charlotte
OCT., 1780

GREENE

⑥ GREENE HARASSES
BRITISH AND
REGAINS MOST OF
THE CAROLINAS
AND GEORGIA
SUMMER, 1781

CAPE FEAR R.

CORNWALLIS

Cowpens

Winnsborough
WINTER
1780-81

HOBKIRK HILL

Camden

③ BRITISH
DEFEAT
GATES
AUG., 1780

Wilmington
APRIL, 1781

CAPE
FEAR

SOUTH   CAROLINA

CORNWALLIS

SANTEE R.

Eutaw
Springs

SAVANNAH R.

CORNWALLIS FROM NEW YORK

ATLANTIC   OCEAN

Charleston

② BRITISH
CAPTURE
CHARLESTON
MAY, 1780

GEORGIA

① BRITISH
CAPTURE
SAVANNAH
1778

Savannah

100 MILES

TRM

French) ". . . we must marry ourselves to the British fleet and nation." Jefferson therefore dispatched James Monroe to Europe with instructions to try to buy New Orleans from the French government.

Before Monroe reached Paris, however, Napoleon had decided to give up the whole of Louisiana. He had sent an army across the Atlantic, with instructions to reconquer the rebellious Negroes in the former French colony of Haiti before occupying Louisiana, but the army was decimated by warfare and yellow fever in Haiti. The European war, which had temporarily ended in 1801, was now about to be resumed; and, having no troops available in America and lacking control of the sea, Napoleon could not hope to defend Louisiana against the British. He therefore decided to sell it while he still had it, believing that it would be advantageous to France to strengthen the United States as a potential rival of Great Britain. Monroe quickly agreed to the purchase of all Louisiana for about $15,000,000. This included not merely the present state of Louisiana, but an immense territory extending northwards as far as Canada and west to the Rocky Mountains, an area of well over 1,000,000 square miles.

According to a strict construction of the Constitution, the Federal government did not have authority to acquire new territory or (as was provided under the treaty with Napoleon) to promise full citizenship rights to its inhabitants. But the treaty was so obviously advantageous to the United States in general, and more particularly to the agricultural interests represented by the Republican Party, that Jefferson swallowed his scruples about the Constitution, became in effect an "implied powers" advocate, and asked the Senate to ratify it.

Another, and more serious, complication was that Monroe was unable to find out from Napoleon the exact boundaries of the territory he had bought. Did Louisiana include Texas and West Florida? Many Americans believed that it did, but the Spanish government insisted that they had not been a part of the areas transferred to France by the Treaty of San Ildefonso. Louisiana itself was formally handed over to the United States in December 1803, but Spain kept control of Texas and Florida and refused to consider suggestions that the United States would pay money in order to secure title to the latter. Yet even without these extra provinces the purchase of Louisiana was the greatest real-estate bargain in history.

The Decline of Federalism.   Nearly everything that happened in Jefferson's first administration added to the popularity of the Republican Party with the electorate. But, meanwhile, the more fanatical New England Federalists, the most active of whom was the former Secretary of State Timothy Pickering, were abandoning the belief in strong national government which had been the main contribution of their party to American development, and were so blinded by their hatred of Jefferson that they even began to discuss secession. It seemed unlikely that they could ever win another national election; western expansion would add steadily to the strength of the agricultural interests, and hence of the Republicans. So some of the Federalists began to plan a separate Northern confederation composed of New England and New York, which would protect commerce, maintain the rule of the wise and rich, and exclude the pernicious doctrines of democracy and the French Revolution. Hamilton gave them no encouragement; although he believed that Jefferson's policies would ruin the country, he was not willing to destroy the Union which he had helped to create. Moreover, he remained hopeful of a popular reaction to sound principles. The Federalists, therefore, looked elsewhere and turned to Aaron Burr, who, though still Vice-President, had lost his standing in the Republican Party as a result of his apparent willingness to make a deal with the opposition during the 1800 election.

In 1804 Burr ran for the governorship of New York, probably hoping that, if elected, he could lead a movement for a Northern confederation. Hamilton, however, plunged into the campaign and brought about Burr's defeat, thus blocking his ambitions for a second time. It was after the election that Burr challenged him to the fatal duel. Hamilton disapproved of dueling and had no intention of shooting Burr, but felt obligated to meet him lest he be accused of cowardice. The encounter took place at Weehawken, across the Hudson River from New York, early on the morning of July 11, 1804. Hamilton was fatally wounded and died thirty hours later.[3]

The factious and disunionist attitude of the Federalists proved to have suicidal effects. In the presidential election of 1804 their candidate, C. C. Pinckney, carried only two states, Connecticut and Delaware. Even Massachusetts voted for Jefferson, who was re-elected President by an electoral vote of 162 to 14.

By its lack of faith in the wisdom of the mass of the American people and its opposition to the irresistible movement towards democracy, the Federalist Party had doomed itself to rapid extinction. Yet in its relatively short career it had made an immense contribution to American development. It had given the United States an effective national government, put her finances on a sound basis, won the respect of European powers, and proved that a republican system was compatible with efficient administration. Although all American governments after the triumph of Jeffersonianism represented very different political ideals, they rested on the foundations so securely laid by the Federalists during the early years of the republic.

[3] Having no further hopes from either political party, Burr went west and engaged in some kind of conspiracy, the purposes of which are still mysterious. He may have planned to detach the Mississippi Valley from the Union; he may have proposed a filibustering expedition against the Spanish colonies; or he may merely have set out to extract money from gullible Westerners. He was arrested and tried for treason in 1807, but was acquitted for lack of sufficient evidence. Burr's later life was spent mostly in New York, where he took no further part in politics. At the age of seventy-seven he married a rich widow, and at the age of seventy-nine was divorced for adultery.

VIII

Emergent Nationalism

1. NEUTRAL RIGHTS

2. THE WAR OF 1812

3. FOREIGN POLICY OF MONROE AND ADAMS

4. NATIONALISM AND SECTIONALISM

F OR a number of years after 1805 political history was dominated by
problems of foreign policy arising from the Napoleonic Wars. The
effect on American internal development was to stimulate an aggressively
nationalist spirit, especially among the younger generation, while the Republican Party, in its efforts to protect American interests, began to
forget its original suspicion of strong central government and to adopt
many of the policies that had been sponsored by its Federalist opponents.

1. NEUTRAL RIGHTS

British and French Blockade Policies.   Jefferson's second administration was occupied almost exclusively with the attempt to maintain
American rights against the warring powers in Europe, where hostilities
between Napoleon and his opponents had been resumed in 1803. Napoleon
was for a long time almost invincible on land, and by 1807 had won control of most of the European continent. Great Britain, on the other hand,

SELECTED BIBLIOGRAPHY: The most useful books on the War of 1812 are J. W.
Pratt, *Expansionists of 1812* (1925), and F. F. Beirne, *The War of 1812* (1949). George
Dangerfield, *The Era of Good Feeling* (1952), covers the Monroe administration. Dexter
Perkins, *Hands Off* (1941), is a general history of the Monroe Doctrine. There are three
excellent books on the origins of the Doctrine: S. F. Bemis, *John Quincy Adams and the
Foundations of American Foreign Policy* (1949); Dexter Perkins, *The Monroe Doctrine, 1823–
1826* (1927); and A. P. Whitaker, *The United States and the Independence of Latin America*
(1941). The work of Chief Justice Marshall can be studied in C. B. Swisher, *American
Constitutional Development* (1943), and in more detail in Charles Warren, *The Supreme Court
in United States History*, Vol. 1 (1922), and in A. J. Beveridge's great four-volume biography
(1916–19).

established command of the sea by destroying the French navy at Tra-
falgar in 1805. Unable to attack each other directly, the two powers then
resorted to economic warfare and tried to starve each other into submission by interfering with commerce. As the leading neutral trading country,
the United States was the chief victim of this process.

As in the 1790's, the British impressed alleged deserters found on
American ships, and after 1805 they again began to seize American ships
trying to do business with the French West Indies. Negotiations with the
British government did not produce any agreement which Jefferson could
regard as satisfactory. Then, in 1806 and 1807, Napoleon issued his Berlin
and Milan Decrees, embodying his "Continental System," the purpose of
which was to bring economic ruin upon Great Britain by destroying her
commerce. Any ship, whether British or neutral, which had sailed to or
from a British port, or had even permitted a British boarding party to
visit it, was declared liable to confiscation by the French. The British
reply to Napoleon's decrees took the form of the Orders in Council of
1807, and was equally drastic. No neutral ship was permitted to trade
with any part of Europe under Napoleon's control unless it cleared from
a British port or secured a British license. Thus, by complying with
French requirements American ships rendered themselves liable to seizure
by the British, while if they obeyed the British Orders in Council, they
would be seized by the French. Neither of the two blockades could be
completely enforced, but the British navy was able to watch the leading
European seaports, while the French sent out privateers to operate in
American waters.

As in 1793 and 1794, American merchants were able to make big
profits in spite of the confiscations. Although they lost a total of 1,500
ships between 1803 and 1812, many of their cargoes slipped through the
blockades and reached British and French ports, fetching prices so high
that they more than compensated for losses. As a result of British preoccupation with the war, moreover, they were able to capture new markets
elsewhere, especially in Asia and South America. Although their treatment
of neutrals left little choice between the two sides, the merchants continued, for reasons both of political sympathy and of economic interest,
to prefer the British. On the other hand, popular opinion in the United
States was much more incensed with Great Britain than with France. This
was largely because of the impressments. There was a particularly outrageous incident in 1807, when an American warship, the *Chesapeake*, was
attacked and forced to surrender by the British ship *Leopard*, after which
four members of the crew (three of them being American citizens) were
impressed into the British navy.

The Embargo.   After the *Chesapeake* affair it was obvious that
something had to be done to defend American rights, although the United
States had no good reason for allying herself with either side in the European war. Jefferson, who was, of course, unsympathetic to mercantile in-

terests, decided to try the weapon which seemed to have won results back
at the time of the Stamp Act. He believed that European countries in
general, and the British especially, were largely dependent upon American imports, particularly of foodstuffs, and that if these were stopped,
the threat of starvation might force them to make concessions. In December 1807, therefore, Congress passed an Embargo Act prohibiting all
ships, except foreign ships in ballast, from leaving the United States for
any foreign port.

This extremely drastic measure did not have the consequences Jefferson had hoped for. He had overestimated the British need for American
goods. The embargo, moreover, had catastrophic effects upon the American economy, leading to commercial stagnation and falling prices all over
the country, and was very difficult to enforce, especially in New England.
American ships already at sea kept away from American ports; merchants
violated the law whenever possible; and in an effort to maintain obedience
Jefferson was compelled to extend the powers of Federal officials far beyond anything attempted by Hamilton. By the beginning of 1809 it was
universally recognized that the measure had been a failure, and Congress
repealed it.

Madison Replaces Jefferson.   By this time the elections of 1808
had been held. Jefferson, declaring that Washington's refusal to accept
a third term was a precedent that ought to be generally followed, refused
to be renominated, and was succeeded in the leadership of the Republican
Party by his closest friend, James Madison. C. C. Pinckney, again the
Federalist candidate, won back most of New England, which had suffered
most acutely from the embargo, but the Republicans retained their control of other sections, and Madison was elected with a vote in the electoral
college of 122 to 47. As President, he proved to be lacking in energy and
administrative efficiency, and allowed policies to be determined largely by
Congress.

For several years the government continued searching for some
effective way of putting pressure on the European powers. The embargo
was followed first by a Non-Intercourse Act prohibiting trade with Great
Britain and France. The prohibition was, as usual, disobeyed by the New
England merchants, and in 1810 was replaced by the so-called Macon's
Bill No. 2. This ended all restrictions for the time being, but declared that
if either Great Britain or France would abandon her blockade policies, the
United States would agree not to trade with the other. Napoleon quickly
saw his opportunity to take advantage of this attempt to bargain, and
informed the American government that the Berlin and Milan Decrees
were being revoked. It soon became apparent that he was lying, but meanwhile Madison, instead of waiting for concrete proof of Napoleon's good
faith, had proclaimed non-intercourse with Great Britain. This went into
effect early in 1811 and was followed by protracted negotiations, during
which the British refused to abandon either impressment or the Orders in

Council, and public opinion in the United States grew steadily more belligerent and willing to accept war.

Western Expansion. It seemed paradoxical that the seaboard merchants, who were the chief victims of the Orders in Council, continued to the end to want peace, while belligerent opposition to Great Britain showed itself most violently among Western frontiersmen, many of whom had never even seen the Atlantic Ocean. The chief reason for this Western aggressiveness was that there was again trouble with the Indians, and the British officials in Canada were held responsible for it. For the Westerners the question of neutral rights of trade was a convenient pretext for a war which they desired on other grounds.

After Wayne's victory at Fallen Timbers in 1794, the Indians had been steadily pushed westwards, and settlers had poured into the Northwest Territory. Ohio became a state in 1803, and territorial governments were afterwards set up in Indiana, Michigan, and Illinois. But the process of grabbing land from the Indians finally met with resistance. A chieftain called Tecumseh appealed to the different tribes to stand together against white expansion, and began to organize an Indian confederacy including not only the tribes in the Northwest Territory but also those to the south in the area now covered by Alabama and Mississippi. Hostilities began in November 1811, when William Henry Harrison, Governor of the Indiana Territory, was attacked by Indians at Tippecanoe. Although Harrison won the battle, he failed to inflict any decisive defeat on Tecumseh, and settlers throughout the West continued to feel themselves in danger. They believed (incorrectly) that the Indians were being armed by the British and (with better reason) that Tecumseh would not have gone to war if he had not expected British assistance. This situation led to a demand throughout the West that Canada be conquered from the British and added to the United States. While this demand was due primarily to fear of Indian attacks, it also appealed to the West for nationalistic and expansionist reasons.

The appetite of the frontiersmen for more land was, in fact, seemingly insatiable. They were hoping that war with Britain would make possible the conquest not only of Canada but also of Florida, held by Britain's ally, Spain.[1] The acquisition of Florida would make it easier for them to deal with the southern Indians, and would also provide convenient seaports along the Gulf of Mexico.

2. THE WAR OF 1812

The Outbreak of War. Western agrarian expansionism found expression in the elections of 1810, which sent to Congress a group of young men who quickly became known as the War Hawks. Having grown up

[1] The Spaniards had changed sides in 1808, when Napoleon tried to take control of their country.

since independence, they displayed an aggressive and often boastful nationalism which had been unknown among the older generation. Their principal leader, Henry Clay, who was elected Speaker of the House of Representatives, was more responsible than any other individual for pushing the somewhat reluctant Madison into war.

War was finally declared by Congress on June 18, 1812, impressment and the Orders in Council being cited as the reasons. Most of the representatives from the maritime states of New England and New York voted against the declaration, while the agrarian West and South were almost unanimously in favor. By one of the many paradoxes associated with the War of 1812, the British, who had been hard-hit by the enforcement of non-intercourse as a result of a series of bad harvests, had announced the suspension of the Orders in Council two days earlier. But news of their surrender did not reach the United States until after military operations had started.

The war was the main issue in the presidential election of 1812, and the country divided along sectional lines. A group of Northern Republicans, who had opposed the war, refused to support Madison for re-election and nominated De Witt Clinton of New York, nephew of George Clinton, after which the Federalists decided not to run a candidate of their own. Clinton carried most of the commercial New England and Middle states, while the agricultural South and West voted unanimously for Madison, giving him a majority of 128 to 89.

In spite of the belligerent speeches of the War Hawks, the United States was totally unprepared for war, and Madison's administration was much too weak to conduct it efficiently. The navy consisted of half a dozen frigates and a number of smaller vessels, none of which dared take on a British ship-of-the-line. The army had less than 7,000 men, and was commanded by elderly survivors of the War of Independence. The War Hawks, who knew nothing about warfare, insisted that the militia could conquer Canada; but the main reason for their optimism was their fond belief that any American militiaman was more than a match for a British regular. In the course of the war the government called up for service more than 400,000 militiamen, but many of them simply ignored the summons. Most of those who responded, moreover, showed the militiaman's usual reluctance to obey orders and usual propensity to desert.

Another difficulty was lack of money. The government could pay only one-third of its expenses by taxation, and was therefore compelled to borrow. Unfortunately, most of the people with capital to spare were opposed to what they called "Mr. Madison's War." Thus loans were smaller than requirements and difficult to arrange even when successful. The Bank of the United States, which might have eased the financial pressure, had ceased to exist in 1811, when the Republican majority in Congress refused to renew its charter. Gallatin, who was still Secretary of the

Treasury, struggled vigorously with these problems, but by the end of the war the government was close to bankruptcy.

Military Operations. During 1812 and 1813 the British were too busy with the war in Europe to send troops across the Atlantic; but the small British army in Canada, aided by Canadian militia, proved at first more than a match for the Americans. In 1812 the United States War Department planned invasions of Canada by way of Lake Champlain, Niagara, and Detroit and actually sent some men across the border. But by the end of the year all the American troops were back on American soil, and, worse still, the British had crossed into Michigan and captured Detroit, thereby winning the support of Tecumseh's confederacy. The year 1813 began in less humiliating fashion, for Captain Oliver Hazard Perry by then had built a fleet which soon won control of Lake Erie, and William Henry Harrison regained Detroit, pursued the British into Ontario, and defeated them at the battle of the Thames, where Tecumseh was killed. But American invasions of Canada from Niagara and Lake Champlain were again easily repulsed.

By 1814, younger and more vigorous American commanders (among them Winfield Scott, who was destined for a long and distinguished career) had replaced the old Revolutionary veterans, and the militia won battles in the Niagara region. But by this time Napoleon had been defeated and forced to abdicate, the war in Europe was over, and a new British army had arrived in Canada, so that all American hopes of conquest had to be abandoned. In the late summer the British invaded northern New York by the Champlain route; but they were unable to win control of Lake Champlain, which was ably defended by a flotilla of boats under Commodore Macdonough. The British then returned to Canada. Thus both sides failed in their offensive efforts, and the honors along the Canadian border remained about evenly divided.

On the sea the Americans at first had more cause for congratulation, since their frigates won a number of naval battles with small British vessels. As in the War of Independence, moreover, American privateers took a heavy toll of British commerce. But in 1813 a large British fleet arrived in American waters and established a successful blockade of the coast. In the summer of 1814, moreover, the British navy landed an invading army on the shores of Chesapeake Bay. This army easily dispersed the defending American militia and marched into the city of Washington. There they set fire to the main buildings and nearly captured President Madison himself. Their next objective was the seizure of Baltimore, but here they failed. It was an episode during the American defense of the city which inspired Francis Scott Key, who watched the battle as a prisoner on a British ship, to write *The Star Spangled Banner*. After this defeat the British departed. The whole Chesapeake venture, though humiliating for the Americans, accomplished little of military importance for the British.

Only in the South could the Americans regard the conduct of the war with any satisfaction. This was due primarily to the emergence of a leader who could impose discipline and obedience upon the militia and inspire them with some of his own courage and indomitable determination. This leader, of course, was Andrew Jackson.

Since Spain did not enter the war on the side of her British ally, Western hopes for the acquisition of Florida had to remain unsatisfied for the time being. The Creek Indians, however, living in the Mississippi Territory, responded to appeals from Tecumseh and in 1813 began to attack American settlements in the area. Jackson, at this time commander of the Tennessee militia, heard the news while convalescing from a pistol shot received during a brawl with the future Senator Thomas Hart Benton and his brother. He promptly left his bed and ordered out the militia against the Indians, and after many months of arduous campaigning inflicted a crushing defeat upon them and compelled them to sign a treaty surrendering most of their lands. After this achievement Jackson was transferred to the regular army and placed in command in the Southwest, in time to deal with a British invasion.

A British army of 10,000 men, all of them veterans of the Napoleonic Wars, arrived in the Gulf of Mexico in the autumn of 1814, and landed near New Orleans, where Jackson was waiting for them. In a battle fought on January 8, 1815, the British army was driven back to its ships with a loss of more than 2,000 men, while the number of Americans killed amounted to precisely 13. In addition to providing the United States with a future president, the battle of New Orleans restored American morale and re-established the credit of Madison's administration. But it had no effect on the terms of peace, for just as this whole war started after one of its ostensible causes—the British Orders in Council—had been removed, so it ended before its most decisive battle was fought. News traveled slowly in those days, and it was learned only after the battle that a peace treaty had been signed in Europe fifteen days earlier.

The Treaty of Ghent.   Peace negotiations began at Ghent in Belgium in the summer of 1814. In addition to the sagacious Albert Gallatin, the most active members of the American delegation were John Quincy Adams (son of the former President) and Henry Clay. They made a strong combination, since Adams, whose working day began at dawn and customarily ended after nightfall, had a thorough knowledge of all relevant facts, while Clay, who spent a large part of his time at the card table, had thereby acquired an equally thorough knowledge of human nature, and could tell when his opponents were bluffing. The British began by demanding territorial cessions and the creation of an independent Indian state in the Northwest; but in the end they agreed to a restoration of the territorial status quo. Nothing whatever was said about impressment or the Orders in Council, the official reasons for the American declaration of war; since the European conflict had ended, it was no longer necessary to argue about them. Various disputed questions were left to be settled later by joint commissions. In the end, therefore, the Treaty of Ghent did little more than declare that the war was over and that neither side had gained anything by it. Possibly this made it a good treaty, since it did not create hard feelings on either side. There continued to be strong popular antagonism to America in Britain and to Britain in America, but since 1814 the governments of the two nations have always been able to settle disputes with each other by agreement.

The End of Federalism. While the Treaty of Ghent was being signed, delegates from the New England states were meeting at Hartford, Connecticut, to discuss the possibility of secession. Most New Englanders hated a war which disrupted their commercial ties with Great Britain and which was being fought primarily to strengthen the agrarian democracy of the West. In consequence, the Federalists had regained control of the whole section from the Republicans, and had opposed the policies of the Federal government by every means in their power. New England refused to place her militia under national authority; her merchants sold goods to the British army and navy; and her political leaders asserted, in language that went even further than the Virginia and Kentucky Resolves, the right of the states to resist Federal usurpations of power.

By the time the Hartford Convention met, however, the war was almost over, and moderate elements were able to win control. Instead of voting for immediate secession, the Convention recommended a number of amendments to the Constitution which would limit the power of Congress to declare war, impose embargoes, or admit new states. The report of the Convention reached Washington at about the same time as the news of the Treaty of Ghent and of the battle of New Orleans. Strengthened by the peace and the victory, Madison's administration could safely ignore it.

In the end, its disunionist attitude brought about the final extinction of the Federalist Party. It had been strong only as long as, under Hamilton's leadership, it had stood for the cause of national unity. It had lost many of its younger supporters, among them being John Quincy Adams, by its factious opposition to Jefferson's foreign policy. And while it profited by the economic distress of the maritime states during the embargo and the war, it quickly lost ground during the resurgence of nationalistic feeling in the post-war period. Controlled by merchants whose minds had been formed in the eighteenth century, the Federalist Party had little to offer to the new generation. Proof came in the election of 1816, when Monroe, the Republican candidate, carried all but three states. Rufus King of New York, who was supported by the Federalists, won only Massachusetts, Connecticut, and Delaware. By 1820 the Federalist Party had virtually ceased to exist, and Monroe was re-elected in that year without any formal opposition at all.

3. FOREIGN POLICY OF MONROE AND ADAMS

FOREIGN policy continued to be important during Monroe's two presidential terms, and a number of decisions were made which have had a lasting effect on American development. The individual primarily responsible was John Quincy Adams, who served as Secretary of State. Adams was perhaps better qualified for the position by education, experience, and native ability than any other Secretary of State in American history. Trained for statesmanship by his father, he had been engaged mainly in diplomacy since boyhood. He was strongly nationalistic, and, like most members of the Adams family, was a man of somewhat austere virtue. He was liable, like other Adamses, to make enemies by speaking his mind too bluntly; but when he became too outspokenly belligerent, he was held in check by President Monroe, who had had considerable diplomatic experience himself as American representative in Europe and as Secretary of State since 1811.

Settlements with Britain.   Thus, between them, Adams and Monroe were able amicably to adjust questions left unsettled by the Treaty of Ghent. Their efforts in this direction were aided by the British Foreign Secretary, Lord Castlereagh, who, although extremely conservative, recognized the value of friendly relations with the United States. Henceforth Great Britain no longer attempted to check American western expansion or to encourage Indian resistance to it. In the United States aggressive patriots continued for a long time to predict that Canada must eventually come under the Stars and Stripes, but more sober statesmen began to realize that there was enough room in North America for both countries.

In 1817, by the Rush-Bagot Agreement, it was provided that neither the United States nor Great Britain should maintain warships on the Great Lakes, except for police purposes. Meanwhile, a series of joint commissions were endeavoring to fix a definitive boundary line between the United States and Canada. The treaty of 1783 had left parts of the boundary vague because of lack of geographical knowledge. Since then, moreover, the Louisiana purchase had extended the territory, and hence the northern border, of the United States from the Mississippi to the Rockies. The boundary commissions succeeded in drawing a line as far west as the Great Lakes, except in a stretch of country where Maine touched New Brunswick. West of the Great Lakes it was agreed, by a convention signed in 1818, that the boundary should run along the 49th parallel as far as the Rockies. Beyond the mountains, between Russian Alaska and Spanish California, was the country then known vaguely as Oregon. This, it was decided, should be left open for the time being to the people of both countries. The Maine–New Brunswick line was not finally settled until the Webster–Ashburton Treaty of 1842. The so-called Oregon Territory was partitioned in 1846, when the present northern border of the far western part of the United States was finally agreed upon.

These agreements gave to both Americans and Canadians a sense of mutual security which could eventually develop into friendship and co-operation. It was more than fifty years before disarmament on the Great Lakes was accompanied by land disarmament along the whole border, but in the end the United States–Canada boundary was left unfortified—the longest such boundary anywhere in the world, and a monument to the wisdom of both American and British diplomacy.

The Acquisition of Florida. In the south the Monroe administration still wanted to round out the territories of the country by acquiring Florida from Spain. Spain was now too weak to present any serious danger, but Florida had become a refuge for runaway slaves from the Georgia plantations and a base for Indian tribes who could cross the border to attack frontier settlements. In 1817 the Seminole Indians began to cause trouble. Andrew Jackson was ordered to deal with them, and authorized by secret instructions to pursue them, if necessary, into Spanish territory. Jackson drove the Seminoles into Florida, and then proceeded to seize two Spanish posts and oust the Spanish officials.

This caused a diplomatic crisis; but Adams (against the wishes of Secretary of War Calhoun and some other members of the Cabinet) persuaded Monroe to give Jackson full support, and dispatched a blistering note to Madrid insisting that Spain was to blame for failing to police the border. In the end Spain decided to give way; the Adams-Onís Treaty was signed in 1819 and finally ratified in 1821. Spain sold Florida to the United States for $5,000,000 (all of which was to be paid to American citizens with claims against the Spanish government), while the United States renounced whatever claim she had to Texas. The treaty also fixed the boundary line between the territories of the two powers across the continent as far as the Pacific.

Non-Colonization. One other European power presented a threat to American interests. Russia, which had planted a colony in Alaska in the eighteenth century, was again showing an interest in the Oregon country. In 1821 the Czar issued a ukase extending Russian territory as far south as the 51st parallel and prohibiting the ships of any other nation from coming within one hundred miles of the coastline. Adams found this disturbing not only because he looked forward to eventual American settlement in Oregon but also because American shipowners were already doing a considerable business in furs with Indians in the Pacific Northwest. He regarded all colonial empires, with their mercantilist trade barriers and monopolies, as obstacles to progress and incentives to war, and felt that the time was approaching when the American hemisphere could be liberated from them. In a speech in 1821, intended partly for Russian consumption, he announced his non-colonization doctrine, declaring that the two

American continents should be closed to further colonization by European powers. In 1824 Russia gave way to the extent of agreeing that her colonizing activities in Alaska should not extend south of the line 54°40'.

The Liberation of Latin America.   In proclaiming the end of colonialism, Adams was referring also to events in South America. The people of the Spanish colonies had been engaged for a dozen years in a struggle for independence, and were now close to final victory. The movement had begun in 1810, and had been made possible initially by the occupation of Spain itself by Napoleon's armies. After the downfall of Napoleon the Spanish government was again able to send troops across the Atlantic, and by the end of 1816 most of the colonies were back under Spanish control. But a number of able leaders, notably Simón Bolívar in Venezuela and José de San Martín in Argentina, continued the struggle, and one area after another was gradually liberated. By 1822 five new states had come into existence: La Plata (the modern Argentina), Chile, Peru, Colombia (which at first included Venezuela and Ecuador), and Mexico (including Central America). The Portuguese colony of Brazil proclaimed her independence in the same year. The last Spanish army was crushed in 1824, so that with the exception of Canada, Alaska, and the Guianas all the American mainland was freed from European control. The only Spanish colonies still left in the New World were the islands of Cuba and Puerto Rico.

The United States had several strong motives for favoring Latin American independence. The expulsion of European imperialisms from the American continent would increase her own security and make it easier for her to remain aloof from the wars and rivalries of the Old World. The destruction of the Spanish Empire, with its rigid trade barriers, would give her new and extensive markets throughout South America. And the spread of republican institutions in other countries would add to the strength and prestige of her own form of government. Thus considerations of military and diplomatic interest, commercial profit, and political and ideological sympathy were all involved in the American attitude. As early as 1808 Jefferson and his Cabinet, discussing the possibility of a Latin American revolt, decided that although the United States should avoid involvement in war, she should encourage any movement tending to destroy European influence in the American hemisphere.

For a long time, however, the United States did nothing to implement Jefferson's decision. In the early stages of the Latin American struggle she was engaged in conflict with Great Britain. Later on, Monroe and Adams were reluctant to antagonize Spain until the Florida treaty was ratified. Meanwhile, public sentiment was aroused by Henry Clay, who made a number of speeches urging cooperation with the new sister republics. In 1822 Monroe and Adams decided to give diplomatic recognition to the five Spanish countries which seemed to have definitely won their independence. The United States was the first power to make this gesture of friend-ship.

Another country with a deep interest in Latin America was Great Britain. The British government disliked the spread of republicanism, and was hostile to any suggestion of a Pan-American system separating the New World from the Old. It was therefore anxious to check the influence of the United States. On the other hand, the British had strong economic reasons for welcoming the destruction of the Spanish colonial system, which they had been trying to break down ever since the time of Queen Elizabeth I. British merchants looking for new commercial opportunities gave help to Bolívar and San Martín, and British soldiers served as vol-unteers in their armies.

While the two English-speaking powers (though to some extent in conflict with each other) thus sympathized with the Spanish Americans, continental Europe supported the Spanish monarchy. Europe since the fall of Napoleon had been dominated largely by the combination of Austria, Russia, and Prussia, usually known as the Holy Alliance, the main purpose of which was to suppress liberal and revolutionary move-ments and make the world safe for kings. Early in 1823 the Holy Alliance authorized the French government to intervene in Spain in order to sup-press a revolutionary movement against the Spanish king. This led to a suggestion that France might also send troops to re-establish monarchical rule in South America, in return for which she would receive commercial privileges and possibly a colony.

The Monroe Doctrine.   Whether there was ever any real danger of intervention in South America is difficult to decide. The Austrian Chan-cellor, Metternich, ablest of the European conservatives, recognized that monarchy could be defended only in Europe and that the American hemisphere must be written off as hopelessly republican. But for a few months the British were seriously alarmed by the threat of French con-trol of South America, and this led the British Foreign Secretary, George Canning, who had succeeded Castlereagh in 1822, to make a startling suggestion. In August, 1823, in a conversation with the American minister, Richard Rush, he proposed that Great Britain and the United States make a joint protest against intervention. The news reached Washington in October, and for the next month Monroe and his Cabinet, along with ex-presidents Jefferson and Madison, debated whether to accept the prop-osition.

Canning was by no means friendly to the United States, and his motives have remained obscure. In any case, he soon dropped the idea and settled the question by means of a direct negotiation with France. In October, after pointing out that British sea power could control the Atlantic, he persuaded the French minister in London, Polignac, to sign a memorandum declaring that the French had no intention of intervening.

Canning, however, did not communicate this information to the United States government, which continued to assume that intervention was possible and that the British were still interested in a joint declaration against it.

From this tangled situation finally emerged the Monroe Doctrine, which formed part of the President's message to Congress on December 2, 1823. Since it was the product of a long series of discussions, it is impossible precisely to allocate responsibility among the men who contributed to it; but Adams undoubtedly deserves the largest share of the credit.

The upshot of these discussions was that Monroe and his Cabinet decided to make a declaration against intervention, but to do so independently and not in association with Great Britain. A joint protest, they felt, would inevitably cause the United States to appear in the role of a junior partner, and would not contribute to that hemispheric separation which was a main objective of American policy. At the same time it was recognized that the British would in any case oppose intervention because of their own economic interests, and that in view of the control of the Atlantic by British sea power, the United States could safely express her sentiments without being required to go to war in order to defend them. One other question was whether, in proclaiming its sympathy for peoples struggling for self-government, the United States should restrict itself to the Western Hemisphere. Some members of the administration originally favored a declaration without any geographic limitation; but they finally accepted Adams's contention that any suggestion of American interference with the affairs of Europe would be unnecessarily provocative.

On December 2, therefore, Monroe informed the world that:

> The political system of the allied powers is essentially different . . . from that of America. . . . We owe it, therefore, to candor and the amicable relations existing between the United States and these powers to declare that we should consider any attempt on their part to extend their system to any portion of this hemisphere as dangerous to our peace and safety. . . . With the Governments who have declared their independence and maintained it, . . . we could not view any interposition for the purpose of oppressing them, or controlling in any other manner their destiny, by any European power in any other light than as the manifestation of an unfriendly disposition towards the United States.

In another part of his message, with specific reference to Russian designs on Oregon, Monroe restated Adams's non-colonization doctrine, declaring "as a principle in which the rights and interests of the United States are involved, that the American continents, by the free and independent condition which they have assumed, and maintain, are henceforth not to be considered subject for future colonization by any European powers."

These positive principles were accompanied by two negative statements, which were added in order to reassure European powers that the United States had no aggressive intentions. The United States would not interfere "with the existing colonies or dependencies of any European power," nor would she take part "in the wars of the European powers in matters relating to themselves."

The Aftermath of the Doctrine.   This bold pronouncement had little influence on the immediate course of events, and was not received with any enthusiasm by the Latin Americans. They had received more valuable aid in establishing their independence from Great Britain than from the United States, and through most of the nineteenth century they remained, economically if not politically, within the British orbit. Through the late 1820's there was considerable diplomatic rivalry between Great Britain and the United States throughout Latin America, most notably in Mexico; but everywhere British influence became predominant. There were a number of reasons for this. The Latin Americans recognized that the British navy was the main guarantee of their independence. They knew that the British could more easily supply the capital and manufactured goods which they needed. Although they adopted forms of government which were—on paper—republican (except in Brazil), they were actually governed for a long time by military dictators or by landowning oligarchies unsympathetic to the democratic ideals of the United States. And some of them, especially the Mexicans, regarded the expansionism of the United States as a threat to their own independence.

There was therefore for a long time very little friendly cooperation between the two parts of the hemisphere. Fortunately, Great Britain was interested primarily in economic control rather than in acquiring territory, although in the 1830's she did annex the Falkland Islands and the area since known as British Honduras and set up a protectorate over the northern part of Nicaragua, known as the Mosquito Coast. The United States did not even protest against these violations of the Monroe Doctrine.

For more than twenty years, in fact, the Doctrine was not regarded even in the United States as more than an expression of opinion by President Monroe. It was not until 1845, when President Polk restated it, that it became a permanent feature of American policy in North America, and not until the Venezuela boundary dispute of 1895 that it was effectively extended to South America. And by that time world conditions had changed so much that the continued relevance of the Doctrine could be fairly disputed. The authors of the Monroe Doctrine had regarded the division of the world into two hemispheres as primarily political: the Old World was monarchical, and the New World would be republican. But by the end of the century there was much more freedom and democracy in western Europe than in Latin America. During the twentieth century the United States has generally been more vitally affected by events in western Europe and eastern Asia than by anything happening in Latin America; and although she has continued to oppose European inter-ference with the American continents, she has found it impossible to conduct her foreign policy on any theory of hemispheric separation.

After 1823 foreign policy was a minor concern for several generations. The United States had acquired a dominating position in the North American continent, and was in no danger of attack across either ocean. The American people could therefore concentrate on their own economic and political development, instead of maintaining large armed forces and becoming involved in the affairs of other parts of the world. This fortunate situation came about largely because of events in Europe and Latin Amer-ica, but was due also to the skill with which such men as Washington, Jefferson, Monroe, and Adams had seized their opportunities. American diplomatic isolation from Europe depended, of course, on European willingness to accept it. But for some seventy-five years after the fall of Napoleon the European countries were occupied primarily with internal changes rather than with external expansion. Not until the revival of European imperialism near the end of the century did foreign affairs again become vitally important to the United States.

4. NATIONALISM AND SECTIONALISM

The Nationalist Program.   For nearly a decade following the War of 1812, there were no clear-cut party divisions in the United States, for which reason this has always been known as the "era of good feeling." Federalism had ceased to be an important political force, but the Repub-lican Party now began to adopt essentially Federalist policies, abandoning much of its original Jeffersonian opposition to centralized power. The younger men in the party, supported by many former Federalists, advo-cated measures designed to strengthen the United States, make her economically more independent of other countries, and promote national unity by binding the different sections more closely together. They argued that the interests of industry and agriculture should be regarded not as hostile to each other but as reciprocal. The principal items in their program were the establishment of a second bank to replace the one which had expired in 1811; the adoption of a tariff to protect American industry against foreign competition; and Federal appropriations for the building of roads, canals, and other "internal improvements."

The chief spokesman of this nationalist program was Henry Clay, advocate of what he called the "American System." Older men, like Presidents Madison and Monroe, accepted it only with considerable mis-givings. The measures advocated by Clay and other young Republicans were similar to those originally advocated by Alexander Hamilton; but, unlike Hamilton, they appealed to the mass of the American people, not merely to the upper class, and sought the support of the agricultural South and West. Clay himself had been born in Virginia and lived in Kentucky, while another strong nationalist was a rising young lawyer from the South Carolina back country, John C. Calhoun. On the other hand, the mercantile interests of New England, which had formerly been the backbone of the Federalist Party, now thought in terms of narrow sectional interest, and their chief Congressional spokesman, Daniel Webster, voted against almost all this nationalist program.

The disappearance of Hamilton's bank had left the currency in a chaotic condition. Since 1791 a large number of state banks had been chartered (88 by 1811, and 208 by 1815); and except in New England and New York, they were allowed to issue notes very much in excess of their capital reserves. Some of these "wildcat" banks in Southern and Western states began business with scarcely any assets except a printing press. The country quickly became flooded with a bewildering multiplicity of bank notes, the value of which varied considerably, and unsound speculation was thereby encouraged. Chiefly in order to provide a more reliable paper currency, Congress in 1816 chartered a second Bank of the United States, once again for a twenty-year period. In organization and functions it resembled Hamilton's bank, but it had a considerably larger capital stock, $35,000,000 instead of $10,000,000.

A protective tariff, which Hamilton had recommended with little success in 1791, now had much stronger support. The War of 1812, which had put a stop to imports from Great Britain, had given a great stimulus to native manufacturing, and a number of textile and other factories were being built in New England and the Middle Atlantic states. When the war ended, the manufacturers began to demand help against British competition. Western farmers, moreover, wanted protection for certain agricultural products, such as wool and hemp. Congress passed a tariff act in 1816. In view of later developments, it was ironical that it was opposed by Daniel Webster, who at this period represented New England shipping interests, while it was strongly supported by John C. Calhoun. Calhoun at this time believed that manufacturing might develop in the South, and also that industrial growth elsewhere in the country would enlarge the market for Southern agricultural products.

The demand for internal improvements came mostly from the Westerners, who wanted roads and canals in order to transport their goods. As early as 1811 the Federal government had begun construction of the Cumberland, or National Road, running westwards from the Potomac to the Ohio River. This was completed as far as Wheeling by 1818, and was afterwards gradually extended across Ohio, Indiana, and Illinois. Madison and Monroe, however, vetoed more elaborate proposals for Federal spending on internal improvements as being unconstitutional, although they would have been willing to support an amendment authorizing the Federal government to assume this function. The building of roads and canals was therefore left chiefly to the state governments.

The Influence of Chief Justice Marshall.   The emergent nationalism that was manifest in Congress during the decade following the War of 1812 was even more strongly exhibited by the judiciary. It was during this period that Chief Justice Marshall wrote his most significant decisions and excercised his greatest influence.

Although Marshall was a Virginian and a cousin of Thomas Jefferson, his point of view was always Hamiltonian. He believed in strong national government and in protection for business enterprise, and had a deep distrust of democracy. He was not a profound legal scholar, but he was able to dominate the Supreme Court by his capacity for clear and forceful reasoning and by the strength and integrity of his character. During his career as Chief Justice he participated in 1,106 decisions, wrote 519 of them, and voted in the minority only eight times. Personally, he was easygoing and unassuming, his manners and way of living being much more democratic than his opinions. Among the Associate Justices, Joseph Story of Massachusetts, although originally appointed as a Republican, gave Marshall most effective assistance.

For a number of years after Marbury v. Madison, few important cases came before the Court. With the growth of nationalism, however, Marshall was called upon to give legal confirmation to the expansion of Federal authority. Particularly significant was the case of McCulloch v. Maryland in 1819. The Maryland legislature, acting in the interests of the state banks, tried to prevent the Bank of the United States from maintaining a branch in Baltimore by imposing heavy taxes upon it. McCulloch, representing the Bank, refused to pay. This gave Marshall an opportunity to develop Hamilton's "implied powers" theory of the Constitution, and incidentally to assert that the Federal government was fully sovereign within its own sphere and not merely the creature of the states. In what was perhaps the most important of all his decisions, he declared that the government of the Union was created by the people, not by the states, and was "supreme within its own sphere of action"; that in pursuing an end that was legitimate and constitutional, the Federal government could adopt any means which might be appropriate, as long as it was not explicitly prohibited; and that the states had no right to impede the Federal government in the exercise of its constitutional powers. Marshall went on to argue that the establishment of a bank, although not explicitly allowed by the Constitution, was within the scope of Federal responsibility, and hence that the states had no right to impede it by taxation.

Another far-reaching affirmation of Federal power came in 1824, in the case of Gibbons v. Ogden. The State of New York had granted to one company a monopoly of steamboat navigation on the waters within the state. Marshall declared that this was a violation of the clause in the Constitution giving the Federal government power over interstate commerce. He defined commerce in the widest possible terms, and asserted that "the power therefore is not to be confined by state lines, but acts upon its subject matter wherever it is to be found." In other cases, notably in Martin v. Hunter's Lessee (1816) and Cohens v. Virginia (1821), the Court asserted the right of the Federal judiciary to review and reverse decisions by state courts whenever rights guaranteed by the Constitution were involved.

In another group of decisions, involving the clause in the Constitution that prohibits states from impairing the obligations of contracts, Marshall interpreted the clause in such a way as to protect property rights against legislative interference. The most important case in this category was Dartmouth College v. Woodward (1819). The New Hampshire legislature had attempted to change the old colonial charter of the college in order to transform it into a state institution. After Daniel Webster, who was a Dartmouth alumnus, had defended the college before the Supreme Court with the highly emotional eloquence for which he was becoming famous, Marshall ruled that a charter of incorporation should be regarded as a contract and hence as inviolable. This decision was important not only because it gave constitutional protection to privately endowed educational and philanthropic institutions, but also through the immunity thereby acquired by business corporations, which were able henceforth to claim that any privileges granted in charters could not afterwards be rescinded.

Marshall regarded the sanctity of contracts almost as a kind of religious dogma, believing that if any violation of it were permitted, the door would be open for confiscatory attacks of all kinds upon the rights of private property. Perhaps the most extreme example of this attitude was his decision in Fletcher v. Peck (1810). This case resulted from one of the most notorious instances of corruption in early American history, the Yazoo lands sale. In 1795 the Georgia legislature had sold 30,000,000 acres in the western part of the state at a price of about one and a half cents an acre. It subsequently became known that all but one of the members of the legislature were themselves stockholders in the company buying the land. At the next election the indignant citizens elected a completely new legislature, after which the sale was declared rescinded. After protracted legal proceedings the question finally reached the Supreme Court, which decided that the sale was legally a contract, and hence that the State of Georgia had no right to invalidate it.[1]

Marshall's solicitude for the protection of contracts, even when they had been acquired by corruption and seemed contrary to public interest, has often been regarded as excessive, both during his lifetime and in later generations. According to the most pungent of his critics, Jefferson's friend John Taylor, Marshall's doctrine "becomes the protector of political fraud; it compels a nation to be an accomplice in its own ruin; it takes from it the right of self-preservation." After Marshall's death the Supreme Court began to allow more legislative regulation of property and con-

---

[1] The purchasers did not actually keep the 30,000,000 acres. The Federal government took over the land and paid them compensation.

tractual rights, chiefly by enlarging the scope of state "police power." On the other hand, Marshall's nationalist interpretation of the Constitution has remained a permanent contribution to the development of the American federal system.

The Revival of Sectional Conflicts.   The hope of Clay, Calhoun, and the other nationalists that their program would diminish sectional and class differences was not realized. The chief beneficiaries of the banking and tariff legislation were business groups in the Northeastern states, and Southern planters and Western farmers were soon insisting that their interests were not receiving enough consideration. The Bank was wholly controlled by seaboard financial interests, who were accused of seeking to dominate and exploit the West. The tariff stimulated industrial development only in the Northeast, and Southerners complained that it increased the prices they had to pay for manufactured goods. Eventually the electorate again became divided along much the same lines as before, and the Republican Party split into two groups similar to the Hamiltonians and Jeffersonians of the 1790's.

The first signs of trouble came in 1819. People had been moving westwards in large numbers since the end of the war. During the decade 1810–19 five new states were added to the Union (Louisiana, Mississippi, and Alabama in the Southwest; Indiana and Illinois in the Northwest), and the trans-Appalachian population more than doubled. Public land sales had been stimulated by a Land Law passed in 1800, which allowed purchasers four years in which to complete payments, and by the flood of notes put into circulation by the state banks. Sales rose from 1,000,000 acres in 1815 to 5,000,000 in 1819. Much of this was for speculative purposes, and many of the purchasers went into debt both to the government and to the banks.

A collapse of the whole speculative structure was probably inevitable. It came in 1819, and was generally attributed throughout the West to the policies of the Bank of the United States. The Bank made a practice of gathering notes issued by state banks and then suddenly presenting them for payment, thereby forcing them to call in their loans to farmers and often driving them into bankruptcy. As a result of the crash, many of the state banks failed; many of the Westerners lost their land through inability to borrow anew to pay their debts; and much Western land became the property of the Bank. This created throughout the West a hatred of the Eastern "money power" that was to remain an influential factor in American politics for a long time to come. The managers of the Bank claimed that, in attacking the state banks, they were trying to check inflation and impose sound financial practices; but the Westerners seem to have had valid reasons for maintaining that the Bank was actually seeking to eliminate its competitors and establish a monopoly.

In the same year there was a political controversy which caused a sectional split between North and South. There were now eleven free and eleven slave states, so that North and South were equally balanced in the Senate. The North, on the other hand, had a majority in the House of Representatives of 105 to 81. Slavery had been prohibited throughout the Northwest Territory by the Ordinance of 1787, but hitherto no restrictions had been placed upon the introduction of slaves into the territories acquired by the Louisiana purchase. In 1819 Missouri applied for admission as a slave state. Alarmed by the prospect of a Southern majority in the Senate, a New York representative, James Tallmadge, proposed that Missouri be required to provide for the gradual abolition of slavery as a condition for admission. The proposal passed the House but not the Senate, and caused very intense feeling, the issue being seen as primarily one of sectional power rather than of the morality of slavery. North and South had divergent economic interests, and whichever section controlled Congress would be able to legislate to its own advantage.

For the time being the dispute was settled by the Missouri Compromise of 1820. Missouri was allowed to retain slavery, but at the same time Maine was detached from Massachusetts and admitted as a new free state, thereby maintaining equality in the Senate. For the future slavery was to be prohibited in territories north of the line 36°30′ (this line ran along the southern border of Missouri, so that Missouri itself was north of it) and allowed in territories south of the line. In the long run the Compromise would prove more favorable to the North; the only territories then available to settlers south of the line were Arkansas and Florida, whereas the area north of it was eventually divided into more than eight states. But everybody was eager to forget about the controversy, and the Compromise was accepted by both sections until the question was reopened as a result of the acquisition of new territory from Mexico in 1848. The alarming potentialities of such a sectional conflict were only too obvious; Jefferson declared that "this momentous question, like a fire bell in the night, awakened and filled me with terror," while John Quincy Adams made the prophetic comment that "the present question is a mere preamble—a title page to a great, tragic volume."

Agrarian Principles. Once Missouri had been admitted, there was little further conflict until the presidential election of 1824. But increasingly strong groups within the Republican Party were complaining about its conversion to Hamiltonian policies and reasserting the original agrarian point of view.

Jefferson himself, now in retirement on his Virginia plantation, had abandoned his conviction that agriculture was the only honest way of life and was willing to recognize that industry ought to be encouraged. He was alarmed, however, by the growth of speculation and the influence of bankers and other monied elements, and felt that, by absorbing most of the Federalists, the Republican Party had lost its own integrity. But the most belligerent champion of agrarian principles was another Virginia planter, John Taylor of Caroline, who wrote a series of books between 1811 and

1822 in which he stated the Jeffersonian point of view much more vigorously than Jefferson himself had ever done.

Taylor argued that the underlying purpose of the Hamiltonian policies was to enrich a small upper class at the expense of the mass of the people. As a result of such "property-transferring" devices as the payment of high rates of interest on the national debt, the issue of paper money by the banks, the protective tariff (which enabled manufacturers to charge high prices), the granting of special privileges in corporation charters, and speculation in stocks and bonds, a new aristocracy of "patronage and paper" was being created, and the planters, farmers, and craftsmen were losing the freedom for which they had fought in the Revolution. If the process continued, he predicted, the whole country would be "turned into one great factory," and all its citizens would "be under the necessity of yielding up the profit of their labors to a combination of legal capitalists." Thus Taylor regarded the growth of capitalism as detrimental to the interests of the independent property-owner, especially the farmer. He called upon "the agricultural and mechanical classes" to combine with each other in abolishing all "property-transferring" laws, limiting the powers of the Federal government, and enforcing an economic policy of strict *laissez faire.*

In the long run, it was the economics of Hamilton and Clay, not of Jefferson and Taylor, that became dominant. The American people preferred to encourage the growth of large-scale industry instead of maintaining an economy of small, independent farmers and craftsmen. But the ideas of John Taylor had a strong appeal to Southern planters and Western farmers and also to men in the Northeast who were disturbed by the growing economic power of the business classes. They helped to provide a program for the Jacksonian movement which triumphed in the election of 1828, and also to shape the Southern states' rights theory that led finally to the Civil War.

Thus, before the end of the Monroe administration, the political pendulum was swinging back again to a new emphasis on sectional conflicts, and the young Republican nationalists had failed to achieve any reconciliation of divergent interests. Antagonisms were greatly accentuated by economic changes, which were causing different parts of the country to develop along different lines. A new agrarian West was emerging as a distinct section with attitudes of its own; the rise of cotton production was transforming the South; and in the North the Industrial Revolution was leading to a new kind of economic system and to the replacement of commerce by manufacturing as the dominant Northern interest. Before proceeding with political trends after 1824, we must examine these changes in more detail.

IX

The Settlement of the Mississippi Valley

1. THE WESTWARD MOVEMENT

2. KENTUCKY AND TENNESSEE

3. THE ROLE OF THE FEDERAL GOVERNMENT

4. THE OLD NORTHWEST

5. THE OLD SOUTHWEST

6. RESULTS OF THE WESTWARD MOVEMENT

PRIOR to the Revolution the movement of population across the Appalachian ranges was blocked first by the French and afterwards by the British authorities. By 1776 only a few scattered groups in Kentucky and Tennessee had made settlements beyond the main watersheds. But the winning of independence opened up the western country and was followed by a steady flow of settlers into the Mississippi Valley. By 1840 ten new Western states had been added to the Federal Union. The frontier line ran through Iowa, Missouri, and Arkansas, on the western side of the river. All parts of the valley except Wisconsin and Minnesota were well populated, and the white inhabitants of the various trans-Appalachian states and territories totaled more than 6,000,000. Thus a whole new

SELECTED BIBLIOGRAPHY: There are several one-volume histories of the westward movement, two excellent examples being R. A. Billington, *Westward Expansion* (1949), and R. I. Riegel, *America Moves West* (revised edition, 1947). F. J. Turner, *The Frontier in American History* (1920), is indispensable, but should be read in conjunction with G. R. Taylor (ed.), *The Turner Thesis* (1949), a volume in the series Amherst College Problems in American Civilization. Two useful books on land policies are B. H. Hibbard, *A History of the Public Land Policies* (1924), and R. M. Robbins, *Our Landed Heritage: The Public Domain, 1776–1936* (1942). The best survey of the development of farming is P. W. Bidwell and J. I. Falconer, *History of Agriculture in the Northern United States, 1620–1860* (1925). The settlement of the Old Northwest is described in B. W. Bond, Jr., *The Civilization of the Old Northwest: A Study of Political, Social and Economic Development, 1788–1812* (1934), and R. C. Buley, *The Old Northwest: Pioneer Period, 1815–1840* (2 vols., 1950).

section had been colonized, with lasting effects on American institutions, ideals, and ways of living. The westward movement, in fact, has often been regarded as the central theme of American history down to the end of the nineteenth century and as the main factor in the shaping of the American nationality.

1. THE WESTWARD MOVEMENT

MOST sections of the West passed through the same phases of development in a regular order. The first white men to enter a new area were usually hunters and fur-trappers who had an extraordinary skill in opening new paths through the wilderness, finding food for themselves, and dealing with the Indians. These men explored the country and brought news of its resources back to the East. In many regions the second phase was cattle ranching, while some also passed through a mining phase. Parts of Missouri and Wisconsin, for example, were first settled by lead-miners. Behind the cattlemen or the miners came the first farmers, who were often squatters with no legal titles to land. These were frequently restless and improvident people, impatient of the restraints of civilized society and not interested in making permanent homes. They would make small clearings in the forests, ringing the trees in order to kill them instead of going through the labor of felling them, and would build cabins and plant corn. Many of them were in the habit of moving every few years, and would follow the frontier line as it was carried farther into the West.

Once a new area had been opened up and shown to be fertile, it would soon attract men of a more sober and ambitious type, who had some capital and more advanced farming techniques and wanted homes where they could settle for the rest of their lives. Bringing with them the habits of civilization, they would develop trade, establish churches, schools, and newspapers, and set up institutions of self-government. The Federal government assumed responsibility for guiding each area through the territorial stage until it was ready for statehood, but there were many parts of the West where the settlers provided for their own government by democratic methods long before the legal establishment of territorial institutions. Thus society gradually became more diversified, and small towns soon sprang up to meet the economic, political, and cultural needs of the farm population. In those areas that did not afterwards become urban and industrial this represented the final phase.

Geographic factors caused some variations in this general pattern. Some mountain regions never fully passed beyond the squatter stage, while fertile country, such as the black belt in Alabama and Mississippi, was sometimes settled at the start by men of the more ambitious type. Geography also determined the order in which different regions were occupied. The early pioneers mostly preferred to make their homes in forest country, or close to it, since they needed timber to provide shelter and warmth and also for fencing; fences were essential in order to keep cattle and hogs out of the corn fields. Forest regions were therefore settled in advance of the open prairies.

Most pioneer groups tended to move almost directly westward. Thus New Englanders migrated into western New York and along the shores of the Great Lakes, Virginians into Kentucky and then into Missouri, and South Carolinians and Georgians into the Gulf territories. Most of the men and women who settled the West had grown up on farms and did not come from the cities; urban workers lacked the skills needed for agriculture, and could not usually obtain the capital needed to buy and equip a farm. And throughout the settlement of the Mississippi Valley most of the pioneers did not travel long distances; as soon as a territory had been fully occupied, families wanting land would begin to move into the adjacent one. This remained the regular practice until the 1840's, when the opening of the Oregon Trail and the migration to the Pacific coast brought a sharp break with previous frontier experience.

In settling the Mississippi Valley the pioneers did not need to learn new techniques. Most of the country was well wooded, well watered, and similar in its general characteristics to the Atlantic seaboard, though nearly everything was richer and on a larger scale. Much of the southern part of the valley was covered with forests and canebrakes much denser than those in the East, interspersed in a few areas with open meadows, as in the Blue Grass region of Kentucky. To the north the trees became thinner until, in central Illinois, they gave place to wide expanses of prairie, beyond which were the pine forests of Wisconsin and Minnesota. Much of the land was extremely fertile, the topsoil in some sections being several feet deep, and the woods were swarming with a great variety of wild animals. The Mississippi River and its tributaries provided an excellent system of navigable waterways. This undeveloped country provided the American people of the post-Revolutionary epoch with opportunities that have rarely been equaled in the history of the human race.

2. KENTUCKY AND TENNESSEE

Early Settlements. The settlement of the trans-Appalachian regions had begun shortly before the Revolution when a few pioneers from the back country of Virginia and North Carolina moved to the western side of the main watershed. Around the year 1769 several families, mostly of Scotch-Irish descent, established themselves along the Watauga River in what is now northeastern Tennessee. Their principal leaders were John Sevier and James Robertson, and until 1777, when North Carolina organized the area as a county, they provided for their own government by democratic methods.

Meanwhile, hunters and explorers, the most notable of whom was Daniel Boone, had found their way to the Blue Grass country of Kentucky and had discovered a relatively easy way of reaching it through the Cumberland Gap. Boone was employed by Richard Henderson, an ambitious but somewhat impractical North Carolina judge who dreamed not only of making a fortune from speculation in western lands but also of building a kind of proprietary colony in the manner of Lord Baltimore or William Penn. Boone cut a wagon trail, known as the Wilderness Road, from Virginia into central Kentucky, and in 1775 Henderson led out a group of settlers and inaugurated a colony which he called Transylvania.

The Transylvania government, however, quickly collapsed; once a road had been opened into this extremely fertile and attractive country, settlers began to arrive in considerable numbers, and most of them were much too individualistic to comply with Henderson's paternalistic and visionary ideas. Henderson, moreover, having acquired the land by direct purchase from the Indians, had no title to it which could be considered valid under British law. In 1777 Virginia organized a regular county government in the region.

Henderson did not give up his ambitions; having bought land in central Tennessee, once again through private negotiations with the Indians, he planned another colony and picked James Robertson of the Watauga region as its leader. His hopes were again frustrated, since North Carolina refused to recognize his claims. But meanwhile, in the winter of 1779–80, Robertson had led a party to the country around Nashville. Thus, before the end of the War of Independence, settlements had been made in three separate regions of Kentucky and Tennessee.

During much of the war the Kentucky settlers were in almost incessant danger from Indian raids. They had to live inside large wooden stockades and remain on guard day and night. Any individual who ventured out into the woods alone was likely to be killed or carried off as a prisoner. Violent death was a constant occurrence, and very few of the original settlers survived for more than a few years. Kentucky had been known to the Indians as "the dark and bloody ground," and it fully deserved this description during the War of Independence.

Statehood.   Even before the end of the war, new groups of pioneers began to cross the mountains, and as soon as the peace treaty had been signed, the stream became a flood. By contrast with Virginia and the Carolinas, where the soil was losing its fertility, and where (in spite of the reforms of the Revolutionary period) the plantation aristocracy was still dominant, Kentucky seemed to the back-country farmers to be a paradise. Having loaded their possessions on to pack horses or piled them into Conestoga wagons, some families made their way along the Wilderness Road, while others crossed southern Pennsylvania to the Ohio River and then built themselves flatboats and floated downstream. By 1790 the population of the Kentucky-Tennessee region amounted to more than 100,000, and by 1800 to more than 300,000.

Although the state-making attempts of the 1780's were abortive, the settlers were, for all practical purposes, largely self-governing from the beginning, and it was not long before this was legally recognized. Kentucky became a state in 1792. The Tennessee region was surrendered by North Carolina in 1790 and was organized as the Southwest Territory. It became a state in 1796, with John Sevier as its first governor and Andrew Jackson as its first member of the House of Representatives.

Social Conditions. Most of the land was transferred to private ownership, by the Southern method of "indiscriminate location and subsequent survey," before Virginia and North Carolina gave up their rights. This method meant that individuals first acquired titles to certain quantities of land, and then went out and picked locations for themselves. In the general scramble for good sites, a few individuals quickly rose to wealth and prominence. A number of large estates, devoted to horse-breeding or the growing of hemp or tobacco, and worked by slave labor, were established in the Blue Grass country, while cotton plantations soon appeared in central Tennessee. Their owners retained much of the aristocratic style of living and (less frequently) the intellectual interests of the Virginia upper class. Lexington, Kentucky, quickly became a cultural center, and was the seat of the first, and for a long time the best, institution of learning west of the Appalachians: Transylvania University. The first two Westerners to become figures of national importance, Henry Clay of Kentucky and Andrew Jackson of Tennessee, both belonged to this frontier upper class.

This slave-owning planter group, however, never became as numerous or as powerful as in other Southern states, and the population consisted mainly of small farmers who raised corn and hogs. In this rural and largely isolated society the primitivism generally characteristic of frontier life was perhaps more conspicuous and more lasting than anywhere else. Men became accustomed to taking the law into their own hands, resorting quickly to shooting or to rough-and-tumble fighting with no holds barred. Illiteracy was more widespread in the second generation than among the original settlers; and religion became narrowly fundamentalist and highly emotional, especially after a series of great revivals at the beginning of the nineteenth century. This was especially true throughout the mountains which covered most of eastern Kentucky and Tennessee. In the twentieth century the inhabitants of the mountain country were still living in much the same fashion as their eighteenth-century ancestors, preserving the folk songs and the superstitions which had been brought from Europe, along with the disregard for official law and government that had been acquired during the frontier period.

3. THE ROLE OF THE FEDERAL GOVERNMENT

MOST other sections of the West were settled under the jurisdiction of the Federal authorities, who fixed the terms by which public land might be occupied and set up territorial governments. Starting with the Land Ordinance of 1785, the public-land policies of the government exercised a profound influence on the whole course of western expansion. Before discussing the settlement of the Northwest Territory and of the Gulf states, it is therefore necessary to trace the evolution of Federal policy. Almost all aspects of American development have involved interplay between private enterprise and government planning, and the westward movement was no exception. Essentially it was a spontaneous migration of free individuals, but this migration was guided and directed through Federal legislation.

The Public-Land Problem.   During the colonial period different systems of land distribution had been adopted. Whereas the South had preferred the method of "indiscriminate location and subsequent survey," in New England land had been divided into townships before being distributed to individuals. The Southern system had obvious disadvantages. It meant that many settlers did not remain members of communities, and hence that there was more likely to be a lowering of moral and cultural standards; and it led to much overlapping and confusion of land titles. The Confederation government therefore wisely adopted the New England system as its principal model when it framed the Land Ordinance of 1785. Each area was to be surveyed and divided into townships before any of it was sold.

Much more controversy was caused by the question of the terms of sale. The Land Ordinance, which provided for the sale of land in square-mile sections for not less than a dollar an acre, meant that land would normally be bought by large companies rather than by actual settlers. Settlers wanted to obtain land on easier terms, and many of them disliked doing business with speculators and preferred to buy directly from the government. Throughout the entire period from the Land Ordinance to the Homestead Act of 1862 there were frequent debates about public-land prices, and both sides recognized that what was at stake was the whole future development of American society.

Conservatives were afraid of the radical and anarchical tendencies which they attributed to the frontiersmen, and wanted the West to be settled slowly, under the supervision of land companies, for which reason they favored relatively high prices. They were supported by speculators who had land of their own to dispose of, and by Eastern business groups who were anxious to prevent too rapid a flow of population westwards. On the other hand, the demand of the settlers for cheaper land was supported by Jeffersonian liberals, who regarded easy access to the public domain as the best foundation for political and economic democracy. The problem was complicated by the fact that many Congressmen and other men in public life were themselves interested in land speculation and therefore not likely to take an impartial view.

Early Federal Legislation.   For some years after the enactment of the Land Ordinance, little was done to put it into effect, and trans-Appalachian settlement took place mostly on the land that had been sold by the Confederation to the Ohio Company or in areas still controlled by state governments. These included parts of the Northwest Territory which had been reserved by the states for distribution to war veterans, although in practice most veterans preferred to sell their warrants to speculators rather than settle in the Territory themselves.

After the establishment of the Federal government, the first change in land policy came in 1796. The Land Act of that year represented the conservative viewpoint of the Federalist Party, its most important provision being an increase in the minimum price to two dollars an acre. Very little land was sold on these terms, so in 1800 Congress consented to make acquisition easier for settlers. The unit of sale was reduced in certain areas to 320 acres, and a purchaser could pay in installments over a four-year period. Public auctions were to be held whenever a new tract was opened, but land left unsold could be bought at other times for the minimum price (which was still two dollars an acre), for which purpose four land offices were set up in different parts of the Northwest Territory. This law of 1800 was largely the work of William Henry Harrison, the first delegate sent by the Territory to Congress. In 1804 Secretary of the Treasury Albert Gallatin persuaded Congress to make a further reduction of the minimum unit to 160 acres. These laws were extended to the Louisiana purchase and all other areas under Federal control.

A settler could now obtain a small farm for a down payment of only $80. Nevertheless, many settlers had difficulty in completing their payments within the four-year period; and much land, especially in locations where towns seemed likely to be built, continued to be bought by speculators. Between 1800 and 1820 no less than 19,000,000 acres of public land were sold. But on twelve occasions Congress gave relief to debtors by extending the period of payment, and one-third of the land eventually reverted to the government because payments were not completed. Finally, the financial crisis of 1819 made a change unavoidable. In 1820 the credit provision was repealed, the minimum unit was reduced to eighty acres, and the minimum price to $1.25. Thus an eighty-acre farm could be obtained for a total cash payment of $100.

Squatters' Rights.   During the 1830's discussion shifted to the problem of the squatters. Much western land was first settled by individuals without legal titles, who moved on to it before it was surveyed and put up for sale. Some of these squatters were shiftless and migratory, but others wanted permanent possession of the land they had cleared and improved and were willing to pay the minimum price for it. Under the auction system, however, there was danger that their farms would be bought out from under them when the land was put on the market. Many of them, moreover, were unable to travel to the appropriate land office, which was often at a considerable distance from their homes.

In order to protect themselves, squatters in many Western communities organized claims clubs or associations. The members of these groups appeared at auctions armed with sticks and guns, prepared to drive out of town any outsider who ventured to bid for land which they were occupying. The squatters claimed that they ought to have a right of pre-emption: in other words, a right to purchase for the minimum price land on which they had settled, without submitting to competitive bidding at an auction.

The lawless proceedings of the claims clubs were denounced by conservatives; but the squatters had their champions in Congress, the most eloquent of whom was Senator Thomas Hart Benton of Missouri. Benton was a thorough Jeffersonian, believing, as he declared, that the public domain belonged to all the people of the United States; and, unlike many of his fellow Congressmen, he was not influenced by any personal interest in land speculation. He was largely instrumental in persuading Congress to pass the Pre-emption Act of 1841. Henceforth settlers could file claims to 160-acre farms and pay for them later at the minimum price.

Another of Benton's proposals was a graduation arrangement, by which the price of land remaining unsold would be gradually reduced. This was accepted by Congress in 1854, in a law providing that the lowest price, to be paid on land not sold after being on the market for thirty years, was to be 12½ cents an acre. Meanwhile, there was growing popular support for the abolition of all prices of small farms, but prior to the Civil War homestead bills were either defeated in Congress or vetoed by the President.

How much of the public domain was actually sold to settlers, and how much to large speculative interests, it is impossible to say. In any event, it is not possible to make any clear differentiation between the settler and the speculator, since many small purchasers were interested in speculative profits and bought more land than they needed for their own use in the expectation of selling it after a few years of occupation and improvement. But even though many farmers acquired land from speculative companies rather than from the government, most of the West was colonized on democratic principles. Outside the plantation South, a wide distribution of landownership, not big estates cultivated by tenants or laborers, was the American pattern.

The Indian Problem.   In addition to controlling the sale of public land, the Federal government also assumed responsibility for dealing with the Indians. Initially, most of the western land was held as hunting-ground by different tribes, and was not opened for white settlement until after the Indians had surrendered their rights through treaties made with Federal officials. These treaties usually provided for money payments to the Indians, and were supposed to be based on agreement.

In actuality the process of treaty-making frequently involved fraud and coercion. Even when the Federal authorities wanted to act justly, they were often prevented from doing so by popular sentiment. The frontier hunters and fur-traders often learned to respect the Indians, and some white people, probably largely of the criminal type, settled among them; but the average frontier farmer regarded them as little better than vermin, worthy only of removal or destruction. In view of the ever-present danger of warfare, with its cruelties and massacres, this attitude is no doubt understandable. Men who wanted land for agriculture, moreover, could hardly be expected to recognize the claim of some small Indian tribe to a large expanse of fertile ground which was being used solely for hunting purposes. Settlers would therefore trespass on Indian lands, in defiance of Federal regulations; the Indians would go on the warpath; Federal troops would suppress them; and then officials would gather together a collection of alleged chieftains whose authority was often highly dubious, give them money which they could spend on liquor, and invite them to sign away most of the land held by the tribe they supposedly represented.

In this fashion almost all the eastern tribes were deprived of their lands before 1840, and were either confined to reservations or moved out into the West. The treatment of the North American Indians does not make a pretty story. Nor is it possible to cast the blame on any particular individuals or groups. It was the mass of the American people who insisted that the Indians had no right to keep their lands, in spite of the fact that some tribes, such as the Cherokees in Georgia, were adopting white ways of living and standards of civilization.

4. THE OLD NORTHWEST

Ohio, Indiana, and Illinois.   French fur-trappers and farmers from Canada had been the first white people to explore and colonize any part of the Mississippi Valley. When the United States after the Revolution acquired jurisdiction over the Northwest Territory, now often known as the Old Northwest and corresponding to part of the present Middle West, there were a few French settlements, mostly in Illinois and Michigan, with a total white population of perhaps 6,000. But this original French influence, unlike that in Louisiana, was quickly obliterated, and has survived only in a number of place names.

Organized settlement of the Territory began in 1788, when the Ohio Company, having obtained its land grant from the Confederation in the previous year, sent out a group of colonists from New England who founded the town of Marietta on the Ohio River. For some years further settlement was blocked by Indian wars, but in 1795 the Ohio tribes were compelled to surrender much of their land by General Anthony Wayne in the Treaty of Greenville. This was followed by a mass movement into Ohio, which had enough inhabitants to qualify for statehood in 1803.

The next two decades saw the extinction of Indian claims in Indiana and Illinois. William Henry Harrison, who was appointed Governor of the Indiana Territory in 1800, was particularly active in signing treaties with groups of thirsty chieftains and persuading them to surrender millions of acres. As we have seen in the previous chapter, this process was temporarily checked by Tecumseh, who urged the Indians to agree with each other that no more land should be ceded and tried to remove the chief inducement for the cessions by persuading them to become teetotalers. But Tecumseh's death at the battle of the Thames in 1813 put an end to effective Indian resistance in this part of the country. There were a few later wars, notably the Black Hawk War of 1832 in Illinois and Wisconsin; but most of the surviving Indians were removed without much difficulty. Meanwhile, Indiana and Illinois had been settled, and were granted statehood in 1816 and 1818 respectively.

Two different streams of migration contributed to the peopling of the Northwest Territory, one of them coming from the Northern states, especially Connecticut, Massachusetts, and Vermont, and the other from the South. The expansion of New England had begun with western New York, where the Iroquois Indians, who had been strong enough during the colonial period to block both English and French advance, were disposed of during the 1780's. Decimated by warfare, some of them moved to Canada, while others gave up their lands in exchange for annuities and small reservations. New Englanders moved in large numbers into western New York in the 1790's, after which the stream of migration flowed along the shores of Lake Erie, where Connecticut had retained its "Western Reserve" to meet the land claims of its war veterans, and thence into northern Indiana and Illinois. The New Englanders brought with them their Congregationalist church system, their faith in education, and their democratic system of township government.

The southern sections of the Northwest, on the other hand, were settled mainly by migrants from Kentucky and Virginia, among them being the parents of Abraham Lincoln. Some of them brought with them a few slaves, and were allowed to keep them through the legal fiction of calling them indentured servants. During the early years there were, in fact, some attempts to bring about the legalization of slavery, though majority opinion throughout the Northwest was always opposed to it. But southern Indiana and Illinois remained for a long time a kind of borderland between South and North; as late as the Civil War many of the inhabitants remembered their original ancestry and retained Southern sympathies.

Michigan, Iowa, Wisconsin, and Minnesota.   The influence of New England was even stronger in some of the later settlements. The westward movement was temporarily checked by the financial crisis of 1819, but regained its impetus within a few years, especially after the completion of the Erie Canal in 1825. This led directly to the colonization of southern Michigan, which was transformed within a few years into a duplicate of

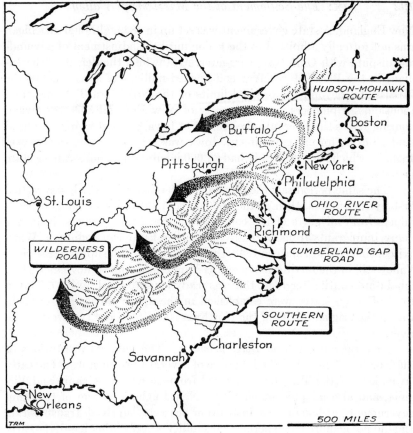

7. Routes to the West, 1760–1840

THE FIRST TRANS-APPALACHIAN REGION TO BE SETTLED WAS THE KENTUCKY-
Tennessee country. Some pioneers made their way through the Cumberland Gap
in southwestern Virginia and followed the Wilderness Road, cut by Daniel Boone,
into the blue-grass region of Kentucky. Others crossed Pennsylvania to the Ohio
River, and then traveled downstream in flatboats.

The Appalachian barrier could be by-passed at its northern and its southern
extremities, but settlement of both the Northwest and the Southwest was delayed by Indian wars. Ohio became safe for settlement when Anthony Wayne
imposed the Treaty of Greenville in 1795. This was followed by a steady stream
of pioneers along the Hudson-Mohawk route. Traffic along this route was intensified by the opening of the Erie Canal in 1825, which made it possible to go as far
as Buffalo by barge.

In the South the Indians of the Alabama-Mississippi country were suppressed
during the War of 1812. After the war there was a heavy migration along the
Southern route, which included many planters and their slaves from South
Carolina and Georgia.

New England. A state government was set up in 1835, although Michigan was not formally admitted to the Union until the adjustment of a boundary dispute with Ohio two years later. Meanwhile, the defeat of the Indians in the Black Hawk War had opened millions of acres west of the Mississippi, beyond the original limits of the Northwest Territory, and thousands of pioneers, predominantly of New England ancestry, began pouring across the river into the prairies of Iowa, without waiting for legal land titles or formal government. Iowa was organized as a territory in 1838, by which time it already had 23,000 inhabitants, and became a state in 1846.

The same period saw the occupation of Wisconsin, which was settled first by fur-traders, then in the 1820's and 1830's by thousands of lead-miners from all parts of the country, and finally by farmers, including many immigrants from Germany and other European countries. When Wisconsin became a state in 1848, the only section of the upper Mississippi Valley still in the territorial stage was Minnesota. Almost devoid of white inhabitants until after 1850, this was ready for statehood by 1857. Thus a total of seven states were established in the upper valley, five of them within the original limits of the Northwest Territory and two west of the river.

Political and Cultural Development.   The political institutions of the Northwest reflected the influence of several Eastern states. The early lawmakers of the Territory borrowed from both Pennsylvania and Virginia, and also adopted much of the New England system of township government, although this institution scarcely survived transplanting and did not acquire much permanent vitality. On the other hand, the early state constitutions of the Northwest were more democratic than those of the East, since they provided from the beginning for universal white manhood suffrage and also imposed severe limitations upon executive authority.

Ohio, the first state carved out of the Territory, set some influential precedents in the constitution which it adopted in 1802. The Governor of the Territory since its organization in 1787 had been Arthur St. Clair, a Pennsylvania soldier and landowner and a strong Federalist, who had aroused violent antagonisms by trying to maintain a conservative and authoritarian form of government. The Ohio constitution was drafted by Jeffersonians and reflected the general opposition to St. Clair's Federalist ideas. In addition to constitutional provisions for white manhood suffrage, the abolition of the governor's veto, and the election of almost all officials, including judges, the democratic tendencies of early Ohio were reflected in such measures as the abolition of imprisonment for debt and the limitation of indentured service to one year. Later Northwestern state constitutions showed a similar faith in popular government.

For a generation after the financial crisis of 1819 the currency was one of the chief political issues in all the Western states, both Northern and Southern. Specie was scarce in the rural sections, and many of the farmers were heavily in debt; so, like their predecessors during the colonial period, they supported inflationary policies, in opposition to the Eastern financial interests represented by the Bank of the United States. Evading the clause in the Constitution forbidding them to issue bills of credit, some Western states set up state-owned banks, authorized them to issue notes without specie backing, and even declared these notes to be legal tender. In the 1830's after disillusioning experiences with both public and private state banks, which were generally mismanaged and sometimes fraudulent, some states swung over to the opposite extreme and severely restricted the powers of all banks or even prohibited banks. Some of them also passed laws making farmers' homesteads immune from seizure on account of unpaid debts.

Closely associated with the democracy of the Northwest was its belief in public education. As the legislature of the Indiana Territory declared in 1806, in a "commonwealth where the humblest citizen may be elected to the highest public office" and where all citizens enjoyed "the heaven-born prerogative" of voting in elections, it was essential that knowledge be "widely diffused." The first constitution of Indiana required the legislature to set up "a general system of education, ascending in a regular gradation from township schools to a state university, where tuition shall be gratis and equally open to all." This statement was echoed by several other states.

As a result of economic difficulties, the ideal could not be quickly achieved. The Land Ordinance of 1785 had provided that public land should be set aside for the support of schools, but in practice most of it was sold too quickly to bring in much money. During the period of settlement, as everywhere on the frontier, illiteracy was widespread, and there were many people who saw no value in book learning and said so in emphatic terms. For a generation after the opening of the Territory there were more institutions of learning and more competent scholars in Kentucky and Tennessee than north of the Ohio.

From the beginning, however, some groups of settlers, both from New England and from Pennsylvania and Virginia, worked to transmit standards of culture to the next generation, while invaluable educational work was done by religious organizations, especially the Congregationalists and the Presbyterians. The first school in the Territory was founded by the colony at Marietta in 1789, and the first library in 1796. Cincinnati quickly developed into a cultural center, having a printing press and a newspaper as early as 1793. The earliest university in the Northwest, at Athens, Ohio, graduated its first class in 1815. Although most of the early schools charged tuition fees, the belief in free public education was gradually put into effect, in most areas before the Civil War. It also bore fruit in the development of the great state universities, the earliest of which, those of Michigan and Wisconsin, were founded in the 1830's.

Economic and Social Characteristics.   Apart from the early fur-trapping, mining, and lumbering activities, agriculture remained for a long time the main occupation throughout the Northwest. And since slavery was illegal and no other source of cheap labor was available, the small family farm, usually about 200 acres in size, became the basic economic unit. Most farmers concentrated on growing corn and wheat and raising cattle and hogs. Since acquiring and equipping a farm cost a considerable sum, the purchase of the land being only a small part of the initial expense, many of them went into debt; and in order to pay their debts, they had to produce more than their subsistence required and find markets for their surplus products. Until the country had been supplied with adequate means of transportation there was no easy way to ship grain except down the Mississippi River to New Orleans. But during the early years of the nineteenth century herds of cattle and hogs were regularly driven across the mountains to the seaboard cities. The early American "razorback" hog, it should be remarked, was a very different animal from his modern successor; he was slim, vigorous, long-legged, and quite capable of going several hundred miles to market on his own feet.

Yet in spite of the pressure of debts, the full transition from subsistence to commercial agriculture came about very slowly, and was not completed until the 1840's and 1850's. This was primarily owing to transportation difficulties, which were partially met by the building of canals in the 1830's and finally and more effectively by railroads in the 1850's. As long as the inhabitants of the Northwest had to ship their grain down the Mississippi, they were at a disadvantage in competing with farmers living closer to New Orleans, and the whole region therefore developed more slowly than the states of the lower Valley. As late as 1839 Kentucky, Tennessee, and Virginia were still the three leading corn-producing states, while wheat was still largely concentrated in Pennsylvania and New York. It was not until the 1850's that the upper valley began the rapid development that soon made it the heartland of the whole United States and the main center of both agriculture and industry. As late as 1840 the population of the seven states and territories in the upper valley amounted to less than 3,000,000. This rose to 4,700,000 in 1850 and to 7,700,000 by 1860.

In spite of prolonged economic difficulties, and in spite also of much frenzied land speculation, fraudulent town-promotion schemes, and the usual lawlessness of the frontier, the society of the upper valley soon began to develop certain characteristic virtues. Settled by small farmers, and free both from the slave plantations of the South and from the aristocratic survivals of the seaboard states, it was perhaps more completely permeated with the spirit of democracy than any other section of the country. Democracy, of course, did not mean any complete equality, and was not incompatible with the competitive struggle for wealth. There were class differences, which often became more marked as society became more stable. Most communities soon acquired an upper class of prosperous business and professional men, a middle class of landowning farmers and small traders, and a lower class of squatter farmers and a few wage-earners. But people had a strong faith in equality of opportunity and admired the man who worked his way up from humble beginnings. Abraham Lincoln of Illinois gave expression to this attitude in his message to Congress in 1861 when he declared that "no men living are more worthy to be trusted than those who toil up from poverty" and described democracy as a system in which the hired laborer was not "fixed to that condition for life."

5. THE OLD SOUTHWEST

The Removal of the Indians.　　After Kentucky and Tennessee, the next Southwestern area to be settled was the country along the Gulf of Mexico. What is now Alabama and Mississippi was organized as the Mississippi Territory in 1798, while the southern part of the Louisiana purchase became the Orleans Territory in 1804. But much of the land in Mississippi and also in western Georgia was held by five powerful Indian tribes, the Cherokees, Creeks, Chickasaws, Choctaws, and Seminoles, who were strong enough to block white advances until after the War of 1812.

During the war, as we have seen, the Creeks were crushed by Andrew Jackson and compelled to cede much of their land. During the next few years similar treaties were extorted from the other tribes, and white settlers began to move into the Gulf country in large numbers. But the Indians still held millions of acres of fertile land, and some of them had adopted many of the institutions of white civilization, including Negro slavery. The 15,000 members of the Cherokee tribe raised cattle and cotton, owned 1,500 slaves, maintained eighteen schools, and even had their own newspaper. Unlike most other Indian groups in the United States, they seemed capable of being assimilated. But this did not save them from the greed of land speculators.

During the 1820's the Federal government came to the conclusion that the only solution to the problem of the Indians was to remove them out into the West. The country beyond the Missouri River, it was generally believed, was mostly desert unsuitable for white settlement and might therefore be reserved as a perpetual home for the Indians. This program was endorsed by humanitarians, as the only way of protecting the Indians themselves from robbery and from alcoholism and the other vices they were learning from the whites. It was publicly announced as the government's policy by President Monroe in 1825.

During the next twenty years almost all the Indians were moved into the West. The removals were supposed to be voluntary, with the Federal government paying the costs and giving the Indians a year's supplies; but, in practice, force had to be used. The Southern tribes made every effort to keep their lands; the Creeks even decreed the death penalty for any chieftain agreeing to sell any part of the tribal domain. But after 1829, when Andrew Jackson became President, they received no protection from the Federal government. The local authorities were allowed to deny the Indians all legal rights, seize their lands, and use fraud and coercion in getting them to sign treaties authorizing removal. When the Supreme Court ruled, in the case of Worcester v. Georgia in 1832, that the state had no jurisdiction over the Indians within its borders, Jackson paid no attention and is said to have made the remark: "John Marshall has made his decision; now let him enforce it."

By 1842, when the last Seminole rising was crushed by troops, the process was completed. Land speculators had taken over millions of acres, and the surviving Indians had been transported to the Oklahoma country. An Indian boundary line had been drawn across the country from Minnesota down to Texas, and the Indians had been promised that they could hold the regions west of it "as long as trees grow and the waters run." Yet it was not much more than a decade before the territories of Kansas and Nebraska were organized west of the boundary line, and the Indians were invited to sign new treaties surrendering more land to the white men.

Settlement and Statehood.   When the Mississippi Territory became safe for settlement after the War of 1812, cotton-growing had become the principal and highly profitable occupation of the Deep South. Much of the Gulf country, being flat, warm, damp, and extremely fertile, was ideally suited for cotton plantations. The land was therefore attractive to wealthy slave-owners in eastern Georgia and South Carolina, where the soil was already badly eroded; and bidding for good locations soon drove prices up to unprecedented figures, in some instances as much as $50 an acre. Many of the seaboard planters bought thousands of acres and brought out their families and possessions in long caravans accompanied by scores of Negro slaves. Alongside these men with upper-class backgrounds, a number of small farmers, among them being the elder brother and guardian of Jefferson Davis, also built up large estates within a few years by hard work or successful speculation. Slaves were acquired by purchase from the worn-out plantations of Virginia and other seaboard states. Other small-farmer settlers, less industrious or less fortunate, were unsuccessful in the scramble for good land, and often moved up into the hill country. Thus in this Gulf country there was from the beginning little of the equality that frequently characterized the frontier elsewhere. There were marked class divisions, and social attitudes were closer to the Southern than to the Western pattern.

Three Gulf States were added to the Union before 1820. Louisiana, which already had a considerable French population, engaged in sugar-planting, commerce, and small farming, was admitted as early as 1812. New Orleans, with its sophisticated French-Catholic traditions and way of life, became the metropolis of the lower Mississippi Valley and the only large city of the Deep South. Mississippi achieved statehood in 1817 and Alabama in 1819, thus balancing the admission of the free states of Indiana and Illinois in 1816 and 1818. The three Gulf states continued to grow rapidly for the next generation, with the population doubling in each decade down to the 1840's.

The period of rapid expansion following the War of 1812 also carried the first wave of pioneers across the Mississippi River into Missouri. The fur trade and the lead mines attracted settlers from all parts of the Union, but a majority of the Missourians were small farmers from Kentucky and Tennessee. With them came a few wealthy slave-owners, who established hemp plantations in the northern part of the Territory. As we have seen, Missouri entered the Union in 1821 as a slave state. But it remained a border area, with strong economic ties with the Northwest; St. Louis was the main entrepôt for the produce which the Northwestern farmers shipped down the Mississippi. Arkansas, on the other hand, the last section of the lower valley to be settled, became an outpost of the Cotton Kingdom. Almost empty until after 1830, it had enough inhabitants to qualify for statehood by 1836. Cotton-planters migrating from the Gulf states settled in the rich bottom lands along the rivers, while small farmers from Tennessee and elsewhere moved up into the Ozark hill country.

Thus seven slave states were established in the lower valley, balancing the seven free states and territories of the upper valley but retaining a preponderance in population until after 1850. And just as the laws and institutions of the Northwest were modeled after New England and the Middle Atlantic seaboard, so those of the Southwest followed the pattern established in Virginia and the Carolinas, the only important exception being in Louisiana, whose legal system was derived from the French Code Napoléon. The new state constitutions, while somewhat more democratic than those of the seaboard South, showed a similar tendency towards upper-class rule, especially in the cotton belt. Perhaps their most significant feature was that the county remained the basic unit of administration and law enforcement; in all plantation regions the county courts were controlled by the slave-owners.

The social and cultural characteristics of the Southwest will be discussed in the next chapter; but one feature of the period of expansion is too interesting to be overlooked. The Southern frontier developed a special tradition of folk humor, usually based on the over statement of the tall tale. Some of the earliest tall tales were associated with the boatmen of the lower Mississippi, who liked to call themselves "ring-tailed roarers" and claimed to be "half-horse, half-alligator, and a little touched with the snapping turtle." The prototype of this lawless, pugnacious, and boastful breed of men was the famous Mike Fink, who claimed that he could "out-run, out-jump, out-shoot, out-brag, out-drink, an' out-fight, rough and tumble, no holts barred, any man on both sides the river from Pittsburgh to New

8. New States, 1789–1850

THE PIONEER MOVEMENT FOR SEVENTY YEARS AFTER THE REVOLUTION CAN BE roughly represented in the form of three parallel streams flowing westward from New England, Virginia, and South Carolina, with the central stream from Virginia well in advance of the others. Movements were not continuous. Boom periods of great activity, during which millions of acres of land were sold, alternated with depression periods during which there was little further expansion of the frontier and many disappointed pioneers back-trailed from west to east.

The first western thrust of the 1780's and 1790's proceeded mainly from Virginia and carried the central stream through Kentucky and Tennessee as far as the Mississippi. During the same period Vermont was separated from New Hampshire and admitted to the Union. In the north the westward movement did not gather momentum until after 1795; Ohio was then settled and was ready for statehood in 1803. In the South much of Georgia was still frontier country until after 1800. Louisiana was admitted in 1812, but its population was largely French.

The half-dozen years following the War of 1812 were a period of rapid expansion. The central pioneer stream crossed the Mississippi into Missouri. Indiana and Illinois were added to the Union in the North, and Mississippi and Alabama in the South. The westward movement was then checked by the financial crisis of 1819 and was gradually resumed during the 1820's. By the middle of the 1830's Michigan and Arkansas were ready for statehood, and settlers had moved into Texas, which became an independent republic in 1836 and was added to the Union in 1845.

After the depression years of 1837–40 the next pioneers moved into Iowa and Wisconsin in the North; in the South the movement turned down into Florida, where settlement had hitherto been blocked by Indian troubles. Meanwhile the central stream was approaching the arid and tree-less plains west of Missouri. Rather than settle in this unattractive region, pioneers from Missouri began to cross the continent to Oregon and California.

Prior to the admission of California as a free state in 1850, free and slave states were admitted roughly in pairs. In 1820 the threat of a slave-state majority through the admission of Missouri was countered by detaching Maine from Massachusetts.

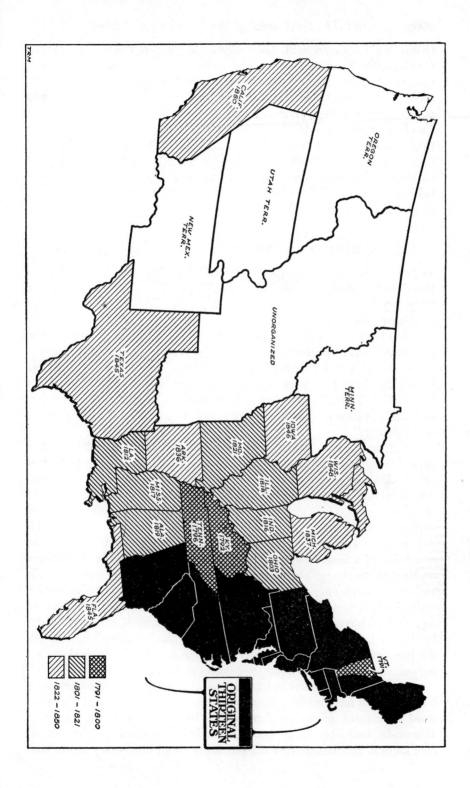

ORIGINAL
THIRTEEN
STATES

1791 – 1800

1801 – 1821

1822 – 1850

Orleans an' back agin to St. Louiee." Another hero of tall tales was David
Crockett, the Tennessee hunter and Indian fighter who served a term in
Congress and died at the Alamo in the Texan war of independence of 1836,
though the Crockett legend was largely built up by Whig journalists who
wished to use him against Andrew Jackson. In later stories of Fink,
Crockett, and other heroes of the lower valley, they could swallow
thunderbolts and ride on streaks of lightning. The imaginative exuberance
displayed in such legends contributed eventually to the growth of an
indigenous American literature. The humor of Mark Twain of Missouri
belonged to the tradition of the Southern frontier, as did that of a number
of writers of the twentieth century.

6. RESULTS OF THE WESTWARD MOVEMENT

ANY discussion of the results of western expansion must begin with the
theories of Frederick Jackson Turner, whose epoch-making paper entitled
"The Significance of the Frontier in American History" was read at a
meeting of the American Historical Association in 1893. Turner's thesis
was that the westward movement had been the central factor in the evolution of American civilization and the chief reason for the differences between America and Europe. "Up to our day," he declared, "American
history has been in a large degree the history of the colonization of the
Great West. The existence of an area of free land, its continuous recession,
and the advance of American settlement westward, explain American
development."

Turner pointed out that each part of the United States in turn had
passed through a frontier stage of development. Each settlement of a new
area had meant at first a return to primitive conditions, so that "American social development has been continually beginning over again on the
frontier"; and each beginning was likely to retain less of the European
heritage and be more deeply affected by the American environment.
According to Turner, the chief effects of the frontier were to promote the
formation of a new, composite nationality and decrease the dependence
on Europe, to strengthen national unity and increase the powers of the
Federal government, and to stimulate individualistic and democratic
attitudes and institutions. The frontier spirit, however, should not be
regarded with complete admiration. "The democracy born of free land,"
he declared, "strong in selfishness and individualism, intolerant of administrative experience and education, and pressing individual liberty
beyond its proper bounds, has its dangers as well as its benefits."

The Turner thesis has had a wide influence on the writing of American
history, but it has also been sharply criticized. In insisting that the westward movement promoted democracy, Turner, who was a native of
Wisconsin, undoubtedly generalized too boldly from the history of his
own section. But the frontier did not bring about democracy in the Gulf

states or in some other parts of the world, such as Latin America. Turner's opponents point out that the new Western state constitutions were modeled after those of the East and that the ideas and institutions which the pioneers carried into the West were more important than their experiences after they settled there. The states of the upper valley became democratic primarily because they were founded by men who already believed in democratic ideals. Thus what "explains American development" is not the frontier so much as the evolution of the East and the trends common to all parts of the Atlantic community of nations. One detail in the Turner thesis has been particularly open to attack. Turner suggested that one of the ways in which the frontier strengthened democracy was by providing a safety valve for urban discontent. "Whenever social conditions tended to crystallize in the East," he declared, "whenever capital tended to press upon labor or political restraints to impede the freedom of the mass, there was this gate of escape to the free conditions of the frontier." In actuality, however, the westward movement was almost wholly a movement from the farms; exploited urban workers had neither the agricultural skill nor the capital needed to settle on the frontier.

Yet, in spite of the exaggerations of the Turner thesis, much of it can be accepted as valid. On the whole, the West was certainly more democratic than the East and had a stronger faith in human equality, although this was probably due not to the frontier experience itself but to the fact that it was settled by men and women who were looking for wider opportunities. Even the safety-valve theory has an element of truth when applied to ambitious young men of the professional class. The urban laborer could not become a frontier farmer; but the young lawyer or journalist beginning his career could move to recently settled territory, grow up with the country, and rise to a position of leadership much more easily than if he had stayed in the East. Without the open frontier, moreover, there would have been a much larger migration of young people from the farms into the cities; thus the frontier helped indirectly to check the exploitation of the working class by preventing it from expanding too rapidly.

Turner was undeniably correct in arguing that the westward movement weakened state and regional loyalties and promoted national unity. The spirit of sectionalism that had taken root in New England and the South could not easily grow up in areas where there was so much mobility. Most Westerners thought of themselves primarily as Americans, and wanted a strong national government with broad powers for developing transportation and promoting the general welfare. This nationalistic attitude was accompanied by a glorification of American achievements and institutions which often became boastful and aggressive. During the War of 1812, and again during the Mexican War of 1846–48, the demand for an expansionist foreign policy came chiefly from the West.

From the colonial period down to the present day, social theorists have held sharply divergent views about the effect of the westward movement on American civilization. While democratic enthusiasts have depicted the pioneer as engaged in creating a new and better society, free from the corruption and oppression of the Old World, conservatives have always pointed with alarm to the loss of high cultural standards and social discipline on the frontier, to its unrestrained individualism and materialistic standards, and to the growth of violence and disrespect for the law. But in actuality the most significant feature of the westward movement was that the pioneers took with them the essential institutions of their civilization. As soon as possible after the occupation of a new area, they set up elective governments, law courts, churches, schools, universities, printing presses, and newspapers. A frontier settlement was often lawless and culturally backward in its early days; but this was only a transitory phase in the adventure of building a new society in the wilderness.

X

The Old South

1. THE RISE OF KING COTTON

2. THE REVIVAL OF SLAVERY

3. SOUTHERN ECONOMIC PROBLEMS

4. SOUTHERN SOCIETY

5. SOUTHERN POLITICAL INTERESTS

W HILE the growth of the West was strengthening the democratic forces within the American Union, the South was turning away from Jeffersonian liberalism and developing attitudes and ideals that ran counter to dominant trends in all other parts of the United States. This was due primarily to the growth of cotton production and the consequent expansion of plantation agriculture and of slavery.

1. THE RISE OF KING COTTON

The Results of the Cotton Gin.   Prior to 1793 little cotton was produced in the United States. This was because the process of separating the fiber from the seeds had to be done by hand and took too much time to be profitable. A few planters grew a variety called sea-island cotton, in

---

SELECTED BIBLIOGRAPHY: C. S. Sydnor, *The Growth of Southern Sectionalism 1819–1848* (1948), and Avery Craven, *The Growth of Southern Nationalism, 1848–1860* (1953), are the relevant volumes in the *History of the South*. Kenneth M. Stampp, *The Peculiar Institution* (1956), is the best study of slavery. U. B. Phillips, *American Negro Slavery* (1918), and *Life and Labor in the Old South* (1929), are based on extensive research but show some Southern bias. J. H. Franklin, *From Slavery to Freedom* (1947), gives the viewpoint of a Negro scholar. The standard study of Southern agriculture is L. C. Gray, *History of Agriculture in the Southern United States to 1860* (2 vols., 1933). Frank L. Owsley, *Plain Folk of the Old South* (1949, stresses the importance of the middle-class farmers. Three useful studies of political and cultural attitudes are J. T. Carpenter, *The South as a Conscious Minority 1789–1861* (1930); Clement Eaton, *Freedom of Thought in the Old South* (1940); and W. S. Jenkins, *Pro-Slavery Thought in the Old South* (1935).

which the process was exceptionally easy; but this plant required special climatic conditions which were found only close to the sea. What was needed was a mechanical contrivance for cleaning out the seeds. The answer to the problem was the cotton gin, and this was invented in 1793 by Eli Whitney, a Connecticut Yankee, recently graduated from Yale, who had come to Georgia to teach school. Whitney hoped to retain ownership of his invention, and planned to set up ginning mills and charge tolls for their use; but he was unable to maintain his patent rights, and after some expensive lawsuits he returned to Connecticut and transferred his energies to the manufacture of firearms.

Few inventions in history have had more far-reaching consequences. Without the cotton gin, plantation agriculture would probably have survived only in a small part of the South. The most important Southern crop of the colonial period, tobacco, was ceasing to be profitable, as a result partly of soil exhaustion and partly of increased production in other countries; before the end of the first quarter of the nineteenth century many of the tobacco-growers were bankrupt or close to it. Some other plantation crops, such as rice and sugar, still brought substantial profits, but rice could be grown only in the low country along the seacoast of Georgia and South Carolina, while sugar was confined to Louisiana. Up to 1793 the general trend in the South seemed to be towards diversified farming and the division of the plantations. Under such conditions it seemed likely that slavery might eventually be abolished by peaceful methods. Most Southern leaders of the late eighteenth century frankly admitted that it was an evil system, although at the same time they were afraid of race equality and therefore insisted that emancipation must be accompanied by a removal of the Negro population.

All this was changed by the cotton gin. Henceforth it was profitable to raise short-staple cotton, and the appropriate soil and climate for this plant existed over a vast area, stretching from Georgia and South Carolina westwards as far as Texas. With the growth of the British textile industry, cotton-growers were assured of a market for whatever they could produce. Cotton-growing, moreover, was suited to slave labor, which is more economical than wage labor only under rather special conditions. It was possible to keep a slave on a cotton plantation occupied throughout the year, with few idle periods. Most of the labor did not require much skill or training; and since the field work could be done by gangs, with one white man overlooking a large number of slaves, the costs of supervision were not excessive.

Nor did efficient cotton-growing necessarily require large plantations. In this respect cotton differed from the two other commercial crops of the Deep South, rice and sugar. Rice-production involved a number of different operations for which a large number of laborers was necessary, while sugar could not be produced without a heavy investment in machinery. But cotton was a more democratic crop. It could be grown successfully both by the wealthy planter who owned thousands of acres and hundreds of slaves and by the small farmer who cultivated a couple of hundred acres with two or three slaves to help him. Actually, right down to the Civil War, about half the total crop was raised by farmers owning less than six slaves apiece, although it was the larger planters who assumed leadership and determined political and social standards throughout the Cotton Kingdom.

Thus the results of the cotton gin were that a large part of the Southern population turned to cotton-growing, any trend towards a more diversified economy was checked, plantation agriculture was revitalized, and slavery began finally to be regarded not as an evil but as a positive good.

The Cotton Kingdom. Cotton spread first through parts of South Carolina and Georgia, and thence into central Tennessee. By 1810 annual production was in excess of 80,000,000 pounds. After the War of 1812 came the invasion of the Gulf regions of Alabama, Mississippi, and part of Louisiana, which by 1830 were producing more than the Atlantic states. This was followed by a movement into southeastern Arkansas and into Florida, which became a state in 1845. Meanwhile, settlers had carried cotton into Texas, which belonged to Mexico until 1836 and was added to the United States in 1845. At its greatest extent the cotton belt covered an area measuring 1,000 miles from east to west and varying from 200 to 700 miles in breadth, and included parts of nine states.

From the War of 1812 down to the Civil War, production continued to double every ten or twelve years. It amounted to 160,000,000 pounds in 1820 and to no less than 2,300,000,000 pounds in 1860. Less than one-fifth of the crop was sold to American factories, the remainder being shipped to Great Britain and the European continent. For more than forty years more than half of the total American exports regularly consisted of cotton. It was this dependence of both the American economy and British industry on Southern cotton that caused planter spokesmen to make such extravagant claims. Senator Hammond of South Carolina proclaimed in 1858: "What would happen if no cotton were furnished for three years? I will not stop to depict what every one can imagine, but this is certain: England would topple headlong and carry the whole civilized world with her, save the South. No, you do not dare to make war on cotton. No power on earth dares to make war upon it. Cotton *is* King."

Cotton, moreover, did not dominate only the area where it was grown; its indirect influence extended also to other areas of the South. The mountain regions of western Virginia and eastern Kentucky and Tennessee remained outside its orbit, as did much of North Carolina; but the seaboard South, especially Virginia, became a kind of tributary of the Cotton Kingdom. Old Virginia families were able to avoid bankruptcy by selling slaves and foodstuffs to the cotton states. This economic dependence was followed by political subordination, so that by the second quarter of the nineteenth century Southern leadership belonged definitely to the

cotton-growers, and the hegemony of the more liberal Virginia planters
had come to an end.

2. THE REVIVAL OF SLAVERY

AS SOON as one leaves the safe ground of statistics, almost everything
about the antebellum South becomes controversial. It is difficult to make
objective judgments about questions involving racial relationships which
still provoke intense emotions. Moreover, it is not easy to decide which features of Southern society were actually caused by slavery and which
were due to climate, to the frontier background, to the lack of large cities,
or to the fact that the Southern economy remained almost wholly agricultural. Even more fundamental is the problem of deciding what standards
to apply. When judged in statistical terms, the South appeared, on the
whole, more backward than the North. But one must remember that the
more important aspects of human life cannot be weighed and measured,
and that reliance on statistical indices is perhaps a weakness of the type of
civilization that developed in the Northern states. The average Northerner had more material goods than the average Southerner; but whether
his life was richer is another question.

One of the most conspicuous aspects of Southern development after
the rise of cotton, and certainly the most productive of controversy, was
the revival of slavery. An institution which in 1793 had few defenders and
was widely believed to be approaching dissolution had come to be
regarded two generations later as the very foundation of Southern society.

The Slave Population.   For the supply of slaves, the South was
dependent mainly upon the natural processes of reproduction. Importation from abroad was prohibited in 1808, as soon as the Constitution permitted it; and although there was some smuggling after this date, it was
not extensive enough to cause any substantial increase.

In some areas outside the cotton belt, especially in tidewater Virginia
and Maryland, planters had more slaves than they could profitably employ, and these were shipped southwards in large numbers. Southerners
never had easy consciences about selling their slaves; and the business of
trading in human beings was left to men of low character and social standing. But many owners in the upper South could not otherwise avoid
bankruptcy. This shift in the slave population from the upper to the lower
South, however, did not satisfy the needs of the expanding cotton economy, and the excess of demand over supply brought about rising prices,
especially after 1830. Before the invention of the cotton gin a young, able-
bodied field hand could be bought for $300 or $400. In the 1850's the price
sometimes rose to $1,500, or even above $2,000 for a skilled craftsman.
The total slave population increased from nearly 800,000 in 1790 to about
4,000,000 in 1860. The rate of increase was somewhat lower than among

the white population because of the higher death rate. The Negro infant mortality rate was twice that of the whites.

Status of the Slaves. It is not easy to generalize about the treatment of the slaves, since conditions varied sharply. There were farmers with two or three slaves, who lived and worked alongside their dependents and often regarded them much as Northern farmers regarded their hired men; middle-class planters who supervised a labor force of ten or twenty; and rich men owning several plantations who kept a retinue of house servants and entrusted the organization of the field to hired overseers. In general, the most favored group among the slaves were the house servants, and the worst exploitation occurred among the field hands subject to overseers.

Southern society expected its members to display a paternalistic attitude towards their slaves, watching over their welfare and tempering justice with mercy; and many planters discovered from experience that excessive severity defeated its own purposes and was less effective in eliciting hard work than was generosity. Enlightened owners often relied on incentives more than on punishments. Another important consideration was that a slave was an expensive piece of property, and his value would deteriorate if he were overworked or inadequately fed. But although the planter had many inducements to display a spirit of *noblesse oblige*, the fact remained that his slaves belonged to him and that he was free to do almost anything he pleased with them. According to Southern legal theory, the property of the owner consisted essentially in the labor of his slave, and only incidentally in his person; and there were therefore laws prohibiting murder and gross ill-treatment. But the law courts were inclined to give owners the benefit of any doubts. Such a situation presented temptations both to cruelty and to illicit sexual relations which many owners and overseers did not resist.

It is equally difficult to generalize about the attitudes held by the slaves themselves. The slave population included, at one extreme, the privileged butlers and nurses of the plantation houses, who were almost part of their owners' families; and a number of skilled craftsmen, who were often hired out by their owners and could sometimes keep their earnings. It included also many field laborers who were close to savagery. Obviously, the system bore hardest on those Negroes who had exceptional talents which they were prohibited from developing. Among the mass of the slave population, running away was not infrequent, but this was mostly a reaction to punishment or ill-treatment. Cases of organized resistance or outright rebellion were rare, even during the Civil War. This was probably due mainly to the lack of opportunities for concerted action among the Negroes, and to the elaborate methods of controlling them adopted by their owners and by the governments of the Southern states.

The maintenance of slavery required the enactment of "black codes" defining the status of Negroes and providing precautions against misbehavior. While the codes varied in different states, they became, in general, more stringent during the 1830's. The slave-owners were alarmed by the growth of the abolitionist movement in the North and by two attempts at rebellion. In 1822 a Charleston Negro called Denmark Vesey made plans for an armed insurrection, but he and his associates were arrested and put to death before they had taken any action. In 1831 Nat Turner in Virginia actually started a rebellion, and nearly sixty white people were killed before the movement was suppressed. After these events night patrols, already customary in the cotton belt, were organized in most other parts of the South in order to make sure that all Negroes were indoors after dark. It was made difficult, or in some states even illegal, for slaves to acquire freedom or become educated, and the free Negroes, who were most numerous in Virginia and Maryland, were subject to severe restrictions.

Justifications of Slavery. The change in Southern sentiment about slavery began to show itself in the 1820's. For the first time political and intellectual leaders began to declare that slavery was not an evil but a positive good and to regard it not as a transitory institution which would be abolished at some future date but as permanent.

A group of South Carolina planters issued a pamphlet in defense of slavery as early as 1822. Perhaps the most influential of early pro-slavery thinkers was Thomas R. Dew, professor at William and Mary College, who published a book on the subject in 1832. Dew was followed by a large number of other writers, one of the most notable being George Fitzhugh, whose *Sociology for the South* appeared in 1854. During the thirty years preceding the Civil War, in fact, a large part of the intellectual energy of the South was devoted, directly or indirectly, to the defense of its peculiar institution.

This pro-slavery propaganda was accompanied by a hardening of public sentiment. The older generation of Southerners mostly continued to believe that slavery was intrinsically wrong, although they also held that abolition would be out of the question for generations to come. But Southerners who grew up after the turn of the century often became militant champions of the institution and unwilling even to allow any discussion of it. As intolerance increased, those individuals who favored abolition often found it necessary either to keep quiet or to leave the South. There was, in fact, an appreciable migration of opponents of slavery across the Ohio, the result being to weaken the liberal forces remaining in the South.

In order to understand these intense emotions, it must be realized that with the growth of liberal ideals, not only in the Northern states but also in most other parts of the world, the South increasingly felt herself isolated and under attack. Slavery had been abolished in the French colonies during the Revolution, throughout the British Empire in 1833, and in almost all the Latin American countries before 1860. By that date,

the only other parts of the civilized world where slavery survived were
Brazil, Cuba, and Dutch Guiana, and in none of these countries was it
accompanied by rigid race barriers. World trends seemed to be leading
towards race equality, and this was something which most white Southerners, particularly those living in areas where they were outnumbered
by Negroes, had been brought up to regard as intolerable.

In defending slavery, Southern leaders used arguments derived from
religion, biology, history, and economics. They asserted that it was in
accord with the will of God as revealed in the Bible, and quoted a few
Biblical passages which appeared to justify it. They tried to prove that
the Negro race was congenitally inferior to the white race, pointed out
that high civilizations in the past, like that of the ancient Greeks, had
been based on slavery, and went on to argue that slavery provided the
best system of economic organization.

The last of these defenses was the most far-reaching in its implications, and showed most clearly how far the South had departed from the
liberalism of the early Virginian leaders. In any society, said Southern
spokesmen, the necessary physical work had to be done, and some class
of men had to be compelled to do it. Cultural achievement and the amenities of civilization were impossible without an upper class which was free
from the burdens of labor. This being the case, American society had to
choose between the Southern system of slavery and the Northern system
of wage labor; and of the two, slavery was both more stable and more
humane. On the one hand, the plantation South was not threatened by
trade unions, strikes, and the growth of radical ideas. On the other hand,
unlike the Northern manufacturers, the slave-owners were responsible for
the welfare of their dependents, seeing that they were adequately fed and
clothed and maintaining them when they were unable to work. Whereas a
Northern wage-earner might be thrown out to starve when he grew old or
whenever business succumbed to a depression, a Southern slave could
always be sure of a home and livelihood.

Thus Southerners took the offensive against the North, scoring some
valid points against the weaknesses of the Northern economic system, and
used arguments that seemed to imply that slavery ought to be extended
throughout the civilized world.

3. SOUTHERN ECONOMIC PROBLEMS

IN SPITE of the profits made by the cotton-planters, the economy of the
South had a number of weaknesses, although it is not easy to decide how
far these were due to slavery and how far to other factors.

Economic Results of Slavery. Even from a narrowly economic
point of view, slavery was not an efficient labor system. In spite of the
practice adopted by the more enlightened planters of awarding bonuses
for good service, the slaves did not generally have enough incentive to do

more than could be extracted from them by compulsion. Their owners normally made money out of them—there is little basis for the suggestion that economic factors alone might eventually have ended the system—but this was due to the low maintenance costs of slave labor, not to its efficiency.

Slavery, moreover, made the whole economic system of the South less flexible and less progressive than that of the North. When an employer had to invest capital in buying his labor force before he could begin operations, and when he could not dispose of his labor force in bad times except by selling it, it became difficult to experiment with new and risky enterprises. One reason for the excessive dependence of the Deep South on cotton was that this was one crop to which slave labor was demonstrably well suited and for which there was always a market. Thus slavery was one of the factors preventing the South from developing a more diversified economy. Another way in which it retarded Southern growth was by discouraging immigration. Newcomers from Europe preferred to settle in regions where they would not have to compete with slave labor. In 1860 only 13.4 per cent of the total foreign-born population were in the South, and most of them were living either in New Orleans or in border states like Maryland and Missouri.

Progress was impeded not only by the economics of the slave system but also by the psychological attitudes associated with it. The way to win prestige was to acquire a plantation and a large number of slaves, and in most parts of the Deep South this meant growing cotton. Ambitious young men set out to grow cotton in the hope that they could one day climb to the top of the social pyramid. Southern society offered little encouragement to any activity not involving the ownership of land and slaves. And since work under another man's supervision was associated with servitude, relatively few white men were willing to become wage laborers, even when the alternative was a meager living on an eroded small farm. The result was that the antebellum South did not produce either a large business class or a large free working class. Society remained preponderantly agricultural and rural.

Dependence on the North.   Agricultural societies throughout history have usually been at a disadvantage in their dealings with business communities, and the South was no exception. Only about half the money paid by British manufacturers for American cotton was actually received by the planters; the remainder went to business firms whose headquarters were usually in the Northern states.

After the cotton had been picked and cleaned, it was transported to the nearest port, New Orleans being the center for much of the Gulf region. Here it was taken over by the factors, most of them representing Northern mercantile firms, who handled the sale, and was loaded on to Northern-owned ships, and often, before being carried to Britain, was shipped first to New York. In exchange for their cotton, the planters bought manufactured goods from Britain or from the North. Most British imports went first to New York instead of directly to the South, and for a number of years after 1816 the prices were raised as a result of the tariffs passed for the protection of Northern industry. Like all farmers, more-over, the planters frequently had to borrow money in anticipation of the harvest; and since there was little banking capital in the South, this meant, directly or indirectly, borrowing from the North. As with most raw materials, moreover, cotton prices fluctuated sharply as a result of busi-ness trends over which the South could exercise no control. Between 1820 and 1860 the price varied between 17½ and 8 cents a pound.

As a result of paying commissions to Northern merchants, transporta-tion charges to Northern shipowners, high prices for manufactured goods due to the tariff protecting Northern industry, and interest to Northern bankers, the South as a whole labored under a growing burden of debt. By 1860 the total debt of the South to the North was probably close to $200,000,000. During periods of 8-cent cotton the planters were likely to develop bitter feelings against their Northern creditors.

Starting in the 1820's, a number of Southern leaders argued that the Cotton Kingdom should make itself independent of the North by ceasing to be exclusively agricultural, and they advocated a program of sectional self-sufficiency. The South should trade directly with Britain, instead of buying and selling through New York, and develop industries of its own. But in spite of many eloquent speeches at public meetings and conven-tions and much newspaper support, little was done to achieve these ob-jectives. Iron foundries were built at Richmond, Virginia, and proved to be invaluable in supplying the Southern need for munitions during the Civil War. Some textile manufacturing developed in Georgia and the Carolinas. William Gregg, who was perhaps the leading Southern cham-pion of industrialism, began manufacturing cotton cloth at Graniteville, Georgia, in 1845. Slaves were successfully employed in many of the South-ern factories and railroads, sometimes replacing white workers who went on strike (as happened in the Richmond iron foundries in 1847). In fact (as Kenneth Stampp observes), "every slave state had industrial estab-lishments which made some use of slave labor." But by 1860 less than 10 per cent of all American industrial production was done by the South.

The chief obstacles to business and industrial development were probably social and psychological rather than strictly economic. The South had the labor and the natural resources, and could have raised the capital. But as long as cotton was king, there was no sufficient incentive for industrial and business development.

4. SOUTHERN SOCIETY

IN SPITE of the pervasive influence of slavery throughout the three or four decades before the Civil War, a large majority of the white population of the South had, in actuality, no direct connection with the institution. In the Southern states as a whole, not more than a quarter of the white heads of families were slave-owners, and even in the cotton states the proportion was less than one-third. Among the slave-owners, moreover, a large majority were small farmers rather than planters. In 1850 there were 348,000 slave-owning families. Half of them owned fewer than five slaves apiece, and nearly three-quarters of them owned fewer than ten slaves apiece. Only 93,000 families (half of them in the cotton states) had ten or more slaves, and only 8,000 (three-quarters of them in the cotton states) had fifty or more.

Thus the typical citizens of the South were not the small minority of wealthy planters but the small farmers who composed the vast mass of the people. These can be divided into several different groups.

Farmers Outside the Plantation South.   Some Southern farmers lived in regions where slavery was almost unknown and none of the plantation crops were raised. These included the western part of Virginia, much of the back country of North Carolina, the mountains of eastern Kentucky and Tennessee, and parts of other states outside the cotton belt. Like their ancestors during the colonial period, the inhabitants of these regions were generally hostile to the plantation aristocracy and to the institution of slavery, although at the same time they had no sympathy for the Negroes.

As late as 1832 a proposal for the gradual abolition of slavery in Virginia, strongly supported by the western counties of the state, failed to pass the legislature by only a small margin. The proposal included a plan for transporting the freed Negroes to Africa. This attitude of hostility to both the planters and the Negroes found expression a generation later in the writings of Hinton R. Helper, who was a native of the back country of North Carolina, although a resident of New York. In 1857 Helper published *The Impending Crisis of the South*, in which he argued that slavery and the rule of the slave-owners were leading the South to economic and cultural ruin. Helper's book infuriated most of the planters, who regarded it as virtually abolitionist propaganda and refused to allow it circulation in the South; but, unlike the abolitionists, Helper was strongly opposed to race equality.

During the Civil War the people of these mountain areas refused, as far as possible, to support the Confederacy. The western counties of Virginia stayed with the North, and were admitted to the Union as the new state of West Virginia, while there was a strong unionist movement in eastern Tennessee, headed by Andrew Johnson.

Poor Whites.   Another group among those who owned no slaves consisted of the so-called "poor whites." In parts of the South, especially in Georgia and Alabama, there were white families who had settled in pine barrens or other infertile areas where successful farming was impossible. Their degenerate way of life was due partly to poverty and partly to devitalization resulting from hookworm, pellagra, or malaria. Both before the Civil War and afterwards they received more publicity than their importance warranted. Abolitionists liked to point to them as proofs of their contention that slavery caused the degeneration of the mass of the white population, while in recent years they have formed the subject-matter of books like *Tobacco Road*. In actuality the genuine "poor whites" of the South were never very numerous, probably little more so than similar groups in the North.

Farmers of the Plantation Country. The majority of the Southern farmers were neither hostile to the institution of slavery nor by any means "poor whites." Throughout the Cotton Kingdom and other plantation sections they composed a vigorous middle class as strongly devoted to Southern ideals as were the large slave-owners. To some extent they suffered from competition with the richer planters, who were able to buy the most fertile lands; but this did not cause them to develop any doubts about the beneficence of slavery. Some of them were indirectly connected with the plantation system, selling food to the planters, or occasionally serving as overseers. Probably a more important reason for their conservatism was that they did not wish to weaken the barriers of race and color which made them superior to the Negroes.

The more ambitious farmers, moreover, hoped to rise into the planter class. The cotton belt had been settled too rapidly for class lines to crystallize; a number of the rich planters had begun with little capital except their energy and ambition, and others hoped to follow their example. But while this attitude prevented class conflicts from developing within Southern society, it also tended in the course of time to generate some dangerously explosive forces. As the cotton belt was settled and most of the fertile land was occupied, and as the price of slaves grew higher, it became more difficult for Southern farmers to climb the economic and social ladder. Their hopes could not be realized unless new territories were made available for settlement, the supply of slaves was increased and the price reduced, and cotton-growing was made more profitable. It was not the richer planters of the cotton belt but the more ambitious middle-class farmers—men who owned a few slaves or none at all—who gave the strongest support to the aggressive and expansionist program of the Southern "fire-eaters" of the 1840's and 1850's.

The Planters. The wealthy planter families who belonged to the Southern upper class comprised, as we have seen, a rather small group. These were the men and women who have been depicted so often in novels and motion pictures that many people suppose that they were typical of the Old South. As everybody knows, they often lived in large white mansions with pillared fronts in the Greek style, were looked after by devoted Negro servants, idealized feminine beauty and purity, expected men to be gallant, courteous, and chivalrous, gave lavish entertainments to their numerous friends and relatives, and liked to drink mint juleps in magnolia-scented gardens. Plantation life was not, in reality, so easygoing or so gracious as popular descriptions suggest; slave labor required incessant supervision and gave everything a disorderly and even slovenly quality. But Southern upper-class society, with its emphasis on social intercourse and on kinship ties, did indeed give its members a rich and rewarding life.

Having achieved dominance through the ownership of land, the planters looked back to earlier landed aristocracies for models with which they could identify themselves. They endeavored to establish an appropriate social ideal and code of conduct, derived from the European upper-class tradition; and some of them liked to believe that they were actually descended from the nobility and gentry of medieval and Tudor England, in contrast to the Northerners, whom they supposed to have sprung from the middle and lower classes. Their wives and daughters read books giving idealized portrayals of life in the age of feudalism, especially the novels by Sir Walter Scott. Based on a belief in the virtues of an aristocracy, the Southern code of chivalry ran counter to the dominant trends of nineteenth-century civilization, and helped in the end to lead the South to the catastrophe of the Civil War. Like all social ideals, it was rooted in the economic system, and was often more honored in the breach than in the observance. Yet, in so far as it inculcated courage, generosity, and a spirit of *noblesse oblige*, there was much about it that was worthy of respect.

The extent to which the South was actually controlled by this upper class cannot easily be defined, since conditions varied in different areas and at different periods. Planter dominance was exercised mainly through the county court system, derived from colonial Virginia and indirectly from Tudor England. The county courts were the main agencies for both administration and law enforcement. The justices were normally chosen from the planter class, and according to the original rule they held office through appointment by the state governor and for life.

During the 1820's and 1830's, however, there was a trend towards more democratic government, with some sharp political conflicts. In five of the Southern states the county court system was not changed, and to a large extent the planters continued to be the ruling class. Elsewhere county officials were henceforth elected for limited terms. But this growth of democracy did not change the prevalent attitudes towards the South's peculiar institution. It meant a transference of political power from the larger planters to the middle-class farmers, who were often even more militant in defending slavery.

Cultural Trends.   Agriculture, politics, and conversation were the chief Southern occupations. Original intellectual activity received, on the whole, little encouragement. Young men of the planter class normally went to college. While the South had a higher rate of illiteracy than the North and did less to provide public education for the mass of its citizens, it also had a higher proportion of college graduates. But Southern college education continued to be based mainly on the study of the classics, which had been associated since the Renaissance with the ideal of the gentleman. Some notable scientific work was done in the South, but less than in the North; and Southern writers were discouraged by general public indifference, and had to depend mainly on Northern publishing houses and Northern audiences. Southerners occasionally made speeches urging greater cultural independence; but, as with the campaigns for economic independence, little was ever done to bring it about. The South did not begin to produce major works of literature until the twentieth century.

As the South grew more conscious of being out of step with the rest of the world, it also became more hostile to current intellectual trends. This was manifest in its religious development. The nineteenth-century South repudiated the rationalism of the early Virginia leaders and returned to a strict belief in revelation and in the Bible as the inspired word of God. Episcopalianism retained its social prestige along the Atlantic seaboard, but most of the wealthy planters in the cotton belt preferred the stricter Presbyterian Church, while the mass of the people were Methodists or Baptists. This rise of religious fundamentalism led to the removal from office of two college presidents, both of them men of wide influence and intellectual distinction who had served for a number of years: Horace Holley of Transylvania University in 1827 and Thomas Cooper of South Carolina College in 1834.

Another quality of Southern life which intensified sectional differences was the propensity towards the use of violence. With the spread of bourgeois ways of life, people in most other parts of the world were becoming more peaceable in their personal relationships, but Southerners continued to believe that violation of a gentleman's code of good behavior could properly be dealt with only through physical combat. The practice of formal dueling survived in the South long after it had been abandoned in the North, as did also the use of fists or bowie knives. Politics in the Deep South was a dangerous occupation, since political leaders were sometimes knifed by their opponents. Public characters who traduced the Southern code were sometimes threatened with hanging by lynch law, and such suggestions were not intended as merely rhetorical.

That the South was culturally less productive and less tolerant than the North has sometimes been attributed to the blighting influence of slavery. But probably it was due much more to the fact that the South had remained rural. The arts and sciences and liberal opinions flourish best in close proximity to urban centers, such as Boston and New York. But south of the border states there was no city except New Orleans with a population in excess of 50,000. Nor did the agricultural economy of the South offer much support for any intellectual class. Much of the South, moreover, was still essentially frontier country, and the planter families in the Gulf states had risen to leadership too quickly to develop much breadth of culture. Another factor which should not be overlooked was the climate. In much of the Deep South the temperature through a large part of the summer exceeded ninety degrees in the shade. Under a Southern sun human beings were likely to be both more easygoing and more prone to violence than in Massachusetts.

5. SOUTHERN POLITICAL INTERESTS

Economic Grievances. The divergent interests of North and South had been a major subject of controversy as early as the Philadelphia Convention of 1787 and had been one of the factors causing the party conflict between the Federalists and the Republicans. The economic changes of the early nineteenth century made the differences more acute. They were an increasingly important factor in Federal politics during the 1820's and 1830's, although it was not until after 1848 that they can be said to have dominated the political scene.

By the 1820's it was becoming apparent that the South would remain predominantly agricultural, and that Federal legislation for economic expansion would benefit only the North. While Northern manufacturers wanted higher tariff rates for protection against foreign competition, Southern planters complained that the tariff compelled them to pay higher prices for what they bought. Southerners also resented Federal protection for American shipping and fisheries, and Federal spending on internal improvements. Relying mainly on its rivers for transportation, the South was slow to build roads and canals, and most of the Federal money voted for such purposes was spent in the North. Southerners began to complain that while, through the tariff, they contributed more than their share of Federal revenues, they received less than their share of the benefits. Thus Federal policy tended to intensify the exploitation of Southern agriculture by Northern business.

In 1845 Southerners were calculating that 78 per cent of all Federal taxes collected since 1791 had been paid by the South, while 85 per cent of all Federal spending on internal improvements had gone to the North. These figures were, no doubt, exaggerated, but the fact that most Southerners believed them was a potent stimulus to sectional hostility.

Southern resentment of Federal policy showed itself first on the Atlantic seaboard. By the 1820's South Carolina was suffering from falling profits and land values, the main causes of which were the declining fertility of her soil and the westward migration of many of her citizens. Being unable to counteract the effects of the rich soil of Alabama and Mississippi, the South Carolinians turned their attention to the Federal government and attributed their troubles to the tariff. Calhoun was the chief political figure in the state. Formerly a strong nationalist, he now changed into a champion of Southern sectional interests, and in the course of time his theories as to the nature of the Federal Union were accepted through a large part of the South.

Calhoun. Born of Scotch-Irish Calvinist ancestry in the South Carolina back country, Calhoun belonged only by marriage, not by birth, to the planter aristocracy; and with his austere manners and mode of life and his narrowly intellectual interests, he seemed in some ways more like a citizen of Massachusetts than of Charleston. It was primarily because of his capacity for uncompromising logic that he became the chief political spokesman of the cotton belt. South and North, he had come to believe, had opposite interests, and the South was a minority section. The North had always had a majority in the House of Representatives, and since immigration was increasing its population faster than that of the South, its preponderance would increase. Thus the rule of a numerical majority meant Northern domination. Southern rights could be safeguarded only if majority rule were checked.

Calhoun was concerned with one of the permanent problems of government; and whatever one may think of the practical results of his logic, it should be recognized that the theoretical analysis which he presented in his *Disquisition on Government* was a contribution to political theory of permanent importance. The protection of minority rights had been one of the main objectives of the American Constitution. The same problem in a different form confronted the men who drafted the Charter of the United Nations, and resulted in the adoption of the veto power. A veto was also Calhoun's solution. The powers of the Federal government must be limited, and a minority section must be allowed to block action detrimental to its interests. In his *South Carolina Exposition and Protest* of 1828 Calhoun adopted a states' rights theory of the Constitution, arguing that sovereignty remained with the states and that any state could nullify an act of the Federal government which it regarded as unconstitutional. In later years he favored adoption of some system of concurrent majorities by which consent of both sections would be needed for Federal legislation. Calhoun was not an advocate of secession; on the contrary, his main objective, as he saw it, was to make it unnecessary for the South to secede. But it is obvious that adoption of his proposals would have fatally weakened the Federal Union.

In so far as Calhoun's purposes were to protect agricultural interests and limit Federal powers, he was the successor of Jefferson and John Taylor. But he did not share Jefferson's liberalism. Defending slavery as a positive good, he frankly repudiated the doctrine of human equality as expressed in the Declaration of Independence. And his theory of nullification was a much more extreme assertion of state sovereignty than Jefferson's Kentucky Resolutions. Nor was Calhoun consistent in his opposition to Federal power. He was against it only in so far as it worked to the detriment of the South. In the 1840's, when he hoped to see Southern control of the Federal government and the spending of Federal money on internal improvements beneficial to the South, he was willing to defend a loose construction of the Constitution.

Thus, under Calhoun's leadership, the South reacted to the threat of Northern domination by adopting a theory of the Federal Union which Northern and Western nationalists regarded as close to treason. After 1830, moreover, the sectional conflict, hitherto due mainly to economic differences, was gradually intensified by the divergence of attitudes towards slavery; the South became increasingly outspoken in the defense of her peculiar institution, while a militant abolitionist movement began to develop in parts of the North.

XI

The Industrial Revolution

1. THE REVOLUTION IN TRANSPORTATION

2. THE REVOLUTION IN MANUFACTURING

3. THE GROWTH OF THE LABORING CLASS

4. FOREIGN TRADE AND SHIPPING

INDUSTRIAL REVOLUTION is the name given to a long series of improvements in methods of production which have, in their total effect, transformed human life more fundamentally than any other change since the adoption of agriculture. Although their beginnings can be traced back to the Middle Ages, it was not until the late eighteenth century that they acquired real momentum. The traditional handicraft methods then began to be revolutionized by the invention of machines and by the use of the steam engine and other sources of power. This meant that work had to be done in factories instead of homes, and the consequent mobilization of factory working forces led to a rapid growth of industrial cities. In order that food and fuel might be brought to the cities and factory products distributed, new forms of transportation had to be developed. And in order that farmers might produce a surplus large enough to feed the new

---

SELECTED BIBLIOGRAPHY: All aspects of the Industrial Revolution are covered in G. R. Taylor, *The Transportation Revolution 1815–1860* (1951). T. C. Cochran and W. Miller, *The Age of Enterprise* (1942), is a stimulating interpretation of industrial and business expansion throughout the nineteenth century. For manufacturing, one can also consult V. S. Clark, *History of Manufactures in the United States 1607–1928* (revised edition, 3 vols., 1929), which gives the facts with little interpretation, while the growth of the most important industry is admirably described in C. F. Ware, *The Early New England Cotton Manufacture* (1931). The standard authority on labor history is J. R. Commons and others, *History of Labor in the United States*, of which Vol. 1 (1918) deals with this period. N. J. Ware, *The Industrial Worker 1840–1860* (1924), is very useful for the decades covered. The standard authority on trade is E. R. Johnson and others, *History of Domestic and Foreign Commerce of the United States* (2 vols., 1915). The best general account of shipping is J. G. B. Hutchins, *The American Maritime Industries and Public Policy 1789–1914* (1941), which can be supplemented with S. E. Morison's delightful *Maritime History of Massachusetts 1783–1860* (1921).

urban populations, agricultural methods had to be improved. The Industrial Revolution thus involved, more or less simultaneously, changes in manufacturing, communication, and agriculture. One of its earliest and most important effects was to bring about a rapid growth of population.

The Industrial Revolution took place initially in Great Britain, whose priority was due largely to her possession of the appropriate natural resources, especially coal and iron, and to a labor scarcity that stimulated manufacturers to turn to machinery. Also important were the establishment of political institutions giving security to individual enterprise and a government favorable to the business class. The movement was, moreover, in harmony with the rationalistic and progressive spirit of the Enlightenment, although in its early stages it was not directly connected with science. The early inventions were the work of practical mechanics, and it was not until the late nineteenth century that scientific research began to have important direct effects upon technology.

Well established in Great Britain by the end of the eighteenth century, the Industrial Revolution then began to spread to other parts of western Europe and across the Atlantic. In the United States industrial growth was favored by vast natural resources, by the maintenance of political unity and stability over a wide area, by government protection and encouragement, and by the fact that the pioneering experience had already created attitudes favorable to individual initiative and economic advancement.

1. THE REVOLUTION IN TRANSPORTATION

THE MOST conspicuous early manifestations of the Industrial Revolution in the United States were a series of new developments in transportation. Some of them, such as canals and hard-surfaced roads, were copied from Great Britain, while others, such as the steamboat, were native inventions. All these innovations raised difficult questions as to the relationship between government and private enterprise. Owing to the urgent need for better means of transportation and to the heavy cost of construction, it was necessary for government to contribute at least part of the capital. Should these enterprises be under public ownership? Or, if they were left to private ownership, how far should government protect the public interest by regulating their rates and services? Throughout the first half of the nineteenth century there was almost continuous discussion of these problems, and a different solution was adopted for each of the new developments.

Roads and Bridges.   The first hard-surfaced road in the United States was completed in 1794 and ran from Philadelphia to Lancaster, Pennsylvania. This inaugurated a period of road-building, about $40,000,-000 being invested in new roads before 1812. With the notable exception of the National Highway, which was built by the Federal government, most of them were constructed and owned by private corporations, which expected to make profits on their investments by charging tolls. State governments chartered these corporations, and frequently contributed a large part of their capital. Most of the early corporations in the United States were, in fact, formed for the purpose of building roads and bridges.

In practice few of the roads brought any substantial profits. Most of the corporations that constructed them quickly went out of business, and ownership then passed to the state governments. Some of the bridge corporations, on the other hand, earned substantial revenues, partly because their initial charters often gave them monopolistic rights. A notorious case was that of the company which had been chartered in 1786 to build a bridge across the Charles River from Boston to Cambridge, Massachusetts. During the next forty years this company made a profit amounting to thirty times its initial investment, while claiming that, according to its charter, no competing bridge could be built.[1] Popular resentment against such privileges, however, caused a gradual change of policy. To an increasing extent charters given to road and bridge corporations included a provision that when the original investment had been paid off, the projected work should become public property.

Steamboats. The second transportation improvement was the steamboat, which was regularly used for inland waterways long before it replaced the sailing ship for ocean traffic. John Fitch had invented a practicable steamboat as early as the 1780's, but the first person to make the idea commercially successful was Robert Fulton. Fulton's *Clermont*, launched in 1807, traveled up the Hudson from New York to Albany and back again in sixty-two hours. But it was on the Mississippi and its tributaries that steamboats were most widely used. The first Mississippi steamboat was built at Pittsburgh in 1811 by Nicholas Roosevelt. A special type of vessel was gradually evolved, capable of navigating in extremely shallow water (in a heavy dew, according to a popular saying) and providing luxurious accommodation for passengers. The period down to the Civil War was the great age of Mississippi steamboating, commemorated for all time in the writings of Mark Twain.

In the age of the steamboat, as in the age of the automobile, it was an American characteristic to prefer speed to safety; fires, boiler explosions, and other catastrophes were not infrequent, particularly when, as often happened, competing vessels raced each other. By 1850 it was estimated that more than a thousand Mississippi steamboats had been destroyed, with a correspondingly heavy loss of life. This caused the steamboat to become the first form of transportation to be subjected to Federal regulation. By the Steamboat Act of 1852, which marked a significant innovation in government policy, a safety code was prescribed and inspectors were to be appointed to enforce it.

---

[1] In 1837 the United States Supreme Court disallowed this claim and authorized the building of another bridge. See page 249.

Canals.   After the steamboat, the next innovation was the canal. The canal-building period was inaugurated by the construction of the Erie, which linked the Hudson River with the Great Lakes and was built between 1817 and 1825 at a cost of about $8,000,000. The individual mainly responsible was De Witt Clinton, Governor of New York from 1816 to 1822 and again from 1824 to 1828.[2] Unlike the roads, this and a number of the later canals were built and owned by the state governments. The completion of the Erie Canal immediately cut freight rates from Buffalo to Albany from $100 to $10 a ton, and within a few years it was bringing in $3,000,000 a year in tolls. It quickly paid for itself, and by providing cheap transportation between the Hudson and the West, caused a rapid growth in the wealth and importance of New York City. By 1850 nearly half of all American foreign trade was passing through New York.

The Erie was so astonishingly successful that other states plunged into a canal-building spree which ended unfortunately. Seaboard states planned competing links with the West, and Northwestern states set out to connect the Great Lakes with the Mississippi. Vast sums were borrowed by state governments, largely from European investors, while the Federal government gave assistance by making grants of public land. But many of these plans were too ambitious; some of the money appears to have been wasted; and during a period of economic depression that began in 1837 several states defaulted on their debts, causing immense indignation in Great Britain, to whose citizens most of these debts were owed. In the end some of these canal projects had to be abandoned, and there was little further building after 1850, by which time about 4,000 miles of canals had been completed. It was partly because of this canal experience that the American people came to believe that private enterprise was generally more efficient and less extravagant than public ownership.

Railroads.   Last and most important of the new internal improvements was the railroad. Practicable engines were devised during the 1820's by both American and British inventors, while the first American railroad was the Baltimore and Ohio, which began construction in 1828 and had enough track completed to run an engine over it by 1830. This was closely followed by the Charleston and Hamburg, which was opened for passenger service in 1831. Trains traveled at the then dizzy rate of about twelve miles an hour.

All the early American railroads were built westwards from Atlantic seaboard cities; Boston, Philadelphia, and Baltimore promoted lines in the hope of offsetting the advantages that New York had acquired from the Erie Canal, while in the South building was spurred by the commercial competition between Charleston and Savannah. By 1850 a total of 8,879

---

[2] Since 1875, when a Federal excise duty was imposed on tobacco, a picture of De Witt Clinton has appeared on every pack of cigarettes sold in the United States. The Treasury Department decided to honor him in this manner because 1875 marked the fiftieth anniversary of the completion of the canal.

miles had been completed, the best coverage being in New England. But almost all the lines were in the Eastern states, almost all of them ran from the coast inland, and except in upper New York, where by traveling on fourteen different systems it was possible to get from New York City to Buffalo, no lines had been completed connecting the Atlantic coast with any part of the trans-Appalachian country. Most of the railroad companies, moreover, controlled only a few miles of track, so that long-distance passengers had to make frequent changes from one line to another. The consolidation of different companies into large systems did not begin until after the middle of the century.

A few of the early railroads were state-owned; but the majority were built by private corporations, although until the financial crisis of 1837 much of the capital was contributed by state and municipal governments. And although the rates and services were subject to considerable state regulation, the railroads were usually allowed to make substantial profits and had little cause for complaint. Thus public policy was swinging back to the encouragement of private enterprise. This was due not only to the unfortunate canal experience but also to propaganda by businessmen and to the fact that capital was becoming more plentiful and could be raised more easily.

Large-scale manufacturing could not develop very far in the United States until after this revolution in transportation. But once freight rates had been cut by the building of roads and canals (the early railroads mostly carried passengers), it became possible for industrial establishments to obtain their raw materials and sell their products over a much wider area. The economy of the whole country then began to be unified into a single interdependent market, and different regions could specialize in particular forms of production.

The Telegraph. Another invention which promoted unification was the electric telegraph. Various people, in both Europe and the United States, had experimented with the sending of messages by electricity; but the first fully effective telegraph was devised in 1837 by Samuel F. B. Morse, who was a painter by profession and only a spare-time scientist. Congress voted money for building a line between Washington and Baltimore, the first message being transmitted in 1844. But the government decided not to retain public ownership, and the telegraph was then taken over by a number of small companies, which gradually became consolidated into one large corporation, Western Union. By 1861 it was possible to send messages to California, and in 1866 a cable was laid across the Atlantic. Thus not only the United States but the whole world was being drawn more closely together.

2. THE REVOLUTION IN MANUFACTURING

PRIOR to the Industrial Revolution most manufacturing in the United States had not been for sale. Farm families made most of what they needed for themselves, while on the Southern plantations some of the slaves were assigned to the various necessary crafts. In the Northern and Middle states, however, there was also some manufacturing for the market. Skilled artisans, some of them migratory and others located in the larger towns, produced various tools, utensils, and articles of clothing, while millers ground wheat and corn into flour. There were also a few relatively large establishments, especially the iron foundries.

Putting Out.   The growth of large-scale industry had two aspects: the development of capitalistic ownership, and the introduction of machinery. Before production was mechanized, some forms of manufacturing came under the control of merchant-capitalists instead of being carried on by independent craftsmen. Capitalists would buy raw materials, distribute it among a number of workers, and then collect and sell the finished product. Initially workers usually did their work in their own homes (this was known as the "domestic" or "putting-out" system), but there was a growing tendency to assemble them in factories.

Soon after the Revolution the putting-out system became well established in New England, where it enabled the wives and daughters of farmers to earn money by weaving. The system was also applied to shoe-making, which during the first half of the nineteenth century ranked as the fourth largest American industry in the value of its products. This industry came quite early under capitalist control, but most of the labor was done by hand and not by machinery until after 1850.

Textile Manufacturing.   The first industry to become fully mechanized was the manufacturing of textiles, particularly cotton goods. The textile industry in Great Britain had been revolutionized by a series of inventions in the course of the eighteenth century, and had become the leading example of the new factory system. It played a similar role in the United States. Until after the Civil War cotton manufacturing ranked second among American industries in the value of its products (the first and third places were occupied by flour-milling and lumbering); but it was first in importance in that it most fully represented the problems and potentialities of the new era.

Southern New England became the principal center of the industry and was the first region of the United States to become predominantly industrial. Probably the most important reason was that both capital and labor were available. New England merchants had made fortunes in foreign trade, and were willing to invest them in the building of factories as soon as they were convinced that this was likely to be more profitable. New England farmers were suffering from competition with the more fertile Mississippi Valley states; and while many of their sons joined the westward movement, many of their daughters were willing to work in industry. New England also had a suitable climate, while its numerous rivers provided water power. The early mills were generally driven by water and not by steam.

Various attempts were made in the late eighteenth century to introduce the new methods of machine production. But before American manufacturers could capture even the home market from their British competitors, a number of obstacles had to be overcome. Investors had to be persuaded to contribute capital; labor had to be found; above all, the necessary managerial and mechanical skills had to be learned by a process of trial and error. The first group to achieve any commercial success was the Rhode Island mercantile firm of Almy and Brown. Almy and Brown employed a mechanic named Samuel Slater, who had emigrated from Great Britain, to construct spinning machines at Pawtucket. Completed in 1791, these forerunners of the American industrial system were very humble contrivances, housed in a small shed, and operated by the labor of seven boys and two girls, none of whom was more than twelve years old.

Manufacturing grew very slowly prior to the War of 1812. But by putting a stop to foreign trade, the war compelled merchants to look for new investment opportunities, and also gave American producers protection, for the time being, against foreign competition. Several wealthy entrepreneurs therefore felt that the time was ripe for transferring their capital into industry. In 1813 Francis Cabot Lowell and a group of other merchants organized the Boston Manufacturing Company with a capital of $300,000, and built a factory at Waltham in which the whole process of making raw cotton into cloth was done by machinery of the then most up-to-date kind. This event may be regarded as the coming-of-age of American industry. An even larger organization, the Merrimack Manufacturing Company, went into business in 1823, establishing its mills in the new industrial city of Lowell. Cotton manufacturing also developed in other areas, especially around Philadelphia, although down to the Civil War four-fifths of the total product was made in New England. Other New England and Pennsylvania companies engaged in the manufacturing of woolen goods, but this developed more slowly, and it was not until after 1840 that more was produced by machinery than by hand.

Other Industries. Meanwhile, changes were occurring in other industries. A more highly mechanized process of flour-milling had been invented by Oliver Evans as early as 1782. As transportation improved, both flour-milling and meat-packing were carried on by larger plants, and became concentrated in cities close to the farm country: flour-milling mainly at Rochester and St. Louis, meat-packing first at Cincinnati and afterwards at Chicago.

The new need for machinery stimulated the iron industry, and this in turn was revolutionized early in the nineteenth century when coal and coke began to replace charcoal for smelting. The industry henceforth had to be located in areas where both coal and iron were available. By 1850 most of the works established along the seaboard during the colonial period had been abandoned, and the industry was becoming concentrated in the valleys of central and western Pennsylvania.

The reproductive metal industries, on the other hand, continued to flourish in New England, and the ingenuity of Yankee craftsmen brought about some important mechanical innovations. In 1798 Eli Whitney, having already revolutionized cotton-production in the South by inventing the cotton gin, began to plan a factory in which firearms, instead of being made separately by skilled gunsmiths, would be manufactured from interchangeable parts made by machinery. It was a quarter of a century before this new method was an assured success, but in the long run Whitney's firearm factory was perhaps even more significant than his cotton gin, since the use of interchangeable parts became one of the basic principles of modern mass production. Two other inventive Yankees were Elias Howe, who devised the first sewing machine in 1846, and A. L. Dennison, who built a factory at Waltham in 1848 by which watches could be made by machinery.

A few figures will illustrate American industrial growth. In 1820 the capital invested in American manufacturing amounted to $50,000,000; by 1850 this had increased to $500,000,000. In 1820 some 349,000 workers were employed; in 1850 the number was 956,000, about three-quarters of them male. The annual value of the product increased during the same period from $200,000,000 to $1,000,000,000. Apart from food-processing, however, industry was still mostly concentrated in the New England and Middle Atlantic states.

The Corporation.   The expansion of industry was accompanied by the development of new legal institutions by which capital might be organized more effectively. The building of a factory was usually beyond the resources of a single individual, and the early entrepreneurs therefore formed partnerships. Capital for any really large-scale enterprise, however, could be obtained only by the formation of a corporation, stock in which could be sold to a large number of investors.

During the 1830's and 1840's state governments gradually revised their laws in order to make incorporation easier. Limited-liability provisions were generally established, so that individual investors could no longer be held responsible for debts incurred by corporations in which they held stock. Another change was the adoption of general incorporation laws, beginning with Connecticut in 1837. Previously the chartering of a corporation required a special legislative act, and entrepreneurs with political influence, corrupt or otherwise, could often obtain monopolistic rights or other special privileges. General incorporation laws were therefore favored by middle-class citizens wishing to prevent monopoly and maintain effective competition. Such laws enabled any group of men to obtain a corporation charter by conforming with the prescribed legal processes; it was no longer necessary to ask the legislature for a special grant.[3] As a result of these legal developments, the corporation gradually

[3] See page 243.

became the favorite method of industrial organization, although it did not become dominant until after the Civil War.

The initial capital for the early American industrial enterprises was supplied mainly by merchants, while expansion was usually financed out of profits. Early entrepeneurs made a regular practice of reinvesting their earnings. British and other European businessmen invested heavily in American securities, but mostly in transportation rather than industry. As the number of corporations increased, there began to be much buying and selling of stocks, with consequent possibilities of speculation. As early as 1792 a group of New York traders, who were accustomed to meet on Wall Street to sell government securities or stock in land companies, had drawn up an informal agreement regulating their procedure—an event which marked the beginning of the New York stock exchange. Corporations gradually adopted the practice of employing banks and brokerage houses to sell new issues of stock, both in the United States and in Europe. By the 1850's the stock market had become an important part of the national economy, and shrewd investors had discovered that it was possible to make a great deal of money simply by buying and selling at the right moments.

These financial developments had important consequences. As industries grew larger, there was a tendency for ownership to become separated from management. When the ownership of stock in a corporation became diffused among a large number of people, most of them were unable or unwilling to maintain any real supervision over its activities. The functions of management had to be left to a few dominant investors. A further development occurred when rich men began to buy control of several corporations. In such cases they could not do more than determine broad policies; all the detailed supervision was entrusted to salaried executives, who might themselves have little or no capital in the companies they directed.

This separation of ownership from management was becoming conspicuous in the Massachusetts textile industry as early as the 1830's. On the one hand, stock-ownership was widely diffused; on the other hand, the Boston merchants who had built up the industry were beginning to invest their profits in a wide variety of enterprises, so that one man sometimes controlled a dozen different companies engaged in completely different occupations. This development had obvious dangers, which soon began to cause controversy. When a corporation was controlled by a few dominant financiers and managed by salaried executives, smaller stockholders were likely to complain that their rights and interests were not properly protected. In the new corporate structure owners were, in fact, beginning to lose their traditional privileges and responsibilities, although the full implications of this transformation did not become apparent until the twentieth century.

3. THE GROWTH OF THE LABORING CLASS

Labor Conditions.   Since there was relatively little immigration between the Revolution and the 1830's, the native farm population, including the women and children, was at first the main source of labor. Small children were employed in the first textile factories. The Boston Manufacturing Company, on the other hand, set out to attract young women, for which purpose it built boarding-houses, carefully supervised the morals of its employees, encouraged them to develop cultural interests, prescribed regular church attendance, and blacklisted anybody who broke any of the rules. This was known as the Waltham System, and received much highly favorable publicity. The mills at Waltham and Lowell became show places, and were much admired by visiting foreigners. Farmers' daughters made a practice of spending a few years as factory workers, often in the hope that if they saved some money, they would have a better chance of securing husbands; the westward movement had caused a shortage of young men in rural New England. In 1831 four-fifths of the New England textile-factory operatives were women.

By modern standards, of course, labor conditions in the early factories were not good. The hours, even for small children, were from sunrise to sunset, with short intervals for breakfast and dinner; and even the adult male worker could not usually earn as much as a dollar a day. But such conditions did not seem bad to most contemporaries, especially when they were contrasted with the much longer hours and much lower wages prevalent in the factories and coal mines of Great Britain. It had always been customary for people on the farms to work through the day and for small children to be required to do their share as soon as possible. It seemed natural to everybody that the same long hours should prevail in the factories, and that children should contribute to the family income. Hard work was regarded as a religious duty, especially in New England, while leisure might lead to sinfulness. Only very gradually was it realized that factory labor, in which conditions were often unhealthful and the pace was set not by the worker but by the machine, was much more exhausting than farm labor.

From the 1830's, immigrants from Europe comprised an increasing proportion of the laboring class. Immigrants now began to pour in from Ireland, which was suffering from overpopulation, aggravated by the ownership of most of the land by English absentee landlords and by discriminatory legislation on the part of the British government. Irish immigrants to the United States numbered 207,000 in the decade of the thirties, 781,000 in the forties, and 914,000 in the fifties. The Irish had been farmers in their homeland, but most of them reached America without financial resources and therefore had to seek jobs in industry. They performed much of the manual labor on the later canals and railroads, worked in the coal and iron fields of Pennsylvania, crowded into New York, Philadelphia,

and Boston, and began to replace native labor in the New England textile
factories. During the 1830's the textile industry was in difficulties owing
to overproduction; wages were reduced and speed-up practices enforced.
The Waltham System no longer seemed so idyllic; the girls actually went
on strike, and the blacklist began to be used not only to enforce moral
standards but also to prevent agitators from getting jobs. Thus the mills
became less attractive to the farm girls, and Irish workers gradually took
their places.

Prior to the Industrial Revolution there had been no large permanent
working class in the United States (apart from the Negro slaves). This
had been a country, unlike Europe, where most people were economically
independent and where the individual wage-earner could always hope to
work his way up and (in Lincoln's words) was not "fixed to that condition
for life." But with the growth of large-scale industry and of capitalist
organization this was no longer true. A large part of the population must
expect to spend their lives as wage-earners and could not achieve economic
independence unless they had exceptional ability or good fortune.

As the factory system expanded, moreover, urban areas sprang up in
which workers were housed in the cheapest manner possible and virtually
nothing was done to protect public health or provide any amenities.
While cities like New York and Philadelphia grew with appalling rapidity,
new industrial towns were built in which factories, houses, and stores were
all owned by a single big corporation. In urban slum areas life was much
harsher and more restricted than on the farms, even though monetary
earnings might be larger.

Another evil of the industrial system was its insecurity. Periods of
high profits and business expansion alternated with depression periods in
which profits shrank and workers were discharged. Throughout the nineteenth century it was generally assumed that little could be done to regulate the business cycle or mitigate its consequences. Unemployed workers
must live on private charity until business improved.

Trade Unions.   The earliest labor unions were formed not among
the factory workers but among skilled craftsmen like the shoemakers
(then known as "cordwainers"), hatters, carpenters, masons, and printers.
Many of these men had formerly been independent but were now becoming employees of merchant-capitalists, so that their economic condition was deteriorating; this gave them a stimulus to organize, of a kind
that was lacking among the textile workers who had no craft tradition
behind them. Since factory workers, moreover, were generally unskilled
and could therefore be easily replaced if they caused trouble, their bargaining power was weak.

Labor organizations appeared in Philadelphia before the end of the
eighteenth century. In 1799, for example, the Philadelphia cordwainers
went on strike in order to obtain wage increases and organized a "tramp-
ing committee" to picket the shops and prevent scabs from going to work.

But the early unions were mostly very short-lived, being formed in response to some specific grievance and dissolving as soon as the issue had been decided.

There was a rapid growth of labor organization between 1828 and 1837. This was in response to the rapid increase of capitalist methods of organization, and was stimulated by the widespread prosperity and business expansion of the period, which made it easier for the workers to insist on better conditions. The Philadelphia craftsmen set up a central organization known as the Mechanics Central Union of Trade Associations and began to issue their own newspaper; similar organizations were formed in thirteen other cities, and in 1834 delegates from six of these city federations held a convention in order to form a National Trades' Union. The four years 1833–37 saw a total of 175 strikes. The year 1837, however, marked the beginning of a long period of depression and widespread unemployment; this brought about a collapse of the whole union movement, which did not begin to revive until the 1850's.

Unions were at first regarded by the law courts as illegal, in accordance with an old British common-law doctrine prohibiting conspiracies and combinations in restraint of trade. In 1806 six leaders of the Philadelphia cordwainers were given prison sentences on the ground that "a combination of workmen to raise their wages" was injurious to society. Judges, however, gradually adopted more tolerant attitudes. In the 1820's there were a number of other union cases, in which the courts no longer considered combination in itself as illegal, although they continued to prohibit almost everything that the unions actually tried to do. The first full recognition of the right to organize came in Massachusetts in 1842, in the case of Commonwealth v. Hunt. In this case Chief Justice Shaw declared that an attempt of the Boston cordwainers to establish a closed shop was not illegal and also affirmed the legality of trade unions in more general terms. This epoch-making decision established a precedent which was gradually followed by the courts of other states.

Labor Objectives.   The main slogan of the trade unions of the 1830's was the ten-hour day. Originating with the carpenters of Boston and Philadelphia in the twenties, the ten-hour movement had assumed national proportions by 1835 and was the objective of a large number of strikes. Among the skilled craftsmen it had considerable success. In 1840 it won the sponsorship of the Federal government, the ten-hour day being adopted for all public works by order of President Van Buren.

Some state governments gradually recognized that children needed special protection. In 1836 Massachusetts limited factory labor for children under fifteen to nine months a year, in order that they might attend school for the other three months, and Rhode Island followed suit in 1840. Children under twelve were limited to a ten-hour day in Massachusetts in 1842, while Pennsylvania in 1848 prohibited child labor in textile factories altogether. New Hampshire and Pennsylvania also passed ten-hour laws for all workers, but with so many loopholes that they could not be enforced. Growing public pressure did, however, induce factory-owners to make some reductions in hours. By 1850 the average working-day appears to have amounted to about eleven and a half hours.

In addition to the ten-hour day, the labor organizations were interested in a number of reforms not directly connected with working conditions. They advocated the removal of property qualifications for voting and other extensions of democracy, the establishment of free universal education, and the abolition of imprisonment for debt, and gave general support to Jacksonian Democracy in national politics. For some years after 1828 there were separate workingmen's political parties in New York and Philadelphia, though they seem to have been controlled by politicians whose claims to represent labor lacked authenticity.

Most of these non-economic labor objectives were quickly achieved. Pressure from organized labor was, in fact, one of the main factors in the widespread reforms brought about in the Northeastern states during the 1830's. But this first labor movement did not become a permanent feature of the American political scene. Mainly representing the skilled craftsmen with a tradition of independence behind them, rather than the factory workers, its objectives had a middle-class rather than a working-class flavor. The craftsman hoped to regain his independence, and was largely interested in making it easier for the poor man to work his way up; he was reluctant to accept the division between employer and employee as permanent.

After 1844 the most popular panacea for the ills of labor was free public land. This was sponsored by the National Reform Union, founded mainly by George Henry Evans, who had been a radical labor journalist for the previous twenty years. This provides a good illustration of the extent to which reformers were still thinking in terms of the old American ideal of economic independence for everybody.

4. FOREIGN TRADE AND SHIPPING

WITH the westward movement and the Industrial Revolution, American energies were increasingly concentrated on internal development, and foreign trade therefore became relatively less important than during the eighteenth century. This was shown by a decrease in its annual per capita value from $22 in the 1790's to $11 in the 1850's. But although foreign trade played a smaller role in the national economy, its absolute volume continued to increase. Prior to 1861, moreover, more than two-thirds of it was carried in American-owned vessels. In fact, the period before the Civil War can fairly be regarded as the golden age of American shipping.

Trade with Britain. The growth of American trade and shipping was aided by the trend towards the removal of trade barriers and economic liberalism in Europe. This was particularly important in the case of Great

Britain. The commercial ties established during the colonial period had not been broken by independence; in fact, as late as 1850 half of American foreign trade was still done with Britain and her colonies. But for nearly half a century Great Britain retained the restrictions on American shipping imposed in 1783, the most important being its exclusion from the trade of the British West Indies. In 1816 and 1818 Congress retaliated by imposing heavy taxes on British ships entering American ports from the West Indies. The movement in British politics towards economic liberalism, however, was steadily gaining ground. In 1830 Great Britain made a commercial treaty with the United States by which the two countries opened their ports to each other on equal terms. In 1846 she removed the tariff on foreign foodstuffs and adopted complete free trade, and in 1849 came the repeal of the British navigation laws. This was paralleled by a movement towards lower tariffs in the United States, which achieved success in the Tariff Acts of 1846 and 1857.

In spite of her industrial growth, the United States continued to import manufactured goods from Great Britain, especially clothing and metal goods. American factories could not supply the whole internal market, and tended to specialize in cheaper products, while the British supplied articles of finer quality. American exports consisted predominantly of raw materials, particularly cotton, meat, and flour. In most years total American imports exceeded exports, the balance being made up mainly through the investment of British money in the United States. American foreign trade, moreover, was largely financed through credits extended by British merchants. Thus the United States was still, as in the colonial period, a debtor country, a status which she retained until World War I.

Contacts with the Far East.   While half of American foreign trade remained within the British orbit, the other half had now become worldwide. American merchants imported fruit and wine from the Mediterranean countries, sugar and coffee from Latin America, and tea, pepper, and silk from the Far East. They exported raw materials, and after about 1830 an increasing proportion of manufactured goods, especially textiles.

Of the various new routes opened after independence, the Far Eastern was the most stirring to the imagination and had the most important consequences, although it accounted for only a small percentage of America's total foreign commerce. It made traders from Puritan New England familiar with exotic places and strange civilizations, and established an American interest in the Pacific and in the mainland of Asia which has had lasting results on American foreign policy.

Although the Far Eastern trade began with the voyage of the *Empress of China* in 1784 from New York, it was developed mainly by New England. The chief initial problem was to find goods which the Chinese and the Indonesians were willing to take in exchange for their tea and pepper. Early American merchants sent out ginseng root, which was believed by the Chinese to promote long life and sexual potency, and various other cargoes, even including ice cut from New England ponds. Furs proved to be the best answer, and this led to the earliest American activity in the Pacific Northwest. In 1788 Robert Gray reached the Oregon country from Boston in the *Columbia* (after which the river was named), and spent the winter gathering otter skins from the Indians before proceeding across the Pacific. This trade continued to be profitable until about 1830, when the supply of otters was nearly exhausted. This Oregon and China trade was a Boston specialty, while Salem merchants sent their ships round Africa and across the Indian Ocean to Java and Sumatra.

Another New England activity pursued mainly in the Pacific was whaling. Whale oil was widely used for illumination, and was one of the chief American exports. New Bedford was the chief whaling port, and the period of greatest activity was from 1815 to 1857, after which whale oil began to be replaced by kerosene. It was from New Bedford in 1841 that Herman Melville shipped as a sailor on the *Acushnet*, on the voyage which gave him the material for his epic celebration of the whaling industry, *Moby Dick*.

These commercial activities in the Pacific soon led to contacts of other kinds. Protestant missionaries from New England went to work in the Hawaiian Islands as early as 1819, establishing connections which were to result eventually in American annexation. In 1830 the first missionaries were dispatched to China, and diplomatic relations were initiated in 1844, when Caleb Cushing negotiated a treaty by which any commercial privileges given by the Chinese to other countries were to be extended on equal terms to the United States, thus foreshadowing the Open Door Policy of the twentieth century. In 1853, Commodore Matthew C. Perry led a naval expedition to Japan, which was followed by the signing of a commercial treaty in the following year. The Perry treaty marked the end of Japan's 200-year isolation and the beginning of a rapid process of transformation by which she adopted Western industrial and military techniques and Western imperialistic ambitions.

The Clippers. All this voyaging to distant countries meant constant stimulus to New England shipbuilders. American ocean-going vessels continued to be driven by sail rather than by steam, but they became larger and faster, a process which culminated in the 1840's with the clippers. This type of vessel was characterized by great length in proportion to breadth and by its enormous sail area. Some of the clippers established records which no other sailing ships have ever equaled: an Atlantic crossing in less than thirteen days, and a day's run of 436 miles. The greatest of the clipper-builders was Donald McKay, a Nova Scotian who worked first in Newburyport and then in Boston. The ships which McKay turned out in the early 1850's, his *Lightning* and *Flying Cloud*,

Great Republic and *Sovereign of the Seas*, were not merely record-breakers; they were also among the most beautiful objects ever created by American craftsmanship.

The clipper proved to be the climax of American shipbuilding and was followed by a rapid decline. A decrease of American interest in the sea had already been manifest for a generation. The young men of New England now preferred to go west for adventure. Ships were still commanded by sons of the old mercantile families, some of whom became captains of vessels in the China trade when they were barely out of their teens; but the crews were increasingly composed of foreigners. But the main reason for the decline was the reluctance to abandon the wood and sails which had produced such satisfying results. As early as the 1830's the British were building steel ships propelled by steam. They did not have the beauty of the clippers, but they were better suited to the needs of an industrial age. During the depression which began in 1857 most of the clipper-owners were driven out of business, and the British captured most of the market. A few years later American shipping suffered another blow with the outbreak of the Civil War, during which Confederate privateers took a heavy toll of Northern commerce. Between 1860 and 1900 the tonnage of American vessels engaged in foreign trade declined from 2,500,000 to 800,000, and the proportion of American imports and exports carried in American ships dropped from two-thirds to less than one-tenth. American shipping sank into a doldrums from which, in spite of lavish government assistance during recent years, it has never really recovered.

Thus it was not until the Civil War that the United States ceased to be one of the world's leading maritime nations. But more than a generation earlier the traditional leadership of the merchant class in the Northeastern states had been replaced by that of the manufacturing interest, as was shown when many Congressmen from this section began to vote consistently for high protective tariffs and other measures to promote industrial development. Becoming firmly established in the Northeast during the first half of the nineteenth century, the new industrial economy was to become after the Civil War the dominant force in the life of the whole nation.

XII

The Jacksonian Period

1. NEW POLITICAL FORCES

2. THE RISE OF JACKSONIAN DEMOCRACY

3. JACKSON'S TWO ADMINISTRATIONS

4. VAN BUREN, HARRISON, AND TYLER

POLITICAL history during the late 1820's and the 1830's was dominated by two main factors: sectional conflicts and the growth of democracy. These caused the Republican Party to split into two rival groups, which eventually became known as Democrats and Whigs, and led to a number of new practices and institutions which became permanent features of the American form of government.

1. NEW POLITICAL FORCES

Sectional Interests. The sectional conflicts were primarily conflicts of economic interest between the dominant elements of each section. Northern merchants and manufacturers, Southern planters, and Western farmers all sought to influence Federal policy to their own advantage; and since none of these main groups was strong enough to control the Federal government by itself, each of them tried to bargain with its competitors.

SELECTED BIBLIOGRAPHY: The most useful one-volume survey of political evolution is W. E. Binkley, *American Political Parties* (1943). For the tariff question. see F. W. Taussig, *The Tariff History of the United States* (revised edition, 1931); for banking and the currency, D. R. Dewey, *Financial History of the United States* (revised edition, 1935). A. M. Schlesinger, Jr., *The Age of Jackson* (1946) is a vivid account of the politics of the period, but is too inclined to interpret Jackson as a forerunner of Franklin D. Roosevelt. C. G. Bowers, *The Party Battles of the Jackson Period* (1922) is lively but biased in favor of Jackson. Among the more useful biographies are those on Jackson by Marquis James (2 vols., 1933–37), on Clay by G. G. Van Deusen (1937), on Webster by C. M. Fuess (1930), on Taney by C. B. Swisher (1935), on Calhoun by C. M. Wiltse (3 vols., 1944–51), on Benton by W. N. Chambers (1956), and on Weed by G. G. Van Deusen (1947). J. M. Blau has edited a useful volume, *Social Theories of Jacksonian Democracy* (1947).

The main issues were the tariff, internal improvements, public-land policy, and banking and currency. The North (excluding the shipping interests) and the Northwest both favored a high protective tariff and Federal spending on internal improvements, and on these issues were able to outvote the South and Southwest. On the other hand, the North wanted to restrict public-land sales, chiefly in order to prevent workers from moving westward, while the West wanted land prices reduced. And whereas Northern business supported the financial policies of the Bank of the United States, the Westerners were hostile to the "money power" and mostly preferred to support the state banks with their inflationary tendencies. This made it possible for the South to bid for Western votes against the tariff and internal improvements by promising, in return, to support the West on the public-land and banking questions.

Thus the political scene presented a very complex picture, with many cross-currents and shifting combinations; and politicians could get bills through Congress only by working out compromises between rival interests. From 1828 until 1856 six out of eight presidential elections were won by the Democrats, who were usually supported by a majority of the voters in the South and West and also by groups in the North who were hostile to the moneyed interests. But this combination was not equally successful in winning control of Congress.

Political Leaders.   This was a great age of political eloquence; and prominent figures, both in Congress and on public platforms, often spoke for several hours at a time, in a style which modern audiences would regard as excessively ornate and emotional. Their speeches were read throughout the country, and had a real influence on popular sentiment. Most of these leading statesmen were primarily the spokesmen of sectional interests. As we have seen in an earlier chapter, John C. Calhoun of South Carolina became the representative of the Southern planters. Similarly, Daniel Webster of Massachusetts was always closely identified with Northern business, while Henry Clay of Kentucky and Thomas Hart Benton of Missouri championed different Western viewpoints. All of these men served for long periods in the Senate and had remarkable intellectual gifts and powers of oratory.

Webster was regarded by many people as the greatest man in America, by virtue both of his eloquence and of the quality of his mind. A massive figure, every inch a statesman (no man, it was said, could be as great as Webster looked), with a Gargantuan appetite for food and liquor, he continued the Federalist tradition of protecting business property rights. A champion of states' rights during the War of 1812, when New England was thinking of secession, and a low-tariff advocate until 1828, he changed into a nationalist and a high-tariff man when manufacturing replaced shipping as the major economic interest of New England. His most famous speeches were made in defense of the Union.

Clay, although a Westerner, was almost equally sympathetic to business interests, and was opposed to the inflationary demands of the Western farmers. His American System, combining a protective tariff with Federal aid for the internal improvements needed for the development of the Mississippi Valley, was an attempt to link the North with the Northwest and the border states in a program of economic expansion. Through much of his career Clay seemed to be primarily a very supple politician. But he had an eloquence and personal charm which won him a large body of devoted adherents; and during times of crisis he could rise to real statesmanship.

While Clay represented the rising business class of the West, Benton was the voice of the farmers. He championed Western expansion, demanded cheaper public land, and denounced the Eastern "money power." But unlike many other Westerners, he was equally hostile to the state banks and insisted that specie was the only safe form of money; his speeches against the issuance of bank notes in any form won him the nickname "Old Bullion." In spite of Benton's limited knowledge of economics, and in spite also of his notorious vanity, few political leaders in American history have displayed a more consistent integrity or a stronger devotion to democratic ideals.

The Growth of Democracy.　　Meanwhile, in all sections of the country, the plain people were beginning to take a more active interest in politics and to insist that leadership and office-holding should no longer be restricted to the wealthier and better-educated classes. This democratic groundswell was perhaps the most important development of the period. The Revolution had brought about a considerable extension of the franchise, but had not by any means made it universal; and leadership had, on the whole, continued hitherto to be the prerogative of the upper classes. Democracy as we know it in the United States today was a product not of the Revolutionary era, but of the 1820's and 1830's.

Most of the new Western states gave the franchise to all white adult males from the beginning. In the older states conservatives continued to oppose extensions of the franchise, but fought a losing battle against popular pressure, as voiced by ambitious politicians who recognized that they could win votes by championing democracy. The removal of property qualifications for voting proceeded by gradual stages and had been completed in a majority of the Eastern states by the 1830's, except that some of them retained poll-tax requirements. The new state constitutions also provided for a considerable increase in the number of positions filled by election rather than by appointment. On the other hand, democratic leaders of this period, unlike those of the Revolution, were no longer suspicious of executive power; governors were given more authority, and elections were no longer held annually.

The growth of democracy led also to the choice of presidential electors by direct popular vote instead of by the state legislatures, and to the abolition of the caucus system by which party candidates had been nominated by members of Congress and of the state legislatures. Since nomination by the caucuses made it difficult for outsiders to break into politics, the system was attacked as undemocratic, and was replaced by the nominating convention, in which representation was given to the rank and file of the party supporters. Conventions became customary in some states during the 1820's. In Federal politics the caucus ceased to be effective in the presidential election of 1824, although the first national nominating conventions were not held until 1831 and 1832.

More important than these technical innovations was the development of new attitudes. There was a great increase in voting, as a result not merely of the extension of the franchise but also of the growth of popular interest, and democratic leaders now began to insist that any honest citizen was qualified for public office. To some extent, in fact, wealth and education began to be regarded no longer as qualifications for leadership but as positive handicaps. Candidates appealing for votes henceforth found it expedient to claim that they belonged to the plain people and to repudiate anything suggestive of higher status. There were also demands for the principle of rotation in office; office-holders, it was suggested, should be replaced at frequent intervals, in order that as many citizens as possible should share in the responsibilities of public administration.

The Party Machines.   These tendencies had some unfortunate consequences. With the expansion of the electorate and the multiplication of non-permanent government jobs, political machines became more elaborate and more powerful. Rotation in office led to the spoils system, under which a victorious party organization distributed government jobs among its chief supporters as a reward for loyalty. These processes developed furthest in state politics. Henceforth there were usually two or more party machines in each state, competing with each other for the support of the voters. Each machine was often organized into a hierarchy of township, county, and state committees, but was usually controlled by a small group or a single leader. Party members who wanted to be nominated as candidates or appointed to the government pay roll had to win the favor of the leaders, and contribute to the party funds. Each party usually had its own newspapers, the editors of which were rewarded by means of contracts for government printing if the party won an election.

New York provided some good examples of machine politics. A group known as the Albany Regency, the chief member of which was Martin Van Buren, built a powerful organization, which controlled the state for some years after the War of 1812 and again after 1828. It was a member of the Albany Regency, William L. Marcy, who made the famous remark, "To the victors belong the spoils," from which the name "spoils system" is derived. Meanwhile, a rival machine, which eventually became affiliated with the Whig Party, was organized by Thurlow Weed. Weed was professionally a newspaper editor, first at Rochester and then at Albany, but his main activity throughout his life was political organization. He captured New York from the Albany Regency in 1838, and then carried his remarkable talents for electioneering into national politics in the presidential campaign of 1840.

The national parties, as they developed during the 1820's and 1830's, were to a large extent coalitions of different state organizations. This meant that neither of them stood for any wholly consistent body of principles, since the same party was sometimes supported by conservative or business elements in one state and by radical or agrarian groups in some other state. And since each party was national in scope, it could not become wholly identified with any one sectional or economic interest. When some strong popular leader won control of a national party, he could largely dictate its policies and use it as an instrument for carrying into effect a coherent program. But when he retired, the party might be captured by some group with different objectives. The organization of a party was usually more permanent than its program.

The unsavory aspects of machine politics were, of course, conspicuous. It brought into existence a class of professional politicians, whose main object in life was to hold public office and who were frequently without any principles and sometimes corrupt. In order to get out the vote and win elections, machines would make demagogic appeals to prejudice, offer special privileges to influential groups, choose candidates on the basis of "availability" rather than ability, and occasionally resort to fraud. But it should be recognized that the party system was a necessary mechanism for eliciting public sentiment and translating it into action, and that many political leaders who worked within a party organization were sincerely and honestly devoted to the public interest. Nor should one suppose that the use of public office for private advantage was a new phenomenon; it had, on the contrary, been frequent during the colonial period, before the advent of democracy. The expansion of the electorate added a new dimension to politics and brought about new political techniques. But although corruption now assumed new forms, there is no valid reason for supposing that it became more prevalent.

2. THE RISE OF JACKSONIAN DEMOCRACY

The Election of 1824.   The Republican Party began to disintegrate in 1824, when it was unable to agree on any one candidate to succeed President Monroe. There were at first five different presidential aspirants, all of whom were Republicans, although they represented somewhat different sectional and economic interests. Four of these had been closely associated with Monroe's administration: John Quincy Adams of Massachusetts as Secretary of State, William H. Crawford of Georgia as Secretary of the Treasury, John C. Calhoun of South Carolina as Secretary

of War, and Henry Clay of Kentucky as Speaker of the House. The fifth
candidate, Andrew Jackson of Tennessee, was a political outsider who
had made his reputation mainly by military leadership. His candidacy
was pushed by democratic politicians in different states who felt that he
would appeal to the mass of new voters and could be presented as a
champion of rule by the plain people rather than by the upper classes.
Jackson thus became the symbol of the new forces in American political
life.

Before the election Crawford's qualifications were weakened by a
physical breakdown; and Calhoun withdrew from the race for the
presidency and was able to make sure of the vice-presidency. In the end
nobody won a majority in the electoral college. Jackson was undoubtedly
the most popular candidate, as was clearly shown in those states where
the presidential electors were now chosen by direct vote; but he won only
99 votes in the electoral college, as against 84 for Adams, 41 for Crawford,
and 37 for Clay. According to the Constitution, the House of Representatives now had to choose among the top three candidates. Clay advised his
followers to vote for Adams, whose viewpoint most closely represented his
own; and Adams was then elected.

The Adams Administration.   Adams had been a great Secretary
of State; but he was not a successful President. Too intellectual and too
scrupulous and high-principled to engage in political maneuvers or make
himself popular with the mass of the electorate, he could not cope with
the rising spirit of democracy or with the politicians who claimed to represent it. He came into office with elaborate plans for using the money
derived from public-land sales on internal improvements and scientific
and educational advancement; but little of his program was accepted by
Congress. The West would have preferred to reduce public-land prices, the
South was opposed to any expansion of Federal responsibilities, and even
in the North there was little enthusiasm for spending money on science.

The most important development during Adams's presidency was
the amalgamation of the different political factions into two main groups.
Adams had appointed Clay as Secretary of State, thereby causing the
Jacksonians to accuse him of obtaining the presidency by means of "a
corrupt bargain," and the followers of the two men began to call themselves the National Republicans. Deriving much of their support from
moneyed groups in the North, they represented somewhat the same elements as the old Federalist Party. Meanwhile, the Jackson, Crawford,
and Calhoun groups came together as the Democratic Republicans or
plain Democrats. It was agreed that Jackson and Calhoun should run for
President and Vice-President on the same ticket against Adams in the
1828 election; and since Crawford was now permanently in retirement,
his principal lieutenant, Martin Van Buren, attached himself to Jackson
and put at Jackson's disposal his remarkable talents for political management. Representing Southern planters, Western farmers, and various

political groups in the North, the Democrats were similar to the original Jeffersonian Republicans.

The Election of 1828. Few specific issues were put before the electorate in the 1828 campaign, and the two parties tried to outdo each other in appeals to prejudice. The Jacksonians represented Adams as an aristocrat, accused him (in spite of the well-known austerity of his private life) of using public funds to transform the White House into a gambling-den, and made other fantastic charges. Adams's supporters elaborated on the circumstances of Jackson's marriage; as a result of an unlucky mis-understanding, Jackson had married his wife before her divorce from a previous husband had been granted, thereby becoming technically guilty of adultery. But probably all this mud-slinging had little influence on the final result. Jackson won a decisive victory, with 178 electoral votes against 83 for Adams, who carried only New England, New Jersey, and parts of New York and Maryland. On the day of Jackson's inauguration many thousands of plain people swarmed into Washington to watch their hero take office, and old-fashioned believers in upper-class rule felt that civilization was coming to an end and were reminded of the French Rev-olution.

Andrew Jackson. In so far as the 1828 election marked the de-finitive victory of the principle of government by, and for, the plain people, it was indeed in some respects the equivalent of a revolution. But there was little reason for the fears of the conservatives. Although Jackson was often biased by personal likes and dislikes and could be vindictive towards his enemies, he was a man of complete integrity and wholly loyal to constitutional government. In choosing "Old Hickory" as the symbol of their aspirations, the plain people of America were following a sound instinct.

Born in 1767 on the border of North and South Carolina, of Scotch-Irish immigrant parents, and left while still a boy to make his own way in the world, Jackson had risen to prominence chiefly by his indomitable courage and determination. After becoming a lawyer, he moved to Ten-nessee while it was still frontier country, plunged into politics and land speculation, often had occasion to defend himself in duels or in rough-and-tumble fighting, and quickly became a leading figure in the state. Soon after the turn of the century he settled down as a cotton-planter and breeder of race horses, and retired from politics. This was partly because he was heavily in debt as a result of the failure of a business firm with which he had had dealings, and partly in order to spare his wife's feelings. Whenever he ran for office, the details of his marriage were publicized by his opponents, in spite of the fact that Jackson wanted to shoot anybody who slandered his wife and succeeded several times in doing so. Of his political positions, he retained only his leadership of the state militia. This brought him out of retirement during the War of 1812 and led to his victory at New Orleans and his transfer to the regular army.

Taking office in his sixty-second year, Jackson was not expected to be a strong president. His exertions during the war had permanently ruined his health; since he had tuberculosis, dropsy, persistent headaches, and chronic indigestion, it was only by a miracle of will power that he was able to pursue any kind of active life. He had just suffered a severe blow, moreover, from the death of his wife—due, he believed, to the slanderous accusations made during the electoral campaign. Nor had he indicated before the election that he would adopt any particular program. Jackson, nevertheless, provided more forceful leadership than any of his predecessors; and his administration was guided, on the whole, by definite principles—those expounded by Thomas Jefferson and John Taylor of Caroline. For the details of policy and wording of his messages to Congress Jackson relied on personal friends, such as Van Buren, who became his first Secretary of State, and Senator Benton,[1] and on a group of assistants, mostly newspapermen, who became known as his "kitchen cabinet." But Jackson himself provided the main impetus. Although he had belonged to the frontier upper class, his own experience had given him a conviction that privileged business interests too often had the upper hand over the average citizen. As with some twentieth-century presidents, moreover, public office made him much more of a liberal than he had been as a private citizen.

Jacksonian Objectives.   The main principles of Jacksonian Democracy were most clearly expressed in the Farewell Address which Jackson issued when he left office in 1837. Government, he declared, should be administered for the benefit of "the planter, the farmer, the mechanic and the laborer" who "form the great body of the people of the United States." These classes "all know that their success depends upon their own industry and economy, and that they must not expect to become suddenly rich by the fruits of their toil." Yet "they are in constant danger of losing their fair influence in the Government" as a result of "the power which the moneyed interest derives from a paper currency, which they are able to control, [and] from the multitude of corporations with exclusive privileges which they have succeeded in obtaining in the different states." Thus the Jacksonians, like John Taylor, believed in a union of the agricultural and laboring classes to curtail the powers of the moneyed interest; and like Taylor, they believed that this could best be accomplished by following a strictly *laissez-faire* program. Small property-owners should be protected; the government should not grant privileges to banking and manufacturing corporations; effective competition should be maintained; and the public lands should be kept open for settlers on easy terms. The functions of the Federal government should, moreover, be limited by a

---

[1] Benton and Jackson had forgiven each other for the dispute that had caused their shooting-match of 1813, and were now close political allies. One of the bullets fired by Benton's brother had remained in Jackson's shoulder, and was removed by a surgeon in 1832. Jackson wished to give it back to Benton, but Benton replied that twenty years' possession had made it Jackson's property.

TONTINE COFFEE HOUSE, by FRANCIS GUY (1760–1820)

The corner of Wall and Water streets in New York City, 1797. Guy, a British immigrant, was one of the first to paint American scenes rather than portraits.

ENGAGEMENT OF THE *United States* AND THE *Macedonian*, by THOMAS BIRCH (1779–1851)
The War of 1812 encouraged marine painting. Birch, a Scotsman living in Philadelphia, was one of its earliest representatives.

FULTON'S *Clermont*
This first commercially successful steamboat, shown on the Hudson in 1810. A lithograph by an unknown artist.

strict construction of the Constitution. Jackson was a nationalist in his attitudes to other countries, and had no patience with the secessionist tendencies developing in South Carolina; but he was also opposed to the expansion of Federal power beyond the words of the Constitution.

Jackson became, in fact, the leader of a broad popular movement provoked by the economic changes going on in the different sections, and deriving its support partly from the Western and Southern farmers and partly from middle-class and working-class groups in the Northeast. Some of its more important manifestations were to be found in state politics, where it led to extensions of democracy, the growth of the public-school system, the abolition of imprisonment for debt, and a number of other humanitarian reforms.

Loco-Focoism. This movement was most vigorous in the Northeast, especially in New York and Massachusetts, where the growth of industry and finance was most conspicuous. Here the more radical Jacksonians became known as "loco-focos." This name originated in 1835, when conservatives tried to break up a radical meeting in New York City by turning off the lights, but the radicals, having been warned in advance, were able to proceed by striking safety matches, then known as loco-focos. The chief spokesman of loco-focoism was the New York journalist William Leggett, who for a long time was editorial writer of the *New York Evening Post,* then edited by the poet William Cullen Bryant.

The loco-focos vigorously supported Jackson in national politics, although in state politics they had to fight against more conservative forces within the Democratic Party. Claiming that the rights of the small property-owner were endangered by the privileges of the moneyed interest, they were responsible for the "general incorporation" and "free banking" laws, by which industrial and banking corporations could be organized by anybody who complied with the legal requirements and no longer depended on special legislation. Their main purpose was to prevent monopoly and establish effective competition. The loco-focos were also hostile to the use of bank notes, arguing that banks should be restricted to the function of keeping people's money and that gold and silver were the only safe currency. Thus loco-focoism (like almost all early American radicalism) was almost diametrically opposed to the radicalism of the twentieth century. Representing the viewpoint of the small property-owners, and championing economic individualism, it was hostile to any form of state intervention.

3. JACKSON'S TWO ADMINISTRATIONS

The Spoils System. Jackson's inauguration was followed by the introduction of the principle of rotation into the Federal civil service. The Jacksonians had asserted during the campaign, with some justice, that there were too many elderly and incompetent office-holders, who should be compulsorily retired; and the new administration therefore undertook a purge. Out of a total of about 10,000 customs collectors, postmasters, clerks, and other Federal employees, Jackson removed about 900, replacing them with men who had supported him during the campaign.

To some extent Jackson could claim that he was following earlier precedents. Washington had given appointments almost exclusively to Federalists; and Jefferson had replaced some of them with Republicans. There had been no reason for replacements since Jefferson's administration, as the same political party had been consistently in power. But it was Jackson's purge that first established the principle that Federal appointments should be based on political services. This principle was enforced much more drastically by later administrations, and for the next half-century each change in the party in power was followed by wholesale removals. Thousands of politicians would swarm into Washington in search of jobs, and each new president had to spend the first few months of his term in fending them off. It was not until after 1881, when a frustrated job-hunter murdered President Garfield, that the movement for civil-service reform became strong enough to achieve results.

The Nullification Crisis.   The chief subject of conflict during Jackson's first term was the tariff. Since the initial protective tariff of 1816, the rates had twice been raised, in 1824 and 1828. Protection was given not only to manufactures but also to Western agricultural products, such as wool and hemp, the bills being passed by a combination of the Middle Atlantic states and the Northwest. New England, where the low-tariff shipping interests were still powerful, was divided, while the South, exclusive of the hemp-growing border states of Kentucky and Missouri, was almost unanimously in opposition. The 1828 rates were so high that they became known in the South as the "Tariff of Abominations." South Carolina was particularly indignant, and in December, 1828, the state legislature adopted Calhoun's *Exposition and Protest* asserting the right of nullification.

Nullification was not put into effect immediately, since South Carolina was waiting to see what would happen under the new administration. It was expected that Calhoun would largely determine its policies and would succeed Jackson in the presidency in 1833. But a series of political and personal disputes led quickly to an open break between the two men. Jackson decided that he would run for a second term and that Van Buren rather than Calhoun should be his choice for the succession. Thus South Carolina could no longer look forward to seeing her favorite son elected President.[2]

[2] Of the various factors causing Calhoun to lose his influence in the administration, the best-known was the Eaton affair. John H. Eaton was a personal friend of Jackson and became Secretary of War in his initial Cabinet. With the approval of Jackson and his wife, he had married the daughter of a Washington tavern-keeper, Peggy O'Neale by name, a girl generally popular with men but regarded with stern disapproval by many women. The Eatons were then cold-shouldered by Washington hostesses, including particularly Mrs.

Meanwhile, the doctrine of nullification was being discussed in Congress, particularly in the debate between Webster and Hayne of January 1830. The subject officially before the Senate was public-land policy, but this gradually broadened into a discussion of fundamental constitutional issues. Senator Augustus Foote of Connecticut, representing the viewpoint of Northern business, proposed a limitation of public-land sales. Benton denounced this as motivated by a desire to keep cheap labor for the East, and appealed to the South for support. Robert Y. Hayne of South Carolina then responded to the challenge by calling for an alliance of West and South not only on public-land policy but also against the tariff, and went on to defend the right of nullification; and this evoked Webster's reply. In one of the most famous speeches ever delivered in the Senate, Webster presented a theory of the Federal Union similar to that expounded by Chief Justice Marshall, asserting that the Federal government was fully sovereign within its own sphere and that the liberties of the American people were inseparably bound up with the preservation of the Union. That Webster himself had been a states' rightist during the War of 1812, when it was New England and not South Carolina that was opposing Federal authority, did not prevent his eloquence from having a great influence on public sentiment.

Jackson agreed with Calhoun in believing that the functions of the Federal government should be limited. He favored tariff-reduction, and believed that construction of internal improvements should, as far as possible, be a state rather than a Federal responsibility. In May 1830 he vetoed a bill granting Federal aid for building a road from Maysville to Lexington in the state of Kentucky. This Maysville veto checked Federal spending on roads and canals in the states for a long time, although money continued to be appropriated for roads in the territories and for river and harbor improvement. But Jackson was determined that the legitimate exercise of Federal authority should be maintained, if necessary by force. He made this plain in April 1830, when a dinner in honor of Jefferson's birthday was organized by leading Democrats. Calhoun and the nullificationists arranged the program and planned a number of speeches in defense of their doctrine. But Jackson was warned of their intentions, and early in the proceedings he rose and (with his eyes on Calhoun) proposed the toast: "Our Federal Union—it must be preserved."

Congress passed a new tariff bill in July, 1832. Although the rates were lower than in the Tariff of Abominations, they were still too high

---

Calhoun. Feeling that his friends were the victims of vicious gossip like that from which he and his own wife had suffered for many years, Jackson vigorously defended them at Cabinet meetings and solemnly pronounced Peggy to be a pure woman, but could not break the united front of the Washington wives. Meanwhile, Van Buren, who was a widower and hence had no domestic opposition to contend with, was able to strengthen his influence with Jackson by entertaining the Eatons. In the end Jackson settled the affair by appointing a new Cabinet (which included no friends of Calhoun) and took care of Eaton by making him Governor of the Florida Territory.

to suit South Carolina; and since no further changes seemed likely, the nullificationists decided that the time had come for action. In November a state convention, especially elected for the purpose, declared that the tariffs of 1828 and 1832 were not binding upon the officials and citizens of South Carolina. Nullification was to go into effect in February 1833. If the Federal government resorted to force, then South Carolina would secede from the Union.

No other Southern state showed any disposition to support South Carolina, and public sentiment rallied behind Federal authority. Jackson promptly issued a proclamation, written mainly by Secretary of State Edward Livingston of Louisiana, in which he asserted that nullification was "incompatible with the existence of the Union, contradicted expressly by the letter of the Constitution, unauthorized by its spirit, inconsistent with every principle on which it was founded, and destructive of the great object for which it was formed." He also asked Congress to pass a Force Bill authorizing him, if necessary, to use troops to compel South Carolina to obey the law.

Meanwhile, proposals for a reduction of the tariff were made in Congress, and Henry Clay, who did not wish Jackson to receive all the credit for maintaining Federal authority, assumed leadership of this movement for appeasement. The Force Bill and the new tariff bill became laws on the same day. South Carolina then withdrew its nullification ordinance, which had never actually gone into effect, and accepted the new tariff, while at the same time it made the gesture of nullifying the Force Bill. Thus the dispute ended in a rather unsatisfactory compromise. Federal authority had been maintained, and no right of nullification had been recognized. On the other hand, Calhoun and his supporters could claim that the threat of nullification had enabled them to win concessions.

The Election of 1832.   For the election of 1832 the Democratic convention renominated Jackson and substituted Van Buren for Calhoun as his running mate, while the National Republicans nominated Henry Clay. There was also a third party in the field, the Anti-Masons. This curious movement originated in 1826, as a result of the mysterious disappearance of a certain William Morgan, a New Yorker who had published a pamphlet purporting to reveal the secrets of Masonry. Popular feeling was aroused by the suggestion that the Masons had murdered him, and a number of ambitious young politicians promptly decided that opposition to secret societies would make an effective platform for getting themselves elected to office. They also calculated that this would undermine the popularity of Jackson, who was a Mason. Although the Anti-Masons adopted William Wirt of Virginia as their presidential candidate, they supported the National Republican ticket in a number of states and advocated much the same program.

The main issue in the campaign was whether the charter of the Bank of the United States should be renewed. Although the existing charter would not expire until 1836, the Bank requested renewal in the spring of 1832. This was done on the advice of Clay, who wanted the question brought before the public and was suffering from the delusion that the Bank was a popular institution. As Clay had expected, the renewal bill was passed by Congress by large majorities and was then vetoed by Jackson. The National Republicans appealed to the electorate as defenders of the Bank, and actually reprinted Jackson's veto message as part of their own campaign literature, declaring that this demonstrated his ignorance of economics. The result was a resounding victory for Jackson, who won 219 electoral votes, as against 49 for Clay and 7 for Wirt.

The War on the Bank. The economics of Jackson's veto message was indeed open to valid criticism; but there was no question about its political effectiveness. The Bank had been hated throughout the West ever since the crisis of 1819. By preventing the state banks from issuing notes and making loans freely, it limited the supply of money and credit in the Western states and thereby, they believed, kept them permanently in debt to Eastern business interests. Thus much of the popular opposition to the Bank was a reflection of that inflationist debtor-class attitude which has often been prevalent among American farmers. But Jackson himself and his closest advisers, such as Senator Benton, were not inflationists. Hostile not only to the Bank of the United States but to all banks, they believed that the only sound currency was gold and silver, and that as long as private corporations were authorized to issue notes, speculation would be encouraged, periods of inflation would be followed by crises and depressions, and honest men would find themselves in debt. In their distrust of current banking practices, the Jacksonians had much justification; but their remedy was not very practical, for American economic growth required a more plentiful and more elastic currency than could have been provided by gold and silver alone.

Jackson also maintained that the Bank was a threat to democratic institutions. Here he was on safer ground. Nicholas Biddle, a member of an upper-class Philadelphia family who had been president of the Bank since 1823, had a thoroughly Hamiltonian contempt for popular government and a dangerously inflated idea of his own abilities. In managing the affairs of the Bank, he did not think it necessary to adhere strictly to the rules and restrictions laid down in the original charter; and after 1829, when Jackson's election made the position of the Bank insecure, he began to seek political support by lending large sums to Congressmen and newspaper editors and not pressing them for repayment. Jackson thus had considerable justification for his belief that the Bank represented a dangerous "concentration of power in the hands of a few men irresponsible to the people."

After the election Jackson decided to attack the Bank immediately instead of waiting until its charter expired, fearing that any delay would enable Biddle to strengthen his influence in Congress. One of the func-

tions of the Bank was to hold deposits of government money; and according to the original charter the Secretary of the Treasury could withdraw
these deposits if he regarded the Bank as unsafe. With some difficulty
Jackson found somebody who was willing to assume this responsibility in
the person of Roger B. Taney of Maryland. Taney took charge of the
Treasury Department, and in September 1833 he began gradually to
transfer government funds from the Bank of the United States to a number of state banks. The Senate, which was controlled by Jackson's opponents, passed a vote of censure on the President, but was unable to stop
the removal of the deposits. The Bank retained its charter until 1836, and
was then reorganized as a state bank under the laws of Pennsylvania.

Boom and Depression.   Whatever criticisms might be made of the
policies of the Bank, it had performed a useful economic function by enforcing sound practices on the small state banks. As soon as the Bank had
been stripped of much of its economic power by the removal of the deposits, the country plunged into an inflationary spree. There was a rapid
increase in the number of banks and in the volume of notes which they
issued; state governments borrowed heavily for internal improvements;
and public-land sales rose from 4,000,000 acres in 1834 to 20,000,000 in
1836. Most of the land was acquired by speculators rather than by settlers,
payments being made in notes borrowed from the state banks.

The boom caused a great increase in government revenue, and in
1835, for the first and last time in the history of the United States, the
public debt was completely paid off, and the Treasury had a mounting
surplus. This proved to be as much of a problem as a deficit would have
been. On the one hand, business interests had enough influence in Congress
to prevent any lowering of public-land prices and tariff rates; on the other
hand, Jackson would not allow the surplus to be spent on internal improvements. In 1836 Congress passed a bill for distributing the surplus
among the states, who could do what they pleased with it.

The crash came early in 1837. While no doubt inevitable, it was
probably hastened by the policies of the government. In July 1836 the
Secretary of the Treasury issued the Specie Circular, declaring that henceforth the government would no longer receive bank notes but only gold
and silver in payment for public land. This was a further move in the campaign of Jackson and his advisers against the banks; having made use of
the state banks in their war with the Bank of the United States, they were
now trying to drive state-bank notes out of circulation. Unfortunately,
the Specie Circular came several years too late. Persons who tried to
obtain gold and silver from the banks found that they had none to lend;
and the position of the banks was further weakened by the Distribution
Act, which required those holding government funds to return them for
distribution among the states. By the spring of 1837 many of the banks
had failed, and their notes had become worthless; farm prices were falling,

and factories were being closed; and the country was plunging into a depression which lasted for several years.

The Election of 1836. It was no doubt fortunate for the Jacksonians that the election of 1836 was held before the end of the boom. Jackson saw to it that Van Buren received the nomination of the Democratic Party. The National Republicans had now combined with the Anti-Masons and some other groups, and assumed the name of Whigs. While Northern business interests were the dominant element in the Whig Party, it was also supported by some of the Southern planters, partly from antagonism to democracy and partly because of Jackson's attitude during the nullification crisis. Since the Northern and Southern Whigs had little in common with each other except their opposition to Jackson, they could not easily agree on a candidate, and in the 1836 election they did not even try. Four different candidates were put forward against Van Buren in different parts of the country, and the Whig leaders hoped that he would thereby be prevented from winning a clear majority, so that the House of Representatives, which had a majority of anti-Jacksonians, could make the final choice. Van Buren, however, was elected with 170 electoral votes, as against 124 for his four opponents.

Jacksonianism and the Supreme Court. The Jacksonian period saw a change in the policies not only of the executive branch of the government but also of the judiciary. Jackson was able to appoint no fewer than eight new Supreme Court justices, including a new Chief Justice, with the result that for the next generation the Court showed a tendency to interpret the Constitution in accordance with agrarian rather than Hamiltonian principles.

The fundamental issues in American politics have often been manifested more clearly and forcefully by changes in judicial attitudes than by debates in Congress or in the press. This was notably exemplified in 1835, when the old Federalist champion, John Marshall, was succeeded as Chief Justice by Roger Taney of Maryland. Whereas Marshall had, whenever possible, extended the powers of the Federal government, Taney believed in protecting those of the states, upholding their right to regulate commerce and work out economic policies of their own. And while Marshall had regarded the sanctity of contracts and the rights of property with a kind of religious reverence, Taney was willing to allow much state regulation of property rights in order to promote the general welfare.

This new trend on the Supreme Court was most clearly exemplified in the Charles River Bridge case of 1837. The Charles River Bridge Company, chartered in 1786 by the Commonwealth of Massachusetts to build a bridge connecting Boston and Cambridge, had made enormous profits from tolls, and claimed that by the terms of its charter no competing bridge could be built. The people of Massachusetts, tired of supporting this monopoly, finally authorized a second bridge, which was to become

free as soon as its costs had been paid off. The stockholders of the original
bridge then brought suit. It is probable that Marshall would have decided
that the building of a second bridge was a breach of contract. Taney, however, in an epoch-making decision, declared that the public interest was
more important than the alleged property rights of the bridge corporation.
"While the rights of private property are sacredly guarded," he said, "we
must not forget that the community also have rights, and that the happiness and well-being of every citizen depends on their faithful preservation."

Conservatives regarded this decision with horror, feeling that all
property rights had become insecure and that the judiciary no longer maintained the sanctity of contracts. Marshall's friend Justice Story declared
that "a case of grosser injustice, or more oppressive legislation, never
existed," while Chancellor Kent of New York, the most famous legal
scholar in the country, asserted that the decision "undermines the foundations of morality, confidence and truth. . . . What destruction of
rights under a contract can be more complete?" he asked. "We can
scarcely avoid being reduced nearly to a state of despair of the Commonwealth." Such statements show what bitter feelings had been aroused by
the Jacksonian struggle to establish effective competition and destroy
monopolies and vested interests.

4. VAN BUREN, HARRISON, AND TYLER

The Van Buren Administration.   The son of a Dutch-speaking
tavern-keeper at Kinderhook, New York, Van Buren had risen to leadership, first in state and afterwards in Federal politics, chiefly through his
skill in political management. Known as "the red fox" and "the little
magician," he lacked Jackson's popular appeal and was widely distrusted.
But in spite of his smoothness, his record shows that he adhered fairly
consistently to Jeffersonianism and Jacksonian principles. On basic issues
he showed more firmness than he has generally received credit for.

The depression lasted throughout Van Buren's term; but as a supporter of *laissez faire* and strict construction of the Constitution, he did
not believe that the Federal government should take measures for assist-
ing business to recover. His main concern was to put the finances of the
government on a sound footing. Since there was no longer a surplus, the
Distribution Act was repealed, an issue of Treasury notes was authorized,
and the government once again went into debt. The widespread failures of
state banks had shown the dangers of entrusting them with government
money, so Van Buren decided that henceforth there should be a complete
"divorce" between the government and private banking. The government
should keep its money in its own Independent Treasury. Vaults, known as
"sub-treasuries," should be constructed in various cities, where government officials would receive and pay out funds on a strictly specie basis.

The struggle for the Independent Treasury lasted through most of Van Buren's term. The project was based on the monetary theories of the loco-focos, and had strong support from opponents of the banking interests in the Northeast; but most Westerners were still inflationists and therefore joined the Whigs in opposing it. Van Buren, however, made a bid for Western support by advocating cheaper public land; and after the danger of an easy-money policy was demonstrated afresh in 1839 by a new crop of bank failures, the bill setting up the Independent Treasury was passed by Congress in 1840. After this the Federal government had no further connections with the banking business until the National Bank Act of 1863. Regulation was left to the state governments. Although business continued to be impeded by the great variety of bank notes in circulation, some of which were not worth the paper they were printed on, banking practices improved during the next two decades, especially in the Northeast and the Middle West. One state after another learned from bitter experience that banks must be prohibited from issuing notes dangerously in excess of their liquid assets.

The Election of 1840. The depression gave the Whigs a good chance of winning the presidential election of 1840, and they made the most of it. Their ablest political organizer was Thurlow Weed, boss of the Whig machine in New York. Weed and the other Whig leaders had a definite program, the main ingredients of which were a higher protective tariff, Federal aid for internal improvements, and the chartering of a third Bank of the United States, but they did not propose to rely solely on its merits. The Jacksonians had shown that the way to win an election was to denounce aristocracy and put forward a candidate who seemed to belong to the plain people and could be presented as a military hero. The Whigs now decided that they could defeat the economics of Jacksonianism by adopting its political methods.

For the 1840 election the Whigs rejected Clay, Webster, and their other outstanding leaders, and gave their nomination to the elderly William Henry Harrison, who had been one of their team of candidates in 1836. Harrison had disappeared into obscurity after the War of 1812, but voters could be reminded about his victories at Tippecanoe and the Thames, which could be played up as equal to Jackson's achievement at New Orleans. And although Harrison was neither poor nor of humble parentage (his father had been Governor of Virginia), he could be portrayed as a spokesman of the plain people. When a disgruntled admirer of Henry Clay remarked that Harrison was a man who would be content to live in a log cabin and drink hard cider, the Whig organizers delightedly appropriated this statement and presented him as the log-cabin and hard-cider candidate. Their vice-presidential choice was John Tyler of Virginia, one of the Southerners who had joined the party because of hostility to Jackson; and their slogan was "Tippecanoe and Tyler too." Log cabins were set up in which hard cider was served to prospective voters; and enormous mass meetings were held at which songs were sung praising the simple virtues of Harrison and denouncing Van Buren as an aristocrat who liked luxurious living and French wines. Although there was more serious discussion of economic issues during the campaign than has often been recognized, the Whigs undoubtedly owed their victory largely to their political tactics. Harrison swept the country with 234 electoral votes, as against only 60 for Van Buren.

In spite of the absurd features of the 1840 election, it had some importance in the evolution of American political methods. It showed conclusively that democracy was now firmly established. Many of the Northern businessmen and rich Southern planters who supported the Whigs had no liking for it; but under the guidance of organizers like Thurlow Weed they had to recognize that no party could now win an election unless it accepted democratic principles. Henceforth all politicians, whatever their real convictions, must at least pretend to believe in popular government and espouse policies which had popular support. Anybody who openly advocated aristocracy, as Hamilton and the early Federalists had done, would immediately be relegated to private life. Another, and less desirable, aspect of the 1840 election was that it marked a decline in the standards of the presidency. The first seven presidents had all been men of distinction; but the Whigs had now discovered that a man with few qualifications for leadership might be a more effective candidate. After 1840 both parties developed a tendency to nominate men about whom little was known, and who therefore had few enemies but could be built up by clever publicity.

Harrison and Tyler.   The Whigs, however, derived little benefit from their victory. Harrison, who was sixty-nine years of age, appointed a Whig Cabinet in which Webster became Secretary of State, spent most of his first month in office fighting off importunate office-seekers, and on April 4, 1841, suddenly died. The presidency then passed to John Tyler, who, as a Southerner, was opposed to most of the program which the dominant Northern wing of the Whig Party had been hoping to put into effect.

Under Clay's leadership the Whigs succeeded in temporarily abolishing the Independent Treasury and raising the tariff, while the West obtained the Pre-emption Act it had long been seeking. But Tyler vetoed a bill setting up a third Bank, vetoed a similar bill in which the proposed bank was called a "fiscal corporation," and vetoed all bills for internal improvements. Tyler's vetoes soon caused him to be read out of the party; and the Cabinet resigned (although Webster remained until 1843 in order to complete the settlement of the Maine boundary dispute in the Webster-Ashburton Treaty). Tyler then appointed Democrats to the Cabinet, and before the end of his term had definitely changed parties. After 1843, however, he was primarily concerned with the question of the annexation of Texas. For the next five years Western expansion was to dominate American politics.

During the 1840's the issues raised by the Jacksonian movement ceased to excite much public interest. But the Jacksonian period had lasting effects on American institutions. The mechanisms of democracy and the party system had been established pretty much as we know them today. And although the agrarian economic ideas of the Jacksonians were obviously unsuited to an industrial society and were quickly forgotten, much had been done to abolish monopolistic privileges and enlarge the opportunities of the middle-class citizen. As will be seen in the next two chapters, moreover, this epoch of American history was important not only for its political changes but for a great variety of humanitarian and intellectual movements.

XIII

The Growth of Social Idealism

1. SOCIAL TRENDS

2. RELIGION

3. MOVEMENTS FOR REFORM

4. EDUCATION AND SCIENCE

T HE ECONOMIC and political growth of the United States was
accompanied, especially in the Northern states, by social changes and
religious expansion, a great variety of humanitarian reform movements,
intellectual ferment and creativity, and a general spirit of nationalistic
optimism and self-confidence. Americans believed that they were creating
a new society, superior to all others in its general well-being and in the
opportunities it offered to the average citizen, and felt that the possibilities of progress were almost limitless. The years between the War of 1812
and the Mexican War were perhaps the happiest epoch in American
history.

1. SOCIAL TRENDS

Foreign Opinions. European visitors did not always see the
United States in such rosy colors. While some of them were enthusiastic

SELECTED BIBLIOGRAPHY: Two volumes in *A History of American Life* cover the
first half of the nineteenth century: J. A. Krout and D. R. Fox, *The Completion of Independence, 1790–1830* (1944), and C. R. Fish, *The Rise of the Common Man, 1830–1850* (1937). Alexis
de Tocqueville's classic *Democracy in America* was reprinted in 1945 with an introduction by
Phillips Bradley. There is much useful information in A. W. Calhoun, *A Social History of the
American Family* (3 vols., 1917–19). W. W. Sweet, *The Story of Religion in America* (revised
edition, 1939), and H. K. Rowe, *The History of Religion in the United States* (1924), are the
best general surveys of this subject. All the humanitarian and reform movements are de-
scribed in A. F. Tyler, *Freedom's Ferment* (1944). The standard history of education is E. P.
Cubberly, *Public Education in the United States* (revised edition, 1934), while Merle Curti,
Social Ideas of American Educators (1935), is a valuable interpretation. F. L. Mott, *American
Journalism, 1690–1941* (1941), is the standard work on newspaper history. B. Jaffe, *Men of
Science in America* (1944), includes biographical essays on several leading scientists of this
period, while intellectual history in general is covered in Merle Curti, *The Growth of American
Thought* (revised edition, 1951).

champions of this experiment in popular government, many were conservatives who crossed the Atlantic largely in order to document their hostility to democracy. English writers like Mrs. Frances Trollope depicted the Americans as an uncultured and materialistic people, and complained of their bad manners, their lack of respect for privacy, and their addiction to nationalistic boasting. One European commentator, however, produced an analysis of American society so penetrating and so dispassionate that it has become a classic. This was the French sociologist Alexis de Tocqueville, whose *Democracy in America* was published in 1836.

In Tocqueville's opinion the "primary fact" about the Americans was their "general equality of condition." Men in America, he declared, were "on a greater equality in point of fortune and intellect, or, in other words, more equal in their strength, than in any other country in the world, or in any age of which history has preserved the remembrance." Tocqueville admired the energy and versatility of the Americans, their high moral standards (due, he believed, to the strength of the Protestant churches), and their ability to achieve desirable social objectives by forming voluntary associations instead of depending on the government. On the other hand, he felt that they were too intent upon making money, and that their culture was, in consequence, too commercialized, and he predicted that their equality might eventually be endangered by the domination of the new industrialist class.

Outside the South, the trend towards equality was indeed the most conspicuous characteristic of American society. It was strengthened especially by the system of landownership, since most Americans in all sections of the country were still independent small farmers. The urban population amounted to only 7.2 per cent of the total in 1820, and to 19.8 per cent in 1860. Even in the cities, moreover, a large number of people were small businessmen, professionals, or independent craftsmen. And while the most obvious manifestation of the equalitarian spirit was the establishment of political democracy, it was also modifying traditional ways of living in more subtle ways. In particular, it was leading to changes in the basic social institution, the family.

The American Family.   The European family had been patriarchal, characterized by the rule of the father over his wife and children. Wives had been denied the power to own property and deprived of other basic legal rights, while the power of a father over his children even included that of deciding whom they should marry. Early American laws regulating family relationships were copied from those of England, but American mores soon began to diverge. The powers of the father decreased, and women and children acquired greater independence. The American family became less monarchical and more democratic.

The change in the status of women was probably due initially to frontier conditions. In new country women had to share equally in the labors and dangers of pioneering, and could no longer remain in the sheltered and submissive position of their European cousins. In frontier communities, moreover, they were often less numerous than the men, so that their value was enhanced by scarcity. Americans, especially in the West, generally admired the woman who was capable of looking after herself.

By the early nineteenth century the difference between the American and the European woman was so conspicuous as to cause frequent comment. Tocqueville, for example, was amazed by the competence and self-assurance of American women, and declared that they were primarily responsible for the prosperity and strength of American civilization. Yet in spite of this change in mores, American law continued for a long time to be based on the traditional patriarchal system. Women began to win a few legal rights from state governments in the early nineteenth century, but they had to fight a long time before they could acquire real economic and political equality.

Both the frontier and the factory also weakened parental control of children. Young people could now become economically independent at a much earlier age, and could therefore marry more quickly, and were in a position to choose their own mates. European visitors were often surprised at the freedom with which boys and girls were allowed to meet each other, without being guarded by chaperons. The European marriage of convenience, arranged by the parents with a view to economic advantage, almost disappeared in America. American marriage was normally based on love. This implied, of course, that if a couple ceased to love each other, the marriage should be dissolved.

Divorce did not become widespread until the twentieth century, but it was already easier to obtain than in Europe and considerably more frequent, especially in the Western states. And although large families continued to be the rule, the birth rate was beginning to decrease. In 1800 there were 1,342 children under five years for every 1,000 women of child-bearing age. After this date there was a gradual decline; by 1850 the corresponding figure had dropped to 892, and by 1900 to 666. The decline was probably due partly to an increase in birth-control, which had been openly advocated in a widely read treatise written by a New England doctor, Charles Knowlton, as early as 1832.

The patriarchal family had always been justified in Europe on moral grounds; it had been argued that both women and children were naturally lacking in self-control and in need of strict discipline. But the weakening of masculine authority in America was not accompanied by any increase in immorality, but rather the reverse. Although the traditional double standard remained in force, and prostitution was a lucrative business in the larger cities, moral standards were definitely stricter than in most European countries. How far these standards were obeyed in practice is an unanswerable question. But among many middle-class families who prided themselves on their respectability, the emphasis on purity became quite excessive. There were taboos on almost anything that might lead to carnal thoughts. Women wore dresses stretching from their necks to their toes, and blushed at any word that suggested a physical function (even the word "legs" was sometimes considered improper; "limbs" had to be substituted). This kind of prudery was a general characteristic of mid-nineteenth-century Western civilization, and was probably associated with the rise of the middle classes to social dominance; but it was carried even further in parts of the United States than in Victorian England. It proved, of course, to be a transitory phenomenon.

2. RELIGION

The Protestant Churches.   The strict moral standards of American society were closely connected with the strength of organized religion. In spite of the separation of church and state, the Protestant churches continued to play a dominant role in shaping American attitudes and ways of living. During the early nineteenth century there was, in fact, a marked increase in their influence. The United States was a more religious country in 1850 than it had been in 1789.

The most important trend in religious history during this period was the expansion of Protestantism into the new communities in the Mississippi Valley. This was mainly the work of three religious groups: the Presbyterians, the Baptists, and the Methodists. The Baptist and Methodist Churches had an especially strong appeal to frontier communities because of their democratic attitudes and their highly emotional ways of preaching.

The Presbyterians and the Baptists had become well established during the colonial period, but the Methodists were more recent arrivals. Methodism had been founded in England during the eighteenth century by the preacher John Wesley. Methodist evangelists, the leader of whom was Francis Asbury, came to America shortly before the outbreak of the War of Independence, and created an independent American organization, the Methodist Episcopal Church, in 1784. Believing in free will instead of in the Calvinist doctrine of predestination, and employing lay preachers as well as ordained ministers, the Methodists were in some respects very liberal; but their system of church organization was highly centralized, and Bishop Asbury exercised almost dictatorial powers. This system made it easy for them to organize missionary activities in the West. A similar advantage was emjoyed by the Presbyterians, who set up a central authority, the General Assembly, in the 1780's.

The other Protestant churches were not so well adapted for expansion. The New England Congregationalists continued to emphasize the independence of each congregation and failed to set up any central governing body. Their intellectual standards, moreover, were apt to be too high for the frontier. For these reasons they had little share in the Western

expansion. The Dutch and German Reformed Churches and the Lutherans, all of which dissolved their European ties and moved towards some
kind of central organization shortly after the Revolution, appealed mainly
to people of Dutch or German descent. The Quakers no longer engaged in
evangelical activities, and were strong only in eastern Pennsylvania.

The church which suffered most acutely from the changes in American life, however, was the Episcopalian. Associated during the colonial
period with British and upper-class rule, it was widely regarded during the
Revolution as a Tory organization. In the 1780's the Episcopalians set up
a national organization, independent of the Church of England, and in
1787 two of the American clergy were ordained as bishops by the Archbishop of Canterbury, thus maintaining the continuity of the apostolic
succession. But for a long time the Protestant Episcopal Church had few
adherents outside the old families of the seaboard states.

Religious Expansion.   The Presbyterian, Baptist, and Methodist
evangelists who followed the frontier line into the West preached a simple
form of religion, well adapted to pioneer communities. They emphasized
chiefly the emotional experience of conversion and strict standards of
personal morality. Many of them were itinerants who were constantly on
the move from one community to another, disdaining comfort and living
lives of heroic self-sacrifice. Their vivid descriptions of hell-fire and promises of salvation caused a number of sensational outbreaks of revivalism,
similar to the Great Awakening of the 1730's and 1740's.

The most famous of the great Western revivals occurred at Cain
Ridge in Logan County, Kentucky, in 1801. It was here that the camp
meeting originated. Many thousands of people would come together in a
forest clearing and remain for several days listening to sermons and singing hymns. Mass excitement caused many strange physical phenomena;
persons in the throes of conviction of sin were irresistibly impelled to start
dancing, barking, or jerking different parts of their bodies, and would fall
to the ground in fits and remain unconscious for hours. The revivals spread
from Kentucky to other parts of the West, and were frequent in less violent form all through the first half of the nineteenth century. In spite of
the hysteria associated with them, they caused many permanent conversions and brought about a rapid increase in church membership.
Perhaps the most successful of the later revivalists was Charles G. Finney,
who was active from the 1820's down to the 1850's, mainly in Ohio and
western New York.

The Protestantism of the early nineteenth century, although still
predominantly Calvinist (except among the Methodists), differed in some
respects from that of the colonial period. On the whole, it was less concerned with the finer points of theology, and had a more practical emphasis, inculcating chiefly good conduct and various forms of social reform.

The morality of the revivals was in many ways stricter than that of
seventeenth-century Calvinism. In fact, the early Puritans are often un-

VERDICT OF THE PEOPLE, by GEORGE CALEB BINGHAM (1811-79)

A resident of Missouri, and himself an occasional candidate for office on the Whig ticket, Bingham's aim as a painter was to "assure us that our social and political characteristics . . . will not be lost in the lapse of time for want of an Art record." This picture was painted in 1854.

A CAMP MEETING

A religious revival meeting portrayed by an English visitor, A. Rider, during the 1830's.

A LYCEUM LECTURE

Sketch of the meteorologist James Pollard Espy lecturing at Clinton Hall, New York, in 1841.

justly blamed for prohibitions which actually originated in the early nineteenth century. In addition to sexual misconduct, many evangelists now denounced as sinful various activities which had been tolerated in early New England—for example, dancing, smoking, and especially the drinking of alcoholic liquor. It was in the early nineteenth century that the leading evangelical churches first began to campaign for "temperance," declaring that anybody who took a drink was not qualified for church membership.

The upsurge of religious enthusiasm found expression in many forms of social action. The churches took a leading part in the promotion of education, especially in the West, where they founded a number of colleges. They set up organizations for the promotion of temperance, sabbath-day observance, Bible-reading, the improvement of morals, and various humanitarian reforms. Beginning in 1812, when the first missionaries were dispatched to India, they carried on missionary work in Asia and the Pacific islands. And in the North they were closely associated with the campaign for the abolition of slavery. The abolitionist movement was largely religious in character and inspiration, especially in the West, where many of its leaders were converts and pupils of Charles G. Finney.

Schisms and Controversies. To some extent the Protestant churches were able to cooperate in the pursuit of common objectives. The Presbyterians and the Congregationalists, for example, formed a Plan of Union in 1801 for joint support of missionary work in the West. But in a period of religious excitement sharp divergencies of opinion were certain to appear. Controversies about Calvinist theology and revivalistic methods and the trend towards more liberal and rationalistic beliefs led to many schisms and the formation of new denominations.

The most important schism occurred in New England. By the end of the eighteenth century Congregationalism in Connecticut and western Massachusetts was permeated with the revised form of Calvinism, known as the "new divinity," which had been developed by Jonathan Edwards and his disciples. Yale College, in particular, became a Calvinist stronghold, largely through the influence of Edwards's grandson Timothy Dwight, who served as president from 1785 to 1817. The lay population of western New England were then converted to the "new divinity" in a long series of revivals running through the first half of the nineteenth century. Meanwhile, many of the clergy in eastern Massachusetts still adhered to the rationalism of the Enlightenment. No longer believing in original sin, predestination, or the eternal damnation of the wicked, they regarded good conduct, not the emotional experience of divine grace, as the essence of religion. The more extreme rationalists were beginning to regard Jesus Christ as a moral teacher rather than as the Son of God, and were thus moving towards Unitarianism.

In 1805 Henry Ware, an avowed Unitarian, was appointed professor of theology at Harvard. This was followed by a bitter controversy and eventually by a permanent division of New England Congregationalism into two groups. Between 1815 and 1820 many of the churches in eastern Massachusetts became officially Unitarian. The leading figure in the movement, William Ellery Channing of Boston, was the most eloquent preacher of his time, and a man of wide culture, liberal sympathies, and moral sensitivity. Theodore Parker, the most prominent Unitarian minister of the 1840's and 1850's, was even more militantly liberal, crusading for the abolition of slavery and many other social reforms. In general, however, Unitarianism appealed to the wealthy and upper-class families, who were conservative in everything except their religious beliefs, and Channing and Parker were by no means typical of the movement.

In their abandonment of the gloomy Calvinist doctrines the Unitarians were responding to the optimistic and progressive spirit of the age. Similar tendencies soon developed in those New England churches that had remained Congregationalist. Edwards's "new divinity" had given a great stimulus to theological speculation, and whole libraries of books were written to expound and develop his theories, with an increasing emphasis on their more liberal implications. By the 1840's and 1850's the more advanced Congregationalist ministers no longer believed that God had deliberately chosen to damn the majority of mankind to Hell and were affirming the freedom of the human will. This movement away from Calvinism was exemplified in the Beecher family. Lyman Beecher of Connecticut, perhaps the most prominent Congregationalist minister of the early nineteenth century, was a vigorous preacher of hell-fire sermons. His son Henry Ward Beecher, on the other hand, minister of the Plymouth Church of Brooklyn and the most popular American preacher of the Civil War period, affirmed a God of love who wished all mankind to be saved.

The other denominations responded less quickly to liberal influences. Many Presbyterians remained rigidly Calvinist until the end of the century, while the Methodists and the Baptists continued to stress emotion rather than doctrine. Differing beliefs caused, nevertheless, a large number of schisms. There were at least half a dozen kinds of Baptists. Early in the century Alexander Campbell led a group of followers out of the Presbyterian Church, and founded the Disciples of Christ; and in 1837 the main body of the Presbyterians split into a conservative Old School and a more liberal New School. Slavery proved to be another cause of religious conflict. By the 1830's most of the churches north of the Ohio had become definitely hostile to slavery, while those in the South were insisting that it was divinely ordained. The Methodists and Baptists split into separate Northern and Southern churches in 1845. Among the Presbyterians, the Old School accepted slavery, while the New School opposed it.

The Sects.   Most of the new religious groups did not deviate far from the traditional beliefs. Some of them, on the other hand, made bold experiments in new ways of living, and even ceased to be recognizably Christian. Although these sects made relatively few converts, they were a picturesque feature of early nineteenth-century American life. They were usually founded by self-appointed prophets or messiahs, some of whom were men of real sincerity, although others were obvious paranoiacs or charlatans. Such men claimed to have special revelations from God, often to the effect that the Kingdom of Heaven was at hand and that men and women could henceforth live perfect and sinless lives. Some of them founded communities organized on cooperative principles which were supposed to be specimens of the Kingdom of Heaven. Thus the sectarian communities reflected not only the religious excitement of this period but also its optimism and its belief that America was destined to be the home of a new and higher mode of life.

Some of the sects were of European origin. George Rapp, for example, brought a group of followers from Germany to western Pennsylvania in 1804. Practicing communism and complete celibacy, the Rappites did not become extinct until 1905. Another German group, the Amana Society, which settled in New York in 1843 and afterwards moved to Iowa, also survived into the twentieth century. The Shakers were founded by an Englishwoman, Ann Lee, who came to America in 1774; but they made few converts until the period of the great revivals a generation later. Regarding Ann Lee as the reincarnation of Jesus Christ in female form, they founded a number of communities in New England and the West where they lived in celibacy, developed fine handicrafts, and worshipped God by engaging in ritualistic dances. At their greatest strength, between 1830 and 1850, they numbered about 6,000.

Of the many American prophets, the one who caused the greatest excitement was William Miller, a sincerely self-deluded Yankee who decided, after a study of Biblical prophecies, that the world would end in 1844. Thousands of people believed Miller's calculations; and when the appointed day came, they sold their property and gathered in white robes on the tops of the hills to wait for Gabriel to blow his horn.

Perhaps the most interesting of the sectarian leaders was John Humphrey Noyes, who founded the Perfectionist colony at Oneida, New York, in 1848. In his search for a perfect way of life Noyes decided that possessiveness was the main cause of evil and that this applied not only to private property, but also to monogamous marriage. The Oneida colony was based not only on communal ownership of property but also on group marriage, every man being regarded as the husband of every woman. Everybody was supposed to love everybody else equally, and any special attachment was considered sinful; this necessitated a severe discipline of sexual impulses, and by no means resulted in promiscuity. Inspired originally by a religious belief in the rapid approach of the Kingdom of Heaven, Noyes's optimism became more secular as he grew older; he became interested in the non-religious forms of socialism, and persuaded

his followers to make experiments in eugenics. The Oneida colony maintained its peculiar institutions with considerable success until 1879, when
it was compelled by the New York legislature to abandon group marriage
and transform itself from a specimen of the Kingdom of Heaven into a
joint-stock business corporation.

The most lasting of the sects was the Church of Jesus Christ of the
Latter Day Saints, better known as the Mormons. Its founder, Joseph
Smith, came from an area in western New York which had been swept so
often by religious revivalism that it was known as the burnt-over district.
In 1830 he published an addition to the Bible which he called the Book of
Mormon. He declared that some of the Israelites had come to America
in early times and had left some sacred writings inscribed on golden plates
which were buried in a hill; through angelic guidance he had found the
plates and translated the writings into English. However one interprets
Smith's claims to divine inspiration, it must be conceded that he had an
infectious gaiety and zest for living; and he soon began to make converts
to his new religion, promising them both prosperity in this life and salvation in the hereafter.

Like most of the other prophets, Smith set out to organize a colony
where the Kingdom of Heaven could be achieved on earth. But wherever
the Mormons settled, his dictatorial assumptions and economic and social
experiments quickly led to conflicts with "gentile" neighbors. After trying
to found his Kingdom of Heaven first in Ohio and then in Missouri, Smith
moved in 1839 to Nauvoo, Illinois, where he added polygamy to the practices of his church. By this time he had about 15,000 disciples, many
of them English immigrants who had been converted by Mormon missionaries. Smith tried to play an ambitious role in Illinois state politics,
hoping that through his control of the Mormon vote he could hold the
balance between Whigs and Democrats, but his ambitions caused so much
resentment that in 1844 he and his brother were seized by a mob and
killed. Brigham Young then succeeded to the leadership of the Church
(and also to a number of Smith's twenty-eight wives), and in 1846 he led
the Mormons to a new and permanent home in Utah, where they could be
free from interference.

The Growth of Catholicism.   Meanwhile, the rich variety of different religious denominations in American communities was further increased through a rapid expansion of Catholicism, a development which
fanatical Protestants viewed with hysterical alarm.

Throughout the colonial period most Americans, especially among
the Calvinist organizations, had been taught to regard the Roman Church
as tyrannical, corrupt, and essentially anti-Christian; and Maryland was
the only part of the country where it had been able to take root. But the
Revolution did much to weaken anti-Catholic prejudice, since Americans
found themselves in alliance with Catholic France; with the arrival of
French troops many parts of the country for the first time saw Catholic

services celebrated by Catholic priests. Catholics benefited, moreover, from the growing spirit of religious toleration. After the Revolution, the Church was able, for the first time, to establish a nation-wide organization.

In 1789 John Carroll, a member of an old Maryland planter family, was ordained as Bishop of Baltimore with jurisdiction over the whole country. At this date the total number of Catholics in the United States was probably about 30,000. Before Carroll's death in 1808 the number had increased very slowly, but firm foundations had been laid for later expansion. The Church established a seminary for training priests at Baltimore, several colleges (the first and most famous being Georgetown), a number of convents for different religious orders, and the first free parochial school at Emmitsburg, Maryland. During this period there were few native-born clergymen, and the Church was largely dependent on the services of French priests.

The Louisiana purchase added appreciably to the Catholic population, but its rapid growth came after 1830 as a result of immigration. The number of Catholics, which amounted to about 200,000 in 1820, had increased by 1850 to 1,750,000 and by 1860 to no less than 3,500,000. The majority of them were Irish, although there were also a number from Germany and some from France and other countries. By 1860 the Church had 1,500 priests and 40 bishoprics. Its main strength was in the big industrial cities of the East, such as New York, Philadelphia, and Boston; but it had also undertaken much successful missionary work in the West, where it had been able to build on foundations established under French and Spanish rule.

The Church had some difficulty in adapting itself to American life without surrendering its basic principles, as was shown especially in the trusteeship controversy. As a matter of legal expediency, the property of the Church was at first placed under the control of lay trustees in the different parishes. In a number of instances these trustees, introducing American democratic ideas into church government, claimed the power of electing priests and even bishops. But clerical authority was finally established in the 1840's, largely through the vigorous leadership of John Hughes, Bishop of New York from 1842 to 1862. Much trouble was also caused by rivalries between the different racial elements within the American Church. The initial leadership of the French clergy was vigorously contested by the Irish, whose control was, in turn, afterwards opposed by the Germans and other groups.

Anti-Catholicism first became a disturbing factor in American life in the 1830's, when Protestant leaders began to declare that the Roman hierarchy was conspiring to win complete control of the United States and eventually to destroy American liberties. Among the most belligerent leaders of the anti-Catholic crusade were the Reverend Lyman Beecher and Samuel F. B. Morse, otherwise known as a portrait-painter and inventor of the telegraph. Their appeals were strengthened by the growing nativist prejudices against the Irish and other immigrant groups. While some of their propaganda consisted of intellectual arguments against Catholic doctrine, much of it appealed to the lowest tastes. A number of pornographic books, describing the alleged immorality of Catholic priests and nuns, had a wide circulation. The most sensational of these was the *Awful Disclosures* of a girl who called herself Maria Monk and claimed to have been brought up in a convent in Montreal. Obviously a psychopathic character, Maria Monk eventually disgraced her clerical sponsors by being arrested for picking pockets while engaged in prostitution. The crusade resulted in several outbreaks of rioting; an Ursuline convent in Charlestown, Massachusetts, was burned by a mob in 1834, and ten years later several Catholic churches were destroyed in a three-day riot in Philadelphia. Anti-Catholic prejudice remained a significant factor in American life for a long time, and occasionally, as in the Know Nothing movement of the 1850's, manifested itself in politics.

3. MOVEMENTS FOR REFORM

ONE of the most important features of nineteenth-century social development, both in the United States and in western Europe, was the growth of humanitarian movements. Enlightened men and women were developing more sensitive consciences about cruelty, injustice, and inequality, and were no longer willing to tolerate forms of misery and suffering which had been accepted as inevitable throughout all previous history.

In the United States the initial impulse for the humanitarian crusade came from the ideals of the Enlightenment and the American Revolution, with their emphasis on the equality of men. Much was contributed also by the Quakers, who had been ahead of most other religious groups in stressing the Christian duty of charity; a number of reform movements originated during the Revolutionary period among the Quakers of Philadelphia. In the early nineteenth century humanitarianism acquired a new impetus from the religious revivals. Most of the reformers were members of different Protestant churches and regarded the improvement of social conditions as Christianity in action.

The reformers pursued their objectives by organizing societies, by carrying on propaganda in newspapers, pamphlets, and public meetings, and by petitioning state and Federal authorities for the appropriate legislation. Some of them were inclined to become intolerant and fanatical; and not all their objectives would be universally regarded as desirable. Yet in spite of their faults they made an immense contribution to human progress.

The most conspicuous manifestation of the humanitarian impulse was the movement for the abolition of slavery, which will be discussed in a later chapter. This won the support of almost all reformers, and tended finally to divert much of their attention from other objectives. Largely because of the association between abolitionism and other forms of humanitarianism, most Southerners after 1830 became hostile to the whole movement in all its phases. In consequence, it had relatively little effect in the South until a later period.

New Attitudes to Crime and Poverty. The treatment of criminals was one of the first causes to attract attention. Down to the late eighteenth century public executions and public floggings were frequent spectacles; and criminals sentenced to prison were herded together in close association with each other and then left to their own devices. The notion that society ought to try to reform the criminal, instead of merely punishing him or keeping him in restraint, was first propounded by humanitarian leaders in Philadelphia during the Revolutionary period, but made little headway until the 1810's and 1820's. State governments then began to accept the ideas of prison reformers. Some of them, such as that of Pennsylvania, built prisons where criminals were kept in solitary confinement in the hope that this would cause them to repent of their sins, while in other state institutions, such as Auburn and Sing Sing, New York, solitary confinement at night was combined with useful labor in gangs during the day. These new systems were far from ideal; solitary confinement often led not to repentance but to insanity. But prison reform was the first manifestation of a new public attitude towards the whole problem of crime. Another improvement was that delinquent children, who had previously been sent to prison, were now entrusted to reform schools; the first such school was built in New York in 1825.

In addition to genuine criminals, early nineteenth-century prisons also contained a large number of debtors, most of whom owed very small sums. In Boston between 1820 and 1822, to cite one example, 3,500 persons were imprisoned for debt, 2,000 of them being convicted for less than $20 apiece, and 500 being women. Conditions were similar in other cities. Agitation against imprisonment for debt had developed by 1820 and quickly achieved results, partly as a result of vigorous support from labor organizations. During the next twenty years almost every state in the Union took action to abolish it.

This was one aspect of a general movement for the relief of the poor. People were coming to believe that indigence was often due to misfortune and not, as previously assumed, to indolence or vice, and that paupers should be assisted to become self-respecting and productive members of society. This change of attitude was partly due to new economic conditions. During the colonial period every able-bodied person had normally been able to find work, so that pauperism had never been a serious problem, but the growth of cities and of the new industrial system with its alternations of prosperity and depression was making indigence and unemployment much more frequent. For the most part, the relief of the poor was left to private charity; and a number of philanthropic agencies, mostly connected with the churches, were formed for this purpose. Organized social work in the United States began early in the nineteenth century. But city and state authorities also gave assistance, chiefly by establishing workhouses, almshouses, and orphanages.

Aid for the Handicapped.   Other humanitarians devoted themselves to helping persons suffering from physical or mental handicaps. Thomas Hopkins Gallaudet of Philadelphia took up the plight of deaf-mutes, showed that it was possible to educate them, and persuaded a number of states to set up institutions for their care. Samuel Gridley Howe of Boston devoted himself with equal fervor to work for the blind, in addition to playing an active part in almost every other humanitarian movement of the period.

Even more in need of help were the insane, who had usually been regarded as incurable and treated like criminals, and had often been considered as objects for ridicule rather than pity. Insane persons who became public charges were kept chained and locked up, beaten whenever they misbehaved, and frequently left naked and half-starved. The first American to advocate more humane treatment and suggest that cure might be possible was Dr. Benjamin Rush of Philadelphia, who carried on a series of experiments with inmates of the Philadelphia Hospital after 1783 and published in 1812 the first book about mental disease by an American author. But the person who did most to improve conditions was Dorothea Dix, a Boston woman who, although already middle-aged and in poor health, took up the cause of the insane in 1841. During the next thirty years she carried on, almost singlehanded, a long and indomitable crusade, visiting one state after another, publicizing bad conditions, and persuading legislatures to vote money for mental hospitals. The reforms which she brought about were by no means either adequate or permanent; a hundred years later the treatment of the insane in many state institutions was still scandalous. But she was the first person to make the American people aware of the problem.

The Temperance Movement.   Crime, pauperism, and insanity seemed to many reformers to be closely connected with the prevalence of alcoholism. Down to the early nineteenth century almost all Americans drank, many of them to excess, with a preference for rum or whisky rather than beer or wine. Any kind of celebration, including even the ordination of a minister, invariably called for a plentiful supply of liquor, and the quantities that individuals were able to consume are, by modern standards, hard to believe. To judge from contemporary records, many Americans must have spent most of their time in a decidedly exhilarated condition.

Dr. Benjamin Rush began to campaign for temperance, mainly on medical grounds, before the end of the eighteenth century. He soon began to win support from Protestant ministers, who were concerned about the connection between liquor and immorality. In its early stages the movement against liquor recommended moderation rather than total abstinence and did not aim at any kind of legislative action. But in the 1820's crusading ministers, especially Lyman Beecher, began to denounce alcohol in any form as an unmitigated evil and to demand total prohibition. The American Society for the Promotion of Temperance was formed in 1826, and in 1833 this and other organizations combined in the Temperance Union. By 1834 temperance advocates could claim that 1,000,000 persons belonged to their societies. The movement was strongest in New England and the Middle West; it won scarcely any support in the South, partly because many of its leading figures were abolitionists.

Temperance advocates issued much lurid and sensational propaganda, well exemplified in T. S. Arthur's famous *Ten Nights in a Bar Room;* and after 1841 the services of reformed drunkards, organized in the Washington Temperance Society, were enlisted with considerable effect. In 1846, mainly through the efforts of Neal Dow, Maine passed a statewide prohibition law; and during the next nine years thirteen other states took similar action. But like the Volstead Act of the twentieth century, the laws proved impossible to enforce, and during the next few years most of them were repealed or declared unconstitutional. The movement for prohibition lost ground during the next generation, and did not make headway again until near the end of the century.

Rights for Women.   A significant feature of all the reform movements was the prominent role played by women. American women had no political and few legal rights, but they were beginning to assert their convictions about social evils with considerable vigor. It was not long before some of them demanded the right to participate in politics, repudiating the conventional belief that woman's place was the home and that she was both physically and mentally weaker than man.

Women were active from the beginning in both the abolitionist and the temperance movement; but when some of them tried to attend conventions or speak at meetings, they invariably encountered vigorous masculine opposition. Most men, even those who prided themselves on their liberalism, were shocked and horrified by the spectacle of a woman on a public platform. Exasperated by such experiences, two of the women most active in the abolitionist movement, Mrs. Lucretia Mott and Mrs. Elizabeth Cady Stanton, summoned a convention at Seneca Falls, New York, in 1848. The convention adopted a Declaration of Sentiments, modeled on that of 1776 but substituting man for King George and listing eighteen grievances against male tyranny. From this time a number of women, especially Mrs. Stanton and Miss Susan B. Anthony, worked tirelessly, in the face of incessant ridicule and abuse, for equality between the sexes. Although the feminist movement did not achieve its main goal, the right to vote, until the twentieth century, a number of states passed laws improving the legal position of women before the Civil War; in particular, they gave women control of their own property after marriage.

Meanwhile, a number of women were successfully disproving the notion of feminine inferiority by becoming highly educated and pursuing professional careers. Emma Willard and Catherine Beecher did pioneer work in establishing academies for girls, and in 1837 Mary Lyon founded the first women's college, Mount Holyoke. Oberlin College, founded in 1834, admitted girl students from the beginning; Antioch became coeducational in 1853, while Iowa led the way among the state universities in 1858. There were a number of prominent women writers, some of whom, like Margaret Fuller, Lydia Maria Child, and Sarah Josepha Hale, were also successful as journalists and magazine editors. In 1849 Elizabeth Blackwell became the first fully qualified American woman doctor; and in 1853 Antoinette Brown was ordained as the first woman minister. One of Elizabeth Blackwell's brothers married Lucy Stone, active as an abolitionist and feminist lecturer, who is remembered for insisting on her right to keep her maiden name. Women engaged in an active life were encumbered by the long flowing gowns imposed upon them by the prudery of the age; and some of them preferred the more convenient costume designed by Amelia Bloomer. Although Miss Bloomer's costume never became widely popular, it added a new word to the language.

Utopianism. The most radical group among the reformers were the advocates of some form of socialism. A number of Europeans, particularly Robert Owen in England and Charles Fourier in France, had argued that the exploitation of labor in the new industrial economy could be remedied through cooperative ownership of the means of production, and unlike the later Marxian socialists, had hoped to achieve this objective not by revolution but by setting up communities which would demonstrate to everybody the virtues of cooperation. A number of such communities were founded in the United States, although none of them lasted for more than a few years, chiefly because their members were too individualistic to submit to the necessary communal discipline. These secular utopian experiments were notably less successful than the communities founded by the Shakers, the Perfectionists, and other religious groups. Experience showed that a cooperative colony was not likely to endure unless its members were animated by a strong religious faith and submitted to the leadership of some strong individual claiming divine inspiration.

In 1825 Owen himself founded a colony at New Harmony, Indiana, which broke up within two years. Fourier had a greater influence in America, especially during the 1840's, when more than forty Fourierist communities were founded. The best-known was Brook Farm, Massachusetts, which was started in 1841 by a group of New England intellectuals and dissolved in 1847. Nathaniel Hawthorne, who lived there for a year, wrote a rather sardonic account of it in his *Blithedale Romance.* The most nearly successful of the colonies was at Red Bank, New Jersey, and lasted from 1843 to 1855. Most of the people who joined the colonies found the atmosphere of plain living and high thinking exhilarating, but were only too glad after a few years to return to a world where there were more physical comforts and more privacy.

4. EDUCATION AND SCIENCE

THE MOST important of all the social advances during the first half of the nineteenth century remains to be discussed. It was during this period that the foundations of the American public-school system were established, and the belief that education ought to be free, universal, and compulsory won general acceptance.

The Movement for Public Schools. In 1800 many people in all parts of the country were illiterate. Education had suffered during the disturbances of the Revolutionary period, and since 1760 there had been some decrease in the proportion of children in school. This was true even in New England, in spite of the laws requiring every township to maintain a school. The average New England school, moreover, was a one-room shack where little was taught except reading, writing, and arithmetic, and the teacher, often a young man earning money to go to college or train for the ministry, had no professional status, and rarely earned more than $10 a month. In the Middle and Southern states some free schools were maintained by the churches or by charity, but there was no public support for education.

All the early spokesmen for democratic ideals recognized that popular government could not succeed without a wide diffusion of literacy, and hoped that the American experiment would eventually justify itself not only by promoting the material well-being of the mass of the people but also by developing their appreciation of culture, learning, and the arts. In advocating universal education they were supported by many conservatives, who believed that public schools could promote social stability by inculcating religious belief and loyalty to established institutions. Nevertheless, it was by no means easy to persuade public authorities to appropriate the necessary money. In the Northwest there was relatively little controversy about the value of public education, although lack of money prevented it from being established quickly. But in the East many people argued that education should be left to private initiative, and that it was contrary to American ideals of individual liberty to compel taxpayers to contribute money for the benefit of other people's children. A number of self-sacrificing public servants had to struggle for many years before universal education became a reality.

Most of the Northern states began to make appropriations for the support of education early in the nineteenth century. New York, for instance, took the initial step in 1812, largely through the efforts of De Witt Clinton. But for a number of years well-to-do parents were required to pay fees; and although the poor could have their children educated free, they were liable to be stigmatized as paupers if they took advantage of this concession. It was not until the middle decades of the century that public education became free for everybody, and not until even later that it was made universal and compulsory. The first compulsory education law was passed in Massachusetts in 1852, and other states did not follow this example until after the Civil War.

The outstanding figure in the fight for universal education was Horace Mann, who became secretary of the Massachusetts Board of Education in 1837. A crusading idealist who declared that "in a republic ignorance is a crime," Mann labored fifteen hours a day for the next eleven years, building schools, raising their standards, establishing normal schools for the training of teachers, and securing higher salaries for them. During the same period Henry Barnard was doing similar work in Connecticut and Rhode Island. Mann and Barnard had a wide influence throughout the country, and did more than anybody else to make teaching into a reputable profession.

By 1850 the nation had a total of 80,000 elementary schools, with nearly 3,500,000 pupils. Most of them were in the North and Northwest, but during the next decade considerable progress was made also in the South, especially in Alabama and North Carolina. Public high schools, however, were still rare, and parents who wished their children to be educated beyond the elementary level usually had to send them to private institutions.

Colleges.   In higher education the United States lagged behind Europe until near the end of the century. Early American leaders had wished to create universities which would be genuine centers of learning on the highest level. Washington, for example, had advocated a national university supported by the Federal government, and Jefferson had spent his old age building the University of Virginia. But American colleges remained for a long time notable more for quantity than for quality. The nine colleges founded during the colonial period increased to twenty-four by 1800 and to 253 by 1860. About twenty of these were state institutions, mostly in the South and West, while most of the remainder were denominational. But almost everywhere standards were low. The college of this period was essentially a glorified high school, which laid all its emphasis on teaching and did little or nothing for the advancement of scholarship and research.

Educational Methods.   In addition to providing an adequate number of schools and colleges, educational reformers sought also to develop a curriculum fitted to American needs and ideals. European educational methods, they felt, were unsuited to a democratic society. Soon after the Revolution, American scholars began to write textbooks for use in primary schools. The most notable of them was Noah Webster, whose *Elementary Spelling Book* had sold 5,000,000 copies by 1818. Webster was a cultural nationalist, who believed that the American language should no longer conform to British spelling and usage, and after making a fortune from his speller, he went on to compile an equally famous dictionary. The expansion of the school system in the 1830's and 1840's produced a new crop of textbooks, written by such authors as Samuel Goodrich, who used the pseudonym Peter Parley, and William H. Mc-Guffey. McGuffey's readers, the first of which appeared in 1836, provided generations of school children with well-chosen excerpts from contemporary literature, along with moral advice and patriotic exhortation. He probably did as much as anybody to form the ideals of late nineteenth-century American society. Apart from the use of new textbooks, teaching methods in the primary schools remained traditional, with strong emphasis on discipline. A few individuals, such as Bronson Alcott in Boston, founded private schools where progressive methods were adopted; but none of them won enough support to last more than a few years.

On the college level there was more controversy about educational aims. Conservatives upheld the merits of the traditional curriculum, based on the study of the classics, which had been established during the Renaissance, while reformers wished to introduce a wider range of subjects and allow students more freedom to choose what they wanted to study. On the whole, the traditional curriculum retained its predominance until near the end of the century; but colleges like Harvard, Yale, and Princeton gave increasing emphasis to science and modern languages, and a few institutions, notably Jefferson's University of Virginia, experimented with an elective system. Another new trend was the foundation of professional schools for medicine, theology, law, and engineering; but since they gave instruction only in theory, without offering practical experience, their value was limited.

Adult Education. Almost as important for democratic institutions as the growth of formal education was the diffusion of culture among the adult population. The first lyceum was founded by Josiah Holbrook at Millbury, Massachusetts, in 1826, and within twenty years there were about 4,000 local organizations of this kind. The lyceums promoted study and discussion, and arranged for lectures by well-known writers and scientists. It was during this period that lecture-going became one of America's favorite occupations. Adult education of a more disciplined kind was provided by mechanics' institutes in a number of cities. Another significant trend was the establishment of free public libraries. Peterborough, New Hampshire, has the distinction of having set up the first tax-supported library in 1833, and within a few years a number of state and city governments had copied this example.

Journalism. The main agency for the spread of information was the newspaper. After the Revolution there was a rapid increase in the number of newspapers; by 1810 there were 350, of which nearly thirty were dailies. But most of them were primarily the organs of political parties, sold at relatively high prices, and were read mainly by the well-to-do classes. Newspapers appealing to a mass audience and independent of political control began in the 1830's. The first newspaper to sell for one cent, the *New York Sun*, began publication in 1833, and two years later came the *New York Herald*, owned and edited by James Gordon Bennett. Specializing in stories of crime and scandal, Bennett probably did more to degrade than to elevate popular taste, and his success showed that universal literacy might be by no means an unmixed blessing. But once he had shown the possibilities of the new mass market, more responsible and enlightened journalists began to appeal to it. In 1841 Horace Greeley began publishing the *New York Tribune*. For the next thirty years he was one of the best-known men in the country; and although his opinions were often eccentric and erratic, he used his wide influence mainly to promote liberal ideals and a respect for culture. More conservative but equally honest and enlightened was Henry J. Raymond, who founded the *New York Times* in 1851. Admirable popular newspapers also appeared in other cities, especially the *Baltimore Sun* and the *Springfield Republican*.

There was a similar proliferation of magazines, of which there were nearly a hundred by 1825. Perhaps the most important was the *North American Review*, founded in Boston in 1815. This remained the leading serious review until 1857, when the *Atlantic Monthly* began publication; but its appeal was limited to intellectual circles. A large number of publications appealed to more popular tastes, many of them, like *Godey's Ladies' Book*, being written primarily for women.

The trend towards a more democratic culture was not peculiar to the United States. Similar developments were taking place in western Europe, and to some extent American reformers could learn from European experience. The American educational system, for example, owed much to Germany, whose schools and universities were then regarded as the best in the world. But by the middle of the century literacy was probably more widely diffused among the American people than elsewhere, and the average citizen had more opportunities for improving his mind.

Scientific Development.   European visitors, however, complained that the United States made few original contributions to science and the arts. In historical retrospect this criticism seems to have only partial validity. The 1840's and 1850's saw much important literature and some good work in the other arts (to be discussed in the next chapter), though it is true that much of it was not adequately appreciated by contemporaries. The United States before the Civil War produced no important professional philosopher or social scientist. On the other hand, some of the men actively engaged in politics, such as Madison and Calhoun, made valuable contributions to social theory. Problems of national policy, moreover, stimulated considerable discussion of economics, some of which was original, although not perhaps of permanent significance. Mathew Carey of Philadelphia and his son Henry, for example, wrote books arguing that the *laissez-faire* theory of Adam Smith was not applicable to American conditions and advocating national planning, through tariffs and internal improvements, to promote a balanced economy.

In the natural sciences the provision of facilities for research had to precede original achievement. The first half of the century saw the foundation of adequately equipped laboratories and observatories at leading universities, of new institutions for scientific training (beginning with the Rensselaer Polytechnic Institute in 1824), of scientific periodicals (especially the *American Journal of Science and the Arts* in 1818), and of scientific societies (such as the American Medical Association in 1847, and the American Association for the Advancement of Science in 1848). The Federal government did much to promote scientific knowledge by its geodetic surveys and through the establishment in 1846 of the Smithsonian Institution, the funds for which were bequeathed by an English chemist.

The leading scientists of this period probably spent more time in promoting public interest and creating the necessary organization and facilities than in original work. Some of them, nevertheless, made important contributions to knowledge. Perhaps the greatest was the physicist Joseph Henry, professor at Princeton and afterwards the first director of the Smithsonian. A close second was Benjamin Silliman, professor of chemistry and natural history at Yale from 1802 to 1853. Other notable figures were the Virginia naval officer Matthew Fontaine Maury, whose great *Physical Geography of the Sea* (1855) founded the science of oceanography, the botanist Asa Gray, and the geologist Edward Hitchcock. Americans could also claim credit for a vast alleviation of human suffering through the discovery that ether could be used as an anesthetic. This was made by two doctors, independently of each other, Crawford Long in Georgia and Charles Jackson in Massachusetts, was first applied by a Boston dentist, William T. G. Morton, in 1846, and was demonstrated during the same year in a major operation at the Massachusetts General Hospital by John C. Warren.

Thus, throughout the first half of the nineteenth century, American democratic idealism found expression in a wide variety of movements seeking to raise the material, moral, and cultural level of all groups in the community. During the same period its spiritual implications were being explored by a group of writers who showed that a democratic society could also produce important works of art.

XIV

American Romanticism

1. FACTORS IN LITERARY DEVELOPMENT

2. EARLY NEW YORK WRITERS

3. THE FLOWERING OF NEW ENGLAND

4. WRITERS OF THE SOUTHERN AND MIDDLE STATES

5. THE OTHER ARTS

THE FIRST attempts to create an American imaginative literature were made during the Revolutionary period, when a number of young men, particularly a Connecticut group known as the "Hartford Wits," were stimulated by the hope of establishing the cultural, as well as the political, independence of their country. But the realization of this ambition proved to be a slow process, and no work of permanent significance was produced until after the turn of the century. By the 1830's and 1840's, however, the United States was beginning to make permanent contributions to world literature.

1. FACTORS IN LITERARY DEVELOPMENT

Literary Economics.   One of the main impediments to the growth of American literature was the lack of economic support. Since there was

SELECTED BIBLIOGRAPHY: The standard history of American literature is Robert Spiller and others (eds.), *Literary History of the United States* (1948); the first volume covers the period down to the Civil War. Van Wyck Brooks, *The Flowering of New England* (1936), *The World of Washington Irving* (1944), and *The Times of Melville and Whitman* (1947), give a fascinating, although uncritical, portrayal of literary life in the United States. V. L. Parrington, *Main Currents in American Thought* (1927–29), of which Vol. 2 deals with the period 1800–60, is a great book which should be read by all students of American history, though its approach to literature is sociological rather than aesthetic. F. O. Matthiessen, *American Renaissance: Art and Expression in the Age of Emerson and Whitman* (1941) is a solid and comprehensive analysis of the work of Emerson, Thoreau, Hawthorne, Melville, and Whitman. O. W. Larkin, *Art and Life in America* (1949), is a comprehensive history of painting, sculpture, and architecture, while J. T. Howard, *Our American Music* (revised edition, 1946) is the most useful book on this subject.

no tradition of patronage by rich men or cultural foundations, writers who lacked private incomes had to rely on the general reading public. But although a considerable proportion of the people were literate, American men mostly preferred to read newspapers rather than books, and showed little appreciation for the more imaginative forms of writing. The audience for fiction and poetry consisted largely of women; and since writers were expected to avoid anything which might bring a blush to the cheeks of an unmarried girl brought up to middle-class standards of refinement, they could not express themselves very freely.

American writers were also handicapped by the refusal of Congress (until 1891) to give copyright protection to foreign authors. Since American publishers did not have to pay royalty fees on English books, they often preferred to reprint them in preference to supporting native talent. To a large extent early American writers relied for financial support on contributing to magazines rather than on book publication. Unfortunately, most magazine editors preferred material that was sentimental or sensational.

Under such conditions any individual determined to devote himself to a serious literary career was likely to have a hard struggle. Of the more important writers of the period before the Civil War, only three, Irving, Cooper, and Hawthorne, succeeded at any time in making an adequate living from literature, and each of them was able to rely on other resources during his period of apprenticeship. Irving and Cooper came from wealthy families, while Hawthorne (who did not achieve success until he published *The Scarlet Letter* at the age of forty-six) had a small private income. Emerson also had a private income, which he supplemented by lecturing. Thoreau and Whitman never married, and kept their personal needs to a minimum. Poe and Melville, less fortunate than the others, were wholly dependent upon their earnings and had families to support. Poe was often close to starvation, while Melville abandoned the struggle halfway through his life and ceased to be more than a spare-time writer. More favorable conditions would probably have produced a much more extensive literary development.

Romanticism. Early American writers began by copying European models, and did not at first display any distinctively national quality. They had to learn their craft from the Europeans before they could effectively handle native themes and work out appropriate new techniques for expressing them. Only gradually did the new American literature become genuinely American. The writers of the Revolutionary period mostly adopted the standards of eighteenth-century classicism. But the main European influence on the later literature was Romanticism.

Developing in England, France, and Germany in the late eighteenth century, and dominating the intellectual life of Western civilization for at least two generations, Romanticism was such a complex and varied movement that it is almost impossible to define. In general, it may be

regarded as a reaction against the rather narrow rationalism of the
Enlightenment. Writers like Rousseau in France and Wordsworth and
Coleridge in England emphasized the emotional, intuitional, and instinctive elements in the human personality, and asserted that man should
trust his feelings rather than his intellect. Whereas the Enlightenment had
regarded man as normally reasonable and self-controlled, the Romanticists
saw him as a creature of intense passions and aspirations. And whereas the
Enlightenment had supposed that ultimate truth could be discovered
through intellectual inquiry, the Romanticists believed that spiritual
intuition had a higher validity. Philosophically, they repudiated the eighteenth-century conception of the universe as a vast machine and regarded
nature as the embodiment of a divine spirit. Aesthetically, they liberated
literature from the restraints imposed by eighteenth-century classicism
and made it more spontaneous and more imaginative. Many of them
turned away from contemporary society, and liked to write about earlier
times (especially the Middle Ages), distant places, and exotic subject
matter. The chief weakness of Romanticist poetry was that it too often
took the form of a relaxed daydreaming, lacking in intellectual content
and in relevance to actual life.

In its earlier phases Romanticism was a highly individualistic movement, with revolutionary implications. Many of its spokesmen believed
that man could achieve virtue and happiness through the spontaneous
expression of his desires and by living close to nature. One of the strongest
elements in Romanticism was a tendency to regard civilization as corrupt
and to idealize simple or primitive people whose lives were supposedly
more natural. But the optimism of the earlier Romanticists quickly faded
away as the incompatibility between man's desires and his environment
became more apparent. Many of the later Romanticist writers felt that
human beings were doomed to frustration and found a morbid satisfaction in describing their misery. Despairing of the possibilities of social
change, they often became extreme conservatives, and ended by glorifying the feudal and Catholic institutions of the Middle Ages.

American Themes. In its more optimistic aspects Romanticism
had an obvious appeal to writers trying to give literary expression to the
American faith in the individual. This faith had originally been based on
the rationalistic philosophy of the Enlightenment. Man had been regarded
as a rational being who could be trusted to follow the laws of nature, which
were identical with those of reason and of God. Under the impact of the
Romantic Movement new conceptions of nature and of the human personality became current, but it was still possible to affirm a confidence in
man's fundamental goodness. He should be guided by his emotions and
intuitions rather than his intellect; but in proportion as he lived naturally
and spontaneously, he would became a vehicle for the divine spirit that
pervaded the universe, and would no longer require the guidance of external authority or tradition. These doctrines of Romantic individualism

were developed by a number of American writers, of whom Emerson was the most important.

Other American writers were more deeply affected by the pessimistic aspects of Romanticism. The Romantic exploration of the individual personality did not always result in an Emersonian optimism. It led also to an emphasis on morbid emotional forces, on a basic contradiction between man's aspirations and the conditions under which he must live, and on his isolation from other human beings. These themes were developed by such writers as Poe, Hawthorne, and Melville, none of whom had much faith in the possibilities of social reform or in man's capacity to dispense with external authority. They were concerned, in particular, with the problem of isolation, which may be regarded as individualism seen in terms not of its opportunities but of its liabilities and dangers.

The more important writers of the period can be roughly classified as optimists or pessimists, according to whether they presented the individualism of American society in bright or dark colors. Emerson, Thoreau, and Whitman clearly belong to the former category, and Poe, Hawthorne, and Melville to the latter. All of them, however, were primarily engaged in exploring the implications of the American doctrine of individualism in the light of Romantic conceptions of the human personality. They were therefore concerned with the emotional experience of the individual and with his place in nature rather than with the social structure or interpersonal relationships. A number of the themes with which European writers have always been largely occupied did not appear in American literature until a later period. Before the Civil War, American novelists, for example, made little attempt to produce realistic portrayals of American society; there were no American equivalents of Dickens or Balzac. What is perhaps even more remarkable is their lack of interest in sexual emotion. Love has, on the whole, been the favorite theme of writers throughout the ages. It was singularly lacking in American fiction until near the end of the nineteenth century (except, rather mildly, in Hawthorne). Most American writers either ignored it or (like Poe and Melville) were concerned with it chiefly in its more morbid forms.

2. EARLY NEW YORK WRITERS

Literary Beginnings.   The literary efforts of the late eighteenth century can be quickly dismissed. The classicist epics of Timothy Dwight, Joel Barlow, and other "Hartford Wits" survive only as names in textbooks. Philip Freneau had real gifts as a lyricist, but the writing of poetry occupied only a small part of a life divided mainly between political journalism, as a militant champion of Jeffersonian ideals, and service as a sea captain. The first American novel, W. H. Brown's *The Power of Sympathy* (1789), was quickly followed by others; but most of them were feeble imitations of the British sentimental fiction of the eighteenth century, dealing mostly with unprotected females at the mercy of wicked seducers. The 1790's, however, produced one more lively work dealing satirically with American political and social conditions: H. H. Bracken-ridge's *Modern Chivalry*.

The first American to devote himself exclusively to a literary career was Charles Brockden Brown, who was born in Philadelphia in 1771 and published six novels before his death in 1810. Brown took his subject-matter from contemporary America, and championed American ideals of freedom and social reform. At the same time he was strongly affected by the more exotic aspects of European Romanticism. One of the most popular literary genres during the Romantic period was the "Gothic" novel, which dealt with morbid emotions and sensational experiences, often occurring in medieval castles and involving elements of the super-natural. Brown's novels showed the influence of the Gothic novel, al-though they were located in Pennsylvania and New York and not in medieval Europe. They communicated a sense of horror by presenting characters addicted to weird crimes or suffering from various forms of neurosis and insanity. It seems significant that the first professional Amer-ican novelist should have shown such a penchant for the darker aspects of the human psyche. Brown began a trend which was developed by Poe and has continued to be one of the dominant characteristics of American fiction down to the present.

Brown's later life was spent in New York, which was now replacing Philadelphia as the chief cultural center in the United States. The first third of the nineteenth century may be regarded as a period of New York dominance in American literature. New York had always been the most cosmopolitan of American cities; and since it was now rapidly developing into the nation's leading seaport, it was becoming even more receptive to foreign influences. Such an environment tended to encourage wit, elegance, and sophistication rather than emotional force or originality.

Irving.   These New York qualities were exemplified in the work of Washington Irving, who published his first book in 1809 and his last in 1859 and was recognized throughout most of his long career, both at home and in Europe, as America's leading man of letters. In both his writings and his personal life, Irving showed himself a man of low emotional pres-sure, who preferred the role of an observer and a dilettante. Uninterested in political and social questions (in spite of the fact that for a few years he held diplomatic posts in Great Britain and Spain), and lacking in strong convictions on any subject, he enjoyed letting his fancy play over pictur-esque scenes and characters, especially in the past. A man with such a temperament found more congenial material in Europe, and Irving spent a total of twenty-three years abroad.

Irving owed his wide popularity to the grace and charm with which he could communicate his idyllic reveries. In addition to essays and short stories, he wrote extensively about Spanish history; and in later life he published several books about the western fur trade (largely in order to glorify the achievements of his friend and patron John Jacob Astor), and ended his career with a five-volume biography of Washington. But he is chiefly remembered for the early works in which he gave a legendary and almost medieval flavor to the history of the Hudson Valley, especially his *History of New York* (allegedly written by Diedrich Knickerbocker) and the stories of Rip Van Winkle and Ichabod Crane published in *The Sketch Book of Geoffrey Crayon.* Irving's purpose, as he defined it, was "to clothe home scenes and places and family names with those imaginative and whimsical associations so seldom met with in our new country, but which live like charms and spells about the cities of the Old World." As this sentence suggests, one cannot turn to Irving for any revelation of the American character and American experience.

Cooper.   The other leading New York writer of this period was a man of very different temperament, though of equally conservative inclinations: the virile and combative James Fenimore Cooper. The son of a wealthy upstate landowner, of strongly Federalist convictions, Cooper spent several years as a naval officer and then married into the aristocratic De Lancey family and settled down as a gentleman farmer. Without any previous literary ambition, he wrote his first novel at the age of thirty, chiefly for the entertainment of his wife. His second book, *The Spy*, published in 1821, was an immediate success, and he was thus launched upon a thirty-year literary career which made him the most widely read American author of his time.

Cooper's books dealt with three subjects: American history, especially the French and Indian Wars and the Revolution; the sea; and social trends in the America of his own time. The popularity which he won from the American public by his historical and sea stories was largely forfeited, in his later life, by his pungent criticisms of contemporary American society. A belligerent champion of American institutions against their European detractors, he was an even more belligerent opponent of forces in American life which he felt to be leading towards degeneration and anarchy. As a landowner and a former naval officer, he believed in leadership by an enlightened upper class, in the maintenance of authority and discipline, and in the rights of property, especially property in land. He was equally hostile, on the one hand, to the growing spirit of commercialism and, on the other hand, to the leveling tendencies of democracy. Cherishing these conservative eighteenth-century convictions, Cooper could scarcely feel at home in the New York of the 1830's and 1840's. Of the novels in which he recorded his social philosophy, the most readable are the Littlepage trilogy (*Satanstoe, The Chainbearer, The Redskins*), in which he commemorated the achievements of a New York landowning family, showing how it built civilization in the wilderness and had to defend its rights against usurpation by squatters from New England (Cooper despised New Englanders, whom he regarded as mostly swindlers, demagogues, and hypocrites).

Cooper had no interest in subtleties of characterization; and most of the figures in his novels, especially the women, are not very clearly individualized. His style had little distinction; and (as Mark Twain pointed out in a devastating critique) his plots were often highly implausible. His main talent was for telling an exciting story. This was most fully displayed in the series of five novels recording the exploits of the frontier hunter and scout, Natty Bumppo, the famous Leatherstocking. In this series he not only communicated the color and drama of the French and Indian Wars; he also created a stock figure which became a part of the American tradition. Natty Bumppo, with his love for the wilderness, his extraordinary skill as hunter and pathfinder, his strong native sense of right and wrong, his modesty, his self-reliance, and his shyness with women, was not a very accurate portrayal of the frontiersman of history, who was usually more self-assertive and less deferential towards his "betters"; but he had a strong appeal to the American imagination. Characters modeled along the same lines still figure prominently in the motion pictures and popular fiction of today.

Other New Yorkers.   Irving and Cooper both belonged to the eighteenth century rather than the nineteenth. The influence of Romanticism was more apparent in the work of William Cullen Bryant, a native of western Massachusetts who became a New Yorker by adoption. Bryant's "Thanatopsis," published in 1817 when he was twenty-three years of age, was the best American poem that had been written up to that time. The central theme of Bryant's poetry was a mystical sense of man's communion with nature, derived from Wordsworth and other English Romanticists but expressed with a power and felicity that made it more than merely imitative. Bryant moved to New York in 1825, and remained one of its most useful citizens until his death in 1878. As the editor for nearly half a century of the *New York Evening Post*, he was the consistent champion of political honesty and morality and of every liberal cause.

None of the other New Yorkers of this period has earned a place among the classics of American literature. Few people still read the historical novels of James Kirke Paulding, the poems of Fitzgreene Halleck, or the essays, stories, and verses of Nathaniel Parker Willis, all of whom were leaders in the cultural life of their time. Nor do they remember the versatile William Dunlap, who was both a portrait-painter and a prolific dramatist and theatrical producer, and wrote the first histories of American art and the American stage. But although such figures are preserved only by the historians of literature, it is important to recognize that they existed. Great writers are never isolated; they can develop only in a favorable milieu. Perhaps the most important aspect of the New York culture of the early nineteenth century was that an increasing number of persons were developing a serious interest in the arts. Most of their work is deservedly forgotten, but they helped to create higher standards, more discriminating audiences, and an atmosphere more conducive to aesthetic creation.

3. THE FLOWERING OF NEW ENGLAND

NEW ENGLAND after the Revolution passed through a period of intellectual stagnation, chiefly because its dominant classes fell into a state of panic about the radicalism of the French Revolution and the religious infidelity associated with it. Throughout the Federalist and Jeffersonian periods they resolutely opposed any introduction of new or alien ideas. This cultural isolation ended after the War of 1812, when young men began to visit Europe and bring back new books and ideas. The seeds of Romanticism, transplanted from Europe and germinating in a soil already well fertilized by the traditional Puritan respect for the life of the mind, eventually flowered into the so-called New England Renaissance. For more than half a century, from the 1830's until near the end of the century, Boston rather than New York was the most vital cultural center in the United States.

The renaissance was almost restricted to the area in which the iron rule of Calvinist orthodoxy had been broken by Unitarianism; it was a flowering of eastern Massachusetts rather than of New England as a whole. And the bolder implications of Romanticism were accepted by only a small number of individuals, although they included the figures most acclaimed by posterity. The New England writers of this period fall fairly clearly into two groups: the radicals who endeavored to break completely with the past and (in Emerson's words) "work out an original relation to the universe"; and the conservatives who remained closer to the "Brahmin" tradition of the old mercantile families and were mostly men of scholarship rather than of creative originality.

Historians.   The earliest manifestations of the New England Renaissance were in the writing of history. In the 1820's the Reverend Jared Sparks began the collection and publication of documents, though he incurred the disapproval of later scholars by correcting George Washington's grammar and spelling. The most ambitious historical writer was George Bancroft, who published in 1834 the first volume of his long *History of the United States*, a work which was not completed until forty years later. Bancroft's central theme was the growth, under divine guidance, of American democracy; he made history, it was said, vote for Jackson on every page. As a result of this strong bias, his work has not had much lasting appeal, in spite of its literary qualities.

Several later and more conservative historians have better chances for permanent survival, especially William H. Prescott, whose works on the Spanish conquest of Mexico and Peru are still sound history as well as good literature, and Francis Parkman. Publishing his first book in 1849, Parkman devoted most of his life to a series of volumes on the conflict between Great Britain and France for North America. Combining thorough scholarship with an ability to tell a dramatic story and a sympathetic understanding of the French and the Indians as well as the American colonists, this series is often regarded as the greatest masterpiece of American historiography.

The Transcendentalists.   The radical aspects of the renaissance were represented chiefly by Transcendentalism. This is the name given to the intellectual attitude developed by a number of young men living in the Boston area in the 1830's. In 1838 they organized a club for philosophical discussion, and between 1840 and 1844 they issued a magazine called the *Dial.* In 1841 some of them were responsible for founding the Brook Farm colony. Among the members of the group were Ralph Waldo Emerson, George Ripley, Bronson Alcott, Margaret Fuller, Henry David Thoreau, and the Unitarian minister Theodore Parker.

The word "transcendentalism" was derived from German Romantic philosophy. Systematizing the Romantic distrust of the intellect and exaltation of intuition, philosophers like Kant, Hegel, Fichte, and Schelling had affirmed that man could apprehend reality by direct spiritual insight. In their phraseology, the "reason" (by which they really meant intuition) knew truths which "transcended" those accessible to the "understanding" (which was the faculty employed in logical argument and scientific inquiry). Emerson and other New Englanders acquired this attitude partly from the Germans directly, and partly from their English interpreters, such as Coleridge and Carlyle. It appealed to them largely because it provided a metaphysical justification for the ideal of individual freedom; if every man could apprehend the truth by direct intuition, then any form of external authority, political or religious, was unnecessary. And they found it easy to think in these terms because of the traditional emphasis of New England Puritanism on man's capacity for direct spiritual insight. The Puritans had believed in original sin, but they had also believed in divine grace; when man was enlightened by the Holy Spirit, he knew the truth by immediate revelation. Transcendentalism may be defined as Calvinism modified by the Romantic doctrine of man's natural goodness. Denying original sin, it affirmed that all men, and not merely the elect few, might achieve a state of grace by casting off external authority and responding to their own spiritual intuitions.

Emerson.   To state the implications of this doctrine was the life-work, in particular, of Emerson. After a brief experience as a Unitarian minister, he settled at Concord in 1834, and this remained his home until his death in 1882. Descended from a long line of Puritan ministers, he devoted himself to the task of intellectual exploration and leadership with the singleminded integrity that his ancestors had given to the worship of God. In his lifetime he propagated his ideas through his public lectures and in his two volumes of *Essays* and other writings. But the quality of his mind can best be appreciated through the private journal he kept for nearly sixty years.

Emerson's central message was self-reliance. Every individual, he believed, shared in the divinity which pervaded the universe and should therefore learn to trust his own intuitions, even when they conflicted with convention and tradition. "In all my lectures," he said, "I have taught one doctrine, namely the infinitude of the private man." In proportion as men acquired a genuine self-reliance, he believed, any form of coercive authority would become unnecessary. He applauded the "gradual casting-off of material aids, and the growing trust in the private self-supplied powers of the individual," and looked forward to a society of free men in which order would be "maintained without artificial restraints as well as the solar system." "The appearance of character," he declared, "makes the state unnecessary. . . . He, who has the law-giver, may with safety not only neglect, but even contravene every written commandment." This was a spiritual reaffirmation of the democratic ideal, and in Emerson's writings it was closely associated with a nationalistic faith in America. In his Phi Beta Kappa address of 1837, *The American Scholar* (which has been called an "intellectual Declaration of Independence"), he urged American writers to abandon the imitation of "the courtly muses of Europe." "Let us have done with Europe and dead cultures, let us explore the possibilities of our own new world."

Emerson was too individualistic to have much faith in institutional changes; while he sympathized with movements for social reform, he did not join them, feeling that the most necessary reform was that of the individual within himself. But the radical implications of his thinking were undeniable, and Emerson underlined them by denouncing the commercialism and the intellectual timidity of the upper classes with the severity of a Hebrew prophet.

Certain aspects of Emerson's thinking have not worn well. Believing that the human spirit and the natural universe were expressions of God, he had a sublime confidence that all things worked together for good. In proportion as man achieved a genuine self-reliance, he would also become virtuous. All natural and social processes developed in conformity with God's moral laws. "An eternal beneficent necessity," he asserted, "is always bringing things right. . . . The league between virtue and nature engages all things to assume a hostile front to vice." A generation which has seen two world wars and the totalitarian state is likely to find this unfailing optimism hard to understand, and to feel that John Calvin and Jonathan Edwards had a more realistic view of human nature. Emersonianism was the product of a society in which the moral discipline of Puritanism had become almost second nature, so that it was easy to equate self-reliance with virtue, and of an epoch in American development when the possibilities of progress seemed limitless. But Emerson was greater than his philosophy. His writings were filled with acute observations of contemporary men and institutions and insights into human psychology. As a critic of the American life of his time he was always shrewd and often profound. And he could express his ideas with a pungency and a poetic vividness which made him one of the great phrasemakers of literature.

Thoreau.   Thoreau probably has a stronger appeal for the twentieth century, although he was a lesser man than Emerson and was regarded during his lifetime merely as one of his disciples. The most rugged and uncompromising of the Transcendentalists, he expressed his individualism in a total rejection of organized society. From one point of view, his life was a catalogue of negations. As Emerson summarized it, "he was bred to no profession; he never married; he lived alone; he never went to church; he never voted; he refused to pay a tax to the state; he ate no flesh; he drank no wine; he never knew the use of tobacco; and though a naturalist he used neither gun nor rod." But Thoreau's refusal to conform was due not to any love of self-denial for its own sake but to a conviction that he could live most fully and richly by devoting himself to contemplation and communion with nature. Most men, he believed, became trapped by their responsibilities and lived "lives of quiet desperation." In order to have time for self-realization, Thoreau repudiated all social obligations and reduced his physical needs to a minimum. *Walden,* describing two years spent in a hut in the woods near Concord, is both a fascinating autobiographical record and a masterpiece of English prose. His essay *On Civil Disobedience,* in which he denounced all organized government and proclaimed the duty of the individual to follow the dictates of his conscience even against the state, was immediately inspired by his opposition to the Mexican War, but has become a classic of philosophic anarchism (both Tolstoi and Gandhi were influenced by it). Obviously, a nation made up of men like Thoreau would be impossible. But every nation, especially at times when individuality is in danger of being crushed by social organization, needs to be leavened by a few such radical nonconformists.

The other members of the group can be more quickly dismissed. Margaret Fuller is remembered chiefly for her championship of the rights of women in *Women in the Nineteenth Century* and other writings. Bronson Alcott, the father of "Little Women," made interesting experiments in progressive education and impressed his contemporaries as a lecturer and conversationalist; but his writings seem today either trite or meaningless. Theodore Parker was more important as a militant champion of abolitionism and other reforms than as a thinker. A number of other people wrote poetry or criticism inspired by Transcendentalism but lacked the vitality of its leading spokesmen.

The Conservatives.   While Concord was the main center of radical individualism, the more conservative figures were mostly associated with Harvard. None of them was wholly untouched by the liberal and reforming spirit of the time; they accepted the optimistic doctrines of Unitarianism, and generally supported the abolitionist movement. But in other respects they adhered to the traditional attitudes of the Boston mercantile oligarchy and disapproved of the Transcendentalists. Regarding American literature as an offshoot of that of England, they did not share Emerson's distrust of "the courtly muses of Europe." While they were influenced by Romanticism, they accepted it as a literary convention rather than as an attitude toward life. After the Civil War their conservatism hardened into the Genteel Tradition.

Henry Wadsworth Longfellow, professor of modern languages at Harvard from 1837 until 1854, resembled Washington Irving in his love for the picturesque and the antique and his desire to give a legendary flavor to American homes and places. He did this with such success that many episodes in colonial history are known to most Americans through Longfellow's retelling of them rather than as they actually occurred. The best-loved of all American poets, he was essentially a writer for young people. His poetry was genuine, but it lacked intellectual force and complexity. James Russell Lowell, who succeeded to Longfellow's professorship at Harvard, almost achieved greatness as both poet and critic. An accomplished craftsman and a man of wide and humane culture, he had every quality needed for intellectual leadership except the one essential element of creative genius. Most modern readers feel that his best work was done in his early life, when he was deeply stirred by abolitionism (especially in *The Biglow Papers*, written against the Mexican War), rather than in his more conservative maturity. A third member of the Harvard group, Oliver Wendell Holmes, doctor of medicine and professor of anatomy, wrote poems and the unique *Autocrat of the Breakfast Table* which preserved much of the wit and the tough-minded rationalism that had characterized the eighteenth century.

Hawthorne. Concord and Harvard comprised between them most aspects of the flowering of New England. But there were other writers who were relatively untouched by ideas and were interested mainly in recording the special flavor of Puritan life and culture, especially in the rural back country. Among them were two individuals whose lives were devoted largely to the abolitionist movement, the Quaker poet John Greenleaf Whittier and the novelist Harriet Beecher Stowe. Mrs. Stowe's New England stories are perhaps of more permanent interest than her best-selling *Uncle Tom's Cabin*. More important was the isolated figure of Nathaniel Hawthorne, the finest artist produced by the New England Renaissance and possibly its most realistic and penetrating mind.

While Emerson may be said to have retained the Puritan belief in divine grace while repudiating original sin, Hawthorne saw human beings as sinners with little hope of grace. And while Emerson glorified American individualism and praised the egotism which enabled men to become self-reliant, Hawthorne regarded egotism as the root of all evil because it separated the individual from his fellows and led to isolation. He was therefore skeptical towards Transcendentalist enthusiasm and towards all social reforms; as long as man's heart was corrupted, little could be accomplished by a change of beliefs or institutions.

Born at Salem of an old but decayed mercantile family, Hawthorne returned to the family home after graduating from Bowdoin College and spent fourteen years in almost complete isolation, writing short stories with little material reward. His obsession with the theme of isolation was therefore rooted in his own experience. A happy marriage to Sophia Peabody, made in his thirty-eighth year, restored his contact with society, and in 1850, when he was forty-six, he became famous as the author of *The Scarlet Letter*, the first American novel which was indisputably a masterpiece. He completed three other novels, *The House of the Seven Gables*, *The Blithedale Romance*, and *The Marble Faun*, before his death in 1864.

From boyhood Hawthorne was steeped in the tradition of New England, and his stories, almost all of which had a New England setting, were an attempt to distill its permanent influence and meaning. Concerned primarily with moral issues, he was uninterested in realistic description for its own sake; like his Puritan ancestors, he saw material things as symbols of spiritual truths, so that his writing had a tendency to degenerate into allegory. His carefully wrought, smooth-flowing style was somewhat deficient in variety and energy. But his analyses of the deeper psychological forces underlying history had an almost inexhaustible depth and complexity and a remarkable objectivity. His central theme was the corruption of the human heart by pride and egotism, and he saw this manifested throughout the history of New England in the Puritan magistrates who imposed their own stern morality upon the New World, in their successors who persecuted the Quakers and hanged the witches, and (in *The Blithedale Romance*) in the social reformers of his own time.

4. WRITERS OF THE SOUTHERN AND MIDDLE STATES

The South.   The South, with its distinctive traditions and way of life, might have been expected to have a flowering comparable to that of New England, but its literary renaissance was delayed until the twentieth century. The society of the antebellum South was too rural, too suspicious of the free play of ideas, and too busy with politics and cotton-growing, to develop an intellectual class. Southern readers preferred the classics, theology, and the novels of Sir Walter Scott to native products. There were therefore few Southern writers, and their books, generally published in New York, received little local patronage.

The South's one professional man of letters was William Gilmore Simms of Charleston, who published no less than eighty works, thirty-five of which were novels or collections of stories. Simms set out to be the

Fenimore Cooper of the Deep South, commemorating the more picturesque episodes of its history as Cooper was doing for New York. His plots
were too melodramatic, and he did not create any character as memorable
as Cooper's Leatherstocking; but his best works, such as *The Yemassee*,
still make exciting reading. No other Southerner was more than a spare-
time novelist. John Pendleton Kennedy and William Alexander Caruthers,
the former a lawyer and the latter a doctor, published novels celebrating
the plantation society of Virginia. Less ambitious, but more original and
of more lasting interest, were some literary expressions of the realistic
humor of the Southern frontier. Notable examples were Judge Augustus
Baldwin Longstreet's *Georgia Scenes* (1835), George W. Harris's *Sut
Lovingood's Yarns* (1845), and Johnson J. Hooper's *Some Adventures of
Captain Simon Suggs* (1846).

    Poe.   Edgar Allan Poe is often regarded as a Southerner, since he
was brought up by foster parents living at Richmond, Virginia. But his
mature life was spent mostly in Baltimore, Philadelphia, and New York,
where from 1831 until his death in 1849 he earned a meager income by
editing and contributing to magazines. It is difficult to find any Southern
influence in his works, which—more than those of any other leading
American writer—were products of fantasy; his environment affected
him only as he reacted against it and tried to escape into a dream world of
his own creation.

    Poe was a deeply neurotic character. Although his neuroses made his
life a torment, they did not prevent him from being astonishingly productive; but they determined the subject-matter of what he wrote. Like a
number of the European Romanticists, he felt like an alien in a hostile
world. Having no sympathy for democracy or the other social ideals of his
time, he believed that the function of art was to create an ideal beauty
which would produce "a pleasurable elevation or excitement of the soul."
Beauty was an end in itself; art did not serve any moral or social purposes,
and should be judged solely by aesthetic standards. Poe's conception of
ideal beauty reflected his neurotic fantasy life. His favorite subject for
poetry was the death of a beautiful woman. The typical character of his
fiction was some young man or woman set apart by aristocratic lineage,
great wealth, extraordinary ability, or an addiction to strange vices, and
often doomed to misery or an untimely death. Like Hawthorne, Poe was
obsessed with the theme of isolation, but he saw it as the result of destiny,
not of sinfulness.

    Poe did important work in three different fields: criticism, poetry, and
the short story. In criticism his insistence that art should be judged by
aesthetic, not moral or political, standards, and his slashing attacks on
writers who were mediocre or merely imitative made him a valuable influence. His judgments of his contemporaries were by no means always
sound, but he was the first American critic to have any clear notion of
aesthetic values. As a poet, his scope was restricted by his belief that the

only function of poetry was to produce an "excitement of the soul." His best poems unquestionably accomplished this, and were superior to anything written previously in America; but they were narrow in scope, deficient in intellectual organization, and excessively dependent on verbal melody. In his short stories he drew his material almost exclusively from fantasy, so that all his work had a hot-house atmosphere; but his best achievements were, in their own way, masterpieces. Incidentally, three of his stories dealt with crime and detection, and he has a good claim to be regarded as the inventor of this astonishingly popular brand of fiction.

Poe had few direct disciples in the United States. In his work, as in his life, he remained an isolated figure. But both his critical theories and his creative writings found enthusiastic admirers in Europe, especially the French poet Baudelaire. As an exponent of art for art's sake and as the creator of a fantasy world expressive of psychic forces rather than of external reality, he had a great influence on literary development in late nineteenth-century France and indirectly, through French intermediaries, on certain American poets of the twentieth century.

Melville.   The two writers of this period who have had the strongest appeal to modern readers were two New Yorkers whose importance was not recognized during their lives: Herman Melville and Walt Whitman.

Born in New York in 1819, of a family with aristocratic pretensions but little money, Melville spent several years as a sailor, taking part in a whaling expedition to the Pacific. He left the sea and settled down to become a writer in 1844. Four of his first five books were straightforward narratives based on his own experiences, although by no means strictly autobiographical: *Typee* and *Omoo* told of adventures in the Pacific, *Redburn* dealt with an early voyage to England, and *White Jacket* described a period of service in the navy. These were widely read, especially *Typee*, with its glamorous account of life among the people of the Marquesan Islands.

But Melville was too concerned with the fundamental problems of human destiny to be content to be merely a writer of adventure stories. His third book was a long allegorical fantasy, *Mardi*, and his sixth, published in 1851, was the massive *Moby Dick*. *Moby Dick* is regarded by modern critics as one of the great books of world literature, but its broodings over the meaning of life and its black pessimism merely bewildered most contemporary readers, who wanted more books like *Typee*. Melville lost the rest of his audience with *Pierre*, which was even gloomier than *Moby Dick* and aesthetically a failure. He did not win it back with *Israel Potter*, a novel of adventure during the American Revolution which deserves more readers than it has ever had, with his short stories (some of which, especially *Benito Cereno*, were masterpieces), or with the bitter and confused *Confidence Man*. In 1867 he gave up the attempt to support his family by literature and took a position in the New York Custom House,

His later writings, which were mostly in verse, were of little interest, with the exception of a novelette, *Billy Budd*, which was not printed until 1924. During his later life Melville was almost forgotten. He was rediscovered after World War I and after World War II he received more critical attention than all his contemporaries put together.

Although all of Melville's prose writings had remarkable qualities, his reputation rests primarily on *Moby Dick*. Superficially the story of how Captain Ahab and the crew of the *Pequod* hunted the white whale and were finally destroyed by it, it was a rendering, in symbolic terms, of human destiny as Melville saw it: of the human will pitted against the powers of nature, and of man's struggle to conquer and eliminate evil and his inevitable defeat. The symbolic meanings to be found in *Moby Dick* are, in fact, almost inexhaustible. It is not surprising that so profoundly pessimistic a writer should have found few appreciative readers in the America of the 1850's. Like Poe and Hawthorne, Melville was oppressed by the loneliness of the individual human being. Throughout his books companionship can be found only among the ship's crew at sea, never with either a man or a woman on shore (except perhaps among the savages of the far-away Marquesan Islands). And for Melville this loneliness was an essential aspect of man's place in the scheme of things; man was doomed to fight against implacable cosmic forces and to be defeated.

Whitman.   Whitman can be regarded as the culminating figure in the literary development of this period, at any rate in his intention, although his achievement fell somewhat short of it. Emerson and his fellow Transcendentalists had made positive affirmations about the spiritual values implicit in American individualism. These had been negated by Hawthorne and Melville, who had regarded Transcendentalism as the expression of a shallow and unrealistic optimism. With Whitman there was a return to the positive, but with a keener awareness of what was lacking in the individualist ideal and what was needed for its consummation.

Born in 1819, Whitman grew up in Brooklyn and in rural Long Island during the period when Jacksonian Democracy was in the ascendant. He was deeply influenced by Jacksonianism and by the loco-foco movement (William Leggett was one of his heroes), sharing their faith in the virtues of the plain people, in equality and popular control of government, and in an economy characterized by a wide diffusion of private property. He believed, as he declared in *Democratic Vistas*, that "the true gravitationhold of liberalism in the United States will be a more universal ownership of property," and that the national welfare depended mainly on "the safety and endurance of the aggregate of its middling property owners." As editor for two years of the *Brooklyn Eagle* and in other journalistic positions, he was a crusader for these ideas. But in his early thirties he passed through some kind of emotional transformation which caused him to see democracy not merely as a political program but also as a spiritual faith. His view of life was henceforth mystical; he felt that the material world and all its inhabitants were emanations of divinity, and therefore sacred, and that man could achieve a sense of unity with God. In arriving at this attitude he was stimulated especially by the writings of Emerson. "I was simmering, simmering, simmering," he declared later; "Emerson brought me to a boil."

The first edition of *Leaves of Grass*, in which Whitman affirmed his faith in the sacredness of man, appeared in 1855. Apart from Emerson and Thoreau, it found few sympathetic readers. Most people were unable to accept as poetry a book written not in conventional metric forms but in a free verse derived mainly from the Bible, and were deeply shocked by its frank celebration of the human body. But Whitman never lost confidence in himself or retreated from the position he had adopted (although he made some decidedly blatant attempts at self-advertisement). For the remainder of his life he continued to add to *Leaves of Grass* and bring out new editions, and to write expositions of the democratic ideal. And to a remarkable extent he not only wrote but also lived as a believer in the essential divinity of every human being. His work during the Civil War, as a kind of one-man Red Cross agency in the army hospitals, was heroic.

Disfigured by much windy and pretentious rhetoric and many lapses of taste, *Leaves of Grass* reached greatness only in brief passages. Yet it was a landmark in the evolution of American culture, even though it had little influence until the twentieth century. Pervaded with a sense of America as a new country demanding appropriate celebration, and filled with loving and precise descriptions of American people and American scenes, it pointed the way to a literature that would be genuinely indigenous and no longer merely imitative of European models. Why such a literature was needed was explained by Whitman in his prose *Democratic Vistas* (1871). Denouncing the materialism and corruption of American society after the Civil War, he affirmed that it was "so far, an almost complete failure in its social aspects, and in really grand religious, moral, literary and asthetic results. In vain do we march with unprecedented strides to empire so colossal, outvying the antique, beyond Alexander's, beyond the proudest sway of Rome. It is as if we were somehow being endow'd with a vast and more and more thoroughly-appointed body, and then left with little or no soul." What was lacking in America, he believed, was a religious and moral faith in democratic values. And it was the function of the writer and the artist to help in creating this faith by clothing it in symbolical and mythological embodiments that would capture the imagination.

Democracy, for Whitman, did not mean individualism alone. It included "individuality, the pride and centripetal isolation of a human being by himself"; but it included also equality, "the leveller, the unyielding principle of the average." These two principles were "confronting and ever modifying the other, often clashing, paradoxical, yet neither of highest avail without the other." They could be reconciled only by the addition of the third element in the revolutionary trinity, the principle of fraternity, "the manly love of comrades." "Loving comradeship" was for Whitman the essential keystone of American democracy, and its celebration was the main purpose of both his writings and his personal life. In so far as he made this principle a reality, he may be said to have supplied what was lacking in the original Transcendentalist doctrine and to have surmounted the pessimism of writers like Poe, Hawthorne, and Melville.

5. THE OTHER ARTS

Painting. In the visual arts the achievement of the period before the Civil War was less impressive. The work of men like Hawthorne, Melville, and Whitman was both universal in its implications and at the same time distinctively American. Among the artists there were no individual masters of comparable importance, nor did any of them succeed to the same degree in transcending the conflict between European forms and American realities. Some of them imitated European styles in the belief that the European cultural heritage was a vast storehouse from which Americans could profitably borrow as they pleased. Others remained more faithful to American experience, but failed to achieve the scope and depth of the greater writers.

The early nineteenth century was a period, nevertheless, of considerable artistic activity. There was a rapid increase in the number of Americans who devoted themselves to painting, sculpture, and architecture, in their technical skill, and in popular interest and appreciation. Although most artists still felt it obligatory to visit Europe, often for extended periods, facilities for study and support were becoming available at home. Academies of fine arts were set up in New York and Philadelphia near the beginning of the century. When they fell under conservative control, a group of younger men, headed by Samuel F. B. Morse, founded the National Academy in 1826.

The early nineteenth century was perhaps the golden age of American portrait-painting. The patrician statesmen and merchants who dominated the republic during its early years wanted their likenesses recorded, and a number of highly skilled craftsmen, mostly trained in Europe, responded to the demand. The ablest and most popular of them was the prolific Gilbert Stuart, whose numerous pictures of Washington became the standard portrayals. A Federalist in his artistic technique as well as his politics, Stuart generally portrayed his sitters as representative members of the upper class. The more democratic American approach, with its more uncompromising emphasis on individual peculiarities, was maintained by Charles Willson Peale (who lived until 1827) and his numerous sons. In the Jacksonian period it reappeared in the work of such men as Samuel F. B. Morse and Chester Harding.

Although portraiture continued to be much the most remunerative form of painting, Americans were now experimenting in a number of new fields. Some of them, like John Trumbull, turned to American history and set out to commemorate important events of the Revolutionary period. Others, like the New Yorker John Vanderlyn, were influenced by the French eighteenth-century classicists and found inspiration in Greek mythology. By the 1820's the Romantic Movement was making itself felt in painting, and artists tried to convey spiritual insights through the portrayal of exotic scenes and episodes. The most ambitious of the Romanticists was Washington Allston, who had been born in South Carolina but lived in Massachusetts. Allston was regarded by his Transcendentalist contemporaries as a great man, although posterity can see him only as a pretentious failure.

Probably the best American work of this period was done in two less ambitious fields: landscape and genre. The first persons to depict American landscapes were several British-born painters who came to the United States in the 1790's; but it was Romanticism, with its emphasis on the spiritual meaning of nature, that made it a significant art form. The first great American landscapists were Thomas Cole, Thomas Doughty, and Asher Durand, all of whom flourished in the 1830's. Their attitude to nature owed something to the writings of their friend William Cullen Bryant. Since they were fond of portraying the Catskills, they are often known as the Hudson River School.

The genre painters depicted characteristic scenes and episodes of American life. The best of them were William S. Mount, who found his subject-matter in the villages of Long Island, and George C. Bingham, who is chiefly remembered for his portrayals of political meetings and fur-traders in his native Missouri. Democratic artists, who set out to paint for the people, and whose work was easily comprehensible to everybody, they made no attempt at aesthetic profundity; but they were excellent craftsmen, and their literal transcriptions of American life had affinities with the poetry of Whitman. A similar desire for realistic portrayal led other artists, most notably George Catlin, to put on canvas the Indians, traders, and scenery of the Far West.

Sculpture.   In sculpture Americans began with wood-carving, of which the finest master was William Rush of Philadelphia. They began to turn to stone and bronze only in the 1830's. There was a demand for monuments commemorating national heroes; but the best specimens were the work of foreigners, and there was little American sculpture of real merit. Nineteenth-century inhibitions about the depiction of the human body were a serious handicap, although Hiram Powers succeeded in creating (in his *Greek Slave*) a nude female so patently lacking in sexual vitality that even clergymen expressed their approval.

Apart from Powers, the most ambitious sculptor of the period was Horatio Greenough, whose immense bare-torsoed statue of Washington once adorned the Capitol but is now hidden in an obscure corner of the Smithsonian Institution. For posterity Greenough's chief importance lies not in his statuary but in his writings. Declaring that an object was beautiful if it was perfectly adapted to its function, and pointing out the beauty of barns, clipper ships, and other things created for utility, Greenough anticipated aesthetic theories which have become widely accepted in the twentieth century.

Architecture. The tendency of Americans to borrow forms from the European past, without sufficiently considering their relevance to American needs, was most evident in architecture. Many excellent buildings were constructed, but certain unhealthy tendencies began to manifest themselves. Art began to lose its vital contact with the realities of daily living and become a mere adornment, restricted to public buildings and to those private families who could afford to pay for it. As different styles proliferated, cities acquired a chaotic appearance and lost the satisfying homogeneity of earlier periods.

Probably the best architecture of the early republic was in New England. Designers like Charles Bulfinch, Samuel McIntire, and Asher Benjamin produced admirable churches, government buildings, and private homes in Boston, Salem, and the small inland towns. Strongly influenced by English architecture of the same period, their work did not mark any sharp break with colonial Georgian, though it was more elaborate and more ornate. Expressive of the conservative self-assurance of the Federalist aristocracy, it prolonged an eighteenth-century dignity and harmony into the early decades of the nineteenth.

Elsewhere the establishment of the republic was followed by a repudiation of the Georgian tradition, owing to its association with British rule, and a search for an architectural style more appropriate to a free people. This resulted finally in the Greek Revival, the exponents of which believed that there was an intimate connection between the building methods of the ancient Athenians and their democratic ideals.

The chief forerunner of the Greek Revival was Thomas Jefferson, although his favorite models were Roman rather than Greek. In addition to all his other accomplishments, he was perhaps the finest architect of his time. Enamored of the Roman buildings he had seen in France and of the work of the Renaissance classicist Palladio, he pioneered in the use of white columns surmounted by triangular pediments and other classical forms. His best work was done in the Virginia Capitol at Richmond, in Virginia plantation houses, and in the buildings of the University of Virginia. Jefferson's classical preferences were continued by the English-born Benjamin Latrobe, the most influential architect of the early nineteenth century and the principal designer of the Capitol in Washington. But it was not until the 1820's that the Greek Revival spread through the whole country. Builders found that the classical style was easy to copy and could easily be adapted to the use of timber instead of stone; and for the next generation it was almost obligatory that public buildings, banks, and the more pretentious private homes should have rows of white pillars like those of the Parthenon. At its best, as in some of the Southern plantation houses, the Greek style achieved an admirable charm and was by no means inappropriate to the needs of American living.

Meanwhile, other Americans were beginning to adopt the pointed style of medieval Gothic, the prestige of which had been revived by Romanticism. Public buildings continued to be classical, but by the 1830's some churches and even a few private homes were beginning to show Gothic influences. This was followed by a borrowing of other European and even oriental styles. By the 1850's American architecture had wholly lost its homogeneity, and standards had become chaotic. All traditions of artistic craftsmanship had disappeared in the tenements, factories, and railroad stations of the rapidly growing industrial cities. The aesthetic and the useful were becoming divorced from each other.

Music.   Music had a very slow development, at least in its more serious forms. There was little opportunity to hear good music. Concerts were given by the Philharmonic Society of New York, founded in 1842, and a few other organizations; but standards were extremely low, and it was apparently considered creditable if all the members of the orchestra finished a piece at the same time. There were also occasional concerts by traveling virtuosi; but, excepting the pianist Louis Moreau Gottschalk, born in New Orleans, all the more popular figures were Europeans. Only three or four Americans attempted to compose orchestral music, and none of their work had any lasting value.

Americans were developing, however, a vigorous tradition of popular music. Much of it was religious. There were many composers of hymns, the ablest being Lowell Mason of Boston. Meanwhile, the more emotional and spontaneous forms of religious music, which had originated among the Baptists and other revivalistic groups, were being taken over by Negroes on the Southern plantations and developed into spirituals. Secular songs, patriotic, narrative, or sentimental, circulated widely in different versions, the original authors being often unknown. The chief vehicles for the spread of popular music were the blackfaced minstrel shows which developed during the 1820's. The performers were white, but they imitated the language and mannerisms of the Negroes. Two of the men associated with these shows were outstanding: Dan Emmett, the composer of "Dixie," and Stephen Collins Foster. In a short and tragically unhappy life Foster composed more than two hundred songs, many of which have become an imperishable part of the American heritage.

9. Trans-Mississippi Routes to the West

THE GREAT WESTWARD MOVEMENT OF THE 1840'S CARRIED CARAVANS OF PIONEERS across the continent to Oregon and California and prepared the way for the establishment of United States sovereignty over those territories in 1846 and 1848. The migration was made possible by the discovery of routes over which ox-drawn wagons could be driven through the Rocky Mountains and across the Western deserts. This was mainly the work of "mountain men" like Jedediah Smith, Jim Bridger, and Kit Carson, who explored the Western country while engaging in fur-trapping during the 1820's and 1830's.

The favorite route to the Pacific was the Oregon Trail. Groups of pioneers usually assembled at Independence, Missouri, near Kansas City, followed the Missouri to Council Bluffs, and then swung westward across Nebraska along the Platte River and up into the arid high plains of Wyoming. Beyond the source of the Platte, shortly before reaching Fort Bridger, they passed through a gap between two mountain chains, known as South Pass, and crossed the continental divide. Close to Fort Hall, in southern Idaho, the trail forked, and pioneers could either follow the Snake River into Oregon or cross the deserts of Nevada into California. If everything went smoothly, the journey took about five months; but many pioneers died along the way from thirst, hunger, or Indian attacks.

The Mormons, driven from their homes at Nauvoo, Illinois, in 1844, traveled along the Oregon Trail in 1846, but turned off at Fort Bridger and crossed the Wasatch Mountains to the basin of the Great Salt Lake.

During the 1820's traders from Missouri began to drive wagons along the Santa Fé Trail to the Mexican province of New Mexico, and some of them afterward followed the Spanish Trail to southern California. During the Mexican War United States troops followed the same route in conquering these provinces.

The discovery of gold near Sacramento in 1848 brought many thousands of "forty-niners" to California, some of whom followed the Oregon and Santa Fé trails. Others made their way across Texas to El Paso and thence through the deserts of Arizona. Many went by boat to Panama or Nicaragua, crossed the isthmus by road, and then took boat to San Francisco or came around Cape Horn by the new, fast clipper ships built by Donald McKay and other New England builders. All these routes were gradually abandoned after 1869 when the Union and Central Pacific railroads were completed. Running from Council Bluffs to Sacramento, the railroad route was close to, but not identical with, the Oregon Trail.

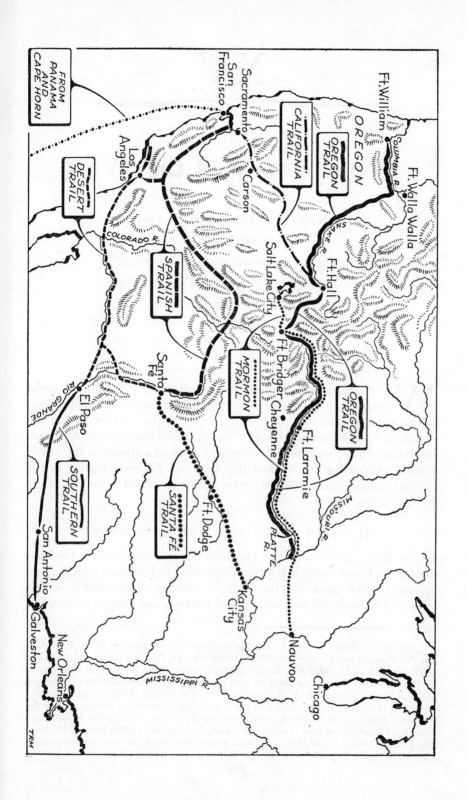

FROM
PANAMA
AND
CAPE HORN

San Francisco

Sacramento

CALIFORNIA
TRAIL

Ft. William

OREGON

COLUMBIA R.

Ft. Walla Walla

OREGON
TRAIL

SNAKE R.

Los Angeles

Carson

DESERT
TRAIL

COLORADO R.

Salt Lake City

Ft. Hall

SPANISH
TRAIL

Ft. Bridger
Cheyenne

MORMON
TRAIL

Ft. Laramie

OREGON
TRAIL

El Paso

RIO GRANDE

Santa Fe

SANTA FÉ
TRAIL

Ft. Dodge

PLATTE R.

MISSOURI R.

SOUTHERN
TRAIL

San Antonio

Galveston

New Orleans

Kansas City

Nauvoo

Chicago

MISSISSIPPI R.

TRM

XV

The Conquest of the West

1. EARLY ACTIVITIES IN THE FAR WEST

2. THE TEXAS QUESTION

3. THE TRANSCONTINENTAL MIGRATION

4. EXPANSIONISM IN AMERICAN POLITICS

5. THE WAR WITH MEXICO

WHILE some Americans were exploring the political and social implications of democracy or pioneering into new spiritual realms, others were penetrating into new territories in the western half of the continent and preparing the way for the establishment of American sovereignty. This expansionist movement reached a climax in the 1840's when American institutions and the American flag were carried to the Pacific and more than 1,000,000 square miles were added to the area of the United States.

1. EARLY ACTIVITIES IN THE FAR WEST

BY THE 1830's, after more than two centuries of steady growth, the frontier line had been carried into Iowa, Missouri, and Arkansas, only about one-third of the way across the continent. Almost all the country settled hitherto had been well wooded and well watered, and pioneer settlers had

---

SELECTED BIBLIOGRAPHY: For the settlement of Oregon, see R. A. Billington, *The Far Western Frontier, 1830–1860* (1956); Oscar Winther, *The Great Northwest* (1950); and D. O. Johanson and C. M. Gates, *Empire of the Columbia* (1956). Bernard De Voto, *Across the Wide Missouri* (1947), is a vivid account of the fur trade. Expansionism in American public opinion is analyzed in A. K. Weinberg, *Manifest Destiny* (1935). N. M. Graebner, *Empire on the Pacific* (1955), gives a new interpretation of American diplomacy. For the war with Mexico, see N. W. Stephenson, *Texas and the Mexican War* (1921). C. G. Sellars is writing a biography of Polk of which one volume has appeared (1957). Bernard De Voto, *The Year of Decision: 1846* (1943), portrays various aspects of the westward movement, while H. N. Smith, *Virgin Land* (1950), is a study of its impact on the American imagination.

not usually found it necessary to travel for long distances; as soon as one area had been settled, population began to flow into the adjacent one. The next phase of the westward movement, however, marked a sharp break with previous experience. The frontier line was now approaching country with very different natural characteristics, where new techniques had to be developed. The Far West was a land of high mountains, deserts, strange rock formations, sagebrush, brilliant colors, and immense distances. And throughout a large part of it there was a scarcity of two of the basic necessities for settlement, water and timber.

The Western Country.   Immediately west of the country watered by the Mississippi and its tributaries was the region of the Great Plains, stretching across the continent through the present states of the Dakotas, Nebraska, Kansas, Oklahoma, and Texas. Four or five hundred miles broad, the Plains sloped gradually upwards towards the Rockies, reaching finally an elevation of about 5,000 feet. In the east the grass grew to a height of several feet; to the west it became shorter and scantier, and finally gave place to sagebrush. There were no trees on the Plains, and rainfall averaged only about fifteen inches a year, which meant that agriculture could not be successfully practiced by the methods prevalent in the East.

The Plains had a great variety of wild life: antelopes, beavers, jack-rabbits, coyotes, and, in particular, millions of buffaloes which roamed in enormous herds sometimes covering sixty square miles. The Indian inhabitants were nomadic and highly warlike. Some of the tribes were partly agricultural, but the majority lived chiefly by hunting buffaloes, whose meat, skins, and droppings provided them with food, clothing, shelter, and fuel. The introduction of the horse during the colonial period had revolutionized the way of life of the Plains Indians, and the men now spent most of their time on horseback. Until the introduction of the Colt revolver in the 1840's a Plains Indian on a horse, with a bow and arrows, was usually more than a match for a white man with a gun; he could move more quickly and discharge several arrows while his adversary was cramming one bullet into his muzzle-loader.

Beyond the Great Plains the way westwards was blocked by two immense mountain systems, one covering parts of Idaho, Montana, and northern Wyoming, and the other in Colorado and New Mexico, which formed the watershed of the entire continent. Although they were inhabited by bears, beavers, and other animals of interest to fur-traders, and were rich in silver, copper, and other minerals, they had few attractions for agricultural settlers. In west-central Wyoming, however, between the two systems, south of the Wind River Range and north of the Uintas, was a broad stretch of relatively level country, though one section of which it was possible to drive wagons into the lowlands west of the Rockies. This became known as South Pass. It was of decisive importance in the American settlement of the West.

The most serious difficulties of a westward journey did not begin until beyond South Pass. West of the Rockies was the region known as the Great Basin, covering Nevada and much of Utah and Arizona. This was all arid country with little wild life or vegetation. Some areas had sagebrush and a few stunted trees, and a few primitive Indian tribes managed to survive by digging up roots and catching small animals and insects. Other sections, especially in parts of Arizona where the rainfall averaged two inches a year, were completely desert. Nor was the Columbia Plateau, north of the Great Basin, much more fertile.

The last lap of a western journey involved a mountain crossing. Pioneers going to the Oregon country had to make their way through the passes of the Cascades, which led them either to the Willamette Valley or farther north to the country around Puget Sound. All this northwestern region was fertile, thickly forested, well watered, and similar in its general characteristics to the Northeast. Farther to the south the Sierra Nevada, barring the way to California, was more difficult to cross, but between the Sierra and the coastal ranges were two attractive and fertile valleys, the Sacramento Valley lying to the north of San Francisco, and the San Joaquin Valley to the south.

Spanish Settlements.   The Spaniards had been the first white men to explore any part of this country, and Spain had thereby acquired sovereignty over the southern half of it. By the Adams-Onís Treaty of 1819 the territories now covered by the states of Texas, New Mexico, Arizona, Utah, Nevada, and California, along with parts of Kansas, Colorado, and Wyoming, had been recognized as Spanish, and in 1821 Spanish rights passed to the newly established government of Mexico. But the only places where the Spaniards had made settlements were New Mexico and parts of Texas and California, and effective Mexican sovereignty was restricted to these areas.

New Mexico and part of Arizona had a large Indian population, including both sedentary agricultural tribes like the Pueblos and Pumas, and partially nomadic tribes like the Navahos. Spanish rule had been established early in the seventeenth century, Santa Fe being the principal settlement. Here alone was the Spanish-speaking population large enough to retain its identity after conquest by the United States. In Texas, a few settlements had been made close to the seacoast during the eighteenth century, but most of the province had been left to unconquered Indians. In California, Spanish friars had built churches and maintained a number of Indian missions, which were brought to an end by the Mexican government in the 1830's. Mexico also gave large land grants to a small number of settlers, so that although California had only a small Spanish-speaking population, much of its land had become private property.

The British in Oregon.   In the Oregon country, to the north of California, American expansion was for a long time threatened by British activities. The British acquired an interest in the region in the eighteenth century. In 1778 James Cook, the discoverer of Australia, reached Vancouver Island, and in 1792 another British expedition, led by George Vancouver, mapped the whole coastline from Alaska southwards. After 1788 ships from Boston engaged in the China trade made a practice of visiting Oregon to buy furs from the Indians, but this did not lead to any permanent American settlement. The first American to plan a colony in Oregon was John Jacob Astor, an immigrant from Germany who became the leading figure in the fur business. Although Astor's American Fur Company operated mainly in northern Michigan and around the Great Lakes, he formed a subsidiary Pacific Fur Company which established a trading-post called Astoria at the mouth of the Columbia River in 1812. But the war with Britain quickly put an end to Astor's plans. Hearing that a British warship was approaching, the men in charge of Astoria sold the whole enterprise to the British and abandoned the country. For the next generation British fur-trading interests, represented after 1821 by the Hudson's Bay Company, dominated the whole of Oregon.

According to the Anglo-American Convention of 1818, Oregon was to be jointly occupied by the two nations. In practice, the area was controlled by the Hudson's Bay Company through its able superintendent, Dr. John McLoughlin. McLoughlin's headquarters were at Fort Vancouver, on the north shore of the Columbia River in what is now the State of Washington. British fur-traders ranged throughout the entire Northwest, and about a thousand British settlers established farms around Puget Sound.

Exploring Expeditions. During the first phase of American expansion into the Far West the initiative was taken by the Federal government, which sent out a number of exploring parties. The first and most famous was the expedition headed by Meriwether Lewis and William Clark, which had been planned by President Jefferson even before the Louisiana purchase. Lewis and Clark were instructed to follow the Missouri River to its source, find, if possible, a good route to the Pacific, investigate natural resources, and study the possibilities of trade with the Indians. Setting out from St. Louis with forty-eight followers in the spring of 1804, they made their way up the Missouri into what is now North Dakota, where they found an Indian woman, Sacajawea, who was able to guide them across the Rockies. They reached the mouth of the Columbia River in November 1805, and were back in St. Louis by September of the following year. Jefferson also dispatched several other parties into the West, the most important of which was led by Lieutenant Zebulon Montgomery Pike. In 1806 and 1807 Pike traveled through the Colorado country, tried to climb the peak that bears his name, and finally reached New Mexico. There he was arrested by Spanish officials, who confiscated his maps and papers and then dumped him across the United States border.

For the next ten years the government was busy with foreign affairs, but exploration was resumed after the War of 1812. Several military expeditions were sent into the Great Plains, and in 1820 Major Stephen H. Long led a party into the Colorado country. But these did not add appreciably to previous geographical knowledge.

On the whole, the official explorations did not accomplish very much. Covering only a small part of the Western country, they did not form any very accurate idea of its resources or discover a practicable route to the Pacific. Most of the West was declared to be valueless for white people and labeled on maps as the "Great American Desert." This notion was due mainly to Major Long, who asserted that the whole country between the Missouri River and the mountains was "almost wholly unfit for cultivation, and of course uninhabitable by a people depending upon agriculture for their subsistence." It was for this reason that American governments during the 1820's and 1830's believed that the West might appropriately be left to the Indians and were willing to promise that they could keep it in perpetuity.

The Fur Trade. A much more important role in the American conquest of the West was played by the fur-trappers. The "mountain men" employed by the fur companies were the first white people to cover most of the Western territories and find routes suitable for pioneer settlers.

The Western fur trade began in 1807, largely as a result of the stories brought back by Lewis and Clark. Its first headquarters were St. Louis, where the Missouri Fur Company was organized in 1809. From the beginning, some of the trappers penetrated into the mountains, notably John Colter, who went into the Yellowstone country as early as 1808. But for a dozen years the main scene of activity was the Great Plains. Intensive exploration and exploitation of the mountain country began in 1822, when Andrew Henry and William Henry Ashley set up a new organization usually known as the Rocky Mountain Fur Company. In 1825 Ashley adopted the rendezvous system. Henceforth, instead of returning to St. Louis, the trappers would meet in the spring of each year in the heart of the mountain country, generally on the Green River near South Pass. Here a motley and colorful group of mountain men, traders, and Indians would come together for several days of business, accompanied by a good deal of heavy drinking and debauchery. Then having disposed of their skins, replenished their supplies, and spent most of their earnings on whisky and Indian women, the trappers would depart for another year of solitude in the mountains.

Several of the mountain men became outstanding figures in the history of Western exploration and in American legend. Perhaps the greatest of them was Jedediah Smith, a New Yorker of Puritan ancestry who felt that his Bible was as indispensable as his gun. Accompanied by Thomas Fitzpatrick, Smith discovered South Pass in 1824. Although not the first white men to go through it, they were the first to make it generally known. In subsequent expeditions, Smith twice crossed the Great Basin into California, discovered two routes which were afterwards followed by settlers, explored a vast area of the Southwest, and was finally killed by Indians at the age of twenty-nine. Other famous mountain men were Jim Bridger, who eventually settled down at a trading-post in southwestern Wyoming, and Kit Carson, who followed Smith in opening routes to California and spent his later life as Indian agent at Taos, New Mexico.

The golden age of the mountain fur trade lasted for about a decade. In 1832 the Rocky Mountain Fur Company began to face competition when a number of rival traders appeared at the annual rendezvous. More serious was the threat presented by Astor's American Fur Company, which was now extending its activities from the Great Lakes country into the West. For several years the rival interests engaged in ruinous price-cutting, sought to gain control over the Indians by giving them free liquor, and encouraged the Indians to attack each other's agents. In 1835 the Rocky Mountain Fur Company retired from the field, and the American Fur Company was left in undisputed control, thereby establishing what seems to have been the first big business monopoly in American history. But by this time the supply of animals in the mountain country had been seriously depleted, and changes of fashion in Europe (notably the growing use of silk instead of fur in the manufacture of men's hats) were diminishing the market. Astor, then the richest man in America, soon sold his holdings in the American Fur Company, and transferred his profits into real estate in New York City. The fur trade, which had been one of the dominant factors in American western expansion since the beginning of the seventeenth century, was henceforth of declining importance.

The Santa Fe Trail.   One other activity contributing to knowledge of the Western country was the overland trade with Mexico. The Spanish-speaking community at Santa Fe, separated from the City of Mexico by more than a thousand miles of mountain trails, were eager for manufactured goods, and could pay for them with silver and furs. After the establishment of Mexican independence in 1821, trade was legally permitted, and was well established after 1824. Every year a caravan of wagons and men on horseback set out from Independence, Missouri, along a 900-mile trail across the plains and through the mountains to Santa Fe. Within a few years some of the traders began to extend the route to California. Smith's expeditions to California had been followed by those of Sylvester and James Pattie, who made their way from Santa Fe to southern California in 1827 and 1828. After 1830 a number of caravans followed the trails which they had opened up, carrying American manufactured goods to Los Angeles and bringing back horses, mules, and Chinese silks. As a result of these commercial activities, Americans learned how to conduct wagons across the Western country, discovered the weaknesses of Mexican authority, and established contacts with New Mexico and California which prepared the way for annexation.

2. THE TEXAS QUESTION

Mexico after Independence.   That the northern provinces of Mexico should eventually come under the control of the United States can fairly be considered to have been inevitable. The Mexican people showed no serious disposition to colonize them, and the Mexican government seemed incapable of establishing any effective sovereignty. As long as they remained almost empty, settlers from the United States were certain to move in, bringing with them their own language and institutions. The only question was whether United States control would be established by a slow process of infiltration or by force. That it eventually came about by force was the fault of dominant groups in both countries. Americans were guilty of an aggressive nationalism which made them eager to hasten the inevitable course of events. The Mexicans, with a lack of realism that was almost equally culpable, refused American offers of purchase and tried to hold the provinces without taking the necessary steps to settle and develop them.

When Mexico achieved independence in 1821, her territories were more than twice as large as today. On the map she looked like an imposing power, and European statesmen who knew little about America believed that she would be strong enough to hold her own against the United States. In reality, Mexico had none of the habits and institutions needed for effective self-government. A small Creole landowning and professional upper class exercised domination over an exploited and illiterate mass of Indian and *mestizo* laborers. There was almost no middle class, and little industry and commerce. In practice, power belonged to the army generals, who had no sense of loyalty to civil government.

In 1824 Mexico adopted a federal constitution closely modeled on that of the United States, the most important difference being that there was no religious freedom for non-Catholics. But constitutional government was quite unworkable, and for the next thirty years the country was dominated by the army and military revolutions became chronic. Between 1824 and 1857 all the presidents were generals, and only one of them completed a full term before being overthrown by a *coup d'état*. The leading figure throughout the period was General Antonio López de Santa Anna, a fantastic character who became dictator four times, twice as a liberal and twice as a conservative, but who was always too greedy for money and power to consolidate his authority and was overthrown on each occasion within a couple of years.

Americans in Texas.   The earliest of the northern provinces to come under the control of Americans was Texas. Moses Austin, a native of Connecticut who had spent a quarter of a century as a trader on the Spanish border, in the course of which he had acquired Spanish citizenship, planned a colony in Texas while it was still under the rule of Spain. When he died, his son Stephen Austin inherited the project, and in 1823 was able to secure authorization from the Mexican government. Austin received a large grant of land for an almost nominal sum, with the understanding that he would bring in three hundred families to settle it. Similar grants were afterwards made by the Mexican authorities to fourteen other *empresarios*, and three additional grants were made to Austin. At this period the Mexican government, already alarmed by the expansionist tendencies of the United States, seems to have had the quaint idea that the best way to keep control of Texas was to settle it as rapidly as possible; the colonists, it was hoped, would become Mexicanized and serve as a barrier to United States annexation.

Immigrants from the lower Mississippi Valley soon began to pour into Texas, some of them settling on the colonies of the *empresarios* and others becoming squatters. The soil was fertile and the climate attractive; and land could be obtained more cheaply than in the United States. Moving to a foreign jurisdiction was, moreover, a convenient way of escaping from creditors. By 1830 there were perhaps 20,000 Americans in Texas. A few of them brought slaves, evading a Mexican law of 1829 abolishing slavery by describing them as indentured servants. Although Texas was part of the Mexican state of Coahuila and therefore under the jurisdiction of the state authorities, the settlers were allowed a considerable measure of local self-government. Austin, who was a man of high integrity and idealism, respected his obligations to his adopted country, and most of the other settlers were willing to follow his leadership.

The Texas Rebellion. In 1826 one of the *empresarios*, who had violated the terms of his contract, was deprived of his land. About twenty of his followers then started a rebellion and paraded through the streets of Nacogdoches proclaiming the independent republic of Fredonia. When Mexican troops arrived, the Fredonians scuttled across the border into Louisiana without fighting. This ludicrous episode was taken more seriously than it deserved by the Mexican officials, and led them to reconsider their whole colonization policy. They soon became alarmed by the obvious United States interest in Texas (American ministers to Mexico had tried to buy it), and were even inclined to suspect a deliberate plan of expansion concocted in Washington. These fears were sedulously encouraged by British diplomats, who were afraid of United States domination over all North America and anxious to stimulate Mexican resistance. By 1830 the Mexican government had come to the conclusion that admitting Americans into Texas had been a serious mistake. On April 6 of that year it was therefore decreed that no more American settlers should be admitted; customs duties should be collected along the border between Texas and the United States; and an army should be posted in Texas to enforce obedience. It was also announced that Texas was to be colonized by Mexicans and Europeans, but nothing was ever done to achieve this objective.

The Texans felt, with considerable justice, that the law of April 6 was a violation of previous agreements, but Austin continued to advocate loyal obedience to Mexican authority. In 1832 the army was withdrawn to take part in a revolution, and the Texans then elected a convention which petitioned for the repeal of the law and for a separate state government of their own within the Mexican federal union. Austin went down to the City of Mexico to lay these requests before the new government, but was unable to win any substantial concessions, and on his way home was arrested and held in prison for several months without trial, on a charge of plotting rebellion. Meanwhile there was another change of government, and Santa Anna proceeded to assume dictatorial powers. Thus the Texans had been deprived of all constitutional liberties and brought under the rule of an arbitrary military government.

Even Austin now felt that the Texans had no alternative but to take up arms. Although they claimed at first to be fighting for their rights under the Mexican constitution of 1824, and received support from a few Mexican liberals, they soon decided that complete independence was the only satisfactory solution. In November 1835 a convention authorized resistance, set up a provisional government, and dispatched Austin to seek help in the United States (where he died shortly afterwards). In March 1836 the convention issued a formal declaration of independence, drafted a constitution for the new republic, and chose Sam Houston as commander-in-chief of the Texan army. Meanwhile, Santa Anna had invaded Texas, had laid siege to the old mission building called the Alamo in San Antonio, which was held by 150 Texans, and after capturing it had slaughtered all its defenders.

Houston, who had entered Texas illegally in 1832, was a picturesque character who had previously been Governor of Tennessee, had been been forced to retire from politics because of a separation from his wife, and had then lived for a period among the Indians, who had given him the nickname "Big Drunk." In spite of a stormy private life, he was a man of unusual sagacity and powers of command. For several weeks Santa Anna, who had a much larger army, pursued the Texans eastwards, and finally came up with them at San Jacinto on April 21. Assuming that they were at his mercy, he and his men settled down for their afternoon siesta, during which Houston ordered an attack. With the loss of only two men, the Texans killed more than 600 of the Mexicans and captured most of the remainder, including Santa Anna himself.

The Lone Star Republic.   After the battle of San Jacinto there was no further fighting, but Mexico refused to concede Texan independence. Santa Anna agreed to recognize it, and was then released and returned to Mexico; but in the interim another military chieftain had assumed control of the government. The Texans were hoping for annexation by the United States, but the suggestion provoked vigorous opposition in the Northern states. The admission of Texas would mean more soil for slavery. Many Northerners had acquired the quite erroneous idea that the Texan rebellion had been planned by the slave-owners and that the main reason for it had been the abolition of slavery in Mexico in 1829. Andrew Jackson was personally in favor of annexation, but officially he maintained a strictly neutral attitude. He gave no help to Texas during the war, and did not recognize its independence until March 1837; and he felt that annexation was politically impossible.

So for the time being the Lone Star Republic remained a republic. The Texans were already characterized by an exuberant self-confidence, and some of them began to dream of a western expansion which would make their republic one of the leading powers in North America. But these ambitious plans were beyond their resources. During the administration of Mirabeau Bonaparte Lamar, President from 1838 to 1842, Texas incurred a heavy debt, most of which was held by citizens of the United States. An attempt by a Texan military expedition to seize Santa Fe was unsuccessful, and destroyed whatever chance there might otherwise have been of securing Mexican recognition. In 1841 Santa Anna again became dictator of Mexico and declared that he would seek vengeance for his defeat at San Jacinto.

Houston, who succeeded Lamar in 1842, decided that Texas needed foreign help and turned to Great Britain and France. One or both of these powers should guarantee Texan independence in return for economic concessions. It was also suggested that, in recompense for British assistance, Texas might be willing to abolish slavery. As Houston had calculated, these proposals caused considerable alarm in the United States. To allow Texas to become a political and economic dependency of a European power would be contrary to the whole tradition of American foreign policy, with its emphasis on continental isolation. Obviously, the United States could prevent European intervention only by taking action herself. In the autumn of 1843, therefore, the Tyler administration took up the Texas question and began to move towards annexation.

Before this was consummated, however, another phase in the western expansion of the United States also reached a point of crisis. The movement for the acquisition of Texas became coupled with demands for the annexation of Oregon.

3. THE TRANSCONTINENTAL MIGRATION

American Interests in Oregon.   For a generation before the great migration of the 1840's a number of individuals were endeavoring to stimulate settlement in Oregon. Their chief motive was nationalistic; the United States, they felt, must not allow the British to acquire permanent control of the Pacific Northwest. In 1820 Dr. John Floyd, a Virginia Congressman, secured the appointment of a committee to consider the question. But although the committee's report emphasized the value of the country and aroused considerable public interest, bills providing for annexation were defeated, largely because of a widespread belief that Oregon was so far away that it would inevitably become an independent country and not an integral part of the United States. Floyd's propagandist efforts were seconded by Hall Jackson Kelley, a Massachusetts schoolteacher who organized a Colonization Society in 1828 and worked assiduously to persuade New Englanders to migrate to Oregon.

The first concrete result came in 1832, when another native of Massachusetts, a Cambridge ice-merchant named Nathaniel Wyeth, led a party of settlers across the continent along what afterwards became known as the Oregon Trail. Wyeth hoped to develop fur-trading, but the Hudson's Bay Company was so strongly entrenched in Oregon that he could not compete with it, and in 1835 he abandoned the enterprise. Public interest, however, continued to increase. In 1836 Andrew Jackson sent W. A. Slacum to study the situation in Oregon. Slacum, on his return, advocated annexation, and this proposal was strongly seconded by Senator Thomas Hart Benton of Missouri.

Another motive for the settlement of Oregon was religious. In 1831 four Indians from the Northwest made a trip to St. Louis, apparently from sheer curiosity. It was reported in the press that they had come to inquire about the Bible, that they all belonged to the Flathead tribe, and that the Flatheads had a barbarous habit of crushing the heads of their babies to flatten them. Actually, all these statements were untrue, but funds were promptly raised for a mission to teach the Indians about the Bible and persuade them to treat their babies more humanely. In 1834 a party of Methodist missionaries, headed by Jason Lee, crossed the continent. On reaching Oregon, they quickly dropped the idea of preaching to the Flatheads (who lived east of the Cascades) and settled instead in the lovely Willamette Valley. In 1836 another mission was founded by Presbyterians and Congregationalists in the country east of the Cascades, around Walla Walla, under the leadership of Marcus Whitman. Neither Lee nor Whitman proved to be very successful in making converts. Catholic priests from French Canada, who began to arrive in 1838, acquired much more influence with the Indians. But the missions were the first permanent American settlements in Oregon, and quickly became centers of agriculture and cattle-raising.

In the 1840's the Federal government again sent out exploring parties. Their leader was John C. Frémont, a young army officer who had eloped with the daughter of Senator Benton and had subsequently acquired his father-in-law's forgiveness and powerful political support. Between 1842 and 1845 Frémont led a series of three expeditions through the Southwest (which still, of course, belonged to Mexico) and mapped the routes to California. There has been a long controversy about Frémont's qualifications as an explorer; his success seems to have been largely due to the expert assistance of Kit Carson and the other mountain men who served as guides. But he described his expeditions in attractively written reports which had a wide circulation and, in addition to making him a popular hero, did much to increase popular knowledge about the West.

The Oregon Trail.   The great migration began in May 1841, when sixty-nine persons assembled at Sapling Grove in eastern Kansas in order to cross the continent. For a number of years thereafter parties set out every spring, usually from Independence, Missouri. The party of 1843 included about a thousand people, and in later years the numbers were much larger. Some groups headed for California, descriptions of which had been brought back by traders and sailors, but prior to the gold rush of 1849 the favorite destination was the Willamette Valley. Twenty years of propaganda had now taken effect, and the rivers, forests, and green fields of Oregon seemed much more attractive than the Kansas and Nebraska prairies, which would normally have been the next area to be settled. The impulse of migration had been stimulated by the depression which began in 1837. Several years of business failures and low prices caused many Americans to become interested in a country where they could make a fresh start. But only people who had some money could actually take the trail to Oregon, since the necessary equipment cost close to $1,000.

Running along the valley of the Platte into the high plains, through South Pass, along the northern edge of the Great Basin to Fort Hall, and thence either northwest to Oregon or southwest to California, the trail covered more than 2,000 miles, and usually required about six months, from May to November. The Conestoga wagons in which the pioneers made the journey were singularly graceful objects, shaped like ships on wheels (hence the name "prairie schooners"), roofed with white canvas for protection against the weather, and usually drawn by oxen. As many motion pictures have demonstrated, there have been few more beautiful spectacles in American history than a line of covered wagons proceeding in single file across the plains. In the course of the six-month journey babies were born, young people fell in love and were married, and older people died and were buried along the way. For most of those who took part in it, it was, no doubt, a great adventure, but many hardships were to be expected. Parties often ran short of food and water while crossing the Great Basin, and some of them, like the Donner party of 1846, met with utter disaster. Bound for California, the seventy-nine members of this group tried to take a short cut beyond South Pass and spent so long in making their way through the Wasatch Mountains and across the deserts south of the Great Salt Lake that they were caught by the winter snows on the wrong side of the Sierra Nevada. Forty-five of them were finally rescued, but not before a few had resorted to cannibalism.

By the end of 1845 there were about 6,000 Americans in Oregon, though almost all of them had settled south of the Columbia River. The Puget Sound region north of the river was still controlled by the British.

The United States government had several times suggested that the country be divided at the 49th parallel (in other words, that the line east of the Rockies should be extended to the Pacific), but the British had been unwilling to surrender the land north of the Columbia. Thus the area now covered by the State of Washington was in dispute. Meanwhile, the American settlers in Oregon, like many earlier frontier groups, had already set up a government of their own. In 1843 they began to hold "wolf meetings" (the original purpose of which was to provide for common protection against wolves and other wild animals), at which they adopted a code of laws and set up an executive committee and a legislature.

In California the American settlers were outnumbered by the Mexicans and were, at least in theory, under the rule of Mexican officials. In practice, however, they were largely left to their own resources for the maintenance of law and order. It was soon evident that the settlers in the Sacramento Valley were likely to follow the example of the Texans in repudiating Mexican sovereignty.

The Mormons in Utah.   While thousands of Americans were moving into Oregon and California, there was another group of pioneers whose main desire was to find a country where they could live in isolation and who therefore chose to settle in the Great Basin itself, in territory which they hoped would remain under Mexican sovereignty. These were the people who called themselves the Latter Day Saints. After Joseph Smith had been lynched in 1844, Brigham Young took over the leadership of the Mormon Church, and decided that they must seek safety beyond the limits of the United States. In 1846 they crossed into Iowa and made preparations for their march into the wilderness. In the spring of 1847 a pioneer band of 146 men and women proceeded to South Pass, and then turned southwards through the Wasatch Mountains to the plain east of the Great Salt Lake. Producing nothing but sagebrush and a single stunted tree, and inhabited only by crickets, lizards, and rattlesnakes, the country seemed utterly desolate. Jim Bridger had told Young that he would pay him a thousand dollars for the first ear of corn the Mormons succeeded in growing there. But Young declared that God had shown him the promised land in a vision and that this was the place. Before the end of the year, four thousand of the Saints had moved to Utah.

What the Mormons succeeded in building in the desert may not have been paradise, but it was a remarkably good imitation of it. All that the land needed to become productive was water, which they were able to obtain by damming the streams flowing down from the Wasatch Mountains. Food was scarce during the first two winters; but within a few years the Mormons transformed much of the country around the lake into fertile farmland and began to build factories and develop a sugar-beet industry. The city which they laid out at the foot of the mountains, close to the lake, not only had one of the most beautiful locations in America; with its broad streets and open spaces and multitude of trees, it was a model example of town-planning.

The Mormon achievement was due mainly to strict religious discipline and enthusiasm and to the able leadership of Brigham Young. Avoiding the unrestricted individualism of most other pioneer groups, they insisted that the welfare of the whole community was always paramount. The leaders of the Church decided where settlements should be made, distributed land to individual families on the basis of need, prohibited land speculation, and maintained control over timber and water rights. Neither the Mormon practice of irrigation nor the legal theory (afterwards incorporated into the laws of Utah) under which the use of water was regulated by the community had any precedents in previous United States history.

4. EXPANSIONISM IN AMERICAN POLITICS

Manifest Destiny.   The movement of the pioneers across the continent led quickly to demands for the annexation of the Pacific territories, if necessary by force. Many Americans, in fact, began to suggest that the whole of the North American continent must eventually come under the Stars and Stripes. The slogan of the expansionists was Manifest Destiny (a phrase first used by a New York journalist, John O'Sullivan). Combining land-grabbing with political idealism, they proclaimed that it was the Manifest Destiny of the United States to extend the benefits of her democratic institutions and way of life over as wide an area as possible. Expansionism was most popular in the Mississippi Valley and along the frontier; the frontiersmen had always believed that they had a right to occupy any empty and attractive territory, with or without legal title. The American government was, however, motivated by commercial and strategic as well as by agrarian interests. It wished to promote American trade and establish American power in the Far East, and was therefore anxious to acquire seaports on the Pacific coast.

Texas in American Politics.   The drive for expansion began to dominate national politics in 1843, when President Tyler and Secretary of State Upshur took up the Texas question. The admission of Texas, however, was delayed by sectional rivalry. Upshur was killed in an accident early in 1844, before the Texas negotiations had been completed, and was succeeded by John C. Calhoun. Calhoun strengthened Northern opposition by identifying the movement for annexation with the cause of slavery. He made it plain that the South wanted Texas admitted in order to obtain more slave soil and prevent the Texans from complying with British proposals that slavery be abolished. There were suggestions, moreover, that Texas be divided into four states, which would have given the South eight more votes in the Senate. The result was that when, in June 1844, a treaty of annexation was submitted to the Senate, it was defeated. The Texas question then became the main issue in the forth-coming presidential election.

Clay and Van Buren, who expected to be nominated by their re-spective parties, both felt that Northern opposition and Mexican hostility made any immediate annexation of Texas unwise and (possibly in collu-sion with each other) issued public statements to that effect. The result was that Van Buren failed to obtain the Democratic nomination. The Democratic convention recognized that expansionism was likely to be popular with the electorate, who would support the admission of Texas if it were combined with a demand for Oregon. The platform called for the "re-annexation" of Texas (on the theory that it had really been part of the Louisiana purchase) and the "re-occupation" of Oregon as far as the line 54 ° 40′, thus resulting in the slogan "Fifty-four Forty or Fight." The nomination went for the first time to a "dark horse" candidate, James K. Polk of Tennessee, a disciple of Andrew Jackson. Clay, who received the Whig nomination, began during the campaign to modify his original statement opposing the annexation of Texas; but the only result was that anti-slavery elements in the North refused to support him and gave their votes to a third-party candidate running on the ticket of the Liberty Party, James G. Birney. Birney won enough votes to prevent Clay from carrying New York and, with it, the election. Polk became President with an electoral vote of 170 to 105.

The election made it certain that Texas would be admitted, and Tyler set out to accomplish this before he left office. In January 1845 annexation was again submitted to Congress, this time in the form not of a treaty but of a joint resolution requiring only a bare majority in each house. Meanwhile, Mexico finally agreed to recognize Texas as independent on condition that she should not join the United States; but like almost every other move by the Mexican government through this period, the offer came too late. The joint resolution was passed by Congress and then accepted by Texas, which became a part of the United States in Decem-ber. The Mexican government had declared that annexation would mean war; after the passage of the joint resolution it broke off diplomatic rela-tions, but did not take any action suggesting that the threat of war must be taken seriously.

Polk and the Oregon Treaty.   Polk, whose administration ran from 1845 to 1849, had neither great intellectual gifts nor an attractive per-sonality. But although he was narrow-minded, unimaginative, and suspicious, he had a strong will and a remarkable capacity for hard work, and knew exactly what he wanted. Few presidents have accomplished more. In accordance with his Jacksonian convictions, he brought about the re-establishment of the Independent Treasury and a reduction of the tariff (by the Tariff Act of 1846, usually named after his Secretary of the Treasury, Robert J. Walker). But his main concern was expansion. He made this plain in his message to Congress of December 1845, in which (with reference to British and French interests in Texas, and British activities in Oregon and elsewhere) he forcefully restated the Monroe Doctrine, and extended it to prohibit European diplomatic interference with American affairs.

The Oregon question was easily settled. The British government recognized that it could not hold the Puget Sound region against American opposition; and since the fur trade was no longer very profitable, the Hudson's Bay Company was willing to withdraw. The British therefore suggested that (in accordance with earlier American proposals) the 49th parallel should be the boundary, and this was agreed to by a treaty concluded in 1846. Thus American sovereignty was established over the area now covered by the states of Washington, Oregon, and Idaho, and the boundary between the United States and Canada was completed from the Atlantic to the Pacific. There was some grumbling at the abandonment of the "Fifty-four Forty or Fight" slogan; but the decision to accept the British offer was obviously wise.

Relations with Mexico.   Relations with Mexico were much more complicated. Polk had to secure Mexican consent to the Texas annexation and to fix a satisfactory boundary line. The Texans claimed that their southern boundary was the Rio Grande, which would give them control over a large part of New Mexico; the Mexicans (with better legal justification) declared that the boundary was the Nueces, which entered the Gulf of Mexico two hundred miles further north.

In spite of the Mexican threats of war, tactful diplomacy would probably have brought about a settlement. But Polk was not a tactful person. Moreover, he also wanted to secure California. British agents were displaying an alarming interest in the province; and it seemed possible that if the United States did not act quickly, Mexico might sell it to Great Britain. The British government was not, in actuality, interested in acquiring it, but this was not known in Washington. Polk therefore hoped to arrange a bargain with Mexico by which all the Southwestern territories would be bought by the United States. Unfortunately, the Mexicans had too much national pride, and too unrealistic a confidence in their own military strength, to consider such a proposition. They believed that the movement of American settlers into Texas had been planned by the American government, that the same process was now being repeated in California, and that if they did not put a stop to it, their country would be devoured by the Yankees, piece by piece.

Another outstanding question between the two countries was the failure of Mexico to pay her debts. American citizens in Mexico had lost property during the innumerable revolutions, and some of them had been arbitrarily shot by Mexican generals. Mexican refusals to pay compensation had caused Andrew Jackson to threaten to send warships to collect it. In 1839 Mexico had finally agreed to pay about $2,000,000, after which she had paid three installments and had then defaulted. The default was due to genuine inability to pay; as a result of almost constant civil war the Mexican government was in a chronic state of bankruptcy. But in the nineteenth century the failure of a country to respect her international obligations was regarded more severely than it has been in more recent years.

In 1845 Polk sent John Slidell, a Democratic politician from Louisiana, to Mexico. Slidell was to offer to cancel the unpaid debt in return for the Rio Grande boundary, and, in addition, to try to buy California. By this time Santa Anna was no longer in power, the president being General Herrera. Slidell found it impossible to do business and when, at the end of the year, Herrera was overthrown by the extremely nationalistic General Paredes, it became plain that the United States could not secure California by negotiation. By the spring of 1846 Polk had come to the conclusion that the refusal of Mexico to negotiate or to pay her debts made war justifiable. He had ordered American troops, under General Zachary Taylor, to occupy the disputed region between the Rio Grande and the Nueces. Paredes sent Mexican troops to hold the region, and on April 25 there was a clash between two patrols, in which sixteen Americans were killed or wounded. When the news reached Washington, Polk sent a message to Congress in which he declared that the Mexicans had "shed American blood on American soil" and that war "existed by act of Mexico." Congress declared war on May 13, and authorized the raising of 50,000 additional troops by voluntary enlistment.

The American people were far from unanimous in supporting the war. There was vigorous opposition in the Northeast, especially in New England. It was still widely believed that the demand for expansion came mostly from the cotton-planters and that the main purpose of the war was to acquire more territories for slavery. This attitude was voiced by New England intellectuals like Emerson, Thoreau, and James Russell Lowell. In actuality, the planters, although eager for Texas, were by no means enthusiastic about further acquisitions; they recognized that areas like New Mexico and California were not suited to slavery and might, in the end, add to the strength of the free states. The war was most popular in the West. It was the people of the Mississippi Valley who were most eager for expansion and who supplied a large majority of the volunteers for the army.

The war has continued to be a controversial subject down to the present day. All Mexicans have continued to feel resentful about an episode which deprived them of more than half their national territory, and many Americans have regarded it as a blot on the national record. It should be recognized, however, that the Mexican government itself welcomed war, that by the standards of international morality then prevalent the United States had ample justification for resorting to force, and that Polk wanted a peaceful settlement. Yet it seems fair to add that his

desire for peace was not so strong as his desire for California, and that a
more enlightened statesman would have displayed greater patience with
the vagaries of the Mexicans.

5. THE WAR WITH MEXICO

THE UNITED STATES had little difficulty in winning the war. She had more
vigorous and enthusiastic soldiers, more competent generals, and—above
all—better guns and equipment. The Mexican regular army was ten times
as large as that of the United States (this was why the Mexican generals
were so confident of winning); but it consisted mostly of underfed and
reluctant Indian conscripts, and was equipped mostly with second-hand
war material bought from Great Britain twenty years earlier.

The Conquest of California. While Zachary Taylor advanced into
northern Mexico, other invading forces seized the northern provinces.
Colonel Stephen W. Kearny led a body of troops along the Santa Fe
trail, took possession of New Mexico, and then set off for California.
As early as 1845 the American consul in California, Thomas O. Larkin,
had been instructed to encourage any movement among the inhabitants
for secession from Mexico, and John C. Frémont, then on his third exploring expedition, had been advised by Senator Benton that war seemed
imminent and he should be ready for action. In July 1846 the Americans
in the Sacramento Valley, in cooperation with Frémont, declared themselves independent of Mexico and raised a white flag with a picture of a
bear on it. Shortly afterwards a detachment of the American fleet entered
the harbor of Monterey. The Americans quickly secured control of the
whole province, but the Mexicans of southern California subsequently
revolted and were not defeated until January 1847. Kearny, after a most
exhausting march across the deserts of Arizona, arrived in time to take
part in the final fighting. The victory was followed by disputes between
the various conquerors of California—the army, the navy, Frémont, and
the bear-flag group—which ended in the establishment of military government by the army.

The Invasion of Mexico. The main American military operations
took the form of two invasions of Mexico, one from Texas under Zachary
Taylor, and the other by way of the Gulf of Mexico under Winfield Scott.
The Mexicans were commanded by Santa Anna, who became dictator
for the third (but not the last) time soon after the war started. Taylor,
although popular with his men (who nicknamed him "Old Rough and
Ready"), was not a very able general. Nevertheless, he won a series of
engagements with small Mexican forces, advanced about two hundred
miles across the Rio Grande, and in February 1847 was victorious over
Santa Anna in a major battle at Buena Vista. After this he was ordered to
remain on the defensive, partly because the government had lost confidence in his leadership, and partly for political reasons; it seemed likely

10. The Mexican War
Mexico City Campaign (inset)

THE BOUNDARY LINE BETWEEN THE UNITED STATES AND THE SPANISH EMPIRE had been fixed by the Adams-Onis Treaty of 1819. When Mexico became independent in 1821, she inherited the Spanish claim to all territories south of the boundary line. But she was too weak to maintain effective authority over most of the country lying between Texas and California. There were small settlements of Spanish-speaking citizens in southern Texas, around Santa Fé in New Mexico, and around San Francisco and Los Angeles in California; but most of the country was inhabited only by unconquered and nomadic Indians. American fur-trappers and traders soon began to move into it and were followed in some areas by agricultural settlers.

Americans settled in Texas in the 1820's; and seceded from Mexico and set up an independent republic in 1836. Mexico, however, refused to recognize the independence of Texas, and her boundary lines remained undetermined. The Texan government actually exercised authority over a relatively small area inhabited almost exclusively by Americans, but its claim extended westward and southward. This would have added to Texas a much larger area, including the valuable trading center of Santa Fé. When the United States admitted Texas to the Union in 1845, she assumed the Texan claim. The refusal of the Mexican government to negotiate a settlement of this question and its decision to defend its right to the disputed territory by force were the chief immediate causes of the war. Meanwhile American pioneers were already moving into northern California; they would probably have seceded from Mexico in imitation of the Texans if the United States had not anticipated events by conquering the province during the war.

In order to compel Mexico to accept defeat, the Americans had to capture her capital city. In 1846 Zachary Taylor invaded northern Mexico from Texas, but the five-hundred-mile march to Mexico City, mainly across mountains and deserts, would have been a hazardous operation. In 1847 Winfield Scott landed at Veracruz and fought his way up to the capital, a distance of about two hundred miles. By the Treaty of Guadalupe Hidalgo of 1848 Mexico surrendered more than half the territories under her sovereignty.

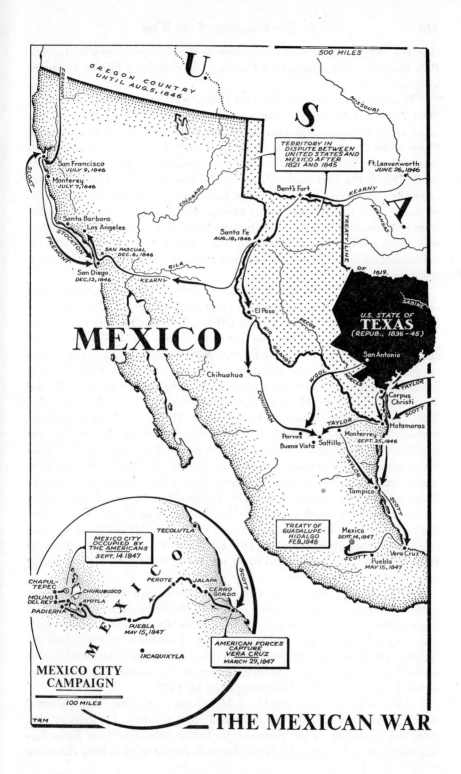

OREGON COUNTRY
UNTIL AUG. 5, 1846

500 MILES

U.

S.

A.

MISSOURI

FREMONT

San Francisco
JULY 9, 1846

Monterey
JULY 7, 1846

SLOAT

STOCKTON

FREMONT

Santa Barbara
Los Angeles

SAN PASCUAL
DEC. 6, 1846

San Diego
DEC. 12, 1846

KEARNY

GILA

COLORADO

Santa Fe
AUG. 18, 1846

Bent's Fort

TERRITORY IN
DISPUTE BETWEEN
UNITED STATES AND
MEXICO AFTER
1821 AND 1845

Ft. Leavenworth
JUNE 26, 1846

KEARNY

ARKANSAS

TREATY LINE OF 1819

SABINE

U.S. STATE OF
TEXAS
(REPUB., 1836–45)

San Antonio

El Paso

PECOS

RIO GRANDE

MEXICO

Chihuahua

DONIPHAN

WOOL

NUECES

TAYLOR

Corpus
Christi

SCOTT

Matamoras

TAYLOR

Parras
Buena Vista

Saltillo

Monterrey
SEPT. 25, 1846

TAYLOR

Tampico

SCOTT

TREATY OF
GUADALUPE–
HIDALGO
FEB. 1848

Mexico
SEPT. 14, 1847

SCOTT

Puebla
MAY 15, 1847

Vera Cruz

MEXICO CITY
OCCUPIED BY
THE AMERICANS
SEPT. 14, 1847

TECOLUTLA

MEXICO

PEROTE

JALAPA

CHAPUL-
TEPEC

CHURUBUSCO

MOLINO
DEL REY

AYOTLA

PADIERNA

PUEBLA
MAY 15, 1847

CERRO
GORDO

SCOTT

IXCAQUIXTLA

MEXICO CITY
CAMPAIGN

100 MILES

AMERICAN FORCES
CAPTURE
VERA CRUZ
MARCH 29, 1847

TRM

THE MEXICAN WAR

that the Whigs would make him their next presidential candidate, and Polk did not wish to strengthen his chances by allowing him to win more victories.

Winfield Scott was an arrogant egotist (his men referred to him as "Old Fuss and Feathers"), but an excellent general. He landed on the coast of Mexico near Veracruz in March 1847, defeated Santa Anna at Cerro Gordo, and then, with an army of only 10,000 men, marched up into the mountains of the interior for an assault on the City of Mexico itself. During the final stages of the war the Americans faced hard fighting, since they were now opposed not by Indian conscripts but by volunteers recruited from the Mexican upper classes; but their guns and generalship were still irresistible. Reaching the outskirts of the city in August, they won a series of battles against Santa Anna, and were in possession of it by September 14. Santa Anna then retired into exile, and organized Mexican resistance ended.

The Treaty of Guadalupe Hidalgo.   Polk had hoped that the Mexicans would be willing to make peace at an earlier stage, and had attached to Scott's army a State Department official, Nicholas Trist by name, who was instructed to offer to buy the territories desired by the United States. Ignoring orders from Polk that he return to Washington, Trist now proceeded, with Scott's approval, to negotiate a settlement with the new Mexican government in accordance with his original instructions. By the Treaty of Guadalupe Hidalgo, signed in February 1848, Mexico ceded Texas with the Rio Grande boundary, New Mexico, California, and the rest of the western territories; the United States was to pay Mexico $15,000,000 and assume the claims of American citizens against the Mexican government (which now amounted to about $3,250,000). By this time many Americans were urging the annexation of the whole of Mexico, but Polk, although indignant with Trist for ignoring his recall, decided to accept the treaty, which was ratified by the Senate in March. The United States could have imposed more severe terms, but her restraint was undoubtedly wise. More extensive annexations would have meant domination over a foreign people who could not easily have been assimilated or reconciled to American rule.

Thus in four years, by three successive acquisitions, well over 1,000,000 square miles had been added to the territories of the United States. One small addition was made in 1853 through the Gadsden purchase, by which the Gila Valley (now part of southern Arizona) was acquired from Mexico for $10,000,000, in order to facilitate the building of a railroad along the southern border. Otherwise the continental boundaries of the United States had been completed by 1848.

The California Gold Rush.   Meanwhile, an event had occurred which greatly accelerated the settlement of California. On January 24, 1848, on an estate in the Sacramento Valley belonging to a Swiss immigrant named Sutter, gold was discovered. Sutter tried to keep the news a secret, but it soon leaked out, and his lands were quickly overrun with fortune-hunters equipped with pickaxes, shovels, and dishpans. Almost every American in California hurried to the diggings. When the news reached the East in the autumn, thousands of persons from every part of the country set out for California, some of them going overland in covered wagons (and in many instances dying of thirst or starvation in the deserts), others traveling by way of Panama or taking clippers round Cape Horn. Before the end of 1849 California had a population of 90,000.

Conditions in the gold fields were chaotic, and prices fantastic; a room rented for $1,000 a month, and eggs cost $10 a dozen. The "forty-niners" included a fair proportion of desperadoes, criminals, and women of easy virtue; but most of them were law-abiding citizens who wanted a government able to maintain order and did not regard their own vigilance committees as adequate substitutes. In August 1849 the military governor of California was induced to authorize elections for a convention. Before the end of the year a constitution had been drafted and a governor and legislature elected, and California was asking Congress for admission as a state.

New Political Problems. As a result of the Mexican acquisitions, two problems confronted the Federal government. One was to provide for some quicker means of transportation to the Pacific coast. There were proposals for the construction of a canal across Panama; and these led to negotiations with Great Britain, which had been deeply involved in the affairs of Central America ever since the area became independent of Spain. By the Clayton-Bulwer Treaty of 1850 the two powers agreed that they would cooperate in building a canal and that neither of them would fortify it or claim exclusive control of it. The treaty also provided that neither power would exercise dominion over any part of Central America, a stipulation which compelled the British (after ten years of controversy) to abandon their protectorate over the Mosquito Coast of Nicaragua, while retaining British Honduras. Although the Clayton-Bulwer Treaty showed that the United States was not yet the dominant power in Central America, it was important in checking British expansion in the area; this was the first time that the non-colonization article in the Monroe Doctrine had been effectively enforced.

But no canal was built at that time, and the project was dropped until near the end of the century, by which time the United States was strong enough to claim exclusive control.[1] Obviously, the most desirable solution to the problem of linking California with the East was the building of a transcontinental railroad. And since such a road would be too expensive to be built by private enterprise alone, the government must take the initiative and offer financial assistance. This resulted in heated debates between the advocates of northern and southern routes.

[1] The Clayton-Bulwer Treaty was finally abrogated by the Hay-Pauncefote Treaty of 1901. See page 529.

The second and more urgent problem was to provide for the government of the newly acquired territories. Should slavery be permitted or prohibited? This question had been raised as early as 1846 when a Pennsylvania Congressman, David Wilmot, proposed a resolution to the effect that slavery should be excluded from any territory that might be acquired from Mexico. This Wilmot Proviso did not pass Congress, but it marked the beginning of a prolonged and bitter controversy about the extension of slavery to new territories. Thus the territorial acquisitions of the 1840's led to new sectional conflict and eventually to the Civil War.

XVI

The Sectional Conflict

1. CAUSES OF THE CONFLICT
2. THE COMPROMISE OF 1850
3. THE RISE OF THE MIDDLE WEST
4. THE CONFLICT REVIVED
5. THE BUCHANAN ADMINISTRATION

F LARING up at the end of the war with Mexico, the sectional conflict was temporarily settled by the Compromise of 1850, broke out again with the Kansas-Nebraska Act of 1854, and was intensified by the long struggle for the control of Kansas and by the Dred Scott decision of 1857. Thus it dominated political life for a dozen years before it finally culminated in the secession of the South and the Civil War. Throughout this period Northerners and Southerners were becoming steadily more hostile to each other and more convinced that their social and political ideals were incompatible.

1. CAUSES OF THE CONFLICT

A FAR-REACHING conflict of this kind cannot be attributed to any single cause or explained by means of any simple formula. In general, there are

SELECTED BIBLIOGRAPHY: Two works by Allan Nevins, *The Ordeal of the Union* (2 vols., 1947) and *The Emergence of Lincoln* (2 vols., 1950), provide a comprehensive history of the United States from 1848 to 1860. The period is covered more briefly in A. C. Cole, *The Irrepressible Conflict* (1934), which is Vol. 7 of *A History of American Life.* H. K. Beale has written a useful essay, "What Historians Have Said about the Causes of the Civil War," published in *Theory and Practise in Historical Study* (1946) by the Social Science Research Council. A. O. Craven, *The Coming of the Civil War* (1942), is a comprehensive study of its causes, somewhat sympathetic to the South. D. L. Dumond, *Anti-Slavery Origins of the Civil War* (1939), emphasizes the role of the abolitionists. Two useful books on politics during the 1850's are G. F. Milton, *The Eve of Conflict: Stephen A. Douglas and the Needless War* (1934), and R. F. Nichols, *The Disruption of American Democracy* (1948).

two main schools of interpretation; some historians emphasize economic factors and regard the Civil War as mainly a clash between two economic systems, while others attribute more influence to moral issues and consider slavery as the primary cause of the conflict. Each view contains aspects of the truth, and a complete analysis must recognize what is valid in both of them.

Economic Interpretations.   Exponents of the economic interpretation point out that South and North had developed divergent economic interests which had resulted in political conflicts ever since the foundation of the republic. The South had remained almost wholly agrarian and exported most of its basic crop. It therefore favored a tariff for revenue only, and was opposed to Federal spending on internal improvements, to a centralized banking system, and to the growth of big industrial and financial corporations. The Northeast, on the other hand, had become a center of capitalist industry and finance. Its businessmen wanted a protective tariff, Federal aid in the development of transportation, and a banking system controlled by Northeastern creditor interests, and looked forward to the organization of the whole national economy by the big corporations which they controlled. For a long period before the Civil War, Southern influences were predominant in the Federal government, and business growth was therefore impeded by a lack of Federal support. The slavery issue, however, brought about a new political combination; Northeastern businessmen and Western farmers joined forces against the South and by the election of 1860 and the subsequent Civil War were able to gain political power. By freeing the slaves they destroyed the planter aristocracy and substituted their own system of wage labor for the Southern system of slave labor.

Thus, according to this economic interpretation, the main underlying significance of the sectional conflict was that power was transferred from the planters of the South to the industrialists and bankers of the Northeast. Some historians, especially Charles A. Beard, have even spoken of the Civil War as a "Second American Revolution."

In the long run the growth of large-scale industry proved indeed to be the most important feature of the Civil War period. But any detailed description of the sectional conflict must also give major emphasis to the controversy about slavery. This was the central subject of discussion for a decade before the Civil War, and was the immediate and explicit cause of Southern secession. Whatever more fundamental economic issues may have been at stake, people certainly believed that they differed chiefly about slavery, and saw this difference in moral and social rather than in narrowly economic terms. While a majority of Southerners believed that slavery was a positive good, deserving the full protection of the Federal government, a growing number of Northerners insisted that it was an evil and a national disgrace. By any interpretation of the Civil War, it is indeed improbable that the two sections would finally have come to blows if they had been divided by economic issues alone.

The Abolitionist Movement. The divergence of attitudes towards slavery did not become acute until the rise of the abolitionist movement. Societies for the abolition of slavery began to increase after the year 1815, their most active leader being a New Jersey Quaker, Benjamin Lundy. They began by advocating gradual emancipation in the hope that the slave-owners themselves could be induced to accept it, and coupled this with proposals for sending the freed Negroes to the African republic of Liberia. By the 1830's, however, it was becoming obvious that the planters would never agree to voluntary abolition. Various individuals in different parts of the North then began to attack slavery in much more militant terms, insisting that it was contrary to both Christian and American ideals, that it ought to be ended immediately, and that the slave-owners had no rights that deserved consideration. Most of them were members of different Protestant churches, and the whole movement was permeated with a spirit of religious idealism.

New England, especially Boston, was one center of abolitionist activity. William Lloyd Garrison began publishing his *Liberator* in Boston in 1831. The movement in New England afterwards gained the active support of the orator Wendell Phillips, the Unitarian minister Theodore Parker, and a number of writers, especially John Greenleaf Whittier. Other abolitionist groups were established in Ohio under the leadership of such men as Theodore Weld and James G. Birney, while Arthur and Lewis Tappan and the wealthy landowner Gerrit Smith were prominent spokesmen in New York. By 1840 there were about 2,000 abolitionist societies, claiming a total membership of nearly 200,000.

The abolitionists were at first regarded even in the North as dangerous radicals and troublemakers, trying to destroy law and order and interfere with business. Their meetings were frequently broken up by mob action, and their printing presses wrecked. In 1837 an abolitionist editor at Alton, Illinois, Elijah Lovejoy, was actually lynched. But after a few years their propaganda began to have some effect. Although only a small proportion of the Northern population ever accepted the full abolitionist program, a much larger number began to develop an uneasy conscience about slavery.

Devoting their lives to a crusade from which they could expect no material rewards, the abolitionist leaders displayed heroic qualities. But many of them were fanatics who saw the problem in dangerously simple terms and were incapable of a realistic appraisal of racial relationships in the South. Insisting that slavery was inherently sinful and elaborating on every case of cruelty and sexual misconduct that came to their attention, they depicted the slave-owners as wicked men motivated solely by the desire for personal profit and pleasure. Emphasizing the doctrine that all men were created equal, they imagined that the Negroes could immediately assume all the responsibilities of a free people in spite of their long heritage of servitude and ignorance. In so far as the abolitionists helped to make any peaceful settlement of the slavery question impossible, it can be argued that, in the long run, they did more harm than good.

Some of the abolitionists refused to participate in ordinary political activity under the Constitution, on the ground that by associating with the Southern states the North became tainted with the sin of slavery. Garrison, who was an impractical idealist with extreme views on many other questions, denounced the Constitution as "a covenant with death and an agreement with hell" and wanted the North to separate from the South. But the New York and Ohio groups hoped to achieve their objective by constitutional methods. As a preliminary measure they advocated the abolition of slavery in areas directly under Federal control: in other words, in the District of Columbia and the territories. In 1840 the abolitionist organizations split into two hostile groups on the question of political action; and the anti-Garrisonians then organized the Liberty Party, which ran Birney for the presidency in 1840 and again in 1844.

All the abolitionists were interested in helping runaway slaves to escape, in defiance of a clause in the Constitution requiring states to cooperate in returning them to their owners. Slaves trying to make their way to Canada (where they automatically became free) were conducted from one hiding-place to another along a series of routes which became known as the Underground Railroad. Between 1830 and 1860 the total number of runaways seems to have averaged about 2,000 a year, although almost all of those who succeeded in reaching the North came from the border states, not from the cotton belt. Northern help for fugitive slaves soon became one of the major grievances of the South, especially after a number of Northern states enacted personal-liberty laws. Designed to give adequate protection to free Negroes accused of being runaway slaves, the laws provided for free legal assistance and for jury trials. Southerners complained that such legislation made it difficult for them to recapture genuine fugitives, and (in spite of their states' rights theory of the Constitution) demanded that the Federal government intervene to protect their property rights.

Southern Reactions.   From the Southern point of view the abolitionist movement was an unwarrantable interference with the South's peculiar institution. Slave-owners became understandably indignant at being incessantly described as criminals who spent most of their time beating their male slaves and begetting mulatto offspring with their female slaves, and often failed to realize that only a small minority of Northerners actually supported the abolitionists. Another and even more potent cause for Southern indignation was their fear lest abolitionist propaganda reach the slaves and lead to rebellions. For this reason they felt that abolitionists were not entitled to the protection of the Bill of Rights.

Throughout most of the South, abolitionist literature could not pass through the mails, and free speech on the slavery question was not usually permitted. In 1836, when Congress was being flooded with petitions from abolitionist organizations, Southerners brought about the adoption of a gag rule prohibiting them from being heard. John Quincy Adams, now a Congressman from Massachusetts, regarded the gag rule as a violation of the constitutional right of petition, and led a fight against it, which was finally successful in 1844. But Southerners continued to feel that, in permitting the abolitionists to speak and write freely, the Northern states were not living up to their responsibilities under the Federal Union.

The Question of Slavery Extension.   After 1848 the main question in dispute between the North and the South was whether slavery should be permitted to spread to new territories. Although relatively few Northerners supported the abolitionist demand for interfering with slavery where it already existed, a much larger number were now convinced that it was an evil institution and should therefore be prevented from expanding. This point of view was supported by Western farmers for economic as well as idealistic reasons; they wanted slavery to be restricted to the South so that they would not have to compete with slave-owning planters in the settlement of the West.

Many Southerners, on the other hand, were now hostile to any proposal implying either that slavery was not a positive good or that the Federal government had any power at all to interfere with it. They argued that the property rights of the slave-owner in his slaves were entitled to Federal protection just as much as those of the Northern farmer in his horses and cattle, and that since the territories were the common property of all the people of the United States, they should be open to Southerners on the same terms as to Northerners. To admit the right of the Federal government to exclude slavery from the territories was, they felt, the first step along the road to complete abolition.

How far Southerners actually believed that new slave states could be established in the West is not easy to decide. Moderate men in both sections argued that the limits of slavery were fixed by soil and climate, that the West was unsuited to slave plantations, and that the whole controversy was therefore unreal. According to this view it was unnecessary for the North to limit slavery by law and futile for the South to protest. But whether this was true or not, Southern spokesmen certainly tried to have slavery legalized in as many areas as possible. This was for political as well as economic and constitutional reasons. They were concerned not only with finding new soil suitable for cotton plantations but also with the balance of power between the sections. Even though a Western territory might not have the right kind of soil for cotton, it was still important that Southerners should try to win control of it, in order to secure more votes for the South in Congress when it became a state.

It must always be remembered that slavery was not merely an economic question. Southerners were determined to keep the Negroes in servitude not only because they profited by it but also because they believed in white supremacy and felt that emancipation would lead eventually to race equality and amalgamation. Any satisfactory solution to this extremely complex and tragic problem could only be reached by a slow evolutionary process. But this was not recognized either by the South or by the North.

The South insisted that slavery was permanent and not temporary, and tried, in defiance of general trends throughout the civilized world, to prevent any change whatever. A growing number of Northerners assumed an attitude of moral condemnation and demanded emancipation without facing the immense problems of readjustment which it would create in Southern society. Yet, as Southerners did not fail to point out, Negroes were denied political rights in most Northern states, and many Northern communities discriminated against them or even totally excluded them.

Armed conflict could have been prevented only by a recognition in both sections that slavery must eventually come to an end but that the emancipation of 4,000,000 uneducated slaves and their admission to the responsibilities of citizenship must inevitably be a slow, difficult, and costly task. Unfortunately, as on so many other occasions in history, men proved in the end more willing to give up their lives and spend their money in war than to make the intellectual effort and material sacrifices needed for working out a just and peaceful settlement.

2. THE COMPROMISE OF 1850

Political Trends.   By the late 1840's, under the impact of the sectional conflict, changes were taking place in each of the national political parties. The Northern Whigs were beginning to split into two groups, often known as the "Conscience" and the "Cotton" Whigs. The Conscience Whigs openly avowed their hostility to slavery, while the Cotton Whigs, supported by textile manufacturers and other groups who did business with the South and had an economic stake in the preservation of slavery, were more conservative and emphasized the protection of the Union. In the South the Whig Party had been supported by a number of the richer planters. These soon became alarmed at the growing influence of the Conscience Whigs, and some of their ablest leaders, notably Alexander Stephens and Robert Toombs of Georgia, eventually joined the Democrats.

While the Whig Party, always a heterogeneous organization, was beginning to break up, the Democratic Party was being transformed into the political instrument of the Southern planters. Calhoun had returned to the party after the retirement of Andrew Jackson and set out to win control of it. The party retained a large body of Northern supporters, most of whom were Jacksonians and nationalists; and as long as they continued to vote the Democratic ticket, it could still win electoral victories. But party policies were now mostly dictated either by Southerners or by "doughfaces," otherwise known as "Northern men with Southern principles." Northern liberal Democrats became increasingly resentful against Southern control—a trend which led finally to their amalgamation with the Conscience Whigs in the new Republican Party in 1854.

Meanwhile, the Southern Democrats, while united in their defense of slavery, were by no means in agreement about methods. The majority wished to remain in the Union on condition that Southern rights and interests were adequately safeguarded. But there was a small but active minority who believed that the formation of a separate Southern confederacy was the only way to preserve Southern institutions and that the sooner the Southern states left the Union, the better would be their chances of success. This secessionist group welcomed sectional conflict and opposed any attempts at solution by compromise. Among its leaders were Robert Barnwell Rhett of South Carolina, publisher of one of the best Southern newspapers, the *Charleston Mercury*; William L. Yancey, an Alabama lawyer famous for his eloquence; and Edmund Ruffin of Virginia, a scientific agriculturist who had written a classic *Essay on Calcareous Manures*.

The Problem of the Territories. The problem of slavery in the territories, temporarily settled by the division of the Louisiana purchase territory in the Missouri Compromise of 1820, was reopened during the Polk administration. In 1848 four newly acquired regions—Oregon, California, New Mexico, and Utah—urgently needed legal government. Polk suggested that the Missouri Compromise line be extended to the Pacific, but this was not acceptable to the more extreme groups in either North or South. Before the end of Polk's administration, Oregon was organized as a territory without slavery, but no settlement could be made about the other areas.

In the 1848 election both major parties sought support in each section and sedulously avoided any commitments about the slavery question. While the Democrats nominated a Jacksonian from Michigan, Lewis Cass, the Whigs adopted Zachary Taylor, who had been born in Virginia and owned a plantation in Louisiana. Taylor had never taken any interest in politics, but his war record made him an attractive candidate; and the Whig organizers, especially Thurlow Weed, had made overtures to him and won his support during the Mexican campaign. Meanwhile, a small group of radical New York Jacksonians, known as the "Barn-burners," [1]

---

[1] They were so called because (according to their opponents) they resembled a farmer who tried to get rid of rats by burning the barn. The rival and more conservative faction among the New York Democrats were called "Hunkers" because they were said to hanker after office.

bolted the Democratic Party and joined forces with Birney and the abolitionists in a new Free-Soil Party, which nominated ex-President Van
Buren. Polling nearly 300,000 votes, the Free-Soilers drew away enough
of the normal Democratic strength in the North to give the election to
Taylor and the Whigs.

In spite of his Southern affiliations, Taylor sought advice mainly from
Conscience Whigs and showed no inclination to conciliate the South. He
proposed that both California and New Mexico be admitted as states and
that they be allowed to decide for themselves about slavery. In November
1849 the Californians adopted a constitution which excluded slavery, and
in the spring of 1850 the people of New Mexico did likewise. Up to this
point free and slave states had been admitted in pairs, so that in spite of
growing Northern preponderance in the House of Representatives, the
two sections had remained equal in the Senate. Adoption of Taylor's
proposals would give the North a majority in both houses; and since there
were no more slave territories to be admitted, this majority would be
permanent. Southern leaders immediately declared that they would never
accept Northern domination, and would prefer to leave the Union if their
rights were not guaranteed. When Congress met in December 1849, there
began one of the greatest debates in American history.

The Compromise Proposed.   Henry Clay, now past seventy,
assumed leadership in the task of working out a settlement which would
satisfy both sections, and in January 1850 he made a series of compromise
proposals. He suggested that California be admitted as a state with its
anti-slavery constitution, and that in the rest of the area acquired from
Mexico territorial governments be set up without any restriction about
slavery. He made it plain that, in his opinion, slavery would never actually
be established in this area because the soil and climate were unsuitable; it
was therefore unnecessary for the North to antagonize the South by
demanding that it be excluded by law. Texas should relinquish her claim
to any part of New Mexico, in return for which the Federal government
should assume the public debt which she had contracted prior to annexation. Clay also proposed that Northern public opinion be conciliated by
the abolition of the slave trade (though not of slavery itself) in the District
of Columbia. So far there was little in Clay's recommendations tending to
reassure the South; but he went on to urge the redress of one of the main
Southern grievances by the enactment of a more stringent fugitive-slave
law.

The discussion of Clay's proposals continued until September, and
for a long time it seemed unlikely that they would pass. Clay had the
powerful support of Daniel Webster, who in a speech delivered on March 7
devoted all his oratorical resources to a plea for restoring sectional harmony and preserving the Union. But the proposals were opposed by
President Taylor and by the more extreme groups in both sections.

Southerners refused to admit California as a free state and demanded either the legalization of slavery in all territories or the extension of the Missouri Compromise line to the Pacific. Calhoun, although too old and ill to participate actively in the debates, was still the leading Southern spokesman, and his views were supported by many disciples, especially by Jefferson Davis, recently elected to the Senate from Mississippi after a brilliant record as an officer in the Mexican War. In the North the suggestion of a new fugitive-slave law aroused bitter indignation. Webster's speech of March 7 was followed by a storm of abuse, and anti-slavery intellectuals declared that he was a traitor who had sold his principles in order to win Southern support for the presidency. The leader of the Conscience Whigs in the Senate, William H. Seward of New York, declared bluntly that slavery was evil and its abolition inevitable and that, in legislating for the territories, Congress should be guided by a "higher law than the Constitution."

The Compromise Accepted. Yet in spite of all the extremist oratory, it gradually became evident that majority opinion in both sections still favored compromise. In the North, businessmen rallied support for Clay and Webster. In the South, a convention from nine states met at Nashville, Tennessee, early in the summer; but its more militant members won little support, and the convention voted to adjourn until after Congress had acted. President Taylor died suddenly in July; and his successor, Millard Fillmore, a little-known lawyer from upstate New York, supported the compromise and worked closely with Clay and Webster. The proposals were split up into five separate bills, and in this form they were passed by Congress during August and September. Relatively few Congressmen voted for all five, but they were supported by Northerners on some issues and by Southerners on others. The final success of Clay's proposals was largely due to the dynamic leadership of the young Democratic Senator from Illinois, Stephen A. Douglas.

As soon as the measures had become law, there was a general feeling of relief that the crisis had passed and of hope that this was a permanent and final settlement of all questions in dispute between North and South. In the North, anti-slavery agitation received, for the time being, markedly less popular support. In the South, the adjourned meeting of the Nashville Convention condemned the compromise, but few people paid any attention to its recommendations. Although conventions were held in four states to consider the advisability of secession, all of them voted in favor of accepting the compromise and taking no further action unless the North failed to abide by its provisions.

The most important items of the Compromise of 1850 were those relating to the territories and to the recapture of fugitive slaves. Apart from California, everything acquired from Mexico was organized into the territories of New Mexico and Utah, with the understanding that the final decision about slavery should be made by their inhabitants when they achieved statehood. Slavery might be permitted during the territorial

11. Slave and Free Territories, 1850–54

MOST AMERICANS BELIEVED THAT THE COMPROMISE OF 1850 WOULD PUT AN END
to all disputes about slavery in the territories. It was assumed that the Missouri
Compromise, under which the area acquired by the Louisiana Purchase was
divided along the line 36°30′, would remain in force. Of the area acquired during
the 1840's, Texas had been admitted as a slave state in 1845, although slavery
was excluded from the Oregon Country, which was organized as a territory in
1848, and from California, admitted as a state under the 1850 Compromise. The
whole of the remaining newly acquired area was organized under the terms of the
Compromise into the territories of Utah and New Mexico. By the new formula
known as popular sovereignty the inhabitants of these territories were left free
to decide for themselves whether they wanted slavery, which was not excluded
by Federal law. Since the soil and climate of Utah and New Mexico were not
suitable for plantation agriculture, it seemed unnecessary for the Federal government to make any decision about the question. In practice, the Territory of
Utah excluded slavery, but a handful of slaves were taken into New Mexico.

With the admission of California the North had, for the first time, a majority
in both Houses of Congress, since there were now sixteen free states and fifteen
slave states. Her preponderance, moreover, was certain to increase. Apart from
New Mexico and Utah, the only remaining territory open to slavery was the
Indian Territory west of Arkansas, whereas a vast region was available for settlement north of 36°30′. Thus the South could expect to be consistently outvoted in
Congress. This led some Southern extremists to advocate immediate secession,
but others sought constitutional limitations on the power of the Federal government to interfere with slavery.

The question was reopened by the Kansas-Nebraska Act of 1854. Repealing
the Missouri Compromise and applying the formula of popular sovereignty to
the country north of 36°30′, this opened a vast new region to slavery. It was
assumed that the Nebraska Territory would be settled by men from the free
states who would exclude slavery, but Northerners were afraid that Kansas,
adjacent to the slave state of Missouri, would come under the control of slave-
owners. Northern anger and alarm found expression in the new Republican party.

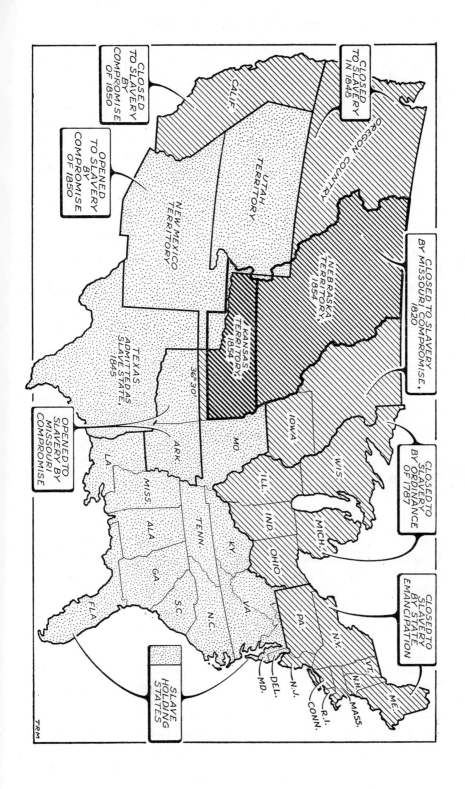

CLOSED TO SLAVERY BY COMPROMISE OF 1850

CLOSED TO SLAVERY IN 1848

OPENED TO SLAVERY BY COMPROMISE OF 1850

CLOSED TO SLAVERY BY MISSOURI COMPROMISE, 1820

OPENED TO SLAVERY BY MISSOURI COMPROMISE

CLOSED TO SLAVERY BY ORDINANCE OF 1787

CLOSED TO SLAVERY BY STATE EMANCIPATION

SLAVE HOLDING STATES

CALIF.

OREGON COUNTRY

UTAH TERRITORY

NEW MEXICO TERRITORY

NEBRASKA TERRITORY 1854

KANSAS TERRITORY 1854

TEXAS ADMITTED AS SLAVE STATE, 1845

36° 30'

LA.

ARK.

MO.

IOWA

WIS.

MICH.

ILL.

IND.

OHIO

MISS.

ALA.

TENN.

KY.

VA.

GA.

S.C.

N.C.

PA.

N.Y.

VT.

N.H.

MASS.

R.I.

CONN.

ME.

FLA.

MD.

DEL.

N.J.

TRM

stage if the inhabitants so desired (actually a small number of slaves were taken into New Mexico, while Utah excluded slavery). This solution to the problem became known as "popular sovereignty." The only other region south of 36°30′ was the so-called Indian Territory (the modern Oklahoma), which was reserved for the tribes removed from Georgia and Alabama during the 1830's. It was assumed, at least in the North, that the Missouri Compromise would remain in force, so that slavery would remain excluded from all territories north of 36°30′. If this assumption was correct, then the question of slavery in the territories had been fully settled, and no further controversy need arise.

In return for an agreement about the territories, the North had been required to accept a new fugitive-slave law, the terms of which were extremely severe. A Negro accused of being a fugitive was denied the right of trial by jury, and his status was to be determined either by a United States judge or by a commissioner appointed by a circuit court. Commissioners were given strong incentives to deliver biased verdicts, since they received a fee of $10 for every Negro sent back to slavery, as against only $5 whenever they declared a Negro to be free. Heavy penalties were prescribed for Federal marshals and their deputies if they failed to display sufficient energy in catching fugitives and for any private citizens who assisted Negroes to escape.

Many Northern intellectuals and humanitarians regarded this law as a disgraceful violation of Christian principles and American ideals, and declared that they had a moral duty to disobey it. In 1851 two Negroes accused of being fugitives, one in Syracuse, New York, and the other in Boston, were rescued from Federal officers by mob action. Yet for the time being most Northerners were prepared to accept the fugitive-slave law, repugnant though it was, if it would lead to a permanent settlement with the South.

3. THE RISE OF THE MIDDLE WEST

EVENTS were to show that the Compromise of 1850 had provided only a breathing-spell. But when the final crisis came a decade later, the North was much better equipped to meet it. Economic developments during the 1850's contributed immensely to the strengthening of the free states, which grew much more rapidly than the South.

The total population of the United States increased during the decade by 8,000,000, from 23,000,000 to 31,000,000; and nearly three-quarters of this increase was in the North. The capital invested in industry almost doubled, rising from $533,000,000 to $1,009,000,000; and almost all of this was in the North. And while the free states were growing with amazing rapidity, they were at the same time developing a much stronger sense of common economic interest. In particular, the Middle Western states of the upper Mississippi Valley, which hitherto had often been allied with the South, were becoming more closely attached to the Northeast.

Railroad Building.   One of the major features of the period was the growth of the railroads. For some years after the collapse of 1837 few new lines were projected, but by 1846 conditions were ripe for another burst of expansion. Between 1846 and 1860 the total mileage increased from about 6,000 to more than 30,000. New Englanders supplied much of the capital and the entrepreneurial skill, John Murray Forbes of Boston being perhaps the chief railroad organizer of this period.

By 1854 four lines were in operation linking the Northeast with the Mississippi Valley: the Baltimore and Ohio, the Pennsylvania, the Erie, and the New York Central. Meanwhile, a network of lines was being constructed throughout the Middle West, and Chicago was emerging as the metropolis of the whole region. As late as 1850 it was still a small town with no railroad connections; but by 1860 it had a population of more than 100,000, and was the terminus of eleven main roads, some of which connected with New York and Philadelphia, while others ran westward into the prairies. In 1850 Stephen A. Douglas and other Westerners steered through Congress a bill granting public land for a projected road linking Chicago with the Gulf of Mexico, to be built partly by the Illinois Central and partly by the Mobile and Ohio; and this was followed by a number of similar grants. By 1860 the railroads had received more than 20,000,000 acres of public land from the Federal government.

One of the most significant results of this railroad building was that it linked the Middle West with the Northeast. Hitherto the Middle West had relied largely on river transportation and had shipped much of its produce by barge and steamboat down the Mississippi to New Orleans. But the railroads provided quicker and safer service, and, unlike the river, were open at all seasons of the year; and until the very eve of the Civil War, when the Mobile and Ohio was finally completed, all the important lines ran east and west, not north and south. The South was also expanding its railroad system, but its major effort was a series of lines connecting the Atlantic seaboard with Chattanooga and Memphis. In consequence, the Middle West now did an increasing proportion of its trade with the Northeast instead of with the South. Chicago and New York took the places of St. Louis and New Orleans as the main entrepôts for its grain and meat.

Population Growth.   While the railroads were solving the transportation problems of the Middle West, its population was growing more rapidly than that of any other section. Between 1850 and 1860 the increase amounted to more than 3,000,000. And whereas many of the original settlers had come from Virginia and Kentucky and had retained strong Southern sympathies, the newcomers came predominantly from New England and New York or from Europe and were often militantly opposed to slavery.

Much the largest of the European groups was the German. A first contingent of 10,000 Germans had arrived in 1832, and had been followed

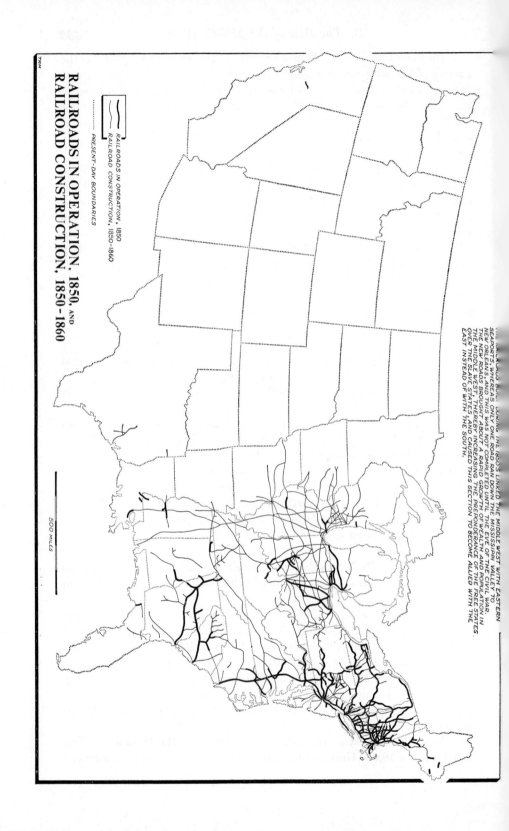

RAILROADS IN OPERATION, 1850, AND
RAILROAD CONSTRUCTION, 1850-1860

RAILROADS IN OPERATION, 1850
RAILROAD CONSTRUCTION, 1850-1860
PRESENT-DAY BOUNDARIES

500 MILES

THE RAILROADS BEGUN DURING THE 1850'S LINKED THE MIDDLE WEST WITH EASTERN SEAPORTS. WHEREAS ONLY ONE ROAD RAN DOWN THE MISSISSIPPI VALLEY TO NEW ORLEANS, AND THIS WAS NOT COMPLETED UNTIL THE EVE OF THE CIVIL WAR. THE NEW ROADS BROUGHT ABOUT A RAPID GROWTH OF WEALTH AND POPULATION IN THE MIDDLE WEST, THEREBY INCREASING THE PREPONDERANCE OF THE FREE STATES OVER THE SLAVE STATES AND CAUSED THIS SECTION TO BECOME ALLIED WITH THE EAST INSTEAD OF WITH THE SOUTH.

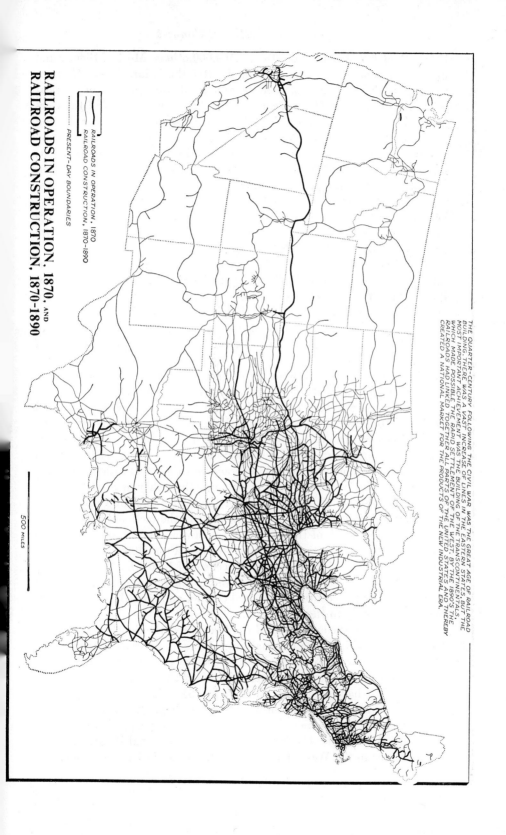

RAILROADS IN OPERATION, 1870, AND
RAILROAD CONSTRUCTION, 1870-1890

500 MILES

THE QUARTER-CENTURY FOLLOWING THE CIVIL WAR WAS THE GREAT AGE OF RAILROAD
BUILDING. THERE WAS A VAST INCREASE OF LINES IN THE EASTERN STATES, BUT THE
MOST IMPORTANT ACHIEVEMENT WAS THE BUILDING OF THE TRANSCONTINENTALS,
WHICH MADE POSSIBLE THE RAPID SETTLEMENT OF THE WEST. BY THE 1890'S THE
RAILROADS HAD LINKED TOGETHER ALL PARTS OF THE UNITED STATES AND THEREBY
CREATED A NATIONAL MARKET FOR THE PRODUCTS OF THE NEW INDUSTRIAL ERA.

before the Civil War by more than 1,500,000 others. Most of them came mainly for economic reasons, although after the failure of the German revolutionary movements of 1848 they included also a number of political refugees with strongly liberal convictions. And well over half of the German immigrants came to the Middle West, becoming farmers or settling in cities like Milwaukee, Chicago, and St. Louis. These and other newcomers were generally welcomed by the Middle Western states, particularly by Wisconsin, which appointed a state Commissioner of Immigration and advertised in European newspapers in order to build up its population. Michigan, Wisconsin, Iowa, and Minnesota grew with especial rapidity, as did also the border state of Missouri, where the influx of Northerners and Europeans was soon large enough to threaten the control of the state government by the slave-owning interests.

Agricultural Expansion.   Even more remarkable than the population growth of the Middle West was the increase of its agricultural production. It now definitely outdistanced every other part of the country in the growing of foodstuffs, particularly wheat and corn. Between 1839 and 1860 Middle Western exports of wheat increased from 2,000,000 to 29,000,000 bushels, of corn from 1,000,000 to 24,000,000 bushels, and of flour from 800,000 to 5,500,000 barrels. By 1860 nearly 90 per cent of these exports were going by railroad across the mountains to the East, and a large proportion were then shipped across the Atlantic. The Middle West was now helping to feed industrial cities not only in New England and New York but also in Great Britain, which was buying increasing quantities of foodstuffs from the United States. This was to be a factor of considerable importance in the Civil War; one of the motives that deterred the British from helping the Confederacy was their realization that they needed Middle Western wheat even more than they needed Southern cotton. There was now a challenger for the throne of King Cotton.

New Political Alignments.   The shift in the sectional balance produced by the growth of the Middle West can be charted in terms of the movement of the country's population center. From 1800 until 1850 the center had been in Virginia. Before the census of 1860 it had moved northwards and westwards into Ohio. And the Southern response to this shift tended further to accentuate sectional conflict and bind the Middle West even more closely to the Northeast.

Alarmed by the expansion of the free states, the South continued to block Federal aid for the internal improvements desired by the Middle West; and it now opposed any liberalization of public-land policy. Hitherto the South and West had generally favored cheaper public land, while the Northeast had opposed it. But by the 1850's it had become obvious that further Western expansion would add to the majority of free states, and Southern Congressmen therefore voted against proposals for a homestead act. Meanwhile, the Northeast had also changed its attitude and drawn closer to the West. The influx of European immigrants ended the fear of a labor shortage; and industrialists were coming to realize that Western growth would enlarge their markets. The result was that Western demands for free public land were now received more sympathetically by the Northeast than by the South. The proposal for a homestead act was to be one of the main planks in the Republican Party platform of 1860.

4. THE CONFLICT REVIVED

The Pierce Administration. For three and a half years after the adoption of the Compromise of 1850 most people tried to forget about slavery. This widespread desire for sectional harmony was very manifest during the election of 1852. The Democrats proclaimed their loyalty to the Compromise; and after a deadlock among several of the party leaders, they gave their nomination to a dark-horse candidate, Franklin Pierce of New Hampshire. Pierce, who was a close friend of the novelist Nathaniel Hawthorne, had few qualifications except good looks and considerable personal charm; as later events revealed, he was fatally lacking in strength of character. The Whigs, who had won the elections of 1840 and 1848 by nominating generals, picked Winfield Scott. While they did not oppose the Compromise, they were less vigorous than the Democrats in its defense. The result was an overwhelming victory for Pierce, who carried all but four states. The decline of anti-slavery feeling was also shown by a drop of nearly 50 per cent in the vote of the Free-Soil Party, which had nominated John P. Hale of New Hampshire.

Pierce picked a Cabinet composed largely of Southerners and Southern sympathizers, Jefferson Davis, who became Secretary of War, being perhaps its strongest member. The new administration apparently hoped to maintain harmony by pursuing an aggressive and expansionist foreign policy. But it was soon obvious that its expansionist plans were designed mainly for the benefit of the South.

Southerners were especially interested in acquiring Cuba, one of the few areas outside the United States where slavery was still legal. Southern adventurers had been making trouble for the Spanish authorities in the island since 1848. The Pierce administration hoped to acquire it, and in 1854 three of its diplomatic representatives in Europe issued the Ostend Manifesto, urging Spain to sell it and declaring that otherwise the United States would be fully justified in taking it by force. Southerners were also interested in Mexico and Central America as areas where new slave states might be created. William Walker, a soldier of fortune from Tennessee, tried to seize part of northern Mexico in 1853, and led an expedition to Nicaragua in 1855. For a short period he was virtual dictator of the country, but he was soon driven out, and his career ended in 1860 when he was shot during a raid on Honduras.

Meanwhile, the great figures who had dominated Congress for more than a generation were disappearing from the scene. Calhoun had died in

1850, and both Clay and Webster in 1852. Benton survived until 1858, but lost his seat in the Senate in 1851. Thus leadership passed to younger men, the most prominent of whom was Stephen A. Douglas of Illinois, known to his admirers as the "Little Giant" (he was not much more than five feet tall). Douglas was the ablest and most aggressive debater in the Senate; and although he often showed a lack of moral sensitivity, his patriotism was unquestionable. He had no strong convictions about slavery, and believed primarily in advancing the unity and greatness of the country. It was Douglas, nevertheless, who was responsible for initiating the next phase in the sectional conflict.

The Kansas-Nebraska Act.   The main issue before the country was the choice of a route for a transcontinental railroad. While Northerners wanted Chicago or St. Louis to be the eastern terminal, Southerners favored a route running from New Orleans along the Mexican border to Los Angeles. Their strongest argument was that the line would be built across the Territory of New Mexico, which had a government and some white inhabitants, whereas any northern line would run across country not yet opened for settlement and inhabited only by nomadic Indian tribes.

As Senator from Illinois, Douglas wanted the line built from Chicago, and in order to remove the main obstacle, he proposed that territorial government be established in the country through which the line would pass. In January 1854, in his capacity as Chairman of the Senate Committee on Territories, he introduced a bill to this effect. In its final form the bill authorized the creation of two new territories, one to be called Kansas and the other Nebraska. Although the whole region was north of the Missouri Compromise line, Douglas recommended that, instead of excluding slavery, the principle of popular sovereignty be adopted. The people who settled in the new territories should decide for themselves whether they wanted slavery or not. In order that the meaning of the bill might be quite clear, Southerners persuaded Douglas to add a clause explicitly stating that the Missouri Compromise was no longer in effect.

Douglas's motives have remained controversial to this day. His opponents declared that he was trying to win Southern support for the next Democratic presidential nomination. Later historians have rejected this view and suggested various alternative explanations. Perhaps the most plausible theory is that since the Southerners were hostile to proposals for a northern railroad, Douglas was afraid that they would block his bill for organizing a new territory unless it was baited with a clause permitting the extension of slavery. It is also possible that Douglas genuinely believed that popular sovereignty, already in effect in Utah and New Mexico, was the ideal solution to the problem.

The Kansas-Nebraska Bill proved to be one of the most catastrophic political blunders in American history. Strongly backed by the Pierce administration, the bill was passed by Congress; but such a storm of indig-

A MOUNTAIN MAN

Long Jakes, one of the fur trappers who explored the Rocky Mountain country. An engraving from the New York Illustrated Magazine *in 1846.*

FUR TRADERS DESCENDING THE MISSOURI, *by* GEORGE CALEB BINGHAM (1811–79)

The picturesque fur traders around St. Louis, the main center of the fur trade, provided Bingham with material for a number of his paintings.

CARAVAN EN ROUTE, by ALFRED JACOB MILLER (1810–74)

A native of Baltimore, Miller traveled across the continent to Oregon in the 1830's. His pictures are an authentic record of early Western life.

nation swept across the North that, as Douglas remarked, he could have traveled from Boston to Chicago by the light of fires kindled to burn him in effigy. Regarding the whole slavery issue as unimportant, he had wholly failed to recognize the depth of the moral conviction now pervading Northern society.

The Struggle for Kansas. There was, moreover, a fatal ambiguity in the theory of popular sovereignty. At what point were the inhabitants of a territory to make their decision about slavery? Southerners declared that the choice was not to be made until the territory became a state and that up to that point slavery should be permitted. Douglas, on the other hand, assumed that the territorial legislature would have power from the start to exclude slavery. This meant that the first settlers would probably determine the whole future of the territory and that the earliest elections might be decisive.

In Utah and New Mexico the whole question had been of little importance, since even Southerners recognized that slavery could not flourish in such arid country. But Kansas might conceivably become slave soil. Slavery was well established in parts of Missouri close to the Kansas border, and the Missouri slave-owners were eager to secure the legalization of slavery in Kansas, chiefly because they were afraid that otherwise their slaves would find it easy to escape; a free state next door to them would mean more runaways. Everybody recognized that Nebraska would become free soil; but the Missourians determined to win Kansas for slavery. And although most Southerners had no interest in Kansas, they were willing, once the issue had been raised, to support the Missourians. Meanwhile, anti-slavery groups, equally aware of the importance of the first elections, set up organizations, particularly the Massachusetts Emigrant Aid Society, to assist Northern free-soilers to go to Kansas and vote for freedom. Under such circumstances fraud and violence were almost inevitable, unless the administration took strong measures to ensure a fair election. Unfortunately, President Pierce was a weak man, wholly under the influence of the Southerners in his Cabinet.

Actually, most of the people who settled in Kansas were ordinary frontier farmers from the Mississippi Valley. Since they did not wish to compete with slave-owning planters, they wanted slavery excluded, but they were also hostile to Negroes and had no sympathy with the abolitionists. The Missourians, however, were alarmed by the activities of the Emigrant Aid Society, assumed that Kansas was in danger of becoming an abolitionist stronghold, and resolved to prevent such a catastrophe.

The first territorial legislature was elected in March 1855. All white adult male residents could vote, but in a territory just opened for settlement it was not easy to distinguish between a genuine resident and a visitor. On election day several thousand Missouri slave-owners paid a visit to Kansas and proceeded to vote. Kansas had only 1,400 qualified voters, yet the number of recorded votes exceeded 6,000, more than 5,000

of which were cast for pro-slavery candidates. The Governor, though far
from hostile to slavery, tried to do his duty by throwing out fraudulent
returns, but President Pierce refused to support him and finally dismissed
him. Thus the pro-slavery party secured control of the legislature, and
then enacted an outrageous code of laws prescribing the death penalty
for helping a slave to escape and a two-year prison sentence for even suggesting that slavery in Kansas was not legally established. The anti-
slavery party retaliated by electing a convention of their own, which met
at Topeka in October 1855, drafted a constitution, and established a
governor and a legislature.

There were now two rival governments in Kansas, and each of them
was well supplied with weapons. Most slave-owners carried guns as a
matter of course. The free-soilers received shipments of rifles from sympathizers in the North; these became known as "Beecher's Bibles" as a
result of a statement by the Brooklyn minister Henry Ward Beecher that
a gun was "a greater moral agency" in Kansas than a Bible. After some
casual shootings, organized violence began in May 1856, when a Federal
marshal collected a posse of Missouri "border ruffians" and raided and
sacked the free-soil headquarters at Lawrence.

This event was followed by the first public appearance of John
Brown, a 56-year-old abolitionist, of Connecticut ancestry, who had tried
a dozen different occupations and failed to achieve any worldly success
in any of them, and had now settled with his family in Kansas. Brown
believed that he had a divine mission to destroy slavery and that the sins
of the slave-owners could be purged only with blood. The most charitable
explanation of his behavior is that he was in an advanced stage of para-
noia, but like many paranoiacs he gave an impression of lucidity. In fact,
many Northerners soon came to regard him as a kind of saint. Having
calculated that five free-soilers had been killed, Brown led his sons in a
raid on a pro-slavery settlement at Pottawatomie Creek and murdered
five of its inhabitants in cold blood.

After this there was a period of open civil war, during which about
two hundred people lost their lives. By the end of the year Federal troops
succeeded in enforcing order; but the only legal legislature was still the
pro-slavery legislature fraudulently elected by the Missourians, and the
question of slavery in Kansas was still unsettled.

Formation of the Republican Party.   Meanwhile, throughout the
North indignation at the Kansas-Nebraska Act continued to increase.
Many Northerners regarded the repeal of the Missouri Compromise as a
wanton repudiation of the Compromise of 1850 and as a proof that there
was a Southern conspiracy to spread slavery as widely as possible. This
view was, of course, incorrect; the Kansas-Nebraska Act had originated
in Douglas's desire for a northern railroad, not in a Southern conspiracy;
in fact, most Southerners had been decidedly lukewarm about it. But
opponents of slavery were much too excited to examine the evidence for

their assertions. And to an increasing extent they resorted to mob action to block enforcement of the Fugitive Slave Act, which they had reluctantly accepted only because it seemed necessary to conciliate the South.

Soon after the passage of the Kansas-Nebraska Act the Federal government was forced to send troops to Boston and spend at least $50,000 in order to recapture a slave named Anthony Burns. Northern states soon began to pass new personal-liberty laws making the recapture of fugitives difficult or even impossible. This resurgence of anti-slavery sentiment was greatly increased by the popularity of *Uncle Tom's Cabin*, written by Harriet Beecher Stowe and first published in 1852. Mrs. Stowe knew almost nothing about slavery at first hand; her book was based on abolitionist propaganda. But its emotional force and dramatic effectiveness made it a best-seller and the most influential book published in America since Tom Paine's *Common Sense*.

In the spring of 1854 Northern opponents of the Kansas-Nebraska Act from both the Whig and the Democratic Party began to hold joint meetings. It soon became evident that a permanent party organization was required, and the name "Republican," with its Jeffersonian associations, was an obvious choice. A mass meeting at Jackson, Michigan, in July 1854, which adopted this name, has often been regarded as the beginning of the new party. Republican organizations were set up in most of the Northern states in the course of the following year.

Combining the bulk of the former Whigs with some of the Democrats, particularly those most closely identified with the liberal Jacksonian tradition, the Republican Party represented both Northeastern business interests and Western farming interests. Having no Southern support except in the border states, it was, of course, the first sectional major party. Its primary objective was the exclusion of slavery from all territories. This issue was presented in moral terms, but to many Northerners important economic interests were involved. Western farmers voted Republican because they did not wish to compete with slave-owners in the Western territories. Eastern businessmen wanted slavery limited in order to prevent the South from acquiring a majority in Congress. Thus the demand for checking the spread of slavery appealed to many Northerners who had no strong convictions about slavery itself.

William H. Seward of New York, who joined the Republicans in 1855, was generally recognized as their principal spokesman. He was able, honest, warmhearted, and free from the fanaticism shown by some of his colleagues, his record for statesmanship being marred only by an occasional lack of discretion and good judgment. Although actually a moderate, he had a propensity for making extreme statements which caused Southerners to regard him as little better than an abolitionist. They were particularly alarmed by his appeal to a "higher law" during the debate of 1850 and by his assertion that there was an "irrepressible conflict" between the sections.

The chief spokesman of the radicals was Salmon P. Chase of Ohio, who had great intellectual gifts, but suffered from inordinate ambition. Even more egotistical was Charles Sumner of Massachusetts. A man of wide learning, Sumner was a favorite with the New England intellectuals, but most other people found his self-righteousness intolerable. The South, however, succeeded in making Sumner into a martyr. In May 1856 he delivered a speech in the Senate which he entitled "The Crime Against Kansas." This was a carefully prepared invective against the South and some of its most respected leaders, modeled after the speeches of Cicero, and in the worst possible taste. A few days later a South Carolina Congressman, Preston Brooks, retaliated by attacking Sumner with a cane while he was sitting at his desk in the Senate, thrashing him so severely that he was a physical and nervous wreck for several years afterwards.

The Know-Nothing Movement.   For a brief period the political scene was further confused by the growth of another new party, the Native Americans, generally known to their opponents as the Know-Nothings. This was the product of years of anti-Catholic propaganda by Protestant clergymen and journalists. A secret society, the Order of the Star-spangled Banner, was formed about the year 1850, with a program of restricting the rights of immigrants, and keeping America Protestant and Anglo-Saxon. It was directed chiefly against the Irish, who were now pouring into the country at the rate of nearly 100,000 a year. The name "Know-Nothing" was derived from the fact that members were instructed, if asked about the society, to assert that they knew nothing about it. Appealing to people who sincerely believed that the growth of Catholicism was a threat to American institutions, to working men who regarded immigrant laborers as dangerous economic competitors, and to politicians who wanted a popular issue for winning elections, the Know-Nothings organized a political party; in 1854 they won control of Massachusetts and made big gains in other Northern states.

Fortunately, the movement died away even more rapidly than it had developed. Once in office, the Know-Nothings did little except demonstrate their lack of integrity. In Massachusetts, for example, they appointed a committee to investigate nunneries. The committeemen toured the state and discovered nothing discreditable about the institutions they visited, but ran up an enormous expense account which the taxpayers were required to pay. In 1855, moreover, the national convention of the Know-Nothings voted to support the Kansas-Nebraska Act. After this the party split into Northern and Southern groups, and most of the Northern Know-Nothings soon joined the Republicans.

The Election of 1856.   For the 1856 election the Democrats nominated James Buchanan, an elderly bachelor from Pennsylvania who had filled many important positions (including that of Secretary of State under Polk) and had been consistently hard-working, discreet, and conscientious, but had never shown any capacity for courageous leadership.

The party platform reaffirmed the doctrine of popular sovereignty, and its Northern supporters were assured that this would be honestly enforced in Kansas; slavery would not be imposed on the Kansans against their wishes.

The Republicans, in their first presidential nomination, went outside the political field and chose John C. Frémont, famous as the "Pathfinder" of California. Frémont was a popular hero, and his name fitted the party slogan ("Free soil, free speech, free men, Frémont"), but he had few qualifications for political leadership. The Know-Nothings nominated ex-President Fillmore, who was also adopted by the surviving Whigs.

The election showed that, in spite of the unpopularity of the Kansas-Nebraska Act, the Democrats still had enough strength in the North to win a national election. Buchanan carried every Southern state except Maryland (which voted for Fillmore), along with Pennsylvania, New Jersey, Indiana, Illinois, and California among the free states, with an electoral college total of 174. Frémont, who was not even on the ballot in eleven Southern states, carried the rest of the North with an electoral vote of 114. The voting indicated that unless the new administration conciliated the Northern element in the Democratic Party by carrying out its promise of genuine popular sovereignty in Kansas, the Republicans might win all the free states in 1860.

5. THE BUCHANAN ADMINISTRATION

THE YEAR 1857 saw a business collapse, the worst since 1837, and the consequent depression lasted through most of the new administration. One of its effects was to intensify the sectional conflict. The South, which suffered less than other parts of the country, interpreted the collapse as another proof that Northern economic institutions were fundamentally unstable, and drew the conclusion that she could safeguard her own prosperity only by separation. Northerners demanded aid from the Federal government, and were infuriated by a further lowering of the tariff in 1857, by Buchanan's veto of a homestead act in 1860, and by the generally Southern orientation of the administration's economic policies.

In dealing with Kansas and other controversial questions, Buchanan proved to be almost as ineffective as Pierce. His chief desire was to avoid any situation calling for decisive action; and since he was terrified lest the Southern states secede from the Union, he sought to appease them by giving way to their demands. His Cabinet, like Pierce's, was dominated by its Southern members, especially by Howell Cobb of Georgia, the Secretary of the Treasury. The result was that Buchanan quickly repudiated his pledges to establish genuine popular sovereignty in Kansas and accepted the Southern viewpoint on slavery in the territories. In so doing, he could claim that he was conforming with the decision of the Su-

preme Court in the Dred Scott case, which was delivered two days after
his inauguration.

The Dred Scott Decision.   Dred Scott was a slave who had belonged
to an army surgeon in Missouri. In 1834 he had been taken by his master
for four years, first to the free state of Illinois and then to the free territory
of Wisconsin, and then had been brought back to Missouri. A number of
years later Scott sued for his freedom on the ground that he had been
taken to territory where slavery was prohibited. His suit was supported
by individuals opposed to slavery who were hoping to receive judicial
confirmation of their belief that a slave automatically became free when he
was taken to free territory. The case eventually reached the Supreme
Court by appeal from a circuit court. Of the nine justices, seven were
Democrats, and five of these (including Chief Justice Taney of Maryland,
now in his eightieth year) were Southerners.

Six members of the Court agreed that Scott's status was determined
by the laws of the state in which he now resided; in other words, that he
was still a slave because he now resided in Missouri. This, of course, was
sufficient to settle the case. Taney, however, took the opportunity to
make assertions of much more far-reaching importance. Supported by two
other justices, he declared that Scott had no right even to bring the suit,
on the ground that no Negro could be a citizen of the United States. And
with the support of five other justices, he went on to affirm that Congress
had no power to prevent slave-owners from taking their slaves into any of
the territories, because to do so would mean depriving citizens of their
property without due process of law. In other words, according to six
members of the Supreme Court, the Missouri Compromise had been
unconstitutional and slavery was legal in all territories, even as far north
as Oregon.

Taney had been a great chief justice, and, at least in his younger
Jacksonian days, a decided liberal. Belonging to the older generation of
Southerners, he did not regard slavery as a positive good and had emancipated his own slaves. Yet he now gave judicial backing to the Southern
contention that slavery could not constitutionally be excluded from any
territory. Both his assertion that no Negro could be a citizen and his
invalidation of the Missouri Compromise were based (as the two non-
Democrats on the Court convincingly argued) on faulty reasoning. Taney,
however, could claim that his denial to Congress of the power to exclude
slavery from the territories was in conformity with the 1850 Compromise
and the Kansas-Nebraska Act, which had superseded the Missouri Compromise, and that many leaders of different shades of opinion had declared
that the whole question should be settled by judicial decision.

The Split in the Democratic Party.   The attempt of the Buchanan
administration to establish slavery in Kansas ended in failure; what it
accomplished instead was to wreck the Democratic Party. The Kansans
were invited to elect a convention to draft a constitution. The free-soilers,

anticipating another fraudulent election, refused to participate, so the pro-slavery group won control of the convention and drafted a constitution legalizing slavery. This, it was decided, should not be submitted to the voters for ratification; a vote was to be taken on a single article allowing the introduction of more slaves, but even if this were rejected, nothing could be done about the slaves already in Kansas. Buchanan then proposed that Kansas be admitted to the Union as a state with this pro-slavery Lecompton constitution.

Meanwhile, a new territorial legislature had been elected; and the new governor appointed by Buchanan, Robert J. Walker, an able and honest man, had taken measures to ensure an honest election and persuaded the free-soilers to vote. After Walker had thrown out several thousand obviously fraudulent ballots, the free-soilers won control of the legislature. Buchanan rewarded Walker for doing his duty by dismissing him from the governorship.

The proposal to admit Kansas with the Lecompton constitution caused an irreparable split between the Northern and Southern wings of the Democratic Party, with Douglas leading the opposition to the administration. Refusing to abandon his principle of popular sovereignty, Douglas insisted that before Kansas could become a state, an honest vote must be taken on the whole constitution. After a bitter struggle, Buchanan's proposal was defeated in the House of Representatives. The administration then made one last attempt. By the English Bill, Kansas was to choose between becoming a state immediately with the pro-slavery Lecompton constitution, and remaining a territory. The bill passed Congress; and the Kansans then voted, 11,812 to 1,926, to remain a territory. Slavery was still legal in Kansas; but the free-soilers kept control of the legislature, and it was obvious that slavery would be abolished as soon as Kansas was allowed to achieve statehood on its own terms. After this the pro-slavery group gave up their struggle to capture the territory.

The split between Douglas and the administration meant that there were now three different attitudes toward the slavery question. The Republicans declared that slavery should be excluded by Federal law from all the territories and that the Supreme Court must be induced to reverse its ruling in the Dred Scott case. The Southern Democrats were now demanding that slavery be protected by Federal law in all the territories. And Douglas and his followers maintained that, by popular sovereignty, the people of a territory could decide for themselves about slavery, and professed to be indifferent whether they voted for or against it. Douglas skillfully sidestepped the Dred Scott decision by pointing out that if the people of a territory did not want slavery, they could exclude it by simply refusing to adopt the necessary police regulations; whatever the Supreme Court might say, slave-owners would not venture to settle in any area where public opinion was hostile and the authorities would not assist them in preventing their slaves from rebelling or escaping. From the Southern point of view, this made Douglas little better than the Republicans. As experience in Kansas had shown, popular sovereignty meant, in practice, the exclusion of slavery from the territories. What difference did it make to the South if it were excluded by popular vote rather than by Federal law?

The Emergence of Lincoln.   Yet there were important differences of principle between Douglas and the Republicans, and these were underlined when Douglas ran for re-election to the Senate in 1858. The Republican candidate was Abraham Lincoln. Born in Kentucky in 1809 and brought by his parents to Illinois at an early age, Lincoln had worked his way up from poverty and was now recognized as one of the ablest and most successful lawyers in the state. He had been one of the leaders of the Illinois Whigs, although apart from one term in the House of Representatives he had not held any important office. A meditative and somewhat melancholy man, with a great fondness for telling humorous stories, he had an innate kindliness and a lack of vanity which made people like and trust him; but he had not hitherto seemed destined for leadership outside his own community.

The two candidates engaged in a series of seven joint debates, which attracted wide attention. Douglas insisted that he was indifferent to the question of slavery and that popular sovereignty was the best way of ending sectional conflict; and in a speech at Freeport, in response to challenging questions from Lincoln, he restated more emphatically his belief that the people of a territory could exclude slavery in spite of the Dred Scott decision. Lincoln's main thesis was that the slavery issue had to be decided one way or the other and could no longer be evaded by compromises. Since Douglas's supporters retained control of the state legislature by a narrow margin, Douglas was re-elected to the Senate; but Lincoln henceforth was a national figure.

Lincoln's speeches revealed him as a man who had thought long and deeply about the central problem confronting the country, had arrived at definite conclusions, and was able to state them lucidly, boldly, and convincingly. As he declared in his speech accepting the senatorial nomination, he believed that "this government cannot endure permanently half slave and half free." Agitation would continue "until a crisis has been reached and passed." "Either the opponents of slavery will arrest the further spread of it, and place it where the public mind shall rest in the belief that it is in the course of ultimate extinction; or its advocates will push it forward until it shall become alike lawful in all the States, old as well as new, North as well as South." This was the main issue, and Lincoln believed that the time had come when it must be faced openly and courageously.

Hostile to the abolitionists, Lincoln did not propose to attack slavery in the South or repeal the Fugitive Slave Law. And although he insisted that Negroes had a right to the life, liberty, and pursuit of happiness

promised to all men by the Declaration of Independence, he declared himself opposed to racial equality. The extinction of slavery, he believed,
could only be a gradual and lengthy process; and if the North adopted an
attitude of moral intolerance and condemnation toward the slave-owners,
the solution of the problem would become more difficult. But it was Lincoln's conviction that a definite decision was now inescapable; the American people should resolve that slavery was contrary to their national
ideals, that it should not be permitted to spread, and that it was their
national policy henceforth to bring it to an end. From this point of view,
Douglas's theory that it could be left to the people of each territory to
decide for themselves was a mere evasion of the issue.

Towards the Final Crisis. Throughout the year 1859 the country
was visibly drifting closer to the crisis which Lincoln had predicted. Congress was so bitterly divided that it was almost incapable of passing any
legislation; and since almost all its members, Northern as well as Southern, now carried guns, there were times when it seemed possible that most
of its members would perish in a general outbreak of shooting. One killing
did indeed occur, though fortunately not in the capital itself; Senator
Broderick of California, a Douglas Democrat, was shot by a Southerner
in a duel. Northerners continued to defy the Fugitive Slave Act, and the
Supreme Court of Wisconsin, in an assertion of states' rights quite as
extreme as that of South Carolina in 1832, actually declared it unconstitutional. In the South the secessionist group of Rhett, Yancey, and Ruffin
were gaining more supporters. The smuggling of slaves from abroad was
increasing, and some people were openly demanding that the slave trade
be legally reopened. Then, in October, came the news that Northern
abolitionists had actually made an armed attack on the South.

John Brown, being no longer able to kill slave-owners in Kansas, had
concocted a plan for a direct attack on slavery. Misled by abolitionist
propaganda, he supposed that the slaves were ready and eager to rebel
and that they would be supported by many of the non-slave-owning white
farmers. After receiving financial aid from certain prominent New England and New York abolitionists, he bought a farm in Maryland under an
assumed name, and on October 16, 1859, with eighteen companions, seized
the Federal arsenal at Harpers Ferry, Virginia. He expected to be joined
by the slaves in the neighborhood, and then to proceed southwards down
the Appalachian chain, waging guerrilla warfare against the planters and
maintaining a kind of independent Negro republic. But nobody, either
white or black, was foolish enough to join Brown and his associates,
and after twenty-four hours of fighting they were captured by Federal
troops under Colonel Robert E. Lee. Convicted of murder, treason, and
conspiracy against the State of Virginia, Brown was hanged on December 2.

In itself the episode was quickly ended; but it was of incalculable
importance in widening the gulf between North and South. Many North-

erners, knowing little about Brown's character or his activities in Kansas but impressed by the eloquence of his final speech at his trial, regarded him as a saint and a martyr. The South, confronted by the threat of race warfare, was swept with something approaching panic, and for a few weeks even the most harmless Northern visitors were in danger of being lynched. Many Southerners concluded that if the abolitionists were going to instigate slave rebellions, then secession was justifiable and necessary.

XVII

The Civil War

1. SECESSION AND WAR

2. BEHIND THE LINES

3. FROM BULL RUN TO GETTYSBURG

4. DIPLOMACY OF THE WAR

5. FROM GETTYSBURG TO APPOMATTOX

6. THE WAR AND THE NORTHERN ECONOMY

B Y 1860 the mounting tension in both sections indicated that the possibilities of compromise had been exhausted. Statesmanship having failed, the South broke her ties with the Union, and in 1861 the United States plunged into a four-year struggle which proved to be the greatest civil war in history and the first modern war in which victory depended primarily on industrial strength. In the end the South was compelled by force of arms to submit to the changes which she had sought to avoid by leaving the Union. Slavery was abolished, and the industrial economy of the North became dominant throughout the nation. Thus the ultimate effect of the Civil War, as of most wars, was not to divert the current of events but to accelerate it.

1. SECESSION AND WAR

The Election of 1860.   The most fateful election campaign in American history began in April, 1860, when the Democratic convention met at

SELECTED BIBLIOGRAPHY: The best one-volume account of the Civil War is J. G. Randall, *The Civil War and Reconstruction* (1937). Of the many lives of Lincoln, the most authoritative is J. G. Randall, *Lincoln the President* (4 vols., 1945–55), and the best-written is Carl Sandburg, *Lincoln: The War Years* (4 vols., 1939), while the best one-volume account is B. P. Thomas, *Abraham Lincoln* (1952). Another outstanding biography is D. S. Freeman, *Robert E. Lee* (4 vols., 1934–35). There are an immense number of books about the military operations. Two useful recent studies are K. P. Williams, *Lincoln Finds a General* (3 vols., 1949–52) and T. H. Williams, *Lincoln and His Generals* (1952). B. I. Wiley, *The Life of Johnny Reb: The Common Soldier of the Confederacy* (1943), and *The Life of Billy Yank: The Common Soldier of the Union* (1952), describe the war as it appeared to those who fought in it.

Charleston, South Carolina. The split between the Northern and Southern wings of the party proved to be irreparable. Delegates from the cotton states demanded a platform repudiating popular sovereignty and calling for the protection of slavery in all territories by Federal law; and when the followers of Douglas refused to agree, a number of them withdrew from the convention. Since no candidate could now obtain the necessary two-thirds majority, the convention arranged to meet again at Baltimore in June. Attempts to re-establish unity were unsuccessful, and the Baltimore convention divided into two groups with two separate tickets. One group nominated Stephen A. Douglas on a popular-sovereignty platform, while the other demanded Federal protection of slavery in all territories and nominated John C. Breckinridge of Kentucky.

The Republicans met at Chicago in May. Declaring that "the normal condition of all the territory of the United States is that of freedom," their platform asserted that neither Congress nor any territorial legislature could legalize slavery in any territory. The platform also included a number of proposals for economic legislation which would benefit both the industrial Northeast and the agricultural West. The most important items were a protective tariff, the building of a transcontinental railroad, and a homestead act. Thus by combining the old Whig program of the tariff and internal improvements with Western demands for free public land, the Republicans appealed to both industrial and agrarian interests. All of these measures had been blocked during the 1850's by Southern control of the Federal government. The tariff had been lowered in 1846, and lowered again in 1857. A transcontinental railroad had been prevented by disputes between supporters of a southern and a northern route. Homestead legislation had been opposed by the South; and when a bill finally passed Congress in 1860, it was vetoed by Buchanan.

Thus the Republican platform indicated that much more was at stake than the limitation of slavery. This new Northern and Western combination wanted a government which would promote economic expansion. "Vote yourself a farm" proved to be the most popular of the Republican slogans.

The presidential nomination went to Abraham Lincoln on the third ballot. Several other party leaders, especially Seward and Chase, were much better known, but precisely for this reason they were more open to attack. Lincoln had made his reputation solely through his speeches about slavery, and little was known about his opinions on other subjects. He came, moreover, from the key state of Illinois, which had voted Democratic at the previous election. Selected because he was the most available candidate, he was not expected, except by those who knew him intimately, to provide strong leadership. Very few men have been nominated for the presidency with such a limited experience of national politics.

A fourth candidate was put into the field by a group who called themselves the Constitutional Union Party. Consisting mainly of former

Whigs, they emphasized the preservation of the Union by compromise and said as little as possible about slavery. In the hope of appealing to both sections, they nominated John Bell of Tennessee for the presidency and Edward Everett of Massachusetts for the vice-presidency.

In the North, where the race was mainly between Lincoln and Douglas, Lincoln ran ahead in every state. He carried all the electoral votes of all the free states except New Jersey, which gave three of its seven votes to Douglas. This meant that, no matter how the South voted, Lincoln had a clear majority of the electoral college. In the South the main contest was between Breckinridge and Bell; Douglas did poorly except in the border state of Missouri, while Lincoln was not even on the ballot in ten Southern states. In general, those people voted for Bell who had most reason for fearing a civil war; he carried Virginia, Kentucky, and Tennessee, the states where such a war would probably be fought, and received strong support from the richer and more conservative planters in the Gulf states. But the mass of the Southern population voted for Breckinridge, who carried eleven states. Thus the election seemed to indicate that a majority of the voters in each section were now opposed to compromise.

The vote in the electoral college was as follows:

Lincoln	180
Breckinridge	72
Bell	39
Douglas	12

On the other hand, the popular vote was:

Lincoln	1,866,352
Douglas	1,375,157
Breckinridge	845,763
Bell	589,581

Thus Lincoln had less than 40 per cent of the popular vote; yet since almost all his support was concentrated in the North, he would still have been elected President even if his opponents had combined their forces behind a single candidate.

The Formation of the Confederacy.   Many Southern leaders had decided long before the election that they would not remain in the Union under a Republican president. They began to take action as soon as the results were announced. The South Carolina legislature ordered the election of a state convention, which adopted an ordinance of secession on December 20. By an unanimous vote it declared that "the Union now subsisting between South Carolina and other States . . . is hereby dissolved." Before the end of February 1861, similar action had been taken by six other states, all of them in the cotton belt: Mississippi, Florida, Alabama, Georgia, Louisiana, and Texas. During February a congress met at Montgomery, Alabama, adopted a provisional constitution for the Confederate States of America, and chose Jefferson Davis of Mississippi and Alexander Stephens of Georgia as provisional President and Vice-President. The eight other slave states, the most important of which was Virginia, took no action at this time and waited to see what the new administration in Washington would decide to do.

Southern leaders regarded secession as legally justifiable because of their states' rights theory of the Constitution; sovereignty, they declared, belonged to the states, not to the Federal Union. This constitutional theory has led to much legal hair-splitting; and since it was never the real issue between North and South, it seems unprofitable to discuss it. In practice, minority sections (such as New England during the War of 1812) have always tried to limit Federal power by adopting a states' rights attitude. The main reason for secession, according to the official statements of the Southern states, was that the North was violating the rights of Southerners by excluding them from the territories, refusing to restore their fugitive slaves, and threatening the institution of slavery itself. It would appear, therefore, that the South seceded because of Northern opposition to slavery. We may suppose that Southerners were also concerned about the threat of a high tariff and other legislation favorable to Northern economic interests; but this was not listed among the reasons for secession.

In every state except South Carolina, secession was opposed by strong minority groups, led by some of the most sagacious Southern statesmen (such as Sam Houston in Texas), who argued that its dangers outweighed any possible advantages. But the dominant elements in the cotton states, swayed more by emotion than by calculation, refused to accept as president a man who had publicly declared slavery to be evil and whom they regarded as little better than an abolitionist. Some of them, moreover, were looking forward to expansionist policies which had been impossible as long as the South remained in the Union; they expected the Confederacy to reopen the African slave trade and thereby lower the price of slaves, and to acquire new land for cotton plantations in Cuba and Central America. Believing Northern society to be inherently unwarlike, interested mainly in making money, and largely dependent upon cotton for its prosperity, they did not expect that any serious effort would be made to prevent secession. They counted also on British assistance, in the belief that Great Britain could not survive without Southern cotton.

Reactions in Washington.   It seemed at first that Southern hopes of peaceful secession were going to be realized. Buchanan was still President until March 4, 1861; and his official attitude was that while secession was unconstitutional, the Federal government had no constitutional power to prevent it. He therefore took no action against the Confederacy and (being a devout Presbyterian) resorted mainly to prayer. In January, however, after several Southerners had left his Cabinet, he replaced them with strong Union men, and the administration then acquired a little more backbone. The Confederacy had assumed control of most Federal property within its borders, but two island forts, Sumter in South Carolina and Pickens in Florida, were still held by Federal troops, and Buchanan refused to surrender them. Public opinion in the North had not yet crystallized, and while some people denounced Buchanan for his weakness and sighed for a few days of Andrew Jackson, others, including some Republican spokesmen and some abolitionists, seemed to favor letting "the erring sisters go in peace." When, on January 11, Confederate batteries fired on a Northern vessel, *The Star of the West*, which was trying to reinforce Fort Sumter, this act of war caused no particular excitement.

Meanwhile, political leaders in Congress were frantically endeavoring to work out some kind of compromise which would induce the Confederate states to change their mind. The most promising of these efforts was primarily the work of Senator John J. Crittenden of Kentucky, a widely respected elder statesman who had inherited the mantle of Henry Clay. Crittenden proposed a series of amendments to the Constitution, the most important of which would have provided for the re-establishment of the Missouri Compromise and the extension of the Missouri line to the Pacific, and for the payment of compensation by the Federal government to owners of uncaptured fugitive slaves. Compromise plans were also put forward by a committee of the House of Representatives and by a peace convention of twenty-one states sponsored by the legislature of Virginia. Crittenden's proposals had considerable popular support in the North; but Lincoln, though willing to promise enforcement of the Fugitive Slave Act and to guarantee the South against any interference with slavery where it was already established, refused to accept any retreat from the Republican position on slavery in the territories. Believing (as he had declared in 1858) that agitation would continue until "a crisis shall have been reached and passed," he was convinced that any further compromises of this basic issue would merely postpone the final showdown; no permanent settlement could be achieved by giving way to Southern demands. The Republicans therefore refused to agree to the restoration of the Missouri Compromise.

Thus no definite action was taken by any branch of the Federal government prior to Lincoln's inauguration. The country waited to see what policy would be adopted by this little-known Illinois lawyer who, with no previous executive experience, assumed the presidency of the United States during the greatest crisis in its history.

The War Begins. In his inaugural address Lincoln was careful not to slam the door against peaceful restoration of the Union. He asserted that the Southern states had no constitutional right to secede, and that the different sections were so closely bound together by geographical and other ties that peaceful separation was impossible, and declared that "the power confided to me will be used to hold, occupy, and possess the property and places belonging to the Government, and to collect the duties and imposts." But he made it plain that the Union government would not commit the first act of war, and urged the Southern states to change their mind before it was too late.

The inauguration was followed by a month of hesitation. The immediate issue before the administration was whether to reinforce Pickens and Sumter, but in spite of his statement that he would hold the places belonging to the government, Lincoln was reluctant to precipitate a crisis. He had also to consider the attitude of the eight slave states still in the Union, which might join the Confederacy if he acted rashly. Nor did he receive much help from his Cabinet. Seward had become Secretary of State and expected to dominate the administration; but Seward's chief contribution at this point was a suggestion that the government immediately pick a quarrel with several European powers and restore the Union by means of a foreign war.

On April 6 Lincoln finally ordered relief expeditions to be sent to the two forts. It was now Jefferson Davis's turn to make up his mind; and after much hesitation he ordered General Pierre G. T. Beauregard, commanding at Charleston, to open fire on Fort Sumter if this was necessary to prevent reinforcement. Beauregard's forces started the shooting on April 12, and two days later the fort surrendered. By this time public opinion in the North was ready to follow Lincoln's leadership, and the firing on Fort Sumter (unlike that on *The Star of the West* in January) provoked a burst of popular indignation. Lincoln, on his own responsibility (Congress was not called into session until July), called for 75,000 volunteers to enforce the laws of the United States and ordered a blockade of Confederate seaports. Thus war had begun.

The eight remaining slave states now had to decide which side they were on. Four of them, Virginia, North Carolina, Tennessee, and Arkansas, voted to join the Confederacy, and the capital was then moved from Montgomery, Alabama, to Richmond, Virginia. The western counties of Virginia, however, refused to go with the rest of the state, and in 1863 were admitted into the Union as the new state of West Virginia. The other four slave states, Maryland, Delaware, Kentucky, and Missouri, remained officially with the North, although a number of their citizens fought on the Southern side. Maryland might, in fact, have seceded if the administration had not sent in Federal troops, suspended habeas corpus, and arrested Confederate sympathizers in the state. This was done in defiance of the Supreme Court, still headed by Roger Taney, which held the suspension of habeas corpus to be a violation of the Constitution.

Reasons for the War.   Why did the North resolve to prevent secession by force? The reasons for the Civil War must be carefully distinguished from the reasons for the secession of the Confederacy, and are

PRESIDENT LINCOLN ON THE BATTLEFIELD OF ANTIETAM

By the famous Civil War photographer, Mathew B. Brady (1823–96). The other figures are Allan Pinkerton, founder of the detective agency, and General J. A. McClernand.

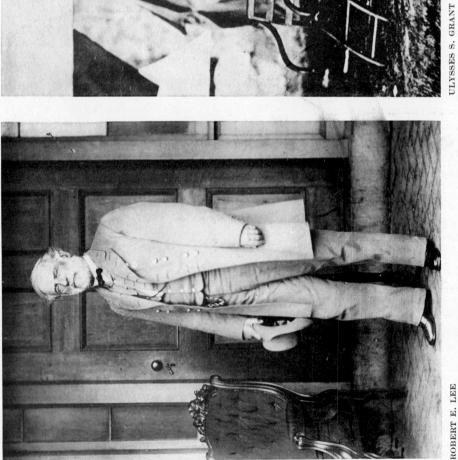

ROBERT E. LEE

These photographs are by Brady. A native of New York, Brady tried to make a complete photographic record of the Civil War as well as portraits of all the famous men of his time. He was one of

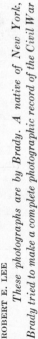

ULYSSES S. GRANT

the first photographers to show the artistic possibilities of this new medium, which had been invented in France in 1837.

less easy to formulate. The Southern states seceded, according to their own statements, to maintain slavery; but the North fought the war in order to preserve the Union. Lincoln was at all times careful to explain that the Union was the central issue and that the North was not fighting to abolish slavery, even though its abolition might be a necessary result of the war.

The North had some economic motives for defending the Union. An independent Confederacy, closely associated with Great Britain, would mean the loss of a profitable market for Northern business. However, it was not the businessmen of the Northeast, but the farmers of the Middle West, who gave most enthusiastic support to Lincoln in defending the Union. The Middle West was strongly nationalistic, and identified American nationalism with the ideals of freedom and democracy. The dissolution of the United States into two separate and probably hostile confederations would prove that popular government was too weak to maintain itself and would put an end to the hopes which had animated the American republic since its foundation.

This was Lincoln's view of the central issue, and this was why, in all his major statements, most memorably in the Gettysburg Address, he insisted that what was at stake was democratic government. As he remarked to his private secretary, "For my own part, I consider the central idea pervading this struggle is the necessity of proving that popular government is not an absurdity. We must settle this question now, whether, in a free government, the minority have the right to break up the government whenever they choose. If we fail, it will go far to prove the incapability of the people to govern themselves."

Resources of the Two Sides. As is usually the case at the beginning of a war, most people on each side underestimated their opponents and expected a quick victory. Yet the struggle was to last four years and cost more than 600,000 lives.

The North had greater potential strength. There were nearly 19,000,000 people in the nineteen free states and another 3,000,000 (including 400,000 slaves) in the four border states. The eleven states in the Confederacy had only 6,500,000 white people, along with 3,500,000 slaves. Nearly 2,000,000 soldiers served in the Northern army, as compared with only about 800,000 in the Confederate army. In industrial equipment and transportation facilities the North had an overwhelming superiority.

On the other hand, the Confederacy had some strong initial advantages. She enjoyed the military advantage of possessing the inner lines; at the outset of the war she had much the better generals; her citizens, being more accustomed to outdoor life and to shooting and horseback riding, required less training to become excellent soldiers; and her armies were fighting on their own territories in defense of their homes and their way of life. But as the struggle continued, the North was increasingly able to make her potential strength effective, while the Confederacy could not replace her losses in man power and supplies.

The North won the war in the end partly because, by controlling the sea, she was able to blockade Confederate ports and impose an economic strangulation, and partly because her armies could afford to take much greater punishment in battle.

2. BEHIND THE LINES

The Confederate Government. Both the Union and the Confederate government faced the problem of organizing all their available resources for war, while at the same time maintaining constitutional processes. Both Lincoln and Davis had to deal with vigorous opposition, and both of them were accused of being dictators.

The constitution of the Confederacy was modeled on that of the United States, with a few minor changes. More emphasis was laid on the rights of states, and slavery was to be protected. The president was limited to one six-year term; the members of his Cabinet were to sit in Congress; and the power of Congress to appropriate money against the wishes of the executive was limited.

The chief political problem in the Confederacy was the conflict between Southern nationalism and states' rights theory. If the war was to be carried on effectively, the Confederate government must assume very broad powers. But Southerners had been accustomed to justify their opposition to Federal extensions of authority by arguing that sovereignty remained with the individual states, and some of them maintained the same attitude under the Confederacy. If the South was fighting for states' rights, then a consolidation of power in Richmond was almost as bad as a Union victory. This view was held by Vice-President Stephens, who was not on speaking terms with Davis through most of the war, and by several state governors, particularly those of North Carolina and Georgia. State opposition made it difficult for the Confederate government to make the most effective use of man power and supplies.

Jefferson Davis did not have the qualities needed for winning loyal cooperation. A man of courage, integrity, and proved administrative ability, he had seemed ideally suited for the presidency. Unfortunately for the Confederacy, he proved to be lacking in the physical and emotional stamina required for leadership in critical times. He was a poor judge of men, and opposition made him increasingly nervous and querulous. Nor did his Cabinet compensate for his deficiencies. After the first few months it contained no members of the planter aristocracy and consisted mostly of obscure figures who inspired little confidence. It was indicative of the strained relations within the Confederate government that Davis vetoed no less than thirty-eight bills passed by the Confederate Congress, and that in thirty-seven instances his veto was overridden.

Conscription in the Confederacy. The Confederate army was raised by voluntary enlistments until March, 1862, when conscription was adopted. Men between the ages of eighteen and thirty-five were then declared subject to the draft, although planters or overseers in charge of twenty or more Negroes might be exempted. By the end of the war the age limits had been expanded to seventeen and fifty. There was considerable opposition to the draft in the Appalachian mountain country, where people were hostile to the planter aristocracy and determined to have as little to do with the war as possible. Some of the state governments, moreover, regarded the draft as an infringement of their rights. The Chief Justice of North Carolina even discharged two deserters who had killed an officer while resisting capture. But throughout most of the South, especially in the plantation regions, public opinion was so enthusiastic for the Confederate cause that conscription was scarcely needed. It was taken as a matter of course that all men of military age would volunteer for service, while the operation of the plantations was largely left to the women.

Confederate Finance. In financing the war, the Confederate government relied mainly on simple inflation. It sold bonds, and collected about $100,000,000 in taxes, some of which were paid in the form not of money but of foodstuffs for army use; but the South, as an agrarian society, had always lacked financial resources. About $1,000,000,000 of paper money was issued by the Confederate government during the war, and much more by the state governments. The paper depreciated steadily in value, and at the end of the war became entirely worthless. As always happens under such circumstances, the sharp price rises encouraged speculation and profiteering. Most Southerners loyally did their duty, and the South as a whole was ruined by the war; but there were a few individuals who grew richer from the catastrophe.

Politics in the North. Few people at the outset of the war would have predicted that the political leadership of the Union would prove superior to that of the Confederacy; yet Lincoln, in spite of his inexperience, was a much better war president than Davis. In his choice of generals and views of war strategy he sometimes made serious mistakes. But unlike Davis, he had an intuitive understanding of the moods and sentiments of the mass of the people, and knew how to inspire confidence and enthusiasm; and his sense of humor and extraordinary selflessness enabled him to accept criticism and tolerate opposition. Knowing when to make decisions and stick by them and when to give way, combining courage and integrity in the defense of principles with suppleness and flexibility in matters of detail, he provided an almost perfect example of leadership in a democratic society.

Lincoln's Cabinet included several men who had been his rivals for the Republican nomination and who continued to feel that they were better qualified for guiding national policy. Although Seward quickly recognized Lincoln's merits, Secretary of the Treasury Chase intrigued with party leaders in Congress in the hope of obtaining the nomination for 1864. Edwin H. Stanton, who became Secretary of War in January 1862, was another troublemaker—hard-working and an excellent administrator, but bad-mannered and outspokenly contemptuous of everybody else in the government. Lincoln showed extraordinary skill in persuading this very inharmonious team to work together and in making the best use of their abilities. After the first few months there was never any doubt that he was the master of his administration.

In Congress, Lincoln's policies were vigorously criticized by a group of Republican leaders who became known as Radicals. Including Thaddeus Stevens of Pennsylvania, Ben Wade of Ohio, and Charles Sumner of Massachusetts, they complained that the war was not being fought with enough vigor. At a later date they opposed Lincoln's mild reconstruction program and demanded stern vengeance upon the South and the destruction of the planter aristocracy. Early in 1862 they brought about the appointment of a Congressional Joint Committee on the Conduct of the War, the purpose of which was to point out the mistakes of the administration and force Lincoln to give Congress greater authority over military affairs. Lincoln, however, insisted that the conduct of the war was an executive responsibility; and although the Radicals continued to denounce him as incompetent, timid, and too lenient toward the South, they were never able to dictate policies.

As soon as the war started, most of the Northern Democrats rallied to the support of the Union, a patriotic example being set by Stephen A. Douglas (who died in June 1861). In the elections of 1862 and 1864, joint Union tickets made up of both Republicans and War Democrats were nominated in a number of states. Some Democratic leaders, on the other hand, advocated a negotiated peace; and a few, especially in those sections of the Middle West that had originally been settled from Virginia and Kentucky, were definitely sympathetic to the Confederacy.

These "Copperheads" were too active to be ignored, although suppressing them meant an infringement of civil liberties. Lincoln decided that men who opposed a war fought in defense of constitutional government were not entitled to be protected by the constitution; and in the autumn of 1862 he proclaimed that persons "guilty of any disloyal practice affording aid and comfort to rebels" should be tried by court-martial and denied the protection of habeas corpus. Under this order more than 13,000 persons were arrested and imprisoned by military authority. The most prominent victim was a Democratic political leader from Ohio, Clement L. Vallandigham. Sentenced to prison, Vallandigham was by Lincoln's orders dumped inside the Confederate lines instead. He then escaped to Canada, where he ran *in absentia* for the governorship of Ohio but was decisively defeated. Yet in spite of the denial of constitutional liberty to Copperheads, the government was very far from being dictatorial, and there was no serious mass hysteria. In most parts of the North men continued to express their opinions freely.

Conscription in the North. After relying for nearly two years on voluntary enlistment, the Union resorted to conscription in March 1863. The country was divided into districts, and each district was responsible for supplying its quota, allowance being made for the volunteers already provided. If a district could fill its quota through volunteering, it was exempt from the draft. Men between the ages of twenty and forty-five were liable to be called, but any individual could avoid service by paying $300 or hiring a substitute.

Thus wealthy men could easily secure exemption, particularly since in the North (unlike the Confederacy) there was no strong pressure from public opinion; young men who evaded service did not generally suffer in the esteem of their neighbors. The hiring of substitutes also led to many abuses. "Bounty-jumpers" would collect the "bounty" paid to a substitute to enlist, desert as soon as possible, and then repeat the process in another district. Meanwhile, poorer districts, unable to hire substitutes, complained that they had to provide more than their share of recruits. Enforcement of the draft in New York City, in July 1863, led to an outbreak of rioting in which hundreds of lives were lost and millions of dollars' worth of damage was done.

The provisions for exemption were afterwards abolished; but throughout the war relatively few individuals were forcibly inducted into the Union army. Many districts were able to fill their quotas by other methods, including not only genuine voluntary enlistment but also wholesale importations of immigrants from Canada and from European countries. During the two years following the Draft Act, the army obtained 835,000 men under the category of voluntary enlistments; 285,000 men evaded service by paying commutation or providing substitutes; and only 46,000 men were actually drafted.

Union Finance. The total cost of the war to the North was about $3,000,000,000. The government raised the tariff, imposed a great variety of excise duties, and collected (for the first time in American history) an income tax; but taxation during the four years of the war brought in only $660,000,000. Between February 1862 and March 1863 some $450,000,000 of paper money was issued. These "greenbacks" quickly depreciated, so that during the gloomiest period of the war a paper dollar was worth only thirty-nine cents in gold. But the main reliance of the Treasury Department was on the sale of war bonds. The later issues were handled by the leading banker in the country, Jay Cooke of Philadelphia, who made a tidy profit for himself but was very successful, through elaborate publicity campaigns, in persuading the public to buy them. Nearly two-thirds of the government's expenses were met by the sale of bonds.

South had better had better generals at start (handwritten margin note)

3. FROM BULL RUN TO GETTYSBURG

Military Leadership and Strategy.   At the beginning of the war the Confederacy could count on the services of most of the ablest officers in the United States army, including particularly Robert E. Lee, who has universally been regarded as one of the greatest soldiers and noblest characters in American history. Lee disapproved of slavery, but felt that he must support his native state of Virginia. Jefferson Davis, however, had an inflated idea of his own military capacity and never gave his generals a free hand. Lee was first military adviser to Davis and then commander of the armies in Virginia; he was not given command of all the Confederate forces until almost the end of the war.

Lincoln, on the other hand, was very willing to give full authority to his generals, but could find able leaders only by a costly process of trial and error. Most of the army officers who had remained loyal to the Union proved to have little competence, and the North had to discover new generals among men who had been in civilian life. The best of them were West Pointers who had served in the Mexican War but had left the army during the 1850's, although high commands were also given to several politicians with no military experience.

From a military point of view, the Confederacy should probably have taken the offensive early in the war, while the North should have remained on the defensive until she had effectively mobilized her man power and economic resources. Political considerations, however, made both these courses of action impossible. Since the Confederacy was fighting not to destroy the North but merely to maintain her independence, her armies waited to be attacked. In the North, on the other hand, public opinion quickly grew impatient and demanded action in the hope that a quick thrust at the Confederate capital at Richmond would end the war. Union armies therefore made a series of invasions of Virginia in which they suffered heavy casualties and for a long time made no substantial gains. In actuality, the more decisive theater of war proved to be the Mississippi Valley, where the Union forces, relatively early in the war, drove deep into the heart of the Confederacy and succeeded eventually in cutting it into two sections. But neither government sufficiently appreciated the importance of these operations in the West.

Operations in 1861.   The first of the attempts to invade Virginia was made in July 1861 under the leadership of General Irvin McDowell. The Northern army met Confederate forces under Beauregard and Joseph Johnston at Bull Run. Both armies consisted mostly of raw recruits, and both of them were quickly thrown into complete confusion. The Confederates, however, held their lines more successfully, largely owing to the firmness of a brigade commanded by Thomas J. Jackson, who earned here his title "Stonewall"; and the battle ended in a disorderly and panic-stricken flight of the Union forces back to Washington.

The North now began to realize for the first time that the war could not be ended in a few days. For the remainder of the year there were no important military operations, and Northern energies were concentrated on the task of training, organizing, and equipping an army. McDowell was replaced by George B. McClellan, who became in November general-in-chief of all Union forces. Only thirty-four years of age, McClellan had served in the Mexican War and had afterwards become a railroad executive. He proved to be admirably suited for the immediate task, and the Army of the Potomac developed into a superb fighting force. But Mc-Clellan's qualifications for military leadership were more open to question; when the time for action came, he seemed reluctant to risk the army he had created by committing it to battle. He made many enemies, moreover, by his arrogance and outspoken contempt for all politicians; Lincoln could tolerate McClellan's insults as long as he felt that he was being useful to the cause, but other men in Washington were less forgiving.

The Blockade. Meanwhile, the North was establishing a blockade of the Confederate coast which became steadily more effective. Almost the whole of the United States navy remained loyal to the Union, and during the war it was greatly enlarged. Northern military forces, moreover, helped to maintain the blockade by seizing a number of bases on islands and headlands in Confederate territory.

The Confederacy was never completely isolated from the rest of the world. Blockade-runners continued to bring supplies from Europe to Southern ports, especially to Charleston and Wilmington. But from the beginning of the war the volume of trade was drastically below peacetime levels, and the Confederacy soon began to suffer from severe scarcities, particularly of clothing and medical supplies. On the other hand, she was able to manufacture or import enough war material, and to grow enough food, although the collapse of her transportation system eventually made it impossible to distribute it where it was needed. In retaliation, Confederate commerce-raiders, the most successful being the *Alabama*, were able to destroy more than 250 Northern merchant ships.

Western Campaigns in 1862. The year 1862 opened with Union successes in the West. Two headquarters had been created, at Cincinnati under Don Carlos Buell and at St. Louis under Henry W. Halleck. Neither Buell nor Halleck displayed much offensive spirit, but each man had an able subordinate. Forces in Buell's command, led by George H. Thomas (a native of Virginia, but loyal to the Union), drove the enemy from eastern Kentucky. Farther to the west a detachment of Halleck's army, led by Ulysses Simpson Grant, captured Fort Henry and Fort Donelson and thereby won control of a large part of western Tennessee. In April, Grant was attacked by Confederate forces at Shiloh, but after a bloody and hard-fought battle succeeded in holding his ground, partly because of the death of the Confederate commander, Albert Sidney Johnston. Grant then occupied Memphis, but was prevented by Halleck from following up

14. The Civil War

WHILE THE BLOCKADE OF THE UNION NAVY PREVENTED THE CONFEDERACY FROM receiving supplies from abroad, Union armies hammered a series of holes in Confederate territories. Much of the fighting centered around three key cities: Vicksburg, Chattanooga, and Richmond.

In the West the Union sought to capture the whole line of the Mississippi, in order to cut off the three Western states of Arkansas, Louisiana, and Texas from the main body of the Confederacy. In the spring of 1862 forces led by Grant won control of western Tennessee, and Admiral Farragut captured New Orleans from the sea and took his ships up the river as far as Vicksburg. But the Confederacy was able to hold Vicksburg for another year and thus maintain communications with the West. Capture of the city in July, 1863, by Grant's army, aided by naval forces under David D. Porter, was the first major Union victory.

Chattanooga, lying on the Tennessee River in southeastern Tennessee, was an even more vital communications center. As long as the Confederates held it, they could hope to advance up the valley of the Tennessee into Kentucky and threaten Ohio. Control of it by the Union would make possible a swing down into the lower South or across the Appalachians into Georgia. Union forces under Buell advanced into Kentucky and eastern Tennessee in 1862 but won no decisive victories. In the summer of 1863 Rosecrans, who had replaced Buell, captured Chattanooga, but was then defeated and besieged. Grant, coming east from the Mississippi, crushed the Confederate offensive and thus prepared the way for Sherman's march across the mountains into Georgia in the following year.

Richmond, the most bitterly contested of the three cities, was valued largely for reasons of prestige, as the capital of the Confederacy, although it was also important as the seat of the Tredegar Iron Works, chief source of Confederate munitions. McClellan's attempt to capture Richmond from the east in the spring and summer of 1862 was unsuccessful. Union armies then tried to fight their way south from Washington. Invasions of Virginia by Pope, Burnside, and Hooker were defeated. Lee made two thrusts into the North and was checked at Antietam in September, 1862, and at Gettysburg, in July, 1863. Richmond was finally captured by Grant in April, 1865.

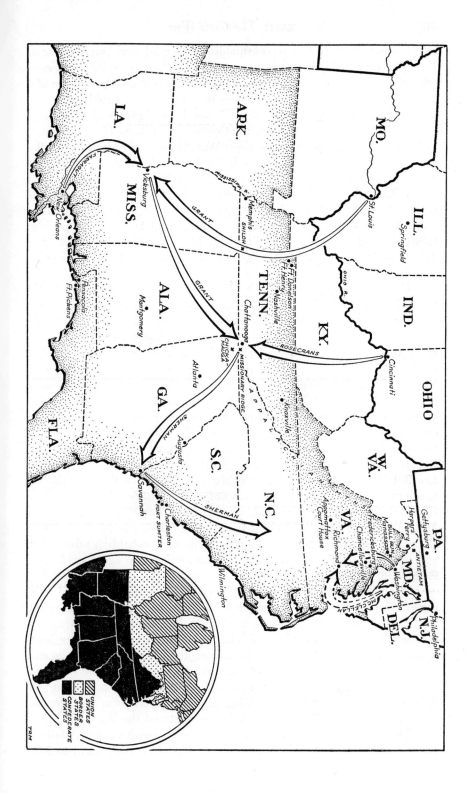

his victories. Meanwhile, a naval squadron under Admiral David Glasgow Farragut captured New Orleans, which was then occupied by Union troops. Thus, within a few months, the North had secured possession of a large part of the Mississippi, although the Confederacy could still maintain communications with the West through the fortress of Vicksburg.

These events attracted public attention to General Grant. A West Pointer and a veteran of the Mexican War, Grant had resigned from the army in 1854, and had subsequently tried several different occupations and failed at all of them. At the outset of the Civil War the need for men with military experience enabled him to obtain the colonelcy of an Illinois regiment, after which his rise was rapid. He soon demonstrated that he understood military strategy and was willing to make decisions quickly, take risks, and accept responsibility, while his aggressive spirit and dogged determination, so unlike the caution of McClellan, made him a popular favorite.

Eastern Campaigns of 1862.   Pressure from the government finally forced McClellan into action in the spring. During the months of March and April 1862 the bulk of the Army of the Potomac landed on the Virginia coast between the York and James Rivers and began an advance westwards toward Richmond which eventually brought them within five miles of the city. Union strategy also called for a simultaneous invasion of Virginia from the north by troops under McDowell. The Confederacy prevented McDowell from moving by sending Stonewall Jackson on raids up the Shenandoah Valley and thereby threatening Washington; and then concentrated on McClellan. In June, Lee took command of the Confederate army in the field, replacing Joseph Johnston, who had been wounded. Between June 26 and July 1 were fought the Seven Days' battles between Lee and McClellan. McClellan was driven back towards the seacoast but was by no means defeated, and the Confederates suffered heavier casualties. But the Union government, by this time thoroughly suspicious of McClellan's will to fight, decided that he had failed, and he was ordered to bring his army back to Washington. This was probably a mistake; it was two and a half years before the Union armies were again so close to Richmond.

McClellan had already been stripped of his command of all Union forces. This position was now given to Halleck, who had received credit for Grant's victories in the West, while John Pope replaced McDowell as commander in northern Virginia. The threat to Richmond having been removed, Lee marched northwards, thoroughly defeated Pope at the end of August in the battle of Manassas, also known as the second battle of Bull Run, and crossed the Potomac west of Washington, hoping to win Maryland for the Confederate cause, invade Pennsylvania, and cut the railroad connections between the Atlantic coast and the West.

The North was now in imminent danger of decisive defeat. Halleck proved incapable of meeting the crisis, so Lincoln turned again to Mc-

Clellan, who was given command of all troops around Washington. On September 17 McClellan met Lee at Antietam; and while neither side could claim a victory, Lee was so hard hit that he had to fall back into Virginia. Failing to pursue him, McClellan again demonstrated (in Lincoln's opinion) his lack of fighting spirit. He was dismissed soon after the battle and never again held a command.

Emancipation. Antietam was followed by the Emancipation Proclamation. Since the outset of the war Lincoln had been under pressure from radicals to make the war a crusade for the abolition of slavery; but he had felt at first that the government would lose more than it would gain by such a policy. An attack on slavery might alienate the four slave states that had not seceded and antagonize many Northern conservatives. As the war progressed, however, it became obvious that Northern victory would, in practice, mean the end of slavery. In any part of the Confederacy that was occupied by Northern troops the slaves promptly left the plantations and became camp-followers of the Northern armies. Emancipation would enable the North to make use of the services of the Negroes. It would also be of great value in winning the support of liberal opinion in Europe.

On September 22, therefore, Lincoln proclaimed, in his capacity as commander-in-chief of the army, that "on the first day of January, A.D. 1863, all persons held as slaves within any state or designated part of a state the people whereof shall then be in rebellion against the United States shall be then, thenceforward, and forever free." This did not mean the complete and final abolition of slavery, which was accomplished by the Thirteenth Amendment in 1865. But henceforth, in all Confederate territories occupied by Northern troops, the slaves were declared free. Ultimately about 150,000 freed Negroes enlisted in the Northern army, and many of them performed good service in some of the later battles.

The proclamation, however, had few immediate good results. Many Northerners felt that, by making a negotiated peace impossible, it would needlessly prolong the war. In the Congressional elections of 1862 the Democrats almost captured the House of Representatives; and while some of them were strong Union men, others had appealed to anti-war sentiment. Meanwhile, the Confederacy continued to win victories.

Campaigns of 1863. McClellan's immediate successor was Ambrose E. Burnside. In December 1862 Burnside invaded Virginia and was decisively defeated by Lee at Fredericksburg. The command was then switched to Hooker, known as "Fighting Joe." Hooker met his fate in May 1863, when Lee crushed him at Chancellorsville (a dearly bought victory for the Confederacy since Stonewall Jackson was killed).

After these two convincing demonstrations of his military genius, Lee for a second time crossed the Potomac in order to carry the war into the North, and before the end of June his army was in Pennsylvania. Hooker was replaced by George G. Meade, who met Lee at Gettysburg. For three days, July 1, 2, and 3, Lee launched a series of attacks on the Northern lines, but failed to break them; and after suffering heavy losses he was compelled to retreat. Although the Union army was too hard hit to pursue him, it had won a decisive victory. This was the last time that the Confederates were able to invade the North or came near to winning the war.

In the West, meanwhile, Grant had been gaining advantages which more than counterbalanced Lee's triumphs at Fredericksburg and Chancellorsville. Succeeding Halleck as Union commander in western Tennessee in the summer of 1862, he defeated a Confederate offensive and, in the following spring, began an attack on Vicksburg, the one remaining Confederate stronghold on the Mississippi River. After several months of arduous campaigning, he succeeded in bottling up the defending Confederate army and surrounding the city, and on July 4 he compelled it to surrender. This meant that the North now had control of the whole river. The Confederacy could no longer obtain troops and supplies from the trans-Mississippi states, which henceforth were virtually out of the war. At the same time General William Rosecrans, who had replaced Buell, was fighting his way down into eastern Tennessee; and though he was unable to defeat his Confederate opponent, Braxton Bragg, he occupied in September the strategically located railroad center of Chattanooga.

Gettysburg and Vicksburg were the main turning-points of the war. The Confederacy had by no means lost her fighting spirit. Nearly two more years of bitter conflict were needed before the Southern armies were willing to accept defeat. But after July 1863 only a miracle could have given them victory.

4. DIPLOMACY OF THE WAR

British Attitudes.   The chief diplomatic question at the outset of the war was whether Great Britain would intervene on behalf of the Confederacy. One-fifth of her population derived their livelihood, directly or indirectly, from the manufacture of cotton textiles, and four-fifths of the raw material was normally imported from the United States. Southerners therefore assumed that Britain's need for cotton would cause her to come to their assistance, or at all events to put pressure on the North to abandon the blockade of Southern ports. In fact, in 1861 they actually stopped the export of cotton themselves and burned a large part of that year's crop, instead of attempting to run it through the blockade.

Cotton, however, proved to be less influential than the Confederacy expected. In 1861 the British manufacturers had a surplus of raw material and were only too glad of the opportunity to dispose of it, particularly since the threat of a shortage enabled them to raise their prices by 300 or 400 per cent. The pinch did not begin until 1863, and by that time it was plain that the Confederacy had already lost the war. Meanwhile, the British were doing a heavy volume of trade with the North. A series of bad harvests caused them to buy increasing quantities of grain from Middle Western farmers, while the war needs of the Union caused a boom in the steel, munitions, and shipbuilding industries. Thus Great Britain had strong economic inducements for remaining neutral.

British opinion agreed, in general, with Lincoln's interpretation of the basic issue of the war, believing that a Union victory would be a victory for democracy. The British upper classes, who were struggling to check the advance of democracy at home, were therefore strongly sympathetic to the Confederacy. The middle and lower classes, on the other hand, mostly favored the North, especially after the Emancipation Proclamation made it plain that a Northern victory would mean the abolition of slavery. British liberal and radical leaders and visitors from the United States (such as Henry Ward Beecher and Harriet Beecher Stowe) aroused mass sentiment on behalf of the North by making speeches and organizing propaganda campaigns. Although the British government at first showed Confederate sympathies, it was soon compelled to recognize that intervention would be very unpopular with the mass of the British people.

The blockade resulted in considerable interference with British shipping. In fact, the Union navy not only prevented British ships from trading directly with Confederate ports but also seized a number of cargoes bound for the Bahamas, claiming that they were ultimately destined for the use of the Confederacy. But British officials did not wish to make an issue of the blockade. Whenever Great Britain was at war, she was accustomed to use her sea power to interfere with neutral trade. Looking ahead to future contingencies, the British felt that it would be unwise to establish precedents which might one day be cited against them. British interests required a broad interpretation of the powers of a blockading navy and a narrow interpretation of neutral rights of trade.

Diplomatic Crises. On two occasions, nevertheless, there seemed to be real danger of war. The first was in November 1861, when James M. Mason and John Slidell, bound for Europe as diplomatic agents for the Confederacy, were removed from the British passenger ship *Trent* by a Union warship. The British government, forgetting how the British navy had treated American merchant ships during the Napoleonic Wars, claimed that this was contrary to international law and demanded the release of the two men. Although Northern public opinion was strongly aroused, Lincoln and Seward wisely decided to give way, and Mason and Slidell were allowed to proceed to Europe. Actually they accomplished little for the Confederacy. The Union minister in London, Charles Francis Adams (son of John Quincy Adams), proved to be a much abler diplomat.

The second crisis was caused by the building, in British shipyards, of warships for the use of the Confederacy. International law prohibited the sale of warships to a belligerent, but not of merchant ships. Most of the Confederate commerce-raiders were built in Britain; but since the ships were not equipped for war until after they had left British waters, the British government claimed that there was no violation of the letter of the law. But Adams repeatedly demanded action on the ground that the ultimate purpose of the ships was common knowledge. Eventually the British authorities accepted Adams's interpretation. They failed to prevent the *Alabama* from sailing in July 1862; [1] but in April 1863 they acted to prevent further building of cruisers. Adams then learned that two warships, known as the Laird Rams, were being constructed for a French company with the understanding that they be sold to the Confederacy after they had gone to sea. In September 1863 he told the British Foreign Secretary: "it would be superfluous in me to point out to your Lordship that this is war." Fortunately, the British government had already given orders to detain the rams.

The French in Mexico.   One other European power had a government strongly sympathetic to the Confederacy. This was France, then under the rule of Emperor Napoleon III. But Napoleon wanted a joint Anglo-French intervention and did not wish to act without the support of the British navy. In 1862, moreover, he took advantage of the temporary inability of the United States to enforce the Monroe Doctrine by sending an army to occupy Mexico. He planned to make Mexico a French dependency, controlled by French troops and exploited by French business interests, while an Austrian prince, Maximilian of Hapsburg, was to be set up as puppet emperor. If he had succeeded in this design, he would have been in a strong position to help the Confederacy.

Fortunately for the Union, the Mexican resistance under the leadership of President Benito Juárez was more vigorous than Napoleon had expected. In May 1862 the French army was defeated at Puebla. It was not until the summer of 1863 that the French were able to win control of any substantial part of the country, and not until the spring of 1864 that Maximilian was actually installed as emperor. Juárez continued to lead resistance forces, and the French troops were kept too busy to do anything for the Confederacy.

When the war in the United States ended, Secretary of State Seward took the Monroe Doctrine out of cold storage and requested the French to leave. Unwilling to risk a war with the United States at a time when France was threatened by the growing power of Prussia, Napoleon complied early in 1867. The Juárez government regained control of Mexico, while Maximilian, who had refused to leave along with the French army, was quickly captured and shot.

5. FROM GETTYSBURG TO APPOMATTOX

Union Victories in the West.   After Gettysburg there was no further fighting in the East until the following spring. Both armies needed

---

[1] By a treaty signed in 1871 Britain agreed to pay damages for this neglect of "due diligence." The amount was fixed by an international arbitration commission and amounted to $15,500,000.

time to recuperate, and Meade's forces were further weakened by the necessity of sending troops to New York to deal with the draft riots. But battles of decisive importance were fought in the West. Having cut the Confederacy in two by capturing Vicksburg, the Union forces now began to swing eastwards with the intention of crossing the mountains into Georgia and carrying the war into the Atlantic states.

Control of Chattanooga was essential to this operation, and for several months this was the main center of activity. A few days after Rosecrans had occupied it, he was defeated by Bragg at the battle of Chickamauga, his army being saved from destruction only by the brilliant leadership of his subordinate, General Thomas. Rosecrans's forces were then surrounded and besieged in the city. In October, Grant was given command of all Union armies in the West. He dismissed Rosecrans and ordered Thomas to hold the city at all costs until he could come to the rescue; and in November, in the battle of Chattanooga, he won a decisive victory over Bragg's army, which was thrown back towards Atlanta.

In March 1864 Grant was called to Washington as general-in-chief of all the Union armies. William T. Sherman became commander in the West, and through the spring and summer was gradually fighting his way across the mountains from Tennessee into the plains of Georgia, skillfully opposed by Joseph Johnston. Sherman finally captured Atlanta in September, after which the Confederate army, now commanded by John B. Hood, made a thrust at his line of communications in Tennessee in the hope that he would be compelled to retreat. But there were enough Union troops in Tennessee, under the command of General Thomas, to deal with this threat, and Hood was crushed at the battle of Nashville.

Meanwhile, Sherman, instead of retreating, boldly cut loose from his communications and began his famous march through Georgia to the sea. Unopposed by any Confederate army, the 60,000 Union troops cut a swath 300 miles long and 60 miles broad in which they systematically destroyed everything that could possibly be of use to the Confederacy. In this ruthless fashion the Atlantic states were cut off from the Gulf states, and the meaning of war was brought home to the civilian population of the Deep South. "I propose," Sherman declared, "to demonstrate the vulnerability of the South and make its inhabitants feel that war and individual ruin are synonymous terms."

Grant and Lee in Virginia. In the East, Grant was discovering that Lee was a much more skillful opponent than the generals he had crushed at Vicksburg and Chattanooga. With a superiority in man power of nearly two to one, he began another invasion of Virginia at the beginning of May 1864. By the middle of June, after a series of hard-fought battles (the Wilderness, Spottsylvania, Cold Harbor), he reached the country east of Richmond where McClellan had stood nearly two years before. But Lee's army, still unbeaten, continued to block the way into the Confederate capital, and Grant's losses, amounting to some 60,000 men, were so heavy that Northern public opinion became seriously alarmed. After futile assaults on Lee's position at Petersburg, the Union army dug entrenchments, and the two armies settled down to watch each other. This period of stalemate lasted for nine months.

The only other operations in the East of any importance were in the Shenandoah Valley. In July, Confederate forces in the valley under Jubal Early raided Maryland and Pennsylvania and nearly captured Washington. In the autumn, Philip Sheridan occupied the valley and made it useless to the Confederacy by completely laying it waste. Not even a crow, he declared, could cross the valley unless it carried its own rations.

The Election of 1864. The summer of 1864 was an unhappy period for the North. Neither Sherman nor Grant was making much progress, and the surrender of the Confederacy seemed as far away as ever. The heavy casualties caused such a widespread spirit of defeatism that the Republicans seemed in danger of losing the autumn elections. The Democratic convention, meeting in August, gave its nomination to General McClellan, and adopted a platform calling for the restoration of the Union by negotiation. This was, of course, impossible; nothing but a decisive victory could bring back the Confederacy into the Union. But the suggestion of a negotiated peace had a strong appeal to war-weary citizens.

Lincoln had been renominated in June by a National Union convention containing both Republicans and War Democrats. In order to demonstrate that this was a genuinely national organization, the convention gave the vice-presidential nomination to a Southern War Democrat, Andrew Johnson of Tennessee. But a number of Republicans were opposed to Lincoln's leadership. The Radicals in Congress had continued to criticize his conduct of the war and were now becoming even more hostile to his policy of post-war reconstruction. Believing that the purpose of the war was to restore the Union, Lincoln wished the Southern states to regain their constitutional rights as quickly as possible. He also insisted that reconstruction be controlled by the president, not by Congress. The Radicals, on the other hand, wanted to wreak vengeance upon the South and impose drastic changes upon Southern society in order to ensure its loyalty in the future.

In December 1863 Lincoln issued a proclamation declaring that whenever 10 per cent of the electorate of 1860 in any Southern state should take an oath of allegiance to the Union, then a civil government should be set up which should be regarded as "the true government of the state." Under this plan three Southern states which had been occupied by Northern armies, Tennessee, Arkansas, and Louisiana, set up civil governments during 1864. But although Lincoln recognized these governments as legal, Congress refused to seat the representatives whom they sent to Washington. In July, Congress passed the Wade-Davis Bill, which laid down more stringent conditions for the re-entry into the Union of the

Southern states and asserted Congressional authority over reconstruction. Lincoln killed this bill by means of a pocket veto.

Before election day Sherman's capture of Atlanta and the obvious demagoguery of the Democratic platform caused public opinion to swing back to support the administration. Lincoln was re-elected with the support of every state in the Union except New Jersey, Delaware, and Kentucky.

The End of the War. During the winter the war came visibly close to a conclusion. In December, Sherman captured Savannah and then, swinging northwards, began to fight his way into the Carolinas, once again opposed by Joseph Johnston. In Virginia, Grant began to extend his lines in the hope of surrounding Lee in Richmond and then starving him into submission. The Confederate government was still determined to continue fighting, as Lincoln discovered in February when he conferred with its vice-president, Alexander Stephens, on a steamer in Hampton Roads; but it was now driven to desperate measures. In March the Confederate Congress voted that slaves should be recruited into the army and given their freedom. The rank and file of the Confederate troops knew that the war was lost and could see no reason for continuing a useless struggle, and the armies of Lee and Johnston began to be decimated by desertions.

On March 4, 1865, Lincoln began his second term, appealing to his fellow-countrymen, in the immortal words of his Second Inaugural, "with malice towards none; with charity for all" to "do all which may achieve and cherish a just and lasting peace." It was obvious that the next few years would be largely occupied by conflict about reconstruction between the executive and the Congressional Radicals.

On April 2 Lee evacuated Richmond in the hope of establishing himself in the mountains. But Sheridan cut off his line of retreat, and on April 9, at Appomattox Court House, Lee met Grant and agreed to terms of surrender. On April 26 Johnston, feeling that further resistance was useless, surrendered to Sherman. Jefferson Davis, who had escaped into the mountains in the hope of continuing the war, was captured soon afterwards; and the last Confederate forces in the field laid down their arms on May 26.

Lincoln did not live to see the end of the war. On April 14, while attending a performance at Ford's Theater in Washington, he was assassinated by a demented Confederate sympathizer, John Wilkes Booth.

6. THE WAR AND THE NORTHERN ECONOMY

THE VICTORY of the North had two obvious consequences: it strengthened the forces making for national unity and meant the final defeat of the principle of states' rights; and it brought about the abolition of slavery.

But it also had indirect effects on American development that in the long run were perhaps even more important. It hastened the growth of large-scale manufacturing and enabled the spokesmen of industrial expansion to shape the policies of the Federal government.

Economic Expansion.   While the war brought ruin to the agrarian economy of the South, its effect on the North was to accelerate business growth. The Federal government made contracts for the purchase of immense quantities of munitions, clothing, foodstuffs, and other goods needed by the armed forces. While prices during the war years jumped to 117 per cent above pre-war levels, wages rose by only 43 per cent, so that profit margins were higher. And since labor was scarce, production could be maintained only through a greatly increased use of machinery. These factors brought about an industrial boom, stimulated the trend towards mass production by improved technological methods, and gave large corporations great advantages over small-scale producers. During the war a vast number of new factories were built in the Northeast; new mines were opened in the West; and there was a general tendency for machinery to replace hand labor, especially in the clothing industries. While the professional and working classes suffered acutely from the inflation, the entrepreneurs who took advantage of the wartime opportunities made enormous profits. There was much frenzied speculation and luxurious living.

Agriculture received a similar stimulus. All through the war years hundreds of thousands of pioneers continued to move westwards; much new land was brought under cultivation; and there was a vast increase in the production of wheat, wool, and other farm commodities. As in industry, scarcity of labor caused a rapid spurt in technological progress. For the first time many farmers began to buy the new mechanical reaper (invented in the 1830's) and adopt other labor-saving devices.

Republican Legislation.   Meanwhile, the Republicans in Congress were passing laws designed to stimulate economic progress. A few days before Lincoln took office, Congress passed, and Buchanan signed, the Morrill Tariff Act, which marked the first increase since 1842. During the war there were further rises, until by 1864 the average ad valorem duty reached 47 per cent, much the highest rate so far in American history. The primary reason for the increases was the need for revenue, but they also protected industry from foreign competition. Industrialists succeeded in keeping the tariff high after the war, although the government no longer needed the revenue it produced.

In 1862, in accordance with the Republican platform of 1860, the Homestead Act was enacted. Any American citizen, or any alien who had declared his intention of becoming a citizen, could obtain 160 acres of public land free; this would become his property for a nominal fee after he had lived on it for five years. In the same year Congress further promoted agricultural development by passing the Morrill Land-Grant Act. This set aside public land in every state for the support of colleges to provide scientific training in agriculture.

The year 1862 also saw the adoption of the long-sought legislation for a transcontinental railroad. With the South out of the Union, there was no longer much controversy about the route to be adopted. The Union Pacific was to build westwards from Nebraska, while the Central Pacific would build eastwards from California. Each company was to receive generous grants of public land and a loan of Federal money for every mile completed. Little track was completed during the war, but after 1865 construction was pushed ahead rapidly, and the two lines met each other in Utah in 1869.

Another measure long desired by business interests was Federal regulation of the banking system. Since the Jacksonian period, supervision had been left to the states, with chaotic results. In 1860 there were more than 1,500 banks, many of which issued their own notes. While some bank notes, especially in the Northeast, were sound, others circulated at a heavy discount; and there were also several hundred varieties of counterfeit notes in circulation. Such a situation was obviously a serious handicap to the transaction of business.

In 1863 Congress passed the National Bank Act. While its immediate purpose was to stimulate the sale of war bonds, it served also to create a stable paper currency. Banks capitalized above a certain minimum were invited to apply for Federal charters. In order to qualify, they had to contribute at least one-third of their capital in the purchase of war bonds. In return, the Treasury would give them national bank notes to the value of 90 per cent of their bond holdings. This measure was profitable to the banks, since with the same initial capital they could buy bonds and collect interest from the government and then put notes into circulation and collect interest from borrowers. But since the quantity of notes in circulation was limited by war-bond purchases, and since the bonds served as backing for the notes, the effect was to establish a reliable paper currency. As long as the credit of the government was good, the notes could not depreciate in value. Banks which continued to operate with state charters were still free to issue notes; but it was expected that their notes would be driven out of circulation, and this objective was achieved in 1866 when a 10-per-cent tax was levied on them.

The new system was far from perfect. The currency it provided was not sufficiently elastic for the needs of an expanding economy. As the government redeemed its bonds, the quantity of notes in circulation decreased, thereby causing deflationary conditions which meant falling prices and severe hardships for debtor groups. Money tended to be concentrated in the Northeast, and Western farming regions continued to suffer from a chronic scarcity of cash and credit. But there was no im-

portant change in the banking system until the Federal Reserve Act of
1913.

This Civil War legislation laid the groundwork for the rapid economic
expansion of the later decades of the nineteenth century. Thus by attempting to secede from the Union, the South had brought about the final
defeat of the agrarian principles in which she professed to believe and the
final victory of industrialism. The ideals of Alexander Hamilton and
Henry Clay had triumphed over those of Thomas Jefferson and Andrew
Jackson.

XVIII

The Post-war South

1. AFTER APPOMATTOX

2. JOHNSON AND THE RADICALS

3. RADICAL RECONSTRUCTION

4. ECONOMIC TRENDS

5. THE POPULIST MOVEMENT

THE WAR was not followed, as Lincoln had hoped, by mutual for-giveness and reconciliation. Most Southerners in 1865 were willing to accept the supremacy of the Federal government and the abolition of slavery, and wanted to concentrate on the immense task of rebuilding their shattered economy. But their desire to forget about the war was not reciprocated in the North, where there was strong sentiment in favor of treating the South as conquered territory and reconstructing her institutions. The hatreds and antagonisms engendered by four years of armed conflict did not quickly subside, and it was not until 1877 that the Union was finally restored on terms acceptable to white Southerners.

SELECTED BIBLIOGRAPHY: The appropriate volumes in the *History of the South* are E. M. Coulter, *The South During Reconstruction, 1865–1877* (1947), and C. Vann Woodward, *Origins of the New South, 1877–1913* (1951). The best study of Johnson and the Radicals is H. K. Beale, *The Critical Year: A Study of Andrew Johnson and Reconstruction* (1930). Most of the general studies of Reconstruction have a somewhat pro-Southern bias; this applies to J. G. Randall, *The Civil War and Reconstruction* (1937), and G. F. Milton, *The Age of Hate: Andrew Johnson and the Radicals* (1930), and more obviously to C. G. Bowers, *The Tragic Era: The Revolution after Lincoln* (1929). For interpretations by Negro scholars, see W. E. B. DuBois, *Black Reconstruction* (1935), and J. H. Franklin, *From Slavery to Freedom* (1947). P. H. Buck, *The Road to Reunion 1865–1900* (1937), deals with the restoration of national unity. For the New South, see Broadus Mitchell and G. S. Mitchell, *The Industrial Revolution in the South* (1930). The most illuminating book about Southern Populism is C. Vann Woodward, *Tom Watson: Agrarian Rebel* (1938). The disfranchisement of the Negroes is analyzed in Paul Lewinson, *Race, Class and Party* (1932).

1. AFTER APPOMATTOX

The Results of Defeat.   As the Confederate soldiers gradually made
their way home, mostly on foot, from the theater of war and from Northern prison camps, they found their section in an indescribable state of
ruin and disorganization. Large areas had been systematically laid waste
by the armies of Sherman and Sheridan. Wherever fighting had taken
place, towns had been destroyed and lines of communication disrupted.
Much of the Southern railroad system had been wrecked. And since almost
all the accumulated savings of the South had been expended during the
war, there was no capital with which to finance rebuilding. The debt
accumulated by the Confederate government was a total loss, and not a
single bank or insurance company was still solvent. The destruction of the
Southern economy did not even end with the cessation of hostilities; the
Federal Treasury Department gave orders for the confiscation of all
property of the Confederate government, and its agents, many of whom
proved dishonest, used this as an excuse for scouring the country and engaging in indiscriminate looting. But the South still had one major asset:
the fertility of her soil. She could hope to begin recovering as soon as the
first cotton crop was gathered.

Large-scale cotton-production, however, was impossible unless order
was re-established and the Negroes returned to work on the plantations. Hundreds of thousands of former slaves had joined the Union armies
or were now wandering aimlessly about the country. Informed that they
were now free, they interpreted this to mean that they were no longer
required to work for their former owners. Many of them believed that the
government was going to give them land of their own. Illiterate, and
totally unprepared for the responsibilities of freedom, they waited hopefully for somebody to explain what their new status meant. In the spring
and summer of 1865 thousands died of starvation and exposure. In March
the Federal government had set up the Freedmen's Bureau, under the
direction of General Oliver O. Howard; and this provided many of the
Negroes with food, shelter, and medical attention. But the government
had nothing to give them more substantial than charity and had no
program for coping with the situation. The conviction of most Southerners
was that the Negroes must be compelled to return to work. To Northern
Radicals this seemed like an intention to re-establish slavery in all but
name.

Johnson's Reconstruction Program.   Meanwhile, the victorious
North was deeply divided in its attitude toward the reconstruction problem. Should full constitutional rights be restored to the Southern states
as quickly and unconditionally as was compatible with the safety of the
Union, as Lincoln had desired? Or should the North take measures to
prevent any recurrence of sectional conflict by destroying the power of the

planters and establishing racial equality, as was demanded by the Radicals?

Congress did not meet until December 1865, and until then reconstruction was under the exclusive control of the executive. Andrew Johnson, who succeeded to the presidency in April, adopted a program similar to Lincoln's. If Lincoln had lived, he would have had a bitter fight with the Radicals in Congress, but it is possible that his prestige and political skill would have given him enough popular support to defeat them. Johnson, however, had fewer advantages. He was to be the most unfortunate and the most unjustly maligned president in American history.

Johnson was a native of the Southern Appalachian region, the inhabitants of which had generally been opposed to the slave-owners and at the same time hostile to the Negroes. He had remained illiterate until past the age of twenty, had worked as a tailor, and had afterwards risen to political leadership in eastern Tennessee as the spokesman of a Jacksonian faith in the rights of the plain people and the preservation of the Union. He had courage and integrity, and was a competent administrator and a forceful stump speaker. Unfortunately, he showed little tact and dexterity in handling political conflicts, did not always display the dignity expected in the nation's chief executive, and had a tendency in his public speeches to denounce his opponents with an indecent lack of restraint. He was also handicapped by his Southern origin, even though he had been a militant champion of the Union throughout the war. He was therefore vulnerable on several counts, and his enemies made the most of them.

Johnson's reconstruction program was put into effect during the summer of 1865. Provisional governors were appointed for the Southern states, with instructions to arrange for the election of constitutional conventions. All persons who had belonged to the electorate in 1860 were eligible to vote, provided they took an oath of allegiance to the Union, with the exception of fourteen specified groups. These disfranchised groups included persons who had held high political or military offices under the Confederacy or who owned property worth more than $20,000. These were required to make personal application to the President for pardons before they could regain political rights. The conventions were required to invalidate the old ordinances of secession, abolish slavery, and repudiate all debts contracted in order to aid the prosecution of the war. Otherwise they were left free to revise their state constitutions as they saw fit. Johnson expressed a hope that the franchise might be given to Negroes who were literate or owned property, but allowed the Southern states to decide about this question for themselves.

The program had been completed in every state except Texas and Florida before the end of the year. The conventions complied with the conditions laid down by the President, and all of them except that in Mississippi ratified the Thirteenth Amendment, which ended slavery everywhere in the United States. This amendment therefore became a part of the Constitution in December. After the conventions had completed their work, regular governors and legislatures were elected, and senators and representatives were sent to Washington. As was to be expected, many of the victorious candidates had been actively associated with the Confederacy; Georgia even selected the former Confederate Vice-President, Alexander Stephens, as one of its senators. Almost all of the Southerners best qualified for leadership had held office during the war, and such men still had the confidence of the mass of the people.

The Black Codes.   The most controversial laws enacted by the new Southern governments were the "black codes" defining the new status of the Negroes. There were considerable variations in the codes, those in states like Virginia and North Carolina, where the Negro population was relatively small, being considerably milder than in the cotton belt. But all the black codes made it plain that the Negro was still to have a subordinate status in Southern society. In spite of Johnson's suggestions, Negroes were wholly prohibited from voting or serving on juries, and were not allowed to carry weapons or appear in all public places. They were given, however, the essential civil rights of owning and inheriting property, making contracts, and suing in court. Most of the codes, moreover, included special provisions to protect them from being cheated and from undue exploitation. Since the most urgent Southern problem was to get them back to work on the land, the codes declared that every Negro must have a steady occupation and included stringent provisions against vagrancy and the violation of labor contracts. Heavier penalties were prescribed for Negro than for white lawbreakers; and in some states individual employers were allowed to give corporal punishment to disobedient servants. In a few states Negroes were excluded from all occupations except agriculture and domestic service.

Widely different opinions have been held about this legislation. Some people have insisted that its intention was to perpetuate slavery in all but name. Others have argued that it represented a statesmanlike approach to the problem of racial relations, giving the four million freedmen both the discipline and the protection they obviously needed. Perhaps the most legitimate criticism of the codes is that they did not offer the Negro population much hope for advancement in the future. For the time being a state of tutelage was obviously necessary. But could the Negroes look forward to a higher status in proportion as they became literate and self-supporting?

2. JOHNSON AND THE RADICALS

The Attitude of the Radicals.   In the opinion of the Radicals, the black codes proved that the war had been fought in vain. Incapable of any realistic appraisal of Southern problems, and convinced that the former slave-owners deserved punishment for their guilt in precipitating the war, they determined, when Congress met in December 1865, to undo Johnson's work and start the reconstruction process afresh along completely new lines. The Federal government, they believed, should treat the Southern states as conquered territory and impose much more drastic conditions before re-admitting them to the Union.

The motives for this program were very mixed. Some of the Radicals were sincere idealists who believed that the main purpose of the war had been to abolish slavery and that the North must now make sure that it remained abolished. Failing to recognize that human beings can never pass directly from slavery to freedom without a period of preparation, they believed that the freedmen would quickly show themselves qualified for political responsibility. But for many of the Radicals, Negro rights were merely a means for securing other objectives. If the South returned to the Union on Johnson's terms, then the pre-war Democratic Party would be re-established and might even win the next national election. Thus the Republicans would lose control of the Federal government. This was alarming not only to all Republican officeholders but also to the economic groups which the party represented. Northern businessmen were afraid that the tariff might be lowered, the national debt partially repudiated, and Federal policy again controlled by the agrarian South. Thus the North, in spite of having won the war, would be deprived of all the benefits of victory. But continued Republican predominance could be ensured if the franchise was given to the Negroes. There was a Negro majority in a number of Southern states; and the Negroes, it was assumed, would give their votes to the party that had emancipated them.

The ablest of the Radicals was Thaddeus Stevens. Throughout his career Stevens had been a consistent advocate of racial equality and the rights of the plain people (he had been a leader in the development of the Pennsylvania public-school system); but he was not a very likable human being. Lame since birth, unmarried, and now past seventy, he was a lonely, embittered, and unforgiving old man, who seemed to be motivated more by hatred of slave-owners than by any positive faith in human rights. But his political shrewdness and sharp tongue enabled him to dominate Congress, while his denunciations of the Southern planters had a strong appeal to Northern public opinion. The hatreds aroused by the war did not quickly subside, and many Northerners responded readily to Stevens's demands for vengeance. Stevens assumed leadership in formulating the Radical program, and before his death in 1868 he had become the most powerful man in the United States.

The Radical Program. The Radicals had a majority in both houses of Congress, and they began their attack on Johnson's program by refusing to admit the representatives of the Southern states. A Joint Committee on Reconstruction with fifteen members (Stevens being its dominant figure) was set up to investigate the whole question. Congress then passed, over Johnson's vetoes, a Freedmen's Bureau Bill, prolonging the life of this agency and giving it larger powers to protect the Negroes, and a Civil Rights Bill, which declared that Negroes should have the same rights as white people.

The joint Committee conducted hearings and collected a vast quantity of evidence designed to prove that the South could not be trusted to remain loyal to the Union. In the spring of 1866 it recommended a Fourteenth Amendment to the Constitution, which, with some changes, was approved by Congress. The first section of the proposed amendment was a restatement of the Civil Rights Bill. It declared that all persons born or naturalized in the United States were "citizens of the United States and of the States wherein they reside." "No states," it went on to say, "shall make or enforce any law which shall abridge the privileges or immunities of the citizens of the United States; nor shall any State deprive any person of life, liberty or property, without due process of law; nor deny to any person within its jurisdiction the equal protection of the laws." This was to become one of the most important parts of the whole Constitution; as afterwards interpreted by the Supreme Court, its effect was to protect the privileges and immunities not only of individual citizens but also of business corporations.

Other sections provided that if states denied the franchise to any adult male citizens, their representation in Congress should be proportionately reduced;[1] declared that no official position might be held by anybody who, after taking an oath of office to the United States, had aided the Confederacy (this disability, which would apply to almost all the political leaders of the South, might be removed by a two-thirds vote of each house of Congress); and affirmed that the debt of the United States should not be questioned, while that of the Confederacy and the Confederate states should not be paid. When the amendment was submitted to the states for ratification, it was promptly rejected everywhere in the South except in Tennessee. Congress therefore declared Tennessee to be back in the Union, but continued to deny recognition to the other Southern governments.

The Elections of 1866.   By this time the Congressional elections of 1866 were approaching, and Johnson hoped to bring about the defeat of the Radicals. He continued to use the name "National Union," which had been used for Lincoln's candidacy in 1864; but he was now supported mainly by Democrats, while the Republican Party machinery was controlled by the Radicals. Voters in most districts had to choose between a Radical and a Democrat who was often a former Copperhead. Johnson made a speaking-tour to appeal for popular support; but in the course of this "swing around the circle" he indulged in so many vituperative

---

[1] With the abolition of slavery, the three-fifths arrangement adopted in the Constitution was no longer in effect. Thus the Civil War had the paradoxical result of increasing the number of congressmen to which the South was entitled. If Negroes were denied the right to vote, a Southern white man would have more political power than a Northerner.

speeches and showed such an unfortunate lack of dignity that he lost more votes than he gained. The Radicals depicted him as an ignorant boor, a Confederate sympathizer, and a habitual drunkard;[2] and these accusations were widely believed. Johnson's position was further weakened by the news of serious race riots at Memphis and New Orleans. The result was a decisive victory for the Radicals, who won increased majorities in both Senate and House. For the last two years of his term Johnson was President in name only.

Immediately after the elections the Radicals set out to deprive Johnson of any power to interfere with their reconstruction program. In defiance of the Constitution, he was to be reduced to a mere figurehead and complete control of the government transferred to Congress. By the Tenure of Office Act the President was prohibited from dismissing civil officeholders without the consent of the Senate; violation of the act was declared to be a misdemeanor, punishable by fine and imprisonment. And by the Command of the Army Act he was deprived of his constitutional powers as commander-in-chief; he was forbidden to remove Grant from his position as general of the army or to issue any military orders except through Grant. Grant had originally favored Johnson, but was now turning to the Radicals, who felt that they could rely on his support.

Starting in March 1867 came a series of Reconstruction Acts. These declared that, except in Tennessee, no legal governments existed anywhere in the former Confederacy. The area was to be divided into five districts, which were to be placed under the rule of army generals backed by Federal troops. The generals were to compile a register of voters, including Negroes and excluding all who had ever been disfranchised for disloyalty, and were to arrange for the election of constitutional conventions. New state constitutions were to be drafted, giving the suffrage to the Negroes. These constitutions had then to be ratified by a majority of the voters and approved by Congress, and the Fourteenth Amendment had to be accepted. Only after all these conditions had been met would representatives of the Southern states be admitted to Congress and the Federal troops withdrawn.

The Impeachment of Johnson. Johnson wrote a forceful veto of the first Reconstruction Act; but after his veto had been overridden, he complied with the provisions of the act, thereby disappointing the Radicals, who were hoping to remove him by impeachment.[3] Before the end of the year, however, he gave them the opportunity for which they were hoping. Goaded beyond endurance by Secretary of War Stanton, who had always

[2] Johnson was drunk once, and that—unfortunately for his reputation—was when he was inaugurated as Vice-President. He was convalescent from an attack of typhoid fever at the time, and drank too much brandy on an empty stomach in order to nerve himself for the ceremony.

[3] According to the law then in force, the succession would have passed to the president of the Senate, Ben Wade, who was a leading Radical. A law passed in 1886 made the secretary of state next in line after the vice-president. This was repealed in 1947, the Speaker of the House being placed after the vice-president.

been a troublemaker and was now working closely with the Radicals, Johnson finally tried to dismiss him. Persisting after the Senate had refused its consent, he could be accused of violating the Tenure of Office Act. In March 1868 the President was impeached, his attempt to dismiss Stanton being the only concrete charge brought against him. Stevens and the other Radical congressmen in charge of the prosecution were unable to prove to the satisfaction of honest men that this constituted a crime or misdemeanor, and relied mainly on appeals to prejudice. By a margin of one vote the Radicals failed to secure the two-thirds majority needed for conviction. Seven of the Republican senators voted with the twelve Democrats for acquittal. All of them were afterwards punished for their disobedience to party discipline by being driven out of politics.

In addition to riding roughshod over the Constitution in their determination to strip Johnson of all executive authority, the Radicals also reduced the power of the Supreme Court. Since the North had fought the war on the assumption that the Southern states could not leave the Union, it followed that Southerners were entitled to the full protection of the Constitution as soon as they were no longer in rebellion, a view subsequently accepted by the Supreme Court in 1869 in the case of Texas v. White. This meant that the military rule established by the Reconstruction Acts of 1867 was a violation of the constitutional liberties of Southerners, particularly since in the case ex parte Milligan in 1866 the Supreme Court had declared that military courts had no jurisdiction over civilians if the civil courts were functioning. The Radicals therefore resolved to prevent the Court from interfering, and Congress voted that it could not hear appeals from lower courts in cases involving the rights of habeas corpus. Fearful of being altogether stripped of its powers, the Court for the next few years found excuses for refusing to accept jurisdiction in cases involving the legality of the reconstruction program. At no other period in American history, in fact, have the rules of the Constitution and the independence of the judiciary been so flagrantly disregarded. No president has come so close to assuming dictatorial powers as did Stevens and his associates in Congress.

The Election of 1868.   That the Republican Party and the economic interests it represented needed the votes of Negroes was very manifest in the presidential election of 1868. The party convention gave its nomination to General Grant by a unanimous vote on the first ballot. Grant's military achievements and unassuming manners had made him a popular hero; and since he was completely ignorant of politics, he could be expected to follow the guidance of the party leaders in Congress. The Radicals therefore regarded him as an ideal candidate. The Democratic candidate was Horatio Seymour of New York, a man of moderate views and little distinction. The main campaign issue was reconstruction, although the Democratic platform also raised an important economic question by calling for the payment of the war debt not in gold but in greenbacks. In the opinion of the bondholders, this, of course, would be equivalent to partial repudiation. Since Grant carried twenty-six states against only eight for Seymour, he had a substantial majority in the electoral college. But his majority in the popular vote was only 300,000, and it was calculated that at least 600,000 Negroes had cast votes for the Republican ticket. The returns showed that since 1866 there had been a marked change in public sentiment. War hatreds were subsiding, and the Radicals had lost much of their support among the Northern white population.

After the election the Radicals determined to safeguard their program by making Negro suffrage a part of the Constitution. By the Fifteenth Amendment it was declared that the right of citizens to vote could not be denied or abridged "on account of race, color, or previous condition of servitude," and that Congress could enforce this article by appropriate legislation. This was ratified by 1870, and proved to be the Radicals' last important achievement. The death of Stevens in 1868 had deprived them of their most forceful leader; and as public sentiment changed, and the obstacles to any complete transformation of Southern society became more apparent, an increasing number of people lost interest in the whole problem. The attempt to establish Negro suffrage in the South was not completely abandoned until 1877; but after the 1868 election most of the Republican leaders no longer defended their reconstruction program with much vigor or sense of conviction.

3. RADICAL RECONSTRUCTION

FOR white Southerners, Radical reconstruction proved to be an even more traumatic experience than the war itself. Its permanent effects were to solidify them against Negro suffrage and against Northern interference with their institutions, and to make any solution of the racial problem even more difficult.

The New Southern Governments. When the generals completed the register of voters in the ten Southern states covered by the Reconstruction Acts of 1867, it was found that 703,000 Negroes and 627,000 whites had been declared eligible for the franchise. Nearly 200,000 whites had been deprived of political rights on the ground that they had voluntarily aided the Confederacy. In five cotton-belt states there were Negro majorities. The process of drafting and ratifying new constitutions, setting up governors and legislatures, and ratifying the Fourteenth Amendment was finished in seven states during 1868, and in all of them by 1870, and they were then declared to be back in the Union. Reconstruction was now officially completed, although this was not followed by the removal of all the Federal troops; it was painfully apparent that armed forces were needed to keep the new governments in power.

Although the Reconstruction governments were based mainly on the votes of Negroes, leadership was assumed everywhere by white men. The most prominent of them were Northerners, many of whom had first seen the South as soldiers in the Union army. Some of them were honest idealists who settled in the South in order to help the Negroes, but others were adventurers hoping for power and plunder. Southerners called them carpetbaggers, alleging that when they first came south they carried all their worldly possessions in a single carpetbag. In the states reconstructed during 1868, four of the seven governors, ten of the fourteen senators, and twenty of the thirty-five representatives were carpetbaggers.

Southern whites who supported the Reconstruction governments were known as scalawags. The motives of this group were similarly mixed. Many of the Southern small farmers, although reluctant to cooperate with the Negroes, were at first inclined to approve of governments that promised to destroy the power of the planters and bring about democratic reforms. But most of the more active scalawags were opportunists interested chiefly in the rewards of office. Although the scalawags came chiefly from the poorer classes, they included a few individuals who had been prominent in Southern affairs before the war. In Georgia, for example, Joseph E. Brown, who had been Governor of the state from 1857 until 1865, became Chief Justice under the Reconstruction government.

The new governments could not survive unless the Negroes not only voted but also voted the Republican ticket. In order to ensure this result, the Freedmen's Bureau became an electioneering agency for the Republican Party; and similar functions were undertaken by a private organization, the Union League, which had been founded in the North during the war in order to promote loyalty. The Union League set up branches throughout the South, where it became a highly organized secret society with an elaborate ritual. Officials of the League instructed the Negroes how to vote, sometimes marking their ballots for them or stuffing the boxes if the necessary majorities could not be obtained by more legal methods.

In spite of the electioneering tactics and dubious motives of many Radical leaders, much of the legislation they sponsored showed a real desire to strengthen democracy in the South. In general, they set out to introduce reforms which had been mostly adopted in the Northern states one or two generations earlier. County government, the judiciary, and the system of taxation were reorganized in order to promote equality and deprive the planter class of its special privileges. Poor-relief and other humanitarian measures became more substantial. Most important of all, laws were passed providing for universal public education. Much was done, also, to repair the damages of the war and bring about the rebuilding of railroads, bridges, and public buildings. All this cost money; and since the Reconstruction governments represented chiefly the poorest classes in Southern society, they had no hesitation about raising tax rates to confiscatory levels and incurring heavy public debts. Between 1868 and 1874 the total debt of the eleven states in the Confederacy increased by no less than $113,000,000.

Unfortunately, the positive achievements of the Reconstruction governments were more than counterbalanced by their corruption. Some of them (that of Mississippi, for example) maintained fairly high standards of honesty. But since the new officeholders were kept in power mainly by force and fraud, they had little but their own consciences to restrain them; and a large number quickly learned how to make the most of their opportunities. While part of the increase in the state debts represented legitimate public expenditures, much of it was the result of outright stealing.

The most notorious cases were in South Carolina and Louisiana. In South Carolina judicial decisions and corporation charters were openly bought and sold; $200,000 was paid for State House furniture actually costing less than $18,000; public printing during a single legislative session cost nearly $500,000; and the members of the legislature acquired furniture, carriages, farm equipment, food, liquor, gold watches, and cuspidors at public expense. The state debt rose in ten years from $7,000,000 to $29,000,000. Louisiana, during Governor Warmouth's term of four and a half years, was systematically looted by the members of the ruling group, who bought public property for trifling sums and obtained contracts at correspondingly inflated figures. The state debt was increased by over $48,000,000, much of which went to members of the legislature and a swarm of other public officials for services never rendered, while the Governor himself (whose official salary was $8,000 a year) amassed a fortune estimated at $500,000.

It should be remembered, however, that corruption during this epoch was by no means restricted to the South. Public morals everywhere had deteriorated after the war, and both in the Federal government during Grant's administration and in some Northern cities, especially New York, the stealing was equally deplorable. Nor should the degeneration of the Reconstruction governments be regarded as a proof that the Negroes were inherently unfitted for political rights. Twenty-eight Negroes represented Southern states in Congress, and many others held minor legislative or administrative positions, some of them being men of distinction who performed good service, while others were illiterate and wholly unfitted for the responsibilities that had been thrust upon them. But in every state leadership remained with the white carpetbaggers and scalawags. Reconstruction was a tragic experience for the Negro people, since they were blamed for evils for which they could not fairly be held responsible.

The Restoration of White Supremacy. For the Southern upper class, all the activities of the Reconstruction governments, whether honest or corrupt, were almost equally deplorable. And in seeking to regain political power, they were soon able to win the support of most of the small farmers, who regarded the Negroes as their economic competitors and were even more strongly opposed to racial equality than were the planters. Thus the white race in the South became almost united in its opposition to the Reconstruction program. This unity found expression in a common adherence to the Democratic Party. Henceforth most white Southerners, whether rich or poor, were Democrats.

Many of the Negroes had returned to work on the plantations and were easily induced to trust their employers rather than the Republican politicians. Since they had not received land of their own and were still economically dependent on their former owners, freedom had proved, on the whole, a disillusioning experience. But the overthrow of the Reconstruction governments was effected by the intimidation of Negro voters as well as by persuasion. White Southerners formed a number of secret societies which used violence against Negroes who misbehaved or were active in politics, the best-known of them being the Ku-Klux. This originated in 1866 among some young men at Pulaski, Tennessee, who dressed up in white robes and pretended to be ghosts in order to frighten the Negroes in the vicinity. Started as a joke, it soon developed serious political objectives and spread rapidly throughout the South.

It should be realized that the abrupt disintegration of the Southern social order at the end of the war had inevitably made persons and property unsafe. Many white Southerners had come to believe that they could not stop thieving and protect their wives and daughters from assault unless they took the law into their own hands. But societies like the Ku-Klux provided many opportunities for indiscriminate criminality, and soon began to attract the most degraded elements among the white population, who used the slogan of white supremacy as an excuse for torturing and murdering any Negroes who incurred their disapproval. More responsible Southern leaders soon tried to disband these secret organizations. The Ku-Klux was formally dissolved as early as 1869, though a number of its constituent units continued to operate. But the use of violence against Negroes who did not "know their place" continued to be endemic in the more backward parts of the South for a long time to come.

The Republicans in Congress responded to this growth of violence by passing in 1870 and 1871 a series of three Enforcement Acts. These provided heavy penalties for anybody who used force or bribery to prevent citizens from voting, declared the secret societies to be criminal organizations, and authorized the President to use troops and suspend the writ of habeas corpus in order to maintain order in the South. For a short period Grant enforced this legislation vigorously, and hundreds of Southern lawbreakers were brought to trial. But by this time Northerners were growing tired of the whole problem and willing to leave Southern problems to be solved by Southern white men. In 1872 an Amnesty Act restored political rights to all but a few hundred Southerners. Subsequently the Enforcement Acts were whittled down by a series of Supreme Court decisions, which declared that the Federal government could intervene to protect the rights of Negroes only when they were restricted by state legislation, not when they were violated by individuals. These and other decisions of the Court made it plain that Southerners need not respect the rights supposedly guaranteed to Negroes by the Fourteenth and Fifteenth Amendments.

By a combination of persuasion and intimidation the Negroes were gradually prevented from casting votes for the Reconstruction governments, and the Democratic Party regained control. White supremacy was re-established in Virginia, North Carolina, Georgia, and Tennessee as early as 1871. These were followed by Alabama, Arkansas, and Texas in 1874, Mississippi in 1876, and Florida at the beginning of 1877. In March 1877, when Hayes succeeded Grant as President, Reconstruction governments survived only in South Carolina and Louisiana, and they were kept in office only by Federal troops. When Hayes removed the troops in April, Democratic administrations immediately assumed power, and the restoration of white supremacy was complete.[4]

The Bourbons. In general, the new governments in the South represented the wealthier classes, and included many individuals who had been prominent in the Confederacy. By analogy with the French royal family which had been restored to power after the fall of Napoleon, these people were often known as "Bourbons." But in reality they were by no means identical with the old plantation aristocracy. Led by men who had usually voted Whig rather than Democratic before the war, they had a business rather than an agrarian orientation. Their economic attitude was, in fact, almost identical with that of the industrialists and financiers represented by the Republican Party in the North.

After assuming control in the South, they set out to promote industrial growth and protect the interests of landlords and factory-owners, while in all other respects they followed strictly *laissez-faire* principles. They reduced taxes and enforced strict economy, repudiated most of the debt incurred during Reconstruction, and cut to the bone all public spending on education and public welfare. In spite of these unprogressive policies, they were able to win much popular support, partly because they could claim to have redeemed the South from the horrors of Reconstruction, and partly because they won a reputation for honesty. By contrast with the excesses of the worst Reconstruction governments, there was, indeed, a decrease in the amount of money stolen by public officials, but in actuality the Bourbons were by no means as pure as they claimed to be, and standards of official conduct remained lamentably low.

4. ECONOMIC TRENDS

The Land System. The recovery of the Southern economy was a slow and painful process, and for a generation following the war poverty

[4] For the Hayes-Tilden election, see page 451.

was the common lot of almost all Southerners, planters and small farmers alike. According to the poet Sidney Lanier, "pretty much the whole of life has been merely not dying." There are many stories of former Confederate generals and high officials working as manual laborers in order to keep their families from starvation. And as always happens during periods of social disintegration and rapid change, it was the men of honor and integrity who suffered most acutely, while those who were more flexible and had fewer scruples found opportunities for advancement.

Nevertheless, there was no fundamental transformation of the Southern social structure. The planter class had lost much of its wealth during the war, and was further impoverished by the high taxes imposed by the Reconstruction governments. Millions of acres were sold for unpaid taxes, and much of this land was bought by the small farmers. Yet on the whole a concentration of landownership continued to prevail in the cotton belt. Some plantations were still owned by the old families, while others were acquired by Northerners or former small farmers who rose to affluence during the post-war period. Although Stevens had wanted to distribute land among the Negroes, the Radicals did not attempt to break up the plantations, probably because this would not have suited the interests of the Northern business groups dominant in the Republican Party.

The plantations, however, could no longer be operated by the old methods. The planters tried at first to employ their former slaves as wage-laborers; but now that the Negroes were legally free, they were no longer willing to work in gangs under the supervision of white men. The planters therefore began to divide their estates into small farms and lease them to Negroes or poor whites. In many instances the planter supplied the tools, animals, and seeds, and the tenant was required, in return, to give him a share (often one-half) of his crop. Under this "share-cropping" arrangement the tenant was obligated to devote himself primarily to the production of cotton, and frequently incurred debts which he was unable ever to pay off. This resulted in a system of peonage which, though an improvement on chattel slavery, kept the Negroes still dependent upon the landowners and attached to the soil.

As a result partly of the sale of land to small farmers and partly of the division of plantations among tenants, the number of separate farm properties in the South rose from 700,000 in 1860 to 2,500,000 in 1900. In the latter year 1,375,000 farms were operated by owners and 1,125,000 by tenants, slightly more than half of whom were Negroes. The average holding of the white tenant farmer was eighty-four acres; that of the Negro was only forty acres.

The Cotton Economy. In the later years of the century cotton-production increased rapidly. By 1894 the crop was twice as large as before the war, and by 1914 it had almost doubled again. New areas were developed in Arkansas and Texas, while the worn-out soils of Georgia and South Carolina were restored with artificial fertilizers. But this did not bring prosperity to the families who grew the cotton. Not only the share-croppers but also many of the cash tenants and the small owners were perpetually in debt and suffered from a crushing poverty unparalleled elsewhere in the United States. They frequently had to ask local merchants to advance them goods on credit, giving them in return a lien on the next cotton crop. The merchants charged high prices, while interest rates often reached 40 per cent. This kept the farmer dependent on the merchant; but the merchant had to take his chances on crop failures or falling prices and was usually himself in debt. Capital was scarce throughout the South, and the chain of debts, tying the farmer to the merchant, and the merchant to the wholesaler, often led finally to Northern banking houses.

This system of indebtedness was vicious not only because the profits of cotton-production were drained off through high interest rates but also because it prevented the growth of a more diversified agriculture. Land-lords and merchants insisted that the farmers should devote themselves exclusively to cotton because this was the one crop for which they were sure of a market. Thus a one-crop system was maintained throughout the cotton belt, even though it resulted in steady depletion of the soil and in falling prices through overproduction. Planting and harvesting continued to be done by hand, without the aid of machinery, and had scarcely changed since the invention of the cotton gin.

Industrial Development. Many Southerners after the war were convinced that their section could find economic salvation only by imi-tating the North and developing her own industries. By the 1880's in-dustrialization was being preached with the fervor of a new religion. Per-haps the most influential prophet of this "New South" was Henry Grady, editor of the *Atlanta Constitution* and the most eloquent Southern orator of the period. The Bourbons who assumed power after Reconstruction mostly shared this viewpoint and granted tax exemptions and other privileges to new industries.

The Southern railroad system was rebuilt and considerably enlarged during the Reconstruction period, the capital being supplied by Northern investors. In the 1880's Northern capital began to be invested also in coal mines in the Appalachian country of Maryland, Virginia, and Kentucky, and in steel mills at Birmingham, Alabama. But the profits from these enterprises did not remain in the South. Southerners succeeded, however, in developing a number of industries of their own, most of which involved the processing of local raw materials, such as tobacco, lumber, cottonseed, and cotton itself.

The most important of Southern industries was the manufacture of cotton goods, which developed chiefly in the piedmont country of North and South Carolina and Georgia. The capital was at first mostly contrib-uted by small local investors, who regarded the encouragement of indus-try as a patriotic duty. The workers were recruited from the small farmers of the hill country and their wives and children. As in the early stages of industrialization all over the world, hours of labor were long and wages were low. In 1900 hours were from 66 to 75 a week, and the family wage (earned jointly by father, mother, and children) was from $15 to $25 a week. Thirty per cent of the workers were children under sixteen. The *laissez-faire* principles of the Bourbon-controlled governments, the wide diffusion of stock-ownership, and the general faith in the gospel of industrialization made any amelioration of labor conditions in the Southern mill towns extremely difficult. Although profits seem to have been almost consistently high, it was argued that welfare legislation would handicap Southern factories in their competition with those of the North and make it more difficult for the section as a whole to achieve economic salvation. There was vigorous public and official opposition to any attempt among the workers to form trade unions. Little was done to limit exploitation until the Federal government began to assume responsibility under the New Deal.

Between 1880 and 1900 the number of workers in the Southern textile mills increased from 17,000 to 98,000, and the capital invested from $102,000 to $1,479,000. By 1904 the South was manufacturing more cotton goods than New England. Yet the relative importance of industry in the South should not be exaggerated. This was a period of rapid industrial growth in the United States as a whole, and the proportion of the nation's manufacturing done in the South was much the same in 1900 as in 1860— in other words, about 10 per cent.

Most Southerners continued to work on the land, and the section as a whole continued to be economically handicapped. In 1900 wealth per capita for the United States as a whole amounted to $1,165, but the figure for the South was only $509. No income statistics are available until 1919, but in that year income per capita in the South was only $405, as contrasted with $929 for New York. The poverty of the rural South brought with it a number of other evils. Many Southern farmers suffered from such devitalizing diseases as hookworm, pellagra, and malaria; and since the South had little money for schools, the rate of illiteracy among the native-born white population amounted in 1900 to 12 per cent. This situation was the result of many different causes, among them being the destruction of Southern wealth in the Civil War, exploitation by Northern industry and finance, decline in the fertility of the soil, excessive dependence on cotton, and concentration of political energies on the race question.

5. THE POPULIST MOVEMENT

The Agrarian Revolt. By the late 1880's the small farmers of the South were beginning to revolt against the leadership of the landlords and industrialists. They wanted more money spent on schools, roads, and other improvements, and a more democratic political system. Their discontent was sharpened by a steady fall in the price of cotton, which dropped from an average of 11.1 cents a pound during the years 1874–77 to 5.8 cents during 1894–97.

The organization which voiced their grievances was the National Farmers' Alliance, more often known as the Southern Alliance, which had been formed in Texas in 1875. After 1886, under the dynamic leadership first of Dr. C. W. Macune of Texas and afterwards of Leonidas L. Polk of North Carolina, it expanded rapidly and was soon claiming a membership of two or three millions. A separate Negro organization, the Colored Farmers' National Alliance, grew to more than a million. The Southern Alliance advocated various measures for the benefit of the farmers, and also appealed to the industrial workers for support. Its abler leaders recognized that the white and colored farmers of the South were suffering from the same forms of exploitation, and urged them to join forces with each other against the landlords and merchants. This seemed to be the most promising liberal movement that the South had known since the time of Thomas Jefferson.

During the same period there was a parallel development of farm insurgency in the West, sponsored by the Northern Alliance.[5] Some of the Southern leaders wanted the two alliances to join forces in a third party; but most Southerners preferred to remain within the Democratic organization in the hope of capturing it from the Bourbons. When the People's (or Populist) Party was launched in 1891, its support came mostly from the West, though the word "populist" was also applied to the insurgents of the South.

During the early 1890's there were bitter political conflicts in most Southern states, with much fraudulent voting, and many shootings, political murders, and even duels. It was the hill country against the plains, and the wool hats against the silk hats. Both sides appealed to the Negroes, who had mostly stopped voting after Reconstruction but had never been legally disfranchised. In this competition for Negro votes the upper classes seem to have been much more successful. Most of the Negro tenant farmers throughout the plantation country were accustomed to rely on their landlords for guidance and protection, and could easily be induced to follow their political leadership.

Populist Victories. In the elections of 1890, 1892, and 1894 a number of candidates sponsored by the Southern Alliance, or professing sympathy with its aims, were victorious in the cotton states. In North Carolina the Alliance leaders joined forces with the Republicans, but elsewhere they mostly worked within the Democratic Party. As a result of these victories, appropriations for education and other social services increased, and some political reforms were made in order to promote democracy. In particular, primary elections were instituted for the choice of party candidates—a measure first adopted by South Carolina in 1896. Except in Kentucky, Tennessee, and North Carolina, where the Republi-

[5] See pages 457–60.

can Party had some strength, the Democratic nomination invariably meant election, so that the real political conflicts henceforth took place in the primary elections.

On the whole, however, the concrete achievements of Southern Populism were meager. There was no fundamental change in the Southern political and social structure. The main reason for this disappointing result was the race question, the South's ancestral curse. In spite of the efforts of the more liberal leaders, most of the poorer whites remained bitterly hostile to the Negroes. This hostility was now sharpened by upper-class control of much of the Negro vote, with the result that the disfranchisement of the Negroes appeared to many of the farmers as necessary in order to put an end to Bourbon domination. It was therefore the spokesmen of the farmers who took the lead in restricting the rights of the Negro population. Yet in the end it was the Southern upper classes who proved to be the chief gainers. Thus Southern Populism was largely diverted from its original objectives and transformed into a crusade for white supremacy.

Negro Disfranchisement.   Direct disfranchisement of the Negroes was prohibited by the Fifteenth Amendment. But the same result could be secured by indirect methods not explicitly contrary to the Constitution. Mississippi led the way in 1890 with a law making payment of a poll tax eight months before the election a prerequisite for voting. In 1892 a literacy test was added, requiring every voter to be able to read and interpret part of the Federal Constitution. During the next decade similar laws were passed in every Southern state. The poll-tax requirements were deliberately made as complicated as possible, in order to discourage Negroes from paying it. The literacy test was even more effective in excluding them, since it was interpreted by white boards of registry which (in the words of Carter Glass in the Virginia Constitutional Convention of 1901) could easily display "discrimination within the letter of the law." Even Negroes with college degrees could be pronounced illiterate if they failed to answer recondite questions about the Constitution. Henceforth the vast majority of the Southern Negroes were legally prohibited from voting. Both the poll tax and the literacy test, however, had the effect of disfranchising many of the poorer whites, and there was a sharp decline in white voting after they went into effect. In 1898 Louisiana evaded this consequence by giving the vote to everybody whose father or grandfather had voted before 1867. A similar "grandfather" clause was subsequently adopted by six other states, but it was invalidated by the Supreme Court in 1915.

Keeping the Negro in his place proved to be such a popular slogan that a number of Southern politicians made it their chief stock-in-trade. One of the most lasting results of Southern Populism was the rise of the rabble-rousing demagogue. Winning power by appealing to all the racial and religious prejudices of the poorer classes, he denounced the rich and was often virulently hostile to Catholics and Jews; but he usually made white supremacy his main campaign issue. The line between the demagogue and the genuine reformer was not easy to draw, and many Southern leaders of the early twentieth century, like "Pitchfork" Ben Tillman in South Carolina, Jeff Davis in Arkansas, and James K. Vardaman in Mississippi, were a little of both. Others, like Cole Blease of South Carolina and Theodore G. Bilbo of Mississippi, represented pure demagoguery with no perceptible trace of idealism. One man, Tom Watson, of Georgia, combined in his own career both the early idealism of the Populist movement and its later degeneration. In the 1880's and 1890's he was one of the ablest and most liberal of the agrarian leaders. Embittered by failure, he gradually turned to demagoguery and in his old age was one of the chief spokesmen of racial and religious hatred. Yet he never wholly forgot his early liberalism, and was a vigorous champion of civil liberties during World War I. Watson's career illustrates the tragic complexity of the South's political problems.

Status of the Negroes. Denied political rights and branded as inherently inferior to all white men, the Negroes could do little to improve their position. In 1900 they numbered 8,834,000, or 11.6 per cent of the total population of the United States; 90 per cent of them lived in the South, and of the Southern Negroes 82.8 per cent were engaged in agriculture. One-quarter of this group owned their own farms, while the remainder were cash tenants or, much more frequently, share-croppers. Thus about 55 per cent of the total Negro population were working on land which they did not own, and were little better off than in 1860. Half of the Southern Negroes were illiterate, and the death rate appears to have been nearly twice that of the white population.

The more restless and ambitious Negroes were beginning to move into the cities, and the twentieth century was to see a considerable migration into the North. But urban job opportunities were limited, since the better-paid occupations were mostly pre-empted by white workers. Many trade unions excluded Negroes. In general, Negroes were restricted to the more menial and insecure occupations. The Negro who "knew his place" and remained dependent upon a white landlord or employer could usually hope for a considerable measure of security; but any expression of initiative or ambition was decidedly hazardous.

Jim Crow laws, enacted in the Southern states between 1900 and 1911, kept the Negro population consistently aware of its inferior status. So also did the prevalence of lynching. This reached a peak during the political disturbances of the 1890's, with 292 cases in the year 1892 alone. During the decade 1889–99 the total number of Negroes lynched was 1,460. Lynchings dropped to 820 during the following ten-year period and continued to decrease thereafter, but have never been wholly eliminated.

The principal spokesman for the Negroes after the failure of Reconstruction was Booker T. Washington. Born into slavery on a Virginia plantation, he was the head of Tuskegee Institute in Alabama from 1881 until his death in 1915. Tuskegee, established as a school for Negroes with funds from the state legislature, gave training chiefly in agriculture and mechanics. Washington believed that the Negroes could improve their position only with the consent of the white race, and therefore urged them not to struggle against the restrictions imposed upon them but to earn approval by displaying industry, sobriety, competence, and obedience to their employers. "The race, like the individual, that makes itself indispensable, has solved many of its problems," he declared. He became nationally famous when he expressed his views in a speech at Atlanta, Georgia, in 1895. A persuasive orator and a man of extraordinary shrewdness and force of character, he wielded immense power in his later years, giving confidential advice to several presidents about all questions involving Negroes and controlling virtually all distributions of money by private philanthropy for their benefit. His conservative program was repudiated by the more militant Negro leaders of the next generation, but in the 1880's and 1890's it was probably realistic.

The Twentieth Century. At the end of the nineteenth century, with the failure of Populism and the increase of restrictions upon the Negroes, the prospect of any solution to the economic and racial problems of the South seemed gloomy. Yet the next half-century was to see steady progress in many directions. There were great advances in agricultural methods, standards of living, public health, education, and cultural achievement. While many Southern leaders continued to be either Bourbon reactionaries or demagogues, enlightened liberalism increased. Racial tensions slowly abated, and Negroes found it easier to achieve business or professional status. The progress often seemed dishearteningly slow, and occasional outbreaks of demagoguery and race hatred were a warning against overconfidence. But a long view, contrasting 1950 with 1900 or with 1860, seemed to justify a sober optimism.

XIX

The Growth of Industry

1. FACTORS IN INDUSTRIAL GROWTH

2. THE EXPANSION OF THE RAILROADS

3. INDUSTRIAL AND FINANCIAL DEVELOPMENT

4. PROBLEMS OF LABOR

THE CENTRAL feature of American history during the later nineteenth century was rapid economic expansion. Between 1860 and 1900 the total railroad mileage increased from 30,000 to 193,000, while the capital invested in manufacturing rose from $1,000,000,000 to nearly $10,000,000,000, the number of workers from 1,300,000 to 5,300,000, and the value of the annual product from less than $2,000,000,000 to more than $13,000,000,000. This amazing industrial growth, combined with a simultaneous and equally remarkable increase in farm production, made the United States the richest and potentially the most powerful country in the world. At the same time it brought about fundamental changes in American social organization and ways of living and thereby created problems the solution of which would require the best efforts of later generations.

SELECTED BIBLIOGRAPHY: Descriptions of industrial growth can be found in a number of one-volume economic histories, among them being H. U. Faulkner, *American Economic History* (revised edition, 1949), E. C. Kirkland, *A History of American Economic Life* (revised edition, 1950), and F. A. Shannon, *America's Economic Growth* (revised edition, 1951), and also in three volumes in the *Chronicles of America* series: John Moody, *The Railroad Builders* (1919) and *The Masters of Capital* (1919), and B. J. Hendrick, *The Age of Big Business* (1921). T. C. Cochran and W. Miller, *The Age of Enterprise* (1942), covers industrial and business expansion through the nineteenth and early twentieth centuries. Matthew Josephson, *The Robber Barons* (1934), is lively muckraking with a radical bias. For the railroads, one can also consult S. H. Holbrook, *The Story of American Railroads* (1947), and R. E. Riegel, *The Story of the Western Railroads* (1926). The trust problem is analyzed in H. R. Seager and C. A. Gulick, *Trust and Corporation Problems* (1929), and M. W. Watkins, *Industrial Combinations and Public Policy* (1927). Herbert Harris, *American Labor* (1939), traces the rise of unionism, while a more detailed account can be found in N. J. Ware, *The Labor Movement in the United States, 1860–1895* (1929). E. Stein and others, *Labor Problems in America* (1940), surveys all aspects of the subject.

1. FACTORS IN INDUSTRIAL GROWTH

THE MATERIAL causes for this economic expansion can easily be summarized. The United States had a rich soil and vast mineral resources. There was no scarcity of capital for their development, since the growth of trade and manufacturing in the Northeast during the previous half-century had resulted in an accumulation of savings, while billions of dollars were contributed by European investors. Labor could be obtained partly from the rapidly expanding native population and partly through the flow of immigrants from Europe. In the United States, moreover, unlike Europe, political unity had been established over a wide area, with no customs barriers or other impediments to the flow of goods. And since the country had no threatening neighbors, its citizens did not need to concern themselves with international politics or maintain large armed forces, and could devote all their energies to internal development.

The rise of industry was not due solely, however, to these material factors. It would have been impossible if the American people had not also possessed the appropriate habits and values, technical skills, and political and legal institutions.

Ever since the first settlements early in the seventeenth century, the Americans had been primarily occupied with the task of subduing the wilderness and compelling nature to serve human needs, and had come to regard economic enterprise and achievement as especially worthy of admiration and encouragement. This attitude had been powerfully reinforced by the beliefs that many early Americans had brought with them from Europe. Calvinism had taught them to develop habits of thrift and hard work, and had given religious sanction to the activities of the businessman, while the optimistic philosophy of the Enlightenment had inculcated faith in individual rights and liberties, in a harmony between private self-interest and the welfare of all, and in the inevitability of progress. In the writings of Adam Smith and other classical economists this was interpreted to mean that the individual could best contribute to the advancement of civilization by devoting himself to the accumulation of wealth. Thus the habits acquired in the settlement of the continent and the values of seventeenth-century Calvinism and eighteenth-century liberalism had combined to shape a national ethos which glorified the successful businessman as the most useful member of society.

The necessary technical skills had been acquired during the earlier stages of the Industrial Revolution. Managerial and technological ability and the kind of unremitting precision and punctuality required for the successful operation of machines cannot be learned quickly. But the growth of industry in the Northeast had produced entrepreneurs who knew how to organize a business efficiently, engineers who understood production, and a working class habituated to the discipline of the machine. As at the beginning of the Industrial Revolution, moreover, important contributions were made by skilled craftsmen emigrating from Great Britain, while American engineers continued to copy new processes developed in European countries, especially in Germany, where industry was now expanding almost as rapidly as in the United States. The advance of technology, as of pure science, was international.

Meanwhile, industrial methods were beginning to be transformed by the progress of chemistry and physics. In the earlier stages of the Industrial Revolution most inventions had been the work of practical mechanics. But after the Civil War science began to have direct applications; after the turn of the century, in fact, a number of business corporations found it profitable to set up their own research laboratories. The partnership between the scientist and the engineer led to an astonishing and apparently endless series of inventions, with revolutionary effects on human living.

Government Support. Another indispensable factor in the industrial growth was the protection and direct assistance given to businessmen by the Federal government. The Constitution protected property-owners in various ways, especially by forbidding states to impair the obligations of contracts. As interpreted by Chief Justice Marshall in the Dartmouth College case of 1819, the word "contract" included the charter of a corporation. A corporation was regarded as an artificial person, which meant that it could not be arbitrarily prevented from doing business or deprived of its property. The Constitution declared, moreover, that "the Citizens of each State shall be entitled to all Privileges or Immunities of Citizens in the several States"; and this statement also was usually extended to corporations. Thus, after obtaining a charter in any one of the states according to whatever rules that state might prescribe, a corporation could do business freely throughout the rest of the Union. Since it was only through the organization of corporations that large accumulations of capital could be brought together, this legal protection was a vital factor in the expansion of industry and transportation.

Prior to the Civil War businessmen had not always received as much political support as they desired. The agrarian leaders who controlled the Federal government for much of the period between 1801 and 1861 had regarded property in land as more worthy of protection than that of merchants, manufacturers, and bankers, and after 1835, when Roger Taney had succeeded Marshall as Chief Justice, a suspicion of business enterprise had also been reflected in some Supreme Court decisions. But with the triumph of the North in the Civil War all branches of the Federal government came under the control of men sympathetic to the business point of view. The Republican Party believed in promoting business expansion, while the Supreme Court showed an increasing eagerness to protect business interests.

Business henceforth received much direct and invaluable assistance, especially while the Republican Party was in power. The tariff enabled

American industrial corporations to charge high prices without fear of being undercut by foreign competition. The banking system set up by the National Bank Act of 1863 and the financial policies pursued by the Treasury Department resulted in a currency deflation which benefited creditors at the expense of debtors. And direct grants and sales of public land, combined with lax administration of the Homestead Act, enabled business corporations to acquire ownership of many of the natural resources of the undeveloped West. Policies like the tariff were, of course, contrary to the *laissez-faire* economic theory in which American businessmen professed to believe. But when they talked in *laissez-faire* terms, all that they really meant was that private enterprise should be free from state interference. What the American business class actually favored was not genuine *laissez faire* but the program of state aid originally propounded by Alexander Hamilton.

Judicial Protection.   Fully as important as this government assistance was the protection given by the law courts, especially through Supreme Court interpretations of the Fourteenth Amendment, which can fairly be regarded as the Magna Carta of the business corporation. Originally added to the Constitution in 1868 in order to protect the rights of Negroes, the amendment declared in its first section that no state might "deprive any person of life, liberty or property, without due process of law." For a number of years this clause seemed to be of little importance, but a new interpretation was given to it in dissenting opinions by Associate Justice Stephen J. Field. Field's views were afterwards accepted by a majority of the Supreme Court in a series of cases beginning in 1886 and culminating in Smyth v. Ames in 1898. In these cases the Court attributed a much broader meaning to the phrase "due process," which had originally been intended merely to prohibit any confiscation of property or other arbitrary violation of individual rights. "Due process" was now extended to prevent any regulation that might prevent a corporation from earning a "reasonable" profit on its investment; and the function of deciding how much profit was reasonable was assumed by the courts.

Thus the right of property no longer meant merely the right of the individual not to be deprived of tangible possessions, as in the agrarian eighteenth century; in accordance with the capitalistic climate of opinion, it now included the right of a corporation to make profits from its properties by engaging in business. What this meant in practical terms was that state laws limiting the rates charged by railroads or public utilities might be declared unconstitutional if the courts decided that they were unreasonable. The importance of this new interpretation of the Fourteenth Amendment was shown by the fact that between 1890 and 1910 there were 528 cases in which it was involved, of which 289 referred to corporations and only 19 to Negroes.

The courts were never wholly consistent in their attitude to business regulation. Laws limiting rates or protecting labor were sometimes accepted as legitimate exercises of police power and sometimes voided as contrary to the Fourteenth Amendment. But for a number of years after the Supreme Court had swung over to this more conservative position in the 1880's and 1890's, its general tendency was to identify the American Constitution with the rules of *laissez-faire* economics, and thereby to create a legal structure very favorable to business. This was accomplished not only through the new interpretation of the due-process clause but also by defining interstate commerce in ways that made it difficult for either the state governments or the Federal government to exercise authority, thereby creating a borderland between the two jurisdictions which seemed to be inhabited chiefly by corporations. As a result of the new attitude of the Supreme Court, it began to restrict legislative power much more narrowly than in the past. Prior to 1870 the Court had invalidated only two acts of Congress, one in the otherwise unimportant case of Marbury v. Madison and the other in the Dred Scott decision. Between 1870 and 1920, on the other hand, the Court struck down thirty-nine acts of Congress, in addition to a number of state laws.

The Role of the Entrepreneur. With these assurances of official support, the task of mobilizing the nation's productive energies and organizing the building of railroads and factories was assumed by entrepreneurs who had the necessary ability, initiative, energy, and driving ambition. They came from all social backgrounds, although relatively few (contrary to popular belief) actually started without hereditary advantages. The more successful—men like Vanderbilt, Carnegie, Rockefeller, and Morgan—ended their lives as multimillionaires, possessed of a wealth and prestige which in earlier times could have been earned only by a military conqueror. At no other period in history, in fact, have such dazzling opportunities been open to men who coveted material success. Alternately awed by the achievements of these men and alarmed by their power, the American people have never quite made up their minds about them. Are they to be praised as "captains of industry" and given credit for the economic growth of modern America? Or should they be regarded as "robber barons" who seized control of the wealth created by the skill of technicians and the labors of the working class and then exacted tribute from the rest of the nation?

Certainly few of these entrepreneurs showed any delicate sense of morality in their business methods. In disposing of their competitors and circumventing any obstacles imposed by politicians or by the laws, they rarely hesitated to employ trickery, seek unfair advantages, and resort, when necessary, to outright bribery and corruption. Much of the wealth they acquired was tainted with fraud at the expense of Federal or state governments or of the smaller stockholders in the corporations they controlled. Nor did they display much concern for the welfare of the workers they employed or of the customers who bought the goods and services they supplied. Most of them could be wholly ruthless in the pursuit of self-interest.

Yet it is important to make certain distinctions. There were some men, like the railroad magnate Jay Gould, who apparently cared only for money and made their fortunes by winning control of enterprises created by other people and then siphoning the profits into their own pockets. But the more typical entrepreneurs, Carnegie and Rockefeller being outstanding examples, were genuine builders with a passion for organizing production more efficiently. Although their methods were often unethical (in which respect they were in no way different from many of their less successful competitors), they believed that they were working for the advancement of civilization and doing the will of God, and that in the pursuit of such noble objectives it would be foolish to display too much moral scruple. American liberals of later generations, justifiably alarmed by the power of the big businessmen and by their disregard for the interest of workers and consumers, have often failed to recognize that, in organizing capital and labor for the building of new enterprises, they made an essential contribution to economic progress.

Business Becomes Big.   In the long run the most significant of the problems caused by the industrial expansion was not the emergence of multimillionaires but the growth of a new kind of economic system in which the principles of *laissez-faire* competition were no longer effective. Before the end of the nineteenth century a few monster corporations were acquiring virtual monopolies in many important branches of manufacturing and transportation. Fields where there had once been many small units engaged in vigorous competition now came under the control of organizations powerful enough to dominate the market, fix their own prices, and charge whatever the traffic would bear. Obviously this meant that the public would be exploited, since there was no guarantee that the benefits of improved methods would be passed on to the consumer through lower prices. Popular indignation against these so-called "trusts" led to a series of attempts to dissolve them into smaller units and enforce competition.

Here again, however, it is necessary to make distinctions. Some of the trusts were formed solely for the purpose of controlling prices. Businessmen normally dislike competition, and during the later nineteenth century they often came together in "pooling" agreements or outright mergers in order to prevent competitive price-cutting and assure themselves of high profits. On the other hand, it must be recognized that the trend towards monopoly was, in large measure, an inevitable result of technological advance. The new methods of production usually required large capital investments, a fact that had important implications. This meant that business had to become big, and in consequence that there was room only for a small number of separate enterprises in many different fields. And when there were only half a dozen different corporations engaged in the same branch of manufacturing, as contrasted with the thousands of small producers characteristic of the pre-industrial era, it was easy for them to make price agreements with each other and virtually impossible for any public authority to enforce competition. And since investors were not willing to contribute capital for new enterprises on a sufficiently vast scale unless they felt assured of substantial long-term profits, the control of prices and the prevention of competitive price-cutting can be justified as necessary for economic progress. Nor should it be forgotten that some corporations achieved monopolistic powers primarily because they were more efficient than their competitors.

Thus the rise of the big corporations created a number of very complex problems, to which there was no easy solution. On the one hand, there was no doubt that they represented alarming concentrations of economic power and were often able to exploit the rest of the community. On the other hand, it was not easy to find a way of controlling them which did not involve either sacrificing the efficiencies of large-scale production or destroying private enterprise and initiative. This dilemma, which first became apparent in the late nineteenth century, has continued throughout the twentieth century to be perhaps the major issue in American internal politics.

2. THE EXPANSION OF THE RAILROADS

THE THIRTY years following the Civil War may well be called the railroad age, since the fivefold increase in mileage and the improvement in services were unquestionably the most important achievements of the period. Railroads dominated the investment market and were the chief source of new fortunes, while their needs set the pace for coal-mining, steel-manufacturing, and other industries. Linking together all parts of the United States, they brought about the rapid settlement of the vast Western territories, created a national market for the products of the new industries, and thereby made possible the mass production of the new era.

Most of the characteristic features and problems of the new economy were first fully exemplified by the railroads. As feats of engineering, they were stupendous. Yet many of the entrepreneurs who organized the railroad corporations were flagrantly guilty of corrupting state legislatures and defrauding stockholders; and after the lines had been built, they claimed unlimited powers to fix rates and services. The railroad corporations incurred so much popular indignation that, in spite of the dominant *laissez-faire* philosophy, they were finally subjected to Federal regulation.

Consolidation of the Eastern Roads.   Before 1860 a network of lines had been built through the Northeastern and Midwestern states, but they were owned by a large number of small companies, so that long-distance passengers had to make frequent changes. After the Civil War most of them were consolidated into a few large systems. The pioneer figure in this process was Cornelius Vanderbilt, a semi-literate and egotistical New Yorker whose first job was operating a ferry between Manhattan and Staten Island. He became a wealthy shipowner, on the strength of which he assumed the title "Commodore"; and in 1862, at the age of sixty-eight, he began to buy railroads. Before his death in 1877 he had expanded the New York Central into a large system providing through transportation between New York and Chicago and bringing about a vast improvement in services and reduction in rates. During his fifteen years as a railroad man he boosted his private fortune from $10,000,000 to more than $100,000,000, and became notorious for his bad grammar, his brutal sayings ("Law, what do I care about law? Haint I got the power?" was perhaps the most characteristic), and a vanity so monumental that he wanted to erect joint statues of George Washington and himself. The Vanderbilts became the first multimillionaire family of the new era, and the rivals of the Astors for leadership in New York society.

The New York Central's principal competitor for the traffic between the eastern seaboard and the Middle West was the Pennsylvania, which was expanded by a series of able managers, J. Edgar Thomson, T. A. Scott, and A. J. Cassatt, and eventually became the largest railroad corporation in the country. The same region was served by the Erie; but for some years in the 1860's and 1870's this road was under the control of three of the most shameless financial pirates of the era, Daniel Drew, Jay Gould, and Jim Fisk, who gave it an unhappy notoriety by speculating in its stock, issuing large quantities of fraudulent securities, and securing legislative and judicial sanction for their activities by wholesale bribery. The process of consolidation also led to the growth of the Baltimore and Ohio, was extended to New England by the New York, New Haven and Hartford and by the Boston and Maine, and spread to the South in 1894 with the creation of the Southern.

These years of expansion also saw railroad travel become quicker, safer, cheaper, and more comfortable. The first sleeping-car was built by George M. Pullman in 1864. In 1868 George Westinghouse invented the air brake, which made it possible for trains to travel safely at high speeds, and the next two or three decades saw the adoption of the standard gauge, steel rails and bridges, the block signaling system, and coal-burning engines. Between 1860 and 1900 the average weight of a freight car increased from 15,000 to 100,000 pounds, and revenue per ton per mile dropped from nearly $2 to 73 cents.

The Western Roads.   The building of the transcontinentals, however, was the most important achievement of this period. This was made possible by lavish help from the Federal government. After the initial grant of 1862 to the Union and Central Pacific lines, similar bills were passed for the benefit of other western roads. Lines were given public land varying between ten and forty square miles for every mile constructed, to be located in alternate sections on each side of the track. The Union and Central Pacific lines also received loans of Federal money, although this form of assistance was not extended to other roads. Altogether, after deducting land forfeited on account of failure to meet the terms of the grants, the railroad corporations received well over 100,000,-000 acres from the Federal government, in addition to an estimated 50,000,000 acres from state governments, amounting to a total area almost as large as the state of Texas. State, county, and municipal governments also aided the railroads by giving them tax exemptions and other privileges, buying their stocks, and contributing considerable sums in outright gifts. Much of this was not altogether voluntary, since the railroad men sometimes blackmailed local authorities by threatening to build their lines elsewhere if they did not receive enough cooperation.

In the long run, land sales by some of the western railroads seem to have more than covered their building costs. It should be realized, however, that most of the land was virtually without value until after the roads had been built, and that without the land grants the railroads would have been unable to obtain enough capital from private investors to finance construction. There was therefore strong justification for the generosity of the Federal government. Many of the lines, however, were left with a heavy burden of indebtedness and watered stock as a result of financial juggling on an immense scale by some of the railroad entrepreneurs. Their favorite device for enriching themselves was to organize construction companies with which the railroad corporations under their control would then do business at excessive prices. The Union Pacific was built by the Crédit Mobilier, which charged a total of $94,000,000 for construction that should have cost less than $50,000,000 and paid dividends of 348 per cent in a single year. In order to prevent embarrassing inquiries, blocks of Crédit Mobilier stock were distributed among Congressmen. The four California merchants who organized the Central Pacific, Leland Stanford, Collis P. Huntington, Charles Crocker, and Mark Hopkins, set up two construction companies which made a profit of $63,-000,000 on an investment of $121,000,000.

The American people ultimately became aware of these facts, although too late to repair the damage. The concrete achievements of the road-builders seemed at first much more important than the financial details. The Union Pacific was carried westwards across the plains and close to South Pass by Irish immigrant laborers under the direction of General Grenville M. Dodge. The Central Pacific, which confronted more serious engineering problems in crossing the Sierra Nevada, was planned by Theodore D. Judah and built mostly by Chinese coolies. Almost all the materials for the two lines had to be brought from the East, while another impediment was the constant danger of Indian attacks. When the roads met in northern Utah on May 10, 1869, a silver spike was driven by

Leland Stanford in the presence of an assembly of notables, and celebrations were held throughout the country.

Four other transcontinental lines were completed during the next quarter of a century, the Southern Pacific and the Northern Pacific in 1883, the Santa Fe in 1884, and the Great Northern in 1893. Of all the western railroad-builders, the greatest was James J. Hill of the Great Northern, whose statesmanlike policies made a refreshing contrast with the chicanery of some other corporation magnates. A small storekeeper in St. Paul until the age of forty, Hill took control of a small Minnesota railroad in 1878 and gradually extended it westwards to Puget Sound. Unlike some other railroad men, Hill realized that the prosperity of his line depended upon that of the people whom it served. Promoting immigration, improving agricultural methods, building schools and churches, and establishing steamboat connections between Seattle and the Orient, he became an empire-builder on a grand scale throughout the Pacific Northwest.

State Regulation.   Meanwhile, popular resentment against abuses of power by the railroads was increasing. When the earliest roads were built in the 1830's, there had been much state regulation, in accordance with the traditional English and American common-law doctrine that enterprises "clothed with a public interest" should be subject to public supervision; but this was contrary to the economic philosophy prevalent after the Civil War, and the Federal legislation endowing the roads with land on a generous scale had left them wholly free to fix their own rates and services.

The chief cause of indignation was the failure of the roads to charge the same rates to all their customers. Where there was competition between different roads, large-scale shippers could often obtain rebates, thereby acquiring great advantages over their smaller competitors. On the other hand, farming communities wholly dependent upon a single line were compelled to pay whatever it chose to demand for both shipping and warehousing, with the result that charges were often much larger for a short haul than for a long one. Another grievance was the formation of pooling agreements between roads supposedly in competition with each other, which enabled them to divide the business and raise their rates.

The railroad men argued that rebates and other forms of discrimination were necessary to secure business, and insisted, in general, that their over-all earnings were barely high enough to meet their financial obligations. This was probably true; during the depression period beginning in 1873, and again after 1893, a large part of the railroad mileage of the country passed through bankruptcy. But these heavy obligations were partly due to excessive construction costs, watering of stock, and other financial malpractices. The railroad men, moreover, sought to make themselves immune from public control by various unethical devices ranging from the giving of free passes to politicians, newspaper-owners, and other influential characters to wholesale bribery. For a long time, in fact, a number of state legislatures, from New Hampshire and Pennsylvania in the East to California in the West, were virtually the private property of big railroad corporations.

Massachusetts led the way towards public control in 1869 by setting up a commission to investigate complaints against the railroads. But the strongest demands for state action came from the rural Middle West, where the attack on the roads was led by a farmers' organization known as the Grange.[1] In 1871 the Illinois legislature passed laws establishing maximum rates, prohibiting discrimination, and setting up a Railway and Warehouse Commission. Similar "Granger laws" were afterwards adopted in Iowa, Minnesota, and Wisconsin. The railroads claimed that the laws were unconstitutional, but in 1876, in Munn v. Illinois and other "Granger Cases," the Supreme Court of the United States upheld the right of a state to regulate public utilities. Reaffirming traditional commonlaw doctrine, Chief Justice Waite declared that "property does become clothed with a public interest when used in a manner to make it of public consequence, and affects the community at large. When, therefore, one devotes his property to a use in which the public has an interest, he, in effect, grants to the public an interest in that use, and must submit to be controlled by the public for the common good, to the extent of the interest he has created." Waite went on to argue that public control included the power to fix maximum charges. "We know that this is a power which may be abused," he declared, "but that is no argument against its existence. For protection against abuses by legislatures, the people must resort to the polls, not to the courts."

Ten years later, however, the Court modified its attitude. In 1886, in the case of Wabash, St. Louis, and Pacific Railway Company v. Illinois, it invalidated an Illinois law prohibiting rate discrimination on the ground that this involved interstate commerce and hence was under the exclusive control of the Federal government, while in the same year, in the case of Santa Clara County v. Southern Pacific Railroad, it agreed that corporations were among the "persons" protected by the Fourteenth Amendment. The meaning of this decision became apparent in 1890 in Chicago, Milwaukee and St. Paul Railroad v. Minnesota, and more fully in 1898 in Smyth v. Ames. In these and other cases the Court declared that a corporation must be allowed a "reasonable" return on its investments, and that rate-fixing regulations were therefore subject to judicial review, thus reversing its decision in Munn v. Illinois.

Federal Regulation. The Wabash decision put an end to all effective state regulation and left a gap which only the Federal government could fill. Although relatively few Congressmen had any genuine belief in effective regulation, public sentiment made some kind of legislation inevitable. The result was the enactment in 1887 of the Interstate Com-

[1] See page 457.

merce Act. This prohibited rebates, lower rates for long hauls than for short hauls, and other forms of discrimination; ordered the railroads to make their rate schedules public; forbade pooling agreements; and declared that all charges should be "reasonable and just" (what these words meant was not explained). An Interstate Commerce Commission (ICC) with five members appointed for six-year terms was to see that the railroads obeyed the act, but it could enforce its rulings only through appeal to the courts.

As the first of the independent administrative boards which have become an important feature of the American government, the ICC proved eventually to be an epoch-making creation. But until its powers were enlarged by the Hepburn Act of 1906 and the Mann-Elkins Act of 1910, it seemed a completely futile body. In the Maximum Freight Rate case of 1897 the Supreme Court declared that it had no power to fix rates, and in the Alabama Midland case of the same year it virtually nullified the prohibition of long and short haul discriminations. The attitude of the courts made the Interstate Commerce Act almost a dead letter for nearly twenty years.

3. INDUSTRIAL AND FINANCIAL DEVELOPMENT

THE EXPANSION of industry was such a varied and complex process that no brief description can do it justice. Certain forms of mining and manufacturing, however, were of peculiar importance. The two most essential needs of the new economy were coal and steel. In fact, the most reliable way to measure industrial progress in general is to watch the increase in the production of these two basic commodities.

Coal and Steel.   The principal coal-mining region was a section of northeastern Pennsylvania where there were beds of the hard coal known as anthracite. Anthracite was not discovered in any other part of the United States, but there were plentiful supplies of soft bituminous coal down the Appalachian plateau and in a number of Middle and Far Western states. The anthracite fields soon passed under the control of half a dozen railroad corporations, but the soft-coal fields continued to be owned by thousands of small operators. During the last forty years of the nineteenth century the annual production of anthracite increased from 10,-000,000 to 60,000,000 tons, and that of bituminous coal from 6,000,000 to nearly 200,000,000 tons.

In 1860 the production of pig iron amounted to 800,000 tons, while that of steel was negligible. By 1900 the United States was producing nearly 14,000,000 tons of pig iron, of which 11,000,000 were made into steel. This was larger than the combined production of the two other leading industrial nations in the world, Great Britain and Germany.

Pennsylvania, which had both coal and iron fields and transportation facilities, had become the chief center of iron production before the Civil

War. Later in the century vast iron fields were developed around Lake Superior, especially the Mesabi range in Minnesota. But since there was no coal in this region, the ore was transported by water through the Soo Canal and across the Great Lakes to the Pennsylvania blast furnaces. Pittsburgh and other Pennsylvania cities thus retained their predominance in heavy industry, although centers of steel-production developed also in Ohio and other Midwestern states and, on a smaller scale, in parts of the South and the Far West.

The dominant figure in the growth of the American steel industry was Andrew Carnegie. Brought to America from Scotland at the age of thirteen, he worked first in a cotton mill and then for the Pennsylvania Railroad, and became an iron-manufacturer at Pittsburgh in 1864. By 1900 the Carnegie Steel Company was making a quarter of all the steel in the United States, and was the owner of coal fields, coke ovens, limestone deposits, iron mines, ore ships, and railroads. Carnegie's success was due primarily to his efficient business methods and driving energy and to his capacity for forming partnerships with men of almost equal ability, such as Henry C. Frick and Charles Schwab. Like most other corporation executives of this period, he enforced a harsh labor policy of long hours and low wages, and was uncompromisingly hostile to trade unions. On the other hand, he did not engage in stock-watering or other financial malpractices, and he felt obligated to use part of his wealth for useful objectives. After he retired in 1901, he contributed large sums to founding public libraries, improving education, and promoting world peace.

Oil.   After coal and iron, the most important mineral product was oil, although this did not become indispensable until internal combustion engines came into general use in the twentieth century. The organizer of the oil business was John D. Rockefeller, who was comparable to Carnegie both as an industrial builder and in the scale of his philanthropies. Establishing the initial trust, he provided the first outstanding example of the tendency towards monopoly.

The first commercial oil well was drilled in western Pennsylvania in 1859 by E. L. Drake, the chief use of oil at this time being for lighting. Mineral oil quickly began to take the place of tallow and whale oil, and a large number of small operators went into the business. The violently competitive conditions caused a great deal of waste, prevented any stability of prices, profits, and wages, and made long-range planning impossible. Rockefeller, then a young merchant at Cleveland, Ohio, became interested in oil in 1862. He left the drilling to other people and set out to win control of refining, through which he could hope to dictate terms to the whole industry and thereby to stabilize production and ensure regular and substantial profits for himself and his associates. Thus his method of making a fortune was to impose order and economy upon a chaotic, wasteful, and uncertain business.

Rockefeller adopted the most efficient methods of production, made

a regular habit of saving part of his profits, and, by forming alliances with
the ablest men in the industry, was able to establish a kind of monopoly
of brains. Operators who were willing to accept his terms were assured of
large profits, but those who insisted on remaining independent were
crushed by means of ruthless price-cutting. Rockefeller showed no pity
in dealing with his competitors, and his methods made him one of the
most unpopular men in the United States. His most remarkable performance was to compel the railroads not merely to give him rebates on the
oil which he shipped but also to pay him drawbacks on shipments of oil
by rival companies. The refiners who were driven into bankruptcy and the
oil drillers who were forced to accept whatever prices Rockefeller chose
to offer them portrayed him as a monster of cold-blooded avarice, although his competitive methods were actually not more unethical than
those of many other businessmen of the time.

In 1870 Rockefeller and his associates formed the Standard Oil
Company of Ohio, which soon acquired a monopoly of refining in the
Cleveland area. He then formed alliances with refiners in other parts of
the country, and by the end of the decade his group controlled 90 per cent
of the oil business in the United States. One of their problems was to find
some legal device for tying together the forty different corporations which
they represented. A pooling agreement was too loose and too easily
violated. The problem was temporarily solved in 1882 when the stock
of the different corporations was turned over to a group of nine trustees.
In this manner Rockefeller created the original "trust," a word which was
afterwards loosely applied to any large combination with monopolistic
powers. Ten years later the State of Ohio, under whose laws the trust
had been organized, ordered its dissolution. In 1889, however, New Jersey
had altered its corporation laws in such a way as to legalize the formation
of a holding company—a company, in other words, which owned a majority of the stock in a number of subsidiary corporations and was set up
for the sole purpose of maintaining unified control. In 1899 the various
properties of the Rockefeller group were legally combined through the
creation of a giant holding company, the Standard Oil Company of New
Jersey.

Meanwhile, the expanding market for oil in its various forms was
rapidly increasing the wealth of the group. They began to acquire ownership of railroads, iron and copper mines, public utilities, and numerous
other industries, representing an enormous concentration of economic
power. Rockefeller himself, however, virtually retired from business
before the end of the century and devoted the last thirty years of his
life to giving a substantial part of his fortune for medicine, science, and
education. He was not a man who could easily be liked; but it must
be recognized that even in his early business career he showed a real
insight into the problems and tendencies of the new industrial economy.

Electricity. The growing use of electricity for light, power, and communication was another notable feature of the period. This had been made possible by the researches of a number of pure scientists, especially Michael Faraday in England and Joseph Henry in the United States. That electricity could be used to provide light had been demonstrated early in the century, but for a long time the materials used for filaments in bulbs were not sufficiently cheap or durable to make general use possible. The problem was then taken up by Thomas Alva Edison, a self-educated man who had little basic scientific knowledge but had a genius for invention. Edison devised a satisfactory filament in 1879, and in 1882 the Edison Electric Company opened a power plant in New York City to supply current for electric lights. In the same year Frank J. Sprague worked out a practical method for using electrical power to provide transportation, and in 1887 he directed the building of the first electrical streetcar service at Richmond, Virginia. The use of electricity for communication, which had already produced the telegraph, was further exemplified in 1876 with the invention of the telephone by Alexander Graham Bell, a Scotch immigrant scientist who had specialized in the study of deafness. Bell's original telephone was afterwards improved by numerous other inventors, the most notable of whom was a Yugoslav immigrant, Michael Pupin. By 1900, 1,355,000 telephones were in use in the United States.

In these public utilities competition meant a wasteful and inconvenient duplication of equipment, and there was therefore strong economic justification for the monopolistic tendencies which quickly developed. The manufacture of much of the essential equipment was controlled partly by Edison Electric, which was expanded into General Electric in 1892, and partly by Westinghouse Electric, which developed the patents taken out by another gifted Yugoslav inventor, Nikola Tesla. The telegraph after 1886 was divided between two companies, Western Union and Postal Telegraph, while most of the nation's telephones were the property of a network of Bell companies which were tied together by a single vast holding company, American Telephone and Telegraph. This eventually became the largest corporation in the United States.

Other Industries. Technological advance was producing equally revolutionary effects in many other human activities. One group of inventors, for example, devised a series of mechanical implements which transformed farming methods. Others speeded up business procedure with appliances like the typewriter (1867), the adding machine (1888), and the cash register (1897). The making of clothes was mechanized by the sewing machine, which had been invented in 1846 but was not generally adopted for factory use until the Civil War period. Food habits were changed by the development of artificial refrigeration and of canning. The number of patents granted by the Federal government, which had reached a total of 36,000 by 1860, increased during the next thirty years by no less than 440,-000.

Some industries continued to be highly competitive. The manufacturing of textiles and clothing, for example, was performed by numerous small or medium corporations. But the tendency towards concentration was by no means restricted to the processing of mineral products and to railroads and public utilities. Entrepreneurs almost as forceful and ambitious as Rockefeller were putting an end to competition in many different fields. Many of the new mechanical appliances were made exclusively by single corporations. The McCormick Harvester Company of Chicago, for example, acquired almost a monopoly of mechanical farm equipment. Even in some of the industries producing goods directly for consumers, where consolidation often had less economic justification, there was the same tendency. James B. Duke's American Tobacco Company, founded in 1890, and Henry O. Havemeyer's American Sugar Refining Company, founded in 1891, were examples of almost complete monopoly, while meat-packing was dominated by a small group of Chicago businessmen headed by Philip D. Armour, Gustavus Swift, and Nelson Morris. Among other consumers' goods notoriously controlled by trusts were salt, whisky, matches, crackers, wire, and nails. Thus the American people could enjoy the benefits of technology only by paying tribute to the overlords of the new industrial economy.

Anti-trust Legislation.   Throughout the 1880's public opinion was becoming increasingly alarmed by the growth of monopoly, its most bitter opponents being the small businessmen who could not compete with the big corporations. In popular parlance any large combination was known as a trust, although actually businessmen secured control of the market in a variety of ways. In addition to forming trusts, they combined different corporations through holding companies or by means of complete mergers. Sometimes one corporation secured so large a share of the market that it could dictate terms to its rivals, and in some of the new industries competition was impossible because one corporation had an exclusive ownership of essential patent rights. As the American people watched the proliferation of millionaires, they became convinced that something must be done to maintain effective competition and thereby bring about lower prices.

During the 1880's a number of state governments passed laws prohibiting trusts and other forms of combination; but such legislation was ineffective as long as other states refused to fall into line. Some of them, however, notably New Jersey, Delaware, and West Virginia, placed very few restrictions upon the issuance of corporation charters. A group of businessmen organizing a combination had only to establish legal headquarters in New Jersey and secure a New Jersey charter, after which their corporation could own property and do business in all the other states. It became obvious, therefore, that only the Federal government could prevent the growth of trusts.

As with the Interstate Commerce Act, few Congressmen regarded legislation as either desirable or practicable, but public opinion demanded some kind of action. In 1890 Congress passed the Sherman Anti-trust Act by an almost unanimous vote. This brief and loosely worded measure was a remarkably crude attempt to cope with a very delicate and complex problem. Giving statutory definition to a traditional common-law doctrine, the act declared that "every contract, combination in the form of trust or otherwise, or conspiracy in restraint of trade or commerce among the several states, or with foreign nations" was illegal. "Every person who shall attempt to monopolize, or combine or conspire with any other person or persons to monopolize, any part of the trade or commerce among the several states or with foreign nations" was declared guilty of a misdemeanor punishable by a fine of not more than $5,000 and/or imprisonment of not more than one year.

If any hopeful citizens expected that John D. Rockefeller would now be sent to jail, they were quickly disillusioned. Prior to the year 1901 neither the Department of Justice nor the law courts showed any honest desire to comply with the Sherman Act. Strict and literal enforcement of its terms would, in fact, have impeded technological progress; it would have been absurd to fine or imprison anybody who established a monopoly without distinguishing between those businessmen who formed combinations solely in order to raise prices and those who dominated an industry through the efficiency of their methods of production. Between 1891 and 1901 the Federal law officers brought eighteen suits under the Sherman Act and won ten of them, while private persons brought twenty-two suits and were successful in three. But none of the victories were won against big business. In the E. C. Knight Company case of 1895 Attorney General Olney showed that the sugar trust controlled 98 per cent of the sugar refined in the United States, but according to the Supreme Court he failed to prove that it had sought "to put a restraint upon trade or commerce," and on this ground the trust was acquitted. The manufacturing business in which it was engaged, declared the Court, "had no direct relation with commerce between the states." But while the Sherman Act was not enforced against the big corporations, it was perverted in several cases into a weapon for attacking trade unions.

The tendency towards combination, in fact, actually became accelerated after the Sherman Act, and did not reach its climax until the turn of the century. In 1904 John Moody calculated that during the period since the Civil War 5,300 separate firms had been combined into 318 large corporations, and that 236 of these combinations had taken place during the period 1898–1903. By 1904, 38 per cent of all manufacturing was done by those firms, 1 per cent of the total, which had an annual output of more than $1,000,000.

The Rise of Investment Banking. Perhaps the most significant feature of the combinations of the 1890's was the growing influence of the investment bankers. Historians sometimes distinguish between three different phases in the development of capitalism, both in Europe and in America; the dominance of mercantile capitalism had been replaced in the early nineteenth century by that of industrial capitalism, and this was now changing into finance capitalism. The influence of the bankers came about through their control of the investment market. A corporation in need of capital would ask a banking house to undertake the function of selling its securities. But if the bankers were to retain the confidence of the customers to whom they sold such securities, they needed some assurance that the corporation was soundly organized and likely to make a profit. As a result of their function of protecting stockholders' interests, the bankers gradually began to assume supervisory powers over corporation management.

The chief banking house of the Civil War period, Jay Cooke and Company of Philadelphia, became insolvent in 1873. Financial supremacy then passed to New York, where the leading firm was Drexel, Morgan and Company, reorganized in 1895 under the name of J. P. Morgan and Company. Other important houses were August Belmont and Kuhn, Loeb of New York and Lee, Higginson and Kidder, Peabody of Boston. But there was relatively little competition between the bankers, and by the 1890's J. P. Morgan was recognized as their leader and, indeed, as the dominant figure in the entire national economy.

The House of Morgan.   Endowed not only with great financial ability but also with an extraordinarily masterful personality, Morgan set out to impose order and stability in one industry after another. His main objective was to ensure a regular flow of dividends to stockholders, in order that they might continue to buy securities and contribute their savings for further expansion. This made it necessary to ensure efficient management and to put an end to the buccaneering of men like Jay Gould, who had made millions by buying control of different corporations, arranging mergers, watering the stock, and then selling out. By promoting higher standards of financial integrity, Morgan performed a very necessary function.[1] At the same time he disliked competition, on the ground that it led to outbreaks of cutthroat price-cutting which were bad for all the businessmen involved, and believed in a policy of "community of interest" by which corporations should make agreements with each about prices and the division of the market. Thus, while Morgan's policies meant more protection for stockholders, they also resulted in higher prices for the consuming public.

Drexel, Morgan and Company was at first occupied chiefly with the sale of American securities in Europe. Since much European capital was

---

[1] Morgan did not always live up to these standards. In 1903, having taken control of the New York, New Haven and Hartford, he set out to secure control of all the transportation facilities of New England. During the next nine years the stock of the railroad was increased from $93,000,000 to $417,000,000, more than half of which seems to have represented water and not genuine capital investment.

invested in railroads, the firm assumed responsibility for reorganizing roads that were no longer paying dividends, scaling down their capitalization and squeezing out the water, installing more efficient management, placing its own representatives on the boards of directors, and promoting combinations. Before the end of the century more than a third of the total railroad mileage of the country had been "Morganized." In the 1890's Morgan extended his activities into a large number of other industries, and was the moving spirit in many of the combinations formed around the turn of the century.

The biggest of the Morgan promotions was United States Steel in 1901, which was made possible by the retirement of Andrew Carnegie. Morgan took the lead in combining the Carnegie Company with ten other steel companies into a single vast corporation capitalized at the then unprecedented figure of $1,018,000,000 plus a bonded debt of $303,450,000. This was scarcely an example of Morgan financing at its best, since the combined assets of all the merged companies were valued at only $682,-000,000 and the remainder of the capitalization therefore represented water, while the House of Morgan itself received the tidy sum of $75,-000,000 for its services. But the investors who bought the stock of United States Steel had no cause to regret their purchases, which usually earned high dividends. United States Steel controlled more than half the entire steel business and was strong enough to fix prices and determine policies for the whole industry. In accordance with Morgan's "community of interest" doctrine, its directors cultivated friendly relations with their competitors, and used their power to maintain high price schedules, which sometimes remained unchanged for a dozen years at a time.

The only financial empire which could compete with the House of Morgan was Standard Oil. But in 1907 the two groups established interlocking directorates in some of the corporations they controlled and became partners in a number of different financial operations. In 1912 the Pujo Committee of the House of Representatives investigated the situation and came to the conclusion that, through the banks, trust companies, and insurance companies under their management, the Morgan-Rockefeller combination had control of financial resources amounting to more than $6,000,000,000, and that members of the group held directorships in 112 corporations with a total capitalization of $22,245,000,000. Many people interpreted these findings as a proof that the House of Morgan had created a monopoly of money and thereby acquired dictatorial powers over American industry. Such fears were exaggerated, since the House of Morgan was a part of the economic system and not a controlling influence over it. Nor should it be forgotten that it had acquired its pre-eminence chiefly because its methods had won the confidence of investors. But such a concentration of money and credit under the control of a few men was certainly a startling contrast to the democratic ideals in which Americans professed to believe.

The Evolution of the Corporation.   The rise of the investment bankers was accompanied by important changes in the management and control of the big corporations. Many of the new industries had been built up by independent entrepreneurs who owned a large proportion of the stocks in the corporations they organized and personally supervised their activities. But after these men died or retired, they did not usually pass on their managerial functions to their heirs, who often preferred to devote themselves to sport, pleasure, politics, or philanthropy. As corporations grew larger, moreover, there was a tendency for ownership to become diffused among large numbers of stokholders, none of whom held a big enough percentage to exercise control. Thus ownership and management began to become divorced from each other, as had happened in the New England textile industry even before the Civil War. Although a corporation was still legally the property of the stockholders, they often ceased to have any effective control over its policies; ownership now meant only the right to receive whatever dividends management chose to distribute. In practice, as we have seen, the function of representing stockholders' interests, including the power to appoint and supervise the managers, was exercised by the investment banking houses. But the actual work of administration was left to salaried executives who understood the business and had usually worked their way up within it.

In this new era of absentee ownership there was less room for personal initiative and willingness to take risks. Bankers were likely to prefer conservative policies and refuse to gamble on new enterprises which offered no assurance of steady profits. It was significant that the chief new industry developed in the twentieth century, the automobile industry, was built up with virtually no financial assistance from Wall Street. The qualities needed to rise to the top in a banker-controlled corporation, moreover, were somewhat different from those that had brought success in the age of Rockefeller and Carnegie. Skill in handling personal contacts and winning other people's approval, and a reputation for caution and sobriety, tended to count for more than brilliance and personal drive. The managers of the big corporations, in fact, began to develop some of the characteristics traditionally associated with government bureaucracies. Thus American industry after the turn of the century was becoming less individualistic and more institutionalized; having passed through its phase of youthful exuberance, it was settling down to a more sober middle age.

4. PROBLEMS OF LABOR

QUITE as essential as the contributions of the entrepreneur and the financier to the building of the new industrial economy was that made by the working man; but his share of the benefits was decidedly smaller. Substantial improvements in working-class standards of living could be brought about only by trade-union organization or by state intervention, neither of which became established until the twentieth century.

The Condition of the Working Class. The fourfold expansion of the wage-earning class that occurred between 1860 and 1900 was made possible partly by the movement into the cities of young people born on American farms and partly by immigration. The heavy immigration from Germany and Ireland which had begun in the 1830's did not appreciably slacken until near the end of the century; and while many of the Germans turned to agriculture, most of the Irish continued to seek urban jobs. In the later decades of the nineteenth century there began a movement from southern and eastern Europe which by 1914 had brought in 10,000,000 persons, most of whom settled in industrial areas. The labor force in the anthracite coal fields and the steel mills of Pennsylvania and the Middle West became a bewildering mixture of Italians, Czechs, Slovaks, Hungarians, Croats, Slovenes, Poles, Ukrainians, and Russians. At the same time there was a steady growth in the number of women gainfully employed, and little decrease in the proportion of children. In 1900 close to 2,000,000 children under the age of sixteen were wage-earners.

In most instances the relations between capital and labor were determined by strictly *laissez-faire* principles. Although businessmen shielded themselves from competition by securing tariff protection from the government and by forming combinations, they were horrified at any suggestion that similar privileges might be claimed by their employees. They believed that any attempt to substitute collective for individual bargaining or to improve the condition of labor through legislation would violate the rights of property-owners and interfere with the processes of supply and demand by which the economic system was regulated. Businessmen believed themselves entitled to decide on what terms they could offer employment and to hire and dismiss workers as they saw fit. They refused to recognize that the worker did not enter into such negotiations on an equal footing, since if he rejected the terms offered him his only alternative was usually to starve. It was widely believed that any deserving worker could always find a job, that poverty was always due to laziness or immorality, and that the laws of economics had been planned by God in such a way as to reward industry and penalize wickedness. It is not going too far to say that many businessmen believed in the divine right of capital.[2]

Any theory of divine right implies responsibilities as well as privileges. Some businessmen, like Rockefeller and Carnegie, were guided by this conviction in the spending of their money; but their sense of trusteeship rarely affected their attitude towards their workers. If they used their

[2] The most famous expression of a divine-right theory was the statement made by George F. Baer, the chief spokesman for the mine-owners during the coal strike of 1902. "The rights and interests of the laboring man," he declared, "will be protected and cared for —not by the labor agitators, but by the Christian men to whom God in His infinite wisdom has given the control of the property interests of the country."

profits to raise wages or shorten hours, they would be encouraging idleness and violating the laws of economics. This was partly due to the fact that as industries became larger and absentee ownership increased, the human factor disappeared and the relation between employer and employee became wholly impersonal. The owner of a small factory might work alongside his men, know them personally, and develop a sense of responsibility for their welfare. In a large corporation, on the other hand, the primary duty of the management was to earn large dividends for the stockholders. Factory-managers had no authority to promote better labor conditions except when this could be justified on grounds of efficiency. The owners, on the other hand, rarely had any direct knowledge of the conditions under which their dividends were earned; and even if a few stockholders developed sensitive consciences, they usually had no way to make their wishes effective.

Real wages slowly increased during the later nineteenth century, while hours of labor for most workers had fallen by 1900 to less than sixty a week, as contrasted with nearly seventy in the 1850's. In some occupations, however, they were much higher, since industrialists claimed that when they invested large sums in machinery, they could not make sufficient profits unless they kept it running constantly; many of the steel workers, for example, had a twelve-hour day and some of them had a seven-day week. Gains in wages and hours, moreover, were offset by a number of other factors.

In many industries more work was required in less time. The pace of the factory worker was regulated by the machinery rather than by the natural rhythms of the human body; and managers were constantly seeking ways of speeding up the process. Much factory labor was extremely monotonous. In many of the new industries the average worker was restricted to the performance of a single function, which could be learned almost at once, and had none of the satisfactions of the old-time skilled craftsman turning out finished products with his own hands and tools. Industrial accidents were frequent. By the end of the century they were causing an average of 20,000 deaths and nearly 1,000,000 injuries every year. Yet the victims and their families were not usually entitled to compensation; according to the accepted legal doctrine, employers had no responsibility for accidents due to the ordinary hazards of the occupation or to negligence on the part of workers. Above all, workers had no job security and were under the constant threat of unemployment, which might easily mean starvation. There were two severe depression periods in the late nineteenth century, one beginning in 1873 and the other in 1893, in each of which millions of workers were dependent for long periods on private charity.

Most of the working class were crowded into the slum areas of big industrial cities, while conditions in some of the smaller factory and mining towns were even worse. A number of towns in the coal fields of Pennsylvania, West Virginia, and Kentucky and in parts of the Middle West were completely dominated by single corporations. The company which owned the factory or the mine also owned the houses where the workers lived and the stores where they did their buying and controlled the local government and the local police force. Completely at the mercy of their employers, the workers had little more freedom and less security than the serfs under the feudal system in medieval Europe.

Beginnings of Labor Organization. Prior to the twentieth century unionism did not make much headway except in those occupations, such as printing and the building trades, which were still carried on by skilled craftsmen. Such workers enjoyed a strong bargaining position because they could not easily be replaced. In the new mass-production industries, on the other hand, most jobs required little training, and if workers demanded better conditions, there was nothing to stop their employers from dismissing them. Immigration was another factor preventing the growth of unions. Labor solidarity was impeded by racial, linguistic, and religious differences and by the prejudices often displayed against immigrant groups by workers of old American stock.

A number of craft unions which had been founded before the Civil War had a continuous existence. But the first attempts to combine them into a united labor movement failed because the objectives were too ambitious and too vague; labor leaders were slow to realize that the only way to build a strong organization was to concentrate on winning concrete improvements in wages and hours. In 1865 William H. Sylvis of the Moulders' Union organized the National Labor Union. This claimed a membership of 600,000 by 1868, but dissipated its energies by advocating various political reforms, and had almost disappeared by 1872.

A similar lack of realism was displayed by the Knights of Labor, which was founded in 1869 by some Philadelphia garment-cutters under the leadership of Uriah Stephens. This organization admitted almost everybody to membership, excluding only lawyers, bankers, stockbrokers, liquor dealers, and professional gamblers; and while its primary purpose was "to secure to the toilers a proper share of the wealth that they create," it hoped to achieve this by organizing cooperatives and through legislation rather than by direct conflict with the employing class. Its leaders believed in the agrarian and Jacksonian individualism of the pre-industrial era, and hoped to make "every man his own master—every man his own employer."

After 1879, when a Pennsylvania machinist named Terence Powderly became Grand Master, the Knights of Labor had a rapid growth. This was a period of rising labor militancy, and workers turned to the only national organization claiming to represent their interests. By 1886 the membership had soared to 700,000. But Powderly and his associates did not know how to organize and guide this sudden flood of new supporters, and were often reluctant to support them in strikes against their employers. In accordance with its somewhat utopian program the Knights of Labor set up more than two hundred producers' cooperatives, but all of them eventually failed as a result either of mismanagement or of business hostility. The result was that most of the workers who joined the organization quickly became disillusioned, and by the end of the century it had almost disappeared.

The American Federation of Labor.   Meanwhile, a "pure and simple" union movement, aiming solely at immediate gains and repudiating more ambitious and remote objectives, had been launched in 1881 under the leadership of a New York cigar-maker, Samuel Gompers. In 1886 this was reorganized and assumed the name of the American Federation of Labor (AFL). Winning the support of every well-established union except the four brotherhoods of railroad workers, it had a slow but steady growth, and by 1900 its membership had reached 550,000. Gompers served as president every year except one until his death in 1924.

This new type of unionism emphasized the value of strict discipline, regular payment of dues, and centralized control under the leadership of salaried officials. Unions must build up reserve funds with which to finance strikes and pay insurance benefits. The main objective of the AFL was to establish collective bargaining and, where possible, the closed shop; in other words, to make union membership a prerequisite for working at particular jobs. Unlike most European labor organizations, it accepted the existing economic system, but insisted that there were conflicts of interest between employers and workers within the system. Refusing to ally itself with any political party, it sought to obtain legislation beneficial to labor by putting pressure on Congressmen; its policy was to reward its friends and oppose its enemies in each of the major parties.

Largely as a result of Gompers's political skill and shrewdness and force of character, the AFL won an influential place in American society. A number of employers were compelled by strikes and other methods to accept collective bargaining, and some of them even recognized its benefits. But while the growth of the AFL brought higher wages and shorter hours for union members, it did little to improve conditions for the vast majority of American workers. The organization represented chiefly the "labor aristocracy" of skilled craftsmen, and made little headway in the basic mass-production industries. Its policies, in fact, were in some respects detrimental to the general welfare. By establishing the closed shop and then restricting their membership through strict apprenticeship rules and high initiation fees, some AFL unions created labor monopolies which enabled them to charge whatever the traffic would bear and, in some instances, to block technological improvements. Some of their salaried officials, moreover, had a tendency to assume dictatorial powers over the rank and file of the membership, and a few of them became corrupt.

Labor and the Courts.   One of the main obstacles to the growth of the unions was the attitude of the law courts, which frequently showed a strong bias in favor of the interests of property. Especially notable was the use of the injunction, the strikebreaking potentialities of which were first discovered during the railroad strike of 1877. An injunction was a court order forbidding certain actions on the ground that they would cause damages which could not afterwards be remedied through legal procedure. Persons who violated an injunction could be convicted of contempt of court, without a jury trial. After the passage of the Sherman Act the courts issued a number of injunctions forbidding strikes and other union activities on the ground that they tended to restrain interstate commerce. In the Bucks Stove and Range Company case of 1907 and the Danbury Hatters case of 1908, for example, AFL officials were enjoined against boycotting the products of firms that had refused to employ union labor. Both these injunctions were upheld, on appeal, by the Supreme Court.

While the courts thus branded as illegal labor's attempts to secure better conditions by direct action, they also had a tendency to block the redress of its grievances through legislative changes. In the late nineteenth century some states passed laws limiting hours of labor for women and children and, in especially arduous occupations, for men. State and Federal courts validated some of these laws but regarded others as violations of the liberty guaranteed by the Fourteenth Amendment. Liberty, declared Justice Peckham in Allgeyer v. Louisiana in 1897, included the right of the individual "to pursue any livelihood or avocation, and for that purpose to enter into all contracts which may be proper, necessary, and essential to the carrying out to a successful conclusion the purpose above mentioned." By this reasoning the courts sometimes reached the conclusion that maximum-hour legislation infringed the right of the worker to contract for as many hours as he chose. In the case of Holden v. Hardy in 1898 the Supreme Court accepted a Utah law fixing an eight-hour day for miners. In Lochner v. New York in 1905, on the other hand, it threw out a law fixing a ten-hour day for bakery workers on the ground that they were "able to assert their rights and care for themselves without the protecting arm of the State interfering with their independence of judgment and action." Lochner v. New York proved to be a high-water mark of judicial conservatism, since in later decisions the Supreme Court allowed maximum-hour laws and other state legislation for the protection of labor; but the courts continued to show themselves unsympathetic to union organization until the 1930's, when the right of collective bargaining was finally legalized by the Wagner Act.

Class Struggles. Meanwhile, the directors of the big corporations remained for a long time uncompromisingly hostile to labor unions. They generally attributed any discontent among the workers to the influence of "agitators" and foreign-born anarchists; and some of them employed labor spies or made use of the services of Pinkerton's Detective Agency, which specialized in dealing with labor disturbances. Denied any legitimate channels of expression, the resentment of the workers broke out occasionally in explosions of terrifying violence. Four episodes in the turbulent labor history of the late nineteenth century were particularly notable.

In 1877 wage-cuts by the railroads led to nation-wide strikes, accompanied by rioting in most of the large industrial cities. Scores of lives were lost, millions of dollars' worth of property was destroyed, and order could be restored only by Federal troops. Lacking effective organization, the railroad workers were forced to accept defeat.

Again, in 1886, there was wide labor unrest, with a number of strikes for an eight-hour day. Employers, however, succeeded in branding the movement as anarchistic as a result of the Haymarket riot. A small group of anarchists organized a demonstration at Haymarket Square, Chicago, in support of the demands of labor. When police attempted to break up the meeting, somebody threw a bomb, and eleven persons were killed. Although there was no evidence connecting the anarchists with the bomb, eight of them were convicted of murder, and four were hanged; and although the anarchists had no appreciable influence among American workers, the impression was created that they had inspired the eight-hour movement.

The bias of the authorities was even more conspicuous in two disturbances of the following decade. In 1892 the workers in the Carnegie steel plant at Homestead, Pennsylvania, went on strike against a wage-cut and took possession of the factory. After they had held their ground in a pitched battle with three hundred Pinkerton detectives, they were ejected by 8,000 militiamen called out by the Governor of the state. In 1894, when the American Railway Union supported a strike against the Pullman Car Company in Chicago, the Federal government intervened on the ground that the mails were being obstructed. An injunction prohibited the workers from interfering with mail shipments, and President Cleveland sent troops to Illinois to enforce it, brushing aside protests by Governor Altgeld that the local authorities were wholly capable of maintaining order. The strike was broken, and the leader of the Railway Union, Eugene Debs, was sent to prison for six months for defying the injunction.

Despite these evidences that the power of the state was enlisted on the side of the employing class, few American workers adopted revolutionary beliefs. Eugene Debs emerged from prison a convert to socialism, and became the leader of the Socialist Party, which was organized in 1901; but the party hoped to achieve its objectives by peaceful and democratic methods, nor did it ever win any wide labor support. One revolutionary organization, however, played a stormy and picturesque role in American society of the early twentieth century, though its concrete achievements were meager. This was the Industrial Workers of the World (IWW), whose members were often known as "Wobblies." The IWW was an outgrowth of the Western Federation of Miners, headed by William D.

Haywood, which was formed in 1893 and organized a number of strikes in mining camps in the Rocky Mountain area. This was still frontier country where men were accustomed to taking the law into their own hands; both strikers and employers resorted quickly to violence, and the workers were easily persuaded that they could secure better conditions only though the revolutionary overthrow of the capitalist system. The IWW was organized in 1905, under Haywood's leadership, with the object of uniting all workers into one big union and waging class war against their employers. During the next decade it led a series of strikes, chiefly among migratory lumber and construction laborers in the West and unskilled workers in Eastern factories. In the course of its career it issued more than a million membership cards, but it won no lasting strength and was crushed during the wave of anti-radical hysteria following World War I.

The Decline of Individualism. The threat of monopoly and the conflicts between capital and labor were the most conspicuous and acute of the problems presented by the growth of industry. But these were merely aspects of the general problem of adapting American ideals and institutions to the new economy. For the rise of the big corporations had transformed the whole social structure of the United States.

In the pre-industrial era the typical citizen had been in business for himself as farmer, craftsman, or small merchant, and the achievement of economic independence had been assumed to be within the reach of everybody. After the growth of big business, small owners by no means disappeared. They still did most of the farming of the country, and much retail trade and even some manufacturing were still carried on by small businessmen. But in the most important branches of industry, transportation, and finance, economic power now belonged to corporations, large or medium-sized, with which small owners could not hope to compete. The typical citizen of the new era was the employee of a large enterprise, either as a wage-earner or as a member of the new salaried middle class which was increasing faster than any other group in the community. The decline of the small owner and the rise of the wage-earning and salary-earning classes had far-reaching effects on the whole national psychology, and eventually necessitated extensions of the power of government to maintain social security and promote economic justice. Principles that had been applicable in the old economy of small owners were no longer valid in a society in which the dominant institution was the big corporation.

Meanwhile, the traditional American ideals of economic individualism were being undermined by developments in another area of national life. For this period of industrial growth was also marked by the closing of the frontier and by a deterioration in the economic position and relative importance of the farm population.

XX

The End of the Frontier

1. THE COMPLETION OF WESTERN SETTLEMENT

2. THE FARMER IN INDUSTRIAL SOCIETY

3. THE CLOSING OF THE FRONTIER

A LONGSIDE the industrial expansion of the post-war years was occurring another transformation, equally momentous and on an equally breath-taking scale: the settlement of the western half of the country. Unbelievable as it may appear, it is literally true that the same generation that built the railroads and new industries also occupied more new land in thirty years than earlier Americans had occupied in two and a half centuries. In view of the rapidity of the process, it is understandable that in agriculture, as in industry, a number of complex problems were left for later generations to solve.

1. THE COMPLETION OF WESTERN SETTLEMENT

IN 1860 the westernmost tier of states consisted of Minnesota, Iowa, Missouri, Arkansas, and Texas. In most sections the frontier line was close to the 95th meridian, and only at two places—in eastern Nebraska and Kansas and in Texas—did it curve appreciably farther to the west. Fifteen hundred miles away there was another line of settlements close to

SELECTED BIBLIOGRAPHY: R. A. Billington, *Westward Expansion* (1949), and R. I. Riegel, *America Moves West* (revised edition, 1947), are excellent one-volume surveys of the westward movement. Indian problems are outlined in John Collier, *The Indians of the Americas* (1947). For the miners' frontier, see T. A. Rickard, *A History of American Mining* (1932), and W. J. Trimble, *The Mining Advance into the Inland Empire* (1914). The best study of the cattle kingdom is E. S. Osgood, *The Day of the Cattlemen* (1929). W. P. Webb, *The Great Plains* (1931), is a fascinating and authoritative study of the influence of environment on social development. The expansion and economic problems of agriculture are described in F. A. Shannon, *The Farmers' Last Frontier: Agriculture, 1860–1897* (1945). Oscar O. Winther, *The Great Northwest* (1950), is a useful regional history.

the Pacific coast. Apart from the Spanish-speaking inhabitants of New Mexico, the only well-established white colony in the whole immense area between the two lines was that of the Mormons in Utah. Yet by 1890 the director of the census could announce that the country's "unsettled area had been so broken into by isolated bodies of settlement that there can hardly be said to be a frontier line." And by 1912 all parts of the western country had been organized into states and admitted into the Union. Between 1607 and 1870 the American people had occupied an area of 407,000,000 acres and had brought 189,000,000 of them under cultivation. During the last three decades of the nineteenth century they occupied an area of 430,000,000 acres, while the area under cultivation increased by 225,000,000 acres. The population of all states and territories west of the 95th meridian rose from 1,370,000 (nearly half of them in Texas) in 1860 to 7,350,000 in 1900.

The western country fell into two main divisions, each of which had been considered by earlier generations of Americans to be virtually uninhabitable by white people. Across the country from the Dakotas down to Texas stretched the Great Plains, comprising almost one-fifth of the area of the United States. The total lack of timber in this region, the scarcity of water, and the militancy of its nomadic Indian inhabitants had hitherto discouraged any attempt at settlement; it had been left to the Indians and to the immense herds of buffaloes on which they lived. West of the Plains, throughout the Rocky Mountains and the desert plateaus between the Rockies and the Pacific ranges, the obstacles to colonization seemed even more insuperable. Artificial irrigation was transforming parts of northern Utah into a garden, but in much of this country water was so scarce that not even the Mormons could have developed successful agriculture. Yet between the 1850's and the end of the century both the Great Plains and the mountain country were effectively colonized.

The Conquest of the Indians. Before white settlers could move in, the Indians had to be subdued, and this required a quarter of a century of almost constant warfare. As at all earlier periods, the story of white-Indian relations was a dreary record of broken treaties and of encroachments by white settlers on Indian lands.

During the Civil War years there was savage fighting with the Apaches and Navahos in the Southwest and with the Arapaho and Cheyenne tribes on the Great Plains. Most of the tribes in the mountain country were induced to give up their land and settle on reservations; but the nomadic Plains tribes were more militant. In 1867 Congress passed a law providing for the removal of all the Indians to reservations, thus definitely repudiating the promises made to the Plains tribes during the 1820's and 1830's that they could keep their hunting-grounds forever. Seven peace commissioners were appointed to negotiate with the different tribes, and these men decided to create two reservations for all the Plains Indians, one in South Dakota and the other in Oklahoma. This was followed by nine years of warfare. Tribal chieftains could usually be induced to sign the necessary treaties, but individual Indian warriors often refused to be bound by them. In 1871 Congress voted to abandon the policy of dealing with the tribes as though they were independent sovereign units. Henceforth government agents dealt with the Indians, as far as possible, as individuals and tried to break down the tribal organization.

By 1875 the United States army, led by Sherman, Sheridan, and other Civil War veterans, had broken the back of Indian resistance, and most of the tribes had settled on the lands assigned to them. But no sooner had the program been completed than gold was discovered in the Black Hills country in the South Dakota reservation, and a flood of white adventurers invaded the lands of the Indians. This led to the last serious Indian conflict, the Sioux War of 1876. In June, Colonel George Custer, in command of a scouting party of some two hundred men, encountered the main Sioux force under Chief Sitting Bull and was rash enough to attack them. Custer and all his party were slaughtered in the battle of the Little Big Horn, but the Sioux gained little by their victory and were forced to submit before the end of the year. The Apaches in New Mexico and the Nez Percés in Oregon continued to give trouble for some years, and there was another Sioux rising, easily suppressed, in 1890. Otherwise, Indian resistance to the white man's conquest of the continent was now ended.

In addition to being driven off most of their land, the Plains Indians had also lost the economic base of their society. For countless centuries they had acquired food, clothing, and shelter from the meat and skins of the buffaloes, who had roamed across the Plains in immense herds totaling perhaps 13,000,000 animals. But the white men almost exterminated them within a quarter of a century. Buffaloes made easy targets, and shooting them, in many instances for pure love of killing, became a popular sport. In 1883 government agents, after scouring the Plains in search of the vanished herds, reported that the number had been reduced to less than 200.

Later Indian Policy.   The enforcement of the reservation program put an end to warfare, but few people regarded it as a satisfactory solution to the Indian problem. On the one hand, Eastern humanitarians insisted that it was the duty of the United States to train the Indians for the rights and responsibilities of white civilization. On the other hand, land-hungry Westerners continued to cast greedy eyes on the territories still held by the Indians. Each group felt that its objectives could be attained by carving up the reservations and making each individual the private owner of a homestead. The result was the enactment in 1887 of the Dawes Severalty Act, which authorized the President to divide the reservation lands. Each Indian head of a family was to be given 160 acres and would receive full title of ownership, along with the rights of citizenship, after a probation period of twenty-five years. The rest of the lands were to be sold, and the funds used by the government for Indian education. With some revisions, this remained the official policy of the government until 1934. Citizenship was given to all Indians in 1924.

The Dawes Act was successfully applied on some of the reservations, especially in Oklahoma, thereby releasing millions of additional acres for white settlement. Some of the Oklahoma Indians became educated and, to a large degree, assimilated into white civilization. But it gradually became apparent that this was not a satisfactory program; the Indians were too easily induced to sell their land (especially if oil was discovered on it) and often succumbed to liquor. A number of the tribes, moreover, especially in Arizona and New Mexico, refused to abandon their old ways. They continued to hold their land in the traditional communal fashion and showed no willingness to accept the attitudes of the conquering white men, retaining their tribal organization and still performing their sun dances and other ancestral rituals, although with a rather thin veneer of Christianity. By the 1930's, partly owing to the work of anthropologists who had studied Indian society in a sympathetic spirit, humanitarians were no longer convinced that the Indians would benefit by abandoning their own traditions. In 1934 the Indian Reorganization Act reversed the program of the Dawes Act and authorized the tribes to hold their land as communal property. By this date the Indians still held 47,000,000 acres, but half of this was desert or semi-desert and most of the remainder over-cropped grassland, so that a long-term program of Federal aid and rehabilitation was essential. By the 1880's warfare, liquor, and disease had reduced the total number of Indians in the United States to about 200,000, as contrasted with perhaps 1,000,000 before the coming of the white men; but after settling on reservations they began to increase, and by 1940 they numbered 334,000.

The Miners' Frontier. After the Pacific coast the mountain country was the next part of the West to be settled, the main stimulus being the search for precious metal. Within a few years of the California gold rush of 1849 the individual prospector, equipped only with a pick ax and a washbowl, could no longer hope to make his fortune in the Sacramento Valley. The rich diggings had all been appropriated; and with the exhaustion of the surface gold, heavy capital investments were required in order to sink mine shafts and install machinery. Corporations took over the fields, and forty-niners who had failed to strike it rich began to look elsewhere. For the next thirty years hopeful prospectors were wandering over the Western mountains in search of gold. They found it in a number of different places, and each new discovery resulted in a rush comparable to that of 1849. Unlike previous frontier movements, this was mainly a migration from west to east.

Within a few months after gold had been reported in a new area, a town would appear, usually consisting of a single street lined by rows of wooden shacks, of which at least half were likely to be saloons, theaters, and gambling-houses. The high prices would attract traders, and a stage-coach service would be organized to provide transportation and bring in supplies. In most instances the miners settled on public land without acquiring any legal title to it, and were dependent upon their own re-sources for the maintenance of law and order. Like many earlier groups of pioneer Americans ever since the *Mayflower* Compact, they organized governments of their own by democratic methods. Every gold rush in-cluded a weird assortment of scoundrels and desperadoes who had to be kept under control. In the early stages of a new settlement the more re-spectable citizens usually held a mass meeting, appointed judges, and adopted a code of rules regulating claims to diggings. Order could be maintained only by setting up a vigilance committee, the most important function of which was to hang a sufficient number of the local criminals. It was often several years before the Federal authorities superseded these improvised methods of enforcing justice by providing for legal govern-ment. These mining settlements of the wild West were the most extreme examples both of frontier individualism and of frontier self-government, and their more picturesque aspects have provided inexhaustible material for the popular fiction and motion pictures of the twentieth century.

In 1858 gold was discovered near Pikes Peak. Within a year 100,000 people set out for Colorado, and those who succeeded in getting there were soon drafting a constitution and petitioning for statehood. Congress refused its assent; but Colorado was given territorial government in 1861, and finally became a state in 1876. Some of the Colorado mining settle-ments were quickly abandoned and became ghost towns; but others, especially Denver, developed into cities.

The year 1859 saw the discovery of the Comstock Lode in the Washoe district of Nevada. This region proved to be enormously rich in both gold and silver, and Virginia City quickly became a thriving metropolis. Becoming a territory in 1861, Nevada was given statehood as early as 1864, chiefly because the Republican Party felt that its vote might be needed to secure the re-election of Abraham Lincoln. Vivid accounts of life in the Washoe mining camps are available for posterity owing to the fortunate fact that the first Governor's secretary, a Missourian named Clemens, brought with him his younger brother Sam, better known by his *nom de plume* of Mark Twain.

During the Civil War years mines were opened around Tucson, Arizona, but the more important discoveries were made in the north. The country between the Cascades and the Rockies, comprising eastern Washington, Idaho, and Montana and often known as the "inland em-pire," was the scene of a number of gold rushes during the 1860's and 1870's, while its fertile valleys were already beginning to attract agri-cultural settlers. A short-lived movement to Wyoming in 1867 left only

PLAINS INDIANS HUNTING BUFFALOES, *by* KARL BODMER (1809–93)
Bodmer, a German artist, visited the West in 1833. Most of the Great Plains country
remained Indian hunting ground until after the Civil War

ACROSS THE CONTINENT

A lithograph, published in 1870, showing one of the first transcontinental trains crossing the Humboldt River, Nevada

the ghost towns of South Pass and Atlantic City. Finally came the discoveries in the Black Hills country of South Dakota in 1875. These caused the last of the big gold rushes, and all the more notorious Western gunmen and gamblers (exclusive of those who had already been shot or hanged) converged upon Deadwood Gulch. For the next few years the town of Deadwood, consisting chiefly of two long rows of saloons frequented by Wild Bill Hickok, Calamity Jane, and other legendary characters, was probably the most lawless spot on the face of the globe, and killings and stagecoach robberies were almost daily occurrences.

By the 1880's the period of the miners' frontier had ended. No important new discoveries were made, and throughout the mountain country the individual prospector began to be replaced by the big corporation, usually controlled by Eastern financiers, which could install machinery and dig deep mine shafts. Between 1860 and 1890, $1,242,000,000 in gold and $901,000,000 in silver was taken out of the Western mines.

But more valuable in the long run were the other mineral resources of the West, particularly its copper, which became vitally important as a result of the development of electricity. Copper-mining quickly came under the control of a few big corporations. The mines at Butte, Montana, known as "the richest hill in the world," became the property of the Anaconda Copper Corporation, which for a long time dominated the government of Montana. Most of the other Western copper mines were eventually acquired by the Guggenheim family. Meyer Guggenheim of Philadelphia, the founder of the family fortune, began to buy mines in 1881, and then set out to control copper by establishing a monopoly of smelting, in the same way that Rockefeller controlled oil by monopolizing refining. After 1901 the Guggenheim-controlled American Smelting and Refining Company dominated the industry.

The Cattle Kingdom. The first white occupants of the Great Plains have proved to be almost as fascinating to the American imagination as the pioneers of the mining frontier. During the 1870's and early 1880's the grasslands from Dakota down to Texas, not yet divided into private properties and fenced in, constituted the Cattle Kingdom. This was the golden age of the cowboy. Wearing the picturesque (though strictly functional) costume which had been developed originally on the ranches of northern Mexico, he was a unique frontier type, with a gallantry and virility and a gift for folk melody which have earned him a special place in the American tradition.

The origins of the Cattle Kingdom were in Texas and, more remotely, in Spanish Mexico. Early in the colonial period the Spaniards had established ranches on the grassy plains of northeastern Mexico, and in the eighteenth century they had brought cattle into Texas. The animals had been left to run wild and multiply in the southern corner of the state, along the Nueces River and the Rio Grande, until by 1865 they numbered about 5,000,000. It then occurred to some enterprising Texans that here was a potential source of profit which might enable the state to recover from the losses of the Civil War. If the cattle could be rounded up and driven to Northern markets, they would fetch $35 or $40 a head. The result was the "long drive."

The first long drive started in the spring of 1866, when herds totaling 260,000 head set off on a 1,000-mile journey to Sedalia, Missouri. Most of them were lost en route, but in the following year a more accessible terminal point was found at Abilene, Kansas, on the Hannibal and St. Joe Railroad. During the next dozen years a total of 4,000,000 Texas cattle were taken over the Chisholm Trail to Abilene, Dodge City, and other Kansas cow towns. After spending months driving thousands of cattle across the plains, the cowboys arrived thirsty and eager for a little celebration; and life in the cow towns at market time was fully as gawdy, and almost as uncertain, as in the Western mining settlements.

The long drive was an unforgettable experience, but it was economically unsound, since the cattle lost too much weight on the way. With the increase of railroad facilities, long drives gradually became unnecessary. Meanwhile, ranching was spreading from Texas northwards, and by 1880 the whole Plains region as far as the Canadian border— western Kansas and Nebraska, part of the Dakotas, and large areas of Colorado, Wyoming, and Montana—had become cattle country.

The ranchers made use of public land, rarely bothering to acquire legal title to more than a homestead; and like the miners, they developed their own code of rules to determine range and water rights. The rules were made by the livestock associations, which assumed virtually governmental powers throughout much of the Cattle Kingdom, and were enforced, when necessary, with six-shooters. An improved breed was developed by the mating of Texas longhorns with Herefords, while the invention of artificial refrigeration and the growth of the meat-packing industries created an expanding market not only in the Eastern states but also in Europe.

Obviously, the open range could not endure for long, but its end was hastened by an economic disaster. For a few years in the early 1880's profits were so high that immense quantities of Eastern and British capital were invested in ranching, with the result that the range became alarmingly overstocked, and prices began to tumble. Finally came the catastrophic winter of 1886–87, with snow falling as early as November and temperatures dropping to nearly seventy below zero, during which millions of animals perished from cold and starvation. Many of the cattlemen were left bankrupt. Those who survived began to fence in their lands in order to make sure of adequate fodder for their own herds and to grow hay. Meanwhile, the Federal government was taking steps to end the open range by enforcing the public-land laws, and the Plains were being invaded both by sheep-herders and by farmers. With the sheep, who were reputed to ruin the grass by close cropping, the cattlemen fought a prolonged civil war, resulting in the deaths of a score of men and many thousands of animals. But before the end of the century the open range had come to an end. Parts of the Great Plains remained cattle country, but the life of the cowboy had lost its original epic quality.

Problems of Agricultural Settlers. Farming in the Great Plains was made possible only by a number of new inventions. The most obvious obstacle to agriculture was the lack of timber. The settler could build himself a house by piling sods on top of each other, and could use hay for fuel, but he still had to devise some method of protecting his crop from wandering cattle. Since all wood had to be brought from elsewhere, a timber fence for a 160-acre homestead cost the prohibitive price of $1,000. The solution to the problem proved to be barbed wire, which was invented by Joseph F. Glidden, a farmer of De Kalb, Illinois, in 1874, and within a few years was being mass-produced at low prices. This discovery was as important to the development of the Great Plains as Eli Whitney's cotton gin had been in the South.

The other main problem was the scarcity of water. This was partially solved when agricultural scientists developed new methods of cultivation, known as "dry farming," by which sub-surface moisture was attracted to plant roots and evaporation was checked. Since dry farming required more labor than ordinary farming, it made the use of machinery imperative. Settlers could also dig wells, but since these were likely to be several hundred feet deep, some mechanical device to draw up the water was desirable. This led to the use of windmills, although it was not until near the end of the century that they were manufactured cheaply enough to be accessible to the average farmer.

Public-Land Legislation. Agriculture in the arid West was different in many ways from what it had been in the East, and much of the experience accumulated by earlier generations of pioneers was no longer applicable. In particular, traditional notions of the proper size of a farm were no longer valid. The 160-acre homestead was based on experience in settling the Mississippi Valley. But in the Great Plains the average farmer required either more land or less: more if he practiced dry farming with the aid of machinery; less if he could obtain sufficient water by artificial irrigation. Congress, however, failed to deal realistically with the question.

The first modification in the Homestead Act was the Timber Culture Act of 1873. This enabled a homesteader to obtain an additional 160 acres on condition that he planted a quarter of it to trees within four years. But growing trees in the arid West was by no means easy, and only 65,000 individuals took advantage of the law during the fifteen years it was in force. Even less beneficial to farmers was the Desert Land Act of 1877. This declared that anyone could secure tentative title to 640 acres in the Great Plains or the Southwest for an initial payment of $160; the land would become his property three years later for an additional $1 an acre

if he could prove that he had irrigated part of it. But in practice the irrigation requirement was generally evaded, and most of the persons who
secured land under the act were cattle ranchers and not farmers.

Other changes in the public-land laws set land of special value outside
the provisions of the Homestead Act, but the chief result was to make it
easy for business corporations to acquire ownership of Western natural
resources. The Mining Act of 1872 set a price of from $2.50 to $5 an acre
for mineral lands, while by the Timber and Stone Act of 1878 forest lands
in the Far West could be bought in 160-acre lots for $2.50 an acre. Under
this latter measure lumber corporations were able to obtain millions of
acres of virgin forest by arranging for dummy entrymen to buy lots and
then transfer the titles. Public-land agents in charge of selling mineral
and timber lands rarely charged more than the minimum prices or in-
quired too closely into the credentials of the purchasers.

In practice the Homestead Act was of relatively little importance in
the settlement of the West. Between 1862 and 1900 no less than 521,000,-
000 acres of public land was acquired by business groups. This area included the grants to the railroads, land bought directly from the Federal
government or from Indian tribes, and land given to the states under the
Morrill Land Grant Act of 1862 and then sold by them. By contrast, only
80,000,000 acres went directly to homesteaders, and a number of these
were, in reality, not bona fide farmers but dummy entrymen employed
by corporations.

Settlement of the Middle Border.   The farmers who settled on the
Great Plains and in other sections of the West mostly bought their land
(at prices varying from $2 to $8 an acre) from the railroads or from real-
estate companies. Such land was usually close to means of transportation,
and credit could be obtained not only for the land itself but also for the
necessary equipment. As at most previous periods in the history of the
frontier, the majority of the settlers came from adjacent states and did
not travel long distances, while others were immigrants from Europe. The
railroads organized elaborate advertising campaigns in European countries, offering easy credit terms and other advantages, and portraying the
Great Plains as a land of milk and honey where farmers could earn substantial fortunes with relatively little labor.

The flow of German immigrants which had begun in the 1830's did
not fall off until near the end of the century, and many of them went
directly to the West. Another important human reservoir was Scandinavia, where many of the peasants were suffering from scarcity of land
and were in disagreement with the religious doctrines taught by the state
churches. During the last forty years of the century almost a million
Scandinavians came to the United States, settling especially at the northern end of the Great Plains, in Minnesota and the Dakotas. Norway
contributed a larger proportion of her population to the settling of the
United States than any other country except Ireland.

Like the promotional literature put out by other immigrant agencies ever since the days of the Virginia and Massachusetts Bay Companies, the railroad advertising did not give an accurate picture of life on the Great Plains. Probably no other section of the United States presented so many hardships to agricultural settlers. With long cold winters, hot dry summers, almost incessant wind, the constant threat of drought, plagues of grasshoppers, and occasional prairie fires, they had to fight an unending battle with the elements. The sod houses built by the early settlers provided shelter, but did little to make life comfortable or cheerful. Population, nevertheless, steadily increased throughout the northern Plains and the adjacent country—a region which became known as the Middle Border. The white inhabitants of Kansas, Nebraska, the Dakotas, Iowa, and Minnesota rose from 992,000 in 1860 to 7,241,000 in 1900.

New States. For twenty-nine years after 1860 only four new Western states were admitted into the Union; the two Plains states of Kansas and Nebraska in 1861 and 1867, and the two mountain states of Nevada and Colorado in 1864 and 1876. Then, in 1889, by an omnibus bill, the two Dakotas, Montana, and Washington were brought in together, and these were followed by Idaho and Wyoming in the following year. There was now for the first time a solid belt of states from the Atlantic to the Pacific, and only four areas within the continental United States remained under territorial government.

Utah was still controlled by the Mormons, in spite of considerable "gentile" settlement, and polygamy was regarded as an insuperable barrier to statehood. But in 1890 the Mormon Church promised to abandon its peculiar institution, and Utah became a state in 1896. Part of Oklahoma, all of which had hitherto been reserved for Indians, was opened for settlement by homesteaders on April 22, 1889. A gun was fired at noon on the appointed day, and 100,000 land-hungry pioneers promptly surged into the territory by railroad, horseback, carriage, bicycle, and foot. Nearly 2,000,000 acres were appropriated within a few hours. Oklahoma became a state in 1907. Arizona and New Mexico followed in 1912, completing the roster of the forty-eight states.

Thus the liberal program originally laid down in the Northwest Ordinance of 1787 had been applied over an area seven times as large as the original thirteen states, and the world's most remarkable experiment in colonial expansion and self-government had been brought to a successful conclusion.

2. THE FARMER IN INDUSTRIAL SOCIETY

THE AGRICULTURAL expansion after the Civil War played an indispensable role in hastening the nation's economic growth. American farmers not only raised enough food to supply the needs of the new industrial cities; they also maintained the country's international balance of payments. A

15. Agricultural Regions of the United States

AS AGRICULTURE BECAME COMMERCIALIZED, DIFFERENT SECTIONS OF THE COUNTRY specialized in particular farm products. Several large regions became clearly defined before 1900 and have not greatly changed since that time. The three main staples were cotton, corn, and wheat.

Cotton was grown over a belt stretching from North Carolina across the Deep South to Texas. As before the Civil War, a large part of the cotton crop was exported to Europe, so that the Southern economy was largely dependent on an open and prosperous world market. Partly for this reason, the South usually favored lower tariffs and an internationalist foreign policy. But cotton prices were too low to bring in large returns, and the profits mostly went to merchants and landlords rather than to the farmers. Intensive cotton-growing, moreover, decreased the fertility of the soil. There was more poverty in the cotton belt than in any other part of the country.

Corn was the basic crop in a block of Midwestern states centering in Iowa. Much of the corn was used to fatten cattle and hogs and reached consumers in the form of meat. The cattle were mostly raised on the high plains of the Rocky Mountain country before being transported eastward for fattening. Wheat become the most important crop in several Middle Atlantic and Border states, including Virginia, early in the nineteenth century, but its two main centers were in sections settled after the Civil War: winter wheat was grown in Kansas, and spring wheat in North Dakota. Except during the two world wars, the foreign market for both meat and grain became relatively less important during the twentieth century, partly because of the growth of production in other countries and partly because Europe preferred to spend its dollar exchange on American manufactured goods. Midwestern farmers mostly sought a better position in the home market, in preference to supporting an internationalist foreign policy designed to maintain a stable world market.

Other sections of the country produced more perishable goods than basic staples. New York, Michigan, and Wisconsin specialized in dairy products; fruit and vegetables were grown in Florida and California; and fruit in the Pacific Northwest. With improved methods of refrigeration and changes in dietary habits during the twentieth century, these became steadily more important.

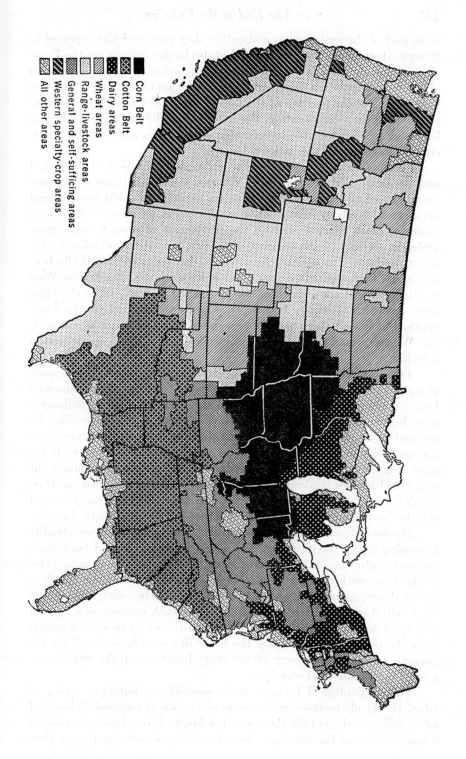

large part of the grain, meat, and cotton they produced was exported to Europe, thereby enabling the United States to pay interest on the European capital invested in her railroads and factories. It was thus the labor of the farm population that made possible the rapid building of the new industries. Yet the position of the farmer in the American economy was at the same time deteriorating. For a number of different reasons he was becoming more vulnerable to economic disturbances and less able to secure his fair share of the national income.

Farming as a Business.   The principle of division of labor had now been extended to agriculture. Whereas the colonial farmer had produced almost all the necessities of life for himself and could usually meet his financial needs by selling only a small surplus, his nineteenth-century successor often concentrated on the production of a single cash crop. Different sections of the country, moreover, tended to specialize in different products. Throughout the newly settled states of the Middle Border, wheat became the basic crop. The older sections of the Middle West mostly produced corn, much of which was fed to hogs, while the third great agricultural staple, cotton, remained concentrated in the Deep South. Cattle and sheep moved westwards into the mountain country, and Wisconsin and parts of New England and New York specialized in dairying.

Thus farming had become a business. From a narrowly economic viewpoint this meant an advance in efficiency. The successful commercial farmer could produce more, attain a higher standard of living, and enjoy more leisure than the old-time subsistence farmer. But by becoming dependent on the market he at the same time became more insecure, since his prosperity depended on the sale of his crops at a good price. If the price was driven down by overproduction or business fluctuation, he might find himself bankrupt. He had no way of controlling the market, which was, in fact, world-wide. Prices were determined by conditions not only in the United States, but also in Europe, Asia, and South America.

Mechanization.   Successful farming, moreover, required steadily increasing capital investments. The simple tools which had been used, generation after generation, almost since the dawn of history gave place in the nineteenth century to machinery. The reaper and the thresher, invented during the 1830's and 1840's, first began to be widely used during the Civil War. The later years of the nineteenth century saw a great variety of new appliances which mechanized the whole process of raising grain. In the twentieth century the horse began to be replaced by the gasoline tractor, while many of the daily farmhouse tasks were transformed by the use of electricity.

This technological progress made possible an immense saving of labor. By the old methods each acre grown to wheat required 61 hours of labor, but as early as 1890 the use of machinery had reduced the time to 3 hours. Whereas the old-time wheat farmer could not plant more than

7½ acres, since this was as much as he could reap during the limited harvesting season, the farmer of 1890 could plant 135 acres. But while mechanization enabled the farmer to produce more, it also increased his dependence upon the market. His life was easier than that of his grandfather, but in order to buy the new appliances he had to obtain much larger sums of money.

Scientific Improvements.   Farming was also becoming more productive through the introduction of new seeds and new techniques. The Federal government played a leading part in stimulating the application of science to agriculture. Congress made an initial appropriation of $1,000 for agricultural research in 1839. A Department of Agriculture was established in 1862, and its head was given Cabinet rank in 1889. The two most important pieces of legislation for the improvement of agriculture were the Morrill Land Grant Act of 1862, which gave public land to the states for setting up agricultural colleges, and the Hatch Act of 1887, which provided for the creation of agricultural experiment stations in each of the states. Largely as a result of this government support, scientists did an immense amount of work in introducing new plants suited to the American soil and climate, creating valuable hybrids, devising methods for curing plant and animal diseases and checking insect pests, and evolving new methods of farming. Federal agencies also worked actively to publicize these discoveries and induce the farm population to abandon its traditional prejudices against new devices.

The result was that American farmland grew not only in size but also in productivity. Agriculture was expanding intensively as well as extensively. In 1850 there had been approximately 1,500,000 farms and plantations with a total area of 290,000,000 acres (about half of it under cultivation). They had produced 100,000,000 bushels of wheat, 590,000,-000 bushels of corn, and 4,590,000 bales of cotton. By 1900 the number of separate farm properties had increased to 5,700,000 and the area to 840,000,000 acres (414,000,000 of them under cultivation). They were now producing 600,000,000 bushels of wheat, 2,662,000,000 bushels of corn, and 20,226,000 bales of cotton. Thus, while both the area in farms and the area under cultivation had nearly tripled, production of wheat had increased by 600 per cent, that of corn by nearly 500 per cent, and that of cotton by more than 400 per cent.

The Farmers' Economic Problems.   Unfortunately, the individuals primarily responsible for this economic advance were those who gained least by it. Unlike the owners of the railroads and the new industries, the farmers were unable to form combinations to control the market and stabilize prices. They had to sell under strictly *laissez-faire* conditions. Nor was the growth of production restricted to the United States; vast new areas of farmland were being opened up in Canada, Argentina, and elsewhere. The result was that during the last two decades of the nineteenth century there was a steady fall in farm prices. Between 1878 and

1881 wheat averaged over $1 a bushel, while corn sold for 43 cents. During the depression period of the 1890's wheat dropped to 63 cents and corn to 30 cents. This meant that the wheat farmer had to sell nearly twice as much grain in order to receive the same amount of money. Yet many American farmers were actually producing less in the 1890's than in the early 1880's, since, starting in 1887, there was nearly a decade of drought in the states of the Middle Border.

Such a situation would have been tolerable only if the farmer's costs had decreased in proportion. But one large item, interest payments on his debts, was actually increasing. Most of the farmers who moved into the Middle Border borrowed money, either to carry them through the period of settlement or to buy equipment, and in the early 1880's there was no lack of lenders. After the depression of the 1870's Easterners with money to spare decided that farm mortgages were a peculiarly safe and profitable investment, and for some years mortgage-company agents were touring the prairie country and positively pleading with the farmers to accept loans on apparently attractive terms. But once the farmer had gone into debt, he usually found it impossible ever to extricate himself. In the late 1880's prices fell, money grew tighter, and drought hit the Middle Border. Many farmers could save their properties from foreclosure only by turning to loan sharks who charged interest rates that were rarely below 20 per cent and sometimes rose as high as 40 per cent. There was thus a rapid growth in the total farm debt and in the proportion of the farmers' income that was paid to creditors.

Nor did other farm costs decrease to anything like the same degree as farm prices. Many of the articles the farmers bought were controlled by trusts. In particular, the market for farm machinery was dominated by the McCormick Harvester Company of Chicago. Even more resentment was caused by the elevator companies which bought and stored the farmers' grain and the railroads which shipped it. In most parts of the farm belt all the storage and transportation facilities were monopolized by single companies, which were able to dictate their own terms. The elevator companies paid the market price for grain, minus transportation costs and a profit for themselves; but they frequently defrauded the farmers—or so it was believed—by means of their practice of grading wheat into different categories with different prices. Wheat which the grower insisted was of No. 1 quality would often be graded as inferior and paid for accordingly. The railroads demanded what seemed to the farmers to be excessive charges and particularly infuriated them by charging more for a short haul than for a long one; for example, it cost as much to ship grain from Fargo to Minneapolis as from Minneapolis to New York. As the wheat farmer saw the situation, the railroads had first enticed him into the prairies by misleading advertising, and now had him at their mercy and could exploit him as they pleased. As a result of heavy storage and transportation costs and other middlemen's charges, only a small part, probably not more than one-fifth, of the price paid for grain by the consumer actually went to the farmer who had produced it.

No doubt the farmers saw their economic problems in excessively simple terms. Many of the practices which seemed to them to be deliberate exploitation were due to the mechanisms of supply and demand. But statistical evidence shows that the economic position of a large number of American farmers was genuinely deteriorating. By the 1890's per capita indebtedness in the Middle Border was higher than in any other part of the country, and a large majority of the farms carried mortgages. Even more disturbing was the growth of tenancy. The tenure ladder sometimes led upwards: young men would begin their careers as tenants and rise finally to ownership. But more often the ladder led downwards, since an increasing number of farmers succumbed to mortgage foreclosures and henceforth had to rent land. In 1880 about a quarter of all American farmers were tenants, but the large majority of them were in the South. The proportion rose to 35 per cent in 1900, and 42 per cent in 1930, and much of this increase was due to a rapid growth of tenancy in the wheat and corn country, especially in Iowa, Kansas, Nebraska, and South Dakota.

The only bright spot in the farmers' economic situation was that real-estate values continued to rise. As a result of the growth of population, the building of towns, the slow westward movement of industry, and the activities of speculators, the price of land in favored areas was sometimes multiplied several times within a few years. The farmer who had settled in the Middle Border during its early years and had succeeded in retaining ownership could normally hope to provide for his old age by selling at a substantial profit. It has sometimes been suggested, in fact, that the rise of land values was the one factor saving the farm belt from total bankruptcy.

Another significant long-term tendency was the growth of economic differentiations among the farmers themselves. A relatively small number of farmers, more efficient or more fortunate than their neighbors, were able to surmount their economic handicaps, expand their farms, and adopt the most modern methods of production. Others slipped down the tenure ladder, making frequent moves from one farm to another, sometimes ending as hired laborers, and never achieving any degree of security. By the 1920's this tendency had progressed so far that half the total farm income was going to only 11 per cent of the nation's farmers, while at the other extreme half the farmers were getting only 11 per cent of the income. Thus the rural population included a vast mass of impoverished farm families who contributed very little to the national income and had living standards far below the national average.

Farm Insurgency.   Throughout all history urban business groups have had the upper hand over the groups producing essential raw materials. Such a situation had already been exemplified in America in

16. The Growth of Farm Tenancy

THE CLEAREST INDICATION THAT ECONOMIC TRENDS AFTER THE CIVIL WAR WERE detrimental to the farm population was the increase of tenancy. The traditional American ideal, as voiced by leaders like Thomas Jefferson, was a society in which most people were independent property owners. But with the rise of industry and the adoption by the Federal government of financial and tariff policies favorable to business interests, a large proportion of the farmers were unable to retain ownership and sank down the tenure ladder.

In 1880 tenancy was extensive throughout the South, but this was because the big plantations, which had been operated as individual units before the Civil War, were now divided up. Most of the tenants were former slaves or poor whites who had formerly been landless. Thus tenancy in the South at this period meant in most instances a step up, rather than down, the economic ladder. But even in 1880 the tenancy ratio was already high in Illinois and half a dozen other Midwestern states.

Economic conditions were bad for the farmers throughout much of the period from 1880 to 1900 and again after World War I. During this period tenancy rose even further. The figures for 1930 showed a marked increase over those for 1880 in almost every part of the country. The only exception was New England, where farming was no longer of much importance. Tenancy had become especially high in the wheat and corn areas of the Middle West, where the soil was richer than in any other section. The same areas also had the highest farm mortgage debts.

Some farmers began as tenants and worked their way up to ownership. A much larger number began as owners but incurred heavy debts and finally lost their land through mortgage foreclosures. Few tenant farmers earned good livings, and a large number of them moved every two or three years. Tenancy was bad for the farmers because they had to pay rents to landlords; it was also bad for the land because tenants had little inducement to conserve its fertility or make long-term improvements.

The growth of tenancy was checked for the first time during the 1930's, when farm prices were raised, partly by the New Deal and partly by bad harvests. During World War II, when hundreds of thousands of tenant farmers moved to jobs in war industries, there was a rapid decrease.

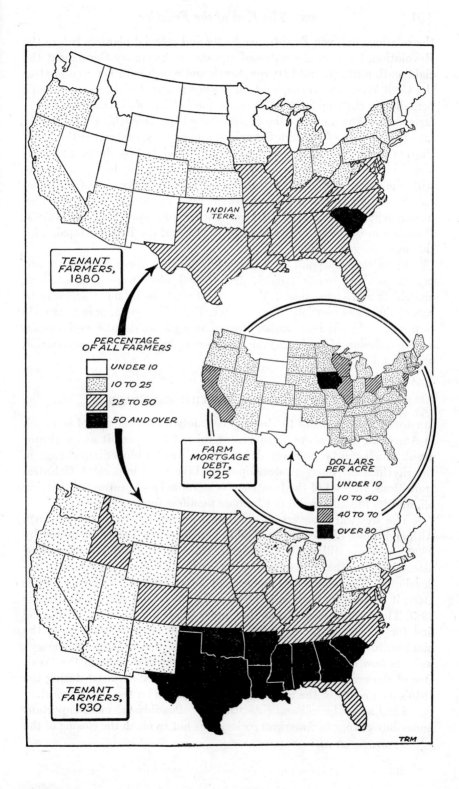

TENANT
FARMERS,
1880

PERCENTAGE
OF ALL FARMERS

UNDER 10

10 TO 25

25 TO 50

50 AND OVER

INDIAN
TERR.

FARM
MORTGAGE
DEBT,
1925

DOLLARS
PER ACRE

UNDER 10

10 TO 40

40 TO 70

OVER 80

TENANT
FARMERS,
1930

TRM

the relations between British merchants and colonial planters before the Revolution, between the seaboard and the back country throughout the eighteenth century, and between North and South both before and after the Civil War. And throughout all history raw-material producers have periodically risen up in revolt against the burden of their debts. As the farmers saw how much of the profits earned by their labors went finally into the pockets of Eastern financiers, and as they contrasted the hardships of life on the prairies with the luxuries enjoyed by the new millionaire families, they became convinced that something had gone wrong with the whole economic system. In the last three decades of the nineteenth century the farm belt was swept by a series of waves of agrarian insurgency; the Granger and Greenbacker movements in the 1870's, Populism in the late 1880's and early 1890's, and the Bryan campaign for the presidency in 1896.[1]

From the viewpoint of Eastern businessmen these movements appeared as dangerously radical, and their leaders were denounced as anarchists and communists. Yet it might perhaps be more accurate to regard them as essentially conservative. Farm insurgency was a struggle to preserve the old Jeffersonian ideal of an agrarian democracy based on a wide diffusion of landownership in the new America of the corporation and the machine.

3. THE CLOSING OF THE FRONTIER

ALTHOUGH the closing of the frontier certainly meant the end of an epoch in American history, one must be careful not to regard it as an abrupt event which can be precisely dated. There was no immediate change in the rhythms of American development. Like most important historical transitions, the end of the frontier was a gradual and protracted tapering off, and its full effects did not become manifest for generations.

The westward movement continued during the twentieth century. Although most of the more valuable locations had been pre-empted by 1890, there was still much public land. Many parts of the West remained astonishingly empty by contrast with the East, and were still largely undeveloped. The number of homestead entries actually increased after 1900; it reached its peak in 1913, and did not fall off sharply until after 1927. The total acreage distributed under the Homestead Act during the first forty years of the twentieth century was twice as much as in the nineteenth. An even more important aspect of the westward movement was the flow of urban workers to the new industrial areas in the West. One of the greatest migrations in American history occurred during the 1940's as a result of the growth of war industries on the Pacific coast.

The End of Agricultural Expansion.   Possibly the most important immediate change in American society was not so much the closing of the

[1] See pages 457–63.

frontier as the fact that economic conditions were unfavorable to further agricultural expansion. After the rapid growth of farmland and productivity in the late nineteenth century the nation had more farmers than were needed. The results were overproduction of foodstuffs, falling farm prices, and agricultural depression. The situation improved during the early years of the twentieth century, but World War I was followed by another collapse of farm prices. Since the population was no longer increasing as rapidly as in the nineteenth century, the domestic market for food products grew only slowly. The farmers, moreover, lost much of their foreign market; foreign countries in the twentieth century preferred to buy the products of American industry rather than of agriculture, and grew more of their own food. After 1920 the farm population began to decrease, not only relatively to the total population but also absolutely; whereas the number of farmers had risen by 5,000,000 between 1850 and 1920, between 1920 and 1950 it dropped by nearly 600,000.

What was the result of this decline in the importance of agriculture in American life? The more extreme exponents of Frederick Jackson Turner's frontier thesis undoubtedly exaggerated it. Believing that frontier agriculture had been a safety valve for urban discontent, they argued that the closing of the frontier would inevitably be followed by a growth of conflicts in the cities. But in actuality there had never been any important movement from the cities into agriculture; discontented urban workers had at no period been able to escape from exploitation by becoming frontier farmers. It is therefore incorrect to regard the closing of the frontier as directly responsible for the conflicts between capital and labor and the other economic problems which the United States has faced in the twentieth century.

Yet there are important indirect connections between these developments. From the first colonization until after the Civil War a majority of all Americans had been independent small farmers, and American ideals of freedom and equality had been expounded mainly by spokesmen for the farmer's point of view. Early champions of human rights, such as Thomas Jefferson, had always regarded the farmer as the typical American citizen, and had suggested that the United States might retain its free institutions only as long as there were western lands available for settlement. But the center of gravity of American society was now shifting to the cities, and the typical citizen was no longer the independent farmer but the employee of a big corporation. The proportion of the total population living on farms dropped from three-fifths in 1860 to less than one-third by 1920 and to less than one-fifth by 1950. Thus the traditional ideals were losing their original economic base, and had to be readapted to new social conditions.

The Conservation Problem. The closing of the frontier had another aspect which was equally momentous. The American people were now faced with the realization that their natural resources were not inexhaustible. During nearly three hundred years wastefulness had been a national habit. As long as farmers could move to new land, they had rarely taken the trouble to conserve soil fertility, with the result that many millions of acres had been irreparably ruined and then abandoned. Lumber companies had destroyed vast areas of virgin forest without planting new trees; and most of the country's mineral wealth had been transferred to private owners interested primarily in immediate profits. But now that all parts of the country were settled, it was necessary to recognize that this reckless process of destruction could not continue indefinitely.

The first steps towards a program of conservation were taken in the late nineteenth century. Pioneer work in demonstrating the need for government action was done by the United States Geological Survey, headed after 1880 by Major J. W. Powell, one of America's truly great public servants. Powell's classic *Lands of the Arid Region*, published in 1878, was a comprehensive study of the whole conservation problem. In 1891 Congress passed the Forest Reserve Act authorizing the president to withdraw timber lands from sale or entry by homesteaders; during the next ten years some 50,000,000 acres were placed in the forest reserve. In 1894 the Carey Act provided that public land should be turned over to Western states for reclamation by irrigation, although little was done to put it into effect. These were moves in the right direction, but they did not go far. Fortunately, some twentieth-century presidents, particularly the two Roosevelts, were keenly aware of the importance of the problem and willing to provide leadership.

The World Perspective.   The full significance of the closing of the frontier can be appreciated only by seeing it in the perspective of world history. The advancing line of settlement in the American West had been the frontier not merely of the United States but of Western civilization. There had been similar frontiers elsewhere: in Latin America, the British Dominions, and parts of Africa, and also (if Russia can be considered as belonging to Western civilization) in Siberia. Ever since the age of the discoveries the Europeans had been expanding across the globe, settling in empty areas and imposing their institutions and techniques upon the peoples of Asia, Africa, and the Americas. By the beginning of the twentieth century this process was close to completion; Western civilization had become virtually world-wide, and except in the tropics and the arctic regions there was little room for any further colonization. Thus the epoch of expansion, which had begun in the late Middle Ages, was drawing to a close, and internal social and economic pressures in the Western nations could no longer be relieved through the migration of discontented groups.

XXI

From Grant to McKinley

1. THE POLITICAL SYSTEM

2. PRESIDENTIAL PARADE

3. THE REVOLT OF THE FARMERS

POLITICAL history during the 1870's and 1880's was no longer of major importance. An uninspiring series of second-rate figures occupied the presidency, and most of the leading men in Congress were equally mediocre. There was a marked decline of political idealism and a growth of cynicism and corruption, especially during the Grant administration. At no other period in American history, in fact, has the moral and intellectual tone of political life been so uniformly low or have political conflicts been concerned so predominantly with patronage rather than principle.

The main reason was that the average citizen was no longer vitally concerned with political questions. After the settlement of the sectional conflict there were for a long time no fundamental issues that aroused public sentiment or demanded statesmanlike leadership. Most people accepted the growth of industry as a beneficent process, and there was little awareness of the new economic problems that were beginning to require solution. Apart from Southern Reconstruction, the chief subjects

SELECTED BIBLIOGRAPHY: Matthew Josephson, *The Politicos* (1938), is a popularly written general account of political history through this period. For specific issues, the following can be consulted: D. R. Dewey, *Financial History of the United States* (revised edition, 1935); C. R. Fish, *The Civil Service and the Patronage* (1905); A. B. Hepburn, *A History of Currency in the United States* (1924); F. W. Taussig, *The Tariff History of the United States* (revised edition, 1931). C. V. Woodward, *Reunion and Reaction* (1951), offers a new interpretation of the events of 1877 following the Hayes-Tilden election. J. D. Hicks, *The Populist Revolt* (1931), is the standard study of agrarian insurgency; it can be supplemented with R. B. Nye, *Midwestern Progressive Politics* (1951). Allan Nevins, *Hamilton Fish: The Inner History of the Grant Administration* (1936) and *Grover Cleveland* (1932), H. J. Eckenrode, *Rutherford B. Hayes* (1930), and D. S. Muzzey, *James G. Blaine* (1934), are among the more useful biographies.

443

of controversy were the tariff, the currency, and civil-service reform; and prior to the rise of Populism in the early 1890's none of these provoked much strong feeling. The result was that politics was largely left to the politicians, and the chief concern of most of them was to be elected or appointed to the government pay roll. The party organizations, instead of being instruments for expressing and enforcing popular decisions, degenerated into independent and irresponsible machines concerned simply with the rewards of office. On all levels of governmental organization few politicians showed much concern for the public interest, and in the state and city governments the real power was assumed by party bosses whose chief function was to decide how jobs should be distributed.

1. THE POLITICAL SYSTEM

Republicans and Democrats.   The two major parties were fairly evenly balanced in popular support, although the Republicans were more often successful in winning national elections. But there was now remarkably little difference between them. In theory the Republican Party stood for a strong national government which would actively promote economic expansion, while the Democratic Party believed in states' rights and a limitation of Federal power. But the states' rights issue no longer had much meaning, except in relation to Southern Reconstruction, and Democratic Congressmen were often willing to support the exercise of Federal power (in maintaining a high tariff, for example) whenever their own constituents were likely to benefit by it. On such basic questions as the currency, the protection of corporate property rights, and the status of labor, the dominant elements in both parties were equally conservative. Many elements within the Democratic Party, although professing allegiance to the principles of Jefferson and Jackson, had in practice largely accepted the Hamiltonian economic philosophy that had triumphed in the Civil War. Orators at election time would, of course, do their best to convince people that vital questions of principle were at stake, pointing with pride to their own accomplishments and viewing with alarm the program of their opponents; but all this was largely shadow-boxing. As most voters cynically recognized, the only real issue in most elections was to determine which group of politicians would enjoy the rewards of public office.

The Republican Party represented primarily a combination of Northern business groups and Western farming groups, originally brought together by a common opposition to the policies of the Southern planters during the 1850's. Throughout most of the North and West this was the party of wealth and respectability. It also had the support of such Negroes as were permitted to vote and of many of the German immigrants, who had been attracted to it because of its opposition to slavery. Since the Northern bankers and industrialists and the Western farmers had sharply divergent views on most economic questions, it was by no means easy for the party leaders to keep all of them satisfied at the same time. Republican orators often found it expedient, therefore, to appeal to memories of the Civil War rather than to contemporary issues. They would remind their constituents that their party had saved the Union and seek to identify the Democrats with the misdeeds of the Confederacy. This technique, known as "waving the bloody shirt," was especially effective among the millions of GAR veterans, the more so since the Republicans showed their gratitude more concretely by voting for generous pension legislation.

The Democratic Party was an even more heterogeneous coalition of different sectional groups. In most parts of the South it was the party of white supremacy, and had the allegiance both of the wealthy and conservative Bourbon landlords and industrialists and of the exploited farmers and wage-earners. Its main strength in the North was among the poorer classes in some of the cities, especially among the Irish, who had joined it during the 1830's and 1840's because of its Jacksonian faith in the plain people. But as a result of local political conflicts or of accidents of heredity and tradition, it also included some Northern businessmen and some Western farmers whose political attitudes were little different from those of their Republican neighbors. The Democrats thus covered almost the whole gamut of political attitudes from radicalism to reaction, and what policies they adopted depended on which group won control of the party machinery. Prior to 1896, however, the party was generally under conservative leadership.

Politics and Business. On all political levels, and no matter which party was in power, it was a recognized fact that individuals could often obtain special privileges if they were willing to pay for them. In city and state governments this normally meant outright bribery. In the Federal government the process was usually more subtle and less manifestly corrupt. Businessmen wanting favors would contribute heavily to party campaign funds and put officials and Congressmen in their debt by various indirect methods not involving actual payments of money. Such transactions might be interpreted either as bribery or as blackmail. Most businessmen regarded them as blackmail, believing that they were entitled to government assistance and complaining that the politicians held them up to ransom and refused to do the right thing unless they were paid for it. There was some truth in this view, since city and state officials would sometimes threaten interference with legitimate business concerns and compel them to pay money for protection. It was thus the politician who took the money, not the businessman who paid it, who was regarded as immoral. Most businessmen cynically agreed with the definition of an honest politician as one who stayed bought.

Although businessmen could usually obtain what they wanted after the Civil War, this does not mean that they controlled America's political development. While most men in politics were more or less conservative in their economic views, they should not be regarded as merely the spokesmen of the business class. It was, in fact, a proof of the independence of the politician that it was necessary for the businessman to bribe him. Businessmen were able to obtain special privileges because they were better organized and had more money at their disposal than any other group in the community. When the farmers and the working classes learned how to organize and put pressure on politicians, they also were able to secure political favors.

The City Machines.   City governments furnished the most flagrant examples of corruption. Most of the large cities after the Civil War came under the control of thoroughly dishonest political machines. Some of them, like Tammany Hall in New York, were Democratic, while others, like the Gas Ring in Philadelphia, were Republican; but their methods were almost identical.

A machine was usually controlled by a boss who preferred to operate behind the scenes, while the mayor and the board of aldermen whom the voters elected to office were likely to be mere puppets. Since the authority of the boss was extra-legal and exercised in private conferences in a back room rather than in public, he constituted an "invisible government." Most of the city bosses were men of little education and recent immigrant stock (frequently Irish), who had worked their way up within the machine. They often started their careers by becoming saloon-keepers, an occupation which had close connections with politics. In spite of their lack of political morality, many of them had substantial virtues; they prided themselves on keeping their word and on their charity to the poor, and were often not particularly interested in enriching themselves.

In order to retain power, a city machine needed votes and money. The votes were contributed mostly by the poorer classes, especially recent immigrants. City bosses would win their support by finding them jobs, protecting them if they were in trouble with the police, distributing turkeys at Christmas, and helping them to become naturalized as quickly as possible, often in advance of the legal time limit. By such methods a machine could earn an unquestioning loyalty in working-class districts which could not be undermined by any proofs of corruption and misgovernment. In addition to winning genuine votes in this way, most machines also resorted to outright electoral frauds. The money came partly from officeholders, who were usually required to contribute part of their salaries in return for being appointed to the city pay roll, and partly from graft. The most lucrative forms of graft were the payments made by streetcar, public-utility, and construction companies in order to obtain franchises, building contracts, and other privileges. Graft also came from lawbreakers in need of police protection, who were numerous in every large city as a result of the enactment of laws reflecting the moral ideals of the community rather than its practices—for example, laws restricting the sale of liquor or prohibiting gambling and prostitution.

Once a machine had acquired complete control of a big city government, its members enjoyed immense opportunities for plunder. Sooner or later it was likely to arouse indignation among decent citizens by raising taxes, protecting criminals, and failing to provide efficient administration; and a good-government crusade would then be organized and a reform mayor would win the next election. But the machine usually had more staying power. Reformers often lacked political shrewdness and experience, were unable to create a permanent organization, and offended many powerful interests by a too rigid enforcement of unpopular laws. Within a few years the machine was likely to return to office, chastened by its temporary separation from the municipal pay roll but not fundamentally changed.

Tammany Hall was the most notorious of the city machines, not because it was fundamentally worse than a dozen others, but because New York, as the richest city in the country, offered the greatest possibilities for plunder. Much the most corrupt of the series of Tammany bosses was William M. Tweed. Tweed and a ring of associates won control of the city in 1869, and their loot during the next three years was probably close to $100,000,000. In 1872 a reform movement, started by the press (especially by *Harper's Weekly*, which printed the famous cartoons of Thomas Nast) and led in its final stages by Samuel J. Tilden, succeeded in forcing out of office all the members of the ring and sending Tweed himself to the penitentiary. But this and subsequent reforms were not permanent, and New York continued to be governed more often than not by Tammany administrations. Eighty years after the overthrow of Boss Tweed its citizens were still wrestling with similar problems of municipal misgovernment.

State and Federal Politics.   Many county governments were even more corrupt and more boss-ridden than the city governments, chiefly because very few people paid any attention to them; but their opportunities for robbing the public were more limited. State governments were less flagrantly dishonest, but often exhibited the same tendency towards machine rule. Many state legislatures, moreover, were notoriously in the pay of railroad corporations. State bosses, unlike city bosses, were usually men of old American stock and well-established families. Instead of running affairs from back rooms, they were generally to be found in the United States Senate, a position which enabled them to control appointments to Federal as well as state offices. In New York, for example, for more than forty years after the Civil War, the Republican Party was controlled first by Senator Roscoe Conkling and afterwards by Senator Thomas C. Platt. Pennsylvania, from the Civil War until after World War I, was dominated by a Republican machine headed successively by Senators Simon Cameron, Matthew Quay, and Boies Penrose.

The Federal government remained more honest than the local governments. No presidents or Supreme Court justices and very few Cabinet members were ever guilty of corruption, and there were always a few men

in national politics who championed high moral principles and did not
hesitate to denounce dishonesty even when their own party was guilty of
it. But the growth of boss and machine rule in cities and states inevitably
infected Federal politics with the same moral laxity. Most Congressmen
had worked their way up within local machines and learned that loyalty
to the organization was the only way to gain preferment. And since prior
to 1883 all Federal jobs were distributed by the spoils system on the basis
of party services, relatively few officials maintained any high standards
of competence and integrity.

2. PRESIDENTIAL PARADE

The Grant Administration.   The level of political morality sank to
its lowest point during the eight-year administration of General Grant
(1869–77). With the possible exception of Warren G. Harding, nobody
ever elected to the presidency has proved to have fewer qualifications.
Totally ignorant of the problems of government, and an extremely poor
judge of men, Grant surrounded himself with a shady group of adventurers, and was genuinely incapable of realizing that they were unworthy
of holding office. A few men of ability and integrity served in his Cabinet
at one time or another; but with the exception of Secretary of State
Hamilton Fish, who provided the administration with its one substantial
claim to respectability, all of them incurred Grant's disapproval and were
dismissed. A man of unassuming manners and great simplicity of character, fond of horses, whisky, and cigars, Grant retained much of the
personal popularity with the mass of the voters that he had earned during
the Civil War, and this made him an invaluable asset to the Republican
Party bosses. But as President he showed none of the energy, determination, and clearheadedness that had made him such a formidable military
leader.

Major questions of policy were now mostly decided by Congress
rather than by the executive. The successful attack of the Radicals on
Andrew Johnson had shifted the balance of power in the Federal government and inaugurated a period of Congressional supremacy. The important work of Congress was mostly done in committees, and the real
power belonged to a few party bosses in the Senate and to the Speaker
of the House of Representatives. Strict party discipline was imposed on
most Congressmen; and rebels could expect to be deprived of their share
of Federal offices for their supporters and favors for their constituents.

Currency and Tariff Policies.   Apart from Southern Reconstruction, the main problems to be settled were financial. During the Civil War
the Treasury had issued greenbacks, which circulated for much less than
their face value in gold; along with national bank notes, these were now
the chief form of currency. As often before in American history, creditor
and debtor groups held sharply opposing views about monetary policy;

creditors wished to return to gold, the effect of which would be to increase the value of money and deflate prices, while debtors favored the continued use of greenbacks.

Creditor interests won a major victory in 1869, when Congress voted that Treasury bonds should be redeemed in coin; this meant that persons who had bought bonds with depreciated greenbacks would now be paid back in gold and would thereby make a profit amounting in many cases to as much as 50 per cent. No final decision was reached about the greenbacks until 1875, when Congress passed a Resumption Act providing that in 1879 they should become redeemable in gold at their face value. This would have the result of making a greenback dollar equivalent in value to a gold dollar. Thus, like the Federalists in the time of Alexander Hamilton, the Republicans adopted financial policies which enriched creditors at the expense of the national Treasury and which, by raising the value of money, increased the obligations of debtors. This proved to be the beginning of a long controversy about the currency which did not reach its climax until 1896.

Another financial question was tax-reduction. There was little dispute about abolishing the income and excise duties imposed during the war, and this was finally done in 1872; but the industrialists wished to retain the high tariff, although this was no longer needed for revenue. Despite considerable popular support for lower duties, the tariff remained high, apart from a small temporary reduction in 1872 in anticipation of the presidential election.

The Republicans had little trouble in spending the consequent Treasury surpluses. The national debt was steadily reduced, and money was distributed throughout the country in ways which would attract votes, chiefly through veterans' pensions and public works. Veterans were entitled to service-disability pensions by a law passed in 1862. In addition, many veterans suffering disabilities not incurred during the war were able to obtain pensions by means of private bills sponsored by their Congressmen. By 1889 there were nearly 500,000 pensioners, who were receiving a total of $89,000,000 a year. Public works included post offices and other Federal office buildings and improvements to rivers and harbors, and were popularly known as "pork-barrel" legislation. Congressmen were anxious to have Federal money spent in their own districts and would therefore support each other in increasing the appropriations, a practice known as "log-rolling." The annual Rivers and Harbors Bill, which covered most of these items, steadily grew larger, and by the 1880's appropriations averaged nearly $12,000,000 a year.

The Election of 1872. By 1872 a number of the more respectable characters in the Republican Party were convinced of Grant's unfitness for the presidency. They included a number of men who had been closely associated with the Lincoln administration, especially Charles Francis Adams, former minister to England, and Carl Schurz, a German immi-

grant who had settled in Missouri and become a major general during the
war, and who was a strong advocate of civil-service reform. Most of them
disapproved of the Reconstruction, financial, and tariff policies of the
administration, and were appalled by the growth of corruption. Since
they were unable to capture the regular Republican machine from the
party bosses, who were determined to bring about Grant's renomination,
they organized a separate Liberal Republican movement and nominated
Horace Greeley, editor of the *New York Tribune,* for the presidency.
Greeley was then endorsed by the Democrats, who had no chance of
winning with a candidate of their own. But the choice of Greeley doomed
the movement to defeat from the outset; although a brilliant liberal
journalist, he was notoriously unreliable and erratic and had a long
record of supporting all kinds of eccentric ideas. Grant won a sweeping
victory, carrying thirty-one states to Greeley's seven, with a popular
majority of 700,000. Greeley was prostrated by his efforts during the
campaign and the slanderous attacks to which he had been exposed, and
died three weeks after the election.

    Political Scandals.   The next four years were filled chiefly with
exposures of corruption, which were vigorously pushed by a few independent Republicans and by the Democrats, who won control of the
House of Representatives in 1874 and held it until 1880. Popular disillusionment with Grant was increased by the business crisis of 1873 and
the acute depression which followed.

    The first major scandal involved Congress rather than the executive.
This was the discovery that the organizers of the Crédit Mobilier had
distributed stock among a number of Congressmen. Crédit Mobilier was
the company that had built the Union Pacific and made immense profits
by charging well over twice the real construction cost, thereby defrauding
the stockholders of the railroad. Afterwards came exposures involving the
Treasury and War Departments and exhibiting the total unfitness for
high office of a number of men who had obtained the President's confidence.

    The biggest of the Treasury scandals was the discovery of a "whisky
ring" composed of tax-collectors and distillers who had conspired to
defraud the government of millions of dollars of excise duties. Secretary
of the Treasury Bristow endeavored to destroy the ring and found that
the trail led to close friends of the President, including his private secretary, Orville E. Babcock. While some members of the ring went to prison,
Grant saw to it that Babcock escaped punishment and rewarded Bristow
for his honesty by forcing him to resign. In the War Department it was
found that Indian-post traders had obtained these very lucrative positions by bribing officials, including Secretary of War William W. Belknap.
Belknap escaped impeachment only because Grant "with great regret"
accepted his resignation. These were only the major items in a series of
revelations which showed that nearly every branch of the government

was honeycombed with corruption. Customs collectors took bribes from importers; Navy Department officials sold business to contractors; officials of the Interior Department allowed speculators to obtain public lands without complying with the legal requirements; and the American minister to Britain had actually used his official position to foist bogus mining-stock on English investors.

The Election of 1876. As the 1876 election approached, the Republican Party began to split into two factions, known as Stalwarts and Halfbreeds. The Stalwarts consisted chiefly of machine politicians and were led by a group of state bosses, including Roscoe Conkling of New York, Simon Cameron of Pennsylvania, Oliver Morton of Indiana, Zechariah Chandler of Michigan, and John Logan of Illinois. These were hard, power-loving, and cynical men who regarded the distribution of offices and privileges as the very essence of politics and derided reformers as impractical or hypocritical. In spite of all the scandals, they would have liked to nominate Grant for a third term.

The Halfbreeds claimed to support higher standards of political morality, although many of them were actually as much concerned with the rewards of office as their opponents. Among these latter was James G. Blaine of Maine, Speaker of the House from 1869 until 1875, who was the chief rival of Roscoe Conkling for party leadership. An eloquent orator and a man of great personal magnetism, Blaine (like Henry Clay half a century earlier) was idolized by a large body of voters, although he never did anything substantial to earn their admiration. Hoping to win the party's presidential nomination, he tried to distract attention from the misdeeds of the administration by vigorously waving the bloody shirt and reviving the Civil War hatreds. But his reputation was somewhat clouded by the publication of letters he had written to a certain James Mulligan which showed that he had helped to secure a land grant for a disreputable railroad corporation by selling its stock on a commission basis to fellow-Congressmen.

The Halfbreeds were strong enough to prevent the renomination of Grant, and the candidate finally selected was Rutherford B. Hayes, Governor of Ohio. The Democrats nominated Samuel J. Tilden, a wealthy corporation lawyer, intellectually gifted but somewhat lacking in courage and forthrightness, who had made his name by breaking the Tweed ring and had then become Governor of New York. Tilden won a majority in the popular vote of 250,000, but the decision in the electoral college depended on four states from which rival returns were received, South Carolina, Florida, Louisiana, and Oregon.

In Oregon only one vote was in dispute as a result of a legal technicality; but in the three Southern states the Democrats had won victories which had afterwards been invalidated by Republican-controlled election boards. On the score of fraud and intimidation there was little to choose between the two parties in these states. Since the Constitution did not provide any means of settling such a dispute, it was agreed that the decision should be made by an electoral commission consisting of five senators, five representatives, and five Supreme Court justices. The original intention was that the commission should include seven Republicans, seven Democrats, and one justice not identified with either party. But the justice finally chosen proved to be a Republican, and the commission, voting along strictly party lines, awarded all the disputed votes to Hayes by eight to seven, thus ensuring his election.

The Democrats talked of blocking the inauguration of Hayes, but after private negotiations between party leaders they decided to give way. It was formerly believed that the principal agreement, reached at a conference at Wormley's Hotel in Washington, was to the effect that if the Democrats would concede the election of Hayes, Federal troops would be withdrawn from the South and the last Reconstruction governments brought to an end. More recent investigations have shown that broader issues were involved. Conservative Southern Democrats were promised that if they would abandon Tilden, the business interests of the South would benefit through land grants for Southern railroads and other economic favors, and white Southerners would be given Federal offices. Thus the Reconstruction episode ended with an understanding behind the scenes between conservative groups in each section; the Southern Bourbons accepted Republican control of the Federal government in return for a share of the benefits.

The Hayes Administration.   Hayes was not a man of outstanding ability or colorful personality, but he had honest intentions and did something to re-establish presidential power and prestige. He fulfilled his part of the bargain with the South by withdrawing the Federal troops and appointing a Tennessee Democrat as head of the Post Office, an office which meant control of considerable patronage. Choosing a strong Cabinet, including Carl Schurz and three other Liberal Republicans who had supported Greeley in 1872, he declared his intention of purging the civil service. "Party leaders," he declared, "should have no more influence in appointments than other equally respectable citizens. No assessments for political purposes on officers or subordinates should be allowed. No useless officer or employee should be retained. No officer should be required or permitted to take part in the management of political organizations, caucuses, conventions or election campaigns." This order struck at the root of the spoils system, and led to a prolonged struggle with Conkling and the Stalwarts. Hayes succeeded in cleaning up some of the more corrupt offices, including the very lucrative New York Custom House, which had been packed with henchmen of Conkling. But he was not strong or shrewd enough to bring about a thorough reform.

The Silver Problem.   The only important legislation during Hayes's term concerned the perennial problem of the currency. American money had originally consisted of both silver and gold, the ratio between them being fixed in the Jacksonian period at sixteen to one. But since an ounce of silver was actually worth more than one-sixteenth of an ounce of gold, people preferred to use silver for other purposes, and silver coins gradually dropped out of use. In 1873 Congress recognized this fact by voting to abandon the coinage of silver dollars. About this time, however, silver mines in Nevada and elsewhere were being developed, and with the increase in production silver's value in relation to gold began to fall. This led to demands for a return to the coinage of silver, especially from the miners, who were hoping to obtain a higher price for it, and from agrarian debtor groups wanting to increase the quantity of money.

In 1878 Congress responded to popular pressure by passing, over Hayes's veto, the Bland-Allison Act. This ordered the Treasury to purchase between $2,000,000 and $4,000,000 worth of silver each month and coin it into dollars at the old ratio of sixteen to one. As enforced by the Treasury Department, this helped to maintain the price of silver but did not satisfy debtor-class demands for inflation. The Treasury bought only the minimum quantities of silver; and since it was at all times willing to change the silver dollars into gold, the country remained for all practical purposes on a gold standard, in spite of the bimetallic currency, and the value of money remained unchanged.

The Election of 1880. Hayes did not seek a second term, and the Republican convention of 1880 was again divided between Stalwarts and Halfbreeds. The Stalwarts almost succeeded in nominating Grant for a third term, but the nomination went finally to a dark-horse candidate favored by the Halfbreeds, James A. Garfield, who had been Congressman from Ohio. In order to conciliate the Stalwarts, the second place on the ticket was given to one of Conkling's closest allies, Chester A. Arthur, who had been head of the New York Custom House until dismissed by Hayes. The Democrats picked a little-known Civil War general, Winfield Scott Hancock of Pennsylvania. After perhaps the dullest election in American history Garfield scraped through by a narrow margin. He won a majority in the electoral college of 59, but was only 9,000 ahead of Hancock in the popular vote.

During the campaign Garfield accepted the aid of the Stalwarts and apparently came to an understanding with them; but as soon as he was inaugurated he became involved in the inevitable conflict with Conkling and the party bosses about civil-service appointments. He also antagonized Conkling by nominating his great rival, James G. Blaine, as Secretary of State. Four months after taking office, he was assassinated by a disappointed office-seeker who proclaimed, after he had fired the fatal bullet: "I am a Stalwart; Arthur is now President of the United States." This event did more than all the exposures of corruption to arouse public opinion to the need for reform and ensure the defeat of the Stalwarts.

The Arthur Administration.   The succession of Chester A. Arthur, known hitherto only as a New York machine politician, seemed to most decent people to be a calamity. But in spite of his unsavory associations, Arthur was personally honest and did not lack ability. He surprised everybody by rising to the occasion and giving the nation perhaps its best administration since the Civil War. Breaking with the Stalwarts, he supported civil-service reform and vigorously prosecuted the "star route" frauds in the Post Office. He also tried to check Federal spending on unnecessary public works and to bring about a lower tariff, but was overruled on both issues by Congress. A tariff commission appointed in 1882 recommended reduction of many excessively high duties; but as a result of lobbying by industrialists and log-rolling by Congressmen the so-called "mongrel tariff" of 1883 was as high as the previous one.

Civil-Service Reform.   The most important event of Arthur's administration was the enactment of the Pendleton Civil Service Act in 1883. For twenty years reformers had been denouncing the spoils system and urging the creation of a permanent civil service based on merit. The distribution of civil-service jobs among politicians of the winning party led inevitably to incompetence, extravagance, and corruption, and meant that, whenever there was a change of administration, the incoming president had to spend most of his time for several months coping with hungry office-seekers. Adoption of a merit system like that of Great Britain had been advocated by political leaders like Charles Sumner and Carl Schurz and by influential magazine editors such as E. L. Godkin of the *Nation* and G. W. Curtis of *Harper's Weekly*. The murder of Garfield finally impelled Congress to take action.

The Pendleton Act authorized the president to appoint a Civil Service Commission of three members to provide "open competitive examinations for testing the fitness of applicants for the public service now classified or to be classified." Only the lowest positions in the civil service were immediately classified by the Pendleton Act, but the president was authorized to extend the list at his discretion. Arthur made excellent appointments to the Commission, and during the first year it was given jurisdiction over 14,000 offices, about 12 per cent of the total. Most subsequent presidents extended the classified list, and by 1932 it included 79 per cent of all Federal offices. With the rapid expansion of the Federal bureaucracy after this date there was some decline in the percentage of classified positions, but their number continued to increase.

Although civil-service reform ended some of the worst evils of the spoils system, it by no means abolished it. There were still many positions where political loyalty rather than merit continued to be the main criterion. The American civil service, moreover, continued to have difficulty in attracting and keeping men of superior talents, partly because it paid relatively low wages and offered little social prestige, and partly because the examination system (unlike that of Great Britain) was designed to test specialized technical training rather than general ability and education.

The Election of 1884. For the election of 1884 James G. Blaine finally captured the Republican nomination he had been seeking for nearly a decade. The Democrats selected Grover Cleveland, who had been an outstandingly honest reform governor of New York. Cleveland was also supported by some liberal Republicans, known as "Mugwumps," who were not impressed by Blaine's spellbinding oratory and regarded him as dishonest, timeserving, and empty of any real ideas. As in 1880, there were few real issues; but whatever else might be said about this election, it cannot be described as dull. The Democrats publicized the Mulligan letters revealing Blaine's unethical business connections, while the Republicans dug up the fact that Cleveland was the father of an illegitimate child. While Cleveland no doubt lost some votes by this embarrassing revelation, he probably gained more by his blunt refusal to deny or evade the truth. Many people agreed with the Mugwump who declared that "we should elect Mr. Cleveland to the public office he is so admirably qualified to fill and remand Mr. Blaine to the private life which he is so eminently fitted to adorn." The best-known episode of the campaign occurred in its final stages. Blaine, who had a Catholic mother and had made anti-British speeches, hoped to capture the vote of the Irish, but lost all chance of doing so when a Republican Protestant clergyman insulted their faith by describing the Democrats as the party of "Rum, Romanism, and Rebellion." But even without this famous *faux pas* it is unlikely that many of the Irish would have abandoned their traditional allegiance to the Democratic Party. Cleveland won the presidency with an electoral college majority of 37 and a popular majority of 23,000.

Cleveland's First Administration. Cleveland was not a man of profound insight or intelligence, and his economic views were as conservative as those of any Republican president; but his courage and integrity made him a most refreshing contrast to the general run of politicians. He genuinely lived up to the aphorism attributed to him by a newspaperman, "A public office is a public trust." Apart from the Interstate Commerce Act, for which he was not responsible, there was little legislation during his term. But he insisted on honest and economical government in defiance of all political pressures. He incurred the wrath of the GAR by vetoing hundreds of pension bills; refused to play up to local demands for Federal spending on unnecessary public works; recovered no less than 81,000,000 acres of public land that had been fraudulently occupied by railroad, lumber, and cattle companies; and alarmed big business by launching a vigorous campaign for a lower tariff, although this was blocked by the Senate.

The Election of 1888. For the 1888 election the Democrats renominated Cleveland, while the Republicans picked a little-known Indiana lawyer, Benjamin Harrison, whose main qualifications were a distinguished ancestry (he was the grandson of William Henry Harrison), an innocuous record, and residence in a doubtful state. Cleveland's stand on the tariff was the main issue, and the Republicans, turning to the big industrialists for support, collected the unprecedented campaign fund of $4,000,000, much of which was spent on outright bribery. They also appealed to the veterans with promises of general pension legislation. After one of the most corrupt elections in American history, Cleveland won a majority in the popular vote of 100,000, but the Republicans captured the crucial states with an electoral college majority of 65.

The Harrison Administration. Although Harrison did not lack ability, he was too colorless to acquire much influence with the electorate; and apart from Blaine, who again became Secretary of State, his Cabinet contained only nonentities. Leadership was assumed mainly by the party bosses in Congress, especially by Nelson W. Aldrich of Rhode Island in the Senate and Thomas B. Reed of Maine as Speaker of the House. Faced with a strong Democratic opposition, Reed forced through the House a revision of the rules which gave the majority leaders almost dictatorial powers over debates and won for himself the title of "czar." The Republicans hastened to pay off their political debts, and the first two years of Harrison's administration saw an unusual amount of important legislation.

Most important was the McKinley Tariff of 1890, which raised rates to higher levels, and gave protection to a wider range of products, than any previous tariff in American history. In the same year, by the Dependent's Pension Act, pensions were given to all GAR veterans suffering from any disability, whether acquired as a result of war service or not, and to all veterans' widows; by 1893 this had increased the number of pensioners to 966,000 and the annual cost to $157,000,000. Meanwhile, the silver-miners were again demanding assistance, and by the Sherman Silver Purchase Act of 1890 the amount of silver to be purchased by the Treasury was increased to 4,500,000 ounces a month; since the Treasury was to pay for it by issuing notes, the amount of currency was substantially increased. According to the terms of the act, the notes were to be redeemable in either gold or silver coin, but the Treasury, faithful to orthodox economic theory, preferred to pay only gold. This Congress also passed the Sherman Anti-trust Act, and appropriated more money than any previous Congress for public works.

According to the rules of American politics, such congressional generosity, beneficial to so many different interests, might have been expected to result in widespread public support. The public reaction, however, was decidedly hostile, and in the congressional elections of 1890 the Democrats won a large majority in the House of Representatives. An even more significant event was the appearance of nine new Congressmen representing farm interests and not affiliated with either of the major parties. A new phase in American political history was beginning.

3. THE REVOLT OF THE FARMERS

THE 1890's were to see the culmination of the movement of farm insurgency which had been slowly gathering strength ever since the Civil War. Suffering from falling farm prices, exploited by the railroads and the trusts, and burdened with heavy debts to bankers and mortgage companies, the farmers were forced to realize that they could secure just treatment only through political action. And since both the Republican and the Democratic Party were dominated by Eastern conservatives, it seemed to many of them that such action must take the form of a third-party organization.

Grangers and Greenbackers. The first expression of farm insurgency was the Granger movement of the 1870's. In 1867 Oliver Hudson Kelley, a government clerk in Washington, had founded an organization known as the Patrons of Husbandry, but more frequently called the Grange. The original purpose of the Grange was to spread information about scientific agriculture, but it soon developed into a vehicle through which the farmers could voice their economic grievances, especially against the railroads. By 1874 the Grange had a membership of 750,000, most of whom were in Iowa and other Middle Western states. The Grangers put up candidates of their own, won control of several state legislatures, and enacted laws regulating the rates charged by railroads and elevators. Unfortunately, the laws proved often to be badly drafted and were not very effective, in spite of the Supreme Court's validation in the Granger Cases of 1876. The Grangers also set up a number of co-operatively owned factories, stores, and selling agencies, but most of these ventures turned out unsuccessfully as a result partly of mismanagement and partly of business opposition. After 1876 the movement quickly subsided, leaving few permanent results. But the farmers had learned lessons about the possibilities of political action which they did not wholly forget.

The immediate heir of the Granger movement was the Greenback Party, which was organized in 1876 in protest against the deflationary financial policies followed during the Grant administration. In 1878 the Greenbackers polled a million votes and elected fifteen Congressmen. But they were unable to prevent the resumption of specie payments in 1879, and their support then rapidly declined. In the presidential election of 1880 their candidate, James B. Weaver of Iowa, received only 300,000 votes, and by 1888 the party was dead. Inflationists were now demanding unlimited coinage of silver and had lost interest in the greenback question.

The Populist Movement. During the early 1880's farm prices remained relatively high, and agrarian discontent subsided. But the year 1887 marked the beginning of a decade of catastrophe. Increased grain-production in other parts of the world brought falling prices, while at the same time the Plains country suffered from a series of droughts, so that the harvests of many American farmers actually declined. As mortgage foreclosures increased, the farm belt was swept with a wave of insurgency which had the emotional fervor of a religious revival. It was strongest in the newly settled wheat country of the Middle Border—Kansas, Nebraska, Minnesota, and the Dakotas. The organization through which it found expression was the National Farmers' Alliance, more often known as the Northern Alliance, which had been founded in 1880. After 1887 the Alliance grew rapidly and began to demand drastic changes in the whole political and economic structure. These were voiced by a number of spellbinding orators, including the former Greenback leader James B. Weaver of Iowa, Ignatius Donnelly of Minnesota, and William A. Peffer, "Sockless" Jerry Simpson, and Mary Elizabeth Lease of Kansas (it was Mrs. Lease who advised the farmers to "raise less corn and more hell"). In 1890, in addition to electing nine Congressmen, the Alliance was strong enough to win the balance of power in a number of Western state legislatures.

After these victories the time seemed ripe for launching a new national political party. The Western agrarian leaders hoped to join forces with the Southern farmers, organized in the Southern Alliance. But most of the Southerners preferred to work within the Democratic Party. The new party was therefore mainly a Western organization, although it had support from some Southern leaders, especially Tom Watson. Formally launched at Cincinnati in May 1891, it was christened the People's Party, while its adherents became known as the Populists. In 1892, in a convention at Omaha, James B. Weaver was nominated for the presidency. A former Civil War general, Weaver had an excellent record and plenty of ability, though he lacked the personal magnetism needed for the leadership of a new political movement.

The Populist platform demanded a long series of reforms, some of which were designed to break the power of political bosses and give the mass of the people more effective control over their government, while others aimed at a more equitable economic system. In the former category were the direct popular election of senators, the initiative, and the referendum. Among the economic reforms were government ownership of railroads, telegraphs, and telephones; a graduated income tax; shorter hours for labor; and currency inflation. To solve the perennial problem of farm credit, the platform proposed a "sub-treasury" plan by which the government would store non-perishable farm produce in national warehouses and give loans to the farmers to whom it belonged up to not more than 80 per cent of its value. In 1892 all these proposals seemed to most Easterners to be positively revolutionary. There was little realization that Populism was essentially a resurgence of the spirit of agrarian democracy which had been the basis of Jeffersonianism and Jacksonianism and had done much to shape American ideals and institutions.

The Question of the Currency.   The issue which aroused most excitement was the currency. The farmers were convinced that the main

WHOLESALE

   Boss Tweed is the central figure in this cartoon from Harper's Weekly *by Thomas Nast (1840–1902). Nast's cartoons helped to send Tweed to the penitentiary in 1873.*

A PAINFUL POSITION
FOR NURSE MCKINLEY

   Hitherto known chiefly for his advocacy of a high tariff, McKinley was believed to have accepted the gold-standard plank in the Republican platform in 1896 for reasons of expediency.

THE WORLD'S CONSTABLE

Theodore Roosevelt's "big stick" Caribbean policy and his role as mediator between Russia and Japan in 1905 inspired this cartoon from Judge.

reason for the fall in farm prices was the policy of deflation adopted by the Federal government after the Civil War and only partially checked by the Bland-Allison and Sherman Silver Purchase Acts. By limiting the quantity of greenbacks and silver dollars and making both of them redeemable in gold, the Treasury had increased the value of money and correspondingly deflated prices. In spite of the rapid growth of business, there had actually been a sharp fall in the per capita quantity of money in circulation, while at the same time there had also been a decrease in the number of bank notes; since, according to the National Bank Act of 1863, these were limited by the quantity of government bonds held by the banks, the Treasury, by paying off 60 per cent of the national debt, had indirectly brought about a considerable contraction of the notes in circulation. Money, moreover, had a tendency to become concentrated in the East, and to be particularly scarce in the farm belt. As the farmers saw the situation, these deflationary policies had forced prices downwards, while at the same time their debts remained unchanged. It seemed to them to be unjust that after borrowing money when wheat sold for $1.00 a bushel, they should be forced to pay back the same amount after wheat had dropped to 63 cents. The Populist program therefore demanded an increase in the quantity of money in the form either of paper issues or of unrestricted coinage of silver at the old ratio of sixteen to one. Of these proposals, the second won much more support, largely because of the propaganda campaign of the silver-miners.

In view of twentieth-century experience with managed currencies and the general abandonment of the gold standard, it is no longer easy to appreciate the intense feelings aroused among both Populists and Easterners by the demands for the coinage of silver. The Populists were convinced that the maintenance of the gold standard was due to a deliberate conspiracy on the part of Eastern financiers who wished to enrich themselves and impoverish the mass of the people. And since most other countries had adopted the gold standard and gold had in consequence become the primary medium of international exchange, many of them concluded that this conspiracy was world-wide and that a sinister group of international bankers were plotting to dominate the human race. This notion had a considerable influence in the rural Middle West for a long time, and was one of the factors in its isolationist attitude to foreign policy during the twentieth century.

But the indignation aroused by the Populist program among almost all respectable people in the East was equally exaggerated. Economists and other makers of public opinion did not regard the gold standard as merely a man-made contrivance for securing a trustworthy and reasonably stable currency. Like the obligations of contracts, it had acquired a kind of religious sanctity, and was supposedly based on the immutable laws of God, nature, and economics. The rise in the value of money, it was believed, was due to factors beyond human control, and any attempt to depreciate it in order to make debts less burdensome was sheer robbery. As the economist J. Lawrence Laughlin declared, "the eagerness of the advocates of free silver is founded on an appeal to dishonesty and cheating on the part of those who would like to repudiate and scale one half of their obligations." On this issue there was little difference between the old-guard politicians and the liberals who had supported Greeley in 1872 and Cleveland in 1884. Men like Godkin of the *Nation*, who had fought valiantly against the spoils system and the pork barrel and the high tariff, were as violently opposed to the Populists as were the bankers and the regular Republicans.

The Election of 1892.   The Republicans and Democrats renominated Harrison and Cleveland for the 1892 campaign, with the tariff again the main issue. For the third time in succession Cleveland had a plurality in the popular vote (amounting on this occasion to 381,000), and he won the presidency with an electoral college majority of 132. The 1,041,000 people who voted for Weaver gave him 22 electoral college votes, all of them from states west of the 95th meridian. This seemed like a promising beginning for a new party, but it was notable that its appeal was narrowly sectional. Weaver's support came almost exclusively from Western farmers and silver-miners; Populist attempts to appeal to labor were not very successful. What proved in the long run to be more significant was the growth of Populist tendencies within the two major parties, especially among the Democrats. A number of the candidates victorious in Western and Southern states were sympathetic to the Populist objectives, although they ran on the Democratic and Republican tickets. The most notable example was John P. Altgeld, a German immigrant who became Democratic governor of Illinois. Attacking the big corporations and promoting the interests of farmers and workers, Altgeld gave the state an outstandingly able, courageous, and progressive administration.

Cleveland's Second Administration.   Populism, however, received no support whatever from Grover Cleveland. In fact, almost everything that happened during his second administration confirmed the silver men in their conviction that the government was controlled by the international bankers, and sharpened the growing conflict between the Eastern and the Populist elements in the Democratic Party. Shortly after Cleveland took office in 1893, the country plunged into a long and severe depression, in which at least 4,000,000 persons were unemployed. Like all earlier presidents, Cleveland did not feel obligated to take any measures for stimulating economic recovery. His main responsibility, he believed, was to maintain the solvency of the Federal government and protect the gold standard by seeing to it that the Treasury could at all times pay out gold dollars in exchange for paper and silver currency. Orthodox economists believed that any suspension of this process would have catastrophic results. But as business confidence declined, gold began to be drawn out of the Treasury in alarming quantities. Cleveland therefore decided that it was essential to diminish the quantity of paper money in circulation, for which reason he asked Congress to repeal the Silver Purchase Act of 1890. This was accomplished by means of support from Eastern Republicans, while most of the Western and Southern Democrats voted against the administration. The Treasury then added to its gold reserve by buying gold and paying for it with bond issues. In particular, gold was bought from the Morgan and Belmont banking houses on terms which gave the bankers a handsome profit. The gold standard was saved (for whatever that was worth), but in the opinion of the Populists the government had capitulated to international finance.

Cleveland failed to bring about any substantial reduction of the tariff. As a result of log-rolling by Democratic senators, in violation of their campaign pledges, the Wilson-Gorman Tariff of 1894 was almost as high as the McKinley Tariff which it superseded. It included provision for an income tax, but in 1895 this was invalidated by the Supreme Court in a five-to-four decision (in spite of the fact that an income tax had been collected during the Civil War). While the main reason for the verdict was that according to the Constitution direct taxes had to be apportioned among the states in proportion to population, the lawyers who had argued the case against the income tax had also represented it as a violation of the rights of property. This decision provided another stimulus to the growth of populism, as did also the use of force by Federal and state authorities in several labor disputes, most notably Cleveland's action in sending troops to Illinois (in spite of protests by Governor Altgeld) in order to break the railroad strike of 1894.

The Election of 1896. The depression years gave a great stimulus to radical thinking of all kinds. A growing number of Americans were becoming convinced that the economic system was fundamentally unsound, and that the Federal government should assume responsibility for the general welfare instead of leaving economic processes to work themselves out. But for the time being the forces of popular discontent concentrated behind the demand for free and unlimited coinage of silver. In spite of its obvious inadequacy as a program of reform, this became the main rallying-point for all who wanted a change in the existing system.

In the 1896 campaign the Republicans met the issue squarely. The leading figure in the Republican convention was Mark Hanna, a wealthy Ohio industrialist who had transferred his energies to politics relatively late in life, and who, like Alexander Hamilton, believed in leadership by an elite group of wealthy men and in a close union between government and business. The platform called for the maintenance of the gold standard and promised opposition to the free coinage of silver unless other leading nations were willing to agree to it. The nomination went to Hanna's close friend, the Ohio Congressman William McKinley.

When the Democratic convention met a few weeks later, it was immediately obvious that the Western and Southern elements were in the

majority and that Cleveland and the Eastern conservatives had lost
control of the party. The platform, written mainly by Altgeld, called
for the free and unlimited coinage of silver without waiting for the consent of any other nation. During the debate on the platform the party
found its candidate. William Jennings Bryan, a thirty-six-year-old ex-
Congressman from Nebraska, stampeded the convention with one of the
most famous speeches in American political history. "There are two ideas
of government," he proclaimed:

> There are those who believe that if you just legislate to make the
> well-to-do prosperous, their prosperity will leak through on those
> below. The Democratic idea has been that if you legislate to make the
> masses prosperous, their prosperity will find its way up and through
> every class that rests upon it. . . . Having behind us the producing
> masses of this nation, and the world, supported by the commercial
> interests, the laboring interests, and the toilers everywhere, we will
> answer their demand for a gold standard by saying to them: You shall
> not press down upon the brow of labor this crown of thorns, you shall
> not crucify mankind upon a cross of gold."

The Democratic nomination of Bryan, who was a Populist in all
but name, meant for all practical purposes the end of Populism as a
separate political force. When the Populist convention met, it could only
endorse Bryan, although it attempted to preserve its independent identity
by rejecting the vice-presidential nominee of the Democrats and supporting Tom Watson in his place. But in this and subsequent elections
most of the former Populists voted for the Democratic ticket.

Thus for the first time since 1860 there was a clear-cut issue, of
major importance, between the two parties. The question of free silver
had become symbolic of the conflict between capitalism and agrarianism.
On one side was the Hamiltonian conception of a society dominated by
the big corporations and the wealthy men who controlled them; on the
other side, the Jeffersonian faith in the small owner, especially the farmer,
as the mainstay of a healthy democracy. But Bryan lacked the stature of
a Jefferson or a Jackson. Handsome, eloquent, and magnetic, he was a
superb popular orator; and his honesty and sincerity were unquestionable. But he was also naïve and provincial, with a limited stock of ideas
and little experience. An old-fashioned Protestant fundamentalist, he
shared the narrow prejudices of the farm belt as well as its aspirations.
He made the most remarkable campaign in American history, traveling
17,000 miles and delivering more than 600 speeches. But meanwhile
Hanna collected from the bankers and industrialists a campaign fund
which probably totaled $16,000,000 and flooded the country with propa-
ganda to the effect that Bryan was no better than an anarchist and his
election would mean economic ruin for everybody. Although Bryan
aroused his audiences to an enthusiasm equaled only in revival meetings,

he was the worst-beaten Democratic candidate since Horace Greeley. The Eastern Democratic machines failed to give him full support, and an upturn in the business cycle brought rising prices, which caused many of the farmers to swing back to the Republicans. McKinley had a popular plurality of 602,000 and an electoral college majority of 95.

The Triumph of the Businessman. McKinley's victory was widely interpreted as the definitive victory of the Hamiltonian ideal. As Henry Adams declared, "the majority at last declared itself, once and for all, in favor of a capitalistic system with all its necessary machinery." For the time being this idea was represented, much more fully than in the past, by the Republican Party. Paralleling the growth of industrial integration under the leadership of the investment bankers there had been a tendency towards the integration of business and politics. An increasing number of Republican senators were now themselves millionaire businessmen who spoke as the direct representatives of powerful economic interests. Instead of buying political support, the industrialists seemed to be moving into politics themselves. Mark Hanna, who entered the Senate in 1897, was a leading representative of this trend. Another was the Republican floor leader, Senator Nelson W. Aldrich, a wealthy Rhode Islander whose daughter married the son of John D. Rockefeller. Such men displayed more integrity and statesmanship than the machine politicians, like Roscoe Conkling, who had dominated the party a generation earlier, but they frankly believed in rule by the wealthy few and had little use for democratic ideals.

By the time McKinley was inaugurated, the depression was ending, and the Republicans could claim to be the party of prosperity. Business was able to obtain the legislation it wanted, and the Dingley Tariff of 1897 outdid all previous tariffs in assuring industrialists of complete protection against foreign competition and enabling them to raise prices in the domestic market. After halfhearted attempts to obtain international agreement for the coinage of silver, as promised in the Republican platform, the currency question was settled for the time being by the Gold Standard Act of 1900. There was no revival of the controversy until the depression of the 1930's, partly because by a happy coincidence the discovery of new mines in South Africa brought a rapid increase in the world's supply of gold and thus produced the currency inflation desired by the silver men.

Thus by the end of the century the forces of big business seemed to have achieved political as well as economic dominance. Nevertheless, the future belonged to the Populists. They had initiated a movement for the revitalization of democracy which expressed the real interests and ideals of a large part of the American people and which, under more realistic leaders, soon became politically effective. Partly during the progressive period prior to World War I and partly during the New Deal, most of the reforms advocated in the Populist platform of 1892 were put into effect.

XXII

Social Changes in the
Industrial Era

1. THE GROWTH OF CITIES

2. IMMIGRATION

3. RELIGIOUS ORGANIZATIONS

4. EDUCATION AND SCIENCE

5. THE PRESS

THE ECONOMIC developments of the period following the Civil War
were accompanied by far-reaching social and cultural changes. A
growing proportion of the population was massed in cities. Increased
immigration from Europe added a wide variety of new ethnic groups to
the American melting pot. Vast sums of money were made available for
the advancement and diffusion of knowledge on all levels, and traditional
mores and beliefs began to disintegrate under the impact of new social
conditions and more rationalistic modes of thought.

Most of these changes can be measured in terms of statistics and

SELECTED BIBLIOGRAPHY: Four volumes in *A History of American Life* deal with
the period between the Civil War and World War I: Allan Nevins, *The Emergence of Modern
America, 1865–1878* (1928); A. M. Schlesinger, *The Rise of the City, 1878–1898* (1933);
Ida Tarbell, *The Nationalizing of Business, 1878–1898* (1936); and H. U. Faulkner, *The
Quest for Social Justice, 1898–1914* (1931). Immigration is described in Carl Wittke, *We Who
Built America* (1939), and M. L. Hansen, *The Immigrant in American History* (1940), while
Oscar Handlin, *The Uprooted* (1951) is a masterly description of experiences of immigrant
families. W. W. Sweet, *The Story of Religion in America* (1930), is the best survey of religious
history, and can be supplemented with C. H. Hopkins, *The Rise of the Social Gospel in
American Protestantism, 1865–1915* (1940), and Theodore Maynard, *The Story of American
Catholicism* (1941). The most useful surveys of educational development are E. P. Cubberly,
Public Education in the United States (revised edition, 1934), and C. F. Thwing, *A History
of Education in the United States Since the Civil War* (1910), which emphasizes the colleges.
Kenneth Stewart and John Tebbel, *Makers of Modern Journalism* (1952) gives vivid accounts
of Hearst and Pulitzer.

documented by pointing to specific facts. But their meaning and implications are less easy to estimate. What kind of society was emerging in the new industrial America? By contrast with the rural and agrarian past, there was less emphasis on individualism and self-reliance, a greater interdependence and a consequent need for more social regulation. Becoming less versatile and more specialized than his grandfather, the new urban man had lost some of his independence. On the other hand, he was less bound by ancestral ways of living, more flexible in his attitudes, and more receptive to new ideas and techniques. And although there was perhaps less scope than in the past for individual distinction and preeminence, higher cultural levels became accessible to the main body of the population.

1. THE GROWTH OF CITIES

ORIGINALLY a rural people, the Americans have been becoming steadily more urbanized ever since the foundation of the republic. In 1790 only 5.1 per cent of the population lived in places with more than 2,500 inhabitants. By 1860 the percentage had risen to 19.8, and by 1900 to 39.7. It passed the halfway mark shortly before 1920.

This standard for measuring urbanization is not wholly adequate, since the inhabitants of many of the smaller towns remained essentially rural in outlook. On the other hand, many commuters living in rural sections outside city limits should be classified as urban. A more significant aspect of urbanization was the concentration of people in a few immense metropolitan areas. The population of the five boroughs of New York (which were brought together under one government in 1898) grew from 1,174,779 in 1860 to 4,766,883 in 1910. Chicago, a mere village as recently as 1850, became the second city in the country, with 2,185,283 inhabitants in 1910, outstripping Philadelphia, which ranked third with 1,549,008. By 1930 more than one-quarter of the people in the United States were massed in seven great urban areas in and around the cities of New York, Chicago, Philadelphia, Boston, Detroit, Los Angeles, and Cleveland.

As the cities grew, municipal authorities were compelled to assume a steadily increasing burden of new responsibilities. The *laissez-faire* conceptions of the rural past could no longer be maintained when millions of human beings were massed together in small congested urban areas. City governments had to protect public health, provide new social services, expand their police forces, and provide citizens with at least a minimum of amenities. But this extension of social control was a slow process, undertaken only under pressure of necessity. *Laissez-faire* traditions were abandoned with reluctance, and governments usually took action only after irreparable harm had already been done.

Virtually no attempt was made to control the process of urban growth in accordance with any enlightened conception of city-planning. Real-estate interests and speculative builders were usually left free to do as they pleased. Cities generally followed the gridiron design with a dreary uniformity; streets were straight, and ran at right angles to each other, and little was done to preserve open spaces or take advantage of rivers and other natural features. A few individuals had broader vision: especially notable was the planning of Central Park in New York by Frederick Law Olmsted in 1868. But city expansion in the late nineteenth century meant chiefly the building of row after row of middle-class homes, often in brownstone, and of working-class tenements that had little or no air or sanitation and were designed on the principle of crowding as many people as possible into the smallest possible space. The congestion in slum areas quickly became appalling. In New York, for example, the crusading journalist Jacob Riis calculated in 1890 that no less than 330,000 persons were living in a single square mile of the Lower East Side.

Urban Problems.   The growth of the cities brought many new hazards. Lack of adequate sanitation and public-health services caused frequent outbreaks of typhoid fever and other epidemic diseases and a rapid growth of diseases associated with bad living conditions, such as tuberculosis. Fires were numerous and sometimes spread over wide areas; in the 1880's it was calculated that they were costing the country $100,-000,000 a year. The spread of slum areas was accompanied, moreover, by a rapid increase in crime and general lawlessness. In New York, Chicago, and other large cities there were "tenderloin" areas given over to gangsterism and prostitution, which were virtually outside the jurisdiction of civilized society.

As conditions grew worse, municipal authorities slowly took action to remedy them. One city after another undertook to remove garbage from its streets, instead of leaving it to be eaten by wandering pigs in accordance with traditional practice, and to dispose of sewage (often, unfortunately, by dumping it into the nearest river). Instead of having to walk several blocks to the nearest pump, householders were provided with fresh water at municipal expense. As late as 1878 only 600 towns and cities had built public waterworks; but the number increased fourfold before the end of the century. Beginning with New York in 1853, cities established uniformed police forces; and the increase in fires led to the employment of professional firemen instead of the picturesque but incompetent volunteer fire brigades.

The assumption of government responsibility for public health was marked by the establishment of the first city board of health in New York in 1866 and the first state board in Massachusetts in 1870. The American Public Health Association was founded in 1872. By the last decade of the century, as a result of sanitary regulations imposed by public authorities and increasing medical knowledge, the death rate from typhoid fever and similar diseases was definitely falling.

Meanwhile, a growing number of private citizens were aroused to action by the poverty and crime of the slums. With the founding of the Charity Organization Society in New York in 1882, followed by similar bodies in most other large cities, social work became more efficient and received more financial support from philanthropists. Before the end of the century nearly a hundred settlement houses had been set up in slum areas, Hull House in Chicago and the Henry Street Settlement in New York being the best-known. Their original function was to enable social workers to become more familiar with the lives of the poor, but they soon developed into social-service agencies on a broad scale and centers of the movement for reform. Social-work leaders like Jane Addams and Lillian D. Wald became active crusaders for government action to improve housing and public health, and limit the exploitation of women and children.

Thus urban America gradually learned new conceptions of social responsibility and interdependence. Yet urban growth continued so rapidly that new problems were constantly being created, and municipal regulation could never quite keep pace with them.

Recreations. A pleasanter aspect of urban development was the growth of new forms of recreation, at least for the middle class. Since the city-dweller, unlike the farmer, usually worked indoors at some specialized occupation, he had a greater need for some outdoor activity. The massing together of large populations, moreover, made it possible for spectator sports to be organized on a more elaborate scale.

Rural Americans had always engaged in a variety of simple games, most of them of European origin. One of these, baseball, gradually acquired more elaborate rules and became professionalized. According to tradition, it assumed its modern form as a result of innovations made by Abner Doubleday of Cooperstown, New York, in 1839, though there is much contradictory evidence. The first baseball club, the New York Knickerbockers, was founded in 1845, and the game acquired national popularity during the Civil War, when it was played in army camps. Professional baseball became fully organized with the founding of the National League in 1876. This attempted to maintain a monopoly, but it was successfully challenged by the American League about the turn of the century, after which the annual world series became the climax of the baseball season. Other spectator sports which gained steadily in popularity, in spite of religious opposition, were horse racing and prize fighting. Prize fights were at first such brutal exhibitions that every state in the Union made them illegal, but they became more respectable in the 1880's with the use of gloves instead of bare fists and the rise of fighters like John L. Sullivan, "Gentleman Jim" Corbett, and James Jeffries, who displayed skill and not merely brute force.

Thus the city-dweller could find a temporary escape from the monotony of his daily job and an outlet for his aggressive impulses by watching professional athletes. He was also beginning to take more open-air exercise himself. Golf and tennis were both introduced in the 1870's and 1880's, though at first they were regarded mainly as games for rich "dudes," while bicycling became widely popular in the 1890's. Meanwhile, urban Americans also enjoyed the theater, which presented mostly cheap melodrama and vaudeville but which flourished all over the country until it was largely displaced by the motion picture early in the twentieth century. Another urban manifestation was the extraordinary growth of fraternal societies, which offered the middle-class male citizen recreation facilities, insurance benefits, business contacts, and an escape from the drabness of daily living through the wearing of brilliant costumes and participation in mystic rites. By 1914 it was calculated that they had a total membership of nearly 16,000,000.

2. IMMIGRATION

A LARGE proportion of the new urban working-class populations consisted of recent immigrants from Europe, along with sizable contingents from French Canada. After the Civil War, with the rapid expansion of the American economy and the increased transportation facilities, the Atlantic migration rose to unprecedented levels, and a growing number of the new arrivals turned to industry instead of to agriculture. In 1910 it was calculated that one-third of the inhabitants of the country's eight largest cities were foreign-born, while considerably more than a third were second-generation Americans. There were even larger concentrations of foreign-born in some of the smaller industrial towns: in the coal and iron towns of Pennsylvania, for example, and in places like Paterson and Passaic, New Jersey, and Hamtramck, Michigan.

Total immigration during the half-century 1870–1920 amounted to 26,277,000—more than three times as much as during the whole of the previous two and a half centuries. Several millions of these were birds of passage who eventually returned to their homelands, but probably more than 20,000,000 remained in the United States as permanent residents. Mounting slowly during the 1870's, immigration reached a peak in the 1880's, dropped back during the depression period of the 1890's, and then rose again in the early twentieth century, until it was checked by the outbreak of World War I. The all-time record was made in 1907, which brought 1,285,349 arrivals. The figures for total immigration for different decades were as follows:

1871–80	2,812,191
1881–90	5,246,613
1891–1900	3,687,564
1901–10	8,795,386
1911–20	5,735,811

The New Immigration. Down to 1890, 85 per cent of the European immigrants came from northern and western Europe, the largest contributors being Germany, Ireland, England, and Scandinavia. But during the 1890's there was a significant change. Immigrants from northern and western Europe began to decrease, while there was a rapid rise in entries from southern and eastern Europe, particularly from Italy, Austria-Hungary, and Russia. This so-called "new immigration" brought a great variety of new ethnic groups: Czechs, Slovaks, Hungarians, Croats, Slovenes, and Jews from the Austro-Hungarian Empire; Poles, Ukrainians, and Jews from the Russian Empire.

Comparative figures for the old and new immigration were as follows:

	From Northern and Western Europe	From Southern and Eastern Europe
1871–80	2,127,000	145,000
1881–90	3,783,000	954,000
1891–1900	1,644,000	1,914,000
1901–10	1,912,000	6,224,000
1911–20	2,001,000	2,370,000

Thus down to 1890 the United States was drawing most of its new citizens from much the same parts of Europe as during the colonial period. Most of the immigrants came from countries which were economically and culturally advanced; most of them were literate; with the exception of the Irish and some of the Germans, they were usually Protestants; and, with the same exceptions, they usually settled on farms after reaching the United States. The "new immigration," on the other hand, came from the more backward parts of Europe. Many of the immigrants were illiterate and accustomed to extremely low living standards; they had no previous experience with any form of democracy, and knew government only as an alien and oppressive force; most of them were not Protestant but Roman Catholic, Greek Orthodox, or Jewish; and most of them settled in the cities, chiefly in the Northeast and the Middle West.

Most of the new immigrants had been peasant farmers in the Old World, with a traditional way of life that had been handed down, generation after generation, since the early Middle Ages. The initial causes of the great folk movement which brought them to America were economic changes somewhat similar to those that had transformed British society in the sixteenth and seventeenth centuries. Population growth and the gradual extension of a monetary economy and machine industry disrupted the traditional village life and made it difficult for the peasants to support themselves as their ancestors had done. Then, in the late nineteenth century, the news began to spread of a land of plenty across the Atlantic. In many areas the news was first brought by the agents of American mining and industrial corporations wanting cheap labor and of steamship companies in quest of passengers. The flow of traffic from eastern Europe mostly carried immigrants first to Hamburg or to the British port of Liverpool. There they took passage across the Atlantic in the steerage class, under conditions almost as squalid and congested as in the ships that had carried indentured servants in the colonial period, and landed at Castle Garden at the foot of Manhattan Island in New York, where (after 1855) the state authorities arranged for them to change money and buy railroad tickets without being cheated. The last lap of the journey carried them to the coal fields or steel mills or clothing factories. Thus they had to adjust themselves to a double change: a change not only from Europe to America but also from the village to the city.

The Immigrant in American Society.   Ignorant of the language and customs of the strange new world, and cold-shouldered by people whose ancestors had arrived at earlier periods, most first-generation Americans continued to live with people of their own ethnic group. Every large industrial city soon acquired a number of colonies of transplanted Europeans; people living in the same area spoke the same European language, worshipped at the same church, tried to preserve their ancestral customs and beliefs, and in the course of time started their own foreign-language newspaper. It was only very gradually that the United States ceased to seem to these immigrant groups like alien territory.

The process of assimilation usually began not with the immigrants themselves but with their children, and was likely to be painful and fraught with problems. The children learned in the public schools to speak English and to adopt as their own the traditions of the *Mayflower* and the Declaration of Independence, forgetting those of their own ancestors. They were quickly made to feel that immigrant customs were signs of inferiority, and that they could be admitted to the full privileges of Americanism only by conforming to the mores of the dominant groups. The result was that in many immigrant families a sharp schism was created between the children and the parents, more especially the father. For while the mother could still perform her traditional functions in the home, the father, ignorant of American life and usually not very successful as a breadwinner, could no longer guide his family or maintain his traditional authority. The result was that many second-generation Americans grew up with little respect for paternal discipline, and with a feeling of alienation from their own ethnic traditions. At the same time they still had a sense of not belonging to the American community and, if they lived in slum areas, often came into contact only with the worst aspects of American life. This situation created many problems of maladjustment, among them being the crime and gangsterism that were sometimes attributed to the immigrants themselves. Relatively few first-generation Americans were criminals; but the proportion was higher than the national average among their children. Crime developed especially in urban areas where old-world traditions were breaking down and no new forms of social integration had replaced them.

Ever since the Germans began flooding into Pennsylvania early in the eighteenth century, each new immigrant group in turn has been the victim of prejudice. And each group in turn has gradually moved upwards in the social and economic scale, become accepted into the American community, and finally acquired the right to display prejudice against later arrivals. With the rapid influx of new ethnic groups in the late nineteenth century, nativist prejudice increased. Many persons of old American stock drew sharp distinctions between the old and the new immigration, and insisted that American traditions would be overwhelmed by the influx from southern and eastern Europe. Repudiating the doctrine that all men had been created equal, they argued that the new immigrants belonged to races that were congenitally inferior, and alleged that a large proportion of them were criminals and anarchists. Prejudice against the Catholic Church increased, and (for the first time in American history) anti-Semitic propaganda began to find an audience.

The large-scale immigration of groups inexperienced in any form of democracy did indeed intensify certain political problems. The presence of large bodies of immigrant voters ignorant of democratic processes presented machine politicians in the big cities with new opportunities, and hence stimulated municipal misgovernment. And in so far as some of the immigrants retained a double loyalty—to their home country as well as to the United States—they created new pressures upon American foreign policy. Candidates in quest of votes were too often tempted to appeal to the attachments and antipathies of ethnic blocs. But most of the accusations made against the new immigrants were mere reflections of prejudice. Nativists ignored the fact that each different immigrant group in turn, from the English and Germans and Scotch-Irish of the colonial period down to the Italians and Slavs and Jews of the twentieth century, had been brought to America by similar hopes of freedom from oppression and of economic opportunity, and had faced similar problems of readjustment after reaching their promised land. Appalled by the squalor and gangsterism of slum areas, they failed to see (as Jacob Riis pointed out) that the significant question was not what the immigrant was doing to America but what America was doing to the immigrant. And in demanding that immigrant groups become assimilated as rapidly as possible, they overlooked the value of cultural diversity and did not recognize that American life might be enriched by the preservation of many immigrant traditions and ways of living.

The Beginning of Restriction. The movement for immigration restriction was slowly gaining strength in the late nineteenth century, though it did not achieve final success until after World War I. While nativist sentiment contributed to its growth, a more important influence was that of organized labor, which had difficulty in maintaining high wage scales as long as new workers continued to pour in from abroad.

Prior to 1875 the Federal government exercised no control at all over immigration. In that year it assumed responsibility for the first time by excluding prostitutes and persons with prison records. In 1882 idiots and persons likely to become public charges were barred, and a small head tax was imposed.

The act of 1882 also set a new precedent by completely prohibiting any further entry of Chinese. During the previous thirty years about 150,000 Chinese laborers had been brought to the United States, mostly to the Pacific coast, where they had originally been employed in building railroads. Their willingness to work for extremely low wages stimulated the color prejudices of their white competitors and brought about a violent anti-Chinese movement among the white workers of California. Their exclusion was at first temporary but was made permanent in 1902. It was repealed as a gesture of friendship during World War II. An influx of Japanese laborers and farmers into California in the 1890's caused similar outbreaks of prejudice. Japanese exclusion was brought about not by legislation but by the Gentlemen's Agreement with the Japanese government of 1907.

After 1882 the list of excluded categories was slowly enlarged, but there was no fundamental change of policy until 1917, when (over President Wilson's veto) a literacy test was imposed. Finally, in 1921, the total number of immigrants permitted was severely restricted, and the traditional American belief that the country had room for all who wished to come was definitely abandoned.[1]

By this time the ethnic composition of the American people had considerably changed since the colonial period. According to the national origins quota, the English, Scotch, and Scotch-Irish element in the white population, which had probably amounted to about 75 per cent in 1790, had dropped by 1920 to 42.7 per cent, while some other estimates made it even lower. The United States had become a new kind of nation, a nation bound together not by common ancestry and memories of the past but by common ideals and hopes for the future.

3. RELIGIOUS ORGANIZATIONS

THE LATE nineteenth century was a difficult period for the Protestant churches. Most of them had always regarded the Bible as the supreme authority, on the assumption that it was the inspired word of God, while their ethical code had been closely associated with the economic individualism of the middle class. Each of these attitudes was now becoming more difficult to maintain. Belief in the authority of the Bible was under-

[1] See page 596.

mined by the Darwinian theory of evolution, which controverted the story of God's creation of the world in seven days,[2] and by the growth of the so-called "Higher Criticism," originating among German scholars who applied historical methods of interpretation to the Biblical narrative. Belief in the virtues of economic individualism was weakened by the rise of big business; the promotion of justice in the new industrial economy seemed to require a different approach to the problems of social ethics.

Modernists and Fundamentalists. During the last two decades of the century a growing number of clergymen accepted the Darwinian hypothesis and found ways of reconciling it with religious belief; they argued that God was ultimately responsible for evolution but that he worked more slowly and less directly than had formerly been believed. Particularly significant was the conversion of the most influential preacher of the time, Henry Ward Beecher, who declared in his *Evolution and Religion*, published in 1885, that evolution was merely "the deciphering of God's thought as revealed in the structure of the world."

Having abandoned belief in the literal truth of the Bible, a few modernist clergymen went on to deny miracles, the Virgin Birth, and other supernatural elements in Christian theology and to reinterpret religion as primarily an ethical attitude rather than a system of beliefs. Conservatives were horrified by this tendency and insisted that the doctrine that every word in the Bible was divinely inspired was the only solid foundation for religious faith. They became known as "Fundamentalists" after a conference at Niagara Falls in 1895 had reaffirmed five "fundamentals" of Christian belief. Several modernists were put on trial for heresy and convicted. In 1893, for example, Charles A. Briggs was expelled from the Presbyterian ministry for declaring that there were a number of errors in the Biblical narrative. But the fundamentalists were fighting a losing battle. The more influential seminaries were gradually captured by the liberals. Before 1900 both Andover in Massachusetts, the main Congregationalist institution, and Union in New York had become modernist strongholds. Fundamentalism, however, continued to be well entrenched in rural communities, especially in the South.

The Social Gospel. Throughout the later nineteenth century a large majority of the Protestant clergy continued to affirm that the existing economic system was basically just and that the poverty of the working class was due mainly to improvidence and laziness. Their critics did not fail to point out that they had strong economic inducements for conservatism, since most of the big businessmen were church members and heavy contributors to church funds. But in the 1880's a few of the Protestant clergy began to preach a new "Social Gospel." Most of them lived in urban communities and were shocked by the living conditions of the working class. They declared that Christianity required more than adherence to strict standards of personal morality, and that business prac-

[2] See page 487.

tices resulting in the exploitation of labor were as unethical as drunkenness and unchastity.

Perhaps the most influential exponent of the Social Gospel was Washington Gladden, who became a Congregationalist minister at Columbus, Ohio, in 1882. In 1887 Gladden joined other Christian reformers in forming the Evangelical Alliance. This was replaced in 1892 by the Brotherhood of the Kingdom, which remained for the next twenty years an important force in American religion, especially among the Congregationalists and the Methodists. In 1908 the General Conference of the Methodist Episcopal Church adopted a progressive social creed calling for the "most equitable division of the products in industry that can ultimately be devised," the reduction of hours of labor, and other economic reforms. This statement was adopted, with only minor changes, by the newly organized Federal Council of Churches. Most of the Social Gospelers favored a reformed capitalism, animated by the principles of the Golden Rule; but a few of them became socialists. Prominent among the latter was Walter Rauschenbusch, whose *A Theology for the Social Gospel* (published in 1917) was one of the most influential documents in the history of American Christianity.

Protestant Growth.   With the increase of more rationalistic conceptions of religion, the Protestant churches were less inclined to seek converts by the use of revivalistic methods. The last great revivalist to win widespread middle-class support was Dwight L. Moody, a Congregationalist of New England origin. Accompanied by the singer Ira D. Sankey, Moody made a series of nation-wide tours in the 1870's and 1880's. In the twentieth century revivalism was still popular in rural areas, but in the cities it was represented chiefly by exhibitionists like the ex-baseball-player Billy Sunday. Instead of appealing to emotion, most urban churches relied to an increasing extent on providing social services for their members. The number of church members continued to increase, though membership probably involved fewer obligations than in the past.

That American Protestantism was still a very vital force in national life was shown by the steady growth of the prohibitionist movement, which derived its main strength from the Methodist, Baptist, and Presbyterian churches. The Women's Christian Temperance Union was founded under the leadership of Frances Willard in 1879, and the Anti-Saloon League in 1895. As a result of pressure from these organizations, one state after another adopted dry legislation, and the Eighteenth Amendment was added to the Constitution in 1919.[3] On the other hand, Protestant attempts to maintain sabbath-day observance and enforce the traditional blue laws were notably unsuccessful. Sunday was becoming increasingly a day devoted to recreation rather than solely to religion.

American Protestantism continued to produce new denominations, though in less profusion than before the Civil War. The chief new church

[3] See page 550.

appealing primarily to the middle class was Christian Science, founded by Mary Baker Eddy, of Lynn, Massachusetts, whose *Science and Health* was published in 1875. Mrs. Eddy's main doctrine was that diseases and other evils were delusions which could be removed by a proper faith in God and did not call for materialistic remedies. At the time of her death in 1910 Christian Science had 1,000 churches and a membership variously estimated at from 300,000 to 1,000,000.

Other new religious groups originated mostly among the poorer classes in rural areas, especially in the Southern mountains, and were usually revivalistic. A number of "Holiness" cults broke away from the Methodist and Baptist churches, conducted wildly emotional religious meetings, and preached various eccentric doctrines. Most of them prohibited the wearing of neckties and other symbols of worldliness, while the more extreme encouraged believers to demonstrate their faith by playing with rattlesnakes. Another growing sect was Jehovah's Witnesses, founded by Pastor Charles T. Russell, and led after his death in 1916 by Judge Joseph F. Rutherford. Like the Millerites in the 1840's, they expected the world to end shortly and declared that "millions now living will never die." Their opposition to saluting the flag in public schools and other patriotic observances led to some delicate problems of religious freedom.

Catholicism. Meanwhile, the immigration of Irish, Italians, Poles, South Germans, and other Catholic peoples was resulting in a steady growth in the size and influence of the Catholic Church. In 1860 there were 3,500,000 American Catholics, 11 per cent of the total population. By 1910 they numbered 16,000,000, or 17 per cent of the total. As the Church expanded, it enlarged its system of parochial schools, and set up new colleges and convents. It was probably more successful than the Protestant churches in retaining the loyalty of the younger generation.

Leadership in the Church continued to be largely Irish, its outstanding American spokesman for many years being James Gibbons, Archbishop of Baltimore from 1877 to 1921, who was appointed the second American cardinal in 1886. Some of the later immigrant groups resented the predominance of the Irish, and a German Catholic, Peter Cahensly, even suggested in 1890 that each group should have priests and bishops of its own. Cahenslyism was opposed by Gibbons and officially condemned by the Pope, but the proposal showed that the Church, like the country as a whole, was having its own assimilation problems.

The Catholic Church found it easier than most Protestant churches to adapt itself to the economic developments of the late nineteenth century. The Church had never been closely identified with economic individualism, and it had its own Social Gospel dating back to the teaching of the medieval Scholastics. This was reaffirmed in 1891 by Pope Leo XIII, in his famous encyclical *De Rerum Novarum*, which condemned the exploitation of labor and affirmed the duty of the state to bring about social justice. While the Church was definitely opposed to socialism, its official economic doctrines gave support to progressivism.

In the United States some Catholic leaders remained economically conservative, but the majority, headed by Cardinal Gibbons, were sympathetic to social reform. Most American Catholics belonged to the working class, and Catholic influence was always strong in the trade-union movement. When some Canadian bishops brought about the condemnation of the Knights of Labor, Gibbons came to its defense and persuaded the Church hierarchy at Rome that the purposes of the organization were in no way antagonistic to Catholic belief. Gibbons was subsequently a strong supporter of the AFL.

Many old-fashioned evangelical Protestants continued to believe that the Pope was Antichrist and was conspiring to dominate America. Dormant since the Know Nothing movement of the 1850's, anti-Catholic prejudice flared up again with the foundation in 1886 of the American Protective Association in Iowa. Within a few years this was claiming more than 1,000,000 adherents, mostly in the rural Middle West. It died away during the 1890's, chiefly because most of its members found the free-silver crusade more absorbing than the fight against the Pope. But the continued strength of anti-Catholicism in rural areas was demonstrated again in the Hoover-Smith campaign of 1928. Smith, the first Catholic to be nominated for the presidency by either major party, failed to carry five of the traditionally Democratic states of the Solid South mainly because of the religious issue.

4. EDUCATION AND SCIENCE

Public-School Expansion.   The ideal of free public education for all, which had won general acceptance in principle before the Civil War, became a reality before the end of World War I. After Massachusetts passed the first compulsory-education law in 1852, the other states and territories gradually fell into line. Thirty-two of them, all in the North and West, had acted by 1900, and all forty-eight (the last being Mississippi) by 1918.

Most of the states began by requiring only two or three years' attendance at a grammar school. But after the initial adoption of compulsory education, the number of years was steadily extended, and states began to assume responsibility for providing secondary as well as primary education. The number of public high schools increased from 500 in 1870 to 2,500 in 1890 and 12,000 in 1915. In 1870 public education cost the American people $63,000,000, the rate per pupil being $9.23. By 1930 the cost had risen to more than $1,000,000,000 and the rate per pupil to $74.38. But facilities varied considerably in different parts of the country, since rich states like New York, New Jersey, and California were able to spend about five times as much per pupil as the more poverty-stricken parts of the South. One of the results of this impressive growth was a fall in the national illiteracy rate from 20 per cent in 1870 to 11 per cent in 1900 and 4.3 per cent in 1930.

The expansion of the public-school system seemed to indicate that the American people had an almost unlimited respect for education. But this did not always extend to the profession responsible for it, which continued to be underpaid and to have a relatively low social status. City and state authorities often seemed to regard expensive buildings and equipment as more important than good instruction, and kept careful watch over teachers lest they express radical opinions or violate established mores. Teachers' salaries remained abysmally low. As late as 1900 the average male teacher earned only $42.14 a month, less than a manual laborer, while women teachers received even less. During the twentieth century there was a considerable improvement in the richer states, but even in New York and California teaching was still underpaid by contrast with other professions. Since it was impossible to support a family on the average teacher's salary, relatively few men cared to enter the profession. The proportion of male teachers dropped from 43 per cent in 1880 to 30 per cent in 1900 and 15 per cent in 1920.

Compulsory education meant that every American child had an opportunity to learn the essentials of literacy and citizenship. In many instances it did not mean much more than this. The vast quantitative expansion of the school system inevitably involved some sacrifice of quality. But possibly the most important functions of the public-school system were not those of education in the narrow sense of the word. The passage of most American children through the same school system promoted national unity and served as a check on the growth of class and race distinctions. It was principally in the schools that children of immigrant parents learned American ways and won acceptance (often by becoming star performers in high-school athletics) into the American community.

College Expansion. The period following the Civil War saw an equally impressive expansion in higher education. The Federal government was a principal contributor through the Morrill Act of 1862, under which 13,000,000 acres of public land were turned over to the states for the support of colleges and universities. State and municipal governments also appropriated large sums of their own, while many private institutions were endowed by wealthy men. Long-established colleges like Harvard, Yale, and Columbia grew into large universities, and new institutions like Chicago, Cornell, Johns Hopkins, Duke, Vanderbilt, and Stanford were founded. By 1900 there were some 500 colleges in the United States, an increase of nearly 100 per cent since 1860. The right of women to higher education was now generally recognized, and by 1900 they comprised about a quarter of the total number of undergraduates. Some 70 per cent of all colleges were now coeducational, while the two decades following the

Civil War had seen the foundation of such women's colleges as Vassar, Wellesley, Smith, and Bryn Mawr.

The quantitative growth of the colleges was accompanied by revolutionary changes in their curricula. Instead of concentrating mainly on classics and mathematics, as in the eighteenth century, they now offered instruction in a vast variety of new courses covering virtually every field of knowledge and including many which seemed very remote from the traditional purposes of higher education. Under the elective system students were then invited to choose for themselves what they proposed to study. This system had originated at the University of Virginia at the time of its foundation in the 1820's, but did not become general until it was adopted at Harvard under the sponsorship of Charles W. Eliot, President from 1869 to 1909. While the elective system served as a useful weapon for breaking down the supremacy of the traditional disciplines, its positive results were much more controversial. Conservatives complained, with considerable justification, that in its more extreme forms it led to educational chaos. Too many students acquired a smattering of information in a bewildering variety of different subjects without gaining real mastery in any of them; and if they made a skillful selection of the snap courses scattered through the college catalogue, they could acquire a B.A. degree with virtually no work at all. The twentieth century saw a number of attempts to limit the elective system and work out some kind of core program, based on the theory that certain subjects should be an essential part of every college education.

Another new development which, though adding to the pleasures of college life, was not always easy to reconcile with high academic standards was the growth of organized athletics. Football was introduced from England after the Civil War, the first intercollegiate game (between Princeton and Rutgers) being played in 1869. American football quickly diverged from English Rugby and became rougher and more complicated, mainly owing to innovations made by Walter Camp, who was coach at Yale during the 1880's. Early in the twentieth century, in fact, so many players were being killed in intercollegiate contests that a number of colleges considered abandoning the game and Theodore Roosevelt even called a White House conference on the problem. Baseball, as we have seen, had become a national sport during the Civil War period, while basketball was invented at the YMCA college at Springfield, Massachusetts, in 1891. In the twentieth century, with the growth of alumni interest that often approached hysteria, some colleges seemed in danger of degenerating into mere adjuncts to stadiums, and an athletic coach sometimes earned a larger salary than anybody else on the campus, even the president.

Graduate and Professional Schools.   One feature of the educational expansion represented an unqualified advance: this was the growth of facilities for post-graduate training and research. Post-graduate training had been virtually non-existent before the Civil War; in 1850 there had been a total of eight graduate students in the whole country. The graduate school, along with the seminar method, was introduced from Germany in the 1870's. Yale and Harvard started graduate schools in 1871 and 1872 respectively, while Johns Hopkins, founded in 1876, was designed primarily as a center for graduate work. By 1900 most of the larger institutions had set up graduate schools, the total registration being more than 5,000.

An even more important branch of post-graduate education was the professional school. Hitherto most American doctors, lawyers, and dentists had acquired their training by working for a few years under the supervision of some experienced practitioner; and while a few professional schools existed, students merely memorized lectures and received no practical experience. The pioneer figure in the growth of professional schools was President Eliot. In the 1870's he reorganized the Harvard schools of medicine and law so that they would give adequate training in practice as well as theory and impose strict standards of attainment. Other university administrators quickly followed his example; and as good professional training became generally accessible, the state governments made regulations preventing unqualified persons from practicing law, medicine, or dentistry.

Scientific Progress. The early American college had been almost exclusively a teaching institution. After the Civil War there was a growing recognition that its function was not merely to transmit existing knowledge to the next generation but also to add to it. Probably an unduly large proportion of the sums devoted to higher education were spent on buildings (many of them in an unfunctional pseudo Gothic), largely because both millionaire contributors and college presidents wanted concrete memorials of their statesmanship handed down to posterity. But increasing sums were also made available for libraries, laboratories, and other research facilities, and some scholars were freed from part of their teaching responsibilities and given more leisure to pursue their own researches. After the Civil War, for the first time, American universities began to add appreciably to the sum of human knowledge.

In philosophy and social studies the new developments were so important that they deserve a separate chapter.[4] In the natural sciences, progress in which bears little or no relation to differences of national background, it is less easy to pick out American contributions. But a few names are too important to be omitted.

Possibly the greatest of all American theoretical scientists was Willard Gibbs, Professor of Mathematical Physics at Yale from 1871 until 1903. Gibbs remained little known until his old age, chiefly because he was so far ahead of other American scientists that none of them were qualified to appreciate his work. His "rule of phase" was a major contribution to the development of modern physics, in addition to having important

[4] See pages 484–502.

practical applications in metallurgy. Another leading physicist was Albert A. Michelson of Chicago, who measured the speed of light in 1879 and afterwards joined Edward Morley of Western Reserve in making a series of ether-drift experiments which led directly to Einstein's relativity theory. Benjamin Pierce of Harvard made important additions to mathematics, Simon Newcomb of the Washington Observatory to astronomy, and Othniel C. Marsh of Yale and Edward D. Cope of Pennsylvania to palaeontology, while genetics was revolutionized by the experiments of T. H. Morgan of Columbia. While major credit for the advance of American science should be given to the universities, the Federal government continued (as before the Civil War) to give valuable stimulation, especially through the foundation of the Weather Bureau in 1870 and of the Geological Survey in 1879.

Especially important in the transformation of human life was the progress of medicine, in which American medical schools, especially that of Johns Hopkins, founded in 1893 under the direction of W. H. Welch, now began to play a leading part. Medicine was revolutionized in the late nineteenth century by the work of Louis Pasteur in France and Robert Koch in Germany in demonstrating the germ theory of disease. Scientists could then track down the specific germs responsible for different diseases and develop techniques for creating immunity. The best-known American contribution was the discovery of the way yellow fever was spread, through the experiments directed by Walter Reed in Cuba after the war with Spain. By the early twentieth century a number of mankind's leading killers were for the first time being brought under effective control. The death rate (especially among infants) was falling, and people were living longer and could expect to remain active for longer periods. In addition to removing much human misery, these developments meant that the proportion of older people in the population was steadily increasing, a change which had important social and political consequences.

Adult Education.   The advance of the sciences and the growing complexity of society made the diffusion of new knowledge among the mass of the adult population even more necessary than in the past. One of the chief agencies in this field was the free public library. By 1900 there were 9,000 libraries containing at least 300 books apiece, as contrasted with a mere handful before the Civil War. This growth owed much to Andrew Carnegie, who contributed $6,000,000 to the building of libraries on condition that municipal authorities undertake to support them.

In organized adult education, the most important new development was the Chautauqua movement, a successor to the lyceum of the 1830's and 1840's. This originated in 1874 when Lewis Miller and John H. Vincent founded a summer school for Sunday School teachers in western New York. Chautauqua soon expanded into a nation-wide organization for all adults interested in educating themselves. In addition to its annual summer schools, it organized study circles (which had 100,000 members by 1892) and sent out itinerant lecturers, among them men like William James, Josiah Royce, and William Jennings Bryan, who were among the nation's intellectual and political leaders. Meanwhile, women's clubs were similarly expanding, and joined forces in a General Federation in 1889.

5. THE PRESS

Newspapers.   American men continued to derive their knowledge of world affairs mainly from their daily or weekly newspapers. The number of newspapers in the United States increased from 7,000 in 1870 to 16,200 in 1900, about as many as in all the rest of the world put together. This quantitative growth was accompanied by a number of technical improvements. Newspapers became larger, were printed more attractively, and contained better illustrations. A more comprehensive news coverage was provided through the establishment in 1892 of the Associated Press, followed by other news-gathering agencies, and through an increasing employment of foreign correspondents. These improvements meant, however, that newspapers cost more to produce and hence needed larger circulations. The result was that journalism began to develop into a big business, and the independent editors who had done so much to shape public opinion during the middle decades of the nineteenth century—men like Greeley of the *Tribune* and Bryant of the *Evening Post*—gave place to journalistic entrepreneurs of a new kind.

The men chiefly associated with the growth of the new mass-circulation newspapers were Joseph Pulitzer and William Randolph Hearst. Pulitzer, an immigrant from Hungary who had reached the United States without financial resources in 1864, became owner of the *St. Louis Post-Dispatch* in 1878, and acquired the *New York World* in 1883. He built up the circulation of the *World* by printing the most lurid news stories, at the same time campaigning in its editorial columns for liberal reforms and public honesty. Hearst, who had inherited a fortune from his father, a California mining millionaire, took control of the *San Francisco Examiner* in 1887, and acquired the *New York Journal* in 1895. The *World* and the *Journal* became bitter rivals, and were soon competing with each other in printing stories of alleged Spanish atrocities in Cuba and stirring up war hysteria. After the nation had been pulled into the war with Spain, each of them ran up its circulation to the unprecedented figure of more than a million. Since they printed rival versions of an early comic strip featuring a character known as the "yellow kid," their sensationalistic methods became known as "yellow journalism." Pulitzer continued to support liberal causes until his death in 1911. Hearst, while always belligerently nationalistic, attacked big business and advocated reforms verging on socialism during the first half of his career, but swung over to conservatism after World War I. He acquired a chain of newspapers and magazines throughout the country, most of which he continued to control until his death in 1951.

The methods of Pulitzer and Hearst were imitated by other entrepreneurs, who established chains and sought mass circulations. Faced with this kind of competition, a number of the smaller papers went out of business or merged with others. After 1900 the number of newspapers in the United States began to decrease; and in some cities the entire press came under the ownership of a single syndicate. These were alarming developments, since they meant that the chief agencies in the formation of public opinion were coming under the control of a small number of wealthy entrepreneurs who might be expected to use their influence to oppose progressive causes. In so far as they slanted news reports and appealed to mass prejudices, they were poisoning public information at its source. On the whole, however, election returns during the twentieth century seemed to indicate that newspapers had less influence over public opinion than might be expected.

A small but distinguished group of papers continued to provide readers with reasonably complete and unbiased news coverage. The *New York Times*, controlled after 1896 by Adolph Simon Ochs, generally lived up to its slogan of giving "all the news that's fit to print," as did a few other journals, most of them in Eastern states. Unfortunately, even the best American newspapers did not circulate widely outside the cities where they were produced. The American press remained primarily local rather than national, and throughout the twentieth century there were many sections of the United States, including some large cities, which remained alarmingly lacking in adequate news coverage of world affairs.

Magazines.   The late nineteenth century was probably the golden age of American magazines. Periodicals like the *Atlantic Monthly, Harper's,* and the *Century* maintained high standards, had a wide influence, and (through the practice of serialization) probably did more than the book-publishing houses to determine the tone of American literature. Among the weeklies, the *Nation* was outstanding. This was founded in 1865 by Edwin L. Godkin, who had come to the United States from Britain nine years earlier. Down to his death in 1902 Godkin probably did more than anybody else to shape middle-class opinion in the Eastern states. A liberal of the old *laissez-faire* vintage and a strong believer in leadership by an enlightened and cultured property-owning class, Godkin crusaded for high moral standards in politics. But having the limitations of his background, he was unable to see the rise of agrarian insurgency and other forms of radicalism as anything but a threat to civilization.

Towards the end of the century the magazines, like the newspapers, began to be transformed by the advent of mass-production methods. Edward L. Bok founded the *Ladies' Home Journal* in 1889, and ran up its circulation to 700,000 within three years. Two other big money-makers were *Munsey's Weekly*, founded in 1889, and *McClure's*, founded in 1893. Even more sensational was the growth of the *Saturday Evening Post*, which achieved a circulation of 2,000,000 early in the twentieth century and held it from that time on. While appealing to a more popular audience than their more sedate predecessors and selling at lower prices, the new magazines printed some good fiction and reliable news stories, and during the first decade of the twentieth century they sponsored the muckraking movement, which did much to stimulate the reforms of the progressive period. Later in the century they generally swung over to a more conservative position, and both their fiction and news stories and their editorials tended to glorify the businessman and the mores of the American middle class.

The growth of the popular press was a vivid illustration of the cultural effects, both good and bad, of urban and industrial growth. On the one hand, the new urban American had many more opportunities than his rural ancestor for acquiring information and entertainment. At the same time, there was danger that the new mass culture would mean general standardization on a relatively low level and result in the manipulation of public opinion by skillful propaganda.

XXIII

New Ways of Thinking

1. THE REIGN OF ORTHODOXY
2. THE IMPACT OF DARWINISM
3. NEW WAYS IN SOCIOLOGY AND ECONOMICS
4. NEW WAYS IN PHILOSOPHY
5. NEW WAYS IN HISTORY

THE NEW industrial economy caused revolutionary changes in the ways in which people lived long before it began to modify their beliefs and thought patterns. The initial reaction of American thinkers to the transformation of their environment was to reaffirm traditional doctrines more rigidly than in the past. During the last two decades of the century, on the other hand, some of them began to propound new answers to social and philosophical problems and set forth new views of life. The new ways of thinking developed by these men have largely shaped the American mind through the twentieth century.

1. THE REIGN OF ORTHODOXY

FOR twenty years after the outbreak of the Civil War there was remarkably little original thinking in the United States. The intellectual ferment

---

SELECTED BIBLIOGRAPHY: Almost all the trends described in this chapter are examined in Richard Hofstadter's excellent *Social Darwinism in American Thought, 1860–1915* (1944), and the later trends are discussed in M. G. White, *Social Thought in America* (1949). V. L. Parrington, *Main Currents in American Thought*, Vol. 3 (1929), deals with some of the earlier social theorists, while H. S. Commager, *The American Mind* (1950), begins at about 1890. More general studies of intellectual history are Merle Curti, *The Growth of American Thought* (1951), and R. H. Gabriel, *The Course of American Democratic Thought* (1940). Economic theory is analyzed in Joseph Dorfman, *The Economic Mind in American Civilization*, Vol. 3 (1949); philosophy in H. W. Schneider, *A History of American Philosophy* (1946); and historiography in Michael Kraus, *A History of American History* (1937).

of the 1830's and 1840's had been brought to an end by the sectional conflict, and for the next generation Americans seemed to be suspicious of new ideas and anxious only to prove that existing conditions were as close to perfection as could be expected. The dominant tendency in all branches of philosophical and social theory was to justify the *status quo* by showing that the strong national government prescribed by the Constitution, the capitalistic economic system, and the traditional religious and ethical beliefs were in accord with the will of God and the laws of nature.

American thinkers still derived their basic conceptions largely from the rationalism of the Enlightenment, and continued to affirm that the human mind had been created by God and was capable of apprehending absolute truths, both in science and in social relationships. Just as Newton had formulated the laws regulating the movements of the stars and planets, so also, it was supposed, man could formulate natural laws of politics, economics, and morality which, like the law of gravitation, were universal and immutable. The intellectual spokesmen of the 1860's and 1870's generally argued that these laws were fully embodied in existing American institutions and that by adhering to them men could achieve happiness and prosperity.

Philosophy. The most important new influence was the German idealistic philosophy of the early nineteenth century, especially that of Hegel, but this also served to justify existing conditions. Hegel had interpreted the whole of history as the working out of a divine purpose which would culminate in the achievement of perfect freedom. The American Hegelians interpreted American institutions, including the *laissez-faire* economic system, as realizations of this perfect freedom and hence as expressions of the divine mind. In so far as Hegelianism introduced any new element into American modes of thought, it did so chiefly by inculcating an especial reverence for the state, which in the United States meant the Federal government. Hegel had regarded a nation as an organic whole, and had insisted that the individual could achieve freedom and self-realization only through an undeviating loyalty to his national government and institutions. Thus what Hegel meant by "freedom" was very different from the traditional American conception, as embodied in the Bill of Rights. This Hegelian glorification of national unity harmonized with the policies of the Republican Party during the Civil War and Reconstruction.

Philosophy was taught almost exclusively by clergymen, who felt that its main purpose was to elucidate the traditional Protestant theology. On the whole, the Scottish common-sense school, first introduced in the late eighteenth century, was still dominant in academic circles. The leading figures of the 1860's and 1870's were the Reverend Noah Porter of Yale and the Reverend James McCosh of Princeton, neither of whom (though men of wide learning) had anything original to contribute.

Social Theory. Political theorists, such as Theodore Dwight Woolsey of Yale, interpreted the Constitution as the embodiment of absolute principles of justice, and recommended particular respect for the Supreme Court as the guardian of these principles. The influence of German nationalist thinking led to a strong emphasis on obedience to the Federal government and to interpretations of the sectional conflict wholly favorable to the North. This tendency was represented during the Civil War period by Francis Lieber, himself an immigrant from Germany, and around the turn of the century by John W. Burgess of Columbia. The same nationalist bias was shown by a number of historians, such as James Schouler and James Ford Rhodes, who wrote about nineteenth-century American development. One of the penalties suffered by the South as a result of losing the Civil War was to see the history of the controversy written by the other side.

Economic theory after the Civil War was wholly dominated by the *laissez-faire* doctrines of Adam Smith and the English classical school. Those American thinkers, such as Henry Carey, who had attempted to modify these doctrines to suit American needs and conditions no longer exerted much influence. Writers like Amasa Walker of Harvard and Amherst argued that competition was the divinely ordained regulator of economic life in the same way that gravitation governed the physical universe. *Laissez faire* would bring about the best possible use of resources, lead to steady progress, and cause each individual to be rewarded according to his deserts. The millionaire earned his wealth by practicing self-denial and saving his money and by displaying ability and industry, while poverty was the appropriate punishment for idleness and wastefulness. In accordance with their *laissez-faire* convictions, most academic economists were opposed to the tariff program of the Republican Party, although, on the other hand, they strongly supported its deflationary currency policies.

Obviously, much of this glorification of the *status quo* was highly unrealistic, especially in the period following the Civil War, with its widespread materialism and corruption. American academic thinking was dangerously out of touch with actuality. What was needed was a stringent criticism of the traditional dogmas in terms of their concrete meaning and application, in order to bring theory and practice into closer relationship with each other. During the 1880's and 1890's a number of original and creative thinkers began to undertake this task, making these two decades perhaps the most intellectually fruitful period in the whole of American history.

2. THE IMPACT OF DARWINISM

The Theory of Evolution. The initial stimulus for this re-examination of accepted beliefs was provided by the new evolutionary theory put forward by the English scientist Charles Darwin. The publication of Darwin's *The Origin of Species* in 1859 was probably the most significant event in the intellectual development of the Western world since the appearance of Newton's *Principia* nearly two centuries earlier.

Darwin presented a mass of evidence in support of the hypothesis that the different species of animals, including man, had not come into existence through an immediate act of divine creation (as affirmed in the *Book of Genesis*) but were instead the products of a slow process of evolution extending through many millions of years. He also went on to argue that the principal factor in evolution was the struggle for existence and the consequent survival of the fittest. Biological variations were constantly occurring (a fact for which he could offer no explanation), so that offspring were slightly different from their parents. Through competition for food and sex those variations which were conducive to successful survival were perpetuated, while others were eliminated. Implying that man had acquired his intellectual and moral capacities not by direct gift from God but as a result of their survival value in the struggle for existence, such a theory revolutionized traditional views of man's place in the universe.

Like most scientific hypotheses, Darwinism was not solely a product of pure thought; it was also a reflection of the spirit of the age. The nineteenth century believed in progress and could see it manifested in the growth of industry and of liberal institutions. It was easy to assume that progress was a law of life and had been in operation since the beginning of time. Other scientists before Darwin had, in fact, propounded theories of evolution, although they had failed to support them with adequate factual evidence. Darwin's emphasis on the competitive struggle for existence, moreover, was obviously suggested by the economics of *laissez-faire* capitalism. Post-Darwinian biologists, while accepting the evolutionary theory in its broad outlines, have found it necessary to modify it in detail. They have shown that Darwin attached too much importance to competition and not enough to cooperation, and that the appearance of new species is due to an accumulation not of small variations but of abrupt jumps known as "mutations."

The first American edition of *The Origin of Species* appeared in 1860. It took about a quarter of a century for the evolutionary hypothesis to win general acceptance, but its victory was decisive. A majority of America's leading scientists, headed by the Harvard botanist Asa Gray, adopted it almost immediately. Philosophers and theologians were harder to convince, but they were sympathetic to a theory which emphasized progress and gradually found ways of reconciling it with their religious beliefs. In popularizing the theory of evolution and showing that it was not inconsistent with a devout belief in God, a leading part was played by John Fiske, a Harvard-trained scholar who wrote and lectured extensively on historical and philosophical subjects.

It seemed at first that Darwinism would not produce any fundamental change in accepted intellectual attitudes. But as thinkers pondered over its significance, its revolutionary implications gradually became apparent. It had formerly been believed that the human mind was created by God with an innate capacity to apprehend objective truths. According to Darwin, however, man had acquired a mind because of its utility in the struggle for existence. This implied that its function was not to discover the truth but to serve as a guide for successful action, and that its formulations should therefore be judged by their practical consequences. Such a conception led to a pragmatic theory of knowledge, and opened the way to a wholesale criticism of all the beliefs that Americans had accepted as absolute truths. When the evolutionary theory was applied to human history, moreover, it led to the conclusion that society was constantly changing and that principles that had been desirable in one stage of development might be detrimental in another. Values and institutions must therefore be judged not by any immutable standards of truth and justice but in relation to specific social situations. This caused social theorists to adopt a historical and relativistic approach. Thus the general effect of Darwinism was to undermine the political, economic, and ethical dogmatism that was prevalent in the 1860's and 1870's and to cause all general principles to be viewed in dynamic rather than static terms.

Social Darwinism.   The initial application of Darwinism to social theory, while leading to a denial of certain cherished American ideals, had conservative rather than radical implications. Darwin's most enthusiastic English exponent was Herbert Spencer, who published in 1864 the first of a series of volumes presenting what he called his "synthetic philosophy." Using Darwinian principles to interpret human history, Spencer affirmed that evolution was leading inevitably to a society in which men would enjoy "the greatest perfection and the most complete happiness," and that competitive struggle was the means by which this evolution was brought about. State action tending to protect the weak and unfit against the strong and better-adapted was therefore an impediment to progress. Men were not created equal, as eighteenth-century Americans had affirmed; they were created unequal, and any attempt to mitigate their inequality was contrary to the laws of nature. Thus, after Darwin had borrowed the belief in competition from economics and applied it to biology, Spencer used the supposed findings of biology as a confirmation of *laissez-faire* economics.

Spencer's "Social Darwinism" provided the big businessmen of America with exactly the justification they needed, and his writings had an enormous American vogue. Industrialists (especially Andrew Carnegie), lawyers, and economists learned from him to apply phrases like "survival of the fittest" to the formation of trusts and monopolies and to regard the millionaire as the finest flower of evolution. When Spencer visited the United States in 1882, most of the leading figures in national life attended a banquet in his honor in New York, and before his death in 1903 Americans had bought nearly 400,000 copies of his books. His more fervent admirers did not hesitate to call him the greatest thinker not merely of the nineteenth century but of all time.

Sumner.   Spencer's ablest American disciple was William Graham Sumner, Professor of Political and Social Science at Yale from 1872 until his death in 1910. A belligerent, trenchant, and epigrammatic lecturer and writer, Sumner devoted much of his life to defending economic individualism and attacking humanitarian reformers who wished to check the struggle for existence in order to protect the weak. This was the theme of essays bearing such titles as "The Absurd Attempt to Make the World Over." Sumner had nothing but scorn for the ideal of equality, which meant in his opinion the survival of the unfittest, and described democracy as the "pet superstition of the age." On the whole, he must be regarded as a defender of big-business capitalism, although he was a thoroughly independent thinker and aroused violent hostility among many industrialists by denouncing the protective tariff, which he correctly regarded as contrary to genuine individualism. There was a strong element of old-fashioned Puritan morality in Sumner, and his favorite character was the so-called "forgotten man," by which he meant the middle-class citizen who worked hard, saved money, and never asked help from the government.

Sumner's defense of millionaires, whom he apparently regarded as men who got rich by thrift and self-denial, now has only historical interest. Of more enduring importance was the demonstration in his *Folkways* and other sociological writings that all human values and institutions were relative to time and place and had no absolute validity. What was considered good in one society appeared immoral in another. Sumner used this fact to support conservative and pessimistic conclusions, arguing that since human attitudes were determined by the mores and customs of society and were products of evolution, they could not be changed by reforming legislation. It followed from this doctrine (although Sumner himself never fully recognized it) that the institutions of nineteenth-century America were also products of their time and place, and that possibly economic individualism was merely a passing phase in the evolution of Western civilization. From this perspective, Sumner's sociology stimulated much searching criticism of accepted beliefs, of a kind which Sumner himself might have deplored.

Racism.   Somewhat inconsistently, Sumner was a vigorous opponent of another form of Social Darwinism, which glorified conflict between races and nations. The notion that mankind was divided into biologically distinct races, some of which were innately more gifted than others, had been popularized by various European writers, especially by the Frenchman Arthur de Gobineau. The total lack of scientific evidence for such a belief did not prevent it from spreading. The racists quickly adopted Darwinism and began to argue that the superior races ought to preserve their biological purity and should have no humanitarian compunctions about conquering and exploiting their weaker neighbors. Somewhat less irrational, though leading to similar conclusions, was the doctrine that conflict between different national states promoted evolution. Both these manifestations of Social Darwinism were particularly prevalent in Germany.

Racist thinking began to spread in the United States in the 1880's, and took the form of claiming some inherent superiority for so-called Anglo-Saxons, or often for all people of Teutonic stock. Two of its leading popular exponents were John Fiske and the Reverend Josiah Strong, both of whom proclaimed in books and lectures that the Anglo-Saxon race was destined by God and evolution to rule the world. Racism influenced a whole generation of American historians. American institutions of self-government, it was supposed, were due to a special political genius possessed by people of Teutonic descent and could be traced back to Anglo-Saxon England and ultimately to the forests of primeval Germany. This genetic approach to American history was inculcated by Herbert Baxter Adams, who trained numerous historians in his famous seminar at Johns Hopkins. At this period, it is interesting to observe, the Teutonic races in general, and not merely the English, were supposed to be endowed with innate political gifts—a doctrine which underwent drastic revision in the twentieth century when the United States went to war with Germany.

These forms of Social Darwinism had some important practical effects. Providing intellectual justification for the demand for restricting the immigration of ethnic groups from southern and eastern Europe, they helped to bring about the quota policy finally adopted in the 1920's. They also stimulated the movement towards imperialism which manifested itself in the war with Spain and the annexation of the Philippines in 1898. Theodore Roosevelt and other expansionists used Darwinian terminology in urging that the United States become a great world power.

3. NEW WAYS IN SOCIOLOGY AND ECONOMICS

IN SO far as Social Darwinism interpreted human development as the product of natural processes which man could not hope to change or control, it had paralyzing effects. Yet this deduction from the evolutionary theory had little intellectual validity, and was patently due to the desire of men like Spencer and Sumner to rationalize their prejudices against reformers. In the animal world the struggle for existence was primarily a struggle between different species; among animals of the same species cooperation often had more survival value than conflict. Moreover, the whole laissez-faire system was not actually a product of nature (in spite of Adam Smith's belief that it had been devised by God's "invisible hand"); realistically considered, it was a mechanism contrived by human intelligence with the purpose of reconciling individual pursuit of self-interest with the welfare of society. It was becoming increasingly plain that this reconciliation was not being wholly achieved in the America of this period, and that perhaps human intelligence might improve the system. In the 1880's a number of sociologists and economists, reacting against the individualism and the fatalism of Spencer and his disciples, began to emphasize the importance of cooperation and of purposive planning in human development.

Lester Ward. The pioneer spokesman of this new tendency was Lester Ward. Born into a poor family in Illinois, Ward suffered severe hardships during his early life and was largely self-educated, thereby acquiring a certain bias against academic conservatism. A man of prodigious industry and varied learning, he worked for many years as a government official. Late in life he became Professor of Sociology at Brown, where he gave a course entitled "A Survey of All Knowledge." Ward's ideas were first expressed in his *Dynamic Sociology*, published in 1882. Written in a clumsy style and filled with long words, many of which Ward invented, this book was never widely read, but it was of epoch-making importance in American intellectual history.

Ward's basic doctrine was that, instead of submitting to natural forces, man must use his intelligence to plan and direct his future. He made a distinction between "telic" phenomena—those governed by human purpose—and "genetic" phenomena—those resulting from blind natural processes, and insisted that there was "no natural harmony between natural law and human advantage." This led him to argue that in many ways a *laissez-faire* economic system did not promote human progress, but rather the reverse, and to recommend positive social planning by the government. Such an approach pointed the way towards the reforms instituted by the Progressive and New Deal movements.

Ward's ideas were developed by a number of gifted younger sociologists, among whom were Albion Small of Illinois, Charles Horton Cooley of Michigan, and Edward Allsworth Ross of Wisconsin. When the American Sociological Society was founded in 1906, Ward was elected as its first president. Although a few scholars, notably Franklin H. Giddings of Columbia, continued to represent the Sumner tradition, American social thinking during the twentieth century was largely dominated by Ward's faith in purposive planning. Herbert Spencer, no longer regarded as the greatest thinker of all time, was now remembered only as a curious specimen of mid-nineteenth-century prejudice.

The Revolt Against Laissez Faire. In the allied science of economics there were similar trends, although they developed more slowly. The most prominent economists of the 1880's and 1890's—men like Francis Amasa Walker of the Massachusetts Institute of Technology and J. Lawrence Laughlin of Harvard and Chicago—remained generally faithful to the classical approach, but they showed a refreshing receptivity to novel ideas and were willing to recognize that the last word had not been spoken by Adam Smith. Some leading members of the classical school, such as John Bates Clark of Columbia, even argued that effective competition required a considerable measure of government intervention—in the control of monopolies, for example.

Meanwhile, a number of men who had studied at German universities brought back with them the doctrines of the German historical school and advocated a more definite break with the classical tradition. Whereas the classical economists had believed that there were absolute economic laws, valid for all societies, from which practical conclusions might be deduced, the historical approach was relative, inductive, and pragmatic. Different economic principles, it was maintained, were valid in different societies and at different phases of development, and the primary task of the economist was not to formulate general laws but to analyze what actually happened.

These younger men were responsible for the foundation in 1885 of the American Economic Association. In the first draft of their statement of principles they boldly affirmed that the state was "an agency whose positive assistance is one of the indispensable conditions of human progress" and that "the doctrine of laissez-faire is unsafe in politics and unsound in morals." One of the leaders of this group was Richard T. Ely, of Johns Hopkins and Wisconsin, who wished economic processes to be modified by Christian ethics. Another was Simon Nelson Patten, of Pennsylvania, who suggested that the United States was moving from an economy of scarcity to a new economy of abundance in which the original classical principles would no longer apply, and argued that the full potentialities of the new era could be realized only by considerable government planning.

The new historical approach gave a great stimulus to the detailed examination of economic realities, much of which tended to show the vast differences between what actually happened and what, according to classical principles, was supposed to happen. The men pursuing such studies mostly belonged to the Middle West rather than the East, and were markedly influenced by Populism and similar movements. One outstanding example was John Rogers Commons, of Wisconsin, who is remembered chiefly for his studies of the history of American labor. Another was Wesley Clair Mitchell, who was born on an Illinois farm, although he spent most of his adult life teaching at Columbia. Mitchell was a pioneer in the use of statistics, and used them to elucidate that baffling phenomenon, the business cycle, which had hitherto been regarded as a kind of act of God which human beings could not hope to control.

Veblen. The most radical and provocative member of the historical school was Thorstein Veblen. Son of Norwegian immigrants who had settled in Wisconsin, Veblen was unable to obtain a university job until he reached the age of thirty-nine, and throughout his life he remained a lonely and maladjusted individual. He taught at Chicago, Stanford, and Missouri, but his intellectual and personal eccentricities and his inability to abide by the accepted rules of monogamous marriage deprived him of academic recognition. He was, moreover, a poor lecturer; only students sitting in the front row could hear what he said, and few even of them could understand it. But Veblen's isolation was a main source of his intellectual originality. He viewed American society with the detachment of an anthropologist studying a tribe of savages.

Veblen's central idea was his distinction between industry and business. Industry, or the production of wealth, was an expression of the chief constructive force in human affairs: the instinct of workmanship. Business, on the other hand, was a series of devices by which acquisitive and predatory characters took possession of the wealth created by the skill and labor of other people. According to Veblen, the millionaire should not be given credit for the creation of the industrial technology; he was essentially the same type of man as the robber baron who had exploited the industrious peasantry of the Middle Ages or as the barbarian conqueror of still earlier periods. Veblen insisted that many aspects of business were positively detrimental to human progress and would become even more so in the future, and he was inclined to predict that as business became more consolidated, it would culminate in the establishment of some kind of militaristic and imperialistic dictatorship. This might be prevented if groups imbued with the instinct of workmanship, especially the technicians and engineers, took control of the economic system; but Veblen did not regard this as very probable. Much of his writing was devoted to showing how deeply modern society was permeated with pecuniary standards of value.

Veblen's analysis of the role of the businessman in American society was presented in *The Theory of the Leisure Class* (1899) and a number of later books. Written in an involved, mordant, and ironical style, without moral indignation or crusading fervor, Veblen's works had little popular appeal, though some of his phrases, such as "conspicuous consumption," passed into common parlance. But he had a widespread influence among intellectuals during the twentieth century, particularly after the depression of 1929 gave confirmation to his criticism of business practices. This influence was not wholly healthful, since Veblen had little that was positive to offer, but he was undoubtedly one of the most stimulating of American thinkers, and his books were filled with illuminating insights.

Henry George. Meanwhile, outside academic circles, a growing number of radical idealists were beginning to denounce the existing system and propound wholly new schemes of economic organization. Many of them were products of the earlier American tradition of democratic protest, heirs of the Jeffersonian and Jacksonian movements and of the loco-focos and the utopian socialists. Others were influenced by the rev-

olutionary socialism developing in Europe. The milder ones had some pet
plan of monetary reform, while the more extreme were often anarchists,
although of the philosophical rather than the bomb-throwing variety.
Their ideas were often dangerously impractical, but they helped to keep
American society in a healthy state of ferment.

Much the most important of these non-academic economists was
Henry George. Born in Philadelphia, George spent twenty years in San
Francisco, where he worked as a printer and a journalist. Living in a
rapidly growing frontier community, he was impressed by the fact that
landowners were able to make fortunes solely through the rise in real-
estate values, and decided that this was the basic flaw in the economic
system. Why was it, he asked, that as civilization progressed, there
seemed to be an increase in the poverty of the masses as well as in the
wealth of the few? He believed that the explanation was the private
ownership of the land and natural resources by a small group of landlords,
who were able to extract a steadily increasing share of the wealth of the
community in the form of rent without contributing any skill or labor in
return. This unearned increment, instead of going to private individuals, should be appropriated by the government as the "single tax." If
this were done, George believed, then no other government intervention
would be needed; individual enterprise could otherwise be left wholly
free, and the *laissez-faire* system would actually function as equitably as
the classical economists said it did.

George expounded his economic theories in *Progress and Poverty*,
published in 1879. Written with remarkable eloquence and clarity, and
presenting a crushing indictment of the evils of the existing economic
system, the book reached a wide audience both in the United States and
in Great Britain. George spent the rest of his life campaigning for the
single-tax program. His theories were probably over-simple. The monopoly of land undoubtedly led to economic injustice in frontier communities,
but in more advanced industrial societies the monopoly of capital was a
more potent cause of inequality. The single-tax program has never been
put into practice, though it has continued to win adherents down to the
present day. But George had an enormous indirect influence in stimulating
an awareness of economic injustice.

Bellamy.   At the opposite pole from George in his economic philosophy, although very similar in his humanitarian idealism, was Edward
Bellamy. Whereas George (like Thomas Jefferson) believed in a maximum
of individual freedom and regarded government as, at best, a necessary
evil, Bellamy advocated a comprehensive state socialism in which everybody would be drafted into a kind of industrial army. This was to be
achieved through the growth of monopolies, which should finally be taken
over by the state, thereby putting an end to private ownership.

Bellamy's program was in some ways similar to that of Karl Marx,
but he was primarily a product of the American tradition of democratic

and religious utopianism. Descended from an old New England family, he regarded socialism as essentially an application of Christian ethics. After working as a journalist at Springfield, Massachusetts, he achieved instantaneous success with his portrayal of an ideal socialist community, *Looking Backward* (1888). But in spite of its popularity, *Looking Backward* had little practical effect. The so-called "nationalist" movement, organized by Bellamy's disciples to achieve his ideals, proved to be short-lived.

Marxism.   By contrast with the Christian socialism of men like Bellamy, the materialistic and revolutionary doctrines of Karl Marx won few American disciples. These doctrines, which insisted that socialism would be achieved only through class conflict and the violent overthrow of capitalism by the industrial proletariat, had first been stated in *The Communist Manifesto* of 1848 and had subsequently been elaborated in the three volumes of *Das Kapital*, published in 1867 and 1882. Marxism was introduced into America by German immigrants before the Civil War, but it remained largely a foreign-language movement and never struck roots in American labor organizations.

A Socialist Labor Party was founded in 1875 with a Marxist program. After 1890 this was controlled by Daniel De Leon, a native of the West Indies who had taught at Columbia. Highly esteemed in later years by Lenin, De Leon maintained an uncompromisingly revolutionary attitude which doomed the party to futility. In 1898 a group of less fanatical Marxists, who believed that capitalism could be ended by peaceful methods and not by revolutionary violence, revolted against De Leon's leadership and founded what became in 1901 the Socialist Party. This never achieved any lasting popular strength, although its leaders, first Eugene Debs and afterwards Norman Thomas, were widely respected for their integrity and idealism even by people who wholly disagreed with their objectives.

4. NEW WAYS IN PHILOSOPHY

Idealism and Materialism.   The intellectual awakening of the 1880's and 1890's was even more strikingly manifested in philosophy. This period saw the emancipation of American academic philosophy from theology and its development into an independent discipline capable of giving its own answers to the mysteries of human existence. As in economics, the initial stimulus towards new ways of thinking came from Germany. Most of the young men who set out to create schools of philosophy in America had studied at German universities and were disciples of Hegel and other German idealists, although they showed a more critical spirit than the nationalistic political theorists of the previous generation who had used German thought chiefly as a justification of conservatism.

The earliest centers of original philosophic thought in the United States were outside the universities. Particularly influential was the

Philosophical Society of St. Louis, which published a *Journal of Specula-tive Philosophy* from 1867 to 1893. Its leading spirit was W. T. Harris, Commissioner of Schools first for St. Louis and afterwards in the Federal government. An offshoot of this society was the Fellowship of the New Life, founded in 1884 by Thomas Davidson, who had been a disciple of Harris. Between 1890 and 1900 Davidson conducted a Summer School for the Cultural Sciences in the Adirondacks, which provided a meeting-place for all Americans seriously interested in the advancement of phi-losophy. Other notable institutions were the Concord Summer School of Philosophy and Literature (1879–88) and the Society for Ethical Culture, founded in 1876 by Felix Adler.

By the 1880's a number of young men in academic life were repu-diating the dreary commonplaces of the common-sense school and giving courses based on German metaphysics. Although the movement was strongest in the New England colleges, where it was represented by men like Josiah Royce at Harvard and C. E. Garman at Amherst, it was not restricted to any one part of the country. Such universities as Columbia, Cornell, Johns Hopkins, Princeton, and California shared in this philo-sophical awakening, and particularly interesting work was done by George Sylvester Morris and Alfred H. Lloyd at Michigan. These men took from the German idealists their belief in the priority of mind over matter and in the fundamental unity of the universe, but modified them in order to justify an American individualism.

Probably the greatest of the American idealists was the California-born Josiah Royce, professor at Harvard and author of *The World and the Individual* (1901–02). Royce taught (like the Germans) that individ-uals were parts of a single absolute mind, but went on to declare (as an American) that each separate individual was a necessary part of this whole and made his own unique and indispensable contribution to it. Thus, while affirming that man finds the meaning of his existence in loyalty to the whole, Royce also asserted the need for individual choice and in-itiative.

One isolated thinker insisted that nothing good could come out of Germany, and turned instead for inspiration to the Mediterranean coun-tries. This was George Santayana, who had been born in Spain but grew up in Boston, and spent the first twenty years of his adult life teaching at Harvard. In his philosophical writings, especially in the five volumes of *The Life of Reason* (1905–06), he espoused a thoroughgoing materi-alism, although this was combined with a sympathetic interest in all the poetic mythologies (as he regarded them) with which man has sought to give meaning to his existence, especially that of the Catholic Church. With his pagan, aristocratic, and disillusioned view of life, Santayana never felt at home in the United States, and in 1912 he resigned from Harvard and settled permanently in Europe, dying in Italy in 1952. But his aesthetic sensitivity, broad culture, and mastery of English prose gave him, in spite of his detachment, a lasting influence among American intellectuals.

Pragmatism.   Meanwhile, a more important and more distinctively American school of philosophy, equally opposed both to Royce's idealism and to Santayana's materialism, was being developed under the name of pragmatism. This was primarily a deduction from the Darwinian theory, while its more remote philosophical pedigree was English rather than German. It displayed the distrust of abstract theory and the feeling that reality cannot be organized into any neat intellectual patterns which have been major characteristics of the English philosophical tradition ever since the Middle Ages. Even more obviously, it reflected the individualism and the practical temper of America.

Unlike most earlier philosophies, pragmatism did not set forth any body of doctrines about God and the universe. Primarily, it was an attitude towards the mind and its processes. The pragmatists declared that thinking, instead of being an end in itself, always served some purpose, and was valid in so far as it enabled this purpose to be realized. The human mind was, in fact, not formed to apprehend ideas that were absolutely and objectively true. An idea was essentially a plan of action, and should therefore be regarded as true to the extent that its practical consequences were desirable.

Pragmatism originated in the discussions of a Metaphysical Club which used to meet in Cambridge during the 1870's. The two men who seem to have contributed most to these discussions were Chauncy Wright and Charles Sanders Peirce, both of whom were primarily interested in mathematics and logic. In 1878 Peirce published a paper entitled "How to Make Our Ideas Clear," which was the first public statement of the pragmatist interpretation of the mind. Peirce was a markedly original and productive philosopher, but most of his other writings were too abstruse for general consumption. Apart from his contribution to the growth of pragmatism, he had little influence during his lifetime, and even today much of his work has not been adequately appreciated and digested.

William James.   The man who did most both to develop and to popularize the pragmatist approach was William James, who was certainly the most lovable, and possibly the greatest, of all American thinkers. James was the son of a well-to-do New Yorker, Henry James, Senior, who devoted his life mainly to expounding certain eccentric religious views which nobody could ever quite understand, but who was also a refreshingly pungent and perceptive critic of contemporary tendencies. The James family grew up in a highly charged intellectual atmosphere, and another of its members, Henry James, Junior, afterwards made contributions to literature as outstanding as those of William to philosophy.

As a young man William James suffered from neurotic fears so acute as to be virtually paralyzing. But he learned finally that he could master them by an effort of the will, and this gave him faith in the freedom and creative powers of the human personality. Throughout his mature life he was conspicuously warmhearted, self-assured, and emotionally healthy. After a scientific training he settled down to teach psychology and philosophy at Harvard. His *Principles of Psychology* (1890) was the first important American contribution to the scientific study of the mind. This was followed by a series of other books dealing with most of the major problems of philosophy. A thorough democrat in his thinking as well as in his personal life, singularly free from any form of dogmatism or pretentiousness, and hospitable to any idea which sounded interesting, James avoided technical jargon and expressed himself in language which the layman could understand.

In both his psychological and his philosophical writings James argued that thinking was subordinate to action and that the meaning and validity of any idea should be judged by its practical applications. Some of James's deductions from this pragmatist view of the mind laid him open to valid criticism. He was at times inclined to suggest that if somebody felt happier or behaved better as a result of believing some idea, that idea should be regarded as true—a deduction which seemed to leave the door open for almost any kind of irrationalism. Moreover, his emphasis on action seemed to leave little room for aesthetic contemplation and other purely mental activities. (Incidentally, pragmatists have always had trouble in explaining why anybody should study history, since ideas about the past do not have any obvious practical application.)

Probably James's most lasting influence on modern thought will come not from his pragmatism but from his general view of the universe. His dominating characteristics were his sense of the uniqueness of every person and every event, and his distrust of all general laws and abstractions, especially those tending to deny man's capacity for free action. He was equally opposed to the disciples of Herbert Spencer, who declared that man should not interfere with natural processes, and to the Hegelians with their conception of the universe as a single organic whole. The future, he insisted, was always uncertain, and the decisions made by human beings would actually influence the course of events. This was an open universe in which anything could happen. James believed in God, but suggested that God was not omnipotent; whether good or evil would finally triumph depended on human choice and intelligence. Such a view of life, with its exhilarating appeal to human beings to repudiate fatalism and accept responsibility for their own destiny, was startlingly different from almost all the philosophies and religions of the past. In its individualism, its spirit of adventurousness, and its acceptance of insecurity, it seemed characteristic of the best aspects of the American spirit.

James made another significant contribution to new ways of thinking by expounding a "radical empiricism" which attempted to break down the distinction between mind and matter that had preoccupied philosophers ever since Descartes. Both mind and matter, he suggested, consisted essentially of streams of events. This notion has had a considerable impact on twentieth-century philosophy, and (by suggesting that mind should be regarded as a "stream of consciousness") has also influenced modern literature.

Dewey.   James's leading disciple was John Dewey, who preferred to call himself an instrumentalist rather than a pragmatist. Born in Vermont in 1859 and teaching successively at Michigan, Chicago, and Columbia, Dewey remained an active force in American thought down to his death in 1952, and made important contributions over a very wide range of subjects. Originally a student of German idealism, from which he derived a sense of the inter-connectedness of everything, he became converted to James's view of the mind during the 1890's. Unfortunately, he was totally lacking in James's ability to write clearly and vividly; but he expounded his theories more carefully and systematically, without the looseness of phrasing that made James open to attack.

Dewey regarded pragmatism-instrumentalism as, above all, a democratic philosophy. Earlier views of the mind, he insisted, reflected the viewpoint of privileged aristocratic or priestly classes who could devote themselves to pure contemplation while supported by the labor of slaves or servants. But in modern America philosophy should be removed from its ivory tower and transformed into a tool for increasing man's mastery of nature and building a better society. In addition to affirming, with James, that ideas must lead to action, Dewey went on to argue that it was only through action that men could acquire valid ideas. One understood things not by contemplating them but by manipulating them, working upon them, and changing them. This "instrumentalist" philosophy was set forth in two general works, *Experience and Nature* (1925) and *The Quest for Certainty* (1929), and in a long series of other books dealing with epistemology, logic, ethics, aesthetics, and social and educational problems.

Results of Pragmatism.   Critics of the new philosophy complained that its view of the mind was so narrow that it seemed to leave no room for mental occupations (such as artistic enjoyment and the study of history) not leading directly to action. They disliked its tendency to brush aside as meaningless most of the metaphysical problems which had occupied the great thinkers of earlier periods. Above all, they declared that it was unable to present a satisfactory theory of values. What should ultimately be regarded as good, and why? James's answer to this question was that we knew by intuition that certain things were good, and that nothing more could be said about the matter. Dewey, on the other hand, argued that men discovered what was good by experience and that general rules of morality were never wholly valid. Such an approach to the problem was a stimulating appeal to avoid dogmatism, but enemies of pragmatism declared that it left the basic questions unanswered, and that the new philosophy offered men only an intellectual method, not a faith to live by.

Yet, in spite of its limitations, pragmatism-instrumentalism had, on the whole, a healthful influence on American development in the early twentieth century. By insisting that all ideas should be judged by consequences, it stimulated a general criticism of traditional beliefs that had ceased to be meaningful and led to much bold experimentation in all areas of political and personal life. Its impact was particularly direct and important in education and in law.

Dewey was an active exponent of new methods of teaching and had a very wide influence on schools of education throughout the country. He insisted that the school must be more directly connected with the community to which it belonged; and in accordance with his theory that valid ideas could be acquired only through action, he urged the abandonment of memorizing by rote and the substitution, wherever possible, of "learning by doing"—a phrase which became the slogan of the progressive educator. The new methods were enthusiastically adopted by many private schools, and began more slowly to affect the public schools, where they led to prolonged and often bitter controversy.

In law, pragmatism-instrumentalism led to a recognition that judges were not actually engaged in simply applying general principles to specific cases in accordance with the rules of logic. As William James's friend Justice Oliver Wendell Holmes declared in his *Common Law* (1881): "The life of the law . . . has not been logic; it has been experience. . . . The felt necessities of the time, the prevalent moral and political theories, intuitions of public policy, avowed or unconscious, even the prejudices which judges share with their fellow men, have had a good deal more to do than the syllogism in determining the rules by which men should be governed." The new school of legal theorists, represented by men like Roscoe Pound of Harvard and Justices Brandeis and Cardozo, argued that justice was more likely to be done if this were frankly recognized, and went on to insist that the meaning of any general legal principle must always be judged by its practical effects. Judges could not effectively maintain the freedoms guaranteed by the Constitution unless they took account of what they meant in concrete economic and social terms.

5. NEW WAYS IN HISTORY

LIKE the economists and the philosophers, American historians of the late nineteenth and the early twentieth century were strongly influenced by their German counterparts, though with less invigorating results. The most obvious effect was an emphasis on the minutiae of exact scholarship, which proved difficult to reconcile with imaginative scope and vividness of presentation. Dissolving its traditional partnership with literature, history set out to become a science. The new methods of historical research led to a flood of studies on different aspects of the past, which added immeasurably to available knowledge. But most historical scholars now wrote for each other rather than for the general public, thereby leaving a gap inadequately filled by journalistic popularizers.

The historian could certainly learn from the scientist to present only ascertainable and verifiable facts. But could he then go on to formulate any general laws and methods of interpretation comparable to those of the natural sciences? The obstacles to such an endeavor were probably insuperable. Yet some of the attempts to find valid generalizations were stimulating and widely influential, though highly debatable.

Social History. Under the influence of the evolutionary concept, historians widened their scope and began to study the development of society as a whole, not merely of its government. American historiography had originally been theological (with the writers of early New England) and political; it now became social, economic, and cultural. The pioneer figure in this trend was John Bach McMaster, of the University of Pennsylvania, who published his *History of the People of the United States, from the Revolution to the Civil War* in a series of volumes between 1883 and 1913. McMaster's work was chiefly an immense compilation of facts, with little organization; but he was the first writer to deal comprehensively with the evolution of American society, and a large number of more recent historians followed in his footsteps. A younger, and perhaps more important, spokesman of the "new history" was James Harvey Robinson, who taught European history at Columbia. In addition to emphasizing cultural history, Robinson was also significant in insisting that the main reason for studying the past was to illuminate the present—an attitude which showed the influence of pragmatism.

New Theories of Causation. Meanwhile, more analytical thinkers were searching for valid theories of historical causation. Earlier historians, such as Bancroft, had seen American society as the product of divine guidance and human idealism. They had been succeeded by the racists, who traced American institutions back to the forests of primeval Germany. The next group looked for more tangible and materialistic explanations and began to study environmental and economic factors. In 1893 Frederick Jackson Turner of the University of Wisconsin presented his frontier thesis, declaring that American democracy was the product not of the forests of Germany but of those of the Middle West. Influenced, like the Midwestern economists, by the Populists, Turner was reacting against the attitudes of the Atlantic seaboard, and there was an element of defiant exaggeration in his insistence that the frontier experience explained American development. But he was a man of genius, and although he wrote relatively little, nobody has had a wider influence on American historiography.

The chief rival of Turner environmentalism was the more strictly economic interpretation, which explained evolution in terms of the interests and conflicts of groups and sections. Its most prominent representative was Charles A. Beard, whose *Economic Interpretation of the Constitution* appeared in 1913. Arguing that the constitution-makers were motivated more by concrete interests than by abstract ideals of justice, Beard's work seemed to all conservatives to be shockingly sacrilegious, while radicals hailed it with delight. Yet Beard by no means intended to attack the Constitution. Believing that any wise statesmanship must be solidly grounded on economic forces, he argued that the Constitution was successful precisely because of the realism of its founders.

Henry Adams.   While men like Turner and Beard were thinking in biological terms, a more boldly speculative thinker attempted to apply to history the concepts of physics. This was Henry Adams, grandson of President John Quincy and great-grandson of President John. As a young man Adams taught at Harvard, where he established German methods of research, and wrote the *History of the United States During the Administrations of Jefferson and Madison*, which combined literary charm with solid scholarship. In middle age he settled in Washington, with intervals of travel, and devoted himself to meditation on more fundamental problems. The results were recorded in *Mont St. Michel and Chartres*, an evocation of the civilization of thirteenth-century Europe, and in his *Education*, which described his own life in nineteenth-century America.

Brooding over the second law of thermodynamics, according to which all the energy in the universe was being dissipated, Adams saw Western history as a process not of evolution towards an ideal society but of decline and eventual dissolution. The change from the unity of the Middle Ages to the multiplicity of modern times was a movement not upwards but downwards. Adams's pessimism was probably due, in part, to personal factors; he was embittered because the values represented by the Adams family had little place in America after the Civil War. His use of physics to interpret history was quite unscientific. But he was an acute and sensitive observer, and much that happened after 1914 made him seem prophetic. His rationalizations might be unsound, but his feeling that Western civilization was rapidly moving not towards utopia but towards catastrophe appeared to have an uncanny and disturbing accuracy.

XXIV

Realism in the Arts

1. LITERATURE AFTER THE CIVIL WAR

2. TWO MASTERS

3. THE MOVEMENT TOWARDS REALISM

4. PAINTING, ARCHITECTURE, AND MUSIC

THE PROCESS of decline and renewal that characterized intellectual development after the Civil War can be traced also in literature and the arts. The transformation of American life was so cataclysmic that writers and artists could not immediately assimilate it. Throughout the 1860's and 1870's there were no creative individuals who were capable of providing vital leadership, and very little work of lasting importance. The last two decades of the century, on the other hand, were a period of important new beginnings, which have had a profound influence on American cultural life during the twentieth century.

1. LITERATURE AFTER THE CIVIL WAR

The Genteel Tradition. The reaction of many writers to the post-war scene was to turn their backs to it. Regarding American society as hopelessly vulgar and materialistic, they tried to escape into an ideal world of romantic imagery. The tendency to divorce art from daily life

---

SELECTED BIBLIOGRAPHY: The history of literature can be followed in R. E. Spiller and others (eds.), *Literary History of the United States*, Vol. 2 (1948); of art and architecture, in O. W. Larkin, *Art and Life in America* (1949); of music, in J. T. Howard, *Our American Music* (revised edition, 1946). V. L. Parrington, *Main Currents in American Thought*, Vol. 3 (1929), deals with the earlier of the post–Civil-War writers, while Oscar Cargill, *Intellectual America* (1941), is a stimulating and provocative discussion of literary trends after 1880. Lewis Mumford, *The Brown Decades* (1931), is a suggestive analysis of American culture in general in the later nineteenth century. The appropriate volumes in Van Wyck Brooks's series are *New England: Indian Summer* (1940) and *The Confident Years, 1885–1915* (1952).

had already been manifest in the more conservative of the New England writers, such as Longfellow and Lowell. Their disciples of the 1860's and 1870's—men like Bayard Taylor, Thomas Bailey Aldrich, Richard Henry Stoddard, Edmund Clarence Stedman, and George Henry Boker—cultivated an even more effete picturesqueness. They failed to realize that great writing, including that of the Romantics, had always been a transmutation of elements derived from experience, even when it dealt with exotic subjects, and never merely an escape.

Yet for a long time men of this kind were regarded as important figures. They dictated editorial and critical standards and were accepted as leading spokesmen of American culture. Since they were horrified by any form of realism, whether about social forces or about sex, and since they were inclined to regard the literature of the United States as an inferior offshoot of that of England, they used their influence mainly to combat the growth of more vital forms of literary expression. Today they are usually dismissed as exponents of a "Genteel Tradition."

Regionalism.   Some other writers, who were equally unable to deal with the central trends of American development, adopted a better solution. They found their subject-matter in the attitudes and customs characteristic of some special region of the country. They were often too strongly inclined to emphasize quaint local color; but though their work in most instances was of minor importance, much of it was genuine. Many of the more interesting later nineteenth-century writers can be roughly classified as regionalists.

The only poet of the first rank who partially bridged the gap between Whitman and the twentieth century was a product of a New England small town where the continuity of the Puritan heritage was still unbroken. This was Emily Dickinson, who spent her life in seclusion in Amherst, Massachusetts, and remained almost unknown until long after her death in 1886. She achieved greatness by distilling into lyric poetry certain aspects of Calvinist tradition—not its gloomy belief in sin and hell-fire but its familiarity with God and eternity and its sense of material things as symbols of divine realities. Her special characteristic was her humorous awareness of the incongruities between matter and spirit. This was expressed in verses that were halting and fragmentary but filled with vivid phrases and sharply etched descriptions. Rural New England also produced some of the finest writers of regional fiction, especially Sarah Orne Jewett, author of the classic *Country of the Pointed Firs* (1896) and Mary E. Wilkins Freeman.

The only other good poet of the later nineteenth century was a Southern regionalist, Sidney Lanier. Lanier fought in the Civil War, supported himself afterwards by playing the flute, wrote critical speculations about the relation between poetry and music, and died in 1881 at the age of thirty-nine. Much of his work was concerned with the conflict between the old Southern code of chivalry and the new commercialism. But his best poetry was inspired by the landscapes of his native Georgia.

The South also produced a whole school of novelists, who more than compensated for the dominance of the North in history and political theory. By the end of the century, in fact, the American reading public were acquiring their notions of slavery and the Civil War mainly from Southern writers, and the legend of the gracious and beneficent plantation life of the Old South had become firmly implanted in the national consciousness. The writers who probably did most to win the war of books for the Confederacy were Thomas Nelson Page and Mary Johnston. The glamour of Southern chivalry also pervaded James Lane Allen's novels of early Kentucky. Some other Southern writers were less sentimental. Joel Chandler Harris's stories of Uncle Remus gave a more lifelike portrayal of the plantation Negro. George Washington Cable wrote some excellent novels about New Orleans, and "Charles Edward Craddock" (the pen-name of Mary Noailles Murfree) discovered the literary potentialities of the mountain folk of eastern Tennessee.

Elsewhere in the United States regional traditions were not yet sufficiently developed for effective literary treatment. There were a few books describing life in Midwestern small towns, but they were written in a tone of bitterness rather than of affection. Notable examples were Edward Eggleston's *Hoosier Schoolmaster* (1871), E. W. Howe's *Story of a Country Town* (1883), and Joseph Kirkland's *Zury* (1887). But the most widely read Midwestern writing was the sentimental verse of James Whitcomb Riley of Indiana.

Other writers, notably Bret Harte, achieved popularity with romanticized descriptions of the lawless life of the mining camps of the Far West. *The Luck of Roaring Camp* (1868) and other California stories made Harte for a few years one of the best-known writers in the United States.

Popular Humor. Probably more significant in the long-range development of American literature was the tradition of journalistic humor. This had originated before the Civil War in several different places, especially in rural New England and on the Southern frontier. The humorous writer or lecturer assumed the role of a simple-minded Yankee or frontiersman, made shrewd comments on national affairs in the style of a "crackerbox philosopher," and sometimes told tall tales.

In the Jacksonian period the genre had been represented by Seba Smith of Maine, author of the *Jack Downing Papers*, and by David Crockett of Tennessee. During and after the Civil War the tradition was maintained by the men who assumed the pseudonyms of Artemus Ward, Petroleum Vesuvius Nasby, and Josh Billings. Reducing apparently complicated questions to common-sense terms and ridiculing sham and pretension, humor of this kind was a true expression of American democracy, while its vivid and colloquial style did much to invigorate the

American language. The tradition was continued into the twentieth
century by Finley Peter Dunne (whose mouthpiece was the Irish saloon-
keeper Mr. Dooley rather than the countryman of earlier generations),
and was represented after World War I by the Oklahoma cowboy Will
Rogers.

2. TWO MASTERS

THE LATER American literature displayed two opposite tendencies. Some
writers plunged into American life, especially that of the new industrial
cities, and set out to record what they experienced with few moral or
aesthetic inhibitions. Others turned back to the European cultural tradition in the hope of finding values and standards applicable to the present
as well as to the past. This dichotomy between the lowbrow and the high-
brow, the "redskin" and the "paleface," is conveniently typified in the
two major writers who were beginning to do their best work in the 1880's:
Mark Twain and Henry James. While Twain knew and enjoyed the
American life of his time on almost every level, James valued experience
only in so far as he could distill moral and aesthetic meanings from it.
And while Twain laughed at the cultural pretensions of European society
and saw it mainly as a horrifying example of feudal oppression, James
was fascinated by the way of life of the European upper class.

Mark Twain.   Samuel Langhorne Clemens, universally known by
the *nom de plume* Mark Twain, grew up in the slave state of Missouri,
spent a few years as a steamboat pilot on the Mississippi, served very
briefly in a Confederate militia regiment at the beginning of the Civil
War, and then went out to the mining camps of Nevada. Here he achieved
fame as a humorous writer and lecturer. His later life was spent in the
East (he settled at Hartford, Connecticut, in 1871), where he was friendly
with leading businessmen and tried occasionally to make a fortune himself. Thus the Old South, the miners' frontier, and the industrial East all
contributed to his development; but primarily he was a product of the
agrarian democracy of the Mississippi Valley. Always on the side of the
underdog, he had a deeply ingrained faith in the equality of man and a
hatred of all injustice and oppression. He began his literary career as a
disciple of Artemus Ward and other popular humorists. Seeing life from
the viewpoint of an untutored but perceptive frontier American, he developed into a satirist of human wickedness and folly in all their manifestations. Writing for a popular audience, he evolved a prose style that was
always simple and smooth-flowing, filled with concrete imagery, and close
to the spoken language. He was more successful than any previous American writer in breaking away from the English literary tradition and
modeling his style on American speech. This made him a most stimulating
influence on the novelists of the twentieth century.

Mark Twain's writings fell into a number of different categories. He wrote travel books (*Innocents Abroad*), reminiscences (*Life on the Mississippi, Roughing It*), stories about boys (*Tom Sawyer*), stories dealing with corruption in contemporary America (*The Gilded Age*), and stories about feudal Europe (*The Connecticut Yankee*). But his masterpiece was undoubtedly *Huckleberry Finn* (1885). In this epic story of the Mississippi, with its rich variety of comic and tragic episodes, he not only gave an unforgettable portrayal of life along the river but also presented a sardonic commentary on human society in general. As everybody knows, the book was written from the viewpoint of a small boy who did not want to be "civilized" and ran away from home in the company of a fugitive slave. Those two outcasts had truer insights and a finer sense of values than any of the white adults they encountered. Civilization, as Mark Twain saw it, meant corruption, and the more elaborate it became, the further it departed from the instinctive goodness of the natural human being.

Like many humorists, in fact, Mark Twain was profoundly pessimistic; and his gloom increased as he grew older. In later years his bitterness exploded in rather naïve philosophical writings attacking religious optimism. He could see little good in organized society or in most grown-up men and women (himself included); and people being what they were, not much could be done to improve things. While his despair was no doubt largely temperamental, some critics have attributed it to the repressive influences of puritanical respectability, while others have seen it as a response to the transformation of American life. Mark Twain was a child of the frontier, and his values were Jeffersonian. These values had disturbingly little relevance to the complex business society of the new America.

Henry James. While Mark Twain judged American society by the standards of the frontier, Henry James contrasted it with that of Europe. Throughout his fifty-year literary career he explored a great number of variations on this international theme; but his basic conceptions remained the same. The American was usually naïve and even crude, but fundamentally good; the European was more cultured and sophisticated but fundamentally corrupt. The American could be culturally enriched through contact with European society but was also in danger of being ruined by it. Thus, in spite of James's long residence in Europe and passionate devotion to its cultural values, he remained essentially American. Only a very superficial reader of his novels could suppose that he regarded upper-class European society as morally admirable. Most of the aristocratic characters in his novels were interested chiefly in getting money by marrying rich girls from America.

James's literary career fell into three distinct phases. From his first appearance in print in 1865 down to 1882 he lived on both sides of the Atlantic and dealt with American subjects as well as with his international theme. The books of this period were simple and straightforward and can be enjoyed by readers who find his later style too ponderous. *Daisy Miller, The Portrait of a Lady*, and others describe Americans in Europe. *The Europeans* is a gay and amusing account of sophisticated continentals in New England, while *The Bostonians* is a decidedly hostile analysis of New England reformers. After 1882 James settled permanently in England, and for the next fifteen years wrote mainly about English upper-class society. This was a period of experimentation, during which he was developing a more sensitive and complex mode of expression but had difficulty in finding appropriate subjects. To unsympathetic readers he seemed to be saying more and more about less and less. Finally, after 1897, he returned to the international theme and produced the three great novels of his maturity: *The Ambassadors, The Wings of the Dove,* and *The Golden Bowl.* Describing the impact of Europe upon American visitors in search of culture, and written in an elaborate metaphorical style, these are regarded by true Jamesians as his three greatest master-pieces.

Giving his whole life to art in a spirit of religious devotion, James was one of the few American novelists who continued to develop over a long period of years. Most other American writers have had relatively short periods of high productivity, after which their work has deteriorated or become repetitive. Some critics, however, have complained that James wasted his genius on subjects that were intrinsically trivial. Why did he turn away from American life and spend his time analyzing the emotions of a few leisure-class cosmopolitans? But it should be recognized that a writer's importance depends not upon his subject-matter but upon what he gets out of it. What James extracted from his studies of wealthy Americans in Europe was by no means trivial. By studying the impact of Europe upon the American visitor he illuminated the whole national tradition. The main motivating force behind all his writing, moreover, was his sense of the profound importance of personal relationships. Most of his major novels dealt with a process of moral growth by which the central character achieved a deeper understanding of the nature of good and evil and learned to act with insight, sympathy, and wisdom. His later books were by no means easy. But those who read them with close attention regard him as one of the greatest writers and most civilized intelligences of modern times.

3. THE MOVEMENT TOWARDS REALISM

William Dean Howells.   Later novelists learned from Twain how to write in the American vernacular, while James taught them the importance of form and sharpened their perceptions. But in their choice of subject-matter they were more deeply influenced by a third writer who was a friend and admirer of both: William Dean Howells. After growing up in a small town in Ohio, Howells settled after the Civil War in Boston, where he was accepted as the heir of the great New Englanders of the previous generation. In 1889 he moved to New York, a change of residence which indicated that this was now replacing Boston as the country's intellectual capital. As editor of leading magazines and adviser of virtually every significant contemporary writer, Howells had a leading position in American literature for nearly half a century. Since he was quick to recognize talent, and was a man of wide sympathies and firm integrity, he made excellent use of his influence.

As a novelist Howells initiated the movement towards realism. Leading European writers, who were wrestling with much the same social problems as the Americans, were declaring that the novelist ought to deal with the typical experiences of ordinary people. Their point of view reflected the growth both of democracy and of science. The novelist, they argued, should write about the masses instead of the aristocracy, and should study society in the same spirit in which the scientist analyzed nature. The more extreme European realists, Emile Zola being the outstanding example, saw the individual as the puppet of social and biological forces and interpreted life in generally pessimistic terms—an approach which was often called naturalism. Howells set out to deal realistically with American society, but did not adopt the fatalism and pessimism of the Europeans. American novelists, he said, should "concern themselves with the more smiling aspects of life, which are the more American."

In a long series of novels, perhaps the best-known being *The Rise of Silas Lapham* (1885), Howells described middle-class Americans confronted by typical dilemmas. Well written and showing considerable psychological insight, his books had every quality except high creative power. If today they seem somewhat pallid, this is largely because of Howells's extreme prudishness about sexual emotions. His plots too often depended on moral scruples which seem merely foolish to most modern readers. But Howells was much less squeamish about economic questions. In later life, in fact, he became a bold defender of economic radicalism and added two books to the rapidly growing number of socialist utopias.

Naturalist Tendencies. A much sharper break with tradition was made by some of the more gifted writers of the next generation. Uninfluenced by any system of thought earlier than Darwinism, they seemed to regard the religious and moral beliefs of earlier generations as no longer worthy of credence or even of respect. Their view of the world was extremely gloomy, since they saw it as a chaos of biological drives without spiritual purpose or direction; but they were fascinated by its color and drama. And since they looked at the new industrial society with fresh eyes, they gave American literature a new vitality and new perceptions.

Hamlin Garland broke fresh ground with *Main-Travelled Roads* (1891) and other early books dealing with the hardships of pioneering in the Middle Border. He was the first American writer to repudiate sentimental idealizations of farm life in the manner of James Whitcomb

Riley. But after 1900 he turned to the writing of popular adventure stories. More important pioneers in literary radicalism were three men born in 1870 and 1871: Stephen Crane, Frank Norris, and Theodore Dreiser.

Crane, the son of a Methodist minister in New Jersey, had a crowded and adventurous life and died at the age of twenty-nine. He was an un-taught genius, whose writings were filled with startling imagery and flashes of profound psychological insight, and who specialized in studies of individuals at moments of crisis. In his best-known work, *The Red Badge of Courage* (1895), he stripped the glamour from war and described the ordinary soldier going into combat for the first time.

The other two members of this group can clearly be classified as naturalists. Norris, a Californian who died at thirty-two, was the first major novelist to grapple with the central socio-economic forces of the new America. He planned a trilogy dealing on a broad canvas with the growing and marketing of wheat, although only two volumes, *The Octopus* (1901) and *The Pit* (1903), were completed. Dreiser, the son of immigrant German parents who had settled in Indiana, probably had fewer natural gifts than Crane or Norris, but he lived to become a leading figure in the literature of the twentieth century. His first book, *Sister Carrie* (1900), was the story of a woman for whom immorality led not to punishment but to emotional fulfillment and worldly success. This violation of con-ventional beliefs was so shocking that the book was withdrawn from circulation, and Dreiser published nothing else until 1911.

The 1890's saw new beginnings also in poetry. William Vaughn Moody wrote poetic dramas filled with a new kind of psychological ex-ploration, but died before his work had come to full fruition. The most important of the new poets was Edwin Arlington Robinson, a native of Maine, who published his first volume in 1897. A lonely and melancholy man, but with enough strength of character to devote himself wholly to poetry in spite of every discouragement, Robinson was an idealist who could find no sanction for his ideals either in the society around him or in the universe as science had revealed it. He wrote lyrics, character studies, and long narrative poems in a style stripped of the romantic ornament fashionable in the nineteenth century. In spite of the admiration of Theodore Roosevelt, who gave him a post in the New York Custom House with instructions to draw a salary and do no work, he had to wait twenty years for recognition, but won acceptance after World War I as one of the greatest American poets.

Novelists of the Early 1900's.   During the first dozen years of the twentieth century these new trends were not carried much further, prob-ably because most intellectuals became preoccupied with the progressive movement and the struggle for reform. Writers like David Graham Phillips and Upton Sinclair dealt with social and economic problems on a relatively superficial level, and were joined by Winston Churchill, who had already won a wide reputation as an author of historical romances. The most widely known novelist of the time was Jack London. Illegitimate son of an astrologer and a spiritualist, London grew up in San Francisco, had a stormy and adventurous life, succumbed to alcoholism, and probably committed suicide. He called himself a revolutionary socialist, but was also influenced by Nietzschean doctrines of master races and supermen. London was significant as a representative of the new trends in American life, and some of his books, like *White Fang* (1906) and *The Call of the Wild* (1903), were exciting stories; but he was too undisciplined to achieve real importance. A writer whose books may last longer was Booth Tarkington of Indiana. Since he was a conservative who generally accepted the standards of the middle-class businessman, critics have not been kind to him; but he was a very skillful craftsman.

The two best novelists whose work belonged mainly to the early twentieth century were both women whose subject-matter was regional rather than national: Edith Wharton and Ellen Glasgow. Mrs. Wharton analyzed the ethical and social standards of old New York families with aristocratic pretensions. In her old age she descended to potboiling, but some of her earlier novels, such as *The House of Mirth* (1905), are classics, somewhat in the manner of Henry James. Ellen Glasgow was also a novelist of manners, who wrote about the old families of Richmond, Virginia. Brought up in a society that sentimentalized the past and deplored the present, she decided that what the South needed was "blood and irony." She supplied the irony in novels that mocked the unreality of Southern ideals of chivalry and gentility. Social comedy of high rank, Miss Glasgow's work was a most effective answer to Thomas Nelson Page and the rest of the school of Confederate writers, and prepared the way for the Southern Renaissance of the 1920's and 1930's.

Another literary trend can be roughly classified as the cult of Bohemia. While most American writers have had a strong social consciousness and liberal sympathies, a few of them, beginning with Edgar Allan Poe, have insisted that art was an end in itself and that the artist had no obligations to society. They have generally condemned American society as Philistine and puritanical and declared that the artist could feel at home only in a place (like Paris) where life was less inhibited. A number of writers of the early twentieth century were primarily Bohemians, Edgar Saltus being perhaps the best example; and those of them who had private incomes mostly sought refuge in Europe. Their work was too thin to have much value, but they were historically important in contributing to the assault on Puritan mores and in introducing a knowledge of new European writers. The critic James Gibbons Huneker, for example, in spite of his superficiality, did much to popularize Nietzsche, Shaw, and other recent or contemporary iconoclasts. Among the expatriates was one, Gertrude Stein, who had a formidable personal influence on the younger writers of the 1920's and 1930's. Most of Miss Stein's own writings consisted of word patterns with little, if any, meaning; but she wrote one book, *Three Lives* (1906), dealing with simple people in deceptively simple language, which had important effects on such later novelists as Sherwood Anderson and Ernest Hemingway.

Many of the writers mentioned in this section received more recognition from later generations than from their contemporaries. Down to World War I critical standards were still dominated by the Genteel Tradition. Professors like Barrett Wendell of Harvard, George Edward Woodberry of Columbia, and Henry Van Dyke of Princeton kept the new literature out of the universities, while editors like Hamilton Wright Mabie excluded it from the more reputable magazines. Although some spokesmen of the Genteel Tradition, especially William Crary Brownell, were discerning and accomplished critics, their influence remained generally repressive.

As for the general public, they mostly preferred either historical romances about chivalrous heroes and beautiful ladies or tales of rural life that dripped with sentimentality. The former were supplied by Charles Major, George B. McCutcheon, and others, and the latter by such writers as Harold Bell Wright, John Fox, Jr., and Gene Stratton Porter. These were the big best-sellers of the early twentieth century.

4. PAINTING, ARCHITECTURE, AND MUSIC

The European Influence in Painting. American painters after the Civil War had a similar difficulty in adjusting themselves to the new environment. With the growth of national wealth, more money was available for the support of art. But the distinctive native trends developed earlier in the century ceased to win support, critical standards became chaotic, and mediocrity was too often rewarded.

European influences, past and present, were now predominant. Almost all American painters studied in Europe, chiefly in Paris, and relatively few of them were strong enough to absorb what they learned without being overwhelmed by it. Meanwhile, a rapidly increasing number of European masterpieces were shipped to the United States. Many of the new millionaires found art-collecting an exciting way of spending their money, and under the tutelage of skillful dealers some of them learned the rudiments of good taste. Most of their acquisitions were eventually made accessible to the general public in museums. The Metropolitan Museum of New York was founded in 1870, and other cities gradually acquired sizable collections. Thus all the varied styles developed by different nations in earlier centuries were now available to American students. But the results of this growth of historical consciousness were not altogether good. The riches of the past were too vast to be easily assimilated.

Official European organizations, like the Royal Academy in England

and the Salon in France, favored elaborate mythological and historical scenes, often featuring idealized nudes. The artist was supposed to produce "beauty," and beauty had nothing to do with reality. Their American disciples, entrenched in the National Academy, produced acres of work of the same kind, most of it now deservedly forgotten except where it survives in the form of murals in public buildings.

Of the newer and more vital European groups, the most important were the French impressionists, who concentrated on effects of light and color rather than on the precise and detailed portrayal of objects. A number of the better American painters came under the influence of the impressionists, among them being Childe Hassam, John Twachtman, and J. Alden Weir. They broke away from the National Academy in 1877 and founded the Society of American Artists, which retained its independence until 1906. The first president was John La Farge, one of the most gifted and versatile artists of the period. Some other American painters became expatriates. Mary Cassatt, also an impressionist, settled in France, while the brilliant and belligerent James MacNeill Whistler and John Singer Sargent, the most popular portrait-painter of the time, spent their later lives mostly in England.

Native Trends.   The impressionists produced much excellent work; but present-day critics see greater significance in a few isolated figures who persisted in going their own way and remained aloof from the different European schools. Thomas Eakins of Philadelphia produced portraits and group studies that had an uncompromising scientific integrity lacking in the more showy work of Sargent. George Inness, originally a disciple of the Hudson River School, developed a power and a lyricism in his portrayals of scenery in the Middle Atlantic states that made him perhaps the greatest American landscapist. Winslow Homer, who spent his later life on the coast of Maine, achieved similar distinction as a painter of the sea. The work of these men had a devotion to objective truth and a lack of sentimentality that linked them with Copley and Peale, along with an emotional depth that was new in American art; but none of them were adequately appreciated by their contemporaries. Even more obscure was Albert Pinkham Ryder, who sought to give pictorial expression to spiritual experience and developed bold new techniques that foreshadowed the abstractionists of the twentieth century. A native of the old whaling port of New Bedford, Massachusetts, Ryder portrayed the sea, but, like Melville, was concerned with its symbolic meanings as well as its visual appearance.

At the end of the century came an abrupt new beginning paralleling the advent of naturalism in literature. A group of young men living in Philadelphia, headed by Robert Henri and John Sloan, began to portray urban scenes and figures with the same harsh fidelity to fact that Garland and Dreiser had introduced into fiction. Their work displayed a strong social consciousness and radical sympathies, and marked a startling break with the conventional belief that art was concerned only with "beauty." The group achieved notoriety in 1908 when eight of them held a joint exhibition in New York. Conservative critics referred to the eight as the "Ash-Can School" and the "Revolutionary Black Gang" and complained that they "deliberately and conscientiously paint the ugly wherever it occurs." But they were excellent craftsmen, and the vigor and the gusto with which they rendered American life made them most stimulating influences on the art of the twentieth century.

Sculpture. The market for sculpture expanded in the late nineteenth century, since cities all over the country began to set up monuments honoring their Civil War dead or commemorating political or military leaders. But the United States did not have any national school capable of meeting the demand. A few individuals, especially John Quincy Adams Ward, displayed an honest realism similar to that of Eakins in painting; but American sculptors usually preferred to copy the Italian neo-classical school and produce allegorical figures with flowing Roman robes in white marble. Nor did most civic officials have any real interest in the aesthetic quality of their statuary. The public monuments of the 1870's and 1880's gave the impression, it was suggested, of being turned out by foundries on a mass-production basis, and almost all of them were of a quite appalling ugliness.

Towards the end of the century a few individuals broke away from the neo-classical tradition and began to produce work with more energy and originality. Probably the greatest of them was the Irish-born Augustus Saint-Gaudens, remembered chiefly for his Sherman and Farragut monuments in New York and for the nameless figure marking the grave of Mrs. Henry Adams in Washington. Some notable statues of American political and intellectual leaders were produced by Daniel Chester French, while the allegorical figures of George Grey Barnard had a refreshing vigor. These men could not wholly transform official tastes, but their influence brought about a slow improvement in the standards of American public statuary.

Architecture of the Gilded Age. In architecture the two decades following the Civil War marked the nadir of bad taste. While aesthetic values were wholly ignored in the construction of factories and tenements, the homes of wealthy families displayed a vulgar ostentation unparalleled before or since. Buildings were decorated with an incredible variety of cupolas, turrets, balconies, and gables, and the whole of architectural history was ransacked for ornamental devices. The notion that the form and appearance of a building should have some connection with its purposes was completely repudiated. The Gothic of medieval Europe was perhaps the favorite source of inspiration, and was applied to private houses as well as to churches and universities. But architects also copied from classical, Arabic, Renaissance, and Georgian styles. Many government buildings, railroad stations, and public libraries were modeled after ancient Roman baths or Italian Renaissance palaces with no consideration whatever for practical convenience. In a few instances the architecture showed competence and good taste. The copies of French châteaux which Richard Morris Hunt designed for millionaire families in Newport and New York were well-proportioned and attractive buildings. But in so far as they represented an attempt to use art not to enrich reality but to escape from it, they were analogous to the poetry sponsored by the critics of the Genteel Tradition and the paintings of the National Academy.

The first architect to rebel against all this florid cake-frosting and assert truer values was Henry Hobson Richardson, who did his best work in the 1880's. Richardson found a personal style by studying the Romanesque buildings of the early Middle Ages, with their heavy structures and appearance of massive strength, and applying it to the construction of churches (such as Trinity in Boston), railroad stations, libraries, and colleges. With the growth of new building methods using steel instead of stonework, the style itself soon became outmoded. But Richardson taught later architects to cultivate simplicity and avoid irrelevant ornamentation and to make the form of a building develop out of its function.

The Rise of Functionalism. Meanwhile, architecture was being revolutionized by technological changes, and pioneers were discovering that structures designed strictly in engineering terms, with little or no decoration, displayed a new kind of austere but breath-taking beauty. One of the first demonstrations of this lyricism of steel was Brooklyn Bridge in New York, designed by John Roebling, built by his son Washington, and completed in 1883. During the next few years the discovery that buildings could be made from steel frames, masonry being used only as a sheath, and the invention of the electric elevator made the skyscraper possible.

A few architects, most of them in Chicago, set out to explore the aesthetic implications of the new methods, repudiating all earlier traditions as irrelevant to the age of steel. Believing that since American democracy was a new social system, it should develop its own aesthetic forms, they dreamed of an architecture that would express New World ideals as truly as the Gothic had expressed those of the Middle Ages. John W. Root was an important pioneer in the development of the new style, but its chief prophet was Louis Sullivan. In his Wainwright Building at St. Louis (designed in 1890) and other office buildings he abandoned all irrelevant ornamentation and allowed the lines of the structures to speak for themselves, while in his writings he elaborated on his famous formula that "form follows function."

During the 1890's, however, there was a reaction against this new "functional" style. The traditionalists rallied their forces and won control of the planning of the Chicago Exposition of 1893, creating a display of buildings in classical and Renaissance modes that dazzled most of the spectators. A few more discerning observers felt that this parade of columns and domes was an indication of artistic sterility and lack of direction, but most people felt that such architecture was a suitable expression of the greatness of America. Classicism was dominant for the next two or three decades, its most gifted exponent being Stanford White of the New York firm of McKim, Mead and White. Its chief rival was Gothic, championed by Ralph Adams Cram of Cram, Goodhue and Ferguson. Both White and Cram were excellent designers, and their buildings were in far better taste than those of the 1870's. But their artistic gifts could not conceal their essential lack of original creative power.

With the rapid rise of real-estate values in urban areas, there were strong economic inducements for skyscraper-building. But few of the designers had learned the lessons taught by Louis Sullivan, and most of the early buildings (like Cass Gilbert's Woolworth Building in New York, designed in 1913) were disfigured with Gothic or classical reminiscences. Although the skyline of New York became an exciting spectacle, very few of the buildings were individually satisfying. The skyscraper, moreover, was socially reprehensible, since it added to the congestion of urban areas. In the words of Louis Sullivan, it was "the eloquent peroration of most bald, most sinister, most forbidding conditions." Although for most people the new American architecture was represented chiefly by the skyscraper, its healthiest manifestations were to be found elsewhere.

During the period of classical and Gothic dominance the ideas of Louis Sullivan were developed by his pupil Frank Lloyd Wright of Wisconsin, one of the few indubitable men of genius of twentieth-century America. Disliking the skyscraper, Wright preferred horizontal to vertical lines, and became known chiefly for his "prairie houses." A disciple of Emerson and Whitman, he speculated about the theory of architecture, emphasized the unity between man and nature, and sought methods of building that would harmonize with the environment and building-materials as well as serve the needs of modern living. In the designing of modern private homes, office buildings, and hotels, he showed an apparently inexhaustible inventiveness and fertility. Until his old age he had little recognition in his own country, but his work was quickly appreciated in Europe, where his innovations were applied (and often perverted) in the so-called "international style."

Music.   In music the United States was accumulating a rich popular tradition but producing little work on higher levels. During the late nineteenth century there were many additions to the country's repertory of folk songs—songs composed by anonymous cowboys, lumberjacks, sailors, railroad workers, Negro plantation hands, even hoboes and convicts. There were also a number of effective composers of light opera, especially the Irish-born Victor Herbert. But there was no serious work on a par with that of the greater novelists, painters, and architects. The first American composer worthy of serious consideration was Edward Mac-

Dowell of New York, who died in 1908. But although some of Mac-Dowell's piano pieces are still played, he was not a major figure.

Nevertheless, the late nineteenth century was an important period in the development of American music because for the first time Americans began to hear good performances. Prior to the Civil War the New York Philharmonic was the only organization that even attempted to give regular orchestral concerts, and its standards were wholly unprofessional. The German immigration of the 1840's and 1850's brought to the United States a number of people who appreciated music, and were willing to support orchestras; and a son of German immigrant parents, Theodore Thomas, set out to supply the need. Beginning to conduct in 1862, Thomas created the first full-time professional orchestra and made a long series of tours which took him to every important city in the country. Down to his death in 1905 he fought an increasingly successful battle to induce Americans to come to concerts where only serious music was played and to listen to it with proper attention. As a direct result of Thomas's leadership, first-class orchestras were established in Boston in 1881 and in Chicago in 1891, while New York and Philadelphia followed suit before 1914. New York also became a center of grand opera, the famous Metropolitan being built in 1883; by 1914, with Caruso as its leading tenor and Toscanini as conductor, it was at the peak of its prestige. Thus a growing number of Americans were at least exposed to good music well played, though both composers and performers remained predominantly European.

XXV

The United States Becomes
a World Power

1. THE NEW POWER POLITICS

2. OVERSEAS EXPANSION

3. THE OPEN DOOR IN CHINA

4. CARIBBEAN AND MEXICAN POLICY

5. RELATIONS WITH JAPAN

FOR a generation following the Civil War American energies were
concentrated on internal development, and foreign relations were of
little importance. This period of isolation came to an end shortly before
the end of the century. In the 1890's the United States became deeply
involved in the affairs of Latin America and of the Far East, and began
to assume the role of a world power. Decisions made during this period
made any future return to isolation almost impossible. Henceforth the
lives of all the people of America were to be affected in increasingly important ways by events in other parts of the world.

Many Americans have continued to deplore this new trend in foreign
policy, arguing that entanglement in the conflicts of Europe and Asia was
not in accord with the true interests of the American people and was due

SELECTED BIBLIOGRAPHY: The best general books on relations with Latin America
are S. F. Bemis, *The Latin American Policy of the United States* (1943), and Dexter Perkins,
Hands Off: A History of the Monroe Doctrine (1941). The influence of naval policy is traced in
Harold and Margaret Sprout, *The Rise of American Naval Power, 1776–1919* (1939). For
the Spanish-American War, see J. W. Pratt, *Expansionists of 1898* (1936), and Walter Millis's
entertaining *The Martial Spirit* (1931). W. H. Haas, *The American Empire* (1940), and
J. W. Pratt, *America's Colonial Experiment* (1950), are useful books on colonial policy.
Tyler Dennett, *Americans in Eastern Asia* (1922), deals with the origins of American policy
in the Far East, while A. W. Griswold, *Far Eastern Policy of the United States* (1938), traces
its development during the twentieth century. H. K. Beale, *Theodore Roosevelt and the Rise
of America to World Power* (1953), is a valuable analysis.

mainly to the blunders or personal ambitions of presidents and secretaries of state. But, in the retrospect of history, the abandonment of isolation appears as a result of broad economic trends, operating in Western civilization as a whole, which were probably too strong to be resisted. Technological development was drawing all parts of the world more closely together and making all countries more interdependent. The end of American isolation was merely one example of a general process, manifest also in all other parts of the world, which seemed to be leading ultimately towards some form of global unification.

1. THE NEW POWER POLITICS

The Growth of Imperialism. The most significant new trend of the late nineteenth century was the need of the leading industrial nations of western Europe for more foreign markets. Industrialists required raw materials not available at home, new customers to buy their products, and new opportunities for the investment of surplus capital. The consequent expansion of the European technological system, although in the long run probably a desirable process, led at first to much exploitation of backward peoples, and was accompanied by increasingly bitter rivalries between the major European powers. Under the pressure of international competition the earlier liberal doctrines of free trade ceased to have much influence on policy. Using their power to secure economic privileges for their citizens, the governments of Great Britain, Germany, France, and other countries now sought exclusive control of colonial areas. As in the seventeenth and eighteenth centuries, this growth of economic imperialism led finally to war.

Since the British controlled India and other possessions and enjoyed a dominant position in the markets of the Dominions, Latin America, and China, they had great initial advantages. But they confronted increasingly formidable competition from Germany. After achieving national unity under Bismarck's leadership in 1871, the Germans were the strongest military power in the world; they created an industrial system more efficient than that of the British; and in the 1890's they began to challenge the traditional British control of the sea by building a navy. Throughout the last two decades of the century there was a three-cornered rivalry for colonies between Britain, France, and Germany, in the course of which most of Africa was partitioned among the three powers. As the supply of backward areas available for annexation diminished, the competition became more intense and war more imminent. Early in the twentieth century Europe became divided into two hostile combinations, Germany being allied with Austria-Hungary and Italy, while Britain reached understandings with France and Russia.

Thus the most conspicuous developments in Europe were the increase of hostilities likely to result in a general war and the rise of Germany. Meanwhile, at the other side of the world another new power was emerging. Most of the Far Eastern nations were unable to resist European penetration, China, in particular, being apparently destined for partition among different European powers. But one Pacific nation, Japan, succeeded not only in retaining her independence but also in adopting European technology. Winning a rapid victory in a war with China in 1894, the Japanese served notice on the rest of the world that a new power was demanding a place in the sun. At the end of the war they annexed Formosa.

Perhaps the chief reason for the trend away from isolation in American foreign policy was that the United States could no longer feel so secure as in the past. Throughout the nineteenth century British sea power had controlled the Atlantic, while the Pacific had been a power vacuum. Although Anglo-American relations had by no means been consistently friendly, all disputes since the War of 1812 had been settled by agreement, and Britain had not threatened any vital American interest. But the revival of imperialism in the late nineteenth century led to a general sense of tension, and after the turn of the century Americans became steadily more disturbed by the threat to the world balance of power presented by the growth of German and Japanese sea power.

American Expansionism.   Meanwhile, the United States also was developing tendencies towards imperialism. American industry was beginning to need new foreign markets; and although the United States remained, on balance, a debtor nation until World War I, surplus capital was beginning to spill over into neighboring countries like Canada, Mexico, and Cuba. The actual economic pressure for an imperialistic foreign policy was never strong. Nevertheless, presidents and secretaries of state became concerned lest, with the partitioning of other parts of the world by European powers, American business be denied access to profitable areas, and felt it necessary to ensure that foreign markets remain open for American capital. While in most instances (notably in China) they supported an "open door" policy, demanding equality rather than special privileges for American business, they also became interested in acquiring overseas possessions.

The building of an American empire was strongly supported by a small but important group of men who believed in a new version of Manifest Destiny. Influenced by Social Darwinism and by European imperialistic writers like Rudyard Kipling, they looked forward to world leadership by the American people. Among the more prominent spokesmen of this imperialist ideology were Theodore Roosevelt, Senator Henry Cabot Lodge of Massachusetts, and Senator Albert J. Beveridge of Indiana. While they never converted many of their fellow-citizens to this version of the national mission, they had considerable influence on American policy, especially when they advocated the acquisition of naval bases overseas. American imperialist expansion in the late nineteenth century was, in fact, probably due more to these strategic considerations than to economic factors. The emphasis on naval bases owed much to the writing of Captain Alfred T. Mahan, especially to his *Influence of Sea Power on History* (1890).

Naval Policy. The first symptom of the change in American attitudes to foreign affairs was the construction of a new navy. During the Grant and Hayes administrations the navy had almost disappeared; the United States had become inferior in naval strength not only to the leading European powers but even to the South American republic of Chile, and such ships as she possessed were intended mainly for coastal defense. But beginning in 1881 Congress began to appropriate large sums for new construction, mainly because of a growing realization of the dangers of national weakness. In disputes with other countries—for example, with Great Britain over the control of a projected isthmus canal—it was painfully apparent that the United States lacked the armed force necessary to support her diplomacy.

During the 1880's the navy was rapidly enlarged and modernized by the building of steel steam-propelled battleships, while its administration became vastly more efficient. Instead of being considered primarily as an instrument for the defense of American shores, the navy henceforth was designed to have enough striking power to meet hostile forces on the high seas. This change from a defensive to a potentially offensive role was made explicit in the Naval Act of 1890. By the end of the century the United States navy was inferior only to those of Britain and Germany. Henceforth its strategic requirements were to have an increasingly important influence on American foreign policy.

2. OVERSEAS EXPANSION

Expansion in the Pacific. The first moves towards overseas expansion had been taken during the Johnson administration at the initiative of Secretary of State Seward. An old advocate of Manifest Destiny, Seward looked forward to the growth of American power across the Pacific. In 1867 he negotiated a treaty with Russia by which Alaska was purchased for $7,200,000, and in the same year he brought about the annexation of Midway Islands. But Seward's interest in expansion had little support from public opinion, which was preoccupied with the Reconstruction problem; and the importance of his acquisitions was not recognized until later generations.

Later in the century the growing emphasis on sea power led to the acquisition of naval bases in the Pacific. As early as 1878 the United States signed a treaty with Samoa by which she received the right to establish a naval base at Pago Pago. Subsequently both Germany and Britain became interested in Samoa, and a conflict among the three powers for control of the island seemed imminent. The aggressive policies of Germany caused an outbreak of nationalist excitement in the United States, and in 1889 Congress voted funds for the protection of American interests in Samoa. The German government then decided to give way, and an agreement was reached for a joint protectorate. Ten years later the island was divided among the three powers, and Tutuila, which included Pago Pago, became an American possession. Though Samoa itself was of no great importance, the episode was significant as the first manifestation of a new imperialist psychology in the United States.

A more useful Pacific acquisition was Hawaii. Guarding the approach to the American coastline, the islands had been considered as strategically important even before the Civil War. As early as 1842 Secretary of State Webster had declared that the United States would oppose annexation by any other power. In 1875 a treaty was concluded making Hawaii virtually an American protectorate, and in 1887 the United States acquired the right to build a naval base at Pearl Harbor.

Meanwhile, American citizens, most of them being the children of missionaries, had developed sugar and pineapple plantations and acquired a dominant position in both the economy and the government of the islands. When a new native queen, who came to the throne in 1891, tried to curtail their privileges, they resolved to bring about annexation by the United States, and won the support of officials of the Harrison administration. In January 1893 they organized a revolution, seized power, and asked the United States for assistance. This was forthcoming in the form of 160 marines, who were landed from an American warship already at Honolulu. But before Congress could act on the request of the new Hawaiian government for annexation, Harrison had been succeeded by Cleveland, who was opposed to imperialist expansion and convinced that most of the inhabitants of Hawaii preferred their own native rulers. The request was therefore rejected; but the Americans in Hawaii retained control of the government and renewed their appeal after Cleveland had been succeeded by McKinley. In July 1898 Congress voted for annexation, and the islands were organized as a territory with a view to eventual statehood. This was during the war with Spain, when the country was in an expansionist mood and becoming more conscious of strategic considerations.

Pan-Americanism.   During the 1880's and 1890's United States foreign policy began also to look southwards as well as westwards. Chiefly in the hope of finding new markets for American industry, American statesmen set out to cultivate closer relations with Latin America in general, while (mainly for strategic rather than economic reasons) they moved also towards the establishment of an American sphere of influence in the Caribbean, control of which appeared necessary for American security.

In 1881 James G. Blaine, Secretary of State under Garfield, suggested a Pan-American conference. The idea was dropped under Arthur, but revived under Cleveland; and a conference was finally held at Washington in 1889, by which time Blaine was again Secretary of State, under Harrison. The conference actually did little to increase United States trade with Latin America; and apart from the founding of the Pan American Union as a clearing-house for disseminating information, its accomplishments were meager. But it was followed by a series of other conferences, mostly at five-year intervals. After World War I the delegates no longer restricted themselves to innocuous expressions of good will and began to deal with serious political and economic problems, and the ideal of hemispheric cooperation gradually assumed more reality.

The Venezuelan Boundary Dispute. The first assertion of American power in the Caribbean came in 1895, as a result of a boundary dispute between Venezuela and the British colony of Guiana. Since ownership of land in the Western Hemisphere was at stake and the British had refused to submit their claims to arbitration, President Cleveland felt that the Monroe Doctrine should be invoked. Secretary of State Olney wrote a most belligerent note, declaring that the United States would resort to force unless the British gave way, and going on to claim suzerainty over the entire hemisphere. In one of the most provocative statements in the annals of diplomacy he declared: "Today the United States is practically sovereign on this continent, and its fiat is law upon the subjects to which it confines its interposition. . . . Its infinite resources combined with its isolated position render it master of the situation and practically invulnerable as against any or all other powers."

The controversy continued for some months, and at one period war seemed imminent; but the British were also involved in disputes in Africa, by comparison with which the ownership of a few square miles of South American jungle was unimportant, and they finally agreed to accept the decision of an international board of arbitration. The Prime Minister, Lord Salisbury, pointed out, however, that if the United States was going to protect the Latin American countries from European intervention, she must, in return, assume responsibility for their good behavior. This implication was afterwards accepted by the United States and led in 1904 to the Roosevelt Corollary to the Monroe Doctrine.

In spite of Olney's belligerence, the Venezuela dispute led in the end to closer relations with Britain. Disturbed by the growing power of Germany, the British were anxious for American friendship and decided that it would be wise to accept American predominance in the Caribbean. Early in the twentieth century British statesmen withdrew most of their armed forces from the Western Hemisphere and began, for the first time, to express approval of the Monroe Doctrine.

The Spanish-American War. The next step in the establishment of American hegemony in the Caribbean was the war with Spain. After losing her possessions on the mainland, Spain had retained ownership of Cuba and Puerto Rico but had failed to reform her methods of government. A ten-year rebellion in Cuba (1868–78) ended unsuccessfully. In 1895 the Cubans rebelled again, and this time the atrocities committed by the Spanish authorities and the general savagery of the struggle soon aroused public opinion in the United States. Journalists demanded intervention in order to liberate the Cubans and restore peace, the Hearst and Pulitzer newspapers in New York being particularly belligerent. By the beginning of 1898 there was considerable popular sentiment in favor of war with Spain, liberal and humanitarian idealism being mingled with a nationalistic eagerness to assert American power.

Meanwhile, the small group of men who looked forward to world leadership by the United States also favored war for more practical reasons. In the process of liberating Cuba the United States could acquire naval bases in the Caribbean. Spain, moreover, also owned the Philippines; and if these were conquered by the United States, they would serve as a valuable foothold in the Far East. Theodore Roosevelt, Assistant Secretary of the Navy in the McKinley administration, was perhaps the most vigorous advocate of this viewpoint. The American business community, on the other hand, was mostly opposed to war. It had relatively little money invested in Cuba, and did not anticipate any particular advantages from its liberation.

In February 1898 the battleship *Maine*, which had been sent to Havana to protect American citizens, was blown up. The causes of the explosion have remained a mystery to this day, but the American public, without adequate reason, immediately decided that the Spanish authorities were responsible, and "Remember the *Maine*" became the slogan of the war party. President McKinley was personally in favor of peace, but he also wanted to be re-elected in 1900 and was not disposed to stick to his private convictions in defiance of the growing pressure for war. He urged Spain to concede an armistice to the insurgents. The Spanish government, concerned about public opinion at home, made up its mind slowly but finally gave way. This would probably have led to the liberation of Cuba without a war; but a peaceful settlement would not have satisfied the popular hysteria, nor would it have enabled the United States to acquire bases overseas. In April, McKinley capitulated to the war party and sent a message to Congress in which he asked for authorization to use force to end the fighting in Cuba and failed to give any adequate recognition of Spain's willingness to give way. Congress promptly declared war.

Although the only official reason for the war was to liberate Cuba, the first operation was in the Far East. On the initiative of Assistant Secretary Roosevelt, the Navy Department had sent orders to Admiral Dewey, in command of the Asiatic Squadron, that if war came, he should proceed to the Phillippines. On May 1, Dewey destroyed a few decrepit Spanish warships in the battle of Manila Bay. Most Americans had never heard of the islands, and McKinley publicly confessed that he did not know where they were within two thousand miles; but Dewey's victory aroused great enthusiasm, and troops were subsequently dispatched to land at Manila and oust the Spanish authorities. In this casual fashion the United States assumed a new major responsibility in the Far East.

Meanwhile, the army was rapidly enlarged by the enlistment of volunteers, and an expedition was prepared for the liberation of Cuba. In July, Admirals Schley and Sampson destroyed the main Spanish fleet outside Santiago. American troops landed on the island, forced the Spanish forces to capitulate after only three weeks of fighting, and then went on to occupy Puerto Rico. American battle casualties amounted to less than 300. Rarely has glory been won at so low a price. By contrast with most other wars, the conflict in Cuba seemed like a holiday jaunt to most of the participants. On the other hand, it revealed gross incompetence in the War Department. American generalship was mediocre or worse; and bad food and lack of medical attention caused nearly 3,000 deaths from disease.

Results of the War. By a peace treaty signed at Paris in December 1898, Spain relinquished Cuba and also ceded the Philippines, Puerto Rico, and the small Pacific island of Guam. Since the United States had not yet conquered the Philippines, she consented to pay $20,000,000 for them. McKinley had hesitated about retaining them, but, as he told a group of Methodist ministers, he had prayed for guidance and decided upon annexation as a result of what he believed to be a message from God. It was the duty of the United States, he declared, "to educate the Filipinos, and uplift and civilize and Christianize them." The Protestant churches had, in fact, worked for annexation in the expectation of developing missionary activities. More mundane considerations, however, probably had more to do with the decision of the administration, since it was hoped that the Philippines would be a base for the expansion of American trade and power throughout the Far East.

Cuba was placed temporarily under American military rule, General Leonard Wood being governor. Meanwhile a convention drafted a constitution, and in 1902 the island assumed self-government, although with some restrictions. Cuba's future relationship with the United States was defined by the Platt Amendment, written mainly by Elihu Root (who had become Secretary of War in 1899) and passed by Congress in the form of an amendment to the Army Appropriation Bill of 1901. The Cubans, much against their will, were then compelled to accept its provisions in the form of a treaty. The new republic was forbidden to incur an excessive national debt or do anything else that might endanger its independence, while the United States was to have the right of intervening, if necessary, to protect life, liberty, and property, and could also buy or lease naval bases. The Platt Amendment indicated clearly the less idealistic and more practical reasons for American entry into war with Spain.

Thus the United States had now, for the first time, become the owner of colonial dependencies. The inhabitants of Puerto Rico and the Philippines, while becoming American nationals, did not receive full rights of citizenship (a position upheld by the Supreme Court in the Insular Cases of 1901); and it was not anticipated that either possession would eventually be granted statehood within the American Union. In these two respects the annexations of 1898 differed sharply from the acquisitions of Louisiana, California, and even Alaska. Many Americans regarded this innovation with grave misgivings, feeling that in abandoning her traditional hostility to imperialism the United States had ceased to be the champion of liberal ideals and become corrupted by the power politics of Europe. Almost every important writer and intellectual in the country was, in fact, outspokenly hostile to the annexations.

Puerto Rico.   Puerto Rico had been granted almost complete self-government by Spain shortly before the war (a fact which very few Americans realized), so that annexation meant less rather than more liberty for its inhabitants. The island was at first given a government roughly modeled on that of the thirteen colonies before 1776, with a governor and a council appointed by the president and an elected legislature. In 1917, by the Jones Act, Puerto Ricans were made United States citizens, and an elective upper house was substituted for the council, although acts of the legislature might still be vetoed by the president of the United States.

Although American rule in Puerto Rico brought a number of improvements, it cannot be regarded as very successful. Much was done to lower the death rate, develop education, and build public works. But the population began to increase rapidly; and since the government failed to solve the consequent economic problems, living standards remained abysmally low. American corporations producing sugar and other tropical crops acquired ownership of much of the land; and a large part of the population worked on the plantations for extremely low wages. Any fall in the sugar market meant economic disaster. During the great depression of the 1930's, 60 per cent of the people were unemployed.

Most Puerto Rican leaders were compelled to recognize that independence would only aggravate their economic problems, but they strongly resented the control exercised by Washington over the destinies of their country; and a vigorous nationalist movement soon developed. The United States responded by giving Puerto Rico the right to elect its own governor in 1947 and making it a self-governing commonwealth in 1952. Under the dynamic leadership of Governor Luis Muñoz Marín, the island then began to make remarkable economic progress. Meanwhile hundreds of thousands of Puerto Ricans had sought better conditions, often in vain, by migrating to New York.

The Philippines.   In the Philippines the United States eventually made a better showing, in spite of initial repressive policies. Some of the Filipinos had hoped for independence; and annexation was followed by a rebellion headed by Emilio Aguinaldo. An army of 70,000 American troops, commanded by General Arthur MacArthur, was engaged for three years in extremely savage and costly fighting. Civil government was set up in 1901, the first governor being William Howard Taft, who served until 1903 with conspicuous success. As in Puerto Rico, an elected legislature was established, public education developed, and public health vastly improved.

Fortunately, unlike Puerto Rico, the Philippines did not suffer from acute overpopulation. Relatively little American capital, moreover, was invested in the islands, and a large part of the population remained small farmers instead of becoming employees of big corporations. Taft encouraged the growth of small holdings, arranging, in particular, for the purchase of 400,000 acres of land held by the Catholic Church and its division into small farms. American rule was not free from criticism. Filipinos continued to ask that control of the government be transferred to them more rapidly than seemed expedient to the American officials. Some American governors were perhaps too inclined to cooperate with the native upper class, to the detriment of the mass of the people. But on the whole, especially by contrast with the record of the British and Dutch in the East Indies, the United States could fairly claim to have shown a real sense of trusteeship. It was ironical that, from the viewpoint of American national interests, the annexation of the Philippines proved to be probably a mistake. They were of little economic value to the United States; the hope that they would serve as a base for trade with other parts of the Far East never materialized; and being more than 6,000 miles from the American coastline, they were a military liability, and the responsibility for defending them in the event of war seriously handicapped American diplomacy.

3. THE OPEN DOOR IN CHINA

THE GROUP of men responsible for taking the Philippines had been dreaming of an American empire in the Far East. The United States had already, of course, had a long history of activity in the Pacific. She had developed commercial relations with China and Indonesia in the late eighteenth century; and American Protestant missionaries had been active in China since 1830. It was now widely believed that there were immense opportunities for profit, power, and idealistic enterprise in the Far East, especially in China, and that it was the duty of the American government to see that they remained open. The next step towards involvement in the Far East was therefore the enunciation of the doctrine of the Open Door in China, which became henceforth one of the guiding principles of American foreign policy.

Sprawling over an immense area, much of it densely populated, China was, in theory, governed by the Manchu dynasty of emperors. In practice, many of its provinces paid only nominal allegiance to the imperial authorities at Peking. In the latter part of the nineteenth century Britain, France, Russia, and Japan annexed or assumed protectorates over a number of outlying areas; and around the turn of the century the central provinces also began to be carved into spheres of interest. Political authority remained, at least in theory, with the Chinese officials, but foreign powers assumed the right to invest capital and exercise economic control, and it seemed likely that their spheres of interest would gradually develop into colonial possessions.

The British were inclined at first to oppose the partition of China. Having formed commercial connections with many parts of the country, they did not wish now to be restricted to a single sphere of interest. In 1898 British officials suggested to the American government that the two countries join each other in sponsoring an Open Door policy, by which all of China, instead of being partitioned, should remain open to businessmen of all nations on equal terms. Although the British made a convert of John Hay, then American minister in London, they failed to convince McKinley, who remained faithful to the tradition of avoiding entangling alliances. When McKinley proved unresponsive, the British dropped the whole idea of the Open Door and set out to make agreements with their competitors for the division of the Chinese market. In 1902, moreover, they formed an alliance with Japan.

In 1899 John Hay became Secretary of State and resolved to give official sponsorship to the Open Door (which was, indeed, in accord with America's earlier Chinese policy, as manifested in the Cushing Treaty of 1844). His main objective was to keep China open for American trade and capital investment. Since the United States did not propose to join the European powers in carving up the country, maintenance of the Open Door was, in fact, the only way by which American citizens could be assured of entry into the Chinese market.

In 1899 Hay circulated a note among the leading powers urging them to maintain commercial equality for citizens of all countries in their spheres of interest. Although their replies were decidedly evasive, he resorted to bluff and declared that all of them had expressed agreement. In 1900 nationalistic resentment among the Chinese people against the privileges of foreigners led to the Boxer Rebellion, and the leading powers (including the United States) sent a joint military expedition to protect their citizens. Fearing lest some of the powers might seize their opportunity to keep troops permanently in China. Hay then circulated a second Open Door note, much more far-reaching than the first in its implications, in which he declared that it was the policy of the United States to "preserve Chinese territorial and administrative entity."

In actuality none of the other powers, not even Britain, was willing to accept the Open Door doctrine. Although China was never carved up into colonies, this was due mainly to the inability of the imperialist powers to come to terms with each other, and eventually to the outbreak of World War I, rather than to the influence of the United States. The United States was probably not strong enough to maintain Chinese independence singlehanded, and certainly not sufficiently interested in the Far East to expend much energy in an attempt to do so. In other words, the Open Door doctrine was merely a pious aspiration not backed by sufficient force.

4. CARIBBEAN AND MEXICAN POLICY

IN THE Caribbean, on the other hand, which was much closer to home than China, the United States was more willing to use sufficient force to protect her interests, although not always wisely or with adequate justification. During the early years of the twentieth century, in fact, United States interference with the affairs of legally independent republics aroused antagonism through all Latin America. It can easily be argued that the essential objectives of American policy would have been attained more successfully if the responsible officials had shown more restraint and more respect for the viewpoint of their neighbors to the south.

Theodore Roosevelt, who succeeded McKinley in 1901, was particularly inclined towards strong-arm methods in foreign policy, the most flagrant example being the method by which he secured the right to build the Panama Canal.

The Panama Canal. After the Clayton-Bulwer Treaty with Great Britain in 1850, the project for a canal across Central America was dropped for a generation. In the 1870's the United States again became interested, but was no longer willing to share control with the British. As President Hayes remarked, the canal would be virtually part of the coastline of the United States. But for a long time the British would not accept any change in the Clayton-Bulwer Treaty. Meanwhile a French company acquired a concession to build a Panama canal from the Republic of Colombia, to which the region then belonged. A few miles were constructed, after which operations were suspended for lack of funds.

The war with Spain made the United States much more security-conscious and was followed by a general recognition of the need for a canal. Otherwise the United States would have to build two navies, one for the Atlantic and one for the Pacific. As a result of the reorientation of their American policy, the British were now willing to surrender their rights, and by the Hay-Pauncefote Treaty of 1901 it was agreed that the United States could build and fortify a canal provided ships of all nations could use it in peacetime on equal terms. The next question was whether to build across Panama or Nicaragua. After a careful investigation Congress voted for the Panama route—a decision applauded by the representatives of the French company, which was anxious to sell its rights and properties.

In 1903, by the Hay-Herrán Treaty with Colombia, the United

17. *The Caribbean since 1895*

INCLUDED IN THE CARIBBEAN REGION ARE THREE MEDIUM-SIZED REPUBLICS (Mexico, Colombia, Venezuela), six small mainland republics (Guatemala, Honduras, Salvador, Nicaragua, Costa Rica, Panama), and three small island republics (Cuba, Haiti, the Dominican Republic), along with a number of possessions of the United States, Britain, France, and Holland. Most of the independent countries in the region are economically and culturally undeveloped and suffer from frequent revolutions. During the nineteenth century European powers claimed the right to intervene by force in order to protect the lives and properties of their citizens.

With the growth of American naval power and the increase of international tensions during the past sixty years, the whole region has become a sphere of influence of the United States. Her primary motivations have been to protect her strategic interests and prevent any potentially hostile power from securing bases there. This became particularly important after the building of the Panama Canal. Henry L. Stimson, Secretary of State from 1929 to 1933, summarized American policy as follows: "The failure therefore of any of these Republics to maintain the responsibilities which go with independence may lead directly to a situation imperiling the vital interests of the United States in its sea-going route through the Panama Canal. Out of this situation has followed our national policy —perhaps the most sensitive and generally held policy that we have—which for half a century has caused us to look with apprehension upon even the perfectly legitimate efforts of European nations to protect their rights within this zone." This statement is sometimes known as the Isthmian Doctrine.

In establishing her predominance in the Caribbean, the United States resorted several times to force or the threat of it. Great Britain, which had formerly claimed at least equal rights in the region, accepted United States supremacy after the Venezuela boundary dispute of 1895. Spain was expelled in 1898. The United States established protectorates or intervened by force in several countries and asserted her responsibility to maintain order throughout the whole region under the Roosevelt Corollary of 1904. After World War I the interventions were gradually terminated and the Roosevelt Corollary was repudiated. But the Caribbean countries, although left free to manage their own internal affairs, continued to follow United States leadership in foreign policy.

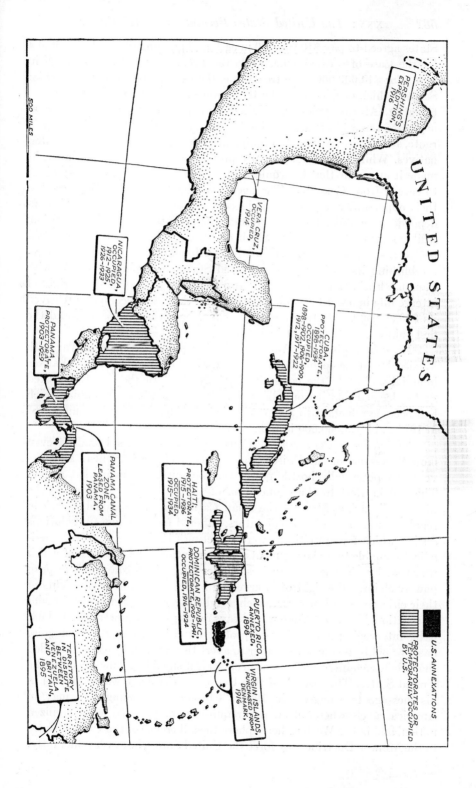

UNITED STATES

500 MILES

PERSHING'S EXPEDITION, 1916

VERA CRUZ, OCCUPIED, 1914

NICARAGUA, OCCUPIED, 1912-1925, 1926-1933

PANAMA PROTECTORATE, 1903-1929

PANAMA CANAL ZONE, LEASED FROM PANAMA, 1903

CUBA, PROTECTORATE, 1898-1934, OCCUPIED, 1898-1902, 1906-1909, 1912, 1917-1922

HAITI, PROTECTORATE, 1915-1936, OCCUPIED, 1915-1934

DOMINICAN REPUBLIC, PROTECTORATE, 1905-1941, OCCUPIED, 1916-1924

PUERTO RICO, ANNEXED, 1898

VIRGIN ISLANDS, PURCHASED FROM DENMARK, 1916

TERRITORY IN DISPUTE BETWEEN VENEZUELA AND BRITAIN, 1895

U.S. ANNEXATIONS

PROTECTORATES OR TEMPORARILY OCCUPIED BY U.S.

States agreed to pay $10,000,000 in cash and an annual rental of $250,000 for the lease of a canal zone, while the French company was to sell its rights for $40,000,000. The treaty was then submitted to the Colombian Senate, which decided that the terms were not good enough and refused to ratify. At this point the United States might have undertaken to negotiate a new treaty with Colombia or have changed to the Nicaraguan route, but Roosevelt was too indignant to consider either of these alternatives. While he did not actually promote a revolution in Panama, he made it apparent that he would support the Panamanians if they chose to secede from Colombia. The agents of the French company grasped their opportunity, and easily induced Panama to declare herself an independent republic. The United States immediately granted recognition, while an American warship, which had been ordered to the scene even before the revolution started, used force to prevent Colombia from reestablishing its authority. The United States then made a treaty with Panama, leasing a canal zone and also assuming (as in Cuba) the right of intervening in order to maintain order, and the French company received its $40,000,000. Construction of the canal began in due course, and the first ship passed through it in 1914.

No other episode in American foreign policy except the War with Mexico has done so much to arouse Latin American fears of "Yankee imperialism" and "the colossus of the North." In the end the United States decided that it would be wise to make amends to Colombia, which had become reluctant to give concessions to American businessmen, and in 1921 paid $25,000,000 in reparation.

The Roosevelt Corollary.   Construction of the canal made it even more necessary for the United States to control the Caribbean and prevent any potentially hostile power from acquiring bases in that region. This led in 1904 to the enunciation of the Roosevelt Corollary to the Monroe Doctrine. Most of the small Caribbean and Central American republics were governed by dictators, suffered from frequent revolutions during which foreign citizens were sometimes in danger, and were periodically unable to make payments on their national debts, much of which was held by European financiers. Under such circumstances European powers claimed the right of intervening by force to protect the rights of their citizens. As a last resort, such a right was recognized as valid under international law. But there was always danger that a power might abuse it by intervening not merely to protect its citizens but also to acquire bases or political control. In order to avert this danger, Roosevelt decided that when such intervention was necessary, it should be done solely by the United States. The essence of this Roosevelt Corollary was expressed in his message to Congress in 1904: "Chronic wrongdoing . . . may in America, as elsewhere, ultimately require intervention by some civilized nation, and in the Western hemisphere the adherence of the United States to the Monroe Doctrine may force the United States, however reluctantly,

The U.S. would be the only nation to step in + settle any disturbances!

in flagrant cases of such wrongdoing or impotence, to the exercise of an international police power."

There has been a long controversy about the motivations of the Roosevelt Corollary. Were they strategic or economic? Was the United States interested primarily in preventing European powers, such as Germany, from acquiring bases in dangerous proximity to the Canal? Or was interventionism due mainly to the desire of American bankers and businessmen to secure protection for investments? Both factors were, no doubt, involved, but probably the economic motives were of secondary importance. The total American capital invested in the region (except in Cuba) was never large, and the initial stimulus for investing it often came not from the bankers themselves but from the State Department, which was anxious to extend American influence throughout the region. There can be no doubt, however, about the reaction of most of the Latin Americans. From their viewpoint, the United States was even more to be feared than the European powers. The Latin American attitude, as formulated in 1903 in the doctrine promulgated by Luis Drago, Argentine Minister of Foreign Affairs, was that any form of intervention should be regarded as a violation of the rights of a sovereign state. For the next generation it was widely believed throughout Latin America that the United States had deliberately embarked on a program of imperialistic expansion and could be stopped only by force.

The first application of the Roosevelt Corollary was in 1905 in the Dominican Republic, which was unable to pay its debts. With the consent of the Dominican government, the United States assumed control of the finances. The foreign debt, after being considerably scaled down, was transferred from European to American bankers; and American officials collected the taxes, allotting the proceeds partly to government expenses and partly to payments on the debt. Otherwise the country retained its autonomy. This was a moderate application of the Corollary, and seems to have brought real benefits to the Dominicans. The only other intervention during Roosevelt's administration was in Cuba under the Platt Amendment. In 1906 revolutionary disturbances were followed by the landing of American troops, who stayed until 1909. Latin American relations improved during Roosevelt's second term (1905–09), largely through the influence of Elihu Root, who had succeeded Hay as Secretary of State. One of the ablest secretaries in American history, Root understood the value of Latin American good will and was able to keep his chief's big-stick proclivities firmly under control.

The Taft-Knox Period.   Relations took another turn for the worse after 1909, when Taft became President, with Philander Knox as Secretary of State. Taft and Knox wanted the kind of financial supervision set up in the Dominican Republic to be extended to other countries, arguing that this would both serve American strategic and financial interests and at the same time promote order and prosperity in the Caribbean. For the same reason they also sought to encourage the investment of American capital—a policy which became known as "dollar diplomacy." Unfortunately, Knox was not very tactful in promoting it.

The chief event during the Taft-Knox regime was an intervention in Nicaragua. In 1911 American bankers took charge of the country's finances, and in 1912 marines were landed to prevent a revolution. This Nicaraguan intervention was not finally liquidated for twenty years. Governments friendly to the United States were kept in power by American marines; and although elections were held at the prescribed intervals, American officials decided in advance who should be the winning candidates. This was, of course, in accord with the traditional political practices of Nicaragua, which had never known a free election. The American-controlled governments were probably more honest than previous regimes, and were not unduly deferential to American business interests; in fact, the American investment in the country decreased during the occupation. But most Nicaraguans resented the loss of their independence.

The Wilson Period.   Woodrow Wilson, who succeeded Taft in 1913, was an avowed enemy of imperialism. In a speech at Mobile in October he declared that the United States would "never again seek one additional foot of territory by conquest" and that its foreign policy should not be determined by "material interest." But in spite of these noble declarations, his administration was responsible for more interventions than those of Roosevelt and Taft combined. Nobody has satisfactorily explained this discrepancy between principle and practice, but it was probably due largely to the outbreak of World War I in 1914. Fear of German victory made American control of the Caribbean seem even more necessary. Caribbean policy was decided mainly by the State and Navy Departments rather than by Wilson himself, who was busy with more important questions. The desire for more naval bases led also to the purchase of the Virgin Islands from Denmark in 1916.

In 1915 there were revolutionary disturbances in Haiti. The President massacred nearly two hundred of his opponents and was then literally torn to pieces by a mob in the main street of the capital city. The country was then occupied by the marines, who stayed until 1934. A native Haitian government continued to function, and the republic was given a new constitution, written mainly by the Assistant Secretary of the Navy (a young man named Franklin D. Roosevelt); but the real authority belonged to the marines. American rule brought material benefits: roads were built, education expanded, and public health improved. On the other hand, opposition to the American occupation was sternly repressed with little regard for civil liberties. In 1918 a rebellion among the peasants, who resented being drafted for forced labor on the building of the roads, was bloodily suppressed, about two thousand of them being shot.

In 1916 the Dominican Republic was similarly occupied. Conflict between the native government and the American officials in charge of the finances led to a deadlock; the marines then took control of the country, and stayed until 1924. The Wilson administration also intervened in Cuba, which was again under American control from 1917 to 1922. Thus, at the end of World War I, American armed forces were in control of four nominally independent republics: Nicaragua, Haiti, the Dominican Republic, and Cuba.

This proved to be the high-water mark of American imperialism in the Caribbean. After World War I the United States gradually abandoned interventionism and began to work out a new relationship with her Latin American neighbors based on cooperation rather than on force. In the long run, in fact, the most significant and unusual feature of the Caribbean policy of the United States was not the imperialism of the Roosevelt-Taft-Wilson era but the reversal of this tendency during the 1920's and 1930's. When the American government sent out the marines, it was acting in accord with the usual methods of power politics, as practiced by all the European powers. But probably no government in history has been so willing to call its forces home again.

The Mexican Revolution. The immediate southern neighbor of the United States presented much more complex diplomatic problems than the smaller Caribbean countries. After the disturbances of the French intervention of 1862–67 the Mexicans had settled down to what seemed to superficial observers to be an era of peace, progress, and prosperity. From 1876 until 1911 Porfirio Díaz held office as president almost continuously. His main policy was to encourage the entry of foreign capital. Perhaps $1,500,000,000 was invested in railroads, public utilities, plantations, mines, and oil fields, about two-thirds of it being contributed by citizens of the United States. Mexico's economic growth caused Díaz to be widely regarded as one of the greatest statesmen in the history of the hemisphere. Unfortunately, it benefited only a small upper class. Díaz allowed the Indian peasants, who composed a large majority of the population, to be robbed of their lands and transformed into peons working at starvation wages for big landowners. The workers in the mines and industries were similarly exploited. Almost all Mexicans, moreover, resented the privileges acquired by foreign businessmen, feeling that an excessive proportion of the national wealth was being drained off to pay dividends to stockholders in Europe and the United States.

Mass discontent exploded finally in a revolution which was to cause far-reaching changes in Mexican society. In the spring of 1911 the eighty-year-old Díaz was driven into exile, and an idealistic but somewhat ineffectual liberal, Francisco Madero, was then elected President. Though he made no substantial reforms, he allowed the peasants and workers to organize and express their grievances, and was distinctly less friendly than Díaz to foreign capital. Many American businessmen were soon hoping for a counter-revolution, and—to the lasting discredit of American diplomacy—they found a spokesman in the United States minister to Mexico, Henry Lane Wilson. In February 1913 Madero was overthrown by a reactionary *coup d'état* headed by General Victoriano Huerta, and was murdered a few days later. Henry Lane Wilson was privy to the coup before it occurred, and tried to secure the prompt recognition of Huerta's government by foreign powers. Yet when asked to intercede with Huerta on behalf of Madero's personal safety, he replied that he could not interfere with Mexico's domestic affairs.

Huerta secured control of most of the country, but in the far north and south there were movements to avenge the death of Madero, restore constitutional government, and bring about land and labor reform. The chief "Constitutionalist" leaders were Venustiano Carranza, Pancho Villa (a former bandit), and the Indian peasant chieftain Emiliano Zapata. Thus, at the time when Woodrow Wilson became President, Mexico was plunged into civil war. Businessmen wanted him to recognize Huerta and intervene for the protection of American investments. But Wilson was determined that the Mexican people should be left free to work out their own destiny. His sympathies, he declared, were with "the submerged eighty-five per cent of the people of that Republic who are now struggling toward liberty." Adopting a policy of "watchful waiting," he tried to persuade Huerta to retire and allow a free election. When Huerta contemptuously rebuffed these suggestions, Wilson allowed the Constitutionalists to buy munitions in the United States, while munitions for Huerta were embargoed. This meant that the United States was taking sides in the Mexican conflict; but some form of indirect participation was inevitable. Whatever attitude the United States adopted would necessarily work to the advantage of one side or the other.

Intervention in Mexico.   Wilson eventually went beyond "watchful waiting." In April 1914 he was informed that a German merchant ship was on its way to the Mexican seaport of Veracruz with arms for Huerta. This threatened to prolong the war and possibly bring German involvement in Mexican affairs. In order to prevent the arms from being landed, Wilson gave orders for the seizure of Veracruz by the marines. Thus American armed forces intervened in Mexico, and Mexican blood was shed on Mexican soil. Although Wilson's action was intended to help the Constitutionalists, it was denounced by them as vigorously as by Huerta. Wilson, however, did much to repair the damage to Latin American relations by arranging for a conference on Mexican problems with the representatives of leading South American countries. This move towards partnership with Latin America in settling hemispheric questions was a significant step towards the later Good Neighbor policy.

In August 1914 Huerta fled into exile, and in November the marines left Veracruz. But the different Constitutionalist factions now came to blows with each other in a war which continued for two more years, and once again the United States was compelled to take sides. Carranza, who was obviously the most respectable of the Mexican leaders and seemed to have the most popular support, was allowed to buy munitions, while shipments to Villa and Zapata were embargoed. By the end of 1915 Carranza was in control of most of Mexico. This was followed by attacks on American citizens on the part of Pancho Villa, who wanted revenge. He shot sixteen Americans in northern Mexico, and in January 1916 he raided the town of Columbus, across the border in New Mexico, and killed sixteen more. Obviously the American government could not ignore this challenge, and General John J. Pershing was ordered down to northern Mexico to capture Villa. Carranza made indignant protests against the presence of American troops on Mexican soil, and the two countries seemed to be drifting steadily closer to outright war. It was probably fortunate for Mexico that the United States was too preoccupied with events in Europe to pay much attention to anything else. Pershing failed to catch Villa and was withdrawn in February 1917.

Meanwhile, Mexico, having achieved some degree of peace and order, adopted a new constitution making provision for radical agrarian and labor reforms. Under Article 27 of this Constitution of 1917 land was to be taken away from the large owners and given back to the Indian village communities, and all minerals and oil fields were declared to be the in-alienable property of the Mexican nation. Under Article 123 numerous rights were guaranteed to organized labor. If these articles were enforced, then American owners of plantations and oil fields could expect to be expropriated, and American businessmen would have to pay higher wages to Mexican laborers. But Mexican constitutions generally represent aspirations rather than immediate realities, and Carranza, who served as President until 1920, made little attempt to put the constitution into effect. It was not until after 1920 that Mexican governments began seriously to curtail the privileges which American investors had acquired during the Díaz era.

5. RELATIONS WITH JAPAN

IN THEIR Far Eastern policy Roosevelt, Taft, and Wilson all professed adherence to Hay's Open Door doctrine, but all of them discovered that little could be done to enforce it. The dominating factor in the situation was the growth of Japanese power and of Japanese ambition to expand on to the mainland at the expense of China.

Theodore Roosevelt's Policies. In 1904 rivalry between Japan and Russia for control of Korea and of the Chinese province of Manchuria led to war. The United States regarded Russia as the more dangerous of the two powers and gave diplomatic support to Japan. The Japanese won a series of victories and then became anxious for peace before their strength was exhausted. At their request Roosevelt acted as mediator and was

18. American and Japanese Expansion in the Pacific

THE PACIFIC OCEAN REMAINED A POWER VACUUM UNTIL THE LATE NINETEENTH century. None of the countries along its shores had a strong navy; and although a number of European powers had Pacific colonies, distance made it impossible for any of them to dominate the ocean.

The United States began to expand her power in the Pacific after the Civil War. She bought Alaska (including the Aleutian Islands) from Russia and acquired Midway in 1867, obtained the right to build naval bases at Pago Pago in Samoa in 1878 and at Pearl Harbor in Hawaii in 1887, and annexed Hawaii in 1898 and part of Samoa in 1899. These moves were primarily defensive. But in 1898 she also acquired the Philippines at the far end of the Pacific, along with Guam. Imperialist Americans began to look forward to United States domination over the entire ocean. Early in the twentieth century, however, it became apparent that Japan would be a formidable competitor.

Japan's ambitions pointed in two directions. While seeking naval supremacy in the western Pacific and looking forward to controlling the East Indies, which had valuable natural resources, she also wanted to acquire territories on the mainland of Asia at the expense of China and Russia. In 1895 she seized Formosa from China. In 1905 she ousted Russia from southern Manchuria and annexed southern Sakhalin, and assumed control over Korea (which she formally annexed in 1910). In 1919, under the Treaty of Versailles, she received mandates over the Mariana, Marshall, and Caroline islands, which had formerly belonged to Germany. And in 1932 she set up the puppet state of Manchukuo, on territory that had formerly been under Chinese sovereignty. Meanwhile her hostility to the United States was sharpened by discrimination against Japanese immigrants, especially in California.

American statesmen were faced with a dilemma. Should they oppose any expansion of the Japanese Empire as a danger to world peace and to the security of the United States? Or should they allow Japan to expand on the Asiatic mainland in the hope that she would then cease to threaten American interests in the Philippines, the East Indies, and the Pacific? This problem confronted each successive president from Theodore Roosevelt to Franklin Roosevelt. American policy remained indecisive until 1941, when the Japanese attack on Pearl Harbor settled the question.

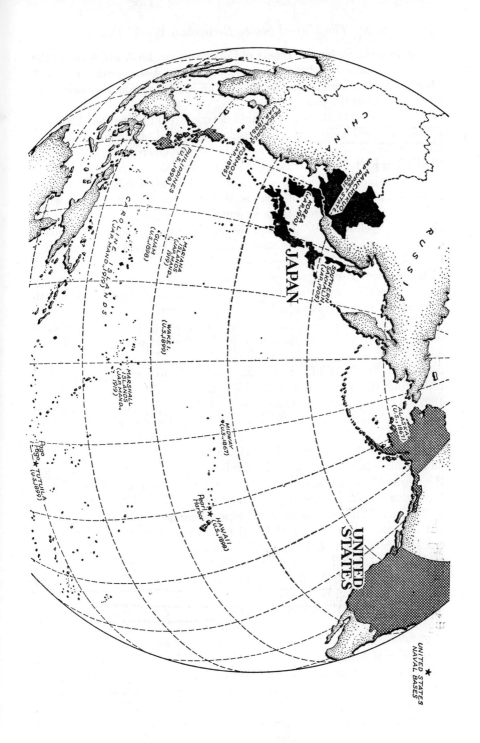

PSSAPOOTS（FORMOSA)
(JAP.,1895)

FORMOSA
(JAP.,1895)

MANCHUKUO
(JAP.,1931)

CHINA

RUSSIA

PHILIPPINES
(U.S.,1898)

CAROLINE ISLANDS
(JAP. MAND.,1919)

KOREA
(JAP.,1910)

SOUTHERN SAKHALIN
(JAP.,1905)

JAPAN

ALASKA
(U.S.,1867)

GUAM
(U.S.,1898)

MARIANA
ISLANDS
(JAP.MAND.,
1919)

WAKE I.
(U.S.,1899)

MARSHALL
ISLANDS
(JAP.MAND.,
1919)

MIDWAY
(U.S.,1867)

Pago
Pago ★ TUTUILA
(U.S.,1899)

Pearl
Harbor ★
HAWAII
(U.S.,1898)

UNITED
STATES

★
UNITED STATES
NAVAL BASES

largely responsible for the Treaty of Portsmouth of 1905, which ended the war. Japan gained exclusive control of Korea and the southern part of Manchuria, but was unable to obtain the indemnity she had originally demanded from Russia.

The war was followed by a rapid deterioration in Japanese-American relations. The Japanese assumed exclusive control of economic development in Manchuria, paying no attention to the Open Door, and blamed the United States for their failure to secure an indemnity. Relations were further strained by racial discrimination in the United States. More than 100,000 Japanese immigrants had settled in California, where their white neighbors refused to treat them as equals and began to talk hysterically about the "yellow peril." In 1906 the San Francisco Board of Education ordered all Oriental pupils to attend a public school specially set aside for them. Understandably conscious of their long tradition of civilization and of their recent rise to great-power status, the Japanese were extremely sensitive to any suggestion that they were an inferior people. On both sides of the Pacific there was talk of eventual war.

Roosevelt met the danger realistically. He had no constitutional power to prevent California from dragging the rest of the Union into a conflict with Japan; but he summoned eight San Francisco officials to a conference at the White House and was able to browbeat them into rescinding the segregation order. By the Gentlemen's Agreement of 1907–08 the Japanese government consented to issue no more passports to coolies wishing to come to the United States, thus stopping the flow of immigrants. American power was advertised by sending the sixteen battleships of the fleet on a tour of the world, in the course of which they stopped off at Yokohama. And finally, by the Root-Takahira Agreement of 1908, the two nations agreed to respect each other's possessions and maintain the *status quo* in the Pacific area. The agreement included affirmations of the Open Door in China and of Chinese "independence and integrity"; but since the *status quo* now included Japanese economic control of southern Manchuria, it would appear that these statements were largely face-saving. Some authorities have argued that what it really meant was that, in return for security for American possessions in the Pacific, Japan was to have a free hand in her penetration of the mainland.

Whatever shortcomings Roosevelt may have had as a diplomat, he understood the danger (as he declared in 1910) of "adopting any position anywhere unless we can make good." "I utterly disbelieve," he said, "in the policy of bluff . . . or in any violation of the old frontier maxim, 'Never draw unless you mean to shoot!' . . . As regards Manchuria, if the Japanese choose to follow a course of conduct to which we are adverse, we cannot stop it unless we are prepared to go to war." He added that "successful war about Manchuria would require a fleet as good as that of England, plus an army as good as that of Germany."

Taft's Policies. This kind of realism was not shared by Taft and Knox, the exponents of dollar diplomacy. Reverting to the original Open Door policy, they tried to keep China open by bringing about American investment in Chinese railroads. This was largely due to the influence of a State Department official, Willard Straight, another of the Americans who have dreamed of an empire in Asia. But American bankers were not particularly eager to invest in China, and the chief result of the efforts of Taft and Knox was that Japan and Russia temporarily drew together in order to resist American penetration. When Wilson became President in 1913, he promptly stopped all government support for American investment in China. Wall Street seems to have hailed this abandonment of economic imperialism with a sigh of relief.

Wilson's Policies. World War I gave Japan opportunities that seemed too good to miss. Entering the war as an ally of Britain, she took possession of the German sphere of interest in the Chinese province of Shantung and the German islands in the northern Pacific. In 1915 she presented China with the "twenty-one demands," asking for complete control of Manchuria and Shantung and extensive powers over the rest of the country. The United States protested, but had no way of making its protests effective. In the end China conceded some of the demands but was able to postpone discussion of others.

In 1917, after the United States entered the war, the Japanese diplomat Ishii came to Washington and, by dropping hints about attractive propositions from Germany, was able to come to terms with Secretary of State Lansing. The Lansing-Ishii Agreement was another face-saving document, which had to be read carefully if its full meaning was to be appreciated. After affirming the Open Door and the territorial integrity of China, it went on to say that "territorial propinquity creates special relations" and that "Japan has special interests in China, particularly in the part to which her possessions are contiguous." The Japanese afterwards insisted that these interests were political as well as economic, and that "special" meant "paramount." Meanwhile, Wilson was becoming alarmed by Japanese ambitions, and in 1918 he reverted to the Taft-Knox policy which he had repudiated and tried to promote American investments in China. But no attempt at a definite Far Eastern settlement could be made until after Germany had been defeated.

Thus the United States continued to affirm the Open Door on paper, while declining to defend it in reality. By this time the motivations for it had changed. Originally an expansionist measure, designed to keep the Chinese market open for the expected growth of American trade and investment, it had now become primarily defensive. The actual American economic interest in China was negligible. In 1913 the United States had only $50,000,000 invested in China, bought from China only 2 per cent of her imports, and sold to China only 1 per cent of her exports. She had much closer economic relations with Japan. On the other hand, the United States feared Japanese aggression, and wished to protect China in order to maintain a balance of power in the Far East. But at no period prior to World War II was she able or willing to support her diplomatic moves in the Far East with adequate armed force.

XXVI

The Progressive Period

1. THE PROGRESSIVE SPIRIT

2. PROGRESSIVISM IN MUNICIPAL AND STATE POLITICS

3. THE ROOSEVELT ADMINISTRATION

4. THE TAFT ADMINISTRATION

5. THE WILSON ADMINISTRATION

DURING the first fourteen years of the twentieth century the intellectual and political ferment of the 1880's and 1890's produced concrete results in the form of a comprehensive movement of reform. This was represented by Presidents Roosevelt, Taft, and Wilson in national politics and by a host of different leaders in state and municipal politics.

1. THE PROGRESSIVE SPIRIT

Purposes of Progressivism. Reformers campaigned against two main evils. In the first place, they were disturbed by the growth of political corruption and by the tendency of government on all levels to give special privileges to organized wealth. Professing faith in the wisdom of the ma-

---

SELECTED BIBLIOGRAPHY: The most useful general surveys of progressivism are John Chamberlain, *Farewell to Reform* (1932), Louis Filler, *Crusaders for American Liberalism* (1939), Eric Goldman, *Rendezvous with Destiny* (1952), and Richard Hofstadter, *The Age of Reform* (1955). R. B. Nye, *Midwestern Progressive Politics* (1951), traces its development from the populist movement. *The Autobiography of Lincoln Steffens* (1931) describes the career of a leading progressive journalist. Of the various books written by intellectual spokesmen of progressivism, Herbert Croly, *The Promise of American Life* (1909), is still worth reading. Mark Sullivan, *Our Times: The United States, 1900–1925* (6 vols., 1926–35), contains masses of interesting information. K. W. Hechler, *Insurgency: Personalities and Politics of the Taft Era* (1940), and G. E. Mowry, *Theodore Roosevelt and the Progressive Movement* (1946), are important studies of political history. F. L. Paxson, *Prewar Years* (1936), deals with the Wilson administration. H. F. Pringle has written the best biographies of Roosevelt (1931) and Taft (2 vols., 1939). A. S. Link is writing a biography of Wilson, of which two volumes have appeared so far (1947–).

jority of the people and insisting that the main secret of good government was to make it possible for the people to make their wishes effective, they worked to destroy the invisible government of bosses and machines, impose higher standards of honesty, and make officials more directly responsible to the electorate. In the second place, they were alarmed by the growth of monopoly and by the exploitation of the farmers and the working class. They believed that it was the function of the government to ensure that the economic system promoted the general welfare, and advocated government regulation of big business and legislation that would give protection to exploited groups.

There was, of course, nothing revolutionary about these objectives. The progressive leaders believed in the traditional American ideals of democratic government, individual liberty, the rule of law, and the protection of private property, but they argued that maintenance of these ideals in the new industrial era required new political techniques. They strongly emphasized ethical, humanitarian, and religious values rather than attempting to stir up economic resentments and class hatreds. Proposals for any thoroughgoing transformation of the traditional political and economic system, such as were put forward by the Socialists, won little support. Progressivism was, in fact, a movement with predominantly middle-class objectives and viewpoint, deriving much of its support from small businessmen, farmers, and professional people. The typical progressive leader was some lawyer, journalist, or businessman who, aroused by corruption or misgovernment in his own community, started a crusade to elect better men to office, and gradually came to the realization that what was needed was a reform of the system as well as a change of men.

Like most earlier reformers in the British and American political tradition, the progressives had a pragmatic approach. Whenever they saw an evil, they attempted to deal with it, without adopting any comprehensive theory or formulating ultimate objectives. This method of piecemeal reform made for a maximum of agreement and prevented conflicts from becoming fanatical or irreconcilable. During the progressive period there was no clear-cut line of division between reformers and conservatives. Popular sentiment so strongly favored reform that most responsible political leaders recognized that it was necessary, although some of them wished to move much further than others. Party labels therefore became even more meaningless than usual. There were progressive Republicans and progressive Democrats, with no perceptible difference in their objectives. And although progressivism was probably strongest in the Middle Western farm belt, where it built on foundations laid by the Populist movement, it spread to all sections of the country.

Attitudes towards Government.   In so far as the progressives had faith in the wisdom of the mass of the people and wished to promote their welfare, they were essentially Jeffersonians. Yet they were agreed that in order to protect the liberties of the average citizen, it was necessary for the government to assume broader responsibilities and more positive economic functions than in the past. Thus their view of government was in many ways Hamiltonian. This change of attitude is a fact of great importance, and unless its causes are clearly understood, American political development presents a very confusing picture.

In the time of Jefferson and Hamilton the United States was primarily a country of small owners, with an abundance of unsettled land. Under such conditions equality and democracy could best be promoted by restricting the powers of government and allowing free play to individual initiative. The establishment of a wealthy upper class, on the other hand, required positive government intervention. Early American liberals were therefore generally suspicious of government and opposed to any extension of its responsibilities, while the exponents of upper-class rule and economic privilege favored strong centralized authority. But as a result of economic developments during the nineteenth century the two groups shifted their positions. With the growth of big corporations, the emergence of a large wage-earning class, and the deterioration in the position of the farmers, the average individual found it more difficult to achieve economic independence by his own unaided efforts, and began to ask for government protection. In consequence, liberal and progressive reformers, representing Jeffersonian ideals, now wanted to increase the powers of the government, while the spokesmen of big business and upper-class rule, the heirs of the Hamiltonian tradition, favored *laissez-faire* principles. Thus the original positions of the two groups were completely reversed. Throughout the twentieth century, in fact, most liberals have adopted a Hamiltonian belief in strong government, while conservatives have emphasized its dangers in language that would have appealed to Thomas Jefferson.

The Problem of Monopoly. While all progressives wished the government to assume broader economic responsibilities, they were not in agreement as to methods. The growth of monopoly was the chief economic problem of the period. What should be the final solution? One school of thought (supported, on the whole, by Theodore Roosevelt) argued that the growth of big corporations was an inevitable economic trend and that government should regulate them instead of trying to dissolve them. Another group (favored by Woodrow Wilson) laid more emphasis on prohibiting monopoly, protecting the small businessman, and enforcing effective competition. The former attitude involved a greater increase in the powers of government, while the latter was more nearly in line with traditional liberalism. On this fundamental question the progressive movement (like the New Deal a generation later) could never quite make up its mind and remained deeply divided.

The most thoroughgoing exposition of the Rooseveltian approach was *The Promise of American Life* (1909), written by the journalist Herbert Croly. Criticizing Jefferson and frankly avowing his admiration for Hamilton, Croly argued that economic injustice should be ended not by dissolving the trusts but by extending the powers of government to control them and also by building up a strong trade-union movement that would counteract the powers of business. The remedy for the special privileges of the rich, he suggested, was not to abolish them in accordance with the old Jeffersonian individualism but to give compensatory privileges to other groups in the community. Perhaps the best representative of the alternative position was the Boston lawyer Louis D. Brandeis, whom Wilson appointed to the Supreme Court in 1916. Disturbed by what he called the "curse of bigness," Brandeis believed that when any organization, whether in business or in government, became too large, it could no longer be managed efficiently, and he suggested that no corporation be allowed to control more than 30 per cent of any industry.

The Muckrakers.   In publicizing the need for reform, a leading part was played by a group of journalists known as the muckrakers, a name applied to them, in a moment of irritation, by Theodore Roosevelt. The muckrakers specialized in carefully documented exposés of fraud and graft, with emphasis on the corrupt connections between business and politics. The first example of muckraking, and one of the best, was Henry Demarest Lloyd's denunciation of trusts, *Wealth Against Commonwealth,* published in 1894; but it was not until 1902 that writing of this kind found a large audience. In that year *McClure's*, a low-priced popular magazine, published an analysis of political corruption in St. Louis by Lincoln Steffens and the first installments of a *History of the Standard Oil Company* by Ida Tarbell. The circulation of the magazine immediately skyrocketed, thereby demonstrating to alert editors that there was a large market for serious studies of current problems. During the next ten years half a dozen popular magazines vied with each other in printing articles that demonstrated the need for reform in almost every area of national life. In addition to Steffens and Ida Tarbell, the leading muckrakers were Ray Stannard Baker, Samuel Hopkins Adams, Charles E. Russell, Norman Hapgood, and Mark Sullivan.

Muckraking died away before 1914. Some of the later muckrakers became sensational and unreliable, and the public finally grew tired of them. But in its early stages the movement was of great importance in winning popular support for progressivism. There had been nothing like it before in the history of American journalism, and there has been nothing like it since.

Almost equally influential were the muckraking novels written by Upton Sinclair, Winston Churchill, David Graham Phillips, and other best-selling authors. Probably the outstanding example was Sinclair's *The Jungle*, published in 1906. The book was written to advocate socialism, but what attracted attention was a lurid (and by no means exaggerated) description of filth in the meat-packing factories in Chicago. The public alarm which it aroused enabled reformers to bring about the enactment of the Meat Inspection Act in the same year.

2. PROGRESSIVISM IN MUNICIPAL AND STATE POLITICS

PROBABLY the most impressive achievements of the progressive movement were in local government. On this level problems were simpler than in Federal politics, the corruption was more obvious, and issues could more easily be dramatized in terms that the average citizen could understand. On the other hand, local governments had limited powers. Municipal authority was often restricted by state laws, while states had to conform with the Federal Constitution as interpreted by the Supreme Court. Most progressives began as local reformers but gradually found it necessary to campaign for changes at higher levels.

City Reformers.   In municipal politics the progressives fought for honest government, city-planning, housing codes to enforce safety and health regulations in slum areas, and larger appropriations for schools, parks, playgrounds, and other improvements. During these battles they usually found that their real enemies were not the grafting politicians in the city hall but powerful streetcar and other public-utility corporations and other business groups that had obtained special privileges by corrupt methods. Organized wealth rather than the boss and the machine seemed to be the chief obstacle to reform. In consequence, many progressives soon began to advocate public ownership of streetcars and other utilities, although they usually found that this was prohibited by state laws.

The best-known of the city reformers was Tom Johnson of Cleveland, who had himself made a fortune as a streetcar owner, but had been converted into a reformer in middle life through reading the books of Henry George. Vigorous, warm-blooded, likable, and a thoroughly realistic politician, he served as Mayor from 1901 to 1907, gathered round him able and enthusiastic disciples (such as Newton D. Baker), and gave Cleveland the reputation for being the best-governed city in the United States.

There were similar reform movements in hundreds of other cities. In many of them an attempt was made to get rid of bosses and machines by abolishing the traditional form of government by a mayor and a board of aldermen and substituting a small non-partisan commission, sometimes accompanied by a city manager. By 1921 some form of commission government had been adopted in perhaps five hundred cities. But the results were unimpressive, since in a number of cities bosses soon found ways of controlling the commissions. Nor did progressivism have much effect in the three largest cities of the country. Despite occasional reform administrations, New York, Chicago, and Philadelphia continued to be governed most of the time by thoroughly corrupt machines.

State Reformers.   Pioneering examples of progressivism in state government had been provided during the 1890's by John P. Altgeld in Illinois and Hazen S. Pingree in Michigan. But the outstanding figure among the state reformers, and possibly the greatest of all the progressives, was Robert Marion La Follette of Wisconsin. An austere, comba-

tive, and somewhat self-righteous man, a little lacking in human warmth
and tolerance, La Follette inspired respect rather than affection; but few
men in the history of the United States have fought more consistently for
democratic ideals. He always showed his faith in the wisdom of the people
by appealing to their reason rather than their prejudices, and could hold
an audience by giving them statistics instead of resorting to oratory.

Entering politics soon after obtaining a law degree at the state university, La Follette from the beginning of his career was the enemy of
machine politicians and of the business interests they represented. By
1900, at the age of forty-five, he had won so much popular support that
he was able to capture the Republican nomination for the governorship
of Wisconsin and to win the election. During his six years as Governor
he provided an outstanding example of progressivism in action by pushing through the state legislature a long series of laws which became
known as the Wisconsin Idea. This included taxation of the railroads,
fixing of railroad rates on the basis of the physical value of the properties,
income and inheritance taxes, regulation of banks and insurance companies, limitation of hours of labor for women and children, a workmen's
compensation law, creation of a forest reserve, and establishment of
primary elections for the choice of party candidates.

One of La Follette's most important contributions to progressivism
was his insistence that effective regulation of business must always be
based on detailed and accurate information, for which reason he drew
scholars into the service of the state and worked closely with economists
and political scientists on the faculty of the state university. Enforcement
of the laws regulating business was entrusted to commissions composed
of experts whose main function was to collect and publicize the relevant
statistics. The main purpose of the whole program, as defined by one of
La Follette's chief allies at the state university, Charles McCarthy, was
"a new individualism" which would "give the individual a better chance
to possess property." It was thus not socialism but an attempt to maintain the original Jeffersonian ideal in the new industrial economy.

The influence of the Wisconsin Idea was felt most strongly in a block
of other Midwestern farm states, including Iowa, Minnesota, Kansas,
Nebraska, and the Dakotas, all of which had strong progressive administrations sometime before 1914. But there were similar trends in almost
every state in the Union. Of the many state governors who earned repu-
tations by sponsoring reforms, two were destined for particularly distinguished careers in national politics: Charles Evans Hughes and Woodrow Wilson. Hughes, a future Secretary of State and Chief Justice, first
attracted attention by serving as counsel for a committee set up in New
York to investigate corruption among the big insurance companies, and
was elected Governor on the Republican ticket in 1906. Wilson, a future
President, served as Democratic Governor of New Jersey from 1910 to
1912.

Extensions of Democracy. All the state reformers supported measures giving the electorate more direct power over the government in the hope of thereby diminishing the influence of political bosses. Most important was the adoption of the primary system allowing popular choice of party candidates. Originating in the South in the 1890's, this was established in thirty-seven states before 1915. A number of states, twenty-nine by 1912, also extended the primary system to the choice of senatorial candidates, and passed laws requiring their legislatures to obey the popular decision. This led to the Seventeenth Amendment, ratified in 1913, which established direct popular election of senators.

Throughout the West there was strong demand for further extensions of democracy. The principal items in this Western program were: the initiative, by which a small number, often 5 per cent, of the citizens of a state could secure consideration of a legislative proposal; the referendum, by which such a proposal could be submitted to direct popular vote; and the recall, by which elected officials could be removed from office by popular vote. The chief advocate of this kind of direct democracy was William S. U'Ren of Oregon. Twenty states eventually adopted the initiative and the referendum, twelve states adopted the recall of elected officials, and eight states adopted the recall of judges. But reformers found the results, on the whole, disappointing, since little significant legislation was ever enacted by these methods.

The Nineteenth Amendment. A much more important extension of democracy was women's suffrage. The feminist movement, initiated before the Civil War, became more vigorous after 1890, when the National American Woman Suffrage Association was founded, Carrie Chapman Catt and Anna Howard Shaw being among its principal leaders. During the progressive period an increasing number of women campaigned actively for social reforms, and most of them went on to demand political rights.

Four Western states—Colorado, Idaho, Wyoming, and Utah—gave the vote to women before 1900 (Wyoming did so as early as 1869, when it was organized as a territory). By 1914 eight more states, all of them west of the Mississippi, followed their example; and in 1916 a woman, Jeanette Rankin of Montana, was elected to Congress. Meanwhile, leaders of the movement were demanding a Federal amendment. They had their way in 1920, when the Nineteenth Amendment was added to the Constitution.

Economic Legislation. In order to curb the powers of business corporations, most of the states set up commissions to regulate (often not very effectively) the rates and practices of railroads and public utilities. Bribery of state officials was diminished by anti-lobbying and corrupt-practice laws and by the establishment of civil-service rules. Many states, moreover, enacted welfare legislation for the protection of wage-earners. Most important were the Workmen's Compensation Acts, adopted before

1920 in forty-three states, which defined more stringently the obligations of employers and set up compulsory insurance plans for the benefit of injured workers.

Attempts to limit hours of labor and fix minimum wages caused more controversy, and such laws were occasionally invalidated by the Supreme Court as contrary to the Fourteenth Amendment. But a large number of states passed maximum-hours laws for women, while two of them, Oregon and Massachusetts, also limited hours of labor for male factory workers. The Oregon law was upheld by the Supreme Court in 1917, which thereby reversed its decision in the Lochner case of 1905. By 1923 minimum-wage laws for women had been adopted in fifteen states and also in the District of Columbia; but in that year the District of Columbia law was voided by the Supreme Court in Adkins v. Children's Hospital, after which several of the state laws were similarly invalidated. The attitude of the Court toward wage and hour laws continued to be uncertain until its swing towards liberalism in 1937.

The Eighteenth Amendment. Another reform movement which won victories in the state governments was the drive for the total prohibition of liquor. After its initial advance early in the nineteenth century, this had subsided during and after the Civil War, but had acquired new impetus with the formation in 1879 of the Women's Christian Temperance Union, led by Frances Willard, and of the Anti-Saloon League in 1895. These organizations worked in close cooperation with the Methodist, Baptist, and Presbyterian churches. The Anti-Saloon League used vigorous pressure politics, and was able to swing so many votes that many politicians who were strongly "wet" in their private lives found it expedient to give public support to "dry" legislation, thereby tainting the whole movement with a political hypocrisy which helped in the end to defeat its objectives.

Rural Protestant Americans were the most responsive to prohibitionist propaganda, while most of the large cities, where Catholic and immigrant influences were strong, remained hostile. In the South the movement was strengthened by the desire of white people to enforce temperance upon the Negroes. By 1916 nineteen states, eight in the South, six in the West, and three in northern New England, had adopted total prohibition, and most of the other states had passed local-option rules allowing counties and municipalities to prohibit the sale of liquor, with the result that three-quarters of the area of the United States, containing half the population, was legally dry.

The final step came during World War I, when the need for economizing foodstuffs gave added strength to the prohibitionist cause. The Eighteenth Amendment, prohibiting the manufacture, sale, and transportation of intoxicating liquors, passed Congress in 1917 and was ratified by January 1919. Congress then passed the Volstead Act, which defined intoxicating liquor as liquor containing more than 0.5 per cent alcohol, and enforcement began on January 1, 1920. The unhappy results of this attempt to police the personal habits of the American people belong in a later chapter.

3. THE ROOSEVELT ADMINISTRATION

THE FIRST of the three progressive presidents achieved power by accident. Born into a New York patrician family and educated at Harvard, Theodore Roosevelt had spent one term in the New York legislature, had ranched in Dakota, had served as a member of the United States Civil Service Commission, as head of the New York City police force, and as Assistant Secretary of the Navy, and had written extensively on American history. His activities in Cuba during the war with Spain as second-in-command of a volunteer regiment of Rough Riders made him a popular hero, and he was then elected Governor of New York. In this position he annoyed the Republican state boss, Senator Tom Platt, by showing too much independence, and Platt determined to remove him from the governorship by having him nominated for the vice-presidency. In the 1900 election Roosevelt therefore became McKinley's running mate, despite the opposition of Mark Hanna, who pointed out that there would be "only one life between that madman and the presidency." Bryan was again the Democratic candidate; and after a campaign in which imperialism was the main issue, McKinley was re-elected with a slightly larger majority than in 1896. In September 1901 McKinley was assassinated by a demented anarchist, and Roosevelt thus succeeded to the presidency.

Roosevelt is one of the most controversial characters in American history. During his lifetime he was idolized by a large personal following. But since his death his reputation has diminished, and many contemporary historians are no longer willing to rank him as one of the great presidents. Possibly the reaction against him has gone too far, and the balance needs to be redressed. His concrete achievements in domestic affairs were, in fact, meager; but there can be no doubt that he introduced a new spirit into Federal politics. He was shocked by the low ethical standards prevalent among businessmen and by their apparent conviction that they were independent of the laws and the government. Although he had no desire to make fundamental changes in the economic system, he believed that business must be compelled to conform to higher standards, since otherwise American institutions might be endangered by a growth of revolutionary sentiment. Roosevelt's main importance was that he was the first president since the rise of the big corporations to insist on the principle of government supremacy over business. He was also the first Republican president since Lincoln to assert strong executive leadership. The infectious gusto with which he went about his duties, his superb showmanship, and his talent for coining pungent phrases did much to stimulate popular interest in politics, while his varied intellectual enthusiasms elevated the whole tone of national life. No other president except Jefferson had been so keenly interested in learning and the arts. It was true, as the more extreme progressives complained, that he was actually much less of a reformer than he sounded; that he would make radical speeches and then come to terms with the conservatives; and that he had a personal vanity and egotism which prevented him from being just to men who disagreed with him. But in spite of his failings he did more than anybody else to arouse and give direction to progressivism.

When Roosevelt became President, conservatism was well entrenched in Congress, under the leadership of Aldrich in the Senate and Speaker Joseph G. Cannon in the House. Roosevelt continued to work with these spokesmen of the business point of view, and retained McKinley's Cabinet. But he quickly showed that he proposed to introduce a new spirit into the administration of the Federal government. While his first term contained little important legislation, it saw the initiation of a campaign to enforce the Sherman Act, intervention in a coal strike to bring about a settlement by negotiation, and strong support for conservation.

Having impressed the electorate, if not the party bosses, with his achievements, Roosevelt had no trouble in 1904 in securing nomination for a second term. The Democrats, deserting Bryan, made a bid for business support by choosing as their candidate an undistinguished New York conservative, Judge Alton B. Parker. But in spite of Roosevelt's trust-busting, big business still preferred the Republicans and contributed generously to their campaign fund. Having the advantage in both money and popular appeal, Roosevelt won the 1904 election with the unprecedented popular plurality of nearly 2,500,000. During his second term he was considerably bolder in support of progressivism, while Congress responded by strengthening the Interstate Commerce Commission through the Hepburn Act and passing the Meat Inspection and Pure Food and Drug Acts.

Enforcement of the Sherman Act.   Roosevelt's trust-busting campaign began in March 1902, when he ordered the Attorney General to bring suit under the Sherman Act against the Northern Securities Company. This had been organized by two railroad magnates, James J. Hill and Edward H. Harriman, with the assistance of the House of Morgan, in order to monopolize the railroad lines of the Northwest. This was the first time that the Federal government had shown any serious intention of enforcing the Sherman Act. The Supreme Court ruled in favor of the government, and Roosevelt then went on to attack a number of other trusts, including Standard Oil. During his seven and a half years in office he was responsible for a total of forty-three cases.

Roosevelt's trust-busting crusade aroused great popular enthusiasm and equally violent indignation among the corporation magnates. Yet its economic results were not impressive. The trusts were compelled by court decisions to dissolve themselves into their component parts, but these parts could not be transferred to different ownership, or compelled to compete with each other. The different sections of Standard Oil and the other trusts made informal "community of interest" agreements with each other for stabilizing prices and production, and there was no real revival of competition. The Supreme Court, moreover, gradually whittled down the Sherman Act. In the Northern Securities case it agreed, contrary to the wording of the act, that the defendants should not be held guilty of a misdemeanor and subject to criminal penalties. In the Standard Oil case (which did not reach the Court until 1911) the justices interpreted the act as prohibiting only "undue" and "unreasonable" restraint of trade. Under what circumstances a monopoly was unreasonable was for the Court to decide.

Roosevelt recognized the inadequacy of trust-busting. Declaring that he was not opposed to big business as such, but making a distinction between good and bad trusts, he said that "we draw the line against misconduct, not against wealth." As an ultimate solution he favored regulation of corporations by the Federal government instead of by the states, and prohibition of various specific forms of misconduct; but bills to this effect were rejected by Congress. But Roosevelt believed that the most important requirement was simply to assert the principle of government supremacy. "These men," he declared in his *Autobiography*, "demanded for themselves an immunity from governmental control which, if granted, would be as wicked and as foolish as immunity to the barons of the twelfth century." "The absolutely vital question was whether the Government had power to control them at all."

Strengthening the ICC. Having made the Sherman Act more than a dead letter, Roosevelt proposed also to strengthen the other main instrument for Federal regulation of business, the Interstate Commerce Act. In 1903 Congress passed the Elkins Act requiring railroads to adhere to their published rates and forbidding them to give rebates. This act had the support of the railroad men and was directed against business corporations like Standard Oil which had obtained competitive advantages by forcing the railroads to ship their goods at preferential rates. During Roosevelt's second term several corporations were fined for securing rebates, but fully effective enforcement of the act proved to be impossible.

A much more important progressive objective was to bring about the reduction of excessive rates. Roosevelt during his second term recommended that broad powers over rates be given to the Interstate Commerce Commission; but when his more drastic proposals were blocked in the Senate, he agreed to compromise. The result was the Hepburn Act of 1906. This authorized the Commission to order a reduction of unreasonable rates; but a railroad could then appeal to the law courts, in which case the reduction could not go into effect until and unless the courts decided that it was reasonable. On the other hand, the burden of proof was now placed upon the railroad and no longer upon the Commission. Possibly the most important feature of the Hepburn Act was that the Commission was empowered to prescribe a uniform system of book-keeping for all railroads and was thus, for the first time, able to find out what they were really doing and whether their profits were excessive.

Most progressives regarded the Hepburn Act as wholly inadequate and blamed Roosevelt for his willingness to compromise with the Senate conservatives. In view of the notorious conservatism of the courts, they were particularly disappointed by the provision for judicial review, and asked for some clear definition of what constituted a "reasonable rate," preferably one based not on the nominal capitalization of the roads but on the real physical value of the properties. Nevertheless, the Hepburn Act, in spite of its obvious weaknesses, was followed by thousands of complaints against high rates by shippers to the Commission, and prepared the way for measures in later administrations giving it full power over rates.

The Coal Strike. Roosevelt's intervention in the coal strike was notable chiefly because it set a new precedent. The miners in the anthracite coal fields were one of the most exploited groups in the United States. In 1902, under the able and dynamic leadership of John Mitchell, they struck for higher wages, a nine-hour day, and union recognition. By the autumn coal was becoming scarce, and the Federal government had to intervene. But whereas previous presidents, like Hayes in 1877 and Cleveland in 1894, had intervened in labor disputes only on the side of the employers and against the workers, Roosevelt intervened in order to bring about a settlement by negotiation. The mine-owners, who had an essentially feudal attitude towards their workers, refused to negotiate with Mitchell, but were finally induced to accept arbitration by a government commission. This included a trade-union representative, who (to get around the stubborn prejudices of the owners) was officially described as an "eminent sociologist." Although union recognition was not accorded until 1916, the workers received higher wages and a nine-hour day.

Conservation. Probably Roosevelt's most important contribution to national welfare was his encouragement of conservation. He was the first president to realize the vital importance of this question. Public-land policies had hitherto been administered by officials in whom (as he declared) "the habit of deciding, wherever possible, in favor of private interests against the public welfare was firmly fixed." With the enthusiastic assistance of Gifford Pinchot, director of the Forest Service, Roosevelt endeavored to inculcate a different attitude. He added about 130,000,000 acres to the forest reserves (as authorized by the act of 1891) and also withdrew from entry (with doubtful legality) nearly 90,000,000 acres of land containing coal, phosphates, and water-power sites. He also helped to secure passage of the Newlands Act of 1902. Superseding the Carey Act of 1894, which had not proved very effective, this authorized the

Federal government directly to establish irrigation projects on arid lands and created a Reclamation Service to supervise them. Since the passage of the act the government has constructed in the Western states a number of dams which are among the most impressive engineering projects in human history. In many other ways, most notably through the White House Conference of 1908, Roosevelt publicized the need for government action to protect and develop the country's natural resources. Thanks largely to his leadership, the American people began to realize that the time had come to establish checks on the wasteful individualism characteristic of the pioneering period.

The only other important laws passed during Roosevelt's administration were the Meat Inspection Act and the Pure Food and Drug Act, both in 1906. The former (inspired by Upton Sinclair's *The Jungle* but pushed through Congress by Roosevelt's leadership) provided for Federal inspection of factories packing meat for interstate commerce. The latter (the product of a long series of startling investigations by chemists working for the Department of Agriculture) prohibited the sale of certain harmful foods and ordered that medicines containing dangerous drugs be correctly labeled. Since few consumers understood the meaning of the labels, and since nothing was done to stop fraudulent advertising, this measure by no means purified the drug industry. Both acts, however, marked another break with strict *laissez-faire* doctrine, according to which consumers were supposed to be capable of protecting themselves. Roosevelt urged upon Congress a number of other, and much more drastic, proposals for political and economic reforms, but was unable to overcome the opposition of the old-guard Republican leadership.

4. THE TAFT ADMINISTRATION

LIKE most strong presidents, Roosevelt was able to choose his own successor. For the 1908 election he secured the Republican nomination for William Howard Taft, who had been his Secretary of War since 1904. The Democrats, for the third and last time, nominated Bryan. Promising to continue faithfully in Roosevelt's footsteps, Taft was elected with a popular plurality of 1,270,000.

A native of Cincinnati, Ohio, Taft had spent thirty years in a wide variety of Federal offices and had served with distinction in all of them. But he was not a very effective president. Anybody who succeeds a Roosevelt in office is likely to seem tame and uninspiring by contrast, and Taft did not have the qualities needed to overcome this initial handicap. A large, friendly, good-humored man, weighing about 350 pounds, he lacked both the dynamic personal force and the political subtlety needed for successful leadership. Temperamentally better suited for a judicial position, he was reluctant to take the initiative or assert executive responsibility, and had none of Roosevelt's capacity for inspiring newspaper headlines. In consequence, he did not receive credit even for what he did accomplish.

Taft was unfortunate, moreover, in taking office at a time when the Republican Party was splitting into two factions. A number of Midwestern progressives had now been elected to Congress. Headed by La Follette in the Senate and George W. Norris of Nebraska in the House, they were rebelling against the old-guard leadership of Senator Aldrich and Speaker Cannon, and hoped for Taft's support. Confronted by a dilemma that was probably insoluble, Taft, like Roosevelt before him, continued to cooperate with the official party leaders rather than with the progressive bloc. In consequence, the progressives soon began to denounce him as a conservative and a tool of predatory business interests. According to Senator Dolliver of Iowa, he was "an amiable man, completely surrounded by men who know exactly what they want."

Progressive Legislation. In reality, more was accomplished during the four years of the Taft administration than in the seven and a half of Roosevelt's. The popular demand for reform was now so strong that even the old-guard leaders recognized the need for making concessions; and Taft loyally supported most progressive proposals except when he felt that he was prevented by legal obstacles. He had more respect than Roosevelt for the letter of the laws and the Constitution and was reluctant to interfere with the prerogatives of Congress.

The Taft administration was responsible for dissolving ninety trusts, as contrasted with Roosevelt's record of forty-four. Meanwhile, Congress passed a long series of progressive laws. The ICC was further strengthened by the Mann-Elkins Act of 1910, which gave it the power to suspend rate increases for ten months pending a decision as to whether they were reasonable. Conservation was promoted by the enactment of laws separating the ownership of minerals in the subsoil from the ownership of the surface and providing for the lease rather than the sale of minerals in public land. Over the protests of private business interests complaining of "socialism," a postal savings bank and a parcel post were instituted. Political corruption was checked by laws requiring that campaign expenditures and contributions to party funds be made public. The Sixteenth Amendment, authorizing an income tax, and the Seventeenth Amendment, providing for popular election of senators, were added to the Constitution. These and other measures made an impressive record; and although in some instances (notably with the Mann-Elkins Act) Congress went further than Taft desired, most of the program had his support.

Conflicts in the Republican Party. On two major issues, however, Taft definitely sided with the conservatives, thereby laying himself open to violent attacks from the progressive bloc in Congress. The first of these was the tariff. All reformers felt that the Dingley Tariff of 1897 was much too high, enabling big business to charge exorbitant prices.

Roosevelt had avoided the problem, but Taft had promised reduction during his campaign for the presidency. But when Congress was asked to draft a new tariff bill, Aldrich and other senatorial conservatives failed to honor this promise. The Payne-Aldrich Tariff of 1909 reduced duties only on articles in which there was no possibility of foreign competition, and actually raised the rates on wool, sugar, and a number of other commodities. Half a dozen progressive senators fought a long battle against the bill, showing in careful detail that it would mean still higher profits for big business, but were unable to prevent it from being passed. Taft sharply disappointed them first by refusing to give them any support and then by signing the bill instead of vetoing it. He made matters worse when he described it as "the best tariff bill that the Republican Party has ever passed."

The other issue involved conservation. Taft sincerely believed in protecting the country's natural resources, but had more respect than Roosevelt for the letter of the law. His Secretary of the Interior, Richard A. Ballinger, restored to public entry certain water-power sites in the Northwest that Roosevelt (with doubtful legality) had placed in the forest reserves, and also threw out charges of fraud that had been made in connection with the acquisition of coal lands in Alaska by private interests. These actions aroused the suspicions of Gifford Pinchot, whose zeal for conservation approached fanaticism, and of an official in the General Land Office, Louis R. Glavis. Having failed to convince Taft, Pinchot and Glavis publicly denounced Ballinger as a tool of predatory business, and were then dismissed from the government service for violating the rules of official discipline. How far Ballinger was actually deferential to business interests, and how far he was motivated simply by respect for the law and the legitimate rights of property-owners, is still a controversial question. But most of the progressives supported Pinchot and Glavis and concluded that Taft's Secretary of the Interior was betraying the public welfare.

In the spring of 1910 the progressives in the House of Representatives won a major victory when, under Norris's leadership, they succeeded in stripping Speaker Cannon of much of his power to control debates. Cannon, like his predecessor "Czar" Reed, had dominated the House by nominating a majority of the members of the Rules Committee, which decided what business should be discussed. Norris won a majority vote for a proposal that the Rules Committee should henceforth be elected by the members of the House.

Meanwhile, progressivism was steadily gaining in popular strength. The elections of 1910 brought impressive Democratic and insurgent victories. The Democrats won a majority in the House of Representatives, while most of the states west of the Mississippi came under the control of Progressive Republicans. It was obvious that in the next presidential election public sentiment would demand a leader much more dynamic and more strongly committed to the progressive cause than Taft had proved to be.

The Fight for the Nomination.   Early in 1911 a National Progressive Republican League was formed with the purpose of winning control of the Republican Party and preventing Taft from being renominated. The most obvious progressive candidate was La Follette, and in the summer he began to campaign for the nomination. But La Follette had little popular support outside the Middle West; despite his impressive accomplishments he had remained a sectional rather than a national leader. Middle-of-the-road reformers, moreover, regarded him as too radical and doctrinaire. It was obvious that Roosevelt, with his magnetic personality and vast popularity and his moderate record as President, would be a much more effective candidate. But would Roosevelt be willing to break with the man whom he had himself chosen as his successor and assume leadership of the progressive bloc?

Roosevelt was willing. Only fifty years of age when he left office, and still brimming with energy and ambition, he found the role of unemployed ex-President extremely irksome. After seeing Taft inaugurated, he had gone on an extended visit to Africa and Europe. After his return to the United States over a year later, he was surrounded by men, such as Pinchot, who told him that Taft was betraying the progressive cause and it was his duty to return to active politics. In the summer of 1910 he made a number of speeches, nominally in order to help the Republicans in the congressional election; but he now advocated reforms much more drastic than any he had sponsored as President, and his position seemed to be almost identical with that of the Midwestern progressives. Conservative criticisms and deviations from his policies on the part of the Taft administration made him steadily more belligerent and more radical. Early in 1912, after a group of Republican state governors had invited him to become a candidate, he announced that his hat was in the ring. La Follette's chances, already weakened by an emotional breakdown during a speech at Philadelphia, were now ended.

Roosevelt was unquestionably the preference of a majority of the Republican voters, but the conservatives controlled the party machinery. When the Republican convention met in Chicago in June 1912, Roosevelt had a majority of the delegates from those states, thirteen in number, which had adopted the presidential primary. But in the other states the delegates had been nominated by the party organizations and were predominantly for Taft. A number of states had sent rival delegations, but the credentials committee, probably with adequate legal justification, seated the Taft groups. Taft was then renominated on the first ballot. Meanwhile Roosevelt had ordered his followers to leave the convention, declaring that he had been tricked out of the nomination by fraud and that Taft had "forfeited the right to win the support of any honest man."

Having lost their fight to capture the Republican machinery, Roosevelt's supporters now organized a third party. The Progressive Party was launched at Chicago in August by a curiously assorted group of delegates, held together by little but a common admiration for the glamour of Roosevelt's personality. Alongside genuine progressives from the Middle West and Far West and social reformers of all kinds, including many from what Roosevelt had once called the "lunatic fringe," there were a number of wealthy Easterners, such as the former Morgan partner George W. Perkins and the newspaper-owner Frank Munsey, who regarded Roosevelt's radical speeches as window-dressing and judged him by his record. After Roosevelt had been nominated for the presidency, the proceedings ended on a religious note with the singing of "Onward, Christian Soldiers." The bull moose became the symbol of the new party.

From the viewpoint of progressive Republicanism the Bull Moose movement was an unhappy mistake. This was clearly recognized by La Follette, who refused to support it. Its only results were to ensure a Democratic victory and leave the conservatives even more firmly in control of the Republican Party. Being chiefly the expression of a single man's ambition, the Progressive Party had no lasting vitality. In 1916 Roosevelt deserted his followers and returned to the Republican fold, and the Progressives were then left with no alternative but to follow his example.

The Democratic Victory. Meanwhile, the Democrats had found a new leader who appeared to have Bryan's eloquence and democratic idealism without his intellectual deficiencies. Woodrow Wilson, native of Virginia, historian and political scientist, and President of Princeton from 1902 to 1910, had first been suggested as presidential timber in 1906 by certain Eastern conservatives who wanted to end Bryan's control of the Democratic Party and re-establish the principles of Grover Cleveland. They were impressed by Wilson's forceful personality and by his stirring (though somewhat vague) appeals for higher standards of political morality. At this period Wilson was avowedly hostile to Bryanism and showed little sympathy for the economic reforms advocated by progressives. In 1910, after being defeated in a struggle to reorganize the university, Wilson resigned from Princeton and was elected Governor of New Jersey. His election was due to a deal between his conservative backers and the bosses who controlled the party machine; but Wilson promptly asserted his independence of both groups, thereby incurring vehement charges of ingratitude, and forced through the state legislature a series of reforms which won the applause of liberals throughout the country. Contact with practical politics had changed him from a preacher of rhetorical generalities into a leader of the progressive movement. When the Democratic convention met at Baltimore, in 1912, the two leading contestants were Wilson and Champ Clark of Missouri. That Wilson was finally nominated was due largely to the support of Bryan.

Progressivism reached its high-water mark in the 1912 campaign. Taft plainly had no chance of re-election, the main contest being between

Roosevelt and Wilson. Both men proposed to revitalize democracy by limiting the powers of big business, but they differed in their remedies. Roosevelt advocated a "square deal" and a "new nationalism"; asserting that large corporations were economically necessary, he proposed that they be regulated by the Federal government. Wilson, as befitted a Southerner and a Democrat, was closer to the Jeffersonian tradition. His "new freedom" called for limiting the powers of big corporations, protecting the rights of small owners, and maintaining effective competition. Such a program had a strong appeal throughout the agricultural sections, and was supported by many progressives even in the industrial East.

Wilson, winning 42 per cent of the popular vote, polled fewer votes than Bryan had done in each of his three unsuccessful campaigns. But with the Republicans split between Taft and Roosevelt, he carried forty states. Six states voted for Roosevelt and only two (Vermont and Utah) for Taft. This election also marked the greatest relative strength ever achieved by socialism in the United States. Eugene Debs, candidate of the Socialist Party, received 900,000 votes, nearly 6 per cent of the total. In no subsequent election did any Socialist candidate even approach this percentage.

5. THE WILSON ADMINISTRATION

DURING his early academic career Wilson had written extensively about the American government and had criticized the division of responsibility between executive and legislative authorities and the consequent lack of coherent, clearly formulated programs. His remedy had been strong presidential leadership, similar to that of the prime minister in the British parliamentary system. When he took office in March 1913, he put his own recommendations into practice. Until his breakdown in 1919 he guided national policy even more decisively than Roosevelt had done. In consequence, both his virtues and his weaknesses had a profound effect on American history.

Descended from Presbyterian ministers of Scotch-Irish stock, Wilson had the strength of will and the moral idealism often associated with this Calvinist heritage. He saw life as a battle between good and evil, and was convinced that the cause of righteousness must eventually triumph and that its champions should never compromise or submit. Appealing always to the noblest motives, never to prejudice or economic interest, he could arouse men to duty and self-sacrifice with speeches that vibrated with a solemn and deeply moving eloquence. During the early years of his administration the American people responded to his rhetoric and his sense of moral purpose, and the whole tone of national life seemed to be elevated and purified. But this lofty note could not be sustained indefinitely. And as opposition increased, Wilson's faith in his own ideals began to degenerate into a self-righteous obstinacy; he seemed to feel that men who opposed him were opposing God. He lacked the suppleness and humility that had enabled Lincoln to work with those who disagreed with him. Wilson had never been very effective in personal contacts; his strength was in the study and on the platform, not in the give-and-take of discussion; although he was capable of gaiety and warm affection with personal friends, he struck most people as cold and reserved. In the end he was to be the most badly defeated president since Andrew Johnson.

Bryan was still the most influential figure in the Democratic Party, and his support was essential. Wilson therefore appointed him Secretary of State, but took charge of foreign affairs himself whenever there was a crisis. But for assistance and advice Wilson relied mainly on a personal friend who held no political office; this was Colonel Edward M. House, a wealthy Texan whom he had first met in 1911. In Congress most of the important committee chairmanships were assigned to Southerners. For the first time since before the Civil War the South seemed to be again in power.

Wilson did not wholly fulfill his campaign promises. Big corporations continued to dominate the American economy. Yet during a period of only a year and a half his administration was responsible for more important legislation than any of its predecessors except those of Washington and Lincoln.

Tariff Revision. The first task that Wilson presented to Congress was revision of the tariff. Lower rates, he declared, would deprive American business of its monopoly of the American market; in order to compete with foreign business, it would have to lower its prices and increase its efficiency. The Underwood Tariff, which became law in October 1913, marked the first real reduction since the Civil War. Duties were abolished on more than a hundred articles, and reduced on nearly a thousand others, the average rate being cut from 37 to 27 per cent. In order to compensate for the expected loss of revenue, the act included a small income tax, recently authorized by the Sixteenth Amendment. But the effect of tariff reduction on the American economy could not be properly assessed, since in 1914 international trade was disrupted by the outbreak of World War I.

The Federal Reserve System. Second on the legislative list came the Glass-Owen Federal Reserve Act, passed in December 1913, which reformed the monetary system. Currency reform had long been demanded by the farmers, and was recognized as necessary even by Eastern conservatives. The system set up by the National Bank Act of 1863 had two major weaknesses. In the first place, since the quantity of bank notes in circulation was limited by the quantity of government bonds held by the banks, the supply of currency had no relation to the need for it. There was no provision for increasing the quantity of notes in proportion to the increase in the volume of business, so that money was likely to be scarce, especially in the South and West. In the second place, each of the nation's 30,000 banking institutions was separate and independent and had to rely solely on its own resources during times of financial pressure, with the result that bankruptcies were distressingly frequent.

Conservatives wanted a central bank controlled by the bankers, along Hamiltonian lines. But the Wilson administration, faithful to the Jacksonian tradition, insisted that banking must be decentralized, so that money would no longer be concentrated in the Northeast, and that control must belong to the government, not to private financiers. Twelve Federal Reserve banks were therefore set up in different regions, while supervision of the whole system was entrusted to a Federal Reserve Board, consisting of the Secretary of the Treasury, the Comptroller of the Currency, and five other members to be appointed by the president for ten-year terms. All national banks were required, and state banks were invited, to become members of the new system.

The bank notes that had circulated under the old system were now to be replaced by Federal Reserve notes. These were to be obtained by member banks from the Federal Reserve banks in exchange not only for bonds or gold but also for eligible commercial paper. This provision, it was hoped, would cause the supply of notes to expand or contract in proportion to the volume of business. And since the reserves of all member banks were to be deposited in the Federal Reserve banks, it now became possible for the country's banking capital to be mobilized in order to give aid to institutions which might be in danger.

One other important objective, it was hoped, would be achieved through the Federal Reserve System. This was to check excessive loan expansion, and thereby prevent a dangerous credit inflation, during boom periods. The Federal Reserve Board could curb inflation in two ways. By selling government bonds and commercial paper and withdrawing from circulation the money so obtained, it could decrease the quantity of currency. And by raising the rediscount rate on the commercial paper given it by member banks, it could indirectly force an increase in the current rate of interest. If the members of the Board used these powers with discretion, they could do much to even out the business cycle. But much depended on the human factor. Contracting the quantity of money and raising interest rates during a boom period were likely to be decidedly unpopular measures, and the Board would have to be capable of resisting political and business pressures in favor of continued easy money.

By 1915 the Federal Reserve System controlled about half the nation's banking capital, and by 1928 the proportion had risen to 80 per cent. But most of the smaller state banks preferred to remain independent. The system proved to be a considerable improvement over previous banking practices, although it did not altogether succeed in preventing bank failures, even of member banks, or in controlling the business cycle. This was partly because the members of the Federal Reserve Board

ALT WHITMAN,
THOMAS EAKINS
844–1916)

Painted in 1887. Eakins
ad much in common with Whit-
an and his Americanism and
und the poet a congenial
bject.

THE GULF STREAM, *by* WINSLOW HOMER (1836–1910)

After an early career as a magazine illustrator, Homer, in 1884, settled in a Maine fishing
lage and became perhaps the greatest of American painters of the sea.

AGRICULTURAL HALL, COLUMBIAN EXPOSITION, CHICAGO, 1893

The Chicago Exposition checked the growth of the new functional style of architecture and restored the vogue of classicism.

ROBIE HOUSE, DESIGNED *by* FRANK LLOYD WRIGHT (1869—)

This house was built in Chicago in 1908 for Frederick Carlton Robie. Its clear simple lines and lack of irrelevant ornamentation are typical of the best functional buildings.

(most notably in the years immediately preceding the crash of 1929) did not always make good use of their power to check credit inflation.

Anti-trust Legislation. The third item on Wilson's program was revision of the Sherman Anti-trust Act. In September and October 1914 Congress passed the Federal Trade Commission Act and the Clayton Anti-trust Act. The Federal Trade Commission (FTC), modeled on the ICC, was to police business practices, with power to issue "cease and desist" orders, against which corporations might, if they chose, appeal to the courts. The Clayton Act specified as illegal a number of practices tending to prevent competition. It also included two sections which Samuel Gompers described as the Magna Carta of labor. Section 6 exempted labor unions from the anti-trust laws, and Section 20 restricted the use of injunctions and declared that strikes, boycotts, and picketing were not contrary to any Federal law. The Wilson administration continued the trust-busting campaign initiated by Roosevelt, bringing a total of ninety-two cases in eight years; but it hoped that, through supervision by the FTC, the problem of monopoly would be solved by prevention rather than by cure. Between 1915 and 1921 the Commission issued 788 formal complaints and 379 cease-and-desist orders.

The later years of the Wilson administration were not wholly devoid of progressive legislation: in 1915 the La Follette Seaman's Act improved labor conditions on board ship; in 1916 the Adamson Act established an eight-hour day for employees of interstate railroads; and in the same year the Federal Farm Loan Act set up twelve Federal Land Banks which were to make mortgage loans available for farmers at relatively low rates of interest. But the progress of reform had been checked by the outbreak of World War I in August 1914. Attention was now concentrated on the economic disturbances caused by the war and on the problems of foreign policy. World War I marked the real end of the progressive movement as a dynamic force in national affairs.

Results of Progressivism. The progressives had not, of course, brought about any major transformation of the political and economic system, nor had such been their intention. They had concentrated on a series of specific reforms, most of which had been achieved by 1914. In politics they had done much to revitalize democracy by making officials more directly responsible to public sentiment. In the economic sphere they had failed to find any solution to the problem of monopoly, but they had extended the power of Federal and state governments to regulate big business (mainly through the appointive commissions, like the ICC and the FTC), to check the exploitation of labor, and to conserve natural resources.

Perhaps more important than any specific reforms was the growth of a new attitude. A notable result of the progressive movement was that both political and business leaders became much more concerned with securing popular approval and support than they had been in the late nineteenth century. It was significant, for example, that business corporations found it necessary henceforth to present their activities in a favorable light by spending large sums on public relations. This meant, of course, that the effectiveness of the progressive reforms, as of democratic institutions in general, depended in the last resort on the enlightenment of the voters and on their capacity for appraising propaganda.

XXVII

The First World War

1. THE ROAD TO BELLIGERENCY
2. THE UNITED STATES AT WAR
3. THE TREATY AND THE LEAGUE

ALTHOUGH the United States had been increasingly concerned with international power politics for a generation prior to 1914, most Americans had continued to assume that they could remain aloof from European alliances and conflicts. But after the outbreak of World War I they discovered that their political, economic, and cultural ties with European countries were stronger than they had realized, and that continued isolation involved risks and sacrifices which a majority of them were unwilling to assume. After nearly three years of precarious neutrality the United States was finally drawn into the conflict as a full belligerent. This proved to be the beginning of a new trend in American foreign policy, only temporarily interrupted by an attempted return to isolation in the 1920's and 1930's, which led finally to American leadership in Western civilization.

1. THE ROAD TO BELLIGERENCY

The Outbreak of the War.   Whole libraries have been written about the causes of World War I, and each side has tried to prove that it was

SELECTED BIBLIOGRAPHY: F. L. Paxson, *Pre-War Years* (1936) and *America at War* (1939), give the general history of the period. The most thorough studies of the causes of the war are S. B. Fay, *Origins of the World War* (1928), and B. E. Schmitt, *The Coming of the War* (1930), the latter being decidedly more anti-German than the former. C. C. Tansill, *America Goes to War* (1938) is the most thorough study of American policy up to 1917, but is strongly isolationist in tone, as also is Walter Millis's very readable *The Road to War* (1935). Charles Seymour, *American Diplomacy During the World War* (1933), is more favorable to Wilson. The most useful study of the Versailles Treaty is Paul Birdsall, *Versailles Twenty Years After* (1941). Wilson's policies and the victory of the isolationists are described in T. A. Bailey, *Woodrow Wilson and the Lost Peace* (1944) and *Woodrow Wilson and the Great Betrayal* (1945).

brought about by its opponents. But from an objective viewpoint the whole long controversy about war guilt appears rather meaningless. The fundamental cause of the war was the division of the world into independent sovereign states and the growth of nationalist and imperialist rivalries among them. Although there were groups in all the major European countries who wanted war, no country can fairly be accused of deliberately planning it.

The immediate precipitating factor was the tension within the Austro-Hungarian Empire, which held dominion over a number of Slavic peoples in the Danube basin who wanted autonomy. On June 28, 1914, the heir to the throne was murdered by a Slav nationalist. The Austrian government believed, with good reason, that the murder had been encouraged by officials of the small Balkan kingdom of Serbia, and demanded extensive powers over Serbian internal affairs. Serbia, fearing the loss of her independence, refused full compliance, and on July 28 Austria declared war. The extension of Austrian power in the Balkans threatened to disturb the whole European balance, and as a result of the system of alliances one country after another was pulled into the controversy.

Russia, supporting Serbia, ordered mobilization, and was in turn supported by France, while Germany sided with Austria. Since the war plans of the German army called for the defeat of France before Russia was ready, Germany could not afford to wait once the Russians had started to mobilize. After failing to obtain assurances of neutrality, Germany therefore declared war on France, and in accordance with previous plans her army marched through Belgium. Up to this point the British had remained uncommitted, though it was obvious that they could not afford to allow the French to be crushed. German violation of Belgian neutrality ended their hesitation, and on August 4 they entered the war in the conviction that they were fighting not merely to preserve the balance of power but also for the rights of small nations and the rule of law in international affairs. Subsequently Bulgaria and Turkey joined the Central Powers, while Japan, Italy, Rumania, and Greece (in return for secret promises of territorial gains) entered the war on the side of the Allies.

The German army almost won the war in the west during the first six weeks, but was stopped in September in the battle of the Marne. After this both sides settled down to four years of dreary trench warfare, during which tens of thousands of young men were often slaughtered to gain a few miles of territory. Neither side was able to win any decisive victory, and the high command on both sides sacrificed human lives on a scale unprecedented in all history. For a long time the same kind of stalemate prevailed on the Russian and Italian fronts. Meanwhile, the British used their sea power to blockade Germany in the hope of starving her into surrender, and the Germans retaliated by sending out submarines to sink Allied merchant ships.

American Attitudes. The war can be regarded as a fusion of two different conflicts, each of which had a thousand years of history behind it: the conflict between the Teutonic and Slavic peoples for domination of eastern Europe, and the conflict between Germany and the Franco-British combination for the domination of western Europe and also for maritime and colonial supremacy. Had the war been fought solely in eastern Europe, American sympathies would probably have been mainly with Germany. Russia was known as a backward and despotic country where Jews and other racial and religious minorities suffered persecution. But American attention was concentrated on the conflict in the west.

Although at the outset of the war almost everybody assumed that the United States would remain neutral, and nobody proposed intervention, a considerable majority of the American people quickly became committed to the cause of Britain and France. This was due not only to the strong ethnic and cultural ties between the United States and Great Britain but also to considerations of national interest. Since the beginning of the century the two nations had drawn steadily closer together, and all outstanding diplomatic differences had been settled by agreement.

On the other hand, Germany's drive for colonies and her aggressive methods of diplomacy had aroused growing alarm and antagonism in the United States. The German government was only partially democratic, and the tradition of Prussian militarism, represented by the Kaiser and the army leaders, appeared as a threat to American ideals of popular government and the rule of law. The fundamental reason for the eventual entry of the United States into the war was the belief of a majority of the American people that a German victory would endanger their interests, institutions, and ideals. The specific diplomatic controversies about the submarine campaign which actually precipitated the entry were of only secondary importance; in fact, as isolationists have frequently pointed out, the American government, from early in the war, treated German violations of international law with much more severity than those committed by the British.

President Wilson assumed direct control over American policy, and his personal convictions were therefore of special importance. To some extent he oscillated between two different attitudes which he could never wholly reconcile. On the one hand he believed that there were rights and wrongs on both sides of the European conflict, that a lasting peace must be a peace without victory for either side, and that the United States should maintain an impartial attitude and act as mediator. On the other hand he had strong personal sympathies for the cause of the Allies, and believed that they were much less to blame than the Germans. He felt that the German government had no respect for international law or the rights of other nations, and that German victory would therefore be a catastrophe which the United States must prevent, if necessary, by entering the war. As early as the autumn of 1914 he was saying privately that

"England is fighting our fight." A German victory, he told the British ambassador, would compel the United States to "give up its present ideals and devote all its energies to defense, which would mean the end of its present system of government." In this statement Wilson summarized the basic motivation of American policy.

While a considerable majority of the American people unquestionably agreed with Wilson in wanting Germany to be defeated, a strong minority —how many it is impossible to say—continued up to the end to advocate strict neutrality. Most of them were pacifist or genuinely isolationist, while a few were pro-German. Ancestry often seemed to be the deciding factor, since, while most Americans of British descent were pro-Ally, those of German, Irish, or Scandinavian origin were often isolationist or pro-German. There was least sympathy for the Allies in the rural Middle West. While this was, in part, a reflection of the feeling of many Midwestern farmers that Europe was far away and her conflicts of no concern to Americans, it was also connected with the fact that many areas had been settled largely by Germans and Scandinavians. Another factor in the Midwestern attitude was the belief, inherited from the Populists, in the sinister powers of international bankers, supposedly located chiefly in London.

Since nobody of any consequence advocated entry into the war on the side of Germany, the debate was between support for the Allies and neutrality. But the isolationist or pacifist was not easy to distinguish from the pro-German; and since the pro-Germans gave money and support to anti-war organizations, many people soon came to the conclusion that anybody who opposed American entry was working for the German government. This was one reason for the intolerance and hysteria that disfigured American life during 1917 and 1918.

Controversies with Britain.   The British blockade of Germany violated several rules of international law and presented Wilson with problems similar to those that had confronted American governments during the French Revolutionary and Napoleonic Wars. According to international law, only goods destined for the use of armed forces were liable to seizure as contraband; yet the British endeavored to stop all trade between Germany and the outside world. They also illegally extended their blockade to cover Holland and Scandinavia, refusing to allow goods to be shipped to these countries unless it could be proved that they were not in "continuous voyage" to Germany. These blockade regulations caused a number of American ships to be stopped and their cargoes confiscated.

Defending the doctrine of freedom of the seas, the American government made protests against the blockade; but they were worded mildly, and it was obvious that the main purpose was to placate indignant American traders rather than win concessions from the British. As Wilson remarked to his private secretary, he would not "take any action to embarrass England when she is fighting for her life and the life of the world." In December 1914, for example, the British were asked not to interfere with American trade "unless such interference is manifestly an imperative necessity to protect their national safety." Wilson never put pressure on Britain by threatening reprisals. Meanwhile, the American minister in London, Walter Hines Page, was so strongly pro-British that he sometimes advised the British Foreign Secretary, Sir Edward Grey, how to answer the American protests. Grey afterwards declared that "Page's advice and suggestions were of the greatest value in warning us when to be careful or encouraging us when we could safely be firm." Throughout the entire war, in fact, Britain did not make a single concession of any importance.

Some of Wilson's critics have argued that he could best have served the cause of humanity by insisting on strict adherence to international rules limiting the powers of belligerents, the main purpose of which had been to protect civilians from the horrors of warfare. But the whole eighteenth-century conception of limited warfare had now become meaningless. World War I was a total war, fought between nations and economic systems; and the traditional distinction between the soldier and the civilian was disappearing. The farmer and the factory worker were as much a part of the war effort as the man in the trenches. In seizing all goods in transit for Germany, whether for armed forces or for civilians, the British were simply responding to the necessities of the situation. The nature of war had changed (very much for the worse) since international law had been formulated.

Controversies with Germany.   The German submarine campaign began in February 1915. Wilson declared that Germany would be held to "strict accountability" if any American ships or lives were lost, and the submarines were given orders not to attack neutral ships. When two American vessels were attacked by accident, Germany at once offered compensation. But the question of American lives was more complicated. British passenger ships as well as freighters were liable to attack; and since they often carried munitions, the Germans could claim that they had valid reasons for sinking them. But among the passengers who lost their lives were some Americans. On March 28 one American was drowned in the sinking of the *Falaba*. And on May 7 the liner *Lusitania* was sunk without warning with a loss of 1,198 lives, of whom 128 were American. The news caused a burst of indignation in the United States, and many people demanded immediate war. Wilson was not yet ready to abandon neutrality, but he took a stand which, more than any other single factor, made American entry into the war ultimately inevitable.

The sinking of the *Lusitania* was a shocking event, but some of the contentions of the American government were of doubtful validity. In the first place, Wilson insisted that Americans who chose to travel on British ships were still under the protection of the American government.

This claim was legally questionable and certainly contrary to common sense. In the second place, he declared that submarines must not sink British merchant ships without giving persons on board time to escape. Wilson overlooked the fact that the merchant ships usually carried guns and had orders to attack any submarines they sighted, and that according to international law ships armed with offensive weapons might be sunk without warning. There were thus serious weaknesses in Wilson's arguments. His misreading of international law was due partly to pro-Ally sympathies and partly to a feeling that the submarine campaign, with its destruction of civilian lives, was a barbarous method of warfare. Each new device for killing people, of course, always seems barbarous until the human race becomes accustomed to it. Wilson, however, had the support of almost all his advisers, the only exception being William Jennings Bryan. Bryan resigned from the State Department in June 1915 and was succeeded by the strongly pro-Ally Robert Lansing.

Controversy about the submarine campaign continued for nearly a year. The German government ordered the submarines not to attack passenger ships, but refused to agree that such sinkings were illegal. Then, in March 1916, a submarine commander violated orders and sank the French passenger ship *Sussex* without warning. This brought matters to a head, and Wilson threatened to break off diplomatic relations unless Germany promised that no more ships would be sunk without warning. The German government gave way and made the required pledge, but added that it might reconsider its decision unless the British modified their blockade rules. Wilson had thus won a diplomatic victory and incidentally, by compelling Germany to abandon unrestricted submarine warfare, had made a substantial contribution to the Allied cause. But he had also deprived the United States of full freedom of action; if the submarines should again start sinking ships without warning, she would be virtually compelled to enter the war.

During the early months of 1916 the United States seemed close to belligerency. Wilson privately discussed entry into the war with congressional leaders at a so-called "sunrise conference." Meanwhile, his friend Colonel House visited Europe to explore the possibility of ending the war through American mediation, and drafted a plan by which Britain would ask the American government to invite both sides to a peace conference, with the understanding that if peace were not obtained on terms favorable to the Allies the United States would probably join them as a belligerent. But the British, who were still hoping for military victory on the western front, refused to adopt any plan involving negotiations with the enemy; and when Germany abandoned unlimited submarine warfare, Wilson swung back to a more neutral position. By the summer and fall of 1916 he was less sympathetic to the Allies than at any previous period.

Belligerent Propaganda.   Meanwhile, the pro-Ally sentiment among the American people was steadily becoming stronger. A growing number of people felt that the United States had a moral obligation to put an end to the slaughter and destruction, and that the only way to end it was by an Allied victory. How far this attitude was due to British propaganda is an unanswerable question. Since the British controlled the Atlantic cables and censored all mail coming out of Germany, they were able to ensure that American newspapers reported the war mainly from the Allied side. They also conducted an elaborate and well-organized propaganda campaign to win over American opinion, the stories of alleged German atrocities committed in Belgium and elsewhere being especially influential. But such propaganda was effective only because many Americans were already emotionally committed to the Allied cause.

Germany also engaged in propaganda, spending a total of $35,000,000 in the United States during the period of American neutrality; but nobody not already pro-German seems to have been favorably influenced by it. German agents, moreover, tried to check American assistance to the Allies by encouraging strikes and sabotage in American factories. Their efforts were often extraordinarily inept, and they also made the mistake of being found out. The most notorious example was in June 1915, when a German agent left a brief case bulging with confidential documents on an elevated train in New York. This was promptly picked up by an American secret service agent, and its contents were made public. These and other examples of German meddling in American internal affairs seemed to all supporters of the Allies to be convincing proof that Germany had no proper respect for the rights of other nations.

Trade with the Allies. Pro-Ally sentiment was greatly strengthened by the growth of close economic ties. While the British blockade kept trade with the Central Powers down to negligible proportions, vast quantities of American goods were shipped to Britain and France. Down to March 1917 the Allies spent more than $2,000,000,000 on munitions in the United States, and even larger sums on civilian goods, especially foodstuffs. Total American exports, which had never reached $2,500,000,000 in any peacetime year, amounted by 1916 to nearly $5,500,000,000. The result was to create a war boom in the United States. The year 1914 had been a depression year, but by 1916 almost every branch of the American economy was in a state of feverish prosperity, and both profits and wages reached unprecedented heights.

Initially the Allies paid for their purchases in cash, partly by shipping gold to the United States and partly by selling American securities owned by their citizens. But by the summer of 1915 their financial reserves were close to exhaustion, and it was obvious that they could not continue buying unless they could borrow money. Wilson, who had originally refused to sanction lending, now gave way, and the Allies floated a series of loans which by April 1917 had reached a total of more than $2,000,000,-000. The House of Morgan handled the operations in return for commissions, but the money was contributed by some 500,000 American citizens.

Thus the United States became an arsenal for the Allies. Without American economic assistance, in fact, it is almost certain that they would have lost the war. Germany protested that the United States was acting unneutrally, and demanded an embargo on munitions. But the American government replied that sales to the Allies were not contrary to international law, and that it would be unfair to change the rules in the middle of a war. This, of course, was true. The economic strength of the United States meant that whatever she did or failed to do would necessarily aid one side or the other, and strict impartiality was impossible.

Thus the United States had acquired a strong economic interest in Allied victory. If the Allies had to stop buying American goods or repudiate their war debts, many Americans would suffer financial losses, and the whole country would probably plunge into a depression. There was serious danger of this by the spring of 1917, by which time the Allies were finding it more difficult to float loans in the United States and were beginning to need direct financial help from the American government. It is therefore possible that economic factors alone might eventually have pulled the United States fully into the war, even if the Germans had not settled the question by adopting unlimited submarine warfare. This does not mean, however, that the isolationists were correct in blaming the bankers and munitions manufacturers for American entry into the war. It was not only a few rich men but a large proportion of the American people who were making more money because of Allied purchases. It should also be realized that these economic ties were the consequences, as well as the causes, of pro-Ally sentiment, since Americans would not have supplied the Allies so extensively, or bought their war bonds, if they had not already wanted them to win the war. The House of Morgan, according to one of its partners, "had never for one moment been neutral; we didn't know how to be. From the very start we did everything we could to contribute to the cause of the Allies." Many other Americans felt the same way.

The Re-election of Wilson.   The year 1916 was an election year; but since there was no essential difference between the Republicans and Democrats in their attitudes towards the war, the campaign had little meaning. The Democrats renominated Wilson, and found that "He kept us out of war" made an effective slogan. Undoubtedly many people regarded this as a promise for the future; but Wilson himself was careful to avoid commitments. "There may at any moment come a time when I cannot preserve both the honor and the peace of the United States," he had declared in January. The Republican candidate was Charles Evans Hughes, who had formerly served as Governor of New York and Associate Justice of the Supreme Court. Theodore Roosevelt, who was now belligerently pro-Ally and had been accusing Wilson of cowardice because he had not yet asked Congress to declare war, refused to head a third-party ticket again and urged his Progressive followers to vote for Hughes. Some

Republican spokesmen appealed to the pro-German vote by denouncing Wilson as too pro-Ally, while others blamed him for remaining neutral and demanded immediate war. In actuality, the attitudes of the two candidates towards the war were virtually identical. In spite of the return of the Progressives to the Republican Party, Wilson was re-elected with a popular plurality of 600,000.

Immediately after the election Wilson set out to explore the possibility of a negotiated peace by asking both sides to state the terms for which they were fighting. But the replies showed clearly that neither side was willing to settle for anything less than total victory. Wilson then formulated his own conception of a satisfactory peace. In a speech delivered on January 22, 1917, he called for a peace without a victory for either side; self-determination for all nationalities; the freedom of the seas; limitation of armaments and abolition of entangling alliances; and a system of collective security to make aggression impossible. He summarized his ideas by asking for a world-wide Monroe Doctrine.

Entry into the War. This was Wilson's last opportunity to assume the role of mediator. On January 31 the German government announced that unlimited submarine warfare would be adopted in the seas around Britain and France, and that neutral as well as belligerent ships entering this war zone would be sunk. The United States was to be permitted to send one passenger ship a week to Britain, provided it carried no contraband and was clearly marked with red and white stripes. This decision was made by the German army and naval leaders, now virtually in control of the government, in the belief that they could starve Britain into submission, and that American entry into the war would make little difference to the military situation. The United States government immediately broke off diplomatic relations, and, rather than allow American ships to be excluded from the war zone, determined to arm them for defense against submarine attacks. This decision, announced on March 12, meant that the shooting was about to begin.

Many Americans, including Wilson himself, though strongly pro-Ally, had hoped that belligerency could somehow be avoided. During February and March they were reluctantly driven to the conclusion that there was no alternative. In February the Zimmermann note, intercepted and decoded by the British, revealed that Germany was inviting Mexico and Japan to join her in an attack on the United States. The first American ship was sunk on March 12. During the next three weeks five more ships were sunk, with the loss of twenty-five American lives.

Meanwhile, one of the major causes of Wilson's indecision was removed by a revolution in Russia. The Czar was forced to abdicate in March, and for the next eight months (for the first and last time in its history) Russia had a liberal government favoring Western ideals of democracy and constitutionalism. Thus Allied victory would no longer lead to the domination of eastern Europe by the reactionary czarist regime. Wilson could now interpret the war as a struggle of the democracies against Prussian autocracy.

On April 2 Wilson sent a message to Congress, declaring that the submarine campaign, the sabotage plots of German agents in the United States, and the Zimmermann note made war unavoidable. War was declared on April 6, the vote being 82–6 in the Senate and 373–50 in the House. The opposition came mostly from Midwestern progressives, such as La Follette and Norris, who believed that Britain was as guilty as Germany and that the United States was being pulled in by bankers and munitions manufacturers. There can be no question that once the decision had been made, a large majority of the American people welcomed it with a sigh of relief.

The Americans entered the war in a somewhat unrealistic frame of mind, largely as a result of the rhetoric with which Wilson rationalized the decision. Many of them believed that they were fighting not only to defeat Germany but also to create a new world order in which war would be abolished. When these hopes were not realized, the sense of disillusionment was acute, and many people drew the conclusion that entry into the war had been a mistake—an attitude which had a pervasive influence on American public opinion for the next twenty years. The wisdom of the American decision is indeed a debatable question, but it is important to recognize the real reasons for it. The basic reason was a conviction that a German victory would endanger the United States.

2. THE UNITED STATES AT WAR

Mobilization of Men and Resources.   The American people now set about mobilizing all their energies and resources for victory. Opposition to the war disappeared, except among a small group of radicals; and almost everybody accepted a regimentation of activities and opinions that would have seemed incredible at any earlier period. People took pride in the fact that a democracy, once it had come to a decision, could discipline itself even more thoroughly and effectively than an autocracy.

War preparation was inevitably a painfully slow process. Although Congress had provided for increases in the army and navy during the summer of 1916, relatively little had been accomplished before the United States became a belligerent. It was therefore more than a year before much military assistance could be given to the Allies. In the end a large part of the American preparation proved to be unnecessary. Plans were made on the assumption that war would continue at least until the end of 1919, and when Germany surrendered in November 1918, the United States was just beginning to fight. The American government drafted at least four times as many men as were actually needed, and spent vast sums on ships and war equipment that were never used.

It was decided to resort immediately to conscription, not because of any lack of enthusiasm for war service but so that the government could select those persons best fitted for it. The Selective Service Act, which became law on May 17, set up the system of registration, followed by winnowing by local draft boards, that was again adopted during World War II and after. Ultimately 2,750,000 persons were drafted into service, all of them men without wives or dependents. Some 750,000 men were in the army, navy, and national guard at the outset of the war, and 1,250,000 men volunteered, so that a total of 4,750,000 served in the armed forces. Persons with religious scruples were exempted or assigned to non-combatant duties.

The most essential American contributions to Allied victory were economic. By 1918 total industrial production was 38 per cent higher than in 1913. Except in the field of airplane-production, where there was serious mismanagement, all the needs of the war program were finally met with remarkable success.

At the outset of the war six major committees were set up to supervise the more vital branches of economic activity, the most important of them being the War Industries Board. These were responsible to the Committee of National Defense, the chairman of which was the Secretary of War, Newton D. Baker. During 1917 there was too much division of authority, and the government was too reluctant to use its coercive powers, so that war production became badly snarled. The situation improved after March 1918, when Bernard M. Baruch became chairman of the War Industries Board. An independent financier who had made a fortune on Wall Street, he had great administrative ability, was free from entangling alliances with other businessmen, and could work in harmony with President Wilson. Efficient production was further promoted by the passage in May of the Overman Act, which gave the government almost unlimited powers over industry.

Since the increase of production now had to take precedence over all other considerations, the government completely reversed its peacetime policies; instead of trying to enforce competition and to police corporation practices, it virtually entered into partnership with big business. In making contracts for munitions and other war materials, it adopted a general policy of paying the cost of production plus a reasonable profit, in the belief that haggling about prices would be too time-consuming. It recognized that corporations would probably make excessive profits by padding their production costs, but hoped that these could be recovered through taxation. As during the Civil War, government purchases stimulated the growth of big business, thereby undoing much of what had been accomplished by the trust-busting of the progressive period. The high profits earned by the big corporations and the advent of a new crop of millionaires evoked criticism; but business was stimulated to speedier production, which was obviously the most immediate objective. Some of the industrialists who entered government service were guilty of feathering their own nests; but on the whole, in spite of the vast sums being spent, there was less corruption than in any previous war in American history.

Although private industry handled most of the production program, there were some vital areas where the government had to assume direct control. The railroads were leased from their owners at the end of 1917 and operated by the government as a single system. And the pressing need of the Allies for ships to replace those sunk by the submarines was met by setting up a government-owned Emergency Fleet Corporation. In 1914 the United States had had less than 1,000,000 tons of shipping engaged in foreign trade. By September 1918 the Emergency Fleet Corporation controlled more than 8,500,000 tons, most of which was obtained through purchases from neutrals and seizure of German vessels interned in American ports. A vast program of new construction was also under way, but little of it was actually completed before the end of the war.

The submarine campaign also made increased food-production a vital necessity. Herbert Hoover, a mining engineer who had earned a great reputation by supervising Belgian relief early in the war, became Food Administrator, and a Government Grain Corporation was set up to buy the total wheat crop at a high fixed price. Assured of a market and substantial profits, farmers increased their wheat acreage from 45,000,000 in 1917 to 75,000,000 in 1919. Total agricultural production increased during the war years by 24 per cent over 1913, while exports of breadstuffs, meat, and sugar more than tripled, but the ultimate effect on the farmers was unfortunate. During the war years many of them incurred heavy debts in order to buy new land, much of it submarginal. After the war, when Europe resumed normal production, the agricultural boom collapsed, and the farmers found themselves compelled to meet wartime debts out of peacetime prices.

The government did not try to control general price levels, and by 1918 they were nearly twice as high as in 1913, which meant severe hardships for middle-class citizens with fixed incomes. On the other hand, labor fared well. Gompers and other union leaders agreed to prevent strikes and keep production running smoothly, and were promised, in return, government support for an eight-hour day, collective bargaining, and wage increases to keep pace with the rise in prices. Corporations engaged in government contracts made little objection to raising wages, since the cost could be passed on to the government. By the end of the war about half the industrial workers had gained a basic forty-eight-hour week, with extra pay for overtime, and union membership had increased by about 25 per cent. While wages lagged behind in some industries, for the country as a whole they actually rose slightly faster than the cost of living, so that the average worker was a little better off than in 1913. After the war, wage rates remained relatively stable, in spite of a sharp fall in prices, so that by 1922 the average real wage was 16 per cent higher than in 1913. This was the most rapid rise in real wages in American history.

Between April 1917 and June 1920 the American government spent on war purposes a total of $32,000,000,000. Of this sum, $10,350,000,000 represented loans to other countries, mainly for purchases in the United States, and was supposed ultimately to be repaid; the remainder was spent directly by the American government. One-third of the cost of the war, roughly the same proportion as in the Civil War, was paid immediately through increased taxes, while the other two-thirds was added to the national debt. A series of five war loans floated by the Treasury brought in a total of nearly $21,000,000,000.

Civil Liberties. The worst effect of the war on American life was the growth of intolerance. As Wilson himself told a friend the evening before he sent his war message to Congress, "to fight you must be brutal and ruthless, and the very spirit of ruthless brutality will enter into the very fibre of our national life." For several years this gloomy prediction seemed to be true. The government itself did much to whip up hysteria through its Committee on Public Information, headed by George Creel. Creel's official purpose was to tell the truth, but the truth, as seen in 1917 and 1918, was very one-sided, and the Committee flooded the country with pamphlets and public speeches accusing the Germans of starting the war and publicizing their alleged atrocities. Popular hostility to everything German assumed the most fantastic forms, including the banning of German music and literature.

Only a handful of radicals opposed the war. Yet popular opinion insisted that anybody who said anything tending to discourage the war effort was a menace and must be suppressed. In June 1917 Congress passed an Espionage Act imposing penalties for making disloyal statements. This was strengthened by the Sedition Act of May 1918. These laws were enforced by agents of the Department of Justice and by judges and juries who seemed to have totally forgotten the American tradition of civil liberties. A total of 1,597 persons were arrested under the Sedition Act, and while the vast majority were eventually released for lack of evidence, some of them (including the Socialist leaders Eugene Debs and Victor Berger) received long prison sentences. An even more alarming manifestation of hysteria was the growth of mob violence against persons suspected of radicalism.

At no earlier period in American history, not even during the worst crises of the Civil War, had public opinion been so thoroughly regimented and controlled. Suppression of anything that volunteer patriots chose to regard as un-American continued, moreover, for more than a year after the end of the war, long after all possible justification for it had disappeared.

A number of cases under the Espionage and Sedition Acts reached the Supreme Court in 1919. While the Court generally affirmed the convictions, thus showing that it could not be relied upon to defend civil liberties in a time of popular hysteria, the cases were made memorable by the dissenting opinions of Justice Holmes. In the Schenck case (involving an attempt to obstruct recruiting) he upheld the conviction but took occasion to declare that only "a clear and present danger" could justify abridgment of free speech. In the Abrams case (in which five persons were sentenced to jail, three of them for twenty years, for circulating a Communist leaflet) he wrote a dissenting opinion which was one of the most eloquent defenses of free speech in American history.

Military Operations.   For more than a year after the United States entered the war the Germans were perilously close to victory. Their submarines sank Allied merchant ships with appalling rapidity, and it was not until the summer of 1918 that the British and American navies definitely won the upper hand and saved Britain from the threat of starvation. German armies overran the Balkans and won smashing victories on the Russian front. In November 1917 the Communists under Lenin's leadership seized power in Russia and began peace negotiations, and by the Treaty of Brest-Litovsk, signed in the following March, the Communist government surrendered to Germany vast stretches of western Russia and dropped out of the war.[1] Germany could now concentrate almost all her forces on the western front in the hope of striking a knock-out blow before the United States was ready. General John J. Pershing, commander of the American Expeditionary Forces, had reached France with a handful of regulars in June 1917, but as late as March 1918 there were still only 300,000 American troops in France.

The Germans began their offensive on March 21, but although they drove deep salients into the Allied lines, they failed to break through completely. Meanwhile, American troops were rushed across the Atlantic and into the battle lines at a rate which soon exceeded 300,000 a month. Used as reinforcements wherever they were needed, they played a major part in checking the German attacks. Then, on July 17, the offensive abruptly came to a standstill before it had won a decisive victory, and the more discerning German leaders knew that the war was lost. General Foch, who had been appointed in April to the supreme command of all the Allied armies, immediately ordered counter-attacks.

The Allies still had nearly four months of hard fighting, but they retained the initiative. The main American contribution was a series of victories in the country north of Verdun, where Pershing took command

[1] The fear that the Germans would take possession of all Russia caused the Allies during 1918 to send expeditionary forces to several parts of the country. The British and French subsequently gave some aid to Russian monarchists fighting against the Communists. American troops participated in expeditions to Siberia and to Murmansk, but had strict orders from Wilson not to take any part in the Russian civil war. The chief function of the contingent sent to Siberia was to watch the Japanese, who were suspected of wanting to appropriate Russian territory for themselves.

WOODROW WILSON

  Taken in 1911 and 1932, shortly before each man was elected to the presidency, these photographs epitomize the difference in character between the two democratic leaders.

FRANKLIN D. ROOSEVELT

BROOKLYN BRIDGE, NEW YORK CITY & HOOVER DAM, NEVADA

Brooklyn Bridge, completed in 1883, remains a lasting example of the aesthetic possibilities of modern engineering.

Initiated during the Hoover administration and completed in 1937. This and other dams, built in Western and Southern states by the Federal government, rank among the largest and most beneficent engineering projects of all time.

of a separate American army, afterwards split into two as its numbers increased. While the British attacked along the line of the Somme and the French up the valley of the Oise, the Americans captured the German fortress of Saint-Mihiel and fought battles in the wooded hill country of the Argonne. By the second week of November the retreat of the enemy was becoming a rout. At the same time other Allied armies were advancing in Turkey and the Balkans and on the Italian front.

The Fourteen Points. Meanwhile, German civilian morale was cracking. This was due primarily to the British blockade and to a realization that victory was now impossible, but Woodrow Wilson also made an important contribution by sponsoring moderate peace terms. In all his speeches he insisted that the United States was fighting against the German government rather than the German people, that her purpose was justice rather than vengeance, and that she wished to make the world safe for democracy. Publicized in all the countries of the world (including Germany) through the efforts of George Creel, Wilson's peace aims were used for psychological warfare.

On January 8, 1918, Wilson (at Creel's suggestion) summarized his objectives in a series of Fourteen Points. This famous statement combined certain broad ideals, expressed in very general terms, with proposals for specific territorial changes. Six of the points presented ideals, which included open covenants of peace, openly arrived at; freedom of the seas; removal of economic barriers between nations; reduction of armaments to the lowest point consistent with domestic safety; an impartial settlement of colonial claims; and a general association of nations. The other eight points declared that Germany must evacuate the Russian, Belgian, and French territories she had occupied, and that the principle of national self-determination must be applied to the Austrian and Turkish empires, the Balkans, and Poland. Having made no agreement with the British and French governments, Wilson spoke only for himself and (presumably) the United States. But the German people could hope that his peace terms represented the program of all the Allies.

The End of the War. In October the German government indicated that it was willing to accept a peace based on the Fourteen Points. Britain and France insisted, however, on two modifications: they could not accept the freedom of the seas; and Germany must pay reparations for damages done to civilians. Meanwhile, Foch was appointed to draw up armistice terms that would make any renewal of the war by Germany impossible. On November 11, 1918, Foch's armistice terms were accepted, and the fighting ended. Revolution had already broken out inside Germany; on November 9 the Kaiser had fled to Holland, and the Social Democrats had taken over the government.

The war had cost mankind 10,000,000 lives and an accumulation of wealth estimated at close to $200,000,000,000. The United States lost relatively little man power; less than 50,000 Americans were killed in action, as contrasted with 1,600,000 Germans, 1,385,000 French, and 950,000 British. But she paid about one-sixth of the economic costs.

Yet the vast material losses caused by the war were quickly repaired. Much more shattering were its psychological effects. The war undermined the confidence of Western man in the ideals of freedom, rationalism, and progress that had guided him since the Enlightenment. In the long run its most significant result proved to be the establishment in Russia of a Communist dictatorship which proposed to create utopia by means of the most savage violence and repression. This first totalitarian state soon had its Fascist and Nazi imitators. Instead of establishing democracy, World War I seemed to have fatally weakened it over large areas of the European continent.

3. THE TREATY AND THE LEAGUE

The Peace Conference.   The peace conference opened at Paris in January 1919. Wilson headed the American delegation, and did not invite any spokesmen of the Senate or any of the leaders of the Republican Party to accompany him. Convinced of the righteousness of his own ideals, he did not wish to be hampered by associates who might disagree with him. He believed that once the treaty had been drafted, the Senate would not dare to refuse ratification. This was a serious error of judgment, particularly in view of the fact that the Republicans had won control of both houses of Congress in the elections of 1918 and had made it plain that they would oppose Wilson's proposal for a League of Nations.

The major decisions of the conference were thrashed out by a council of four, consisting of Wilson, Clemenceau of France, Lloyd George of Britain, and Orlando of Italy. Their meetings consisted largely of a long battle between the American and the Frenchman, with the British and Italian representatives playing minor roles. Clemenceau was a match for Wilson in force of character, and was equally devoted to human freedom; but he had radically different ideas about the peace settlement. Wilson, with his American faith in the binding force of moral and juridical principles, believed that if a just settlement were made, satisfying the legitimate claims of both sides, the peoples of all nations would be willing to defend it. No aggressor would then dare to challenge the collective will and conscience of mankind, so that war could be prevented forever. Clemenceau, on the other hand, with Gallic pessimism, was convinced that no settlement, however just, would be voluntarily accepted by the Germans, who would always want to dominate Europe. Peace could therefore be maintained only by force, and the conference must weaken Germany and strengthen France. While liberal idealists throughout the world looked to Wilson for leadership, the mass of the British and French peoples, embittered by the deaths of two million of their young men, supported Clemenceau and demanded a peace of vengeance.

Wilson's main victory was the establishment of a League of Nations. A number of different Allied statesmen had been advocating a league since the beginning of the war, but Wilson was the principal author of the League Covenant, which was drafted during February. The basic principle of the Covenant was that all the nations of the world should promise to settle disputes peacefully and protect each other against aggression. Article 10 guaranteed each member-nation against loss of territory or independence through aggression; Article 12 provided machinery for the peaceful settlement of disputes; and Article 16 prescribed economic sanctions, followed if necessary by military action, against any state resorting to war in violation of the Covenant. The authority of the League was divided between an Assembly representing all member-nations and a Council consisting of five great powers and four other states to be elected by the Assembly. There was, of course, no transfer of sovereignty; the League was essentially a league and not a world government, and had no coercive power of its own. Its effectiveness would therefore depend, in practice, on the willingness of nations to accept the existing distribution of power and territory and to prevent it from being changed except by peaceful methods.

The details of the settlement were worked out in March and April. Clemenceau did not secure all his objectives, but the peace was closer to his ideas than to Wilson's. Germany was stripped of her navy and her colonies, forbidden to maintain an army of more than 100,000 men, deprived of Alsace-Lorraine in the west and the Polish territories in the east, declared guilty of having caused the war and ordered to pay the Allies the full cost of it. The total amount of reparations was left undecided until two years later, when it was fixed at $33,000,000,000. The German colonies were divided among the victorious powers, Britain getting the major share; in theory they were to be held as mandates under League supervision, but in practice this differed little from outright annexation. In separate treaties made with Germany's allies, the Austrian and Turkish empires were broken up, and a number of new or newly enlarged states established in eastern Europe.

The territorial items in the Fourteen Points were, on the whole, fulfilled (though some of the new states contained large ethnic minorities who were denied the right of self-determination). But the severe treatment of Germany, especially the confiscation of her colonies and the requirement that she pay the complete cost of the war, was clearly contrary to Wilson's program. Nothing was done to carry out his more general ideas, such as disarmament and the removal of economic barriers, nor did Wilson himself put forward any practicable plan for doing so.

The Debate in the Senate.   The treaty with Germany was signed at Versailles in June 1919 and submitted to the United States Senate during July. The Senate was divided three ways. Forty of its members, all of them Democrats, favored unconditional ratification. At the other extreme were thirteen or fourteen thoroughgoing isolationists, headed by William E. Borah of Idaho and Hiram Johnson of California. The remainder, most of them Republicans, were for ratification with reservations. Many members of this last group were by no means isolationists, but had a number of plausible objections to the Covenant of the League. They felt chiefly that the United States should not limit her freedom of action by pledging herself, in all instances, to adopt sanctions against aggressors. But mingled with these valid doubts about the Covenant were some less legitimate motivations. Many of the reservationists wanted to assert the authority of the Senate, humiliate Woodrow Wilson, and discredit the Democratic Party in order to assure a Republican victory at the next election. Thus a vital question of national policy became a football of party politics. The leader of the reservationists was Henry Cabot Lodge of Massachusetts, Chairman of the Foreign Relations Committee, whose distrust of the principles embodied in the League of Nations was sharpened by a strong personal antagonism to Woodrow Wilson.

While the Foreign Relations Committee gave a hearing to anybody who objected to any aspect of the treaty, Wilson carried his case to the people. Leaving Washington for the West on September 3, he delivered thirty-seven speeches and traveled eight thousand miles during the next twenty-two days. On September 26, while crossing Kansas, he had a paralytic stroke which left him a sick man for the remainder of his term of office. Thus the cause of the League was left without effective leadership.

In November the Foreign Relations Committee recommended ratification with fourteen reservations. The most important were that the United States could not undertake to apply economic or military sanctions against aggressors without the consent of Congress, and that the United States alone could interpret her powers and responsibilities under the Monroe Doctrine. Wilson believed that these reservations would fatally weaken the League and urged the Democrats in the Senate to vote against them. This refusal to accept compromises was probably a mistake. The defeat of the treaty was due, in the end, not only to the political skill of its opponents but also to the obstinacy of its supporters.

The division of the Senate into three groups made it impossible to secure a two-thirds majority either for the treaty with reservations or for the treaty without reservations. In the final vote, in March 1920, there was actually a majority of 49 to 35 for ratification with reservations (some of the Democrats having refused to follow Wilson's advice); but this was still seven votes short of the necessary two-thirds majority. Thus it was the small group of isolationists, who voted consistently against ratification in any form, whose views ultimately prevailed. Since it was the whole treaty, not merely the Covenant of the League, that had been defeated, the United States was still legally at war with Germany, and it was not until the summer of 1921 that peaceful relations were officially resumed.

The Election of 1920. In the presidential election of 1920 the Democrats gave their nomination to James A. Cox, former Governor of Ohio, with the young Franklin D. Roosevelt, Assistant Secretary of the Navy, as his running-mate, and called for unconditional adherence to the League. But the Republican position was much less definite, since the party contained both isolationists and reservationists. The platform repudiated Wilson's League but promised support, in vague terms, for some kind of "association of nations" which would fulfill the same purposes while safeguarding American sovereignty. After the Republican convention had been deadlocked by the leading contestants, the nomination went to a dark-horse candidate picked by a small group of party bosses, Senator Warren G. Harding of Ohio.

As in many American elections, the issues were by no means clear. While Johnson and Borah urged the election of Harding because he would keep America out of the League, anti-isolationist Republicans promised that he would take America into the League on the basis laid down by the Senate reservationists. Harding himself gave utterance only to soothing generalities which his supporters could interpret as meaning almost anything they pleased. "America's present need," he explained, "is not heroics but healing; not nostrums but normalcy; not revolution but restoration; . . . not surgery but serenity." The result was an overwhelming victory for the Republicans, with the unprecedented popular plurality of 7,000,000.

In spite of the Republican double talk, it seems probable that the immense vote for Harding was largely an expression of isolationist sentiment. The American people, having entered the war in the belief that it was a crusade for international righteousness, were disillusioned by its results and beginning to feel that perhaps they should never have abandoned neutrality. Victory was followed by a general moral let-down, a distrust of all idealisms, and hostility towards the British and French and foreigners in general. All the European powers now seemed equally greedy and imperialistic. Why should the United States undertake to protect a settlement so plainly unjust as the Versailles Treaty or become involved again in the apparently interminable cycle of European wars? She could best serve the cause of humanity by refusing to be drawn into other people's quarrels and building a higher civilization within her own borders. In 1920 this attitude, as expressed by men like Senator Borah, had great popular appeal. After Harding became President, no more was heard about any "association of nations." The United States would assume no commitments to protect the Versailles settlement or oppose aggression, nor could Britain and France count on American assistance in any future conflict with Germany.

Results of the American Decision.   In retrospect, it does not seem likely that American membership in the League of Nations would have made that organization effective. Although this was not appreciated in 1919, the really important underlying question was whether the United States would continue to act with Britain and France in defense of the settlement her armed forces had helped to win. By her refusal to assume commitments, the United States helped to create a general sense of instability that led in the end to another division of the world into two hostile alliances.

The ultimate effect of the Treaty of Versailles was to create a sharp division between those powers that were satisfied with the settlement and those that wanted to revise it. The settlement was supported mainly by Britain and France in western Europe and by four of the new states in eastern Europe—Poland, Czechoslovakia, Rumania, and Yugoslavia. In addition, one of the defeated powers, Turkey, eventually joined this *status quo* group. Germany remained the chief revisionist power, since Austria and Hungary were left too small to cause trouble. But two of the victorious powers, Italy and Japan, were unsatisfied with the gains they had made at Versailles; they also became revisionist, and eventually joined forces with Germany. Another potential troublemaker was Communist Russia, although her expansionist ambitions did not become manifest until 1939. Thus a number of powerful nations were unwilling to abide by the principles of the League of Nations, and were determined to overthrow the Versailles settlement, if necessary by force.

The central European problem was that Germany, owing to her population, resources, and industrial development, was potentially strong enough to dominate the continent and by no means willing to accept an inferior, or even an equal, position. There was no solution to this problem unless the United States continued to throw her weight into the European balance by supporting Britain and France, as she had done during the war. If Britain and France had been assured of American support during the 1920's, they could have safely removed Germany's more legitimate grievances against the Versailles settlement (such as reparations), thereby strengthening those groups among the German people who wanted peace and friendship with other nations. Lacking such support, the French were left in a state of insecurity which made them unwilling to consider any revision of the Versailles Treaty; and by trying to keep Germany in an inferior status, they stimulated a nationalistic indignation which led in the end to the establishment of the Nazi dictatorship.

19. America's Expanding Population

THE MAP IN THE CENTER OF THE PAGE INDICATES THE FRONTIER LINE AT DIFFERENT periods from 1800 to 1880. In 1800 the settled area included the Atlantic seaboard states, except for Florida and part of Georgia in the South and parts of Maine and New York in the North. By 1830 the frontier had been carried into southern Illinois, Missouri, Arkansas, and Louisiana, but the Ozark hill country in southern Missouri and northern Arkansas remained unsettled. By 1860 most of the Eastern half of the country had been occupied, and there were also pockets of settlement in Colorado and New Mexico, in Utah, and around San Francisco. By 1880 these pockets had expanded, and a number of new settlements were scattered over the West. After 1880 it soon became impossible to trace definite frontier lines, since pioneers were moving into all parts of the West. The Indians had now been removed to reservations, so that white control had been effectively established over the whole country. The frontier, which had been such an important factor in the growth of American civilization for nearly three hundred years, soon became only a memory. This did not bring any abrupt change in the rhythms of American development, since people continued to move into the thinly populated western states. But the end of the frontier, combined with the growth of cities and the declining importance of agriculture, had important effects on American character and ideals.

The maps at the top and bottom of the page mark the growth of population. In 1790, 95 per cent of the people were still rural, but parts of the Northeastern states were already thickly settled, especially round the urban centers of Boston, New York, and Philadelphia. In 1830 the main urban centers were still in the Northeast, where industry was rapidly expanding, and the South had remained agricultural and rural. A hundred years later most of the Eastern half of the country was thickly settled, and urban centers had also grown up on the Pacific coast. Fifty-five per cent of the population now lived in places with more than 2,500 inhabitants. To an increasing extent the big cities determined the attitudes and mores of the whole country.

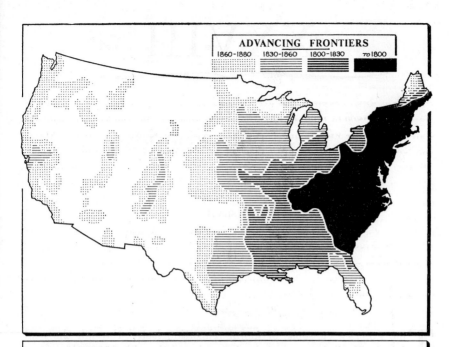

ADVANCING FRONTIERS

1860-1880   1830-1860   1800-1830   TO 1800

AMERICA'S EXPANDING POPULATION

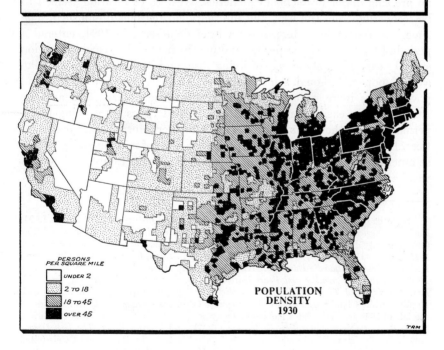

PERSONS
PER SQUARE MILE

UNDER 2

2 TO 18

18 TO 45

OVER 45

POPULATION
DENSITY
1930

TRM

XXVIII

Post-war Politics

1. FROM HARDING TO HOOVER
2. LEGISLATION
3. PROBLEMS OF INDIVIDUAL LIBERTY
4. FOREIGN POLICY

T HE POST-WAR sense of moral relaxation lasted through the next
decade. Until the onset of the depression at the end of 1929 there were
no pressing major problems or anxieties. Western civilization seemed to
be recovering from the war, and international tensions diminished. The
American economic system, after a brief depression in 1921, entered a
period of unexampled prosperity, and for the next eight years production
steadily expanded, standards of living rose, and it seemed easy to make
a lot of money. Although some groups did not share in the prosperity, and
poverty was more widespread than most people realized, the average
American was easily persuaded that the good times were going to be
permanent and there was no need for any further reform of business practices. He could settle down to the congenial tasks of making and spending
as much money as possible, in the confidence that the established system
was basically sound.

SELECTED BIBLIOGRAPHY: The most useful general history of the period is L. M.
Hacker, *American Problems of Today: A History of the United States Since the World War*
(1938). Society during the 1920's is described in P. W. Slosson, *The Great Crusade and After,
1914–1928* (1931), and in a more popular style in F. L. Allen, *Only Yesterday* (1931), and
H. M. Robinson, *Fantastic Interim: A Hindsight History of American Manners, Morals and
Mistakes Between Versailles and Pearl Harbor* (1943). Samuel Hopkins Adams, *Incredible
Era: The Life and Times of Warren Gamaliel Harding* (1939), deals entertainingly with
Harding, while Claude M. Fuess, *Calvin Coolidge* (1940), is more sober. Useful studies on
special subjects are Zechariah Chafee, Jr., *Free Speech in the United States* (revised edition,
1941), R. L. Garis, *Immigration Restriction* (1927), and Charles Merz, *The Dry Decade*
(1931). For foreign policy, in addition to the general histories by Bailey and Bemis (cited
earlier), one can consult D. F. Fleming, *The United States and World Organization, 1920–1933*
(1938), and Frank H. Simonds, *American Foreign Policy in the Post-War Years* (1935).

In retrospect the decade of the 1920's seems like a golden age. It was the last age of apparent security that the Western world was to know for an indefinite period to come. But many things went on in the United States that were obviously unhealthy. Standards of honesty declined, in both politics and business, and there was almost as much corruption as after the Civil War. There was also an extraordinary increase of organized crime, due largely to the fact that in 1920 it had become illegal to sell liquor. Meanwhile, many Americans indulged in a complacent and uncritical glorification of things as they were, accompanied by an intolerance of anything that seemed radical or alien. A number of artists and intellectuals, in fact, repudiated American civilization as hopelessly materialistic and repressive and sought refuge as expatriates in Europe. In the end, the sense of security proved to be an illusion, and the American people paid heavily for indulging it. The events of the 1930's and 1940's would have been less catastrophic if there had been more foresight and sense of responsibility in the 1920's.

1. FROM HARDING TO HOOVER

WHAT most people wanted during the 1920's was well expressed by Harding's word "normalcy." In politics this seemed to mean a return to conditions as they had been in the late nineteenth century. There was no revival of progressivism; although a group of Midwestern senators continued to champion reform, they now won little support outside the farm belt. Conservative Republicans controlled the Federal government, with a program of promoting business expansion. As long as this resulted in prosperity, there was little effective opposition, since the Democratic Party had become almost as conservative as the Republicans.

The Harding Administration. Harding had been picked for the presidency by the Republican bosses largely because he was as unlike Woodrow Wilson as possible. Since he was amiable, unassuming, and thoroughly conservative, they believed that he would make a popular figurehead and would allow Congress to regain the supremacy it had lost during the progressive period. Unfortunately, Harding was so abysmally lacking in both intelligence and force of character that he almost brought catastrophe upon his party. A native of Marion, Ohio, he had spent most of his adult life as the editor of the local newspaper. The ambitions of his wife and his friend Harry Daugherty had pushed him into politics, and he had served in the Senate since 1914. He had good intentions and a warm heart; but mentally he seemed to exist in a perpetual fog. His speeches were an astonishing mixture of sonorous platitudes, meaningless verbiage, and bad grammar, from which it was usually impossible to derive any concrete meaning except that he was a patriotic American. And since he liked to be generous to his friends and chose them very unwisely, he could easily be tricked by men who knew what they wanted. During the

Harding regime an extraordinary collection of shady adventurers descended upon Washington and were made welcome at White House parties
and at more intimate drinking and poker sessions with the President.

Harding appointed three strong men to his Cabinet. Charles Evans
Hughes made an outstandingly successful Secretary of State; Andrew
Mellon, a Pittsburgh millionaire who took charge of the Treasury Department, showed a financial ability which caused his admirers to call
him the greatest Secretary since Alexander Hamilton; and Herbert
Hoover was a highly efficient Secretary of Commerce. Most of the other
members were mediocre, and two of them, Secretary of the Interior
Albert B. Fall and Attorney General Daugherty, soon disgraced themselves. A number of other friends whom Harding appointed to high offices
were equally unworthy.

The most sensational of the many scandals that discredited the
Harding administration had to do with oil. Previous presidents had set
aside some oil fields on public land for the use of the navy. After Harding
took office, control over these fields was transferred to the Interior Department, and during 1922 they were secretly leased, without competitive
bidding, to men in the oil business. Two fields at Elk Hills, California,
went to Harry F. Sinclair, and one at Teapot Dome, Wyoming, to Edward L. Doheny. About the same time the Secretary of the Interior was
observed to be spending money more freely than formerly. As a result of
the suspicions of La Follette and other progressive senators, a formal
investigation was launched in the autumn of 1923, and a committee
headed by Senator Thomas J. Walsh of Montana extracted from a series
of very unwilling witnesses irrefutable proofs of corruption, showing that
Fall had received $260,000 from Sinclair and $100,000 from Doheny. Fall
was eventually sentenced to a fine of $100,000 and a year in prison,
thereby becoming the first Cabinet minister in American history to be
convicted of criminal charges.

Other branches of the government where there were major scandals
were the Department of Justice and the Veterans' Bureau. A Senate committee found evidences of corruption against Daugherty (who loudly proclaimed that he was the victim of a Communist smear); but when he
was put on trial, the jury could not reach a unanimous verdict. But
Daugherty's closest friend, Jess Smith, committed suicide, and one of his
chief subordinates, Thomas W. Miller, Alien Property Custodian, went
to prison for taking bribes. In the Veterans' Bureau some $200,000,000 of
the sums appropriated for hospital services was stolen or wasted. The
director, Colonel Charles R. Forbes, eventually went to the penitentiary,
and the legal adviser, Charles F. Cramer, committed suicide.

It was no doubt fortunate for Harding that he died before there
was any public knowledge of what had been going on. In August 1923 he
succumbed suddenly to a blood clot on the brain. He seems to have

realized during the last weeks of his life that he had been betrayed by his friends and might himself face impeachment charges.

The Coolidge Administration. Luckily for the Republican Party, Vice-President Calvin Coolidge, who succeeded Harding, was a man of unimpeachable integrity. Born in Vermont of old Puritan stock, Coolidge had settled at Northampton, Massachusetts, and had risen by regular stages to the governorship of the state. He owed his place on the Republican ticket to the Boston police strike of 1919. Through most of the strike Coolidge had displayed a characteristic inactivity, but after it had been broken he supported the city authorities in refusing to reinstate the strikers, declaring that there was "no right to strike against the public safety by anybody, anywhere, any time." This one brief sentence captured the popular imagination and won him the vice-presidency. Parsimonious and taciturn, hostile to new ways and suspicious of any attempt to improve the world, Coolidge had all the less lovable qualities of the New England Yankee without the idealism or the zeal for reform of the Puritan tradition. Like his ancestors, he believed in hard work, thrift, individual initiative, and as little government as possible. But in spite of his narrow mind and chilly personality, he had great political shrewdness. Oddly enough, he became one of the most popular of American presidents, and his wry sayings, which were often ill-mannered or even cruel, were passed around like bons mots. In an age of dizzy speculation and feverish business expansion it was reassuring to have in the White House a man who seemed like a throwback to the vanished age of agrarian individualism.

Although the new President did not engage in any thorough housecleaning, Harding's friends gradually disappeared from office, and there was a salutary change in the quality of the guests invited to the White House. Coolidge had no trouble in securing the Republican nomination for the 1924 election. When the Democratic convention met, the long-standing division between the Southern and Northeastern wings of the party, which had originated back in 1791, flared into open conflict. The Southerners, mostly rural, Protestant, and of old American stock, supported William G. McAdoo, who had been Wilson's Secretary of the Treasury. The Northeastern wing, predominantly urban and Catholic and composed of recent immigrant groups, had for the first time a candidate of its own, Alfred E. Smith, an Irish Catholic and a member of Tammany Hall, who was making an excellent record as Governor of New York. Not until the 103rd ballot did the convention finally agree on a compromise nominee, John W. Davis, a New York corporation lawyer who had been born in West Virginia.

Since both Coolidge and Davis were conservatives, the surviving progressives tried again to launch a third party. With the support of organized labor and some farm groups, they organized a Progressive Party (not connected with the Bull Moose Party of 1912). La Follette, now sixty-nine years of age but still a belligerent opponent of special privilege, became its candidate, with Burton K. Wheeler, Democratic Senator from Montana, as his running-mate.

There was never any doubt that Coolidge would be elected. Carrying every Northern and Western state except Wisconsin (which supported its favorite son, La Follette), he won crushing popular and electoral majorities. Under the circumstances the Progressive popular vote of nearly 5,000,000 seemed like a creditable beginning, but in the following year La Follette died and the organization was dissolved.

The Election of 1928.   The economic climate continued rosy throughout Coolidge's second term, and political history was uneventful. For the 1928 election the Republican nomination went to Herbert Hoover. Among the Democrats the sectional split had by no means been healed, but Al Smith, who had been twice re-elected Governor of New York since 1924, was now recognized as much the strongest candidate, and he was nominated on the first ballot.

Smith was a moderate progressive, and promised reforms for the benefit of farmers and organized labor. But there was little popular interest in any questions of economic policy. The campaign, which was one of the most bitter in American history, revolved around issues more highly charged with emotion. The two candidates typified two conflicting elements in American society, arousing hostilities which only once before, during the Know Nothing movement of the 1850's, had played a major role in Federal politics. Hoover was Protestant, of old American stock, and had been born on a farm in Iowa. Smith was Catholic, of Irish descent, and had grown up on the Lower East Side of New York. While Hoover's less scrupulous supporters assiduously appealed to all the racial and religious prejudices of rural and small-town Americans, Smith evoked in the big cities of the Northeast a popular acclaim that approached hysteria. The two men, moreover, disagreed about prohibition. Hoover described it as "a great social and economic experiment, noble in nature and far-reaching in purpose"—a platitudinous statement which apparently meant that he was in favor of it. Smith, on the other hand, boldly called for repeal of the Eighteenth Amendment and return of liquor-control to the states.

Although Smith won a larger popular vote than any previous Democratic candidate, he was defeated in the electoral college by an unprecedented margin. In view of the business prosperity, there can be little doubt that any Republican could have beaten any Democrat; but the size of Hoover's victory seems to have been due mainly to the religious issue. Smith carried only six Southern states, along with Massachusetts and Rhode Island, and for the first time five of the former Confederate states voted Republican.

2. LEGISLATION

THE DOMINANT economic theory during the 1920's was that if business were assisted in making steady profits and expanding production, there would be jobs for everybody and prosperity would percolate down to all sections of the population. Such a program meant a sharp reversal of most of the policies adopted during the progressive era. There was no revival of trust-busting, and the Sherman and Clayton Acts became almost dead letters. While the ICC and the FTC continued to function, their members interpreted their duties in a new spirit and were now more concerned with aiding business than with policing it. Meanwhile, the Department of Commerce, under Hoover's direction, encouraged the growth of trade associations which limited competition and adopted "codes of fair practice." A similar trend was shown by the law courts. The Supreme Court ruled in 1925 that trade associations were not illegal as long as they did not make agreements fixing prices and limiting production, and judges once again issued injunctions in order to break strikes, a practice supposedly prohibited by Section 20 of the Clayton Act.

Finance. Mellon, who served as Secretary of the Treasury until 1931, strongly urged tax-reductions in the upper brackets, arguing that wealthy men would then have more capital to invest. Congress preferred to begin at the other end, and the Revenue Acts of 1921 and 1924 lowered taxes for the average citizen. But in the end Mellon had his way, and in 1926 and 1929 substantial relief was given to millionaires and corporations. As a result of the tax-reductions, the national debt was not decreased as much as might fairly have been expected in a period of such unexampled prosperity; the actual reduction was from $24,298,000,000 in 1920 to $16,185,000,000 in 1930. A long-overdue reform was the establishment in 1921 of the Bureau of the Budget, which made possible more effective coordination of Federal expenditures.

The Tariff. As during earlier periods of Republican rule, the demands of industrialists for tariff increases received sympathetic consideration. The Underwood Tariff of 1913 proved to be a war casualty, and in 1922 the Fordney-McCumber Tariff pushed rates up again, roughly, to the levels of 1909. This provoked complaints from farmers and from business groups interested in foreign trade, and in the 1928 campaign Hoover (like Taft in 1908) promised revision. But when the question was submitted to Congress, Taft's unhappy experience with the Payne-Aldrich Tariff was repeated. The Hawley-Smoot Tariff of 1930 was mostly written by the spokesmen of big business, and almost all the duties were raised. It was, in fact, the highest tariff in American history. Hoover then signed the bill in spite of protests from almost all the country's leading economists. Going into effect during the depression, it hastened the collapse of international trade.

The Railroads. The government divested itself of its wartime control of the railroads before Harding took office. By the Esch-Cummins Act of 1920 the roads were returned to private operation, but the powers of the ICC were considerably enlarged; it was for the first time given full authority to fix rates, with the understanding that they should yield a "fair return" (5½ per cent was the amount indicated) "upon the aggregate value of the railway property of the country." This left undetermined the important question of how the capital value of the railroads was to be calculated. Whereas the ICC proposed to use their reproduction cost in 1914 as its yardstick, the railroads argued for the year 1920, when prices were considerably higher and the capital value proportionately greater. In the St. Louis and O'Fallon Railway Company case, decided in 1929, the Supreme Court supported the position of the railroads.

Shipping. Getting out of the shipping business proved to be more difficult. By the Merchant Marine Act of 1920 the vast fleet of merchant ships operated by the government-owned Emergency Fleet Corporation was to be sold. Under the Harding administration ships were turned over to private companies at the rate of $30 a ton, which was about one-eighth of their cost. This led to charges of corruption, though the low prices were largely due to the fact that many of the ships were slow and poorly constructed. This official generosity did not enable operators to hold their own against foreign competition, and by 1928 less than a third of American foreign trade was carried in American ships. In that year the government came to the rescue with another Merchant Marine Act, by which companies were loaned money for new construction and given subsidies in the guise of mail-carrying contracts. Meanwhile, the government continued to operate about a quarter of all American ocean-going vessels. This was one area where private enterprise did not seem to be very effective.

Power. Another economic activity calling for Federal regulation was the production of electric power. A Federal Power Commission was set up in 1920, and in 1930 it was reorganized and given powers similar to those of the ICC and FTC. Its chief functions were to give licenses to corporations wishing to build plants on navigable rivers and to regulate their rates. Progressives, especially Senator Norris of Nebraska, wanted the government to go further and regulate all interstate power corporations. The industry was growing rapidly, and was notoriously under the control of unscrupulous financiers. Norris argued that the American people could derive immense benefits from cheap power, and that since effective competition in this field was obviously impossible, only government intervention could ensure low rates. He was especially concerned with the question of Muscle Shoals, Alabama, where the government during the war had begun to build dams and nitrate plants for the manufacture of explosives on the Tennessee River. Whereas the administration proposed to transfer the whole enterprise to private ownership, Norris suggested that the dams be completed and operated by a government corporation, which would then have a yardstick for the measurement of electricity rates. Congress passed bills embodying Norris's proposals in 1928 and 1931, but both of them were killed by executive vetoes. Hoover's veto message was particularly bitter; this, he declared, "is not liberalism; it is degeneration."

Farm Relief. The administration was not much more sympathetic to the demands of the farmers. The foreign market for American farm produce was shrinking, and the farmers were again beginning to suffer from chronic overproduction. At first it was hoped that the problem might be solved through the organization of cooperatives for the more efficient marketing of farm products. The Capper-Volstead Act of 1922 exempted cooperatives from the anti-trust laws, while the Intermediate Credits Act of 1923 set up banks to lend them money; crops stored in warehouses were to be accepted as collateral (this was similar to the subtreasury plan of the Populists thirty years earlier). But the farmers continued to have difficulty in disposing of all they produced, and their spokesmen asked for government help in regaining their foreign markets. By the McNary-Haugen plan cooperatives were to have help in keeping surpluses off the domestic market (so that high prices would be maintained at home) and in selling them abroad for whatever they would fetch. Bills embodying this plan were twice vetoed by Coolidge.

Hoover recognized the need for some kind of farm relief, and in 1929 Congress, at his recommendation, passed the Agricultural Marketing Act. This set up a Federal Farm Board with a fund of $500,000,000, which was to be used for keeping surpluses off the market. Hoover optimistically assumed that overproduction was occasional rather than chronic, and that the surpluses could be sold at some later date. Beginning operations during the depression, agencies set up by the Farm Board bought up vast quantities of surplus grain and cotton, were unable to find any purchasers, and finally had to stop buying and leave the farmers to their fate.

Benefits for Veterans. As after the Civil War, Congressmen were very responsive to the demands of veterans, and the American Legion became one of the most powerful pressure groups in Washington. During the war the government had made what it regarded as adequate provision for veterans' needs, arranging that men disabled through war service should receive hospitalization and pensions, while all veterans were to receive a bonus when they left the army. But during the 1920's veterans who developed disabilities after being discharged demanded support, and these were brought under the pension system by laws passed in 1924 and 1930.

Veterans also asked for an additional bonus to compensate them for the difference between their pay as soldiers and the high wages they would have received if they had not been drafted. In 1924 Congress passed a bonus bill giving twenty-year endowment policies to all veterans. In

1931 veterans were allowed to borrow half of the value of their policies, and in 1936 it was voted that the full value should be paid immediately. All these bonus measures were passed over successive vetoes by Presidents Coolidge, Hoover, and Roosevelt. By the end of 1930 the total cost of veterans' relief, including the bonus policies, amounted to $5,500,-000,000.

Immigration Restriction.   Much the most important legislation passed during the 1920's remains to be discussed. For the first time in American history immigration was limited. For a number of years various organizations had been pointing with alarm to the increase of immigration from the backward countries of southern and eastern Europe. Opposition to unrestricted immigration grew stronger during the war, with its intolerance and hysteria, and in 1917, for the first time, a literacy test was imposed. When the war ended, poverty and unrest in Europe led quickly to a flood of new arrivals. Demands for restriction were then voiced by labor organizations fearful of competition with cheap immigrant labor.

Congress responded with the Emergency Quota Act of 1921, which limited immigration from the Old World to 350,000 a year. The Immigration Quota Act of 1924 provided for an immediate reduction of this figure to 165,000 and laid down a permanent program, which went into effect in 1929. After this date total immigration from the Old World was limited to 150,000 a year, and a quota was allotted to each national group in proportion to the estimated number of persons descended from that group in the American population of 1920. The effect, of course, was to give preference to immigrants from western and northern Europe. This was done deliberately, in the belief that persons of British, Irish, German, and Scandinavian origin could more easily be assimilated.

The quota system applied only to the countries of the Old World; immigration from Canada and Latin America was not restricted, and during the 1920's some 900,000 Canadians and 450,000 Mexicans entered the United States. Certain Asiatic countries, including China and Japan, were not given quotas, the entry of immigrants for permanent residence being totally prohibited. This insult to the Oriental peoples, passed by Congress over the protests of the State Department, was strongly resented in Japan.

There can be no question that some kind of restriction was necessary, particularly since during and after World War I most of the other countries of the world were adopting similar policies. Yet it is impossible not to regard restriction, however necessary, as a step backward from the liberalism of earlier generations. One of the essential freedoms, almost as important as freedom of speech, is freedom of movement. This had been almost universal in the nineteenth century, and had been limited only by notoriously backward countries such as Russia. But after World War I all the nations of the world, the United States included, began to build walls around themselves, so that human beings were imprisoned within national boundaries. The full tragic effects became apparent with the growth of totalitarian dictatorships in the 1930's and 1940's, when millions of victims of political, religious, and racial persecution found themselves unable to escape and everywhere unwanted.

3. PROBLEMS OF INDIVIDUAL LIBERTY

Prohibition.   When prohibition went into effect in 1920, its supporters optimistically predicted that the next generation of Americans would grow up unacquainted with liquor. But in the end all but a few fanatics had to recognize that the "noble experiment" had done more harm than good. Nobody knows how many Americans were personally (not merely politically) dry during the 1920's. Certainly a large minority had never accepted the theory that intoxicating liquor was intrinsically harmful and regarded the Eighteenth Amendment as an unwarrantable violation of personal liberty. Among them were many men in high office, from President Harding downwards, who supported the dry cause for political reasons. Many Americans proposed to go on drinking, and a sufficient number of bootleggers were willing to undertake the very lucrative business of keeping them supplied.

Enforcement was ludicrously inadequate from the start. For the whole country there were only 1,520 prohibition agents in 1920 and 2,836 in 1930; and since their salaries were generally less than $2,000 a year, they were under strong temptation to increase them illicitly. Prohibition was fairly well obeyed in small towns and rural areas, where it had the support of public opinion, but most of the larger cities remained wide open. Bootlegged liquor was either brewed at home or smuggled in from abroad, and sold in speakeasies. The quality was often doubtful; much of it, in fact, was positively dangerous. But outside rural areas any American who wanted a drink could usually get one.

Gangsterism.   The most harmful result of prohibition was to stimulate crime. Since selling liquor was illegal, the persons engaged in it could not ask the police to protect them against theft and assault, and had to provide for their own defense. This was the main cause for the growth of gangsterism. Gangs set out to organize the liquor business in different areas, acquiring arsenals of bombs and machine guns, fighting pitched battles with highjackers who tried to steal their liquor, murdering competitors who muscled in on their territory, and beating up speakeasy proprietors who refused to work with them. A gangster's life was hazardous, but the profits were enormous. The gangs often had corrupt connections with local politicians, and were too strong to be controlled by the police. In Chicago, which became the most notorious criminal center, "Scarface" Al Capone headed a gang which by 1927 was earning an annual revenue estimated at $60,000,000, out of which Capone himself accumulated a private fortune of $20,000,000. During the 1920's there were more than five hundred gang murders in the city, many of which occurred on public streets in broad daylight; yet there were virtually no convictions. Conditions in many other cities were not much better.

Many of the liquor gangs soon branched out into other activities. Some of them established rackets by which retail storekeepers were compelled to pay for "protection," while smaller groups of criminals specialized in bank robberies or in kidnapping members of wealthy families and holding them for ransom. Criminal statistics during the 1920's showed a real breakdown of law and order. Homicides averaged 10,500 a year, a figure which (in proportion to population) was sixteen times as large as in England. Thefts cost the American people a direct loss of $250,000,000 a year, while the indirect costs ran into billions.

Public opinion during the 1920's was alarmingly tolerant towards criminals. The Americans had always been a rather lawless people, possibly as a result of their frontier background. The "bad men" of the early West had been romanticized, and a similar glamour now became attached to the thoroughly vicious characters who dominated the urban underworld. It was not until the onset of the depression that more responsible attitudes began to prevail.

Repeal of Prohibition.   After Al Smith had called for the repeal of prohibition in the 1928 campaign, a number of other political leaders began publicly to call it a failure. President Hoover appointed the Wickersham Commission to consider the whole problem of crime; and although the Commission as a whole was pressured into recommending continuance of prohibition, seven of its eleven members came out individually for modification or repeal. Meanwhile, the decrease of Federal revenues during the depression gave the wets a new argument; legalization of liquor would enable the government to tax it. In the 1932 campaign the Democratic platform called for repeal; and with the election of Franklin D. Roosevelt the "noble experiment" was brought to an end. The Twenty-first Amendment, repealing the Eighteenth, was added to the Constitution before the end of 1933. Henceforth control was left to the states. Although they adopted various restrictions on the sale of liquor, only a small part of the country remained legally dry.

Repeal of prohibition deprived the gangs of their chief source of revenue, while at the same time the Federal government had begun to take action against them. Most of the crimes they committed came under the jurisdiction of local authorities, who often seemed powerless to deal with them; but some of their offenses were covered by Federal law. During the early 1930's the Federal Bureau of Investigation, founded in 1924 and headed by J. Edgar Hoover, succeeded in hunting down and eliminating most of the leading public enemies, though it sometimes had to resort to legal technicalities. Capone, for example, went to prison for nine years not for the murders he had plotted but for falsifying his income-tax returns. But this salutary housecleaning had only temporary effects, and World War II was followed by another breakdown of law enforcement, associated chiefly with the growth of illegal gambling.

Communism and Civil Liberty. Another disturbing feature of the post-war decade was the growth of intolerance. The hysteria stirred up during the war seemed to have done lasting damage to the American tradition of intellectual freedom.

In 1919 a group of radicals, seceding from the Socialist Party, established the American Communist Party, which became affiliated with the Russian-controlled Third International, and proposed to bring about a violent revolution and a proletarian dictatorship in the United States. Throughout the 1920's, however, the Communists remained a negligible force in American life. Although they assumed leadership in a few strikes, they won no lasting strength in the labor movement. They included a hard core of fanatics who were beyond the reach of rational argument, but most of their supporters were misguided idealists or rebellious adolescents who quickly became disillusioned. But they presented American liberalism with a wholly new problem. How far was it right or expedient to grant civil liberty to groups who were working to destroy the civil liberties of everybody else?

The government's initial response to the formation of the Communist Party was to resort to repression. The year 1919 was stormy. Aroused by a rapid rise in the cost of living, 4,000,000 workers took part in strikes; and many middle-class citizens, failing to recognize that the workers had real grievances, attributed their unrest to revolutionary agitators. In the autumn the Department of Justice deported 250 alien radicals to Russia, and on New Year's Day 1920 it raided all Communist Party offices and placed 6,000 alleged Communists under temporary arrest. During the same period a number of state governments passed criminal-syndicalism laws imposing penalties for any advocacy of revolution. As a result of the popular fear of revolution, radicals of all kinds, including many who had no sympathy whatever with Communism, came under suspicion. The most notorious case was that of two Italian-born anarchists in Massachusetts: Sacco and Vanzetti. These men, arrested in 1920 on charges of murder and robbery, were convicted on what seemed to be inadequate evidence by a judge and a jury who were obviously influenced by political prejudice. Champions of civil liberty came to their defense, but could not save them from being finally executed in 1927.

After 1920 it became obvious that there was no real danger of revolution, and the hysteria began to subside. President Harding pardoned most of the people convicted on political charges during and after the war. The existence of the Communist Party was one reason for the refusal of the United States, prior to 1933, to establish diplomatic relations with the Soviet Union, but the party was henceforth allowed to pursue its activities more or less openly.

The Ku Klux Klan.   A much more serious threat to liberal traditions was the growth of organized movements of intolerance with reactionary rather than radical objectives. The most formidable of these was a new Ku Klux Klan, unconnected except by name with the Ku Klux of the Reconstruction period, which was dedicated to the suppression of Negroes, Catholics, and Jews. Founded in 1915, with headquarters at Atlanta, Georgia, it had achieved by 1924 a membership approaching 5,000,000, and had acquired an alarming political power not only in parts of the South but also in some Midwestern and Pacific states. Like Hitlerism in Germany, it appealed chiefly to members of the lower middle class, who felt economically insecure and frustrated. Masked and wearing white robes, groups of Klansmen would assault persons whom they chose to regard as un-American. Fortunately, internal disputes and corruption among its leaders caused the organization to disintegrate within a few years, and by 1929 it had ceased to exercise much influence, except in some parts of the rural South.

Restrictions on Intellectual Freedom.   Liberalism was also endangered by a widespread tendency to enforce intellectual and moral conformity by law. There was much censorship of books and plays which police departments chose to regard as immoral, especially in Boston, and on numerous occasions customs officials tried to protect the morals of American citizens by refusing to allow the importation of European classics. In three Southern states where religious fundamentalism was still dominant, Tennessee, Oklahoma, and Mississippi, the teaching of the Darwinian theory in the public schools was prohibited. In 1925 a teacher in Dayton, Tennessee, John Thomas Scopes, was tried for violating the law. This was one of the *causes célèbres* of the 1920's, with William Jennings Bryan appearing for the prosecution [1] and a famous Chicago liberal lawyer, Clarence Darrow, for the defense. Scopes was convicted, although the Supreme Court of the state later remitted his penalty on technical grounds.

4. FOREIGN POLICY

THROUGHOUT the 1920's and 1930's a majority of the American people remained unwilling to assume binding commitments to take action against an aggressor or give support to other countries in the event of war. But this attitude did not mean that the United States refrained from seeking international agreements. In spite of the repudiation of Wilson's program in 1919 and 1920, American foreign policy never became narrowly isolationist. In many ways, in fact, the Harding, Coolidge, and Hoover administrations assumed world leadership in the promotion of disarmament, peaceful settlement of disputes, and economic stabilization. This even included some cooperation with the League of Nations on non-

[1] This was Bryan's last appearance. He died a week after the trial.

political questions; although the United States refused to become a member, she sent delegates to more than forty League conferences between 1924 and 1930. Her concern with world affairs was due not only to a general interest in peace but also to a rapid expansion of her foreign trade and overseas capital investment. Unfortunately, attempts made during the 1920's to bring about international harmony had only temporary results, perhaps because they dealt with symptoms rather than basic causes.

The Washington Treaties. The first and most successful American gesture in the cause of peace was the Washington Conference of 1921–22, which was concerned partly with naval disarmament and partly with the Far East. All powers interested in these two questions were represented, except the Soviet Union, which was not invited. Responsibility for calling the conference was shared between the Americans and the British, but its dominating figure was Secretary of State Hughes. In his opening speech Hughes proposed that the different powers scrap a total of sixty-six capital ships, thereby, it was said, sinking more tonnage in thirty-four minutes than all the admirals had sunk in centuries. Hughes's bold recommendations were substantially accepted, and the conference agreed on a Five-Power Naval Treaty, by which the United States and Britain accepted the principle of naval equality, and the capital-ship tonnage of the world's naval powers was fixed by a system of ratios: 5 for the United States and Britain, 3 for Japan, and 1.75 for France and Italy. No agreement could be made about smaller ships, but as a result of the treaty there was no further battleship construction by any power until the 1930's. This was the only one of the various post-war disarmament conferences which actually brought about any disarming.

With reference to the Far East, the purpose of the conference was to bring about a settlement with Japan, which had taken advantage of World War I to acquire a number of Pacific islands from Germany and to expand her power on the mainland of Asia. Japan was willing, for the time being, to come to terms, so once again the *status quo* in the Pacific and the Open Door and the territorial integrity of China were reaffirmed, though more forcefully than in previous agreements. A Four-Power Treaty, signed by the United States, Britain, France, and Japan, and a Nine-Power Treaty, signed by all powers with Pacific interests, stabilized the Far East as completely as any documents could. In the long run the signatures of the Japanese delegates proved to be worthless, but the treaties did result in a breathing-spell of nearly ten years before there was any further Japanese aggression.

Reparations and War Debts. Throughout the 1920's the American government used its influence to promote the stabilization of Europe. In 1923, when Germany defaulted on the reparations payments stipulated by the Versailles Treaty, the French army occupied the German industrial region in the Ruhr Valley. Hughes offered American help in working out a settlement, and a commission headed by a Chicago banker, Charles G. Dawes, then fixed a new scale of payments more nearly adjusted to German capacity. This led in 1925 to the Locarno Treaties by which Germany, France, and Britain pledged themselves to maintain peace with each other. In 1928 the reparations payments were again modified by a commission headed by another American, Owen D. Young, the year 1988 being fixed as the date when payments were to be completed.

The question of reparations was involved with that of war debts. During and after the war the United States had loaned a total of $10,-350,000,000 to European countries at 5 per cent interest. This had been regarded by many people as a contribution to the common cause, especially since there was little American military participation until the summer of 1918. But with the swing back toward isolation, Congress asked for repayment. Between 1923 and 1930 agreements were made with all the debtor countries except the Soviet Union. Rates of interest were considerably reduced, and payments were to go on for more than sixty years. While most Americans regarded the terms as generous, many Europeans felt that the debts should have been canceled and began to speak of "Uncle Shylock."

In the end the whole system of reparation and debt agreements proved to be utterly unrealistic. Debtor countries could obtain enough gold to make payments only by expanding their exports and capturing new foreign markets, which the businessmen of creditor countries were by no means willing to allow. In practice the system of payments could be maintained only through extensive private lending. Down to 1933, when the whole structure collapsed, private investors loaned the Germans about $6,000,000,000, nearly half of which was contributed by Americans. This made it possible for Germany to pay $4,470,000,000 in reparations, and of this sum $2,606,000,000 came back to the United States in the form of war-debt payments. In the end most of the $6,000,000,000 invested in Germany was never repaid and had to be written off as a total loss. Thus the final paradoxical result was that Germany paid out considerably less than she received, while the sums received by the United States Treasury were considerably less than the sums sunk in Europe by private American investors.

In Quest of Peace.   The Locarno Treaties of 1925 looked like the dawn of a new day in Europe. They were followed in 1928 by a more comprehensive attempt to exorcise the threat of war. This was the Pact of Paris, better known by the names of its two leading sponsors, Frank B. Kellogg, who had succeeded Hughes as Secretary of State in 1925, and Aristide Briand, French Foreign Minister. Actually neither the American nor the French government was particularly enthusiastic about the pact; they were impelled to support it by pressure from a number of influential Americans, especially the isolationist leader Senator Borah, who argued that the way to abolish war was to abolish it. By the Pact of Paris virtually all the nations of the world, totaling fifty-nine, pledged themselves to outlaw war as an instrument of national policy. But the pact did not provide any method for enforcing obedience upon any nation violating its pledge and did not rule out defensive war, for which reasons it proved to be wholly futile. It illustrated in its most extreme form the illusion cherished by many Americans that noble moral gestures, not backed by force, could put an end to international power politics.

Obviously, the abolition of war should have been followed by general disarmament. But none of the great powers had enough faith in the Kellogg-Briand Pact to scrap its armed forces. After the Washington Conference, competition had continued in the building of smaller ships, and naval conferences at Rome in 1924 and Geneva in 1927 had failed to agree on any program of limitation. In 1930, at the London Conference, the United States, Britain, and Japan adopted ratios for smaller ships; but the agreement allowed considerable extra construction by all three powers. Nothing was done to limit land and air forces. A conference met at Geneva in 1932 in order to discuss general disarmament, but could reach no agreement. In the following year, Hitler became ruler of Germany, and all hope of disarmament had to be abandoned. It soon became obvious that the only way to preserve peace was not by disarmament but by the rapid rearmament of all peace-loving nations.

Dropping the Big Stick. The most lasting diplomatic achievement of the 1920's was the improvement of relations with Latin America. At the end of World War I, American armed forces were occupying four Caribbean countries: Cuba, Haiti, the Dominican Republic, and Nicaragua. This big-stick policy had antagonized all of Latin America, and made it difficult for United States businessmen to secure markets and investment opportunities. But with the defeat of Germany and the decrease of international tension in the 1920's, the United States could afford to relax her vigilance in the Caribbean. Secretary Hughes therefore set out to conciliate Latin America by initiating a process of withdrawal. His policy was not wholly followed by Kellogg, but was continued by Henry L. Stimson, who served as Secretary of State under Hoover.

Since the occupations could not be terminated until stable governments had been installed, getting out was a more complicated process than getting in. Cuba was evacuated in 1922 and the Dominican Republic in 1924, but American forces could not be wholly withdrawn from Haiti until 1934. Nicaragua was evacuated in 1925, but the administration left in power was promptly overthrown by revolution, so in 1926 marines were landed again to restore order and protect American property. This was probably a mistake, especially since the American officials tried to establish as provisional president of Nicaragua a candidate who had little legal claim or popular support. The renewed intervention was opposed by many of the Nicaraguans, and by 1927 some 5,000 American troops had been sent to the country. This led to vigorous protests in the United States

Senate, which complained that the executive was involving the country in war without congressional authorization. Coolidge then sent Henry L. Stimson to Nicaragua to find a way out of the impasse. Stimson persuaded almost all the different factions to agree to a free election, and promised that the results would be accepted by the United States. A candidate strongly opposed to the intervention won the election and took office in 1928. The American troops were then gradually withdrawn, the evacuation being completed in 1933.

Relations with Mexico.   Mexico, as usual, proved to be the chief test of United States sincerity in seeking Latin American good will. In 1920 Álvaro Obregón had assumed power by revolution. This proved to be the beginning of a new era of political stability, economic reform, and progress towards democracy. But since Obregón and his successors began to put into effect the revolutionary Constitution of 1917, with its promises of land and labor reform, their policies were decidedly unpopular with the Americans owning property in Mexico. How far would the United States government support the claims of its citizens?

Obregón was not given recognition until 1923, after he had given assurances that American property-owners, especially the oil companies, would not be disturbed. In 1926 a serious crisis developed when President Plutarco Elías Calles ordered the oil companies to exchange their titles of ownership for fifty-year leases. He pointed out that, according to the Constitution of 1917, private ownership of the subsoil was prohibited, and argued that since the fields could certainly be exhausted in less than fifty years, the companies would not lose anything. The companies refused and were supported by the Coolidge administration, which seemed for a few months to be moving towards intervention, especially when Kellogg (with no evidence whatever) accused the Mexican government of being Communistic. But after the Senate, already aroused by the Nicaraguan imbroglio, had passed a resolution calling for a settlement by negotiation, Coolidge sent Dwight Morrow to Mexico with instructions to work out a compromise.

Morrow showed great tact and skill in conciliating Mexican national pride and was scrupulously careful to avoid any suggestion of intimidation. The oil dispute was settled in 1927 with the understanding that the companies should have perpetual leases for fields on which drilling had started prior to 1917. This satisfied everybody but the oil companies, who were reluctant to make the slightest concession to the Mexican point of view. In the end the oil settlement proved to be transitory, but the atmosphere of friendship which Morrow had created was more lasting. Since 1927 relations between the United States and her southern neighbor have become increasingly close and harmonious.

The End of the Roosevelt Corollary.   It took time to convince the Latin Americans that the United States had genuinely dropped the big stick. Throughout the 1920's they continued to ask what American troops were doing in Haiti and Nicaragua and whether they really intended to leave. In particular, at the Pan-American Conference of Havana in 1928, the United States faced outspoken and belligerent criticism from the rest of the hemisphere. Although the administration was not willing to give up interventionism completely, it went a long way to meet these criticisms. An official *Memorandum on the Monroe Doctrine*, written by J. Reuben Clark of the State Department and published in 1930, repudiated the Roosevelt Corollary and declared that the sole purpose of the doctrine was to protect Latin America from Europe. This meant that while the United States still claimed the right of intervening, under international law, to protect her own citizens, she was no longer assuming (as under Roosevelt, Taft, and Wilson) the responsibilities of a hemispheric policeman. The final step—repudiation of intervention on any ground whatever —was taken by the administration of Franklin D. Roosevelt a few years later.

The Chinese Situation. In the Far East the most important developments during the 1920's were in China, although it was not until after World War II that their full importance became apparent. The Manchu empire had been overthrown in 1911, but the republican regime that succeeded it failed to provide effective central government, and large parts of the country fell under the control of local military chieftains. An idealistic liberal leader, Sun Yat-sen, then began to build a new political organization, the Kuomintang, with a three-point program of national independence, democratic government, and social welfare. Meanwhile, the Soviet government sent agents to China to establish a Communist movement, and Sun Yat-sen, although critical of Marxist doctrine, was willing to cooperate with them.

When Sun Yat-sen died in 1925, his disciple Chiang Kai-shek became leader of the Kuomintang. In 1926 Chiang established a government at Nanking and set out to extend the authority of the Kuomintang over the rest of China. The United States, wanting a strong and independent China in accordance with her traditional Open Door policy, quickly accepted Chiang Kai-shek's claims to leadership and gave him diplomatic recognition. By this time he had become convinced that cooperation with the Communists was impossible, and in 1927 he expelled them from the Kuomintang and set out to destroy them. But a number succeeded in escaping and establishing themselves in a north-central region, where they built up a strong organization among the peasants. Henceforth the dominant elements in the Kuomintang grew steadily more conservative, and civil war between Chiang Kai-shek and the Communists became chronic.

The Crisis in Manchuria. The rise of the Kuomintang presented a serious threat to the ambitions of Japan, whose rulers had looked forwards to the gradual absorption of China, province by province, into their empire. In particular, it endangered the Japanese position in southern Manchuria, which was still legally under Chinese sovereignty, although Japan controlled its government and economy. When the Kuomintang took steps to reassert Chinese authority in Manchuria, the Japanese army resorted to force. In September 1931 the Japanese ousted the Chinese officials and put an end to Chinese sovereignty, afterwards reorganizing the province into the puppet state of Manchukuo. China promptly appealed to the League of Nations and to the United States.

Japan had real grievances in Manchuria, but the action of her army was clearly an act of aggression. This was a breach of the Washington treaties of 1922 and a major challenge to both the League concept of collective security and the American faith in the outlawry of war. Much would depend upon how the challenge was met.

The League took no action except to appoint the Lytton Commission to investigate the dispute. No attempt was made to invoke Article 16, according to which economic sanctions against an aggressor were supposed to be mandatory. This was largely due to Britain, whose government disliked Chinese nationalism, was somewhat sympathetic to Japan, and had no desire to become embroiled in a conflict at the other end of the world.

In the United States, Secretary Stimson felt strongly that Japan must be stopped. While he was disturbed by the threat to the balance of power in the Pacific, he was motivated chiefly by a conviction that if aggression was not prevented, international relations would quickly become anarchical and the world would drift into another general war. But since Stimson's convictions were not shared either by Congress or by President Hoover, who was opposed to any action which might lead to war with Japan, he had to battle for the principle of collective security almost singlehanded. Through the autumn of 1931 he tried to persuade the League to take action and promised American cooperation; but it was obviously impossible for the United States to guide the proceedings of an organization which she had refused to join. Early in 1932, after failing to prod the League into action, Stimson announced that the United States would not recognize any territorial changes made by force in violation of treaties (this became known as the Stimson Doctrine). But this diplomatic gesture had no effect on Japan.

In the autumn of 1932 the League accepted the report of the Lytton Committee, which branded Japan as an aggressor; and Japan was expelled from membership. But Japan kept control of Manchukuo. Early in 1933 she signed a truce with China, and the Far East settled down to a few years of relative peace, apart from intermittent fighting between Chiang Kai-shek and the Communists. Thus it had been demonstrated that the peace-loving nations of the world were not willing to stop aggression by collective action—a fact that was appreciated in Rome and Berlin as well as Tokyo.

Thus the early 1930's saw the rise of Hitler and the end of all hope of permanent stability in Europe and a war in the Far East. The Versailles settlement was breaking down, and the world was entering a new period of international conflict. Some Americans believed that the United States ought to assume broader responsibilities for the defense of peace by promising help to victims of aggression. A larger number argued that if the rest of the world proved to be obstinately bent on suicide, the United States could best serve the cause of civilization by isolating herself from other people's quarrels. American opinion on foreign policy thus became more deeply divided, and for a few years isolationist sentiment became much stronger than during the 1920's.

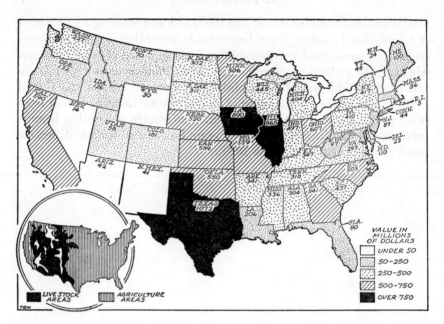

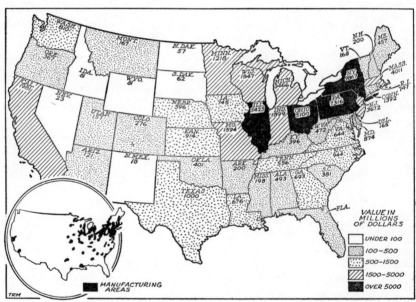

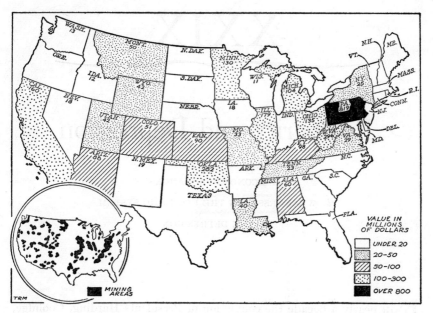

20. American Productive Capacity, 1920

THE THREE LARGE MAPS SHOW THE PRODUCTION OF EACH STATE IN FARMING, manufacturing, and mining, respectively, in the year 1920. The three small maps show areas of concentration in livestock, manufacturing, and mining in 1935. It will be noted that the figures for manufacturing are much larger than those for farming and mining. Although the United States was one of the world's great agricultural nations, the value of its industrial output was four times that of its farm produce.

The maps also indicate that in 1920 the Northeastern quarter of the country still retained the economic supremacy it had established during the nineteenth century. With the exception of Texas, Iowa and Illinois were the richest farming states; and both manufacturing and mining were largely concentrated in a block of states around the Great Lakes from New York to Minnesota, in spite of the opening of mining areas in many other parts of the country. A significant trend of American life since 1920 has been the rapid economic development of the South and the West, especially of Texas and California, and the growth of a better balance of economic power between the different sections.

XXIX

Prosperity and Depression

1. ECONOMIC ADVANCES

2. WEAKNESSES IN THE ECONOMIC SYSTEM

3. THE DEPRESSION

FOR nearly a decade the conviction of Presidents Harding, Coolidge, and Hoover that the primary economic function of government was to assist business in making higher profits, not to police business practices, seemed to be triumphantly justified. Business did indeed make profits on an unexampled scale; investing them in industrial expansion, it rapidly increased the national wealth and productive capacity; and some of the benefits percolated down to wage-earners in the form of new consumers' goods, steady employment, and higher standards of living. Although a considerable part of the population did not share at all in the prosperity, scarcely anybody, whether conservative or liberal, was acute enough to realize that the policy of stimulating the accumulation of profits, which had had strong economic justification in the age of Alexander Hamilton and after the Civil War, must lead eventually to disaster in the new era of abundance. Not until over-production, over-speculation, and under-consumption had brought about the worst depression in American history

SELECTED BIBLIOGRAPHY: Two volumes in *The Economic History of the United States* provide the best survey of economic developments during the 1920's and 1930's: George Soule, *Prosperity Decade: From War to Depression, 1917–1929* (1947), and Broadus Mitchell, *Depression Decade: From New Era Through New Deal, 1929–1941* (1947). A. A. Berle and G. C. Means, *The Modern Corporation and Private Property* (1932), which analyzes the separation between ownership and control in the big corporations, has had a wide influence on economic thinking. Monopoly and oligopoly are described in A. R. Burns, *The Decline of Competition* (1936). For foreign investment, see Cleona Lewis, *America's Stake in International Investments* (1938). One of the best of the many studies of the cause of the depression is J. M. Blair, *Seeds of Destruction* (1938). The depression itself is described in popular style in Gilbert Seldes, *Years of the Locust* (1933), and J. N. Leonard, *Three Years Down* (1939). A. H. Hansen, *Fiscal Policy and Business Cycles* (1941), is a good example of Keynesian thinking.

did it become apparent that throughout the 1920's there had been serious weaknesses in the whole economic structure and that, in failing to take action to rectify them, government had abdicated its proper functions.

1. ECONOMIC ADVANCES

THE MOST conspicuous feature of economic development during the 1920's was the growth of production resulting from the application of new scientific inventions, new sources of power, and new techniques for promoting efficiency. By 1929 sixty-nine workers could produce as much as a hundred workers in 1920. Total production in all branches of the economic system increased between 1920 and 1929 by no less than 46 per cent. In 1929 the national income amounted to $82,000,000,000. Allowing for changes in the value of money, this represented an increase of 31 per cent over 1922, while population during the same period increased by only 11 per cent.

With the steady improvement of productive methods, relatively fewer workers were needed for basic necessities, such as food and clothing. In 1899 these had amounted to 57.9 per cent of all production, but by 1929 the proportion had dropped to 43.6 per cent. Meanwhile there was a rapid increase in new buildings and machinery and in durable consumption goods, such as cars, refrigerators, telephones, and electrical appliances. What this meant, in concrete terms, was that articles originally regarded as luxuries for the upper class were becoming available for the average American family. The middle-class American, in fact, now had a standard of living which would have seemed incredible even to the very rich at any earlier period of history.

Another aspect of economic progress was the rapid growth of service, distribution, and white-collar occupations. Fewer people were employed in making goods, while more people were engaged in administration and in providing amenities for consumers. Between 1920 and 1929, in fact, in spite of the growth of population, the number of industrial workers employed in manufacturing, mining, and transportation actually decreased by more than 500,000, while the number of farmers fell off by nearly 250,-000. According to the census of 1930, only 58 per cent of the employed population were directly engaged in production. Of the remainder, 8 per cent were businessmen, 5.5 per cent were domestic servants, and no less than 30.5 per cent were engaged in professional, clerical, and service occupations.

The Automobile. The industrial expansion of the late nineteenth century had centered on railroads and steel. The expansion of the 1920's was dominated by a building-boom and by a number of new durable-consumption-goods industries. Much the most important of these was the manufacture of automobiles, in which the leading pioneer figure was Henry Ford, of Detroit, Michigan.

The first gasoline-driven vehicles were made in Europe in the 1870's, and in the United States in the early 1890's. At first only the very rich could afford to buy these new contraptions, but by 1909, after sixteen years of experimentation, Henry Ford evolved his famous Model T, which could be produced at a price that made it accessible to middle-class Americans. Ford owned a majority of the stock in the Ford Motor Company and consistently refused to surrender his independence to bankers and stockholders, so that he was free to carry out his own ideas. More fully than any of his contemporaries, he grasped the essential elements of the new era of abundance—standardization and the division of labor in order to cut costs, high wages in order to increase purchasing power, and mass production at low prices for a popular market. Largely as a result of his leadership, the automobile after 1909 ceased to be a toy for the rich and became an essential ingredient in the American standard of living. Ford was an eccentric character, who supervised his employees with a paternalism that sometimes became oppressive and expressed views on world affairs that were often remarkably naïve. But he was one of the key figures in American economic development, and the assembly lines in his factories around Detroit attracted awed pilgrims from all over the world.

After Ford had shown the way, a number of other companies began to make low-cost cars, the most successful of them being General Motors. Controlled by the Du Pont family, this corporation was the most spectacular moneymaker of the 1920's, and anybody who invested $25,000 in it in 1921 was a millionaire by 1929. By 1928 a total of 24,500,000 cars had been manufactured, and nearly 4,000,000 workers were directly or indirectly dependent on the industry. Meanwhile, Federal and state governments cooperated by spending vast sums, in excess of $1,000,000,000 a year, on hard-surfaced highways.

Thus the Americans became a people on wheels. Every big city was soon suffering from apparently insoluble traffic problems; the rhythms of living grew quicker, and death more imminent (by 1950 the automobile had claimed 1,000,000 victims—a figure larger than the total number of battle deaths in all American wars, both foreign and civil); and the nation's oil resources were consumed at a dizzy and alarming rate. But there was no question that the life of the average American, especially in rural areas, had become vastly richer and more varied.

Other Industries.   In many other ways the progress of the sciences was now having revolutionary effects on daily living. Apart from the automobile, perhaps the most significant economic advance of the 1920's was the rapid increase in the use of electricity. This made many forms of manufacturing and transportation cheaper and more efficient, and also brought new comforts to the home and lightened the labors of housewives in their kitchens. Measured in terms of horsepower, the production of electric power grew from 7,500,000,000 in 1912 to 20,300,000,000 in 1922 and 43,200,000,000 in 1930, an expansion of nearly 600 per cent in eighteen years.

While physicists were working wonders with light and power, chemists were creating astonishing new materials for building, clothing, decoration, and innumerable other purposes. Outstanding in this field was the Delaware firm of E. I. Du Pont de Nemours. This had been founded back in 1802 by a French immigrant for the purpose of manufacturing gunpowder, and had been controlled ever since by the same family. After making millions in World War I, the Du Ponts branched out into other forms of industrial chemistry, especially coal tar and cellulose products. During the 1920's the firm earned larger net profits than any other corporation except American Telephone and Telegraph and General Motors.

Meanwhile, other inventions had led to the growth of vast new entertainment industries. The motion picture had been invented during the 1880's, as a result of a series of contributions by different individuals, especially Thomas Edison. But the possibilities of the new medium did not become apparent until 1903, when the first picture to tell a story was made. Before World War I the industry had become concentrated in Hollywood, and the first popular stars, such as Mary Pickford and Charlie Chaplin, had emerged. In the 1920's movie-going became a national habit, and Hollywood captured the entertainment market of the world. By 1926 there were 20,000 movie theaters in the United States, with an average attendance of 100,000,000 persons a week, a figure only slightly smaller than the total population. In 1927, with *The Jazz Singer* (starring Al Jolson), came the victory of the talking picture. Radio was made possible early in the century by the inventions of the Italian Guglielmo Marconi and the American Lee De Forest. It began to be a part of American life on November 2, 1920, when Station KDKA in Pittsburgh started regular broadcasts. By 1927 there were 732 different stations, and a receiving set had become a normal feature in the American home.[1]

Another triumph of technology, aviation, was expanding during the later 1920's, though the air did not become a generally accepted mode of travel until the 1940's. Human beings had dreamed of flying for thousands of years; but the first persons to construct a successful flying machine were two obscure young men who kept a bicycle shop at Dayton, Ohio: Wilbur and Orville Wright. They began to study flying in 1896, choosing for their experiments the desolate sand dunes of Kitty Hawk on the coast of North Carolina. Their first flight was made on December 17, 1903, although they were so uninterested in publicity, and newspapermen were so skeptical, that there was no general realization that the air had been conquered until five years later. World War I stimulated aviation in all leading countries, but after the war the United States failed to maintain

[1] Authority to allot wave lengths to different stations was exercised at first by the Department of Commerce, and was entrusted in 1934 to a new Federal Communications Commission (FCC).

an efficient air force, and there was little industrial development. Then, in 1925, Congress passed the Air Mail Act, empowering the government to subsidize the industry through mail contracts, and in 1927 Charles A. Lindbergh's solo flight across the Atlantic aroused popular enthusiasm. After this there was a steady growth both in the manufacture of airplanes and in air travel and transportation.

 Towards an Economy of Abundance. Many of the new inventions of the early twentieth century, unlike those associated with the beginnings of machine production, directly enriched the lives of the average citizen. Their combined effect upon human life was so momentous that they can fairly be described as a Second Industrial Revolution. The age of coal and steam was being replaced by an age of oil and electricity. With the use of the new sources of power and forms of transportation, it was no longer necessary for human beings to be massed in vast industrial cities. Urban areas, no longer overshadowed by smoking factory chimneys, could become cleaner and more healthful. The farmer no longer lived in isolation, and the barriers between the city and the country began to disappear.

 It was widely believed during the 1920's, moreover, that the United States had entered a new era of permanent abundance, and that mass production, combined with high wage levels, was abolishing poverty and creating, for the first time in history, a high standard of living for everybody. This belief was widely held by businessmen, who no longer spoke in the "public-be-damned" terms characteristic of the period following the Civil War, and liked to describe themselves as engaged in serving the public. Service and high ethical standards were preached by the Rotary Clubs and other businessmen's organizations. Most big corporations now felt a need for popular support, and spent large sums on new and more subtle forms of advertising, known as "public relations." It is easy, of course, to be cynical about the talk of service—obviously business was still carried on to make profits—yet the increasing willingness of business leaders to recognize that they had social responsibilities, and to appreciate the dependence of prosperity upon mass purchasing power, was a significant trend, although practice often fell short of precept.

2. WEAKNESSES IN THE ECONOMIC SYSTEM

UNFORTUNATELY, the high hopes of the 1920's were destined to be frustrated by the great depression of the 1930's. Although the American economy could produce goods in an astonishing quantity and variety, it had not solved the problem of distribution. An analysis of how industry was organized and controlled and income distributed shows that there were serious weaknesses in the mechanisms of the market. In retrospect, it is easy to see why these led finally to a financial crisis and made the ensuing depression unusually prolonged and intense.

Monopoly and Oligopoly.   With each decade since the Civil War the big corporations had achieved a greater dominance in the economic system. In 1929 there were 1,349 corporations with annual incomes in excess of $1,000,000. These earned 80 per cent of all corporate profits, leaving only 20 per cent to the remaining 455,000 corporations. In fact, almost half of all corporate wealth, and almost a quarter of the total national wealth, was the property of only 200 firms. Big corporations controlled transportation and public utilities, did most of the nation's manufacturing, and (with the growth of chain stores) were rapidly moving ahead in retail trade. Small ownership remained strong only in agriculture, some consumers' goods industries (such as clothing), some forms of retail trade, and service occupations.

Probably there was less outright monopoly in 1929 than in 1901. This was due partly to trust-busting, and partly to the vast economic expansion, which had made it more difficult for a single firm to dominate an entire industry. But the decrease of monopoly had not brought much revival of price competition. The characteristic situation in most key industries was now "oligopoly"—control of the market not by one corporation but by a few. Under oligopoly corporations usually cooperated with each other in maintaining uniform prices, either by agreement or by following a "price leader," while they competed through improvements in quality and through advertising. This was true in many basic capital goods industries, such as steel, and in some consumer goods industries; the four or five leading cigarette companies, for example, always charged the same prices.

There were, of course, strong arguments in favor of managed prices, since they facilitated long-range planning and expansion. But it is probable that price-control enabled the big corporations to take more than their fair share of the consumers' dollars, and certain that it made it more difficult for the economy to weather a depression. Under a fully competitive system any decrease in purchasing power would have been quickly counteracted by a cut in prices. But when the depression started, the big corporations found it more profitable to keep their prices stable and cut production, thereby increasing unemployment and intensifying the crisis. Price rigidity was thus one major weakness in the economic system.

Corporate Organization.   Some of the newer industries were controlled by entrepreneurs who, like Carnegie, Rockefeller, and their contemporaries, combined ownership with management. Such men as Henry Ford and the Du Pont brothers were genuinely creative builders and organizers. Other business leaders were primarily financial promoters seeking speculative profits; this type was especially prevalent in the electric power industries, Samuel Insull being a notorious example. But in the older and better-established industries, with the steady trend towards the separation of ownership from management, there was no longer so much room for individual drive and ambition. Ownership was diffused among large numbers of stockholders, while management was assumed by salaried executives who had often worked their way up within the corporation hierarchy. This tendency was most fully exemplified in the country's largest organization, American Telephone and Telegraph, which by 1930 was "owned" by no fewer than 570,000 stockholders, none of whom held as much as 1 per cent. Among the 200 largest corporations, there were 88, controlling nearly 30 per cent of all corporate wealth, in which ownership and management were now completely divorced from each other. Many other large and medium-sized corporations were evolving rapidly in the same direction.

With the rapid increase in the number of stockholders, it was sometimes asserted that the United States was becoming a nation of capitalists. This was unduly optimistic. Nobody knows how many different individuals owned stock, but certainly the major share of the profits of industry went to a relatively small group. In 1929 more than one-third of all dividends was paid to only 17,000 owners, and more than three-fifths to only 150,000 owners. Some of the recipients were insurance companies, colleges, and other endowed institutions, but the majority were individuals belonging to a wealthy upper class.

The Distribution of Income.   A trend of major significance in the prosperity period of the 1920's was that salaries and profits increased much more rapidly than wages. It is true that American workers made substantial gains. Many corporations (partly in order to check the growth of unionism) gave substantial wage increases, adopted pension plans, and spent large sums on welfare and recreation. Nevertheless, the wage increases failed to keep pace with the growth of production. Between 1922 and 1929 the real wages of industrial workers rose, on an average, by 1.4 per cent a year, whereas production per capita was increasing by 2.4 per cent a year. During these years the total money wages paid to industrial workers increased by 33 per cent, as contrasted with a rise in salaries of 42 per cent, in corporation net profits of 76 per cent, and in stockholders' dividends of 108 per cent. Thus, while the wage-earners were earning larger incomes, they were at the same time receiving a smaller share of the national income.

An appreciable part of the population, moreover, definitely had no share in the prosperity. This was true of the workers in certain depressed occupations, such as textile manufacturing and the mining of bituminous coal. More significantly, it was true for many of the farmers. The expanded production of the war years was followed in 1921 by a catastrophic drop in farm prices of no less than 44 per cent. Throughout the 1920's agriculture never fully recovered. With the loss of foreign markets, overproduction was more or less chronic, and farm prices remained low. In 1929, in terms of the ratio of farm prices to other prices, the farmers were 11 per cent worse off than in 1913. Few of them were able to pay off the heavy debts they had incurred during the boom years of the war, and mortgages and tenancy continued to increase. A relatively small number of prosperous commercial farmers had no real cause for complaint, but millions of farm families, especially in the South, lived close to starvation. Half of all the farm families, numbering more than 3,000,000, had annual incomes (including what they raised for their own consumption) of less than $1,000 apiece.

In 1929, according to figures compiled by the Brookings Institution, more than 70 per cent of the employed population were receiving less than $2,500 a year, and more than 40 per cent were receiving less than $1,500 a year. Thus, in spite of the progress made during the 1920's, the country still fell far short of giving all its citizens a high standard of living. The degree of inequality, moreover, had become so acute that the 631,000 families at the top of the economic ladder were earning substantially more than the 16,000,000 families at the bottom of the ladder. This is shown in the following table:

Income Group	Families in Thousands	Per Cent	Income in Millions	Per Cent
Under $1,000	5,899	21.5	$2,900	3.8
$1,000–1,999	10,455	38.0	$15,364	19.9
$2,000–2,999	5,192	18.9	$12,586	16.3
$3,000–4,999	3,672	13.4	$13,866	18.0
$5,000–9,999	1,625	5.9	$10,820	14.0
$10,000 and above	631	2.3	$21,580	28.0

Savings and Purchasing Power. Since the richer classes save a large part of their incomes, while the poor save little or nothing, inequality of income distribution leads to a rapid growth of savings. This is desirable in so far as the savings can then be invested in industrial expansion. But the purpose of expansion is to produce more goods for consumers, and it is profitable only to the extent that people are able and willing to buy them. For this reason an economic system is likely to run into difficulties if savings are allowed to run too far ahead of consumers' purchasing power. This happened during the later 1920's, which differed in this respect from earlier boom periods. Large sums were laid aside by people in the upper income brackets. Most of the big corporations, moreover, were accumulating savings instead of distributing all their profits to stockholders.[2] The result was that the building and industrial expansion of the later 1920's was in excess of the effective needs of the economy, while at the same time additional billions of dollars of savings were diverted into speculation in real estate and the stock market instead of being invested in production.

Why did the deficiency of purchasing power fail to become manifest before 1929? The answer can be found in the growth of debt. A consider-

[2] This growth of corporate saving was a development of considerable importance, since it diminished the importance of the investment market and the influence of the banking houses.

able proportion of the goods sold during the 1920's, especially of the durable consumers' goods that formed so important a part of industrial production, were not paid for immediately. But the process of piling up debts could not continue indefinitely. Borrowing money and buying on credit enlarged the market for the time being, but sooner or later the debts would have to be paid and the market would then contract.

The Growth of Debt.   One form of debt was installment buying. Between 1923 and 1929 this is estimated to have averaged $5,000,000,000 a year. The average American family bought its car and its refrigerator by making a small down payment and contracting to pay the remainder over a period of years. There was also a rapid increase in other forms of private debts. By 1930 the total farm mortgage debt amounted to $9,200,-000,000, while the urban mortgage debt had reached the colossal sum of $26,000,000,000. Businessmen, particularly those owning small or medium-sized firms, were also borrowing heavily for expansion. By the end of the 1920's a most intricate system of debt obligations had developed. The total amount of private debts, long-term and short-term, was well in excess of $200,000,000,000, and nearly everybody seemed to be in debt to somebody else. This made the whole economy more vulnerable to depressions, since whenever any group became unable to meet its obligations, the whole structure would start collapsing like a house of cards.

There was a considerable increase also in the public debt. Although the Federal government was reducing the national debt, states and municipalities were piling up bond issues for the building of roads, bridges, offices, and hospitals. Spending on public works during the 1920's averaged $3,000,000,000 a year. This was partly paid out of taxes, but by 1930 the total debt of local governments had reached $16,000,000,000.

Foreign Investments.   Another influential factor in prolonging the prosperity was investment in foreign countries. Prior to World War I the United States had remained, on balance, a debtor country; foreigners had invested more money in the United States than Americans had invested abroad. During the war much of the investment held by foreigners was liquidated, and the United States emerged as the world's leading creditor nation, taking the place formerly held by Britain in the world's money market. American bankers and businessmen then began to invest heavily abroad. By 1929 the total American long-term foreign investments (not counting the war debts due to the American government) amounted to nearly $15,400,000,000. Of this sum, $7,800,000,000 represented American holdings of foreign securities, while $7,600,000,000 represented American ownership of properties in foreign countries. A total of $5,400,000,000 had been invested in Latin America, $4,600,000,000 in Europe, $3,700,000,000 in Canada, and $1,400,000,000 in Asia and the Pacific. Since foreigners held $5,700,000,000 worth of investments in the United States, America's credit balance was $9,700,000,000.

One of the effects of foreign investment was to make it possible for foreign countries to buy more American goods. The United States continued to export some agricultural products, especially cotton (more than half of which was shipped abroad), tobacco, and wheat. She was also flooding the rest of the world with manufactured goods, capturing markets that had formerly been held by the British and the Germans. Between 1922 and 1929 American exports exceeded imports by a figure averaging $700,000,000 a year. In other words, the American economy was disposing of part of its surplus products by shipping them abroad and was at the same time lending foreign countries the money with which to pay for them.

If a creditor country invests its capital constructively in undeveloped areas (in the building of railroads and utilities, for example) and looks for moderate long-term profits rather than for quick speculative gains, then the process benefits everybody concerned. Some of the American foreign investment of the 1920's was of this nature. Unfortunately, much of it was badly mishandled. This was particularly true of the purchase of the securities of foreign governments. Although the State Department in 1922 asked for advance information about foreign loans, there was no effective government supervision. The process was left to Wall Street bankers, some of whom were more interested in collecting commissions than in finding sound investments for the savings entrusted to them by American citizens.

It would perhaps be unfair to blame the bankers for sinking vast sums in Germany; they could hardly foresee Hitler and World War II. But they can fairly be accused of irresponsibility in lending nearly $2,000,-000,000 to governments, most of them dictatorships, in Latin America. The bankers were, in fact, so eager for business that they paid large gratuities to influential citizens in those countries in order to bring about more borrowing.[3] Two billion dollars, wisely invested, could have done much for the people of Latin America. Actually the money was largely wasted on unnecessary public buildings, war materials, and other unproductive purposes. The dictators got the money, Wall Street got its commissions, and the bill was paid by gullible investors throughout the United States. During the depression all but two of the Latin American countries stopped payment on their foreign debts, and two-thirds of these loans have remained permanently in default ever since.[4]

The recklessness with which the bankers disposed of other people's money was the most sensational feature of the foreign lending but not the most important one. America's rise to creditor status raised some fundamental questions of national policy. Loans were made to foreign countries

[3] For example, the son of the President of Peru was paid $415,000; the son-in-law of the President of Cuba received $500,000 along with an annual salary of $19,000.

[4] Argentina continued payments, while Venezuela, which had a large revenue from oil royalties, never ran up a foreign debt.

on the assumption that interest would be paid back. But in the long run
countries could meet these financial obligations only by selling goods in
the American market. Yet, at the same time that the United States was
investing capital abroad, she was also maintaining a tariff policy designed
to reserve as much as possible of the American market for native producers and was continuing to export more goods than she imported. Her
economic policy was thus schizophrenic. The United States could not
permanently go on disposing of both her surplus money and her surplus
goods in foreign markets unless she was willing to forgo repayment. What
actually happened was that by 1929 interest payments by foreign countries on earlier loans amounted to a larger sum than the new foreign
loans. This could result only in a drop in American exports, and was a
contributory cause of the great depression.

Causes of the Depression.   The weaknesses in the system of distribution can now be summarized. Relatively too much money was saved,
while not enough was available for spending by consumers. Part of the
accumulation of savings was invested in expansion; but sooner or later
a time had to come when the supply of new factories, machinery, office
buildings, and apartment houses was in excess of the actual possibilities of
the market. Throughout the 1920's the market was stimulated through
the growth of debt, both internal and foreign. But debt is like a drug; the
doses have to be increased, and cannot safely go on indefinitely. As
the debts began to be repaid, the market contracted. And once the period
of expansion ended and the capital goods industries slowed down, there
were a number of reasons why the economy could not easily or quickly
readjust itself.

One reason was the extremely intricate system of debt obligations.
As soon as one group became unable to meet its obligations, everybody
else ran into difficulties. A second reason was price-fixing by the big corporations. This deprived the economy of the necessary flexibility and capacity for quick readjustment. Instead of cutting prices and maintaining
production, the corporations during the depression maintained prices and
cut production, thereby creating large-scale unemployment. And a third
reason was the dependence of the economy on the sale of durable goods.
Even in bad times people have to eat, but they can easily refrain from
buying new cars and refrigerators and moving into new houses. Recovery
in these industries was therefore extremely slow.

These material factors, however, do not present the whole picture.
For the inner motor which keeps the wheels rolling in a modern industrial
community is psychological. Prosperity depends upon that mysterious
thing known as "confidence," which causes businessmen to expand their
activities, incur debts on the assumption that they can repay them,
produce new goods in the expectation that somebody will buy them, and
keep money and goods in circulation. And while the state of mind of the
business community depends upon objective factors, it has a tendency to

run to extremes. During the boom period of the 1920's confidence led to frenzied over-production, speculation, and piling up of debts. When the crash came, on the other hand, confidence suddenly disappeared, and businessmen immediately became reluctant to undertake any new enterprises whatever.

3. THE DEPRESSION

The Collapse of 1929. By the summer of 1929 there were already symptoms of a coming depression. Production was declining in the building, steel, and automobile industries, and workmen were being laid off. But scarcely anybody realized the significance of these facts, since attention was concentrated on the dizzy rise in the price of stocks. In retrospect, in fact, the great bull market of 1929 can only be regarded as a case of temporary mass insanity.

That the proper function of the stock market was to provide facilities for the investment of capital in productive enterprise was now almost forgotten. It had become a place where a large proportion of the American people expected to make fortunes by gambling on the price of stocks. People bought stocks not because they wanted sound investments but in the hope that they could sell them to other people a few weeks later at substantial profits. Wall Street financiers had been making money in this fashion for generations, but in the late 1920's millions of ordinary American citizens engaged in speculation, and many of them began to buy stocks on margin; in other words, they actually paid only a small fraction of the price and were given credit by their brokers for the remainder. As a result of mass speculation, stock prices went on rising and ceased to bear any relation whatever to the companies' real capacity for earning dividends. But this process could not continue indefinitely, and as soon as prices began to turn downwards, the millions of people who had bought on margin stocks which they could not genuinely afford would be forced to sell in a hurry.

Catastrophe was therefore inevitable. Nevertheless, many bankers, economists, and public officials reiterated that stock prices were not too high; and since experts viewed the situation so optimistically, the general public could scarcely be expected to show more foresight. Some of the bankers, notably Charles E. Mitchell of the National City Bank, were, in fact, doing everything possible to stimulate stock-buying by as many people as possible. The Federal Reserve Board had powers to limit speculation and curtail brokers' loans, but it took no action until March, 1929, and when it finally tried to check buying on margin, some of the bankers violently denounced it and refused to comply with its recommendations. By this time, of course, it was too late to save the situation; any public recognition that speculation was excessive would in itself precipitate the crash.

On October 19, 1929, stock prices passed their peak, and began to fall. The first bad day was October 24, but the real catastrophe came on October 29. Some 16,500,000 shares were traded; prices dropped in some cases as much as 80 per cent below their September levels; no buyers at all could be found for many of them; and hundreds of thousands of margin accounts were wiped out. These events marked the beginning of a depression which spread to every country in the world except the Soviet Union and rocked to its foundations the whole structure of Western civilization.

Obviously, the American people had as much real wealth in November 1929 as in September. Most people therefore supposed that prosperity would continue. But the catastrophe on the stock exchange disrupted the whole process of circulation and distribution. Although there was as much real wealth, some $30,000,000,000 of paper wealth had been wiped out. The result was that businessmen stopped investing money in expansion, and consumers began to buy fewer goods, particularly of the durable goods that had been so important throughout the 1920's. Production of capital goods and durable consumers' goods therefore declined; workers in those industries were laid off; and the growth of unemployment resulted in further contractions of purchasing power, which led, in turn, to more unemployment. Meanwhile, with the contraction of American loans and American purchases, depression spread to Europe and Latin America, and in 1931 the collapse of their economies reacted upon the United States. Thus for three long and dreary years the economic system continued to spiral downwards, and the lowest point was not reached until July 1932.

The Course of the Depression.   Between 1929 and 1932 the national income decreased from $82,000,000,000 to $40,000,000,000. Allowing for the fall in prices, this represented a drop in production of 37 per cent. Exports sank from $5,240,000,000 to $1,611,000,000, and imports from $4,399,000,000 to $1,322,000,000.

The general reaction of industry, wherever prices were not determined competitively, was to cut production rather than prices. Total industrial production fell by 48 per cent, the result being a rapid growth of unemployment. Total wages paid by industry fell from $10,909,000,000 to $4,608,000,000, while factory employment fell off by 38 per cent. Wage rates were not sharply reduced, and as a result of the fall in the cost of living those workers who succeeded in keeping full-time jobs were actually better off than before the depression. But many people were put on part time, and by the summer of 1932 the total number of unemployed was variously estimated at between 12,000,000 and 16,000,000. This represented more than one-quarter of the nation's total labor force.

In 1929 corporations had earned total net profits of $8,740,000,000. In 1932 they reported a net deficit of $5,640,000,000. There were 4,377 bank failures, with a loss to depositors of $2,752,000,000. But by no means all corporations operated at a loss. Many of the more powerful ones continued to make small profits all through the depression, while there were a few, such as the cigarette companies, which were able to take advantage of the fall in raw material prices and actually earned higher dividends than before 1929.

The farmers, on the other hand, could not control prices and had to continue producing. Total farm production dropped by only 6 per cent, while prices fell by the catastrophic figure of 63 per cent. The total farm income declined from $12,791,000,000 to $5,562,000,000. At its lowest point in 1932 the purchasing power of the farmers was exactly one-half of what it had been ten years earlier.

These grim statistics tell a story of mass misery on a scale unequaled in earlier American history. There had been five major depressions during the nineteenth century, and on each occasion business had eventually recovered without direct help from the government. But the depression of the 1930's involved a larger proportion of the population and lasted for a longer period. Its psychological effects, moreover, were more shocking because of the contrast with the high hopes of permanent prosperity that had been entertained during the 1920's.

For almost a year after the crash it was assumed that the economy would quickly recover, and the growing number of the unemployed were left to depend on private charity. During the winter of 1930–31 the cities began giving direct relief, and jobless persons selling apples at street corners became a familiar sight. By the following winter the resources of charity and of the city governments were almost exhausted, and most of the states were appropriating money for relief. Yet economic conditions continued to deteriorate, with no end in sight, and each year saw more banks and business corporations tumbling into bankruptcy. By 1932 hundreds of thousands of people had become homeless migrants and were drifting aimlessly about the country. Hundreds of thousands more were living in huts built out of refuse timber on vacant city lots (these colonies were known ironically as Hoovervilles). Half a million city workers had gone back into agriculture. The remainder of the vast army of the unemployed were being supported by relatives or on the tiny sums doled out in relief by the city or state governments. For a substantial part of the American people, the depression meant the deprivation of homes and savings, prolonged malnutrition, and a loss of self-respect and of confidence in their own capacity to support themselves.

Yet perhaps the most remarkable feature of the depression was the patience displayed by most of its victims. Throughout these bitter years the American people displayed an extraordinary respect for law and order and the rights of property. Among the farmers there were a few outbreaks of organized violence. In the summer of 1931 starving cotton-growers in Arkansas seized food from local storekeepers. Early in 1933 law courts throughout the Middle West were forcibly prevented from ordering the seizure of farms on account of unpaid debts and taxes, an episode remi-

niscent of Shays's Rebellion 146 years earlier. Some groups of workers,
notably the bituminous coal-miners, went on strike against wage-cuts,
and in a few instances demonstrations of the unemployed became riotous,
largely because of interference by the police. But on the whole the country
remained astonishingly peaceful.

Political Repercussions.   In parts of Europe the depression struck
a fatal blow at liberalism, democracy, and private-enterprise capitalism.
A growing number of people were willing to give up freedom in the hope
of achieving economic security. Many of them turned to communism, with
its promise of a classless society and a planned economy. A larger number
responded to the propaganda of fascist organizations that sought power
by stirring up racial and religious hatreds, particularly in Germany, where
the social structure had already been weakened by defeat in war and the
post-war inflation. Appealing primarily to the middle class and to the
unemployed, and attributing the crisis partly to the Jews and partly to
the Versailles Treaty, the Nazis rapidly gained strength and finally took
control of the government in January 1933. Even in those countries which
retained their faith in democracy, governments assumed much wider
powers of economic regulation. Each country tried to protect its own
economy from crises elsewhere, and tariffs and other impediments to
world trade increased. The general trend was towards an economic nationalism resembling the mercantilism of the seventeenth and eighteenth
centuries. Latin America, largely dependent on the sale of its raw materials in the world market, suffered as acutely as Europe. There were revolutions in Argentina, Brazil, Chile, and nine other countries, followed by
attempts to promote national self-sufficiency and to stimulate native
industries.

Only the Soviet Union, largely isolated from the rest of the world
and operating on different economic principles, seemed immune from
crises and unemployment. Its first Five Year Plan, initiated in 1928, was
rapidly approaching completion. The statistics of Russian industrial
growth and the contrast with conditions under capitalism were indeed
thought-provoking. There was as yet little awareness in western countries
of the inefficiency of Communist planning, the growth of a new privileged
ruling class, the repressiveness of Stalin's government, and the "liquida-
tion" of millions of peasant farmers.

In the United States, as also in Britain, democracy had more solid
foundations, and totalitarian movements made little headway. The only
large-scale change of popular sentiment was from the Republicans to the
Democrats. In less obvious ways, however, the depression tended to
weaken faith in the American tradition. This was especially noticeable
among intellectuals. The shock of World War I, followed by the feverish
moneymaking of the 1920's, had already given many of them a feeling of
being alienated from their society, unable to participate in its activities

or believe in its values. This sense of not belonging was now reinforced by the economic collapse.

Socialism and Communism.   The depression caused many idealistic Americans—writers, professors, ministers of religion, and college students—to feel that economic salvation could be found only through a planned economy, and to become sympathetically interested in the Soviet experiment and willing to believe that it was moving, on the whole, in the right direction. Few of them became definitely converted to Socialism or Communism. In spite of the able leadership of Norman Thomas, the Socialist Party polled less than 900,000 votes in the 1932 election and dropped below 200,000 in 1936. The Communist Party remained a small organization with a membership which by 1934 had risen to only 25,000. But although only a handful of Americans joined the Communist Party or voted for its candidates at elections, a much larger number were willing to cooperate with it in the pursuit of common objectives.

The Communists adopted a policy of setting up "front" organizations to work for trade-union rights, racial equality, an anti-fascist foreign policy, friendship with the Soviet Union, and other aims which would win liberal support. The result was that during the 1930's the Communist Party achieved a much wider influence than its actual voting strength seemed to indicate, and was able to infiltrate trade unions, departments of the Federal government, and other positions of power. This period of liberal-Communist collaboration ended in the later 1930's, when the series of Moscow trials, followed by the Stalin-Hitler pact of 1939, made it apparent that the Soviet Union did not actually stand for peace or justice. Most of the front organizations were then dissolved because of lack of popular support, but Communism retained a small body of fanatical adherents, including a few in influential positions.

Fascist Tendencies.   Fascism had very little appeal to Americans, at least in its fully developed form. A number of would-be Hitlers and Mussolinis offered to save the country from Catholics, Communists, Jews, and foreigners in general; but only a handful of mentally unbalanced characters joined their organizations. The depression, however, produced three mass leaders whose irrational and hysterical propaganda had a disturbingly fascist flavor: Huey Long, Dr. Francis Townsend, and Father Charles E. Coughlin.

Long was elected Governor of Louisiana in 1928, and went on to the United States Senate in 1930. A cross between a Populist spellbinder and a Caribbean dictator, he acquired virtually absolute powers over the State of Louisiana, but used them for the benefit not only of himself and his friends but also of the poorer classes, who received better schools and roads. During the depression he began to build a national organization for the redistribution of property, with the slogans "Share Our Wealth" and "Every Man a King." With his inordinate ambition, great ability, and talent for mob oratory, he seemed like a real threat to American liberties. Except among his followers, there was little regret when he was assassinated at Baton Rouge in 1935. Dr. Townsend, a retired California physician, conceived the idea that depressions could be prevented by paying a pension of $200 a month to everybody above the age of sixty. Townsend himself seems to have been an honest man, but no competent economist approved of his plan, and the methods used by his associates to promote it were decidedly demagogic. Father Coughlin, a Catholic priest attached to the Shrine of the Little Flower at Royal Oak, Michigan, won a vast audience by his highly emotional radio oratory. He denounced bankers, demanded inflation, advocated isolationism, and became steadily more sympathetic to Hitlerism. As the pro-Nazi implications of his program became more explicit, he lost much of his popular support, although he did not abandon his political activities until after the United States entered World War II.

Conservatives and Liberals.   Although Long, Townsend, and Coughlin all made claims (probably exaggerated) to millions of followers, and certainly had some influence on legislation during the 1930's, the large majority of the American people retained their sense of reality. What they wanted was to bring about full production and employment without at the same time destroying the essential liberty of the individual to choose his own occupation, accumulate property, and save or spend his money as he pleased. When individuals had no rights, it was easy to put all of them to work, as both Stalin and Hitler demonstrated, but the economic problems confronting a democratic people were more complex.

During the darkest period of the depression virtually everybody demanded vigorous action by the Federal government, but there was considerable disagreement about its objectives. Conservatives regarded government intervention as a temporary expedient, and insisted that the economic system was basically sound. They attributed the crisis partly to the disturbing effects of the war and the post-war debt and reparations payments, and partly to errors of financial policy. According to Winthrop W. Aldrich, Chairman of the Board of the Chase National Bank, "the real trouble in 1928 and 1929 was . . . an excess of bank credit going into capital uses and speculative uses due to the cheap money policies of the Federal Reserve System during the nineteen-twenties." Liberals, on the other hand, emphasized the restricted purchasing power of the farmers and many of the wage-earners, and called for government action to diminish inequalities of income and raise mass living standards.

The most influential liberal economist of the 1930's was the Englishman John Maynard Keynes. Keynes believed that the accumulation of surplus savings was due to more fundamental causes than errors of financial policy. He argued that this was bound to happen in a mature economy and could not be rectified by the automatic processes of supply and demand. The remedy, he suggested, was for the government to put these savings into circulation through a public works program and thereby compensate for the decline of private investment. Thus the traditional belief in a constantly balanced budget ought to be abandoned; in times of prosperity the government could impose heavy taxes and start reducing the national debt, but during a depression it ought to spend more than it took in. According to Keynes, government financial policy, if wisely managed, could serve as a control over the workings of the economy, evening out business cycles and maintaining full employment. The Keynesian theory was adopted by a number of influential American economists, such as Alvin Hansen of Harvard, and had largely permeated American liberal thought by the later 1930's.

Thus almost all Americans were agreed that, contrary to nineteenth-century practice, the Federal government should take positive steps to restore prosperity; and most of them accepted the traditional American system of constitutional government and private enterprise, rejecting both fascistic calls for a dictator and Socialist and Communist programs for the abolition of private ownership. But throughout the 1930's and 1940's there were violent controversies between budget-balancers and Keynesians, and between those who proposed to bring about recovery by restoring business confidence and those who laid more emphasis on the need for mass purchasing power. These conflicts became, in fact, so virulent that they obscured the important fact that both sides were essentially in agreement about their basic objectives. The United States, unlike many European countries, was in no danger either of civil war or of revolution.

XXX

The New Deal

1. THE HOOVER ADMINISTRATION

2. ROOSEVELT AND HIS NEW DEAL

3. NEW DEAL LEGISLATION

4. FOREIGN POLICY DURING THE NEW DEAL PERIOD

T HE ECONOMIC crisis dominated American politics for nearly a decade. Both Hoover and Roosevelt, unlike nineteenth-century presidents during depression periods, attempted to bring about recovery. Government encouragement and supervision of economic growth had been, of course, established practices ever since the time of Alexander Hamilton. But the measures adopted during the 1930's were of unprecedented scope and involved far-reaching changes in the relation between government and business.

1. THE HOOVER ADMINISTRATION

Hoover's Attitude. Hoover accepted this expansion of government responsibility with obvious reluctance. He was a strong believer in

---

SELECTED BIBLIOGRAPHY: Among the more useful general surveys of the period are D. W. Brogan, *The Era of Franklin D. Roosevelt* (1951), a volume in the *Chronicles of America* series; Broadus Mitchell, *Depression Decade* (1947); and Dixon Wecter, *The Age of the Great Depression* (1948). Ex-President Hoover has told his own story in *The Memoirs of Herbert Hoover:* Vol. 2, *The Cabinet and the Presidency* (1951), and Vol. 3, *The Great Depression* (1952). The best general account of the Roosevelt administration is Basil Rauch, *The History of the New Deal* (1944). Merle Fainsod and Lincoln Gordon, *Government and the American Economy* (1941), analyzes the various New Deal agencies. S. I. Rosenman (ed.), *The Public Papers and Addresses of Franklin D. Roosevelt* (9 vols., 1938–40), is an indispensable source of information. Frank Friedel is writing a biography of Roosevelt, of which three volumes have appeared (1952–). One volume has been published of *The Age of Roosevelt* (1957–) by A. M. Schlesinger, Jr. The rise of organized labor can be studied in Herbert Harris, *American Labor* (1939), and *Labor's Civil War* (1940). For Latin-American relations, see F. O. Guerrant, *Roosevelt's Good Neighbor Policy* (1950).

the virtues of private enterprise and of what he called "rugged individ-ualism." Afraid of the growth of a "superstate where every man becomes the servant of the State and real liberty is lost," he was convinced that relief for the unemployed must be left to private charity and the local authorities; if needy persons acquired the habit of looking to Washington for support, liberty would be destroyed and the country would come under the dictatorship of "a remote bureaucracy." On the other hand, the Federal government, he felt, might legitimately give financial help to business in order to shore up private enterprise and save it from total collapse.

Hoover had a clearly integrated philosophy of government, and showed considerable courage in sticking to it through the depression. But his willingness to give Federal aid to corporations, while denying it to starving people, inevitably caused him to appear as callously indifferent to human suffering. Nor did he have the ebullience and showmanship needed for successful leadership in a time of crisis. He was a man of high integrity, an efficient administrator, and extremely hard-working. Un-fortunately, he resented criticism, was inclined to see every problem in the gloomiest possible terms, lacked political skill and experience, and was totally incapable of dramatizing his personality and program in such a way as to appeal to the mass of the people. No president has taken office under apparently more favorable auspices; none except Andrew Johnson has left it more widely distrusted and disliked.

The Hoover Program. During the first two years after the Wall Street debacle Hoover doubled Federal spending on public works, urged businessmen not to cut wages, and sponsored monetary policies making possible an expansion of credit. Feeling that what was chiefly needed was a revival of business confidence, he went on reiterating that prosperity would soon return (according to his opponents he said it was "just around the corner"). But by the summer of 1931, with the spread of the depres-sion throughout the world and the collapse of the financial structure of central Europe, it became obvious that there would be no quick recovery in the United States. Hoover then persuaded the European powers to accept a moratorium on all war-debt and reparations payments (this was supposed to last for a year only, but actually the payments were never resumed), while at home he proposed a comprehensive program of aid for property-owners threatened with bankruptcy.

Congress, now controlled by Democrats and farm-belt progressives, did not respond very quickly. Many members asked for generous appro-priations for direct relief and public works, to which Hoover refused to agree. But after bitter and prolonged debates most of the program was adopted. A Reconstruction Finance Corporation was set up to lend money to business corporations. Home-owners in danger of losing their homes could have their mortgages refinanced by twelve Federal Home Loan Banks, while farmers could receive help from the Federal Land Banks.

These measures, it was hoped, would stop the chain of disaster. At the same time a large extension of bank credit was made possible through changes in the Federal Reserve System, and taxes were increased to compensate for the decrease in Federal revenue, in the hope of balancing the budget. Whether these measures would have restored business confidence and started an upswing is, of course, debatable. By the time they went into effect the presidential election of 1932 was rapidly approaching.

The Election of 1932.   Renominated by the Republicans, Hoover argued that the severity of the depression was due to world conditions over which the United States had no control, and that his program was already producing results. The Democratic platform promised a balanced budget, a cut in Federal expenditures, a sound currency, and no interference with legitimate private enterprise, but at the same time called for reform of certain business abuses and Federal spending on relief and public works. The candidate was Franklin Delano Roosevelt, Governor of New York since 1928. While Roosevelt promised to adhere to the party platform, and castigated Hoover on several occasions for his failure to keep the budget balanced, he also gave expression to the main principles of what afterwards became the New Deal, though in somewhat vague and general terms. There was never any doubt that the Democrats would win a sweeping victory, and Roosevelt carried no fewer than forty states.

The election was followed by a deterioration of financial conditions which threatened to ruin every bank in the country. By February 1933 alarmed depositors were removing their money in such quantities that the state governments were compelled to intervene. Michigan decreed a bank holiday on February 14, and by the time Roosevelt took office on March 4 nearly every other state had taken similar action.

2. ROOSEVELT AND HIS NEW DEAL

The New Dealers.   Prior to his election to the presidency few people regarded Franklin D. Roosevelt as endowed with any unusual qualities of leadership. He was destined, nevertheless, to become one of the great world-figures of modern times and to inspire both admiration and hatred on a scale unparalleled in recent American history.

In seeking first to end the depression and afterwards to defeat the Axis and establish world peace, Roosevelt adopted an essentially pragmatic approach, and was guided by experience rather than by doctrine; he was willing to try almost any expedient that sounded promising and to abandon it if it turned out unsuccessfully. Recognizing that all civilization was in a state of crisis, he thought in large, bold, and imaginative terms. Devoted to American democratic ideals, he was temperamentally on the side of the underdog and the enemy of privilege and exploitation. And in fighting for his objectives, he showed stubborn courage and a political skill unsurpassed by any of his predecessors. He was unequaled in intuitive grasp of popular sentiment and in capacity for giving it expression and direction. His radio speeches, written in language that everybody could understand, made him more intimately known to more people than any other living man. These qualities, along with his Rooseveltian gusto and self-assurance, made him a refreshing contrast to his gloomy predecessor. In the opinion of his admirers they entitled him to rank with the greatest of American presidents. His enemies, on the other hand, could argue, with considerable justice, that he was too inclined to concentrate authority in his own hands, that his careless methods of administration caused waste and confusion, that his political tactics were sometimes tricky and disingenuous, and that, in the pursuit of ends which he regarded as desirable, he sometimes resorted to short cuts and abandoned basic principles. It is still too early to decide how the books will finally be balanced and to what extent Roosevelt's services to democracy were nullified by some of the methods he employed.

The New Deal was a continuation of the progressive movement, combining policies derived from both Theodore Roosevelt and Woodrow Wilson. Roosevelt, however, had been elected as the candidate of the Democratic Party, which was by no means dedicated to progressive ideals. The party organization was still largely controlled by Southern conservatives and machine politicians from the Northern cities. The strongest support for Roosevelt's policies came from elements not hitherto identified with the party—from organized labor and many of the farmers and from middle-class reformers. To keep these different groups working together required extraordinary political dexterity. The election of 1932 marked the beginning of a long period of Democratic ascendancy in all branches of the Federal government. Yet there was constant conflict between conservative and progressive factions within the party, and some of the bitterest opponents of the New Deal were Democrats.

From the beginning Roosevelt turned to people outside the party organization. His Cabinet included several Southerners, the most important being Cordell Hull of Tennessee, who became Secretary of State, while the Northern political machines were represented by his campaign-manager, Postmaster General James A. Farley. But of the three members most closely identified with the New Deal, Harold Ickes, Secretary of the Interior, and Henry A. Wallace, Secretary of Agriculture, were former progressive Republicans, while Frances Perkins, Secretary of Labor, was a social worker. For advice about legislation and assistance in writing speeches, Roosevelt relied on a group of college professors whom newspapermen called the "brain trust." The original Brain Trust did not last very long, but throughout the administration various scholars, writers, lawyers, and social workers had an entree into the White House and exercised considerable influence on national policy. With the establishment of new agencies to administer New Deal legislation, moreover, men of a similar type were brought into the lower levels of government service in large numbers. These people were New Dealers rather than Democrats and gave a unique flavor to the Roosevelt administration. Their enemies claimed that most of them were starry-eyed doctrinaires, lacking in practical experience and dangerously radical. Such accusations were justifiable in some instances; but both their idealism and their high standards of integrity made them refreshingly different from the traditional type of politician.

The New Deal in Operation. Delivering his first inaugural address at a moment when the American people, for the first time in their history, were close to despair, Roosevelt in bold and confident tones declared that "the only thing we have to fear is fear itself" and promised action against the depression on a broad front. Congress was immediately called into special session to put into effect the program recommended by the administration, and during the next three months it enacted a series of laws so varied and important that in earlier periods they would have occupied the legislative energies of a generation. For the time being almost everybody in the country rallied enthusiastically to the President's support and hailed him as a great national leader. Whatever may be the final verdict of history on Franklin D. Roosevelt, one achievement must always stand to his credit: during his first hundred days in office he restored the faith of the American people in their capacity to control their destiny.

Although enemies of the New Deal soon began to describe it as socialistic, its central purpose was to preserve the capitalist system by bringing about recovery. The main intention of the early New Deal legislation was to check the process of deflation and bankruptcy and restore business confidence by bringing about a general and simultaneous increase in prices, wages, and consumer purchasing power. Roosevelt argued that the economy had fallen out of balance and that this must be rectified by government action. "What we seek," he declared in 1934, "is balance in our economic system—balance between agriculture and industry and balance between the wage earner, the employer and the consumer." The New Deal therefore continued and extended the Hoover program of lending money to business and saving property-owners from foreclosure, and adopted a number of new measures to aid different groups in the community. In particular, the National Industrial Recovery Act was intended to stabilize industrial prices, raise wages, and promote collective bargaining, while the Agricultural Adjustment Act was to raise farm prices. These were combined with measures for reforming banking and financial practices and increasing the supply of money and credit.

In addition to trying to stimulate private enterprise, Congress also appropriated large sums for direct relief and for an ambitious public-works program. This made continued Treasury deficits inevitable, though Roosevelt himself would apparently have preferred to keep the budget balanced and did not fully accept the Keynesian theory of compensatory government spending until several years later. Yet the large appropriations for relief were perhaps the most significant feature of the early New Deal. It was now recognized for the first time that if people were starving, and no help was available from other sources, the Federal government ought to assume responsibility. The public-works program, moreover, included some of the New Deal's most imaginative and constructive achievements.

The main lines of the New Deal were blocked out in the spring of 1933, and later Congresses did little more than make necessary changes and fill in details. The chief later additions were social-security legislation and the Wagner Act guaranteeing the right of collective bargaining, both passed in 1935. The two main pillars of the original recovery program, the National Industrial Recovery Act and the Agricultural Adjustment Act, however, were struck down by Supreme Court vetoes in 1935 and 1936.

Meanwhile, the whole program, which had been intended to promote the welfare of the people as a whole, soon began to evoke bitter class conflict. Many businessmen quickly became violently hostile to it, complaining that it meant too much government interference with private enterprise and too much support for organized labor, while industrial workers, farmers, and the unemployed enthusiastically supported it. The reasons for these diverse attitudes were clearly indicated by statistics. By 1937 the real income of the farmers was as high as in 1929, while the average employed worker earned a real wage that was nearly 10 per cent higher than in 1929 and also worked considerably shorter hours. On the other hand, corporation net profits after taxes, though much higher than during the worst period of the depression, were scarcely more than half the figure for 1929. Thus, in seeking to restore balance to the economic system, the New Deal had benefited some groups in the community much more than others.

The Election of 1936.   While Roosevelt's more enthusiastic supporters were soon hailing him as the equal of Washington and Lincoln, his business opponents, along with conservative-minded citizens in all income brackets, insisted that the New Deal had delayed rather than stimulated recovery and that most of its legislation had been devised by impractical theorists who knew nothing about meeting pay rolls. The more extreme haters of "that man in the White House" declared that he was destroying private enterprise, bringing about financial ruin, building up an omnipotent bureaucracy, using relief as a vast electioneering agency, and making himself a dictator, and that many of his advisers were virtually Communists. The weakness of the opposition to the New Deal, however, was that it was almost wholly negative. There was obvious room for constructive criticism, but conservatives often talked as though the depression had been invented by Franklin D. Roosevelt, and all would be well if the country could go back to the days of Calvin Coolidge. When required to formulate an election program, they could, in fact, do little more than promise to keep most of the New Deal reforms and administer them more efficiently.

For the 1936 election the Republicans adopted a decidedly New Dealish platform and gave their nomination to Alfred M. Landon, Governor of Kansas and a former 1912 Progressive. Roosevelt ran on his record and promised more of the same kind of thing, but avoided specific commitments. Most of the country's newspapers were belligerently hostile to the administration; but the New Deal combination of the South, the city machines, the labor vote, and the farm vote was unbeatable. Roosevelt was re-elected with the most overwhelming majority for more than a century. Although Landon won 16,680,000 popular votes, as against 27,476,000 for Roosevelt, he carried only two states, Maine and Vermont.

The Supreme Court Fight.   Roosevelt began his second term by calling for a reform of the judiciary. Supreme Court opposition to the New Deal had been manifest for two years, but the President (with a deplorable lack of frankness) did not indicate what he proposed to do about it until after he had been re-elected. Of the nine members of the Supreme Court, four were extreme conservatives, interpreting the Constitution to give maximum protection to property rights in accordance with the precedents established in the 1880's. Three were liberals, following Justice Holmes (who had retired in 1932) in allowing more leeway to legislatures and showing more concern for freedom of speech. Charles Evans Hughes, who had succeeded Taft as Chief Justice in 1930, inclined more to the liberal side, while Roberts stood squarely in the middle. In practice, what the government could do seemed to depend upon the wavering opinions of Justice Roberts. In addition to ending the NIRA and the AAA, the Court by a five-to-four decision had recently voided a New York law fixing a minimum wage for women. This meant that as long as Roberts voted with the conservatives, no authority in the country, state or Federal, could regulate wages and hours.

What Roosevelt proposed was that whenever a judge passed the age of seventy without retiring, the President should be allowed to appoint an extra judge to assist him. Since six Supreme Court justices were over seventy, this meant that the membership of that body might be increased to fifteen. This "court-packing" plan aroused the most intense opposition, which was by no means restricted to conservatives. Many progressives felt that it would undermine the independence of the judiciary, and wanted some more straightforward method of bringing the Supreme Court into line with the election returns, preferably an amendment to the Constitution. A long and bitter fight started in Congress. While it was in progress, Roberts changed his mind and validated a Washington minimum-wage law; the Court accepted the Wagner and Social Security Acts; and with the resignation of one of the conservatives, Roosevelt was able to add to the liberal bloc by appointing Hugo Black, Senator from Alabama. These developments made any reform of the Court unnecessary, and Roosevelt (for the first time) had to accept defeat.

Yet in the end Roosevelt gained his objectives. During his second and third terms he was able to make eight appointments to the Court, thus completely changing its character. Originally much more conservative than the electorate, the judiciary now became a stronghold of liberalism.

Roosevelt's Second Administration. During the first two years of his second term Roosevelt seemed to be moving further to the left, while political conflicts were embittered by the Court plan, by the rapid growth of trade unionism, and by another economic tailspin. For five years production had been slowly increasing, though without reaching the levels of 1929; but in the summer of 1937 there was a sudden downward plunge, described by the administration as a "recession," and unemployment shot up by 4,000,000. While the main purpose of the New Deal was still to bring about recovery, it no longer attempted to cooperate with business. Roosevelt blamed monopolistic price-fixing for the recession, lashed out at "economic royalists," and launched a trust-busting program against big business. At the same time he now fully adopted, for the first time, the Keynesian theory of compensatory government spending, and asked Congress for large new appropriations for relief and public works.

Production figures soon began another slow climb; but public confidence in the administration had been weakened by the Court fight and the recession. In the 1938 election the Republicans made substantial gains, and the combination of Republicans and conservative Democrats in Congress was strong enough to prevent any further extension of the New Deal. It was obvious, moreover, that another war in Europe was rapidly approaching, so that the administration was henceforth increasingly preoccupied with foreign affairs. Thus the New Deal period ended in 1938.

3. NEW DEAL LEGISLATION

Industry and Labor. In its industrial and labor policies the New Deal began by trying to cooperate with business. The National Industrial Recovery Act of 1933 was intended to revive business enterprise by stabilizing prices and restricting competition, while in return for government protection business was asked to make concessions to labor. This was the most widely publicized of all the early New Deal measures, and also one of the least successful.

The act set up a National Recovery Administration (NRA), which was authorized to draft for each industry a code of fair competition that would have the force of law. The codes were to provide for higher wages and shorter hours and prevent competitive price-cutting, while Section 7A declared that workers might "bargain collectively through representatives of their own choosing." In so far as the act legalized price-fixing and restricted competition, it meant an abandonment of the traditional liberal belief in trust-busting and an acceptance of oligopoly. The New Dealers at this period were close to the program of Theodore Roosevelt in the 1912 election and the doctrines of Herbert Croly.

Hugh S. Johnson, a former army general with a colorful personality and a talent for pungent phrase-making, was the first head of NRA, and under his supervision the trade associations representing big business were, to a large extent, allowed to make their own terms about prices. The initial enthusiasm for the NRA did not last very long. Effective enforcement of the codes was almost impossible. Since many of them raised prices, they were unpopular with consumers, while big business disliked Section 7A and became increasingly disturbed by the possible implications of government control. Labor, on the other hand, made substantial gains: the NRA brought about higher wages and shorter hours and gave a great spurt to trade-union membership. Probably the NRA did not do much to promote recovery. Few people expressed much regret when, in the Schechter case of May 1935, the Supreme Court unanimously voided the original act on the twofold ground that legislative power had been transferred to the executive and its scope had been extended beyond interstate commerce.

The history of the NRA illustrated the dangers of allowing business price-fixing, and showed also that business was unwilling to accept collective bargaining except under compulsion. After it failed, the administration no longer attempted to regulate prices directly, and gradually swung over to the traditional trust-busting approach. During the recession of 1938 Congress appointed a Temporary National Economic Committee to investigate monopoly, and Thurman Arnold, as head of the anti-trust division of the Department of Justice, started legal proceedings against corporations that engaged in price-fixing, although this campaign did not last long enough to produce important results.

Meanwhile, the administration had continued to give direct protection to labor. In July 1935 Congress passed the Wagner Act reaffirming the right of workers to join unions and bargain collectively and setting up a National Labor Relations Board (NLRB) to see that this right was respected. Since the Wagner Act was concerned only with the rights of workers, and not with those of employers, it was vehemently denounced by many businessmen as discriminatory class legislation. Another objective of the NRA, the improvement of labor conditions in especially backward industries, was partially achieved by the Fair Labor Standards Act of 1938. This fixed minimum wages and maximum hours and prohibited child labor for all industries engaged in interstate commerce.

Agriculture.   The other main pillar of the original recovery program was the Agricultural Adjustment Act (AAA), which sought to reduce farm production and raise farm prices. Farmers who accepted the program were to reduce the acreage they devoted to basic products; in return they would receive cash payments from the government, the money for which would be raised through excise taxes levied on processors. Critics of the AAA declared that it was economic insanity to pay people for producing less, and wept tears over the ploughing under of 10,000,000 acres already planted to cotton and the slaughter of 6,000,000 young pigs in the spring of 1933. But a large majority of the farmers voted their approval, in spite of some grumbling about bureaucratic regimentation, and nobody seemed to have any alternative plan for coping with the chronic problem of over-production. Essentially, the AAA meant the extension to the farmers of the power to fix prices and limit production already enjoyed by the big corporations.

In January 1936 the AAA was voided by the Supreme Court in a six-to-three decision which declared that the rights of the states had been impaired and that the excise taxes were an unconstitutional misuse of the taxing power. Congress immediately filled the gap by passing a Soil Conservation and Domestic Allotment Act, under which the government would subsidize farmers who agreed to use part of their land for soil-conserving rather than commercial crops. In February 1938 this was replaced by a second Agricultural Adjustment Act. Its general purposes were to control production and achieve what Henry Wallace called an "ever-normal granary" and to raise the ratio between farm prices and other prices to the levels of 1909–14 (this was known as "parity"). The government was to allot acreage quotas among the producers of five basic crops; farmers were not compelled to keep to the quotas, but those who did so would receive subsidies. The act included a number of other provisions for the maintenance of farm incomes, including cash payments by the government if prices fell too far below parity.

The farmers made substantial gains after 1933, partly because over-production was remedied not only by the AAA but also by the droughts of 1934 and 1936. By 1937 prices were 86 per cent higher than in 1932, and the farmers' real income was about the same as in 1929. But these gains were not wholly maintained in 1938 and 1939, and it was not until World War II that real prosperity returned to the farm belt.

Probably the most legitimate criticism of the two AAA's was that most of the benefits went to the more prosperous commercial farmers. With the cut in production, the millions of impoverished tenant farmers and farm laborers were probably worse off, especially in the cotton belt. This vast mass of human misery continued to be a heavy national liability. The administration wanted to do something about it, but Congress was not very cooperative, perhaps because many of its leaders were spokesmen of the Southern landlord class. A Resettlement Administration, set up in 1935, removed a few destitute farmers from submarginal land and settled them in semi-rural cooperative communities. And in 1937 a Farm Security Administration was established to lend money to tenant farmers and assist them to become owners. But the money appropriated for these purposes was a mere drop in the bucket. Nevertheless, the tenancy percentage began for the first time to decrease. Between 1930 and 1940 it dropped from 42.4 to 38.7. By 1945, as a result of a mass movement of tenant farmers into war industries, it had fallen to 31.7, the lowest figure for half a century.

  Credit, Currency, and Banking. These measures for raising price and wage levels were accompanied by aid for debtors along the lines already laid down by the Hoover administration. The RFC continued to lend money to business corporations. A Farm Credit Administration took over a large number of farm mortgages, and a Home Owners' Loan Corporation performed the same function for urban mortgages. Creditors were paid off, debtors benefited through a considerable reduction in interest rates, and the total amount of debt was substantially reduced. Incidentally, this meant that the Federal government seemed to be taking the place of private banking as the nation's principal source of credit.

  Taking office during the bank "holiday," the administration immediately assumed control over the whole national banking system. Public confidence was quickly restored, and most of the banks were authorized to resume business within a few weeks. By the Banking Act of 1933 deposits were henceforth to be guaranteed by the Federal Deposit Insurance Corporation. The Securities Act of 1933 and the Securities and Exchange Act of 1934 endeavored to regulate the stock exchanges and prevent any repetition of the events of 1929. Speculation was limited in various ways, particularly by a rule forbidding the buying of stocks on margin unless at least 55 per cent of the price was paid immediately. The issuance of new securities was henceforth to be regulated by a Securities and Exchange Commission (SEC).

  Roosevelt's monetary policies were reminiscent of nineteenth-century agrarian insurgency. He hoped that by managing the currency and controlling the value of the dollar the government could first raise prices and then keep them stable. In practice (though not in theory) this meant an abandonment of the gold standard; all gold was withdrawn from circulation, and the government began buying both gold and silver and storing them away. Meanwhile the paper dollar was devalued to less than 60 per cent of its former value. These and other measures brought about a considerable increase in the quantity of money in circulation, while interest rates were reduced to the lowest point in American history.

  Roosevelt's monetary experiments evoked dire predictions of national ruin from bankers and orthodox economists, while inflationists hoped for an upsurge of prosperity. But the concrete effects on prices and business movements seemed to be insignificant. Probably the gold standard had now gone forever, and the only currency henceforth would consist of paper not redeemable in gold. Thus the long controversy going on ever since the colonial period between the champions of specie and the advocates of irredeemable paper had come to an anticlimactic conclusion. In retrospect, it was not easy to see why the question had ever caused such strong feelings.

Public Works and the TVA. The first New Deal Congress appropriated large sums for public works in the hope that this would speed recovery. By June 1940 the Roosevelt administration had spent on large-scale public works a total sum of $7,032,000,000. The money was entrusted to a Public Works Administration (PWA), headed by Secretary of the Interior Ickes, under whose direction it was spent too slowly to have much "pump-priming" effect. But although the program did little to stimulate business, it included some of the New Deal's most significant and controversial activities.

The PWA invested some of its money in the development of electric power. In continuance of the public-works program instituted by the Hoover administration, a number of immense dams were constructed on rivers in the Western states. A Rural Electrification Administration (REA) built generating plants and power lines in rural areas throughout the country. And a project was undertaken on the Tennessee River which aroused more enthusiasm among progressives than anything else done by the New Deal.

The long fight conducted by Senator Norris during the 1920's to retain public ownership of the Muscle Shoals power site now ended victoriously. In May 1933 Congress set up the Tennessee Valley Authority (TVA). The TVA was to build and operate dams along the river and sell the power, thus creating a yardstick for measuring the rates charged by private power companies. It was also to manufacture fertilizer, carry out flood-control and conservation operations, and promote the economic and social welfare of the communities living in the valley. The area covered by the TVA included parts of seven states, with a population of 2,000,000, and was one of the most poverty-stricken regions in the United States. This was regional planning of a kind unprecedented in American history. According to David Lilienthal, one of the TVA directors, "For the first time since the trees fell before the settlers' axe, America set out to command nature not by defying her, as in that wasteful past, but by understanding and acting upon her first law—the oneness of men and natural resources."

By 1940 the TVA had completed seven dams and brought about marked improvements in standards of living throughout the valley. It sought voluntary cooperation for all its activities, working directly with local farmers and businessmen, avoiding remote control from Washington, and—as far as possible—steering clear of politics. Progressives hailed the TVA as the forerunner of a new kind of economic order, and wanted similar authorities set up elsewhere. Defenders of private enterprise, on the other hand, declared that the TVA yardstick was unfair on the ground that, in fixing rates, it did not sufficiently allow for the fact that it was financed with government money and paid no interest or taxes. The government, they maintained, was driving the private power companies out of business. Most of the companies in the region were a part of the Commonwealth and Southern system, the president of which was Wendell Willkie. In 1939 the TVA ended the controversy by buying their properties for a generous price. But the campaign conducted by Willkie and other power-company executives, combined with the fact that many Congressmen resented the political independence of the TVA, prevented any extension of the idea to other parts of the country.

Conservation.   In addition to the TVA, the New Deal spent money in other ways to promote conservation. A series of natural disasters had now forced a general realization that unless the United States adopted a new attitude towards her remaining natural resources, she could not survive as a great power for more than a few generations. After three centuries of incredible wastefulness, no less than one-sixth of all the land available for agriculture had been totally ruined, and an additional one-third was seriously damaged. With the cutting of forests and the loss of topsoil, rainwater, instead of remaining in the soil, flowed down into the river valleys, producing catastrophic floods on the Ohio, the Mississippi, and other rivers. Wind erosion created a dust bowl in part of Kansas and Oklahoma and left it virtually a desert. In the great dust storm of 1934 millions of tons of irreplaceable topsoil were blown into the Atlantic Ocean.

A Soil Conservation Service, set up in 1934, set out to persuade farmers to adopt terraced farming and other conservation practices. The government added extensively to its forest reserves and restricted the grazing of cattle on public land. And much of the money spent on relief and public works was used for conservation. Especially notable was the Civilian Conservation Corps (CCC), set up in 1933 to provide temporary work for boys between the ages of 18 and 25, many of whom had never had jobs before. By 1940 the CCC had employed a total of 2,000,000 boys, mainly on reforestation and other activities. The AAA was also a conservation measure, since it required that soil-conserving crops be planted in the land withdrawn from commercial use.

Railroads, Shipping, and Housing.   The New Deal also contributed public money to some forms of industrial expansion. In most industries, as a result of the over-expansion of the 1920's, there seemed to be little room for further growth until the consumers' market had caught up. But in three major fields, where private enterprise had not functioned very effectively, there was obvious need for new construction. These were railroads, shipping, and housing.

The railroads had run into serious difficulties with the advent of the automobile; and during the depression a large number of them had become bankrupt. The New Deal could do little to reduce their heavy indebtedness; but extensive lending by the RFC enabled them to modernize much of their equipment and win back some of their lost customers. Shipping was directly subsidized by the Merchant Marine Act of 1936. This set up a Maritime Commission which undertook to build fifty ships a year and then turn them over to private companies for operation. In housing, the crying need was for slum-clearance and low-cost apartment buildings. Owing partly to heavy real-estate and material costs and partly to the restrictive practices of the building unions, it was apparently impossible for private enterprise to provide new homes at prices that working-class families could afford to pay. The New Deal set up a Federal Housing Authority (FHA) in 1934, which gave some stimulus to private building by underwriting mortgage loans at low rates of interest. And in 1937 a United States Housing Authority (USHA) began lending money to local governments for the construction of low-cost housing. But the total amount of cheap housing constructed during the 1930's fell far short of what was needed, and it was not until after World War II that public authorities made a serious effort to cope with the scarcity.

Social Security. The only attempt to provide a permanent unemployment program was the Social Security Act of 1935. This provided for unemployment insurance, to be financed by a tax on pay rolls. While the Federal government collected the money, administration was left to the states, which were to have considerable leeway in experimenting with different plans. But benefits were payable for short periods only, and workers unemployed for long periods had to apply for relief. The Social Security Act also provided for payment of pensions to workers past the age of sixty-five. Various categories of workers were not covered by the act, which applied to about half the total working population.

Unemployment Relief. Meanwhile, large sums were appropriated for relief. The first New Deal Congress created the Federal Emergency Relief Administration (FERA), supplemented for a few months by the Civil Works Administration (CWA). The FERA was to distribute funds to the local authorities, and was placed under the direction of a New York social worker, Harry Hopkins, who soon became one of Roosevelt's closest friends and advisers. But by the beginning of 1935, in spite of a considerable business revival, 5,500,000 persons were still living on relief, and they and their dependents comprised no less than 17 per cent of the total population. Unemployment was apparently going to be permanent. Congress then set up the Works Progress Administration (WPA) to provide work for the unemployed, while direct relief was left to the local authorities.

The WPA lasted until World War II, the greatest number of persons on its rolls at any one time being 3,300,000. It operated under severe hardships, since it had to find jobs that would be useful but would not interfere with private enterprise. Many of its employees, moreover, were unskilled, and morale and discipline were low. In view of these obstacles, the WPA appears to have made a very creditable record. Some of its projects took the form of "boondoggling" (a word used by its opponents to describe activities which were obviously valueless). But the WPA built or improved vast numbers of roads, schools, other public buildings, and conservation projects, and conducted many enterprises in the field of adult education, while the projects set up for professional workers in literature, painting, music, and the theater were outstandingly successful examples of government patronage of the arts.

The Federal Budget.   Down to June 1940 the Roosevelt administration spent on relief agencies a total sum of $16,231,000,000. Combined with its spending on public works, this was the main reason for its inability to balance the budget. Apart from a liquor tax, made possible by the repeal of prohibition, and an increase in the income taxes paid by corporations and by individuals in the upper brackets, adopted in the Revenue Acts of 1935 and 1936, there was little change in the tax system. Every year the Roosevelt administration spent more than it took in, and during its first seven years it was responsible for an increase in the gross national debt from $22,539,000,000 to $44,458,000,000.

Growth of Unionism.   Possibly even more important than any of the specific reforms sponsored by the New Deal was the support which it gave to labor, and the consequent rise of a militant union movement. Union membership, which had reached a peak of more than 5,000,000 in 1919, had dropped to less than 3,000,000 by 1932. The AFL, headed after the death of Gompers in 1924 by William Green, failed to provide dynamic leadership. Still organized largely on craft lines, it represented chiefly the skilled workers and had made no progress in the big mass-production industries. Its officials spent their time adjusting jurisdictional disputes between different craft unions and representing labor at public meetings. But when the Roosevelt administration gave support to collective bargaining, millions of workers began flocking into the unions and enforcing their demands by going on strike. Many of them were factory workers and not skilled craftsmen, and wanted a new system of organization by which all workers in the same industry would belong to the same union.

The AFL failed to respond to the demand for industrial unionism. In 1935 a group of more militant union leaders, including John L. Lewis of the United Mine Workers, Sidney Hillman of the Amalgamated Clothing Workers, and David Dubinsky of the International Ladies' Garment Workers, broke away and set up a Committee for Industrial Organization (CIO). Headed by the belligerent and egotistical Lewis, the CIO expanded rapidly, and won notable successes in steel and automobiles.

In March 1937 United States Steel, hitherto a stronghold of the open shop, accepted collective bargaining. The smaller steel companies refused to follow suit; and during the summer their workers went on strike. Tom Girdler of Republic Steel, Eugene Grace of Bethlehem Steel, and other company executives stubbornly refused all concessions, blasting Roosevelt and the CIO and displaying attitudes more appropriate to the 1870's. On Memorial Day a group of strikers picketing a plant in Chicago was attacked by the police, ten of them being killed and seventy-five injured by gunfire or clubbing. The strike ended in defeat, but the NLRB, in a decision upheld by the Supreme Court, subsequently ordered the companies to accept collective bargaining. The years 1936 and 1937 also saw a series of strikes by the automobile workers, in which, instead of merely picketing, they occupied the factories and adopted a new "sit-down" technique. In the end all the leading automobile companies were forced to agree to collective bargaining. But the "sit-down" seemed to conservatives a most alarming violation of property rights, and was finally declared illegal by the Supreme Court in 1939.

Meanwhile, the AFL had also made big gains and, in fact, retained a slight edge over its rival. By 1940 total union membership, including groups not affiliated with either federation, amounted to about 9,000,000. Although only about a quarter of all wage-earners were organized, unionism was now strongly entrenched in all basic industries and was beginning to spread to professional and white-collar workers. Conservatives continued to oppose it, and many of their specific criticisms had considerable validity. Union leaders often had too much power, and sometimes used it corruptly. Some AFL unions were led by racketeers; some CIO unions were controlled by Communists. In seeking benefits for their members, unions sometimes flouted the national interest; and some of them sought to safeguard jobs by blocking technological progress. But the fundamental reason for the growth of unions was the conviction of the workers that they could not otherwise obtain their just rights.

Henceforth the unions were certain to play an increasingly important role in American economic, social, and political life. The abler and more statesmenlike union leaders—men like Hillman, Dubinsky, Philip Murray, George Meany, and Walter Reuther—ranked among the most influential national figures. The split in the labor movement ended in December, 1955, when the AFL and the CIO were united in one federation claiming a membership of close to 16,000,000.

Results of the New Deal. What had the New Deal accomplished? In its primary objective, the revival of full employment and production, it had obviously failed. Even at the peak period in 1937 there were still 7,500,000 persons unemployed, and the national product had reached only $71,853,000,000, as compared with the 1929 figure of $82,691,000,-000. While the consumer goods industries had recovered, there had been little new investment. The function of putting the savings of the community back into circulation, which had formerly been performed by private investors, seemed now to have been assumed by the government. When the government cut down on its spending, as it did in 1937, there was an immediate recession.

The facts were obvious, but what did they mean? Opponents of the New Deal insisted that the lack of new investment was the fault of the government. They declared that by attacking private enterprise, imposing bureaucratic regulations, increasing the national debt, and giving too many privileges to labor, it had created a state of uncertainty in which business expansion was impossible. Progressives, on the other hand, argued that the New Deal had failed because it had not gone far enough. They called for a more drastic redistribution of income in order to expand the purchasing power of the mass of the people, and also argued, in Keynesian terms, that a falling off of private investment was inevitable in a mature economy. The country, they suggested, had substantially as many factories and office buildings as would be needed for a long time to come. Public investment must henceforth be a permanent policy, and if the money was spent in ways that added to the national wealth—on low-cost housing, schools, hospitals, and other public buildings, for example—then budget deficits and a steady increase in the national debt should not cause alarm.

Both opponents and admirers of the New Deal sometimes described it as revolutionary. This was, of course, a great exaggeration. There was no change in the ownership and control of basic economic enterprises; in fact, the big corporations were even bigger and more powerful in the 1940's than they had been in the 1920's. But the New Deal had made two general changes in the economic system. In the first place, it had given direct protection to farmers and wage-earners, and had thereby built up big agriculture and big labor as checks on the power of big business. And, in the second place, it had given the Federal government much broader responsibilities than in the past for regulating the movements of the economy, providing security, and protecting underprivileged groups. There were obvious dangers in these developments. Big agriculture and big labor, no less than big business, could exploit the public. Government officials could abuse their powers for personal advantage. But the main reason for the New Deal reforms was the conviction of a majority of the American people that unrestricted private enterprise, of the kind that had prevailed during the 1920's, did not sufficiently promote the general welfare. Since the Republicans in each successive election accepted the basic New Deal legislation, it can be assumed that it has become a permanent addition to the American system.

Although the New Deal did not restore prosperity, it introduced a new spirit into public affairs. By its forward-looking and adventurous attitude, it restored American morale. By insisting that the government must find work for starving men, it changed despair into hope. And through its public-works program it added immeasurably to the national heritage. Probably the most satisfying achievements of the New Deal were not its direct attempts to promote recovery but some of its peripheral activities, such as the TVA, the dams built in the Western states, rural electrification, the promotion of soil conservation, and the varied cultural projects sponsored by the WPA.

4. FOREIGN POLICY DURING THE NEW DEAL PERIOD

Early Roosevelt and Hull Policies. During the early years of his administration Roosevelt was absorbed in domestic problems and seemed to have abandoned his earlier belief in Wilsonian internationalism. In some ways, in fact, he was even more isolationist than the Republicans. The Hoover administration had agreed to American participation in an International Economic Conference, to be held in London in June 1933. But when the Conference met, Roosevelt refused to agree to currency stabilization, since this would interfere with his plans for devaluing the dollar; this killed the Conference, though it is doubtful if it would have accomplished anything anyway. The only innovation in American foreign policy during the early New Deal period was the recognition given to the Soviet Union in 1933. While the main reason was that it seemed foolish not to have diplomatic relations with a government that was obviously well established, it was hoped also that the recognition would stimulate trade and would have a restraining influence on Japan.

Secretary of State Hull hewed closer than Roosevelt to the Wilsonian line. His integrity and persistence made him widely respected, especially among conservatives who disliked much of the New Deal, though he was extremely cautious and too inclined to believe that moralistic pronouncements actually produced results. Hull's strongest conviction was that barriers to international trade were the chief cause of war. In 1934 Congress passed the Trade Agreements Act, authorizing the executive to negotiate treaties with other countries for the reciprocal lowering of tariffs. By 1939 the State Department had negotiated twenty-one such treaties. They helped to remove the bad feelings provoked in the rest of the world by the Smoot-Hawley Tariff of 1930, but the concrete economic results were not impressive, and world trade remained far below the levels of the 1920's.

The Good Neighbor Policy. The most constructive diplomatic achievements of the 1930's were in Latin American relations, where Roosevelt and Hull built on foundations laid by the Republicans during the 1920's. The United States now completely repudiated interventionism and promised to respect the sovereign independence of all her neighbors and to take no action involving them without consultation. In return, Roosevelt and Hull hoped to gain economic advantages and to persuade all the Latin American nations to promise united action against aggression. Thus the Monroe Doctrine was to become a joint hemispheric responsibility. This was the essence of the Good Neighbor policy.

Pan-American conferences at Montevideo (1933), Buenos Aires (1936), and Lima (1938) worked out new principles of inter-American law which developed after World War II into the Organization of American States. With reservations at Montevideo, but fully at Buenos Aires, the United States agreed that no state had the right to intervene in the internal or external affairs of any other. The Buenos Aires conference affirmed that any threat to the peace of the hemisphere was the concern of all the American states and agreed that if such a threat arose, their foreign ministers should immediately meet for consultation.

Meanwhile, the United States gave practical demonstrations of her sincerity. When there was a revolution in Cuba in 1933, she did not intervene; and in 1934 she negotiated a new treaty dropping the Platt Amendment. During the next few years she also gave up her right to intervene in Panama and terminated her financial supervision over Haiti and the Dominican Republic. Thus the small Caribbean countries again became fully independent. The United States proposed henceforth to defend her strategic interests in the region not by wielding the big stick but by relying on good will and economic influence. Inevitably the Caribbean remained a United States sphere of influence, but the relationship now established between the dominant power and her smaller neighbors set a novel and admirable precedent in international relations.

Mexican relations provided an even more convincing demonstration of good-neighborliness. Lázaro Cárdenas, President from 1934 to 1940, put new vigor into the revolutionary program of land and labor reform and limitations on the rights of foreign capital. This meant losses for American investors. In particular, in March 1938, the oil companies were expropriated, after they had balked at a government order for wage increases. Unlike Coolidge in 1926, Roosevelt and Hull did not protest against the expropriation and asked only that adequate compensation be paid. In the end, by an agreement reached in 1942, Mexico paid a relatively small sum, representing the value of the machinery and equipment. By accepting this economic loss, the United States gained a more important political objective: strong Mexican support during and after World War II.

The Good Neighbor policy was not completely successful. Argentina, retaining close economic and cultural ties with Europe and hoping to lead a Latin American bloc in opposition to the United States, was consistently hostile to hemispheric unity. Nazi Germany was alarmingly successful in her drive for trade and influence in South America. The traditional fear of Yankee imperialism did not wholly disappear. But throughout the Roosevelt administration the United States was definitely more trusted in Latin America than at any earlier period.

Neutrality Legislation.   Meanwhile, isolationist and pacifist sentiment in the United States had reached its high-water mark. With Hitler in power in Germany, Europe was plainly heading for another war; but the initial American reaction was to stay neutral at almost any cost. Books and motion pictures emphasized the horrors and futility of World War I, and students in colleges throughout the country took pledges never to fight. This attitude was greatly strengthened by the revisionist interpretations of the events of 1917, according to which the United States had been pulled into the war by British propaganda and by the sinister machinations of bankers and "merchants of death." This interpretation was publicized in 1934 by a Senate committee, headed by Gerald Nye of North Dakota, which investigated the munitions industry. A large part of the American people resolved to learn the apparent lesson of history and legislate against any recurrence of the 1917 situation.

With the seeming approval of the administration, Congress passed a series of neutrality acts, culminating in the act of May 1937. This prohibited the sale of munitions or the lending of money to any nation at war, made it illegal for Americans to travel on belligerent-owned ships, and authorized the president to apply cash-and-carry rules to goods other than munitions; this meant that a belligerent would be required to pay for such goods on delivery and transport them in her own ships. Since the legislation implied that if Britain and France went to war they would get no help from the United States, its effect was to encourage Hitler and thereby hasten World War II.

The Threat of War. In the summer of 1937 Japan resumed her attempt to conquer China, occupying a large part of the seacoast and eventually forcing the Chiang Kai-shek government to take refuge in the interior at Chungking. Henceforth Roosevelt was increasingly concerned about the drift towards another world war. In October, in a speech at Chicago, he startled everybody (including Secretary Hull) by calling upon all peace-loving nations to "quarantine" the aggressor nations. What this meant was never explained; the public reaction was so hostile that Roosevelt said no more about it. But American spokesmen vigorously affirmed their belief in the Open Door and their disapproval of Japanese aggresson; and in 1938 credits were given, through the RFC, to the Chinese government. Meanwhile, Congress voted $1,000,000,000 for expanding the navy. It was obvious that, in spite of the neutrality legislation, few Americans really believed that they could remain aloof from another world war.

XXXI

The Second World War

1. THE END OF NEUTRALITY
2. THE UNITED STATES AT WAR
3. PLANNING A NEW WORLD ORDER

T HE ULTIMATE causes of World War II were the same international tensions that had led to World War I. But during the intervening twenty years they had been greatly strengthened by the rise of totalitarian dictatorships in Germany and Italy. Hitler and Mussolini sought to get rid of internal dissensions and economic difficulties by organizing racial and religious persecutions, preaching hatred of foreign peoples, and pursuing aggressive foreign policies. Thus much more fundamental issues were at stake. The United States entered World War II not only to maintain the balance of power but also to protect the traditional ideals of Western civilization against the new and sinister doctrines of Nazism and Fascism.

SELECTED BIBLIOGRAPHY: Three recent additions to the *Chronicles of America* series give a general account of America's role in the war: Allan Nevins, *The New Deal and World Affairs* (1950); Eliot Janeway, *The Struggle for Survival* (1950); and Fletcher Pratt, *The War for the World* (1951). The events leading up to the war are related in C. G. Haines and R. J. S. Hoffman, *The Origins and Background of World War II* (1943). Two volumes by W. L. Langer and J. E. Gleason, *The Challenge to Isolation* (1952), and *The Undeclared War* (1953), give a comprehensive account of American policy before Pearl Harbor. Useful shorter books are *Peace and War, United States Foreign Policy, 1931–1941* (published by the State Department, 1942); Forrest Davis and E. K. Lindley, *How War Came* (1942); and Basil Rauch, *Roosevelt, From Munich to Pearl Harbor* (1950). There is no comprehensive history of the war, but all students of the period should read Winston S. Churchill, *The Second World War* (6 vols., 1948–53). Among the more important memoirs and biographies are Omar Bradley, *A Soldier's Story* (1951); Dwight D. Eisenhower, *Crusade in Europe* (1946); E. J. King and N. M. Whitehill, *Fleet Admiral King* (1952); R. E. Sherwood, *Roosevelt and Hopkins* (1948); and H. L. Stimson and M. Bundy, *On Active Service in Peace and War*, (1947).

1. THE END OF NEUTRALITY

The Outbreak of the War.   Through the disastrous 1930's Europe had traveled the road to ruin with appalling rapidity. The first milestone had been the Japanese seizure of Manchuria in 1931 and the failure of the League of Nations to prevent it. In 1935 Mussolini attacked Ethiopia, while Britain and France again showed their lack of faith in the principles of the League by allowing only a half-hearted and ineffectual adoption of economic sanctions. Meanwhile, Hitler abrogated the checks on German militarism established at Versailles, announcing rearmament in 1935 and remilitarizing the Rhineland in 1936. In Spain, in 1936, after a leftist government had been elected to office, General Francisco Franco launched a rebellion with support from Italy and Germany, while in the same year Germany and Japan formed the Berlin-Tokyo Axis, being joined by Italy in 1937. In the spring of 1938 Hitler seized Austria, and in the autumn, by the Munich settlement with Britain and France, he was allowed to occupy a large part of Czechoslovakia. In the spring of 1939 he seized Prague, destroying what remained of Czechoslovakia, after which he made threats against Poland and obviously planned to dominate the whole of eastern Europe.

During several dreary years France and Britain did nothing to stop the destruction of the Versailles settlement. France was weakened by internal conflicts, while the British Prime Minister, Neville Chamberlain, obstinately insisted that if Hitler were sufficiently appeased, he would finally settle down. These illusions were finally shattered by the seizure of Prague. Forced by public indignation to abandon appeasement, Chamberlain promised, in April 1939, to aid Poland against German aggression. This made war inevitable. And since the British had now committed themselves, the Soviet government, which had hitherto advocated collective security on account of its fear of German attack, began to bargain with both sides. The Germans were more receptive to Soviet demands for expansion, and on August 23 Stalin and Hitler came to terms. Germany invaded Poland on September 1, and by September 3 Britain and France had declared war. Poland was crushed within three weeks, and was then partitioned between Germany and Russia. The Russians then went on to seize the three Baltic states (Estonia, Latvia, and Lithuania) and the Rumanian province of Bessarabia, and launched an attack on Finland. On the western front the German and Allied armies watched each other through the winter, and there were no important movements until April.

American Attitudes.   For nearly two years before the actual outbreak, Roosevelt and Hull had been looking for ways of checking the drift towards war. They saw the futility of appeasement; but since their hands were tied by the neutrality legislation and the isolationism of American opinion, they could do little to stiffen the British attitude. In July, after

Chamberlain had finally dropped appeasement, they asked Senate leaders of both parties to consider revising the neutrality legislation, but Senator Borah, still the main isolationist spokesman, insisted that there would be no war and won enough support to prevent action.

When the war came, however, American sentiment immediately began to change. To a much greater extent than in World War I it was preponderantly pro-Ally from the beginning, since Hitlerism was obviously a menace to everything that Americans believed in. Congress passed a new Neutrality Act in November, allowing the sale of munitions to belligerents under cash-and-carry rules, while at the same time American merchant ships were forbidden to enter the combat zone. Thus Britain and France could buy munitions in the United States as long as they had enough money and ships. But almost all Americans believed that Britain and France could win the war without their aid, and nobody proposed intervention. There was, in fact, some criticism of the Allied inactivity through the winter, and Senator Borah suggested that the war was "phony" and might end in more appeasement.

The Fall of France.   In the spring of 1940 came a series of cataclysmic events which shocked the American people more profoundly than anything in their whole previous history. Exhibiting a frightening offensive power, German forces seized Denmark and Norway in April, overran Holland and Belgium in May, and quickly inflicted a crushing defeat on the French army, hitherto believed by most Americans to be the best in the world. Mussolini then entered the war. And on June 25 a new French government, headed by the semi-fascist Marshal Pétain, signed an armistice, agreeing to German occupation of a large part of France. Britain was the only remaining barrier to complete German domination of western Europe. And although the British in the moment of crisis had found a new leader in Winston Churchill, whose defiant speeches aroused the enthusiasm of free men throughout the world, their ability to resist the expected German invasion seemed decidedly questionable. It was not until September, when in a series of battles over British cities the Royal Air Force inflicted devastating losses upon the Luftwaffe, that Hitler met his first defeat.

If Hitler conquered Britain, he would control all the eastern Atlantic and could outbuild the United States in any race for military and naval supremacy. He could also take possession of West Africa, whence he could move easily into South America. America south of the bulge of Brazil was a military liability, and the United States could not possibly defend it. Meanwhile, Japan was showing an obvious interest in the French, Dutch, and British possessions in Asia and Indonesia, with their invaluable rubber, oil, tin, and other natural resources, and threatened to take control of all the western Pacific. Thus the United States might be hemmed in by two aggressive and dictatorial powers, and could hold only North America and the Caribbean. Even if she were never directly attacked, it seemed unlikely that under such circumstances she could preserve her way of life and democratic institutions unimpaired. This view of the situation was the determining influence on American foreign policy after the spring of 1940.

Interventionists and Isolationists. The fall of France precipitated one of the great debates in American history, a debate conducted not only in Congress and in the press but among private citizens all over the country. Of the various organizations which undertook to influence public opinion, two were outstanding: the Committee to Defend America by Aiding the Allies, headed by a veteran Kansas newspaper editor, William Allen White of the *Emporia Gazette;* and the isolationist America First Committee. While few of the interventionists advocated full entry into the war, they argued that the security of the American people required the defeat of Hitler, for which reason they should give Britain all possible aid short of war. The isolationists maintained, in reply, that Hitler could never consolidate his conquests, that even if he were victorious it would be possible to come to terms with him, and that under no conceivable circumstances would the United States be in danger of attack.

The results of the debate are still a subject of bitter controversy. It has been maintained that a majority of the American people continued to favor neutrality, and that Roosevelt, eager to retain power and conceal the failure of the New Deal, pulled the country into war against its will. But the election returns and public-opinion polls do not support this interpretation. According to the available evidence, a majority of the people (probably about two-thirds) repudiated isolationism during the summer of 1940, and (while continuing to hope that full belligerency could be avoided) felt that defeating Hitler was more important than staying out of war. Roosevelt, in fact, being anxious to avoid conflict with the congressional isolationists, seems to have moved more slowly than majority sentiment would have wished.

While there were many honest and patriotic Americans in the America First Committee, it was also supported by elements that were much more questionable. Reactionaries who felt that Hitler was better than the New Deal, fascistic and anti-Semitic agitators, mentally unbalanced characters who regarded any form of liberalism as Communistic, peddlers of hate of all kinds—all the most sinister elements in American life were in the isolationist camp. Some isolationists were motivated simply by a love for peace and a conviction that the United States was in no danger, but others (like similar groups in every other country) displayed a narrowly nationalistic suspicion of all foreign peoples and a conviction that they would always take advantage of American generosity. Many isolationists, in fact, while opposed to cooperation with any other nation, favored the expansion of American power overseas, especially in the Far East.

American Policy. As opinion crystallized, the policy of the administration became firmer. The most obvious necessity was defense. In May, Roosevelt declared that the aviation industry must be expanded to the point where it could construct 50,000 war planes a year. His enemies declared that the figure was astronomical, though by 1944 production reached nearly double that figure. By October, Congress had appropriated no less than $17,692,000,000 for defense. And in September, for the first time in peacetime, the United States adopted military conscription.

Meanwhile, American diplomacy had tried, without success, to deter Italy from entering the war and France from accepting the armistice. After the fall of France the War Department released "surplus" guns and planes for sale to Britain. And in September the United States leased bases on British territory in Newfoundland and the West Indies, and gave the British fifty destroyers in return. Plans were made for taking over any European colonies in the American hemisphere which might be in danger of German occupation, the assent of Latin America being secured at a conference at Havana in July. This Havana Conference also produced the strongest statement so far of hemispheric unity, with the passage of a resolution stating that an attack on any one of the American states from outside the hemisphere should be considered as an attack on all. Thus the administration had definitely abandoned neutrality. American policy henceforth was to bring about the defeat of Hitler.

The Election of 1940.   For the 1940 election the Democrats, violating tradition, nominated Roosevelt for a third term. Very few Democrats were isolationists, and the South, as always, was the most interventionist section of the country. The Republicans, on the other hand, were deeply divided, as they had been for a generation. Most Eastern Republicans followed the tradition of Theodore Roosevelt and Elihu Root, and were even more interventionist than the administration. Two of Theodore Roosevelt's disciples, Henry L. Stimson and Frank Knox, had, in fact, entered the Cabinet in June to take charge, respectively, of the War and Navy Departments. Many Midwestern Republicans, on the other hand, were still inclined towards isolationism. But the interventionists had found a dynamic candidate in Wendell Willkie, who had made a national reputation, while president of Commonwealth and Southern, as a forceful and lucid champion of private enterprise, and after an exciting battle in the Republican convention he was nominated on the sixth ballot.

Although the two candidates were in essential agreement about foreign policy, they fought a deplorable campaign. Willkie appealed to the isolationist vote by asserting that if Roosevelt were re-elected, the country would be at war by April. Roosevelt reiterated in a number of speeches ("again and again and again," as he said in Boston) that American boys were "not going to be sent into any foreign wars." Both candidates insisted that their main objective would be to keep America out of war. Obviously, if this had been true, they would have been betraying their duty; the president's first responsibility is to protect America's vital interests, by force if necessary. The only extenuation of this "campaign oratory" (as Willkie frankly described it a few months later) was that nobody believed it. In the end Roosevelt was re-elected, though by a reduced majority. Willkie won 6,000,000 more popular votes than Landon in 1936, and carried ten New England and Midwestern states. Probably the chief reason for Roosevelt's victory was the feeling of many independent voters that it was wise to keep an experienced man in office in a time of crisis, and that his defeat would be regarded as a repudiation of his foreign policy.

Aid Short of War. Roosevelt interpreted the election result as a mandate for all-out support of Britain. In a speech on December 29 he declared that "the Axis powers are not going to win this war" and that the United States "must be the great arsenal of democracy." Implementation of this program obviously meant dropping the cash-and-carry requirements of the Neutrality Act, since the British needed supplies far in excess of what they could pay for and transport.

In order to solve the financial problem, Roosevelt devised the lend-lease program. Anxious to avoid any repetition of the war loans of World War I, he proposed that goods rather than money be lent to Britain, with the understanding that repayment be made in kind after the war. The United States, he suggested, should think of herself as like a man lending his garden hose to a neighbor whose house was on fire. This momentous and imaginative proposition was approved by Congress in March 1941 with substantial majorities in both houses. Goods might be lent to any country "whose defense the President deems vital to the defense of the United States."

The shipping problem was more complex. As in World War I, German submarines were sinking British freighters with appalling rapidity. But if the United States herself undertook to transport war material across the Atlantic, she would almost certainly become involved in a shooting war, which the administration was still hoping to avoid. As a halfway measure, assistance was given to the British convoys. In April, American naval and air patrols in the North Atlantic were instructed to watch for hostile submarines and give warnings to the British. Greenland was occupied in the same month. In July, American forces occupied Iceland, and American destroyers began to escort British vessels as far as that point, watching for German submarines and giving warning of their whereabouts to British warships.

Shooting quickly followed. In September the destroyer *Greer* was attacked by a submarine, and Roosevelt promptly ordered that any submarines sighted in American-patrolled waters be sunk on sight. In October two more destroyers were attacked, one of them, the *Reuben James*, being sunk. In November, Congress swept away what was left of the Neutrality Act, authorizing the arming of merchant vessels and their entry into the combat zone. Thus the United States was engaged in an undeclared naval war in the North Atlantic. This was probably as close to full belligerency as it was possible to go without taking the final plunge.

The growing partnership between the United States and the British Commonwealth had become more intimate in August, when Roosevelt and Churchill held a conference on a battleship near the coast of Newfoundland. Their main purpose was to discuss Britain's need for supplies, although they also issued an eight-point statement of war aims which became known as the Atlantic Charter. The statement declared that Britain and the United States sought no aggrandizement for themselves, wished to see no territorial changes contrary to the wishes of the people concerned, and would respect the right of peoples to choose their own forms of government. It promised access by all nations to trade and raw materials, and international collaboration for economic advancement and social security. And it called for a peace which would give all men security and freedom from fear and want, and ("pending the establishment of a wider and permanent system of general security") for the disarmament of aggressor nations.

Meanwhile, the Nazis, unable to conquer Britain, had turned eastwards. Hungary, Rumania, and Bulgaria were absorbed into Hitler's "new order" without resistance; and in the spring of 1941 the German army overran Yugoslavia and Greece. The Soviet government, which also aspired to dominate the Balkans, regarded these events with obvious displeasure. They were followed, on June 22, by a German invasion of Russia, which proved to be the beginning of a four-year struggle on a scale unequaled in all history. Both the British and the American government, convinced that the defeat of Hitler was more important than any other consideration, immediately undertook to send war material to the Soviets. Incidentally, the break between Hitler and Stalin caused Communist organizations throughout the world, hitherto somewhat pro-German, to become belligerent advocates of war against the Axis.

Pearl Harbor.   Whether the American people would ever have become full belligerents of their own accord is an interesting but unanswerable question. In the end the decision was taken out of their hands. The Nazi victories gave Japan an opportunity which seemed too good to miss. She was still fighting China, but only part of her forces were engaged, and the East Indies looked like an easy conquest. In September 1940 she signed a treaty with Germany by which the two powers agreed to assist each other if either were attacked by the United States. Japanese forces then began to infiltrate into Indo-China, where the French officials, obeying orders from the Pétain government, offered no resistance. Statements by Japanese leaders made it plain that the "new order" of the Japanese "co-prosperity sphere" was to include Indonesia as well as China and Manchukuo.

The American government responded by giving further credits to China and restricting sales of scrap iron to Japan. But it was anxious to avoid a showdown as long as possible, since the United States was by no means ready for a Pacific war. Roosevelt and his advisers felt that the United States could not allow Japan to take over the East Indies, but hoped that if they refrained from provocation, there would be no immediate attack. For this reason they did not immediately embargo sales of gasoline to Japan. But by the summer of 1941 troop movements made it obvious that Japan was preparing to attack anyway. Gasoline shipments were then stopped, and Japanese assets in the United States were frozen.

Meanwhile, the Japanese ambassador in Washington, Kichisaburo Nomura, joined in November by Saburo Kurusu, had a series of meetings with Secretary Hull. They promised that Japan would refrain from attacking Indonesia if, in return, the United States would leave her a free hand in China and drop all trade restrictions. Whether the United States could have had peace on these terms is extremely doubtful. In any event the administration was not willing to abandon China or to repudiate the traditional American policy of the Open Door and the maintenance of the *status quo* in the Pacific. Thus the negotiations broke down before the end of November.

Undoubtedly the Japanese made a mistake in not attacking only the British and Dutch possessions and leaving the American people to debate what, if anything, they should do about it. But they decided to take no chances on the American decision and to cripple the American fleet at the outset. On December 7, 1941, while Japanese forces began an invasion of the East Indies (including the Philippines), Japanese planes raided Pearl Harbor and scored hits on all the eight battleships of the Pacific fleet.

Pearl Harbor united the American people more fully than ever before in history. For the time being even those groups most bitterly opposed to Roosevelt's foreign policy recognized that the time for debate had ended. Congress declared that a state of war existed with Japan; and three days later Germany and Italy, removing any doubts as to the common purposes of the Axis powers, declared war on the United States. The European and Asiatic conflicts had now become merged into a single global war.

On January 1, 1942, representatives of the United States, Britain, the Soviet Union, China, and twenty-two other countries signed a Declaration of the United Nations, by which they accepted the Atlantic Charter and pledged themselves not to make peace until the enemy had been defeated.

2. THE UNITED STATES AT WAR

War Production. All the more important of the United Nations made indispensable contributions to the defeat of the Axis, but the greatest single factor was unquestionably American production. The achievements of American industry were, in fact, almost beyond belief. The total national product increased by no less than 125 per cent, so that by 1944 the government was able to spend on war purposes alone a larger sum than the whole national income in any peacetime year. In addition to shipping lend-lease goods worth $49,000,000,000 to other countries, mainly to Britain and Russia, the United States created a navy, army, and air force equipped with terrific striking power, and fought two major wars, one in Europe and one in the Pacific, at the same time. And although there was little new construction of durable consumers' goods and some serious shortages developed, especially of housing, the general standard of living of the civilian population actually grew higher. During the war the American people as a whole ate more food, bought more clothing, and spent more money on goods for immediate consumption than they had ever done in peacetime. All this took place in spite of the withdrawal of 12,000,000 able-bodied workers into the armed forces. This technological miracle has implications for the future that have not yet been fully appreciated.

The production achievement does not appear to have been due to any particularly efficient central direction. Although planning for war began in the summer of 1939, nothing concrete was done until nearly a year later. An advisory commission with seven members was then appointed to supervise the armament program, but was not given adequate powers. In December 1940 this was replaced by the Office of Production Management (OPM) under the dual control of William S. Knudsen, president of General Motors, and Sidney Hillman, president of the Amalgamated Clothing Workers. Finally, in January 1942, the War Production Board (WPB) was set up, with Donald Nelson, formerly of Sears Roebuck, as director. Nelson was apparently slated to become the Bernard Baruch of World War II, but he never exercised any comparable authority, and was eased out in 1944. Other segments of the home front were entrusted to other officials with independent and often overlapping powers, which led to considerable bickering and feuding in Washington. In 1942 James F. Byrnes, formerly Senator from South Carolina and Supreme Court Justice, was appointed to head the Office of Economic Stabilization. He was succeeded in 1943 by Fred M. Vinson, and promoted to the new Office of War Mobilization. For the remainder of the war Byrnes acted as assistant president with authority over the whole home front. He was chosen mainly because his special skill lay in mediating conflicts.

Critics of the administration declared that all the same mistakes had been made as in World War I, along with some new ones, and complained of favoritism in the awarding of contracts and of the wasting of billions of dollars on goods that were not needed or were already obsolete. Progressives were alarmed by the close cooperation of the government with business, especially big business, and its willingness to allow large profits without haggling about prices. No doubt many of these criticisms were justified, yet the fact remains that the job was done. By 1943 war materials were pouring off the assembly lines in quantities sufficient to overwhelm the Axis. As early as October of that year, long before any of the decisive battles had been fought, the government could actually begin cutting its orders and preparing for reconversion to peace.

The original Selective Training and Service Act of September 1940 made men between the ages of 21 and 35 liable to the draft. Those not deferred on account of occupation, support of dependents, or physical disability were to be called first, the order being determined (as in World War I) by lottery. Acts passed after Pearl Harbor extended the age limits to 18 and 45, but in the autumn of 1942 deferment was given to men over 38. Some men with dependent wives and children were drafted during the last two years of the war.

With 12,000,000 men serving in the armed forces before the end of the war, a serious man-power shortage might have been expected. But as the young men were drafted, their places were taken by women, boys under 18, and men who had previously retired. In 1940 some 50,000,000 people had been gainfully employed, and another 4,000,000 were looking for work. By 1945 the nation's total labor force (including those in the armed forces) had risen to 64,000,000. The needs of industry were also met by a mass migration into the cities of farm families, both white and colored, who had previously lived close to starvation levels and now, for the first time, earned decent incomes.

The two most vital needs of the war program were ships and planes. In 1940 production of new merchant shipping amounted to little more than 600,000 tons. Yet the country produced no less than 19,000,000 tons in 1943, and 16,000,000 in 1944. During the same period naval tonnage rose from 1,825,000 to 5,000,000, and the number of combat vessels from 380 to 1,100. Plane-production increased from 2,100 in 1939 to 96,356 in 1944. The output of tanks, guns, and innumerable other items was equally fantastic, while whole new industries, like synthetic rubber, sprang into existence.

In agriculture there was less need for rapid expansion. There was little increase in the acreage under cultivation, and the farm-labor supply decreased by nearly 10 per cent. Yet by making use of improved methods, the nation's farmers increased food production by about one-third, which was more than enough to cover what the United States was shipping to her allies. There were food shortages at home in the later war years, but the main reason was that people were eating more. Millions of war workers, for the first time in their lives, could now afford to buy steaks.

Prices, Wages, and Taxes.   With the national income jumping by the end of the war to $198,000,000,000 (as contrasted with $72,000,000,-000 in 1939), there was an enormous excess of purchasing power over available goods. This made price-control essential. The Office of Price Administration (OPA) was set up in April 1941, but Congress refused at first to give it full authority to fix ceilings, chiefly because the farm bloc wanted higher prices for farm products. By 1942 there was danger of a runaway inflation, and in October Congress passed the Stabilization of the Cost of Living Act, which authorized the OPA to freeze prices and wages at the September levels. After this the OPA was, on the whole, remarkably successful in holding the line. The total increase in the cost of living between 1939 and 1945 was only 31 per cent. The OPA also rationed a number of essential goods, although it was only in the case of gasoline and rubber tires that rationing meant any serious cut in normal levels of consumption. Part of the excess purchasing power was taken in higher taxes, but much of it was saved until after the war, thereby helping to make possible the remarkable boom period of 1945–49.

Labor disputes were arbitrated by a National War Labor Board. It alarmed conservatives by allowing 15 per cent wage increases in 1942, but was successful in stabilizing wages during the later war years. Hours of labor rose to an average of 45 a week, but overtime rates were generally paid above 40. Almost all union leaders cooperated with the government; and although opponents of the administration insisted that strikes were seriously obstructing the war effort, there were actually few serious labor troubles. The chief exception was in the coal fields, where twice during 1943 the government assumed control in order to prevent strikes. John L. Lewis, who had turned over the leadership of the CIO to Philip Murray in 1940 but still led the United Mine Workers, was violently denounced by conservatives as a threat to national security; and Congress passed, over Roosevelt's veto, the Smith-Connally Act providing penalties for labor leaders who instigated strikes against companies working on government contracts.

Total government spending on war purposes from 1939 to 1945 amounted to about $300,000,000,000, so that World War II was ten times as expensive as World War I. About two-fifths was paid out of taxes (as contrasted with one-third in World War I). These rose to much the highest levels in American history, and the number of persons liable to income taxes rose from 4,000,000 in 1939 to 30,000,000 in 1943. The national debt by the end of the war had risen to $247,000,000,000. In 1939, when the debt had been only one-sixth as large, conservatives had insisted that the country was heading straight for bankruptcy; yet the astronomical post-war debt caused little alarm and seemed to present no insoluble difficulties.

Civil Liberties. One of the most satisfying features of the war period was the absence of the intolerance associated with World War I. Isolationists had gloomily predicted that war would mean the end of American liberties. Actually there was remarkably little interference with civil rights, partly because most radicals were as anxious for the defeat of the Axis as anybody else. The government set up an Office of War Information (OWI), headed by a former newspaperman, Elmer Davis; but unlike George Creel's Committee on Public Information in World War I, it did not stir up hysteria. Genuine Axis agents were taken into custody by the FBI, which was very successful in preventing sabotage and fifth-column activities. Public opinion remained calm, and critics of the government continued to express their opinions openly.

The only blot on the record was the treatment of Americans of Japanese descent. Some 110,000 of them, including many who had been born in the United States and were therefore citizens, were removed from the Pacific coast to other parts of the country. The authorities were afraid that some of them might be Japanese agents. Yet certainly the overwhelming majority of them were wholly loyal to the United States and entitled to the protection of the Constitution.

Events of 1942. Apart from Roosevelt and his personal advisers (the most influential of whom were Harry Hopkins and Admiral William D. Leahy), the men mainly responsible for American war planning were George C. Marshall, Chief of Staff of the Army, Ernest J. King, Commander in Chief of the Navy, and Henry H. Arnold, head of the American Army Air Force. But the final authority remained with the President, whose bold and imaginative mind made him peculiarly well qualified for directing global strategy. In the considered judgment of Henry L. Stimson, his Republican Secretary of War, he proved himself the greatest of all America's war presidents.

Throughout the war every effort was made to establish a close partnership with Britain. Roosevelt and Churchill, who fortunately found each other personally congenial, held six major conferences and were in constant communication. Joint boards were set up to establish coordination of war planning and production, and single commanders, sometimes American and sometimes British, were appointed in the different theaters of war. But relations with the other United Nations were much less intimate, and global unity of command was, of course, impossible. The Russians, and to a less extent the Chinese, fought separate wars.

In spite of eighteen months of preparation, the United States was still not strong enough for offensive action when war came. Axis victories, possibly decisive ones, were therefore to be expected in 1942. In the spring the Germans resumed their advance in southern Russia, hoping to sweep across to the Caspian and capture the Caucasian oil fields upon which Russian resistance depended. In North Africa, meanwhile, another German army, having taken over the Italian colony of Libya, attacked the British in Egypt. If these drives had been successful, and if at the same time the Japanese had crushed the Allied forces in the western Pacific, then the two ends of the Axis might have met each other in India or the Middle East and made their position virtually invincible.

For five months after Pearl Harbor the Japanese continued to win victories, and the American people could find encouragement only in the resistance of the small army defending the Philippines under the command first of Douglas MacArthur and then (after MacArthur was ordered to Australia by the War Department) of Jonathan Wainwright. By May the Japanese had conquered all the East Indies except the southern part of New Guinea, along with Thailand, Malaya, and Burma on the mainland, and were threatening India and Australia. They also occupied a vast circle of Pacific islands stretching from Kiska near the Alaskan coast to the Solomons south of the equator. What was left of the American army in the Philippines finally surrendered on May 6. But already the tide was turning. A Japanese naval force was defeated by American planes in the Coral Sea, near Australia, early in May; and a month later, when the Japanese fleet made a direct thrust across the Pacific towards Pearl Harbor, it was defeated again by carrier-based planes in the battle of Midway. In August, American forces launched an attack on enemy positions at Guadalcanal in the Solomons, in order to safeguard the supply route to Australia. Henceforth the Japanese won no more victories, except in China.

On the other side of the globe November was the decisive month. In North Africa, General Bernard L. Montgomery defeated the Germans in the battle of El Alamein, concluded on November 4. In Russia the Germans had for two months been assaulting the city of Stalingrad on the Volga, where the Russians were making a final stand. But the defenses held, and by the third week in November the Germans were retreating. Although the United Nations had not yet won the war, the Axis had already lost it. And meanwhile the American forces in Europe were undertaking their first offensive operation.

The Mediterranean Campaigns. American war strategy was to deal with Hitler first. While relatively small forces were assigned to the Pacific war, troops were shipped to Britain as rapidly as possible, and in June 1942 Dwight D. Eisenhower was appointed to command them. The Soviet government wanted the British and Americans to open a second front by a direct invasion of the mainland of western Europe; but they were obviously not yet strong enough to undertake such a hazardous operation with any reasonable chance of success. It was decided instead that Eisenhower's forces should seize the French North African colonies, in the hope of winning control of the Mediterranean and knocking Italy out of the war.

On November 7, 1942, British and American troops landed in Morocco and Algeria. The French officials, under orders from the Pétain government, offered some resistance, but agreed to support the United Nations five days later. Unfortunately, Tunisia was seized by German forces ferried across from Italy, and it took several months of heavy fighting before they were dislodged. Eisenhower and Montgomery finally completed the liberation of North Africa in May 1943. This was quickly followed by an assault on Sicily, which was fully conquered by August 17, and by landings in southern Italy early in September. These successes brought about the fall of Mussolini, whose alliance with Germany had always been hated by most of the Italian people. The new government signed armistice terms on September 8. But meanwhile the Germans had occupied northern and central Italy, and the British and Americans could hold only the southern end of the peninsula.

Nevertheless, the Allies had made substantial gains from the year's campaigns. They had ended the German threat to the Middle East, won control of the Mediterranean, and toppled over one fascist dictatorship. What was perhaps even more important was that the Americans had acquired combat experience and had discovered an army leader in Omar Bradley and a field commander in George S. Patton who were the equals of any in their past history.

There were now long debates as to how and where the next attack should be launched. Some people, though not in the top echelons, were arguing that the war could be won by air power alone. Starting in the spring of 1942, British and American bombers subjected German cities to constant and devastating air attacks; but the military results were scarcely commensurate with the costs. The British took an understandable satisfaction in paying back the Germans in their own coin and reducing their chief cities to piles of rubble. But the raids did relatively little damage to German war production, which actually went on increasing until 1944. World War II proved that the more extreme advocates of air power had very much exaggerated its potentialities. Bombing civilian populations did not win wars.

It was obvious that Germany had to be invaded; but whereas the Americans wanted to concentrate all their efforts on an assault from the west, Churchill favored further diversionary operations in the Mediterranean. According to his own account, this was solely for military reasons though it has often been alleged that he was motivated also by a suspicion of the Russians, who by the spring of 1944 had regained all their own territory and were advancing into Poland and Rumania. In the end Churchill had his way to the extent that the Italian campaign was continued. Throughout 1944 the Allied forces were fighting their way northwards,

21. Western Fronts, 1942–45

THE NAZI "FORTRESS-EUROPE" CONSISTED OF GERMANY AND A RING OF SATELLITE and occupied states. The main problem confronting Anglo-American strategists was whether to direct their main assault against Germany herself or to concentrate on what Churchill called "the soft under-belly of the Axis." Inasmuch as Italy and the small satellite states in eastern Europe were militarily weak and resentful of German domination, quick victories at relatively little cost might be won by invading them from the Mediterranean. On the other hand, the conquest of Italy and the Balkans would leave German strength unimpaired; and in view of the mountainous terrain, Allied forces could not hope to advance into central Europe very rapidly. The Soviet Union, which had begun to drive back the German invaders from her soil in the autumn of 1942, insistently demanded a "second front," by which she meant a direct attack on Germany; and when the Western Powers did not immediately launch such an attack, she suggested that they were deliberately letting her bear the main brunt of the war in order to weaken her. This allegation was unfounded, for the primary motivation of Anglo-American strategy was to win the war as fast as possible.

The initial Anglo-American campaigns were fought in the Mediterranean. Forces under General Eisenhower occupied the French colonies of Morocco and Algeria in November, 1942, but had to fight until the following May before capturing Tunisia, which had been seized by German troops ferried across from Italy. The Allies then occupied Sicily and southern Italy; but after the fall of Naples in October, 1943, they were met by strong German forces and did not capture Rome until June, 1944.

The main Allied invasion of Europe was launched from England against the shores of northern France on June 6, 1944. All of France was liberated within three months, but the assault on Germany herself was more difficult. It was not until the spring of 1945 that the Allies fought their way across the Rhine and the German resistance crumbled. Of great importance for the future was the fact that in the meantime Russian armies had occupied eastern Germany and all the satellite and occupied countries in the east except Greece. Thus a large area of eastern Europe became a Soviet sphere of influence.

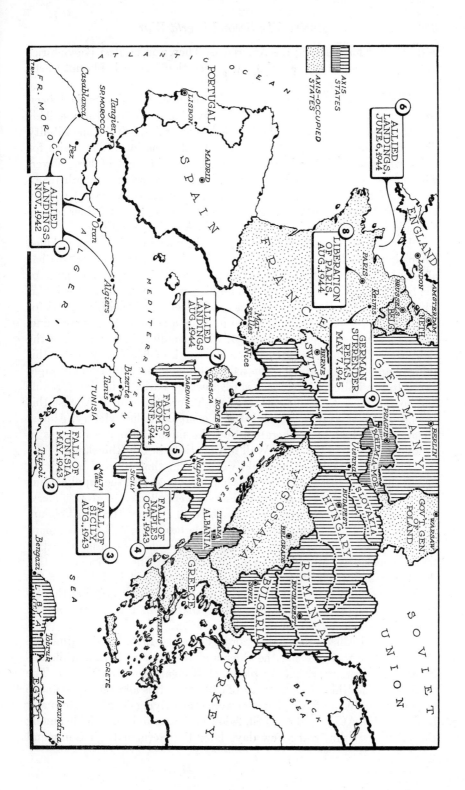

with Mark Clark leading the Americans. They won no decisive victories until the spring of 1945, and the whole operation was probably not worth what it cost.

The Campaign in the West.   Meanwhile, Eisenhower had been transferred to Britain to command the invasion of western Europe. This was planned as a joint Anglo-American enterprise, with responsibility divided as equally as possible between the two nations. The desire for unity was one of the main reasons for the appointment of Eisenhower, whose most obvious qualification was his ability to secure smooth team-work. Unfortunately, some of his leading subordinates were not equally tactful, and disputes between Montgomery and Bradley and their respective admirers soon began to disturb Anglo-American relations.

D-day was June 6, 1944. On the early morning of that day Allied troops began to land on the Normandy beachheads. Invasion by sea has always been extremely hazardous; and this was the largest, and perhaps the boldest, operation of its kind in all history. In its initial stages it was wholly successful. But the Germans quickly reformed their lines, and for seven weeks the Allies were hemmed in along a narrow strip of coastline. The breakthrough began on July 25, when Bradley, in command of the right wing, launched an offensive to the south of Cherbourg. After this things happened quickly. Patton led his tanks in an astonishingly rapid sweep to the Loire and then eastwards towards Paris, while the Germans had to fall back to avoid encirclement. Before the end of August this second battle of France had ended in a complete Allied victory. Almost all of France had been liberated, and the main German army was in headlong retreat to the West Wall fortifications in the Rhineland.

Patton believed that he could win the war that autumn by driving across the Rhine before the Germans had recovered. But the supply of fuel was running low, and the available reserves were allotted to Montgomery, in command of the left wing, who proposed to advance through Belgium and Holland. Unfortunately, he made little headway, and the Germans had time to consolidate their positions. This episode has caused more bitter arguments than anything else in the entire war. The two armies settled down to watch each other through the autumn, and in December the Germans actually launched a surprise offensive, nearly splitting the Allied lines and reaching Antwerp. The situation in this "battle of the bulge" remained critical for more than a week.

The final Allied offensive began in February 1945. By this time one Russian army was crossing the Oder and threatening Berlin, while another was sweeping across the plains of Hungary towards Vienna. The crossing of the Rhine began on March 13. After this all enemy resistance began to crumble, and Allied armies were soon driving deep into Germany from all sides. At the end of April, Adolf Hitler committed suicide among the ruins of Berlin, and a few days later the German High Command agreed to unconditional surrender. The terms were signed at Reims on May 7, and the war officially ended on May 8.

Operations in the Pacific. In the Pacific it had originally been expected that the American forces could not undertake much more than holding operations until Hitler had been disposed of. In actuality, American war production was so immense that major offensives were under way against Japan even before Eisenhower landed in France. Long before VE-day the United States navy was considerably stronger than those of all other countries in the world combined, and could control the Pacific right up to the coast of Japan herself.

Through the latter part of 1942 and most of 1943 the Americans were engaged in minor operations on the periphery of Japan's island empire. MacArthur attacked Japanese forces in northern New Guinea, and a prolonged and bloody struggle was fought in the Solomons. The stubborn Japanese resistance, the deadly tropical climate, and the prospect of hopping from one island to another across the world's largest ocean caused many gloomy predictions about the length of the war. But before the end of 1943 the Americans were ready for bolder tactics. Henceforth they struck at key points inside the Japanese circle, and thereby isolated the garrisons on the periphery, many of which were left to themselves until the war ended. "Leap-frog" replaced "island-hopping," and the vast extent of the Japanese empire was turned to American advantage.

In a series of jumps, each of them involving a few days of extremely savage fighting, with heavy casualties for the Marine Corps, the American navy drove steadily closer to Japan. In November 1943 the marines seized Tarawa in the Gilbert Islands. In January they attacked Kwajalein in the Marshall Islands, whence it was possible to make destructive air raids on the big Japanese naval base at Truk. In June came the capture of Saipan in the Mariana Islands, only 1,500 miles from the Japanese coast. This brought out a large part of the Japanese navy, which was put to flight in the battle of the Philippine Sea.

This was followed by the boldest of all the American advances. In October, MacArthur, hitherto occupied in New Guinea and the Bismarck Islands, led his army back to the Philippines and landed on the island of Leyte, in the very center of the archipelago, 1,500 miles from the nearest American bases. The Japanese navy could not ignore this audacious challenge and came south in the hope of cutting off the invading forces. The result was the battle for Leyte Gulf of October 23–25, the greatest sea engagement in all history. American leadership was faulty, and at one point the Japanese were close to victory, but fortunately they failed to grasp their opportunity. The battle ended in a decisive American triumph and the virtual end of Japanese sea power. MacArthur landed on Luzon, largest and most northerly of the Philippines, in January, and fought his way into Manila in February. Meanwhile, the marines carried the

22. Pacific Theater, 1941–45

BY THE SPRING OF 1942 THE JAPANESE AMBITION TO CREATE A "NEW ORDER" IN eastern Asia and the Pacific seemed close to realization. Japan controlled large areas on the mainland of Asia, all of the East Indies except southern New Guinea, and a vast island empire in the Pacific. Her forces could make thrusts eastward against the American bases in the Hawaiian Islands, southward against Australia, or westward against the British in India. Part of her army was still engaged in fighting the Chinese, whose leader, Chiang Kai-shek, maintained headquarters at Chungking; but by winning control of Burma and blocking the Burma Road she prevented him from receiving American assistance, except by air over the Himalayas on the northern border of India. Short of military equipment and engaged in a losing struggle since 1937 the Chinese could not maintain effective resistance on any large scale. The Soviet Union, preoccupied with the defense of her territories against German invasion, remained officially neutral toward the Pacific war. Thus Japan's position appeared to be alarmingly strong, and was to become more so as she developed the vast natural resources of the East Indies.

In May, 1942, a Japanese naval thrust southward was checked at the Battle of the Coral Sea, east of Australia; and in June, when the Japanese navy turned eastward against Hawaii, it was defeated at Midway. For the next eighteen months American forces were engaged in minor offensive operations on the periphery of the Japanese Empire, in New Guinea, the Solomon Islands, and the Aleutian Islands. But by the autumn of 1943 the United States was strong enough for more ambitious moves, and her forces began to drive straight toward the Japanese mainland. In a series of jumps the American navy seized bases in the Gilberts, the Marshalls, and the Marianas; the American army moved from New Guinea to the Philippines; and early in 1945, came the capture of Iwo Jima and Okinawa between Japan and Formosa. Thus Japanese garrisons in the East Indies and the Pacific islands were cut off and rendered useless to the defense of the Japanese mainland. Plans for an invasion of Japan were cut short by her surrender in August, 1945.

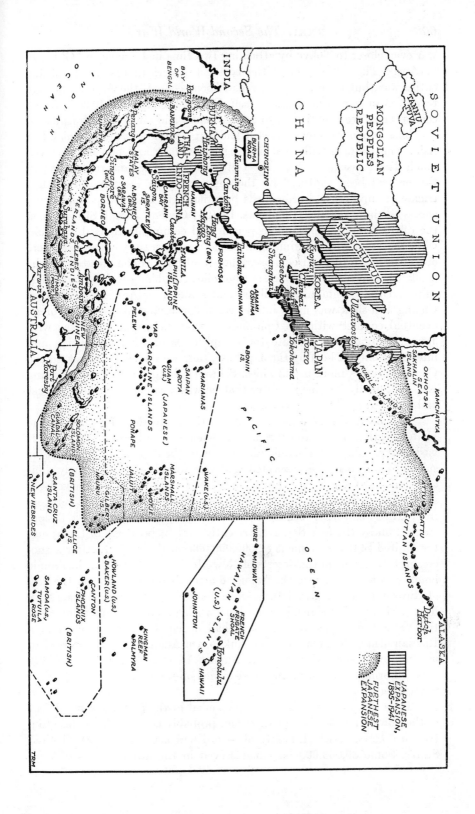

war even closer to Tokyo by attacking Iwo Jima in January and Okinawa in April. These were much the costliest American operations of the entire war; but once these bases had been secured, the Americans were ready for an assault on Japan herself. During the spring of 1945 Japanese coastal cities were subjected to intense naval and air bombardments.

The Japanese, however, still had large armies on the mainland of Asia. The Chinese had been fighting since 1937, and had not received much direct assistance from the United States. The land route through Burma had been captured by the Japanese early in 1942, although a trickle of supplies had afterwards been flown to Chungking from India across the hump of the Himalayas. In 1944 General Joseph Stilwell took the offensive in Burma and reopened land communications; but meanwhile the Japanese were winning more victories over the Chinese, who were obviously close to total collapse. The situation was complicated by the conflict between the Nationalists who followed Chiang Kai-shek's leadership and the Communists. Stilwell and some other Americans felt that Chiang Kai-shek was more interested in conserving his strength for an eventual conflict with the Communists than in winning the war with Japan. Failing to appreciate the complexities of Chinese politics, and interested only in beating the Japanese, they were inclined to regard the Communists as more useful allies. Stilwell's disagreements with Chiang Kai-shek finally became so bitter that he was recalled from the Far East and replaced by Albert Wedemeyer.

The Surrender of Japan.   After the surrender of Germany the United Nations began to concentrate their forces in the Pacific for an invasion of the Japanese mainland. In view of the Japanese reputation for suicidal resistance, they expected that this would be an extremely difficult and costly enterprise. It proved, however, to be unnecessary. Ever since 1942 an international group of physicists, many of them refugees from Hitler, had been secretly working on the problem of atomic fission, spurred on by the fear that Nazi scientists might be ahead of them; and the United States had spent $2,000,000,000 on the project. After a successful experiment in the deserts of New Mexico in June 1945, the atomic bomb was ready for use. On August 6 a bomb was dropped on the city of Hiroshima. Three days later a second bomb was dropped on Nagasaki. Meanwhile, the Russians, in accordance with a secret agreement made at the Yalta Conference in February, had declared war on Japan and a Russian army was invading Manchukuo. On August 10 Japan agreed to unconditional surrender, and on August 14 the Pacific war officially ended. Formal surrender terms were signed on the battleship *Missouri* on September 2.

Thus the greatest war in history ended in the overwhelming defeat of the powers responsible for it. It had probably cost mankind close to a trillion dollars, of which nearly one-third had been paid by the United States. Some 80,000,000 men had served in the armed forces of their respective countries, and perhaps 14,000,000 of them had been killed, 375,000 being Americans. In Europe and Asia millions of civilians had been slaughtered, and millions more had been deported from their homes to serve as slave laborers, or had fled from persecution, and were now "displaced persons." Much of the accumulated wealth of mankind had been destroyed, and many irreplaceable natural resources had been consumed. It was obvious that if the human species continued to settle its disputes by war, its days would eventually be numbered. This fact was brought home to all thinking people by the unparalleled destructivity of the atomic bomb.

3. PLANNING A NEW WORLD ORDER

American Peace Plans. Relatively early in the conflict the United States government took the lead in drafting peace plans. Everybody remembered that when Wilson had assumed a similar leadership, he had been repudiated by the American people; but it soon became obvious that his experience was not going to be repeated. In the autumn of 1943 resolutions calling for American membership in a world organization were introduced into Congress by Representative J. William Fulbright and Senator Tom Connally and passed both houses by overwhelming majorities. In the later stages of the war the State Department cooperated with senators of both political parties in working out a bipartisan foreign policy. Especially important was the conversion of Senator Arthur Vandenberg, chief Republican spokesman on foreign affairs, into a strong internationalist. Isolationism was not dead; it now took the form of opposition to various forms of economic cooperation. But for the time being a large majority of Americans seemed to favor political cooperation for the maintenance of peace.

In the hope of avoiding any repetition of Wilson's unhappy experience at the peace conference of 1919, Roosevelt and Hull tried to secure agreement about the main features of the peace settlement while the war was still going on. They also sharply separated the treatment of the enemy powers from the planning of a new world order. Germany and Japan were to be required to surrender unconditionally (a decision announced at the Casablanca Conference between Roosevelt and Churchill in January 1943), and were to be occupied by Allied troops for a long period afterwards. Meanwhile, it was hoped that the wartime association among the United Nations could be perpetuated and expanded into a permanent security organization.

Relations with the Soviet Union. World War II changed the balance of power much more drastically than World War I. Of the eight great powers existing in 1914 (Britain, France, Germany, Austria-Hungary, Italy, Russia, the United States, and Japan), only one—Austria-Hungary —had been eliminated by 1919. But World War II ended, at least for the time being, the great-power status of Germany, Italy, and Japan, and gravely weakened Britain and France. Only the United States and the Soviet Union were still undubitably first-class powers. All of Europe was exhausted, while countries on the periphery of Western civilization, such as Argentina and the four British dominions, were rapidly rising in the power scale. The most important result was that the Soviet Union was left as the main center of power in the whole Eurasian continent. Would the Soviet government be willing to join the United States in maintaining peace?

At no period in the war was there much evidence of Soviet coopera-tion. The Russians refused to share military information, did not acknowl-edge the $11,000,000,000 worth of lend-lease aid given by the United States, and recognized Communist groups instead of the official govern-ments-in-exile of Poland and Yugoslavia. Roosevelt, nevertheless, was willing to go to great lengths in meeting Soviet demands. He argued that their uncooperativeness was due to fear and could be removed by a dis-play of friendship. This was a gamble, and in the end it failed. In retro-spect it became obvious that Soviet policy was determined not by fear, but by the expansionist ambitions of the Stalinist dictatorship, and by its conviction that communism was intrinsically opposed to capitalism and must in the end become world-wide. But in fairness to Roosevelt it must be remembered that a large part of the American people, including many Republicans, were equally hopeful of winning Soviet cooperation and ready to find excuses for Stalin's policies. If the experiment had not been made, moreover, public opinion throughout the world would have blamed the United States for Soviet intransigence.

Top-level peace-planning began in October 1943, when Secretary Hull met the British and Russian foreign ministers, Anthony Eden and Vyache-slav Molotov, in a conference in Moscow. They signed a declaration prom-ising permanent cooperation and the establishment of a "general inter-national organization, based on the principle of the sovereign equality of all peace-loving states." This was followed in November by meetings of Roosevelt, Churchill, and Chiang Kai-shek at Cairo and of Roosevelt, Churchill, and Stalin at Teheran. Although these conferences were con-cerned mainly with the conduct of the war, it was agreed at Cairo that Japan should be deprived of whatever she had conquered since 1894, and at Teheran that Russia should retain some, at least, of the territories she had appropriated in 1939 and 1940.

Yalta and Potsdam.   During 1944 the cooperation promised at the Moscow Conference was conspicuously absent. As the Russians drove the German armies out of Poland and the Balkan countries, they pro-ceeded to install Communist-controlled governments, without consulting Britain and the United States. Meanwhile, the British stepped into Greece and set up a conservative regime. These and other evidences of conflict led Roosevelt to make his last and most vigorously criticized attempt to reach an understanding with Russia at the Yalta Conference of February 1945. This eight-day meeting in the Crimea was attended by most of the top brass of the United States, Britain, and the Soviet Union.

Germany, it was decided, was to be divided into four zones, to be occupied by American, British, Russian, and French armies, and was to pay reparations in kind for the damages she had inflicted upon other countries. In the smaller liberated and Axis nations interim governments were to be set up which would be "broadly representative of all democratic elements in the population and pledged to the earliest possible establishment through free elections of governments responsive to the will of the people." Poland was to be compensated for the loss of her eastern territories by receiving a slice of eastern Germany. By a secret agreement the Soviet Union promised to enter the war against Japan, in return for which she was to regain the territories she had lost to Japan in 1905 and also to recover her paramount position in the Chinese province of Manchuria. In making these concessions, Roosevelt was acting at the request of American military leaders who were convinced that Russian assistance would save hundreds of thousands of American lives. Since Stalin also promised to make a treaty of friendship and alliance with Chiang Kai-shek, it was hoped that the agreement would lead to permanent peace for the Far East.

The last of the wartime conferences took place at Potsdam in July, with President Truman representing the United States. This was mainly concerned with filling in the details of decisions made at Yalta. The occupation policies of the four powers in Germany were to be coordinated through a central Control Council, the general purposes being to bring about disarmament and promote democracy. The western border of Poland was fixed provisionally, and the German city of Königsberg was to be transferred to the Soviet Union.

The agreements about the Polish border and about Königsberg were, of course, clear violations of the Atlantic Charter, which had promised that there should be no territorial changes except by the wishes of the people concerned, while the restoration to the Soviet Union of her control over Manchuria was equally indefensible. The promises of democracy and free elections in Poland and the Balkans were never honored, nor was there ever any coordination of occupation policies in Germany; from the beginning the Russians set out to establish communism in the zone assigned to them. There can be little doubt that the Yalta and Potsdam agreements weakened the moral position of the United States. But whether they also weakened her power position is a much more debatable question. Russian armies were already in control of eastern Europe, and it is not apparent that Roosevelt gave them anything which they would not have taken in any case.

Building the United Nations. Meanwhile, another series of conferences had been drafting blueprints for a new world order. The main structure of the United Nations was to resemble that of the League of Nations, with changes in detail. But Roosevelt and Hull laid great emphasis on the creation of specialized agencies to promote economic and cultural cooperation. They hoped that through these agencies nations would acquire the habit of working together, so that political conflicts and the whole question of sovereignty would gradually lose their importance.

The process began in May 1943, with a conference at Hot Springs, Virginia, at which representatives of forty-four nations drew up a plan for a Food and Agriculture Organization. In November a conference at Atlantic City, New Jersey, set up the United Nations Relief and Rehabilitation Administration, and in April 1944 the International Labor Organization of the League of Nations was reconstituted. In July a conference on monetary questions was held at Bretton Woods, New Hampshire. This agreed to establish an International Bank for Reconstruction, which would lend money for the development of backward areas, and an International Monetary Fund, which would promote currency stabilization. The participating nations were not to change the values of their currencies without the consent of the committee in charge of the fund. This provision was applauded by internationalists as indicating a real surrender of sovereignty. Other agencies, set up after the war, included the United Nations Educational, Scientific and Cultural Organization, the International Refugee Organization, and the World Health Organization.

The main task confronting the architects of the United Nations, that of planning a security organization for the maintenance of peace, began with a series of conferences among American, Russian, British, and Chinese representatives at Dumbarton Oaks, in the District of Columbia, in the late summer and autumn of 1944. The proposals drawn up at Dumbarton Oaks were then considerably amended by a general conference, attended by delegates of fifty nations, which met at San Francisco between April 25 and June 26, 1945. The two main authors of the United Nations were missing from the scene, since Roosevelt had died in April and Hull had been compelled by ill health to resign. The United States delegation, which included leaders of both parties from both houses of Congress, was headed by the new Secretary of State, Edward R. Stettinius.

The Charter of the United Nations, as adopted by the San Francisco Conference, provided for an Assembly representing all member states and meeting at least once a year, and for a Security Council of eleven members which was to be able to function continuously and have the main responsibility for preventing war. The United States, the Soviet Union, Britain, China, and France were to be permanent members of the Security Council, and each of them was to have a right of veto on substantive (though not on "procedural") matters. The other six members were to be chosen by the Assembly for two-year terms. The Security Council was to investigate any dispute that might lead to war and take any action that might be necessary to maintain peace. All member nations were to pledge themselves to settle disputes by peaceful means and to assist the United Nations in any action undertaken in accordance with the Charter. The Charter also provided for an Economic and Social Council with eighteen members to control the various specialized agencies; a Trusteeship Council to supervise the government of colonial territories; an International Court of Justice; and a Secretariat. Regional agencies for the settlement of local disputes were to be encouraged, and Article 51 specified that "nothing in the present Charter shall impair the inherent right of individual or collective self-defense."

Pan-American Relations.   The only regional agency actually established was in the Western Hemisphere. During World War II the American nations were more nearly united than ever before. A Pan-American Conference at Rio de Janeiro in January 1942 recommended breaking diplomatic relations with the Axis; all the American states except Chile and Argentina complied immediately, and Chile did so within a year. Mexico, Brazil, and a number of smaller nations declared war within a few months of Pearl Harbor, and most of the others followed their example later. Their military assistance was, of course, unimportant, though Brazil sent troops to the Italian campaign and a Mexican air squadron took part in MacArthur's invasion of the Philippines. But Latin American cooperation was valuable in three ways: Axis agents were prevented from maintaining centers of espionage; and the United States obtained naval and air bases, and received aid in the development of essential raw materials. Unfortunately, the unity of the hemisphere was broken by Argentina, traditionally hostile to the United States and governed by extreme conservatives somewhat sympathetic to fascism. Argentinian uncooperativeness became even more pronounced in 1943, when army leaders staged a *coup d'état* and seized power. In 1944 the United States broke off diplomatic relations and began to threaten economic reprisals; but effective action was prevented by the need of the United Nations for Argentinian foodstuffs.

Another Pan-American Conference was held at Chapultepec in Mexico in February 1945. Under pressure from the Latin Americans, who were disturbed by anything suggestive of the "big stick" of earlier periods, the United States agreed that if Argentina would declare war on the Axis, all would be forgiven. Argentina duly went through the motions of entering the war (now almost over), and hemispheric unity was officially re-established. The Chapultepec Conference also voted that any act of aggression against an American state, whether from within or without the hemisphere, should "be considered as an act of aggression against the other states which sign this declaration." Thus the Pan-American system was to become a security organization for the maintenance of peace in the Western Hemisphere. A conference at Rio de Janeiro in 1947 reaffirmed this promise of collective defense against aggression in the form of a treaty of reciprocal assistance, and a conference at Bogotá in 1948 set up the Organization of American States as a regional agency within the United Nations.

The Hope of Peace.   Thus for a second time idealists throughout the world hoped to bring about the rule of law in international affairs. Resembling the League of Nations in its organization and functions, the United Nations was in no sense a world government. It was "based on the principle of the sovereign equality of all its members," and had no authority to "intervene in matters which are essentially within the domestic jurisdiction of any state." Its efficacy would thus depend on the willingness of the member nations to support its purposes. It would depend, in particular, on the attitudes of the United States and the Soviet Union, each of which could wreck the organization by refusing to support it. The great powers had authority to prevent other countries from committing acts of aggression; but if they themselves resorted to aggression, they could not be disciplined, unless the rest of the world was willing to start World War III. The right of veto assumed by the great powers was merely a legal recognition of this practical reality.

The whole structure of the United Nations was, in fact, grounded on the supposition that the wartime cooperation between its leading members would continue in the post-war world. This hope quickly proved, of course, to be a delusion. And when it became apparent that the United Nations could not be relied upon to maintain peace, member nations fearing Soviet aggression had to look for other means of self-defense, as authorized by Article 51.

XXXII

Since the War

1. DOMESTIC AFFAIRS

2. TWO WORLDS

3. THE EISENHOWER ADMINISTRATION

T HE DEFEAT of the Axis left the United States endowed with a power and prestige unparalleled in all history. Yet no nation has ever been less interested in glory or more reluctant to assume an imperial role. Hating militarism in all its forms, the American people had gone to war only under pressure of necessity and were now eager to return to their peacetime occupations. But the course of events after 1945 quickly made it apparent that the crisis of modern civilization was not yet over. Both the movement towards international unity and the drive of underprivileged classes and races towards a fairer distribution of the world's goods had to work themselves out to some kind of conclusion before there could be any lasting peace. The United States could hope to win security for herself and the ideals in which she believed only by recognizing the irresistible trends of history and accepting the full responsibilities of world leadership.

1. DOMESTIC AFFAIRS

The Truman Administration. The Americans faced their post-war problems under an inexperienced chief executive. Roosevelt had been

---

SELECTED BIBLIOGRAPHY: Eric F. Goldman, *The Crucial Decade* (1956), is a lively survey of the first ten postwar years. President Truman has described his own administration in *Year of Decisions* (1955), and *Years of Trial and Hope* (1956). He is sympathetically portrayed in Jonathan Daniels, *Man of Independence* (1950). The best account of Eisenhower's first three years is R. J. Donovan, *Eisenhower, The Inside Story* (1956). Three of the most thought-provoking of recent books on internal affairs are J. K. Galbraith, *American Capitalism, The Concept of Countervailing Power* (1952), and Samuel Lubell, *The Future of American Politics* (1952), and *The Revolt of the Moderates* (1956). For foreign affairs during the Truman period, F. O. Wilcox and T. V. Kalijarvi, *Recent American Foreign Policy* (1952) is a useful reference book. Two of the better books on the Chinese catastrophe are Herbert Feis, *The China Tangle* (1953) and K. S. Latourette, *The American Record in the Far East* (1952).

re-elected in 1944, his Republican opponent being Thomas E. Dewey, Governor of New York. But his fourth term lasted for only four months. He died suddenly on April 12, 1945, and the presidency passed to Vice-President Harry S. Truman. Like many of his predecessors, Truman owed his nomination mainly to his political availability. In the Democratic convention of 1944 the traditional conflicts between Southerners and Northerners, conservatives and progressives, had again come into the open. After Southern and conservative groups had prevented the nomination of Henry Wallace, who had served as vice-president since 1941, Truman, from the border state of Missouri, had been chosen as the most acceptable compromise candidate.

Senator from Missouri since 1934, Truman had done valuable work as head of a committee investigating waste and inefficiency in war production. But he seemed hardly qualified to lead the world's most powerful nation at one of the most critical periods in human history. Until his election to the Senate at the age of fifty, he had been a farmer, a small businessman, and a holder of minor political offices, and had had substantially the same experiences and way of life as millions of other middle-class Americans. Of all the presidents of the United States, in fact, it was perhaps Harry Truman who came closest to being an average citizen, with all his characteristic virtues and limitations. His record in office proved, on the whole, to be a reassuring demonstration of the vitality of American ideals. He made serious errors. When led astray by explosive emotions, he could be stubbornly wrong-headed, and was sometimes much too loyal to unworthy friends. But on major issues, especially in foreign affairs, he rose to the responsibilities of his high office and provided by no means ineffectual leadership.

Although Truman declared that he would continue Roosevelt's policies, his direction during his early years in office was very uncertain, with a number of abrupt shifts between conservatism and progressivism. In the end he settled to a definitely progressive course, advocating a Fair Deal as a sequel to the New Deal, appealing (like Roosevelt) to organized labor, the farmers, and the middle-class liberals, and fighting the Southern conservatives in the Democratic Party.[1] But during the first eighteen months of his presidency almost all the surviving New Dealers left the government and were replaced by men of a different type, many of them being machine politicians or small-town lawyers and businessmen with little experience of national affairs.

Truman made some of his worst mistakes in his appointments to departments concerned with domestic administration. Given responsible positions in a government which had immense powers over the national economy and which was spending between thirty and forty billion dollars

---

[1] Strong support for the continuance of the New Deal was provided by Americans for Democratic Action, an organization founded in 1947 which combined advocacy of progressive reforms with militant opposition to Communism.

a year, a catastrophically large number of officials took advantage of their opportunities. Within a few years standards of honesty in the lower brackets of some departments, especially the Bureau of Internal Revenue, declined to levels perhaps as low as during the Grant administration. Probably the most disturbing trend was not so much the amount of actual bribery and theft but the spread of lax ethical attitudes. Many officials, while technically honest, saw nothing wrong in doing favors for friends. In consequence, Washington was soon swarming with unsavory characters, known as "five-per-centers," who made fortunes by cultivating influence in government circles and fixing contacts for businessmen who wanted special privileges. The personal integrity and good intentions of Harry Truman were unquestionable; but the sprawling Federal bureaucracy was soon in need of drastic purification.

Reconversion Problems. For about two years after the surrender of the Axis, domestic affairs were dominated by the gradual removal of controls and the return to peacetime ways of living. Industry reconverted to production for civilian use; and the government, fearing that the process would be accompanied by large-scale unemployment, made every effort to ease the transition. Taxes were reduced, loans were made to business through the RFC, money remained plentiful and interest rates low, and billions of dollars' worth of government-owned war plants and surplus war material were sold off at bargain rates. Actually all the fears of a depression proved to be baseless, and the country soon entered upon the most remarkable prosperity period in its entire history.

As soon as the war ended, men in the services and their relatives at home put pressure on the authorities for rapid demobilization, and the dissolution of American armed forces proceeded so rapidly that the country had difficulty in meeting its occupation obligations in Germany and Japan. This made it necessary for Congress to continue selective service until 1947. By January of that year the country had a total of only about 1,000,000 men in the army and navy. Thus the United States rapidly ceased to be a first-class military power—a change which had potentially catastrophic effects in world politics. Discharged veterans were given educational opportunities and some economic assistance under the G.I. Bill of Rights, which had become law in 1944.

As after World War I, reconversion was accompanied by widespread labor disputes. Labor had been able to maintain its standards of living during the war through overtime pay. The unions now demanded increases in regular wage rates in order to compensate for the expected loss of overtime, and during the eighteen months following VJ-Day there were a series of strikes in major industries—automobiles, steel, coal, and railroads. In most instances, the unions gained substantial wage increases, while the government authorized the industries involved to pass on the costs to the consumer through higher prices.

These price and wage increases soon endangered the whole price-control program. This was the chief subject of domestic controversy through 1946. Whereas the administration wanted the powers of OPA continued until the supply of civilian goods caught up with the demand, conservatives in Congress and elsewhere argued that if price-controls were immediately abandoned and business was allowed to make higher profits, production would be stimulated and the scarcities would quickly disappear. They also pointed out that the growth of the black market showed that price regulations could no longer be effectively enforced. In June 1946 Congress passed a bill extending OPA for another year but emasculating its powers and permitting a number of price increases. Truman vetoed the bill; but after a month without controls, during which prices shot up alarmingly, he accepted a similar bill, which included a clause authorizing the administration to end controls when it saw fit. But when OPA attempted to force price-reductions, many producers, especially of meat, withdrew their goods from the market; and public indignation then became so intense that the administration surrendered. In October, Truman announced the gradual abandonment of all controls except on rent.

After this, prices began a steady and apparently inexorable rise, and within a year the cost of living had risen more than during the whole of the war period. Prices slowly began to level off in 1948 and 1949, but shot up again in 1950 with the rearmament program and the Korean war. Inflation had apparently come to stay; and while labor was able, on the whole, to win wage increases which kept its living standards level, middle-class citizens with relatively rigid incomes suffered acutely.

Legislation.   Apart from the fight about price-controls, Congress was largely occupied through 1945 and 1946 with ratifying the various United Nations agreements. The only significant law dealing with domestic affairs was the Maximum Employment Act of February 1946. The administration had wanted a measure based on Keynesian principles which would establish government responsibility for maintaining "full employment" and provide, when necessary, for Federal spending on a sufficient scale to prevent depression. The bill as finally passed fell far short of these hopes, though it represented a significant innovation in Federal policy. It set a goal of "maximum" rather than "full" employment, and provided for a board of three economists who were to prepare annual reports on the state of the national economy and make recommendations to the President.

The administration's surrender on price-control was followed by defeat at the polls, and in 1946, when the 80th Congress was elected, the Republicans won control of both houses for the first time since 1930. Under the leadership of Senator Taft of Ohio, their chief spokesman on internal policy, they set out to revise the Wagner Act and limit the powers of labor unions. The Taft-Hartley Act, passed over Truman's veto, became law in June 1947. According to its sponsors, its purpose was to bring about legal equality between employers and employees and to safeguard the community against abuses of power on the part of labor unions. Labor leaders, on the other hand, bitterly denounced it as an attempt to destroy collective bargaining. The act declared that unions could be sued if they violated contracts, outlawed the closed shop, declared illegal a long list of practices in which unions had frequently engaged, and authorized the government to obtain an eighty-day injunction against any strike that would endanger national safety. The NLRB, which had been set up by the Wagner Act to protect the rights of labor, was now to be reorganized as a court for the enforcement of collective bargaining rules upon both employers and unions.

Apart from the Taft-Hartley Act, the 80th Congress made no drastic revisions in New Deal legislation. The Republican majority, supported by many conservative Democrats, paid no attention to Truman's recommendations for further reforms; but, on the other hand, they showed no serious desire to return to the 1920's. Much was heard about the dangers of the "welfare state" and the virtues of unrestricted free enterprise. But such basic New Deal measures as social security and support for farm prices underwent only minor changes, and the government continued to exercise broad powers over the economy through its currency and credit policies.

The Election of 1948. The year 1948 seemed like a Republican year. Governor Dewey won the nomination for the second time; and apparently anticipating an easy victory if he avoided damaging mistakes, he largely restricted himself to generalities in his speeches. Truman was renominated by the Democrats in spite of opposition from both the right and the left wing of the party, after which two splinter groups broke away and chose candidates of their own. Southern "Dixiecrats," hostile to Truman's demands for Federal legislation to protect the rights of Negroes, nominated Governor J. Strom Thurmond of South Carolina, while Northern radicals who were not yet convinced that the Soviet Union was a threat to peace and who disliked the administration's foreign policies nominated Henry Wallace and assumed the name "Progressive."

Virtually everybody but Truman himself assumed that his defeat was inevitable. But the President conducted a fighting campaign, making speeches at every whistle stop on cross-country tours and lambasting the 80th Congress for its refusal to accept his Fair Deal program. As a result of the Progressive and Dixiecrat secessions, he won slightly less than half the popular vote, but he had a popular majority over Dewey of more than 2,000,000, with a substantial lead in the electoral college. Even with the loss of part of the South, the combination of groups won to the Democratic Party by the New Deal was still unbeatable. In fact, a number of liberals campaigning in state elections ran well ahead of the President.

Truman's remarkable triumph had few political results. The 81st Congress, though controlled by the Democrats, was not much more receptive to his recommendations than the 80th. It extended the social-security system to cover more groups of citizens, raised minimum-wage scales, and voted money for low-cost housing. But it refused to enact laws for national health insurance, Federal enforcement of civil rights for Negroes, Federal subsidies for education, and the rest of the Fair Deal program. Meanwhile, international tensions were increasing, and the growing Soviet threat soon brought a return to war production. In actuality, in spite of the popularity of the Fair Deal with a large part of the electorate, there was no strong popular pressure for further reform legislation. Production was booming, jobs were easy to find, and almost everybody in the country was earning far more than ever before.

The Post-war Boom.   Almost everybody had expected a post-war depression, and the administration had planned its economic program on the assumption that the economy would need to be stimulated rather than restrained. And as the boom developed, scarcely anybody believed that it would continue. There were, in truth, a number of causes for anxiety. The boom was largely set in motion by the pent-up demand and accumulated savings of the war years, and was accompanied by inflationary price increases which might end in a sudden deflationary collapse. Nevertheless, the fact remained that the years 1947 and 1948 saw production and consumption on a scale unexampled in all earlier history. By 1948 some 60,000,000 people were gainfully employed, as contrasted with 47,000,000 in 1939, and goods were being produced at the rate of $225,-000,000,000 a year, as contrasted with $72,000,000,000 in 1939. Even allowing for the 70 per cent rise in price levels, this was an astonishing increase.

Eventually a few bold economists began to suggest that perhaps the system was in better shape than all the prophets of gloom had believed. Perhaps the lessons learned by business and the reforms made by government since the debacle of 1929 had created a basis for more lasting prosperity. Professor J. K. Galbraith of Harvard argued that the country had gone a long way towards checking the power of big corporations, not by the uneconomic method of dissolving them into smaller units, as the trust-busters had wanted, but by the development of "countervailing power." Manufacturing corporations, for example, were prevented from charging excessive prices by the big chain stores, while the share of the national income going to big business in general was limited through the rise of strong labor unions and government aid for agriculture. Statisticians, moreover, showed that since 1929 there had been a remarkable improvement in the living standards of the poorer classes. This had been accomplished not by directly decreasing the earnings of the richer classes but by expanding production and distributing it more equitably.

Figures collected by the National Bureau of Economic Research showed that whereas in 1929 the richest 1 per cent of the population had received 16 per cent of the national income, in 1948 they received only

8 per cent. But since the national income (even allowing for price increases) had considerably more than doubled, this did not mean that the rich were actually worse off, in spite of the drastic change in their relative share. During the same period the proportion going to the next highest 6 per cent of the population had dropped from 15 per cent to 13 per cent, while the share of the remaining 93 per cent had jumped from 69 per cent to 79 per cent. Nor did these figures allow for income-tax payments, which reduced still further the share of the richer classes. Between 1939 and 1949 the median family income rose from $1,231 to $2,949. Whereas in 1939 as many as 75 per cent of all families were earning less than $2,000 a year, by 1949 the proportion had dropped to about 25 per cent These changes had been brought about by the industrial expansion of the war years, by the rise of organized labor, and by New Deal legislation for the benefit of wage-earners and farmers. They meant that industry had a much larger market for its products than during the 1920's, so that there was less danger of a collapse.

Thus the United States, without any change in its basic institutions, had made greater strides towards a more equitable system of distribution than other countries had accomplished by violence and revolution. Unfortunately, the American people were not permitted to enjoy this peacetime prosperity for more than a few years, since industry was soon required to reconvert again to war production.

2. TWO WORLDS

EVEN before the war ended, it was becoming apparent that Roosevelt's attempt to win Soviet cooperation in building a new world order had failed. The old Russian imperialism and the new Communist program of world revolution had become fused into a single dynamic and expansionist force. The Soviet government sought to control as much as possible of the Eurasian continent, while its Communist supporters throughout the world stopped calling for democratic collaboration against fascism and were soon denouncing "Yankee imperialism." But the American people were slow to recognize that one world conflict had been succeeded by another. As a result of the rapid demobilization of American armed forces, the free world was left with no check on the Communist advance in eastern Europe and the Far East, except the American monopoly of the atomic bomb. It was not until the spring of 1947 that the United States undertook a positive program of resistance to Communist pressure.

Post-war Europe. In accordance with the Yalta and Potsdam agreements, Germany and Austria after the war were split into different zones and occupied by American, British, French, and Russian armies, which were supposed to wipe out Hitlerism and promote democracy. The surviving Nazi leaders were put on trial at Nuremberg in the autumn of 1945; and after judicial proceedings lasting for nearly a year, twelve of

them were sentenced to be hanged. But it was doubtful whether any of
the occupying armies actually did much to strengthen democracy. From
the beginning the provision for coordination agreed upon at Potsdam
proved to be unworkable. The Russians established Communism in their
zone, made it politically and economically subsidiary to the Soviet Union,
and sealed it off from the western zones. As the American and British
authorities came to the realization that they might need German help
against Soviet aggression, they gradually adopted less stringent policies
and began to forget about the crimes committed by the Nazis. In 1949
the three western zones were united into a new German federal republic,
and a government was set up at Bonn.

In eastern Europe, in addition to annexing 273,000 square miles of
territory, the Russians by the summer of 1945 had set up Communist-
controlled governments in Poland, Rumania, Bulgaria, Yugoslavia, and
Albania, were working towards the same objective in Hungary and
Czechoslovakia, and were encouraging rebellion against the royalist
regime in Greece and making territorial demands on Turkey. The task of
drafting peace treaties with Italy and the smaller Axis countries in eastern
Europe began in the autumn. James F. Byrnes, who had been appointed
Secretary of State a few weeks after Truman's accession to the presidency,
was the chief American spokesman. As a result of Russian intransigence
the negotiations were prolonged through no less than six different conferences over a period of fourteen months, and were finally completed in
November 1946. Leaders of liberal groups opposed to Communism were
added to the Bulgarian and Rumanian governments, but on most issues
the Russians got what they wanted. The only important exceptions were
that the city of Trieste, formerly Italian, was internationalized, and
that the Russians got no share of control over the former Italian colonies
in Africa, most of which were eventually to become self-governing.

After the treaties the Communists seized power in Hungary and
Czechoslovakia; and except in Finland, which retained a precarious independence, an "iron curtain" descended upon all the countries in the
Soviet sphere of influence. Liberal leaders were lucky if they escaped with
their lives; some of them were shot, and others disappeared or committed
suicide. The promises of free elections, made at Yalta and other conferences, proved to be worthless. The free world could take comfort only
from two things: the Communists failed to win control of Greece; and in
1948 the Communist government of Yugoslavia refused to continue
taking orders from Moscow.

The Far East.   In the Pacific the United States retained control
of the islands that her armed forces had wrested from Japan, and also
kept naval and air bases in the Philippines, which became an independent
republic in 1946. Japan was occupied by American troops commanded by
MacArthur, who exercised a proconsular authority without precedent in
American history. Under MacArthur's supervision Japan democratized

her government and economy and repudiated aggressive policies. Most observers felt that the occupation forces were remarkably successful in reforming the institutions of the Japanese and winning their friendship; but whether this conversion was more than skin-deep remained to be seen. Korea was divided between the Americans and the Russians, with the same results as in Germany. North Korea was organized as a Communist state; in South Korea the Americans endeavored, not very successfully, to establish democracy.

Meanwhile, events in China led to a major catastrophe. In 1945 the long civil war between the Nationalist government of Chiang Kai-shek and the Communists, which had been suspended during the struggle with Japan, began to break out again. The men in charge of America's Far Eastern policy felt that such a war must, if possible, be prevented, both because of the danger of American and Russian involvement on opposite sides, and because they had no confidence in Chiang Kai-shek's capacity to win it. They regarded his regime as thoroughly corrupt, reactionary, and unrepresentative of the mass of the people. The American program was to bring the two sides together in a coalition government which would adopt liberal policies but would leave political and military predominance with the Nationalists. It was hoped that the Russians, in accordance with their pledge at Yalta to make a treaty of friendship and alliance with the Nationalist government, would refrain from supporting the Communists.

General George C. Marshall was sent to China at the end of 1945 to try to mediate between the two sides, and pressure was put upon Chiang Kai-shek to prevent him from attacking the Communists. But neither side was willing to come to terms, and after a year of futile negotiation Marshall gave up and returned home. The civil war then began in earnest. The American government sent some supplies to Chiang Kai-shek, but its attitude continued to be decidedly halfhearted. The Communists won a rapid series of victories; and by 1949 they had gained control of most of the mainland of China, while what was left of the Nationalist forces took refuge on the island of Formosa. Thus 450,000,000 people were added to the Communist world, and the United States suffered the most serious diplomatic defeat in her entire history.

The ensuing controversy about these events was long and bitter, but produced more heat than light. Opponents of the Truman administration insisted that China had been lost because of the American failure to give more effective assistance to Chiang Kai-shek, and even suggested that American policy had been directed by secret Communist agents in the State Department. Its supporters replied that the basic reason for Chiang Kai-shek's defeat was that he had lost the support of the mass of the Chinese people, that the United States could have prevented it only by intervening on a vast scale and fighting a long and costly war, and that the administration had acted wisely in refusing to become too deeply involved with a leader so thoroughly discredited. Obviously, only experts who knew China at first hand were qualified to appraise American policy; but the experts disagreed among themselves.

The United Nations.   With the world splitting into two spheres and "cold war" developing between them, the United Nations could not function according to the intentions of its founders. The first meeting of the General Assembly was held in London in January 1946. It was decided that permanent headquarters should be established in the United States, a site being chosen later in the year in New York City. The Soviet Union and her satellites refused to join almost all the specialized agencies, and these were able to settle down to the task of promoting economic and cultural progress throughout the free world. But the Security Council was reduced almost to paralysis by the obstructive tactics of the Soviet representatives and their unrestrained use of the veto power. It became plain that if the other nations wanted effective international organization for the maintenance of peace, they would have to by-pass the Security Council and invoke the right of collective self-defense under Article 51 of the Charter.

The United States could feel confident that the Russians would not start World War III as long as she had a monopoly of the atomic bomb. But how long would its construction remain a secret? In 1946 a committee headed by Bernard Baruch drafted a plan for putting it under international control. The United Nations was to set up an International Atomic Energy Commission, which would supervise the use of atomic energy throughout the world and have rights of inspection in all countries in order to prevent any unauthorized manufacture of weapons. The United States would then turn over her secrets to the Commission and destroy her stockpile of bombs. This seemed a remarkably bold and enlightened proposal for preventing mankind from committing suicide, and would have meant a decisive step towards real world government. But the Russians opposed it, making it plain that they would never allow international inspectors to wander freely inside Soviet territory. Apparently the chief reason for their hostility was that they expected to make bombs themselves. They had, in fact, acquired the essential information by means of espionage during the war, although it is reasonably certain that Russian scientists would soon have discovered it independently. As early as 1949 President Truman announced that an atomic bomb had been successfully exploded within the Soviet Union. Meanwhile the United States continued to manufacture atomic bombs, while an Atomic Energy Commission was set up to explore the various uses of atomic fission.

The Containment Policy.   Obviously, the United States could not allow the rest of the world to be dominated by Stalin, any more than by Hitler. But Communism presented more complex problems than Nazism. Hitler had relied mainly on force, but Stalin's most dangerous weapon was the belief of exploited groups that the triumph of Communism would mean the establishment of a utopian commonwealth. While the Soviet advance had to be checked by force, it was equally important to check the spread of Communism in the minds of men by offering them a better alternative. Freedom could be safeguarded only by showing that it meant justice, progress, and prosperity.[2]

Beginning in 1947, the United States began to undertake the double task of maintaining enough force to check any further Soviet advance and at the same time promoting prosperity throughout the free world. In addition to President Truman, American foreign policy was directed by General Marshall, who had succeeded Byrnes as Secretary of State in January. Marshall resigned on account of failing health early in 1949, and was replaced by Dean Acheson. Marshall and Acheson believed that if the United States "contained" the Soviet Union by checking any aggression wherever it occurred, and in the meantime built up her own strength and that of the free world, it might eventually be possible to negotiate a general settlement by which World War III could be prevented. This was a difficult and dangerous program, and required the American people to display a patience unique in their experience; but any alternative policy seemed to present even greater dangers.

Every major move was made only after long and often bitter debates. While the Truman administration regarded Europe as the most vital area, many Republicans wanted more emphasis placed on the Far East. And while most Democrats and some Republicans (headed until his death in 1951 by Senator Vandenberg) favored generous appropriations for aid to other countries, a large body of Congressmen insisted that the United States was in danger of overtaxing her resources and that other countries could not be trusted. This attitude reflected the old isolationist suspicion of the rest of the world (especially the European part of it), although the kind of isolationism that had prevailed in the 1930's was now obviously untenable. There was, in fact, a marked revival of the old ultra-nationalist lunatic fringe; men who in 1940 and 1941 had insisted that Roosevelt was a war-monger, and that it would be easy to do business with a victorious Hitler, now declared that both the Truman administration and most of America's foreign allies were tainted with Communism, and apparently wanted the United States to fight a crusade against the Soviet Union almost singlehanded.

Aid to Europe. The initial step in the development of the containment policy was taken in March 1947. The British had been giving financial help to Greece and Turkey; but being in serious difficulties themselves, they wanted to transfer the responsibility to the United States. On March 12, Truman asked Congress to appropriate $400,000,000 for mili-

---

[2] In Point Four of his inaugural address of 1949, Truman suggested that the United States give technical assistance to backward nations for economic development. Progressives received this "Bold New Program" with enthusiasm, but Congress voted only small sums to implement it. By 1952, however, projects had been launched in thirty-seven countries.

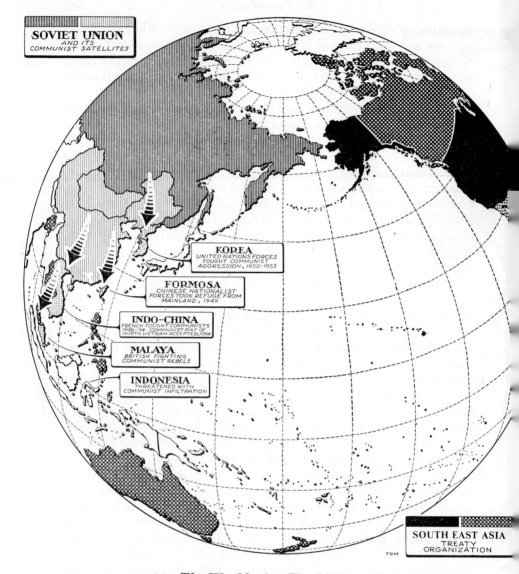

KOREA
UNITED NATIONS FORCES FOUGHT COMMUNIST AGGRESSION, 1950-1953

FORMOSA
CHINESE NATIONALIST FORCES TOOK REFUGE FROM MAINLAND, 1949

INDO-CHINA
FRENCH FOUGHT COMMUNISTS 1946-54. COMMUNIST RULE OF NORTH VIETNAM ACCEPTED, 1954

MALAYA
BRITISH FIGHTING COMMUNIST REBELS

INDONESIA
THREATENED WITH COMMUNIST INFILTRATION

TRM

SOUTH EAST ASIA TREATY ORGANIZATION

23. *The World after World War II*

CONTROLLING THE VAST HEARTLAND OF THE EURASIAN CONTINENT, COMMUNIST Russia after World War II extended its influence over a number of satellite states and then sought to advance at various points around the perimeter of its dominions. In Europe the major center of conflict was Germany, with its great industrial resources and military potential. In the Middle East, most of which was held by weak and backward states incapable of self-defense, strategic interests and ownership of immense oil reserves were at stake. In the Far East Communism was able to capitalize on the growing nationalistic spirit of the Asiatic peoples and their resentment against Western imperialism. Having won mastery of all China by

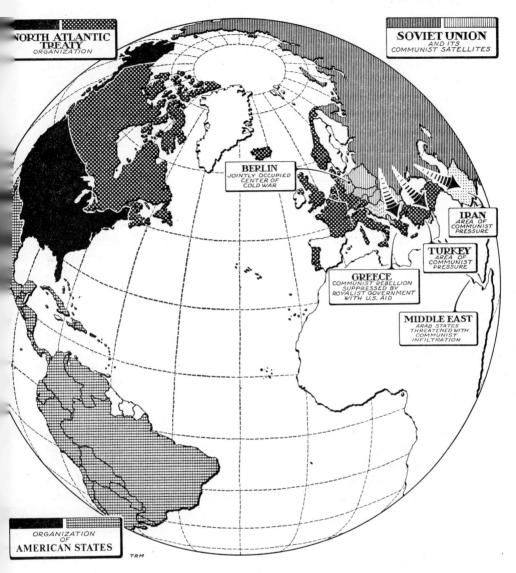

NORTH ATLANTIC TREATY ORGANIZATION

SOVIET UNION AND ITS COMMUNIST SATELLITES

BERLIN JOINTLY OCCUPIED CENTER OF COLD WAR

IRAN AREA OF COMMUNIST PRESSURE

TURKEY AREA OF COMMUNIST PRESSURE

GREECE COMMUNIST REBELLION SUPPRESSED BY ROYALIST GOVERNMENT WITH U.S. AID

MIDDLE EAST ARAB STATES THREATENED WITH COMMUNIST INFILTRATION

ORGANIZATION OF AMERICAN STATES

TRM

1949, Communism launched a war for the conquest of southern Korea in 1950, while insurgent groups tried to drive the French from Indo-China and the British from Malaya.

After reluctantly abandoning the hope of a permanent settlement that had guided her policy during World War II, the United States began in 1947 to give aid to countries threatened by Communist aggression. As the strongest power among the free nations, she took the lead in building three defense groups. In 1948 all the republics of the Western hemisphere set up the Organization of American States, by which they were pledged to assist each other against attack. In 1949 the United States and Canada joined ten of the free nations of western Europe in

[CONTINUED ON FOLLOWING PAGE]

the North Atlantic Treaty Organization, to which Greece and Turkey were added in 1952 and West Germany in 1954. In the Far East the United States made separate defense pacts with Japan, South Korea, and the Chinese Nationalists, and in 1954 she sponsored the formation of the South East Asia Treaty Organization, which was joined by Australia, New Zealand, the Philippines, Thailand, and Pakistan. Meanwhile a fourth group, the Middle East Defense Organization (better known as the Baghdad Pact), was formed by the British in association with four Middle Eastern countries.

During the Truman administration the United States adopted a defensive policy, based on the thesis that if the Communist advance were "contained" and aggression checked wherever it occurred, the Soviet Union would eventually abandon its expansionist ambitions or be weakened by internal conflicts. Critics of the administration complained that this policy left the initiative to the Russians and was likely to be too costly in American men and resources, and advocated a more positive program aiming at the liberation of countries under Communist control. The Eisenhower administration, however, continued the containment program with only minor changes, though for the protection of the free world it proposed to rely more on America's capacity to deter aggression by the threat of "massive retaliation" and less on local defensive power.

The whole world situation was a remarkable fulfillment of a prediction made more than a century earlier by the French sociologist, Alexis de Tocqueville. In 1834 Tocqueville ended the first volume of his great *Democracy in America* with the following words: "The Anglo-American relies upon personal interest to accomplish his ends and gives free scope to the unguided strength and common sense of the people; the Russian centers all the authority of society in a single arm. The principal instrument of the former is freedom; of the latter, servitude. Their starting-point is different and their courses are not the same; yet each of them seems marked out by the will of Heaven to sway the destinies of half the globe."

tary and economic aid to the two countries. Pointing out that "Totalitarian regimes imposed on free peoples by direct or indirect aggression, undermine the foundations of international peace and hence the security of the United States," he declared: "It must be the policy of the United States to support free peoples who are resisting attempted subjugation by armed minorities or by outside pressure." This statement quickly became known as the Truman Doctrine. Congress voted the appropriation, which appears to have been well spent. The Communist rebellion in Greece was brought to an end, and both Greece and Turkey remained securely outside the Soviet orbit.

It was obvious that this was only a beginning. All of western Europe, devastated and exhausted by nearly six years of warfare, was in economic straits, and poverty and instability were leading to an alarming growth of Communism, especially in France and Italy. The United States had already spent large sums on relief and in 1946 had made a loan of $3,750,-000,000 to Britain. But Europe could not get back on its feet without more substantial help, designed to expand industrial and agricultural production rather than merely provide relief. In June 1947 General Marshall suggested in a speech delivered at Harvard University that if the European countries worked out a joint program of economic reconstruction, the United States would assist them. The western nations quickly complied with this recommendation in a conference at Paris. Invitations were sent to the Soviet Union and her satellites, but they preferred to boycott the conference, declaring that its real purpose was to bring about the subjugation of Europe by American capitalism.

In November 1947 Truman asked Congress to appropriate money for the Marshall Plan, officially known as the European Recovery Program. Congress voted the first appropriation in April 1948, with the understanding that the program should continue until 1952. In the course of this four-year period total ERP appropriations exceeded $14,000,000,000. The money was spent under the direction of an Economic Cooperation Administration, headed by a Republican business executive, Paul G. Hoffman.

The logical sequel to economic cooperation was military alliance. In March 1948 five countries of western Europe signed a pact at Brussels promising to aid each other against aggression. The United States Senate then passed the Vandenberg resolution affirming American support for regional security pacts. With this encouragement, the State Department sponsored negotiations for the expansion of the Brussels pact. In April 1949 the North Atlantic Treaty was signed by the United States, Canada, Britain, France, Italy, Belgium, the Netherlands, Luxemburg, Norway, Denmark, Iceland, and Portugal. Its most important article affirmed (on the model of the Organization of American States) that "an armed attack against one or more of them in Europe or North America shall be considered an attack against them all." This epoch-making agreement was

approved by the Senate by an overwhelming majority, and was followed
by the passage of a Mutual Defense Assistance Act under which military
aid was given to the countries in the North Atlantic Treaty Organization
and also to Greece, Turkey, Iran, Korea, the Philippines, and the Chinese
Nationalists on Formosa. In December 1950 the treaty partners agreed
to create a united army to defend western Europe, and at their request
General Eisenhower was appointed as Supreme Allied Commander in
Europe.

The Marshall Plan and subsequent measures stopped the advance of
Communism in Europe, at least for the time being. After the rape of
Czechoslovakia in 1947 no more countries were pulled behind the Iron
Curtain. There was a remarkable improvement in economic conditions
in western Europe, and Communistic sentiment in France, Italy, and else-
where, though still alarmingly extensive, began to decrease.

The Korean War. In the Far East, on the other hand, where the
American position was considerably weaker, the Truman administration
failed to adopt any coherent or consistent policy. In 1949 American occupation forces were withdrawn from South Korea, leaving in power a
native government headed by Syngman Rhee. This was followed, on
June 24, 1950, by a full-scale invasion of South Korea by Communist
armies from North Korea. On the next day the Security Council of the
United Nations (then being boycotted by the Russians because of their
opposition to the continued membership of Nationalist China) condemned
this act of aggression, called for an immediate cease-fire, and asked all
member-nations to "render every assistance" to bring it about. And on
June 26 President Truman ordered General MacArthur to give military
assistance to the South Koreans. The Security Council quickly endorsed
this decision, and MacArthur became officially the United Nations commander.

The invaders routed the South Korean forces, but failed to conquer
the whole country. On September 15, in a remarkably bold and well-
planned operation, MacArthur landed marines at Inchon behind the
Communist lines; and this was followed by a general United Nations advance. Early in October, having driven the enemy out of South Korea,
MacArthur advanced into North Korea—a move which was authorized
by the administration and by the United Nations General Assembly, but
which was widely criticized in Europe as unnecessarily provocative. By
November 23 he was confidently predicting that all enemy resistance
would soon be crushed and that American troops would be home by
Christmas. Two days later came the black news that Chinese Communist
armies had intervened on a large scale. For the next few weeks a military
catastrophe seemed to be imminent. But by the end of January 1951 the
United Nations forces, after falling back into South Korea, had re-formed
their lines, and the war changed into a dreary and apparently interminable process of mutual attrition.

By this time acute differences of opinion had developed between MacArthur and the administration. MacArthur, supported by many Republicans, argued that, in order to win the Korean war, it was advisable to bomb bases and industrial installations on Chinese soil and to make use of the Nationalist forces on Formosa. But the administration, supported by its military advisers in Washington, preferred to fight only a limited war in Korea. In accordance with its general containment policy, it proposed merely to hold Communism in check, not to risk provoking World War III by undertaking offensive operations. It regarded the Far East as secondary in importance to Europe, and felt that it would be a catastrophic mistake to become involved in what General Bradley, chairman of the Joint Chiefs of Staff, described as "the wrong war at the wrong place at the wrong time and with the wrong enemy." After MacArthur had violated official discipline by making a series of public pronouncements indicating his disagreement with this policy, he was abruptly dismissed by President Truman on April 11, 1951. He was replaced by General Matthew B. Ridgway, who had shown brilliant leadership as ground commander in Korea since December.

Returning to the United States for the first time since 1935, MacArthur received a tumultuous popular reception, which was followed by a series of hearings conducted by the Senate Military Affairs Committee. Through May and June 1951 most of the men responsible for America's policy laid bare their calculations and objectives with a frankness which probably proved very illuminating to the Soviet government but which was also a remarkable demonstration of democracy in action. The hearings showed again that many Republicans were deeply distrustful of the Truman-Acheson Far Eastern policies, but did not result in any change. The United States continued to fight a limited war in Korea; and in spite of protracted truce negotiations, there seemed to be no way of bringing it to a satisfactory conclusion.

After the outbreak of the Korean war the rearmament program was stepped up. Selective service, which had been reintroduced in 1948, claimed young men in increasing numbers; and Congress once again voted heavy appropriations for defense, raised taxes, and adopted price-control legislation. The country seemed to be back where it had been ten years earlier.

Problems of Civil Liberty.   The need for defense against the external enemy aroused little controversy. Only insignificant groups of Communist sympathizers continued to argue that the Soviet Union was no threat to peace and security. But the problems of the internal enemy were much more complex. Was it possible to deal with Communist agents in the United States without impairing the legitimate exercise of civil liberties? On the one hand, many dogmatic liberals, failing to recognize the dangers of Communist espionage and infiltration into positions of power, had a tendency to regard any security program as "witch-hunting." On the other hand, ultra-nationalist Congressmen and newspapers seemed to regard anybody left of center as virtually a Russian agent.

In 1949 ten officials of the Communist Party were convicted of advocating the overthrow of the government by violence and given prison sentences. Similar proceedings were then taken against second-string Communist leaders. The government had set up machinery for investigating the loyalty of public servants in 1947, and under Congressional prodding its standards became steadily more stringent. Meanwhile, the House Committee on Un-American Activities had heard testimony from a series of ex-Communists to the effect that several individuals who had held office under the Roosevelt administration had been secret supporters of the Communist Party. Truman, Acheson, and most liberals at first dismissed these stories as incredible. But in 1950 Alger Hiss, a former State Department official, after denying charges that in 1938 he had given confidential information to Russia, was put on trial for perjury and convicted on evidence which the defense could not controvert.

Hiss's conviction enabled ultra-nationalists to claim that the whole New Deal had been tainted with Communism, and that American foreign policy, especially in China, had been directed by Communist agents. Vociferous enemies of the Truman administration, especially Senator Joseph McCarthy of Wisconsin, insisted that the State Department was still honeycombed with Communists; and although most of their accusations were wholly unsubstantiated, and some of them were (in the words of Paul Hoffman) "fantastically false," they aroused considerable popular hysteria. As a result of a new theory of "guilt by association," officials, teachers, writers, actors, and other prominent citizens who had ever in their lives been friendly with Communists or supported left-wing causes began to fall under suspicion, and some of them lost their jobs. Although the actual suppression of civil liberties by the government was less than in 1798 or 1918, there was an alarming growth of pressure by organized reactionary groups seeking to impose conformity of opinion.

The Election of 1952.   The Far Eastern policy of the Truman administration and its alleged softness with Communists at home were vigorously debated throughout the presidential campaign of 1952. The Republican Party, however, was again deeply divided, along much the same lines as in 1940. The more liberal and internationalist wing of the party, with a mainly European orientation in foreign policy, picked General Eisenhower as its candidate. In June, Eisenhower turned over his European command to General Ridgway (who was replaced in the Far East by Mark Clark), and came home to campaign for the nomination. More conservative Republicans, with a greater interest in the Far East, supported Senator Taft. After a bitter fight the Eisenhower forces won control of the Republican convention, and nominated their candidate by a narrow margin. The Democrats, substantially in agreement about foreign policy but violently divided about domestic issues, found a leader whom almost all groups in the party were willing to support in Adlai Stevenson, Governor of Illinois since 1948.

In his campaign speeches Stevenson displayed a comprehension of the issues and a moral idealism unequaled by any previous presidential candidate since Woodrow Wilson, and even many of his opponents admitted that he spoke with the accents of greatness. But he could not counteract the immense personal prestige of General Eisenhower or the accumulated popular resentment against the corruption of the Truman administration, its failure to prevent high prices, and its inability to end the Korean war. Running far ahead of the rest of the Republican ticket in nearly every state, Eisenhower was swept into office by a record-breaking popular vote of 33,936,252 as against 27,314,992 for Stevenson. By much smaller margins the Republicans also won control of both houses of Congress.

Thus twenty years of Democratic ascendancy had come to an end. But even though the American people had decided that it was time for a change in Washington, they had not voted to put the clock back to the 1920's. During the campaign Eisenhower had pledged himself to maintain, and even extend, all the major reforms of the New Deal; and he had won the Republican nomination as the spokesman of an internationalist foreign policy. The victorious party had been asked to purify the Federal administration and to bring more vigor and efficiency to the execution of its programs; it had not been given a mandate for any fundamental change of objectives, either at home or abroad.

3. THE EISENHOWER ADMINISTRATION

IN SPITE of his long army career, the new president was by temperament a man of peace, his most conspicuous qualification for leadership being his capacity for smoothing discords and evoking cooperation. Conciliation was therefore the keynote of the Eisenhower administration, in both its domestic and its foreign programs. Although its critics complained that some essential issues were being evaded rather than solved, there can be no doubt that it was remarkably successful in reducing the political tensions that had characterized the Roosevelt and Truman periods. Eisenhower's middle-of-the-road policies won the support of moderate men in each political party and decreased the strength of both the right-wing Republicans and the left-wing Democrats.

Economic Policies. It was, of course, to be expected that the new administration would be more friendly to business than its Democratic predecessors. Big business was strongly represented in the cabinet, its outstanding spokesmen being George M. Humphreys, Secretary of the Treasury, and Charles E. Wilson, Secretary of Defense. Most of the price-control regulations that had been imposed during the Korean war were quickly removed, while the administration's inclination to promote private rather than public ownership of power and natural resources soon began to cause liberals to complain of a "give-away program." The most obvious changes from the Truman period, however, were in fiscal policy. As soon as it assumed office, the new administration began to make deep cuts in government spending, especially on defense and foreign aid, with the ultimate intention of both reducing taxes and balancing the budget. These objectives were achieved by the fiscal year 1955–56: spendings were down to 64 billion dollars (nearly 60 per cent of which was for defense), as contrasted with 73 billion in the last Truman year, while revenues slightly exceeded this figure although there were considerable tax reductions.

Yet in spite of the administration's firm belief in the superiority of private enterprise, its spokesmen made it plain that, in the event of an economic recession, they would make use of all the methods of controlling the economy which had been worked out under the New Deal. Nor did they propose to repeal any of the basic measures of the previous twenty years. Although the hopes of union leaders for a revision of the Taft-Hartley Act were not fulfilled, there was no attempt to diminish further the rights and powers of organized labor. In 1954 the social security system was expanded to cover ten million additional workers, and the scale of payments was increased; further extensions were voted by Congress in 1956. Eisenhower advocated legislation calling for new government spending on public health, housing, education, and other needs, especially notable being a sixteen-year 33-billion-dollar highway program, which was accepted by Congress in 1956. After 1955, expenditures again began to rise, reaching almost 72 billion dollars in the fiscal year 1957–58.

The only area of economic legislation where the administration favored any substantial change of program was agriculture. Under the existing laws the government was obligated to keep farm surpluses off the market in order to maintain prices at 90 per cent of parity, with the result that it was compelled to keep in storage vast quantities of unsalable farm commodities. The Agricultural Adjustment Act of 1954, which was based on the recommendations of Secretary of Agriculture Ezra Taft Benson, substituted flexible for rigid price supports, allowing price drops to 75 per cent of parity where there was overproduction. It was hoped that this would induce farmers to reduce the production of basic crops. Overproduction, however, continued; the government accumulated more farm surpluses at heavy expense; and farm prices, which had reached a peak in 1951, continued to decline for two more years. Total farm income dropped from 17 billion dollars in 1951 to 13 billion in 1955. Meanwhile there was little change in the prices paid by consumers, the difference being absorbed in higher marketing costs. Confronted by growing farm discontent, the administration continued to insist on flexible rather than rigid price supports, and proposed to end the surplus by paying farmers to take more than forty million acres out of production and plant them with trees or soil-conserving crops. This "soil bank" plan, which differed only in detail from the original New Deal agricultural program, was adopted by Congress in 1956.

For all other important sectors of the economy, Eisenhower's first term was characterized by high prosperity. After a brief recession in the autumn and winter of 1953–54, figures for national production, income, and employment continued to soar to new record levels. There were remarkably few labor disputes, and even the mutterings of revolt in the farm belt died away in 1956 when farm prices began to rise again. It was obvious that most Americans had strong reasons for satisfaction with existing conditions.

McCarthyism. One of the chief obstacles to Eisenhower's program of moderation was the continuing anti-Communist hysteria. Its most prominent spokesman, Senator McCarthy, was elevated by the Republican victory to the chairmanship of the Senate Committee on Government Operations. Liberals were disappointed by Eisenhower's failure to repudiate McCarthy during the presidential campaign and by the willingness of the administration to make concessions to him in the hope of avoiding an open break.

During 1953 and the early months of 1954, McCarthy presided over a series of public hearings into alleged subversive activities in the State and Defense Departments, browbeating unsympathetic witnesses, flinging accusations of Communism against anybody who dared to oppose him, and persistently interfering with the policies of executive officials; and although he did not unearth a single case of subversion not already known to the appropriate authorities, his apparent zeal for national security won alarmingly wide popular support. A long series of public servants were smeared with charges of subversion, while an unsavory group of ex-Communists enjoyed new careers as professional witnesses with every encouragement to make their evidence as sensational as possible. For a long period neither the administration nor any appreciable number of his fellow Senators were willing to oppose McCarthy, although it was obvious that if his activities were not checked they would wreck the efficiency of the whole government and do irreparable harm to the American tradition of civil liberties and to America's good name abroad. Particularly damaging to her reputation in other countries were the activities of McCarthy's two young aides, Roy Cohn and David Schine, who toured Europe in the spring of 1953 in order to remove all Communistic books from United States Information Service libraries.

In the spring of 1954, however, McCarthy finally overreached himself by accusing respected officers of the United States army of being soft with Communists. The War Department retaliated by making public charges that McCarthy and Cohn had used threats to secure special privileges for Schine, who had by this time been drafted. During April and May the charges and countercharges were investigated by a Senate committee, and the proceedings were televised. The conflict of personalities at the hearings made a fascinatingly dramatic spectacle, which was watched by a large proportion of the American people, and for weeks the issues of whether Private Schine had performed his fair share of KP, and how he had managed to combine army service with so many visits to New York night clubs, were main subjects of national conversation. The committee was unable to agree on its findings, but there can be no doubt that this exhibition of McCarthy's personality and methods brought his power to an end. Millions of Americans who had hitherto supposed him to be a valiant crusader against Communism could now see for themselves his arrogance, brutality, and disregard for the truth. In the autumn, following a denunciation of McCarthy by Senator Ralph E. Flanders of Vermont and an investigation by another committee headed by Senator Arthur V. Watkins of Utah, his colleagues voted 67 to 22 to condemn him for abuse of the Senate, after which he rapidly subsided into obscurity. He died in May, 1956.

When McCarthy's name disappeared from the newspaper headlines, liberty-loving Americans could breathe more easily, but the problem of which McCarthyism had been a symptom remained unsolved. How could the government take adequate precautions against Communist agents without impairing civil liberties and undermining the morale of the government service? The Truman administration had failed to find a satisfactory answer, and the Eisenhower administration did not make a better record. Before the 1952 election the Republicans had denounced Truman for allowing Communists to remain on the public payroll, and after their victory it was to be expected that they would adopt more rigorous security regulations. By 1955 government spokesmen were claiming that 3,614 persons had been dismissed as security risks. The Democrats pointed out, in reply, that this figure did not include a single proven Communist and that the phrase "security risks" had been extended to cover persons suspected of moral rather than political misconduct. Undoubtedly many persons were condemned on trivial or unproved charges: contrary to traditional principles of justice the burden of proof was on the accused, and the government did not reveal the sources of its information, so that individuals about whom suspicions had arisen were compelled to spend an exorbitant amount of time and money in the often impossible task of clearing themselves. Meanwhile private citizens with left-wing records found their liberties restricted, most notably by the Passport Office, which arbitrarily assumed the power of denying them the right of foreign travel.

There was no reasonable doubt that during the 1930's and 40's Communists had been active in some branches of the government and that many liberals had failed to appreciate the Communist threat. But during the hysteria of the early fifties many Americans failed to recognize that total security was an unattainable objective and that the attempt to achieve it would do more harm than good. By impairing the efficiency of two crucial branches of government activity, its foreign service and its scientific research, the security investigations did more to weaken than to strengthen the United States.

Political Trends. Party labels during the Eisenhower period were even more meaningless than usual, since each party was still sharply divided. Eisenhower was unable to reunite the Republicans and his program consistently encountered more vigorous opposition from the right wing of his own party than from the official leaders of the Democratic opposition. The former supporters of Senator Taft (who died in July, 1955) continued to display a deep nostalgia for the lost simplicities of the nineteenth century, remaining suspicious of government paternalism at home and internationalism abroad. Eisenhower endeavored to work with the party organization, supporting all Republican candidates for election, but in private conversations he even considered breaking with the right wing and forming a new centrist political party. Meanwhile the Democrats were still split between Northern progressives and Southern conservatives, the question of civil rights for Negroes being the most acute cause of dissension. A majority of the electorate, however, were plainly in favor of continued moderation, and showed it by combining support for Eisenhower with a preference for Democratic control of Congress.

The Republicans lost control of both houses of Congress in the elections of 1954. This made relatively little difference in the functioning of the government, since the Democratic leaders eschewed partisan politics, maintained a middle-of-the-road attitude, and in some ways gave more effective support to Eisenhower's program than the Republicans had done. But this indication that the Democrats were still the majority party meant that the Republicans could have little hope of winning the next presidential election unless Eisenhower could be persuaded to run again. This seemed improbable when he suffered a coronary thrombosis in September, 1955, but he made a remarkable recovery from this attack and also from an abdominal operation for ileitis in June, 1956. After his doctors had pronounced him fit for a second term, his renomination became a certainty. The Republican convention also retained Richard Nixon as his running mate, despite some suggestions that he lacked the experience and personal qualities needed for possible succession to the highest office.

Adlai Stevenson was again chosen by the Democrats, after some bitter primary contests with Senator Estes Kefauver of Tennessee. The campaign was unexciting and there was never any serious doubt about the outcome. Stevenson was unable to find any election issues that aroused much popular interest, and his speeches failed to arouse as much enthusiasm among liberals as in 1952. Eisenhower and Nixon were re-elected by overwhelming majorities, winning 33,212,325 popular votes and 457 electoral votes, as against 24,192,953 and 74 for Stevenson. The Democrats, however, retained their lead in both houses of Congress.

After this remarkable political triumph the administration no longer had such smooth sailing. The national economy went into a tailspin in the later months of 1957. There was a sharp increase in unemployment, and the federal budget for 1957–58 incurred a deficit of nearly three billion dollars; but in marked contrast with its attitude four years earlier, the administration preferred to deal with the recession by conservative methods. At the same time it was facing new difficulties at home in the field of race relations,[1] while its foreign policies were impeded by an apparent growth of anti-American sentiment in various parts of the world. In consequence, there was a marked increase in public criticism and congressional opposition. As had happened during the later years of many previous administrations, it seemed likely that political conflicts would prevent the adoption of any important new measures until after the next presidential election.

Foreign Policy.   The moderation of the Eisenhower wing of the Republican Party was also manifested in its conduct of international relations. Before the 1952 election Republican spokesmen had denounced the Truman-Acheson containment program as too mild and too negative and had called for positive steps towards the liberation of the peoples behind the Iron Curtain and for a militant policy towards Communist China. Once in office, however, the administration quickly showed that it proposed to continue the containment program with only minor modifications and had no intention of risking World War III by trying to roll back the Iron Curtain. Ignoring the warnings of right-wing Republicans, its spokesmen were willing to accept compromise agreements, such as that ending the Korean war, which would have evoked loud outcries of surrender to Communism if they had been made by Truman and Acheson. Meanwhile they maintained and expanded the system of defense pacts on which the containment program depended, and Congress continued to appropriate several billion dollars a year for assistance, primarily military, to other countries. The detailed execution of these policies was entrusted to a New York lawyer with considerable diplomatic experience, John Foster Dulles. Displaying a physical energy that would have been astonishing in a much younger man, Dulles was inexhaustible in his attendance at conferences, being almost constantly in flight between Europe, Washington, and the Far East; and although his propensity for making blunt statements aroused considerable resentment in other countries, his admirers claimed that it produced substantial results.

Only one significant change of method could fairly be attributed to the new administration. In order to bring about agreements, it sometimes "walked to the brink" of war, as Dulles described it, threatening to resort to "massive retaliation" if the Communists refused to come to terms. Early in his term of office Dulles declared that the protection of the free world should be based primarily on America's "great capacity to retaliate . . . instantly, by means and at places of our own choosing," with more reliance on deterrent power and less on local defensive power

[1] See page 733.

than in the past. Such a policy had obvious dangers, but Dulles believed that it would prevent further local wars like that in Korea, reduce the need for American ground forces, and make possible the substantial cuts in defense spending which the Republicans wished to accomplish. According to an article published in *Life* early in 1956, Dulles claimed that by warning Communist China of America's willingness to use her deterrent power, he had three times prevented further aggression in the Far East.

The Far East. The first concern of the administration in the Far East was to bring to an end the war in Korea. Protracted negotiations resulted, in June, 1953, in an agreement for the exchange of prisoners of war and finally, on July 26, in an armistice. Korea was to be divided in accord with the existing military situation, which meant that the South Koreans were left in possession of about fifteen hundred square miles more territory than before the war. One of the chief obstacles to an agreement had been the insistence of the North Koreans that all prisoners must be returned (the United Nations forces held more than 20,000 prisoners who did not wish to be sent back to Communism); but it was finally agreed that prisoners were not to be returned against their will, the exchange being supervised by five countries not involved in the war.

Thus ended a dreary and protracted struggle which had cost the United States 25,000 lives and 117,000 other casualties. The compromise by which it ended was bitterly denounced by Syngman Rhee, who continued to hope for the reunification of all Korea and even threatened to continue the war unaided. But most Americans felt only relief that the fighting had finally stopped. The United States and her associates in the United Nations had, in fact, achieved their original objective, which was simply to protect South Korea from aggression, although the issues had afterwards been confused by the attempt to end Communist control of North Korea and by the demands of some American leaders for total victory over the Chinese Communists.

Meanwhile another war had been continuing in the French colony of Indo-China ever since 1946. The Vietminh Communist forces were steadily gaining ground and now controlled most of northern Vietnam. Communist control of all Indo-China had to be prevented if possible, and in the spring of 1954 Dulles warned the Chinese Communists not to come to the aid of the Vietminh. The United States was, however, unwilling to intervene more directly, and the French government of Mendes-France therefore resolved to end an obviously futile struggle. In July, 1954, a truce was signed by which the Communists retained control of northern Vietnam, more than 60 per cent of the whole, while southern Vietnam and the two other Indo-Chinese states of Laos and Cambodia became independent. It seemed likely that this was a prelude to Communist control of all Indo-China. With the departure of the French, however, the struggle against Communism was no longer complicated by native resentment against foreign rule. Southern Vietnam found a reputable leader in Ngo Dienh Diem. Aided and advised by the United States, he sought to create an effective democratic regime, apparently with fair prospects of success.

A third object of American concern in the Far East was Formosa, where it was hoped that the Chinese Nationalists would demonstrate that they had learnt from their earlier failures and could now provide a better government than their Communist opponents. The Eisenhower administration began by "unleashing" Chiang Kai-shek, announcing that the United States would abandon the policy (initiated by the Truman administration) of preventing the Nationalists from attacking the mainland. This was welcomed by those Americans, mainly right-wing Republicans, who believed that the Nationalists had been defeated because of lack of support from Washington, not because of their intrinsic weaknesses. But it soon became apparent that continued hostilities between the two Chinese groups might result only in the loss of Formosa. There were repeated threats of a Communist invasion of the island, and in January, 1955, Eisenhower asked for, and received, authority from Congress to use force, if necessary, to protect it. The situation was complicated by the Nationalist control of the islands of Quemoy and Matsu, which are close to the mainland. Whether the American commitment included these offshore islands remained at first uncertain, but in September, 1958, when the islands were under bombardment from the mainland, the administration made it plain that it was prepared to defend them. Meanwhile the United States continued to deny diplomatic recognition to Communist China and to oppose her admission to the United Nations, where China's seat on the Security Council was still held by the Nationalists.

In order to prevent any further Communist advance in Asia, the American government hoped to build a defense system comparable to NATO in Europe. Unfortunately some of the more important Asiatic countries, especially India, remained deeply suspicious of the Western powers because of their past record of imperialism, and preferred to adopt a neutralist position. In 1953 and 1954, the United States concluded mutual defense treaties with South Korea, Japan, and the Chinese Nationalists, and in September, 1954, she sponsored the formation of the South East Asia Treaty Organization. This was accompanied by the adoption of a Pacific Charter calling for equal rights for all races and for independence by peaceful means for all colonial peoples ready to assume its responsibilities. But only three Asiatic countries—Pakistan, Thailand and the Philippines—were willing to become members of SEATO, which remained largely a paper organization.

Europe and the Middle East.   In Western Europe the chief problem left unsolved by the Truman administration was that of bringing West Germany into the defense system. American military leaders were convinced that the protection of western Europe against the Russians required effective German co-operation, but this had hitherto been blocked by French opposition to German rearmament. Germany had made a remarkable recovery from the war, and in view of past experience it was not hard to understand that the French should feel nervous about renewed German attempts at domination. Dulles provoked some bitter complaints by declaring that continued French opposition would compel the United States to make an "agonizing reappraisal" of her European commitments, but after prolonged negotiations the objective was achieved. On October 23, 1954, a series of treaties was signed in Paris by which the German Federal Republic regained full sovereign rights, was admitted to NATO, and was to contribute troops to a collective West European army.

Meanwhile changes within the Soviet sphere had been precipitated by the death of Stalin in March, 1953. The expected struggle for the succession within the Communist hierarchy ended in the victory of Nikita Khrushchev. The new rulers of Russia dissociated themselves from Stalin's regime by publicly denouncing his errors and promised liberal reforms, though it was uncertain how far this represented a real change of policy and how far it was merely a new and perhaps more dangerous propaganda technique. In international relations the only tangible evidence of conciliation was the conclusion of a peace treaty with Austria in May, 1955. This was followed in July by a "summit" meeting of heads of governments at Geneva, the first such meeting since Potsdam a decade earlier, but in spite of public assurances of better relations there were no concrete results. In 1956, attempts by peoples behind the Iron Curtain to throw off the Soviet yoke were met with armed repression, the treatment of the Hungarians being especially murderous. The failure of the United States to come to their aid demonstrated the abandonment of the liberationist slogans of the 1952 election. The only American action was to give hospitality to a number of Hungarian refugees.

During 1956 the main concern of American foreign policy began to shift to the Middle East, an area which was important both for strategic reasons and because of its immense oil reserves. Like so many other backward peoples, the Arabs were becoming fanatically nationalistic, and American attempts to win their friendship were complicated by their hostility against Israel, which had won her independence with American approval in 1947, and by their antagonism to Britain and France, which had formerly been the dominant powers in the region. In 1955 the British sponsored a Middle East Defense Organization; but Iraq was the only Arab state to join the group, its other members being Turkey, Iran, and Pakistan. The other Arab countries remained aloof and some of them showed an alarming propensity to play with both sides; Nasser, the dictator of Egypt, was the chief trouble-maker.

In July, 1956, Secretary Dulles, disturbed by Nasser's willingness to accept Russian offers of military and economic aid, abruptly announced that the United States would not proceed with a project for financing the building of the Aswan dam on the Nile. Nasser retaliated by seizing the Suez Canal, hitherto owned by an international corporation under the control of British and French stockholders. During the subsequent negotiations the United States refused to join Britain and France in putting effective pressure on Nasser. In October the Israelis, denied the use of the canal and harassed by Egyptian raids and threats of invasion, invaded Egyptian territory. Britain and France promptly dispatched armed forces to seize the canal, claiming that their purpose was to enforce peace between the Egyptians and the Israelis. These actions met with American disapproval, and were condemned by the United Nations, which passed resolutions demanding an immediate cease-fire. Complying with world opinion, the Israelis, British, and French quickly withdrew their forces from Egyptian territory, while Nasser, who had refused to make any concessions whatever, regained control of the canal. This unfortunate series of events gave new stimulus to Arab nationalism, further weakened British influence in the Middle East, and seriously impaired the good relations between Britain and the United States.

With the decline of British power the United States was compelled to assume new responsibilities. In March, 1957, at Eisenhower's request, Congress declared that the United States was prepared to use force to protect Middle Eastern peoples against armed aggression by international Communism, and appropriated 200 million dollars for military and economic aid to all Middle Eastern states which were willing to receive it. This extension of American leadership to a new region became known as the Eisenhower Doctrine. But by what means the United States could curb the explosive nationalism of the Arab states, prevent them from accepting Soviet offers, and persuade them to make peace with the Israelis remained to be seen. Nasser and his supporters apparently hoped to unite the whole Arab world, and pursued this objective by fomenting rebellions and revolutions against any Arab governments that refused to join them. In July, 1958, American and British forces were sent to the Middle East to give support to friendly governments in Lebanon and Jordan.

Meanwhile both the Americans and the Russians continued to invent and manufacture new weapons of war, some of which were many times more destructive than the atomic bombs dropped on Hiroshima and Nagasaki. The confidence of the American people in their technological leadership was rudely shaken by a series of demonstrations of Soviet scientific advance, the most disturbing being the launching of two artificial earth satellites in October and November, 1957. It became increasingly apparent that the two powers could now inflict such widespread destruction on each other that neither of them could afford to invoke the threat of "massive retaliation." War had ceased to be a practical instrument of national policy, unless it could be limited and localized as had been done in Korea. The obvious conclusion was that some agreement for the limitation of armaments was the only alternative to race suicide, especially since continued experiments with new atomic weapons threatened eventually to pollute the whole atmosphere of the earth. Disarmament negotiations through the spring and summer of 1957 failed, however, to produce any result. Meanwhile the Soviet Union continued to work for world domination, and while the more advanced nations of Europe and Latin America showed little disposition to respond to Communist propaganda, further Communist gains were probably to be expected among the peoples of Asia and perhaps of Africa. As the leader of the free world the United States could not afford to be complacent. While the mood of relaxation that characterized the Eisenhower era was a welcome change from the bitter conflicts of the previous administrations, one could fairly ask whether the American people were not becoming too intent on the enjoyment of material prosperity and forgetful of their world responsibilities.

XXXIII

The Arts in a
Business Civilization

1. LITERARY TRENDS

2. CRITICISM

3. THE NOVEL

4. POETRY

5. THE THEATER

6. PAINTING AND SCULPTURE

7. ARCHITECTURE

8. MUSIC

T HE MOST productive period in American literary and artistic history began shortly before World War I. During the years 1912–15 a number of important figures made their first appearance, and new trends began to attract greater critical support and popular interest. As during the previous three hundred years, much of the initial stimulus came from Europe; Americans copied the techniques of European innovators, and throughout the next generation they were deeply affected by European systems of ideas, especially by the Marxist critique of capitalist society and the Freudian interpretation of man's emotional conflicts. But the transit of influences across the Atlantic soon ceased to

SELECTED BIBLIOGRAPHY: Most of the books listed on page 503 are useful also for this chapter. Alfred Kazin, *On Native Ground* (1942), deals enthusiastically with the leading prose-writers since 1900. The leading critics are presented in M. D. Zabel, *Literary Opinion in America* (revised edition, 1951). For poetry, see Horace Gregory and Marya Zaturenska, *A History of American Poetry, 1900–1940* (1946); and for the leading dramatists J. W. Krutch, *American Drama since 1918* (1939). Two volumes by Maxwell Geismar, *The Last of the Provincials* (1947) and *Writers in Crisis* (1942), analyze the work of the leading novelists. J. I. H. Baur, *Revolution and Tradition in Modern American Art* (1951), is an excellent study of twentieth-century painting.

be a one-way passage; after World War I, possibly for the first time, the creative writers and artists of the United States displayed as much vitality and originality as those of any European country, and younger Europeans began to imitate the Americans.

1. LITERARY TRENDS

THE NEW American literature was predominantly realistic in method and critical in tone. Writers set out to show social forces in operation and describe the lives of typical Americans; and they emphasized the deficiencies rather than the virtues of American society, insisting that its values were too materialistic and its atmosphere too repressive. They generally showed little respect for traditional religious beliefs and moral taboos, and suggested that the individual could find fulfillment through emotional liberation rather than through ethical discipline. These tendcies had originated back in the 1880's and 1890's, but it was not until the second decade of the twentieth century that they began to dominate the literary scene. They were opposed by the surviving spokesmen of the Genteel Tradition, and, at a later period, by a number of younger men, the most influential being T. S. Eliot, who reasserted the values of religious and moral discipline. But throughout the 1920's and 1930's the strongest currents in American intellectual life were libertarian or radical rather than conservative.

The United States, as presented in its literature, seemed to be inhabited largely by unhappy and lonely men and women whose aspirations were frustrated by the materialistic values of a business civilization. Unquestionably the writers of the 1920's and 1930's did not give a balanced portrayal of all aspects of American life. During World War II, in fact, some critics, such as Archibald MacLeish and Bernard De Voto, accused them of weakening the faith of the American people by portraying their society in such negative terms. But if the writers criticized America as it was, this was, in most instances, on the ground that it fell short of American ideals. Their work constituted a kind of minority report on American culture; and although the indictment was overstated, it cannot simply be dismissed.

Economic Factors. It was probably easier than in the nineteenth century for the American writer to make a living. The number of people in the habit of reading books, though still only a tiny fraction of the total population, was increasing, and there was now a considerable audience for novels and studies of current problems.[1] But the effects of this expansion of the market were not wholly good. Publishing and book-reviewing became more commercialized, and the writer was under considerable pressure to lower his standards in order to appeal to the general reading

---

[1] This was enlarged during the 1940's by the remarkable growth of the cheap reprints known as pocketbooks.

public. If he produced a best-seller or conformed to the editorial requirements of the popular magazines, he could become a relatively wealthy
man. He could also earn a large salary by ceasing altogether to be an
independent creator and going to Hollywood. Thus mass-production
methods began to spread to the arts; and while the tastes of the general
public probably improved, there was perhaps less room for the exercise
of individual discrimination. Serious magazines had a smaller circulation,
in proportion to population, than in the nineteenth century.

While some writers combined high standards with popular success,
others appealed only to small intellectual audiences and therefore needed
some non-commercial outlet. With the high cost of printing and publishing, this was more difficult in the United States than in Europe. But
subsidies from universities or wealthy patrons made it possible to produce
non-commercial magazines for the publication of experimental poetry and
fiction. One of the earliest of these so-called "little magazines" was *Poetry,*
edited by Harriet Monroe, which began in 1912. It was followed by a
host of others, outstanding examples being the *Dial,* the *Little Review,*
and *Transition* in the 1920's, *Hound and Horn* and the *Southern Review*
in the 1930's, and the *Partisan Review* and the *Sewanee Review* in the
1940's. The little magazines performed an indispensable function in the
development of modern American literature, since they printed the early
work of almost all the more original writers of the period. The economic
problems of writers were also eased by the growth of patronage through
foundations, the Guggenheim Foundation, which awarded annual fellow-
ships for creative or scholarly work, being particularly important. For a
few years during the 1930's thousands of creative writers and artists
were assisted by the Federal government through the WPA. On the whole,
however, the United States did less than most European countries to
encourage the more serious art forms. While vast sums were spent on
popular entertainment, the proportion of the national income going to
the higher arts was infinitesimal.

2. CRITICISM

The Rebels.   Of the critics who defined the standards and fought
the battles of the new literature, the most important were probably
H. L. Mencken and Van Wyck Brooks. Both men published their first
books before World War I and achieved their greatest influence during
the 1920's.

Mencken, a journalist of German descent who spent his life in his
native Baltimore, had great limitations. He had no use whatever for religion, philosophy, politics, or any kind of idealism, was hostile to democracy, and felt that the intelligent individual could only entertain himself
by watching the follies of the world instead of trying to improve it. The

one value for which he was prepared to fight was personal freedom. But he had no equal as a slashing antagonist of anything stuffy, pretentious, or hypocritical. He was important because he recognized the talents of some of the new writers and did more than anybody else to publicize them. His influence, exercised chiefly through the *American Mercury,* which he edited from 1924 to 1933, was not altogether healthy; he encouraged too many undergraduates to regard most other people as moronic. But he earned a place in literary history not only as a master of invective but also by his learned studies of the American language.

Brooks wrote a series of books accusing American society of materialism and puritanical repressiveness and arguing that frustration had been the usual experience of the American intellectual. Whitman alone, he felt, had achieved full self-expression. He wanted writers to follow Whitman in asserting the right of the individual to a richer and freer life and in condemning business values. Brooks's positive beliefs were never clearly defined; but he felt in general that literature had a social function and should be on the side of liberalism. Similar ideas were expressed by the brilliant but short-lived Randolph Bourne and by such critics as Lewis Mumford, Paul Rosenfeld, and Waldo Frank. Brooks's destructive analyses of American society influenced a whole generation of writers. In the 1930's, however, he underwent an emotional transformation; and whereas formerly he had emphasized only the negative aspects of the American heritage, he now saw only the positive. He settled down to write a five-volume history of American literary life from 1789 to 1915, glorifying its achievements and ignoring all its shortcomings.

Brooks's belief that literature should support progressive ideals was carried further by Vernon Louis Parrington, of the University of Washington, whose three-volume *Main Currents in American Thought* was published in 1927 and 1929. One of the most influential interpretations of American history ever written, this presented liberalism as the chief main current in American intellectual development; according to Parrington, writers like Poe and Henry James, who were not clearly on the progressive side, were scarcely entitled to consideration. The popularity of this sociological approach to literature was increased by the depression. Throughout the 1930's a large majority of the younger writers insisted that the function of the creative artist was to expose exploitation and advocate radicalism, and flirted with Communism. This literary Marxism was essentially a naïve manifestation of American idealism, being based on a passionate belief in the equality of man and a sense of hopelessness about existing institutions; but it was not until the Stalin-Hitler pact of 1939 that most of its exponents woke up to the fact that the Soviet system, instead of being a fulfillment of the Declaration of Independence, was actually a complete negation of it. Marxism in its more dogmatic manifestations had a paralyzing effect on intellectual life; but there were a number of excellent critics—men like Edmund Wilson, Kenneth Burke, Newton Arvin, and Lionel Trilling—who combined leftist political sympathies with a comprehensive appreciation of aesthetic values.

The Conservatives.   Most of the surviving spokesmen of the Genteel Tradition had been quickly routed by Mencken, Brooks, and their disciples. But two of them were of tougher grain and continued the battle against the literary radicals into the 1930's. These were Irving Babbitt and Paul Elmer More, who called themselves Humanists. Both were men of wide learning, but Babbitt was a more belligerent controversialist, while More had more literary sensitivity. They insisted that civilization depended on the maintenance of strict ethical prohibitions, manifested in man's "inner check" and "will to refrain," and condemned virtually all literature since the Romantic movement because it encouraged the free expression of emotional drives. Politically, they were uncompromisingly conservative, upholding the rights of property and arguing that humanitarian reforms tended to weaken moral restraints. Although they had no appreciable influence on creative writers, they won some adherents among academic critics.

Meanwhile, a broader and more formidable conservative movement was taking shape. Its most influential representative was T. S. Eliot, a poet and critic who settled in England after graduating from Harvard. Eliot's criticisms of modern culture paralleled those of the Humanists, but he had a more discriminating intelligence and could appreciate good writing even when he disliked its moral tendencies. Believing in the Christian doctrine of original sin, he agreed with Henry Adams in regarding the Catholic and authoritarian society of the Middle Ages as the high point of Western civilization. Somewhat similar attitudes were developed by a group of Southern writers, most of them graduates of Vanderbilt University, whose leaders were John Crowe Ransom and Allen Tate. This group argued (not very plausibly) that Southern society before the Civil War had been based on conservative principles; they were hostile to industrialism, and wanted to recreate an agrarian society of small propertyowners. Both Eliot and the Vanderbilt agrarians had a growing influence on American intellectual life during the 1930's and 1940's. Though they made few converts to their political ideas, they helped to create a climate of opinion more favorable to religious dogma, while their skepticism about progress had only too much corroboration from the trend of world affairs.

The new conservatism was associated with a form of criticism which analyzed content and construction in great detail and judged work by its internal organization rather than its political implications. The function of art, it was asserted, was to present experience in its totality, not to impel towards any kind of action. Exponents of this approach were likely to admire writing in proportion to its complexity and dislike almost anything romantic. In addition to Eliot, Ransom, and Tate, they included such critics as Yvor Winters, R. P. Blackmur, and Cleanth Brooks. In the 1940's they began to be widely known as the "New Critics"—an oddly inappropriate title, since most of them had begun writing in the 1920's. The New Critics were anathematized by progressives of the older generation like Van Wyck Brooks, and their standards were undeniably narrow and highly intellectual; but their re-evaluations of the literature of the past showed remarkable subtlety and aesthetic discrimination. The 1930's and 1940's, although less productive in original writing than the 1920's, were, in fact, a great age of criticism.

3. THE NOVEL

OUT of the many thousands of twentieth-century Americans who have written novels, a small number have seemed to their contemporaries to be gifted with real creative power. Posterity will probably evaluate them differently; but there can be little question as to which of them have so far attracted the most critical attention. They include Theodore Dreiser, Sinclair Lewis, Sherwood Anderson, and Willa Cather among those who began writing before World War I, and F. Scott Fitzgerald, Ernest Hemingway, John Dos Passos, Thomas Wolfe, and William Faulkner among those whose first books appeared during the 1920's.

The Older Group. Dreiser, after ten years of silence following the suppression of *Sister Carrie*, renewed his assault on traditional moral beliefs with *Jennie Gerhardt* (1911) and a series of other books culminating in *An American Tragedy* (1925). In spite of a clumsy style, he communicated a deep sense of pity for his main characters, whom he saw as the victims of their own biological drives. Dreiser himself searched incessantly for some meaning to the riddle of existence, and was drawn towards both Communism and religious mysticism, but could find no final belief. American society, as presented in his books, was a jungle governed by a Darwinian struggle for existence; and men were divided not into the good and the bad but into the strong and the weak. Such a portrayal perhaps revealed more about Dreiser than about America. But his massive integrity and his insistence on his right to tell the truth as he saw it made him the chief pioneer of the new literature.

Lewis, the most widely read of the new novelists, achieved fame with *Main Street* (1920) and added a new word to the language with *Babbitt* (1922). His special talent was for conveying, usually with more than a touch of caricature, the speech patterns and daily habits of the average middle-class American. His earlier books were generally regarded as denunciations of American society. *Main Street* exposed the limitations of a Middle Western small town, while *Babbitt* showed a typical small businessman as misinformed, prejudiced, and frustrated. But while Lewis laughed at his average Americans, he also felt a real affection for them.

In his later (and weaker) books he defended them against the attacks of radicals and bohemians.

Lewis's businessmen derived little satisfaction from their daily lives but had no way of escape. In Anderson's novels escape was the main theme. Anderson had himself been in business in a small Ohio town and turned to writing only after prolonged emotional conflicts in middle life. Most of his books dealt with middle-class men and women who were in revolt against the materialism and puritanism of their environment and were groping for something different. What they were looking for was never defined; all of Anderson's writings seemed imperfectly realized. But in books like *Winesburg, Ohio* (1919), a collection of sketches of small-town life, he conveyed a sense of the pathos of unfulfilled potentialities which was echoed by many young people of the 1920's.

The other leading novelist of this generation, Willa Cather, eschewed sociological description and achieved a more classic artistry. While she felt that contemporary American life was too often mean and impoverished, she was more interested in stressing affirmation, as represented by the creative artist (*The Song of the Lark*, 1915), by the pioneer farmer (*My Ántonia*, 1918), and above all by the builders of the American past (*The Lost Lady*, 1923; *The Professor's House*, 1925). Her admiration for the courage and generosity of earlier periods led her back finally to the French and Spanish explorers and to an espousal of Catholicism.

The Younger Group.   The next group of novelists developed the same themes with even more bitterness. Like Dreiser, they regarded American society as a jungle; like Lewis and Anderson, they presented the average American as emotionally frustrated; and like Willa Cather, they felt that earlier generations had displayed virtues that had disappeared from the present. Some of them had been involved in World War I, and this had sharpened their hostility to modern civilization.

Fitzgerald was accepted during the 1920's as the voice of a new generation in revolt against its parents. His best-selling *This Side of Paradise* (1920) was a mere expression of juvenile ebullience; but he had immense natural gifts as a novelist, as he showed in *The Great Gatsby* (1925), a novel about a bootlegger romantically in love with an upper-class girl, and in *Tender Is the Night* (1934), a study of the moral disintegration of wealthy expatriates. Fitzgerald was both fascinated by the glamour of wealth and social position and at the same time aware of its hollowness; and this conflict was so typical of the America of the 1920's that he became one of its most sensitive recorders. Almost forgotten during the 1930's, his books were rediscovered after World War II.

Fitzgerald's only superior in technical skill was Ernest Hemingway, whose simple staccato style, filled with concrete images, was widely imitated. Probably the finest of all American masters of the short story, Hemingway specialized in studies of simple characters confronting inevitable defeat. His world was mysterious and terrifying; and men could strive only to enjoy the pleasures of physical exercise and love, to respect good craftsmanship, and to be prepared to confront death with a stoical courage. In some of his later books, such as his best-selling novel of the Spanish Civil War, *For Whom the Bell Tolls* (1940), he showed more faith in the possibilities of collective action; but these were inferior to his short stories.

Dos Passos's world was even gloomier. In his panoramic studies of American civilization, especially his trilogy *U. S. A.* (1930–36), he insisted that all sound values were destroyed by the drive for material success; only the dishonest prospered, and everybody with decent instincts was either crushed or corrupted. Originally he had faith in some form of radicalism, but in a later trilogy dealing with American politics during the 1930's (*The Adventures of a Young Man*, 1939; *Number One*, 1943; *Grand Design*, 1949), he discovered that the reformers were just as corrupt and power-hungry as the reactionaries.

Two of the more prominent novelists who appeared in the 1920's were natives of the South, which was now producing more good writing than any other section of the country. But there was little that seemed characteristically Southern in the work of Thomas Wolfe, who grew up in the mountain country of North Carolina. In four sprawling autobiographical novels he poured out a young man's hunger for experience and his search for reality. He was undisciplined and shamelessly egotistical; but he had a gusto and a hopefulness that were lacking in many of his contemporaries, and his books contained unforgettable renderings of many areas of American life.

William Faulkner, on the other hand, remained rooted in his ancestral soil, and wrote specifically about the South. Most of his novels dealt with a mythical Mississippi county, Yoknatapawpha, and presented an interpretation of the whole history of the black belt: the coming of the planter aristocracy, who respected courage and generosity but who brought an ancestral curse upon the South by their seizure of the land from the Indians and by their enslavement of the Negroes; their decline after the Civil War and the rise of a new ruling class interested only in money and power; and the final working out of the curse in crime, insanity, and suicide, apparently leaving the Negro as the ultimate possessor of the land. This symbolic history of the South was developed with such an exuberant virtuosity in the use of language and such a fondness for macabre and grotesque episodes (Faulkner was influenced by both Poe and the frontier humorists) that many readers missed its main drift and accused him of lacking serious intentions. But he had a clear grasp of moral values, as he showed in his speech accepting the Nobel Prize for 1949, though they were never made very explicit in his novels.

The 1930's and the 1940's.   The depression made as sharp a break in literary as in political history. Novelists who had found their own mode of expression before 1929 continued writing with relatively little change.

But the generation that reached maturity in the 1930's was obsessed with the collapse of the economy and the threat of fascism and easily seduced by Communism. Only a few of them managed to produce work of much importance. James T. Farrell's long denunciations of lower-middle-class Irish society in Chicago achieved power through the accumulation of sordid details. Richard Wright gave a terrifying portrayal of American society as seen by a talented and sensitive Negro. John Steinbeck wrote movingly about rural laborers in California, and his *The Grapes of Wrath* (1939), dealing with the migration of farmers from the Oklahoma dust bowl, was the most powerful of the many novels of social significance. Perhaps the most gifted writer of this generation was Robert Penn Warren, one of the Vanderbilt agrarians, whose novels about Southern politics presented a wide range of characters and were rich both in descriptive power and in metaphysical overtones. But none of the novelists who published their first work after 1930 was the equal of the major figures who had emerged in the 1920's.

Nor did the 1940's bring any improvement. There was nothing comparable after World War II to the outburst of creative energy that had followed World War I. A few novelists, such as Norman Mailer, wrote sensationally frank descriptions of army life. A number of the more talented younger men, such as Truman Capote, seemed to be obsessed with sexual abnormality. Apparently the political problems of the 1940's and the insecurity of the whole of modern civilization were too immense for literary masterpieces to be possible.

Shifting critical tastes will no doubt cause some of the writers who loomed large during the 1920's and 1930's to be forgotten by later generations. Certain re-evaluations have already taken place. Critics of the 1920's admired the historical romances of Joseph Hergesheimer, and attributed major importance to James Branch Cabell, who wrote a series of fantasies on the theme that only poetic illusions gave meaning to life. There were a number of writers whose work lacked bulk but had an artistic perfection which may ensure their survival: for example, two Southern women, Elizabeth Madox Roberts and Katherine Anne Porter. Some critics enjoyed the polished sophistication of Thornton Wilder, while others liked John P. Marquand's analyses of upper-middle-class society in Boston and New York, or praised the solid craftsmanship and social perceptiveness of James Gould Cozzens.

Meanwhile, the reading public, while giving a warm reception to some of the better novelists of the period, liked the same kinds of books as the public of 1900, although it preferred them to be more sophisticated and less obviously sentimental than in the past. Hervey Allen's *Anthony Adverse* (1933) and Margaret Mitchell's *Gone with the Wind* (1936) started a fashion for long historical romances which differed from those of thirty years earlier only in that the heroines had larger bosoms and looser morals. There were also wide markets for religious novels, such as those of Lloyd Douglas, and for the light entertainment provided by detective stories, some of which, like those of the hard-boiled school represented especially by Dashiell Hammett, had some literary and sociological significance.

4. POETRY

THE NEW poets who began appearing after 1912 broke even more sharply with their immediate predecessors than the new novelists. Among writers of the older generation only Edwin Arlington Robinson was accepted as a valuable influence. Repudiating the mellifluous daydreaming favored by the Genteel Tradition, some members of the new generation set out to deal with the contemporary scene in somewhat the same realistic fashion as Dreiser in the novel and Henri and Sloan in painting, while others went back to earlier pre-Romantic traditions in an effort to give their work a more comprehensive scope and tighter intellectual organization. Under the influence both of Whitman and of recent French writers, most of them experimented with difficult free-verse forms and abandoned conventional rhymes and meters. Since their work did not conform with accepted notions either in subject-matter or in form, it seemed to many early readers to be not poetry at all.

Some of the new poets (like Walt Whitman earlier) would have liked to write for the mass of the people. But since most Americans were not in the habit of reading poetry, except possibly the newspaper verses of Eddie Guest, they could find audiences only among the small minority of cultivated readers. Long critical battles were fought before they gained attention even among this minority group. In these battles two women played important roles: Harriet Monroe of Chicago printed most of the new poets in her magazine *Poetry;* and Amy Lowell of Boston, who was herself the author of mediocre "imagist" poetry, devoted all the resources of a distinguished social background and a formidable personality to winning publicity for them.

Of the poets who appeared after 1912, three quickly stood out as recorders of the American scene, though none of them proved to have much capacity for development. Vachel Lindsay captured attention with the stirring new rhythms of *The Congo* (1913). Carl Sandburg celebrated Chicago in poems that exhibited a Whitmanian delight in American life and faith in democracy. Edgar Lee Masters contributed to the revolt against the small town with the acrid character sketches of *Spoon River Anthology* (1915). Meanwhile, a quieter and more meditative writer proved to have more staying-power and gradually won a reputation as assured as that of Robinson. This was Robert Frost, who, though born in San Francisco, identified himself with New Hampshire, where he spent much of his life as a farmer. Writing in a deceptively simple style based on colloquial speech patterns, he produced realistic transcriptions of rural people and places which were also philosophical commentaries on the meaning of human life.

The return to the pre-Romantic past was exemplified chiefly by two expatriates: Ezra Pound and T. S. Eliot. Pound, who settled in Europe in 1908, carried on a long critical crusade against Romanticism, and also denounced American lack of appreciation for the arts in diatribes which grew increasingly embittered and hysterical. His own poetry influenced other poets because of its technical innovations and mastery of language, but its content never seemed very important. After World War I he moved to Italy, began to record his view of life in a long series of *Cantos*, and became an ardent admirer of Mussolini. He was saved from being tried for treason after World War II only by being diagnosed as paranoiac. T. S. Eliot, on the other hand, who learned his verse technique from Pound, had something significant to say, although many people profoundly disagreed with it. In his poetry, as in his criticism, he expressed a sense of the decadence of modern civilization and a conviction that it could be revitalized only by a revival of religious belief. His *The Waste Land* (1922), with its abrupt changes of subject, broken rhythms, and obscure references, bewildered most of its early readers, but gradually won recognition as one of the masterpieces of modern literature.

The 1920's produced a great variety of good poetry, though most of it was in a minor key. One man, Hart Crane, attempted in *The Bridge* (1930) to convey the spiritual meaning of American civilization as a whole; but although he had great rhetorical power, he failed to find the unity for which he was searching. Other writers were less ambitious. But serious readers enjoyed the epicurean monologues of Wallace Stevens, the love poems of E. E. Cummings, the witty and elegant character studies of John Crowe Ransom, the metaphysical lyrics of Allen Tate, the precise observations of Marianne Moore, the Freudian reveries of Conrad Aiken, and William Carlos Williams's notations on the American scene. Middle-brow readers who found these too difficult turned to Archibald MacLeish, who combined the technical innovations of Pound and Eliot with a more popular appeal, to Edna St. Vincent Millay, whose love lyrics were closer to traditional forms, and to the verse narratives of Stephen Vincent Benét. Some others liked Robinson Jeffers of California, whose work expressed an extreme pessimism about human society and a conviction of the coming triumph of nature over man.

As with the novel, there was little further development in American poetry after the onset of the depression. The many young men and women of the 1930's who denounced the capitalist system in verse have mostly been deservedly forgotten. A few new figures of the World War II generation seemed more promising: Karl Shapiro and Robert Lowell, for example. But, on the whole, American poetry in the early 1950's was still dominated by writers who had emerged in the 1920's.

5. THE THEATER

THROUGHOUT most of its history the American theater has been dominated too exclusively by commercial standards to have much room for work requiring some intellectual effort on the part of its audience. At the beginning of the twentieth century, however, a few dramatists, notably Bronson Howard, Augustus Thomas, and Clyde Fitch, were writing social comedies of some merit. And in 1915 two important non-commercial theatrical groups were organized: the Washington Square Players, which later became the Theater Guild; and the Provincetown Playhouse.

These groups produced one outstanding figure, Eugene O'Neill, whose first play, *Bound East for Cardiff*, was staged at the Provincetown Playhouse in 1916. O'Neill became the only American dramatist who can be ranked with the leading novelists and poets. Throughout his long career he experimented ceaselessly with new techniques, yet was usually able to hold the attention of popular audiences. Many of his early plays were brutally realistic, and were often interpreted as denunciations of social injustice. In his later works, especially in such long psychological dramas as *Strange Interlude* (1928) and *Mourning Becomes Electra* (1931), it became more apparent that his primary concern was not sociological but religious and that he was preoccupied with the most fundamental questions of man's relationship with God and the universe. Testing one view of life after another, he never came to rest in any system of beliefs. But his work as a whole was a comprehensive exploration of what he called "the sickness of today . . . the death of the old God and the failure of science and materialism to give any new one."

It was not until the middle of the 1920's that other important dramatists began to appear, and none of them had O'Neill's power or scope. Probably the best of them were the authors of comedy and satire from the viewpoint of a sophisticated liberalism, such as S. N. Behrman, Sidney Howard, Philip Barry, and George Kelly. Maxwell Anderson boldly attempted to revive poetic tragedy, while men like Elmer Rice and John Howard Lawson experimented with symbolic rather than realistic methods of presenting social problems. The radicalism of the 1930's produced one talented dramatist, Clifford Odets, though his portrayals of middle-class futility were more convincing than his affirmations of faith in revolution.

In spite of a series of attempts by young enthusiasts to reform the theater, it cannot be said that it has ever become in America an established vehicle for the expression of ideas, as it has been occasionally in other countries. Reformers have usually blamed the commercialism of Broadway, and have insisted that the theater could never be really healthy as long as it was concentrated in a few blocks of the West Forties of New York and that it could be redeemed by the organization of little theaters in other parts of the country. But although a few such theaters have occasionally done interesting work, they have generally preferred to give their audiences warmed-over Broadway successes rather than providing a hearing for dramatists with something new to say.

Thus the main function of the American theater has been to provide popular entertainment, with the musical comedy as its most characteristic expression. Perhaps the most encouraging feature of theatrical history has been the steady improvement in the aesthetic and intellectual standards of Broadway musicals. Some of the more popular shows of the 1940's and 1950's, such as *Oklahoma* and *South Pacific*, may not have been great art; but the music and choreography could be enjoyed on all levels of discrimination, and showed a great advance over the sentimentality of twenty years earlier.

There has also been a remarkable development of another art form associated with the theater: the dance. At the beginning of the twentieth century the United States produced one of the greatest figures in choreographic history in Isadora Duncan. Impulsive, undisciplined, and egotistical, Miss Duncan had a tempestuous and in some ways tragic life; but she transformed the technique of the dance, in Europe as well as the United States, by making it a vehicle for spontaneous emotional expression. Partly as a result of her innovations, the ballet developed into one of the most interesting art forms of twentieth-century civilization. During the past thirty years there has been a rapid growth of interest in the ballet in the United States, and American audiences have enjoyed the dancing of such individual figures as Martha Graham and Ruth St. Denis and the choreography of Agnes De Mille.

6. PAINTING AND SCULPTURE

THE PERIOD immediately preceding World War I was as significant in the development of American painting as in that of literature. Two new trends, both of which marked a revolutionary change from nineteenth-century traditions, were spreading among the younger men. One of them was the realistic movement, including a strong element of radical social consciousness, which had been initiated by Henri, Sloan, and the rest of the "Eight" who collaborated in the exhibition of 1908.

Even more influential was the growth of a wholly new theory of the artist's function derived from the new post-impressionist groups in Europe. Certain European painters and critics were now repudiating the conception, dominant since the Renaissance, that the artist should copy nature; they declared instead that his proper task was to create significant forms, not necessarily resembling anything in the external world, which would be expressive of emotional states and spiritual experiences. A series of European masters, beginning with Cézanne and culminating with Picasso, produced pictures which simplified or distorted visual appearances or which were wholly abstract and non-representational. While enthusiasts hailed the new men as among the greatest artists of all time, the average citizen, accustomed to easily recognizable portraits and land-scapes, found their work completely bewildering, so that in painting, as in poetry, the contrast between cultivated and popular tastes became ever sharper than in the past.

The new movements in painting were given wide publicity in 1913 when all of them, both American and European, were represented at an exhibition held at the 69th Regiment Armory in New York. The most famous art display ever organized in the United States, this made critics and collectors aware that a decisive change of standards was occurring. Henceforth there was a growing market for the work of modernists, and the traditional work favored by the National Academy gradually fell into disrepute. The individual who probably did most to hasten the change was Alfred Stieglitz, himself a pioneer in the development of photography into a fine art, whose New York gallery was a center for all the more interesting new trends.

American painting since 1913 has been much too varied and too vast to be covered in any short summary, and it is possible only to indicate a few of the more conspicuous tendencies. Most of the original Eight continued to be productive down to the 1940's, and their delight in recording the vigor and color of the new urban America was communicated to a number of younger men, especially to George Bellows, who is remembered especially for his lithographs of prize fights, and to Reginald Marsh. At the opposite extreme painters like Max Weber followed the European post-impressionists in breaking completely with representational art. Probably the most satisfying work was done by men and women who set out to record American landscapes but who had also learned some of the lessons of significant form and were able to achieve a fusion of the descriptive with the expressive. John Marin, whose favorite subjects were found on the coast of Maine, was regarded by some critics as the greatest of all American painters. Almost equally satisfying were the landscapes and seascapes of Marsden Hartley, the flower studies of Georgia O'Keeffe, and the pictures in which Edward Hopper and Charles Burchfield used urban scenes as vehicles for communicating emotional states.

The 1920's and 1930's brought some new developments, one of which was a nationalistic emphasis. Some painters and critics were disturbed by the continued influence of the Europeans, especially of the non-representationalists, and were inclined to regard them as decadent. Turning back to the American past, they began to discover that their own country had a rich and largely unexplored tradition of her own, embodied both in the masters of the eighteenth and nineteenth centuries, from Copley and Peale down to Eakins and Ryder, and also in a great variety of folk arts. Scholars and collectors gave increasing attention to this native tradition, while a number of painters, repudiating the cosmopolitanism of the

Atlantic seaboard, set out to record the life of other sections of the country, especially the rural Middle West. Thus Thomas Hart Benton (a
descendant of the statesman) became identified with Missouri, John
Steuart Curry with Kansas, and Grant Wood with Iowa. Another new
trend, resulting from the depression and the subsequent growth of radicalism among the intellectuals, was towards political propaganda. Artists
like Ben Shahn, William Gropper, and Philip Evergood devoted their
talents to satirizing economic privilege and glorifying the working class.

As the new schools won critical acceptance, there were improvements
in the economic status of the American artist. New galleries like the
Whitney Museum and the Museum of Modern Art in New York bought
American pictures, while the older institutions were increasingly receptive,
and private collectors no longer concentrated on European old masters.
For a few years under the New Deal, for the first time in American history,
the Federal government became an art patron on a large scale; the WPA
art project, launched in 1935 and wound up in 1940, gave employment to
5,000 artists in forty states, mostly in the painting of murals in public
buildings. While some of their work was mediocre, the project was highly
valuable both in enabling painters to continue painting and in stimulating
popular interest in art in all parts of the country. Yet in spite of increasing
manifestations of both private and public interest, most American painters continued to find it difficult to earn a living. A statistical survey in
1940 showed that average annual earnings amounted to $1,150 for each
man and only $500 for each woman.

During the 1940's new forms of patronage developed as both business
firms and trade unions began to commission good painters to decorate the
walls of their office buildings with murals, while magazines and advertising agencies employed some of them for illustrations. It was estimated, in
fact, that more money was paid to American artists after 1940 than during the whole of previous history. Growing popular interest in art, moreover, was shown by a rapid increase in the number of amateurs who took
up painting as a spare-time occupation; between 1940 and 1950 sales of
painters' materials increased by no less than 1,000 per cent. But whether
the new generation of American artists were equal to their predecessors
was a debatable question. A visit to any gallery showing the work of
younger men indicated that most of them seemed to be turning away from
the tensions and insecurities of the period into a world of pure abstraction
or adopting surrealist techniques which purported to reveal, often in
terrifying forms, the emotional forces of the subconscious. While their
work was often technically excellent, it seemed to indicate a somewhat unhealthy retreat from the realism characteristic of the earlier American
tradition.

The twentieth century was less productive in sculpture than in
painting, and probably none of the younger men equaled the work of
Saint-Gaudens. Nineteenth-century representational traditions were con-

tinued by men like Lorado Taft and Paul Manship, while William Zorach
and others experimented with abstract forms. Perhaps the best achievements were the long series of portrait busts by Jo Davidson and the
opulent and powerful nudes of Gaston Lachaise. A new invention, which
was at first regarded as merely amusing but which some critics, especially
in Europe, considered to have real aesthetic importance, was the "mobile"
of Alexander Calder. By twisting metal into queer shapes strung on wires,
Calder devised a series of lyrical or satiric commentaries on the life around
him.

7. ARCHITECTURE

IN ARCHITECTURE the new methods of design, developed in the later
nineteenth century by such men as Louis Sullivan and Frank Lloyd
Wright, were slow to win popular acceptance. Architects, unlike poets and
painters, normally work only on commission; and throughout the 1920's
commissions continued to be given mainly to men who were not too
radical or experimental. Sullivan died in 1924 in poverty and obscurity
in a cheap Chicago hotel, and Wright, who had won considerable recognition before World War I, was for a long time unemployed and almost forgotten. The most prominent architects of the 1920's were men like Cass
Gilbert and Raymond Hood, who had picked up the more superficial
ideas of the functionalists without understanding their spirit.

Skyscrapers were built in increasing numbers in most large cities;
and there was a marked improvement in their designs after municipal
authorities began to make zoning ordinances requiring set-backs above a
certain number of floors. But most of them continued to be disfigured
with irrelevant ornamentation, and all of them, by increasing urban congestion, made humane living more difficult. Government buildings, like
the Supreme Court building designed by Gilbert, often continued to be
classical, with rows of columns, and were almost always ponderous and
unfunctionally wasteful in their use of space and material. Gothic continued to be predominant on many university campuses. The new buildings designed for Yale by James Gamble Rogers, for example, were pains-
taking imitations of medieval colleges, even including windowpanes
broken and mended in the medieval manner, while the library was
modeled after a Gothic cathedral.

During the 1930's and 1940's there was a slow improvement. Wright
was rediscovered, and his Johnson Wax Company building at Racine,
Wisconsin, completed in 1939, was widely recognized as a masterpiece.
While too many official edifices continued to recall the Parthenon, it was
possible to take pleasure in the clear forceful lines and simple harmonies
of many of the bridges, dams and power plants built by the PWA. Young
architects with new ideas found it easier to secure commissions for private
houses in all sections of the country; and while some of them seemed

intent simply on unconventionality for its own sake, their best work was genuinely in the modern idiom. In other words, they sought to design houses adapted to twentieth-century needs and in harmony with their environment, and made a bold and imaginative use of the new building materials supplied by modern technology. Even more significant were a few examples of enlightened town-planning, like Radburn, New Jersey, and Greenbelt, Maryland, which provided whole communities with facilities for humane living unknown in congested cities. Unfortunately, these were still exceptional cases. After World War II a considerable part of the urban population was rehoused, and many of the new apartment buildings were barrack-like structures, oppressively monotonous, which crowded even more people on to each acre of ground space than the slum tenements had ever done. The critic Lewis Mumford aptly described them as totalitarian architecture. Twentieth-century America was well on the way to developing its own appropriate building style; but it was plain that the doctrines of the functionalists had not yet penetrated official minds.

8. MUSIC

THE HISTORY of music in America has differed from that of the other arts in that the most significant achievements have been on a popular rather than a cultivated level. The United States has a remarkably rich tradition of folk music; on the other hand, she has produced no serious composers equal to the best of her writers, painters, and architects.

Popular music includes the ballads brought across during the colonial period, the hymns composed by the revivalist sects and developed by the Negroes into spirituals, and the folk songs devised by cowboys, lumberjacks, sailors, and other groups during the nineteenth century. During the past twenty years, with the growth of interest in all aspects of the American past, these have been intensively collected by students and made widely known by singers like Burl Ives and John Jacob Niles. Another form of popular music is the work of the commercial composers for the theater—men like Irving Berlin, Jerome Kern, Cole Porter, and Richard Rodgers—whose most effective melodies are known all over the world and seem likely to be remembered for generations.

The most peculiarly American form of popular music, however, has been the idiom variously known as ragtime, jazz, and swing. Though there have been long controversies about its origins, it has been established that it began towards the end of the nineteenth century in cabarets in New Orleans and other Southern cities, and that it represented a Negro contribution to the American folk heritage. In its early form it was essentially extemporaneous; while one musician played a tune on a piano or cornet, another would improvise counter-melodies on a clarinet. The national vogue of jazz began during World War I when Southern bands brought it to Northern cities, after which it was commercialized, made more respectable, and sweetened and sentimentalized by white orchestra leaders like Paul Whiteman. True enthusiasts, however, reject the "sweet" variety, and prefer their jazz to be "hot" and extemporaneous, speaking of masters like Louis Armstrong and Bix Beiderbecke in tones that other people reserve for Bach or Beethoven. The musical importance of jazz has been debated with considerable violence, but its admirers believe that composers can use it as a foundation for serious work, in much the same way that Mark Twain developed the tradition of popular humor into great literature. Something like this was almost achieved by George Gershwin, who, before his untimely death in 1937 at the age of thirty-nine, had become the most widely known of American composers through his *Rhapsody in Blue* and his score for the opera *Porgy and Bess*.

Meanwhile, there has been a steady increase in the number of serious composers in the United States and in the proportion of native works played at concerts by the leading orchestras. Among the older and more traditional group, perhaps the best-known have been Deems Taylor and Howard Hanson. Among the younger men Aaron Copland has assumed a position of leadership, while at least a dozen others seem potentially important. But much of their work is pervaded with echoes from contemporary European composers like Stravinsky and Schönberg, and no definite native idiom has become established.

On the whole, the history of serious music in the United States has remained largely a history of appreciation. Here the progress made during the twentieth century has been remarkable. The invention first of the phonograph and then of the radio made good music accessible to the average citizen, and his response surprised those who had supposed that the arts could be appreciated only by a cultivated minority. Appreciation courses increased in high schools and colleges, while an important contribution was made during the 1930's by the WPA music project, which organized unemployed musicians into orchestras and gave thousands of concerts all over the country. One proof of the growth of popular interest was the increase in the number of symphony orchestras; whereas in 1900 there had been fewer than half a dozen in the whole country, by the 1940's there were hundreds. And while the fact that, from Toscanini and Koussevitzky downwards, most of the better conductors were Europeans seemed to indicate that American professional standards had not yet reached the highest level, it also meant that American audiences demanded the best possible performances.

24. Continental United States in the Mid-twentieth Century

POPULATION CHANGES DURING THE FIFTH DECADE OF THE TWENTIETH CENTURY showed that the westward movement, which had been one of the central themes in American history since the founding of the colonies, had by no means lost its momentum. The largest gains were made by the three western states of California, Oregon, and Nevada; and Washington and Arizona also were expanding rapidly. Especially notable was the influx into California, due mainly to the building of war industries. This state registered a population growth of nearly 4,000,000 above the figure for 1940. The only Atlantic state showing a large increase was Florida, which had remained frontier country until the 1840's and had been the last area east of the Mississippi to be admitted to the Union.

Unlike the westward movement of earlier epochs, however, this was an expansion of cities and industries, not of agriculture. The country had contained a surplus of farmers beyond its real economic needs ever since the end of the nineteenth century, and the industrial growth of the war years resulted in a large-scale movement of farm tenants and laborers into factories. Most of the states that had remained predominantly agricultural either made insignificant gains or actually lost population. There was a significant migration away from the Great Plains region, stretching across the center of the United States from Montana and North Dakota down to Oklahoma. In this arid country, settled during the last three decades of the nineteenth century, the economic problems of the farmers were intensified by a decline in soil fertility. Plowing of the grasslands had been followed by wind and water erosion; topsoil was blown away in dust storms or carried down into the Mississippi by rain water; and much of the land was reduced virtually to desert.

The farm population, which had reached a peak of 32,440,000 in 1916, dropped to 30,547,000 in 1940, and to only 25,058,000 in 1950. By this date the proportion of the total population living in towns and cities, which had amounted to 5.1 per cent in the first census of 1790, had risen to 64.0 per cent.

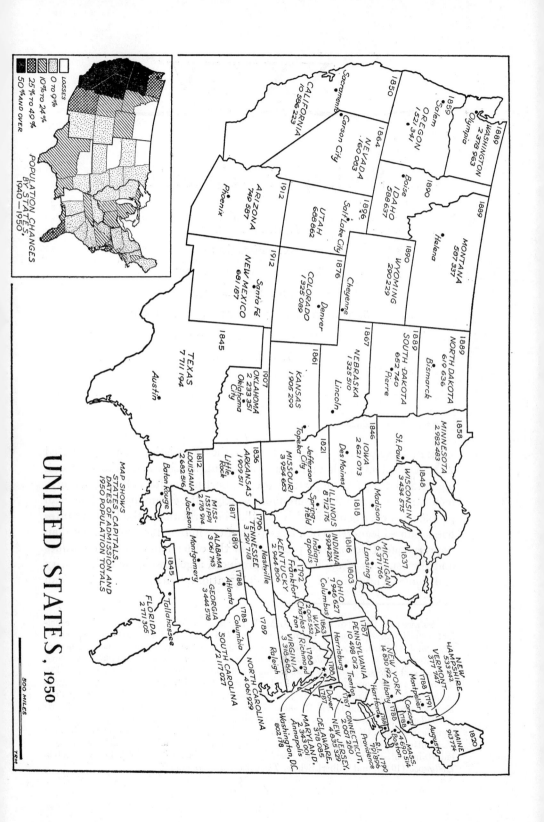

UNITED STATES, 1950

MAP SHOWS STATES, CAPITALS, AND DATES OF ADMISSION AND 1950 POPULATION TOTALS

500 MILES

POPULATION CHANGES BY STATES, 1940–1950.

LOSSES
50% AND OVER
25% TO 49%
10% TO 24%
0 TO 9%

XXXIV

Society at Midcentury

1. THE CHURCHES

2. EDUCATION

3. PROBLEMS OF EQUALITY

4. CHANGING MORALS

5. THREATS TO INDIVIDUAL INDEPENDENCE

6. THE ADVANCE OF THE SCIENCES

7. CONCLUSION

AMERICAN society halfway through the twentieth century presented its students with a number of apparent paradoxes. On the one hand, high standards of living, with varied opportunities for cultural advancement and for recreation, were more widely diffused among the American people than ever before in history, while in world affairs the United States had assumed leadership of a large part of the human race and achieved an unprecedented power and prestige. On the other hand, changing values and the tensions of modern living produced a general sense of insecurity and some symptoms of social disintegration. Critics of the American

SELECTED BIBLIOGRAPHY: R. M. Williams, *American Society* (1951), is an excellent overall analysis. Some of the more useful of the many studies of particular communities are: J. Dollard, *Caste and Class in a Southern Town* (revised edition, 1949); Robert S. Lynd and Helen M. Lynd, *Middletown* (1929) and *Middletown in Transition* (1937); W. Lloyd Warner and others, *Democracy in Jonesville* (1949); James West, *Plainville U. S. A.* (1945). There are an immense number of general appraisals of social trends, among the more stimulating being Erich Fromm, *Escape from Freedom* (1941), Margaret Mead, *And Keep Your Powder Dry* (1943), and David Riesman, *The Lonely Crowd* (1950). Gunnar Myrdal, *American Dilemma* (2 vols., 1944), is a comprehensive examination of the place of the Negro in American society. Of the many studies of educational problems, the Report of the Harvard Committee, *General Education in a Free Society* (1945), is outstanding. For the mass media of entertainment, see Lewis Jacobs, *The Rise of the American Film* (1939), Leo C. Rosten, *Hollywood* (1941), and Gilbert Seldes, *The Great Audience* (1950).

scene pointed with alarm to internal conflicts caused by the failure to conform to democratic ideals, to the decline of traditional moral standards and the increase of emotional maladjustment, and to the growth of a cultural standardization which threatened the independence of the individual. It is therefore by no means easy to present a balanced picture. But it should be emphasized at the beginning that, in order to undermine complacency and stimulate reform, most social critics, like most novelists, have always exaggerated the evils to which they wished to call attention. While American society in 1950 was far from perfect, it was undoubtedly healthier than many of the books written about it seemed to suggest.

In spite of certain shifts of value, the basic attitudes and institutions which had given American society its distinctive character in the past retained their vitality. Change and conflict developed within a general cultural pattern which remained relatively stable, and were caused mainly by new emphases or interpretations. Most of the observations made about Americans in the early nineteenth century by acute foreign visitors, such as Tocqueville, were still true in 1950. Almost all Americans, for example, accepted the general ideals of liberty and equality which had been formulated in the eighteenth century, even though they disagreed about their applications. Similarly, most Americans were oriented towards the active control and improvement of material conditions rather than the passive and fatalistic acceptance of their environment. American society continued to emphasize a high average level of attainment rather than the production of individual geniuses. These and other fundamental qualities of American civilization, acquired partly from its European inheritance and partly through the historical experience of settling the continent, were as conspicuous in 1950 as at any earlier period.

1. THE CHURCHES

ONE of the more obvious examples of stability and continuity in the American heritage was the vitality of organized religion. Defying the arguments of innumerable agnostics and materialists, Americans remained a churchgoing people, while continuing also to believe in freedom for people of all faiths and in separation of church and state. In the early years of the twentieth century it was widely asserted that religion was incompatible with rational views of life and concepts of morality; and down to the 1930's the churches seemed, on the whole, to be losing influence with the younger generation. But the anxieties evoked by the economic and political problems of the 1930's and 1940's weakened confidence in the unaided capacity of the human race and strengthened the plausibility of the doctrine of original sin. Numerous books presenting religious answers to personal conflicts became best-sellers; a number of individuals prominent in intellectual or political life became converted; and there was a rapid rise in church membership. By 1950 some 77,000,-

000 Americans, slightly over one-half of the total population of all ages, were affiliated with churches. While reliable figures for earlier periods are not available, this probably represented the highest percentage since before the Civil War.

Protestantism.   Nearly two-thirds of American church-members belonged to different Protestant organizations, with the Methodists and the various Baptist groups far in the lead. On the whole, the trends that had developed in the period following the Civil War remained dominant in American Protestantism throughout the twentieth century. While some groups continued to preach strict fundamentalism, the more influential clergymen in all the leading denominations no longer believed in the verbal inspiration of the Bible and emphasized ethics and social service rather than dogma. And while many churches maintained a conservative attitude to economic questions, the Federal Council of Churches and other important bodies continued to preach a social gospel. In 1932, for example, the Federal Council adopted a revised social creed in which it called for extensive measures of social and economic planning along the lines afterwards put into effect by the New Deal. As theological controversies subsided, there was a strong tendency towards unification. Different groups of Lutherans, Congregationalists, and Methodists combined into single organizations, and in 1950 most of the Protestant churches came together to set up the National Council of Churches in order to coordinate their educational and welfare activities.

Perhaps the most significant new trend in American Protestantism was a reaction against the optimism of the modernists and back to the more pessimistic doctrines of Luther and Calvin. Originating with such German theologians as Karl Barth, it was expounded in the United States by Reinhold Niebuhr, of Union Theological Seminary, New York. In his massive *Nature and Destiny of Man* (1941–43) and numerous other books Niebuhr emphasized the sinfulness of man and the corrupting influences of pride and self-love in all human activities. But unlike most earlier believers in original sin, Niebuhr was neither a fundamentalist nor a conservative. Insisting that corruption was peculiarly inherent in all forms of authority and privilege, he was an active and militant liberal and one of the founders of Americans for Democratic Action.

Catholicism.   The Catholic Church in 1950 claimed 25,000,000 members, as compared with 16,000,000 in 1910. Thus, despite the decrease in immigration, its expansion was more than keeping pace with that of the population as a whole. With the steady growth of its educational and cultural institutions and its continuing influence in city governments and in the trade-union movement, it was an increasingly important factor in American society.

The fanatical anti-Catholicism that had flared up on several occasions in the nineteenth century now seemed to have subsided. During the 1940's most exponents of prejudice preferred to concentrate on the

Communist menace or on anti-Semitism. On the other hand, the growing power of the Church alarmed many non-Catholic liberals, whose viewpoint was expressed with considerable violence by Paul Blanshard in his *American Freedom and Catholic Power* (1949).

There were two main issues on which Catholics and many non-Catholics were so vigorously in disagreement that no settlement by mutual consent seemed to be possible. Whereas the Church believed that the state should support strict moral standards, particularly with reference to birth-control, divorce, and the censorship of books, plays, and motion pictures, non-Catholic liberals felt that questions of personal morality should be left to individuals to decide for themselves and complained that Catholics were trying to impose their own principles on the whole community. And whereas the Church was expanding its system of parochial schools and asking for state assistance, most non-Catholics insisted that one of the essential foundations of American democracy was a secular public-school system in which children of all faiths would learn to live together. There were prolonged controversies as to whether public money might be used to provide free transportation for children going to parochial schools. This was allowed in a number of states, and prohibited in others. In 1947 the Supreme Court validated a New Jersey law to this effect by a five-to-four decision, but many non-Catholics continued to argue that such legislation was a violation of the first article of the Bill of Rights. These and other conflicts showed that the relationship between church and state was still an unsettled question and that no *modus vivendi* between Catholic and non-Catholic viewpoints had yet been established.

2. EDUCATION

School and College Expansion. The expansion of education on all levels was another example of the continuity of the American heritage. It was an article of faith for most Americans that as much education as possible should be given to as many people as possible. After the final establishment of compulsory education in all states in 1918, the process of extending the years of attendance and enlarging the number of public high schools went on steadily. By 1948 nearly 80 per cent of all children between the ages of 5 and 17 were in school. High-school attendance rose from 700,000 in 1900 to 6,800,000 in 1949.

Facilities varied considerably, however, in different parts of the country. In 1940 the national expenditure per pupil amounted to $88, but eight of the Southern states were spending less than $50 per pupil. This discrepancy was due not to any lack of enthusiasm in the South but simply to poverty; actually most Southern states devoted considerably larger proportions of their budgets to education than did most Northern states. There were also wide variations between urban and rural areas. In 1942 there were still more than 100,000 one-teacher rural schools, most of them meagerly financed and equipped.

A steadily increasing proportion of the American people went on to college. College attendance, which had amounted to 250,000 in 1900, rose to 600,000 in 1920, and jumped to 1,100,000 by 1930. By 1940 it had risen to 1,500,000, about 16 per cent of all persons of the college age group, while in 1948 the addition of more than 1,000,000 veterans carried it to the record figure of 2,600,000. As the number of graduates expanded, a college degree became a prerequisite for an increasing number of occupations, including virtually all professions.

Educational Controversies.   Unfortunately the quality of the American school system did not keep pace with its quantitative expansion. As the educational ladder became longer, the curriculum became thinner; subjects that could not be mastered without disciplined effort, such as foreign languages, mathematics, and the sciences, were taught less intensively; and the growth of athletics and of such commercialized entertainments as motion pictures, radio, and television increasingly cut into the time and energy available for study. While there were more educational opportunities available for more of the population than at earlier periods, there could be little doubt that the middle decades of the twentieth century saw a serious decline in academic standards. American society was not doing enough to develop the abilities of those more gifted students on whom it depended for continued cultural and scientific progress. In the 1950's, with Soviet schools giving their pupils a much more thorough training in mathematics and science and producing many more qualified engineers and technicians, the United States was in serious danger of losing her technological leadership.

These educational deficiencies provoked vigorous and incessant controversy. Progressives continued to support the ideas of John Dewey and his disciples. More conservative critics of the school system insisted that the application of this philosophy was undermining the necessary educational disciplines, and pointed with alarm to the growing influence of the Schools of Education, mainly on the ground that they concentrated on training prospective teachers in pedagogical methods and gave little attention to the knowledge of subject matter. The most convincing statement of this attitude was Arthur E. Bestor's *Restoration of Learning* (1955). But effective educational reform required a change of attitude not only among school administrators but also among the American people as a whole. The ultimate reason for the weaknesses of the school system was the widespread lack of respect for intellectual achievement. This was reflected in the low social status of American teachers and their inadequate salaries, which lagged far behind the rise in living costs after World War II. The abrupt realization of the Soviet scientific advance after the launching of the earth satellites in the autumn of 1957 seemed likely to result in a healthy reappraisal of American education, though there was danger that it might lead to too exclusive a concentration on the sciences. Effective citizenship in a democratic society required humanistic as well as scientific training.

There were similar controversies about the methods of college education. Most college reformers were disturbed by the proliferation of different courses, many of which seemed to have little or no connection with a liberal arts education, and by the excessive freedom permitted under the elective system. One of their most influential spokesmen was Dr. Abraham Flexner, whose *Universities, American, German, English* (1930) was a devastating attack on the deterioration of the American college. One extreme group, headed by Robert M. Hutchins, Chancellor of the University of Chicago, felt that college education should be based on the "great tradition" of Western civilization, as embodied in its great books. Hutchins's ideas were tried out in St. John's College, at Annapolis, Maryland. At the other extreme the disciples of John Dewey declared that there were reactionary implications in this emphasis on the "great tradition," that education should be oriented round the problems of the contemporary world, and that students should be free to work out their own programs in accordance with their own special interests. A number of small colleges, such as Bennington, in Vermont, and Sarah Lawrence, in New York, provided the best examples of this progressive philosophy.

Most of the larger universities tried to strike a balance between these two positions, retaining some of the freedom advocated by the progressives but laying increasing emphasis on some kind of core program which all students should be required to take. Probably the most influential statement of this central position was the report of a Harvard committee issued in 1945: *General Education in a Free Society*. The report emphasized the differences, which had been largely forgotten after the growth of the elective system, between "general education," meaning "that part of a student's whole education which looks first of all to his life as a responsible human being and citizen," and "special education," referring to "that part which looks to the student's competence in some occupation." The central trend in American colleges in the 1930's and 1940's was to re-emphasize the importance of general education, with a recognition that their primary function was not to turn out skilled specialists but to produce men and women capable of responsible and enlightened citizenship.

3. PROBLEMS OF EQUALITY

CONFLICT is to be expected where there is a marked discrepancy between the official values of a society and its actual practices. The most obvious examples of such a conflict in American society related to the value of equality. The traditional American belief was that all men had been created equal and were entitled to equal opportunities for developing their talents and achieving success. Americans liked to believe that the social and economic status of each individual in their society was roughly commensurate to his merits and that the poor man could always work his way to the top if he had enough ability and initiative. In actuality, however, equality of opportunity was a social myth rather than a reality, since it was restricted by distinctions of both class and race.

Class Divisions.   The class structure of twentieth-century American society was the subject of a number of sociological analyses, which showed that it had become more complex and more rigid than had generally been recognized. The most obvious differentiating line in urban America was between the business and professional class and the working class. The lower categories of white-collar workers formed an intermediate class, while a number of different grades could be distinguished within the business class. According to studies made by W. Lloyd Warner, of the University of Chicago, the average medium or small town, where society was more tightly patterned than in the large cities, contained no less than six distinct classes. The status of any family could be determined by considering such criteria as its social and religious affiliations, the location of its house, the clubs to which its members belonged, and its general prestige in the community. Perhaps the most significant conclusion emphasized in these studies was that class status was by no means dependent solely on wealth and occupation but that heredity was an even more important factor. While members of the upper class were normally wealthy, they owed their position primarily to being born into long-established families.

Although the differences in living standards between upper-class and working-class families were markedly less than in earlier periods, the lines between them were not easy to cross. Children born into wealthy families had great initial advantages and access to educational and professional opportunities not open to children born on the wrong side of the tracks. Statistical evidence showed that heredity was a much more important factor in determining success than Americans liked to think. Most business executives were the sons of executives, most sons of workers became workers, and the individuals who actually succeeded in climbing the social ladder constituted only a tiny fraction of the total population.

The discrepancy between these class differentiations and the ideals and political institutions of democracy was an obvious source of social tensions, and did much to embitter political conflicts during the Roosevelt and Truman administrations. But its importance should not be exaggerated. While American society had less mobility than democratic idealists would have desired, it had not become as rigidly stratified as that of most European countries down to the twentieth century. Although it was difficult for ambitious individuals to climb the social ladder, it was not impossible. And while the upper class had more political, economic, and social power than other groups in the community, it was very far from being a ruling class.

The Race Problem.   A much sharper deviation from the professed American ideal of equality was represented by the emphasis on distinctions of race and national origin. Many of these proved to be transitory; each new immigrant group in turn encountered initial hostility, but was usually well on the way to assimilation after one or two generations. After large-scale immigration from Europe ended, the pattern of prejudice was repeated in the 1930's and 1940's with the Mexican laborers who moved into Texas and California and the Puerto Ricans who settled in New York. But one group among the nineteenth-century immigrants, the Jews, continued to suffer from social discrimination as a result of the importation into the United States of European anti-Semitic traditions; and one group who had arrived during the colonial period, the Negroes, were never permitted to move up the social ladder or become fully integrated into the American community.

At the beginning of the twentieth century 90 per cent of the Negroes still lived in the South, and more than three-quarters of them were engaged in agriculture. With a few exceptions, they were not permitted to vote or sit on juries, and a policy of segregation was enforced by law. Negroes in the South went to different schools, and were kept apart from white people by Jim Crow rules. Theoretically, the educational and other facilities provided for the two races were supposed to be equal, but in practice those allotted to the Negroes were far inferior. As late as 1930, for example, the South was spending $45.63 on public education for each white child and only $14.95 for each Negro child. In the North segregation never became an official program, but it was enforced in practice by popular pressure, especially in housing and access to jobs. Severely restricted in their employment and educational opportunities, Negroes suffered from great economic handicaps. Nor should it be forgotten that in addition to the material problems of poverty, they were burdened by the even more difficult problems of emotional adjustment to a society in which they were branded as inferior to all white people.

The twentieth century saw a considerable improvement in the position of the Negro people. Negroes moved in large numbers from the farms to the cities and from the South to the North, especially during the two world wars; and although they were confined to congested slum areas, the migration brought some gains in living standards and cultural levels. By 1950 more than half of them were living in cities and more than a third of them were outside the South. In spite of opposition from some white trade unions, new job opportunities in industry and transportation became available. Educational facilities steadily expanded, with a drop in the rate of Negro illiteracy from 30 per cent in 1910 to only 8 per cent in 1940. A considerable Negro business and professional class emerged, and a few gifted individuals achieved national fame in athletics, entertainment, and the arts. Most Negro leaders of the twentieth century repudiated the conservative program of Booker T. Washington and, with the aid of white sympathizers, formed organizations like the National Association for the Advancement of Colored People to fight militantly for the rights supposedly guaranteed them by the Constitution.

Gains were especially rapid during and after World War II. By this time an appreciable number of white people had developed uneasy con-sciences about color prejudice, and had become acutely aware that as long as the United States practiced discrimination at home, her claim to be the champion of freedom abroad would be regarded in other countries as blatantly hypocritical. Another influential factor was the growing im-portance of the Negro vote in several large Northern states; after the coming of the New Deal the Negroes had abandoned their traditional Republicanism and were now willing to support whatever party seemed most likely to give them concrete assistance.

In 1941 Roosevelt set up a Fair Employment Practices Committee to end discrimination in industries working on government contracts, and some Northern states subsequently passed legislation to promote the same objective. During the 1940's a series of Supreme Court decisions affirmed the right of Negroes in the South to vote in primary elections, sit on juries, and secure admission to white educational institutions where the facilities allotted to Negroes were plainly inadequate. A long list of items showed that real progress was being made: the appointment during the war for the first time of a Negro brigadier general; the appointment of Ralph Bunche as Director of the Department of Trusteeship in the United Nations; the increasing number of Negro members of college fac-ulties, and of Negro employees in industries formerly restricted to white people; several successful battles against discrimination in housing; the admission of Negroes to professional baseball in 1948 (when Jackie Robin-son joined the Brooklyn Dodgers). Although gains were most conspicuous in the North, there were visible changes in the South also. More than 1,000,000 Southern Negroes voted in the elections of 1952 and 1956.

During the 1950's Negro leaders, assured of support from the judicial and executive branches of the Federal government, made bolder moves to secure their civil rights, and there were some impressively orderly and well-organized protests against discrimination. There was growing resist-ance to the Jim Crow laws still enforced in the Southern states, especially notable being a prolonged boycott of the local bus system by the Negro population of Montgomery, Alabama. In April, 1956, the Supreme Court affirmed that enforced segregation on all public transportation, intrastate as well as interstate, was unconstitutional. The main storm center, how-ever, was the maintenance of segregation in the public schools. Seventeen states, along with the District of Columbia, had established separate school systems, which theoretically offered equal educational opportu-nities, though in practice the Negro schools were much more poorly financed and equipped. This "separate but equal" doctrine had been accepted by the Supreme Court in 1896 in the case of *Plessy* v. *Ferguson,* in which the contention that segregation meant inequality had been brushed aside as a mere subjective opinion without factual support. But in spite of this judicial reasoning it was obvious that Negro children were handicapped by the material deficiencies of the Negro schools and also by the stigma of inferiority necessarily implied by the mere fact of segregation. Legal proceedings in the Federal courts were initiated by Negro parents in South Carolina in order to secure adequate schooling for their children, and on May 27, 1954, the Supreme Court ruled by a unanimous vote that segregation in the public schools was a violation of the legal equality guaranteed to all citizens by the Fourteenth Amendment. The Court recognized that the abolition of segregation would necessarily be a long and difficult process, but declared that the Southern states were obligated to begin moving in that direction.

During the next four years segregation was ended only in the District of Columbia. Ten states, in varying degrees, made some progress towards integration. Seven states took no action whatever. Extremist white leaders in Virginia and the Deep South threatened to abolish their public school systems altogether rather than accept integration, and hysterically predicted that any attempt to enforce the Supreme Court decision could lead only to a repetition of the Reconstruction experience, when the South had been occupied by Federal troops. The only actual use of troops, however, was precipitated by the behavior of a Southern governor. In September, 1957, the educational authorities of Little Rock, Arkansas, proposed to admit nine Negro students to Central High School, hitherto attended only by whites. When classes opened, the Negroes were barred from the school by state troopers under orders from Governor Orval E. Faubus, on the ground that their attendance would lead to rioting. This defiance of the Supreme Court ruling was so flagrant that President Eisenhower was compelled to intervene; and after private negotiations had produced no satisfactory result, Federal troops were sent to Little Rock to protect the right of the Negro students to attend the high school. Meanwhile another victory for race equality had been scored in August, 1957, when Congress passed a Civil Rights Bill giving the Federal judiciary power to protect, by the use of injunctions, the Negroes' right to vote. The Eisenhower administration had proposed a more extensive measure covering all civil rights, but even in its final diluted form the enactment of the bill was a notable step forward. Ever since the Reconstruction period Southern congressmen had consistently blocked all proposals for civil rights legislation.

Thus the United States had made considerable strides toward its professed ideal of equality of opportunity. Another cause for satisfaction was that, in spite of the growth of race tensions during the 1950's, there was relatively little violence. While lynchings had been decreasing fairly steadily since the 1890's, they had never wholly disappeared, and during the 1940's they still averaged 3.6 a year. During the 1950's, on the other hand, there were only two cases, one in Florida in 1951 and one in Georgia in 1957. But when and how the problem of race relations would finally be solved remained an unanswerable question. Color discrimination was still part of the behavior pattern of most white Americans, Northern as well as Southern; and it would be a long time before the Negro people could feel secure in the enjoyment of their constitutional rights.

4. CHANGING MORALS

SOME of the most conspicuous changes in twentieth-century American society were in the field of sexual relationships. The actual extent of the transformation was often exaggerated; probably actual sexual practices have not varied as much between different periods as might appear on the surface. But undeniably overt attitudes underwent a minor revolution.

New Attitudes to Sex. While American legal codes continued to reflect the strict standards and taboos characteristic of the nineteenth century, public opinion permitted much greater freedom and frankness. The most obvious change, particularly marked during the 1920's, was that young women began to repudiate some of the restrictions imposed during earlier periods, so that the line between the respectable and the immoral woman was no longer drawn so sharply. Girls asserted their right to smoke in public, began to discuss subjects hitherto tabooed, and wore fewer clothes (somebody calculated that the yards of material needed to dress a woman dropped from $19\frac{1}{4}$ in 1913 to 7 in 1928). Among some members of the younger generation—probably fewer than most people supposed—the traditional double standard of sexual morality was abandoned, and inhibitions were considered as positively harmful. This revolt was partly stimulated by the writings of Europeans who had studied sex in a spirit of scientific inquiry, especially Havelock Ellis and Sigmund Freud. During the depression the interests of persons who considered themselves emancipated shifted from sex to economics, but the attitudes developed during the 1920's were not repudiated and continued to spread among wider segments of the population.

Except among the Catholics and other religious groups who continued to inculcate strict standards, the American people by the 1940's had largely adopted a new sexual code, not fundamentally different from that of the past but allowing considerably more flexibility. While the double standard had by no means disappeared, young people of both sexes were allowed a wide range of experimentation before marriage (the dating customs of American adolescents interested anthropologists, who found parallels with the rituals of primitive tribes). Monogamous marriage and mutual fidelity continued to be standard, but marriages could be dissolved easily, and children were limited. Sexual problems, moreover, were discussed with considerable frankness, with more tolerance for aberrations, and with the assumption (which had not been accepted during the nineteenth century) that people of both sexes had a right to fulfillment.

More Divorces and Fewer Children. Some of the consequences of such a code gave reason for alarm, especially the rapid rise in the divorce rate. This grew from 0.7 for every thousand people in 1900 to 2.6 in 1949. almost a fourfold increase. In 1946, a year which saw the dissolution of many hasty war marriages, the rate was 4.3. What this meant was that during the 1940's almost one marriage in every four was ending in divorce. However, a high divorce rate did not mean that Americans had a low opinion of marriage but rather that they expected too much from it. As one humorist remarked, to be divorced meant that one had flunked the course the first time and had to take it again.

Another theme for pessimistic speculation was the fall in the birth rate, presumably due mainly to the growing use of contraceptives. While the Catholic Church continued to regard birth-control as sinful, most non-Catholic groups gradually came to accept it. By the 1920's, and probably earlier, it had become customary with couples in the upper income levels, and appliances could be bought in any drugstore. Rural and working-class families, on the other hand, continued to have large families, and there were long controversies as to whether it was right to give them advice about contraceptive methods. Margaret Sanger, who had been arrested in 1914 under the laws of New York for circulating a pamphlet about birth-control, founded the American Birth Control League in 1921 and was a leader in the campaign for free clinics. By 1950 there were nearly 800 such clinics; and although most of them were privately financed, seven Southern states were supporting clinics as part of their public-health programs. In Massachusetts and Connecticut, on the other hand, where Catholic influence was strong, it remained illegal even for physicians to advise their patients about birth-control methods.

In actuality, the birth rate did not follow a consistent trend. From the beginning of the nineteenth century it had dropped fairly steadily, being less than half as high in 1900 as in 1800. In 1910 it amounted to 27 per thousand, and by 1935, after several years of depression, it had dropped to 16.9. But this was followed by a rise, especially after World War II, and by 1947 the figure was back to 25.8. Obviously, most young Americans still wanted children.

A more legitimate cause for alarm was that the birth rate remained much higher among the poorer classes, especially in rural areas, than in those professional groups that presumably included the most talented members of the population. While professional people often had only one or two children or none at all, large families continued to be customary on the lower income levels. If heredity counted for as much as was generally believed, this meant that there would be a serious decline in the average intelligence of the American people in later generations.

Male and Female Roles. Probably the main factor making for instability in marriage relationships was the shift in the relative status of men and women. Women had acquired more independence in American society than they had usually been permitted in Europe, the most obvious reasons being the active role they had been required to play in frontier communities, the decline in the authority of the father in many immigrant families, the democratic tendencies of American society, and the struggle conducted by militant feminists. By the 1920's women had established their right to do almost anything that men did, and it was no longer considered unusual for married middle-class women to work outside their homes. At the same time the mother in the normal American family had the main responsibility for bringing up the children, and the father had ceased to be the awe-inspiring figure of earlier periods.

There were many indications that the American male, having lost his traditional dominance, felt uncertain of his status; and a note of anti-feminism began to appear in literature and art on all levels, from serious fiction to the comic strip. Male social critics occasionally declared that America had become a matriarchy, and some of them, such as Philip Wylie, even suggested that American boys were being emasculated by maternal domination. But by the 1940's there were indications that a new balance was being achieved. Having won their fight for equality, women were no longer so concerned with asserting their independence, and some of them explicitly repudiated the feminism of earlier generations—an attitude expressed by the psychiatrist Marynia Farnham in *Modern Woman: The Lost Sex* (1947). Most women still wanted chiefly to raise families, and the rise in the birth rate showed that they were doing it.

Psychoneurotic Diseases.   A period of instability and rapid change is likely to see an increase in psychological maladjustments of all kinds, and this seemed to be true of American society during and after World War II. There was a marked growth of crime, especially among juveniles, and of alcoholism and drug addiction, though possibly this was a temporary war and post-war phenomenon. More alarming was the apparent increase of emotional disorders varying from mild neuroses to outright insanity. By 1948 there were 540,000 inmates of mental institutions; this represented a proportion of 3.7 for every thousand people, as contrasted with only 1.1 per thousand in 1910. Among young men of draft age in World War II, 1,825,000 were rejected and 600,000 were discharged because of psychoneurotic disturbances. Possibly the increase was more apparent than real, and due largely to a better understanding of what constituted emotional disease. Many people who in the nineteenth century would have been considered normal were now diagnosed as having neurotic tendencies. But although mental diseases may not actually have increased, neurotic patterns seemed to be changing. Whereas maladjusted characters in the nineteenth century had mostly settled into rigid patterns of eccentricity, in the twentieth century they were more likely to suffer from pervasive feelings of anxiety.

The new science of psychiatry was one of the major intellectual influences of the twentieth century, and by the 1940's some understanding of its basic concepts had spread to most educated Americans. But the science was still in its infancy; the number of trained psychiatrists remained far less than the demand; and treatment continued to be long and expensive, and cures very uncertain. The profession, moreover, split into a number of rival schools with different theoretical approaches; while some psychiatrists followed Freud in laying their main emphasis on the patient's early sexual development, other groups, represented by such spokesmen as Harry Stack Sullivan, Karen Horney, and Erich Fromm, gave more attention to social factors and stressed the patient's problems of adjustment to society in adolescence and maturity. A growing number of psychiatric clinics became available for individuals who could not afford to pay the fees of private practitioners, but many people ended in state mental institutions, which were often understaffed and underfinanced and sometimes almost as backward and barbarous in their methods as in the days of Dorothea Dix. Meanwhile, vast numbers of quack healers flourished by promising easy cures to persons suffering from phobias and nervous tensions.

5. THREATS TO INDIVIDUAL INDEPENDANCE

THE APPARENT growth of emotional disorders seemed to indicate that human beings found it more difficult to adjust to society than in earlier periods. This was no doubt related to another general trend which pessimistic observers of the American scene stressed even more frequently. Machine industry and mass production seemed to be leading to a cultural standardization on a relatively low level and to a decrease in individual independence.

The "Lonely Crowd." One aspect of this trend was the spread of the same big-city way of life to all groups and all sections of the country. By the twentieth century the national market had become a market not only for material goods but also for attitudes and ideas. To an increasing extent people in all sections saw the same motion pictures, listened to the same radio programs, read the same newspaper columnists, and responded to the same advertising. Except in a few relatively isolated areas, such as the German country of Pennsylvania and the Tennessee and Ozark mountains, all Americans were coming to resemble each other more closely, and cultural differences between the city and the farm, and between North, South, and West, were steadily diminishing.

While individuals all over the country were exposed to the same mass media of communication, economic changes were at the same time limiting the opportunities for personal initiative. The modern economy had relatively little room for the kind of aggressive individualist who could often rise to the top in the nineteenth century; it now set a greater premium on qualities making for group harmony and offered high rewards to persons with a talent for smooth handling of personal contacts.[1] In spite

[1] One illustration of this trend was the abrupt change in the tone of how-to-get ahead books. Such books had been written since the sixteenth century, and for more than 300 years the formula never varied much, the main emphasis being placed on individual drive, thrift, and hard work. But the 1920's and 1930's saw the introduction of a new note. The most popular success manual of the period was Dale Carnegie's *How to Win Friends and Influence People.*

of the continued emphasis on free enterprise and competition, most modern enterprises, however free from government control, were essentially cooperative. The central economic institution, the corporation, was a device for bringing together the labor and resources of different individuals and enabling them to work together for a common objective. There were similar trends towards teamwork in science and scholarship and in the popular arts. Except in the higher arts, it was becoming increasingly unusual for one man working alone to accomplish anything of value. And perhaps one of the main factors in the economic and military achievements of the United States was that, as a result of the informality of manners, the lack of emphasis on distinctions of class and rank, and the democratic tone of society, Americans had a special capacity for working together without personal friction.

Thus, while the American of 1950 was likely to be less strict in his moral standards than his grandfather, he often had less individual independence and was more responsive to popular currents of thought and emotion. In *The Lonely Crowd* David Riesman, of the University of Chicago, summarized the change by suggesting that Americans were becoming less "inner-directed" and more "other-directed." While the old-fashioned inner-directed character was guided by strong internal convictions of right and wrong, usually implanted by his parents during childhood, the modern other-directed character was less rigid, more flexible, and more readily influenced by his associates, regarding the approval of the group as more important than the approval of his private conscience. This apparent decline in individual moral integrity was the theme of numerous sociological and psychological studies (such as the books of Erich Fromm) and of popular novels and plays, like Arthur Miller's *Death of a Salesman.* Modern Americans, it was suggested, especially in the professional and salaried middle class, had lost the inner strength and security that come from adherence to fixed moral values and were spending their lives in a ceaseless search for other people's approval.

Journalistic Trends.   The dangers of cultural standardization were most apparent in the growth of the mass media of communication: newspapers, magazines, motion pictures, radio, and television. Since they generally required large capital investments, and most of them were largely financed by advertising, they had to appeal to large popular audiences and therefore could not run the risk of puzzling or antagonizing any part of their clientele.

The number of separate newspapers was, on the whole, diminishing, in spite of a rise in the later 1930's following a sharp drop during the depression. In 1950 there were about 10,000, as contrasted with 16,000 in 1900. Papers that championed liberal principles found it especially difficult to stay in business; the *New York World,* for example, was a depression casualty, and was merged with the *Telegram* in 1930. While a small number of responsible papers continued to flourish, much the largest circulations were enjoyed by journals that relied largely on scandals and comic strips and inculcated ultra-nationalist and reactionary political attitudes. Thus there was reason for thinking that the press was becoming less liberal and catering to lower tastes, while outside a few large cities it continued to leave the American people dangerously uninformed about world affairs. One counteracting tendency, however, was the growth of syndicated columns by well-known commentators, some of whom were liberals; this revived in a new form the personal tradition represented by the Greeleys and Leggetts of a century earlier. Election returns, moreover, indicated that the newspapers had less influence than might have been expected; the Democratic victories of 1936, 1940, 1944, and 1948 were won in spite of the opposition of a large proportion of the press.

One reason for the inability of the press to control opinion was that, with the growth of the radio, it no longer had a monopoly of public information. Government regulation, exercised through the FCC, prohibited radio stations from giving the candidates of any one party exclusive access to the air, so that—at least during election campaigns—the American people did not hear only one point of view. A single radio speech by President Roosevelt undoubtedly had more effect than thousands of newspaper editorials. But with a few notable exceptions, most radio commentators were as nationalistic and as anti-progressive as most newspapers.

In the magazine field, similarly, increasingly high costs and the growth of mass-production methods meant some loss of quality. During the 1930's there was a high death rate among the more serious monthlies and quarterlies; and apart from those that were subsidized by universities, the only survivors were *Harper's* and the *Atlantic*. Four serious weeklies appeared regularly, but all of them had small circulations: the *Nation* and the *New Republic* were too far to the left to exert much influence; the *Commonweal* was addressed primarily to Catholics with progressive political views; and the *Saturday Review* was concerned mainly with the arts. Meanwhile, vast circulations were achieved by magazines of a new type catering to middle-class citizens with not much time for reading.

Time, founded in 1923, presented busy Americans with spiced and predigested summaries of the weekly news. Its principal founder, Henry R. Luce, scored another circulation triumph with *Life*, founded in 1936, and became one of the most influential figures in American society as the spokesman of an up-to-date sophisticated conservatism and of a strong foreign policy. The other big journalistic success of this period was the *Reader's Digest*, founded in 1922 by DeWitt Wallace; this claimed to present summaries of the best articles in the current magazines, though its editorial policies were strongly slanted in favor of conservative viewpoints. The lower levels of literacy were tapped by other journalistic entrepreneurs; millions of Americans read magazines about the love lives of motion-picture stars, and millions of others derived their main intellectual sustenance from comics which were not only devoid of any artistic quality but also remarkably sadistic in tone.

Motion Pictures and Radio.   In the entertainment field the dangers of cultural deterioration were even more strikingly manifest. The twentieth century saw the growth of vast new entertainment industries appealing to nation-wide, and even world-wide, popular audiences, dominated by commercial standards, and making little attempt to discriminate between different intellectual levels.

The motion picture was both a business and an art. As a business, it was dominated by a few corporation executives, most of whom had come in on the ground floor before World War I and worked their way to the top. Interested primarily in the box office, they were generally inclined to avoid risky experiments and prefer well-established formulas. Some directors and writers, on the other hand, had high aesthetic standards, and fought long battles to secure financial backing for their ideas. A few Hollywood pictures were artistically satisfying, and some of these also made money. Probably the greatest figure in motion-picture history was D. W. Griffith, whose *Birth of a Nation* (1915) first revealed the artistic possibilities of this new medium though its subject was deplorable, since it glorified the Ku-Klux of the Reconstruction Period. During the 1920's the comedies of Charlie Chaplin, mingling humor and tenderness with bitter commentary on modern life, pleased audiences on all levels. Some distinguished work was produced during the 1930's and 1940's: dramas directed by such men as John Ford and John Huston, for example, the comedies of Preston Sturges, and the screwball humor of the Marx brothers. But few American pictures could be considered as more than good entertainment, and the majority of them were not even that. Probably the most nauseating were the epic spectacles upon which millions were lavished. *Ben Hur* was the most expensive picture of the 1920's and also one of the worst; it was topped in both respects by *Quo Vadis* in the 1950's.

Hollywood developed into a fantastic community, apparently almost insulated from real life; money flowed more freely than anywhere else in the world; and thousands of stars and would-be stars, qualified mainly by their good looks (few of them knew anything about acting), lived and loved almost as publicly as goldfish. Its main function was to provide people with vicarious pleasures and an escape from the monotony of daily living. Controversial subjects were usually avoided, since they might antagonize some groups in Hollywood's vast audience; and most pictures remained faithful to the well-worn formulas of love and adventure, with a strong preference for characters in the upper income brackets. Although the industry adopted a self-imposed censorship, with rigid rules prohibiting bad language, provocative displays of sexuality, and any condonation of crime or immorality, the moral standards implicit in the average picture were low; sexual allure, material success, and the use of violence were generally glorified, while any character who displayed intellectual interests was portrayed as either ludicrous or sinister. While the social influence of the American motion picture cannot be estimated with any accuracy, it probably did more harm than good; frequent excursions to the dream world created in Hollywood probably made it more difficult for the average citizen to adjust to actuality. For pictures about real people confronting real problems, one generally had to turn to European producers.

On the whole, similar criticisms might be made of American radio and television. One did not know how low the human intelligence could sink unless one listened to the soap operas produced over the radio during day-time hours for the edification of housewives, while the willingness of Americans to tolerate the unctuous inanities of the commercials suggested that they had become alarmingly sheep-like. On the other hand, the lead-ing radio corporations, partly as a result of pressure from the FCC, made some attempt to provide educational programs and good music as well as popular entertainment. But since radio and television required large in-vestments and were financed by advertising, they could not afford to forget box-office considerations or move too far ahead of their mass audi-ences.

Sociologists often expressed alarm at this growth of mechanized entertainment. Unlike the recreational activities of earlier generations, they did not require the individual to participate but reduced him to the role of a passive spectator or auditor. The same trend was exhibited in the continued popularity of professional athletics. But in considering how twentieth-century Americans spent their leisure hours, important com-pensating tendencies should not be overlooked. People on all economic levels had many more opportunities for outdoor vacations than their ancestors, and they made the most of them. With the development of the automobile and the general decrease in working hours, families traveled in steadily increasing numbers. A notably valuable and imaginative contri-bution was made by the Federal government through the development of the national parks. Anybody who felt that Americans were becoming too passive and too gregarious could take comfort in the fact that their favor-ite recreation, as determined by the amount of money spent on it, was fishing.

6. THE ADVANCE OF THE SCIENCES

WHATEVER validity there may have been in these widely expressed fears of cultural standardization, there was certainly no decrease in intellectual progress. On the contrary, the twentieth century was a period of rapid development in virtually every form of human knowledge. All leading American universities now encouraged research, and vast sums of money were devoted to its promotion by foundations, by business corporations, and by the Federal government. In consequence, the United States was now beginning to assume world leadership in science and scholarship, especially after 1933, when the growth of totalitarianism compelled many of Europe's most gifted intellectuals to seek refuge in American univer-sities. The growth of American pre-eminence was indicated by the distri-bution of the Nobel prizes for the sciences. Between 1930 and 1950 one-third of them went to American citizens, as contrasted with less than 6 per cent from 1901 to 1929, while Britain and Germany together received another third, and the remainder were distributed over the rest of the world.

Physics.   Although the frontiers of knowledge were being rapidly carried forward in every branch of science, unquestionably the most important developments, in both theory and practical application, were in physics. New experimental data and new hypotheses presented mankind with a view of the universe radically different from common-sense conceptions. The principles of relativity and indeterminacy undermined traditional certainties, and made matter more insubstantial, laws of causation less universal, and all human knowledge more subjective. Possibly there was little justification for the argument, advanced by some scientists, that the new physics corroborated religious beliefs, but there was no doubt that it had made untenable the kind of dogmatic materialism popular in the nineteenth century. Probably it would be generations before mankind could fully digest it. The problem of coping with its applications, however, was urgent and inescapable, since the new physics led directly to the atomic bomb.

While most of the major new hypotheses were formulated by Europeans, Americans like Robert A. Millikan, Arthur Compton, Harold C. Urey, Ernest O. Lawrence, and Robert Van de Graaff made important additions, particularly in finding experimental validations. But even more than in the past science required international collaboration and knew no distinctions of race or national origin, as was most fully demonstrated in the invention of the atomic bomb. Physicists from half a dozen different countries helped to formulate the theories on which it was based, while the most essential American contributions were the money and resources, the practical know-how, and the capacity for organizing effective teamwork.

Medicine.   While science was making it easier to kill, it was also enabling human life to be prolonged. From the viewpoint of the average man, its most important achievements were in medicine. The main medical advances during the 1920's, 1930's, and 1940's were a series of new drugs which proved remarkably efficacious in dealing with infections, a number of discoveries in nutrition, and a growing understanding of the importance of psychic factors in somatic disorders. While relatively little progress was made in fighting the degenerative diseases of middle and old age, such as cancer and heart trouble, most of the infections could now definitely be kept under control.

Medical progress intensified the practical problem of making the best treatment available to families in the lower income brackets. Proposals by the Truman administration for compulsory health insurance were opposed as socialistic by conservative spokesmen for the medical profession, though a rapid growth of private insurance plans helped to make sickness less catastrophic. But even though many people could not afford adequate care, the general progress of medical knowledge and the activities of public-health authorities had remarkable results. Between 1900 and 1949 the death rate dropped from 17.2 to 9.7 per thousand, male life expectancy increased from 45 to 64, and the median age of the population rose from 22.9 to 30.1.

The Social Sciences. Alongside the development of the physical sciences there was an even more rapid expansion of social studies, as scholars in increasing numbers explored every aspect of the past and present of their society.

Although men like Samuel Eliot Morison of Harvard and Allan Nevins of Columbia showed that the apparatus of modern scholarship did not necessarily deprive history of its literary qualities, the main impetus in American historiography continued to be scientific. While there were no new general hypotheses comparable in importance to Turner's frontier thesis or to the theory of economic determinism, accepted interpretations of the American past were subject to constant revision in the light of new data, and it could safely be said that American historians had accumulated more knowledge about the development of their country than those of any other nation. Since it was increasingly difficult for any one man to master all the available material, there was more emphasis on teamwork, as shown in cooperative works like *A History of American Life*, *The History of the South*, and the *Economic History of the United States*.

Meanwhile, another group of scholars had carried their researches back to primitive man. The proximity of the Indians had always given Americans a special interest in anthropology, and in the 1870's Lewis H. Morgan, deriving his material mainly from a study of the Indians of western New York, had pioneered in the application of the Darwinian theory to early social development. Under the leadership of Franz Boas of Columbia, later anthropologists no longer supposed that all societies passed through the same evolutionary stages, and they began to interpret primitive ways of living in terms of different patterns of culture. This led to a long series of analyses of the various patterns exemplified among Indian tribes and Pacific islanders, and to the formulation of techniques and hypotheses which could afterwards be extended to the society of the United States. Using the methods of the anthropologists, Robert and Helen Lynd made a pioneer investigation of life in a Midwestern town (Muncie, Indiana), the results being published under the title *Middletown* in 1929. This was followed by many similar studies of American attitudes, behavior patterns, and social organization, the findings of which were often surprising and disconcerting to complacent citizens.

By the 1950's considerable progress had been made towards a comprehensive interpretation of American culture patterns, with significant contributions from many different sources. As a result of the work of historians and political scientists, sociologists and economists, public-opinion analysts and students of social and clinical psychology, Americans now knew more about themselves than any other people in history. If knowledge alone could solve social problems, they could look forward to their future with optimism.

7. CONCLUSION

KNOWLEDGE was essential, but plainly it was not sufficient. Continued progress depended also on sound values and a willingness to live by them, not only among the groups to which society looked for guidance but also among the mass of the population. The United States had staked her destiny on the proposition that the people as a whole, and not merely a ruling elite, had enough wisdom to determine the policies of their government and that (in the words of Justice Holmes) "the ultimate good desired is better reached by free trade in ideas" than by persecution of unpopular opinions and enforced conformity. After more than a century and a half of government under the Constitution the success of the experiment was still not assured. Democracy could not be regarded as firmly established in a country where nearly half the adult population did not even take the trouble to vote in presidential elections; and continuing attempts to limit free speech and compel teachers and other opinion-makers to express only conservative views showed that many Americans did not believe in free trade in ideas. It was probable, moreover, that the most decisive tests were still ahead.

The first half of the twentieth century had been a period of crises on a scale unprecedented in human history, and the second half might well prove to be even more turbulent and momentous and possibly even more catastrophic. The growth of the sciences had given mankind almost limitless powers for either good or evil; and both the destruction of all civilization and the creation of a world which earlier generations would have regarded as utopian were well within human capacity. The fate of mankind now depended largely on the people of the United States, who, after seeking throughout their history primarily to make a better life for themselves, were now required to assume the unwelcome responsibilities of leadership in a civilization that had become world-wide. It was impossible for them to regard the future without anxiety. But if they looked back over the amazing story of their own past development, seeing how their society had evolved from the first small settlements of the seventeenth century into the world power of the twentieth, and how one advance after another had been made through faith in the principles of freedom and the exercise of idealism, intelligence, and good will, they could feel confident that the problems ahead of them were capable of solution. As long as Americans retained the pioneering, enterprising, and adventurous spirit that had made them a great people, and as long as they continued to display this spirit both in solving material problems and in adapting their institutions and ideas to meet the challenge of new conditions, they had no valid cause for fear.

APPENDIX I

The Declaration of Independence

W HEN, in the course of human events, it becomes necessary for one people to dissolve the political bands which have connected them with another, and to assume, among the powers of the earth, the separate and equal station to which the laws of nature and of nature's God entitle them, a decent respect to the opinions of mankind requires that they should declare the causes which impel them to the separation.

We hold these truths to be self-evident, that all men are created equal; that they are endowed by their Creator with certain unalienable rights; that among these, are life, liberty, and the pursuit of happiness. That, to secure these rights, governments are instituted among men, deriving their just powers from the consent of the governed; that, whenever any form of government becomes destructive of these ends, it is the right of the people to alter or to abolish it, and to institute a new government, laying its foundation on such principles, and organizing its powers in such form, as to them shall seem most likely to effect their safety and happiness. Prudence, indeed, will dictate that governments long established, should not be changed for light and transient causes; and, accordingly, all experience hath shown, that mankind are more disposed to suffer, while evils are sufferable, than to right themselves by abolishing the forms to which they are accustomed. But, when a long train of abuses and usurpations, pursuing invariably the same object, evinces a design to reduce them under absolute despotism, it is their right, it is their duty, to throw off such government and to provide new guards for their future security. Such has been the patient sufferance of these colonies, and such is now the necessity which constrains them to alter their former systems of government. The history of the present King of Great Britain is a history of repeated injuries and usurpations, all having, in direct object, the establishment of an absolute tyranny over these States. To prove this, let facts be submitted to a candid world:—

He has refused his assent to laws the most wholesome and necessary for the public good.

He has forbidden his governors to pass laws of immediate and pressing importance, unless suspended in their operation till his assent should be obtained; and, when so suspended, he has utterly neglected to attend to them.

He has refused to pass other laws for the accommodation of large districts of people, unless those people would relinquish the right of representation in the legislature: a right inestimable to them, and formidable to tyrants only.

He has called together legislative bodies at places unusual, uncomfortable, and distant from the depository of their public records, for the sole purpose of fatiguing them into compliance with his measures.

He has dissolved representative houses repeatedly for opposing, with manly firmness, his invasions on the rights of the people.

He has refused, for a long time after such dissolutions, to cause others to be elected; whereby the legislative powers, incapable of annihilation, have returned to the people at large for their exercise; the state remaining, in the meantime, exposed to all the danger of invasion from without, and convulsions within.

He has endeavored to prevent the population of these States; for that purpose, obstructing the laws for naturalization of foreigners, refusing to pass others to encourage their migration hither, and raising the conditions of new appropriations of lands.

He has obstructed the administration of justice, by refusing his assent to laws for establishing judiciary powers.

He has made judges dependent on his will alone, for the tenure of their offices, and the amount and payment of their salaries.

He has erected a multitude of new offices, and sent hither swarms of officers to harass our people, and eat out their substance.

He has kept among us, in time of peace, standing armies, without the consent of our legislatures.

He has affected to render the military independent of, and superior to, the civil power.

He has combined, with others, to subject us to a jurisdiction foreign to our Constitution, and unacknowledged by our laws; giving his assent to their acts of pretended legislation:

For quartering large bodies of armed troops among us:

For protecting them by a mock trial, from punishment, for any murders which they should commit on the inhabitants of these States:

For cutting off our trade with all parts of the world:

For imposing taxes on us without our consent:

For depriving us, in many cases, of the benefit of trial by jury:

For transporting us beyond seas to be tried for pretended offences:

For abolishing the free system of English laws in a neighboring province, establishing therein an arbitrary government, and enlarging its boundaries, so as to render it at once an example and fit instrument for introducing the same absolute rule into these colonies:

For taking away our charters, abolishing our most valuable laws, and altering, fundamentally, the powers of our governments:

For suspending our own legislatures, and declaring themselves invested with power to legislate for us in all cases whatsoever.

He has abdicated government here, by declaring us out of his protection, and waging war against us.

He has plundered our seas, ravaged our coasts, burnt our towns, and destroyed the lives of our people.

He is, at this time, transporting large armies of foreign mercenaries to complete the works of death, desolation, and tyranny, already begun, with circumstances of cruelty and perfidy scarcely paralleled in the most barbarous ages, and totally unworthy the head of a civilized nation.

He has constrained our fellow citizens, taken captive on the high seas, to bear arms against their country, to become the executioners of their friends, and brethren, or to fall themselves by their hands.

He has excited domestic insurrections amongst us, and has endeavored to bring on the inhabitants of our frontiers, the merciless Indian savages, whose known rule of warfare is an undistinguished destruction of all ages, sexes, and conditions.

In every stage of these oppressions, we have petitioned for redress, in the most humble terms; our repeated petitions have been answered only by repeated injury. A prince, whose character is thus marked by every act which may define a tyrant, is unfit to be the ruler of a free people.

Nor have we been wanting in attention to our British brethren. We have warned them, from time to time, of attempts made by their legislature to extend an unwarrantable jurisdiction over us. We have reminded them of the circumstances of our emigration and settlement here. We have appealed to their native justice and magnanimity, and we have conjured them, by the ties of our common kindred, to disavow these usurpations, which would inevitably interrupt our connections and correspondence. They, too, have been deaf to the voice of justice and consanguinity. We must, therefore, acquiesce in the necessity which denounces our separation, and hold them, as we hold the rest of mankind, enemies in war, in peace, friends.

We, therefore, the representatives of the United States of America, in general Congress assembled, appealing to the Supreme Judge of the world for the rectitude of our intentions, do, in the name, and by the authority of the good people of these colonies, solemnly publish and declare, that these united colonies are, and of right ought to be, free and independent states: that they are absolved from all allegiance to the British Crown, and that all political connection between them and the state of Great Britain is, and ought to be, totally dissolved; and that, as free and independent states, they have full power to levy war, conclude peace, contract alliances, establish commerce, and to do all other acts and things which independent states may of right do. And, for the support of this declaration, with a firm reliance on the protection of Divine Providence, we mutually pledge to each other our lives, our fortunes, and our sacred honor.

APPENDIX II

The Constitution of the United States of America

Preamble to the Constitution

WE THE people of the United States, in order to form a more perfect union, establish justice, insure domestic tranquillity, provide for the common defense, promote the general welfare, and secure the blessings of liberty to ourselves and our posterity, do ordain and establish this Constitution for the United States of America. *6 MAIN Parts*

ARTICLE I

SECTION 1. All legislative powers herein granted shall be vested in a Congress of the United States, which shall consist of a Senate and House of Representatives.

SECTION 2. 1. The House of Representatives shall be composed of members chosen every second year by the people of the several States, and the electors in each State shall have the qualifications requisite for electors of the most numerous branch of the State legislature.

2. No person shall be a representative who shall not have attained to the age of twenty-five years, and been seven years a citizen of the United States, and who shall not, when elected, be an inhabitant of that State in which he shall be chosen.

3. Representatives and direct taxes [1] shall be apportioned among the several States which may be included within this Union, according to their respective numbers, which shall be determined by adding to the whole number of free persons, including those bound to service for a term of years, and excluding Indians not taxed, *three fifths of all other persons*.[2] The actual enumeration shall be made within three years after the first meeting of the Congress of the United States, and

[1] See the 16th Amendment.
[2] See the 14th Amendment.

within every subsequent term of ten years, in such manner as they shall by law direct. The number of representatives shall not exceed one for every thirty thousand, but each State shall have at least one representative; and until such enumeration shall be made, the State of New Hampshire shall be entitled to choose three, Massachusetts eight, Rhode Island and Providence Plantations one, Connecticut five, New York six, New Jersey four, Pennsylvania eight, Delaware one, Maryland six, Virginia ten, North Carolina five, South Carolina five, and Georgia three.

4. When vacancies happen in the representation from any State, the executive authority thereof shall issue writs of election to fill such vacancies.

5. The House of Representatives shall choose their speaker and other officers; and shall have the sole power of impeachment.

SECTION 3. 1. The Senate of the United States shall be composed of two senators from each State, *chosen by the legislature thereof*,[1] for six years; and each senator shall have one vote.

2. Immediately after they shall be assembled in consequence of the first election, they shall be divided as equally as may be into three classes. The seats of the senators of the first class shall be vacated at the expiration of the second year, of the second class at the expiration of the fourth year, and of the third class at the expiration of the sixth year, so that one third may be chosen every second year; and if vacancies happen by resignation, or otherwise, during the recess of the legislature of any State, the executive thereof may make temporary appointments until the next meeting of the legislature, which shall then fill such vacancies.

3. No person shall be a senator who shall not have attained to the age of thirty years, and been nine years a citizen of the United States, and who shall not when elected, be an inhabitant of that State for which he shall be chosen.

4. The Vice President of the United States shall be President of the Senate, but shall have no vote, unless they be equally divided.

5. The Senate shall choose their other officers, and also a president *pro tempore*, in the absence of the Vice President, or when he shall exercise the office of the President of the United States.

6. The Senate shall have the sole power to try all impeachments. When sitting for that purpose, they shall be on oath or affirmation. When the President of the United States is tried, the chief justice shall preside: and no person shall be convicted without the concurrence of two thirds of the members present.

7. Judgment in cases of impeachment shall not extend further than to removal from office, and disqualifications to hold and enjoy any office of honor, trust or profit under the United States: but the party convicted shall nevertheless be liable and subject to indictment, trial, judgment and punishment, according to law.

SECTION 4. 1. The times, places, and manner of holding elections for senators and representatives, shall be prescribed in each State by the legislature thereof; but the Congress may at any time by law make or alter such regulations, except as to the places of choosing senators.

2. The Congress shall assemble at least once in every year, and such meeting shall be on the first Monday in December, unless they shall by law appoint a different day.

SECTION 5. 1. Each House shall be the judge of the elections, returns and qualifications of its own members, and a majority of each shall constitute a quorum

[1] See the 17th Amendment.

to do business; but a smaller number may adjourn from day to day, and may be authorized to compel the attendance of absent members, in such manner, and under such penalties as each House may provide.

2. Each House may determined the rules of its proceedings, punish its members for disorderly behavior, and, with the concurrence of two thirds, expel a member.

3. Each House shall keep a journal of its proceedings, and from time to time publish the same, excepting such parts as may in their judgment require secrecy; and the yeas and nays of the members of either House on any question shall, at the desire of one fifth of those present, be entered on the journal.

4. Neither House, during the session of Congress, shall, without the consent of the other, adjourn for more than three days, nor to any other place than that in which the two Houses shall be sitting.

Section 6. 1. The Senators and Representatives shall receive a Compensation for their Services, to be ascertained by Law, and paid out of the Treasury of the United States. They shall in all Cases, except Treason, Felony, and Breach of the Peace, be privileged from Arrest during their Attendance at the Session of their respective Houses, and in going to and returning from the same; and for any Speech or Debate in either House, they shall not be questioned in any other Place.

2. No Senator or Representative shall, during the Time for which he was elected, be appointed to any civil Office under the Authority of the United States, which shall have been created, or the Emoluments whereof shall have been increased, during such time; and no Person holding any Office under the United States shall be a Member of either House during his continuance in Office.

Section 7. 1. All Bills for raising Revenue shall originate in the House of Representatives; but the Senate may propose or concur with Amendments as on other bills.

2. Every Bill which shall have passed the House of Representatives and the Senate, shall, before it become a Law, be presented to the President of the United States; If he approve he shall sign it, but if not he shall return it, with his Objections, to that House in which it shall have originated, who shall enter the Objections at large on their Journal, and proceed to reconsider it. If after such Reconsideration two thirds of that House shall agree to pass the bill, it shall be sent, together with the objections, to the other House, by which it shall likewise be reconsidered, and if approved by two thirds of that House, it shall become a Law. But in all such Cases the Votes of both Houses shall be determined by Yeas and Nays, and the Names of the Persons voting for and against the Bill shall be entered on the Journal of each House respectively. If any Bill shall not be returned by the President within ten Days (Sundays excepted) after it shall have been presented to him, the Same shall be a Law, in like Manner as if he had signed it, unless the Congress by their Adjournment prevent its Return, in which Case it shall not be a Law.

3. Every Order, Resolution, or Vote to which the Concurrence of the Senate and House of Representatives may be necessary (except on a question of Adjournment) shall be presented to the President of the United States; and before the Same shall take Effect, shall be approved by him, or being disapproved by him, shall be repassed by two thirds of the Senate and House of Representatives, according to the rules and limitations prescribed in the case of a bill.

SECTION 8. The Congress shall have the power

1. To lay and collect taxes, duties, imposts, and excises, to pay the debts and provide for the common defense and general welfare of the United States; but all duties, imposts, and excises shall be uniform throughout the United States;

2. To borrow money on the credit of the United States;

3. To regulate commerce with foreign nations, and among the several States, and with the Indian tribes;

4. To establish a uniform rule of naturalization, and uniform laws on the subject of bankruptcies throughout the United States;

5. To coin money, regulate the value thereof, and of foreign coin, and fix the standard of weights and measures;

6. To provide for the punishment of counterfeiting the securities and current coin of the United States;

7. To establish post offices and post roads;

8. To promote the progress of science and useful arts, by securing for limited times to authors and inventors the exclusive right to their respective writings and discoveries;

9. To constitute tribunals inferior to the Supreme Court;

10. To define and punish piracies and felonies committed on the high seas, and offenses against the law of nations;

11. To declare war, grant letters of marque and reprisal, and make rules concerning captures on land and water;

12. To raise and support armies, but no appropriation of money to that use shall be for a longer term than two years;

13. To provide and maintain a navy;

14. To make rules for the government and regulation of the land and naval forces;

15. To provide for calling forth the militia to execute the laws of the Union, suppress insurrections and repel invasions;

16. To provide for organizing, arming, and disciplining the militia, and for governing such part of them as may be employed in the service of the United States, reserving to the States respectively, the appointment of the officers, and the authority of training the militia according to the discipline prescribed by Congress;

17. To exercise exclusive legislation in all cases whatsoever, over such district (not exceeding ten miles square) as may, by cession of particular States, and the acceptance of Congress, become the seat of the government of the United States, and to exercise like authority over all places purchased by the consent of the legislature of the State in which the same shall be, for the erection of forts, magazines, arsenals, dockyards, and other needful buildings; and

18. To make all laws which shall be necessary and proper for carrying into execution the foregoing powers, and all other powers vested by this Constitution in the government of the United States, or in any department or officer thereof.

SECTION 9. 1. The migration or importation of such persons as any of the States now existing shall think proper to admit, shall not be prohibited by the Congress prior to the year one thousand eight hundred and eight, but a tax or duty may be imposed on such importation, not exceeding ten dollars for each person.

2. The privilege of the writ of *habeas corpus* shall not be suspended, unless when in cases of rebellion or invasion the public safety may require it.

3. No bill of attainder or *ex post facto* law shall be passed.

4. No capitation, or other direct, tax shall be laid, unless in proportion to the census or enumeration hereinbefore directed to be taken.[1]

5. No tax or duty shall be laid on articles exported from any State.

6. No preference shall be given by any regulation of commerce or revenue to the ports of one State over those of another: nor shall vessels bound to, or from, one State be obliged to enter, clear, or pay duties in another.

7. No money shall be drawn from the treasury, but in consequence of appropriations made by law; and a regular statement and account of the receipts and expenditures of all public money shall be published from time to time.

8. No title of nobility shall be granted by the United States: and no person holding any office of profit or trust under them, shall, without the consent of the Congress, accept of any present, emolument, office, or title, of any kind whatever, from any king, prince, or foreign State.

SECTION 10. 1. No State shall enter into any treaty, alliance, or confederation; grant letters of marque and reprisal; coin money; emit bills of credit; make anything but gold and silver coin a tender in payment of debts; pass any bill of attainder, *ex post facto* law, or law impairing the obligation of contracts, or grant any title of nobility.

2. No State shall, without the consent of the Congress, lay any imposts or duties on imports or exports, except what may be absolutely necessary for executing its inspection laws: and the net produce of all duties and imposts laid by any State on imports or exports, shall be for the use of the treasury of the United States; and all such laws shall be subject to the revision and control of the Congress.

3. No State shall, without the consent of the Congress, lay any duty of tonnage, keep troops, or ships of war in time of peace, enter into any agreement or compact with another State, or with a foreign power, or engage in war, unless actually invaded, or in such imminent danger as will not admit of delay.

ARTICLE II

SECTION 1. 1. The executive power shall be vested in a President of the United States of America. He shall hold his office during the term of four years, and, together with the Vice President, chosen for the same term, be elected as follows:

2. Each State shall appoint, in such manner as the legislature thereof may direct, a number of electors, equal to the whole number of senators and representatives to which the State may be entitled in the Congress: but no senator or representative, or person holding an office of trust or profit under the United States, shall be appointed an elector.

The electors shall meet in their respective States, and vote by ballot for two persons, of whom one at least shall not be an inhabitant of the same State with themselves. And they shall make a list of all the persons voted for, and of the number of votes for each; which list they shall sign and certify, and transmit sealed to the seat of the government of the United States, directed to the president of the Senate. The president of the Senate shall, in the presence of the Senate and House

[1] See the 16th Amendment.

of Representatives, open all the certificates, and the votes shall then be counted. The person having the greatest number of votes shall be the President, if such number be a majority of the whole number of electors appointed; and if there be more than one who have such majority, and have an equal number of votes, then the House of Representatives shall immediately choose by ballot one of them for President; and if no person have a majority, then from the five highest on the list the said House shall in like manner choose the President. But in choosing the President, the votes shall be taken by States, the representation from each State having one vote; a quorum for this purpose shall consist of a member or members from two thirds of the States, and a majority of all the States shall be necessary to a choice. In every case, after the choice of the President, the person having the greatest number of votes of the electors shall be the Vice President. But if there should remain two or more who have equal votes, the Senate shall choose from them by ballot the Vice President.[1]

3. The Congress may determine the time of choosing the electors, and the day on which they shall give their votes; which day shall be the same throughout the United States.

4. No person except a natural born citizen, or a citizen of the United States, at the time of the adoption of this Constitution, shall be eligible to the office of President; neither shall any person be eligible to that office who shall not have attained to the age of thirty-five years, and been fourteen years a resident within the United States.

5. In case of the removal of the President from office, or of his death, resignation, or inability to discharge the powers and duties of the said office, the same shall devolve on the Vice President, and the Congress may by law provide for the case of removal, death, resignation, or inability, both of the President and Vice President, declaring what officer shall then act as President, and such officer shall act accordingly, until the disability be removed, or a President shall be elected.

6. The President shall, at stated times, receive for his services a compensation, which shall neither be increased nor diminished during the period for which he shall have been elected, and he shall not receive within that period any other emolument from the United States, or any of them.

7. Before he enter on the execution of his office, he shall take the following oath or affirmation:—"I do solemnly swear (or affirm) that I will faithfully execute the office of President of the United States, and will to the best of my ability, preserve, protect and defend the Constitution of the United States."

Section 2. 1. The President shall be commander in chief of the army and navy of the United States, and of the militia of the several States, when called into the actual service of the United States; he may require the opinion, in writing, of the principal officer in each of the executive departments, upon any subject relating to the duties of their respective offices, and he shall have power to grant reprieves and pardons for offenses against the United States, except in cases of impeachment.

2. He shall have power, by and with the advice and consent of the Senate, to make treaties, provided two thirds of the senators present concur; and he shall nominate, and by and with the advice and consent of the Senate, shall appoint ambassadors, other public ministers and consuls, judges of the Supreme Court, and all other officers of the United States, whose appointments are not herein

[1] Superseded by the 12th Amendment.

otherwise provided for, and which shall be established by law: but the Congress may by law vest the appointment of such inferior officers, as they think proper, in the President alone, in the courts of law, or in the heads of departments.

3. The President shall have power to fill up all vacancies that may happen during the recess of the Senate, by granting commissions which shall expire at the end of their next session.

SECTION 3. He shall from time to time give to the Congress information of the state of the Union, and recommend to their consideration such measures as he shall judge necessary and expedient; he may, on extraordinary occasions, convene both Houses, or either of them, and in case of disagreement between them with respect to the time of adjournment, he may adjourn them to such time as he shall think proper; he shall receive ambassadors and other public ministers; he shall take care that the laws be faithfully executed, and shall commission all the officers of the United States.

SECTION 4. The President, Vice President, and all civil officers of the United States, shall be removed from office on impeachment for, and conviction of, treason, bribery, or other high crimes and misdemeanors.

ARTICLE III

SECTION 1. The judicial power of the United States shall be vested in one Supreme Court, and in such inferior courts as the Congress may from time to time ordain and establish. The judges, both of the Supreme and inferior courts, shall hold their offices during good behavior, and shall, at stated times, receive for their services, a compensation, which shall not be diminished during their continuance in office.

SECTION 2. 1. The judicial power shall extend to all cases, in law and equity, arising under this Constitution, the laws of the United States, and treaties made, or which shall be made, under their authority;—to all cases affecting ambassadors, other public ministers and consuls;—to all cases of admiralty and maritime jurisdiction;—to controversies to which the United States shall be a party;—to controversies between two or more States;—between a State and citizens of another State; [1]—between citizens of different States;—between citizens of the same State claiming lands under grants of different States, and between a State, or the citizens thereof, and foreign States, citizens or subjects.

2. In all cases affecting ambassadors, other public ministers and consuls, and those in which a State shall be party, the Supreme Court shall have original jurisdiction. In all the other cases before mentioned, the Supreme Court shall have appellate jurisdiction, both as to law and to fact, with such exceptions, and under such regulations as the Congress shall make.

3. The trial of all crimes, except in cases of impeachment, shall be by jury; and such trial shall be held in the State where the said crimes shall have been committed; but when not committed within any State, the trial shall be at such place or places as the Congress may by law have directed.

SECTION 3. 1. Treason against the United States shall consist only in levying war against them, or in adhering to their enemies, giving them aid and comfort. No person shall be convicted of treason unless on the testimony of two witnesses to the same overt act, or on confession in open court.

[1] See the 11th Amendment.

2. The Congress shall have power to declare the punishment of treason, but no attainder of treason shall work corruption of blood, or forfeiture except during the life of the person attained.

ARTICLE IV

SECTION 1. Full faith and credit shall be given in each State to the public acts, records, and judicial proceedings of every other State. And the Congress may by general laws prescribe the manner in which such acts, records and proceedings shall be proved, and the effect thereof.

SECTION 2. 1. The citizens of each State shall be entitled to all privileges and immunities of citizens in the several States.[1]

2. A person charged in any State with treason, felony, or other crime, who shall flee from justice, and be found in another State, shall on demand of the executive authority of the State from which he fled, be delivered up to be removed to the State having jurisdiction of the crime.

3. No person held to service or labor in one State under the laws thereof, escaping into another, shall, in consequence of any law or regulation therein, be discharged from such service or labor, but shall be delivered up on claim of the party to whom such service or labor may be due.[2]

SECTION 3. 1. New States may be admitted by the Congress into this Union; but no new State shall be formed or erected within the jurisdiction of any other State; nor any State be formed by the junction of two or more States, or parts of States, without the consent of the legislatures of the States concerned as well as of the Congress.

2. The Congress shall have power to dispose of and make all needful rules and regulations respecting the territory or other property belonging to the United States; and nothing in this Constitution shall be so construed as to prejudice any claims of the United States, or of any particular State.

SECTION 4. The United States shall guarantee to every State in this Union a republican form of government, and shall protect each of them against invasion; and on application of the legislature, or of the executive (when the legislature cannot be convened) against domestic violence.

ARTICLE V

The Congress, whenever two thirds of both Houses shall deem it necessary, shall propose amendments to this Constitution, or, on the application of the legislatures of two thirds of the several States, shall call a convention for proposing amendments, which in either case, shall be valid to all intents and purposes, as part of this Constitution when ratified by the legislatures of three fourths of the several States, or by conventions in three fourths thereof, as the one or the other mode of ratification may be proposed by the Congress; Provided that no amendment which may be made prior to the year one thousand eight hundred and eight shall in any manner affect the first and fourth clauses in the ninth section of the first article; and that no State, without its consent, shall be deprived of its equal suffrage in the Senate.

[1] See the 14th Amendment, Sec. 1.
[2] See the 13th Amendment.

ARTICLE VI

1. All debts contracted and engagements entered into, before the adoption of this Constitution, shall be as valid against the United States under this Constitution, as under the Confederation.[1]

2. This Constitution, and the laws of the United States which shall be made in pursuance thereof; and all treaties made, or which shall be made, under the authority of the United States, shall be the supreme law of the land; and the Judges in every State shall be bound thereby, anything in the Constitution or laws of any State to the contrary notwithstanding.

3. The senators and representatives before mentioned, and the members of the several State legislatures, and all executive and judicial officers, both of the United States and of the several States, shall be bound by oath or affirmation to support this Constitution; but no religious test shall ever be required as a qualification to any office or public trust under the United States.

ARTICLE VII

The ratification of the conventions of nine States shall be sufficient for the establishment of this Constitution between the States so ratifying the same.

Done in Convention by the unanimous consent of the States present the seventeenth day of September in the year of our Lord one thousand seven hundred and eighty-seven, and of the independence of the United States of America the twelfth. In witness whereof we have hereunto subscribed our names.

[Names omitted]

* * *

Articles in addition to, and amendment of, the Constitution of the United States of America, proposed by Congress, and ratified by the legislatures of the several States pursuant to the fifth article of the original Constitution.

Amendments

FIRST TEN AMENDMENTS PASSED BY CONGRESS SEPT. 25, 1789.
RATIFIED BY THREE-FOURTHS OF THE STATES DECEMBER 15, 1791.

ARTICLE I

Congress shall make no law respecting an establishment of religion, or prohibiting the free exercise thereof; or abridging the freedom of speech, or of the press; or the right of the people peaceably to assemble, and to petition the government for a redress of grievances.

ARTICLE II

A well regulated militia, being necessary to the security of a free State, the right of the people to keep and bear arms, shall not be infringed.

[1] See the 14th Amendment, Sec. 4.

ARTICLE III

No soldier shall, in time of peace be quartered in any house, without the consent of the owner, nor in time of war, but in a manner to be prescribed by law.

ARTICLE IV

The right of the people to be secure in their persons, houses, papers, and effects, against unreasonable searches and seizures, shall not be violated, and no warrants shall issue, but upon probable cause, supported by oath or affirmation, and particularly describing the place to be searched, and the persons or things to be seized.

ARTICLE V

No person shall be held to answer for a capital, or otherwise infamous crime, unless on a presentment or indictment of a grand jury, except in cases arising in the land or naval forces, or in the militia, when in actual service in time of war or public danger; nor shall any person be subject for the same offense to be twice put in jeopardy of life or limb; nor shall be compelled in any criminal case to be a witness against himself, nor be deprived of life, liberty, or property, without due process of law; nor shall private property be taken for public use without just compensation.

ARTICLE VI

In all criminal prosecutions, the accused shall enjoy the right to a speedy and public trial, by an impartial jury of the State and district wherein the crime shall have been committed, which district shall have been previously ascertained by law, and to be informed of the nature and cause of the accusation; to be confronted with the witnesses against him; to have compulsory process for obtaining witnesses in his favor, and to have the assistance of counsel for his defense.

ARTICLE VII

In suits at common law, where the value in controversy shall exceed twenty dollars, the right of trial by jury shall be preserved, and no fact tried by a jury shall be otherwise reëxamined in any court of the United States, than according to the rules of the common law.

ARTICLE VIII

Excessive bail shall not be required, nor excessive fines imposed, nor cruel and unusual punishments inflicted.

ARTICLE IX

The enumeration in the Constitution of certain rights shall not be construed to deny or disparage others retained by the people.

ARTICLE X

The powers not delegated to the United States by the Constitution, nor prohibited by it to the States, are reserved to the States respectively, or to the people.

ARTICLE XI

PASSED BY CONGRESS MARCH 5, 1794. RATIFIED JANUARY 8, 1798.

The judicial power of the United States shall not be construed to extend to any suit in law or equity, commenced or prosecuted against one of the United States by citizens of another State, or by citizens or subjects of any foreign State.

ARTICLE XII

PASSED BY CONGRESS DECEMBER 12, 1803. RATIFIED SEPTEMBER 25, 1804.

The electors shall meet in their respective States, and vote by ballot for President and Vice President, one of whom, at least, shall not be an inhabitant of the same State with themselves; they shall name in their ballots the person voted for as President, and in distinct ballots the person voted for as Vice President, and they shall make distinct lists of all persons voted for as President and of all persons voted for as Vice President, and of the number of votes for each, which lists they shall sign and certify, and transmit sealed to the seat of the government of the United States, directed to the President of the Senate;—The President of the Senate shall, in the presence of the Senate and House of Representatives, open all the certificates and the votes shall then be counted;—The person having the greatest number of votes for President, shall be the President, if such number be a majority of the whole number of electors appointed; and if no person have such majority, then from the persons having the highest numbers not exceeding three on the list of those voted for as President, the House of Representatives shall choose immediately, by ballot, the President. But in choosing the President, the votes shall be taken by States, the representation from each State having one vote; a quorum for this purpose shall consist of a member or members from two thirds of the States, and a majority of all the States shall be necessary to a choice. And if the House of Representatives shall not choose a President whenever the right of choice shall devolve upon them, before the fourth day of March next following, then the Vice President shall act as President, as in the case of the death or other constitutional disability of the President. The person having the greatest number of votes as Vice President shall be the Vice President, if such number be a majority of the whole number of electors appointed, and if no person have a majority, then from the two highest numbers on the list, the Senate shall choose the Vice President; a quorum for the purpose shall consist of two thirds of the whole number of Senators, and a majority of the whole number shall be necessary to a choice. But no person constitutionally ineligible to the office of President shall be eligible to that of Vice President of the United States.

ARTICLE XIII

PASSED BY CONGRESS FEBRUARY 1, 1865. RATIFIED DECEMBER 18, 1865.

SECTION 1. Neither slavery nor involuntary servitude, except as punishment for crime whereof the party shall have been duly convicted, shall exist within the United States, or any place subject to their jurisdiction.

Section 2. Congress shall have power to enforce this article by appropriate legislation.

ARTICLE XIV
PASSED BY CONGRESS JUNE 16, 1866. RATIFIED JULY 23, 1868.

Section 1. All persons born or naturalized in the United States, and subject to the jurisdiction thereof, are citizens of the United States and of the State wherein they reside. No State shall make or enforce any law which shall abridge the privileges or immunities of citizens of the United States; nor shall any State deprive any person of life, liberty, or property, without due process of law; nor deny to any person within its jurisdiction the equal protection of the laws.

Section 2. Representatives shall be apportioned among the several States according to their respective numbers, counting the whole number of persons in each State, excluding Indians not taxed. But when the right to vote at any election for the choice of electors for President and Vice President of the United States, representatives in Congress, the executive and judicial officers of a State, or the members of the legislature thereof, is denied to any of the male inhabitants of such State, being twenty-one years of age, and citizens of the United States, or in any way abridged, except for participation in rebellion, or other crime, the basis of representation therein shall be reduced in the proportion which the number of such male citizens shall bear to the whole number of male citizens twenty-one years of age in such State.

Section 3. No person shall be a senator or representative in Congress, or elector of President and Vice President, or hold any office, civil or military, under the United States, or under any State, who having previously taken an oath, as a member of Congress, or as an officer of the United States, or as a member of any State legislature, or as an executive or judicial officer of any State, to support the Constitution of the United States, shall have engaged in insurrection or rebellion against the same, or given aid or comfort to the enemies thereof. But Congress may by a vote of two thirds of each House, remove such disability.

Section 4. The validity of the public debt of the United States, authorized by law, including debts incurred for payment of pensions and bounties for services in suppressing insurrection or rebellion, shall not be questioned. But neither the United States nor any State shall assume or pay any debt or obligation incurred in aid of insurrection or rebellion against the United States, or any claim for the loss or emancipation of any slave; but all such debts, obligations, and claims shall be held illegal and void.

Section 5. The Congress shall have power to enforce, by appropriate legislation, the provisions of this article.

ARTICLE XV
PASSED BY CONGRESS FEBRUARY 27, 1869. RATIFIED MARCH 30, 1870.

Section 1. The right of citizens of the United States to vote shall not be denied or abridged by the United States or by any State on account of race, color, or previous condition of servitude.

Section 2. The Congress shall have power to enforce this article by appropriate legislation.

ARTICLE XVI
PASSED BY CONGRESS JULY 12, 1909 RATIFIED FEBRUARY 25, 1913.

The Congress shall have power to lay and collect taxes on incomes, from whatever source derived, without apportionment among the several States, and without regard to any census or enumeration.

ARTICLE XVII
PASSED BY CONGRESS MAY 16, 1912. RATIFIED MAY 31, 1913.

The Senate of the United States shall be composed of two senators from each state, elected by the people thereof, for six years; and each senator shall have one vote. The electors in each State shall have the qualifications requisite for electors of the most numerous branch of the State legislature.

When vacancies happen in the representation of any State in the Senate, the executive authority of such State shall issue writs of election to fill such vacancies: *Provided,* That the legislature of any State may empower the executive thereof to make temporary appointments until the people fill the vacancies by election as the legislature may direct.

This amendment shall not be so construed as to affect the election or term of any senator chosen before it becomes valid as part of the Constitution.

ARTICLE XVIII
PASSED BY CONGRESS DECEMBER 17, 1917. RATIFIED JANUARY 29, 1919.

After one year from the ratification of this article, the manufacture, sale, or transportation of intoxicating liquors within, the importation thereof into, or the exportation thereof from the United States and all territory subject to the jurisdiction thereof for beverage purposes is hereby prohibited.

The Congress and the several States shall have concurrent power to enforce this article by appropriate legislation.

This article shall be inoperative unless it shall have been ratified as an amendment to the Constitution by the legislatures of the several States, as provided in the Constitution, within seven years from the date of the submission hereof to the states by Congress.

ARTICLE XIX
PASSED BY CONGRESS JUNE 5, 1919. RATIFIED AUGUST 26, 1920.

The right of citizens of the United States to vote shall not be denied or abridged by the United States or by any State on account of sex.

The Congress shall have power by appropriate legislation to enforce the provisions of this article.

ARTICLE XX
PASSED BY CONGRESS MARCH 3, 1932. RATIFIED JANUARY 23, 1933.

SECTION 1. The terms of the President and Vice President shall end at noon on the 20th day of January, and the terms of Senators and Representatives at noon on the 3d day of January, of the years in which such terms would have ended if this article had not been ratified; and the terms of their successors shall then begin.

SECTION 2. The Congress shall assemble at least once in every year, and such meeting shall begin at noon on the 3d day of January, unless they shall by law appoint a different day.

SECTION 3. If, at the time fixed for the beginning of the term of the President, the President-elect shall have died, the Vice President-elect shall become President. If a President shall not have been chosen before the time fixed for the beginning of his term, or if the President-elect shall have failed to qualify, then the Vice President-elect shall act as President until a President shall have qualified; and the Congress may by law provide for the case wherein neither a President-elect nor a Vice President-elect shall have qualified, declaring who shall then act as President, or the manner in which one who is to act shall be selected, and such person shall act accordingly until a President or Vice President shall have qualified.

SECTION 4. The Congress may by law provide for the case of the death of any of the persons from whom the House of Representatives may choose a President whenever the right of choice shall have devolved upon them, and for the case of the death of any of the persons from whom the Senate may choose a Vice President whenever the right of choice shall have devolved upon them.

SECTION 5. Sections 1 and 2 shall take effect on the 15th day of October following the ratification of this article.

SECTION 6. This article shall be inoperative unless it shall have been ratified as an amendment to the Constitution by the legislatures of three-fourths of the several States within seven years from the date of its submission.

ARTICLE XXI

PASSED BY CONGRESS FEBRUARY 20, 1933. RATIFIED DECEMBER 5, 1933.

SECTION 1. The Eighteenth Article of amendment to the Constitution of the United States is hereby repealed.

SECTION 2. The transportation or importation into any State, Territory, or possession of the United States for delivery or use therein of intoxicating liquors in violation of the laws thereof, is hereby prohibited.

SECTION 3. This article shall be inoperative unless it shall have been ratified as an amendment to the Constitution by conventions in the several States, as provided in the Constitution, within seven years from the date of the submission thereof to the States by the Congress.

ARTICLE XXII

PASSED BY CONGRESS MARCH 12, 1947. RATIFIED FEBRUARY 26, 1951.

No person shall be elected to the office of the President more than twice, and no person who has held the office of President, or acted as President, for more than two years of a term to which some other person was elected President shall be elected to the office of the President more than once.

But this article shall not apply to any person holding the office of President when this article was proposed by the Congress, and shall not prevent any person who may be holding the office of President, or acting as President, during the term within which this article becomes operative from holding the office of President or acting as President during the remainder of such term.

This article shall be inoperative unless it shall have been ratified as an amendment to the Constitution by the legislatures of three-fourths of the several states within seven years from the date of its submission to the states by the Congress.

TABLE I

Admission of States to the Union

STATE	ENTERED UNION	STATE	ENTERED UNION
Alabama	1819	Nebraska	1867
Alaska	1959	Nevada	1864
Arizona	1912	New Hampshire	1788
Arkansas	1836	New Jersey	1787
California	1850	New Mexico	1912
Colorado	1876	New York	1788
Connecticut	1788	North Carolina	1789
Delaware	1787	North Dakota	1889
Florida	1845	Ohio	1803
Georgia	1788	Oklahoma	1907
Idaho	1890	Oregon	1859
Illinois	1818	Pennsylvania	1787
Indiana	1816	Rhode Island	1790
Iowa	1846	South Carolina	1788
Kansas	1861	South Dakota	1889
Kentucky	1792	Tennessee	1796
Louisiana	1812	Texas	1845
Maine	1820	Utah	1896
Maryland	1788	Vermont	1791
Massachusetts	1788	Virginia	1788
Michigan	1837	Washington	1889
Minnesota	1858	West Virginia	1863
Mississippi	1817	Wisconsin	1848
Missouri	1821	Wyoming	1890
Montana	1889		

TABLE II

United States Population, 1790–1950

DIVISION & STATE	1790	1800	1810	1820	1830	1840	1850	1860
UNITED STATES	3,929,214	5,308,483	7,239,881	9,638,453	12,866,020 *	17,069,453	23,191,976	31,443,321
NEW ENGLAND	1,009,408	1,233,011	1,471,973	1,660,071	1,954,717	2,234,822	2,728,116	3,135,283
MAINE	96,540	151,719	228,705	298,335	399,455	501,793	583,169	628,279
NEW HAMPSHIRE	141,885	183,858	214,460	244,161	269,328	284,574	317,976	326,073
VERMONT	85,425	154,465	217,895	235,981	280,652	291,948	314,120	315,098
MASSACHUSETTS	378,787	422,845	472,040	523,287	610,408	737,699	994,514	1,231,066
RHODE ISLAND	68,824	69,122	76,931	83,059	97,199	108,830	147,545	174,620
CONNECTICUT	237,946	251,002	261,942	275,248	297,675	309,978	370,792	460,147
MIDDLE ATLANTIC	958,632	1,402,565	2,014,702	2,699,845	3,587,664	4,526,260	5,898,735	7,458,985
NEW YORK	340,120	589,051	959,049	1,372,812	1,918,608	2,428,921	3,097,394	3,880,735
NEW JERSEY	184,139	211,149	245,562	277,575	320,823	373,306	489,555	672,035
PENNSYLVANIA	434,373	602,365	810,091	1,049,458	1,348,233	1,724,033	2,311,786	2,906,215

* Includes persons on public ships in the service of the United States not credited to any geographic division.

	1	2	3	4	5	6	7	8
EAST NORTH CENTRAL		51,006	272,324	792,719	1,470,018	2,924,728	4,523,260	6,926,884
OHIO		45,365	230,760	581,434	937,903	1,519,467	1,980,329	2,339,511
INDIANA		5,641	24,520	147,178	343,031	685,866	988,416	1,350,428
ILLINOIS			12,282	55,211	157,445	476,183	851,470	1,711,951
MICHIGAN			4,762	8,896	31,639	212,267	397,654	749,113
WISCONSIN						130,945	305,391	775,881
WEST NORTH CENTRAL			19,783	66,586	140,455	426,814	880,335	2,169,832
MINNESOTA							6,077	172,023
IOWA						43,112	192,214	674,913
MISSOURI			19,783	66,586	140,455	383,702	682,044	1,182,012
NORTH DAKOTA								4,837
SOUTH DAKOTA								28,841
NEBRASKA								107,206
KANSAS								
SOUTH ATLANTIC	1,851,806	2,286,494	2,674,891	3,061,063	3,645,752	3,925,299	4,679,090	5,364,703
DELAWARE	59,096	64,273	72,674	72,749	76,748	78,085	91,532	112,216
MARYLAND	319,728	341,548	380,546	407,350	447,040	470,019	583,034	687,049
DISTRICT OF COLUMBIA		14,093	24,023	33,039	39,834	43,712	51,687	75,080
VIRGINIA	747,610	880,200	974,900	1,065,366	1,211,405	1,239,797	1,421,661	1,596,318
WEST VIRGINIA								
NORTH CAROLINA	393,751	478,103	555,500	638,829	737,987	753,419	869,039	992,622
SOUTH CAROLINA	249,073	345,591	415,115	502,741	581,185	594,398	668,507	703,708
GEORGIA	82,548	162,680	252,433	340,989	516,823	691,392	906,185	1,057,286
FLORIDA					34,730	54,477	87,445	140,424
EAST SOUTH CENTRAL	109,368	335,407	708,590	1,190,489	1,815,969	2,575,445	3,363,271	4,020,991
KENTUCKY	73,677	220,955	406,511	564,317	687,917	779,828	982,405	1,155,684
TENNESSEE	35,691	105,602	261,727	422,823	681,904	829,210	1,002,717	1,109,801
ALABAMA		8,850	40,352	127,901	309,527	590,758	771,623	964,201
MISSISSIPPI				75,448	136,621	375,651	606,526	791,305

TABLE II (*Continued*)

United States Population, 1790–1950

DIVISION & STATE	1790	1800	1810	1820	1830	1840	1850	1860
WEST SOUTH CENTRAL			77,618	167,680	246,127	449,985	940,251	1,747,667
ARKANSAS			1,062	14,273	30,388	97,574	209,897	435,450
LOUISIANA			76,556	153,407	215,739	352,411	517,762	708,002
OKLAHOMA								
TEXAS							212,592	604,215
MOUNTAIN							72,927	174,923
MONTANA								
IDAHO								
WYOMING								
COLORADO								34,277
NEW MEXICO							61,547	93,516
ARIZONA								
UTAH							11,380	40,273
NEVADA								6,857
PACIFIC							105,891	444,053
WASHINGTON								11,594
OREGON							13,294	52,465
CALIFORNIA							92,597	379,994

DIVISION & STATE	1870	1880	1890	1900	1910	1920	1930	1940	1950
UNITED STATES	39,818,449	50,155,783	62,947,714	75,994,575	91,972,266	105,710,620	122,775,046	131,669,275	150,697,361
NEW ENGLAND	3,487,924	4,010,529	4,700,749	5,592,017	6,552,681	7,400,909	8,166,341	8,437,290	9,314,453
MAINE	626,915	648,936	661,086	694,466	742,371	768,014	797,423	847,226	913,774
NEW HAMPSHIRE	318,300	346,991	376,530	411,588	430,572	443,083	465,293	491,524	533,242
VERMONT	330,551	332,286	332,422	343,641	355,956	352,428	359,611	359,231	377,747
MASSACHUSETTS	1,457,351	1,783,085	2,238,947	2,805,346	3,366,416	3,852,356	4,249,614	4,316,721	4,690,514
RHODE ISLAND	217,353	276,531	345,506	428,556	542,610	604,397	687,497	713,346	791,896
CONNECTICUT	537,454	622,700	746,258	908,420	1,114,756	1,380,631	1,606,903	1,709,242	2,007,280
MIDDLE ATLANTIC	8,810,806	10,496,878	12,706,220	15,454,678	19,315,892	22,261,144	26,260,750	27,539,487	30,163,533
NEW YORK	4,382,759	5,082,871	6,003,174	7,268,894	9,113,614	10,385,227	12,588,066	13,479,142	14,830,192
NEW JERSEY	906,096	1,131,116	1,444,933	1,883,669	2,537,167	3,155,900	4,041,334	4,160,165	4,835,329
PENNSYLVANIA	3,521,951	4,282,891	5,258,113	6,302,115	7,665,111	8,720,017	9,631,350	9,900,180	10,498,012
EAST NORTH CENTRAL	9,124,517	11,206,668	13,478,305	15,985,581	18,250,621	21,475,543	25,297,185	26,626,342	30,399,368
OHIO	2,665,260	3,198,062	3,672,329	4,157,545	4,767,121	5,759,394	6,646,697	6,907,612	7,946,627
INDIANA	1,680,637	1,978,301	2,192,404	2,516,462	2,700,876	2,930,390	3,238,503	3,427,796	3,934,224
ILLINOIS	2,539,891	3,077,871	3,826,352	4,821,550	5,638,591	6,485,280	7,630,654	7,897,241	8,712,176
MICHIGAN	1,184,059	1,636,937	2,093,890	2,420,982	2,810,173	3,668,412	4,842,325	5,256,106	6,371,766
WISCONSIN	1,054,670	1,315,497	1,693,330	2,069,042	2,333,860	2,632,067	2,939,006	3,137,587	3,434,576
WEST NORTH CENTRAL	3,856,594	6,157,443	8,932,112	10,347,423	11,637,921	12,544,249	13,296,915	13,516,990	14,061,394
MINNESOTA	439,706	780,773	1,310,283	1,751,394	2,075,708	2,387,125	2,563,953	2,792,300	2,982,483
IOWA	1,194,020	1,624,615	1,912,297	2,231,853	2,224,771	2,404,021	2,470,939	2,538,268	2,621,073
MISSOURI	1,721,295	2,168,380	2,679,185	3,106,665	3,293,335	3,404,055	3,629,367	3,784,664	3,954,653
NORTH DAKOTA	2,405	36,909	190,983	319,146	577,056	646,872	680,845	641,935	619,636
SOUTH DAKOTA	11,776	98,268	348,600	401,570	583,888	636,547	692,849	642,961	652,740
NEBRASKA	122,993	452,402	1,062,656	1,066,300	1,192,214	1,296,372	1,377,963	1,315,834	1,325,510
KANSAS	364,399	996,096	1,428,108	1,470,495	1,690,949	1,769,257	1,880,999	1,801,028	1,905,299

TABLE II (*Continued*)

United States Population, 1790–1950

DIVISION & STATE	1870	1880	1890	1900	1910	1920	1930	1940	1950
SOUTH ATLANTIC	5,853,610	7,597,197	8,857,922	10,443,480	12,194,895	13,990,272	15,793,589	17,823,151	21,182,335
DELAWARE	125,015	146,608	168,493	184,735	202,322	223,003	238,380	266,505	318,085
MARYLAND	780,894	934,943	1,042,390	1,188,044	1,295,346	1,449,661	1,631,526	1,821,244	2,343,001
DIST. OF COLUMBIA	131,700	177,624	230,392	278,718	331,069	437,571	486,869	663,091	802,178
VIRGINIA	1,225,163	1,512,565	1,655,980	1,854,184	2,061,612	2,309,187	2,421,851	2,677,773	3,318,680
WEST VIRGINIA	442,014	618,457	762,794	958,800	1,221,119	1,463,701	1,729,205	1,901,974	2,005,552
NORTH CAROLINA	1,071,361	1,399,750	1,617,949	1,893,810	2,206,287	2,559,123	3,170,276	3,571,623	4,061,929
SOUTH CAROLINA	705,606	995,577	1,151,149	1,340,316	1,515,400	1,683,724	1,738,765	1,599,804	2,117,027
GEORGIA	1,184,109	1,542,180	1,837,353	2,216,331	2,609,121	2,895,832	2,908,506	3,123,723	3,444,578
FLORIDA	187,748	269,493	391,422	528,542	752,619	968,470	1,468,211	1,897,414	2,771,305
EAST SOUTH CENTRAL	4,404,445	5,585,151	6,429,154	7,547,757	8,409,901	8,893,307	9,887,214	10,778,225	11,477,181
KENTUCKY	1,321,011	1,648,690	1,858,635	2,147,174	2,289,905	2,416,630	2,614,589	2,845,627	2,944,806
TENNESSEE	1,258,520	1,542,359	1,767,518	2,020,616	2,184,789	2,337,885	2,616,556	2,915,841	3,291,718
ALABAMA	996,992	1,262,505	1,513,401	1,828,697	2,138,093	2,348,174	2,646,248	2,832,961	3,061,743
MISSISSIPPI	827,922	1,131,597	1,289,600	1,551,270	1,797,114	1,790,618	2,009,821	2,183,796	2,178,914

WEST SOUTH CENTRAL	2,029,965	3,334,220	4,740,983	6,532,290	8,784,534	10,242,224	12,176,830	13,064,525	14,537,572
ARKANSAS	484,471	802,525	1,128,211	1,311,564	1,574,449	1,752,204	1,854,482	1,949,387	1,909,511
LOUISIANA	726,915	939,946	1,118,588	1,381,625	1,656,388	1,798,509	2,101,593	2,363,880	2,683,516
OKLAHOMA			258,657	790,391	1,657,155	2,028,283	2,396,040	2,336,434	2,233,351
TEXAS	818,579	1,591,749	2,235,527	3,048,710	3,896,542	4,663,228	5,824,715	6,414,824	7,711,194
MOUNTAIN	315,385	653,119	1,213,935	1,674,657	2,633,517	3,336,101	3,701,789	4,150,003	5,074,998
MONTANA	20,595	39,159	142,924	243,329	376,053	548,889	537,606	559,456	591,024
IDAHO	14,999	32,610	88,548	161,772	325,594	431,866	445,032	524,873	588,637
WYOMING	9,118	20,789	62,555	92,531	145,965	194,402	225,565	250,742	290,529
COLORADO	39,864	194,327	413,249	539,700	799,024	939,629	1,035,791	1,123,296	1,325,089
NEW MEXICO	91,874	119,565	160,282	195,310	327,301	360,350	423,317	531,818	681,187
ARIZONA	9,658	40,440	88,243	122,931	204,354	334,162	435,573	499,261	749,587
UTAH	86,786	143,963	210,779	276,749	373,351	449,396	507,847	550,310	688,862
NEVADA	42,491	62,266	47,355	42,335	81,875	77,407	91,058	110,247	160,083
PACIFIC	675,125	1,114,578	1,888,334	2,416,692	4,192,304	5,566,871	8,194,433	9,733,262	14,486,527
WASHINGTON	23,955	75,116	357,232	518,103	1,141,990	1,356,621	1,563,396	1,736,191	2,378,963
OREGON	90,923	174,768	317,704	413,536	672,765	783,389	953,786	1,089,684	1,521,341
CALIFORNIA	560,247	864,694	1,213,398	1,485,053	2,377,549	3,426,861	5,677,251	6,907,387	10,586,223

TABLE III

Presidents of the United States

TENURE OF OFFICE	PRESIDENT	RESIDENCE
1789–97	*George Washington*	Virginia
1797–1801	*John Adams*	Massachusetts
1801–09	*Thomas Jefferson*	Virginia
1809–17	*James Madison*	Virginia
1817–25	*James Monroe*	Virginia
1825–29	*John Quincy Adams*	Massachusetts
1829–37	*Andrew Jackson*	Tennessee
1837–41	*Martin Van Buren*	New York
1841	*William Henry Harrison*	Ohio
1841–45	*John Tyler*	Virginia
1845–49	*James K. Polk*	Tennessee
1849–50	*Zachary Taylor*	Louisiana
1850–53	*Millard Fillmore*	New York
1853–57	*Franklin Pierce*	New Hampshire
1857–61	*James Buchanan*	Pennsylvania
1861–65	*Abraham Lincoln*	Illinois
1865–69	*Andrew Johnson*	Tennessee
1869–77	*Ulysses S. Grant*	Ohio
1877–81	*Rutherford B. Hayes*	Ohio
1881	*James A. Garfield*	Ohio
1881–85	*Chester A. Arthur*	New York
1885–89	*Grover Cleveland*	New York
1889–93	*Benjamin Harrison*	Indiana
1893–97	*Grover Cleveland*	New York
1897–1901	*William McKinley*	Ohio
1901–09	*Theodore Roosevelt*	New York
1909–13	*William H. Taft*	Ohio
1913–21	*Woodrow Wilson*	New Jersey
1921–23	*Warren G. Harding*	Ohio
1923–29	*Calvin Coolidge*	Massachusetts
1929–33	*Herbert C. Hoover*	California
1933–45	*Franklin D. Roosevelt*	New York
1945–53	*Harry S. Truman*	Missouri
1953–	*Dwight D. Eisenhower*	New York

TABLE IV

Chief Justices of the Supreme Court

TENURE OF OFFICE	CHIEF JUSTICE	RESIDENCE
1789–95	*John Jay*	New York
1795	*John Rutledge*	South Carolina
1796–99	*Oliver Ellsworth*	Connecticut
1801–35	*John Marshall*	Virginia
1835–64	*Roger B. Taney*	Maryland
1864–73	*Salmon P. Chase*	Ohio
1874–88	*Morrison R. Waite*	Ohio
1888–1910	*Melville W. Fuller*	Illinois
1910–21	*Edward D. White*	Louisiana
1921–30	*William H. Taft*	Ohio
1930–41	*Charles E. Hughes*	New York
1941–46	*Harlan F. Stone*	New York
1946–53	*Fred M. Vinson*	Kentucky
1953–	*Earl Warren*	California

TABLE V

Presidential Elections*

Before the adoption of the Twelfth Amendment in 1804 each member of the Electoral College voted for two presidential candidates instead of casting separate ballots for president and vice-president. Prior to the election of 1824 the members of the Electoral College were chosen by the state legislatures, not by popular vote.

ELECTION	CANDIDATES	PARTIES	POPULAR VOTE	ELECTORAL VOTE
1789	GEORGE WASHINGTON	No party designations		69
	John Adams			34
	Minor Candidates			35
1792	GEORGE WASHINGTON	No party designation		132
	John Adams	Federalist		77
	George Clinton	Republican		50
	Minor Candidates			5
1796	JOHN ADAMS	Federalist		71
	Thomas Jefferson	Republican		68
	Thomas Pinckney	Federalist		59
	Aaron Burr	Republican		30
	Minor Candidates			48
1800	THOMAS JEFFERSON	Republican		73
	Aaron Burr	Republican		73
	John Adams	Federalist		65
	Charles C. Pinckney	Federalist		64
	John Jay	Federalist		1
1804	THOMAS JEFFERSON	Republican		162
	Charles C. Pinckney	Federalist		14
1808	JAMES MADISON	Republican		122
	Charles C. Pinckney	Federalist		47
	George Clinton	Republican		6
1812	JAMES MADISON	Republican		128
	DeWitt Clinton	Federalist		89
1816	JAMES MONROE	Republican		183
	Rufus King	Federalist		34
1820	JAMES MONROE	Republican		183
	John Q. Adams	Republican		1

* Candidates receiving less than one per cent of the popular vote are omitted.

TABLE V (*Continued*)

Election	Candidates	Parties	Popular Vote	Electoral Vote
1824 †	JOHN Q. ADAMS	Republican	108,740	84
	Andrew Jackson	Republican	153,544	99
	William H. Crawford	Republican	46,618	41
	Henry Clay	Republican	47,136	37
1828	ANDREW JACKSON	Democratic	647,231	178
	John Q. Adams	National Republican	509,097	83
1832	ANDREW JACKSON	Democratic	687,502	219
	Henry Clay	National Republican	530,189	49
	William Wirt	Anti-Mason	} 33,108	7
	John Floyd	National Republican		11
1836	MARTIN VAN BUREN	Democratic	761,549	170
	William H. Harrison	Whig		73
	Hugh L. White	Whig	} 736,656	26
	Daniel Webster	Whig		14
	W. P. Mangum	Whig		11
1840	WILLIAM H. HARRISON	Whig	1,275,016	234
	Martin Van Buren	Democratic	1,129,102	60
1844	JAMES K. POLK	Democratic	1,337,243	170
	Henry Clay	Whig	1,299,062	102
	James G. Birney	Liberty	62,300	
1848	ZACHARY TAYLOR	Whig	1,360,099	163
	Lewis Cass	Democratic	1,220,544	127
	Martin Van Buren	Free Soil	291,263	
1852	FRANKLIN PIERCE	Democratic	1,601,274	254
	Winfield Scott	Whig	1,386,580	42
	John P. Hale	Free Soil	155,825	
1856	JAMES BUCHANAN	Democratic	1,838,169	174
	John C. Frémont	Republican	1,341,264	114
	Millard Fillmore	American	874,534	8
1860	ABRAHAM LINCOLN	Republican	1,866,452	180
	Stephen A. Douglas	Democratic	1,375,157	12
	John C. Breckinridge	Democratic	847,953	72
	John Bell	Union	590,631	39
1864	ABRAHAM LINCOLN	Republican	2,213,665	212
	George B. McClellan	Democratic	1,802,237	21
1868	ULYSSES S. GRANT	Republican	3,012,833	214
	Horatio Seymour	Democratic	2,703,249	80
1872	ULYSSES S. GRANT	Republican	3,597,132	286
	Horace Greeley	Democratic and Liberal Republican	2,834,125	66
1876	RUTHERFORD B. HAYES	Republican	4,036,298	185
	Samuel J. Tilden	Democratic	4,300,590	184
1880	JAMES A. GARFIELD	Republican	4,454,416	214
	Winfield S. Hancock	Democratic	4,444,952	155
	James B. Weaver	Greenback	308,578	

† Since no candidate had a majority in the Electoral College, the final choice was made by the House of Representatives.

TABLE V (*Continued*)

Election	Candidates	Parties	Popular Vote	Electoral Vote
1884	GROVER CLEVELAND	Democratic	4,874,986	219
	James G. Blaine	Republican	4,851,981	182
	Benjamin F. Butler	Greenback	175,370	
	John P. St. John	Prohibition	150,369	
1888	BENJAMIN HARRISON	Republican	5,439,853	233
	Grover Cleveland	Democratic	5,540,309	168
	Clinton B. Fisk	Prohibition	249,506	
	Anson J. Streeter	Union Labor	146,935	
1892	GROVER CLEVELAND	Democratic	5,556,918	277
	Benjamin Harrison	Republican	5,176,108	145
	James B. Weaver	People's	1,041,028	22
	John Bidwell	Prohibition	264,133	
1896	WILLIAM McKINLEY	Republican	7,104,779	271
	William J. Bryan	Democratic	6,502,925	176
1900	WILLIAM McKINLEY	Republican	7,207,923	292
	William J. Bryan	Democratic	6,358,133	155
	John C. Woolley	Prohibition	208,914	
1904	THEODORE ROOSEVELT	Republican	7,623,486	336
	Alton B. Parker	Democratic	5,077,911	140
	Eugene V. Debs	Socialist	402,283	
	Silas C. Swallow	Prohibition	258,536	
1908	WILLIAM H. TAFT	Republican	7,678,908	321
	William J. Bryan	Democratic	6,409,104	162
	Eugene V. Debs	Socialist	420,793	
	Eugene W. Chafin	Prohibition	253,840	
1912	WOODROW WILSON	Democratic	6,293,454	435
	Theodore Roosevelt	Progressive	4,119,538	88
	William H. Taft	Republican	3,484,980	8
	Eugene V. Debs	Socialist	900,672	
	Eugene W. Chafin	Prohibition	206,275	
1916	WOODROW WILSON	Democratic	9,129,606	277
	Charles E. Hughes	Republican	8,538,221	254
	A. L. Benson	Socialist	585,113	
	J. F. Hanly	Prohibition	220,506	
1920	WARREN G. HARDING	Republican	16,152,200	404
	James M. Cox	Democratic	9,147,353	127
	Eugene V. Debs	Socialist	919,799	
	P. P. Christensen	Farmer-Labor	265,411	
1924	CALVIN COOLIDGE	Republican	15,725,016	382
	John W. Davis	Democratic	8,386,503	136
	Robert M. LaFollette	Progressive	4,822,856	13
1928	HERBERT C. HOOVER	Republican	21,391,381	444
	Alfred E. Smith	Democratic	15,016,443	87
1932	FRANKLIN D. ROOSEVELT	Democratic	22,821,857	472
	Herbert C. Hoover	Republican	15,761,841	59
	Norman Thomas	Socialist	881,951	

TABLE V (*Continued*)

Election	Candidates	Parties	Popular Vote	Electoral Vote
1936	FRANKLIN D. ROOSEVELT	Democratic	27,751,597	523
	Alfred M. Landon	Republican	16,679,583	8
	William Lemke	Union	882,479	
1940	FRANKLIN D. ROOSEVELT	Democratic	27,244,160	449
	Wendell L. Willkie	Republican	22,305,198	82
1944	FRANKLIN D. ROOSEVELT	Democratic	25,602,504	432
	Thomas E. Dewey	Republican	22,006,285	99
1948	HARRY S. TRUMAN	Democratic	24,105,695	303
	Thomas E. Dewey	Republican	21,969,170	189
	J. Strom Thurmond	States' Rights	1,169,021	39
	Henry A. Wallace	Progressive	1,156,103	
1952	DWIGHT D. EISENHOWER	Republican	33,936,252	442
	Adlai E. Stevenson	Democratic	26,314,992	89
1956	DWIGHT D. EISENHOWER	Republican	33,212,325	457
	Adlai E. Stevenson	Democratic	24,192,953	74

TABLE VI

Public Elementary and Secondary Schools—Summary, 1870–1947

Item	1870	1880	1890	1900	1910	1920	1930	1940	1944	1946	1947
Total population	38,558,371	50,155,783	62,622,250	75,602,515	91,972,266	105,710,620	122,775,046	131,669,275	138,083,449	139,893,406	143,405,000
Population 5-17 years, inclusive	12,055,443	15,065,767	18,543,201	21,404,322	24,239,948	27,728,788	31,571,322	29,745,246	28,930,000	28,944,000	29,317,000
Percent of total population	31.3	30.0	29.6	28.3	26.4	26.2	25.7	22.6	21.0	20.7	20.4
Pupils enrolled in public schools	6,871,532	9,867,395	12,722,631	15,503,110	17,813,852	21,578,316	25,678,015	25,433,542	23,266,616	23,299,941	23,659,158
Percent of total population	17.82	19.67	20.32	20.51	19.37	20.4	20.9	19.3	16.9	16.7	16.5
Percent of population 5-17, inclusive	57.00	65.50	68.61	72.43	73.49	77.8	81.3	85.5	80.4	80.5	80.7
Average daily attendance	4,077,347	6,144,143	8,153,635	10,632,772	12,827,307	16,150,035	21,264,886	22,042,151	19,602,772	19,848,507	20,448,656
Percent of pupils enrolled	59.3	62.3	64.1	68.6	72.0	74.8	82.8	86.7	84.3	85.2	86.4
Average number of days schools in session	132.2	130.3	134.7	144.3	157.5	161.9	172.7	175.0	175.5	176.8	176.2
Average number of days attended per enrolled pupil	78.4	81.1	86.3	99.0	113.0	121.2	143.0	151.7	147.9	150.6	152.3
Number of teachers	200,515	286,593	363,922	423,062	523,210	679,533	854,263	875,477	827,990	831,096	833,512
Male	77,529	122,795	125,525	126,588	110,481	95,666	141,771	194,725	126,672	138,209	153,297
Female	122,986	163,798	238,397	296,474	412,729	583,867	712,492	680,752	701,318	692,817	680,215
Percent male teachers	38.7	42.8	34.5	29.9	21.1	14.1	16.6	22.2	15.3	16.6	18.4
Salaries: Teachers, supervisors, and principals (thousands of dollars)	37,833	55,943	91,836	137,688	253,915	590,120	1,250,427	1,314,342	1,494,507	1,730,563	1,979,657
Average annual salary per teacher	$189	$195	$252	$325	$485	$871	$1,420	$1,441	$1,728	$1,995	$2,254
Total expenditure for education (thousands of dollars)	63,397	78,095	140,507	214,965	426,250	1,036,151	2,316,790	2,344,049	2,452,581	2,906,886	3,419,994
Per capita of total population	$1.64	$1.56	$2.24	$2.84	$4.63	$9.80	$18.87	$17.76	$17.76	$20.78	$23.85
Per capita of population 5-17, inclusive	$5.26	$5.18	$7.58	$10.04	$17.58	$37.37	$73.38	$78.65	$84.78	$100.43	$116.66
Per pupil enrolled	$9.23	$7.91	$11.04	$13.87	$23.93	$48.02	$89.84	$91.64	$105.04	$124.27	$143.77
Per pupil in average attendance	$15.55	$12.71	$17.23	$20.22	$33.23	$64.16	$108.49	$105.74	$124.68	$145.88	$166.34

TABLE VII

Recipients of the Nobel Prize

Chemistry		Literature		Medicine and Physiology		Physics		Peace	
T. W. Richards	1914	Sinclair Lewis	1930	A. Carrel	1912	A. A. Michelson	1907	Theodore Roosevelt	1906
I. Langmuir	1932	Eugene O'Neill	1936	K. Landsteiner	1930	R. A. Millikan	1923	Elihu Root	1912
H. C. Urey	1934	Pearl Buck	1938	T. H. Morgan	1933	A. Compton	1927	Woodrow Wilson	1919
J. B. Sumner }	1946	T. S. Eliot	1948	G. R. Minot }	1934	C. A. Anderson	1936	C. G. Dawes	1925
J. Northrop }		William Faulkner	1949	P. Murphy }		C. J. Davison	1937	F. B. Kellogg	1929
W. M. Stanley }		Ernest Hemingway	1954	G. H. Whipple }		E. O. Lawrence	1939	N. M. Butler }	1931
W. F. Giauque	1949			E. Doisy	1943	O. Stern	1943	Jane Addams }	
E. M. McMillan }	1951			J. Erlanger }	1944	I. I. Rabi	1944	Cordell Hull	1945
G. T. Seaborg }				H. Gasser }		P. W. Bridgman	1946	J. R. Mott }	1946
L. Pauling	1954			H. J. Muller	1946	F. Bloch }	1952	Emily Balch }	
V. Du Vigneaud	1955			S. A. Waksman	1952	E. M. Purcell }		Ralph Bunche	1950
				F. A. Lipmann }	1953	W. E. Lamb }	1955	G. C. Marshall	1953
				H. A. Krebs }		P. Kusch }			
				T. H. Weller }		J. Bardeen }			
				F. C. Robbins }	1954	W. H. Brattain }	1956		
				J. F. Enders }		W. B. Shockley }			
				D. W. Richards }	1956				
				A. F. Cournand }					

A Student's Reading List
on Major Subjects

WORKS OF REFERENCE. Every student should know Allen Johnson and Dumas Malone (eds.), *Dictionary of American Biography* (20 vols., 1928–36). Other outstanding works of reference are J. T. Adams and R. V. Coleman (eds.), *Dictionary of American History* (6 vols., 1940), and E. R. A. Seligman (ed.), *Encyclopaedia of the Social Sciences* (15 vols., 1930–35). Many publications of the Federal government give useful statistical information, especially the annual *Statistical Abstracts of the United States*.

PERIODICALS. *The American Historical Review* (1895—) appears quarterly and contains important articles, as well as reviews of all new books on history. Among other outstanding periodicals are *American Quarterly* (1947—); *Journal of Economic History* (1941—); *Journal of Southern History* (1935—); *Journal of Negro History* (1916—); *Mississippi Valley Historical Review* (1915—); *The New England Quarterly* (1928—); *Pennsylvania Magazine of History and Biography* (1877—); and *The William and Mary Quarterly* (1892—). The *Proceedings* and *Collections* of the Massachusetts Historical Society (1791—), and the *Proceedings* of the American Antiquarian Society (1812—), are particularly valuable collections of source materials.

ANTHOLOGIES OF SOURCE MATERIALS. Among the more useful collections are H. S. Commager (ed.), *Documents of American History* (rev. ed., 1949); H. S. Commager and Allan Nevins (eds.), *The Heritage of America* (rev. ed., 1949); Louis M. Hacker and H. S. Zahler, *The Shaping of the American Tradition* (1947); Willard Thorp, Merle Curti, and Carlos Baker, *American Issues* (2 vols., 1941). A. B. Hart (ed.), *American History Told by Contemporaries* (5 vols., 1897–1929), is still useful. More specialized studies include R. J. Bartlett, *The Record of American Diplomacy* (1947); F. Flugel and H. U. Faulkner, *Readings in the Economic and Social History of the United States* (1929); L. B. Schmidt and E. D. Ross, *Readings in the Economic History of American Agriculture* (1925); I. F. Woestemeyer and J. M. Gambrill. *The Westward Movement* (1939). The Amherst *Problems in American Civilization* and the Yale *Select Problems in Historical Interpretation for American History* are two series that present conflicting viewpoints on various aspects of American history.

GEOGRAPHY. There are a number of excellent books on the geographic background, among them, Isaiah Bowman, *The New World* (1928); R. H. Brown, *Historical Geography of the United States* (1948); E. C. Semple, *American History and Its Geographic Conditions* (rev. ed., 1933); J. R. Smith and M. Phillips, *North America* (rev. ed., 1940). The most convenient collections of maps are C. L. and E. H. Lord, *Historical Atlas of the United States* (1944); and C. O. Paullin, *Atlas of the Historical Geography of the United States* (1932).

GENERAL AND POLITICAL HISTORY. Earlier historians like George Bancroft, Richard Hildreth, Hermann Von Holst, J. B. McMaster, James Schouler, J. R. Rhodes, and E. P. Oberholtzer wrote comprehensive histories of the United States, although much of their work has been superseded by more recent research. The last of these was Edward Channing, whose *History of the United States* (6 vols., 1905–25), goes as far as 1865 and is still generally dependable. An outstanding shorter and more interpretive work is Charles and Mary Beard,

The Rise of American Civilization (2 vols., rev. ed., 1933), which ends at 1929. Two later volumes, *America in Midpassage* (1939), and *The American Spirit* (1942), fall below the standards set in the first study. Henry Steele Commager and Richard B. Morris, *The New American Nation Series*, is an excellent collection by different authors, still in process of publication. Many of the volumes in A. B. Hart, *The American Nation: a History* (28 vols., 1904–28), are still useful. Allen Johnson and Allan Nevins (eds.), *Chronicles of America* (56 vols., 1918–51), is an uneven collection, but all the volumes are easy to read, and some are excellent. A. M. Schlesinger and D. R. Fox (eds.), *A History of American Life* (13 vols., 1927–48), stresses social and cultural development and maintains high standards. R. H. Gabriel (ed.), *The Pageant of America* (15 vols., 1925–29), describes American development largely through pictures.

W. E. Binkley, *American Political Parties: Their Natural History* (1943), and Richard Hofstadter, *The American Political Tradition and the Men Who Made It* (1948), are recommended for political history. A. M. Schlesinger, *New Viewpoints in American History* (1922), is a stimulating collection of essays.

ECONOMIC DEVELOPMENT. Henry David *et al.* (eds.), *The Economic History of the United States* (1945—), to be completed in nine volumes, is first-rate. There are a number of excellent one-volume surveys, among them, H. U. Faulkner, *American Economic History* (rev. ed., 1949); E. C. Kirkland, *A History of American Economic Life* (rev. ed., 1939); B. and L. M. Mitchell, *American Economic History* (1947); F. A. Shannon, *America's Economic Growth* (rev. ed., 1951); C. W. Wright, *Economic History of the United States* (rev. ed., 1949). T. C. Cochran and W. Miller, *The Age of Enterprise: a Social History of Industrial America* (1942); and L. M. Hacker, *The Triumph of American Capitalism* (1940), are more interpretive.

Works on special phases of American economy are P. W. Bidwell and J. A. Falconer, *History of Agriculture in the Northern United States: 1620–1860* (1925); V. S. Clark, *History of Manufactures in the United States* (3 vols., 1929); D. R. Dewey, *Financial History of the United States* (rev. ed., 1936); L. C. Gray, *History of Agriculture in the Southern United States to 1860* (2 vols., 1933); E. R. Johnson *et al.*, *History of Domestic and Foreign Commerce of the United States* (2 vols., 1915); B. H. Meyer *et al.*, *History of Transportation in the United States before 1860* (1917); F. W. Taussig, *The Tariff History of the United States* (rev. ed., 1931). All of these are severely factual. Two shorter and more interpretive works on agriculture are E. E. Edwards, *American Agriculture: the First Three Hundred Years*, which is contained in the *1940 Yearbook of Agriculture*, and Joseph Schafer, *Social History of American Agriculture* (1936). Seymour Dunbar, *A History of Travel in America* (4 vols., 1915), is particularly readable.

The standard work on labor history is J. R. Commons (ed.), *History of Labor in the United States* (4 vols., 1918–35); and his *Documentary History of American Industrial Society* (11 vols., 1910–11), which stops at 1880, is recommended.

IMMIGRATION. The most recent general accounts are M. L. Hansen, *The Atlantic Migration, 1607–1860* (1940), and *The Immigrant in American History* (1940); and Carl Wittke, *We Who Built America* (1939). Oscar Handlin, *Uprooted: the Epic Story of the Great Migrations That Made the American People* (1951), describes typical immigrant experiences. Edith Abbott (ed.), *Immigration: Select Documents and Case Records* (1924), and *Historical Aspects of the Immigration Problem* (1926), are two collections of documentary material on this subject.

Some of the better studies on the different ethnic groups include A. B. Faust, *The German Element in the United States* (2 vols., 1909); H. J. Ford, *The Scotch-Irish in America* (1916); J. H. Franklin, *From Slavery to Freedom: a History of American Negroes* (1948); and Herbert Aptheker (ed.), *Documentary History of the Negro People in the United States* (1951).

THE WESTWARD MOVEMENT. R. A. Billington, *Westward Expansion* (1949); D. E. Clark, *The West in American History* (1937); F. L. Paxson, *History of the American Frontier: 1763–1893* (1924); and R. E. Riegel, *America Moves West* (1947), are one-volume surveys. All students of American history should read F. J. Turner, *The Frontier in American History* (1920). Land policies are described in B. H. Hibbard, *A History of the Public Land Policies* (1924), and R. M. Robbins, *Our Landed Heritage; the Public Domain: 1776–1936* (1942). There is much interesting material in R. G. Thwaites (ed.), *Early Western Travels: 1748–1846* (32 vols., 1904–07).

CONSTITUTIONAL DEVELOPMENT. Among the more useful general surveys are H. C. Hockett, *The Constitutional History of the United States: 1776–1876* (2 vols., 1939); A. H. Kelly and W. A. Harbison, *The American Constitution: Its Origins and Development* (1948); A. C. McLaughlin, *A Constitutional History of the United States* (1935); R. L. Schuyler, *The Constitution of the United States* (1923); C. B. Swisher, *American Constitutional Development* (1943); B. F. Wright, *The Growth of American Constitutional Law* (1942). More specialized volumes are Charles A. Beard, *The Supreme Court and the Constitution* (1912); L. Boudin, *Government by Judiciary* (2 vols., 1932); E. S. Corwin, *The Doctrine of Judicial Review* (1914), and *The President, Office and Powers: 1787–1948* (rev. ed., 1948); G. H. Haynes, *The Senate of the United States: Its History and Practice* (2 vols., 1938); A. N. Holcombe, *State Government in the United States* (rev. ed., 1926); Charles Warren, *The Supreme Court in United States History* (2 vols., rev. ed., 1932); B. F. Wright, *The Contract Clause of the Constitution* (1938).

FOREIGN POLICY. T. A. Bailey, *Diplomatic History of the American People* (rev. ed., 1955), and S. F. Bemis, *Diplomatic History of the United States* (rev. ed., 1955), are excellent one-volume surveys. S. F. Bemis (ed.), *The American Secretaries of State and Their Diplomacy* (10 vols., 1927–29), is also recommended.

Specific areas of American foreign policy are dealt with in S. F. Bemis, *The Latin American Policy of the United States* (1943); J. M. Callahan, *American Foreign Policy in Canadian Relations* (1937), and *American Foreign Policy in Mexican Relations* (1932); A. W. Griswold, *The Far Eastern Policy of the United States* (1938); J. F. Rippy, *The United States and Mexico* (1931).

INTELLECTUAL DEVELOPMENT. The most comprehensive general work is Merle Curti, *The Growth of American Thought* (rev. ed., 1951). V. L. Parrington, *Main Currents in American Thought* (3 vols., 1927–30), is primarily an interpretation of the American liberal tradition. R. H. Gabriel, *The Course of American Democratic Thought* (1940), is uneven, but contains much useful material. Philosophy is covered in H. W. Schneider, *A History of American Philosophy* (1946). Joseph Dorfman, *The Economic Mind in American Civilization* (3 vols., 1946–49), deals with economic theory. R. G. Gettel, *History of American Political Theories* (1928), and C. E. Merriam, *American Political Theories* (1910), and *American Political Ideals: 1865–1917* (1920), are recommended studies in the development of political thinking.

SCIENCE. There is no general history of American science, but there is useful material in B. Jaffe, *Men of Science in America* (1944); W. Kaempffert, *A Popular History of American Inventions* (2 vols., 1924); F. R. Packard, *History of Medicine in the United States* (2 vols., 1931); and M. S. C. Smallwood, *Natural History and the American Mind* (1941).

EDUCATION. The standard work on education is E. P. Cubberly, *Public Education in the United States* (1919). Of particular interest, too, is Merle Curti, *Social Ideas of American Educators* (1935).

RELIGION. H. K. Rowe, *The History of Religion in the United States* (1924); W. L. Sperry, *Religion in America* (1946); and W. W. Sweet, *The Story of Religions in America* (1930), are the best short surveys written on this subject to date. W. W. Sweet is engaged in a more extensive work, of which three volumes have been completed: *Religion in Colonial America* (1942), and *Religion in the Development of American Culture*, 1765–1840 (2 vols., 1952). P. Schaff (ed.), *The American Church History Series* (13 vols., 1893–1901) is an informative general guide. For the relations between church and state, see E. B. Greene, *Religion and the State: the Making and Testing of an American Tradition* (1941), and A. P. Stokes, *Church and State in the United States* (3 vols., 1950).

LITERATURE AND THE ARTS. R. E. Spiller *et al.* (eds.), *Literary History of the United States* (3 vols., 1948) is the standard work on literature. One of the best one-volume surveys is W. F. Taylor, *A History of American Letters* (1936). Van Wyck Brooks, *Makers and Finders: A History of the Writer in America, 1800–1915* (6 vols., 1936–51) is an imaginative examination of the American cultural tradition. J. W. Krutch *et al.* (eds.), *American Men of Letters* (1948—) is a valuable series, still in course of publication. H. L. Mencken, *The American Language* (rev. ed., 1936) is a standard authority.

Painting, sculpture, and architecture are covered in O. W. Larkin, *Art and Life in America* (1949). This can be supplemented with Alan Burroughs, *Limners and Likenesses: Three Centuries of American Painting* (1936); Vergil Barker, *American Painting* (1950); Samuel Isham and Royal Cortissoz, *The History of American Painting* (rev. ed., 1936); Jerome Mellquist, *The Emergence of an American Art* (1942); Lorado Taft, *The History of American Sculpture* (rev. ed., 1924).

J. T. Howard, *Our American Music* (rev. ed., 1946), is the only comprehensive work on this subject. See also Sigmund Spaeth, *A History of Popular Music in America* (1948).

JOURNALISM. F. L. Mott, *History of American Magazines* (3 vols., 1930–38), and *American Journalism, 1690–1940* (1941), are standard authorities. W. G. Bleyer, *Main Currents in the History of American Journalism* (1927), and Kenneth Stewart and John Tebbel, *Makers of Modern Journalism* (1952), are shorter studies.

SOCIAL DEVELOPMENT. A. M. Schlesinger and D. R. Fox (eds.), *The History of American Life* (13 vols., 1927–48), is the main authority in this field. N. M. Blake, *A Short History of American Life* (1952), is a one-volume survey. Marshall Davidson, *Life in America* (2 vols., 1951), is primarily a collection of pictures. Other works dealing with social development are A. W. Calhoun, *A Social History of the American Family* (3 vols., 1917–19); F. R. Dulles, *America Learns to Play* (1940); Dixon Wecter, *The Saga of American Society* (1937).

THE ARMY AND NAVY. Useful in this field are C. S. Alden and A. Westcott, *The United States Navy* (1943); D. W. Knox, *A History of the United States Navy* (1948); C. H. Metcalf, *A History of the United States Marine Corps* (1939); O. L. Spaulding, *The United States Army in War and Peace* (1937); H. and M. Sprout, *The Rise of American Naval Power, 1776–1918* (1939).

REGIONAL HISTORY. W. H. Stephenson and E. M. Coulter (eds.), *A History of the South* (1947), which will eventually be completed in twelve volumes, is an outstanding cooperative enterprise. J. T. Adams's *History of New England* (3 vols., 1921–26), is a lively but unsympathetic study. Other regional histories are J. W. Caughey, *History of the Pacific Coast* (1933), Oscar Winther, *The Great Northwest* (rev. ed., 1950), and D. O. Johansen and C. M. Gates, *Empire of the Columbia* (1957). An outstanding state history is A. C. Flick (ed.), *History of the State of New York* (10 vols., 1933–37).

DESCRIPTIONS BY FOREIGN VISITORS. A large number of foreigners have written accounts of American society at different periods. These can be sampled in H. S. Commager, *America in Perspective* (1947); Oscar Handlin, *This Was America* (1949); Frank Monaghan, *French Travellers in the United States: 1762–1832* (1933); Allan Nevins, *America Through British Eyes* (1948). Two books by foreigners have become classics: Alexis de Tocqueville, *Democracy in America* (2 vols., 1945), with a preface by Phillips Bradley; and James Bryce, *The American Commonwealth* (2 vols., 1888). Two others that are worth reading are Harriet Martineau, *Society in America* (1837), and Frances E. Trollope, *Domestic Manners of the Americans*

(2 vols., 1832). Three stimulating recent books of the same kind are Denis W. Brogan, *The American Character* (1944); Alistair Cooke, *One Man's America* (1952); and H. J. Laski, *The American Democracy* (1948).

*   *   *

For the student who wishes to extend his reading beyond the basic works noted here, the outstanding bibliographical guide is Oscar Handlin and others, *The Harvard Guide to American History* (1954). Also valuable is the American Historical Association series edited by Grace G. Griffin, *Writings on American History* (1906–38). Edward Channing and others, *Guide to the Study and Reading of American History* (1912), is still useful. Two excellent bibliographies in special fields are S. F. Bemis and Grace G. Griffin, *Guide to the Diplomatic History of the United States* (1935), and E. E. Edwards, *A Bibliography of the History of Agriculture in the United States* (1930). R. E. Spiller and others, *Literary History of the United States*, Vol. III (1948), is a comprehensive bibliography of American literature. Other bibliographical information can be found by consulting H. P. Beers, *Bibliographies in American History: Guide to Materials for Research* (1942).

INDEX

Abolitionist movement, 259, 264–5, 323–6
Abrams case, 578
Acadia, 26, 72; *see also* Nova Scotia
Acheson, Dean, 685
Adams, Charles Francis, 367, 368, 449
Adams, Henry, 463, 502
Adams, Herbert Baxter, 490
Adams, John, 101, 102, 103, 108, 114, 128, 140; President, 149–53
Adams, John Quincy, 166, 167, 179, 325; Secretary of State, 168–74; President, 239–41
Adams, Samuel, 65, 98, 99, 100, 101, 103, 108, 117, 144
Adams, Samuel Hopkins, 546
Adams-Onís Treaty (1819), 169, 300, 316
Adamson Act (1916), 563
Addams, Jane, 467
Adkins v. Children's Hospital, 550
Adler, Felix, 496
Agricultural Adjustment Act (1933), 632, 633, 636; (1938), 637; (1954), 694
Agricultural Marketing Act (1929), 595
Agriculture: in colonies, 31–2, 37–8, 58–9; in Old Northwest, 194, 336; in Old South, 203–11; in New South, 387–9; during later nineteenth century, 429–42; during World War I, 576; during 1920's, 595, 616–17; under New Deal, 636–8; during World War II, 657–8; in 1950's, 694–5
Aguinaldo, Emilio, 526
Aiken, Conrad, 714
Air Mail Act (1925), 614
Alabama, settlement of, 182, 195, 197, 198
Alabama, the, 361, 368
Alabama Midland case, 406
Alamance, battle of, 67
Alamo, siege of the, 306
Alaska: Russians in, 69, 169–170; acquisition of, 521
Albany Congress (1754), 73
Albany Regency, 238
Alcott, Bronson, 271, 282, 284
Aldrich, Nelson W., 456, 463, 552, 556

Aldrich, Thomas Bailey, 504
Aldrich, Winthrop W., 626
Alien Act (1798), 151, 154
Allen, Ethan, 81, 125
Allen, Hervey, 712
Allen, James Lane, 505
Allgeyer v. Louisiana, 419
Almy and Brown, 225
Altgeld, John P., 420, 460, 461, 462, 547
Amana Society, 261
America First Committee, 651
American Association for the Advancement of Science, 273
American Economic Association, 492
American Federation of Labor, 418, 642–3
American Fur Company, 301, 303
American Journal of Science and the Arts, 273
American Magazine, 80
American Medical Association, 273
American Mercury, 707
American Philosophical Society, 85
American Protective Association, 476
American Railway Union, 420
American Smelting and Refining Company, 427
American Sociological Society, 491
American Sugar Refining Company, 410
American Telephone and Telegraph Company, 409, 616
American Tobacco Company, 410
Americans for Democratic Action, 676, 726
Amherst, Lord, 73
Amish, 50
Amnesty Act (1872), 386
Anaconda Copper Company, 427
Anderson, Maxwell, 715
Anderson, Sherwood, 512, 710
Andros, Sir Edmund, 54–5
anesthesia, invention of, 273
Anglican Church: in England, 12, 13; in colonies, 30, 31, 42, 54, 63, 81; during Revolution, 121; in early nineteenth century, 215, 258

i

Annapolis convention (1786), 128
Anthony, Susan B., 267
anthropology, study of, 743
Antietam, battle of, 365
Anti-Masonic Party, 246, 249
Antioch College, 268
Anti-Saloon League, 474, 550
Apache Indians, 423, 424
Arabs, 701–2
Arapaho Indians, 423
Architecture: in colonies, 90–1; nineteenth
  century, 293–4, 514–16; twentieth cen-
  tury, 719–20
Argentina, 646, 673
Arizona, settlement of, 300, 318, 426, 431
Arkansas, settlement of, 197, 205
Arminianism, 81, 82
Armour, Philip D., 410
Armstrong, Louis, 721
Arnold, Benedict, 111, 112, 113
Arnold, General Henry H., 659
Arnold, Thurman, 636
Art. *See* Painting
Arthur, Chester A., 453, 454
Arthur, T. S., 267
Arvin, Newton, 708
Asbury, Bishop Francis, 257
Ashley, William H., 302
Astor, John Jacob, 279, 301, 303
athletics, 467–8, 478
Atlantic Charter, 654, 655, 671
Atlantic Monthly, 272, 482, 739
atomic bomb, 668, 684, 702
Atomic Energy Commission, 684
Austin, Stephen, 304–6
automobile industry, 414, 611–12
aviation industry, 613–14, 657

Babbitt, Irving, 708
Babcock, Orville E., 450
Bacon's rebellion, 32, 61
Baer, George F., 415
Baker, Newton D., 547, 575
Baker, Ray Stannard, 546
Ballinger, Richard A., 557
Baltimore, Lord, 30
Baltimore and Ohio Railroad, 222, 333, 402
Bancroft, George, 281
Bank of the United States: first, 142–3, 164;
  second, 175, 176, 178, 193, 236, 246–248
banking: colonial period, 62; during Con-
  federation, 123; during Washington's
  administration, 142–3, early nineteenth
  century, 175, 178, 193; Jacksonian period,

banking (*continued*)
  236, 246–8, 250–1; National Bank Act,
  373; later nineteenth century, 411–14;
  Federal Reserve System, 561–3; under
  New Deal, 630, 638
Banking Act (1933), 638
Baptist Church, 474, 716; in England, 13;
  in colonies, 37, 41, 63, 65; in early nine-
  teenth century, 215, 257–60
Barlow, Joel, 277
Barnard, George Grey, 514
Barnard, Henry, 270
Barnburners, 327
Barry, Philip, 715
Bartram, John, 86
Bartram, William, 86
Baruch, Bernard M., 575, 684
baseball, 467, 478
basketball, 478
Beard, Charles A., 322, 502
Beauregard, General Pierre G. T., 354, 360
Beecher, Catharine, 268
Beecher, Henry Ward, 260, 340, 367, 473
Beecher, Lyman, 260, 263
Behrman, S. N., 715
Belknap, W. W., 450
Bell, Alexander Graham, 409
Bell, John, 351
Bellamy, Edward, 494–5
Bellamy, Joseph, 83
Bellows, George, 717
Belmont, August, 412, 461
Benet, Stephen Vincent, 714
Benjamin, Asher, 293
Bennett, James Gordon, 272
Bennington College, 729
Benson, Ezra Taft, 694
Benton, Thomas Hart (statesman), 166,
  188, 236, 237, 242, 245, 247, 308, 315, 338
Benton, Thomas Hart (painter), 718
Berger, Victor, 577
Berlin, Irving, 720
Bestor, Arthur E., 728
Beveridge, Albert J., 520
Beverly, Robert, 88
Biddle, Nicholas, 247
Bilbo, Theodore G., 393
Bill of Rights: English, 55; American, 135
Billings, Josh, 505
Billings, William, 91
bills of credit, 62–5
Bingham, George Caleb, 292
Birney, James G., 312, 323, 324, 328
birth control, 256, 735

birth rate: colonial, 49; in nineteenth century, 256; in twentieth century, 735
Black, Hugo, 634
black codes: before Civil War, 207–08; after Civil War, 378
Black Hawk War, 190, 192
Blackmur, R. P., 709
Blackwell, Elizabeth, 268
Blaine, James G., 451, 453, 455, 456, 522–3
Bland-Allison Act (1878), 453
Blanshard, Paul, 727
Blease, Cole, 393
Bloomer, Amelia, 268
Boas, Franz, 743
Bogota conference (1948), 674
Bok, Edward L., 482
Boker, G. H., 504
bonus, for World War I veterans, 595–6
Boone, Daniel, 183, 184
Booth, John Wilkes, 371
Borah, William E., 582, 583, 602, 650
Boston and Maine Railroad, 402
Boston Manufacturing Company, 225, 228
Boston Massacre, 99
Boston Teaparty, 100
Bourbons (in Southern states), 387, 389
Bourne, Randolph, 707
Brackenridge, H. H., 278
Braddock, General Edward, 72
Bradford, William, 34, 88
Bradley, General Omar, 661, 664, 691
Bradstreet, Anne, 87
Bragg, General Braxton, 366, 369
"brain trust," 631
Brandeis, Louis D., 500, 546
Brandywine, battle of, 112
Breckinridge, John C., 350–1
Bretton Woods Conference (1944), 672
Bridger, Jim, 296, 303, 310
Briggs, C. A., 473
Bristow, B. H., 450
Brook Farm, 268, 282
Brookings Institution, 617
Brooklyn Bridge, 515
Brooks, Cleanth, 709
Brooks, Preston, 342
Brooks, Van Wyck, 707
Brotherhood of the Kingdom, 474
Brown, Antoinette, 268
Brown, Charles Brockden, 278
Brown, John, 340, 347–8
Brown, Joseph E., 384
Brown, William Hill, 87, 277
Brown University, 79

Brownell, W. C., 512
Bryan, William Jennings, 440, 481, 559, 600; 1896 campaign, 462; later campaigns, 551, 555; Secretary of State, 561, 570
Bryant, William Cullen, 243, 280, 292
Bryn Mawr College, 478
Buchanan, James, 342–5, 352–3
Bucks Stove and Range Company case, 419
Buell, General D. C., 361, 362, 366
Buena Vista, battle of, 315
Buenos Aires conference (1936), 645–6
Bulfinch, Charles, 293
Bull Moose Party. *See* Progressive Party (1912)
Bull Run, battle of, 360
Bunche, Ralph, 732
Bunker Hill, battle of, 111
Burchfield, Charles, 717
Bureau of the Budget, 593
Burgess, John W., 486
Burgoyne, General John, 106, 112
Burke, Edmund, 95, 102
Burke, Kenneth, 708
Burns, Antony, 341
Burnside, General Ambrose E., 362, 365
Burr, Aaron, 144, 145, 152, 159
Byrd, William, 80, 88
Byrnes, James F., 656, 682, 685

Cabell, James Branch, 712
Cable, George Washington, 505
Cabot, John, 24
Cahensly, Peter, 475
Cairo Conference (1943), 670
Cajuns, 72
Calder, Alexander, 719
Calhoun, John C.: early career, 169, 175, 178; political theory, 216–18; Vice-President, 239–40; during Jackson's administration, 244–6; Secretary of State, 311; Southern leader, 326, 329; death, 337
California: early settlers, 309, 310; acquisition of, 313, 315–18; gold rush, 318–19; statehood, 327–8, 330
Calles, Plutarco Elias, 604
Calvin, John, 9, 40
Calvinism: in Europe, 9–12; in colonies, 39–41, 50–1, 63, 81–3; in early nineteenth century, 258–60; economic influence, 396
Camden, battle of, 113
Cameron, Simon, 447, 451
Camp, Walter, 478
Campbell, Alexander, 260

Canada: French in, 26–7, 37, 68–74; Quebec Act, 97, 100; during War of 1812, 163–5; settlement of boundaries, 156, 168–9, 313; immigration from, 468, 596
canals, building of, 222
Canning, George, 171, 172
Cannon, Joseph G., 552, 556, 557
Capone, Al, 597, 598
Capote, Truman, 712
Capper-Volstead Act (1922), 595
Cárdenas, Lázaro, 646
Cardozo, Benjamin, 500
Carey, Henry, 272, 486
Carey, James B., 643
Carey, Matthew, 272
Carey Act (1894), 442, 554
Carnegie, Andrew, 399, 400, 407, 413, 415, 480, 488
Carnegie, Dale, 737
carpetbaggers, 384–5
Carranza, Venustiano, 536, 537
Carroll, Bishop John, 263
Carson, Kit, 296, 303, 308
Cartier, Jacques, 26
Caruthers, W. A., 287
Casablanca Conference (1943), 669
Cass, Lewis, 327
Cassatt, A. J., 402
Cassatt, Mary, 513
Castlereagh, Viscount, 168, 171
Cather, Willa, 710
Catholic Church: in Europe, 4, 8; in Canada, 26; in Maryland, 30; during early nineteenth century, 262–4; during later nineteenth century, 475–6; during twentieth century, 726–7; hostility to, 263–4, 342, 476, 727
Catlin, George, 292
Catt, Carrie Chapman, 549
caucus system, 145, 237–8
Cecilia Society, 91
Central Pacific Railroad, 373, 402–3
Century, The, 482
Chamberlain, Neville, 649
Champlain, Samuel de, 26
Chancellorsville, battle of, 365
Chandler, Zechariah, 451
Channing, William Ellery, 260
Chaplin, Charles, 613, 740
Chapultepec Conference (1945), 673
Charity Organization Society, 467
Charles I, king of England, 13, 42
Charles II, king of England, 42, 54
Charles River Bridge case, 221, 249–50

Charleston and Hamburg Railroad, 222
Chase, Salmon P., 342, 350, 358
Chase, Samuel, 98, 155
Chatauqua movement, 480
Chatham, William Pitt, earl of, 73, 95, 98, 102
Chattanooga, battle of, 369
Chauncy, Charles, 81
Cherokee Indians, 189, 195
Cheyenne Indians, 423
Chiang Kai-shek, 605, 606, 647, 666, 668, 670, 683–4, 700
Chicago Exposition, 515
Chicago, Milwaukee and St. Paul Railroad v. Minnesota, 405
Chicago, University of, 477
Chickamauga, battle of, 369
Chickasaw Indians, 195
Child, Lydia Maria, 268
child labor: during Industrial Revolution, 225, 228, 230–1; in later nineteenth century, 390, 415; prohibited in interstate commerce, 636
China: early commercial relations, 123, 232, 233; relations before World War I, 520, 527–9, 541–2; during 1920's, 596, 605–6; war with Japan, 647, 666, 668, 672; since World War II, 683–4, 699–700
Chinese immigrants, 472
Chisholm Trail, 428
Choctaw Indians, 195
Christian Science, 475
Church of England. *See* Anglican Church
Churchill, Winston (novelist), 510, 546
Churchill, Winston (statesman), 650, 659, 661, 670
cities: growth of, 139, 229, 255, 466–7, 725–6; government of, 139, 446–7, 547
Civil Rights Bill (1866), 380; (1957), 733
civil service: under Washington, 140; spoils system, 238–9; reform, 454–5
Civil Works Administration, 641
Civilian Conservation Corps, 640
claims clubs, 188
Clark, Champ, 559
Clark, George Rogers, 113
Clark, John Bates, 492
Clark, J. Reuben, 605
Clark, General Mark, 664, 692
Clark, William, 301
Clay, Henry, 170, 185; during War of 1812, 164, 166; nationalist program of, 174–5, 178; character, 236–7; in campaign of 1824, 240; Whig Party leader, 246, 247,

Clay, Henry (*continued*)
251, 252, 312; proposes Compromise of
1850, 328–9; death, 338
Clayton Act (1914), 563
Clayton-Bulwer Treaty (1850), 319, 529
Clemenceau, Georges, 580, 581
Clemens, Samuel L. *See* Twain, Mark
Cleveland, Grover: first administration, 455;
second administration, 420, 456, 460, 461,
522, 523
Clinton, De Witt, 164, 222, 269
Clinton, George, 121, 126, 144, 147, 164
Clinton, Sir Henry, 106, 112, 114
clipper ships, 233–4
coal mining, 225, 389, 406, 554
Cobb, Howell, 343
"coercive acts" (1774), 100
Cohens v. Virginia, 177
Cohn, Roy, 695
Cold Harbor, battle of, 369
Colden, Cadwallader, 86, 87, 88
Cole, Thomas, 292
Colombia, Panama Canal dispute, 529, 532
Colorado, settlement of, 426, 431
Colored Farmers' National Alliance, 391
Colter, John, 302
Columbia University, 79, 81, 477
Columbus, Christopher, 14, 18
Command of the Army Act (1867), 381
commerce: in medieval Europe, 4; in Eng-
land, 12; during colonial period, 38, 54–7,
64; under Confederation, 123; during
early nineteenth century, 231–3
Committee for Industrial Organization,
642–3
Committee to Defend America by Aiding
the Allies, 651
committees of correspondence, 100, 101
Commons, John R., 492
Commonweal, The, 739
Commonwealth and Southern Company,
640
Commonwealth v. Hunt, 230
Communist Party, 599, 625, 654, 691–2, 696
Compton, Arthur, 742
Conestoga wagons, 51, 309
Confederation, Articles of, 108, 122, 126
Congregationalist Church, 474, 726; in
early New England, 39; during later
colonial period, 63, 65, 83; separated from
state, 121; during early nineteenth cen-
tury, 193, 257–60
Conkling, Roscoe, 447, 451, 452, 453
Connally, Tom, 669

Connecticut, settlement of, 36
conservation, of natural resources, 441–2,
554–5, 556, 557, 640
Constitution of the United States, 128–34;
first ten amendments, 135; twelfth, 133,
152; thirteenth, 365, 377; fourteenth, 380,
383, 398–9, 405, 419; fifteenth, 383; six-
teenth, 556; seventeenth, 549, 556;
eighteenth, 550, 598; nineteenth, 549;
twenty-first, 598; *see also* Appendix II
Constitutional Union Party, 350
Continental Congress, 101–2, 103–5, 108,
122
conventions, nominating, 238
Cooke, Jay, 359, 412
Cooley, C. H., 491
Coolidge, Calvin, 591–2, 595, 596, 604
Cooper, James Fenimore, 275, 279–80
Cooper, Thomas, 215
Cope, E. D., 480
Copland, Aaron, 721
Copley, John Singleton, 89, 90
Copperheads, 358
Coral Sea, battle of the, 660, 666
Corbett, James J., 467
Cornell University, 477
Cornwallis, Lord, 106, 113, 114
Coronado, Francisco Vásquez de, 15
corporations: growth during early nine-
teenth century, 220–3, 226–7; after Civil
War, 397, 414; twentieth-century, 615–16
Cortés, Hernán, 15
Cotton, John, 37, 39
cotton cultivation: in Old South, 203–6,
209–11; after Civil War, 388–9, 432
Coughlin, Charles E., 625, 626
cowboys, 427–9
Cox, James A., 583
Cozzens, James Gould, 712
Craddock, C. E., 505
Cram, Ralph Adams, 516
Cramer, C. F., 590
Crane, Hart, 714
Crane, Stephen, 510
Crawford, William H., 239–40
Crédit Mobilier, 403, 450
Creek Indians, 166, 195, 196
Creel, George, 577, 579
Crèvecoeur, St. Jean de, 52, 60
crime, 265, 466, 470, 597–9, 736
Crittendon, John J., 353
Crocker, Charles, 403
Crockett, David, 200, 505
Croly, Herbert, 545

Cromwell, Oliver, 42, 54

Cuba, 15, 170, 209; Southern interest in, 337; liberation of, 520, 523–5; intervention in, 533, 535, 603; Good Neighbor policy towards, 646

Cummings, E. E., 714

currency: during colonial period, 62–5, 85; during Revolution, 109; under Confederation, 143; during Washington administration, 193; controversy, 236; during Jackson administration, 247–9; during Civil War, 359, 373; in later nineteenth century, 448–9, 452–3, 456–63; during Wilson administration, 561–3; under New Deal, 638–9

Curry, John Steuart, 718

Curtis, George W., 454

Cushing, Caleb, 233

Custer, George, 424

Danbury Hatters case, 419

dancing, 91, 716

Darrow, Clarence, 600

Dartmouth College, 79, 177

Dartmouth College case, 132, 177, 397

Darwin, Charles, influence of, 487–490

Davenport, John, 36, 39

Dougherty, Harry, 589, 590

Davidson, Jo, 719

Davidson, Thomas, 496

Davis, Elmer, 659

Davis, Jeff, 393

Davis, Jefferson, 196, 329, 337, 352, 354, 356, 360, 371

Davis, John W., 591

Dawes, Charles G., 602

Dawes, William, 103

Dawes Severalty Act (1887), 424–5

Debs, Eugene, 420, 495, 560, 577

debt, imprisonment for, 62; abolition of, 231, 243, 265

Declaration of Independence, 105; _see also_ Appendix I

Declaratory Act (1766), 98

DeForest, Lee, 613

deism, 76, 80

Delaware, settlement of, 44

De Leon, Daniel, 495

De Mille, Agnes, 716

Democratic Party, 144; in Jacksonian period, 240; after Mexican War, 326–7; before Civil War, 344–6; in North during Civil War, 358; in South after Civil War, 386, 391–3; in national politics during

Democratic Party (_continued_) later nineteenth century, 444–5; during New Deal, 631; in 1950's, 697

Dennison, A. L., 226

Dependent's Pension Act (1890), 456

Desert Land Act (1877), 429

Dew, Thomas R., 208

Dewey, Admiral George, 524

Dewey, John, 499

Dewey, Thomas E., 676, 679

De Voto, Bernard, 705

Dial (Transcendentalist), 282; (twentieth century), 706

Díaz, Porfirio, 535

Dickinson, Emily, 504

Dickinson, John, 99, 101, 122

Dingley Tariff (1897), 463

Disciples of Christ, 260

Distribution Act (1836), 248, 250

divorce, 256, 734–5

Dix, Dorothea, 266

Dixiecrats, 679

Dodge, Grenville M., 403

Doheny, Edward L., 590

dollar diplomacy, 533–4, 541

Dolliver, Jonathan P., 556

Dominican Republic, intervention in, 533, 534, 603, 646

Donnelly, Ignatius, 458

Donner party, 309

Dos Passos, John, 710

Doubleday, Abner, 467

Doughty, Thomas, 292

Douglas, Lloyd, 712

Douglas, Stephen A., 329, 333, 338, 339, 345–7, 350–1, 358

Douglass, Dr. William, 86, 87, 88

Dow, Neal, 267

draft: Confederate, 357; Union, 359; World War I, 575; World War II, 652, 657; since 1945, 677, 691

Drago, Luis, 533

Drake, E. L., 407

drama: colonial period, 87–8; twentieth century, 715

Dred Scott case, 344

Dreiser, Theodore, 510, 709

Drew, Daniel, 402

Dubinsky, David, 642, 643

Duke, James B., 410

Duke University, 477

Dulles, John Foster, 698–703

Dumbarton Oaks Conference (1944), 672

Dummer, Jeremiah, 91

Duncan, Isadora, 716
Dunkers, 50, 91
Dunlap, William, 280
Dunne, Finley Peter, 506
Du Pont family, 612, 613, 615
Durand, Asher, 292
Dutch colonists, 27–8, 43, 46
Dutch Reformed Church, 258
Dwight, Timothy, 259, 277

Eakins, Thomas, 513
Early, General Jubal, 370
East Indies. *See* Indonesia
Eaton, Peggy, 244–5
Economic Cooperation Administration, 689
economic theory, study of: colonial period,
　77, 84–5; early nineteenth century, 272;
　later nineteenth century, 486, 491–5
Eddy, Mary Baker, 475
Edison, Thomas A., 409, 613
education: in colonies, 41, 79–80; in Old
　Northwest, 193; in Old South, 214–15;
　early nineteenth century, 269–71; later
　nineteenth century, 476–9; influence of
　John Dewey, 500; twentieth century,
　727–9
Edwards, Jonathan, 64–5, 82–3, 259
Eggleston, Edward, 505
Eisenhower, Dwight D., 660–5, 690–703, 733
Eisenhower Doctrine, 702
El Alamein, battle of, 660
electrical industries, 409, 544–5, 612–13,
　615, 639–40
Eliot, Charles W., 478, 479
Eliot, Jared, 86
Eliot, T. S., 705, 708, 714
Elizabeth I, queen of England, 10, 12, 24–5
Elkins Act (1903), 553
Ely, Richard T., 392
Embargo Act (1807), 161–2
Emergency Fleet Corporation, 576, 594
Emergency Quota Act (1921), 596
Emerson, Ralph Waldo, 275, 277, 281, 282–
　4, 290
Emigrant Aid Society, 339
Emmett, Daniel, 294
Endicott, John, 35
Enforcement Acts (1870–1), 386
England: political development of, 10–13,
　42, 54; beginnings of colonial expansion,
　24–6, 28; policy towards early colonies,
　53–5; *see also* Great Britain
English Bill (1858), 345
entail, abolition of, 121

Episcopal Church. *See* Anglican Church
Erie Canal, 190, 222
Erie Railroad, 333, 402
Esch-Cummins Act (1920), 594
Espionage Act (1917), 577
Ethical Culture Society, 496
European Recovery Program, 689
Evangelical Alliance, 474
Evans, George Henry, 231
Evans, Oliver, 225
Everett, Edward, 351
Evergood, Philip, 718
evolution, theory of, 473, 486–90

Fair Employment Practices Committee, 732
Fair Labor Standards Act (1938), 636
Fall, Albert B., 590
Fallen Timbers, battle of, 148
family, development of American, 255–7,
　470, 734–6
Farley, James A., 631
Farm Credit Administration, 638
Farm Security Administration, 637
Farnham, Marynia, 736
Farragut, Admiral David G., 362, 364
Farrell, James T., 712
Fascism (in United States), 625
Faubus, Orval E., 733
Faulkner, William, 711
Federal Bureau of Investigation, 598, 659
Federal Communications Commission, 613,
　739, 741
Federal Council of Churches, 474, 726
Federal Deposit Insurance Corporation, 638
Federal Emergency Relief Administration,
　641
Federal Farm Board, 595
Federal Farm Loan Act (1916), 563
Federal Home Loan Banks, 629
Federal Housing Authority, 641
Federal Power Commission, 594
Federal Reserve System, 561–3, 621, 630
Federal Trade Commission, 563, 593
Federalist Party: organization, 144–6; de-
　cline, 158–9, 167
Feke, Robert, 89
Fellowship of the New Life, 496
Field, Justice Stephen J., 398
Fillmore, Millard, 329, 343
finance, government: during Revolution,
　109; under Confederation, 127; in Wash-
　ington administration, 141–3; in Jefferson
　administration, 154; during War of 1812,

finance (*continued*)
164; in Jacksonian period, 248, 250; of Confederacy, 357; of Union, 359; after Civil War, 449; during World War I, 577; during 1920's, 593, 618; during 1930's, 630, 632, 642; during World War II, 658; during 1950's, 694, 698
Fink, Mike, 197
Finney, Charles G., 258, 259
Fish, Hamilton, 448
fisheries (New England), 33, 38, 114, 233
Fisk, Jim, 402
Fiske, John, 487, 490
Fitch, Clyde, 715
Fitch, John, 221
Fitzgerald, F. Scott, 710
Fitzhugh, George, 208
Fitzpatrick, Thomas, 302
Flanders, Ralph E., 696
Flathead Indians, 308
Fletcher v. Peck, 177
Flexner, Abraham, 729
Florida: under Spanish rule, 15, 68, 70, 73, 115, 125; American interest in, 156, 158, 163, 166; acquisition of, 169; settlement of, 198, 205
flour-milling, 224, 225
Floyd, John, 307
folksongs, 91, 294, 516, 720
football, 478
Foote, Augustus, 245
Forbes, Charles R., 590
Forbes, John Murray, 333
Ford, Henry, 611–12, 615
Ford, John, 740
Fordney-McCumber Tariff (1922), 593
Forest Reserve Act (1891), 442
Foster, Stephen C., 294
Fourier, Charles, influence of, 268
Fourteen Points, 579
Fox, John, 512
France: settlement of Canada, 26–7; French in United States, 50, 189, 263; colonial rivalry with Great Britain, 68–74; during War of Independence, 109, 111, 113, 114; relations during Washington and Adams administrations, 146–51; relations during Jefferson and Madison administrations, 155–8, 160–3; intervention in Mexico, 368; during World War I, 566–7, 580–1, 584; during 1920's, 601–3; during World War II, 649–50, 664, 672; in 1950's, 701–2
Frank, Waldo, 707

Franklin, Benjamin, 59, 60, 73, 94; intellectual activities, 78–9, 80, 84–5, 86, 88; during Revolution, 102, 103, 111, 114
fraternal societies, 468
Fredericksburg, battle of, 365
Freedmen's Bureau, 376, 380, 384
Freeman, Mary E. Wilkins, 504
Free Soil Party, 328, 337
Frémont, John C., 308, 315, 343
French, Daniel Chester, 514
Freneau, Philip, 87, 145, 277
Frick, Henry Clay, 407
Friends, Society of. *See* Quakers
Fromm, Erich, 737, 738
Frost, Robert, 713–14
Fugitive Slave Act (1850), 328, 332, 341, 347
fugitive slaves, 324
Fulbright, J. William, 669
Fuller, Margaret, 268, 282, 284
Fulton, Robert, 221
functionalism (in architecture), 515–16, 719
fundamentalism, 473, 600, 726
fur trade: colonial period, 21, 26, 34, 42, 68, 69, 96; in Far West, 301–3

Gadsden, Christopher, 98
Gadsden Treaty (1853), 156, 318
Gage, General Thomas, 100, 102, 103
Galbraith, J. K., 680
Gallatin, Albert, 144, 154, 164, 166, 187
Gallaudet, Thomas Hopkins, 266
Galloway, Joseph, 102
Garden, Alexander, 86
Garfield, James A., 244, 453
Garland, Hamlin, 509
Garman, C. E., 496
Garrison, William Lloyd, 323, 324
Gates, General Horatio, 110, 112, 113
General Electric Company, 409
General Motors Company, 612
Genêt, Edmond Charles, 147
Geneva Conference (1927), 603; (1932), 603; (1955), 701
"Genteel Tradition," 285, 503–4, 512, 705
Gentlemen's Agreement (1907–08), 472, 540
Geological Survey, 442, 480
George III, king of England, 96, 102, 105, 114
George, Henry, 494
Georgetown University, 263
Georgia, settlement of, 49–50, 51, 52, 205
German immigrants: during colonial period, 44, 46, 50–1, 66, 91; before Civil War, 263,

German immigrants (*continued*) 333, 336; during later nineteenth century, 415, 430, 469

German Reformed Church, 258

Germantown, battle of, 112

Germany, 519, 521; during World War I, 566–74, 578–81, 584; during 1920's, 601–3, 618; during 1930's, 624, 646, 647; during World War II, 649–55, 659–65, 671; since 1945, 681–2, 700–1

Gerry, Elbridge, 150

Gershwin, George, 721

Gettysburg, battle of, 365–6

Ghent, Treaty of (1814), 166

Gibbons, Cardinal James, 475, 476

Gibbons v. Ogden, 176

Gibbs, Willard, 479

Giddings, Franklin H., 491

Gilbert, Cass, 516, 719

Gilbert, Sir Humphrey, 25

Girdler, Tom, 642

Gladden, Washington, 474

Glasgow, Ellen, 511

Glass, Carter, 392

Glass-Owen Act (1913), 561

Glavis, Louis R., 557

Glidden, Joseph F., 429

Godey's Ladies' Book, 272

Godfrey, Thomas, 88

Godkin, Edwin L., 454, 460, 482

Gold Standard Act (1900), 463

golf, 468

Gompers, Samuel, 418, 563, 576

Good Neighbor policy, 645–6

Goodrich, Samuel, 271

Gottschalk, Louis Moreau, 294

Gould, Jay, 400, 402, 412

Grace, Eugene, 642

Graduation Act (1854), 188

Grady, Henry, 389

Graham, Martha, 716

Grand Army of the Republic, 445, 455, 456

"grandfather" clause, 392

"Granger cases," 405

Granger movement, 405, 440, 457

Grant, Ulysses S.: during Civil War, 361, 362, 364, 366, 369–71; during Reconstruction, 381, 386; President, 382–3, 448–51

Grasse, Comte de, 106

Graves, Admiral Thomas, 106

Gray, Asa, 273, 487

Gray, Captain Robert, 233

Great Awakening, 64–5, 81–2

Great Britain: policies during colonial period, 53–7, 64, 68–74; policies during Revolution, 93–115; relations during Confederation, 123, 125; relations during 1790's, 146–51; War of 1812, 160–7; settlement of Canadian boundary, 168-9, 300–1, 309–10, 313; role in Monroe Doctrine, 171–3; trade relations, 231–3; interest in Texas, 305, 307; interest in Central America, 173, 319; during Civil War, 336, 366–8; Venezuela boundary dispute, 523; during World War I, 566–74, 578–81, 584; during 1920's, 601, 606; during World War II, 649–55, 659–65, 672; loan to, 689; in 1950's, 701–2

Great Meadows, battle of, 70, 72

Great Northern Railroad, 404

Great Plains, 299, 423; settlement of, 427–31

Greek Revival (in architecture), 293–4

Greeley, Horace, 272, 450

Green, William, 642

Greenback Party, 440, 457

Greenbacks, 359, 449

Greene, General Nathanael, 110, 113

Greenough, Horatio, 292

Greenville, Treaty of (1795), 189

Gregg, William, 211

Grenville, George, 97, 98

Griffith, D. W., 740

Gropper, William, 718

Guadalcanal, battles of, 660

Guadalupe Hidalgo, Treaty of (1848), 316, 318

Guam, acquisition of, 525

Guest, Edgar, 713

Guggenheim, Meyer, 427

Guggenheim Foundation, 706

Guilford Court House, battle of, 113

Haiti, 158; intervention in, 534, 603, 646

Hakluyt, Richard, 25

Hale, John P., 337

Hale, Sara Josepha, 268

halfbreeds, 451, 453

Halleck, Fitzgreene, 280

Halleck, General Henry W., 361, 364

Hamilton, Alexander, 117–19, 126, 128, 129, 135; Secretary of the Treasury, 140–3; Federalist leader, 143–52; death, 159

Hammett, Dashiell, 713

Hammond, James H., 205

Hancock, John, 99, 102, 103

Hancock, Winfield Scott, 453

Hanna, Mark, 461–3, 551
Hansen, Alvin H., 627
Hanson, Howard, 712
Hapgood, Norman, 546
Harding, Chester, 291
Harding, Warren G., 583, 589–91, 599
Harper's, 447, 482, 739
Harriman, Edward H., 552
Harris, George W., 287
Harris, Joel Chandler, 505
Harris, W. T., 496
Harrison, Benjamin, 455, 456, 460, 522
Harrison, William Henry, 163, 165, 187, 190, 251, 252
Harte, Bret, 505
Hartford Convention, 167
Hartford Wits, 274, 277
Hartley, Marsden, 717
Harvard College, 41, 79, 85, 86, 259, 271, 477, 478, 479
Hassam, Childe, 513
Hatch Act (1887), 435
Havana conference (1928), 605; (1940), 650
Havemeyer, Henry O., 410
Hawaii, 233; acquisition of, 522
Hawley-Smoot Tariff (1930), 593
Hawthorne, Nathaniel, 268, 275, 277, 285–6, 337
Hay, John, 528, 533
Hay-Herran Treaty (1903), 529
Hay-Pauncefote Treaty (1901), 529
Hayburn case, 141
Hayes, Rutherford B., 387, 451–3, 529
Haymarket riot, 420
Hayne, Robert Y., 245
Haywood, William D., 420–1
health, public, 139, 466, 480, 742–3
Hearst, William Randolph, 481, 524
Helper, Hinton R., 212
Hemingway, Ernest, 512, 710
Henderson, Richard, 184
Henri, Robert, 513
Henry IV, king of France, 26
Henry VII, king of England, 24
Henry VIII, king of England, 10
Henry, Andrew, 302
Henry, Joseph, 273, 409
Henry, Patrick, 67, 98, 100, 101, 117, 121, 126, 128, 134
Henry Street Settlement, 467
Henry the Navigator, 13
Hepburn Act (1906), 406, 553
Herbert, Victor, 516
Hergesheimer, Joseph, 712

Hill, James J., 404, 552
Hillman, Sidney, 642, 643, 656
Hispanic America: colonization, 14–16, 18; independence, 170–4; relations during 1880's and 1890's, 522–6; during early twentieth century, 529–37; during 1920's, 603–5, 619; during 1930's, 624, 645–6; during and after World War II, 652, 673–4
Hiss, Alger, 692
history, study of: during colonial period, 88; in New England, 281–2; during later nineteenth century, 486, 490, 500–2; contemporary tendencies, 743
Hitchcock, Edward, 273
Hitler, Adolf, 603, 649–55, 664
Hoffman, Paul G., 689, 692
Holbrook, Josiah, 271
Holden v. Hardy, 419
holding companies, 408, 410
"Holiness" cults, 475
Holley, Horace, 215
Holmes, Dr. Oliver Wendell, 285
Holmes, Justice Oliver Wendell, 500, 578, 634, 744
Holy Alliance, 171
Home Owners Loan Corporation, 638
Homer, Winslow, 513
Homestead Act (1862), 372, 429–30, 440
Homestead strike, 420
Hood, General John B., 369
Hood, Raymond, 719
Hooker, General Joseph, 362, 365
Hooker, Thomas, 36, 39
Hooper, J. J., 287
Hoover, Herbert, 576, 590, 593; President, 592, 595, 596, 598, 606, 628–30
Hoover, J. Edgar, 598
Hopkins, Harry, 641, 659
Hopkins, Mark, 403
Hopkins, Samuel, 83
Hopkinson, Francis, 91
Hopper, Edward, 717
Horney, Karen, 737
horse racing, 467
Hot Springs Conference (1943), 672
Hound and Horn, 706
House, Edward M., 561, 570
Houston, Samuel, 306, 307, 352
Howard, Bronson, 715
Howard, General Oliver O., 376
Howard, Sidney, 715
Howe, Elias, 226

Howe, E. W., 505
Howe, Samuel Gridley, 266
Howe, Sir William, 106, 108, 111, 112
Howells, William Dean, 508–9
Hudson, Henry, 24, 27
Hudson River School, 292, 513
Hudson's Bay Company, 301, 308, 313
Huerta, Victoriano, 536
Hughes, Charles Evans, 548, 572; Secretary of State, 590, 601–3; Chief Justice, 634
Hughes, Bishop John, 263
Hull, Cordell, 631, 645–7, 649, 655, 669, 670, 672
Hull House, 467
humor, in American literature, 197, 200, 287, 505–6
Humphreys, George M., 693
Huneker, James Gibbons, 511
Hunkers, 327
Hunt, Richard M., 515
Huntington, Collis P., 403
Huston, John, 740
Hutchins, Robert M., 729
Hutchinson, Anne, 36
Hutchinson, Thomas, 88, 98, 100
hymns, 91, 294

Ickes, Harold, 631, 639
Idaho, settlement of, 313, 426, 431
Illinois, settlement of, 163, 178, 189–90, 198
Illinois Central Railroad, 333
immigration: colonial period, 49–52; early nineteenth century, 210, 228–9, 333, 336; later nineteeth century, 415, 430, 468–71; restriction of, 471–2, 596–7
Immigration Quota Act (1924), 596
Impressionism (in painting), 513
income tax, 359, 449, 461, 561
Independent Treasury, 250–1, 252, 312
Indiana, settlement of, 163, 178, 189–90, 193, 198
Indian Reorganization Act (1934), 425
Indians, 23–4; during colonial period, 32, 33, 37, 44, 68, 70, 72, 73, 96–7; Federal policy towards, 188–9; in Old Northwest, 148, 163, 190; in Old Southwest, 169, 184, 195–6; in Far West, 299, 303, 423–5; during twentieth century, 425
Indo-China, 699–700
Indonesia: commercial relations with, 123, 232, 233; in World War II, 654, 660
Industrial Workers of the World, 420–1
industry: colonial period, 38, 64, 66; in Old South, 211; growth in Northern states,

industry (*continued*)
223–6, 332; during Civil War, 372; in New South, 389–90; during later nineteenth century, 395–401, 406–10; during 1920's, 611–14; after World War II, 680
initiative, the, 549
injunctions, 419, 563
Inness, George, 513
insanity, treatment of, 266, 736–7
instrumentalism (in philosophy), 499–500
Insular Cases, 526
Insull, Samuel, 615
Intermediate Credits Act (1923), 595
internal improvements, controversy about, 175, 216, 220–3, 236, 245
Interstate Commerce Act (1887), 405–6
Interstate Commerce Commission, 406, 553–4, 556, 593, 594
Iowa, settlement of, 192, 198, 336
Iowa, University of, 268
Irish immigrants, 52, 228–9, 263, 342, 415
iron industry, 56, 64, 225, 406
Iroquois Indians, 23, 26, 27, 68, 190
Irving, Washington, 275, 278–9
Israel, 701–2
Isthmian Doctrine, 530
Ives, Burl, 720
Iwo Jima, battle of, 666, 668

Jackson, Andrew, 166, 169, 185, 195, 196; President, 240–50, 307, 308, 313
Jackson, Charles, 273
Jackson, Richard, 88
Jackson, General Thomas J., 360, 364, 365
James I, king of England, 29, 30
James II, king of England, 54–5
James, Henry, Sr., 497
James, Henry, 497, 507–8
James, William, 481, 497–9
Japan: commercial treaty with, 233; rise of, 520, 528; relations before World War I, 537–41; during World War I, 542, 566, 578, 584; during 1920's, 596, 601, 603; during 1930's, 605–6, 647; during World War II, 649–55, 660, 665–9; since 1945, 682, 700
Japanese immigrants, 472, 540, 659
jazz, 720–1
Jay, John, 108, 114, 126, 128, 134, 135, 140, 148
Jay-Gardoqui Treaty (1786), 126, 134
Jay Treaty (1794), 148
Jeffers, Robinson, 714
Jefferson, Thomas, 170, 171, 179; ideals and character, 117–19, 153–4; during Revolu-

Jefferson, Thomas (*continued*)
tion, 100, 102, 105, 121, 122; during
Confederation, 124, 128; Secretary of
State, 140; Republican leader, 142–6, 149,
151; President, 152–62, 301; as architect,
293
Jeffries, James, 467
Jehovah's Witnesses, 475
Jewett, Sarah Orne, 504
Jim Crow laws, 393
Johns Hopkins University, 477, 479, 480
Johnson, Andrew, 212, 370, 377–82
Johnson, Hiram, 582, 583
Johnson, Hugh S., 636
Johnson, Samuel, 81, 87
Johnson, Tom, 547
Johnston, General Albert Sidney, 361
Johnston, General Joseph E., 360, 364, 369,
371
Johnston, Mary, 505
Joliet, Louis, 68
Jolson, Al, 613
Jones Act (1917), 526
journalism: in colonial period, 80; in early
nineteenth century, 238, 271–2; in later
nineteenth century, 481–3; in twentieth
century, 738–9
Juárez, Benito, 368
Judah, Theodore D., 403
judicial review, theory of, 140–1, 398–9
Judiciary Act (1789), 140; (1801), 152

Kansas, settlement of, 196, 339–40, 344–6,
431
Kansas-Nebraska Act (1854), 330, 338
Kearny, Stephen W., 315
Kefauver, Estes, 697
Kelley, Hall Jackson, 308
Kelley, Oliver H., 457
Kellogg, Frank B., 602, 603, 604
Kelly, George, 715
Kennedy, John P., 287
Kent, Chancellor James, 250
Kentucky, settlement of, 97, 125, 181, 183–
5, 198
Kentucky Resolutions (1798), 151, 217
Kern, Jerome, 720
Key, Francis Scott, 165
Keynes, John Maynard, influence of, 626–7,
635
Kidder, Peabody and Company, 412
King, Admiral Ernest J., 659
King, Rufus, 167
King's Mountain, battle of, 106, 113

Kirkland, Joseph, 505
Knight Company case, 411
Knights of Labor, 417–18, 476
Knowlton, Charles, 256
Know Nothing movement, 264, 342
Knox, Frank, 652
Knox, Henry, 140
Knox, Philander, 533–4, 541
Knudsen, William S., 656
Korea, 520, 537, 540, 683; war in, 690–1,
699
Kuhn, Loeb and Company, 412
Ku-Klux Klan (after Civil War), 386; (in
1920's), 600
Kwajalein, battle of, 665

labor, condition of: early nineteenth century, 228–31; later nineteenth century,
389–90, 414–21
labor unions: early nineteenth century, 229–
31; later nineteenth and twentieth cen-
turies, 417–21; under New Deal, 635–6,
642 3
Lachaise, Gaston, 719
Ladies' Home Journal, 482
La Farge, John, 513
Lafayette, Marquis de, 111
La Follette, Robert M., 547–8, 556, 558,
574, 590, 592
La Follette Seamen's Act (1915), 563
Laird rams, 368
laissez faire, economic theory of, 77, 118,
143, 242, 398, 415, 486, 490–5
Lamar, Mirabeau Bonaparte, 307
Lamb, John, 98
Land Act (1796), 187; (1800), 178, 187;
(1820), 187
land banks, 62–3, 64
Land Ordinance (1785), 124, 186, 193
Landon, Alfred M., 634
landownership, systems of: in Southern
colonies, 29, 42, 67; in New England, 34,
38, 64–5; in middle colonies, 43, 44, 65–6;
later colonial period, 61–2; changes during
Revolution, 121; policy of Confederation,
123–5; policy of Federal government, 178,
185–8, 236, 336; in South after Civil War,
387–8; in West, 429–30; growth of tenancy, 437, 438
Lanier, Sidney, 388, 504
Lansing, Robert, 541, 570
Lansing-Ishii Agreement (1917), 541
Larkin, Thomas O., 315
La Salle, Sieur de, 68

Latin America. *See* Hispanic America
Latrobe, Benjamin, 293
Latter Day Saints. *See* Mormon Church
Laughlin, J. Lawrence, 460, 491
Lawrence, Ernest O., 742
Lawson, John Howard, 715
League of Nations, 580–4, 600–1, 606
Leahy, Admiral William D., 659
Lease, Mary Elizabeth, 458
Lee, Ann, 261
Lee, Charles, 110, 112
Lee, Higginson and Company, 412
Lee, Jason, 308
Lee, Richard Henry, 67, 101, 105, 108, 126, 134
Lee, General Robert E., 347, 360, 362, 364–6, 369–71
Leggett, William, 243, 289
Leisler, Jacob, 55, 61
Lend-Lease Act (1941), 653, 656
Lewis, John L., 642, 658
Lewis, Meriwether, 301
Lewis, Sinclair, 709
Lexington, battle of, 103
Leyte Gulf, battle of, 665
Liberal Republican movement, 450
Liberator, 323
Liberia, 323
Liberty Party, 312, 324
libraries, growth of, 80, 193, 271, 480
Lieber, Francis, 486
Life, 739
Lilienthal, David, 639
Lima conference (1938), 645
Lincoln, Abraham, 190, 195, 229, 346–7; President, 350–71
Lindbergh, Charles A., 614
Lindsay, Vachel, 713
literature: colonial period, 77–8, 87–8; before Civil War, 274–91; after Civil War, 503–12; since 1912, 704–15
Little Big Horn, battle of, 424
Little Review, 706
Livingston, Edward, 246
Lloyd, Alfred H., 496
Lloyd, Henry Demarest, 546
Locarno Treaties (1925), 602
Lochner v. New York, 419
Locke, John, influence of, 76, 82, 83, 84, 105
Loco-foco movement, 243, 251, 289
Lodge, Henry Cabot, 520, 582
Logan, James, 86
Logan, John A., 451
"log-rolling," 449

London, Jack, 511
London Conference (1930), 603; (1933), 645
Long, Dr. Crawford, 273
Long, Huey P., 625–6
Long, Major Stephen H., 302
Longfellow, Henry Wadsworth, 285
Longstreet, Augustus Baldwin, 287
Louis XIV, king of France, 50, 69
Louisiana: French and Spanish in, 68, 72, 73, 125; purchase of, 155–8; settlement of, 178, 195, 196, 198
Lovejoy, Elijah, 323
Lowell, Amy, 713
Lowell, Francis C., 225
Lowell, James Russell, 285, 314
Lowell, Robert, 714
Loyalists (in American Revolution), 103–4, 108, 111, 113, 114, 120
Luce, Henry R., 739
Lundy, Benjamin, 323
Lusitania, sinking of, 569
Luther, Martin, 8–9
Lutheran Church, 8–9, 50–1, 258, 726
lyceum movement, 271
lynching, 393, 733
Lynd, Robert and Helen, 743
Lyon, Mary, 268

McAdoo, William G., 591
MacArthur, General Arthur, 527
MacArthur, General Douglas, 660, 665, 682, 690–1
McCarthy, Charles, 548
McCarthy, Joseph, 692, 695–6
McClellan, General George B., 361, 362, 364, 365, 370
McClure's, 483, 546
McCormick Harvester Company, 410, 436
McCosh, James, 485
McCulloch v. Maryland, 176
McCutcheon, George B., 512
Macdonough, Captain Thomas, 165
MacDowell, Edward A., 516
McDowell, General Irvin, 360, 364
McGuffey, William H., 271
McIntire, Samuel, 293
McKay, Donald, 233
McKinley, William, 456, 461–3, 522, 524, 525, 528, 551
MacLeish, Archibald, 705, 714
McLoughlin, Dr. John, 301
McMaster, John B., 301
McNary-Haugen plan, 595
Macon's Bill (1810), 162

Macune, C. W., 391

Madero, Francisco, 535, 536

Madison, James, 171, 174, 175; role in making Constitution, 126, 128, 129, 130, 132, 133, 134, 135; Congressman, 140; leader in Republican Party, 144, 145, 149, 151; Secretary of State, 154, 155; President, 162, 164, 165

magazines, 80, 272, 275, 482–3, 739

Magellan, Ferdinand, 14

Mahan, Alfred T., 521

Mailer, Norman, 712

Maine: settlement, 37; statehood, 179, 198

Maine, sinking of, 524

Major, Charles, 512

Manassas, battle of, 364

Manchuria, 537, 540, 605–6, 668, 671

Manifest Destiny, 311

Manila Bay, battle of, 524

Mann, Horace, 270

Mann-Elkins Act (1910), 406, 556

Manship, Paul, 719

Marbury v. Madison, 141, 154–5

Marcy, William L., 238

Marin, John, 717

Marion, Francis, 113

Marne, battle of the, 566

Marquand, John P., 712

Marquette, Jacques, 68

Marsh, Othniel C., 480

Marsh, Reginald, 717

Marshall, General George C., 659, 683, 685, 689

Marshall, John, 132, 150, 152, 154–5, 176–8, 196

Marshall Plan, 689

Martin v. Hunter's Lessee, 177

Marx brothers, 740

Marxism, influence of, 495, 707–8

Maryland, settlement of, 30–2

Mason, George, 134

Mason, James M., 367

Mason, Lowell, 294

Massachusetts: settlement, 34–41; deprived of charter, 54–5; conflicts during early eighteenth century, 62, 63, 64–5; Shays's Rebellion, 128

Masters, Edgar Lee, 713

Mather, Cotton, 40, 41, 80, 81, 84, 85, 86, 88

Mather, Increase, 40, 41, 55, 81, 84, 85

Maury, Matthew Fontaine, 273

Maximum Employment Act (1946), 678

Maximum Freight Rate case, 406

Mayhew, Jonathan, 81, 84

Maysville road veto, 245

Meade, General George G., 365–6

Meat Inspection Act (1906), 546, 555

meat-packing industry, 225, 410

medicine, progress of, 86–7, 480, 742

Mellon, Andrew W., 590, 593

Melville, Herman, 233, 275, 288–9

Memorial Day massacre, 643

Mencken, H. L., 706–7

Mennonites, 44, 50

Mercantilism, 7, 53–7, 94

Merchant Marine Act (1920), 594; (1928), 594; (1936), 641

Merrimack Manufacturing Company, 225

Methodist Church, 215, 257–60, 474, 726

Mexico: conquest by Spaniards, 15, 18; independence, 170, 173; events leading to war, 304–7, 312, 313–15; war with United States, 315–18; French intervention, 368; relations during Wilson administration, 535–7; during 1920's, 604; during Franklin Roosevelt administration, 646, 673

Michelson, Albert A., 480

Michigan, settlement of, 163, 189, 190, 192

Michigan, University of, 193

Middle East Defence Organization, 701

Midway: acquistion of, 521; battle of, 660, 666

militia, 59, 69, 109, 164

Millay, Edna St. Vincent, 714

Miller, Arthur, 738

Miller, Lewis, 480

Miller, Thomas W., 590

Miller, William, 261

Milligan, ex parte, 382

Millikan, Robert A., 742

Mining Act (1872), 430

missions, foreign, 233, 259, 525, 527

Mississippi, settlement of, 178, 182, 195, 196, 197, 198

Missouri, settlement of, 179, 182, 197, 198

Missouri Compromise, 179, 330, 332, 338, 344

Missouri Fur Company, 302

Mitchell, Charles E., 621

Mitchell, John, 554

Mitchell, Margaret, 712

Mitchell, Wesley C., 492

Mobile and Ohio Railroad, 333

modernism (in religion), 473, 726

Molasses Act (1733), 56, 97

Monk, Maria, 264

Monmouth, battle of, 112

Monroe, Harriet, 706, 713

Monroe, James, 158, 167, 168–74, 175, 195

Monroe Doctrine, 169–74, 313, 319, 368, 523, 532, 605, 645–6

Montana, settlement of, 426, 431

Montcalm, Marquis de, 73

Montevideo conference (1933), 645

Montgomery, General Bernard L., 660, 661, 664

Moody, Dwight L., 474

Moody, John, 411

Moody, William Vaughn, 510

Moore, Marianne, 714

Moravians, 91

More, Paul Elmer, 708

Morgan, J. Pierpont, 399, 412–13, 461, 552, 571, 572

Morgan, Dr. John, 86

Morgan, Lewis, H., 743

Morgan, T. H., 480

Morison, Samuel Eliot, 743

Morley, Edward, 480

Mormon Church, 262, 295, 310–11, 431

Morrill Land-Grant Act (1862), 373, 430, 435, 477

Morrill Tariff (1861), 372

Morris, George S., 496

Morris, Nelson, 410

Morris, Robert, 108, 126

Morrow, Dwight, 604

Morse, Samuel F. B., 223, 263, 291

Morton, Oliver, 451

Morton, William T. G., 273

Moscow Conference (1943), 670

motion-picture industry, 613, 740–1

Mott, Lucretia, 267

Mount, William S., 292

Mount Holyoke College, 268

Muckrakers, 546

Mugwumps, 455

Mulligan letters, 451, 455

Mumford, Lewis, 707, 720

Munich Conference (1938), 649

Munn v. Illinois, 405

Munsey, Frank, 559

Munsey's, 483

Murfree, Mary N., 505

Murray, Philip, 643, 658

music: colonial period, 91–2; early nineteenth century, 294; later nineteenth century, 516–17; twentieth century, 720–1

Mutual Defense Assistance Act (1948), 690

Napoleon I, emperor of France, 146, 158, 160–2, 165, 170

Napoleon III, emperor of France, 368

Nasby, Petroleum Vesuvius, 505

Nashville, battle of, 369

Nashville Convention (1850), 329

Nast, Thomas, 447

Nation, the, 482, 739

National Academy of Design, 291, 513

National Association for the Advancement of Colored People, 732

National Bank Act (1863), 373, 459

National Bureau of Economic Research, 680

National Council of Churches, 726

National Farmers' Alliance, 391, 458

National Industrial Recovery Act (1933), 632, 633, 635

National Labor Relations Board, 636, 643, 679

National Labor Union, 417

National Recovery Administration, 635–6

National Reform Union, 231

National Republicans, 240

National War Labor Board, 658

Native American Party, 342

naturalism (in literature), 509

Navaho Indians, 300, 423

Naval Act (1890), 521

Navigation Acts (British), 53–7, 232; (American), 143, 232

Navy, United States: in War of Independence, 114; in War of 1812, 164–5; in Civil War, 361; expansion in later nineteenth century, 521; limitation during 1920's, 601, 603; expansion during Roosevelt administration, 647, 657; in World War II, 665–9

Nebraska, settlement of, 196, 431

Negroes: during colonial period, 31–2, 42, 50, 52–3; in Old South, 206–9; emancipation, 365; during Reconstruction period, 376, 378, 382–3, 384–7; after Reconstruction, 388, 391, 392–4; in twentieth century, 731–4

Nelson, Donald, 656

Neutrality Act (1937), 647; (1939), 650, 654

Nevada, settlement of, 426, 431

Nevins, Allan, 743

New England: settlement of, 33–41; in later colonial period, 64–5; in War of 1812, 167; migration from, 190; industrial expansion, 224–5; trade and shipping, 232–4; intellectual flowering, 281–6

New Hampshire, settlement of, 37, 46, 65

New Haven, colony of, 36
New Jersey, settlement of, 43-4; internal conflicts, 66
New Mexico: settled by Spaniards, 68; acquired by United States, 318; territorial government, 327-9, 330; statehood, 431
New Netherland, 27, 37, 43
New Orleans, battle of, 166
New Republic, the, 739
New Sweden, 28
New York: under English rule, 43, 54, 55; internal conflicts, 65-6; political machines, 238-9; literary development in, 277-8
New York Central Railroad, 333, 402
New York Journal, 481
New York, New Haven and Hartford Railroad, 402, 412
New York Times, 272, 482
New York Tribune, 272
New York World, 481, 738
Newcomb, Simon, 480
Newlands Act (1902), 554
newspapers: colonial period, 80; early nineteenth century, 145, 193, 238, 271-2; later nineteenth century, 481-2; twentieth century, 738-9
Newton, Sir Isaac, 76, 82
Nez Percés Indians, 424
Nicaragua: British in, 173, 319; Walker expedition, 337; intervention in, 534, 603-4
Niebuhr, Reinhold, 726
Niles, John Jacob, 710
Nixon, Richard, 697
non-colonization doctrine, 169-70, 172
Non-Intercourse Act (1809), 162
Norris, Frank, 510
Norris, George W., 556, 557, 574, 594, 639
North, Lord, 96, 99-101, 114
North American Review, 272
North Atlantic Treaty Organization, 689-90, 701
North Carolina, settlement of, 42-3; Regulator movement, 67
North Dakota, settlement of, 428, 430, 431
Northern Alliance, 391, 458
Northern Pacific Railroad, 404
Northern Securities Company case, 552, 553
Northwest Ordinance (1787), 124
Northwest Territory, settlement of, 122, 123-6, 187, 189-95
Norwegian immigrants, 430

Nova Scotia, 72, 97, 111
Noyes, John Humphrey, 261-2
nullification, doctrine of, 217, 244-6
Nuremburg trials, 681-2
Nye, Gerald P., 647

Oberlin College, 268
Obregón, Álvaro, 604
Ochs, Adolph S., 482
Odets, Clifford, 715
Office of Price Administration, 658, 678
Office of Production Management, 656
Office of War Information, 659
Oglethorpe, James, 49
Ohio, settlement of, 163, 189-90, 192
Ohio Company, 124, 187, 189
oil industry, 407-8, 604
O'Keeffe, Georgia, 717
Okinawa, battle of, 666, 668
Oklahoma: reserved for Indians, 196, 424, 425; white settlement, 431
oligopoly, 615
Olmsted, F. L., 466
Olney, Richard, 411, 523
Oneida community, 261-2
O'Neill, Eugene, 715
Open Door in China, 233, 520, 527-9, 537-42, 601
Oregon: Russian interest, 69, 169; British activities, 168, 300-1; American activities, 233, 307-10; acquisition, 312-13; territorial government, 327
Organization of American States, 674
Ostend Manifesto (1854), 337
O'Sullivan, John, 311
Otis, James, 96
Overman Act (1918), 575
Owen, Robert, 268

Pacific Charter, 700
Pacific Fur Company, 301
Page, Thomas N., 505
Page, Walter H., 569
Paine, Thomas, 52, 104
painting: colonial period, 88-90; early nineteenth century, 291-2; later nineteenth century, 512-14; twentieth century, 717-19
Panama, 532, 646
Panama Canal, 529, 532
Pan American conferences, 522-3, 645-6, 652, 673-4
Paris, Pact of (1928), 602-3

Paris, Treaty of (1763), 70, 73; (1783), 114–15; (1898), 525
Parker, Theodore, 260, 282, 284, 323
Parkman, Francis, 282
Parrington, Vernon Louis, 707
Partisan Review, 706
Patten, Simon N., 492
Pattie, James, 303
Pattie, Sylvester, 303
Patton, General George S., 661, 664
Patrons of Husbandry. *See* Granger movement
Paulding, James Kirke, 280
Payne-Aldrich Tariff (1909), 557
Peale, Charles Willson, 90, 291
Pearl Harbor, attack on, 655
Peckham, Justice Rufus W., 419
Peffer, William A., 458
Peirce, Charles S., 497
Pendleton Act (1883), 454
Penn, William, 44–5
Pennsylvania: settlement of, 44–5, 46, 51, 52; internal conflicts, 66
Pennsylvania Railroad, 333, 402
Pennsylvania, University of, 79
Penrose, Boies, 447
pensions, for veterans: after Civil War, 449, 455, 456; after World War I, 595–6
People's Party, 391, 458
Pequot War, 37
Perfectionism, 261–2
Perkins, Frances, 631
Perkins, George W., 559
Perry, Commodore Matthew C., 233
Perry, Captain Oliver H., 165
Pershing, General John J., 537, 578
Petersburg, battle of, 370
Philip, King, war with, 37
Philippine Islands: acquisition of, 524, 525, 526–7; during World War II, 655, 660, 665; independence, 682
Philippine Sea, battle of the, 665
Phillips, David Graham, 510, 546
Phillips, Wendell, 323
philosophy: scholastic, 7; in colonial period, 76, 87; since Civil War, 485, 495–500
physiocrats, influence of, 77, 85
Pickens, Andrew, 113
Pickering, Timothy, 146, 151, 153, 158
Pickford, Mary, 613
Pierce, Benjamin, 480
Pierce, Franklin, 337, 338, 339, 340
Pike, Zebulon M., 301
Pilgrim Fathers, 33–4

Pinchot, Gifford, 554, 557
Pinckney, Charles Cotesworth, 150, 152, 159, 162
Pinckney, Thomas, 149
Pingree, Hazen S., 547
Pinkerton detectives, 419, 420
Plan of Union (1801), 259
Platt, Thomas C., 447, 551
Platt Amendment, 525, 646
Plessy v. Ferguson, 732
Plymouth, settlement of, 33–4; united to Massachusetts, 55
Pocahontas, 29
Poe, Edgar Allan, 275, 277, 287–8
Poetry, 706, 713
Point Four program, 685
Polignac memorandum (1823), 171
Polk, James K., 173, 312–18, 327
Pontiac, 73, 96
Pope, General John, 362, 364
popular sovereignty, 332, 338, 339, 345–6
Populist Party, 391–3, 440, 457–62
"pork-barrel" legislation, 449
Porter, Cole, 720
Porter, Captain David D., 362
Porter, Gene Stratton, 512
Porter, Katherine Anne, 712
Porter, Noah, 485
Portsmouth, Treaty of (1905), 540
Postal Telegraph Company, 409
Potsdam Conference (1945), 671
Pound, Ezra, 714
Pound, Roscoe, 500
Powderly, Terence, 417
Powell, John W., 442
Powers, Hiram, 292
pragmatism (in philosophy), 497–500
Pre-emption Act (1841), 188, 252
Presbyterian Church, 39, 51–2, 63, 83, 193, 215, 257–60, 474
Prescott, W. H., 281
primary elections, 391, 549
primogeniture, abolition of, 121
Prince, Thomas, 88
Princeton, battle of, 112
Princeton University, 79, 478
prisons, reform of, 265
prize fighting, 467
Progressive Party (1912), 559, 573; (1924), 591–2; (1948), 679
Prohibitionists, 259, 266–7, 474, 592, 597–9
psychiatry, development of, 736–7
public land. *See* Landownership
Public Works Administration, 639, 719

Pueblo Indians, 300
Puerto Rico, 525–6
Pujo Committee, 413
Pulitzer, Joseph, 481, 524
Pullman, George M., 402
Pullman strike, 420
Puma Indians, 300
Pupin, Michael, 409
Pure Food and Drug Act (1906), 555
Puritanism: in England, 12–13; in New England, 39–41

Quakers: in England, 13; in the colonies, 41, 43–5, 53, 66, 81; humanitarian activities, 264
Quay, Matthew S., 447
Quebec Act (1774), 97, 100
quitrents, 29, 30

Radical Republicans, 358, 370, 378–83
radio industry, 613, 739, 741
railroads: before Civil War, 222–3, 333, 334; after Civil War, 389, 401–6, 413; regulation by state governments, 223, 404–5; regulation by Federal government, 405–6, 553, 556, 594, 640–1
Raleigh, Sir Walter, 25
Randolph, Edmund, 129, 140, 146
Randolph, John, of Roanoke, 155
Rankin, Jeanette, 549
Ransom, John Crowe, 708, 714
Rapp, George, 261
Rauschenbusch, Walter, 474
Raymond, Henry J., 272
Reader's Digest, 739
recall, the, 549
Reclamation Service, 555
Reconstruction Acts (1867), 381
Reconstruction Finance Corporation, 629, 638, 640, 677
recreations, 467–8, 741
Reed, Thomas B., 456
Reed, Dr. Walter, 480
referendum, the, 549
Regulators, 67, 104
religion: in Europe, 7–10; in England, 12–13; in New England, 39–41; during later colonial period, 63, 64–5, 76, 80–3, 86; separation of church and state, 121; in Old South, 215; expansion during early nineteenth century, 257–64; during later nineteenth century, 472–6; during twentieth century, 725–7
Rensselaer, Kiliaen Van, 27

Rensselaer Polytechnic Institute, 273
reparations, after World War I, 579, 581, 601–2, 629
Republican Party: (first), formation during 1790's, 144–6; development after War of 1812, 174, 179–80; division of, 235, 239–40; (second), formation during 1850's, 327, 330, 340–2; character after Civil War, 444–5; association with big business, 463; conflict between conservatives and progressives, 556–9; in 1950's, 692, 697
Resettlement Administration, 637
Resumption Act (1875), 449
Reuther, Walter, 643
Revere, Paul, 91, 103
Rhee, Syngman, 699
Rhett, Robert Barnwell, 327, 347
Rhode Island, settlement of, 36–7; inflation in, 63, 64, 127
Rhodes, James Ford, 486
Rice, Elmer, 715
rice cultivation, 42, 50, 204
Richardson, Henry Hobson, 515
Ridgway, General Matthew B., 691, 692
Riesman, David, 738
Riis, Jacob, 466, 471
Riley, James Whitcomb, 505
Rio de Janeiro conference (1942), 673; (1947), 673
Ripley, George, 282
Rittenhouse, David, 86
Rivers and Harbors Bill, 449
road-building, 123, 175, 220–1, 612
Roberts, Elizabeth Madox, 712
Roberts, Justice Owen J., 634
Robertson, James, 183, 184
Robinson, Edwin Arlington, 510, 713
Robinson, Jackie, 732
Robinson, James Harvey, 501
Rockefeller, John D., 399, 400, 407–8, 415, 463
Rockingham, marquis of, 98, 114
Rocky Mountain Fur Company, 302, 303
Rodgers, Richard, 720
Roebling, John, 515
Roebling, Washington, 515
Rogers, James Gamble, 719
Rolfe, John, 29
Roman Catholic Church. *See* Catholic Church
Rome Conference (1924), 603
Roosevelt, Franklin D., 534, 583, 596; President, 630–5; foreign policy, 645–55;

Roosevelt, Franklin (*continued*)
  during World War II, 659, 669–71, 672;
  death, 675
Roosevelt, Nicholas, 221
Roosevelt, Theodore, 478, 490, 520, 524,
  545, 546, 572; President, 551–5; foreign
  policy, 529, 532–3, 537, 540; in campaign
  of 1912, 558–60
Roosevelt Corollary (to Monroe Doctrine),
  523, 532–3, 604–05
Root, Elihu, 525, 533, 540
Root, John W., 515
Root-Takahira Agreement (1908), 540
Rosecrans, General William, 362, 366, 369
Rosenfeld, Paul, 707
Ross, Edward A., 491
Rotary Clubs, 614
Royce, Josiah, 481, 496
Ruffin, Edmund, 327, 347
Rural Electrification Administration, 639
Rush, Dr. Benjamin, 266
Rush, Richard, 171
Rush, William, 292
Rush-Bagot Agreement (1817), 168
Russell, Charles E., 546
Russell, Pastor Charles T., 475
Russia: activities on Pacific coast, 68–9,
  169–70; purchase of Alaska from, 521;
  activities in Far East, 528, 537, 540;
  in World War I, 566, 567; Revolution of
  1917, 573; Allied intervention in, 578;
  see also Soviet Union
Rutgers University, 79, 478
Rutherford, Judge Joseph F., 475
Ryder, Albert Pinkham, 513
Ryswick, Treaty of (1697), 72

St. Clair, Arthur, 168, 192
St. Denis, Ruth, 716
Saint-Gaudens, Augustus, 514
St. John's College, 729
St. Louis and O'Fallon Railroad case, 594
St. Louis Post-Dispatch, 481
Sacajawea, 301
Sacco and Vanzetti case, 599
Saipan, battle of, 665
Salisbury, marquis of, 523
Saltus, Edgar, 511
Samoa, acquisition of, 521
Sampson, Admiral William T., 525
San Francisco Conference (1945), 672
San Ildefonso, Treaty of (1800), 155
San Jacinto, battle of, 306
Sandburg, Carl, 713

Sandys, Sir Edwin, 29
Sanger, Margaret, 735
Sankey, Ira D., 474
Santa Anna, Antonio López de, 304, 306,
  307, 315, 318
Santa Clara County v. Southern Pacific
  Railroad, 405
Santa Fe Railroad, 404
Santayana, George, 496
Santiago, battle of, 525
Sarah Lawrence College, 729
Saratoga, battle of, 106, 112
Sargent, John Singer, 513
Saturday Evening Post, 483
Saturday Review, 739
scalawags, 384–5
Schechter case, 636
Schenck case, 578
Schine, David, 695–6
Schley, Admiral Winfield S., 525
schools. *See* education
Schouler, James S., 486
Schurz, Carl, 449, 452, 454
Schwab, Charles, 407
science, progress of: in Europe, 8, 76; in
  colonial period, 85–7; before Civil War,
  272–3; after Civil War, 479–80; in twenti-
  eth century, 741–4
Scioto Company, 124
Scopes trial, 600
Scotch-Irish immigrants, 46, 51–2, 66
Scott, Dred. *See* Dred Scott case.
Scott, T. A., 402
Scott, General Winfield, 165, 315, 316, 318,
  337
sculpture: before Civil War, 292–3; after
  Civil War, 514; in twentieth century,
  718–19
Sears, Isaac, 98
Securities Act (1933), 658
Securities and Exchange Commission, 638
Sedition Act (1798), 151, 154; (1918), 577
Selective Service Act (1917), 575
Selective Training and Service Act (1940),
  657
Seminole Indians, 169, 195, 196
Separatists: in England, 13, 33; in New
  England, 63, 65
servants, indentured, 31, 49, 51
settlement houses, 467
Seven Days' battles, 364
Sevier, John, 183, 185
Sewall, Samuel, 88
Sewanee Review, 706

Seward, William H., 329, 341, 350, 354, 358, 367, 369, 521
sexual mores, 255–7, 734–5
Seymour, Horatio, 382
Shahn, Ben, 718
Shakers, 261
Shapiro, Karl, 714
share-cropping, 388
Shaw, Anna Howard, 549
Shaw, Justice Lemuel, 230
Shays's Rebellion, 128
Sheridan, General Philip, 370, 371, 424
Sherman, General William T., 362, 369–71, 424
Sherman Anti-trust Act (1890), 411, 419, 552–3, 563
Sherman Silver Purchase Act (1890), 456, 461
Shiloh, battle of, 361
shipping industry: in colonial New England, 38, 64; in New England before Civil War, 233–4; government aid for, 594, 641; in World War II, 657
shoe industry, 224
Silliman, Benjamin, 273
silver-mining, 425–7
Simms, William Gilmore, 286
Simpson, Jerry, 458
Sinclair, Harry F., 590
Sinclair, Upton, 510, 546, 555
Sioux Indians, 424
sit-down strikes, 643
Sitting Bull, 424
skyscrapers, 516, 719
Slacum, W. A., 308
Slater, Samuel, 225
Slavery: in Southern colonies, 31–2, 42, 50, 52–3, 64; movement against during Revolution, 121–2; in Old South, 204, 206–10; in Texas, 305–6; as cause of Civil War, 322–6; abolition, 365
Slidell, John, 314, 367
Sloan, John, 513
Small, Albion, 491
Smibert, John, 89
Smith, Adam, influence of, 77, 143, 396, 486
Smith, Alfred E., 476, 591, 592, 598
Smith, Gerrit, 323
Smith, Jedediah, 296, 302–3
Smith, Jess, 590
Smith, Joseph, 262, 310
Smith, Seba, 505
Smith, Sir Thomas, 28
Smith, William (of New York), 88

Smith, William (of Pennsylvania), 80, 87, 91
Smith College, 478
Smith-Connally Act (1943), 658
Smithsonian Institution, 273
Smyth v. Ames, 398, 405
social contract, theory of, 76, 83–4, 135
Social Darwinism, 488–90
Social Gospel, 473–4
Social Security Act (1935), 633, 634, 641, 694
social work, development of, 265–6, 467
Socialism, influence of, 268–9, 494–5, 625
Socialist Labor Party, 495
Socialist Party, 420, 495, 560, 599, 625
sociology, study of, 486, 488–91, 743
Soil Conservation and Domestic Allotment Act (1936), 637
Soil Conservation Service, 640
Sons of Liberty, 98, 99, 100, 117
Soto, Hernando de, 15
South Carolina: settlement of, 42–3, 46; nullification crisis, 244–6
South Carolina Exposition, 217, 244
South Dakota, settlement of, 427, 428, 430, 431
South-East Asia Treaty Organization, 700
Southern Alliance, 391, 458
Southern Pacific Railroad, 404
Southern Railway, 404
Southern Review, 706
Soviet Union: 599, 605, 624, 625, 645; during World War II, 649, 654, 660–5, 668; negotiations with, 669–73; since 1945, 681–91, 700–3
Spain: colonial expansion, 14–16, 18; conflicts with, during colonial period, 68, 70, 72, 73; in War of Independence, 111, 115; problem of the Mississippi, 125–6, 149; Florida question, 158, 163, 166, 169; loss of colonial empire, 170–4; war with, 523–5
Sparks, Jared, 281
Specie Circular (1836), 248
Spencer, Herbert, influence of, 488–9
spirituals, Negro, 91, 294
spoils system, 238–9, 243–4, 448, 452, 454
Spottsylvania, battle of, 369
Sprague, Frank J., 409
Springfield Republican, 272
Stalwarts, 451, 453
Stamp Act (1765), 97–8
Standard Oil Company, 408, 413, 552, 553
Stanford, Leland, 403, 404
Stanford University, 477
Stanton, Edwin H., 358, 381

Stanton, Elizabeth Cady, 267
Staple Act (1663), 54
steamboats, 176, 221
Steamboat Act (1852), 221
Stedman, Edmund Clarence, 504
steel industry, 389, 406–7
Steffens, Lincoln, 546
Stein, Gertrude, 511
Steinbeck, John, 712
Stephens, Alexander, 326, 352, 356, 371, 378
Stephens, Uriah, 417
Stettinius, Edward R., 672
Stevens, Thaddeus, 358, 379, 382, 383, 388
Stevens, Wallace, 714
Stevenson, Adlai E., 693, 697
Stieglitz, Alfred, 717
Stilwell, General Joseph, 668
Stimson, Henry L., 530, 603–4, 606, 652, 659
Stith, William, 88
Stoddard, Richard Henry, 504
Stone, Lucy, 268
Story, Justice Joseph, 176, 250
Stowe, Harriet Beecher, 285, 341, 367
Straight, Willard, 541
Strong, Josiah, 490
Stuart, Gilbert, 291
Sturges, Preston, 740
Suffolk Resolves, 101
suffrage: during colonial period, 61; changes during Revolution, 120; growth of universal manhood, 192, 237; restrictions on Negro, 392; women's, 549
Sugar Act (1764), 97
Sullivan, Harry Stack, 737
Sullivan, John L., 467
Sullivan, Louis, 515, 516, 719
Sullivan, Mark, 546
Sumner, William Graham, 489
Sumter, Thomas, 113
Sunday, William A. (Billy), 474
Supreme Court: established, 140; in Jefferson administration, 154–5; Marshall's decisions, 176–8; Taney as Chief Justice, 249–50, 344; in later nineteenth century, 398–9; in administration of Franklin Roosevelt, 634–5
Sussex, sinking of the, 570
Sutter, Johann A., 318
Swedish colonists, 28, 43, 46
Swift, Gustavus, 410
Swiss immigrants, 50–1
Sylvis, William H., 417
Symmes, John Cleves, 124

Taft, Lorado, 709
Taft, Robert A., 678, 692, 697
Taft, William H., 527, 533–4, 541, 555–60, 634
Taft-Hartley Act (1947), 678–9, 693
Tallmadge, James, 179
Tammany Society, 144, 446–7
Taney, Roger B., 248, 249–50, 344, 354, 397
Tappan, Arthur, 323
Tappan, Lewis, 323
Tarawa, battle of, 665
Tarbell, Ida, 546
tariff acts: of 1789, 140; of 1816, 175; of 1824, 244; of 1828 (of abominations), 244; of 1832, 245; of 1833, 246; of 1842, 252; of 1846 (Walker), 232, 312; of 1857, 232, 343; of 1861 (Morrill), 372; of 1872, 449; of 1883 (mongrel), 454; of 1890 (McKinley), 456; of 1894 (Wilson-Gorman), 461; of 1897 (Dingley), 463; of 1909 (Payne-Aldrich), 557; of 1913 (Underwood), 561; of 1922 (Fordney-McCumber), 593; of 1930 (Hawley-Smoot), 593; of 1934 (Trade Agreements Act), 645
Tarkington, Booth, 511
Tate, Allen, 708, 714
Taylor, Bayard, 504
Taylor, Deems, 721
Taylor, Edward, 87
Taylor, John, of Caroline, 177, 179–80, 217, 242
Taylor, Zachary, 314, 315, 316, 327–9
Tecumseh, 163, 165, 166, 190
Teheran Conference (1943), 670
telegraph, invention of, 223
telephone, invention of, 409
temperance movement, 259, 266–7
Temporary National Economic Committee, 656
Tennessee, settlement of, 97, 123, 125, 181, 183–5, 198, 205
Tennessee Valley Authority, 639–40
tennis, 468
Tenure of Office Act (1867), 381, 383
Tesla, Nikola, 409
Texas: under Spanish rule, 68, 158, 169; settled by Americans, 304–5; independent republic, 305–7; admitted to Union, 311–12, 316, 318
Texas v. White, 382
textile industry: before Civil War, 224–5; in South, 389–90
Thames, battle of the, 165, 190

theater: colonial period, 87–8; nineteenth century, 468; twentieth century, 715–16
Thomas, Augustus, 715
Thomas, General George H., 361, 369
Thomas, Norman, 495, 625
Thomas, Theodore, 517
Thomson, Charles, 98
Thomson, J. Edgar, 402
Thoreau, Henry David, 275, 277, 284, 290, 314
Thurmond, J. Strom, 679
Tilden, Samuel J., 447, 451–2
Tillman, Benjamin, 393
Timber and Stone Act (1878), 430
Timber Culture Act (1873), 429
Time, 739
Tippecanoe, battle of, 163
tobacco cultivation, 29, 31, 67
Tocqueville, Alexis de, 255, 256
Toombs, Robert, 326
Tordesillas, Treaty of (1494), 15, 18
Toscanini, Arturo, 517, 721
Townsend, Dr. Francis, 625, 626
Townshend, Charles, 99
Trade Agreements Act (1934), 645
Trade and Plantations, Board of, 56, 57
trade associations, 593
trade unions. *See* labor unions
transcendentalism, 282
Transition, 706
Transylvania University, 185, 215
Trent affair, 367
Trenton, battle of, 112
Trilling, Lionel, 708
Trist, Nicholas, 318
Trollope, Frances, 255
Truman, Harry S., 671, 675–7, 679, 690, 691
Truman Doctrine, 689
Trumbull, John, 292
trusts: growth of, 400–1, 408, 411–13; Federal action against, 410–11, 545–6, 552–3, 563
Turner, Frederick Jackson, 200–2, 441, 501
Turner, Nat, 208
Tuskegee Institute, 394
Tutuila, acquisition of, 522
Twachtman, John, 513
Twain, Mark, 200, 221, 280, 426, 506–7
Tweed, William M., 447
Tyler, John, 251, 252, 307, 311–12

underground railroad, 324
Underwood Tariff (1913), 561
Union League, 384

Union Pacific Railroad, 373, 402–03
Unitarian Church, 259–60
United Nations, 655, 671–4, 684, 690, 700, 702
United States Housing Authority, 641
United States Steel Company, 413, 642
Upshur, A. P., 311
U'Ren, William S., 549
Urey, Harold C., 742
Utah: settlement of, 310–11; organized as territory, 327–9; admitted to Union, 431
Utrecht, Treaty of (1713), 72

Vallandigham, Clement L., 358
Van Buren, Martin, 230, 238, 240, 242, 244, 246, 249, 312, 328; President, 250–2
Vancouver, George, 301
Van de Graaf, Robert, 742
Vandenberg, Arthur, 669, 685
Vanderbilt, Cornelius, 399, 402
Vanderbilt University, 477
Vanderlyn, John, 292
Van Dyke, Henry, 512
Vardaman, James K., 393
Vassar College, 478
Veblen, Thorstein, 492–3
Venezuela boundary dispute, 523
Vermont, settlement of, 46, 65, 125
Versailles, Treaty of (1919), 580–1, 584
Vesey, Denmark, 208
Vicksburg, siege of, 366
Vietnam, 699–700
Villa, Pancho, 536, 537
Vincent, John H., 480
Vinson, Fred M., 656
Virgin Islands, acquisition of, 534
Virginia: colonization of, 25–6; economic and social conditions, 28–33; internal conflicts, 32–3, 66–7; economic decline, 212
Virginia Resolutions (1798), 151
Virginia, University of, 154, 270, 271, 293
Volstead Act (1919), 550

Wabash, St. Louis and Pacific Railway Company v. Illinois, 405
Wade, Benjamin, 358, 381
Wade-Davis Bill (1864), 370
Wagner Act (1935), 633, 634, 636, 678
Wainwright, General Jonathan, 660
Waite, Chief Justice Morrison R., 405
Wald, Lillian D., 467
Walker, Amasa, 486
Walker, Francis A., 491
Walker, Robert J., 312, 345

Walker, William, 337
Wallace, DeWitt, 739
Wallace, Henry A., 631, 637, 676, 679
Walsh, Thomas J., 590
Waltham System, 228, 229
war debts (after World War I), 601–2, 629
War Hawks, 163
War Industries Board, 575
War Production Board, 656
Ward, Artemus, 505
Ward, Lester, 491
Ward, John Quincy Adams, 514
Ware, Henry, 259
Warmouth, H. C., 385
Warner, W. Lloyd, 730
Warren, Dr. John C., 273
Warren, Robert Penn, 712
wars: French and Indian, 68–74; of Independence, 103–15; of 1812, 164–7; with Mexico, 304–8; Civil, 354–71; with Indians, 423–4; with Spain, 523–5; First World, 574–80; Second World, 659–69; Korean, 690–1, 699
Washington, Booker T., 393–4
Washington, George, 67, 70, 72, 90, 127, 128, 133, 136, 270; in War of Independence, 103–15; President, 140–9
Washington: acquisition of, 310, 313; settlement and statehood, 426, 431
Washington Conference (1921–22), 601
Washington Temperance Society, 267
Watkins, Arthur V., 696
Watson, Thomas Edward, 393, 458, 462
Wayne, General Anthony, 148, 189
Weather Bureau, 480
Weaver, James B., 457, 458, 460
Weber, Max, 717
Webster, Daniel, 156, 175, 177, 236, 245, 251, 252, 328, 329, 338, 522
Webster, Noah, 270
Webster-Ashburton Treaty (1842), 156, 168, 252
Wedemeyer, General Albert, 668
Weed, Thurlow, 238, 251, 252, 327
Weir, J. Alden, 513
Welch, Dr. W. H., 480
Weld, Theodore, 323
Wellesley College, 478
Wendell, Barrett, 512
West, Benjamin, 90
West Indies: settlement of, 14–15; colonial trade with, 38, 56, 64; British trade restrictions, 123, 232; British and French blockades, 147–8, 150, 161

West Virginia, 212, 354
Western Federation of Miners, 420–1
Western Union, 223, 409
Westinghouse, George, 402
Westinghouse Electric Company, 409
whaling industry, 233
Wharton, Edith, 511
Wheeler, Burton K., 592
Whig Party, 249, 251, 326–7
Whiskey Rebellion, 142
Whistler, James McNeill, 513
White, John, 25
White, Stanford, 516
White, William Allen, 651
Whitefield, George, 63, 64–5
Whiteman, Paul, 721
Whitman, Marcus, 308
Whitman, Walt, 275, 277, 289–91
Whitney, Eli, 204, 226
Whittier, John Greenleaf, 285, 323
Wickersham Commission, 598
Wilder, Thornton, 712
Wilderness, battle of the, 369
Willard, Emma, 268
Willard, Frances, 474, 550
William III, king of England, 55
William and Mary College, 79
Williams, Roger, 36–7, 84
Williams, William Carlos, 714
Willis, N. P., 280
Willkie, Wendell L., 640, 652–3
Wilmot Proviso, 320
Wilson, Charles E., 693
Wilson, Edmund, 708
Wilson, Henry Lane, 536
Wilson, James, 102
Wilson, Woodrow, 534, 541, 545, 548, 559–63, 567–82
Winters, Yvor, 709
Winthrop, John, Sr., 34, 35, 38, 88
Winthrop, John, Jr., 85
Winthrop, John, IV, 85
Wirt, William, 246, 247
Wisconsin, settlement of, 182, 192, 198, 336
Wisconsin, University of, 193, 548
Wise, John, 83, 84
witchcraft, 40
Wolfe, General James, 73
Wolfe, Thomas, 711
women: role in American society, 255–7, 734–6; movement for political rights, 267–8, 549
Women's Christian Temperance Union, 474, 550

Wood, Grant, 718
Wood, General Leonard, 525
Woodberry, George E., 512
Woollen Act (1699), 56
Woolman, John, 81
Woolsey, Theodore Dwight, 486
Worcester v. Georgia, 196
Workmen's Compensation Acts, 549–50
Works Progress Administration, 641–2, 706, 718, 721
Wright, Chauncy, 497
Wright, Frank Lloyd, 516, 719
Wright, Harold Bell, 512
Wright, Orville, 613
Wright, Richard, 712
Wright, Wilbur, 613
writs of assistance, 96
Wyeth, Nathaniel, 308

Wylie, Philip, 736
Wyoming, settlement of, 426, 431

X.Y.Z. affair, 150

Yale College, 79, 259, 271, 477, 478, 479
Yalta Conference (1945), 671
Yancey, William L., 327, 347
Yazoo lands fraud, 177
York, duke of, 43, 44; *see also* James II
Yorktown, battle of, 113, 114
Young, Brigham, 262, 310–11
Young, Owen D., 602

Zapata, Emiliano, 536
Zenger case, 80
Zimmermann note, 573
Zorach, William, 719